W9-CET-591

# *Complete Solutions Guide*

# CALCULUS
## SEVENTH EDITION
## Larson/Hostetler/Edwards

## Volume II
## Chapters 6-10

## Bruce H. Edwards
University of Florida

**HOUGHTON MIFFLIN COMPANY**     Boston   New York

Printed in the United States of America

ISBN 0-618-14932-5

123456789-VG-05 04 03 02 01

# CONTENTS

# PREFACE

The *Complete Solutions Guide* for *Calculus*, Seventh Edition, is a supplement to the text by Ron Larson, Robert P. Hostetler, and Bruce H. Edwards. Solutions to every exercise in the text are given with all essential algebraic steps included. There are three volumes in the complete set of solutions guides. Volume I contains Chapters P-5, Volume II contains Chapters 6-10, and Volume III contains Chapters 10-14.

I have made every effort to see that the solutions are correct. However, I would appreciate hearing about any errors or other suggestions for improvement.

I would like to thank the staff at Larson Texts, Inc. for their help in the production of this guide.

Bruce H. Edwards
University of Florida
Gainesville, Florida 32611
(be@math.ufl.edu)

# C H A P T E R   6
## Applications of Integration

# C H A P T E R 6
## Applications of Integration

## Section 6.1    Area of a Region Between Two Curves

Solutions to Odd-Numbered Exercises

**1.** $A = \int_0^6 [0 - (x^2 - 6x)]\, dx = -\int_0^6 (x^2 - 6x)\, dx$

**3.** $A = \int_0^3 [(-x^2 + 2x + 3) - (x^2 - 4x + 3)]\, dx = \int_0^3 (-2x^2 + 6x)\, dx$

**5.** $A = 2\int_{-1}^0 3(x^3 - x)\, dx = 6\int_{-1}^0 (x^3 - x)\, dx \quad$ or $\quad -6\int_0^1 (x^3 - x)\, dx$

**7.** $\int_0^4 \left[(x + 1) - \dfrac{x}{2}\right] dx$

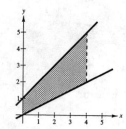

**9.** $\int_0^6 \left[4(2^{-x/3}) - \dfrac{x}{6}\right] dx$

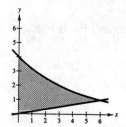

**11.** $\int_{-\pi/3}^{\pi/3} [2 - \sec x]\, dx$

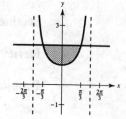

**13.** $f(x) = x + 1$

$g(x) = (x - 1)^2$

$A \approx 4$

Matches (d)

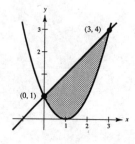

**15.** $A = \int_0^2 \left[\left(\dfrac{1}{2}x^3 + 2\right) - (x + 1)\right] dx$

$\quad = \int_0^2 \left(\dfrac{1}{2}x^3 - x + 1\right) dx$

$\quad = \left[\dfrac{x^4}{8} - \dfrac{x^2}{2} + x\right]_0^2$

$\quad = \left(\dfrac{16}{8} - \dfrac{4}{2} + 2\right) - 0 = 2$

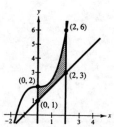

**17.** The points of intersection are given by:

$$x^2 - 4x = 0$$

$$x(x - 4) = 0 \quad \text{when} \quad x = 0, 4$$

$$A = \int_0^4 [g(x) - f(x)]\, dx$$

$$= -\int_0^4 (x^2 - 4x)\, dx$$

$$= -\left[\frac{x^3}{3} - 2x^2\right]_0^4$$

$$= \frac{32}{3}$$

**19.** The points of intersection are given by:

$$x^2 + 2x + 1 = 3x + 3$$

$$(x - 2)(x + 1) = 0 \quad \text{when} \quad x = -1, 2$$

$$A = \int_{-1}^2 [g(x) - f(x)]\, dx$$

$$= \int_{-1}^2 [(3x + 3) - (x^2 + 2x + 1)]\, dx$$

$$= \int_{-1}^2 (2 + x - x^2)\, dx$$

$$= \left[2x + \frac{x^2}{2} - \frac{x^3}{3}\right]_{-1}^2 = \frac{9}{2}$$

**21.** The points of intersection are given by:

$$x = 2 - x \quad \text{and} \quad x = 0 \quad \text{and} \quad 2 - x = 0$$

$$x = 1 \qquad\qquad x = 0 \qquad\qquad x = 2$$

$$A = \int_0^1 [(2 - y) - (y)]\, dy = \left[2y - y^2\right]_0^1 = 1$$

Note that if we integrate with respect to x, we need two integrals. Also, note that the region is a triangle.

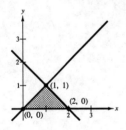

**23.** The points of intersection are given by:

$$\sqrt{3x} + 1 = x + 1$$

$$\sqrt{3x} = x \quad \text{when} \quad x = 0, 3$$

$$A = \int_0^3 [f(x) - g(x)]\, dx$$

$$= \int_0^3 [(\sqrt{3x} + 1) - (x + 1)]\, dx$$

$$= \int_0^3 [(3x)^{1/2} - x]\, dx$$

$$= \left[\frac{2}{9}(3x)^{3/2} - \frac{x^2}{2}\right]_0^3 = \frac{3}{2}$$

**25.** The points of intersection are given by:

$$y^2 = y + 2$$

$$(y - 2)(y + 1) = 0 \quad \text{when} \quad y = -1, 2$$

$$A = \int_{-1}^2 [g(y) - f(y)]\, dy$$

$$= \int_{-1}^2 [(y + 2) - y^2]\, dy$$

$$= \left[2y + \frac{y^2}{2} - \frac{y^3}{3}\right]_{-1}^2 = \frac{9}{2}$$

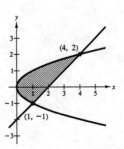

**27.** $A = \displaystyle\int_{-1}^{2} [f(y) - g(y)] \, dy$

$= \displaystyle\int_{-1}^{2} [(y^2 + 1) - 0] \, dy$

$= \left[ \dfrac{y^3}{3} + y \right]_{-1}^{2} = 6$

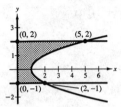

**29.** $y = \dfrac{10}{x} \implies x = \dfrac{10}{y}$

$A = \displaystyle\int_{2}^{10} \dfrac{10}{y} \, dy$

$= \left[ 10 \ln y \right]_{2}^{10}$

$= 10(\ln 10 - \ln 2)$

$= 10 \ln 5 \approx 16.0944$

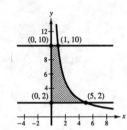

**31.** The points of intersection are given by:

$x^3 - 3x^2 + 3x = x^2$

$x(x - 1)(x - 3) = 0$   when   $x = 0, 1, 3$

$A = \displaystyle\int_{0}^{1} [f(x) - g(x)] \, dx + \int_{1}^{3} [g(x) - f(x)] \, dx$

$= \displaystyle\int_{0}^{1} [(x^3 - 3x^2 + 3x) - x^2] \, dx + \int_{1}^{3} [x^2 - (x^3 - 3x^2 + 3x)] \, dx$

$= \displaystyle\int_{0}^{1} (x^3 - 4x^2 + 3x) \, dx + \int_{1}^{3} (-x^3 + 4x^2 - 3x) \, dx$

$= \left[ \dfrac{x^4}{4} - \dfrac{4}{3}x^3 + \dfrac{3}{2}x^2 \right]_{0}^{1} + \left[ \dfrac{-x^4}{4} + \dfrac{4}{3}x^3 - \dfrac{3}{2}x^2 \right]_{1}^{3} = \dfrac{37}{12}$

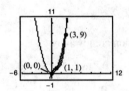

Numerical Approximation: $0.417 + 2.667 \approx 3.083$

**33.** The points of intersection are given by:

$x^2 - 4x + 3 = 3 + 4x - x^2$

$2x(x - 4) = 0$   when   $x = 0, 4$

$A = \displaystyle\int_{0}^{4} [(3 + 4x - x^2) - (x^2 - 4x + 3)] \, dx$

$= \displaystyle\int_{0}^{4} (-2x^2 + 8x) \, dx$

$= \left[ -\dfrac{2x^3}{3} + 4x^2 \right]_{0}^{4} = \dfrac{64}{3}$

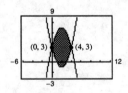

Numerical Approximation: 21.333

**35.** $f(x) = x^4 - 4x^2, \quad g(x) = x^2 - 4$

The points of intersection are given by:

$$x^4 - 4x^2 = x^2 - 4$$

$$x^4 - 5x^2 + 4 = 0$$

$$(x^2 - 4)(x^2 - 1) = 0 \quad \text{when} \quad x = \pm 2, \pm 1$$

By symmetry,

$$A = 2 \int_0^1 \left[ (x^4 - 4x^2) - (x^2 - 4) \right] dx + 2 \int_1^2 \left[ (x^2 - 4) - (x^4 - 4x^2) \right] dx$$

$$= 2 \int_0^1 (x^4 - 5x^2 + 4) \, dx + 2 \int_1^2 (-x^4 + 5x^2 - 4) \, dx$$

$$= 2 \left[ \frac{x^5}{5} - \frac{5x^3}{3} + 4x \right]_0^1 + 2 \left[ -\frac{x^5}{5} + \frac{5x^3}{3} - 4x \right]_1^2$$

$$= 2 \left[ \frac{1}{5} - \frac{5}{3} + 4 \right] + 2 \left[ \left( -\frac{32}{5} + \frac{40}{3} - 8 \right) - \left( -\frac{1}{5} + \frac{5}{3} - 4 \right) \right] = 8.$$

Numerical Approximation: $5.067 + 2.933 = 8.0$

**37.** The points of intersection are given by:

$$\frac{1}{1 + x^2} = \frac{x^2}{2}$$

$$x^4 + x^2 - 2 = 0$$

$$(x^2 + 2)(x^2 - 1) = 0$$

$$x = \pm 1$$

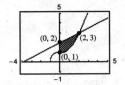

$$A = 2 \int_0^1 \left[ f(x) - g(x) \right] dx$$

$$= 2 \int_0^1 \left[ \frac{1}{1 + x^2} - \frac{x^2}{2} \right] dx$$

$$= 2 \left[ \arctan x - \frac{x^3}{6} \right]_0^1$$

$$= 2 \left( \frac{\pi}{4} - \frac{1}{6} \right) = \frac{\pi}{2} - \frac{1}{3} \approx 1.237$$

Numerical Approximation: 1.237

**39.** $\sqrt{1 + x^3} \le \frac{1}{2}x + 2$ on $[0, 2]$

Numerical approximation: 1.759

$$A = \int_0^2 \left[ \frac{1}{2}x + 2 - \sqrt{1 + x^3} \right] dx \approx 1.759$$

**41.** $A = 2 \int_0^{\pi/3} \left[ f(x) - g(x) \right] dx$

$$= 2 \int_0^{\pi/3} (2 \sin x - \tan x) \, dx$$

$$= 2 \left[ -2 \cos x + \ln|\cos x| \right]_0^{\pi/3}$$

$$= 2(1 - \ln 2) \approx 0.614$$

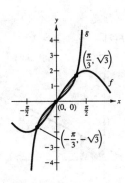

**43.** $A = \displaystyle\int_0^{2\pi} [(2 - \cos x) - \cos x]\, dx$

$= 2 \displaystyle\int_0^{2\pi} (1 - \cos x)\, dx$

$= 2\Big[ x - \sin x \Big]_0^{2\pi} = 4\pi \approx 12.566$

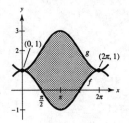

**45.** $A = \displaystyle\int_0^1 [xe^{-x^2} - 0]\, dx$

$= \Big[ -\frac{1}{2}e^{-x^2} \Big]_0^1 = \frac{1}{2}\Big( 1 - \frac{1}{e} \Big) \approx 0.316$

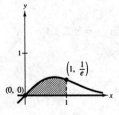

**47.** $A = \displaystyle\int_0^{\pi} [(2\sin x + \sin 2x) - 0]\, dx$

$= \Big[ -2\cos x - \frac{1}{2}\cos 2x \Big]_0^{\pi} = 4.0$

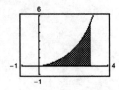

**49.** $A = \displaystyle\int_1^3 \Big[ \frac{1}{x^2} e^{1/x} - 0 \Big]\, dx$

$= \Big[ -e^{1/x} \Big]_1^3 = e - e^{1/3} \approx 1.323$

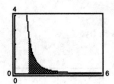

**51.** (a) $y = \sqrt{\dfrac{x^3}{4 - x}}, \quad y = 0, \quad x = 3$

(b) $A = \displaystyle\int_0^3 \sqrt{\frac{x^3}{4 - x}}\, dx,$

　　No, it cannot be evaluated by hand.

(c) 4.7721

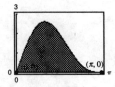

**53.** $F(x) = \displaystyle\int_0^x \Big( \frac{1}{2}t + 1 \Big)\, dt = \Big[ \frac{t^2}{4} + t \Big]_0^x = \frac{x^2}{4} + x$

(a) $F(0) = 0$

(b) $F(2) = \dfrac{2^2}{4} + 2 = 3$

(c) $F(6) = \dfrac{6^2}{4} + 6 = 15$

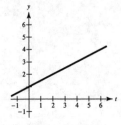

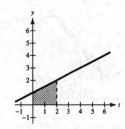

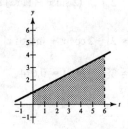

**55.** $F(\alpha) = \int_{-1}^{\alpha} \cos\frac{\pi\theta}{2}\,d\theta = \left[\frac{2}{\pi}\sin\frac{\pi\theta}{2}\right]_{-1}^{\alpha} = \frac{2}{\pi}\sin\frac{\pi\alpha}{2} + \frac{2}{\pi}$

(a) $F(-1) = 0$     (b) $F(0) = \frac{2}{\pi} \approx 0.6366$     (c) $F\left(\frac{1}{2}\right) = \frac{2 + \sqrt{2}}{\pi} \approx 1.0868$

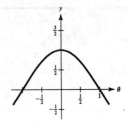
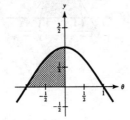
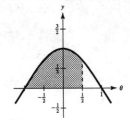

**57.** $A = \int_0^c \left[\left(\frac{b-a}{c}y + a\right) - \frac{b}{c}y\right] dy$

$= \int_0^c \left(-\frac{a}{c}y + a\right) dy$

$= \left[-\frac{a}{2c}y^2 + ay\right]_0^c$

$= -\frac{ac}{2} + ac = \frac{ac}{2} \quad \left(= \frac{1}{2}(\text{base})(\text{height})\right)$

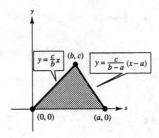

**59.** $f(x) = x^3$

$f'(x) = 3x^2$

At $(1, 1)$, $f'(1) = 3$.

Tangent line:

$y - 1 = 3(x - 1)$ or $y = 3x - 2$

The tangent line intersects $f(x) = x^3$ at $x = -2$.

$A = \int_{-2}^{1} [x^3 - (3x - 2)]\,dx = \left[\frac{x^4}{4} - \frac{3x^2}{2} + 2x\right]_{-2}^{1} = \frac{27}{4}$

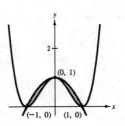

**61.** The variable is $y$.

**63.** $x^4 - 2x^2 + 1 \le 1 - x^2$ on $[-1, 1]$

$A = \int_{-1}^{1} [(1 - x^2) - (x^4 - 2x^2 + 1)]\,dx$

$= \int_{-1}^{1} (x^2 - x^4)\,dx$

$= \left[\frac{x^3}{3} - \frac{x^5}{5}\right]_{-1}^{1} = \frac{4}{15}$

You can use a single integral because $x^4 - 2x^2 + 1 \le 1 - x^2$ on $[-1, 1]$.

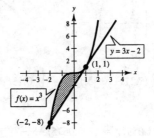

**65.** Offer 2 is better because the accumulated salary (area under the curve) is larger.

**67.**     $A = \displaystyle\int_{-3}^{3} (9 - x^2)\, dx = 36$

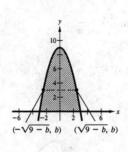

$$\int_{-\sqrt{9-b}}^{\sqrt{9-b}} [(9 - x^2) - b]\, dx = 18$$

$$\int_{0}^{\sqrt{9-b}} [(9 - b) - x^2]\, dx = 9$$

$$\left[ (9 - b)x - \frac{x^3}{3} \right]_{0}^{\sqrt{9-b}} = 9$$

$$\frac{2}{3}(9 - b)^{3/2} = 9$$

$$(9 - b)^{3/2} = \frac{27}{2}$$

$$9 - b = \frac{9}{\sqrt[3]{4}}$$

$$b = 9 - \frac{9}{\sqrt[3]{4}} \approx 3.330$$

**69.**     $\displaystyle\lim_{\|\Delta\| \to 0} \sum_{i=1}^{n} (x_i - x_i^2)\, \Delta x$

where $x_i = \dfrac{i}{n}$ and $\Delta x = \dfrac{1}{n}$ is the same as

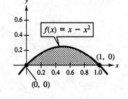

$$\int_{0}^{1} (x - x^2)\, dx = \left[ \frac{x^2}{2} - \frac{x^3}{3} \right]_{0}^{1} = \frac{1}{6}.$$

**71.** $\displaystyle\int_{0}^{5} \big[(7.21 + 0.58t) - (7.21 + 0.45t)\big]\, dt = \int_{0}^{5} 0.13t\, dt = \left[ \frac{0.13t^2}{2} \right]_{0}^{5} = \$1.625 \text{ billion}$

**73.** (a) $y_1 = (275.0675)(1.0537)^t = (275.0675)e^{0.0523t}$]

(b) $y_2 = (239.9407)(1.0417)^t = (239.9407)e^{0.0408t}$

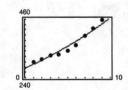

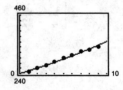

(c) $\displaystyle\int_{10}^{15} (y_1 - y_2)\, dt \approx 649.5$ billion dollars

(d) No, model $y_1 > y_2$ forever because $1.0537 > 1.0417$.

No, these models are not accurate. According to news reports, $E > R$ eventually.

**75.** The total area is 8 times the area of the shaded region to the right. A point $(x, y)$ is on the upper boundary of the region if

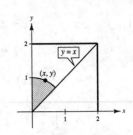

$$\sqrt{x^2 + y^2} = 2 - y$$

$$x^2 + y^2 = 4 - 4y + y^2$$

$$x^2 = 4 - 4y$$

$$4y = 4 - x^2$$

$$y = 1 - \frac{x^2}{4}.$$

We now determine where this curve intersects the line $y = x$.

$$x = 1 - \frac{x^2}{4}$$

$$x^2 + 4x - 4 = 0$$

$$x = \frac{-4 \pm \sqrt{16 + 16}}{2} = -2 \pm 2\sqrt{2} \implies x = -2 + 2\sqrt{2}$$

$$\text{Total area} = 8 \int_0^{-2+2\sqrt{2}} \left(1 - \frac{x^2}{4} - x\right) dx$$

$$= 8\left[x - \frac{x^3}{12} - \frac{x^2}{2}\right]_0^{-2+2\sqrt{2}} = \frac{16}{3}\left(4\sqrt{2} - 5\right) \approx 8(0.4379) = 3.503$$

**77. (a)** $A = 2\left[\int_0^5 \left(1 - \frac{1}{3}\sqrt{5 - x}\right) dx + \int_5^{5.5} (1 - 0)\, dx\right]$

$$= 2\left(\left[x + \frac{2}{9}(5 - x)^{3/2}\right]_0^5 + \left[x\right]_5^{5.5}\right) = 2\left(5 - \frac{10\sqrt{5}}{9} + 5.5 - 5\right) \approx 6.031 \text{ m}^2$$

**(b)** $V = 2A \approx 2(6.031) \approx 12.062 \text{ m}^3$        **(c)** $5000\,V \approx 5000(12.062) = 60{,}310$ pounds

**79.** True

**81.** False. Let $f(x) = x$ and $g(x) = 2x - x^2$. $f$ and $g$ intersect at $(1, 1)$, the midpoint of $[0, 2]$. But

$$\int_a^b [f(x) - g(x)]\, dx = \int_0^2 [x - (2x - x^2)]\, dx = \frac{2}{3} \neq 0.$$

## Section 6.2    Volume: The Disk Method

**1.** $V = \pi \int_0^1 (-x + 1)^2\, dx = \pi \int_0^1 (x^2 - 2x + 1)\, dx = \pi\left[\frac{x^3}{3} - x^2 + x\right]_0^1 = \frac{\pi}{3}$

**3.** $V = \pi \int_1^4 (\sqrt{x})^2\, dx = \pi \int_1^4 x\, dx = \pi\left[\frac{x^2}{2}\right]_1^4 = \frac{15\pi}{2}$

**5.** $V = \pi \int_0^1 [(x^2)^2 - (x^3)^2]\, dx = \pi \int_0^1 (x^4 - x^6)\, dx = \pi\left[\frac{x^5}{5} - \frac{x^7}{7}\right]_0^1 = \frac{2\pi}{35}$

**7.** $y = x^2 \implies x = \sqrt{y}$

$$V = \pi \int_0^4 (\sqrt{y})^2\, dy = \pi \int_0^4 y\, dy$$

$$= \pi\left[\frac{y^2}{2}\right]_0^4 = 8\pi$$

**9.** $y = x^{2/3} \implies x = y^{3/2}$

$$V = \pi \int_0^1 (y^{3/2})^2\, dy = \pi \int_0^1 y^3\, dy = \pi\left[\frac{y^4}{4}\right]_0^1 = \frac{\pi}{4}$$

**11.** $y = \sqrt{x}$, $y = 0$, $x = 4$

(a) $R(x) = \sqrt{x}$, $r(x) = 0$

$$V = \pi \int_0^4 \left(\sqrt{x}\right)^2 dx$$

$$= \pi \int_0^4 x \, dx = \left[\frac{\pi}{2}x^2\right]_0^4 = 8\pi$$

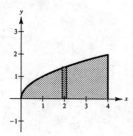

(b) $R(y) = 4$, $r(y) = y^2$

$$V = \pi \int_0^2 (16 - y^4) \, dy$$

$$= \pi \left[16y - \frac{1}{5}y^5\right]_0^2 = \frac{128\pi}{5}$$

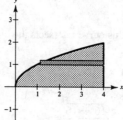

(c) $R(y) = 4 - y^2$, $r(y) = 0$

$$V = \pi \int_0^2 (4 - y^2)^2 \, dy$$

$$= \pi \int_0^2 (16 - 8y^2 + y^4) \, dy$$

$$= \pi \left[16y - \frac{8}{3}y^3 + \frac{1}{5}y^5\right]_0^2 = \frac{256\pi}{15}$$

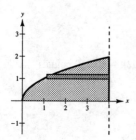

(d) $R(y) = 6 - y^2$, $r(y) = 2$

$$V = \pi \int_0^2 \left[(6 - y^2)^2 - 4\right] dy$$

$$= \pi \int_0^2 (32 - 12y^2 + y^4) \, dy$$

$$= \pi \left[32y - 4y^3 + \frac{1}{5}y^5\right]_0^2 = \frac{192\pi}{5}$$

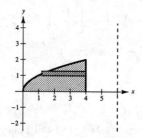

**13.** $y = x^2$, $y = 4x - x^2$ intersect at $(0, 0)$ and $(2, 4)$.

(a) $R(x) = 4x - x^2$ $r(x) = x^2$

$$V = \pi \int_0^2 \left[(4x - x^2)^2 - x^4\right] dx$$

$$= \pi \int_0^2 (16x^2 - 8x^3) \, dx$$

$$= \pi \left[\frac{16}{3}x^3 - 2x^4\right]_0^2 = \frac{32\pi}{3}$$

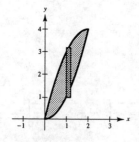

(b) $R(x) = 6 - x^2$, $r(x) = 6 - (4x - x^2)$

$$V = \pi \int_0^2 \left[(6 - x^2)^2 - (6 - 4x + x^2)^2\right] dx$$

$$= 8\pi \int_0^2 (x^3 - 5x^2 + 6x) \, dx$$

$$= 8\pi \left[\frac{x^4}{4} - \frac{5}{3}x^3 + 3x^2\right]_0^2 = \frac{64\pi}{3}$$

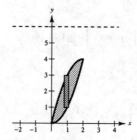

**15.** $R(x) = 4 - x, \; r(x) = 1$

$$V = \pi \int_0^3 [(4-x)^2 - (1)^2] \, dx$$

$$= \pi \int_0^3 (x^2 - 8x + 15) \, dx$$

$$= \pi \left[ \frac{x^3}{3} - 4x^2 + 15x \right]_0^3 = 18\pi$$

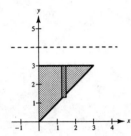

**17.** $R(x) = 4, \; r(x) = 4 - \dfrac{1}{1+x}$

$$V = \pi \int_0^3 \left[ 4^2 - \left( 4 - \frac{1}{1+x} \right)^2 \right] dx$$

$$= \pi \int_0^3 \left[ \frac{8}{1+x} - \frac{1}{(1+x)^2} \right] dx$$

$$= \pi \left[ 8 \ln(1+x) + \frac{1}{1+x} \right]_0^3$$

$$= \pi \left[ 8 \ln 4 + \frac{1}{4} - 1 \right]$$

$$= \left( 8 \ln 4 - \frac{3}{4} \right) \pi \approx 32.485$$

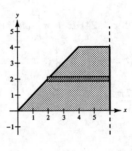

**19.** $R(y) = 6 - y, \; r(y) = 0$

$$V = \pi \int_0^4 (6-y)^2 \, dy$$

$$= \pi \int_0^4 (y^2 - 12y + 36) \, dy$$

$$= \pi \left[ \frac{y^3}{3} - 6y^2 + 36y \right]_0^4$$

$$= \frac{208\pi}{3}$$

**21.** $R(y) = 6 - y^2, \; r(y) = 2$

$$V = \pi \int_{-2}^2 [(6-y^2)^2 - (2)^2] \, dy$$

$$= 2\pi \int_0^2 (y^4 - 12y^2 + 32) \, dy$$

$$= 2\pi \left[ \frac{y^5}{5} - 4y^3 + 32y \right]_0^2$$

$$= \frac{384\pi}{5}$$

**23.** $R(x) = \dfrac{1}{\sqrt{x+1}}, \; r(x) = 0$

$$V = \pi \int_0^3 \left( \frac{1}{\sqrt{x+1}} \right)^2 dx$$

$$= \pi \int_0^3 \frac{1}{x+1} \, dx$$

$$= \left[ \pi \ln|x+1| \right]_0^3 = \pi \ln 4$$

**25.** $R(x) = \dfrac{1}{x}, \; r(x) = 0$

$$V = \pi \int_1^4 \left(\dfrac{1}{x}\right)^2 dx$$

$$= \pi \left[-\dfrac{1}{x}\right]_1^4$$

$$= \dfrac{3\pi}{4}$$

**27.** $R(x) = e^{-x}, \; r(x) = 0$

$$V = \pi \int_0^1 (e^{-x})^2 \, dx$$

$$= \pi \int_0^1 e^{-2x} \, dx$$

$$= \left[-\dfrac{\pi}{2} e^{-2x}\right]_0^1$$

$$= \dfrac{\pi}{2}(1 - e^{-2}) \approx 1.358$$

**29.** $V = \pi \int_0^2 \left[(5 + 2x - x^2)^2 - (x^2 + 1)^2\right] dx + \pi \int_2^3 \left[(x^2 + 1)^2 - (5 + 2x - x^2)^2\right] dx$

$$= \pi \int_0^2 (-4x^3 - 8x^2 + 20x + 24) \, dx + \pi \int_2^3 (4x^3 + 8x^2 - 20x - 24) \, dx$$

$$= \pi \left[-x^4 - \dfrac{8}{3}x^3 + 10x^2 + 24x\right]_0^2 + \pi \left[x^3 + \dfrac{8}{3}x^3 - 10x^2 - 24x\right]_2^3$$

$$= \pi \dfrac{152}{3} + \pi \dfrac{125}{3} = \dfrac{277\pi}{3}$$

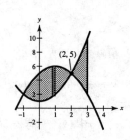

**31.** $y = 6 - 3x \implies x = \dfrac{1}{3}(6 - y)$

$$V = \pi \int_0^6 \left[\dfrac{1}{3}(6 - y)\right]^2 dy$$

$$= \dfrac{\pi}{9} \int_0^6 [36 - 12y + y^2] \, dy$$

$$= \dfrac{\pi}{9} \left[36y - 6y^2 + \dfrac{y^3}{3}\right]_0^6$$

$$= \dfrac{\pi}{9} \left[216 - 216 + \dfrac{216}{3}\right]$$

$$= 8\pi$$

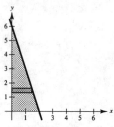

**33.** $V = \pi \int_0^\pi [\sin x]^2 \, dx \approx 4.9348$

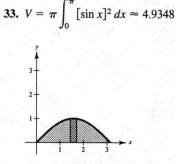

**35.** $V = \pi \int_0^2 [e^{-x^2}]^2 \, dx \approx 1.9686$

**37.** $V = \pi \int_{-1}^2 [e^{x/2} + e^{-x/2}]^2 \, dx \approx 49.0218$

**39.** $A \approx 3$

Matches (a)

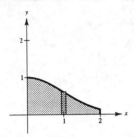

**41.** Disk Method:

$$V = \pi \int_a^b [R(x)]^2 \, dx \quad \text{or} \quad V = \pi \int_c^d [R(y)]^2 \, dy$$

Washer Method:

$$V = \pi \int_a^b ([R(x)]^2 - [r(x)]^2) \, dx \quad \text{or}$$

$$V = \pi \int_c^d ([R(y)]^2 - [r(y)]^2) \, dy$$

**43.**

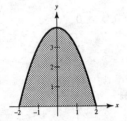

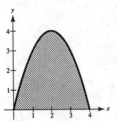

The volumes are the same because the solid has been translated horizontally.

**45.** $R(x) = \dfrac{1}{2}x, \ r(x) = 0$

$V = \pi \int_0^6 \dfrac{1}{4}x^2 \, dx$

$= \left[ \dfrac{\pi}{12}x^3 \right]_0^6 = 18\pi$

**Note:** $V = \dfrac{1}{3}\pi r^2 h$

$= \dfrac{1}{3}\pi(3^2)6$

$= 18\pi$

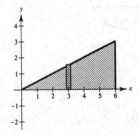

**47.** $R(x) = \sqrt{r^2 - x^2}, \ r(x) = 0$

$V = \pi \int_{-r}^r (r^2 - x^2) \, dx$

$= 2\pi \int_0^r (r^2 - x^2) \, dx$

$= 2\pi \left[ r^2 x - \dfrac{1}{3}x^3 \right]_0^r$

$= 2\pi \left( r^3 - \dfrac{1}{3}r^3 \right) = \dfrac{4}{3}\pi r^3$

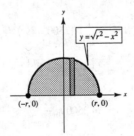

**49.** $x = r - \dfrac{r}{H}y = r\left(1 - \dfrac{y}{H}\right),\ R(y) = r\left(1 - \dfrac{y}{H}\right),\ r(y) = 0$

$$V = \pi \int_0^h \left[r\left(1 - \frac{y}{H}\right)\right]^2 dy = \pi r^2 \int_0^h \left(1 - \frac{2}{H}y + \frac{1}{H^2}y^2\right) dy$$

$$= \pi r^2 \left[y - \frac{1}{H}y^2 + \frac{1}{3H^2}y^3\right]_0^h$$

$$= \pi r^2 \left(h - \frac{h^2}{H} + \frac{h^3}{3H^2}\right)$$

$$= \pi r^2 h\left(1 - \frac{h}{H} + \frac{h^2}{3H^2}\right)$$

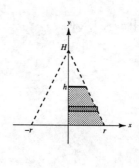

**51.** $V = \pi \int_0^2 \left(\dfrac{1}{8}x^2 \sqrt{2 - x}\right)^2 dx = \dfrac{\pi}{64}\int_0^2 x^4(2 - x)\,dx = \dfrac{\pi}{64}\left[\dfrac{2x^5}{5} - \dfrac{x^6}{6}\right]_0^2 = \dfrac{\pi}{30}$

**53.** (a) $R(x) = \dfrac{3}{5}\sqrt{25 - x^2},\ r(x) = 0$

$$V = \frac{9\pi}{25}\int_{-5}^{5}(25 - x^2)\,dx$$

$$= \frac{18\pi}{25}\int_0^5 (25 - x^2)\,dx$$

$$= \frac{18\pi}{25}\left[25x - \frac{x^3}{3}\right]_0^5 = 60\pi$$

(b) $R(y) = \dfrac{5}{3}\sqrt{9 - y^2},\ r(y) = 0,\ x \geq 0$

$$V = \frac{25\pi}{9}\int_0^3 (9 - y^2)\,dy$$

$$= \frac{25\pi}{9}\left[9y - \frac{y^3}{3}\right]_0^3 = 50\pi$$

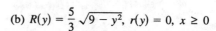

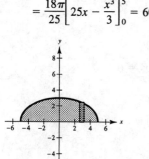

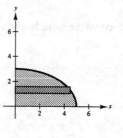

**55.** Total volume: $V = \dfrac{4\pi(50)^3}{3} = \dfrac{500,000}{3}$ ft$^3$

Volume of water in the tank:

$$\pi \int_{-50}^{y_0} \left(\sqrt{2500 - y^2}\right)^2 dy = \pi \int_{-50}^{y_0} (2500 - y^2)\,dy$$

$$= \pi\left[2500y - \frac{y^3}{3}\right]_{-50}^{y_0}$$

$$= \pi\left(2500y_0 - \frac{y_0^3}{3} + \frac{250,000}{3}\right)$$

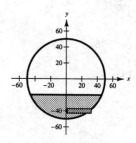

When the tank is one-fourth of its capacity:

$$\frac{1}{4}\left(\frac{500,000\pi}{3}\right) = \pi\left(2500y_0 - \frac{y_0^3}{3} + \frac{250,00}{3}\right)$$

$$125,000 = 7500y_0 - y_0^3 + 250,000$$

$$y_0^3 - 7500y_0 - 125,000 = 0$$

$$y_0 \approx -17.36$$

Depth: $-17.36 - (-50) = 32.64$ feet

When the tank is three-fourths of its capacity the depth is $100 - 32.64 = 67.36$ feet.

**57. (a)** $\pi \int_0^h r^2 \, dx$   (ii)

is the volume of a right circular cylinder with radius $r$ and height $h$.

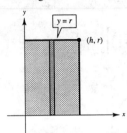

**(b)** $\pi \int_{-b}^b \left( a \sqrt{1 - \dfrac{x^2}{b^2}} \right)^2 dx$   (iv)

is the volume of an ellipsoid with axes $2a$ and $2b$.

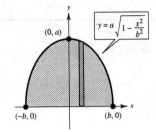

**(c)** $\pi \int_{-r}^r \left( \sqrt{r^2 - x^2} \right)^2 dx$   (iii)

is the volume of a sphere with radius $r$.

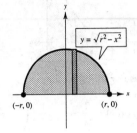

**(d)** $\pi \int_0^h \left( \dfrac{rx}{h} \right)^2 dx$  (i)

is the volume of a right circular cone with the radius of the base as $r$ and height $h$.

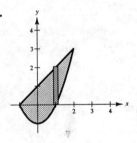

**(e)** $\pi \int_{-r}^r \left[ \left( R + \sqrt{r^2 - x^2} \right)^2 - \left( R - \sqrt{r^2 - x^2} \right)^2 \right] dx$   (v)

is the volume of a torus with the radius of its circular cross section as $r$ and the distance from the axis of the torus to the center of its cross section as $R$.

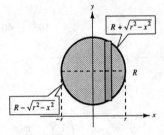

**59.**

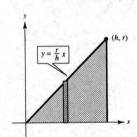

Base of Cross Section $= (x + 1) - (x^2 - 1) = 2 + x - x^2$

**(a)** $A(x) = b^2 = (2 + x - x^2)^2$

$\qquad = 4 + 4x - 3x^2 - 2x^3 + x^4$

$V = \displaystyle\int_{-1}^2 (4 + 4x - 3x^2 - 2x^3 + x^4) \, dx$

$\qquad = \left[ 4x + 2x^3 - x^3 - \dfrac{1}{2}x^4 + \dfrac{1}{5}x^5 \right]_{-1}^2 = \dfrac{81}{10}$

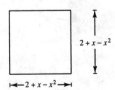

**(b)** $A(x) = bh = (2 + x - x^2)1$

$V = \displaystyle\int_{-1}^2 (2 + x - x^2) \, dx = \left[ 2x + \dfrac{x^2}{2} - \dfrac{x^3}{3} \right]_{-1}^2 = \dfrac{9}{2}$

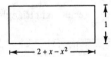

**61.**

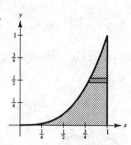

Base of Cross Section $= 1 - \sqrt[3]{y}$

(a) $A(y) = b^2 = \left(1 - \sqrt[3]{y}\right)^2$

$$V = \int_0^1 \left(1 - \sqrt[3]{y}\right)^2 dy$$

$$= \int_0^1 \left(1 - 2y^{1/3} + y^{2/3}\right) dy$$

$$= \left[y - \frac{3}{2}y^{4/3} + \frac{3}{5}y^{5/3}\right]_0^1 = \frac{1}{10}$$

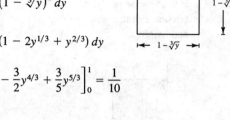

(b) $A(y) = \frac{1}{2}\pi r^2 = \frac{1}{2}\pi\left(\frac{1 - \sqrt[3]{y}}{2}\right)^2 = \frac{1}{8}\pi\left(1 - \sqrt[3]{y}\right)^2$

$$V = \frac{1}{8}\pi \int_0^1 \left(1 - \sqrt[3]{y}\right)^2 dy = \frac{\pi}{8}\left(\frac{1}{10}\right) = \frac{\pi}{80}$$

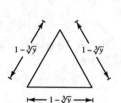

(c) $A(y) = \frac{1}{2}bh = \frac{1}{2}(1 - \sqrt[3]{y})\left(\frac{\sqrt{3}}{2}\right)(1 - \sqrt[3]{y})$

$$= \frac{\sqrt{3}}{4}(1 - \sqrt[3]{y})^2$$

$$V = \frac{\sqrt{3}}{4}\int_0^1 (1 - \sqrt[3]{y})^2 dy = \frac{\sqrt{3}}{4}\left(\frac{1}{10}\right) = \frac{\sqrt{3}}{40}$$

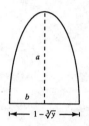

(d) $A(y) = \frac{1}{2}\pi ab = \frac{\pi}{2}(2)(1 - \sqrt[3]{y})\frac{1 - \sqrt[3]{y}}{2}$

$$= \frac{\pi}{2}(1 - \sqrt[3]{y})^2$$

$$V = \frac{\pi}{2}\int_0^1 (1 - \sqrt[3]{y})^2 dy = \frac{\pi}{2}\left(\frac{1}{10}\right) = \frac{\pi}{20}$$

**63.** Let $A_1(x)$ and $A_2(x)$ equal the areas of the cross sections of the two solids for $a \le x \le b$. Since $A_1(x) = A_2(x)$, we have

$$V_1 = \int_a^b A_1(x)\,dx = \int_a^b A_2(x)\,dx = V_2$$

Thus, the volumes are the same.

**65.** $\frac{4}{3}\pi(25 - r^2)^{3/2} = \frac{1}{2}\left(\frac{4}{3}\right)\pi(125)$

$$(25 - r^2)^{3/2} = \frac{125}{2}$$

$$25 - r^2 = \left(\frac{125}{2}\right)^{2/3}$$

$$25 - \frac{25}{(2^{2/3})} = r^2$$

$$25(1 - 2^{-2/3}) = r^2$$

$$r = 5\sqrt{1 - 2^{-2/3}} \approx 3.0415$$

**67.** (a) Since the cross sections are isosceles right triangles:

$$A(x) = \frac{1}{2}bh = \frac{1}{2}\left(\sqrt{r^2 - y^2}\right)\left(\sqrt{r^2 - y^2}\right) = \frac{1}{2}(r^2 - y^2)$$

$$V = \frac{1}{2}\int_{-r}^r (r^2 - y^2)\,dy = \int_0^r (r^2 - y^2)\,dy = \left[r^2 y - \frac{y^3}{3}\right]_0^r = \frac{2}{3}r^3$$

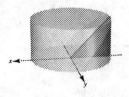

(b) $A(x) = \frac{1}{2}bh = \frac{1}{2}\sqrt{r^2 - y^2}\left(\sqrt{r^2 - y^2}\tan\theta\right) = \frac{\tan\theta}{2}(r^2 - y^2)$

$$V = \frac{\tan\theta}{2}\int_{-r}^r (r^2 - y^2)\,dy = \tan\theta\int_0^r (r^2 - y^2)\,dy = \tan\theta\left[r^2 y - \frac{y^3}{3}\right]_0^r = \frac{2}{3}r^3\tan\theta$$

As $\theta \to 90°$, $V \to \infty$.

# Section 6.3    Volume:  The Shell Method

**1.** $p(x) = x$

$h(x) = x$

$V = 2\pi \int_0^2 x(x)\, dx = \left[\frac{2\pi x^3}{3}\right]_0^2 = \frac{16\pi}{3}$

$= \left[\frac{2\pi x^3}{3}\right]_0^2 = \frac{16\pi}{3}$

**3.** $p(x) = x$

$h(x) = \sqrt{x}$

$V = 2\pi \int_0^4 x\sqrt{x}\, dx$

$= 2\pi \int_0^4 x^{3/2}\, dx$

$= \left[\frac{4\pi}{5} x^{5/2}\right]_0^4 = \frac{128\pi}{5}$

**5.** $p(x) = x$

$h(x) = x^2$

$V = 2\pi \int_0^2 x^3\, dx$

$= \left[\frac{\pi}{2} x^4\right]_0^2 = 8\pi$

**7.** $p(x) = x$

$h(x) = (4x - x^2) - x^2 = 4x - 2x^2$

$V = 2\pi \int_0^2 x(4x - 2x^2)\, dx$

$= 4\pi \int_0^2 (2x^2 - x^3)\, dx$

$= 4\pi \left[\frac{2}{3}x^3 - \frac{1}{4}x^4\right]_0^2 = \frac{16\pi}{3}$

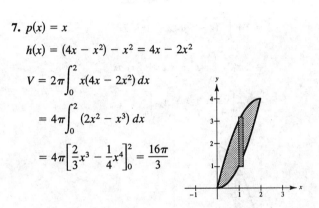

**9.** $p(x) = x$

$h(x) = 4 - (4x - x^2) = x^2 - 4x + 4$

$V = 2\pi \int_0^2 (x^3 - 4x^2 + 4x)\, dx$

$= 2\pi \left[\frac{x^4}{4} - \frac{4}{3}x^3 + 2x^2\right]_0^2 = \frac{8\pi}{3}$

**11.** $p(x) = x$

$h(x) = \frac{1}{\sqrt{2\pi}} e^{-x^2/2}$

$V = 2\pi \int_0^1 x\left(\frac{1}{\sqrt{2\pi}} e^{-x^2/2}\right) dx$

$= \sqrt{2\pi} \int_0^1 e^{-x^2/2} x\, dx$

$= \left[-\sqrt{2\pi}\, e^{-x^2/2}\right]_0^1 = \sqrt{2\pi}\left(1 - \frac{1}{\sqrt{e}}\right) \approx 0.986$

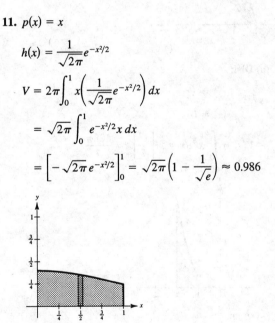

**13.** $p(y) = y$

$h(y) = 2 - y$

$V = 2\pi \int_0^2 y(2 - y)\, dy$

$= 2\pi \int_0^2 (2y - y^2)\, dy$

$= 2\pi \left[y^2 - \frac{y^3}{3}\right]_0^2 = \frac{8\pi}{3}$

**15.** $p(y) = y$ and $h(y) = 1$ if $0 \le y < \dfrac{1}{2}$.

$p(y) = y$ and $h(y) = \dfrac{1}{y} - 1$ if $\dfrac{1}{2} \le y \le 1$.

$V = 2\pi \displaystyle\int_0^{1/2} y \, dy + 2\pi \int_{1/2}^1 (1 - y) \, dy$

$= 2\pi \left[ \dfrac{y^2}{2} \right]_0^{1/2} + 2\pi \left[ y - \dfrac{y^2}{2} \right]_{1/2}^1 = \dfrac{\pi}{4} + \dfrac{\pi}{4} = \dfrac{\pi}{2}$

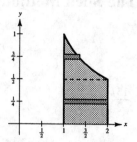

**17.** $p(x) = 4 - x$

$h(x) = 4x - x^2 - x^2 = 4x - 2x^2$

$V = 2\pi \displaystyle\int_0^2 (4 - x)(4x - 2x^2) \, dx$

$= 2\pi(2) \displaystyle\int_0^2 (x^3 - 6x^2 + 8x) \, dx$

$= 4\pi \left[ \dfrac{x^4}{4} - 2x^3 + 4x^2 \right]_0^2 = 16\pi$

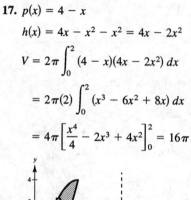

**19.** $p(x) = 5 - x$

$h(x) = 4x - x^2$

$V = 2\pi \displaystyle\int_0^4 (5 - x)(4x - x^2) \, dx$

$= 2\pi \displaystyle\int_0^4 (x^3 - 9x^2 + 20x) \, dx$

$= 2\pi \left[ \dfrac{x^4}{4} - 3x^3 + 10x^2 \right]_0^4 = 64\pi$

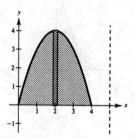

**21. (a) Disk**

$R(x) = x^3$

$r(x) = 0$

$V = \pi \displaystyle\int_0^2 x^6 \, dx = \pi \left[ \dfrac{x^7}{7} \right]_0^2 = \dfrac{128\pi}{7}$

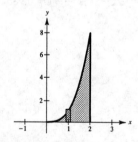

**(b) Shell**

$p(x) = x$

$h(x) = x^3$

$V = 2\pi \displaystyle\int_0^2 x^4 \, dx = 2\pi \left[ \dfrac{x^5}{5} \right]_0^2 = \dfrac{64\pi}{5}$

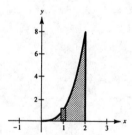

**(c) Shell**

$p(x) = 4 - x$

$h(x) = x^3$

$V = 2\pi \displaystyle\int_0^2 (4 - x)x^3 \, dx$

$= 2\pi \displaystyle\int_0^2 (4x^3 - x^4) \, dx$

$= 2\pi \left[ x^4 - \dfrac{1}{5}x^5 \right]_0^2 = \dfrac{96\pi}{5}$

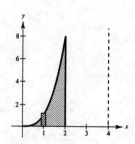

**23.** (a) **Shell**

$$p(y) = y$$

$$h(y) = (a^{1/2} - y^{1/2})^2$$

$$V = 2\pi \int_0^a y(a - 2a^{1/2}y^{1/2} + y)\, dy$$

$$= 2\pi \int_0^a (ay - 2a^{1/2}y^{3/2} + y^2)\, dy$$

$$= 2\pi \left[ \frac{a}{2}y^2 - \frac{4a^{1/2}}{5}y^{5/2} + \frac{y^3}{3} \right]_0^a$$

$$= 2\pi \left[ \frac{a^3}{2} - \frac{4a^3}{5} + \frac{a^3}{3} \right] = \frac{\pi a^3}{15}$$

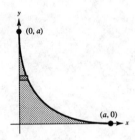

(b)  Same as part (a) by symmetry

**25.**  $V = 2\pi \int_x^d p(y)h(y)\, dy$    or    $V = 2\pi \int_a^b p(x)h(x)\, dx$

**27.**  $\pi \int_1^5 (x - 1)\, dx = \pi \int_1^5 \left(\sqrt{x - 1}\right)^2 dx$

This integral represents the volume of the solid generated by revolving the region bounded by $y = \sqrt{x - 1}$, $y = 0$, and $x = 5$ about the $x$-axis by using the Disk Method.

$$2\pi \int_0^2 y[5 - (y^2 + 1)]\, dy$$

represents this same volume by using the Shell Method.

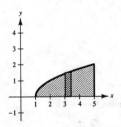

Disk Method

(c) **Shell**

$$p(x) = a - x$$

$$h(x) = (a^{1/2} - x^{1/2})^2$$

$$V = 2\pi \int_0^a (a - x)(a^{1/2} - x^{1/2})^2\, dx$$

$$= 2\pi \int_0^a (a^2 - 2a^{3/2}x^{1/2} + 2a^{1/2}x^{3/2} - x^2)\, dx$$

$$= 2\pi \left[ a^2x - \frac{4}{3}a^{3/2}x^{3/2} + \frac{4}{5}a^{1/2}x^{5/2} - \frac{1}{3}x^3 \right]_0^a = \frac{4\pi a^3}{15}$$

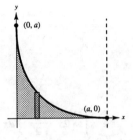

**29.** (a)

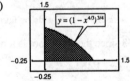

(b)  $x^{4/3} + y^{4/3} = 1,\ x = 0,\ y = 0$

$$y = (1 - x^{4/3})^{3/4}$$

$$V = 2\pi \int_0^1 x(1 - x^{4/3})^{3/4}\, dx \approx 1.5056$$

**31.** (a)

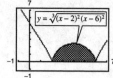

$y = \sqrt[3]{(x-2)^2(x-6)^2}$

(b) $V = 2\pi \displaystyle\int_2^6 x\sqrt[3]{(x-2)^2(x-6)^2}\,dx \approx 187.249$

**33.** $y = 2e^{-x}, \; y = 0, \; x = 0, \; x = 2$

Volume $\approx 7.5$

Matches (d)

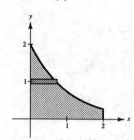

**35.** $p(x) = x$

$h(x) = 2 - \dfrac{1}{2}x^2$

$V = 2\pi \displaystyle\int_0^2 x\left(2 - \dfrac{1}{2}x^2\right)dx = 2\pi \int_0^2 \left(2x - \dfrac{1}{2}x^3\right)dx = 2\pi\left[x^2 - \dfrac{1}{8}x^4\right]_0^2 = 4\pi \text{ (total volume)}$

Now find $x_0$ such that

$$\pi \doteq 2\pi \int_0^{x_0}\left(2x - \dfrac{1}{2}x^3\right)dx$$

$$1 = 2\left[x^2 - \dfrac{1}{8}x^4\right]_0^{x_0}$$

$$1 = 2x_0^2 - \dfrac{1}{4}x_0^4$$

$$x_0^4 - 8x_0^2 + 4 = 0$$

$$x_0^2 = 4 \pm 2\sqrt{3} \quad \text{(Quadratic Formula)}$$

Take $x_0 = \sqrt{4 - 2\sqrt{3}}$ since the other root is too large.

Diameter: $2\sqrt{4 - 2\sqrt{3}} \approx 1.464$

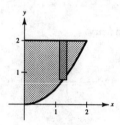

**37.** $V = 4\pi \displaystyle\int_{-1}^1 (2 - x)\sqrt{1 - x^2}\,dx$

$= 8\pi \displaystyle\int_{-1}^1 \sqrt{1 - x^2}\,dx - 4\pi \int_{-1}^1 x\sqrt{1 - x^2}\,dx$

$= 8\pi\left(\dfrac{\pi}{2}\right) + 2\pi \displaystyle\int_{-1}^1 x(1 - x^2)^{1/2}(-2)\,dx$

$= 4\pi^2 + \left[2\pi\left(\dfrac{2}{3}\right)(1 - x^2)^{3/2}\right]_{-1}^1 = 4\pi^2$

**39. Disk Method**

$R(y) = \sqrt{r^2 - y^2}$

$r(y) = 0$

$V = \pi \displaystyle\int_{r-h}^r (r^2 - y^2)\,dy$

$= \pi\left[r^2 y - \dfrac{y^3}{3}\right]_{r-h}^r = \dfrac{1}{3}\pi h^2(3r - h)$

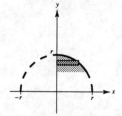

**41.** (a) $2\pi \int_0^r hx\left(1 - \dfrac{x}{r}\right) dx$  (ii)

is the volume of a right circular cone with the radius of the base as $r$ and height $h$.

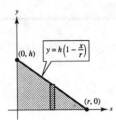

(c) $2\pi \int_0^r 2x\sqrt{r^2 - x^2}\, dx$  (iii) is the

volume of a sphere with radius $r$.

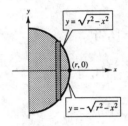

(e) $2\pi \int_0^b 2ax\sqrt{1 - (x^2/b^2)}\, dx$  (iv)

is the volume of an ellipsoid with axes $2a$ and $2b$.

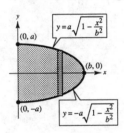

(b) $2\pi \int_{-r}^r (R - x)\left(2\sqrt{r^2 - x^2}\right) dx$  (v)

is the volume of a torus with the radius of its circular cross section as $r$ and the distance from the axis of the torus to the center of its cross section as $R$.

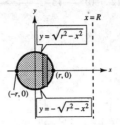

(d) $2\pi \int_0^r hx\, dx$  (i) is the volume of a

right circular cylinder with a radius of $r$ and a height of $h$.

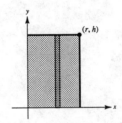

**43.** (a) $V = 2\pi \int_0^{200} xf(x)\, dx$

$\approx \dfrac{2\pi(200)}{3(8)}[0 + 4(25)(19) + 2(50)(19) + 4(75)(17) + 2(100)15 + 4(125)(14) + 2(150)(10) + 4(175)(6) + 0]$

$\approx 1,366,593$ cubic feet

(b) $d = -0.000561x^2 + 0.0189x + 19.39$

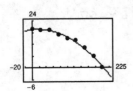

(c) $V \approx 2\pi \int_0^{200} xd(x)\, dx \approx 2\pi(213,800) = 1,343,345$ cubic feet

(d) Number gallons $\approx V(7.48) = 10,048,221$ gallons

# Section 6.4     Arc Length and Surfaces of Revolution

**1.** $(0, 0), (5, 12)$

   (a) $d = \sqrt{(5 - 0)^2 + (12 - 0)^2} = 13$

   (b) $y = \dfrac{12}{5}x$

      $y' = \dfrac{12}{5}$

      $s = \displaystyle\int_0^5 \sqrt{1 + \left(\dfrac{12}{5}\right)^2}\, dx = \left[\dfrac{13}{5}x\right]_0^5 = 13$

**3.** $y = \dfrac{2}{3}x^{3/2} + 1$

   $y' = x^{1/2}, [0, 1]$

   $s = \displaystyle\int_0^1 \sqrt{1 + x}\, dx$

    $= \left[\dfrac{2}{3}(1 + x)^{3/2}\right]_0^1$

    $= \dfrac{2}{3}\left(\sqrt{8} - 1\right) \approx 1.219$

**5.** $y = \dfrac{3}{2}x^{2/3}$

   $y' = \dfrac{1}{x^{1/3}}, [1, 8]$

   $s = \displaystyle\int_1^8 \sqrt{1 + \left(\dfrac{1}{x^{1/3}}\right)^2}\, dx$

    $= \displaystyle\int_1^8 \sqrt{\dfrac{x^{2/3} + 1}{x^{2/3}}}\, dx$

    $= \dfrac{3}{2}\displaystyle\int_1^8 \sqrt{x^{2/3} + 1}\left(\dfrac{2}{3x^{1/3}}\right) dx$

    $= \dfrac{3}{2}\left[\dfrac{2}{3}(x^{2/3} + 1)^{3/2}\right]_1^8$

    $= 5\sqrt{5} - 2\sqrt{2} \approx 8.352$

**7.** $\qquad y = \dfrac{x^4}{8} + \dfrac{1}{4x^2}$

   $y' = \dfrac{1}{2}x^3 - \dfrac{1}{2x^3}, [1, 2]$

   $1 + (y')^2 = \left(\dfrac{1}{2}x^3 + \dfrac{1}{2x^3}\right)^2, [1, 2]$

   $s = \displaystyle\int_a^b \sqrt{1 + (y')^2}\, dx$

    $= \displaystyle\int_1^2 \left(\dfrac{1}{2}x^3 + \dfrac{1}{2x^3}\right) dx$

    $= \left[\dfrac{1}{8}x^4 - \dfrac{1}{4x^2}\right]_1^2 = \dfrac{33}{16} \approx 2.063$

**9.** $\qquad y = \ln(\sin x), \left[\dfrac{\pi}{4}, \dfrac{3\pi}{4}\right]$

    $y' = \dfrac{1}{\sin x}\cos x = \cot x$

  $1 + (y')^2 = 1 + \cot^2 x = \csc^2 x$

    $s = \displaystyle\int_{\pi/4}^{3\pi/4} \csc x\, dx$

     $= \Big[\ln|\csc x - \cot x|\Big]_{\pi/4}^{3\pi/4}$

     $= \ln\left(\sqrt{2} + 1\right) - \ln\left(\sqrt{2} - 1\right) \approx 1.763$

**11.** (a) $y = 4 - x^2, 0 \le x \le 2$

   (b) $\qquad y' = -2x$

      $1 + (y')^2 = 1 + 4x^2$

      $L = \displaystyle\int_0^2 \sqrt{1 + 4x^2}\, dx$

   (c) $L \approx 4.647$

**13.** (a) $y = \dfrac{1}{x}, 1 \le x \le 3$

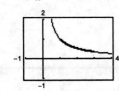

(b) $y' = -\dfrac{1}{x^2}$

$$1 + (y')^2 = 1 + \dfrac{1}{x^4}$$

$$L = \int_1^3 \sqrt{1 + \dfrac{1}{x^4}}\, dx$$

(c) $L \approx 2.147$

**15.** (a) $y = \sin x, 0 \le x \le \pi$

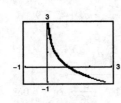

(b) $y' = \cos x$

$$1 + (y')^2 = 1 + \cos^2 x$$

$$L = \int_0^\pi \sqrt{1 + \cos^2 x}\, dx$$

(c) $L \approx 3.820$

**17.** (a) $x = e^{-y}, 0 \le y \le 2$

$y = -\ln x$

$1 \ge x \ge e^{-2} \approx 0.135$

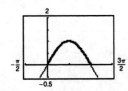

(b) $y' = -\dfrac{1}{x}$

$$1 + (y')^2 = 1 + \dfrac{1}{x^2}$$

$$L = \int_{e^{-2}}^1 \sqrt{1 + \dfrac{1}{x^2}}\, dx$$

(c) $L \approx 2.221$

Alternatively, you can do all the computations with respect to $y$.

(a) $x = e^{-y}\ 0 \le y \le 2$

(b) $\dfrac{dx}{dy} = -e^{-y}$

$$1 + \left(\dfrac{dx}{dy}\right)^2 = 1 + e^{-2y}$$

$$L = \int_0^2 \sqrt{1 + e^{-2y}}\, dy$$

(c) $L \approx 2.221$

**19.** (a) $y = 2\arctan x, 0 \le x \le 1$

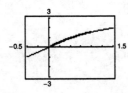

(b) $y' = \dfrac{2}{1 + x^2}$

$$L = \int_0^1 \sqrt{1 + \dfrac{4}{(1 + x^2)^2}}\, dx$$

(c) $L \approx 1.871$

**21.** $\displaystyle\int_0^2 \sqrt{1 + \left[\frac{d}{dx}\left(\frac{5}{x^2+1}\right)\right]^2}\, dx$

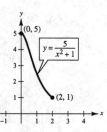

$s \approx 5$

Matches (b)

**23.** $y = x^3, \, [0, 4]$

(a) $d = \sqrt{(4-0)^2 + (64-0)^2} \approx 64.125$

(b) $d = \sqrt{(1-0)^2 + (1-0)^2} + \sqrt{(2-1)^2 + (8-1)^2} + \sqrt{(3-2)^2 + (27-8)^2} + \sqrt{(4-3)^2 + (64-27)^2}$

$\approx 64.525$

(c) $s = \displaystyle\int_0^4 \sqrt{1 + (3x^2)^2}\, dx = \int_0^4 \sqrt{1 + 9x^4}\, dx \approx 64.666$

(d) $64.672$

**25.** (a)

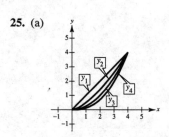

(c) $y_1' = 1, \, L_1 = \displaystyle\int_0^4 \sqrt{2}\, dx \approx 5.657$

$y_2' = \dfrac{3}{4}x^{1/2}, \, L_2 = \displaystyle\int_0^4 \sqrt{1 + \frac{9x}{16}}\, dx \approx 5.759$

$y_3' = \dfrac{1}{2}x, \, L_3 = \displaystyle\int_0^4 \sqrt{1 + \frac{x^2}{4}}\, dx \approx 5.916$

$y_4' = \dfrac{5}{16}x^{3/2}, \, L_4 = \displaystyle\int_0^4 \sqrt{1 + \frac{25}{256}x^3}\, dx \approx 6.063$

(b) $y_1, y_2, y_3, y_4$

**27.** $y = \dfrac{1}{3}[x^{3/2} - 3x^{1/2} + 2]$

When $x = 0$, $y = \frac{2}{3}$. Thus, the fleeting object has traveled $\frac{2}{3}$ units when it is caught.

$$y' = \frac{1}{3}\left[\frac{3}{2}x^{1/2} - \frac{3}{2}x^{-1/2}\right] = \left(\frac{1}{2}\right)\frac{x-1}{x^{1/2}}$$

$$1 + (y')^2 = 1 + \frac{(x-1)^2}{4x} = \frac{(x+1)^2}{4x}$$

$$s = \int_0^1 \frac{x+1}{2x^{1/2}}\, dx = \frac{1}{2}\int_0^1 (x^{1/2} + x^{-1/2})\, dx = \frac{1}{2}\left[\frac{2}{3}x^{3/2} + 2x^{1/2}\right]_0^1 = \frac{4}{3} = 2\left(\frac{2}{3}\right)$$

The pursuer has traveled twice the distance that the fleeing object has traveled when it is caught.

**29.** $\quad y = 20\cosh\dfrac{x}{20}, \; -20 \le x \le 20$

$y' = \sinh\dfrac{x}{20}$

$1 + (y')^2 = 1 + \sinh^2\dfrac{x}{20} = \cosh^2\dfrac{x}{20}$

$L = \displaystyle\int_{-20}^{20} \cosh\frac{x}{20}\, dx = 2\int_0^{20} \cosh\frac{x}{20}\, dx = 2(20)\sinh\frac{x}{20}\Big]_0^{20}$

$= 40\sinh(1) \approx 47.008 \text{ m.}$

**31.**
$$y = \sqrt{9 - x^2}$$

$$y' = \frac{-x}{\sqrt{9 - x^2}}$$

$$1 + (y')^2 = \frac{9}{9 - x^2}$$

$$s = \int_0^2 \sqrt{\frac{9}{9 - x^2}}\, dx$$

$$= \int_0^2 \frac{3}{\sqrt{9 - x^2}}\, dx$$

$$= \left[ 3 \arcsin \frac{x}{3} \right]_0^2$$

$$= 3 \left( \arcsin \frac{2}{3} - \arcsin 0 \right)$$

$$= 3 \arcsin \frac{2}{3} \approx 2.1892$$

**33.**
$$y = \frac{x^3}{3}$$

$$y' = x^2,\ [0, 3]$$

$$S = 2\pi \int_0^3 \frac{x^3}{3} \sqrt{1 + x^4}\, dx$$

$$= \frac{\pi}{6} \int_0^3 (1 + x^4)^{1/2}(4x^3)\, dx$$

$$= \left[ \frac{\pi}{9}(1 + x^4)^{3/2} \right]_0^3$$

$$= \frac{\pi}{9}\left(82\sqrt{82} - 1\right) \approx 258.85$$

**35.**
$$y = \frac{x^3}{6} + \frac{1}{2x}$$

$$y' = \frac{x^2}{2} - \frac{1}{2x^2}$$

$$1 + (y')^2 = \left( \frac{x^2}{2} + \frac{1}{2x^2} \right)^2,\ [1, 2]$$

$$S = 2\pi \int_1^2 \left( \frac{x^3}{6} + \frac{1}{2x} \right)\left( \frac{x^2}{2} + \frac{1}{2x^2} \right) dx$$

$$= 2\pi \int_1^2 \left( \frac{x^5}{12} + \frac{x}{3} + \frac{1}{4x^3} \right) dx$$

$$= 2\pi \left[ \frac{x^6}{72} + \frac{x^2}{6} - \frac{1}{8x^2} \right]_1^2 = \frac{47\pi}{16}$$

**37.**
$$y = \sqrt[3]{x} + 2$$

$$y' = \frac{1}{3x^{2/3}},\ [1, 8]$$

$$S = 2\pi \int_1^8 x \sqrt{1 + \frac{1}{9x^{4/3}}}\, dx$$

$$= \frac{2\pi}{3} \int_1^8 x^{1/3} \sqrt{9x^{4/3} + 1}\, dx$$

$$= \frac{\pi}{18} \int_1^8 (9x^{4/3} + 1)^{1/2}(12x^{1/3})\, dx$$

$$= \left[ \frac{\pi}{27}(9x^{4/3} + 1)^{3/2} \right]_1^8$$

$$= \frac{\pi}{27}\left(145\sqrt{145} - 10\sqrt{10}\right) \approx 199.48$$

**39.** $y = \sin x$

$$y' = \cos x,\ [0, \pi]$$

$$S = 2\pi \int_0^\pi \sin x \sqrt{1 + \cos^2 x}\, dx$$

$$\approx 14.4236$$

**41.** A rectifiable curve is one that has a finite arc length.

**43.** The precalculus formula is the surface area formula for the lateral surface of the frustum of a right circular cone. The representative element is

$$2\pi f(d_i)\sqrt{\Delta x_i^2 + \Delta y_i^2} = 2\pi f(di) \sqrt{1 + \left( \frac{\Delta y_i}{\Delta x_i} \right)^2}\, \Delta x_i.$$

**45.**
$$y = \frac{hx}{r}$$

$$y' = \frac{h}{r}$$

$$1 + (y')^2 = \frac{r^2 + h^2}{r^2}$$

$$S = 2\pi \int_0^r x\sqrt{\frac{r^2 + h^2}{r^2}}\, dx$$

$$= \left[\frac{2\pi\sqrt{r^2 + h^2}}{r}\left(\frac{x^2}{2}\right)\right]_0^r = \pi r\sqrt{r^2 + h^2}$$

**47.**
$$y = \sqrt{9 - x^2}$$

$$y' = \frac{-x}{\sqrt{9 - x^2}}$$

$$\sqrt{1 + (y')^2} = \frac{3}{\sqrt{9 - x^2}}$$

$$S = 2\pi \int_0^2 \frac{3x}{\sqrt{9 - x^2}}\, dx$$

$$= -3\pi \int_0^2 \frac{-2x}{\sqrt{9 - x^2}}\, dx$$

$$= \left[-6\pi\sqrt{9 - x^2}\right]_0^2$$

$$= 6\pi\left(3 - \sqrt{5}\right) \approx 14.40$$

See figure in Exercise 48.

**49.**
$$y = \frac{1}{3}x^{1/2} - x^{3/2}$$

$$y' = \frac{1}{6}x^{-1/2} - \frac{3}{2}x^{1/2} = \frac{1}{6}(x^{-1/2} - 9x^{1/2})$$

$$1 + (y')^2 = 1 + \frac{1}{36}(x^{-1} - 18 + 81x) = \frac{1}{36}(x^{-1/2} + 9x^{1/2})^2$$

$$S = 2\pi \int_0^{1/3} \left(\frac{1}{3}x^{1/2} - x^{3/2}\right)\sqrt{\frac{1}{36}(x^{-1/2} + 9^{1/2})^2}\, dx = \frac{2\pi}{6}\int_0^{1/3}\left(\frac{1}{3}x^{1/2} - x^{3/2}\right)(x^{-1/2} + 9x^{1/2})\, dx$$

$$= \frac{\pi}{3}\int_0^{1/3}\left(\frac{1}{3} + 2x - 9x^2\right)dx = \frac{\pi}{3}\left[\frac{1}{3}x + x^2 - 3x^3\right]_0^{1/3} = \frac{\pi}{27}\ \text{ft}^2 \approx 0.1164\ \text{ft}^2 \approx 16.8\ \text{in}^2$$

Amount of glass needed: $V = \frac{\pi}{27}\left(\frac{0.015}{12}\right) \approx 0.00015\ \text{ft}^3 \approx 0.25\ \text{in}^3$

**51.** (a) $y = f(x) = 0.0000001953x^4 - 0.0001804x^3 + 0.0496x^2 - 4.8323x + 536.9270$

(b) Area $= \displaystyle\int_0^{400} f(x)\, dx \approx 131{,}734.5$ square feet

$$\approx 3.0\ \text{acres}$$

(Answers will vary.)

(c) $L = \displaystyle\int_0^{400} \sqrt{1 + f'(x)^2}\, dx \approx 794.9$ feet

(Answers will vary.)

**53.** (a) $V = \pi \displaystyle\int_1^b \frac{1}{x^2}\, dx = \left[-\frac{\pi}{x}\right]_1^b = \pi\left(1 - \frac{1}{b}\right)$

(b) $S = 2\pi \displaystyle\int_1^b \frac{1}{x}\sqrt{1 + \left(-\frac{1}{x^2}\right)^2}\, dx$

$$= 2\pi \int_1^b \frac{1}{x}\sqrt{1 + \frac{1}{x^4}}\, dx$$

$$= 2\pi \int_1^b \frac{\sqrt{x^4 + 1}}{x^3}\, dx$$

**—CONTINUED—**

**53. —CONTINUED—**

(c) $\lim\limits_{b\to\infty} V = \lim\limits_{b\to\infty} \pi\left(1 - \frac{1}{b}\right) = \pi$

(d) Since

$$\frac{\sqrt{x^4 + 1}}{x^3} > \frac{\sqrt{x^4}}{x^3} = \frac{1}{x} > 0 \text{ on } [1, b]$$

we have

$$\int_1^b \frac{\sqrt{x^4 + 1}}{x^3}\, dx > \int_1^b \frac{1}{x}\, dx = \Big[\ln x\Big]_1^b = \ln b$$

and $\lim\limits_{b\to\infty} \ln b \to \infty$. Thus,

$$\lim\limits_{b\to\infty} 2\pi \int_1^b \frac{\sqrt{x^4 + 1}}{x^3}\, dx = \infty.$$

**55.** (a) Area of circle with radius $L$: $A = \pi L^2$

Area of sector with central angle $\theta$ (in radians)

$$S = \frac{\theta}{2\pi} A = \frac{\theta}{2\pi}(\pi L^2) = \frac{1}{2} L^2 \theta$$

(b) Let $s$ be the arc length of the sector, which is the circumference of the base of the cone. Here, $s = L\theta = 2\pi r$, and you have

$$S = \frac{1}{2} L^2 \theta = \frac{1}{2} L^2 \left(\frac{s}{L}\right) = \frac{1}{2} Ls = \frac{1}{2} L(2\pi r) = \pi r L$$

(c) The lateral surface area of the frustum is the difference of the large cone and the small one.

$$S = \pi r_2 (L + L_1) - \pi r_1 L_1$$
$$= \pi r_2 L + \pi L_1 (r_2 - r_1)$$

By similar triangles, $\dfrac{L + L_1}{r_2} = \dfrac{L_1}{r_1} \Rightarrow Lr_1 = L_1(r_2 - r_1)$

Hence,

$$S = \pi r_2 L + \pi L_1 (r_2 - r_1) = \pi r_2 L + \pi L r_1$$
$$= \pi L(r_1 + r_2).$$

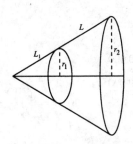

# Section 6.5    Work

**1.** $W = Fd = (100)(10) = 1000 \text{ ft} \cdot \text{lb}$

**3.** $W = Fd = (112)(4) = 448 \text{ joules } \text{(newton-meters)}$

**5.** Work equals force times distance, $W = FD$.

**7.** Since the work equals the area under the force function, you have $(c) < (d) < (a) < (b)$.

**9.** $F(x) = kx$

$5 = k(4)$

$k = \dfrac{5}{4}$

$W = \displaystyle\int_0^7 \frac{5}{4} x\, dx = \left[\frac{5}{8} x^2\right]_0^7$

$= \dfrac{245}{8} \text{ in} \cdot \text{lb}$

$= 30.625 \text{ in} \cdot \text{lb} \approx 2.55 \text{ ft} \cdot \text{lb}$

**11.** $F(x) = kx$

$250 = k(30) \Rightarrow k = \dfrac{25}{3}$

$W = \displaystyle\int_{20}^{50} F(x)\, dx = \int_{20}^{50} \frac{25}{3} x\, dx = \frac{25x^2}{6}\bigg]_{20}^{50}$

$= 8750 \text{ n} \cdot \text{cm} = 87.5 \text{ joules or Nm}$

**13.** $F(x) = kx$

$20 = k(9)$

$k = \dfrac{20}{9}$

$W = \displaystyle\int_0^{12} \dfrac{20}{9}x\,dx = \left[\dfrac{10}{9}x^2\right]_0^{12} = \dfrac{40}{3}\ \text{ft}\cdot\text{lb}$

**15.** $W = 18 = \displaystyle\int_0^{1/3} kx\,dx = \dfrac{kx^2}{2}\Big]_0^{1/3} = \dfrac{k}{18} \Rightarrow k = 324$

$W = \displaystyle\int_{1/3}^{7/12} 324x\,dx = 162x^2\Big]_{1/3}^{7/12} = 37.125\ \text{ft}\cdot\text{lbs}$

$\Big[$**Note:** 4 inches $= \tfrac{1}{3}$ foot$\Big]$

**17.** Assume that Earth has a radius of 4000 miles.

$F(x) = \dfrac{k}{x^2}$

$s = \dfrac{k}{(4000)^2}$

$k = 80,000,000$

$F(x) = \dfrac{80,000,000}{x^2}$

(a) $W = \displaystyle\int_{4000}^{4100} \dfrac{80,000,000}{x^2}\,dx = \left[\dfrac{-80,000,000}{x}\right]_{4000}^{4100} \approx 487.8\ \text{mi}\cdot\text{tons}$

$\approx 5.15\times10^9\ \text{ft}\cdot\text{lb}$

(b) $W = \displaystyle\int_{4000}^{4300} \dfrac{80,000,000}{x^2}\,dx \approx 1395.3\ \text{mi}\cdot\text{ton}$

$\approx 1.47\times10^{10}\ \text{ft}\cdot\text{lb}$

**19.** Assume that the earth has a radius of 4000 miles.

$F(x) = \dfrac{k}{x^2}$

$10 = \dfrac{k}{(4000)^2}$

$k = 160,000,000$

$F(x) = \dfrac{160,000,000}{x^2}$

(a) $W = \displaystyle\int_{4000}^{15,000} \dfrac{160,000,000}{x^2}\,dx = \left[-\dfrac{160,000,000}{x}\right]_{4000}^{15,000} \approx -10,666.667 + 40,000$

$= 29,333.333\ \text{mi}\cdot\text{ton}$

$\approx 2.93\times10^4\ \text{mi}\cdot\text{ton}$

$\approx 3.10\times10^{11}\ \text{ft}\cdot\text{lb}$

(b) $W = \displaystyle\int_{4000}^{26,000} \dfrac{160,000,000}{x^2}\,dx = \left[-\dfrac{160,000,000}{x}\right]_{4000}^{26,000} \approx -6,153.846 + 40,000$

$= 33,846.154\ \text{mi}\cdot\text{ton}$

$\approx 3.38\times10^4\ \text{mi}\cdot\text{ton}$

$\approx 3.57\times10^{11}\ \text{ft}\cdot\text{lb}$

**21.** Weight of each layer: $62.4(20)\,\Delta y$

Distance: $4 - y$

(a) $W = \displaystyle\int_2^4 62.4(20)(4-y)\,dy = \left[4992y - 624y^2\right]_2^4 = 2496\ \text{ft}\cdot\text{lb}$

(b) $W = \displaystyle\int_0^4 62.4(20)(4-y)\,dy = \left[4992y - 624y^2\right]_0^4 = 9984\ \text{ft}\cdot\text{lb}$

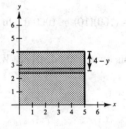

**23.** Volume of disk: $\pi(2)^2\,\Delta y = 4\pi\,\Delta y$

Weight of disk of water: $9800(4\pi)\,\Delta y$

Distance the disk of water is moved: $5 - y$

$W = \displaystyle\int_0^4 (5-y)(9800)4\pi\,dy = 39,200\pi\int_0^4 (5-y)\,dy$

$= 39,200\pi\left[5y - \dfrac{y^2}{2}\right]_0^4$

$= 39,200\pi(12) = 470,400\pi\ \text{newton–meters}$

**25.** Volume of disk: $\pi\left(\dfrac{2}{3}y\right)^2 \Delta y$

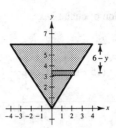

Weight of disk: $62.4\pi\left(\dfrac{2}{3}y\right)^2 \Delta y$

Distance: $6 - y$

$$W = \frac{4(62.4)\pi}{9}\int_0^6 (6-y)y^2\,dy = \frac{4}{9}(62.4)\pi\left[2y^3 - \frac{1}{4}y^4\right]_0^6 = 2995.2\pi \text{ ft} \cdot \text{lb}$$

**27.** Volume of disk: $\pi\left(\sqrt{36-y^2}\right)^2 \Delta y$

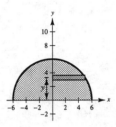

Weight of disk: $62.4\pi(36-y^2)\Delta y$

Distance: $y$

$$W = 62.4\pi\int_0^6 y(36-y^2)\,dy$$

$$= 62.4\pi\int_0^6 (36y - y^3)\,dy = 62.4\pi\left[18y^2 - \frac{1}{4}y^4\right]_0^6$$

$$= 20{,}217.6\pi \text{ ft} \cdot \text{lb}$$

**29.** Volume of layer: $V = lwh = 4(2)\sqrt{(9/4)-y^2}\,\Delta y$

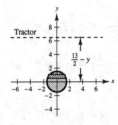

Weight of layer: $W = 42(8)\sqrt{(9/4)-y^2}\,\Delta y$

Distance: $\dfrac{13}{2} - y$

$$W = \int_{-1.5}^{1.5} 42(8)\sqrt{(9/4)-y^2}\left(\frac{13}{2}-y\right)dy$$

$$= 336\left[\frac{13}{2}\int_{-1.5}^{1.5}\sqrt{(9/4)-y^2}\,dy - \int_{-1.5}^{1.5}\sqrt{(9/4)-y^2}\,y\,dy\right]$$

The second integral is zero since the integrand is odd and the limits of integration are symmetric to the origin. The first integral represents the area of a semicircle of radius $\frac{3}{2}$. Thus, the work is

$$W = 336\left(\frac{13}{2}\right)\pi\left(\frac{3}{2}\right)^2\left(\frac{1}{2}\right) = 2457\pi \text{ ft} \cdot \text{lb}$$

**31.** Weight of section of chain: $3\,\Delta y$

Distance: $15 - y$

$$W = 3\int_0^{15} (15-y)\,dy$$

$$= \left[-\frac{3}{2}(15-y)^2\right]_0^{15}$$

$$= 337.5 \text{ ft} \cdot \text{lb}$$

**33.** The lower 5 feet of chain are raised 10 feet with a constant force.

$$W_1 = 3(5)(10) = 150 \text{ ft} \cdot \text{lb}$$

The top 10 feet of chain are raised with a variable force.

Weight per section: $3\,\Delta y$

Distance: $10 - y$

$$W_2 = 3\int_0^{10} (10-y)\,dy = \left[-\frac{3}{2}(10-y)^2\right]_0^{10}$$

$$= 150 \text{ ft} \cdot \text{lb}$$

$$W = W_1 + W_2 = 300 \text{ ft} \cdot \text{lb}$$

**35.** Weight of section of chain: $3 \Delta y$

Distance: $15 - 2y$

$$W = 3 \int_0^{7.5} (15 - 2y) \, dy = \left[ -\frac{3}{4}(15 - 2y)^2 \right]_0^{7.5}$$

$$= \frac{3}{4}(15)^2 = 168.75 \text{ ft} \cdot \text{lb}$$

**37.** Work to pull up the ball: $W_1 = 500(15) = 7500 \text{ ft} \cdot \text{lb}$

Work to wind up the top 15 feet of cable: force is variable

Weight per section: $1 \Delta y$

Distance: $15 - x$

$$W_2 = \int_0^{15} (15 - x) \, dx = \left[ -\frac{1}{2}(15 - x)^2 \right]_0^{15}$$

$$= 112.5 \text{ ft} \cdot \text{lb}$$

Work to lift the lower 25 feet of cable with a constant force:

$$W_3 = (1)(25)(15) = 375 \text{ ft} \cdot \text{lb}$$

$$W = W_1 + W_2 + W_3 = 7500 + 112.5 + 375$$

$$= 7987.5 \text{ ft} \cdot \text{lb}$$

**39.**    $p = \dfrac{k}{V}$

$$1000 = \frac{k}{2}$$

$$k = 2000$$

$$W = \int_2^3 \frac{2000}{V} \, dV = \left[ 2000 \ln |V| \right]_2^3$$

$$= 2000 \ln \left( \frac{3}{2} \right) \approx 810.93 \text{ ft} \cdot \text{lb}$$

**41.**    $F(x) = \dfrac{k}{(2 - x)^2}$

$$W = \int_{-2}^1 \frac{k}{(2 - x)^2} \, dx = \left[ \frac{k}{2 - x} \right]_{-2}^1 = k \left( 1 - \frac{1}{4} \right)$$

$$= \frac{3k}{4} \text{(units of work)}$$

**43.** $W = \displaystyle\int_0^5 1000 [1.8 - \ln(x + 1)] \, dx \approx 3249.44 \text{ ft} \cdot \text{lb}$

**45.** $W = \displaystyle\int_0^5 100x \sqrt{125 - x^3} \, dx \approx 10{,}330.3 \text{ ft} \cdot \text{lb}$

# Section 6.6    Moments, Centers of Mass, and Centroids

**1.** $\bar{x} = \dfrac{6(-5) + 3(1) + 5(3)}{6 + 3 + 5} = -\dfrac{6}{7}$

**3.** $\bar{x} = \dfrac{1(7) + 1(8) + 1(12) + 1(15) + 1(18)}{1 + 1 + 1 + 1 + 1} = 12$

**5.** (a) $\bar{x} = \dfrac{(7 + 5) + (8 + 5) + (12 + 5) + (15 + 5) + (18 + 5)}{5} = 17 = 12 + 5$

(b) $\bar{x} = \dfrac{12(-6 - 3) + 1(-4 - 3) + 6(-2 - 3) + 3(0 - 3) + 11(8 - 3)}{12 + 1 + 6 + 3 + 11} = \dfrac{-99}{33} = -3$

**7.**    $50x = 75(L - x) = 75(10 - x)$

$50x = 750 - 75x$

$125x = 750$

$x = 6$ feet

**9.**    $\bar{x} = \dfrac{5(2) + 1(-3) + 3(1)}{5 + 1 + 3} = \dfrac{10}{9}$

$\bar{y} = \dfrac{5(2) + 1(1) + 3(-4)}{5 + 1 + 3} = -\dfrac{1}{9}$

$(\bar{x}, \bar{y}) = \left( \dfrac{10}{9}, -\dfrac{1}{9} \right)$

**11.**
$$\bar{x} = \frac{3(-2) + 4(-1) + 2(7) + 1(0) + 6(-3)}{3 + 4 + 2 + 1 + 6} = -\frac{7}{8}$$

$$\bar{y} = \frac{3(-3) + 4(0) + 2(1) + 1(0) + 6(0)}{3 + 4 + 2 + 1 + 6} = -\frac{7}{16}$$

$$(\bar{x}, \bar{y}) = \left(-\frac{7}{8}, -\frac{7}{16}\right)$$

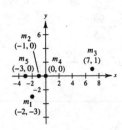
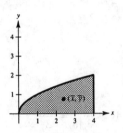

**13.**
$$m = \rho \int_0^4 \sqrt{x}\, dx = \left[\frac{2\rho}{3} x^{3/2}\right]_0^4 = \frac{16\rho}{3}$$

$$M_x = \rho \int_0^4 \frac{\sqrt{x}}{2}\left(\sqrt{x}\right) dx = \left[\rho \frac{x^2}{4}\right]_0^4 = 4\rho$$

$$\bar{y} = \frac{M_x}{m} = 4\rho\left(\frac{3}{16\rho}\right) = \frac{3}{4}$$

$$M_y = \rho \int_0^4 x\sqrt{x}\, dx = \left[\rho \frac{2}{5} x^{5/2}\right]_0^4 = \frac{64\rho}{5}$$

$$\bar{x} = \frac{M_y}{m} = \frac{64\rho}{5}\left(\frac{3}{16\rho}\right) = \frac{12}{5}$$

$$(\bar{x}, \bar{y}) = \left(\frac{12}{5}, \frac{3}{4}\right)$$

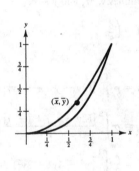

**15.**
$$m = \rho \int_0^1 (x^2 - x^3)\, dx = \rho\left[\frac{x^3}{3} - \frac{x^4}{4}\right]_0^1 = \frac{\rho}{12}$$

$$M_x = \rho \int_0^1 \frac{(x^2 + x^3)}{2}(x^2 - x^3)\, dx = \frac{\rho}{2} \int_0^1 (x^4 - x^6)\, dx = \frac{\rho}{2}\left[\frac{x^5}{5} - \frac{x^7}{7}\right]_0^1 = \frac{\rho}{35}$$

$$\bar{y} = \frac{M_x}{m} = \frac{\rho}{35}\left(\frac{12}{\rho}\right) = \frac{12}{35}$$

$$M_y = \rho \int_0^1 x(x^2 - x^3)\, dx = \rho \int_0^1 (x^3 - x^4)\, dx = \rho\left[\frac{x^4}{4} - \frac{x^5}{5}\right]_0^1 = \frac{\rho}{20}$$

$$\bar{x} = \frac{M_y}{m} = \frac{\rho}{20}\left(\frac{12}{\rho}\right) = \frac{3}{5}$$

$$(\bar{x}, \bar{y}) = \left(\frac{3}{5}, \frac{12}{35}\right)$$

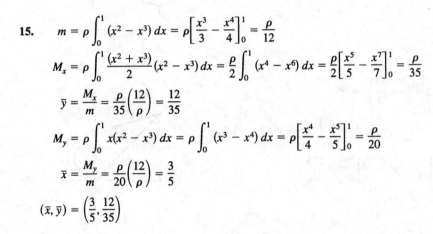

**17.**
$$m = \rho \int_0^3 [(-x^2 + 4x + 2) - (x + 2)]\, dx = -\rho\left[\frac{x^3}{3} + \frac{3x^2}{2}\right]_0^3 = \frac{9\rho}{2}$$

$$M_x = \rho \int_0^3 \left[\frac{(-x^2 + 4x + 2) + (x + 2)}{2}\right][(-x^2 + 4x + 2) - (x + 2)]\, dx$$

$$= \frac{\rho}{2} \int_0^3 (-x^2 + 5x + 4)(-x^2 + 3x)\, dx = \frac{\rho}{2} \int_0^3 (x^4 - 8x^3 + 11x^2 + 12x)\, dx$$

$$= \frac{\rho}{2}\left[\frac{x^5}{5} - 2x^4 + \frac{11x^3}{3} + 6x^2\right]_0^3 = \frac{99\rho}{5}$$

$$\bar{y} = \frac{M_x}{m} = \frac{99\rho}{5}\left(\frac{2}{9\rho}\right) = \frac{22}{5}$$

$$M_y = \rho \int_0^3 x[(-x^2 + 4x - 2) - (x + 2)]\, dx = \rho \int_0^3 (-x^3 + 3x^2)\, dx = \rho\left[-\frac{x^4}{4} + x^3\right]_0^3 = \frac{27\rho}{4}$$

$$\bar{x} = \frac{M_y}{m} = \frac{27\rho}{4}\left(\frac{2}{9\rho}\right) = \frac{3}{2}$$

$$(\bar{x}, \bar{y}) = \left(\frac{3}{2}, \frac{22}{5}\right)$$

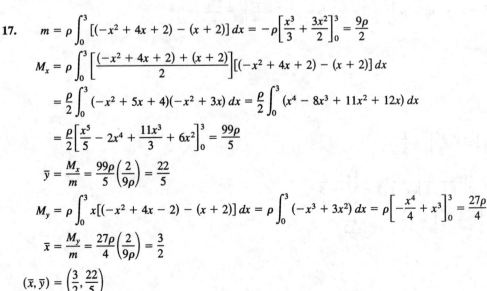

**19.** $m = \rho \int_0^8 x^{2/3}\, dx = \rho\left[\frac{3}{5}x^{5/3}\right]_0^8 = \frac{96\rho}{5}$

$M_x = \rho \int_0^8 \frac{x^{2/3}}{2}(x^{2/3})\, dx = \frac{\rho}{2}\left[\frac{3}{7}x^{7/3}\right]_0^8 = \frac{192\rho}{7}$

$\bar{y} = \frac{M_x}{m} = \frac{192\rho}{7}\left(\frac{5}{96\rho}\right) = \frac{10}{7}$

$M_y = \rho \int_0^8 x(x^{2/3})\, dx = \rho\left[\frac{3}{8}x^{8/3}\right]_0^8 = 96\rho$

$\bar{x} = \frac{M_y}{m} = 96\rho\left(\frac{5}{96\rho}\right) = 5$

$(\bar{x}, \bar{y}) = \left(5, \frac{10}{7}\right)$

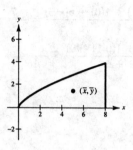

**21.** $m = 2\rho \int_0^2 (4 - y^2)\, dy = 2\rho\left[4y - \frac{y^3}{3}\right]_0^2 = \frac{32\rho}{3}$

$M_y = 2\rho \int_0^2 \left(\frac{4 - y^2}{2}\right)(4 - y^2)\, dy = \rho\left[16y - \frac{8}{3}y^3 + \frac{y^5}{5}\right]_0^2 = \frac{256\rho}{15}$

$\bar{x} = \frac{M_y}{m} = \frac{256\rho}{15}\left(\frac{3}{32\rho}\right) = \frac{8}{5}$

By symmetry, $M_x$ and $\bar{y} = 0$.

$(\bar{x}, \bar{y}) = \left(\frac{8}{5}, 0\right)$

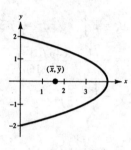

**23.** $m = \rho \int_0^3 [(2y - y^2) - (-y)]\, dy = \rho\left[\frac{3y^2}{2} - \frac{y^3}{3}\right]_0^3 = \frac{9\rho}{2}$

$M_y = \rho \int_0^3 \frac{[(2y - y^2) + (-y)]}{2}[(2y - y^2) - (-y)]\, dy = \frac{\rho}{2}\int_0^3 (y - y^2)(3y - y^2)\, dy$

$\quad = \frac{\rho}{2}\int_0^3 (y^4 - 4y^3 + 3y^2)\, dy = \frac{\rho}{2}\left[\frac{y^5}{5} - y^4 + y^3\right]_0^3 = -\frac{27\rho}{10}$

$\bar{x} = \frac{M_y}{m} = -\frac{27\rho}{10}\left(\frac{2}{9\rho}\right) = -\frac{3}{5}$

$M_x = \rho \int_0^3 y[(2y - y^2) - (-y)]\, dy = \rho \int_0^3 (3y^2 - y^3)\, dy = \rho\left[y^3 - \frac{y^4}{4}\right]_0^3 = \frac{27\rho}{4}$

$\bar{y} = \frac{M_x}{m} = \frac{27\rho}{4}\left(\frac{2}{9\rho}\right) = \frac{3}{2}$

$(\bar{x}, \bar{y}) = \left(-\frac{3}{5}, \frac{3}{2}\right)$

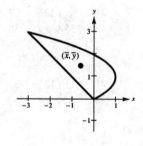

**25.** $A = \int_0^1 (x - x^2)\, dx = \left[\frac{1}{2}x^2 - \frac{x^3}{3}\right]_0^1 = \frac{1}{6}$

$M_x = \frac{1}{2}\int_0^1 (x^2 - x^4)\, dx = \frac{1}{2}\left[\frac{x^3}{3} - \frac{x^5}{5}\right]_0^1 = \frac{1}{2}\left(\frac{1}{3} - \frac{1}{5}\right) = \frac{1}{15}$

$M_y = \int_0^1 (x^2 - x^3)\, dx = \left[\frac{x^3}{3} - \frac{x^4}{4}\right]_0^1 = \left(\frac{1}{3} - \frac{1}{4}\right) = \frac{1}{12}$

**27.**  $A = \int_0^3 (2x + 4)\, dx = \left[ x^2 + 4x \right]_0^3 = 9 + 12 = 21$

$M_x = \frac{1}{2} \int_0^3 (2x + 4)^2\, dx = \int_0^3 (2x^2 + 8x + 8)\, dx = \left[ \frac{2x^3}{3} + 4x^2 + 8x \right]_0^3 = 18 + 36 + 24 = 78$

$M_y = \int_0^3 (2x^2 + 4x)\, dx = \left[ \frac{2x^3}{3} + 2x^2 \right]_0^3 = 18 + 18 = 36$

**29.**  $m = \rho \int_0^5 10x\sqrt{125 - x^3}\, dx \approx 1033.0\rho$

$M_x = \rho \int_0^5 \left( \frac{10x\sqrt{125 - x^3}}{2} \right)\left( 10x\sqrt{125 - x^3} \right) dx = 50\rho \int_0^5 x^2(125 - x^3)\, dx = \frac{3{,}124{,}375\rho}{24} \approx 130{,}208\rho$

$M_y = \rho \int_0^5 10x^2\sqrt{125 - x^3}\, dx = -\frac{10\rho}{3} \int_0^5 \sqrt{125 - x^3}\,(-3x^2)\, dx = \frac{12{,}500\sqrt{5}\rho}{9} \approx 3105.6\rho$

$\bar{x} = \dfrac{M_y}{m} \approx 3.0$

$\bar{y} = \dfrac{M_x}{m} \approx 126.0$

Therefore, the centroid is (3.0, 126.0).

**31.**  $m = \rho \int_{-20}^{20} 5\sqrt[3]{400 - x^2}\, dx \approx 1239.76\rho$

$M_x = \rho \int_{-20}^{20} \frac{5\sqrt[3]{400 - x^2}}{2}\left( 5\sqrt[3]{400 - x^2} \right) dx$

$= \frac{25\rho}{2} \int_{-20}^{20} (400 - x^2)^{2/3}\, dx \approx 20064.27$

$\bar{y} = \dfrac{M_x}{m} \approx 16.18$

$\bar{x} = 0$ by symmetry. Therefore, the centroid is (0, 16.2).

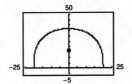

**33.**  $A = \frac{1}{2}(2a)c = ac$

$\frac{1}{A} = \frac{1}{ac}$

$\bar{x} = \left( \frac{1}{ac} \right)\frac{1}{2} \int_0^c \left[ \left( \frac{b - a}{c}y + a \right)^2 - \left( \frac{b + a}{c}y - a \right)^2 \right] dy$

$= \frac{1}{2ac} \int_0^c \left[ \frac{4ab}{c}y - \frac{4ab}{c^2}y^2 \right] dy$

$= \frac{1}{2ac} \left[ \frac{2ab}{c}y^2 - \frac{4ab}{3c^2}y^3 \right]_0^c = \frac{1}{2ac}\left( \frac{2}{3}abc \right) = \frac{b}{3}$

$\bar{y} = \frac{1}{ac} \int_0^c y\left[ \left( \frac{b - a}{c}y + a \right) - \left( \frac{b + a}{c}y - a \right) \right] dy$

$= \frac{1}{ac} \int_0^c y\left( -\frac{2a}{c}y + 2a \right) dy = \frac{2}{c} \int_0^c \left( y - \frac{y^2}{c} \right) dy$

$= \frac{2}{c}\left[ \frac{y^2}{2} - \frac{y^3}{3c} \right]_0^c = \frac{c}{3}$

$(\bar{x}, \bar{y}) = \left( \dfrac{b}{3}, \dfrac{c}{3} \right)$

In Exercise 566 of Section P.2, you found that $(b/3, c/3)$ is the point of intersection of the medians.

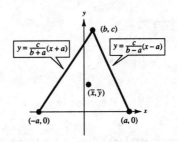

**35.** $A = \dfrac{c}{2}(a + b)$

$$\frac{1}{A} = \frac{2}{c(a + b)}$$

$$\bar{x} = \frac{2}{c(a + b)}\int_0^c x\left(\frac{b - a}{c}x + a\right) dx = \frac{2}{c(a + b)}\int_0^c \left(\frac{b - a}{c}x^2 + ax\right) dx = \frac{2}{c(a + b)}\left[\frac{b - a}{c}\frac{x^3}{3} + \frac{ax^2}{2}\right]_0^c$$

$$= \frac{2}{c(a + b)}\left[\frac{(b - a)c^2}{3} + \frac{ac^2}{2}\right] = \frac{2}{c(a + b)}\left[\frac{2bc^2 - 2ac^2 + 3ac^2}{6}\right] = \frac{c(2b + a)}{3(a + b)} = \frac{(a + 2b)c}{3(a + b)}$$

$$\bar{y} = \frac{2}{c(a + b)}\frac{1}{2}\int_0^c \left(\frac{b - a}{c}x + a\right)^2 dx = \frac{1}{c(a + b)}\int_0^c \left[\left(\frac{b - a}{c}\right)^2 x^2 + \frac{2a(b - a)}{c}x + a^2\right] dx$$

$$= \frac{1}{c(a + b)}\left[\left(\frac{b - a}{c}\right)^2 \frac{x^3}{3} + \frac{2a(b - a)}{c}\frac{x^2}{2} + a^2 x\right]_0^c = \frac{1}{c(a + b)}\left[\frac{(b - a)^2 c}{3} + ac(b - a) + a^2 c\right]$$

$$= \frac{1}{3c(a + b)}\left[(b^2 - 2ab + a^2)c + 3ac(b - a) + 3a^2 c\right]$$

$$= \frac{1}{3(a + b)}\left[b^2 - 2ab + a^2 + 3ab - 3a^2 + 3a^2\right] = \frac{a^2 + ab + b^2}{3(a + b)}$$

Thus, $(\bar{x}, \bar{y}) = \left(\dfrac{(a + 2b)c}{3(a + b)}, \dfrac{a^2 + ab + b^2}{3(a + b)}\right)$.

The one line passes through $(0, a/2)$ and $(c, b/2)$. It's equation is $y = \dfrac{b - a}{2c}x + \dfrac{a}{2}$.

The other line passes through $(0, -b)$ and $(c, a + b)$. It's equation is $y = \dfrac{a + 2b}{c}x - b$.

$(\bar{x}, \bar{y})$ is the point of intersection of these two lines.

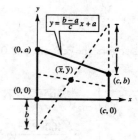

**37.** $\bar{x} = 0$ by symmetry

$$A = \frac{1}{2}\pi ab$$

$$\frac{1}{A} = \frac{2}{\pi ab}$$

$$\bar{y} = \frac{2}{\pi ab}\frac{1}{2}\int_{-a}^a \left(\frac{b}{a}\sqrt{a^2 - x^2}\right)^2 dx$$

$$= \frac{1}{\pi ab}\left(\frac{b^2}{a^2}\right)\left[a^2 x - \frac{x^3}{3}\right]_{-a}^a = \frac{b}{\pi a^3}\left[\frac{4a^3}{3}\right] = \frac{4b}{3\pi}$$

$(\bar{x}, \bar{y}) = \left(0, \dfrac{4b}{3\pi}\right)$

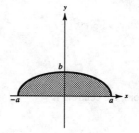

**39. (a)**

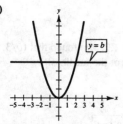

**(b)** $\bar{x} = 0$ by symmetry

**(c)** $M_y = \displaystyle\int_{-\sqrt{b}}^{\sqrt{b}} x(b - x^2)\, dx = 0$ because $bx - x^3$ is odd

**(d)** $\bar{y} > \dfrac{b}{2}$ since there is more area above $y = \dfrac{b}{2}$ than below

**(e)** $M_x = \displaystyle\int_{-\sqrt{b}}^{\sqrt{b}} \frac{(b + x^2)(b - x^2)}{2}\, dx$

$$= \int_{-\sqrt{b}}^{\sqrt{b}} \frac{b^2 - x^4}{2}\, dx = \frac{1}{2}\left[b^2 x - \frac{x^5}{5}\right]_{-\sqrt{b}}^{\sqrt{b}}$$

$$= b^2\sqrt{b} - \frac{b^2\sqrt{b}}{5} = \frac{4b^2\sqrt{b}}{5}$$

$$A = \int_{-\sqrt{b}}^{\sqrt{b}} (b - x^2)\, dx = \left[bx - \frac{x^3}{3}\right]_{-\sqrt{b}}^{\sqrt{b}}$$

$$= \left(b\sqrt{b} - \frac{b\sqrt{b}}{3}\right)2 = 4\frac{b\sqrt{b}}{3}$$

$$\bar{y} = \frac{M_x}{A} = \frac{4b^2\sqrt{b}/5}{4b\sqrt{b}/3} = \frac{3}{5}b.$$

**41.** (a) $\bar{x} = 0$ by symmetry

$$A = 2 \int_0^{40} f(x)\,dx = \frac{2(40)}{3(4)}[30 + 4(29) + 2(26) + 4(20) + 0] = \frac{20}{3}(278) = \frac{5560}{3}$$

$$M_x = \int_{-40}^{40} \frac{f(x)^2}{2}\,dx = \frac{40}{3(4)}[30^2 + 4(29)^2 + 2(26)^2 + 4(20)^2 + 0] = \frac{10}{3}(7216) = \frac{72160}{3}$$

$$\bar{y} = \frac{M_x}{A} = \frac{72160/3}{5560/3} = \frac{72160}{5560} \approx 12.98$$

$(\bar{x}, \bar{y}) = (0, 12.98)$

(b) $y = (-1.02 \times 10^{-5})x^4 - 0.0019x^2 + 29.28$

(c) $\bar{y} = \frac{M_x}{A} \approx \frac{23697.68}{1843.54} \approx 12.85$

$(\bar{x}, \bar{y}) = (0, 12.85)$

**43.** Centroids of the given regions: $(1, 0)$ and $(3, 0)$

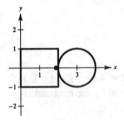

Area: $A = 4 + \pi$

$$\bar{x} = \frac{4(1) + \pi(3)}{4 + \pi} = \frac{4 + 3\pi}{4 + \pi}$$

$$\bar{y} = \frac{4(0) + \pi(0)}{4 + \pi} = 0$$

$$(\bar{x}, \bar{y}) = \left(\frac{4 + 3\pi}{4 + \pi}, 0\right) \approx (1.88, 0)$$

**45.** Centroids of the given regions: $\left(0, \frac{3}{2}\right)$, $(0, 5)$, and $\left(0, \frac{15}{2}\right)$

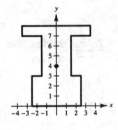

Area: $A = 15 + 12 + 7 = 34$

$$\bar{x} = \frac{15(0) + 12(0) + 7(0)}{34} = 0$$

$$\bar{y} = \frac{15(3/2) + 12(5) + 7(15/2)}{34} = \frac{135}{34}$$

$$(\bar{x}, \bar{y}) = \left(0, \frac{135}{34}\right)$$

**47.** Centroids of the given regions: $(1, 0)$ and $(3, 0)$

Mass: $4 + 2\pi$

$$\bar{x} = \frac{4(1) + 2\pi(3)}{4 + 2\pi} = \frac{2 + 3\pi}{2 + \pi}$$

$$\bar{y} = 0$$

$$(\bar{x}, \bar{y}) = \left(\frac{2 + 3\pi}{2 + \pi}, 0\right) \approx (2.22, 0)$$

**49.** $V = 2\pi r A = 2\pi(5)(16\pi) = 160\pi^2 \approx 1579.14$

**51.** $A = \frac{1}{2}(4)(4) = 8$

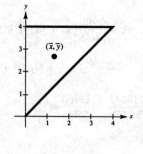

$$\bar{y} = \left(\frac{1}{8}\right)\frac{1}{2}\int_0^4 (4 + x)(4 - x)\,dx = \frac{1}{16}\left[16x - \frac{x^3}{3}\right]_0^4 = \frac{8}{3}$$

$$r = \bar{y} = \frac{8}{3}$$

$$V = 2\pi rA = 2\pi\left(\frac{8}{3}\right)(8) = \frac{128\pi}{3} \approx 134.04$$

**53.** $m = m_1 + \cdots + m_n$

$M_y = m_1 x_1 + \cdots + m_n x_n$

$M_x = m_1 y_1 + \cdots + m_n y_n$

$$\bar{x} = \frac{M_y}{m}, \bar{y} = \frac{M_x}{m}$$

**55.** (a) Yes. $(\bar{x}, \bar{y}) = \left(\frac{5}{6}, \frac{5}{18} + 2\right) = \left(\frac{5}{6}, \frac{41}{18}\right)$

(b) Yes. $(\bar{x}, \bar{y}) = \left(\frac{5}{6} + 2, \frac{5}{18}\right) = \left(\frac{17}{6}, \frac{5}{18}\right)$

(c) Yes. $(\bar{x}, \bar{y}) = \left(\frac{5}{6}, -\frac{5}{18}\right)$

(d) No.

**57.** The surface area of the sphere is $S = 4\pi r^2$. The arc length of $C$ is $s = \pi r$. The distance traveled by the centroid is

$$d = \frac{S}{s} = \frac{4\pi r^2}{\pi r} = 4r.$$

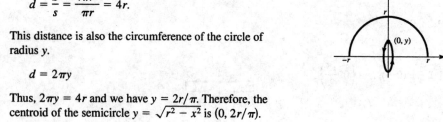

This distance is also the circumference of the circle of radius $y$.

$$d = 2\pi y$$

Thus, $2\pi y = 4r$ and we have $y = 2r/\pi$. Therefore, the centroid of the semicircle $y = \sqrt{r^2 - x^2}$ is $(0, 2r/\pi)$.

**59.** $A = \int_0^1 x^n\,dx = \left[\frac{x^{n+1}}{n+1}\right]_0^1 = \frac{1}{n+1}$

$$m = \rho A = \frac{\rho}{n+1}$$

$$M_x = \frac{\rho}{2}\int_0^1 (x^n)^2\,dx = \left[\frac{\rho}{2}\cdot\frac{x^{2n+1}}{2n+1}\right]_0^1 = \frac{\rho}{2(2n+1)}$$

$$M_y = \rho\int_0^1 x(x^n)\,dx = \left[\rho\cdot\frac{x^{n+2}}{n+2}\right]_0^1 = \frac{\rho}{n+2}$$

$$\bar{x} = \frac{M_y}{m} = \frac{n+1}{n+2}$$

$$\bar{y} = \frac{M_x}{m} = \frac{n+1}{2(2n+1)} = \frac{n+1}{4n+2}$$

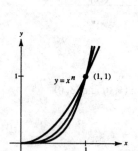

Centroid: $\left(\frac{n+1}{n+2}, \frac{n+1}{4n+2}\right)$

As $n \to \infty$, $(\bar{x}, \bar{y}) \to \left(1, \frac{1}{4}\right)$.

The graph approaches the $x$-axis and the line $x = 1$ as $n \to \infty$.

## Section 6.7    Fluid Pressure and Fluid Force

**1.** $F = PA = [62.4(5)](3) = 936$ lb

**3.** $F = 62.4(h + 2)(6) - (62.4)(h)(6)$

$\quad = 62.4(2)(6) = 748.8$ lb

**5.** $h(y) = 3 - y$

$\quad L(y) = 4$

$\quad F = 62.4 \int_0^3 (3 - y)(4) \, dy$

$\quad = 249.6 \int_0^3 (3 - y) \, dy$

$\quad = 249.6 \left[ 3y - \dfrac{y^2}{2} \right]_0^3 = 1123.2$ lb

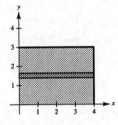

**7.** $h(y) = 3 - y$

$\quad L(y) = 2 \left( \dfrac{y}{3} + 1 \right)$

$\quad F = 2(62.4) \int_0^3 (3 - y) \left( \dfrac{y}{3} + 1 \right) dy$

$\quad = 124.8 \int_0^3 \left( 3 - \dfrac{y^2}{3} \right) dy$

$\quad = 124.8 \left[ 3y - \dfrac{y^3}{9} \right]_0^3 = 748.8$ lb

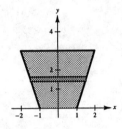

**9.** $h(y) = 4 - y$

$\quad L(y) = 2\sqrt{y}$

$\quad F = 2(62.4) \int_0^4 (4 - y)\sqrt{y} \, dy$

$\quad = 124.8 \int_0^4 (4y^{1/2} - y^{3/2}) \, dy$

$\quad = 124.8 \left[ \dfrac{8y^{3/2}}{3} - \dfrac{2y^{5/2}}{5} \right]_0^4 = 1064.96$ lb

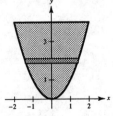

**11.** $h(y) = 4 - y$

$\quad L(y) = 2$

$\quad F = 9800 \int_0^2 2(4 - y) \, dy$

$\quad = 9800 \left[ 8y - y^2 \right]_0^2 = 117{,}600$ Newtons

**13.** $h(y) = 12 - y$

$L(y) = 6 - \dfrac{2y}{3}$

$F = 9800 \displaystyle\int_0^9 (12 - y)\left(6 - \dfrac{2y}{3}\right) dy$

$= 9800\left[72y - 7y^2 + \dfrac{2y^3}{9}\right]_0^9 = 2{,}381{,}400$ Newtons

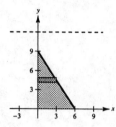

**15.** $h(y) = 2 - y$

$L(y) = 10$

$F = 140.7 \displaystyle\int_0^2 (2 - y)(10) \, dy$

$= 1407 \displaystyle\int_0^2 (2 - y) \, dy$

$= 1407\left[2y - \dfrac{y^2}{2}\right]_0^2 = 2814$ lb

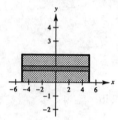

**17.** $h(y) = 4 - y$

$L(y) = 6$

$F = 140.7 \displaystyle\int_0^4 (4 - y)(6) \, dy$

$= 844.2 \displaystyle\int_0^4 (4 - y) \, dy$

$= 844.2\left[4y - \dfrac{y^2}{2}\right]_0^4 = 6753.6$ lb

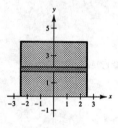

**19.** $h(y) = -y$

$L(y) = 2\left(\dfrac{1}{2}\right)\sqrt{9 - 4y^2}$

$F = 42 \displaystyle\int_{-3/2}^0 (-y)\sqrt{9 - 4y^2} \, dy$

$= \dfrac{42}{8} \displaystyle\int_{-3/2}^0 (9 - 4y^2)^{1/2}(-8y) \, dy$

$= \left[\left(\dfrac{21}{4}\right)\left(\dfrac{2}{3}\right)(9 - 4y^2)^{3/2}\right]_{-3/2}^0 = 94.5$ lb

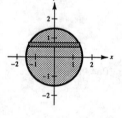

**21.** $h(y) = k - y$

$L(y) = 2\sqrt{r^2 - y^2}$

$F = w \displaystyle\int_{-r}^r (k - y)\sqrt{r^2 - y^2}\,(2) \, dy$

$= w\left[2k \displaystyle\int_{-r}^r \sqrt{r^2 - y^2}\, dy + \int_{-r}^r \sqrt{r^2 - y^2}\,(-2y)\, dy\right]$

The second integral is zero since its integrand is odd and the limits of integration are symmetric to the origin. The first integral is the area of a semicircle with radius $r$.

$F = w\left[(2k)\dfrac{\pi r^2}{2} + 0\right] = wk\pi r^2$

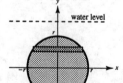

**23.** $h(y) = k - y$

$L(y) = b$

$$F = w \int_{-h/2}^{h/2} (k - y)b \, dy$$

$$= wb \left[ ky - \frac{y^2}{2} \right]_{-h/2}^{h/2} = wb(hk) = wkhb$$

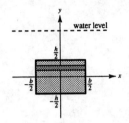

**25.** From Exercise 22:

$$F = 64(15)(1)(1) = 960 \text{ lb}$$

**27.** $h(y) = 4 - y$

$$F = 62.4 \int_0^4 (4 - y)L(y) \, dy$$

Using Simpson's Rule with $n = 8$ we have:

$$F \approx 62.4 \left( \frac{4 - 0}{3(8)} \right)[0 + 4(3.5)(3) + 2(3)(5) + 4(2.5)(8) + 2(2)(9) + 4(1.5)(10) + 2(1)(10.25) + 4(0.5)(10.5) + 0]$$

$$= 3010.8 \text{ lb}$$

**29.** $h(y) = 12 - y$

$L(y) = 2(4^{2/3} - y^{2/3})^{3/2}$

$$F = 62.4 \int_0^4 2(12 - y)(4^{2/3} - y^{2/3})^{3/2} \, dy$$

$$\approx 6448.73 \text{ lb}$$

**31. (a)** If the fluid force is one half of 1123.2 lb, and the height of the water is $b$, then

$$h(y) = b - y$$

$$L(y) = 4$$

$$F = 62.4 \int_0^b (b - y)(4) \, dy = \frac{1}{2}(1123.2)$$

$$\int_0^b (b - y) \, dy = 2.25$$

$$\left[ by - \frac{y^2}{2} \right]_0^b = 2.25$$

$$b^2 - \frac{b^2}{2} = 2.25$$

$$b^2 = 4.5 \implies b \approx 2.12 \text{ ft.}$$

**(b)** The pressure increases with increasing depth.

**33.** $F = Fw = w \int_c^d h(y)L(y) \, dy$, see page 471.

# Review Exercises for Chapter 6

**1.** $A = \int_1^5 \frac{1}{x^2}\, dx = \left[-\frac{1}{x}\right]_1^5 = \frac{4}{5}$

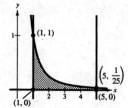

**3.** $A = \int_{-1}^1 \frac{1}{x^2 + 1}\, dx$

$= \left[\arctan x\right]_{-1}^1$

$= \frac{\pi}{4} - \left(-\frac{\pi}{4}\right) = \frac{\pi}{2}$

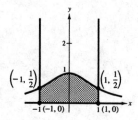

**5.** $A = 2\int_0^1 (x - x^3)\, dx$

$= 2\left[\frac{1}{2}x^2 - \frac{1}{4}x^4\right]_0^1$

$= \frac{1}{2}$

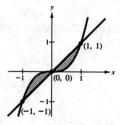

**7.** $A = \int_0^2 (e^2 - e^x)\, dx$

$= \left[xe^2 - e^x\right]_0^2$

$= e^2 + 1$

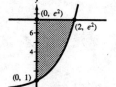

**9.** $A = \int_{\pi/4}^{5\pi/4} (\sin x - \cos x)\, dx$

$= \left[-\cos x - \sin x\right]_{\pi/4}^{5\pi/4}$

$= \left(\frac{1}{\sqrt{2}} + \frac{1}{\sqrt{2}}\right) - \left(-\frac{1}{\sqrt{2}} - \frac{1}{\sqrt{2}}\right)$

$= \frac{4}{\sqrt{2}} = 2\sqrt{2}$

**11.** $A = \int_0^8 \left[(3 + 8x - x^2) - (x^2 - 8x + 3)\right] dx$

$= \int_0^8 (16x - 2x^2)\, dx$

$= \left[8x^2 - \frac{2}{3}x^3\right]_0^8 = \frac{512}{3} \approx 170.667$

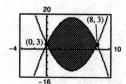

**13.** $y = \left(1 - \sqrt{x}\right)^2$

$$A = \int_0^1 \left(1 - \sqrt{x}\right)^2 dx$$

$$= \int_0^1 (1 - 2x^{1/2} + x)\, dx$$

$$= \left[x - \frac{4}{3}x^{3/2} + \frac{1}{2}x^2\right]_0^1 = \frac{1}{6} \approx 0.1667$$

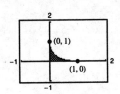

**15.** $x = y^2 - 2y \Rightarrow x + 1 = (y - 1)^2 \Rightarrow y = 1 \pm \sqrt{x + 1}$

$$A = \int_{-1}^0 \left[\left(1 + \sqrt{x + 1}\right) - \left(1 - \sqrt{x + 1}\right)\right] dx = \int_{-1}^0 2\sqrt{x + 1}\, dx$$

$$A = \int_0^2 \left[0 - (y^2 - 2y)\right] dy = \int_0^2 (2y - y^2)\, dy = \left[y^2 - \frac{1}{3}y^3\right]_0^2 = \frac{4}{3}$$

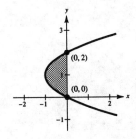

**17.** $A = \int_0^2 \left[1 - \left(1 - \frac{x}{2}\right)\right] dx + \int_2^3 \left[1 - (x - 2)\right] dx$

$$= \int_0^2 \frac{x}{2}\, dx + \int_2^3 (3 - x)\, dx$$

$$y = 1 - \frac{x}{2} \Rightarrow x = 2 - 2y$$

$$y = x - 2 \Rightarrow x = y + 2,\ y = 1$$

$$A = \int_0^1 \left[(y + 2) - (2 - 2y)\right] dy$$

$$= \int_0^1 3y\, dy = \left[\frac{3}{2}y^2\right]_0^1 = \frac{3}{2}$$

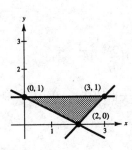

**19.** Job 1 is better. The salary for Job 1 is greater than the salary for Job 2 for all the years except the first and 10th years.

**21. (a) Disk**

$$V = \pi \int_0^4 x^2\, dx = \left[\frac{\pi x^3}{3}\right]_0^4 = \frac{64\pi}{3}$$

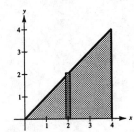

**(b) Shell**

$$V = 2\pi \int_0^4 x^2\, dx = \left[\frac{2\pi}{3}x^3\right]_0^4 = \frac{128\pi}{3}$$

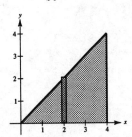

**—CONTINUED—**

**21.** **—CONTINUED—**

(c) **Shell**

$$V = 2\pi \int_0^4 (4 - x)x\, dx$$

$$= 2\pi \int_0^4 (4x - x^2)\, dx$$

$$= 2\pi \left[ 2x^2 - \frac{x^3}{3} \right]_0^4 = \frac{64\pi}{3}$$

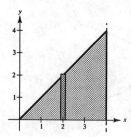

(d) **Shell**

$$V = 2\pi \int_0^4 (6 - x)x\, dx$$

$$= 2\pi \int_0^4 (6x - x^2)\, dx$$

$$= 2\pi \left[ 3x^2 - \frac{1}{3}x^3 \right]_0^4 = \frac{160\pi}{3}$$

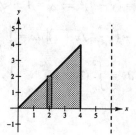

**23.** (a) **Shell**

$$V = 4\pi \int_0^4 x\left(\frac{3}{4}\right)\sqrt{16 - x^2}\, dx$$

$$= \left[ 3\pi\left(-\frac{1}{2}\right)\left(\frac{2}{3}\right)(16 - x^2)^{3/2} \right]_0^4 = 64\pi$$

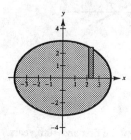

(b) **Disk**

$$V = 2\pi \int_0^4 \left[ \frac{3}{4}\sqrt{16 - x^2} \right]^2 dx$$

$$= \frac{9\pi}{8}\left[ 16x - \frac{x^3}{3} \right]_0^4 = 48\pi$$

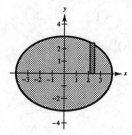

**25.** **Shell**

$$V = 2\pi \int_0^1 \frac{x}{x^4 + 1}\, dx$$

$$= \pi \int_0^1 \frac{(2x)}{(x^2)^2 + 1}\, dx$$

$$= \left[ \pi \arctan(x^2) \right]_0^1$$

$$= \pi\left[ \frac{\pi}{4} - 0 \right] = \frac{\pi^2}{4}$$

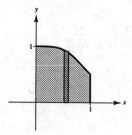

**27. Shell**

$$u = \sqrt{x - 2}$$

$$x = u^2 + 2$$

$$dx = 2u \, du$$

$$V = 2\pi \int_2^6 \frac{x}{1 + \sqrt{x - 2}} \, dx = 4\pi \int_0^2 \frac{(u^2 + 2)u}{1 + u} \, du$$

$$= 4\pi \int_0^2 \frac{u^3 + 2u}{1 + u} \, du = 4\pi \int_0^2 \left(u^2 - u + 3 - \frac{3}{1 + u}\right) du$$

$$= 4\pi \left[\frac{1}{3}u^3 - \frac{1}{2}u^2 + 3u - 3\ln(1 + u)\right]_0^2 = \frac{4\pi}{3}(20 - 9\ln 3) \approx 42.359$$

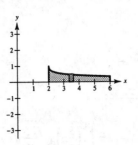

**29.** Since $y \le 0$, $A = -\int_{-1}^0 x\sqrt{x + 1} \, dx$.

$$u = x + 1$$

$$x = u - 1$$

$$dx = du$$

$$A = -\int_0^1 (u - 1)\sqrt{u} \, du = -\int_0^1 (u^{3/2} - u^{1/2}) \, du$$

$$= -\left[\frac{2}{5}u^{5/2} - \frac{2}{3}u^{3/2}\right]_0^1 = \frac{4}{15}$$

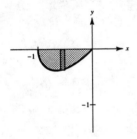

**31.** From Exercise 23(a) we have:   $V = 64\pi \text{ ft}^3$

$$\frac{1}{4}V = 16\pi$$

**Disk:**   $\pi \int_{-3}^{y_0} \frac{16}{9}(9 - y^2) \, dy = 16\pi$

$$\frac{1}{9}\int_{-3}^{y_0} (9 - y^2) \, dy = 1$$

$$\left[9y - \frac{1}{3}y^3\right]_{-3}^{y_0} = 9$$

$$\left(9y_0 - \frac{1}{3}y_0^3\right) - (-27 + 9) = 9$$

$$y_0^3 - 27y_0 - 27 = 0$$

By Newton's Method, $y_0 \approx -1.042$ and the depth of the gasoline is $3 - 1.042 = 1.958$ ft.

**33.**   $f(x) = \frac{4}{5}x^{5/4}$

$$f'(x) = x^{1/4}$$

$$1 + [f'(x)]^2 = 1 + \sqrt{x}$$

$$u = 1 + \sqrt{x}$$

$$x = (u - 1)^2$$

$$dx = 2(u - 1) \, du$$

$$s = \int_0^4 \sqrt{1 + \sqrt{x}} \, dx = 2\int_1^3 \sqrt{u}(u - 1) \, du$$

$$= 2\int_1^3 (u^{3/2} - u^{1/2}) \, du$$

$$= 2\left[\frac{2}{5}u^{5/2} - \frac{2}{3}u^{3/2}\right]_1^3 = \frac{4}{15}\left[u^{3/2}(3u - 5)\right]_1^3$$

$$= \frac{8}{15}(1 + 6\sqrt{3}) \approx 6.076$$

**35.**   $y = 300 \cosh\left(\frac{x}{2000}\right) - 280, \quad -2000 \le x \le 2000$

$$y' = \frac{3}{20} \sinh\left(\frac{x}{2000}\right)$$

$$s = \int_{-2000}^{2000} \sqrt{1 + \left[\frac{3}{20} \sinh\left(\frac{x}{2000}\right)\right]^2} \, dx$$

$$= \frac{1}{20}\int_{-2000}^{2000} \sqrt{400 + 9 \sinh^2\left(\frac{x}{2000}\right)} \, dx$$

$$\approx 4018.2 \text{ ft (by Simpson's Rule or graphing utility)}$$

**37.** $y = \dfrac{3}{4}x$

$$y' = \dfrac{3}{4}$$

$$1 + (y')^2 = \dfrac{25}{16}$$

$$S = 2\pi \int_0^4 \left(\dfrac{3}{4}x\right)\sqrt{\dfrac{25}{16}}\, dx = \left[\left(\dfrac{15\pi}{8}\right)\dfrac{x^2}{2}\right]_0^4 = 15\pi$$

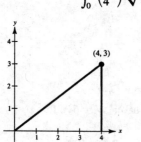

**39.** $F = kx$

$$4 = k(1)$$

$$F = 4x$$

$$W = \int_0^5 4x\, dx = \left[2x^2\right]_0^5$$

$$= 50 \text{ in} \cdot \text{lb} \approx 4.167 \text{ ft} \cdot \text{lb}$$

**41.** Volume of disk: $\pi\left(\dfrac{1}{3}\right)^2 \Delta y$

Weight of disk: $62.4\pi\left(\dfrac{1}{3}\right)^2 \Delta y$

Distance: $175 - y$

$$W = \dfrac{62.4\pi}{9} \int_0^{150} (175 - y)\, dy = \dfrac{62.4\pi}{9}\left[175y - \dfrac{y^2}{2}\right]_0^{150}$$

$$= 104{,}000\pi \text{ ft} \cdot \text{lb} \approx 163.4 \text{ ft} \cdot \text{ton}$$

**43.** Weight of section of chain: $5\,\Delta x$

Distance moved: $10 - x$

$$W = 5 \int_0^{10} (10 - x)\, dx = \left[-\dfrac{5}{2}(10 - x)^2\right]_0^{10}$$

$$= 250 \text{ ft} \cdot \text{lb}$$

**45.** $W = \displaystyle\int_a^b F(x)\, dx$

$$80 = \int_0^4 ax^2\, dx = \dfrac{ax^3}{3}\bigg]_0^4 = \dfrac{64}{3}a$$

$$a = \dfrac{3(80)}{64} = \dfrac{15}{4} = 3.75$$

**47.** $A = \displaystyle\int_0^a \left(\sqrt{a} - \sqrt{x}\right)^2 dx = \int_0^a \left(a - 2\sqrt{a}\, x^{1/2} + x\right) dx = \left[ax - \dfrac{4}{3}\sqrt{a}\, x^{3/2} + \dfrac{1}{2}x^2\right]_0^a = \dfrac{a^2}{6}$

$$\dfrac{1}{A} = \dfrac{6}{a^2}$$

$$\bar{x} = \dfrac{6}{a^2} \int_0^a x\left(\sqrt{a} - \sqrt{x}\right)^2 dx = \dfrac{6}{a^2} \int_0^a \left(ax - 2\sqrt{a}\, x^{3/2} + x^2\right) dx$$

$$\bar{y} = \left(\dfrac{6}{a^2}\right)\dfrac{1}{2} \int_0^a \left(\sqrt{a} - \sqrt{x}\right)^4 dx$$

$$= \dfrac{3}{a^2} \int_0^a \left(a^2 - 4a^{3/2}x^{1/2} + 6ax - 4a^{1/2}x^{3/2} + x^2\right) dx$$

$$= \dfrac{3}{a^2}\left[a^2 x - \dfrac{8}{3}a^{3/2}x^{3/2} + 3ax^2 - \dfrac{8}{5}a^{1/2}x^{5/2} + \dfrac{1}{3}x^3\right]_0^a = \dfrac{a}{5}$$

$$(\bar{x}, \bar{y}) = \left(\dfrac{a}{5}, \dfrac{a}{5}\right)$$

**49.** By symmetry, $x = 0$.

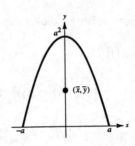

$$A = 2 \int_0^1 (a^2 - x^2)\, dx = 2 \left[ a^2 x - \frac{x^3}{3} \right]_0^a = \frac{4a^3}{3}$$

$$\frac{1}{A} = \frac{3}{4a^3}$$

$$\bar{y} = \left( \frac{3}{4a^3} \right) \frac{1}{2} \int_{-a}^a (a^2 - x^2)^2\, dx$$

$$= \frac{6}{8a^3} \int_0^a (a^4 - 2a^2 x^2 + x^4)\, dx$$

$$= \frac{6}{8a^3} \left[ a^4 x - \frac{2a^2}{3} x^3 + \frac{1}{5} x^5 \right]_0^a$$

$$= \frac{6}{8a^3} \left( a^5 - \frac{2}{3} a^5 + \frac{1}{5} a^5 \right) = \frac{2a^2}{5}$$

$$(\bar{x}, \bar{y}) = \left( 0, \frac{2a^2}{5} \right)$$

**51.** $\bar{y} = 0$ by symmetry

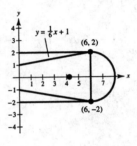

For the trapezoid:

$$m = [(4)(6) - (1)(6)]\rho = 18\rho$$

$$M_y = \rho \int_0^6 x \left[ \left( \frac{1}{6} x + 1 \right) - \left( -\frac{1}{6} x - 1 \right) \right] dx$$

$$= \rho \int_0^6 \left( \frac{1}{3} x^2 + 2x \right) dx = \rho \left[ \frac{x^3}{9} + x^2 \right]_0^6 = 60\rho$$

For the semicircle:

$$m = \left( \frac{1}{2} \right)(\pi)(2)^2 \rho = 2\pi\rho$$

$$M_y = \rho \int_6^8 x \left[ \sqrt{4 - (x - 6)^2} - \left( -\sqrt{4 - (x - 6)^2} \right) \right] dx = 2\rho \int_6^8 x \sqrt{4 - (x - 6)^2}\, dx$$

Let $u = x - 6$, then $x = u + 6$ and $dx = du$. When $x = 6$, $u = 0$. When $x = 8$, $u = 2$.

$$M_y = 2\rho \int_0^2 (u + 6) \sqrt{4 - u^2}\, du = 2\rho \int_0^2 u\sqrt{4 - u^2}\, du + 12\rho \int_0^2 \sqrt{4 - u^2}\, du$$

$$= 2\rho \left[ \left( -\frac{1}{2} \right)\left( \frac{2}{3} \right)(4 - u^2)^{3/2} \right]_0^2 + 12\rho \left[ \frac{\pi(2)^2}{4} \right] = \frac{16\rho}{3} + 12\pi\rho = \frac{4\rho(4 + 9\pi)}{3}$$

Thus, we have:

$$\bar{x}(18\rho + 2\pi\rho) = 60\rho + \frac{4\rho(4 + 9\pi)}{3}$$

$$\bar{x} = \frac{180\rho + 4\rho(4 + 9\pi)}{3} \cdot \frac{1}{2\rho(9 + \pi)} = \frac{2(9\pi + 49)}{3(\pi + 9)}$$

The centroid of the blade is $\left( \dfrac{2(9\pi + 49)}{3(\pi + 9)}, 0 \right)$.

**53.** Let $D$ = surface of liquid; $\rho$ = weight per cubic volume.

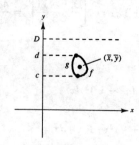

$$F = \rho \int_c^d (D - y)[f(y) - g(y)] \, dy$$

$$= \rho \left[ \int_c^d D[f(y) - g(y)] \, dy - \int_c^d y[f(y) - g(y)] \, dy \right]$$

$$= \rho \left[ \int_c^d [f(y) - g(y)] \, dy \right] \left[ D - \frac{\int_c^d y[f(y) - g(y)] \, dy}{\int_c^d [f(y) - g(y)] \, dy} \right]$$

$$= \rho(\text{Area})(D - \bar{y})$$

$$= \rho(\text{Area})(\text{depth of centroid})$$

# Problem Solving for Chapter 6

**1.** $T = \dfrac{1}{2}c(c^2) = \dfrac{1}{2}c^3$

$$R = \int_0^c (cx - x^2) \, dx = \left[ \frac{cx^2}{2} - \frac{x^3}{3} \right]_0^c = \frac{c^3}{2} - \frac{c^3}{3} = \frac{c^3}{6}$$

$$\lim_{c \to 0^+} \frac{T}{R} = \lim_{c \to 0^+} \frac{\frac{1}{2}c^3}{\frac{1}{6}c^3} = 3$$

**3.** (a) $\dfrac{1}{2}V = \displaystyle\int_0^1 \left[ \pi\left(2 + \sqrt{1 - y^2}\right)^2 - \pi\left(2 - \sqrt{1 - y^2}\right)^2 \right] dy$

$$= \pi \int_0^1 \left[ \left(4 + 4\sqrt{1 - y^2} + (1 - y^2)\right) - \left(4 - 4\sqrt{1 - y^2} + (1 - y^2)\right) \right] dy$$

$$= 8\pi \int_0^1 \sqrt{1 - y^2} \, dy \quad \text{(Integral represents 1/4 (area of circle))}$$

$$= 8\pi\left(\frac{\pi}{4}\right) = 2\pi^2 \implies V = 4\pi^2$$

(b) $(x - R)^2 + y^2 = r^2 \implies x = R \pm \sqrt{r^2 - y^2}$

$$\frac{1}{2}V = \int_0^r \left[ \pi\left(R + \sqrt{r^2 - y^2}\right)^2 - \pi\left(R - \sqrt{r^2 - y^2}\right)^2 \right] dy$$

$$= \pi \int_0^r 4R\sqrt{r^2 - y^2} \, dy$$

$$= \pi(4R)\frac{1}{4}\pi r^2 = \pi^2 r^2 R$$

$$V = 2\pi^2 r^2 R$$

**5.** $V = 2(2\pi) \displaystyle\int_{\sqrt{r^2 - (h^2/4)}}^r x\sqrt{r^2 - x^2} \, dx$

$$= -2\pi \left[ \frac{2}{3}(r^2 - x^2)^{3/2} \right]_{\sqrt{r^2 - (h^2/4)}}^r$$

$$= \frac{-4\pi}{3}\left[ -\frac{h^3}{8} \right] = \frac{\pi h^3}{6} \text{ which does not depend on } r!$$

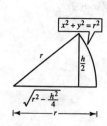

**7. (a)** Tangent at $A$: $y = x^3$, $y' = 3x^2$

$$y - 1 = 3(x - 1)$$
$$y = 3x - 2$$

To find point $B$:
$$x^3 = 3x - 2$$
$$x^3 - 3x + 2 = 0$$
$$(x - 1)^2(x + 2) = 0 \implies B = (-2, -8)$$

Tangent at $B$: $\quad y = x^3$, $y' = 3x^2$
$$y + 8 = 12(x + 2)$$
$$y = 12x + 16$$

To find point $C$: $\qquad x^3 = 12x + 16$
$$x^3 - 12x - 16 = 0$$
$$(x + 2)^2(x - 4) = 0 \implies C = (4, 64)$$

Area of $R = \displaystyle\int_{-2}^{1} (x^3 - 3x + 2)\, dx = \dfrac{27}{4}$

Area of $S = \displaystyle\int_{-2}^{4} (12x + 16 - x^3)\, dx = 108$

Area of $S = 16(\text{area of } R)$ $\quad \left[ \dfrac{\text{area } S}{\text{area } R} = 16 \right]$

**(b)** Tangent at $A(a, a^3)$: $\quad y - a^3 = 3a^2(x - a)$
$$y = 3a^2x - 2a^3$$

To find point $B$: $\quad x^3 - 3a^2x + 2a^3 = 0$
$$(x - a)^2(x + 2a) = 0 \implies$$
$$B = (-2a, -8a^3)$$

Tangent at $B$: $\quad y + 8a^3 = 12a^2(x + 2a)$
$$y = 12a^2x + 16a^3$$

To find point $C$: $\quad x^3 - 12a^2x - 16a^3 = 0$
$$(x + 2a)^2(x - 4a) = 0 \implies$$
$$C = (4a, 64a^3)$$

Area of $R = \displaystyle\int_{-2a}^{a} [x^3 - 3a^2x + 2a^3]\, dx = \dfrac{27}{4}a^4$

Area of $S = \displaystyle\int_{-2a}^{4a} [12a^2x + 16a^3 - x^3]\, dx = 108a^4$

Area of $S = 16(\text{area of } R)$

---

**9.** $s(x) = \displaystyle\int_{\alpha}^{x} \sqrt{1 + f'(t)^2}\, dt$

**(a)** $s'(x) = \dfrac{ds}{dx} = \sqrt{1 + f'(x)^2}$

**(b)** $\quad ds = \sqrt{1 + f'(x)^2}\, dx$

$$(ds)^2 = [1 + f'(x)^2](dx)^2 = \left[1 + \left(\dfrac{dy}{dx}\right)^2\right](dx)^2 = (dx)^2 + (dy)^2$$

**(c)** $s(x) = \displaystyle\int_{1}^{x} \sqrt{1 + \left(\dfrac{3}{2}t^{1/2}\right)^2}\, dt = \int_{1}^{x} \sqrt{1 + \dfrac{9}{4}t}\, dt$

**(d)** $s(2) = \displaystyle\int_{1}^{2} \sqrt{1 + \dfrac{9}{4}t}\, dt = \left[\dfrac{8}{27}\left(1 + \dfrac{9}{4}t\right)^{3/2}\right]_{1}^{2} = \dfrac{22}{27}\sqrt{22} - \dfrac{13}{27}\sqrt{13} \approx 2.0858$

This is the length of the curve $y = x^{3/2}$ from $x = 1$ to $x = 2$.

---

**11. (a)** $\bar{y} = 0$ by symmetry

$$M_y = \int_{1}^{6} x\left(\dfrac{1}{x^3} - \left(-\dfrac{1}{x^3}\right)\right) dx = \int_{1}^{6} \dfrac{2}{x^2}\, dx = \left[-2\dfrac{1}{x}\right]_{1}^{6} = \dfrac{5}{3}$$

$$m = 2\int_{1}^{6} \dfrac{1}{x^3}\, dx = \left[-\dfrac{1}{x^2}\right]_{1}^{6} = \dfrac{35}{36}$$

$$\bar{x} = \dfrac{5/3}{35/36} = \dfrac{12}{7} \qquad (\bar{x}, \bar{y}) = \left(\dfrac{12}{7}, 0\right)$$

**(b)** $m = 2\displaystyle\int_{1}^{b} \dfrac{1}{x^3}\, dx = \dfrac{b^2 - 1}{b^2}$

$$M_y = 2\int_{1}^{b} \dfrac{1}{x^2}\, dx = \dfrac{2(b - 1)}{b}$$

$$\bar{x} = \dfrac{2(b - 1)/b}{(b^2 - 1)/b^2} = \dfrac{2b}{b + 1} \qquad (\bar{x}, \bar{y}) = \left(\dfrac{2b}{b + 1}, 0\right)$$

**(c)** $\displaystyle\lim_{b \to \infty} \bar{x} = \lim_{b \to \infty} \dfrac{2b}{b + 1} = 2 \qquad (\bar{x}, \bar{y}) = (2, 0)$

**13.** (a) $W = \text{area} = 2 + 4 + 6 = 12$

  (b) $W = \text{area} = 3 + (1 + 1) + 2 + \dfrac{1}{2} = 7\dfrac{1}{2}$

**15.** Point of equilibrium: $50 - 0.5x = 0.125x$

$$x = 80, p = 10$$

$(P_0, x_0) = (10, 80)$

Consumer surplus $= \displaystyle\int_0^{80} [(50 - 0.5x) - 10]\, dx = 1600$

Producer surplus $= \displaystyle\int_0^{80} [10 - 0.125x]\, dx = 400$

**17.** (a) Wall at shallow end

  From Exercise 22: $F = 62.4(2)(4)(20) = 9984$ lb

  (b) Wall at deep end

  From Exercise 22: $F = 62.4(4)(8)(20) = 39{,}936$ lb

  (c) Side wall

  From Exercise 22: $F_1 = 62.4(2)(4)(40) = 19{,}968$ lb

$$F_2 = 62.4 \int_0^4 (8 - y)(10y)\, dy$$

$$= 624 \int_0^4 (8y - y^2)\, dy = 624\left[ 4y^2 - \frac{y^3}{3} \right]_0^4$$

$$= 26{,}624 \text{ lb}$$

  Total force: $F_1 + F_2 = 46{,}592$ lb

# C H A P T E R  7
## Integration Techniques, L'Hôpital's Rule, and Improper Integrals

# C H A P T E R   7
# Integration Techniques, L'Hôpital's Rule, and Improper Integrals

## Section 7.1    Basic Integration Rules

Solutions to Odd-Numbered Exercises

1. (a) $\dfrac{d}{dx}\left[2\sqrt{x^2+1}+C\right]=2\left(\dfrac{1}{2}\right)(x^2+1)^{-1/2}(2x)=\dfrac{2x}{\sqrt{x^2+1}}$

(b) $\dfrac{d}{dx}\left[\sqrt{x^2+1}+C\right]=\dfrac{1}{2}(x^2+1)^{-1/2}(2x)=\dfrac{x}{\sqrt{x^2+1}}$

(c) $\dfrac{d}{dx}\left[\dfrac{1}{2}\sqrt{x^2+1}+C\right]=\dfrac{1}{2}\left(\dfrac{1}{2}\right)(x^2+1)^{-1/2}(2x)=\dfrac{x}{2\sqrt{x^2+1}}$

(d) $\dfrac{d}{dx}[\ln(x^2+1)+C]=\dfrac{2x}{x^2+1}$

$\displaystyle\int\dfrac{x}{\sqrt{x^2+1}}\,dx$ matches (b).

3. (a) $\dfrac{d}{dx}\left[\ln\sqrt{x^2+1}+C\right]=\dfrac{1}{2}\left(\dfrac{2x}{x^2+1}\right)=\dfrac{x}{x^2+1}$

(b) $\dfrac{d}{dx}\left[\dfrac{2x}{(x^2+1)^2}+C\right]=\dfrac{(x^2+1)^2(2)-(2x)(2)(x^2+1)(2x)}{(x^2+1)^4}=\dfrac{2(1-3x^2)}{(x^2+1)^3}$

(c) $\dfrac{d}{dx}[\arctan x+C]=\dfrac{1}{1+x^2}$

(d) $\dfrac{d}{dx}[\ln(x^2+1)+C]=\dfrac{2x}{x^2+1}$

$\displaystyle\int\dfrac{1}{x^2+1}\,dx$ matches (c).

5. $\displaystyle\int(3x-2)^4\,dx$

$u=3x-2,\,du=3\,dx,\,n=4$

Use $\displaystyle\int u^n\,du$.

7. $\displaystyle\int\dfrac{1}{\sqrt{x}(1-2\sqrt{x})}\,dx$

$u=1-2\sqrt{x},\,du=-\dfrac{1}{\sqrt{x}}\,dx$

Use $\displaystyle\int\dfrac{du}{u}$.

9. $\displaystyle\int\dfrac{3}{\sqrt{1-t^2}}\,dt$

$u=t,\,du=dt,\,a=1$

Use $\displaystyle\int\dfrac{du}{\sqrt{a^2-u^2}}$.

11. $\displaystyle\int t\sin t^2\,dt$

$u=t^2,\,du=2t\,dt$

Use $\displaystyle\int\sin u\,du$.

13. $\displaystyle\int\cos xe^{\sin x}\,dx$

$u=\sin x,\,du=\cos x\,dx$

Use $\displaystyle\int e^u\,du$.

**15.** Let $u = -2x + 5$, $du = -2\,dx$.

$$\int (-2x + 5)^{3/2}\,dx = -\frac{1}{2}\int (-2x + 5)^{3/2}(-2)\,dx$$

$$= -\frac{1}{5}(-2x + 5)^{5/2} + C$$

**17.** Let $u = z - 4$, $du = dz$.

$$\int \frac{5}{(z - 4)^5}\,dz = 5\int (z - 4)^{-5}\,dx = 5\frac{(z - 4)^{-4}}{-4} + C$$

$$= \frac{-5}{4(z - 4)^4} + C$$

**19.** Let $u = t^3 - 1$, $du = 3t^2\,dt$.

$$\int t^2 \sqrt[3]{t^3 - 1}\,dt = \frac{1}{3}\int (t^3 - 1)^{1/3}(3t^2)\,dt$$

$$= \frac{1}{3}\frac{(t^3 - 1)^{4/3}}{4/3} + C$$

$$= \frac{(t^3 - 1)^{4/3}}{4} + C$$

**21.** $\displaystyle\int\left[v + \frac{1}{(3v - 1)^3}\right]dv = \int v\,dv + \frac{1}{3}\int (3v - 1)^{-3}(3)\,dv$

$$= \frac{1}{2}v^2 - \frac{1}{6(3v - 1)^2} + C$$

**23.** Let $u = -t^3 + 9t + 1$, $du = (-3t^2 + 9)\,dt = -3(t^2 - 3)\,dt$.

$$\int \frac{t^2 - 3}{-t^3 + 9t + 1}\,dt = -\frac{1}{3}\int \frac{-3(t^2 - 3)}{-t^3 + 9t + 1}\,dt = -\frac{1}{3}\ln|-t^3 + 9t + 1| + C$$

**25.** $\displaystyle\int \frac{x^2}{x - 1}\,dx = \int (x + 1)\,dx + \int \frac{1}{x - 1}\,dx$

$$= \frac{1}{2}x^2 + x + \ln|x - 1| + C$$

**27.** Let $u = 1 + e^x$, $du = e^x\,dx$.

$$\int \frac{e^x}{1 + e^x}\,dx = \ln(1 + e^x) + C$$

**29.** $\displaystyle\int (1 + 2x^2)^2\,dx = \int (4x^4 + 4x^2 + 1)\,dx = \frac{4}{5}x^5 + \frac{4}{3}x^3 + x + C = \frac{x}{15}(12x^4 + 20x^2 + 15) + C$

**31.** Let $u = 2\pi x^2$, $du = 4\pi x\,dx$.

$$\int x(\cos 2\pi x^2)\,dx = \frac{1}{4\pi}\int (\cos 2\pi x^2)(4\pi x)\,dx$$

$$= \frac{1}{4\pi}\sin 2\pi x^2 + C$$

**33.** Let $u = \pi x$, $du = \pi\,dx$.

$$\int \csc(\pi x)\cot(\pi x)\,dx = \frac{1}{\pi}\int \csc(\pi x)\cot(\pi x)\pi\,dx = -\frac{1}{\pi}\csc(\pi x) + C$$

**35.** Let $u = 5x$, $du = 5\,dx$.

$$\int e^{5x}\,dx = \frac{1}{5}\int e^{5x}(5)\,dx = \frac{1}{5}e^{5x} + C$$

**37.** Let $u = 1 + e^x$, $du = e^x\,dx$.

$$\int \frac{2}{e^{-x} + 1}\,dx = 2\int\left(\frac{1}{e^{-x} + 1}\right)\left(\frac{e^x}{e^x}\right)dx$$

$$= 2\int \frac{e^x}{1 + e^x}\,dx = 2\ln(1 + e^x) + C$$

**39.** $\int \dfrac{\ln x^2}{x}\, dx = 2\int (\ln x)\dfrac{1}{x}\, dx = 2\dfrac{(\ln x)^2}{2} + C = (\ln x)^2 + C$

**41.** $\int \dfrac{1 + \sin x}{\cos x}\, dx = \int (\sec x + \tan x)\, dx = \ln|\sec x + \tan x| + \ln|\sec x| + C = \ln|\sec x(\sec x + \tan x)| + C$

**43.**
$$\dfrac{1}{\cos\theta - 1} = \dfrac{1}{\cos\theta - 1} \cdot \dfrac{\cos\theta + 1}{\cos\theta + 1} = \dfrac{\cos\theta + 1}{\cos^2\theta - 1} = \dfrac{\cos\theta + 1}{-\sin^2\theta}$$

$$= -\csc\theta \cdot \cot\theta - \csc^2\theta$$

$$\int \dfrac{1}{\cos\theta - 1}\, d\theta = \int (-\csc\theta\cot\theta - \csc^2\theta)\, d\theta$$

$$= \csc\theta + \cot\theta + C$$

$$= \dfrac{1}{\sin\theta} + \dfrac{\cos\theta}{\sin\theta} + C$$

$$= \dfrac{1 + \cos\theta}{\sin\theta} + C$$

**45.**
$$\int \dfrac{3z + 2}{z^2 + 9}\, dz = \dfrac{3}{2}\int \dfrac{2z}{z^2 + 9}\, dz + 2\int \dfrac{dz}{z^2 + 9}$$

$$= \dfrac{3}{2}\ln(z^2 + 9) + \dfrac{2}{3}\arctan\left(\dfrac{z}{3}\right) + C$$

**47.** Let $u = 2t - 1$, $du = 2\, dt$.

$$\int \dfrac{-1}{\sqrt{1 - (2t - 1)^2}}\, dt = -\dfrac{1}{2}\int \dfrac{2}{\sqrt{1 - (2t - 1)^2}}\, dt$$

$$= -\dfrac{1}{2}\arcsin(2t - 1) + C$$

**49.** Let $u = \cos\left(\dfrac{2}{t}\right)$, $du = \dfrac{2\sin(2/t)}{t^2}\, dt$.

$$\int \dfrac{\tan(2/t)}{t^2}\, dt = \dfrac{1}{2}\int \dfrac{1}{\cos(2/t)}\left[\dfrac{2\sin(2/t)}{t^2}\right]\, dt$$

$$= \dfrac{1}{2}\ln\left|\cos\left(\dfrac{2}{t}\right)\right| + C$$

**51.** $\int \dfrac{3}{\sqrt{6x - x^2}}\, dx = 3\int \dfrac{1}{\sqrt{9 - (x - 3)^2}}\, dx = 3\arcsin\left(\dfrac{x - 3}{3}\right) + C$

**53.** $\int \dfrac{4}{4x^2 + 4x + 65}\, dx = \int \dfrac{1}{[x + (1/2)]^2 + 16}\, dx = \dfrac{1}{4}\arctan\left[\dfrac{x + (1/2)}{4}\right] + C = \dfrac{1}{4}\arctan\left(\dfrac{2x + 1}{8}\right) + C$

**55.** $\dfrac{ds}{dt} = \dfrac{t}{\sqrt{1 - t^4}}$, $\left(0, -\dfrac{1}{2}\right)$

(a)

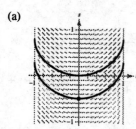

(b) $u = t^2$, $du = 2t\, dt$

$$\int \dfrac{t}{\sqrt{1 - t^4}}\, dt = \dfrac{1}{2}\int \dfrac{2t}{\sqrt{1 - (t^2)^2}}\, dt = \dfrac{1}{2}\arcsin t^2 + C$$

$$\left(0, -\dfrac{1}{2}\right): \; -\dfrac{1}{2} = \dfrac{1}{2}\arcsin 0 + C \implies C = -\dfrac{1}{2}$$

$$s = \dfrac{1}{2}\arcsin t^2 - \dfrac{1}{2}$$

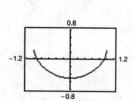

**57.**

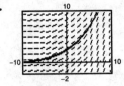

$y = 3e^{0.2x}$

**59.** $y = \displaystyle\int (1 + e^x)^2\, dx = \int (e^{2x} + 2e^x + 1)\, dx$

$= \dfrac{1}{2}e^{2x} + 2e^x + x + C$

**61.** $\dfrac{dy}{dx} = \dfrac{\sec^2 x}{4 + \tan^2 x}$

Let $u = \tan x,\, du = \sec^2 x\, dx.$

$y = \displaystyle\int \dfrac{\sec^2 x}{4 + \tan^2 x}\, dx = \dfrac{1}{2}\arctan\!\left(\dfrac{\tan x}{2}\right) + C$

**63.** Let $u = 2x,\, du = 2\, dx.$

$\displaystyle\int_0^{\pi/4} \cos 2x\, dx = \dfrac{1}{2}\int_0^{\pi/4} \cos 2x(2)\, dx$

$= \left[\dfrac{1}{2}\sin 2x\right]_0^{\pi/4} = \dfrac{1}{2}$

**65.** Let $u = -x^2,\, du = -2x\, dx.$

$\displaystyle\int_0^1 xe^{-x^2}\, dx = -\dfrac{1}{2}\int_0^1 e^{-x^2}(-2x)\, dx = \left[-\dfrac{1}{2}e^{-x^2}\right]_0^1$

$= \dfrac{1}{2}(1 - e^{-1}) \approx 0.316$

**67.** Let $u = x^2 + 9,\, du = 2x\, dx.$

$\displaystyle\int_0^4 \dfrac{2x}{\sqrt{x^2 + 9}}\, dx = \int_0^4 (x^2 + 9)^{-1/2}(2x)\, dx$

$= \left[2\sqrt{x^2 + 9}\right]_0^4 = 4$

**69.** Let $u = 3x,\, du = 3\, dx.$

$\displaystyle\int_0^{2/\sqrt{3}} \dfrac{1}{4 + 9x^2}\, dx = \dfrac{1}{3}\int_0^{2/\sqrt{3}} \dfrac{3}{4 + (3x)^2}\, dx$

$= \left[\dfrac{1}{6}\arctan\!\left(\dfrac{3x}{2}\right)\right]_0^{2/\sqrt{3}}$

$= \dfrac{\pi}{18} \approx 0.175$

**71.** $\displaystyle\int \dfrac{1}{x^2 + 4x + 13}\, dx = \dfrac{1}{3}\arctan\!\left(\dfrac{x + 2}{3}\right) + C$

The antiderivatives are vertical translations of each other.

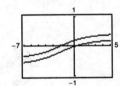

**73.** $\displaystyle\int \dfrac{1}{1 + \sin\theta}\, d\theta = \tan\theta - \sec\theta + C\left(\text{or } \dfrac{-2}{1 + \tan(\theta/2)}\right)$

The antiderivatives are vertical translations of each other.

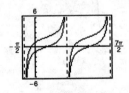

**75.** Power Rule: $\displaystyle\int u^n\, du = \dfrac{u^{n+1}}{n + 1} + C,\, n \neq -1.$

$u = x^2 + 1,\, n = 3$

**77.** Log Rule: $\displaystyle\int \dfrac{du}{u} = \ln|u| + C,\, u = x^2 + 1.$

**79.** The are equivalent because

$e^{x + C_1} = e^x \cdot e^{C_1} = Ce^x,\, C = e^{C_1}$

**81.** $\sin x + \cos x = a \sin(x + b)$

$\sin x + \cos x = a \sin x \cos b + a \cos x \sin b$

$\sin x + \cos x = (a \cos b) \sin x + (a \sin b) \cos x$

Equate coefficients of like terms to obtain the following.

$1 = a \cos b$ and $1 = a \sin b$

Thus, $a = 1/\cos b$. Now, substitute for $a$ in $1 = a \sin b$.

$$1 = \left(\frac{1}{\cos b}\right) \sin b$$

$$1 = \tan b \implies b = \frac{\pi}{4}$$

Since $b = \dfrac{\pi}{4}$, $a = \dfrac{1}{\cos(\pi/4)} = \sqrt{2}$. Thus, $\sin x + \cos x = \sqrt{2} \sin\left(x + \dfrac{\pi}{4}\right)$.

$$\int \frac{dx}{\sin x + \cos x} = \int \frac{dx}{\sqrt{2}\sin(x + (\pi/4))} = \frac{1}{\sqrt{2}} \int \csc\left(x + \frac{\pi}{4}\right) dx = -\frac{1}{\sqrt{2}} \ln\left|\csc\left(x + \frac{\pi}{4}\right) + \cot\left(x + \frac{\pi}{4}\right)\right| + C$$

**83.** $\displaystyle\int_0^2 \frac{4x}{x^2 + 1}\, dx \approx 3$

Matches (a).

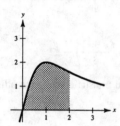

**85.** Let $u = 1 - x^2$, $du = -2x\, dx$.

$$A = 4\int_0^1 x\sqrt{1 - x^2}\, dx$$

$$= -2\int_0^1 (1 - x^2)^{1/2}(-2x)\, dx$$

$$= \left[-\frac{4}{3}(1 - x^2)^{3/2}\right]_0^1 = \frac{4}{3}$$

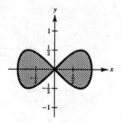

**87.** $\displaystyle\int_0^{1/a} (x - ax^2)\, dx = \left[\frac{1}{2}x^2 - \frac{a}{3}x^3\right]_0^{1/a}$

$$= \frac{1}{6a^2}$$

Let $\dfrac{1}{6a^2} = \dfrac{2}{3}$, $12a^2 = 3$, $a = \dfrac{1}{2}$.

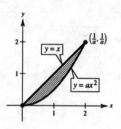

**89. (a) Shell Method:**

Let $u = -x^2$, $du = -2x\, dx$.

$$V = 2\pi \int_0^1 xe^{-x^2}\, dx$$

$$= -\pi \int_0^1 e^{-x^2}(-2x)\, dx$$

$$= \left[-\pi e^{-x^2}\right]_0^1$$

$$= \pi(1 - e^{-1}) \approx 1.986$$

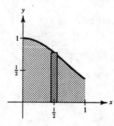

**(b) Shell Method:**

$$V = 2\pi \int_0^b xe^{-x^2}\, dx$$

$$= \left[-\pi e^{-x^2}\right]_0^b$$

$$= \pi(1 - e^{-b^2}) = \frac{4}{3}$$

$$e^{-b^2} = \frac{3\pi - 4}{3\pi}$$

$$b = \sqrt{\ln\left(\frac{3\pi}{3\pi - 4}\right)}$$

$$\approx 0.743$$

**91.** $A = \int_0^4 \dfrac{5}{\sqrt{25 - x^2}}\,dx = \left[5\arcsin\dfrac{x}{5}\right]_0^4 = 5\arcsin\dfrac{4}{5}$

$\bar{x} = \dfrac{1}{A}\int_0^4 x\left(\dfrac{5}{\sqrt{25 - x^2}}\right)dx$

$\quad = \dfrac{1}{5\arcsin(4/5)}\left(-\dfrac{5}{2}\right)\int_0^4 (25 - x^2)^{-1/2}(-2x)\,dx$

$\quad = \dfrac{1}{5\arcsin(4/5)}(-5)\left[(25 - x^2)^{1/2}\right]_0^4$

$\quad = -\dfrac{1}{\arcsin(4/5)}[3 - 5]$

$\quad = \dfrac{2}{\arcsin(4/5)} \approx 2.157$

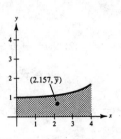

**93.**    $y = \tan(\pi x)$

$\qquad y' = \pi\sec^2(\pi x)$

$1 + (y')^2 = 1 + \pi^2\sec^4(\pi x)$

$\qquad s = \int_0^{1/4}\sqrt{1 + \pi^2\sec^4(\pi x)}\,dx$

$\qquad\quad \approx 1.0320$

# Section 7.2    Integration by Parts

**1.** $\dfrac{d}{dx}[\sin x - x\cos x] = \cos x - (-x\sin x + \cos x) = x\sin x.$ Matches (b)

**3.** $\dfrac{d}{dx}[x^2 e^x - 2xe^x + 2e^x] = x^2 e^x + 2xe^x - 2xe^x - 2e^x + 2e^x = x^2 e^x.$ Matches (c)

**5.** $\displaystyle\int xe^{2x}\,dx$

$u = x,\, dv = e^{2x}\,dx$

**7.** $\displaystyle\int (\ln x)^2\,dx$

$u = (\ln x)^2,\, dv = dx$

**9.** $\displaystyle\int x\sec^2 x\,dx$

$u = x,\, dv = \sec^2 x\,dx$

**11.** $dv = e^{-2x}\,dx \;\Rightarrow\; v = \displaystyle\int e^{-2x}\,dx = -\dfrac{1}{2}e^{-2x}$

$\quad u = x \qquad \Rightarrow du = dx$

$\displaystyle\int xe^{-2x}\,dx = -\dfrac{1}{2}xe^{-2x} - \int -\dfrac{1}{2}e^{-2x}\,dx$

$\qquad = -\dfrac{1}{2}xe^{-2x} - \dfrac{1}{4}e^{-2x} + C = \dfrac{-1}{4e^{2x}}(2x + 1) + C$

**13.** Use integration by parts three times.

(1) $dv = e^x\,dx \implies v = \displaystyle\int e^x\,dx = e^x$    (2) $dv = e^x\,dx \implies v = \displaystyle\int e^x\,dx = e^x$    (3) $dv = e^x\,dx \implies v = \displaystyle\int e^x\,dx = e^x$

$u = x^3 \implies du = 3x^2\,dx$    $u = x^2 \implies du = 2x\,dx$    $u = x \implies du = dx$

$$\int x^3 e^x\,dx = x^3 e^x - 3\int x^2 e^x\,dx = x^3 e^x - 3x^2 e^x + 6\int x e^x\,dx$$

$$= x^3 e^x - 3x^2 e^x + 6x e^x - 6e^x + C = e^x(x^3 - 3x^2 + 6x - 6) + C$$

**15.** $\displaystyle\int x^2 e^{x^3}\,dx = \frac{1}{3}\int e^{x^3}(3x^2)\,dx = \frac{1}{3}e^{x^3} + C$

**17.** $dv = t\,dt \implies v = \displaystyle\int t\,dt = \frac{t^2}{2}$

$u = \ln(t + 1) \implies du = \dfrac{1}{t + 1}\,dt$

$$\int t \ln(t + 1)\,dt = \frac{t^2}{2}\ln(t + 1) - \frac{1}{2}\int \frac{t^2}{t + 1}\,dt$$

$$= \frac{t^2}{2}\ln(t + 1) - \frac{1}{2}\int\left(t - 1 + \frac{1}{t + 1}\right)dt$$

$$= \frac{t^2}{2}\ln(t + 1) - \frac{1}{2}\left[\frac{t^2}{2} - t + \ln(t + 1)\right] + C$$

$$= \frac{1}{4}[2(t^2 - 1)\ln|t + 1| - t^2 + 2t] + C$$

**19.** Let $u = \ln x,\ du = \dfrac{1}{x}\,dx$.

$$\int \frac{(\ln x)^2}{x}\,dx = \int (\ln x)^2\left(\frac{1}{x}\right)dx = \frac{(\ln x)^3}{3} + C$$

**21.** $dv = \dfrac{1}{(2x + 1)^2}\,dx \implies v = \displaystyle\int (2x + 1)^{-2}\,dx$

$$= -\frac{1}{2(2x + 1)}$$

$u = xe^{2x} \implies du = (2xe^{2x} + e^{2x})\,dx$

$$= e^{2x}(2x + 1)\,dx$$

$$\int \frac{xe^{2x}}{(2x + 1)^2}\,dx = -\frac{xe^{2x}}{2(2x + 1)} + \int \frac{e^{2x}}{2}\,dx$$

$$= \frac{-xe^{2x}}{2(2x + 1)} + \frac{e^{2x}}{4} + C$$

$$= \frac{e^{2x}}{4(2x + 1)} + C$$

**23.** Use integration by parts twice.

(1) $dv = e^x\,dx \implies v = \displaystyle\int e^x\,dx = e^x$    (2) $dv = e^x\,dx \implies v = \displaystyle\int e^x\,dx = e^x$

$u = x^2 \implies du = 2x\,dx$    $u = x \implies du = dx$

$$\int (x^2 - 1)e^x\,dx = \int x^2 e^x\,dx - \int e^x\,dx = x^2 e^x - 2\int x e^x\,dx - e^x$$

$$= x^2 e^x - 2\left[xe^x - \int e^x\,dx\right] - e^x = x^2 e^x - 2xe^x + e^x + C = (x - 1)^2 e^x + C$$

**25.** $dv = \sqrt{x-1}\,dx \implies v = \int (x-1)^{1/2}\,dx = \frac{2}{3}(x-1)^{3/2}$

$u = x \qquad\qquad \implies du = dx$

$\int x\sqrt{x-1}\,dx = \frac{2}{3}x(x-1)^{3/2} - \frac{2}{3}\int (x-1)^{3/2}\,dx$

$\qquad\qquad = \frac{2}{3}x(x-1)^{3/2} - \frac{4}{15}(x-1)^{5/2} + C$

$\qquad\qquad = \frac{2(x-1)^{3/2}}{15}(3x+2) + C$

**27.** $dv = \cos x\,dx \implies v = \int \cos x\,dx = \sin x$

$u = x \qquad\qquad \implies du = dx$

$\int x \cos x\,dx = x \sin x - \int \sin x\,dx = x \sin x + \cos x + C$

**29.** Use integration by parts three times.

(1) $u = x^3,\ du = 3x^2,\ dv = \sin x\,dx,\ v = -\cos x$

$\int x^3 \sin dx = -x^3 \cos x + 3\int x^2 \cos x\,dx$

(2) $u = x^2,\ du = 2x\,dx,\ dv = \cos x\,dx,\ v = \sin x$

$\int x^3 \sin x\,dx = -x^3 \cos x + 3\left[x^2 \sin x - 2\int x \sin x\,dx\right]$

$\qquad\qquad = -x^3 \cos x + 3x^2 \sin x - 6\int x \sin x\,dx$

(3) $u = x,\ du = dx,\ dv = \sin x\,dx,\ v = -\cos x$

$\int x^3 \sin x\,dx = -x^3 \cos x + 3x^2 \sin x - 6\left[-x \cos x + \int \cos x\,dx\right]$

$\qquad\qquad = -x^3 \cos x + 3x^2 \sin x + 6x \cos x - 6 \sin x + C$

**31.** $u = t,\ du = dt,\ dv = \csc t \cot t\,dt,\ v = -\csc t$

$\int t \csc t \cot t\,dt = -t \csc t + \int \csc t\,dt$

$\qquad\qquad = -t \csc t - \ln|\csc t + \cot t| + C$

**33.** $dv = dx \qquad \implies v = \int dx = x$

$u = \arctan x \implies du = \frac{1}{1+x^2}\,dx$

$\int \arctan x\,dx = x \arctan x - \int \frac{x}{1+x^2}\,dx$

$\qquad\qquad = x \arctan x - \frac{1}{2}\ln(1+x^2) + C$

**35.** Use integration by parts twice.

(1) $dv = e^{2x}\,dx \implies v = \int e^{2x}\,dx = \frac{1}{2}e^{2x}$

$u = \sin x \implies du = \cos x\,dx$

(2) $dv = e^{2x}\,dx \implies v = \int e^{2x}\,dx = \frac{1}{2}e^{2x}$

$u = \cos x \implies du = -\sin x\,dx$

$\int e^{2x} \sin x\,dx = \frac{1}{2}e^{2x} \sin x - \frac{1}{2}\int e^{2x} \cos x\,dx = \frac{1}{2}e^{2x} \sin x - \frac{1}{2}\left(\frac{1}{2}e^{2x} \cos x + \frac{1}{2}\int e^{2x} \sin x\,dx\right)$

$\frac{5}{4}\int e^{2x} \sin x\,dx = \frac{1}{2}e^{2x} \sin x - \frac{1}{4}e^{2x} \cos x$

$\int e^{2x} \sin x\,dx = \frac{1}{5}e^{2x}(2 \sin x - \cos x) + C$

**37.** $y' = xe^{x^2}$

$$y = \int xe^{x^2}\, dx = \frac{1}{2}e^{x^2} + C$$

**39.** Use integration by parts twice.

(1) $dv = \dfrac{1}{\sqrt{2+3t}}\, dt \implies v = \int (2+3t)^{-1/2}\, dt = \dfrac{2}{3}\sqrt{2+3t}$

$\quad u = t^2 \qquad\qquad \implies du = 2t\, dt$

(2) $dv = \sqrt{2+3t}\, dt \implies v = \int (2+3t)^{1/2}\, dt = \dfrac{2}{9}(2+3t)^{3/2}$

$\quad u = t \qquad\qquad\;\; \implies du = dt$

$$\begin{aligned}
y &= \int \frac{t^2}{\sqrt{2+3t}}\, dt = \frac{2t^2\sqrt{2+3t}}{3} - \frac{4}{3}\int t\sqrt{2+3t}\, dt \\
&= \frac{2t^2\sqrt{2+3t}}{3} - \frac{4}{3}\left[\frac{2t}{9}(2+3t)^{3/2} - \frac{2}{9}\int (2+3t)^{3/2}\, dt\right] \\
&= \frac{2t^2\sqrt{2+3t}}{3} - \frac{8t}{27}(2+3t)^{3/2} + \frac{16}{405}(2+3t)^{5/2} + C \\
&= \frac{2\sqrt{2+3t}}{405}(27t^2 - 24t + 32) + C
\end{aligned}$$

**41.** $(\cos y)y' = 2x$

$$\int \cos y\, dy = \int 2x\, dx$$

$$\sin y = x^2 + C$$

**43.** (a)

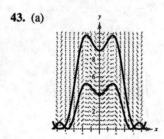

(b) $\qquad \dfrac{dy}{dx} = x\sqrt{y}\cos x,\ (0, 4)$

$$\int \frac{dy}{\sqrt{y}} = \int x\cos x\, dx$$

$$\int y^{-1/2}\, dy = \int x\cos x\, dx \qquad (u = x, du = dx, dv = \cos x\, dx, v = \sin x)$$

$$2y^{1/2} = x\sin x - \int \sin x\, dx$$

$$= x\sin x + \cos x + C$$

$(0, 4)$: $2(4)^{1/2} = 0 + 1 + C \implies C = 3$

$$2\sqrt{y} = x\sin x + \cos x + 3$$

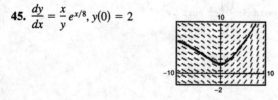

**45.** $\dfrac{dy}{dx} = \dfrac{x}{y}e^{x/8},\ y(0) = 2$

**47.** $u = x$, $du = dx$, $dv = e^{-x/2}\,dx$, $v = -2e^{-x/2}$

$$\int xe^{-x/2}\,dx = -2xe^{-x/2} + \int 2e^{-x/2}\,dx = -2xe^{-x/2} - 4e^{-x/2} + C$$

Thus, $\displaystyle\int_0^4 xe^{-x/2}\,dx = \left[-2xe^{-x/2} - 4e^{-x/2}\right]_0^4$

$$= -8e^{-2} - 4e^{-2} + 4$$

$$= -12e^{-2} + 4 \approx 2.376.$$

**49.** See Exercise 27.

$$\int_0^{\pi/2} x\cos x\,dx = \Big[x\sin x + \cos x\Big]_0^{\pi/2} = \frac{\pi}{2} - 1$$

**51.** $u = \arccos x$, $du = -\dfrac{1}{\sqrt{1 - x^2}}\,dx$, $dv = dx$, $v = x$

$$\int \arccos x\,dx = x\arccos x + \int \frac{x}{\sqrt{1 - x^2}}\,dx = x\arccos x - \sqrt{1 - x^2} + C$$

Thus, $\displaystyle\int_0^{1/2} \arccos x = \left[x\arccos x - \sqrt{1 - x^2}\right]_0^{1/2}$

$$= \frac{1}{2}\arccos\left(\frac{1}{2}\right) - \sqrt{\frac{3}{4}} + 1$$

$$= \frac{\pi}{6} - \frac{\sqrt{3}}{2} + 1 \approx 0.658.$$

**53.** Use integration by parts twice.

(1) $dv = e^x\,dx \implies v = \displaystyle\int e^x\,dx = e^x$ 　　　(2) $dv = e^x\,dx \implies v = \displaystyle\int e^x\,dx = e^x$

　　$u = \sin x \implies du = \cos x\,dx$ 　　　　　　　$u = \cos x \implies du = -\sin x\,dx$

$$\int e^x \sin x\,dx = e^x \sin x - \int e^x \cos x\,dx = e^x \sin x - e^x \cos x - \int e^x \sin x\,dx$$

$$2\int e^x \sin x\,dx = e^x(\sin x - \cos x)$$

$$\int e^x \sin x\,dx = \frac{e^x}{2}(\sin x - \cos x) + C$$

Thus, $\displaystyle\int_0^1 e^x \sin x\,dx = \left[\frac{e^x}{2}(\sin x - \cos x)\right]_0^1 = \frac{e}{2}(\sin 1 - \cos 1) + \frac{1}{2} = \frac{e(\sin 1 - \cos 1) + 1}{2} \approx 0.909.$

**55.** $dv = x^2\,dx$, $v = \dfrac{x^3}{3}$, $u = \ln x$, $du = \dfrac{1}{x}\,dx$

$$\int x^2 \ln x\,dx = \frac{x^3}{3}\ln x - \int \frac{x^3}{3}\left(\frac{1}{x}\right)dx$$

$$= \frac{x^3}{3}\ln x - \frac{1}{3}\int x^2\,dx$$

Hence, $\displaystyle\int_1^2 x^2 \ln x\,dx = \left[\frac{x^3}{3}\ln x - \frac{1}{9}x^3\right]_1^2$

$$= \frac{8}{3}\ln 2 - \frac{8}{9} + \frac{1}{9} = \frac{8}{3}\ln 2 - \frac{7}{9} \approx 1.071.$$

**57.** $dv = x\,dx,\ v = \dfrac{x^2}{2},\ u = \text{arcsec } x,\ du = \dfrac{1}{x\sqrt{x^2-1}}\,dx$

$$\int x \text{ arcsec } x\,dx = \frac{x^2}{2}\text{arcsec } x - \int \frac{x^2/2}{x\sqrt{x^2-1}}\,dx$$

$$= \frac{x^2}{2}\text{arcsec } x - \frac{1}{4}\int \frac{2x}{\sqrt{x^2-1}}\,dx$$

$$= \frac{x^2}{2}\text{arcsec } x - \frac{1}{2}\sqrt{x^2-1} + C$$

Hence,

$$\int_2^4 x \text{ arcsec } x\,dx = \left[\frac{x^2}{2}\text{arcsec } x - \frac{1}{2}\sqrt{x^2-1}\right]_2^4$$

$$= \left(8\text{ arcsec }4 - \frac{\sqrt{15}}{2}\right) - \left(\frac{2\pi}{3} - \frac{\sqrt{3}}{2}\right)$$

$$= 8\text{ arcsec }4 - \frac{\sqrt{15}}{2} + \frac{\sqrt{3}}{2} - \frac{2\pi}{3}$$

$$\approx 7.380.$$

**59.** $\displaystyle\int x^2 e^{2x}\,dx = x^2\left(\frac{1}{2}e^{2x}\right) - (2x)\left(\frac{1}{4}e^{2x}\right) + 2\left(\frac{1}{8}e^{2x}\right) + C$

$$= \frac{1}{2}x^2 e^{2x} - \frac{1}{2}xe^{2x} + \frac{1}{4}e^{2x} + C$$

$$= \frac{1}{4}e^{2x}(2x^2 - 2x + 1) + C$$

| Alternate signs | $u$ and its derivatives | $v'$ and its antiderivatives |
|---|---|---|
| + | $x^2$ | $e^{2x}$ |
| − | $2x$ | $\frac{1}{2}e^{2x}$ |
| + | $2$ | $\frac{1}{4}e^{2x}$ |
| − | $0$ | $\frac{1}{8}e^{2x}$ |

**61.** $\displaystyle\int x^3 \sin x\,dx = x^3(-\cos x) - 3x^2(-\sin x) + 6x\cos x - 6\sin x + C$

$$= -x^3\cos x + 3x^2\sin x + 6x\cos x - 6\sin x + C$$

$$= (3x^2 - 6)\sin x - (x^3 - 6x)\cos x + C$$

| Alternate signs | $u$ and its derivatives | $v'$ and its antiderivatives |
|---|---|---|
| + | $x^3$ | $\sin x$ |
| − | $3x^2$ | $-\cos x$ |
| + | $6x$ | $-\sin x$ |
| − | $6$ | $\cos x$ |
| + | $0$ | $\sin x$ |

**63.** $\displaystyle\int x\sec^2 x\,dx = x\tan x + \ln|\cos x| + C$

| Alternate signs | $u$ and its derivatives | $v'$ and its antiderivatives |
|---|---|---|
| + | $x$ | $\sec^2 x$ |
| − | $1$ | $\tan x$ |
| + | $0$ | $-\ln|\cos x|$ |

**65.** Integration by parts is based on the product rule.

**67.** No. Substitution.

**69.** Yes. $u = x^2,\ dv = e^{2x}\,dx$

**71.** Yes. Let $u = x$ and $du = \dfrac{1}{\sqrt{x+1}},\ dx$.

(Substitution also works. Let $u = \sqrt{x+1}$.)

**73.** $\displaystyle\int t^3 e^{-4t}\,dt = -\frac{e^{-4t}}{128}(32t^3 + 24t^2 + 12t + 3) + C$

**75.** $\displaystyle\int_0^{\pi/2} e^{-2x}\sin 3x\,dx = \left[\frac{e^{-2x}(-2\sin 3x - 3\cos 3x)}{13}\right]_0^{\pi/2} = \frac{1}{13}(2e^{-\pi} + 3) \approx 0.2374$

**77.** (a) $dv = \sqrt{2x - 3}\, dx \implies v = \int (2x - 3)^{1/2}\, dx = \frac{1}{3}(2x - 3)^{3/2}$

$u = 2x \qquad\qquad \implies du = 2\, dx$

$$\int 2x\sqrt{2x - 3}\, dx = \frac{2}{3}x(2x - 3)^{3/2} - \frac{2}{3}\int (2x - 3)^{3/2}\, dx$$

$$= \frac{2}{3}x(2x - 3)^{3/2} - \frac{2}{15}(2x - 3)^{5/2} + C$$

$$= \frac{2}{15}(2x - 3)^{3/2}(3x + 3) + C = \frac{2}{5}(2x - 3)^{3/2}(x + 1) + C$$

(b) $u = 2x - 3 \implies x = \dfrac{u + 3}{2}$ and $dx = \dfrac{1}{2}\, du$

$$\int 2x\sqrt{2x - 3}\, dx = \int 2\left(\frac{u + 3}{2}\right)u^{1/2}\left(\frac{1}{2}\right) du = \frac{1}{2}\int (u^{3/2} + 3u^{1/2})\, du = \frac{1}{2}\left[\frac{2}{5}u^{5/2} + 2u^{3/2}\right] + C$$

$$= \frac{1}{5}u^{3/2}(u + 5) + C = \frac{1}{5}(2x - 3)^{3/2}[(2x - 3) + 5] + C = \frac{2}{5}(2x - 3)^{3/2}(x + 1) + C$$

**79.** (a) $dv = \dfrac{x}{\sqrt{4 + x^2}}\, dx \implies v = \int (4 + x^2)^{-1/2}x\, dx = \sqrt{4 + x^2}$

$u = x^2 \implies du = 2x\, dx$

$$\int \frac{x^3}{\sqrt{4 + x^2}}\, dx = x^2\sqrt{4 + x^2} - 2\int x\sqrt{4 + x^2}\, dx$$

$$= x^2\sqrt{4 + x^2} - \frac{2}{3}(4 + x^2)^{3/2} + C = \frac{1}{3}\sqrt{4 + x^2}\,(x^2 - 8) + C$$

(b) $u = 4 + x^2 \implies x^2 = u - 4$ and $2x\, dx = du \implies x\, dx = \dfrac{1}{2}\, du$

$$\int \frac{x^3}{\sqrt{4 + x^2}}\, dx = \int \frac{x^2}{\sqrt{4 + x^2}}x\, dx = \int \frac{u - 4}{\sqrt{u}}\frac{1}{2}\, du$$

$$= \frac{1}{2}\int (u^{1/2} - 4u^{-1/2})\, du = \frac{1}{2}\left(\frac{2}{3}u^{3/2} - 8u^{1/2}\right) + C$$

$$= \frac{1}{3}u^{1/2}(u - 12) + C = \frac{1}{3}\sqrt{4 + x^2}\,[(4 + x^2) - 12] + C = \frac{1}{3}\sqrt{4 + x^2}\,(x^2 - 8) + C$$

**81.** $n = 0$: $\displaystyle\int \ln x\, dx = x(\ln x - 1) + C$

$n = 1$: $\displaystyle\int x \ln x\, dx = \frac{x^2}{4}(2 \ln x - 1) + C$

$n = 2$: $\displaystyle\int x^2 \ln x\, dx = \frac{x^3}{9}(3 \ln x - 1) + C$

$n = 3$: $\displaystyle\int x^3 \ln x\, dx = \frac{x^4}{16}(4 \ln x - 1) + C$

$n = 4$: $\displaystyle\int x^4 \ln x\, dx = \frac{x^5}{25}(5 \ln x - 1) + C$

In general, $\displaystyle\int x^n \ln x\, dx = \frac{x^{n+1}}{(n + 1)^2}[(n + 1)\ln x - 1] + C.$ (See Exercise 85.)

**83.** $dv = \sin x\, dx \implies v = -\cos x$

$u = x^n \qquad \implies du = nx^{n-1}\, dx$

$$\int x^n \sin x\, dx = -x^n \cos x + n\int x^{n-1}\cos x\, dx$$

**85.** $dv = x^n\, dx \implies v = \dfrac{x^{n+1}}{n+1}$

$u = \ln x \implies du = \dfrac{1}{x}\, dx$

$$\int x^n \ln x\, dx = \frac{x^{n+1}}{n+1}\ln x - \int \frac{x^n}{n+1}\, dx$$

$$= \frac{x^{n+1}}{n+1}\ln x - \frac{x^{n+1}}{(n+1)^2} + C$$

$$= \frac{x^{n+1}}{(n+1)^2}[(n+1)\ln x - 1] + C$$

**87.** Use integration by parts twice.

(1) $dv = e^{ax}\, dx \implies v = \dfrac{1}{a}e^{ax}$

$\quad u = \sin bx \implies du = b\cos bx\, dx$

$$\int e^{ax}\sin bx\, dx = \frac{e^{ax}\sin bx}{a} - \frac{b}{a}\int e^{ax}\cos bx\, dx$$

(2) $dv = e^{ax}\, dx \implies v = \dfrac{1}{a}e^{ax}$

$\quad u = \cos bx \implies du = -b\sin bx\, dx$

$$= \frac{e^{ax}\sin bx}{a} - \frac{b}{a}\left[\frac{e^{ax}\cos bx}{a} + \frac{b}{a}\int e^{ax}\sin bx\, dx\right] = \frac{e^{ax}\sin bx}{a} - \frac{b^2}{a^2}\int e^{ax}\sin bx\, dx$$

Therefore, $\left(1 + \dfrac{b^2}{a^2}\right)\displaystyle\int e^{ax}\sin bx\, dx = \dfrac{e^{ax}(a\sin bx - b\cos bx)}{a^2}$

$$\int e^{ax}\sin bx\, dx = \frac{e^{ax}(a\sin bx - b\cos bx)}{a^2 + b^2} + C.$$

**89.** $n = 3$ (Use formula in Exercise 85.)

$$\int x^3 \ln x\, dx = \frac{x^4}{16}[4\ln x - 1] + C$$

**91.** $a = 2, b = 3$ (Use formula in Exercise 88.)

$$\int e^{2x}\cos 3x\, dx = \frac{e^{2x}(2\cos 3x + 3\sin 3x)}{13} + C$$

**93.** $dv = e^{-x}\, dx \implies v = -e^{-x}$

$u = x \qquad \implies du = dx$

$$A = \int_0^4 xe^{-x}\, dx = \left[-xe^{-x}\right]_0^4 + \int_0^4 e^{-x}\, dx = \frac{-4}{e^4} - \left[e^{-x}\right]_0^4$$

$$= 1 - \frac{5}{e^4} \approx 0.908$$

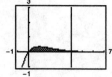

**95.** $A = \displaystyle\int_0^1 e^{-x}\sin(\pi x)\, dx$

$$= \left[\frac{e^{-x}(-\sin \pi x - \pi \cos \pi x)}{1 + \pi^2}\right]_0^1$$

$$= \frac{1}{1 + \pi^2}\left(\frac{\pi}{e} + \pi\right) = \frac{\pi}{1 + \pi^2}\left(\frac{1}{e} + 1\right)$$

$$\approx 0.395 \quad \text{(See Exercise 87.)}$$

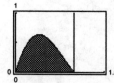

**97.** (a) $A = \int_1^e \ln x \, dx = \left[ -x + x \ln x \right]_1^e = 1$ (See Exercise 4.)

(b) $R(x) = \ln x, r(x) = 0$

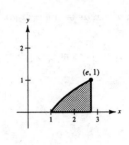

$$V = \pi \int_1^e (\ln x)^2 \, dx$$

$$= \pi \left[ x(\ln x)^2 - 2x \ln x + 2x \right]_1^e \text{ (Use integration by parts twice, see Exercise 7.)}$$

$$= \pi(e - 2) \approx 2.257$$

(c) $p(x) = x, h(x) = \ln x$

$$V = 2\pi \int_1^e x \ln x \, dx = 2\pi \left[ \frac{x^2}{4}(-1 + 2 \ln x) \right]_1^e$$

$$= \frac{(e^2 + 1)\pi}{2} \approx 13.177 \text{ (See Exercise 85.)}$$

(d) $\bar{x} = \dfrac{\int_1^e x \ln x \, dx}{1} = \dfrac{e^2 + 1}{4} \approx 2.097$

$\bar{y} = \dfrac{\frac{1}{2}\int_1^e (\ln x)^2 dx}{1} = \dfrac{e - 2}{2} \approx 0.359$

$(\bar{x}, \bar{y}) = \left( \dfrac{e^2 + 1}{4}, \dfrac{e - 2}{2} \right) \approx (2.097, 0.359)$

**99.** Average value $= \dfrac{1}{\pi} \int_0^\pi e^{-4t}(\cos 2t + 5 \sin 2t) \, dt$

$$= \frac{1}{\pi} \left[ e^{-4t} \left( \frac{-4 \cos 2t + 2 \sin 2t}{20} \right) + 5e^{-4t} \left( \frac{-4 \sin 2t - 2 \cos 2t}{20} \right) \right]_0^\pi \text{ (From Exercises 87 and 88)}$$

$$= \frac{7}{10\pi}(1 - e^{-4\pi}) \approx 0.223$$

**101.** $c(t) = 100{,}000 + 4000t, r = 5\%, t_1 = 10$

$$P = \int_0^{10} (100{,}000 + 4000t)e^{-0.05t} \, dt = 4000 \int_0^{10} (25 + t)e^{-0.05t} \, dt$$

Let $u = 25 + t, dv = e^{-0.05t} dt, du = dt, v = -\dfrac{100}{5}e^{-0.05t}$

$$P = 4000 \left\{ \left[ (25 + t)\left( -\frac{100}{5}e^{-0.05t} \right) \right]_0^{10} + \frac{100}{5} \int_0^{10} e^{-0.05t} \, dt \right\}$$

$$= 4000 \left\{ \left[ (25 + t)\left( -\frac{100}{5}e^{-0.05t} \right) \right]_0^{10} - \left[ \frac{10{,}000}{25}e^{-0.05t} \right]_0^{10} \right\} \approx \$931{,}265$$

**103.** $\displaystyle\int_{-\pi}^{\pi} x \sin nx \, dx = \left[ -\frac{x}{n} \cos nx + \frac{1}{n^2} \sin nx \right]_{-\pi}^{\pi}$

$$= -\frac{\pi}{n} \cos \pi n - \frac{\pi}{n} \cos(-\pi n)$$

$$= -\frac{2\pi}{n} \cos \pi n$$

$$= \begin{cases} -(2\pi/n), & \text{if } n \text{ is even} \\ (2\pi/n), & \text{if } n \text{ is odd} \end{cases}$$

**105.** Let $u = x, dv = \sin\left(\dfrac{n\pi}{2}x\right)dx, du = dx, v = -\dfrac{2}{n\pi}\cos\left(\dfrac{n\pi}{2}x\right)$.

$$I_1 = \int_0^1 x\sin\left(\frac{n\pi}{2}x\right)dx = \left[\frac{-2x}{n\pi}\cos\left(\frac{n\pi}{2}x\right)\right]_0^1 + \frac{2}{n\pi}\int_0^1 \cos\left(\frac{n\pi}{2}x\right)dx$$

$$= -\frac{2}{n\pi}\cos\left(\frac{n\pi}{2}\right) + \left[\left(\frac{2}{n\pi}\right)^2 \sin\left(\frac{n\pi}{2}x\right)\right]_0^1$$

$$= -\frac{2}{n\pi}\cos\left(\frac{n\pi}{2}\right) + \left(\frac{2}{n\pi}\right)^2 \sin\left(\frac{n\pi}{2}\right)$$

Let $u = (-x + 2), dv = \sin\left(\dfrac{n\pi}{2}x\right)dx, du = -dx, v = -\dfrac{2}{n\pi}\cos\left(\dfrac{n\pi}{2}x\right)$.

$$I_2 = \int_1^2 (-x + 2)\sin\left(\frac{n\pi}{2}x\right)dx = \left[\frac{-2(-x+2)}{n\pi}\cos\left(\frac{n\pi}{2}x\right)\right]_1^2 - \frac{2}{n\pi}\int_1^2 \cos\left(\frac{n\pi}{2}x\right)dx$$

$$= \frac{2}{n\pi}\cos\left(\frac{n\pi}{2}\right) - \left[\left(\frac{2}{n\pi}\right)^2 \sin\left(\frac{n\pi}{2}x\right)\right]_1^2$$

$$= \frac{2}{n\pi}\cos\left(\frac{n\pi}{2}\right) + \left(\frac{2}{n\pi}\right)^2 \sin\left(\frac{n\pi}{2}\right)$$

$$h(I_1 + I_2) = b_n = h\left[\left(\frac{2}{n\pi}\right)^2 \sin\left(\frac{n\pi}{2}\right) + \left(\frac{2}{n\pi}\right)^2 \sin\left(\frac{n\pi}{2}\right)\right] = \frac{8h}{(n\pi)^2}\sin\left(\frac{n\pi}{2}\right)$$

**107. Shell Method:**

$$V = 2\pi\int_a^b x f(x)\,dx$$

$$dv = x\,dx \implies v = \frac{x^2}{2}$$

$$u = f(x) \implies du = f'(x)\,dx$$

$$V = 2\pi\left[\frac{x^2}{2}f(x) - \int\frac{x^2}{2}f'(x)dx\right]_a^b$$

$$= \pi\left[(b^2 f(b) - a^2 f(a)) - \int_a^b x^2 f'(x)dx\right]$$

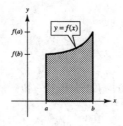

**Disk Method:**

$$V = \pi\int_0^{f(a)}(b^2 - a^2)\,dy + \pi\int_{f(a)}^{f(b)}[b^2 - [f^{-1}(y)]^2]\,dy$$

$$= \pi(b^2 - a^2)f(a) + \pi b^2(f(b) - f(a)) - \pi\int_{f(a)}^{f(b)}[f^{-1}(y)]^2\,dy$$

$$= \pi\left[(b^2 f(b) - a^2 f(a)) - \int_{f(a)}^{f(b)}[f^{-1}(y)]^2\,dy\right]$$

Since $x = f^{-1}(y)$, we have $f(x) = y$ and $f'(x)dx = dy$. When $y = f(a), x = a$. When $y = f(b), x = b$. Thus,

$$\int_{f(a)}^{f(b)}[f^{-1}(y)]^2\,dy = \int_a^b x^2 f'(x)\,dx$$

and the volumes are the same.

**109.** $f'(x) = xe^{-x}$

(a) $f(x) = \displaystyle\int xe^{-x}\,dx = -xe^{-x} - e^{-x} + C$

(b)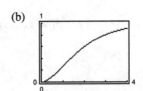

(Parts: $u = x,\ dv = e^{-x}\,dx$)

$f(0) = 0 = -1 + C \implies C = 1$

$f(x) = -xe^{-x} - e^{-x} + 1$

(c) You obtain the points

| $n$ | $x_n$ | $y_n$ |
|---|---|---|
| 0 | 0 | 0 |
| 1 | 0.05 | 0 |
| 2 | 0.10 | $2.378 \times 10^{-3}$ |
| 3 | 0.15 | 0.0069 |
| 4 | 0.20 | 0.0134 |
| $\vdots$ | $\vdots$ | $\vdots$ |
| 80 | 4.0 | 0.9064 |

(d) You obtain the points

| $n$ | $x_n$ | $y_n$ |
|---|---|---|
| 0 | 0 | 0 |
| 1 | 0.1 | 0 |
| 2 | 0.2 | 0.0090484 |
| 3 | 0.3 | 0.025423 |
| 4 | 0.4 | 0.047648 |
| $\vdots$ | $\vdots$ | $\vdots$ |
| 40 | 4.0 | 0.9039 |

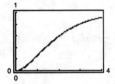

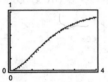

(e) $f(4) = 0.9084$

The approximations are tangent line approximations. The results in (c) are better because $\Delta x$ is smaller.

# Section 7.3    Trigonometric Integrals

**1.** $f(x) = \sin^4 x + \cos^4 x$

(a) $\sin^4 x + \cos^4 x = \left(\dfrac{1 - \cos 2x}{2}\right)^2 + \left(\dfrac{1 + \cos 2x}{2}\right)^2$

$\qquad\qquad\qquad\quad = \dfrac{1}{4}[1 - 2\cos 2x + \cos^2 2x + 1 + 2\cos 2x + \cos^2 2x]$

$\qquad\qquad\qquad\quad = \dfrac{1}{4}\left[2 + 2\dfrac{1 + \cos 4x}{2}\right]$

$\qquad\qquad\qquad\quad = \dfrac{1}{4}[3 + \cos 4x]$

(b) $\sin^4 x + \cos^4 x = (\sin^2 x)^2 + \cos^4 x$

$\qquad\qquad\qquad\quad = (1 - \cos^2 x)^2 + \cos^4 x$

$\qquad\qquad\qquad\quad = 1 - 2\cos^2 x + 2\cos^4 x$

(c) $\sin^4 x + \cos^4 x = \sin^4 x + 2\sin^2 x \cos^2 x + \cos^4 x - 2\sin^2 x \cos^2 x$

$\qquad\qquad\qquad\quad = (\sin^2 x + \cos^2 x)^2 - 2\sin^2 x \cos^2 x$

$\qquad\qquad\qquad\quad = 1 - 2\sin^2 x \cos^2 x$

**—CONTINUED—**

**1. —CONTINUED—**

(d)  $1 - 2 \sin^2 x \cos^2 x = 1 - (2 \sin x \cos x)(\sin x \cos x)$

$$= 1 - (\sin 2x)\left(\frac{1}{2} \sin 2x\right)$$

$$= 1 - \frac{1}{2} \sin^2(2x)$$

(e)  Four ways. There is often more than one way to rewrite a trigonometric expression.

**3.** Let $u = \cos x$, $du = -\sin x\, dx$.

$$\int \cos^3 x \sin x\, dx = -\int \cos^3 x (-\sin x)\, dx$$

$$= -\frac{1}{4} \cos^4 x + C$$

**5.** Let $u = \sin 2x$, $du = 2 \cos 2x\, dx$.

$$\int \sin^5 2x \cos 2x\, dx = \frac{1}{2} \int \sin^5 2x (2 \cos 2x)dx$$

$$= \frac{1}{12} \sin^6 2x + C$$

**7.** Let $u = \cos x$, $du = -\sin x\, dx$.

$$\int \sin^5 x \cos^2 x\, dx = \int \sin x (1 - \cos^2 x)^2 \cos^2 x\, dx$$

$$= -\int (\cos^2 x - 2 \cos^4 x + \cos^6 x)(-\sin x)\, dx = \frac{-1}{3} \cos^3 x + \frac{2}{5} \cos^5 x - \frac{1}{7} \cos^7 x + C$$

**9.**  $\displaystyle\int \cos^3 \theta \sqrt{\sin \theta}\, d\theta = \int \cos \theta (1 = \sin^2 \theta)(\sin \theta)^{1/2}\, d\theta$

$$= \int [(\sin \theta)^{1/2} - (\sin \theta)^{5/2}]\cos \theta\, d\theta$$

$$= \frac{2}{3}(\sin \theta)^{3/2} - \frac{2}{7}(\sin \theta)^{7/2} + C$$

**11.**  $\displaystyle\int \cos^2 3x\, dx = \int \frac{1 + \cos 6x}{2}\, dx$

$$= \frac{1}{2}\left(x + \frac{1}{6} \sin 6x\right) + C$$

$$= \frac{1}{12} (6x + \sin 6x) + C$$

**13.**  $\displaystyle\int \sin^2 \alpha \cdot \cos^2 \alpha\, d\alpha = \int \frac{1 - \cos 2\alpha}{2} \cdot \frac{1 + \cos 2\alpha}{2}\, d\alpha$

$$= \frac{1}{4}\int (1 - \cos^2 2\alpha)\, d\alpha$$

$$= \frac{1}{4}\int \left(1 - \frac{1 + \cos 4\alpha}{2}\right) d\alpha$$

$$= \frac{1}{8}\int (1 - \cos 4\alpha)\, d\alpha$$

$$= \frac{1}{8}\left[\alpha - \frac{1}{4} \sin 4\alpha\right] + C$$

$$= \frac{1}{32}[4\alpha - \sin 4\alpha] + C$$

**15.** Integration by parts.

$$dv = \sin^2 x \, dx = \frac{1 - \cos 2x}{2} \implies v = \frac{x}{2} - \frac{\sin 2x}{4} = \frac{1}{4}(2x - \sin 2x)$$

$$u = x \implies du = dx$$

$$\int x \sin^2 x \, dx = \frac{1}{4} x(2x - \sin 2x) - \frac{1}{4} \int (2x - \sin 2x) \, dx$$

$$= \frac{1}{4} x(2x - \sin 2x) - \frac{1}{4}\left(x^2 + \frac{1}{2}\cos 2x\right) + C = \frac{1}{8}(2x^2 - 2x \sin 2x - \cos 2x) + C$$

**17.** Let $u = \sin x$, $du = \cos x \, dx$.

$$\int_0^{\pi/2} \cos^3 x \, dx = \int_0^{\pi/2} (1 - \sin^2 x) \cos x \, dx$$

$$= \left[ \sin x - \frac{1}{3}\sin^3 x \right]_0^{\pi/2} = \frac{2}{3}$$

**19.** Let $u = \sin x$, $du = \cos x \, dx$.

$$\int_0^{\pi/2} \cos^7 x \, dx = \int_0^{\pi/2} (1 - \sin^2 x)^3 \cos x \, dx = \int_0^{\pi/2} (1 - 3\sin^2 x + 3\sin^4 x - \sin^6 x) \cos x \, dx$$

$$= \left[ \sin x - \sin^3 x + \frac{3}{5}\sin^5 x - \frac{1}{7}\sin^7 x \right]_0^{\pi/2} = \frac{16}{35}$$

**21.** $\displaystyle \int \sec(3x) \, dx = \frac{1}{3} \ln|\sec 3x + \tan 3x| + C$

**23.** $\displaystyle \int \sec^4 5x \, dx = \int (1 + \tan^2 5x) \sec^2 5x \, dx$

$$= \frac{1}{5}\left( \tan 5x + \frac{\tan^3 5x}{3} \right) + C$$

$$= \frac{\tan 5x}{15}(3 + \tan^2 5x) + C$$

**25.** $dv = \sec^2 \pi x \, dx \implies v = \dfrac{1}{\pi} \tan \pi x$

$u = \sec \pi x \implies du = \pi \sec \pi x \tan \pi x \, dx$

$$\int \sec^3 \pi x \, dx = \frac{1}{\pi} \sec \pi x \tan \pi x - \int \sec \pi x \tan^2 \pi x \, dx = \frac{1}{\pi} \sec \pi x \tan \pi x - \int \sec \pi x (\sec^2 \pi x - 1) \, dx$$

$$2 \int \sec^3 \pi x \, dx = \frac{1}{\pi}(\sec \pi x \tan \pi x + \ln|\sec \pi x + \tan \pi x|) + C_1$$

$$\int \sec^3 \pi x \, dx = \frac{1}{2\pi}(\sec \pi x \tan \pi x + \ln|\sec \pi x + \tan \pi x|) + C$$

**27.** $\displaystyle \int \tan^5 \frac{x}{4} \, dx = \int \left( \sec^2 \frac{x}{4} - 1 \right) \tan^3 \frac{x}{4} \, dx$

$$= \int \tan^3 \frac{x}{4} \sec^2 \frac{x}{4} \, dx - \int \tan^3 \frac{x}{4} \, dx$$

$$= \tan^4 \frac{x}{4} - \int \left( \sec^2 \frac{x}{4} - 1 \right) \tan \frac{x}{4} \, dx$$

$$= \tan^4 \frac{x}{4} - 2 \tan^2 \frac{x}{4} - 4 \ln\left| \cos \frac{x}{4} \right| + C$$

**29.** $u = \tan x$, $du = \sec^2 x \, dx$

$$\int \sec^2 x \tan x \, dx = \frac{1}{2} \tan^2 x + C$$

**31.** $\int \tan^2 x \sec^2 x \, dx = \dfrac{\tan^3 x}{3} + C$

**33.** $\int \sec^6 4x \tan 4x \, dx = \dfrac{1}{4} \int \sec^5 4x (4 \sec 4x \tan 4x) \, dx$

$$= \dfrac{\sec^6 4x}{24} + C$$

**35.** Let $u = \sec x$, $du = \sec x \tan x \, dx$.

$$\int \sec^3 x \tan x \, dx = \int \sec^2 x (\sec x \tan x) \, dx$$

$$= \dfrac{1}{3} \sec^3 x + C$$

**37.** $\int \dfrac{\tan^2 x}{\sec x} \, dx = \int \dfrac{(\sec^2 x - 1)}{\sec x} \, dx$

$$= \int (\sec x - \cos x) \, dx$$

$$= \ln|\sec x + \tan x| - \sin x + C$$

**39.** $r = \int \sin^4(\pi\theta) \, d\theta = \dfrac{1}{4} \int [1 - \cos(2\pi\theta)]^2 \, d\theta$

$$= \dfrac{1}{4} \int [1 - 2\cos(2\pi\theta) + \cos^2(2\pi\theta)] \, d\theta$$

$$= \dfrac{1}{4} \int \left[ 1 - 2\cos(2\pi\theta) + \dfrac{1 + \cos(4\pi\theta)}{2} \right] d\theta$$

$$= \dfrac{1}{4} \left[ \theta - \dfrac{1}{\pi} \sin(2\pi\theta) + \dfrac{\theta}{2} + \dfrac{1}{8\pi} \sin(4\pi\theta) \right] + C$$

$$= \dfrac{1}{32\pi} [12\pi\theta - 8\sin(2\pi\theta) + \sin(4\pi\theta)] + C$$

**41.** $y = \int \tan^3 3x \sec 3x \, dx$

$$= \int (\sec^2 3x - 1) \sec 3x \tan 3x \, dx$$

$$= \dfrac{1}{3} \int \sec^2 3x (3 \sec 3x \tan 3x) \, dx - \dfrac{1}{3} \int 3 \sec 3x \tan 3x \, dx$$

$$= \dfrac{1}{9} \sec^3 3x - \dfrac{1}{3} \sec 3x + C$$

**43.** (a)

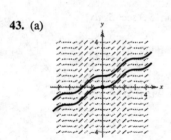

(b) $\dfrac{dy}{dx} = \sin^2 x$, $(0, 0)$

$$y = \int \sin^2 x \, dx = \int \dfrac{1 - \cos 2x}{2} \, dx$$

$$= \dfrac{1}{2} x - \dfrac{\sin 2x}{4} + C$$

$(0, 0)$: $0 = C$, $y = \dfrac{1}{2} x - \dfrac{\sin 2x}{4}$

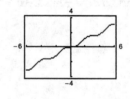

**45.** $\dfrac{dy}{dx} = \dfrac{3 \sin x}{y}$, $y(0) = 2$

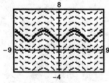

**47.** $\int \sin 3x \cos 2x \, dx = \dfrac{1}{2} \int (\sin 5x + \sin x) \, dx$

$$= \dfrac{-1}{2} \left( \dfrac{1}{5} \cos 5x + \cos x \right) + C$$

$$= \dfrac{-1}{10} (\cos 5x + 5 \cos x) + C$$

**49.** $\int \sin \theta \sin 3\theta \, d\theta = \dfrac{1}{2} \int (\cos 2\theta - \cos 4\theta) \, d\theta$

$$= \dfrac{1}{2} \left( \dfrac{1}{2} \sin 2\theta - \dfrac{1}{4} \sin 4\theta \right) + C$$

$$= \dfrac{1}{8} (2 \sin 2\theta - \sin 4\theta) + C$$

**51.** $\int \cot^3 2x \, dx = \int (\csc^2 2x - 1) \cot 2x \, dx$

$$= -\dfrac{1}{2} \int \cot 2x (-2\csc^2 2x) \, dx - \dfrac{1}{2} \int \dfrac{2 \cos 2x}{\sin 2x} \, dx$$

$$= -\dfrac{1}{4} \cot^2 2x - \dfrac{1}{2} \ln|\sin 2x| + C$$

$$= \dfrac{1}{4} (\ln|\csc^2 2x| - \cot^2 2x) + C$$

**53.** Let $u = \cot \theta$, $du = -\csc^2 \theta \, d\theta$.

$$\int \csc^4 \theta \, d\theta = \int \csc^2 \theta (1 + \cot^2 \theta) \, d\theta$$

$$= \int \csc^2 \theta \, d\theta + \int \csc^2 \theta \cot^2 \theta \, d\theta$$

$$= -\cot \theta - \frac{1}{3} \cot^3 \theta + C$$

**55.** $\displaystyle\int \frac{\cot^2 t}{\csc t} \, dt = \int \frac{\csc^2 t - 1}{\csc t} \, dt$

$$= \int (\csc t - \sin t) \, dt$$

$$= \ln|\csc t - \cot t| + \cos t + C$$

**57.** $\displaystyle\int \frac{1}{\sec x \tan x} \, dx = \int \frac{\cos^2 x}{\sin x} \, dx = \int \frac{1 - \sin^2 x}{\sin x} \, dx$

$$= \int (\csc x - \sin x) \, dx$$

$$= \ln|\csc x - \cot x| + \cos x + C$$

**59.** $\displaystyle\int (\tan^4 t - \sec^4 t) \, dt = \int (\tan^2 t + \sec^2 t)(\tan^2 t - \sec^2 t) \, dt$     $(\tan^2 t - \sec^2 t = -1)$

$$= -\int (\tan^2 t + \sec^2 t) \, dt = -\int (2\sec^2 t - 1) \, dt = -2\tan t + t + C$$

**61.** $\displaystyle\int_{-\pi}^{\pi} \sin^2 x \, dx = 2 \int_0^{\pi} \frac{1 - \cos 2x}{2} \, dx$

$$= \left[ x - \frac{1}{2} \sin 2x \right]_0^{\pi} = \pi$$

**63.** $\displaystyle\int_0^{\pi/4} \tan^3 x \, dx = \int_0^{\pi/4} (\sec^2 x - 1) \tan x \, dx$

$$= \int_0^{\pi/4} \sec^2 x \tan x \, dx - \int_0^{\pi/4} \frac{\sin x}{\cos x} \, dx$$

$$= \left[ \frac{1}{2} \tan^2 x + \ln|\cos x| \right]_0^{\pi/4}$$

$$= \frac{1}{2} (1 - \ln 2)$$

**65.** Let $u = 1 + \sin t$, $du = \cos t \, dt$.

$$\int_0^{\pi/2} \frac{\cos t}{1 + \sin t} \, dt = \Big[ \ln|1 + \sin t| \Big]_0^{\pi/2} = \ln 2$$

**67.** Let $u = \sin x$, $du = \cos x \, dx$.

$$\int_{-\pi/2}^{\pi/2} \cos^3 x \, dx = 2 \int_0^{\pi/2} (1 - \sin^2 x) \cos x \, dx$$

$$= 2 \left[ \sin x - \frac{1}{3} \sin^3 x \right]_0^{\pi/2} = \frac{4}{3}$$

**69.** $\displaystyle\int \cos^4 \frac{x}{2} \, dx = \frac{1}{16} [6x + 8 \sin x + \sin 2x] + C$

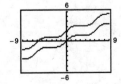

**71.** $\displaystyle\int \sec^5 \pi x \, dx = \frac{1}{4\pi} \left\{ \sec^3 \pi x \tan \pi x + \frac{3}{2} [\sec \pi x \tan \pi x + \ln|\sec \pi x + \tan \pi x|] \right\} + C$

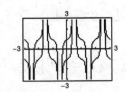

**73.** $\displaystyle\int \sec^5 \pi x \tan \pi x \, dx = \frac{1}{5\pi} \sec^5 \pi x + C$

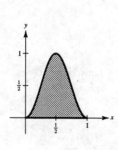

**75.** $\displaystyle\int_0^{\pi/4} \sin 2\theta \sin 3\theta \, d\theta = \frac{1}{2}\left[ \sin \theta - \frac{1}{5} \sin 5\theta \right]_0^{\pi/4} = \frac{3\sqrt{2}}{10}$

**77.** $\displaystyle\int_0^{\pi/2} \sin^4 x \, dx = \frac{1}{4}\left[ \frac{3x}{2} - \sin 2x + \frac{1}{8} \sin 4x \right]_0^{\pi/2}$

$\qquad\qquad\qquad = \dfrac{3\pi}{16}$

**79.** (a) Save one sine factor and convert the remaining sine factors to cosine. Then expand and integrate.

     (b) Save one cosine factor and convert the remaining cosine factors to sine. Then expand and integrate.

     (c) Make repeated use of the power reducing formula to convert the integrand to odd powers of the cosine.

**81.** (a) Let $u = \tan 3x$, $du = 3 \sec^2 3x \, dx$.

$$\int \sec^4 3x \tan^3 3x \, dx = \int \sec^2 3x \tan^3 3x \sec^2 3x \, dx$$

$$= \frac{1}{3} \int (\tan^2 3x + 1) \tan^3 3x (3 \sec^2 3x) \, dx$$

$$= \frac{1}{3} \int (\tan^5 3x + \tan^3 3x)(3 \sec^2 3x) \, dx$$

$$= \frac{\tan^6 3x}{18} + \frac{\tan^4 3x}{12} + C_1$$

Or let $u = \sec 3x$, $du = 3 \sec 3x \tan 3x \, dx$.

$$\int \sec^4 3x \tan^3 3x \, dx = \int \sec^3 3x \tan^2 3x \sec 3x \tan 3x \, dx$$

$$= \frac{1}{3} \int \sec^3 3x (\sec^2 3x - 1)(3 \sec 3x \tan 3x) \, dx$$

$$= \frac{\sec^6 3x}{18} - \frac{\sec^4 3x}{12} + C$$

(c) $\dfrac{\sec^6 3x}{18} - \dfrac{\sec^4 3x}{12} + C = \dfrac{(1 + \tan^2 3x)^3}{18} - \dfrac{(1 + \tan^2 3x)^2}{12} + C$

$\qquad\qquad = \dfrac{1}{18} \tan^6 3x + \dfrac{1}{6} \tan^4 3x + \dfrac{1}{6} \tan^2 3x + \dfrac{1}{18} - \dfrac{1}{12} \tan^4 3x - \dfrac{1}{6} \tan^2 3x - \dfrac{1}{12} + C$

$\qquad\qquad = \dfrac{\tan^6 3x}{18} + \dfrac{\tan^4 3x}{12} + \left( \dfrac{1}{18} - \dfrac{1}{12} \right) + C$

$\qquad\qquad = \dfrac{\tan^6 3x}{18} + \dfrac{\tan^4 3x}{12} + C_2$

(b)

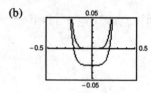

**83.** $A = \displaystyle\int_0^1 \sin^2(\pi x) \, dx$

$\quad = \displaystyle\int_0^1 \dfrac{1 - \cos(2\pi x)}{2} \, dx$

$\quad = \left[ \dfrac{x}{2} - \dfrac{1}{4\pi} \sin(2\pi x) \right]_0^1$

$\quad = \dfrac{1}{2}$

**85.** (a) $V = \pi \int_0^\pi \sin^2 x \, dx = \frac{\pi}{2} \int_0^\pi (1 - \cos 2x) \, dx = \frac{\pi}{2} \left[ x - \frac{1}{2} \sin 2x \right]_0^\pi = \frac{\pi^2}{2}$

(b) $A = \int_0^\pi \sin x \, dx = \left[ -\cos x \right]_0^\pi = 1 + 1 = 2$

Let $u = x, \, dv = \sin x \, dx, \, du = dx, \, v = -\cos x.$

$$\bar{x} = \frac{1}{A} \int_0^\pi x \sin x \, dx = \frac{1}{2} \left[ \left[ -x \cos x \right]_0^\pi + \int_0^\pi \cos x \, dx \right] = \frac{1}{2} \left[ -x \cos x + \sin x \right]_0^\pi = \frac{\pi}{2}$$

$$\bar{y} = \frac{1}{2A} \int_0^\pi \sin^2 x \, dx$$

$$= \frac{1}{8} \int_0^\pi (1 - \cos 2x) \, dx$$

$$= \frac{1}{8} \left[ x - \frac{1}{2} \sin 2x \right]_0^\pi = \frac{\pi}{8}$$

$$(\bar{x}, \bar{y}) = \left( \frac{\pi}{2}, \frac{\pi}{8} \right)$$

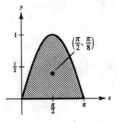

**87.** $dv = \sin x \, dx \implies v = -\cos x$

$u = \sin^{n-1} x \implies du = (n - 1)\sin^{n-2} x \cos x \, dx$

$$\int \sin^n x \, dx = -\sin^{n-1} x \cos x + (n - 1) \int \sin^{n-2} x \cos^2 x \, dx$$

$$= -\sin^{n-1} x \cos x + (n - 1) \int \sin^{n-2} x (1 - \sin^2 x) \, dx$$

$$= -\sin^{n-1} x \cos x + (n - 1) \int \sin^{n-2} x \, dx - (n - 1) \int \sin^n x \, dx$$

Therefore, $n \int \sin^n x \, dx = -\sin^{n-1} x \cos x + (n - 1) \int \sin^{n-2} x \, dx$

$$\int \sin^n x \, dx = \frac{-\sin^{n-1} x \cos x}{n} + \frac{n - 1}{n} \int \sin^{n-2} x \, dx.$$

**89.** Let $u = \sin^{n-1} x, \, du = (n - 1)\sin^{n-2} x \cos x \, dx, \, dv = \cos^m x \sin x \, dx, \, v = \frac{-\cos^{m+1} x}{m + 1}.$

$$\int \cos^m x \sin^n x \, dx = \frac{-\sin^{n-1} x \cos^{m+1} x}{m + 1} + \frac{n - 1}{m + 1} \int \sin^{n-2} x \cos^{m+2} x \, dx$$

$$= \frac{-\sin^{n-1} x \cos^{m+1} x}{m + 1} + \frac{n - 1}{m + 1} \int \sin^{n-2} x \cos^m x (1 - \sin^2 x) \, dx$$

$$= \frac{-\sin^{n-1} x \cos^{m+1} x}{m + 1} + \frac{n - 1}{m + 1} \int \sin^{n-2} x \cos^m x \, dx - \frac{n - 1}{m + 1} \int \sin^n x \cos^m x \, dx$$

$$\frac{m + n}{m + 1} \int \cos^m x \sin^n x \, dx = \frac{-\sin^{n-1} x \cos^{m+1} x}{m + 1} + \frac{n - 1}{m + 1} \int \sin^{n-2} x \cos^m x \, dx$$

$$\int \cos^m x \sin^n x \, dx = \frac{-\cos^{m+1} x \sin^{n-1}}{m + n} + \frac{n - 1}{m + n} \int \cos^m x \sin^{n-2} x \, dx$$

**91.** $\displaystyle\int \sin^5 x \, dx = -\frac{\sin^4 x \cos x}{5} + \frac{4}{5}\int \sin^3 x \, dx$

$\displaystyle = -\frac{\sin^4 x \cos x}{5} + \frac{4}{5}\left[-\frac{\sin^2 x \cos x}{3} + \frac{2}{3}\int \sin x \, dx\right]$

$\displaystyle = -\frac{1}{5}\sin^4 x \cos x - \frac{4}{15}\sin^2 x \cos x - \frac{8}{15}\cos x + C$

$\displaystyle = -\frac{\cos x}{15}[3 \sin^4 x + 4 \sin^2 x + 8] + C$

**93.** $\displaystyle\int \sec^4\!\left(\frac{2\pi x}{5}\right) dx = \frac{5}{2\pi}\int \sec^4\!\left(\frac{2\pi x}{5}\right)\frac{2\pi}{5}\, dx$

$\displaystyle = \frac{5}{2\pi}\left[\frac{1}{3}\sec^2\!\left(\frac{2\pi x}{5}\right)\tan\!\left(\frac{2\pi x}{5}\right) + \frac{2}{3}\int \sec^2\!\left(\frac{2\pi x}{5}\right)\frac{2\pi}{5}\, dx\right]$

$\displaystyle = \frac{5}{6\pi}\left[\sec^2\!\left(\frac{2\pi x}{5}\right)\tan\!\left(\frac{2\pi x}{5}\right) + 2\tan\!\left(\frac{2\pi x}{5}\right)\right] + C$

$\displaystyle = \frac{5}{6\pi}\tan\!\left(\frac{2\pi x}{5}\right)\left[\sec^2\!\left(\frac{2\pi x}{5}\right) + 2\right] + C$

**95.** (a) $\displaystyle f(t) = a_0 + a_1 \cos\frac{\pi t}{6} + b_1 \sin\frac{\pi t}{6}$ where:

$\displaystyle a_0 = \frac{1}{12}\int_0^{12} f(t)\, dt$

$\displaystyle a_1 = \frac{1}{6}\int_0^{12} f(t)\cos\frac{\pi t}{6}\, dt$

$\displaystyle b_1 = \frac{1}{6}\int_0^{12} f(t)\sin\frac{\pi t}{6}\, dt$

$\displaystyle a_0 \approx \frac{12-0}{3(12)^2}[30.9 + 4(32.2) + 2(41.1) + 4(53.7) + 2(64.6) + 4(74.0) + 2(78.2) + 4(77.0) + 2(71.0) +$

$\displaystyle 4(60.1) + 2(47.1) + 4(35.7) + 30.9] \approx 55.46$

$\displaystyle a_1 \approx \frac{12-0}{6(3)(12)}\left[30.9\cos 0 + 4\!\left(32.2\cos\frac{\pi}{6}\right) + 2\!\left(41.1\cos\frac{\pi}{3}\right) + 4\!\left(53.7\cos\frac{\pi}{2}\right) + 2\!\left(64.6\cos\frac{2\pi}{3}\right) + \right.$

$\displaystyle 4\!\left(74.0\cos\frac{5\pi}{6}\right) + 2(78.2\cos\pi) + 4\!\left(77.0\cos\frac{7\pi}{6}\right) + 2\!\left(71.0\cos\frac{4\pi}{3}\right) +$

$\displaystyle \left. 4\!\left(60.1\cos\frac{3\pi}{2}\right) + 2\!\left(47.1\cos\frac{5\pi}{3}\right) + 4\!\left(35.7\cos\frac{11\pi}{6}\right) + 30.9\cos 2\pi\right] \approx -23.88$

$\displaystyle b_1 \approx \frac{12-0}{6(3)(12)}\left[30.9\sin 0 + 4\!\left(32.2\sin\frac{\pi}{6}\right) + 2\!\left(41.1\sin\frac{\pi}{3}\right) + 4\!\left(53.7\sin\frac{\pi}{2}\right) + 2\!\left(64.6\sin\frac{2\pi}{3}\right) + \right.$

$\displaystyle 4\!\left(74.0\sin\frac{5\pi}{6}\right) + 2(78.2\sin\pi) + 4\!\left(77.0\sin\frac{7\pi}{6}\right) + 2\!\left(71.0\sin\frac{4\pi}{3}\right) +$

$\displaystyle \left. 4\!\left(60.1\sin\frac{3\pi}{2}\right) + 2\!\left(47.1\sin\frac{5\pi}{3}\right) + 4\!\left(35.7\sin\frac{11\pi}{6}\right) + 30.9\sin 2\pi\right] \approx -3.34$

$\displaystyle H(t) \approx 55.46 - 23.88\cos\frac{\pi t}{6} - 3.34\sin\frac{\pi t}{6}$

**—CONTINUED—**

**95. —CONTINUED—**

(b) $a_0 \approx \dfrac{12 - 0}{3(12)^2}[18.0 + 4(17.7) + 2(25.8) + 4(36.1) + 2(45.4) + 4(55.2) + 2(59.9) + 4(59.4) + 2(53.1) +$

$$4(43.2) + 2(34.3) + 4(24.2) + 18.0] \approx 39.34$$

$a_1 \approx \dfrac{12 - 0}{6(3)(12)}\Bigg[18.0 \cos 0 + 4\left(17.7 \cos \dfrac{\pi}{6}\right) + 2\left(25.8 \cos \dfrac{\pi}{3}\right) + 4\left(36.1 \cos \dfrac{\pi}{2}\right) + 2\left(45.4 \cos \dfrac{2\pi}{3}\right) +$

$$4\left(55.2 \cos \dfrac{5\pi}{6}\right) + 2(59.9 \cos \pi) + 4\left(59.4 \cos \dfrac{7\pi}{6}\right) + 2\left(53.1 \cos \dfrac{4\pi}{3}\right) +$$

$$4\left(43.2 \cos \dfrac{3\pi}{2}\right) + 2\left(34.3 \cos \dfrac{5\pi}{3}\right) + 4\left(24.2 \cos \dfrac{11\pi}{6}\right) + 18 \cos 2\pi\Bigg] \approx -20.78$$

$b_1 \approx \dfrac{12 - 0}{6(3)(12)}\Bigg[18.0 \sin 0 + 4\left(17.7 \sin \dfrac{\pi}{6}\right) + 2\left(25.8 \sin \dfrac{\pi}{3}\right) + 4\left(36.1 \sin \dfrac{\pi}{2}\right) + 2\left(45.4 \sin \dfrac{2\pi}{3}\right) +$

$$4\left(55.2 \sin \dfrac{5\pi}{6}\right) + 2(59.9 \sin \pi) + 4\left(59.4 \sin \dfrac{7\pi}{6}\right) + 2\left(53.1 \sin \dfrac{4\pi}{3}\right) +$$

$$4\left(43.2 \sin \dfrac{3\pi}{2}\right) + 2\left(34.3 \sin \dfrac{5\pi}{3}\right) + 4\left(24.2 \sin \dfrac{11\pi}{6}\right) + 18 \sin 2\pi\Bigg] \approx -4.33$$

$$L(t) \approx 39.34 - 20.78 \cos \dfrac{\pi t}{6} - 4.33 \sin \dfrac{\pi t}{6}$$

(c) The difference between the maximum and minimum temperatures is greatest in the summer.

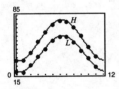

**97.** $\displaystyle\int_{-\pi}^{\pi} \cos(mx)\cos(nx)\, dx = \dfrac{1}{2}\left[\dfrac{\sin(m + n)x}{m + n} + \dfrac{\sin(m - n)x}{m - n}\right]_{-\pi}^{\pi} = 0, \ (m \neq n)$

$\displaystyle\int_{-\pi}^{\pi} \sin(mx)\sin(nx)\, dx = \dfrac{1}{2}\int_{-\pi}^{\pi}[\cos(m - n)x - \cos(m + n)x]\, dx$

$$= \dfrac{1}{2}\left[\dfrac{\sin(m - n)x}{m - n} - \dfrac{\sin(m + n)x}{m + n}\right]_{-\pi}^{\pi} = 0, \ (m \neq n)$$

$\displaystyle\int_{-\pi}^{\pi} \sin(mx)\cos(nx)\, dx = \dfrac{1}{2}\int_{-\pi}^{\pi}[\sin(m + n)x + \sin(m - n)x]\, dx$

$$= -\dfrac{1}{2}\left[\dfrac{\cos(m + n)x}{m + n} + \dfrac{\cos(m - n)x}{m - n}\right]_{-\pi}^{\pi}, \ (m \neq n)$$

$$= -\dfrac{1}{2}\left[\left(\dfrac{\cos(m + n)\pi}{m + n} + \dfrac{\cos(m - n)\pi}{m - n}\right) - \left(\dfrac{\cos(m + n)(-\pi)}{m + n} + \dfrac{\cos(m - n)(-\pi)}{m - n}\right)\right]$$

$$= 0, \text{ since } \cos(-\theta) = \cos\theta.$$

$\displaystyle\int_{-\pi}^{\pi} \sin(mx)\cos(mx)\, dx = \dfrac{1}{m}\dfrac{\sin^2(mx)}{2}\Bigg]_{-\pi}^{\pi} = 0$

# Section 7.4    Trigonometric Substitution

**1.** $\dfrac{d}{dx}\left[4\ln\left|\dfrac{\sqrt{x^2+16}-4}{x}\right| + \sqrt{x^2+16} + C\right] = \dfrac{d}{dx}\left[4\ln\left|\sqrt{x^2+16}-4\right| - 4\ln|x| + \sqrt{x^2+16} + C\right]$

$$= 4\left[\dfrac{x/\sqrt{x^2+16}}{\sqrt{x^2+16}-4}\right] - \dfrac{4}{x} + \dfrac{x}{\sqrt{x^2+16}}$$

$$= \dfrac{4x}{\sqrt{x^2+16}\left(\sqrt{x^2+16}-4\right)} - \dfrac{4}{x} + \dfrac{x}{\sqrt{x^2+16}}$$

$$= \dfrac{4x^2 - 4\sqrt{x^2+16}\left(\sqrt{x^2+16}-4\right) + x^2\left(\sqrt{x^2+16}-4\right)}{x\sqrt{x^2+16}\left(\sqrt{x^2+16}-4\right)}$$

$$= \dfrac{4x^2 - 4(x^2+16) + 16\sqrt{x^2+16} + x^2\sqrt{x^2+16} - 4x^2}{x\sqrt{x^2+16}\left(\sqrt{x^2+16}-4\right)}$$

$$= \dfrac{\sqrt{x^2+16}(x^2+16) - 4(x^2+16)}{x\sqrt{x^2+16}\left(\sqrt{x^2+16}-4\right)}$$

$$= \dfrac{(x^2+16)\left(\sqrt{x^2+16}-4\right)}{x\sqrt{x^2+16}\left(\sqrt{x^2+16}-4\right)} = \dfrac{\sqrt{x^2+16}}{x}$$

Indefinite integral: $\displaystyle\int \dfrac{\sqrt{x^2+16}}{x}\,dx$     Matches (b)

**3.** $\dfrac{d}{dx}\left[8\arcsin\dfrac{x}{4} - \dfrac{x\sqrt{16-x^2}}{2} + C\right] = 8\dfrac{1/4}{\sqrt{1-(x/4)^2}} - \dfrac{x(1/2)(16-x^2)^{-1/2}(-2x) + \sqrt{16-x^2}}{2}$

$$= \dfrac{8}{\sqrt{16-x^2}} + \dfrac{x^2}{2\sqrt{16-x^2}} - \dfrac{\sqrt{16-x^2}}{2}$$

$$= \dfrac{16}{2\sqrt{16-x^2}} + \dfrac{x^2}{2\sqrt{16-x^2}} - \dfrac{(16-x^2)}{2\sqrt{16-x^2}} = \dfrac{x^2}{\sqrt{16-x^2}}$$

Matches (a)

**5.** Let $x = 5\sin\theta$, $dx = 5\cos\theta\,d\theta$, $\sqrt{25-x^2} = 5\cos\theta$.

$$\int \dfrac{1}{(25-x^2)^{3/2}}\,dx = \int \dfrac{5\cos\theta}{(5\cos\theta)^3}\,d\theta$$

$$= \dfrac{1}{25}\int \sec^2\theta\,d\theta$$

$$= \dfrac{1}{25}\tan\theta + C$$

$$= \dfrac{x}{25\sqrt{25-x^2}} + C$$

**7.** Same substitution as in Exercise 5

$$\int \dfrac{\sqrt{25-x^2}}{x}\,dx = \int \dfrac{25\cos^2\theta\,d\theta}{5\sin\theta} = 5\int \dfrac{1-\sin^2\theta}{\sin\theta}\,d\theta = 5\int (\csc\theta - \sin\theta)\,d\theta$$

$$= 5[\ln|\csc\theta - \cot\theta| + \cos\theta] + C = 5\ln\left|\dfrac{5-\sqrt{25-x^2}}{x}\right| + \sqrt{25-x^2} + C$$

**9.** Let $x = 2 \sec \theta$, $dx = 2 \sec \theta \tan \theta \, d\theta$, $\sqrt{x^2 - 4} = 2 \tan \theta$.

$$\int \frac{1}{\sqrt{x^2 - 4}} \, dx = \int \frac{2 \sec \theta \tan \theta \, d\theta}{2 \tan \theta} = \int \sec \theta \, d\theta = \ln|\sec \theta + \tan\theta| + C_1$$

$$= \ln\left|\frac{x}{2} + \frac{\sqrt{x^2 - 4}}{2}\right| + C_1$$

$$= \ln\left|x + \sqrt{x^2 - 4}\right| - \ln 2 + C_1 = \ln\left|x + \sqrt{x^2 - 4}\right| + C$$

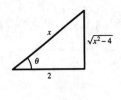

**11.** Same substitution as in Exercise 9

$$\int x^3 \sqrt{x^2 - 4} \, dx = \int (8 \sec^3 \theta)(2 \tan \theta)(2 \sec \theta \tan \theta) \, d\theta = 32 \int \tan^2 \theta \sec^4 \theta \, d\theta$$

$$= 32 \int \tan^2 \theta(1 + \tan^2 \theta) \sec^2 \theta \, d\theta = 32\left(\frac{\tan^3 \theta}{3} + \frac{\tan^5 \theta}{5}\right) + C$$

$$= \frac{32}{15} \tan^3 \theta[5 + 3 \tan^2 \theta] + C = \frac{32}{15} \frac{(x^2 - 4)^{3/2}}{8}\left[5 + 3\frac{(x^2 - 4)}{4}\right] + C$$

$$= \frac{1}{15}(x^2 - 4)^{3/2}[20 + 3(x^2 - 4)] + C = \frac{1}{15}(x^2 - 4)^{3/2}(3x^2 + 8) + C$$

**13.** Let $x = \tan \theta$, $dx = \sec^2 \theta \, d\theta$, $\sqrt{1 + x^2} = \sec \theta$.

$$\int x\sqrt{1 + x^2} \, dx = \int \tan \theta(\sec \theta) \sec^2 \theta \, d\theta = \frac{\sec^3 \theta}{3} + C = \frac{1}{3}(1 + x^2)^{3/2} + C$$

**Note:** This integral could have been evaluated with the Power Rule.

**15.** Same substitution as in Exercise 13

$$\int \frac{1}{(1 + x^2)^2} \, dx = \int \frac{1}{(\sqrt{1 + x^2})^4} \, dx$$

$$= \int \frac{\sec^2 \theta \, d\theta}{\sec^4 \theta}$$

$$= \int \cos^2 \theta \, d\theta = \frac{1}{2}\int (1 + \cos 2\theta) \, d\theta$$

$$= \frac{1}{2}\left[\theta + \frac{\sin 2\theta}{2}\right]$$

$$= \frac{1}{2}[\theta + \sin \theta \cos \theta] + C$$

$$= \frac{1}{2}\left[\arctan x + \left(\frac{x}{\sqrt{1 + x^2}}\right)\left(\frac{1}{\sqrt{1 + x^2}}\right)\right] + C$$

$$= \frac{1}{2}\left[\arctan x + \frac{x}{1 + x^2}\right] + C$$

**17.** Let $u = 3x$, $a = 2$, and $du = 3 \, dx$.

$$\int \sqrt{4 + 9x^2} \, dx = \frac{1}{3}\int \sqrt{(2)^2 + (3x)^2} \, 3 \, dx$$

$$= \frac{1}{3}\left(\frac{1}{2}\right)\left(3x\sqrt{4 + 9x^2} + 4 \ln\left|3x + \sqrt{4 + 9x^2}\right|\right) + C$$

$$= \frac{1}{2}x\sqrt{4 + 9x^2} + \frac{2}{3} \ln\left|3x + \sqrt{4 + 9x^2}\right| + C$$

**19.** $\displaystyle\int \frac{x}{\sqrt{x^2+9}}\,dx = \frac{1}{2}\int (x^2+9)^{-1/2}(2x)\,dx$

$$= \sqrt{x^2+9} + C$$

(Power Rule)

**21.** $\displaystyle\int \frac{1}{\sqrt{16-x^2}}\,dx = \arcsin\!\left(\frac{x}{4}\right) + C$

**23.** Let $x = 2\sin\theta$, $dx = 2\cos\theta\,d\theta$, $\sqrt{4-x^2} = 2\cos\theta$.

$$\int \sqrt{16-4x^2}\,dx = 2\int \sqrt{4-x^2}\,dx$$

$$= 2\int 2\cos\theta(2\cos\theta\,d\theta)$$

$$= 8\int \cos^2\theta\,d\theta$$

$$= 4\int (1+\cos 2\theta)\,d\theta$$

$$= 4\!\left[\theta + \frac{1}{2}\sin 2\theta\right] + C$$

$$= 4\theta + 4\sin\theta\cos\theta + C$$

$$= 4\arcsin\!\left(\frac{x}{2}\right) + x\sqrt{4-x^2} + C$$

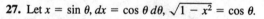

**25.** Let $x = 3\sec\theta$, $dx = 3\sec\theta\tan\theta\,d\theta$,

$\sqrt{x^2-9} = 3\tan\theta$.

$$\int \frac{1}{\sqrt{x^2-9}}\,dx = \int \frac{3\sec\theta\tan\theta\,d\theta}{3\tan\theta}$$

$$= \int \sec\theta\,d\theta$$

$$= \ln|\sec\theta + \tan\theta| + C_1$$

$$= \ln\left|\frac{x}{3} + \frac{\sqrt{x^2-9}}{3}\right| + C_1$$

$$= \ln\left|x + \sqrt{x^2-9}\right| + C$$

**27.** Let $x = \sin\theta$, $dx = \cos\theta\,d\theta$, $\sqrt{1-x^2} = \cos\theta$.

$$\int \frac{\sqrt{1-x^2}}{x^4}\,dx = \int \frac{\cos\theta(\cos\theta\,d\theta)}{\sin^4\theta}$$

$$= \int \cot^2\theta\csc^2\theta\,d\theta$$

$$= -\frac{1}{3}\cot^3\theta + C$$

$$= \frac{-(1-x^2)^{3/2}}{3x^3} + C$$

**29.** Same substitutions as in Exercise 28

$$\int \frac{1}{x\sqrt{4x^2+9}}\,dx = \int \frac{(3/2)\sec^2\theta\,d\theta}{(3/2)\tan\theta\,3\sec\theta}$$

$$= \frac{1}{3}\int \csc\theta\,d\theta = -\frac{1}{3}\ln|\csc\theta + \cot\theta| + C = -\frac{1}{3}\ln\left|\frac{\sqrt{4x^2+9}+3}{2x}\right| + C$$

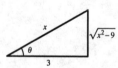

**31.** Let $x = \sqrt{5} \tan \theta$, $dx = \sqrt{5} \sec^2 \theta \, d\theta$, $x^2 + 5 = 5 \sec^2 \theta$.

$$\int \frac{-5x}{(x^2 + 5)^{3/2}} \, dx = \int \frac{-5\sqrt{5} \tan \theta}{(5 \sec^2 \theta)^{3/2}} \sqrt{5} \sec^2 \theta \, d\theta$$

$$= -\sqrt{5} \int \frac{\tan \theta}{\sec \theta} \, d\theta$$

$$= -\sqrt{5} \int \sin \theta \, d\theta$$

$$= \sqrt{5} \cos \theta + C$$

$$= \sqrt{5} \frac{\sqrt{5}}{\sqrt{x^2 + 5}} + C$$

$$= \frac{5}{\sqrt{x^2 + 5}} + C$$

**33.** Let $u = 1 + e^{2x}$, $du = 2e^{2x} \, dx$.

$$\int e^{2x} \sqrt{1 + e^{2x}} \, dx = \frac{1}{2} \int (1 + e^{2x})^{1/2} (2e^{2x}) \, dx = \frac{1}{3} (1 + e^{2x})^{3/2} + C$$

**35.** Let $e^x = \sin \theta$, $e^x \, dx = \cos \theta \, d\theta$, $\sqrt{1 - e^{2x}} = \cos \theta$.

$$\int e^x \sqrt{1 - e^{2x}} \, dx = \int \cos^2 \theta \, d\theta$$

$$= \frac{1}{2} \int (1 + \cos 2\theta) \, d\theta$$

$$= \frac{1}{2} \left[ \theta + \frac{\sin 2\theta}{2} \right]$$

$$= \frac{1}{2} (\theta + \sin \theta \cos \theta) + C = \frac{1}{2} \left( \arcsin e^x + e^x \sqrt{1 - e^{2x}} \right) + C$$

**37.** Let $x = \sqrt{2} \tan \theta$, $dx = \sqrt{2} \sec^2 \theta \, d\theta$, $x^2 + 2 = 2 \sec^2 \theta$.

$$\int \frac{1}{4 + 4x^2 + x^4} \, dx = \int \frac{1}{(x^2 + 2)^2} \, dx$$

$$= \int \frac{\sqrt{2} \sec^2 \theta \, d\theta}{4 \sec^4 \theta}$$

$$= \frac{\sqrt{2}}{4} \int \cos^2 \theta \, d\theta$$

$$= \frac{\sqrt{2}}{4} \left( \frac{1}{2} \right) \int (1 + \cos 2\theta) \, d\theta$$

$$= \frac{\sqrt{2}}{8} \left( \theta + \frac{1}{2} \sin 2\theta \right) + C$$

$$= \frac{\sqrt{2}}{8} (\theta + \sin \theta \cos \theta) + C$$

$$= \frac{1}{4} \left[ \frac{x}{x^2 + 2} + \frac{1}{\sqrt{2}} \arctan \frac{x}{\sqrt{2}} \right] + C$$

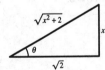

**39.** Since $x > \dfrac{1}{2}$,

$$u = \operatorname{arcsec} 2x, \implies du = \frac{1}{x\sqrt{4x^2 - 1}}\, dx,\, dv = dx \implies v = x$$

$$\int \operatorname{arcsec} 2x \, dx = x \operatorname{arcsec} 2x - \int \frac{1}{\sqrt{4x^2 - 1}}\, dx$$

$$2x = \sec\theta,\, dx = \frac{1}{2}\sec\theta \tan\theta \, d\theta,\, \sqrt{4x^2 - 1} = \tan\theta$$

$$\int \operatorname{arcsec} 2x \, dx = x \operatorname{arcsec} 2x - \int \frac{(1/2)\sec\theta \tan\theta \, d\theta}{\tan\theta} = x \operatorname{arcsec} 2x - \frac{1}{2}\int \sec\theta \, d\theta$$

$$= x \operatorname{arcsec} 2x - \frac{1}{2}\ln|\sec\theta + \tan\theta| + C = x \operatorname{arcsec} 2x - \frac{1}{2}\ln\left|2x + \sqrt{4x^2 - 1}\right| + C.$$

**41.** $\displaystyle \int \frac{1}{\sqrt{4x - x^2}}\, dx = \int \frac{1}{\sqrt{4 - (x - 2)^2}}\, dx = \arcsin\!\left(\frac{x - 2}{2}\right) + C$

**43.** Let $x + 2 = 2\tan\theta,\, dx = 2\sec^2\theta \, d\theta,\, \sqrt{(x + 2)^2 + 4} = 2\sec\theta$.

$$\int \frac{x}{\sqrt{x^2 + 4x + 8}}\, dx = \int \frac{x}{\sqrt{(x + 2)^2 + 4}}\, dx = \int \frac{(2\tan\theta - 2)(2\sec^2\theta)\, d\theta}{2\sec\theta}$$

$$= 2\int (\tan\theta - 1)(\sec\theta)\, d\theta$$

$$= 2[\sec\theta - \ln|\sec\theta + \tan\theta|] + C_1$$

$$= 2\left[\frac{\sqrt{(x + 2)^2 + 4}}{2} - \ln\left|\frac{\sqrt{(x + 2)^2 + 4}}{2} + \frac{x + 2}{2}\right|\right] + C_1$$

$$= \sqrt{x^2 + 4x + 8} - 2\left[\ln\left|\sqrt{x^2 + 4x + 8} + (x + 2)\right| - \ln 2\right] + C_1$$

$$= \sqrt{x^2 + 4x + 8} - 2\ln\left|\sqrt{x^2 + 4x + 8} + (x + 2)\right| + C$$

**45.** Let $t = \sin\theta,\, dt = \cos\theta \, d\theta,\, 1 - t^2 = \cos^2\theta$.

(a) $\displaystyle \int \frac{t^2}{(1 - t^2)^{3/2}}\, dt = \int \frac{\sin^2\theta \cos\theta \, d\theta}{\cos^3\theta}$

$$= \int \tan^2\theta \, d\theta$$

$$= \int (\sec^2\theta - 1)\, d\theta$$

$$= \tan\theta - \theta + C$$

$$= \frac{t}{\sqrt{1 - t^2}} - \arcsin t + C$$

Thus, $\displaystyle \int_0^{\sqrt{3}/2} \frac{t^2}{(1 - t^2)^{3/2}}\, dt = \left[\frac{t}{\sqrt{1 - t^2}} - \arcsin t\right]_0^{\sqrt{3}/2} = \frac{\sqrt{3}/2}{\sqrt{1/4}} - \arcsin\frac{\sqrt{3}}{2} = \sqrt{3} - \frac{\pi}{3} \approx 0.685.$

(b) When $t = 0$, $\theta = 0$. When $t = \sqrt{3}/2$, $\theta = \pi/3$. Thus,

$$\int_0^{\sqrt{3}/2} \frac{t^2}{(1 - t^2)^{3/2}}\, dt = \left[\tan\theta - \theta\right]_0^{\pi/3} = \sqrt{3} - \frac{\pi}{3} \approx 0.685.$$

**47.** (a) Let $x = 3\tan\theta$, $dx = 3\sec^2\theta\,d\theta$, $\sqrt{x^2+9} = 3\sec\theta$.

$$\int \frac{x^3}{\sqrt{x^2+9}}\,dx = \int \frac{(27\tan^3\theta)(3\sec^2\theta\,d\theta)}{3\sec\theta}$$

$$= 27\int (\sec^2\theta - 1)\sec\theta\tan\theta\,d\theta$$

$$= 27\left[\frac{1}{3}\sec^3\theta - \sec\theta\right] + C = 9[\sec^3\theta - 3\sec\theta] + C$$

$$= 9\left[\left(\frac{\sqrt{x^2+9}}{3}\right)^3 - 3\left(\frac{\sqrt{x^2+9}}{3}\right)\right] + C = \frac{1}{3}(x^2+9)^{3/2} - 9\sqrt{x^2+9} + C$$

Thus, $\displaystyle\int_0^3 \frac{x^3}{\sqrt{x^2+9}}\,dx = \left[\frac{1}{3}(x^2+9)^{3/2} - 9\sqrt{x^2+9}\right]_0^3$

$$= \left(\frac{1}{3}(54\sqrt{2}) - 27\sqrt{2}\right) - (9 - 27)$$

$$= 18 - 9\sqrt{2} = 9(2 - \sqrt{2}) \approx 5.272.$$

(b) When $x = 0$, $\theta = 0$. When $x = 3$, $\theta = \pi/4$. Thus,

$$\int_0^3 \frac{x^3}{\sqrt{x^2+9}}\,dx = 9\left[\sec^3\theta - 3\sec\theta\right]_0^{\pi/4} = 9(2\sqrt{2} - 3\sqrt{2}) - 9(1 - 3) = 9(2 - \sqrt{2}) \approx 5.272.$$

**49.** (a) Let $x = 3\sec\theta$, $dx = 3\sec\theta\tan\theta\,d\theta$, $\sqrt{x^2-9} = 3\tan\theta$.

$$\int \frac{x^2}{\sqrt{x^2-9}}\,dx = \int \frac{9\sec^2\theta}{3\tan\theta}\,3\sec\theta\tan\theta\,d\theta$$

$$= 9\int \sec^3\theta\,d\theta$$

$$= 9\left[\frac{1}{2}\sec\theta\tan\theta + \frac{1}{2}\int \sec\theta\,d\theta\right] \qquad \text{(7.3 Exercise 90)}$$

$$= \frac{9}{2}[\sec\theta\tan\theta + \ln|\sec\theta + \tan\theta|]$$

$$= \frac{9}{2}\left[\frac{x}{3}\cdot\frac{\sqrt{x^2-9}}{3} + \ln\left|\frac{x}{3} + \frac{\sqrt{x^2-9}}{3}\right|\right]$$

Hence,

$$\int_4^6 \frac{x^2}{\sqrt{x^2-9}}\,dx = \frac{9}{2}\left[\frac{x\sqrt{x^2-9}}{9} + \ln\left|\frac{x}{3} + \frac{\sqrt{x^2-9}}{3}\right|\right]_4^6$$

$$= \frac{9}{2}\left[\left(\frac{6\sqrt{27}}{9} + \ln\left|2 + \frac{\sqrt{27}}{3}\right|\right) - \left(\frac{4\sqrt{7}}{9} + \ln\left|\frac{4}{3} + \frac{\sqrt{7}}{3}\right|\right)\right]$$

$$= 9\sqrt{3} - 2\sqrt{7} + \frac{9}{2}\left(\ln\left(\frac{6 + \sqrt{27}}{3}\right) - \ln\left(\frac{4 + \sqrt{7}}{3}\right)\right)$$

$$= 9\sqrt{3} - 2\sqrt{7} + \frac{9}{2}\ln\left(\frac{6 + 3\sqrt{3}}{4 + \sqrt{7}}\right)$$

$$= 9\sqrt{3} - 2\sqrt{7} + \frac{9}{2}\ln\left(\frac{(4 - \sqrt{7})(2 + \sqrt{3})}{3}\right) \approx 12.644.$$

—CONTINUED—

**49. —CONTINUED—**

(b) When $x = 4$, $\theta = \operatorname{arcsec}\left(\dfrac{4}{3}\right)$.

When $x = 6$, $\theta = \operatorname{arcsec}(2) = \dfrac{\pi}{3}$.

$$\int_4^6 \frac{x^2}{\sqrt{x^2 - 9}}\, dx = \frac{9}{2}\Big[\sec\theta\tan\theta + \ln|\sec\theta + \tan\theta|\Big]_{\operatorname{arcsec}(4/3)}^{\pi/3}$$

$$= \frac{9}{2}\Big[2\cdot\sqrt{3} + \ln|2 + \sqrt{3}|\Big] - \frac{9}{2}\left[\frac{4}{3}\frac{\sqrt{7}}{3} + \ln\left|\frac{4}{3} + \frac{\sqrt{7}}{3}\right|\right]$$

$$= 9\sqrt{3} - 2\sqrt{7} + \frac{9}{2}\ln\left(\frac{6 + 3\sqrt{3}}{4 + \sqrt{7}}\right) \approx 12.644$$

**51.** $\displaystyle\int \frac{x^2}{\sqrt{x^2 + 10x + 9}}\, dx = \frac{1}{2}\sqrt{x^2 + 10x + 9}\,(x - 15) + 33\ln\left|(x + 5) + \sqrt{x^2 + 10x + 9}\right| + C$

**53.** $\displaystyle\int \frac{x^2}{\sqrt{x^2 - 1}}\, dx = \frac{1}{2}\left(x\sqrt{x^2 - 1} + \ln\left|x + \sqrt{x^2 - 1}\right|\right) + C$  **55.** (a) $u = a\sin\theta$  (b) $u = a\tan\theta$  (c) $u = a\sec\theta$

**57.** $A = 4\displaystyle\int_0^a \frac{b}{a}\sqrt{a^2 - x^2}\, dx$

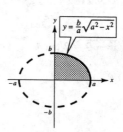

$$= \frac{4b}{a}\int_0^a \sqrt{a^2 - x^2}\, dx$$

$$= \left[\frac{4b}{a}\left(\frac{1}{2}\right)\left(a^2\arcsin\frac{x}{a} + x\sqrt{a^2 - x^2}\right)\right]_0^a$$

$$= \frac{2b}{a}\left(a^2\left(\frac{\pi}{2}\right)\right)$$

$$= \pi ab$$

**Note:** See Theorem 7.2 for $\int \sqrt{a^2 - x^2}\, dx$.

**59.** $x^2 + y^2 = a^2$

$\quad\quad x = \pm\sqrt{a^2 - y^2}$

$$A = 2\int_h^a \sqrt{a^2 - y^2}\, dy = \left[a^2\arcsin\left(\frac{y}{a}\right) + y\sqrt{a^2 - y^2}\right]_h^a \quad \text{(Theorem 7.2)}$$

$$= \left(a^2\frac{\pi}{2}\right) - \left(a^2\arcsin\left(\frac{h}{a}\right) + h\sqrt{a^2 - h^2}\right)$$

$$= \frac{a^2\pi}{2} - a^2\arcsin\left(\frac{h}{a}\right) - h\sqrt{a^2 - h^2}$$

**61.** Let $x - 3 = \sin\theta$, $dx = \cos\theta\, d\theta$, $\sqrt{1 - (x - 3)^2} = \cos\theta$.

**Shell Method:**

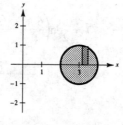

$$V = 4\pi\int_2^4 x\sqrt{1 - (x - 3)^2}\, dx$$

$$= 4\pi\int_{-\pi/2}^{\pi/2} (3 + \sin\theta)\cos^2\theta\, d\theta$$

$$= 4\pi\left[\frac{3}{2}\int_{-\pi/2}^{\pi/2} (1 + \cos 2\theta)\, d\theta + \int_{-\pi/2}^{\pi/2} \cos^2\theta\sin\theta\, d\theta\right]$$

$$= 4\pi\left[\frac{3}{2}\left(\theta + \frac{1}{2}\sin 2\theta\right) - \frac{1}{3}\cos^3\theta\right]_{-\pi/2}^{\pi/2} = 6\pi^2$$

**63.** $y = \ln x$, $y' = \dfrac{1}{x}$, $1 + (y')^2 = 1 + \dfrac{1}{x^2} = \dfrac{x^2 + 1}{x^2}$

Let $x = \tan\theta$, $dx = \sec^2\theta\,d\theta$, $\sqrt{x^2 + 1} = \sec\theta$.

$$s = \int_1^5 \sqrt{\frac{x^2 + 1}{x^2}}\,dx = \int_1^5 \frac{\sqrt{x^2 + 1}}{x}\,dx$$

$$= \int_a^b \frac{\sec\theta}{\tan\theta}\sec^2\theta\,d\theta = \int_a^b \frac{\sec\theta}{\tan\theta}(1 + \tan^2\theta)\,d\theta$$

$$= \int_a^b (\csc\theta + \sec\theta\tan\theta)\,d\theta$$

$$= \Big[-\ln|\csc\theta + \cot\theta| + \sec\theta\Big]_a^b$$

$$= \left[-\ln\left|\frac{\sqrt{x^2 + 1}}{x} + \frac{1}{x}\right| + \sqrt{x^2 + 1}\right]_1^5$$

$$= \left[-\ln\left(\frac{\sqrt{26} + 1}{5}\right) + \sqrt{26}\right] - \left[-\ln\left(\sqrt{2} + 1\right) + \sqrt{2}\right]$$

$$= \ln\left[\frac{5(\sqrt{2} + 1)}{\sqrt{26} + 1}\right] + \sqrt{26} - \sqrt{2} \approx 4.367 \text{ or } \ln\left[\frac{\sqrt{26} - 1}{5(\sqrt{2} - 1)}\right] + \sqrt{26} - \sqrt{2}$$

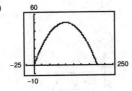

**65.** Length of one arch of sine curve: $y = \sin x$, $y' = \cos x$

$$L_1 = \int_0^\pi \sqrt{1 + \cos^2 x}\,dx$$

Length of one arch of cosine curve: $y = \cos x$, $y' = -\sin x$

$$L_2 = \int_{-\pi/2}^{\pi/2} \sqrt{1 + \sin^2 x}\,dx$$

$$= \int_{-\pi/2}^{\pi/2} \sqrt{1 + \cos^2\left(x - \frac{\pi}{2}\right)}\,dx \qquad u = x - \frac{\pi}{2},\, du = dx$$

$$= \int_{-\pi}^0 \sqrt{1 + \cos^2 u}\,du$$

$$= \int_0^\pi \sqrt{1 + \cos^2 u}\,du = L_1$$

**67.** (a)

(b) $y = 0$ for $x = 200$  (range)

(c) $y = x - 0.005x^2$, $y' = 1 - 0.01x$, $1 + (y')^2 = 1 + (1 - 0.01x)^2$

Let $u = 1 - 0.01x$, $du = -0.01\,dx$, $a = 1$. (See Theorem 7.2.)

$$s = \int_0^{200} \sqrt{1 + (1 - 0.01x)^2}\,dx = -100\int_0^{200} \sqrt{(1 - 0.01x)^2 + 1}\,(-0.01)\,dx$$

$$= -50\left[(1 - 0.01x)\sqrt{(1 - 0.01x)^2 + 1} + \ln\left|(1 - 0.01x) + \sqrt{(1 - 0.01x)^2 + 1}\right|\right]_0^{200}$$

$$= -50\left[\left(-\sqrt{2} + \ln\left|-1 + \sqrt{2}\right|\right) - \left(\sqrt{2} + \ln\left|1 + \sqrt{2}\right|\right)\right]$$

$$= 100\sqrt{2} + 50\ln\left(\frac{\sqrt{2} + 1}{\sqrt{2} - 1}\right) \approx 229.559$$

**69.** Let $x = 3\tan\theta$, $dx = 3\sec^2\theta\,d\theta$, $\sqrt{x^2 + 9} = 3\sec\theta$.

$$A = 2\int_0^4 \frac{3}{\sqrt{x^2+9}}\,dx = 6\int_0^4 \frac{dx}{\sqrt{x^2+9}} = 6\int_a^b \frac{3\sec^2\theta\,d\theta}{3\sec\theta}$$

$$= 6\int_a^b \sec\theta\,d\theta = \left[6\ln|\sec\theta + \tan\theta|\right]_a^b = \left[6\ln\left|\frac{\sqrt{x^2+9}+x}{3}\right|\right]_0^4 = 6\ln 3$$

$\bar{x} = 0$ (by symmetry)

$$\bar{y} = \frac{1}{2}\left(\frac{1}{A}\right)\int_{-4}^4 \left(\frac{3}{\sqrt{x^2+9}}\right)^2 dx$$

$$= \frac{9}{12\ln 3}\int_{-4}^4 \frac{1}{x^2+9}\,dx$$

$$= \frac{3}{4\ln 3}\left[\frac{1}{3}\arctan\frac{x}{3}\right]_{-4}^4$$

$$= \frac{2}{4\ln 3}\arctan\frac{4}{3} \approx 0.422$$

$$(\bar{x}, \bar{y}) = \left(0, \frac{1}{2\ln 3}\arctan\frac{4}{3}\right) \approx (0, 0.422)$$

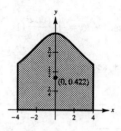

**71.** $y = x^2$, $\qquad y' = 2x$, $\qquad 1 + (y') = 1 + 4x^2$

$2x = \tan\theta$, $dx = \frac{1}{2}\sec^2\theta\,d\theta$, $\sqrt{1+4x^2} = \sec\theta$

(For $\int\sec^5\theta\,d\theta$ and $\int\sec^3\theta\,d\theta$, see Exercise 80 in Section 7.3)

$$S = 2\pi\int_0^{\sqrt{2}} x^2\sqrt{1+4x^2}\,dx = 2\pi\int_a^b \left(\frac{\tan\theta}{2}\right)^2(\sec\theta)\left(\frac{1}{2}\sec^2\theta\right)d\theta$$

$$= \frac{\pi}{4}\int_a^b \sec^3\theta\tan^2\theta\,d\theta = \frac{\pi}{4}\left[\int_a^b \sec^5\theta\,d\theta - \int_a^b \sec^3\theta\,d\theta\right]$$

$$= \frac{\pi}{4}\left\{\frac{1}{4}\left[\sec^3\theta\tan\theta + \frac{3}{2}(\sec\theta\tan\theta + \ln|\sec\theta+\tan\theta|)\right] - \frac{1}{2}(\sec\theta\tan\theta + \ln|\sec\theta+\tan\theta|)\right\}\bigg]_a^b$$

$$= \frac{\pi}{4}\left[\frac{1}{4}[(1+4x^2)^{3/2}(2x)] - \frac{1}{8}[(1+4x^2)^{1/2}(2x) + \ln\left|\sqrt{1+4x^2}+2x\right|]\right]_0^{\sqrt{2}}$$

$$= \frac{\pi}{4}\left[\frac{54\sqrt{2}}{4} - \frac{6\sqrt{2}}{6} = \frac{1}{8}\ln(3+2\sqrt{2})\right]$$

$$= \frac{\pi}{4}\left(\frac{51\sqrt{2}}{4} - \frac{\ln(3+2\sqrt{2})}{8}\right) = \frac{\pi}{32}\left[102\sqrt{2} - \ln(3+2\sqrt{2})\right] \approx 13.989$$

**73.** (a) Area of representative rectangle: $2\sqrt{1-y^2}\,\Delta y$

Pressure: $2(62.4)(3-y)\sqrt{1-y^2}\,\Delta y$

$$F = 124.8\int_{-1}^1 (3-y)\sqrt{1-y^2}\,dy$$

$$= 124.8\left[3 + \int_{-1}^1 \sqrt{1-y^2}\,dy - \int_{-1}^1 y\sqrt{1-y^2}\,dy\right]$$

$$= 124.8\left[\frac{3}{2}\left(\arcsin y + y\sqrt{1-y^2}\right) + \frac{1}{2}\left(\frac{2}{3}\right)(1-y^2)^{3/2}\right]_{-1}^1$$

$$= (62.4)3[\arcsin 1 - \arcsin(-1)] = 187.2\pi\text{ lb}$$

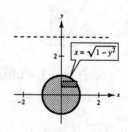

(b) $F = 124.8\int_{-1}^1 (d-y)\sqrt{1-y^2}\,dy = 124.8d\int_{-1}^1 \sqrt{1-y^2}\,dy - 124.8\int_{-1}^1 y\sqrt{1-y^2}\,dy$

$$= 124.8\left(\frac{d}{2}\right)\left[\arcsin y + y\sqrt{1-y^2}\right]_{-1}^1 - 124.8(0) = 62.4\pi d\text{ lb}$$

**75.** (a) $m = \dfrac{dy}{dx} = \dfrac{y - \left(y + \sqrt{144 - x^2}\right)}{x - 0}$

$\qquad = -\dfrac{\sqrt{144 - x^2}}{x}$

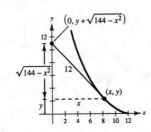

(b) $y = -\displaystyle\int \dfrac{\sqrt{144 - x^2}}{x}\, dx$

Let $x = 12 \sin \theta$, $dx = 12 \cos \theta\, d\theta$, $\sqrt{144 - x^2} = 12 \cos \theta$.

$y = -\displaystyle\int \dfrac{12 \cos \theta}{12 \sin \theta}\, 12 \cos \theta\, d\theta = -12 \int \dfrac{1 - \sin^2 \theta}{\sin \theta}\, d\theta$

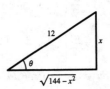

$\qquad = -12 \displaystyle\int (\csc \theta - \sin \theta)\, d\theta = -12 \ln|\csc \theta - \cot \theta| - 12 \cos \theta + C$

$\qquad = -12 \ln\left|\dfrac{12}{x} - \dfrac{\sqrt{144 - x^2}}{x}\right| - 12\left(\dfrac{\sqrt{144 - x^2}}{12}\right) + C$

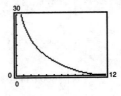

$\qquad = -12 \ln\left|\dfrac{12 - \sqrt{144 - x^2}}{x}\right| - \sqrt{144 - x^2} + C$

When $x = 12$, $y = 0 \Rightarrow C = 0$. Thus, $y = -12 \ln\left(\dfrac{12 - \sqrt{144 - x^2}}{x}\right) - \sqrt{144 - x^2}$.

**Note:** $\dfrac{12 - \sqrt{144 - x^2}}{x} > 0$ for $0 < x \le 12$

(c) Vertical asymptote: $x = 0$

(d) $y + \sqrt{144 - x^2} = 12 \Rightarrow y = 12 - \sqrt{144 - x^2}$

Thus,

$$12 - \sqrt{144 - x^2} = -12 \ln\left(\dfrac{12 - \sqrt{144 - x^2}}{x}\right) - \sqrt{144 - x^2}$$

$$-1 = \ln\left(\dfrac{12 - \sqrt{144 - x^2}}{x}\right)$$

$$xe^{-1} = 12 - \sqrt{144 - x^2}$$

$$\left(xe^{-1} - 12\right)^2 = \left(-\sqrt{144 - x^2}\right)^2$$

$$x^2 e^{-2} - 24xe^{-1} + 144 = 144 - x^2$$

$$x^2(e^{-2} + 1) - 24xe^{-1} = 0$$

$$x\left[x(e^{-2} + 1) - 24e^{-1}\right] = 0$$

$$x = 0 \text{ or } x = \dfrac{24e^{-1}}{e^{-2} + 1} \approx 7.77665.$$

Therefore,

$$s = \int_{7.77665}^{12} \sqrt{1 + \left(-\dfrac{\sqrt{144 - x^2}}{x}\right)^2}\, dx = \int_{7.77665}^{12} \sqrt{\dfrac{x^2 + (144 - x^2)}{x^2}}\, dx$$

$$= \int_{7.77665}^{12} \dfrac{12}{x}\, dx = \Big[\, 12 \ln|x| \,\Big]_{7.77665}^{12} = 12(\ln 12 - \ln 7.77665) \approx 5.2 \text{ meters.}$$

**77.** True

$$\int \frac{dx}{\sqrt{1-x^2}} = \int \frac{\cos\theta\,d\theta}{\cos\theta} = \int d\theta$$

**79.** False

$$\int_0^{\sqrt{3}} \frac{dx}{(\sqrt{1+x^2})^3} = \int_0^{\pi/3} \frac{\sec^2\theta\,d\theta}{\sec^3\theta} = \int_0^{\pi/3} \cos\theta\,d\theta$$

**81.** Let $u = a\sin\theta$, $du = a\cos\theta\,d\theta$, $\sqrt{a^2-u^2} = a\cos\theta$.

$$\int \sqrt{a^2-u^2}\,du = \int a^2\cos^2\theta\,d\theta = a^2 \int \frac{1+\cos 2\theta}{2}\,d\theta$$

$$= \frac{a^2}{2}\left(\theta + \frac{1}{2}\sin 2\theta\right) + C = \frac{a^2}{2}(\theta + \sin\theta\cos\theta) + C$$

$$= \frac{a^2}{2}\left[\arcsin\frac{u}{a} + \left(\frac{u}{a}\right)\left(\frac{\sqrt{a^2+u^2}}{a}\right)\right] + C = \frac{1}{2}\left[a^2\arcsin\frac{u}{a} + u\sqrt{a^2-u^2}\right] + C$$

Let $u = a\sec\theta$, $du = a\sec\theta\tan\theta\,d\theta$, $\sqrt{u^2-a^2} = a\tan\theta$.

$$\int \sqrt{u^2-a^2}\,du = \int a\tan\theta(a\sec\theta\tan\theta)\,d\theta = a^2 \int \tan^2\theta\sec\theta\,d\theta$$

$$= a^2 \int (\sec^2\theta - 1)\sec\theta\,d\theta = a^2 \int (\sec^3\theta - \sec\theta)\,d\theta$$

$$= a^2\left[\frac{1}{2}\sec\theta\tan\theta + \frac{1}{2}\int \sec\theta\,d\theta\right] - a^2\int \sec\theta\,d\theta = a^2\left[\frac{1}{2}\sec\theta\tan\theta - \frac{1}{2}\ln|\sec\theta + \tan\theta|\right]$$

$$= \frac{a^2}{2}\left[\frac{u}{a} \cdot \frac{\sqrt{u^2-a^2}}{a} - \ln\left|\frac{u}{a} + \frac{\sqrt{u^2-a^2}}{a}\right|\right] + C_1$$

$$= \frac{1}{2}\left[u\sqrt{u^2-a^2} - a^2\ln|u + \sqrt{u^2-a^2}|\right] + C$$

Let $u = a\tan\theta$, $du = a\sec^2\theta\,d\theta$, $\sqrt{u^2+a^2} = a\sec\theta\,d\theta$.

$$\int \sqrt{u^2+a^2}\,du = \int (a\sec\theta)(a\sec^2\theta)\,d\theta$$

$$= a^2\int \sec^3\theta\,d\theta = a^2\left[\frac{1}{2}\sec\theta\tan\theta + \frac{1}{2}\ln|\sec\theta + \tan\theta|\right] + C_1$$

$$= \frac{a^2}{2}\left[\frac{\sqrt{u^2+a^2}}{a} \cdot \frac{u}{a} + \ln\left|\frac{\sqrt{u^2+a^2}}{a} + \frac{u}{a}\right|\right] + C_1 = \frac{1}{2}\left[u\sqrt{u^2+a^2} + a^2\ln|u + \sqrt{u^2+a^2}|\right] + C$$

# Section 7.5    Partial Fractions

**1.** $\dfrac{5}{x^2-10x} = \dfrac{5}{x(x-10)} = \dfrac{A}{x} + \dfrac{B}{x-10}$

**3.** $\dfrac{2x-3}{x^3+10x} = \dfrac{2x-3}{x(x^2+10)} = \dfrac{A}{x} + \dfrac{Bx+C}{x^2+10}$

**5.** $\dfrac{16x}{x^3-10x^2} = \dfrac{16x}{x^2(x-10)} = \dfrac{A}{x} + \dfrac{B}{x^2} + \dfrac{C}{x-10}$

**7.** $\dfrac{1}{x^2-1} = \dfrac{1}{(x+1)(x-1)} = \dfrac{A}{x+1} + \dfrac{B}{x-1}$

$$1 = A(x-1) + B(x+1)$$

When $x = -1$, $1 = -2A$, $A = -\frac{1}{2}$.

When $x = 1$, $1 = 2B$, $B = \frac{1}{2}$.

$$\int \frac{1}{x^2-1}\,dx = -\frac{1}{2}\int \frac{1}{x+1}\,dx + \frac{1}{2}\int \frac{1}{x-1}\,dx$$

$$= -\frac{1}{2}\ln|x+1| + \frac{1}{2}\ln|x-1| + C$$

$$= \frac{1}{2}\ln\left|\frac{x-1}{x+1}\right| + C$$

**9.** $\dfrac{3}{x^2 + x - 2} = \dfrac{3}{(x-1)(x+2)} = \dfrac{A}{x-1} + \dfrac{B}{x+2}$

$$3 = (x+2) + B(x-1)$$

When $x = 1, 3 = 3A, A = 1$.

When $x = -2, 3 = -3B, B = -1$.

$$\int \frac{3}{x^2 + x - 2}\, dx = \int \frac{1}{x-1}\, dx - \int \frac{1}{x+2}\, dx$$

$$= \ln|x-1| - \ln|x+2| + C$$

$$= \ln\left|\frac{x-1}{x+2}\right| + C$$

**11.** $\dfrac{5-x}{2x^2 + x - 1} = \dfrac{5-x}{(2x-1)(x+1)} = \dfrac{A}{2x-1} + \dfrac{B}{x+1}$

$$5 - x = A(x+1) + B(2x-1)$$

When $x = \frac{1}{2}, \frac{9}{2} = \frac{3}{2}A, A = 3$.

When $x = -1, 6 = -3B, B = -2$.

$$\int \frac{5-x}{2x^2 + x - 1}\, dx = 3\int \frac{1}{2x-1}\, dx - 2\int \frac{1}{x+1}\, dx$$

$$= \frac{3}{2}\ln|2x-1| - 2\ln|x+1| + C$$

**13.** $\dfrac{x^2 + 12x + 12}{x(x+2)(x-2)} = \dfrac{A}{x} + \dfrac{B}{x+2} + \dfrac{C}{x-2}$

$$x^2 + 12x + 12 = A(x+2)(x-2) + Bx(x-2) + Cx(x+2)$$

When $x = 0, 12 = -4A, A = -3$. When $x = -2, -8 = 8B, B = -1$. When $x = 2, 40 = 8C, C = 5$.

$$\int \frac{x^2 + 12x + 12}{x^3 - 4x}\, dx = 5\int \frac{1}{x-2}\, dx - \int \frac{1}{x+2}\, dx - 3\int \frac{1}{x}\, dx$$

$$= 5\ln|x-2| - \ln|x+2| - 3\ln|x| + C$$

**15.** $\dfrac{2x^3 - 4x^2 - 15x + 5}{x^2 - 2x - 8} = 2x + \dfrac{x+5}{(x-4)(x+2)} = 2x + \dfrac{A}{x-4} + \dfrac{B}{x+2}$

$$x + 5 = A(x+2) + B(x-4)$$

When $x = 4, 9 = 6A, A = \frac{3}{2}$. When $x = -2, 3 = -6B, B = -\frac{1}{2}$.

$$\int \frac{2x^3 - 4x^2 - 15x + 5}{x^2 - 2x - 8}\, dx = \int \left[2x + \frac{3/2}{x-4} - \frac{1/2}{x+2}\right] dx$$

$$= x^2 + \frac{3}{2}\ln|x-4| - \frac{1}{2}\ln|x+2| + C$$

**17.** $\dfrac{4x^2 + 2x - 1}{x^2(x+1)} = \dfrac{A}{x} + \dfrac{B}{x^2} + \dfrac{C}{x+1}$

$$4x^2 + 2x - 1 = Ax(x+1) + B(x+1) + Cx^2$$

When $x = 0, B = -1$. When $x = -1, C = 1$. When $x = 1, A = 3$.

$$\int \frac{4x^2 + 2x - 1}{x^3 + x^2}\, dx = \int \left[\frac{3}{x} - \frac{1}{x^2} + \frac{1}{x+1}\right] dx = 3\ln|x| + \frac{1}{x} + \ln|x+1| + C$$

$$= \frac{1}{x} + \ln|x^4 + x^3| + C$$

**19.** $\dfrac{x^2 + 3x - 4}{x^3 - 4x^2 + 4x} = \dfrac{x^2 + 3x - 4}{x(x-2)^2} = \dfrac{A}{x} + \dfrac{B}{(x-2)} + \dfrac{C}{(x-2)^2}$

$$x^2 + 3x - 4 = A(x-2)^2 + Bx(x-2) + Cx$$

When $x = 0, -4 = -4A \Rightarrow A = -1$. When $x = 2, 6 = 2C \Rightarrow C = 3$. When $x = 1, 0 = -1 - B + 3 \Rightarrow B = 2$.

$$\int \frac{x^2 + 3x - 4}{x^3 - 4x^2 + 4x}\, dx = \int \frac{-1}{x}\, dx + \int \frac{2}{(x-2)}\, dx + \int \frac{3}{(x-2)^2}\, dx$$

$$= -\ln|x| + 2\ln|x-2| - \frac{3}{(x-2)} + C$$

**21.** $\dfrac{x^2 - 1}{x(x^2 + 1)} = \dfrac{A}{x} + \dfrac{Bx + C}{x^2 + 1}$

$$x^2 - 1 = A(x^2 + 1) + (Bx + C)x$$

When $x = 0, A = -1$. When $x = 1, 0 = -2 + B + C$. When $x = -1, 0 = -2 + B + C$.
Solving these equations we have $A = -1, B = 2, C = 0$.

$$\int \frac{x^2 - 1}{x^3 + x}\, dx = -\int \frac{1}{x}\, dx + \int \frac{2x}{x^2 + 1}\, dx$$

$$= \ln|x^2 + 1| - \ln|x| + C$$

$$= \ln\left|\frac{x^2 + 1}{x}\right| + C$$

**23.** $\dfrac{x^2}{x^4 - 2x^2 - 8} = \dfrac{A}{x - 2} + \dfrac{B}{x + 2} + \dfrac{Cx + D}{x^2 + 2}$

$$x^2 = A(x + 2)(x^2 + 2) + B(x - 2)(x^2 + 2) + (Cx + D)(x + 2)(x - 2)$$

When $x = 2, 4 = 24A$. When $x = -2, 4 = -24B$. When $x = 0, 0 = 4A - 4B - 4D$, and when $x = 1$,
$1 = 9A - 3B - 3C - 3D$. Solving these equations we have $A = \frac{1}{6}, B = -\frac{1}{6}, C = 0, D = \frac{1}{3}$.

$$\int \frac{x^2}{x^4 - 2x^2 - 8}\, dx = \frac{1}{6}\left[\int \frac{1}{x - 2}\, dx - \int \frac{1}{x + 2}\, dx + 2\int \frac{1}{x^2 + 2}\, dx\right]$$

$$= \frac{1}{6}\left[\ln\left|\frac{x - 2}{x + 2}\right| + \sqrt{2}\,\arctan\frac{x}{\sqrt{2}}\right] + C$$

**25.** $\dfrac{x}{(2x - 1)(2x + 1)(4x^2 + 1)} = \dfrac{A}{2x - 1} + \dfrac{B}{2x + 1} + \dfrac{Cx + D}{4x^2 + 1}$

$$x = A(2x + 1)(4x^2 + 1) + B(2x - 1)(4x^2 + 1) + (Cx + D)(2x - 1)(2x + 1)$$

When $x = \frac{1}{2}, \frac{1}{2} = 4A$. When $x = -\frac{1}{2}, -\frac{1}{2} = -4B$. When $x = 0, 0 = A - B - D$, and when $x = 1$,
$1 = 15A + 5B + 3C + 3D$. Solving these equations we have $A = \frac{1}{8}, B = \frac{1}{8}, C = -\frac{1}{2}, D = 0$.

$$\int \frac{x}{16x^4 - 1}\, dx = \frac{1}{8}\left[\int \frac{1}{2x - 1}\, dx + \int \frac{1}{2x + 1}\, dx - 4\int \frac{x}{4x^2 + 1}\, dx\right]$$

$$= \frac{1}{16}\ln\left|\frac{4x^2 - 1}{4x^2 + 1}\right| + C$$

**27.** $\dfrac{x^2 + 5}{(x + 1)(x^2 - 2x + 3)} = \dfrac{A}{x + 1} + \dfrac{Bx + C}{x^2 - 2x + 3}$

$$x^2 + 5 = A(x^2 - 2x + 3) + (Bx + C)(x + 1)$$

$$= (A + B)x^2 + (-2A + B + C)x + (3A + C)$$

When $x = -1, A = 1$. By equating coefficients of like terms, we have $A + B = 1, -2A + B + C = 0$,
$3A + C = 5$. Solving these equations we have $A = 1, B = 0, C = 2$.

$$\int \frac{x^2 + 5}{x^3 - x^2 + x + 3}\, dx = \int \frac{1}{x + 1}\, dx + 2\int \frac{1}{(x - 1)^2 + 2}\, dx$$

$$= \ln|x + 1| + \sqrt{2}\,\arctan\left(\frac{x - 1}{\sqrt{2}}\right) + C$$

**29.** $\dfrac{3}{(2x + 1)(x + 2)} = \dfrac{A}{2x + 1} + \dfrac{B}{x + 2}$

$$3 = A(x + 2) + B(2x + 1)$$

When $x = -\frac{1}{2}$, $A = 2$. When $x = -2$, $B = -1$.

$$\int_0^1 \frac{3}{2x^2 + 5x + 2}\, dx = \int_0^1 \frac{2}{2x + 1}\, dx - \int_0^1 \frac{1}{x + 2}\, dx$$

$$= \left[ \ln|2x - 1| - \ln|x + 2| \right]_0^1$$

$$= \ln 2$$

**31.** $\dfrac{x + 1}{x(x^2 + 1)} = \dfrac{A}{x} + \dfrac{Bx + C}{x^2 + 1}$

$$x + 1 = A(x^2 + 1) + (Bx + C)x$$

When $x = 0$, $A = 1$. When $x = 1$, $2 = 2A + B + C$. When $x = -1$, $0 = 2A + B - C$. Solving these equations we have $A = 1$, $B = -1$, $C = 1$.

$$\int_1^2 \frac{x + 1}{x(x^2 + 1)}\, dx = \int_1^2 \frac{1}{x}\, dx - \int_1^2 \frac{x}{x^2 + 1}\, dx + \int_1^2 \frac{1}{x^2 + 1}\, dx$$

$$= \left[ \ln|x| - \frac{1}{2}\ln(x^2 + 1) + \arctan x \right]_1^2$$

$$= \frac{1}{2}\ln \frac{8}{5} - \frac{\pi}{4} + \arctan 2$$

$$\approx 0.557$$

**33.** $\displaystyle\int \frac{3x\, dx}{x^2 - 6x + 9} = 3\ln|x - 3| - \dfrac{9}{x - 3} + C$

$(4, 0)$: $\quad 3\ln|4 - 3| - \dfrac{9}{4 - 3} + C = 0 \Rightarrow C = 9$

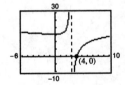

**35.** $\displaystyle\int \frac{x^2 + x + 2}{(x^2 + 2)^2}\, dx = \dfrac{\sqrt{2}}{2}\arctan \dfrac{x}{\sqrt{2}} - \dfrac{1}{2(x^2 + 2)} + C$

$(0, 1)$: $\quad 0 - \dfrac{1}{4} + C = 1 \Rightarrow C = \dfrac{5}{4}$

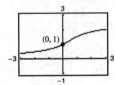

**37.** $\displaystyle\int \frac{2x^2 - 2x + 3}{x^3 - x^2 - x - 2}\, dx = \ln|x - 2| + \dfrac{1}{2}\ln|x^2 + x + 1| - \sqrt{3}\arctan\!\left(\dfrac{2x + 1}{\sqrt{3}}\right) + C$

$(3, 10)$: $\quad 0 + \dfrac{1}{2}\ln 13 - \sqrt{3}\arctan \dfrac{7}{\sqrt{3}} + C = 10 \Rightarrow C = 10 - \dfrac{1}{2}\ln 13 + \sqrt{3}\arctan \dfrac{7}{\sqrt{3}}$

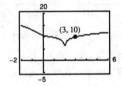

**39.** $\displaystyle\int \frac{1}{x^2 - 4}\, dx = \dfrac{1}{4}\ln\left|\dfrac{x - 2}{x + 2}\right| + C$

$(6, 4)$: $\quad \dfrac{1}{4}\ln\left|\dfrac{4}{8}\right| + C = 4 \Rightarrow C = 4 - \dfrac{1}{4}\ln \dfrac{1}{2} = 4 + \dfrac{1}{4}\ln 2$

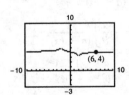

**41.** Let $u = \cos x \ du = \sin x \, dx$.

$$\frac{1}{u(u-1)} = \frac{A}{u} + \frac{B}{u-1}$$

$$1 = A(u-1) + Bu$$

When $u = 0$, $A = -1$. When $u = 1$, $B = 1$, $u = \cos x$, $du = -\sin x \, dx$.

$$\int \frac{\sin x}{\cos x(\cos x - 1)} \, dx = -\int \frac{1}{u(u-1)} \, du$$

$$= \int \frac{1}{u} \, du - \int \frac{1}{u-1} \, du$$

$$= \ln|u| - \ln|u-1| + C$$

$$= \ln\left|\frac{u}{u-1}\right| + C$$

$$= \ln\left|\frac{\cos x}{\cos x - 1}\right| + C$$

**43.** $\displaystyle\int \frac{3 \cos x}{\sin^2 x + \sin x - 2} \, dx = 3\int \frac{1}{u^2 + u - 2} \, du$

$$= \ln\left|\frac{u-1}{u+2}\right| + C$$

$$= \ln\left|\frac{-1 + \sin x}{2 + \sin x}\right| + C$$

(From Exercise 9 with $u = \sin x$, $du = \cos x \, dx$)

**45.** Let $u = e^x$, $du = e^x \, dx$.

$$\frac{1}{(u-1)(u+4)} = \frac{A}{u-1} + \frac{B}{u+4}$$

$$1 = A(u+4) + B(u-1)$$

When $u = 1$, $A = \frac{1}{5}$. When $u = -4$, $B = -\frac{1}{5}$, $u = e^x$, $du = e^x \, dx$.

$$\int \frac{e^x}{(e^x - 1)(e^x + 4)} \, dx = \int \frac{1}{(u-1)(u+4)} \, du$$

$$= \frac{1}{5}\left(\int \frac{1}{u-1} \, du - \int \frac{1}{u+4} \, du\right)$$

$$= \frac{1}{5} \ln\left|\frac{u-1}{u+4}\right| + C$$

$$= \frac{1}{5} \ln\left|\frac{e^x - 1}{e^x + 4}\right| + C$$

**47.** $\displaystyle\frac{1}{x(a+bx)} = \frac{A}{x} + \frac{B}{a+bx}$

$$1 = A(a+bx) + Bx$$

When $x = 0$, $1 = aA \Rightarrow A = 1/a$.
When $x = -a/b$, $1 = -(a/b)B \Rightarrow B = -b/a$.

$$\int \frac{1}{x(a+bx)} \, dx = \frac{1}{a}\int \left(\frac{1}{x} - \frac{b}{a+bx}\right) dx$$

$$= \frac{1}{a}\left(\ln|x| - \ln|a+bx|\right) + C$$

$$= \frac{1}{a} \ln\left|\frac{x}{a+bx}\right| + C$$

**49.** $\displaystyle\frac{x}{(a+bx)^2} = \frac{A}{a+bx} + \frac{B}{(a+bx)^2}$

$$x = A(a+bx) + B$$

When $x = -a/b$, $B = -a/b$.
When $x = 0$, $0 = aA + B \Rightarrow A = 1/b$.

$$\int \frac{x}{(a+bx)^2} \, dx = \int \left(\frac{1/b}{a+bx} + \frac{-a/b}{(a+bx)^2}\right) dx$$

$$= \frac{1}{b}\int \frac{1}{a+bx} \, dx - \frac{a}{b}\int \frac{1}{(a+bx)^2} \, dx$$

$$= \frac{1}{b^2} \ln|a+bx| + \frac{a}{b^2}\left(\frac{1}{a+bx}\right) + C$$

$$= \frac{1}{b^2}\left(\frac{a}{a+bx} + \ln|a+bx|\right) + C$$

**51.** $\displaystyle\frac{dy}{dx} = \frac{6}{4 - x^2}$, $y(0) = 3$

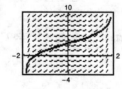

**53.** Dividing $x^3$ by $x - 5$.

**55.** (a) Substitution: $u = x^2 + 2x - 8$

    (b) Partial fractions

    (c) Trigonometric substitution (tan) or inverse tangent rule

**57.** Average Cost $= \dfrac{1}{80 - 75} \displaystyle\int_{75}^{80} \dfrac{124p}{(10 + p)(100 - p)}\, dp$

$$= \frac{1}{5} \int_{75}^{80} \left( \frac{-124}{(10 + p)11} + \frac{1240}{(100 - p)11} \right) dp$$

$$= \frac{1}{5} \left[ \frac{-124}{11} \ln(10 + p) - \frac{1240}{11} \ln(100 - p) \right]_{75}^{80}$$

$$\approx \frac{1}{5}(24.51) = 4.9$$

Approximately \$490,000.

**59.** $A = \displaystyle\int_{1}^{3} \dfrac{10}{x(x^2 + 1)}\, dx \approx 3$

Matches (c)

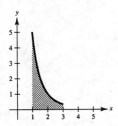

**61.**

$$\frac{1}{(x + 1)(n - x)} = \frac{A}{x + 1} + \frac{B}{n - x}, A = B = \frac{1}{n + 1}$$

$$\frac{1}{n + 1} \int \left( \frac{1}{x + 1} + \frac{1}{n - x} \right) dx = kt + C$$

$$\frac{1}{n + 1} \ln \left| \frac{x + 1}{n - x} \right| = kt + C$$

When $t = 0, x = 0, C = \dfrac{1}{n + 1} \ln \dfrac{1}{n}$.

$$\frac{1}{n + 1} \ln \left| \frac{x + 1}{n - x} \right| = kt + \frac{1}{n + 1} \ln \frac{1}{n}$$

$$\frac{1}{n + 1} \left[ \ln \left| \frac{x + 1}{n - x} \right| - \ln \frac{1}{n} \right] = kt$$

$$\ln \frac{nx + n}{n - x} = (n + 1)kt$$

$$\frac{nx + n}{n - x} = e^{(n + 1)kt}$$

$$x = \frac{n \left[ e^{(n + 1)kt} - 1 \right]}{n + e^{(n + 1)kt}} \qquad \textbf{Note:} \ \lim_{t \to \infty} x = n$$

**63.** $\dfrac{x}{1 + x^4} = \dfrac{Ax + B}{x^2 + \sqrt{2}\,x + 1} + \dfrac{Cx + D}{x^2 - \sqrt{2}\,x + 1}$

$\qquad x = (Ax + B)\big(x^2 - \sqrt{2}\,x + 1\big) + (Cx + D)\big(x^2 + \sqrt{2}\,x + 1\big)$

$\qquad\quad = (A + C)x^3 + \big(B + D - \sqrt{2}\,A + \sqrt{2}\,C\big)x^2 + \big(A + C - \sqrt{2}\,B + \sqrt{2}\,D\big)x + (B + D)$

$0 = A + C \Rightarrow C = -A$

$\left. \begin{array}{l} 0 = B + D - \sqrt{2}\,A + \sqrt{2}\,C \\[6pt] 1 = A + C - \sqrt{2}\,B + \sqrt{2}\,D \end{array} \right\}$  $\begin{array}{l} -2\sqrt{2}\,A = 0 \Rightarrow A = 0 \text{ and } C = 0 \\[6pt] -2\sqrt{2}\,B = 1 \Rightarrow B = -\dfrac{\sqrt{2}}{4} \text{ and } D = \dfrac{\sqrt{2}}{4} \end{array}$

$0 = B + D \Rightarrow D = -B$

Thus,

$\displaystyle \int_0^1 \frac{x}{1 + x^4}\,dx = \int_0^1 \left[ \frac{-\sqrt{2}/4}{x^2 + \sqrt{2}\,x + 1} + \frac{\sqrt{2}/4}{x^2 - \sqrt{2}\,x + 1} \right] dx$

$\displaystyle \qquad\qquad\qquad = \frac{\sqrt{2}}{4} \int_0^1 \left[ \frac{-1}{\big[x + (\sqrt{2}/2)\big]^2 + (1/2)} + \frac{1}{\big[x - (\sqrt{2}/2)\big]^2 + (1/2)} \right] dx$

$\displaystyle \qquad\qquad\qquad = \frac{\sqrt{2}}{4} \cdot \frac{1}{1/\sqrt{2}} \left[ -\arctan\!\left( \frac{x + (\sqrt{2}/2)}{1/\sqrt{2}} \right) + \arctan\!\left( \frac{x - (\sqrt{2}/2)}{1/\sqrt{2}} \right) \right]_0^1$

$\displaystyle \qquad\qquad\qquad = \frac{1}{2} \left[ -\arctan\!\big( \sqrt{2}\,x + 1 \big) + \arctan\!\big( \sqrt{2}\,x - 1 \big) \right]_0^1$

$\displaystyle \qquad\qquad\qquad = \frac{1}{2} \Big[ \big( -\arctan(\sqrt{2} + 1) + \arctan(\sqrt{2} - 1) \big) - \big( -\arctan 1 + \arctan(-1) \big) \Big]$

$\displaystyle \qquad\qquad\qquad = \frac{1}{2} \left[ \arctan(\sqrt{2} - 1) - \arctan(\sqrt{2} + 1) + \frac{\pi}{4} + \frac{\pi}{4} \right].$

Since $\arctan x - \arctan y = \arctan[(x - y)/(1 + xy)]$, we have:

$\displaystyle \int_0^1 \frac{x}{1 + x^4}\,dx = \frac{1}{2} \left[ \arctan\!\left( \frac{(\sqrt{2} - 1) - (\sqrt{2} + 1)}{1 + (\sqrt{2} - 1)(\sqrt{2} + 1)} \right) + \frac{\pi}{2} \right] = \frac{1}{2} \left[ \arctan\!\left( \frac{-2}{2} \right) + \frac{\pi}{2} \right] = \frac{1}{2} \left[ -\frac{\pi}{4} + \frac{\pi}{2} \right] = \frac{\pi}{8}$

# Section 7.6    Integration by Tables and Other Integration Techniques

**1.** By Formula 6: $\displaystyle \int \frac{x^2}{1 + x}\,dx = -\frac{x}{2}(2 - x) + \ln|1 + x| + C$

**3.** By Formula 26: $\displaystyle \int e^x \sqrt{1 + e^{2x}}\,dx = \frac{1}{2} \Big[ e^x \sqrt{e^{2x} + 1} + \ln\big| e^x + \sqrt{e^{2x} + 1} \big| \Big] + C$

$\qquad\qquad\qquad u = e^x,\ du = e^x\,dx$

**5.** By Formula 44: $\displaystyle \int \frac{1}{x^2 \sqrt{1 - x^2}}\,dx = -\frac{\sqrt{1 - x^2}}{x} + C$

**7.** By Formulas 50 and 48: $\displaystyle\int \sin^4(2x)\,dx = \frac{1}{2}\int \sin^4(2x)(2)\,dx$

$$= \frac{1}{2}\left[\frac{-\sin^3(2x)\cos(2x)}{4} + \frac{3}{4}\int \sin^2(2x)(2)\,dx\right]$$

$$= \frac{1}{2}\left[\frac{-\sin^3(2x)\cos(2x)}{4} + \frac{3}{8}(2x - \sin 2x \cos 2x)\right] + C$$

$$= \frac{1}{16}(6x - 3\sin 2x \cos 2x - 2\sin^3 2x \cos 2x) + C$$

**9.** By Formula 57: $\displaystyle\int \frac{1}{\sqrt{x}(1 - \cos\sqrt{x})}\,dx = 2\int \frac{1}{1 - \cos\sqrt{x}}\left(\frac{1}{2\sqrt{x}}\right)dx$

$$= -2\left(\cot\sqrt{x} + \csc\sqrt{x}\right) + C$$

$$u = \sqrt{x},\, du = \frac{1}{2\sqrt{x}}\,dx$$

**11.** By Formula 84:

$$\int \frac{1}{1 + e^{2x}}\,dx = x - \frac{1}{2}\ln(1 + e^{2x}) + C$$

**13.** By Formula 89:

$$\int x^3 \ln x\,dx = \frac{x^4}{16}(4\ln|x| - 1) + C$$

**15.** (a) By Formulas 83 and 82: $\displaystyle\int x^2 e^x\,dx = x^2 e^x - 2\int xe^x\,dx$

$$= x^2 e^x - 2[(x - 1)e^x + C_1]$$

$$= x^2 e^x - 2xe^x + 2e^x + C$$

(b) Integration by parts: $u = x^2,\, du = 2x\,dx,\, dv = e^x\,dx,\, v = e^x$

$$\int x^2 e^x\,dx = x^2 e^x - \int 2xe^x\,dx$$

Parts again: $u = 2x,\, du = 2\,dx,\, dv = e^x\,dx,\, v = e^x$

$$\int x^2 e^x\,dx = x^2 e^x - \left[2xe^x - \int 2e^x\,dx\right] = x^2 e^x - 2xe^x + 2e^x + C$$

**17.** (a) By Formula: 12, $a = b = 1$, $u = x$, and

$$\int \frac{1}{x^2(x + 1)}\,dx = \frac{-1}{1}\left(\frac{1}{x} + \frac{1}{1}\ln\left|\frac{x}{1 + x}\right|\right) + C$$

$$= \frac{-1}{x} - \ln\left|\frac{x}{1 + x}\right| + C$$

$$= \frac{-1}{x} + \ln\left|\frac{x + 1}{x}\right| + C$$

(b) Partial fractions:

$$\frac{1}{x^2(x + 1)} = \frac{A}{x} + \frac{B}{x^2} + \frac{C}{x + 1}$$

$$1 = Ax(x + 1) + B(x + 1) + Cx^2$$

$x = 0$: $1 = B$

$x = -1$: $1 = C$

$x = 1$: $1 = 2A + 2 + 1 \Rightarrow A = -1$

$$\int \frac{1}{x^2(x + 1)}\,dx = \int \left[\frac{-1}{x} + \frac{1}{x^2} + \frac{1}{x + 1}\right]dx$$

$$= -\ln|x| - \frac{1}{x} + \ln|x + 1| + C$$

$$= -\frac{1}{x} - \ln\left|\frac{x}{x + 1}\right| + C$$

**19.** By Formula 81: $\int xe^{x^2} = \frac{1}{2}e^{x^2} + C$

**21.** By Formula 79: $\int x \operatorname{arcsec}(x^2 + 1)\, dx = \frac{1}{2}\int \operatorname{arcsec}(x^2 + 1)(2x)\, dx$

$$= \frac{1}{2}\Big[(x^2 + 1)\operatorname{arcsec}(x^2 + 1) - \ln\big((x^2 + 1) + \sqrt{x^4 + 2x^2}\big)\Big] + C$$

$u = x^2 + 1,\, du = 2x\, dx$

**23.** By Formula 89: $\int x^2 \ln x\, dx = \frac{x^3}{9}\big(-1 + 3\ln|x|\big) + C$    **25.** By Formula 35: $\int \frac{1}{x^2\sqrt{x^2 - 4}}\, dx = \frac{\sqrt{x^2 - 4}}{4x} + C$

**27.** By Formula 4: $\int \frac{2x}{(1 - 3x)^2}\, dx = 2\int \frac{x}{(1 - 3x)^2}\, dx = \frac{2}{9}\Big(\ln|1 - 3x| + \frac{1}{1 - 3x}\Big) + C$

**29.** By Formula 76:

$\int e^x \arccos e^x\, dx = e^x \arccos e^x - \sqrt{1 - e^{2x}} + C$

$u = e^x,\, du = e^x\, dx$

**31.** By Formula 73:

$\int \frac{x}{1 - \sec x^2}\, dx = \frac{1}{2}\int \frac{2x}{1 - \sec x^2}\, dx$

$$= \frac{1}{2}(x^2 + \cot x^2 + \csc x^2) + C$$

**33.** By Formula 23: $\int \frac{\cos x}{1 + \sin^2 x}\, dx = \arctan(\sin x) + C$

$u = \sin x,\, du = \cos x\, dx$

**35.** By Formula 14: $\int \frac{\cos \theta}{3 + 2\sin \theta + \sin^2 \theta}\, d\theta = \frac{\sqrt{2}}{2}\arctan\Big(\frac{1 + \sin \theta}{\sqrt{2}}\Big) + C$

$u = \sin \theta,\, du = \cos \theta\, d\theta$

**37.** By Formula 35: $\int \frac{1}{x^2\sqrt{2 + 9x^2}}\, dx = 3\int \frac{3}{(3x)^2 \sqrt{\big(\sqrt{2}\big)^2 + (3x)^2}}\, dx$

$$= -\frac{3\sqrt{2 + 9x^2}}{6x} + C$$

$$= -\frac{\sqrt{2 + 9x^2}}{2x} + C$$

**39.** By Formulas 54 and 55:

$\int t^3 \cos t\, dt = t^3 \sin t - 3\int t^2 \sin t\, dt$

$$= t^3 \sin t - 3\Big[-t^2 \cos t + 2\int t \cos t\, dt\Big]$$

$$= t^3 \sin t + 3t^2 \cos t - 6\Big[t \sin t - \int \sin t\, dt\Big]$$

$$= t^3 \sin t + 3t^2 \cos t - 6t \sin t - 6\cos t + C$$

**41.** By Formula 3: $\displaystyle\int \frac{\ln x}{x(3 + 2\ln x)}\,dx = \frac{1}{4}\big(2\ln|x| - 3\ln|3 + 2\ln||x|\big) + C$

$$u = \ln x,\; du = \frac{1}{x}\,dx$$

**43.** By Formulas 1, 25, and 33: $\displaystyle\int \frac{x}{(x^2 - 6x + 10)^2}\,dx = \frac{1}{2}\int \frac{2x - 6 + 6}{(x^2 - 6x + 10)^2}\,dx$

$$= \frac{1}{2}\int (x^2 - 6x + 10)^{-2}(2x - 6)\,dx + 3\int \frac{1}{[(x - 3)^2 + 1]^2}\,dx$$

$$= -\frac{1}{2(x^2 - 6x + 10)} + \frac{3}{2}\left[\frac{x - 3}{x^2 - 6x + 10} + \arctan(x - 3)\right] + C$$

$$= \frac{3x - 10}{2(x^2 - 6x + 10)} + \frac{3}{2}\arctan(x - 3) + C$$

**45.** By Formula 31: $\displaystyle\int \frac{x}{\sqrt{x^4 - 6x^2 + 5}}\,dx = \frac{1}{2}\int \frac{2x}{\sqrt{(x^2 - 3)^2 - 4}}\,dx$

$$= \frac{1}{2}\ln\left|x^2 - 3 + \sqrt{x^4 - 6x^2 + 5}\right| + C$$

$$u = x^2 - 3,\; du = 2x\,dx$$

**47.** $\displaystyle\int \frac{x^3}{\sqrt{4 - x^2}}\,dx = \int \frac{8\sin^3\theta(2\cos\theta\,d\theta)}{2\cos\theta}$

$$= 8\int (1 - \cos^2\theta)\sin\theta\,d\theta$$

$$= 8\int \big[\sin\theta - \cos^2\theta(\sin\theta)\big]\,d\theta$$

$$= -8\cos\theta + \frac{8\cos^3\theta}{3} + C$$

$$= \frac{-\sqrt{4 - x^2}}{3}(x^2 + 8) + C$$

$$x = 2\sin\theta,\; dx = 2\cos\theta\,d\theta,\; \sqrt{4 - x^2} = 2\cos\theta$$

**49.** By Formula 8: $\displaystyle\int \frac{e^{3x}}{(1 + e^x)^3}\,dx = \int \frac{(e^x)^2}{(1 + e^x)^3}(e^x)\,dx$

$$= \frac{2}{1 + e^x} - \frac{1}{2(1 + e^x)^2} + \ln|1 + e^x| + C$$

$$u = e^x,\; du = e^x\,dx$$

**51.** $\displaystyle\frac{u^2}{(a + bu)^2} = \frac{1}{b^2} - \frac{(2a/b)u + (a^2/b^2)}{(a + bu)^2} = \frac{1}{b^2} + \frac{A}{a + bu} + \frac{B}{(a + bu)^2}$

$$-\frac{2a}{b}u - \frac{a^2}{b^2} = A(a + bu) + B = (aA + B) + bAu$$

Equating the coefficients of like terms we have $aA + B = -a^2/b^2$ and $bA = -2a/b$. Solving these equations we have $A = -2a/b^2$ and $B = a^2/b^2$.

$$\int \frac{u^2}{(a + bu)^2}\,du = \frac{1}{b^2}\int du - \frac{2a}{b^2}\Big(\frac{1}{b}\Big)\int \frac{1}{a + bu}b\,du + \frac{a^2}{b^2}\Big(\frac{1}{b}\Big)\int \frac{1}{(a + bu)^2}b\,du = \frac{1}{b^2}u - \frac{2a}{b^3}\ln|a + bu| - \frac{a^2}{b^3}\Big(\frac{1}{a + bu}\Big) + C$$

$$= \frac{1}{b^3}\Big(bu - \frac{a^2}{a + bu} - 2a\ln|a + bu|\Big) + C$$

**53.** When we have $u^2 + a^2$:

$$u = a \tan \theta$$

$$du = a \sec^2 \theta \, d\theta$$

$$u^2 + a^2 = a^2 \sec^2 \theta$$

$$\int \frac{1}{(u^2 + a^2)^{3/2}} \, du = \int \frac{a \sec^2 \theta \, d\theta}{a^3 \sec^3 \theta}$$

$$= \frac{1}{a^2} \int \cos \theta \, d\theta$$

$$= \frac{1}{a^2} \sin \theta + C$$

$$= \frac{u}{a^2 \sqrt{u^2 + a^2}} + C$$

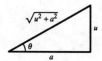

When we have $u^2 - a^2$:

$$u = a \sec \theta$$

$$du = a \sec \theta \tan \theta \, d\theta$$

$$u^2 - a^2 = a^2 \tan^2 \theta$$

$$\int \frac{1}{(u^2 - a^2)^{3/2}} \, du = \int \frac{a \sec \theta \tan \theta \, d\theta}{a^3 \tan^3 \theta}$$

$$= \frac{1}{a^2} \int \frac{\cos \theta}{\sin^2 \theta} \, d\theta$$

$$= -\frac{1}{a^2} \csc \theta + C$$

$$= \frac{-u}{a^2 \sqrt{u^2 - a^2}} + C$$

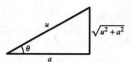

**55.** $\displaystyle\int (\arctan u) \, du = u \arctan u - \frac{1}{2} \int \frac{2u}{1 + u^2} \, du$

$$= u \arctan u - \frac{1}{2} \ln(1 + u^2) + C$$

$$= u \arctan u - \ln \sqrt{1 + u^2} + C$$

$$w = \arctan u, \, dv = du, \, dw = \frac{du}{1 + u^2}, \, v = u$$

**57.** $\displaystyle\int \frac{1}{x^{3/2} \sqrt{1 - x}} \, dx = \frac{-2\sqrt{1 - x}}{\sqrt{x}} + C$

$\left(\dfrac{1}{2}, 5\right)$: $\dfrac{-2\sqrt{1/2}}{\sqrt{1/2}} + C = 5 \Rightarrow C = 7$

$$y = \frac{-2\sqrt{1 - x}}{\sqrt{x}} + 7$$

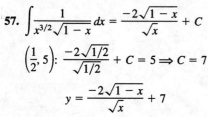

**59.** $\displaystyle\int \frac{1}{(x^2 - 6x + 10)^2} \, dx = \frac{1}{2}\left[ \tan^{-1}(x - 3) + \frac{x - 3}{x^2 - 6x + 10} \right] + C$

$(3, 0)$: $\dfrac{1}{2}\left[ 0 + \dfrac{0}{10} \right] + C = 0 \Rightarrow C = 0$

$$y = \frac{1}{2}\left[ \tan^{-1}(x - 3) + \frac{x - 3}{x^2 - 6x + 10} \right]$$

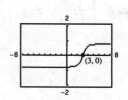

**61.** $\displaystyle\int \frac{1}{\sin \theta \tan \theta} \, d\theta = -\csc \theta + C$

$\left(\dfrac{\pi}{4}, 2\right)$: $-\dfrac{2}{\sqrt{2}} + C = 2 \Rightarrow C = 2 + \sqrt{2}$

$$y = -\csc \theta + 2 + \sqrt{2}$$

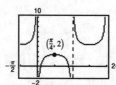
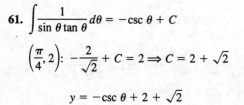
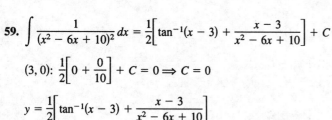
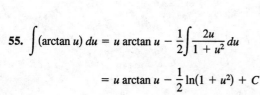

**63.** $\displaystyle\int \frac{1}{2 - 3\sin\theta}\, d\theta = \int \left[ \dfrac{\dfrac{2\,du}{1 + u^2}}{2 - 3\left(\dfrac{2u}{1 + u^2}\right)} \right]$

$\displaystyle= \int 2 \frac{2}{(1 + u^2) - 6u}\, du$

$\displaystyle= \int \frac{1}{u^2 - 3u + 1}\, du$

$\displaystyle= \int \frac{1}{\left(u - \dfrac{3}{2}\right)^2 - \dfrac{5}{4}}\, du$

$\displaystyle= \frac{1}{\sqrt{5}} \ln \left| \frac{\left(u - \dfrac{3}{2}\right) - \dfrac{\sqrt{5}}{2}}{\left(u - \dfrac{3}{2}\right) + \dfrac{\sqrt{5}}{2}} \right| + C$

$\displaystyle= \frac{1}{\sqrt{5}} \ln \left| \frac{2u - 3 - \sqrt{5}}{2u - 3 + \sqrt{5}} \right| + C$

$\displaystyle= \frac{1}{\sqrt{5}} \ln \left| \frac{2\tan\left(\dfrac{\theta}{2}\right) - 3 - \sqrt{5}}{2\tan\left(\dfrac{\theta}{2}\right) - 3 + \sqrt{5}} \right| + C$

$u = \tan\dfrac{\theta}{2}$

**65.** $\displaystyle\int_0^{\pi/2} \frac{1}{1 + \sin\theta + \cos\theta}\, d\theta = \int_0^1 \left[ \dfrac{\dfrac{2\,du}{1 + u^2}}{1 + \dfrac{2u}{1 + u^2} + \dfrac{1 - u^2}{1 + u^2}} \right]$

$\displaystyle= \int_0^1 \frac{1}{1 + u}\, du$

$\displaystyle= \Big[ \ln|1 + u| \Big]_0^1$

$= \ln 2$

$u = \tan\dfrac{\theta}{2}$

**67.** $\displaystyle\int \frac{\sin\theta}{3 - 2\cos\theta}\, d\theta = \frac{1}{2} \int \frac{2\sin\theta}{3 - 2\cos\theta}\, d\theta$

$\displaystyle= \frac{1}{2} \ln|u| + C$

$\displaystyle= \frac{1}{2} \ln(3 - 2\cos\theta) + C$

$u = 3 - 2\cos\theta,\, du = 2\sin\theta\, d\theta$

**69.** $\displaystyle\int \frac{\cos\sqrt{\theta}}{\sqrt{\theta}}\, d\theta = 2 \int \cos\sqrt{\theta} \left( \frac{1}{2\sqrt{\theta}} \right) d\theta$

$\displaystyle= 2 \sin\sqrt{\theta} + C$

$u = \sqrt{\theta},\, du = \dfrac{1}{2\sqrt{\theta}}\, d\theta$

**71.** $\displaystyle A = \int_0^8 \frac{x}{\sqrt{x + 1}}\, dx$

$\displaystyle= \left[ \frac{-2(2 - x)}{3} \sqrt{x + 1} \right]_0^8$

$\displaystyle= 12 - \left( -\frac{4}{3} \right)$

$\displaystyle= \frac{40}{3} \approx 13.333$ square units

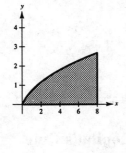

**73.** Arctangent Formula, Formula 23,

$$\int \frac{1}{u^2 + 1}\, du,\, u = e^x$$

**75.** Substitution: $u = x^2,\, du = 2x\, dx$
Then Formula 81.

**77.** Cannot be integrated.

**79.** Answers will vary. For example,

$$\int (2x)e^{2x}\, dx$$

can be integrated by first letting $u = 2x$ and then using Formula 82.

**81.** $W = \int_0^5 2000xe^{-x}\,dx$

$\qquad = -2000\int_0^5 -xe^{-x}\,dx$

$\qquad = 2000\int_0^5 (-x)e^{-x}(-1)\,dx$

$\qquad = 2000\Big[(-x)e^{-x} - e^{-x}\Big]_0^5$

$\qquad = 2000\left(-\dfrac{6}{e^5} + 1\right)$

$\qquad \approx 1919.145 \text{ ft} \cdot \text{lbs}$

**83.** (a) $V = 20(2)\int_0^3 \dfrac{2}{\sqrt{1+y^2}}\,dy$ $\qquad\qquad\qquad W = 148\big(80\ln\big(3 + \sqrt{10}\big)\big)$

$\qquad\quad = \Big[80\ln\big|y + \sqrt{1+y^2}\big|\Big]_0^3$ $\qquad\qquad\quad = 11{,}840\ln\big(3 + \sqrt{10}\big)$

$\qquad\quad = 80\ln\big(3 + \sqrt{10}\big)$ $\qquad\qquad\qquad\qquad \approx 21{,}530.4 \text{ lb}$

$\qquad\quad \approx 145.5 \text{ cubic feet}$

$\qquad$ (b) By symmetry, $\bar{x} = 0$.

$\qquad\qquad M = \rho(2)\int_0^3 \dfrac{2}{\sqrt{1+y^2}}\,dy = \Big[4\rho\ln\big|y + \sqrt{1+y^2}\big|\Big]_0^3 = 4\rho\ln\big(3 + \sqrt{10}\big)$

$\qquad\qquad M_x = 2\rho\int_0^3 \dfrac{2y}{\sqrt{1+y^2}}\,dy = \Big[4\rho\sqrt{1+y^2}\Big]_0^3 = 4\rho\big(\sqrt{10} - 1\big)$

$\qquad\qquad \bar{y} = \dfrac{M_x}{M} = \dfrac{4\rho\big(\sqrt{10} - 1\big)}{4\rho\ln\big(3 + \sqrt{10}\big)} \approx 1.19$

$\qquad$ Centroid: $(\bar{x}, \bar{y}) \approx (0, 1.19)$

**85.** (a) $\int_0^4 \dfrac{k}{2 + 3x}\,dx = 10$ $\qquad\qquad\qquad\qquad$ (b) $\int_0^4 \dfrac{15.417}{2 + 3x}\,dx$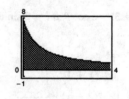

$\qquad\qquad k = \dfrac{10}{\displaystyle\int_0^4 \dfrac{1}{2+3x}\,dx} \approx \dfrac{10}{0.6486}$

$\qquad\qquad\quad = 15.417 \ \left(= \dfrac{30}{\ln 7}\right)$

**87.** False. You might need to convert your integral using substitution or algebra.

# Section 7.7   Indeterminate Forms and L'Hôpital's Rule

**1.** $\displaystyle\lim_{x\to 0} \dfrac{\sin 5x}{\sin 2x} \approx 2.5\left(\text{exact: } \dfrac{5}{2}\right)$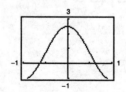

| $x$ | $-0.1$ | $-0.01$ | $-0.001$ | $0.001$ | $0.01$ | $0.1$ |
|------|--------|---------|----------|---------|--------|-------|
| $f(x)$ | 2.4132 | 2.4991 | 2.500 | 2.500 | 2.4991 | 2.4132 |

**3.** $\lim\limits_{x \to \infty} x^5 e^{-x/100} \approx 0$

| $x$ | 1 | 10 | $10^2$ | $10^3$ | $10^4$ | $10^5$ |
|---|---|---|---|---|---|---|
| $f(x)$ | 0.9901 | 90,484 | $3.7 \times 10^9$ | $4.5 \times 10^{10}$ | 0 | 0 |

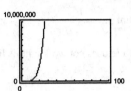

**5.** (a) $\lim\limits_{x \to 3} \dfrac{2(x - 3)}{x^2 - 9} = \lim\limits_{x \to 3} \dfrac{2(x - 3)}{(x + 3)(x - 3)} = \lim\limits_{x \to 3} \dfrac{2}{x + 3} = \dfrac{1}{3}$

(b) $\lim\limits_{x \to 3} \dfrac{2(x - 3)}{x^2 - 9} = \lim\limits_{x \to 3} \dfrac{(d/dx)[2(x - 3)]}{(d/dx)[x^2 - 9]} = \lim\limits_{x \to 3} \dfrac{2}{2x} = \dfrac{2}{6} = \dfrac{1}{3}$

**7.** (a) $\lim\limits_{x \to 3} \dfrac{\sqrt{x + 1} - 2}{x - 3} = \lim\limits_{x \to 3} \dfrac{\sqrt{x + 1} - 2}{x - 3} \cdot \dfrac{\sqrt{x + 1} + 2}{\sqrt{x + 1} + 2} = \lim\limits_{x \to 3} \dfrac{(x + 1) - 4}{(x - 3)[\sqrt{x + 1} + 2]} = \lim\limits_{x \to 3} \dfrac{1}{\sqrt{x + 1} + 2} = \dfrac{1}{4}$

(b) $\lim\limits_{x \to 3} \dfrac{\sqrt{x + 1} - 2}{x - 3} = \lim\limits_{x \to 3} \dfrac{(d/dx)[\sqrt{x + 1} - 2]}{(d/dx)[x - 3]} = \lim\limits_{x \to 3} \dfrac{1/(2\sqrt{x + 1})}{1} = \dfrac{1}{4}$

**9.** (a) $\lim\limits_{x \to \infty} \dfrac{5x^2 - 3x + 1}{3x^2 - 5} = \lim\limits_{x \to \infty} \dfrac{5 - (3/x) + (1/x^2)}{3 - (5/x^2)} = \dfrac{5}{3}$

(b) $\lim\limits_{x \to \infty} \dfrac{5x^2 - 3x + 1}{3x^2 - 5} = \lim\limits_{x \to \infty} \dfrac{(d/dx)[5x^2 - 3x + 1]}{(d/dx)[3x^2 - 5]} = \lim\limits_{x \to \infty} \dfrac{10x - 3}{6x} = \lim\limits_{x \to \infty} \dfrac{(d/dx)[10x - 3]}{(d/dx)[6x]} = \lim\limits_{x \to \infty} \dfrac{10}{6} = \dfrac{5}{3}$

**11.** $\lim\limits_{x \to 2} \dfrac{x^2 - x - 2}{x - 2} = \lim\limits_{x \to 2} \dfrac{2x - 1}{1} = 3$

**13.** $\lim\limits_{x \to 0} \dfrac{\sqrt{4 - x^2} - 2}{x} = \lim\limits_{x \to 0} \dfrac{-x/\sqrt{4 - x^2}}{1} = 0$

**15.** $\lim\limits_{x \to 0} \dfrac{e^x - (1 - x)}{x} = \lim\limits_{x \to 0} \dfrac{e^x + 1}{1} = 2$

**17.** Case 1: $n = 1$

$$\lim\limits_{x \to 0^+} \dfrac{e^x - (1 + x)}{x} = \lim\limits_{x \to 0^+} \dfrac{e^x - 1}{1} = 0$$

Case 2: $n = 2$

$$\lim\limits_{x \to 0^+} \dfrac{e^x - (1 + x)}{x^2} = \lim\limits_{x \to 0^+} \dfrac{e^x - 1}{2x} = \lim\limits_{x \to 0^+} \dfrac{e^x}{2} = \dfrac{1}{2}$$

Case 3: $n \geq 3$

$$\lim\limits_{x \to 0^+} \dfrac{e^x - (1 + x)}{x^n} = \lim\limits_{x \to 0^+} \dfrac{e^x - 1}{nx^{n-1}} = \lim\limits_{x \to 0^+} \dfrac{e^x}{n(n - 1)x^{n-2}} = \infty$$

**19.** $\lim\limits_{x \to 0} \dfrac{\sin 2x}{\sin 3x} = \lim\limits_{x \to 0} \dfrac{2 \cos 2x}{3 \cos 3x} = \dfrac{2}{3}$

**21.** $\lim\limits_{x \to 0} \dfrac{\arcsin x}{x} = \lim\limits_{x \to 0} \dfrac{1/\sqrt{1 - x^2}}{1} = 1$

**23.** $\lim\limits_{x \to \infty} \dfrac{3x^2 - 2x + 1}{2x^2 + 3} = \lim\limits_{x \to \infty} \dfrac{6x - 2}{4x}$

$= \lim\limits_{x \to \infty} \dfrac{6}{4} = \dfrac{3}{2}$

**25.** $\lim\limits_{x \to \infty} \dfrac{x^2 + 2x + 3}{x - 1} = \lim\limits_{x \to \infty} \dfrac{2x + 2}{1} = \infty$

**27.** $\lim\limits_{x \to \infty} \dfrac{x^3}{e^{x/2}} = \lim\limits_{x \to \infty} \dfrac{3x^2}{(1/2)e^{x/2}}$

$= \lim\limits_{x \to \infty} \dfrac{6x}{(1/4)e^{x/2}} = \lim\limits_{x \to \infty} \dfrac{6}{(1/8)e^{x/2}} = 0$

**29.** $\displaystyle\lim_{x\to\infty}\frac{x}{\sqrt{x^2+1}} = \lim_{x\to\infty}\frac{1}{\sqrt{1+(1/x^2)}} = 1$

**Note:** L'Hôpital's Rule does not work on this limit.
See Exercise 79.

**31.** $\displaystyle\lim_{x\to\infty}\frac{\cos x}{x} = 0$ by Squeeze Theorem

$$\left(\frac{\cos x}{x} \le \frac{1}{x}\right)$$

**33.** $\displaystyle\lim_{x\to\infty}\frac{\ln x}{x^2} = \lim_{x\to\infty}\frac{1/x}{2x} = \lim_{x\to\infty}\frac{1}{2x^2} = 0$

**35.** $\displaystyle\lim_{x\to\infty}\frac{e^x}{x^2} = \lim_{x\to\infty}\frac{e^x}{2x} = \lim_{x\to\infty}\frac{e^x}{2} = \infty$

**37.** (a) $\displaystyle\lim_{x\to0^+}(-x\ln x) = (-0)(-\infty) = (0)(\infty)$

    (b) $\displaystyle\lim_{x\to0^+}(-x\ln x) = \lim_{x\to0^+}\frac{\ln x}{-1/x}$

$$= \lim_{x\to0^+}\frac{1/x}{1/x^2}$$

$$= \lim_{x\to0^+} x = 0$$

    (c)

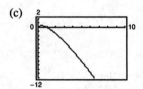

**39.** (a) $\displaystyle\lim_{x\to\infty}\left(x\sin\frac{1}{x}\right) = (\infty)(0)$

    (b) $\displaystyle\lim_{x\to\infty}x\sin\frac{1}{x} = \lim_{x\to\infty}\frac{\sin(1/x)}{1/x}$

$$= \lim_{x\to\infty}\frac{(-1/x^2)\cos(1/x)}{-1/x^2}$$

$$= \lim_{x\to\infty}\cos\left(\frac{1}{x}\right) = 1$$

    (c)

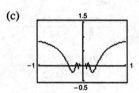

**41.** (a) $\displaystyle\lim_{x\to0^+} x^{1/x} = 0^\infty = 0$, not indeterminant
    (See Exercise 95)

    (b) Let   $y = x^{1/x}$

$$\ln y = \ln x^{1/x} = \frac{1}{x}\ln x.$$

    Since $x\to0^+$, $\dfrac{1}{x}\ln x\to(\infty)(-\infty) = -\infty$. Hence,

$$\ln y\to-\infty \implies y\to0^+.$$

    Therefore, $\displaystyle\lim_{x\to0^+} x^{1/x} = 0.$

    (c)

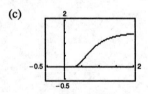

**43.** (a) $\displaystyle\lim_{x\to\infty} x^{1/x} = \infty^0$

    (b) Let $y = \displaystyle\lim_{x\to\infty} x^{1/x}$.

$$\ln y = \lim_{x\to\infty}\frac{\ln x}{x} = \lim_{x\to\infty}\left(\frac{1/x}{1}\right) = 0$$

    Thus, $\ln y = 0 \implies y = e^0 = 1$. Therefore,

$$\lim_{x\to\infty} x^{1/x} = 1.$$

    (c)

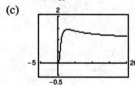

**45.** (a) $\displaystyle\lim_{x\to0^+}(1+x)^{1/x} = 1^\infty$

    (b) Let $y = \displaystyle\lim_{x\to0^+}(1+x)^{1/x}$.

$$\ln y = \lim_{x\to0^+}\frac{\ln(1+x)}{x}$$

$$= \lim_{x\to0^+}\left(\frac{1/(1+x)}{1}\right) = 1$$

    Thus, $\ln y = 1 \implies y = e^1 = e.$

    Therefore, $\displaystyle\lim_{x\to0^+}(1+x)^{1/x} = e.$

    (c)

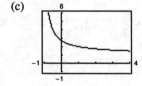

**47. (a)** $\lim\limits_{x\to0^+} [3(x)^{x/2}] = 0^0$

(c)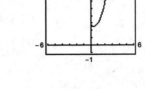

**(b)** Let $y = \lim\limits_{x\to0^+} 3(x)^{x/2}$.

$$\ln y = \lim\limits_{x\to0^+} \left[\ln 3 + \frac{x}{2}\ln x\right]$$

$$= \lim\limits_{x\to0^+} \left[\ln 3 + \frac{\ln x}{2/x}\right]$$

$$= \lim\limits_{x\to0^+} \ln 3 + \lim\limits_{x\to0^+} \frac{1/x}{-2/x^2}$$

$$= \lim\limits_{x\to0^+} \ln 3 - \lim\limits_{x\to0^+} \frac{x}{2}$$

$$= \ln 3$$

Hence, $\lim\limits_{x\to0^+} 3(x)^{x/2} = 3$.

**49. (a)** $\lim\limits_{x\to1^+} (\ln x)^{x-1} = 0^0$

**(b)** Let $y = \lim\limits_{x1^+} (\ln x)^{x-1}$

$$= \lim\limits_{x\to1^+} (x-1)\ln x = 0$$

Hence, $\lim\limits_{x\to1^+} (\ln x)^{x-1} = 1$

(c)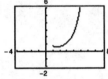

**51. (a)** $\lim\limits_{x\to2^+} \left(\frac{8}{x^2-4} - \frac{x}{x-2}\right) = \infty - \infty$

**(b)** $\lim\limits_{x\to2^+} \left(\frac{8}{x^2-4} - \frac{x}{x-2}\right) = \lim\limits_{x\to2^+} \frac{8 - x(x+2)}{x^2-4}$

$$= \lim\limits_{x\to2^+} \frac{(2-x)(4+x)}{(x+2)(x-2)}$$

$$= \lim\limits_{x\to2^+} \frac{-(x+4)}{x+2} = \frac{-3}{2}$$

(c)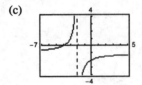

**53. (a)** $\lim\limits_{x\to1^+} \left(\frac{3}{\ln x} - \frac{2}{x-1}\right) = \infty - \infty$

**(b)** $\lim\limits_{x\to1^+} \left(\frac{3}{\ln x} - \frac{2}{x-1}\right) = \lim\limits_{x\to1^+} \frac{3x - 3 - 2\ln x}{(x-1)\ln x}$

$$= \lim\limits_{x\to1^+} \frac{3 - (2/x)}{[(x-1)/x] + \ln x} = \infty$$

(c)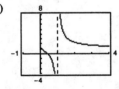

**55. (a)**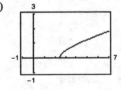

**(b)** $\lim\limits_{x\to3} \frac{x-3}{\ln(2x-5)} = \lim\limits_{x\to3} \frac{1}{2/(2x-5)}$

$$= \lim\limits_{x\to3} \frac{2x-5}{2} = \frac{1}{2}$$

**57. (a)**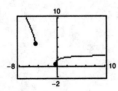

**(b)** $\lim\limits_{x\to\infty} \left(\sqrt{x^2+5x+2} - x\right) = \lim\limits_{x\to\infty} \left(\sqrt{x^2+5x+2} - x\right)\frac{\left(\sqrt{x^2+5x+2} + x\right)}{\left(\sqrt{x^2+5x+2} + x\right)}$

$$= \lim\limits_{x\to\infty} \frac{(x^2+5x+2) - x^2}{\sqrt{x^2+5x+2} + x}$$

$$= \lim\limits_{x\to\infty} \frac{5x+2}{\sqrt{x^2+5x+2} + x}$$

$$= \lim\limits_{x\to\infty} \frac{5 + (2/x)}{\sqrt{1 + (5/x) + (2/x^2)} + 1} = \frac{5}{2}$$

**59.** $\dfrac{0}{0}, \dfrac{\infty}{\infty}, 0 \cdot \infty, 1^{\infty}, 0^0, \infty - \infty$

**61.** (a) Let $f(x) = x^2 - 25$ and $g(x) = x - 5$.

(b) Let $f(x) = (x - 5)^2$ and $g(x) = x^2 - 25$.

(c) Let $f(x) = x^2 - 25$ and $g(x) = (x - 5)^3$.

**63.** $\displaystyle\lim_{x \to \infty} \dfrac{x^2}{e^{5x}} = \lim_{x \to \infty} \dfrac{2x}{5e^{5x}} = \lim_{x \to \infty} \dfrac{2}{25e^{5x}} = 0$

**65.** $\displaystyle\lim_{x \to \infty} \dfrac{(\ln x)^3}{x} = \lim_{x \to \infty} \dfrac{3(\ln x)^2(1/x)}{1}$

$= \displaystyle\lim_{x \to \infty} \dfrac{3(\ln x)^2}{x}$

$= \displaystyle\lim_{x \to \infty} \dfrac{6(\ln x)(1/x)}{1}$

$= \displaystyle\lim_{x \to \infty} \dfrac{6(\ln x)}{x} = \lim_{x \to \infty} \dfrac{6}{x} = 0$

**67.** $\displaystyle\lim_{x \to \infty} \dfrac{(\ln x)^n}{x^m} = \lim_{x \to \infty} \dfrac{n(\ln x)^{n-1}/x}{mx^{m-1}}$

$= \displaystyle\lim_{x \to \infty} \dfrac{n(\ln x)^{n-1}}{mx^m}$

$= \displaystyle\lim_{x \to \infty} \dfrac{n(n - 1)(\ln x)^{n-2}}{m^2 x^m}$

$= \cdots = \displaystyle\lim_{x \to \infty} \dfrac{n!}{m^n x^m} = 0$

**69.**

| $x$ | 10 | $10^2$ | $10^4$ | $10^6$ | $10^8$ | $10^{10}$ |
|---|---|---|---|---|---|---|
| $\dfrac{(\ln x)^4}{x}$ | 2.811 | 4.498 | 0.720 | 0.036 | 0.001 | 0.000 |

**71.** $y = x^{1/x}, \; x > 0$

Horizontal asymptote: $y = 1$  (See Exercise 37)

$\ln y = \dfrac{1}{x} \ln x$

$\dfrac{1}{y}\dfrac{dy}{dx} = \dfrac{1}{x}\left(\dfrac{1}{x}\right) + (\ln x)\left(-\dfrac{1}{x^2}\right)$

$\dfrac{dy}{dx} = x^{1/x}\left(\dfrac{1}{x^2}\right)(1 - \ln x) = x^{(1/x)-2}(1 - \ln x) = 0$

Critical number:    $x = e$

Intervals:    $(0, e)$       $(e, \infty)$

Sign of $dy/dx$:       $+$            $-$

$y = f(x)$:  Increasing    Decreasing

Relative maximum: $(e, e^{1/e})$

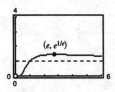

**73.** $y = 2xe^{-x}$

$\displaystyle\lim_{x \to \infty} \dfrac{2x}{e^x} = \lim_{x \to \infty} \dfrac{2}{e^x} = 0$

Horizontal asymptote: $y = 0$

$\dfrac{dy}{dx} = 2x(-e^{-x}) + 2e^{-x}$

$= 2e^{-x}(1 - x) = 0$

Critical number:    $x = 1$

Intervals:    $(-\infty, 1)$       $(1, \infty)$

Sign of $dy/dx$:       $+$            $-$

$y = f(x)$:  Increasing    Decreasing

Relative maximum: $\left(1, \dfrac{2}{e}\right)$

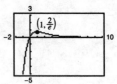

**75.** $\displaystyle\lim_{x \to 0} \dfrac{e^{2x} - 1}{e^x} = \dfrac{0}{1} = 0$

Limit is not of the form $0/0$ or $\infty/\infty$.

L'Hôpital's Rule does not apply.

**77.** $\displaystyle\lim_{x \to \infty} x \cos \dfrac{1}{x} = \infty(1) = \infty$

Limit is not of the form $0/0$ or $\infty/\infty$.

L'Hôpital's Rule does not apply.

**79.** (a) $\displaystyle\lim_{x\to\infty} \frac{x}{\sqrt{x^2+1}} = \lim_{x\to\infty} \frac{x/x}{\sqrt{x^2+1}/x}$

$\displaystyle\qquad\qquad = \lim_{x\to\infty} \frac{1}{\sqrt{x^2+1}/\sqrt{x^2}}$

$\displaystyle\qquad\qquad = \lim_{x\to\infty} \frac{1}{\sqrt{1+(1/x^2)}}$

$\displaystyle\qquad\qquad = \frac{1}{\sqrt{1+0}} = 1$

(b) $\displaystyle\lim_{x\to\infty} \frac{x}{\sqrt{x^2+1}} = \lim_{x\to\infty} \frac{1}{x/\sqrt{x^2+1}}$

$\displaystyle\qquad\qquad = \lim_{x\to\infty} \frac{\sqrt{x^2+1}}{x} = \lim_{x\to\infty} \frac{x/\sqrt{x^2+1}}{1}$

$\displaystyle\qquad\qquad = \lim_{x\to\infty} \frac{x}{\sqrt{x^2+1}}$

Applying L'Hôpital's rule twice results in the original limit, so L'Hôpital's rule fails.

(c)

**81.** $\displaystyle\lim_{k\to 0} \frac{32\left(1 - e^{-kt} + \dfrac{v_0 k e^{-kt}}{32}\right)}{k} = \lim_{k\to 0} \frac{32(1 - e^{-kt})}{k} + \lim_{k\to 0} (v_0 e^{-kt})$

$\displaystyle\qquad\qquad = \lim_{k\to 0} \frac{32(0 + te^{-kt})}{1} + \lim_{k\to 0} \left(\frac{v_0}{e^{kt}}\right) = 32t + v_0$

**83.** Area of triangle: $\dfrac{1}{2}(2x)(1 - \cos x) = x - x\cos x$

Shaded area: Area of rectangle − Area under curve

$\displaystyle 2x(1 - \cos x) - 2\int_0^x (1 - \cos t)\,dt = 2x(1 - \cos x) - 2\left[t - \sin t\right]_0^x$

$\displaystyle\qquad\qquad\qquad = 2x(1 - \cos x) - 2(x - \sin x) = 2\sin x - 2x\cos x$

Ratio: $\displaystyle\lim_{x\to 0} \frac{x - x\cos x}{2\sin x - 2x\cos x} = \lim_{x\to 0} \frac{1 + x\sin x - \cos x}{2\cos x + 2x\sin x - 2\cos x}$

$\displaystyle\qquad\qquad = \lim_{x\to 0} \frac{1 + x\sin x - \cos x}{2x\sin x}$

$\displaystyle\qquad\qquad = \lim_{x\to 0} \frac{x\cos x + \sin x + \sin x}{2x\cos x + 2\sin x}$

$\displaystyle\qquad\qquad = \lim_{x\to 0} \frac{x\cos x + 2\sin x}{2x\cos x + 2\sin x} \cdot \frac{1/\cos x}{1/\cos x}$

$\displaystyle\qquad\qquad = \lim_{x\to 0} \frac{x + 2\tan x}{2x + 2\tan x}$

$\displaystyle\qquad\qquad = \lim_{x\to 0} \frac{1 + 2\sec^2 x}{2 + 2\sec^2 x} = \frac{3}{4}$

**85.** $f(x) = x^3,\ g(x) = x^2 + 1,\ [0, 1]$

$\displaystyle\frac{f(b) - f(a)}{g(b) - g(a)} = \frac{f'(c)}{g'(c)}$

$\displaystyle\frac{f(1) - f(0)}{g(1) - g(0)} = \frac{3c^2}{2c}$

$\displaystyle\frac{1}{1} = \frac{3c}{2}$

$\displaystyle c = \frac{2}{3}$

**87.** $f(x) = \sin x,\ g(x) = \cos x,\ \left[0, \dfrac{\pi}{2}\right]$

$\displaystyle\frac{f(\pi/2) - f(0)}{g(\pi/2) - g(0)} = \frac{f'(c)}{g'(c)}$

$\displaystyle\frac{1}{-1} = \frac{\cos c}{-\sin c}$

$-1 = -\cot c$

$\displaystyle c = \frac{\pi}{4}$

**89.** False. L'Hôpital's Rule does not apply since                    **91.** True

$$\lim_{x \to 0} (x^2 + x + 1) \neq 0.$$

$$\lim_{x \to 0} \frac{x^2 + x + 1}{x} = \lim_{x \to 0} \left( x + 1 + \frac{1}{x} \right) = 1 + \infty = \infty$$

**93.** (a)  $\sin \theta = BD$

$\cos \theta = DO \implies AD = 1 - \cos \theta$

Area $\triangle ABD = \frac{1}{2} bh = \frac{1}{2}(1 - \cos \theta) \sin \theta = \frac{1}{2} \sin \theta - \frac{1}{2} \sin \theta \cos \theta$

(b) Area of sector: $\frac{1}{2} \theta$

Shaded area: $\frac{1}{2} \theta - $ Area $\triangle OBD = \frac{1}{2} \theta - \frac{1}{2}(\cos \theta)(\sin \theta) = \frac{1}{2} \theta - \frac{1}{2} \sin \theta \cos \theta$

(c) $R = \dfrac{(1/2) \sin \theta - (1/2) \sin \theta \cos \theta}{(1/2)\theta - (1/2) \sin \theta \cos \theta} = \dfrac{\sin \theta - \sin \theta \cos \theta}{\theta - \sin \theta \cos \theta}$

(d) $\lim_{\theta \to 0} R = \lim_{\theta \to 0} \dfrac{\sin \theta - (1/2) \sin 2\theta}{\theta - (1/2) \sin 2\theta}$

$= \lim_{\theta \to 0} \dfrac{\cos \theta - \cos 2\theta}{1 - \cos 2\theta} = \lim_{\theta \to 0} \dfrac{-\sin \theta + 2 \sin 2\theta}{2 \sin 2\theta} = \lim_{\theta \to 0} \dfrac{-\cos \theta + 4 \cos 2\theta}{4 \cos 2\theta} = \dfrac{3}{4}$

**95.** $\lim_{x \to a} f(x)^{g(x)}$

$y = f(x)^{g(x)}$

$\ln y = g(x) \ln f(x)$

$\lim_{x \to a} g(x) \ln f(x) = (\infty)(-\infty) = -\infty$

As $x \to a$, $\ln y \implies -\infty$, and hence $y = 0$. Thus,

$\lim_{x \to a} f(x)^{g(x)} = 0.$

**97.** $f'(a)(b - a) - \displaystyle\int_a^b f''(t)(t - b) \, dt = f'(a)(b - a) - \left\{ \left[ f'(t)(t - b) \right]_a^b - \int_a^b f'(t) \, dt \right\}$

$$= f'(a)(b - a) + f'(a)(a - b) + \left[ f(t) \right]_a^b = f(b) - f(a)$$

$dv = f''(t)dt \implies v = f'(t)$

$u = t - b \implies du = dt$

# Section 7.8    Improper Integrals

**1.** Infinite discontinuity at $x = 0$.

$$\int_0^4 \frac{1}{\sqrt{x}} \, dx = \lim_{b \to 0^+} \int_b^4 \frac{1}{\sqrt{x}} \, dx$$

$$= \lim_{b \to 0^+} \left[ 2\sqrt{x} \right]_b^4$$

$$= \lim_{b \to 0^+} \left( 4 - 2\sqrt{b} \right) = 4$$

Converges

**3.** Infinite discontinuity at $x = 1$.

$$\int_0^2 \frac{1}{(x-1)^2}\, dx = \int_0^1 \frac{1}{(x-1)^2}\, dx + \int_1^2 \frac{1}{(x-1)^2}\, dx$$

$$= \lim_{b \to 1^-} \int_0^b \frac{1}{(x-1)^2}\, dx + \lim_{c \to 1^+} \int_c^2 \frac{1}{(x-1)^2}\, dx$$

$$= \lim_{b \to 1^-} \left[ -\frac{1}{x-1} \right]_0^b + \lim_{c \to 1^+} \left[ -\frac{1}{x-1} \right]_c^2 = (\infty - 1) + (-1 + \infty)$$

Diverges

**5.** Infinite limit of integration.

$$\int_0^\infty e^{-x}\, dx = \lim_{b \to \infty} \int_0^b e^{-x}\, dx$$

$$= \lim_{b \to \infty} \left[ -e^{-x} \right]_0^b = 0 + 1 = 1$$

Converges

**7.** $\displaystyle \int_{-1}^1 \frac{1}{x^2}\, dx \neq -2$

because the integrand is not defined at $x = 0$.
Diverges

**9.** $\displaystyle \int_1^\infty \frac{1}{x^2}\, dx = \lim_{b \to \infty} \int_1^b \frac{1}{x^2}\, dx$

$$= \lim_{b \to \infty} \left[ -\frac{1}{x} \right]_1^b = 1$$

**11.** $\displaystyle \int_1^\infty \frac{3}{\sqrt[3]{x}}\, dx = \lim_{b \to \infty} \int_1^b 3x^{-1/3}\, dx$

$$= \lim_{b \to \infty} \left[ \frac{9}{2} x^{2/3} \right]_1^b = \infty$$

Diverges

**13.** $\displaystyle \int_{-\infty}^0 xe^{-2x}\, dx = \lim_{b \to -\infty} \int_b^0 xe^{-2x}\, dx = \lim_{b \to -\infty} \frac{1}{4} \left[ (-2x - 1)e^{-2x} \right]_b^0 = \lim_{b \to -\infty} \frac{1}{4} \left[ -1 + (2b+1)e^{-2b} \right] = -\infty$   (Integration by parts)

Diverges

**15.** $\displaystyle \int_0^\infty x^2 e^{-x}\, dx = \lim_{b \to \infty} \int_0^b x^2 e^{-x}\, dx = \lim_{b \to \infty} \left[ -e^{-x}(x^2 + 2x + 2) \right]_0^b = \lim_{b \to \infty} \left( -\frac{b^2 + 2b + 2}{e^b} + 2 \right) = 2$

Since $\displaystyle \lim_{b \to \infty} \left( -\frac{b^2 + 2b + 2}{e^b} \right) = 0$ by L'Hôpital's Rule.

**17.** $\displaystyle \int_0^\infty e^{-x} \cos x\, dx = \lim_{b \to \infty} \frac{1}{2} \left[ e^{-x}(-\cos x + \sin x) \right]_0^b$

$$= \frac{1}{2}[0 - (-1)] = \frac{1}{2}$$

**19.** $\displaystyle \int_4^\infty \frac{1}{x(\ln x)^3}\, dx = \lim_{b \to \infty} \int_4^b (\ln x)^{-3} \frac{1}{x}\, dx$

$$= \lim_{b \to \infty} \left[ -\frac{1}{2}(\ln x)^{-2} \right]_4^b$$

$$= -\frac{1}{2}(\ln b)^{-2} + \frac{1}{2}(\ln 4)^{-2}$$

$$= \frac{1}{2} \frac{1}{(2 \ln 2)^2} = \frac{1}{8(\ln 2)^2}$$

**21.** $\displaystyle \int_{-\infty}^\infty \frac{2}{4 + x^2}\, dx = \int_{-\infty}^0 \frac{2}{4 + x^2}\, dx + \int_0^\infty \frac{2}{4 + x^2}\, dx$

$$= \lim_{b \to -\infty} \int_b^0 \frac{2}{4 + x^2}\, dx + \lim_{c \to \infty} \int_0^c \frac{2}{4 + x^2}\, dx$$

$$= \lim_{b \to -\infty} \left[ \arctan\left(\frac{x}{2}\right) \right]_b^0 + \lim_{c \to \infty} \left[ \arctan\left(\frac{x}{2}\right) \right]_0^c$$

$$= \left( 0 - \left(-\frac{\pi}{2}\right) \right) + \left( \frac{\pi}{2} - 0 \right) = \pi$$

**23.** $\displaystyle\int_0^\infty \frac{1}{e^x + e^{-x}}\,dx = \lim_{b\to\infty}\int_0^b \frac{e^x}{1 + e^{2x}}\,dx$

$\qquad\qquad = \lim_{b\to\infty}\left[\arctan(e^x)\right]_0^b$

$\qquad\qquad = \dfrac{\pi}{2} - \dfrac{\pi}{4} = \dfrac{\pi}{4}$

**25.** $\displaystyle\int_0^\infty \cos \pi x\,dx = \lim_{b\to\infty}\left[\frac{1}{\pi}\sin \pi x\right]_0^b$

Diverges since $\sin \pi x$ does not approach a limit as $x \to \infty$.

**27.** $\displaystyle\int_0^1 \frac{1}{x^2}\,dx = \lim_{b\to 0^+}\left[\frac{-1}{x}\right]_b^1 = -1 + \infty$

Diverges

**29.** $\displaystyle\int_0^8 \frac{1}{\sqrt[3]{8-x}}\,dx = \lim_{b\to 8^-}\int_0^b \frac{1}{\sqrt[3]{8-x}}\,dx = \lim_{b\to 8^-}\left[\frac{-3}{2}(8-x)^{2/3}\right]_0^b = 6$

**31.** $\displaystyle\int_0^1 x\ln x\,dx = \lim_{b\to 0^+}\left[\frac{x^2}{2}\ln|x| - \frac{x^2}{4}\right]_b^1 = \lim_{b\to 0^+}\left[\frac{-1}{4} - \frac{b^2\ln b}{2} + \frac{b^2}{4}\right] = \frac{-1}{4}$ since $\lim_{b\to 0^+}(b^2\ln b) = 0$ by L'Hôpital's Rule.

**33.** $\displaystyle\int_0^{\pi/2} \tan \theta\,d\theta = \lim_{b\to(\pi/2)^-}\left[\ln|\sec \theta|\right]_0^b = \infty$

Diverges

**35.** $\displaystyle\int_2^4 \frac{2}{x\sqrt{x^2-4}}\,dx = \lim_{b\to 2^+}\int_b^4 \frac{2}{x\sqrt{x^2-4}}\,dx$

$\qquad\qquad = \lim_{b\to 2^+}\left[\operatorname{arcsec}\left|\frac{x}{2}\right|\right]_b^4$

$\qquad\qquad = \lim_{b\to 2^+}\left(\operatorname{arcsec} 2 - \operatorname{arcsec}\left(\frac{b}{2}\right)\right)$

$\qquad\qquad = \dfrac{\pi}{3} - 0 = \dfrac{\pi}{3}$

**37.** $\displaystyle\int_2^4 \frac{1}{\sqrt{x^2-4}} = \lim_{b\to 2^+}\left[\ln\left|x + \sqrt{x^2-4}\right|\right]_b^4$

$\qquad\qquad = \ln\left(4 + 2\sqrt{3}\right) - \ln 2$

$\qquad\qquad = \ln\left(2 + \sqrt{3}\right) \approx 1.317$

**39.** $\displaystyle\int_0^2 \frac{1}{\sqrt[3]{x-1}}\,dx = \int_0^1 \frac{1}{\sqrt[3]{x-1}}\,dx + \int_1^2 \frac{1}{\sqrt[3]{x-1}}\,dx$

$\qquad\qquad = \lim_{b\to 1^-}\left[\frac{3}{2}(x-1)^{2/3}\right]_0^b + \lim_{c\to 1^+}\left[\frac{3}{2}(x-1)^{2/3}\right]_c^2 = \frac{-3}{2} + \frac{3}{2} = 0$

**41.** $\displaystyle\int_0^\infty \frac{4}{\sqrt{x}(x+6)}\,dx = \int_0^1 \frac{4}{\sqrt{x}(x+6)}\,dx + \int_1^\infty \frac{4}{\sqrt{x}(x+6)}\,dx$

Let $u = \sqrt{x}$, $u^2 = x$, $2u\,du = dx$.

$\displaystyle\int \frac{4}{\sqrt{x}(x+6)}\,dx = \int \frac{4(2u\,du)}{u(u^2+6)} = 8\int \frac{du}{u^2+6} = \frac{8}{\sqrt{6}}\arctan\left(\frac{4}{\sqrt{6}}\right) + C = \frac{8}{\sqrt{6}}\arctan\left(\frac{\sqrt{x}}{\sqrt{6}}\right) + C$

Thus, $\displaystyle\int_0^\infty \frac{4}{\sqrt{x}(x+6)}\,dx = \lim_{b\to 0^+}\left[\frac{8}{\sqrt{6}}\arctan\left(\frac{\sqrt{x}}{\sqrt{6}}\right)\right]_b^1 + \lim_{c\to\infty}\left[\frac{8}{\sqrt{6}}\arctan\left(\frac{\sqrt{x}}{\sqrt{6}}\right)\right]_1^c$

$\qquad\qquad = \left(\frac{8}{\sqrt{6}}\arctan\left(\frac{1}{\sqrt{6}}\right) - \frac{8}{\sqrt{6}}0\right) + \left(\frac{8}{\sqrt{6}}\frac{\pi}{2} - \frac{8}{\sqrt{6}}\arctan\left(\frac{1}{\sqrt{6}}\right)\right)$

$\qquad\qquad = \dfrac{8\pi}{2\sqrt{6}} = \dfrac{2\pi\sqrt{6}}{3}.$

**43.** If $p = 1$, $\displaystyle\int_1^\infty \frac{1}{x}\,dx = \lim_{b\to\infty}\int_1^b \frac{1}{x}\,dx = \lim_{b\to\infty} \ln x\Big]_1^b$.

Diverges. For $p \neq 1$,

$$\int_1^\infty \frac{1}{x^p}\,dx = \lim_{b\to\infty}\left[\frac{x^{1-p}}{1-p}\right]_1^b = \lim_{b\to\infty}\left[\frac{b^{1-p}}{1-p} - \frac{1}{1-p}\right].$$

This converges to $\dfrac{1}{p-1}$ if $1 - p < 0$ or $p > 1$.

**45.** For $n = 1$ we have

$$\int_0^\infty xe^{-x}\,dx = \lim_{b\to\infty}\int_0^b xe^{-x}\,dx$$

$$= \lim_{b\to\infty}\left[-e^{-x}x - e^{-x}\right]_0^b \qquad \text{(Parts: } u = x, dv = e^{-x}\,dx\text{)}$$

$$= \lim_{b\to\infty}\left[-e^{-b}b - e^{-b} + 1\right]$$

$$= \lim_{b\to\infty}\left[\frac{-b}{e^b} - \frac{1}{e^b} + 1\right] = 1 \quad \text{(L'Hôpital's Rule)}$$

Assume that $\displaystyle\int_0^\infty x^n e^{-x}\,dx$ converges. Then for $n + 1$ we have

$$\int x^{n+1}e^{-x}\,dx = -x^{n+1}e^{-x} + (n+1)\int x^n e^{-x}\,dx$$

by parts ($u = x^{n+1}$, $du = (n+1)x^n\,dx$, $dv = e^{-x}\,dx$, $v = -e^{-x}$).

Thus,

$$\int_0^\infty x^{n+1}e^{-x}\,dx = \lim_{b\to\infty}\left[-x^{n+1}e^{-x}\right]_0^b + (n+1)\int_0^\infty x^n e^{-x}\,dx = 0 + (n+1)\int_0^\infty x^n e^{-x}\,dx, \text{ which converges.}$$

**47.** $\displaystyle\int_0^1 \frac{1}{x^3}\,dx$ diverges.

(See Exercise 44, $p = 3 \not< 1$.)

**49.** $\displaystyle\int_1^\infty \frac{1}{x^3}\,dx = \frac{1}{3-1} = \frac{1}{2}$ converges.

(See Exercise 43, $p = 3$.)

**51.** Since $\dfrac{1}{x^2 + 5} \leq \dfrac{1}{x^2}$ on $[1, \infty)$ and $\displaystyle\int_1^\infty \frac{1}{x^2}\,dx$ converges by Exercise 43, $\displaystyle\int_1^\infty \frac{1}{x^2 + 5}\,dx$ converges.

**53.** Since $\dfrac{1}{\sqrt[3]{x(x-1)}} \geq \dfrac{1}{\sqrt[3]{x^2}}$ on $[2, \infty)$ and $\displaystyle\int_2^\infty \frac{1}{\sqrt[3]{x^2}}\,dx$ diverges by Exercise 43, $\displaystyle\int_2^\infty \frac{1}{\sqrt[3]{x(x-1)}}\,dx$ diverges.

**55.** Since $e^{-x^2} \leq e^{-x}$ on $[1, \infty)$ and $\displaystyle\int_0^\infty e^{-x}\,dx$ converges (see Exercise 5), $\displaystyle\int_0^\infty e^{-x^2}\,dx$ converges.

**57.** Answers will vary. See pages 540, 543.

**59.** $\displaystyle\int_{-1}^1 \frac{1}{x^3}\,dx = \int_{-1}^0 \frac{1}{x^3}\,dx + \int_0^1 \frac{1}{x^3}\,dx$

These two integrals diverge by Exercise 44.

**61.** $f(t) = 1$

$$F(s) = \int_0^\infty e^{-st}\,dx = \lim_{b\to\infty}\left[-\frac{1}{s}e^{-st}\right]_0^b = \frac{1}{s}, s > 0$$

**63.** $f(t) = t^2$

$$F(s) = \int_0^\infty t^2 e^{-st}\,dx = \lim_{b\to\infty}\left[\frac{1}{s^3}(-s^2t^2 - 2st - 2)e^{-st}\right]_0^b$$

$$= \frac{2}{s^3}, s > 0$$

**65.** $f(t) = \cos at$

$$F(s) = \int_0^\infty e^{-st} \cos at\, dt$$

$$= \lim_{b \to \infty} \left[ \frac{e^{-st}}{s^2 + a^2}(-s \cos at + a \sin at) \right]_0^b$$

$$= 0 + \frac{s}{s^2 + a^2} = \frac{s}{s^2 + a^2}, \, s > 0$$

**67.** $f(t) = \cosh at$

$$F(s) = \int_0^\infty e^{-st} \cosh at\, dt = \int_0^\infty e^{-st}\left( \frac{e^{at} + e^{-at}}{2} \right) dt = \frac{1}{2}\int_0^\infty \left[ e^{t(-s+a)} + e^{t(-s-a)} \right] dt$$

$$= \lim_{b \to \infty} \frac{1}{2}\left[ \frac{1}{(-s+a)}e^{t(-s+a)} + \frac{1}{(-s-a)}e^{t(-s-a)} \right]_0^b = 0 - \frac{1}{2}\left[ \frac{1}{(-s+a)} + \frac{1}{(-s-a)} \right]$$

$$= \frac{-1}{2}\left[ \frac{1}{(-s+a)} + \frac{1}{(-s-a)} \right] = \frac{s}{s^2 - a^2}, \, s > |a|$$

**69.** (a) $A = \int_0^\infty e^{-x}\, dx$

$$= \lim_{b \to \infty}\left[ -e^{-x} \right]_0^b = 0 - (-1) = 1$$

(b) **Disk:**

$$V = \pi \int_0^\infty (e^{-x})^2\, dx$$

$$= \lim_{b \to \infty} \pi \left[ -\frac{1}{2}e^{-2x} \right]_0^b = \frac{\pi}{2}$$

(c) **Shell:**

$$V = 2\pi \int_0^\infty xe^{-x}\, dx$$

$$= \lim_{b \to \infty}\left\{ 2\pi \left[ -e^{-x}(x + 1) \right]_0^b \right\} = 2\pi$$

**71.**

$$x^{2/3} + y^{2/3} = 4$$

$$\frac{2}{3}x^{-1/3} + \frac{2}{3}y^{-1/3}y' = 0$$

$$y' = \frac{-y^{1/3}}{x^{1/3}}$$

$$\sqrt{1 + (y')^2} = \sqrt{1 + \frac{y^{2/3}}{x^{2/3}}} = \sqrt{\frac{x^{2/3} + y^{2/3}}{x^{2/3}}} = \sqrt{\frac{4}{x^{2/3}}} = \frac{2}{x^{1/3}}$$

$$s = 4\int_0^8 \frac{2}{x^{1/3}}\, dx = \lim_{b \to 0^+}\left[ 8 \cdot \frac{3}{2}x^{2/3} \right]_b^8 = 48$$

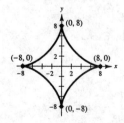

**73.** $\Gamma(n) = \displaystyle\int_0^\infty x^{n-1}e^{-x}\, dx$

    **(a)** $\Gamma(1) = \displaystyle\int_0^\infty e^{-x}\, dx = \lim_{b\to\infty}\left[-e^{-x}\right]_0^b = 1$

        $\Gamma(2) = \displaystyle\int_0^\infty xe^{-x}\, dx = \lim_{b\to\infty}\left[-e^{-x}(x+1)\right]_0^b = 1$

        $\Gamma(3) = \displaystyle\int_0^\infty x^2e^{-x}\, dx = \lim_{b\to\infty}\left[-x^2e^{-x} - 2xe^{-x} - 2e^{-x}\right]_0^b = 2$

    **(b)** $\Gamma(n+1) = \displaystyle\int_0^\infty x^ne^{-x}\, dx = \lim_{b\to\infty}\left[-x^ne^{-x}\right]_0^b + \lim_{b\to\infty} n\int_0^b x^{n-1}e^{-x}\, dx = 0 + n\Gamma(n)$    $(u = x^n,\ dv = e^{-x}\, dx)$

    **(c)** $\Gamma(n) = (n-1)!$

**75.** **(a)** $\displaystyle\int_{-\infty}^\infty \frac{1}{7}e^{-t/7}\, dt = \int_0^\infty \frac{1}{7}e^{-t/7}\, dt = \lim_{b\to\infty}\left[-e^{-t/7}\right]_0^b = 1$      **(b)** $\displaystyle\int_0^4 \frac{1}{7}e^{-t/7}\, dt = \left[-e^{-t/7}\right]_0^4 = -e^{-t/7} + 1$

                                                                                      $\approx 0.4353 = 43.53\%$

    **(c)** $\displaystyle\int_0^\infty t\left[\frac{1}{7}e^{-t/7}\right]dt = \lim_{b\to\infty}\left[-te^{-t/7} - 7e^{-t/7}\right]_0^b$

                         $= 0 + 7 = 7$

**77.** **(a)** $C = 650{,}000 + \displaystyle\int_0^5 25{,}000\, e^{-0.06t}\, dt = 650{,}000 - \left[\frac{25{,}000}{0.06}e^{-0.06t}\right]_0^5 \approx \$757{,}992.41$

    **(b)** $C = 650{,}000 + \displaystyle\int_0^{10} 25{,}000e^{-0.06t}\, dt \approx \$837{,}995.15$

    **(c)** $C = 650{,}000 + \displaystyle\int_0^\infty 25{,}000e^{-0.06t}\, dt = 650{,}000 - \lim_{b\to\infty}\left[\frac{25{,}000}{0.06}e^{-0.06t}\right]_0^b \approx \$1{,}066{,}666.67$

**79.** Let $x = a\tan\theta$, $dx = a\sec^2\theta\, d\theta$, $\sqrt{a^2 + x^2} = a\sec\theta$.

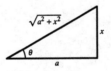

    $\displaystyle\int \frac{1}{(a^2 + x^2)^{3/2}}\, dx = \int \frac{a\sec^2\theta\, d\theta}{a^3\sec^3\theta} = \frac{1}{a^2}\int \cos\theta\, d\theta$

                         $= \frac{1}{a^2}\sin\theta = \frac{1}{a^2}\frac{x}{\sqrt{a^2 + x^2}}$

    Hence,

    $P = k\displaystyle\int_1^\infty \frac{1}{(a^2 + x^2)^{3/2}}\, dx = \frac{k}{a^2}\lim_{b\to\infty}\left[\frac{x}{\sqrt{a^2 + x^2}}\right]_1^b$

       $= \frac{k}{a^2}\left[1 - \frac{1}{\sqrt{a^2 + 1}}\right] = \frac{k\left(\sqrt{a^2 + 1} - 1\right)}{a^2\sqrt{a^2 + 1}}.$

**81.** $\dfrac{10}{x^2 - 2x} = \dfrac{10}{x(x-2)} \Rightarrow x = 0, 2.$

    You must analyze three improper integrals, and each must converge in order for the original integral to converge.

    $\displaystyle\int_0^3 f(x)\, dx = \int_0^1 f(x)\, dx + \int_1^2 f(x)\, dx + \int_2^3 f(x)\, dx$

**83.** For $n = 1$,

$$I_1 = \int_0^\infty \frac{x}{(x^2 + 1)^4} \, dx = \lim_{b \to \infty} \frac{1}{2} \int_0^b (x^2 + 1)^{-4}(2x \, dx) = \lim_{b \to \infty} \left[ -\frac{1}{6} \frac{1}{(x^2 + 1)^3} \right]_0^b = \frac{1}{6}.$$

For $n > 1$,

$$I_n = \int_0^\infty \frac{x^{2n-1}}{(x^2 + 1)^{n+3}} \, dx = \lim_{b \to \infty} \left[ \frac{-x^{2n-2}}{2(n + 2)(x^2 + 1)^n} + 2 \right]_0^b + \frac{n - 1}{n + 2} \int_0^\infty \frac{x^{2n-3}}{(x^2 + 1)^{n+2}} \, dx = 0 + \frac{n - 1}{n + 2}(I_{n-1})$$

$$u = x^{2n-2}, \, du = (2n - 2)x^{2n-3} \, dx, \, dv = \frac{x}{(x^2 + 1)^{n+3}} \, dx, \, v = \frac{-1}{2(n + 2)(x^2 + 1)^{n+2}}$$

(a) $\displaystyle \int_0^\infty \frac{x}{(x^2 + 1)^4} \, dx = \lim_{b \to \infty} \left[ -\frac{1}{6(x^2 + 1)^3} \right]_0^b = \frac{1}{6}$

(b) $\displaystyle \int_0^\infty \frac{x^3}{(x^2 + 1)^5} \, dx = \frac{1}{4} \int_0^\infty \frac{x}{(x^2 + 1)^4} \, dx = \frac{1}{4}\left(\frac{1}{6}\right) = \frac{1}{24}$

(c) $\displaystyle \int_0^\infty \frac{x^5}{(x^2 + 1)^6} = \frac{2}{5} \int_0^\infty \frac{x^3}{(x^2 + 1)^5} \, dx = \frac{2}{5}\left(\frac{1}{24}\right) = \frac{1}{60}$

**85.** False. $f(x) = 1/(x + 1)$ is continuous on $[0, \infty)$, $\displaystyle \lim_{x \to \infty} 1/(x + 1) = 0$, but $\displaystyle \int_0^\infty \frac{1}{x + 1} \, dx = \lim_{b \to \infty} \left[ \ln|x + 1| \right]_0^b = \infty$.

Diverges

**87.** True

# Review Exercises for Chapter 7

**1.** $\displaystyle \int x\sqrt{x^2 - 1} \, dx = \frac{1}{2} \int (x^2 - 1)^{1/2}(2x) \, dx$

$\qquad\qquad\qquad = \frac{1}{2} \frac{(x^2 - 1)^{3/2}}{3/2} + C$

$\qquad\qquad\qquad = \frac{1}{3}(x^2 - 1)^{3/2} + C$

**3.** $\displaystyle \int \frac{x}{x^2 - 1} \, dx = \frac{1}{2} \int \frac{2x}{x^2 - 1} \, dx$

$\qquad\qquad\qquad = \frac{1}{2} \ln|x^2 - 1| + C$

**5.** $\displaystyle \int \frac{\ln(2x)}{x} \, dx = \frac{(\ln 2x)^2}{2} + C$

**7.** $\displaystyle \int \frac{16}{\sqrt{16 - x^2}} \, dx = 16 \arcsin\left(\frac{x}{4}\right) + C$

**9.** $\displaystyle \int e^{2x} \sin 3x \, dx = -\frac{1}{3} e^{2x} \cos 3x + \frac{2}{3} \int e^{2x} \cos 3x \, dx$

$\qquad\qquad\qquad = -\frac{1}{3} e^{2x} \cos 3x + \frac{2}{3}\left(\frac{1}{3} e^{2x} \sin 3x - \frac{2}{3} \int e^{2x} \sin 3x \, dx\right)$

$\displaystyle \frac{13}{9} \int e^{2x} \sin 3x \, dx = -\frac{1}{3} e^{2x} \cos 3x + \frac{2}{9} e^{2x} \sin 3x$

$\displaystyle \int e^{2x} \sin 3x \, dx = \frac{e^{2x}}{13}(2 \sin 3x - 3 \cos 3x) + C$

(1) $dv = \sin 3x \, dx \implies v = -\frac{1}{3} \cos 3x$ $\qquad$ (2) $dv = \cos 3x \, dx \implies v = \frac{1}{3} \sin 3x$

$\qquad u = e^{2x} \qquad\qquad \implies du = 2e^{2x} \, dx$ $\qquad\qquad u = e^{2x} \qquad\qquad \implies du = 2e^{2x} \, dx$

**11.** $u = x, du = dx, dv = (x - 5)^{1/2} dx, v = \frac{2}{3}(x - 5)^{3/2}$

$$\int x\sqrt{x - 5}\, dx = \frac{2}{3}x(x - 5)^{3/2} - \int \frac{2}{3}(x - 5)^{3/2}\, dx$$

$$= \frac{2}{3}x(x - 5)^{3/2} - \frac{4}{15}(x - 5)^{5/2} + C$$

$$= (x - 5)^{3/2}\left[\frac{2}{3}x - \frac{4}{15}(x - 5)\right] + C$$

$$= (x - 5)^{3/2}\left[\frac{6}{15}x + \frac{4}{3}\right] + C$$

$$= \frac{2}{15}(x - 5)^{3/2}[3x + 10] + C$$

**13.** $\int x^2 \sin 2x\, dx = -\frac{1}{2}x^2 \cos 2x + \int x \cos 2x\, dx$

$$= -\frac{1}{2}x^2 \cos 2x + \frac{1}{2}x \sin 2x - \frac{1}{2}\int \sin 2x\, dx$$

$$= -\frac{1}{2}x^2 \cos 2x + \frac{x}{2}\sin 2x + \frac{1}{4}\cos 2x + C$$

(1) $dv = \sin 2x\, dx \implies v = -\frac{1}{2}\cos 2x$

$\quad u = x^2 \qquad\qquad \implies du = 2x\, dx$

(2) $dv = \cos 2x\, dx \implies v = \frac{1}{2}\sin 2x$

$\quad u = x \qquad\qquad \implies du = dx$

**15.** $\int x \arcsin 2x\, dx = \frac{x^2}{2}\arcsin 2x - \int \frac{x^2}{\sqrt{1 - 4x^2}}\, dx$

$$= \frac{x^2}{2}\arcsin 2x - \frac{1}{8}\int \frac{2(2x)^2}{\sqrt{1 - (2x)^2}}\, dx$$

$$= \frac{x^2}{2}\arcsin 2x - \frac{1}{8}\left(\frac{1}{2}\right)\left[-(2x)\sqrt{1 - 4x^2} + \arcsin 2x\right] + C \quad \text{(by Formula 43 of Integration Tables)}$$

$$= \frac{1}{16}\left[(8x^2 - 1)\arcsin 2x + 2x\sqrt{1 - 4x^2}\right] + C$$

$dv = x\, dx \quad \implies \quad v = \frac{x^2}{2}$

$u = \arcsin 2x \implies du = \frac{2}{\sqrt{1 - 4x^2}}\, dx$

**17.** $\int \cos^3(\pi x - 1)\, dx = \int [1 - \sin^2(\pi x - 1)]\cos(\pi x - 1)\, dx$

$$= \frac{1}{\pi}\left[\sin(\pi x - 1) - \frac{1}{3}\sin^3(\pi x - 1)\right] + C$$

$$= \frac{1}{3\pi}\sin(\pi x - 1)[3 - \sin^2(\pi x - 1)] + C$$

$$= \frac{1}{3\pi}\sin(\pi x - 1)[3 - (1 - \cos^2(\pi x - 1))] + C$$

$$= \frac{1}{3\pi}\sin(\pi x - 1)[2 + \cos^2(\pi x - 1)] + C$$

**19.** $\int \sec^4\left(\frac{x}{2}\right) dx = \int \left[\tan^2\left(\frac{x}{2}\right) + 1\right]\sec^2\left(\frac{x}{2}\right) dx$

$$= \int \tan^2\left(\frac{x}{2}\right)\sec^2\left(\frac{x}{2}\right) dx + \int \sec^2\left(\frac{x}{2}\right) dx$$

$$= \frac{2}{3}\tan^3\left(\frac{x}{2}\right) + 2\tan\left(\frac{x}{2}\right) + C = \frac{2}{3}\left[\tan^3\left(\frac{x}{2}\right) + 3\tan\left(\frac{x}{2}\right)\right] + C$$

**21.** $\int \frac{1}{1 - \sin\theta}\, d\theta = \int \frac{1 + \sin\theta}{\cos^2\theta}\, d\theta = \int (\sec^2\theta + \sec\theta\tan\theta)\, d\theta = \tan\theta + \sec\theta + C$

**23.** $\displaystyle\int \frac{-12}{x^2\sqrt{4-x^2}}\,dx = \int \frac{-24\cos\theta\,d\theta}{(4\sin^2\theta)(2\cos\theta)}$

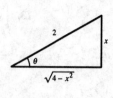

$\displaystyle = -3\int \csc^2\theta\,d\theta$

$\displaystyle = 3\cot\theta + C$

$\displaystyle = \frac{3\sqrt{4-x^2}}{x} + C$

$x = 2\sin\theta,\, dx = 2\cos\theta\,d\theta,\, \sqrt{4-x^2} = 2\cos\theta$

**25.**     $x = 2\tan\theta$

$dx = 2\sec^2\theta\,d\theta$

$4 + x^2 = 4\sec^2\theta$

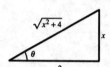

$\displaystyle\int \frac{x^3}{\sqrt{4+x^2}}\,dx = \int \frac{8\tan^3\theta}{2\sec\theta}\,2\sec^2\theta\,d\theta$

$\displaystyle = 8\int \tan^3\theta\sec\theta\,d\theta$

$\displaystyle = 8\int (\sec^2\theta - 1)\tan\theta\sec\theta\,d\theta$

$\displaystyle = 8\left[\frac{\sec^3\theta}{3} - \sec\theta\right] + C$

$\displaystyle = 8\left[\frac{(x^2+4)^{3/2}}{24} - \frac{\sqrt{x^2+4}}{2}\right] + C$

$\displaystyle = \sqrt{x^2+4}\left[\frac{1}{3}(x^2+4) - 4\right] + C$

$\displaystyle = \frac{1}{3}x^2\sqrt{x^2+4} - \frac{8}{3}\sqrt{x^2+4} + C$

$\displaystyle = \frac{1}{3}(x^2+4)^{1/2}(x^2-8) + C$

**27.** $\displaystyle\int \sqrt{4-x^2}\,dx = \int (2\cos\theta)(2\cos\theta)\,d\theta$

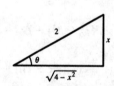

$\displaystyle = 2\int (1 + \cos 2\theta)\,d\theta$

$\displaystyle = 2\left(\theta + \frac{1}{2}\sin 2\theta\right) + C$

$\displaystyle = 2(\theta + \sin\theta\cos\theta) + C$

$\displaystyle = 2\left[\arcsin\left(\frac{x}{2}\right) + \frac{x}{2}\left(\frac{\sqrt{4-x^2}}{2}\right)\right] + C$

$\displaystyle = \frac{1}{2}\left[4\arcsin\left(\frac{x}{2}\right) + x\sqrt{4-x^2}\right] + C$

$x = 2\sin\theta,\, dx = 2\cos\theta\,d\theta,\, \sqrt{4-x^2} = 2\cos\theta$

**29. (a)** $\displaystyle\int \frac{x^3}{\sqrt{4 + x^2}}\,dx = 8\int \frac{\sin^3\theta}{\cos^4\theta}\,d\theta$

$\displaystyle\qquad\qquad = 8\int (\cos^{-4}\theta - \cos^{-2}\theta)\sin\theta\,d\theta$

$\displaystyle\qquad\qquad = \frac{8}{3}\sec\theta(\sec^2\theta - 3) + C$

$\displaystyle\qquad\qquad = \frac{\sqrt{4 + x^2}}{3}(x^2 - 8) + C$

$x = 2\tan\theta,\ dx = 2\sec^2\theta\,d\theta$

**(b)** $\displaystyle\int \frac{x^3}{\sqrt{4 + x^2}}\,dx = \int (u^2 - 4)\,du$

$\displaystyle\qquad\qquad = \frac{1}{3}u^3 - 4u + C$

$\displaystyle\qquad\qquad = \frac{u}{3}(u^2 - 12) + C$

$\displaystyle\qquad\qquad = \frac{\sqrt{4 + x^2}}{3}(x^2 - 8) + C$

$u^2 = 4 + x^2,\ 2u\,du = 2x\,dx$

**(c)** $\displaystyle\int \frac{x^3}{\sqrt{4 + x^2}}\,dx = x^2\sqrt{4 + x^2} - \int 2x\sqrt{4 + x^2}\,dx$

$\displaystyle\qquad\qquad = x^2\sqrt{4 + x^2} - \frac{2}{3}(4 + x^2)^{3/2} + C = \frac{\sqrt{4 + x^2}}{3}(x^2 - 8) + C$

$\displaystyle dv = \frac{x}{\sqrt{4 + x^2}}\,dx \implies v = \sqrt{4 + x^2}$

$u = x^2 \qquad\qquad \implies du = 2x\,dx$

**31.** $\displaystyle \frac{x - 28}{x^2 - x - 6} = \frac{A}{x - 3} + \frac{B}{x + 2}$

$x - 28 = A(x + 2) + B(x - 3)$

$x = -2 \implies -30 = B(-5) \implies B = 6$

$x = 3 \ \implies -25 = A(5) \ \implies A = -5$

$\displaystyle\int \frac{x - 28}{x^2 - 6 - 6}\,dx = \int\left(\frac{-5}{x - 3} + \frac{6}{x + 2}\right)dx = -5\ln|x - 3| + 6\ln|x + 2| + C$

**33.** $\displaystyle \frac{x^2 + 2x}{(x - 1)(x^2 + 1)} = \frac{A}{x - 1} + \frac{Bx + C}{x^2 + 1}$

$x^2 + 2x = A(x^2 + 1) + (Bx + C)(x - 1)$

Let $x = 1$: $3 = 2A \implies A = \dfrac{3}{2}$

Let $x = 0$: $0 = A - C \implies C = \dfrac{3}{2}$

Let $x = 2$: $8 = 5A + 2B + C \implies B = -\dfrac{1}{2}$

$\displaystyle\int \frac{x^2 + 2x}{x^3 - x^2 + x - 1}\,dx = \frac{3}{2}\int \frac{1}{x - 1}\,dx - \frac{1}{2}\int \frac{x - 3}{x^2 + 1}\,dx$

$\displaystyle\qquad\qquad = \frac{3}{2}\int \frac{1}{x - 1}\,dx - \frac{1}{4}\int \frac{2x}{x^2 + 1}\,dx + \frac{3}{2}\int \frac{1}{x^2 + 1}\,dx$

$\displaystyle\qquad\qquad = \frac{3}{2}\ln|x - 1| - \frac{1}{4}\ln|x^2 + 1| + \frac{3}{2}\arctan x + C$

$\displaystyle\qquad\qquad = \frac{1}{4}\left[6\ln|x - 1| - \ln(x^2 + 1) + 6\arctan x\right] + C$

**35.** $\dfrac{x^2}{x^2 + 2x - 15} = 1 + \dfrac{15 - 2x}{x^2 + 2x - 15}$

$\dfrac{15 - 2x}{(x - 3)(x + 5)} = \dfrac{A}{x - 3} + \dfrac{B}{x + 5}$

$15 - 2x = A(x + 5) + B(x - 3)$

Let $x = 3$:  $9 = 8A \implies A = \dfrac{9}{8}$

Let $x = -5$: $25 = -8B \implies B = -\dfrac{25}{8}$

$\displaystyle\int \dfrac{x^2}{x^2 + 2x - 15}\,dx = \int dx + \dfrac{9}{8}\int \dfrac{1}{x - 3}\,dx - \dfrac{25}{8}\int \dfrac{1}{x + 5}\,dx$

$\qquad\qquad\qquad\qquad = x + \dfrac{9}{8}\ln|x - 3| - \dfrac{25}{8}\ln|x + 5| + C$

**37.** $\displaystyle\int \dfrac{x}{(2 + 3x)^2}\,dx = \dfrac{1}{9}\left[\dfrac{2}{2 + 3x} + \ln|2 + 3x|\right] + C$

(Formula 4)

**39.** $\displaystyle\int \dfrac{x}{1 + \sin x^2}\,dx = \dfrac{1}{2}\int \dfrac{1}{1 + \sin u}\,du$  $(u = x^2)$

$\qquad\qquad\qquad\qquad = \dfrac{1}{2}[\tan u - \sec u] + C$  (Formula 56)

$\qquad\qquad\qquad\qquad = \dfrac{1}{2}[\tan x^2 - \sec x^2] + C$

**41.** $\displaystyle\int \dfrac{x}{x^2 + 4x + 8}\,dx = \dfrac{1}{2}\left[\ln|x^2 + 4x + 8| - 4\int \dfrac{1}{x^2 + 4x + 8}\,dx\right]$  (Formula 15)

$\qquad\qquad\qquad\qquad = \dfrac{1}{2}[\ln|x^2 + 4x + 8|] - 2\left[\dfrac{2}{\sqrt{32 - 16}}\arctan\left(\dfrac{2x + 4}{\sqrt{32 - 16}}\right)\right] + C$  (Formula 14)

$\qquad\qquad\qquad\qquad = \dfrac{1}{2}\ln|x^2 + 4x + 8| - \arctan\left(1 + \dfrac{x}{2}\right) + C$

**43.** $\displaystyle\int \dfrac{1}{\sin \pi x \cos \pi x}\,dx = \dfrac{1}{\pi}\int \dfrac{1}{\sin \pi x \cos \pi x}(\pi)\,dx$  $(u = \pi x)$

$\qquad\qquad\qquad\qquad = \dfrac{1}{\pi}\ln|\tan \pi x| + C$  (Formula 58)

**45.** $dv = dx \implies v = x$

$u = (\ln x)^n \implies du = n(\ln x)^{n-1}\dfrac{1}{x}dx$

$\displaystyle\int (\ln x)^n\,dx = x(\ln x)^n - n\int (\ln x)^{n-1}\,dx$

**47.** $\displaystyle\int \theta \sin \theta \cos \theta\,d\theta = \dfrac{1}{2}\int \theta \sin 2\theta\,d\theta$

$\qquad\qquad = -\dfrac{1}{4}\theta \cos 2\theta + \dfrac{1}{4}\int \cos 2\theta\,d\theta = -\dfrac{1}{4}\theta \cos 2\theta + \dfrac{1}{8}\sin 2\theta + C = \dfrac{1}{8}(\sin 2\theta - 2\theta \cos 2\theta) + C$

$dv = \sin 2\theta\,d\theta \implies v = -\dfrac{1}{2}\cos 2\theta$

$u = \theta \qquad\qquad \implies du = d\theta$

**49.** $\displaystyle\int \frac{x^{1/4}}{1+x^{1/2}}\,dx = 4\int \frac{u(u^3)}{1+u^2}\,du$

$\displaystyle\qquad = 4\int\left(u^2 - 1 + \frac{1}{u^2+1}\right)du$

$\displaystyle\qquad = 4\left(\frac{1}{3}u^3 - u + \arctan u\right) + C$

$\displaystyle\qquad = \frac{4}{3}\left[x^{3/4} - 3x^{1/4} + 3\arctan(x^{1/4})\right] + C$

$y = \sqrt[4]{x},\ x = u^4,\ dx = 4u^3\,du$

**51.** $\displaystyle\int \sqrt{1+\cos x}\,dx = \int \frac{\sin x}{\sqrt{1-\cos x}}\,dx$

$\displaystyle\qquad = \int (1-\cos x)^{-1/2}(\sin x)\,dx$

$\displaystyle\qquad = 2\sqrt{1-\cos x} + C$

$u = 1 - \cos x,\ du = \sin x\,dx$

**53.** $\displaystyle\int \cos x\,\ln(\sin x)\,dx = \sin x\,\ln(\sin x) - \int \cos x\,dx$

$\displaystyle\qquad = \sin x\,\ln(\sin x) - \sin x + C$

$dv = \cos x\,dx \implies v = \sin x$

$u = \ln(\sin x) \implies du = \frac{\cos x}{\sin x}\,dx$

**55.** $\displaystyle y = \int \frac{9}{x^2-9}\,dx = \frac{3}{2}\ln\left|\frac{x-3}{x+3}\right| + C$

(by Formula 24 of Integration Tables)

**57.** $\displaystyle y = \int \ln(x^2+x)\,dx = x\ln|x^2+x| - \int \frac{2x^2+x}{x^2+x}\,dx$

$\displaystyle\qquad = x\ln|x^2+x| - \int \frac{2x+1}{x+1}\,dx$

$\displaystyle\qquad = x\ln|x^2+x| - \int 2\,dx + \int \frac{1}{x+1}\,dx$

$\displaystyle\qquad = x\ln|x^2+x| - 2x + \ln|x+1| + C$

$dv = dx \qquad \implies v = x$

$u = \ln(x^2+x) \implies du = \frac{2x+1}{x^2+x}\,dx$

**59.** $\displaystyle\int_2^{\sqrt{5}} x(x^2-4)^{3/2}\,dx = \left[\frac{1}{5}(x^2-4)^{5/2}\right]_2^{\sqrt{5}} = \frac{1}{5}$

**61.** $\displaystyle\int_1^4 \frac{\ln x}{x}\,dx = \left[\frac{1}{2}(\ln x)^2\right]_1^4 = \frac{1}{2}(\ln 4)^2 = 2(\ln 2)^2 \approx 0.961$

**63.** $\displaystyle\int_0^\pi x\sin x\,dx = \left[-x\cos x + \sin x\right]_0^\pi = \pi$

**65.** $\displaystyle A = \int_0^4 x\sqrt{4-x}\,dx = \int_2^0 (4-u^2)u(-2u)\,du$

$\displaystyle\qquad = \int_2^0 2(u^4 - 4u^2)\,du$

$\displaystyle\qquad = \left[2\left(\frac{u^5}{5} - \frac{4u^3}{3}\right)\right]_2^0 = \frac{128}{15}$

$u = \sqrt{4-x},\ x = 4 - u^2,\ dx = -2u\,du$

**67.** By symmetry, $\bar{x} = 0,\ A = \frac{1}{2}\pi$.

$\displaystyle\bar{y} = \frac{2}{\pi}\left(\frac{1}{2}\right)\int_{-1}^1 \left(\sqrt{1-x^2}\right)^2 dx = \frac{1}{\pi}\left[x - \frac{1}{3}x^3\right]_{-1}^1 = \frac{4}{3\pi}$

$\displaystyle(\bar{x}, \bar{y}) = \left(0, \frac{4}{3\pi}\right)$

**69.** $\displaystyle s = \int_0^\pi \sqrt{1+\cos^2 x}\,dx \approx 3.82$

**71.** $\displaystyle\lim_{x\to 1}\left[\frac{(\ln x)^2}{x-1}\right] = \lim_{x\to 1}\left[\frac{2(1/x)\ln x}{1}\right] = 0$

**73.** $\displaystyle\lim_{x\to\infty}\frac{e^{2x}}{x^2} = \lim_{x\to\infty}\frac{2e^{2x}}{2x} = \lim_{x\to\infty}\frac{4e^{2x}}{2} = \infty$

**75.** $\displaystyle y = \lim_{x\to\infty}(\ln x)^{2/x}$

$\displaystyle\ln y = \lim_{x\to\infty}\frac{2\ln(\ln x)}{x} = \lim_{x\to\infty}\left[\frac{2/(x\ln x)}{1}\right] = 0$

Since $\ln y = 0$, $y = 1$.

**77.** $\lim\limits_{n \to \infty} 1000\left(1 + \dfrac{0.09}{n}\right)^n = 1000 \lim\limits_{n \to \infty} \left(1 + \dfrac{0.09}{n}\right)^n$

Let $y = \lim\limits_{n \to \infty} \left(1 + \dfrac{0.09}{n}\right)^n$.

$\ln y = \lim\limits_{n \to \infty} n \ln\left(1 + \dfrac{0.09}{n}\right) = \lim\limits_{n \to \infty} \dfrac{\ln\left(1 + \dfrac{0.09}{n}\right)}{\dfrac{1}{n}} = \lim\limits_{n \to \infty} \left(\dfrac{\dfrac{-0.09/n^2}{1 + (0.09/n)}}{-\dfrac{1}{n^2}}\right) = \lim\limits_{n \to \infty} \dfrac{0.09}{1 + \left(\dfrac{0.09}{n}\right)} = 0.09$

Thus, $\ln y = 0.09 \implies y = e^{0.09}$ and $\lim\limits_{n \to \infty} 1000\left(1 + \dfrac{0.09}{n}\right)^n = 1000e^{0.09} \approx 1094.17$.

**79.** $\displaystyle\int_0^{16} \dfrac{1}{\sqrt[4]{x}}\, dx = \lim\limits_{b \to 0^+} \left[\dfrac{4}{3}x^{3/4}\right]_b^{16} = \dfrac{32}{3}$

Converges

**81.** $\displaystyle\int_1^{\infty} x^2 \ln x\, dx = \lim\limits_{b \to \infty} \left[\dfrac{x^3}{9}(-1 + 3\ln x)\right]_1^b = \infty$

Diverges

**83.** $\displaystyle\int_0^{t_0} 500{,}000e^{-0.05t}\, dt = \left[\dfrac{500{,}000}{-0.05}e^{-0.05t}\right]_0^{t_0}$

$\qquad = \dfrac{-500{,}000}{0.05}(e^{-0.05t_0} - 1)$

$\qquad = 10{,}000{,}000(1 - e^{-0.05t_0})$

(a) $t_0 = 20$:  \$6,321,205.59

(b) $t_0 \to \infty$:  \$10,000,000

**85.** (a) $P(13 \le x < \infty) = \dfrac{1}{0.95\sqrt{2\pi}} \displaystyle\int_{13}^{\infty} e^{-(x - 12.9)^2/2(0.95)^2}\, dx \approx 0.4581$

(b) $P(15 \le x < 20) = \dfrac{1}{0.95\sqrt{2\pi}} \displaystyle\int_{15}^{\infty} e^{-(x - 12.9)^2/2(0.95)^2}\, dx \approx 0.0135$

## Problem Solving for Chapter 7

**1.** (a) $\displaystyle\int_{-1}^{1} (1 - x^2)\, dx = \left[x - \dfrac{x^3}{3}\right]_{-1}^{1} = 2\left(1 - \dfrac{1}{3}\right) = \dfrac{4}{3}$

$\displaystyle\int_{-1}^{1} (1 - x^2)^2\, dx = \int_{-1}^{1} (1 - 2x^2 + x^4)\, dx = \left[x - \dfrac{2x^3}{3} + \dfrac{x^5}{5}\right]_{-1}^{1} = 2\left(1 - \dfrac{2}{3} + \dfrac{1}{5}\right) = \dfrac{16}{15}$

(b) Let $x = \sin u$, $dx = \cos u\, du$, $1 - x^2 = 1 - \sin^2 u = \cos^2 u$.

$\displaystyle\int_{-1}^{1} (1 - x^2)^n\, dx = \int_{-\pi/2}^{\pi/2} (\cos^2 u)^n \cos u\, du$

$\qquad = \displaystyle\int_{-\pi/2}^{\pi/2} \cos^{2n+1} u\, du$

$\qquad = 2\left[\dfrac{2}{3} \cdot \dfrac{4}{5} \cdot \dfrac{6}{7} \cdots \dfrac{(2n)}{(2n + 1)}\right]$   (Wallis's Formula)

$\qquad = 2\left[\dfrac{2^2 \cdot 4^2 \cdot 6^2 \cdots (2n)^2}{2 \cdot 3 \cdot 4 \cdot 5 \cdots (2n)(2n + 1)}\right]$

$\qquad = \dfrac{2(2^{2n})(n!)^2}{(2n + 1)!} = \dfrac{2^{2n+1}(n!)^2}{(2n + 1)!}$

**3.**
$$\lim_{x \to \infty} \left(\frac{x + c}{x - c}\right)^x = 9$$

$$\lim_{x \to \infty} x \ln\left(\frac{x + c}{x - c}\right) = \ln 9$$

$$\lim_{x \to \infty} \frac{\ln(x + c) - \ln(x - c)}{1/x} = \ln 9$$

$$\lim_{x \to \infty} \frac{\dfrac{1}{x + c} - \dfrac{1}{x - c}}{-\dfrac{1}{x^2}} = \ln 9$$

$$\lim_{x \to \infty} \frac{-2c}{(x + c)(x - c)}(-x^2) = \ln 9$$

$$\lim_{x \to \infty} \left(\frac{2cx^2}{x^2 - c^2}\right) = \ln 9$$

$$2c = \ln 9$$

$$2c = 2 \ln 3$$

$$c = \ln 3$$

**5.** $\sin \theta = \dfrac{PB}{OP} = PB$, $\cos \theta = OB$

$AQ = \widehat{AP} = \theta$

$BR = OR + OB = OR + \cos \theta$

The triangles $\triangle AQR$ and $\triangle BPR$ are similar:

$$\frac{AR}{AQ} = \frac{BR}{BP} \Rightarrow \frac{OR + 1}{\theta} = \frac{OR + \cos \theta}{\sin \theta}$$

$$\sin \theta(OR) + \sin \theta = (OR)\theta + \theta \cos \theta$$

$$OR = \frac{\theta \cos \theta - \sin \theta}{\sin \theta - \theta}$$

$$\begin{aligned}
\lim_{\theta \to 0^+} OR &= \lim_{\theta \to 0^+} \frac{\theta \cos \theta - \sin \theta}{\sin \theta - \theta} \\
&= \lim_{\theta \to 0^+} \frac{-\theta \sin \theta + \cos \theta - \cos \theta}{\cos \theta - 1} \\
&= \lim_{\theta \to 0^+} \frac{-\theta \sin \theta}{\cos \theta - 1} \\
&= \lim_{\theta \to 0^+} \frac{-\sin \theta - \theta \cos \theta}{-\sin \theta} \\
&= \lim_{\theta \to 0} \frac{\cos \theta + \cos \theta - \theta \sin \theta}{\cos \theta} \\
&= 2
\end{aligned}$$

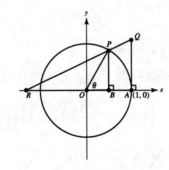

**7. (a)**

Area $\approx 0.2986$

**(b)** Let $x = 3 \tan \theta, dx = 3 \sec^2 \theta \, d\theta, x^2 + 9 = 9 \sec^2 \theta$.

$$\int \frac{x^2}{(x^2+9)} \, dx = \int \frac{9 \tan^2 \theta}{(9 \sec^2 \theta)^{3/2}} (3 \sec^2 \theta \, d\theta)$$

$$= \int \frac{\tan^2 \theta}{\sec \theta} \, d\theta$$

$$= \int \frac{\sin^2 \theta}{\cos \theta} \, d\theta$$

$$= \int \frac{1 - \cos^2 \theta}{\cos \theta} \, d\theta$$

$$= \ln|\sec \theta + \tan \theta| - \sin \theta + C$$

$$\text{Area} = \int_0^4 \frac{x^2}{(x^2+9)^{3/2}} \, dx = \left[ \ln|\sec \theta + \tan \theta| - \sin \theta \right]_0^{\tan^{-1}(4/3)}$$

$$= \left[ \ln\left( \frac{\sqrt{x^2+9}}{3} + \frac{x}{3} \right) - \frac{x}{\sqrt{x^2+9}} \right]_0^4$$

$$= \ln\left( \frac{5}{3} + \frac{4}{3} \right) - \frac{4}{5} = \ln 3 - \frac{4}{5}$$

**(c)** $x = 3 \sinh u, dx = 3 \cosh u \, du, x^2 + 9 = 9 \sinh^2 u + 9 = 9 \cosh^2 u$

$$A = \int_0^4 \frac{x^2}{(x^2+9)^{3/2}} \, dx = \int_0^{\sin^{-1}(4/3)} \frac{9 \sinh^2 u}{(9 \cosh^2 u)^{3/2}} (3 \cosh u \, du)$$

$$= \int_0^{\sinh^{-1}(4/3)} \tanh^2 u \, du$$

$$= \int_0^{\sinh^{-1}(4/3)} (1 - \text{sech}^2 u) \, du$$

$$= \left[ u - \tanh u \right]_0^{\sinh^{-1}(4/3)}$$

$$= \sinh^{-1}\left( \frac{4}{3} \right) - \tanh\left( \sinh^{-1}\left( \frac{4}{3} \right) \right)$$

$$= \ln\left( \frac{4}{3} + \sqrt{\frac{16}{9} + 1} \right) - \tanh\left[ \ln\left( \frac{4}{3} + \sqrt{\frac{16}{9} + 1} \right) \right]$$

$$= \ln\left( \frac{4}{3} + \frac{5}{3} \right) - \tanh\left( \ln\left( \frac{4}{3} + \frac{5}{3} \right) \right)$$

$$= \ln 3 - \tanh(\ln 3)$$

$$= \ln 3 - \frac{3 - (1/3)}{3 + (1/3)}$$

$$= \ln 3 - \frac{4}{5}$$

**9.** $y = \ln(1 - x^2)$, $y' = \dfrac{-2x}{1 - x^2}$

$$1 + (y')^2 = 1 + \frac{4x^2}{(1 - x^2)^2} = \frac{1 - 2x^2 + x^4 + 4x^2}{(1 - x^2)^2} = \left(\frac{1 + x^2}{1 - x^2}\right)^2$$

$$\text{Arc length} = \int_0^{1/2} \sqrt{1 + (y')^2}\, dx$$

$$= \int_0^{1/2} \left(\frac{1 + x^2}{1 - x^2}\right) dx$$

$$= \int_0^{1/2} \left(-1 + \frac{2}{1 - x^2}\right) dx$$

$$= \int_0^{1/2} \left(-1 + \frac{1}{x + 1} + \frac{1}{1 - x}\right) dx$$

$$= \left[-x + \ln(1 + x) - \ln(1 - x)\right]_0^{1/2}$$

$$= \left(-\frac{1}{2} + \ln\frac{3}{2} - \ln\frac{1}{2}\right)$$

$$= -\frac{1}{2} + \ln 3 - \ln 2 + \ln 2$$

$$= \ln 3 - \frac{1}{2} \approx 0.5986$$

**11.** Consider $\displaystyle\int \frac{1}{\ln x}\, dx$.

Let $u = \ln x$, $du = \dfrac{1}{dx}\, dx$, $x = e^u$. Then $\displaystyle\int \frac{1}{\ln x}\, dx = \int \frac{1}{u} e^u\, du = \int \frac{e^u}{u}\, du$.

If $\displaystyle\int \frac{1}{\ln x}\, dx$ were elementary, then $\displaystyle\int \frac{e^u}{u}\, du$ would be too, which is false.

Hence, $\displaystyle\int \frac{1}{\ln x}\, dx$ is not elementary.

**13.** $x^4 + 1 = (x^2 + ax + b)(x^2 + cx + d)$

$$= x^4 + (a + c)x^3 + (ac + b + d)x^2 + (ad + bc)x + bd$$

$a = -c$, $b = d = 1$, $a = \sqrt{2}$

$$x^4 + 1 = \left(x^2 + \sqrt{2}x + 1\right)\left(x^2 - \sqrt{2}x + 1\right)$$

$$\int_0^1 \frac{1}{x^4 + 1}\, dx = \int_0^1 \frac{Ax + B}{x^2 + \sqrt{2}x + 1}\, dx + \int_0^1 \frac{Cx + D}{x^2 - \sqrt{2}x + 1}\, dx$$

$$= \int_0^1 \frac{\frac{1}{2} + \frac{\sqrt{2}}{4}x}{x^2 + \sqrt{2}x + 1}\, dx - \int_0^1 \frac{-\frac{1}{2} + \frac{\sqrt{2}}{4}x}{x^2 + \sqrt{2}x + 1}\, dx$$

$$= \frac{\sqrt{2}}{4}\left[\arctan\left(\sqrt{2}x + 1\right) + \arctan\left(\sqrt{2}x - 1\right)\right]_0^1 + \frac{\sqrt{2}}{8}\left[\ln\left(x^2 + \sqrt{2}x + 1\right) - \ln\left(x^2 - \sqrt{2}x + 1\right)\right]_0^1$$

$$= \frac{\sqrt{2}}{4}\left[\arctan\left(\sqrt{2} + 1\right) + \arctan\left(\sqrt{2} - 1\right)\right] + \frac{\sqrt{2}}{8}\left[\ln\left(2 + \sqrt{2}\right) - \ln\left(2 - \sqrt{2}\right)\right] - \frac{\sqrt{2}}{4}\left[\frac{\pi}{4} - \frac{\pi}{4}\right] - \frac{\sqrt{2}}{8}[0]$$

$$\approx 0.5554 + 0.3116$$

$$\approx 0.8670$$

**15.** Using a graphing utility,

(a) $\lim\limits_{x \to 0^+} \left( \cot x + \dfrac{1}{x} \right) = \infty$

(b) $\lim\limits_{x \to 0^+} \left( \cot x - \dfrac{1}{x} \right) = 0$

(c) $\lim\limits_{x \to 0^+} \left( \cot x + \dfrac{1}{x} \right)\left( \cot x - \dfrac{1}{x} \right) \approx -\dfrac{2}{3}.$

Analytically,

(a) $\lim\limits_{x \to 0^+} \left( \cot x + \dfrac{1}{x} \right) = \infty + \infty = \infty$

(b) $\lim\limits_{x \to 0^+} \left( \cot x - \dfrac{1}{x} \right) = \lim\limits_{x \to 0^+} \dfrac{x \cot x - 1}{x} = \lim\limits_{x \to 0^+} \dfrac{x \cos x - \sin x}{x \sin x}$

$$= \lim\limits_{x \to 0^+} \dfrac{\cos x - x \sin x - \cos x}{\sin x + x \cos x} = \lim\limits_{x \to 0} \dfrac{-x \sin x}{\sin x + x \cos x}$$

$$= \lim\limits_{x \to 0^+} \dfrac{-\sin x - x \cos x}{\cos x + \cos x - x \sin x} = 0.$$

(c) $\left( \cot x + \dfrac{1}{x} \right)\left( \cot x - \dfrac{1}{x} \right) = \cot^2 x - \dfrac{1}{x^2}$

$$= \dfrac{x^2 \cot^2 x - 1}{x^2}$$

$$\lim\limits_{x \to 0^+} \dfrac{x^2 \cot^2 x - 1}{x^2} = \lim\limits_{x \to 0^+} \dfrac{2x \cot^2 x - 2x^2 \cot x \csc^2 x}{2x}$$

$$= \lim\limits_{x \to 0^+} \dfrac{\cot^2 x - x \cot x \csc^2 x}{1}$$

$$= \lim\limits_{x \to 0^+} \dfrac{\cos^2 x \sin x - x \cos x}{\sin^3 x}$$

$$= \lim\limits_{x \to 0^+} \dfrac{(1 - \sin^2 x)\sin x - x \cos x}{\sin^3 x}$$

$$= \lim\limits_{x \to 0^+} \dfrac{\sin x - x \cos x}{\sin^3 x} - 1$$

Now, $\lim\limits_{x \to 0^+} \dfrac{\sin x - x \cos x}{\sin^3 x} = \lim\limits_{x \to 0^+} \dfrac{\cos x - \cos x + x \sin x}{3 \sin^2 x \cos x}$

$$= \lim\limits_{x \to 0^+} \dfrac{x}{3 \sin x \cdot \cos x}$$

$$= \lim\limits_{x \to 0^+} \left( \dfrac{x}{\sin x} \right)\dfrac{1}{3 \cos x} = \dfrac{1}{3}.$$

Thus, $\lim\limits_{x \to 0^+} \left( \cot x + \dfrac{1}{x} \right)\left( \cot x - \dfrac{1}{x} \right) = \dfrac{1}{3} - 1 = -\dfrac{2}{3}.$

The form $0 \cdot \infty$ is indeterminant.

**17.** $\dfrac{x^3 - 3x^2 + 1}{x^4 - 13x^2 + 12x} = \dfrac{P_1}{x} + \dfrac{P_2}{x-1} + \dfrac{P_3}{x+4} + \dfrac{P_4}{x-3} \Rightarrow c_1 = 0,\ c_2 = 1,\ c_3 = -4,\ c_4 = 3$

$N(x) = x^3 - 3x^2 + 1$

$D'(x) = 4x^3 - 26x + 12$

$P_1 = \dfrac{N(0)}{D'(0)} = \dfrac{1}{12}$

$P_2 = \dfrac{N(1)}{D'(1)} = \dfrac{-1}{-10} = \dfrac{1}{10}$

$P_3 = \dfrac{N(-4)}{D'(-4)} = \dfrac{-111}{-140} = \dfrac{111}{140}$

$P_4 = \dfrac{N(3)}{D'(3)} = \dfrac{1}{42}$

Thus, $\dfrac{x^3 - 3x^2 + 1}{x^4 - 13x^2 + 12x} = \dfrac{1/12}{x} + \dfrac{1/10}{x-1} + \dfrac{111/140}{x+4} + \dfrac{1/42}{x-3}$.

**19.** By parts,

$$\int_a^b f(x)g''(x)\,dx = \left[ f(x)g'(x) \right]_a^b - \int_a^b f'(x)g'(x)\,dx$$

$$= -\int_a^b f'(x)g'(x)\,dx$$

$$= \left[ -f'(x)g(x) \right]_a^b + \int_a^b g(x)f''(x)\,dx$$

$$= \int_a^b f''(x)g(x)\,dx.$$

# C H A P T E R  8
## Infinite Series

# C H A P T E R  8
## Infinite Series

## Section 8.1    Sequences

Solutions to Odd-Numbered Exercises

**1.** $a_n = 2^n$

$a_1 = 2^1 = 2$

$a_2 = 2^2 = 4$

$a_3 = 2^3 = 8$

$a_4 = 2^4 = 16$

$a_5 = 2^5 = 32$

**3.** $a_n = \left(-\dfrac{1}{2}\right)^n$

$a_1 = \left(-\dfrac{1}{2}\right)^1 = -\dfrac{1}{2}$

$a_2 = \left(-\dfrac{1}{2}\right)^2 = \dfrac{1}{4}$

$a_3 = \left(-\dfrac{1}{2}\right)^3 = -\dfrac{1}{8}$

$a_4 = \left(-\dfrac{1}{2}\right)^4 = \dfrac{1}{16}$

$a_5 = \left(-\dfrac{1}{2}\right)^5 = -\dfrac{1}{32}$

**5.** $a_n = \sin \dfrac{n\pi}{2}$

$a_1 = \sin \dfrac{\pi}{2} = 1$

$a_2 = \sin \pi = 0$

$a_3 = \sin \dfrac{3\pi}{2} = -1$

$a_4 = \sin 2\pi = 0$

$a_5 = \sin \dfrac{5\pi}{2} = 1$

**7.** $a_n = \dfrac{(-1)^{n(n+1)/2}}{n^2}$

$a_1 = \dfrac{(-1)^1}{1^2} = -1$

$a_2 = \dfrac{(-1)^3}{2^2} = -\dfrac{1}{4}$

$a_3 = \dfrac{(-1)^6}{3^2} = \dfrac{1}{9}$

$a_4 = \dfrac{(-1)^{10}}{4^2} = \dfrac{1}{16}$

$a_5 = \dfrac{(-1)^{15}}{5^2} = -\dfrac{1}{25}$

**9.** $a_n = 5 - \dfrac{1}{n} + \dfrac{1}{n^2}$

$a_1 = 5 - 1 + 1 = 5$

$a_2 = 5 - \dfrac{1}{2} + \dfrac{1}{4} = \dfrac{19}{4}$

$a_3 = 5 - \dfrac{1}{3} + \dfrac{1}{9} = \dfrac{43}{9}$

$a_4 = 5 - \dfrac{1}{4} + \dfrac{1}{16} = \dfrac{77}{16}$

$a_5 = 5 - \dfrac{1}{5} + \dfrac{1}{25} = \dfrac{121}{25}$

**11.** $a_n = \dfrac{3^n}{n!}$

$a_1 = \dfrac{3}{1!} = 3$

$a_2 = \dfrac{3^2}{2!} = \dfrac{9}{2}$

$a_3 = \dfrac{3^3}{3!} = \dfrac{27}{6}$

$a_4 = \dfrac{3^4}{4!} = \dfrac{81}{24}$

$a_5 = \dfrac{3^5}{5!} = \dfrac{243}{120}$

**13.** $a_1 = 3,\ a_{k+1} = 2(a_k - 1)$

$a_2 = 2(a_1 - 1)$

$\quad = 2(3 - 1) = 4$

$a_3 = 2(a_2 - 1)$

$\quad = 2(4 - 1) = 6$

$a_4 = 2(a_3 - 1)$

$\quad = 2(6 - 1) = 10$

$a_5 = 2(a_4 - 1)$

$\quad = 2(10 - 1) = 18$

**15.** $a_1 = 32,\ a_{k+1} = \dfrac{1}{2}a_k$

$a_2 = \dfrac{1}{2}a_1 = \dfrac{1}{2}(32) = 16$

$a_3 = \dfrac{1}{2}a_2 = \dfrac{1}{2}(16) = 8$

$a_4 = \dfrac{1}{2}a_3 = \dfrac{1}{2}(8) = 4$

$a_5 = \dfrac{1}{2}a_4 = \dfrac{1}{2}(4) = 2$

**17.** Because $a_1 = 8/(1 + 1) = 4$ and $a_2 = 8/(2 + 1) = \frac{8}{3}$, the sequence matches graph (d).

**19.** This sequence decreases and $a_1 = 4$, $a_2 = 4(0.5) = 2$. Matches (c).

**21.**

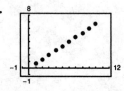

$$a_n = \frac{2}{3}n, \, n = 1, \ldots, 10$$

**23.**

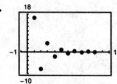

$$a_n = 16(-0.5)^{n-1}, \, n = 1, \ldots, 10$$

**25.**

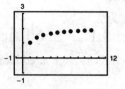

$$a_n = \frac{2n}{n + 1}, \, n = 1, 2, \ldots, 10$$

**27.** $a_n = 3n - 1$

$a_5 = 3(5) - 1 = 14$

$a_6 = 3(6) - 1 = 17$

Add 3 to preceeding term.

**29.** $a_n = \dfrac{3}{(-2)^{n-1}}$

$a_n = \dfrac{3}{(-2)^4} = \dfrac{3}{16}$

$a_6 = \dfrac{3}{(-2)^5} = -\dfrac{3}{32}$

Multiply the preceeding term by $-\frac{1}{2}$.

**31.** $\dfrac{10!}{8!} = \dfrac{8!(9)(10)}{8!}$

$= (9)(10) = 90$

**33.** $\dfrac{(n + 1)!}{n!} = \dfrac{n!(n + 1)}{n!}$

$= n + 1$

**35.** $\dfrac{(2n - 1)!}{(2n + 1)!} = \dfrac{(2n - 1)!}{(2n - 1)!(2n)(2n + 1)}$

$= \dfrac{1}{2n(2n + 1)}$

**37.** $\displaystyle\lim_{n \to \infty} \dfrac{5n^2}{n^2 + 2} = 5$

**39.** $\displaystyle\lim_{n \to \infty} \dfrac{2n}{\sqrt{n^2 + 1}} = \lim_{n \to \infty} \dfrac{2}{\sqrt{1 + (1/n^2)}}$

$= \dfrac{2}{1} = 2$

**41.** $\displaystyle\lim_{n \to \infty} \sin\left(\dfrac{1}{n}\right) = 0$

**43.**

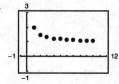

The graph seems to indicate that the sequence converges to 1. Analytically,

$$\lim_{n \to \infty} a_n = \lim_{n \to \infty} \dfrac{n + 1}{n} = \lim_{x \to \infty} \dfrac{x + 1}{x} = \lim_{x \to \infty} 1 = 1.$$

**45.**

The graph seems to indicate that the sequence diverges. Analytically, the sequence is

$$\{a_n\} = \{0, -1, 0, 1, 0, -1, \ldots\}.$$

Hence, $\displaystyle\lim_{n \to \infty} a_n$ does not exist.

**47.** $\displaystyle\lim_{n \to \infty} (-1)^n \left(\dfrac{n}{n + 1}\right)$

does not exist (oscillates between $-1$ and 1), diverges.

**49.** $\displaystyle\lim_{n \to \infty} \dfrac{3n^2 - n + 4}{2n^2 + 1} = \dfrac{3}{2}$, converges

**51.** $\displaystyle\lim_{n \to \infty} \dfrac{1 + (-1)^n}{n} = 0$, converges

**53.** $\displaystyle\lim_{n \to \infty} \dfrac{\ln(n^3)}{2n} = \lim_{n \to \infty} \dfrac{3}{2} \dfrac{\ln(n)}{n}$

$= \displaystyle\lim_{n \to \infty} \dfrac{3}{2}\left(\dfrac{1}{n}\right) = 0$, converges

(L'Hôpital's Rule)

**55.** $\lim\limits_{n\to\infty} \left(\frac{3}{4}\right)^n = 0$, converges

**57.** $\lim\limits_{n\to\infty} \frac{(n+1)!}{n!} = \lim\limits_{n\to\infty} (n+1) = \infty$, diverges

**59.** $\lim\limits_{n\to\infty} \left(\frac{n-1}{n} - \frac{n}{n-1}\right) = \lim\limits_{n\to\infty} \frac{(n-1)^2 - n^2}{n(n-1)}$

$\qquad\qquad = \lim\limits_{n\to\infty} \frac{1-2n}{n^2-n} = 0$, converges

**61.** $\lim\limits_{n\to\infty} \frac{n^p}{e^n} = 0$, converges

$\quad (p > 0, n \geq 2)$

**63.** $a_n = \left(1 + \frac{k}{n}\right)^n$

$\qquad \lim\limits_{n\to\infty} \left(1 + \frac{k}{n}\right)^n = \lim\limits_{u\to 0} [(1+u)^{1/u}]^k = e^k$

where $u = \dfrac{k}{n}$, converges

**65.** $\lim\limits_{n\to\infty} \frac{\sin n}{n} = \lim\limits_{n\to\infty} (\sin n)\frac{1}{n} = 0$, converges

**67.** $a_n = 3n - 2$

**69.** $a_n = n^2 - 2$

**71.** $a_n = \dfrac{n+1}{n+2}$

**73.** $a_n = \dfrac{(-1)^{n-1}}{2^{n-2}}$

**75.** $a_n = 1 + \dfrac{1}{n} = \dfrac{n+1}{n}$

**77.** $a_n = \dfrac{n}{(n+1)(n+2)}$

**79.** $a_n = \dfrac{(-1)^{n-1}}{1 \cdot 3 \cdot 5 \cdots (2n-1)} = \dfrac{(-1)^{n-1} 2^n n!}{(2n)!}$

**81.** $a_n = 4 - \dfrac{1}{n} < 4 - \dfrac{1}{n+1} = a_{n+1}$,

monotonic; $|a_n| < 4$ bounded.

**83.** $\dfrac{n}{2^{n+2}} \overset{?}{\geq} \dfrac{n+1}{2^{(n+1)+2}}$

$\quad 2^{n+3}n \overset{?}{\geq} 2^{n+2}(n+1)$

$\qquad 2n \overset{?}{\geq} n+1$

$\qquad\quad n \geq 1$

Hence, $\quad n \geq 1$

$\qquad\qquad 2n \geq n+1$

$\qquad\quad 2^{n+3}n \geq 2^{n+2}(n+1)$

$\qquad\qquad \dfrac{n}{2^{n+2}} \geq \dfrac{n+1}{2^{(n+1)+2}}$

$\qquad\qquad a_n \geq a_{n+1}$

True; monotonic; $|a_n| \leq \frac{1}{8}$, bounded

**85.** $a_n = (-1)^n\left(\dfrac{1}{n}\right)$

$\quad a_1 = -1$

$\quad a_2 = \dfrac{1}{2}$

$\quad a_3 = -\dfrac{1}{3}$

Not monotonic; $|a_n| \leq 1$, bounded

**87.** $a_n = \left(\frac{2}{3}\right)^n > \left(\frac{2}{3}\right)^{n+1} = a_{n+1}$

Monotonic; $|a_n| \leq \frac{2}{3}$, bounded

**89.** $a_n = \sin\left(\dfrac{n\pi}{6}\right)$

$\quad a_1 = 0.500$

$\quad a_2 = 0.8660$

$\quad a_3 = 1.000$

$\quad a_4 = 0.8660$

Not monotonic; $|a_n| \leq 1$, bounded

**91.** (a) $a_n = 5 + \dfrac{1}{n}$

$\left| 5 + \dfrac{1}{n} \right| \le 6 \implies \{a_n\}$ bounded

$a_n = 5 + \dfrac{1}{n} > 5 + \dfrac{1}{n+1}$

$\qquad = a_{n+1} \implies \{a_n\}$ monotonic

Therefore, $\{a_n\}$ converges.

(b)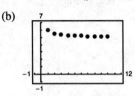

$\lim\limits_{n\to\infty} \left( 5 + \dfrac{1}{n} \right) = 5$

**93.** (a) $a_n = \dfrac{1}{3}\left( 1 - \dfrac{1}{3^n} \right)$

$\left| \dfrac{1}{3}\left( 1 - \dfrac{1}{3^n} \right) \right| < \dfrac{1}{3} \implies \{a_n\}$ bounded

$a_n = \dfrac{1}{3}\left( 1 - \dfrac{1}{3^n} \right) < \dfrac{1}{3}\left( 1 - \dfrac{1}{3^{n+1}} \right)$

$\qquad = a_{n+1} \implies \{a_n\}$ monotonic

Therefore, $\{a_n\}$ converges.

(b)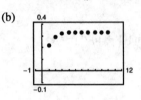

$\lim\limits_{n\to\infty} \left[ \dfrac{1}{3}\left( 1 - \dfrac{1}{3^n} \right) \right] = \dfrac{1}{3}$

**95.** $A_n = P\left[ 1 + \dfrac{r}{12} \right]^n$

(a) $\lim\limits_{n\to\infty} A_n = \infty$, divergent. The amount will grow arbitrarily large over time.

(b) $A_n = 9000\left[ 1 + \dfrac{0.115}{12} \right]^n$

$A_1 = \$9086.25 \qquad A_6 = \$9530.06$

$A_2 = \$9173.33 \qquad A_7 = \$9621.39$

$A_3 = \$9261.24 \qquad A_8 = \$9713.59$

$A_4 = \$9349.99 \qquad A_9 = \$9806.68$

$A_5 = \$9439.60 \qquad A_{10} = \$9900.66$

**97.** (a) A sequence is a function whose domain is the set of positive integers.

(b) A sequence converges if it has a limit.

(c) A bounded monotonic sequence is a sequence that has nondecreasing or nonincreasing terms, and an upper and lower bound.

**99.** $a_n = 10 - \dfrac{1}{n}$

**101.** $a_n = \dfrac{3n}{4n+1}$

**103.** (a) $A_n = (0.8)^n (2.5)$ billion

(b) $A_1 = \$2$ billion

$A_2 = \$1.6$ billion

$A_3 = \$1.28$ billion

$A_4 = \$1.024$ billion

(c) $\lim\limits_{n\to\infty} (0.8)^n (2.5) = 0$

**105.** (a) $a_n = -3.7262n^2 + 75.9167n + 684.25$

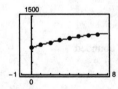

(b) For 2004, $n = 14$ and $a_{14} \approx 1017$, or $\$1017$.

**107.** $a_n = \dfrac{10^n}{n!}$

    (a) $a_9 = a_{10} = \dfrac{10^9}{9!}$

                 $= \dfrac{1{,}000{,}000{,}000}{362{,}880}$

                 $= \dfrac{1{,}562{,}500}{567}$

    (b) Decreasing

    (c) Factorials increase more rapidly than exponentials.

**109.** $\{a_n\} = \{\sqrt[n]{n}\} = \{n^{1/n}\}$

$a_1 = 1^{1/1} = 1$

$a_2 = \sqrt{2} \approx 1.4142$

$a_3 = \sqrt[3]{3} \approx 1.4422$

$a_4 = \sqrt[4]{4} \approx 1.4142$

$a_5 = \sqrt[5]{5} \approx 1.3797$

$a_6 = \sqrt[6]{6} \approx 1.3480$

Let $y = \lim\limits_{n\to\infty} n^{1/n}$.

$$\ln y = \lim_{n\to\infty}\left(\frac{1}{n}\ln n\right)$$

$$= \lim_{n\to\infty}\frac{\ln n}{n} = \lim_{n\to\infty}\frac{1/n}{1} = 0$$

Since $\ln y = 0$, we have $y = e^0 = 1$.  Therefore, $\lim\limits_{n\to\infty} \sqrt[n]{n} = 1$.

**111.** $a_{n+2} = a_n + a_{n+1}$

    (a)

| | |
|---|---|
| $a_1 = 1$ | $a_7 = 8 + 5 = 13$ |
| $a_2 = 1$ | $a_8 = 13 + 8 = 21$ |
| $a_3 = 1 + 1 = 2$ | $a_9 = 21 + 13 = 34$ |
| $a_4 = 2 + 1 = 3$ | $a_{10} = 34 + 21 = 55$ |
| $a_5 = 3 + 2 = 5$ | $a_{11} = 55 + 34 = 89$ |
| $a_6 = 5 + 3 = 8$ | $a_{12} = 89 + 55 = 144$ |

    (b) $b_n = \dfrac{a_{n+1}}{a_n}, n \geq 1$

| | |
|---|---|
| $b_1 = \frac{1}{1} = 1$ | $b_6 = \frac{13}{8}$ |
| $b_2 = \frac{2}{1} = 2$ | $b_7 = \frac{21}{13}$ |
| $b_3 = \frac{3}{2}$ | $b_8 = \frac{34}{21}$ |
| $b_4 = \frac{5}{3}$ | $b_9 = \frac{55}{34}$ |
| $b_5 = \frac{8}{5}$ | $b_{10} = \frac{89}{55}$ |

    (c) $1 + \dfrac{1}{b_{n-1}} = 1 + \dfrac{1}{a_n/a_{n-1}}$

                 $= 1 + \dfrac{a_{n-1}}{a_n}$

                 $= \dfrac{a_n + a_{n-1}}{a_n} = \dfrac{a_{n+1}}{a_n} = b_n$

    (d) If $\lim\limits_{n\to\infty} b_n = \rho$, then $\lim\limits_{n\to\infty}\left(1 + \dfrac{1}{b_{n-1}}\right) = \rho$.

    Since $\lim\limits_{n\to\infty} b_n = \lim\limits_{n\to\infty} b_{n-1}$ we have,

    $1 + (1/\rho) = \rho$.

    $\rho + 1 = \rho^2$

    $0 = \rho^2 - \rho - 1$

    $\rho = \dfrac{1 \pm \sqrt{1+4}}{2} = \dfrac{1 \pm \sqrt{5}}{2}$

    Since $a_n$, and thus $b_n$, is positive,

    $\rho = (1 + \sqrt{5})/2 \approx 1.6180$.

**113.** True

**115.** True

**117.** $a_1 = \sqrt{2} \approx 1.4142$

$a_2 = \sqrt{2 + \sqrt{2}} \approx 1.8478$

$a_3 = \sqrt{2 + \sqrt{2 + \sqrt{2}}} \approx 1.9616$

$a_4 = \sqrt{2 + \sqrt{2 + \sqrt{2 + \sqrt{2}}}} \approx 1.9904$

$a_5 = \sqrt{2 + \sqrt{2 + \sqrt{2 + \sqrt{2 + \sqrt{2}}}}} \approx 1.9976$

$\{a_n\}$ is increasing and bounded by 2, and hence converges to $L$. Letting $\lim\limits_{n\to\infty} a_n = L$ implies that $\sqrt{2 + L} = L \Rightarrow L = 2$. Hence, $\lim\limits_{n\to\infty} a_n = 2$.

# Section 8.2    Series and Convergence

**1.** $S_1 = 1$

$S_2 = 1 + \frac{1}{4} = 1.2500$

$S_3 = 1 + \frac{1}{4} + \frac{1}{9} \approx 1.3611$

$S_4 = 1 + \frac{1}{4} + \frac{1}{9} + \frac{1}{16} \approx 1.4236$

$S_5 = 1 + \frac{1}{4} + \frac{1}{9} + \frac{1}{16} + \frac{1}{25} \approx 1.4636$

**3.** $S_1 = 3$

$S_2 = 3 - \frac{9}{2} = -1.5$

$S_3 = 3 - \frac{9}{2} + \frac{27}{4} = 5.25$

$S_4 = 3 - \frac{9}{2} + \frac{27}{4} - \frac{81}{8} = -4.875$

$S_5 = 3 - \frac{9}{2} + \frac{27}{4} - \frac{81}{8} + \frac{243}{16} = 10.3125$

**5.** $S_1 = 3$

$S_2 = 3 + \frac{3}{2} = 4.5$

$S_3 = 3 + \frac{3}{2} + \frac{3}{4} = 5.250$

$S_4 = 3 + \frac{3}{2} + \frac{3}{4} + \frac{3}{8} = 5.625$

$S_5 = 3 + \frac{3}{2} + \frac{3}{4} + \frac{3}{8} + \frac{3}{16} = 5.8125$

**7.** $\sum_{n=0}^{\infty} 3\left(\frac{3}{2}\right)^n$    Geometric series

$r = \frac{3}{2} > 1$

Diverges by Theorem 8.6

**9.** $\sum_{n=0}^{\infty} 1000(1.055)^n$    Geometric series

$r = 1.055 > 1$

Diverges by Theorem 8.6

**11.** $\sum_{n=1}^{\infty} \frac{n}{n+1}$

$\lim_{n \to \infty} \frac{n}{n+1} = 1 \neq 0$

Diverges by Theorem 8.9

**13.** $\sum_{n=1}^{\infty} \frac{n^2}{n^2+1}$

$\lim_{n \to \infty} \frac{n^2}{n^2+1} = 1 \neq 0$

Diverges by Theorem 8.9

**15.** $\sum_{n=0}^{\infty} \frac{2^n + 1}{2^{n+1}}$

$\lim_{n \to \infty} \frac{2^n + 1}{2^{n+1}} = \lim_{n \to \infty} \frac{1 + 2^{-n}}{2} = \frac{1}{2} \neq 0$

Diverges by Theorem 8.9

**17.** $\sum_{n=0}^{\infty} \frac{9}{4}\left(\frac{1}{4}\right)^n = \frac{9}{4}\left[1 + \frac{1}{4} + \frac{1}{16} + \cdots\right]$

$S_0 = \frac{9}{4}, S_1 = \frac{9}{4} \cdot \frac{5}{4} = \frac{45}{16}, S_2 = \frac{9}{4} \cdot \frac{21}{16} \approx 2.95, \ldots$

Matches graph (c).

Analytically, the series is geometric:

$$\sum_{n=0}^{\infty} \left(\frac{9}{4}\right)\left(\frac{1}{4}\right)^n = \frac{9/4}{1 - 1/4} = \frac{9/4}{3/4} = 3$$

**19.** $\sum_{n=0}^{\infty} \frac{15}{4}\left(-\frac{1}{4}\right)^n = \frac{15}{4}\left[1 - \frac{1}{4} + \frac{1}{16} - \cdots\right]$

$S_0 = \frac{15}{4}, S_1 = \frac{45}{16}, S_2 \approx 3.05, \ldots$

Matches graph (a).

Analytically, the series is geometric:

$$\sum_{n=0}^{\infty} \frac{15}{4}\left(-\frac{1}{4}\right)^n = \frac{15/4}{1 - (-1/4)} = \frac{15/4}{5/4} = 3$$

**21.** $\sum_{n=1}^{\infty} \frac{1}{n(n+1)} = \sum_{n=1}^{\infty} \left(\frac{1}{n} - \frac{1}{n+1}\right) = \left(1 - \frac{1}{2}\right) + \left(\frac{1}{2} - \frac{1}{3}\right) + \left(\frac{1}{3} - \frac{1}{4}\right) + \left(\frac{1}{4} - \frac{1}{5}\right) + \cdots$

$\sum_{n=1}^{\infty} \frac{1}{n(n+1)} = \lim_{n \to \infty} S_n = \lim_{n \to \infty} \left(1 - \frac{1}{n+1}\right) = 1$

**23.** $\sum_{n=0}^{\infty} 2\left(\frac{3}{4}\right)^n$

Geometric series with $r = \frac{3}{4} < 1$.

Converges by Theorem 8.6

**25.** $\sum_{n=0}^{\infty} (0.9)^n$

Geometric series with $r = 0.9 < 1$.

Converges by Theorem 8.6

**27.** (a) $\displaystyle\sum_{n=1}^{\infty} \frac{6}{n(n+3)} = 2\sum_{n=1}^{\infty}\left(\frac{1}{n} - \frac{1}{n+3}\right)$

$$= 2\left[\left(1 - \frac{1}{4}\right) + \left(\frac{1}{2} - \frac{1}{5}\right) + \left(\frac{1}{3} - \frac{1}{6}\right) + \left(\frac{1}{4} - \frac{1}{7}\right) + \cdots\right]$$

$$= 2\left[1 + \frac{1}{2} + \frac{1}{3}\right] = \frac{11}{3} \approx 3.667$$

(b)

| $n$ | 5 | 10 | 20 | 50 | 100 |
|---|---|---|---|---|---|
| $S_n$ | 2.7976 | 3.1643 | 3.3936 | 3.5513 | 3.6078 |

(c)

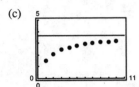

(d) The terms of the series decrease in magnitude slowly. Thus, the sequence of partial sums approaches the sum slowly.

**29.** (a) $\displaystyle\sum_{n=1}^{\infty} 2(0.9)^{n-1} = \sum_{n=0}^{\infty} 2(0.9)^n = \frac{2}{1 - 0.9} = 20$

(c)

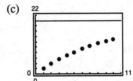

(b)

| $n$ | 5 | 10 | 20 | 50 | 100 |
|---|---|---|---|---|---|
| $S_n$ | 8.1902 | 13.0264 | 17.5685 | 19.8969 | 19.9995 |

(d) The terms of the series decrease in magnitude slowly. Thus, the sequence of partial sums approaches the sum slowly.

**31.** (a) $\displaystyle\sum_{n=1}^{\infty} 10(0.25)^{n-1} = \frac{10}{1 - 0.25} = \frac{40}{3} \approx 13.3333$

(c)

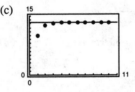

(b)

| $n$ | 5 | 10 | 20 | 50 | 100 |
|---|---|---|---|---|---|
| $S_n$ | 13.3203 | 13.3333 | 13.3333 | 13.3333 | 13.3333 |

(d) The terms of the series decrease in magnitude rapidly. Thus, the sequence of partial sums approaches the sum rapidly.

**33.** $\displaystyle\sum_{n=2}^{\infty} \frac{1}{n^2 - 1} = \sum_{n=2}^{\infty}\left(\frac{1/2}{n-1} - \frac{1/2}{n+1}\right) = \frac{1}{2}\sum_{n=2}^{\infty}\left(\frac{1}{n-1} - \frac{1}{n+1}\right)$

$$= \frac{1}{2}\left[\left(1 - \frac{1}{3}\right) + \left(\frac{1}{2} - \frac{1}{4}\right) + \left(\frac{1}{3} - \frac{1}{5}\right) + \left(\frac{1}{4} - \frac{1}{6}\right) + \cdots\right]$$

$$= \frac{1}{2}\left(1 + \frac{1}{2}\right) = \frac{3}{4}$$

**35.** $\displaystyle\sum_{n=1}^{\infty} \frac{8}{(n+1)(n+2)} = 8\sum_{n=1}^{\infty}\left(\frac{1}{n+1} - \frac{1}{n+2}\right) = 8\left[\left(\frac{1}{2} - \frac{1}{3}\right) + \left(\frac{1}{3} - \frac{1}{4}\right) + \left(\frac{1}{4} - \frac{1}{5}\right) + \cdots\right] = 8\left(\frac{1}{2}\right) = 4$

**37.** $\displaystyle\sum_{n=0}^{\infty} \left(\frac{1}{2}\right)^n = \frac{1}{1 - (1/2)} = 2$

**39.** $\displaystyle\sum_{n=0}^{\infty} \left(-\frac{1}{2}\right)^n = \frac{1}{1 - (-1/2)} = \frac{2}{3}$

**41.** $\displaystyle\sum_{n=0}^{\infty} \left(\frac{1}{10}\right)^n = \frac{1}{1 - (1/10)} = \frac{10}{9}$

**43.** $\displaystyle\sum_{n=0}^{\infty} 3\left(-\frac{1}{3}\right)^n = \frac{3}{1 - (-1/3)} = \frac{9}{4}$

**45.** $\displaystyle\sum_{n=0}^{\infty}\left(\frac{1}{2^n}-\frac{1}{3^n}\right)=\sum_{n=0}^{\infty}\left(\frac{1}{2}\right)^n-\sum_{n=0}^{\infty}\left(\frac{1}{3}\right)^n$

$\displaystyle\qquad\qquad\qquad=\frac{1}{1-(1/2)}-\frac{1}{1-(-1/3)}$

$\displaystyle\qquad\qquad\qquad=2-\frac{3}{2}=\frac{1}{2}$

**47.** $\displaystyle 0.\overline{4}=\sum_{n=0}^{\infty}\frac{4}{10}\left(\frac{1}{10}\right)^n$

Geometric series with $a=\frac{4}{10}$ and $r=\frac{1}{10}$

$\displaystyle S=\frac{a}{1-r}=\frac{4/10}{1-(1/10)}=\frac{4}{9}$

**49.** $\displaystyle 0.07\overline{5}\overline{7}\overline{5}=\sum_{n=0}^{\infty}\frac{3}{40}\left(\frac{1}{100}\right)^n$

Geometric series with $a=\frac{3}{40}$ and $r=\frac{1}{100}$

$\displaystyle S=\frac{a}{1-r}=\frac{3/40}{99/100}=\frac{5}{66}$

**51.** $\displaystyle\sum_{n=1}^{\infty}\frac{n+10}{10n+1}$

$\displaystyle\lim_{n\to\infty}\frac{n+10}{10n+1}=\frac{1}{10}\neq 0$

Diverges by Theorem 8.9

**53.** $\displaystyle\sum_{n=1}^{\infty}\left(\frac{1}{n}-\frac{1}{n+2}\right)=\left(1-\frac{1}{3}\right)+\left(\frac{1}{2}-\frac{1}{4}\right)+\left(\frac{1}{3}-\frac{1}{5}\right)+\left(\frac{1}{4}-\frac{1}{6}\right)+\cdots=1+\frac{1}{2}=\frac{3}{2}$, converges

**55.** $\displaystyle\sum_{n=1}^{\infty}\frac{3n-1}{2n+1}$

$\displaystyle\lim_{n\to\infty}\frac{3n-1}{2n+1}=\frac{3}{2}\neq 0$

Diverges by Theorem 8.9

**57.** $\displaystyle\sum_{n=0}^{\infty}\frac{4}{2^n}=4\sum_{n=0}^{\infty}\left(\frac{1}{2}\right)^n$

Geometric series with $r=\frac{1}{2}$

Converges by Theorem 8.6

**59.** $\displaystyle\sum_{n=0}^{\infty}(1.075)^n$

Geometric series with $r=1.075$

Diverges by Theorem 8.6

**61.** $\displaystyle\sum_{n=2}^{\infty}\frac{n}{\ln n}$

$\displaystyle\lim_{n\to\infty}\frac{n}{\ln n}=\lim_{n\to\infty}\frac{1}{1/n}=\infty$

(by L'Hôpital's Rule) Diverges by Theorem 8.9

**63.** See definition, page 567.

**65.** The series given by

$$\sum_{n=0}^{\infty}ar^n=a+ar+ar^2+\cdots+ar^n+\cdots,\,a\neq 0$$

is a geometric series with ratio $r$. When $0<|r|<1$, the series converges to $\dfrac{a}{1-r}$. The series diverges if $|r|\geq 1$.

**67.** (a) $x$ is the common ratio.

(b) $\displaystyle 1+x+x^2+\cdots=\sum_{n=0}^{\infty}x^n=\frac{1}{1-x},\,|x|<1$

Geometric series: $a=1,\,r=x,\,|x|<1$

(c) $y_1=\dfrac{1}{1-x}$

$\quad y_2=1+x$

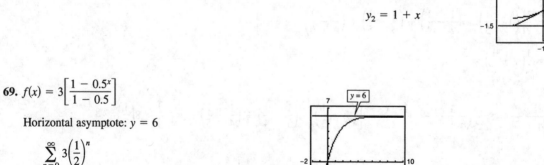

**69.** $f(x)=3\left[\dfrac{1-0.5^x}{1-0.5}\right]$

Horizontal asymptote: $y=6$

$\displaystyle\sum_{n=0}^{\infty}3\left(\frac{1}{2}\right)^n$

$S=\dfrac{3}{1-(1/2)}=6$

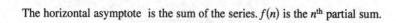

The horizontal asymptote is the sum of the series. $f(n)$ is the $n^{\text{th}}$ partial sum.

**71.** $\dfrac{1}{n(n + 1)} < 0.001$

$\qquad 10,000 < n^2 + n$

$\qquad\quad 0 < n^2 + n - 10,000$

$\qquad n = \dfrac{-1 \pm \sqrt{1^2 - 4(1)(-10,000)}}{2}.$

Choosing the positive value for $n$ we have $n \approx 99.5012$. The first *term* that is less than 0.001 is $n = 100$.

$\qquad \left(\dfrac{1}{8}\right)^n < 0.001$

$\qquad 10,000 < 8^n$

This inequality is true when $n = 5$. This series converges at a faster rate.

**73.** $\displaystyle\sum_{i=0}^{n-1} 8000(0.9)^i = \dfrac{8000[1 - (0.9)^{(n-1)+1}]}{1 - 0.9}$

$\qquad\qquad\qquad\qquad = 80,000(1 - 0.9^n), \ n > 0$

**75.** $\displaystyle\sum_{i=0}^{n-1} 100(0.75)^i = \dfrac{100[1 - 0.75^{(n-1)+1}]}{1 - 0.75}$

$\qquad\qquad\qquad\qquad = 400(1 - 0.75^n)$ million dollars.

Sum = 400 million dollars

**77.** $D_1 = 16$

$\quad D_2 = \underbrace{0.81(16)}_{\text{up}} + \underbrace{0.81(16)}_{\text{down}} = 32(0.81)$

$\quad D_3 = 16(0.81)^2 + 16(0.81)^2 = 32(0.81)^2$

$\quad \vdots$

$\quad D = 16 + 32(0.81) + 32(0.81)^2 + \cdots = -16 + \displaystyle\sum_{n=0}^{\infty} 32(0.81)^n = -16 + \dfrac{32}{1 - 0.81} = 152.42 \text{ ft}$

**79.** $P(n) = \dfrac{1}{2}\left(\dfrac{1}{2}\right)^n$

$\quad P(2) = \dfrac{1}{2}\left(\dfrac{1}{2}\right)^2 = \dfrac{1}{8}$

$\quad \displaystyle\sum_{n=0}^{\infty} \dfrac{1}{2}\left(\dfrac{1}{2}\right)^n = \dfrac{1/2}{1 - (1/2)} = 1$

**81.** (a) $\displaystyle\sum_{n=1}^{\infty}\left(\dfrac{1}{2}\right)^n = \sum_{n=0}^{\infty} \dfrac{1}{2}\left(\dfrac{1}{2}\right)^n = \dfrac{1}{2}\dfrac{1}{(1 - (1/2))} = 1$

$\quad$ (b) No, the series is not geometric.

$\quad$ (c) $\displaystyle\sum_{n=1}^{\infty} n\left(\dfrac{1}{2}\right)^n = 2$

**83.** Present Value $= \displaystyle\sum_{n=1}^{19} 50,000\left(\dfrac{1}{1.06}\right)^n$

$\qquad\qquad\qquad = \displaystyle\sum_{n=0}^{18} \dfrac{50,000}{1.06}\left(\dfrac{1}{1.06}\right)^n \qquad , \ r = \dfrac{1}{1.06}$

$\qquad\qquad\qquad = \dfrac{50,000}{1.06}\left(\dfrac{1 - 1.06^{-19}}{1 - 1.06^{-1}}\right)$

$\qquad\qquad\qquad \approx \$557,905.82$

The present value is less than \$1,000,000. After accruing interest over 20 years, it attains its full value.

**85.** $w = \displaystyle\sum_{i=0}^{n-1} 0.01(2)^i = \dfrac{0.01(1 - 2^n)}{1 - 2} = 0.01(2^n - 1)$

$\quad$ (a) When $n = 29$: $w = \$5,368,709.11$

$\quad$ (b) When $n = 30$: $w = \$10,737,418.23$

$\quad$ (c) When $n = 31$: $w = \$21,474,836.47$

**87.** $P = 50, r = 0.03, t = 20$

    (a) $A = 50\left(\dfrac{12}{0.03}\right)\left[\left(1 + \dfrac{0.03}{12}\right)^{12(20)} - 1\right] \approx \$16{,}415.10$

    (b) $A = \dfrac{50 - (e^{0.03(20)} - 1)}{e^{0.03/12} - 1} \approx \$16{,}421.83$

**89.** $P = 100, r = 0.04, t = 40$

    (a) $A = 100\left(\dfrac{12}{0.04}\right)\left[\left(1 + \dfrac{0.04}{12}\right)^{12(40)} - 1\right] \approx \$118{,}196.13$

    (b) $A = \dfrac{100(e^{0.04(40)} - 1)}{e^{0.04/12} - 1} \approx \$118{,}393.43$

**91.** (a) $a_n = 6110.1832(1.0544)^x = 6110.1832e^{0.05297n}$

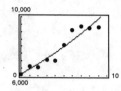

    (b) 78,530 or \$78,530,000,000

    (c) Total $= \displaystyle\sum_{n=0}^{9} a_n \approx 78{,}449$ or \$78,449,000,000

**93.** $x = 0.749999\ldots = 0.74 + \displaystyle\sum_{n=0}^{\infty} 0.009(0.1)^n$

    $= 0.74 + \dfrac{0.009}{1 - 0.1}$

    $= 0.74 + 0.01 = 0.75$

**95.** By letting $S_0 = 0$, we have $a_n = \displaystyle\sum_{k=1}^{n} a_k - \sum_{k=1}^{n-1} a_k = S_n - S_{n-1}$. Thus,

$$\sum_{n=1}^{\infty} a_n = \sum_{n=1}^{\infty} (S_n - S_{n-1}) = \sum_{n=1}^{\infty} (S_n - S_{n-1} + c - c) = \sum_{n=1}^{\infty} [(c - S_{n-1}) - (c - S_n)].$$

**97.** Let $\displaystyle\sum a_n = \sum_{n=0}^{\infty} 1$ and $\displaystyle\sum b_n = \sum_{n=0}^{\infty} (-1)$.

Both are divergent series.

$$\sum (a_n + b_n) = \sum_{n=0}^{\infty} [1 + (-1)] = \sum_{n=0}^{\infty} [1 - 1] = 0$$

**99.** False. $\displaystyle\lim_{n \to \infty} \frac{1}{n} = 0$, but $\displaystyle\sum_{n=1}^{\infty} \frac{1}{n}$ diverges.

**101.** False

$$\sum_{n=1}^{\infty} ar^n = \left(\frac{a}{1 - r}\right) - a$$

The formula requires that the geometric series begins with $n = 0$.

**103.** Let $H$ represent the half-life of the drug. If a patient receives $n$ equal doses of $P$ units each of this drug, administered at equal time interval of length $t$, the total amount of the drug in the patient's system at the time the last dose is administered is given by

    $T_n = P + Pe^{kt} + Pe^{2kt} + \cdots + Pe^{(n-1)kt}$

where $k = -(\ln 2)/H$. One time interval *after* the last dose is administered is given by

    $T_{n+1} = Pe^{kt} + Pe^{2kt} + Pe^{3kt} + \cdots + Pe^{nkt}$.

Two time intervals *after* the last dose is administered is given by

    $T_{n+2} = Pe^{2kt} + Pe^{3kt} + Pe^{4kt} + \cdots + Pe^{(n+1)kt}$

and so on. Since $k < 0$, $T_{n+s} \to 0$ as $s \to \infty$, where $s$ is an integer.

# Section 8.3    The Integral Test and *p*-Series

**1.** $\sum\limits_{n=1}^{\infty} \dfrac{1}{n+1}$

Let $f(x) = \dfrac{1}{x+1}$.

$f$ is positive, continuous and decreasing for $x \geq 1$.

$$\int_1^{\infty} \frac{1}{x+1}\, dx = \Big[\ln(x+1)\Big]_1^{\infty} = \infty$$

Diverges by Theorem 8.10

**3.** $\sum\limits_{n=1}^{\infty} e^{-n}$

Let $f(x) = e^{-x}$.

$f$ is positive, continuous, and decreasing for $x \geq 1$.

$$\int_1^{\infty} e^{-x}\, dx = \Big[-e^{-x}\Big]_1^{\infty} = \frac{1}{e}$$

Converges by Theorem 8.10

**5.** $\sum\limits_{n=1}^{\infty} \dfrac{1}{n^2+1}$

Let $f(x) = \dfrac{1}{x^2+1}$.

$f$ is positive, continuous, and decreasing for $x \geq 1$.

$$\int_1^{\infty} \frac{1}{x^2+1}\, dx = \Big[\arctan x\Big]_1^{\infty} = \frac{\pi}{4}$$

Converges by Theorem 8.10

**7.** $\sum\limits_{n=1}^{\infty} \dfrac{\ln(n+1)}{n+1}$

Let $f(x) = \dfrac{\ln(x+1)}{x+1}$.

$f$ is positive, continuous, and decreasing for $x \geq 2$ since

$$f'(x) = \frac{1 - \ln(x+1)}{(x+1)^2} < 0 \text{ for } x \geq 2.$$

$$\int_1^{\infty} \frac{\ln(x+1)}{x+1}\, dx = \left[\frac{\ln^2(x+1)}{2}\right]_1^{\infty} = \infty$$

Diverges by Theorem 8.10

**9.** $\sum\limits_{n=1}^{\infty} \dfrac{n^{k-1}}{n^k+c}$

Let $f(x) = \dfrac{x^{k-1}}{x^k+c}$.

$f$ is positive, continuous, and decreasing for $x > \sqrt[k]{c(k-1)}$ since

$$f'(x) = \frac{x^{k-2}\big[c(k-1) - x^k\big]}{(x^k+c)^2} < 0$$

for $x > \sqrt[k]{c(k-1)}$.

$$\int_1^{\infty} \frac{x^{k-1}}{x^k+c}\, dx = \left[\frac{1}{k}\ln(x^k+c)\right]_1^{\infty} = \infty$$

Diverges by Theorem 8.10

**11.** $\sum\limits_{n=1}^{\infty} \dfrac{1}{n^3}$

Let $f(x) = \dfrac{1}{x^3}$.

$f$ is positive, continuous, and decreasing for $x \geq 1$.

$$\int_1^{\infty} \frac{1}{x^3}\, dx = \left[-\frac{1}{2x^2}\right]_1^{\infty} = \frac{1}{2}$$

Converges by Theorem 8.10

**13.** $\sum\limits_{n=1}^{\infty} \dfrac{1}{\sqrt[5]{n}} = \sum\limits_{n=1}^{\infty} \dfrac{1}{n^{1/5}}$

Divergent $p$-series with $p = \frac{1}{5} < 1$

**15.** $\sum\limits_{n=1}^{\infty} \dfrac{1}{n^{1/2}}$

Divergent $p$-series with $p = \frac{1}{2} < 1$

**17.** $\sum\limits_{n=1}^{\infty} \dfrac{1}{n^{3/2}}$

Convergent $p$-series with $p = \frac{3}{2} > 1$

**19.** $\sum\limits_{n=1}^{\infty} \dfrac{1}{n^{1.04}}$

Convergent $p$-series with $p = 1.04 > 1$

**21.** $\displaystyle\sum_{n=1}^{\infty} \frac{2}{\sqrt[4]{n^3}} = \frac{2}{1} + \frac{2}{2^{3/4}} + \frac{2}{3^{3/4}} + \cdots$

$S_1 = 2$

$S_2 \approx 3.189$

$S_3 \approx 4.067$

Matches (a)

Diverges—$p$-series with $p = \frac{3}{4} < 1$

**23.** $\displaystyle\sum_{n=1}^{\infty} \frac{2}{n\sqrt{n}} = 2 + 2/2^{3/2} + 2/3^{3/2} + \cdots$

$S_1 = 2$

$S_2 \approx 2.707$

$S_3 \approx 3.092$

Matches (b)

Converges—$p$-series with $p = 3/2 > 1$

**25.** No. Theorem 8.9 says that if the series converges, then the terms $a_n$ tend to zero. Some of the series in Exercises 21-24 converge because the terms tend to 0 very rapidly.

**27.** $\displaystyle\sum_{n=1}^{N} \frac{1}{n} = 1 + \frac{1}{2} + \frac{1}{3} + \frac{1}{4} + \cdots + \frac{1}{N} > M$

(a)

| $M$ | 2 | 4 | 6 | 8 |
|---|---|---|---|---|
| $N$ | 4 | 31 | 227 | 1674 |

(b) No. Since the terms are decreasing (approaching zero), more and more terms are required to increase the partial sum by 2.

**29.** $\displaystyle\sum_{n=2}^{\infty} \frac{1}{n(\ln n)^p}$

If $p = 1$, then the series diverges by the Integral Test. If $p \neq 1$,

$$\int_2^{\infty} \frac{1}{x(\ln x)^p}\, dx = \int_2^{\infty} (\ln x)^{-p} \frac{1}{x}\, dx = \left[ \frac{(\ln x)^{-p+1}}{-p+1} \right]_2^{\infty}.$$

Converges for $-p + 1 < 0$ or $p > 1$.

**31.** Let $f$ be positive, continuous, and decreasing for $x \geq 1$ and $a_n = f(n)$. Then,

$$\sum_{n=1}^{\infty} a_n \text{ and } \int_1^{\infty} f(x)\, dx$$

either both converge or both diverge (Theorem 8.10).
See Example 1, page 578.

**33.** Your friend is not correct. The series

$$\sum_{n=10,000}^{\infty} \frac{1}{n} = \frac{1}{10,000} + \frac{1}{10,001} + \cdots$$

is the harmonic series, starting with the $10,000^{\text{th}}$ term, and hence diverges.

**35.** Since $f$ is positive, continuous, and decreasing for $x \geq 1$ and $a_n = f(n)$, we have,

$$R_N = S - S_N = \sum_{n=1}^{\infty} a_n - \sum_{n=1}^{N} a_n = \sum_{n=N+1}^{\infty} a_n > 0.$$

Also, $\displaystyle R_N = S - S_N = \sum_{n=N+1}^{\infty} a_n \leq a_{N+1} + \int_{N+1}^{\infty} f(x)\, dx \leq \int_N^{\infty} f(x)\, dx$. Thus,

$$0 \leq R_N \leq \int_N^{\infty} f(x)\, dx.$$

**37.** $S_6 = 1 + \dfrac{1}{2^4} + \dfrac{1}{3^4} + \dfrac{1}{4^4} + \dfrac{1}{5^4} + \dfrac{1}{6^4} \approx 1.0811$

$R_6 \leq \displaystyle\int_6^{\infty} \frac{1}{x^4}\, dx = \left[ -\frac{1}{3x^3} \right]_6^{\infty} \approx 0.0015$

$1.0811 \leq \displaystyle\sum_{n=1}^{\infty} \frac{1}{n^4} \leq 1.0811 + 0.0015 = 1.0826$

**39.** $S_{10} = \frac{1}{2} + \frac{1}{5} + \frac{1}{10} + \frac{1}{17} + \frac{1}{26} + \frac{1}{37} + \frac{1}{50} + \frac{1}{65} + \frac{1}{82} + \frac{1}{101} \approx 0.9818$

$R_{10} = \leq \int_{10}^{\infty} \frac{1}{x^2 + 1} \, dx = \left[ \arctan x \right]_{10}^{\infty} = \frac{\pi}{2} - \arctan 10 \approx 0.0997$

$0.9818 \leq \sum_{n=1}^{\infty} \frac{1}{n^5} \leq 0.9818 + 0.0997 = 1.0815$

**41.** $S_4 = \frac{1}{e} + \frac{2}{e^4} + \frac{3}{e^9} + \frac{4}{e^{16}} \approx 0.4049$

$R_4 \leq \int_{4}^{\infty} xe^{-x^2} \, dx = \left[ -\frac{1}{2} e^{-x^2} \right]_{4}^{\infty} = 5.6 \times 10^{-8}$

$0.4049 \leq \sum_{n=1}^{\infty} ne^{-n^2} \leq 0.4049 + 5.6 \times 10^{-8}$

**43.** $0 \leq R_N \leq \int_{N}^{\infty} \frac{1}{x^4} \, dx = \left[ -\frac{1}{3x^3} \right]_{N}^{\infty} = \frac{1}{3N^3} < 0.001$

$\frac{1}{N^3} < 0.003$

$N^3 > 333.33$

$N > 6.93$

$N \geq 7$

**45.** $R_N \leq \int_{N}^{\infty} e^{-5x} \, dx = \left[ -\frac{1}{5} e^{-5x} \right]_{N}^{\infty} = \frac{e^{-5N}}{5} < 0.001$

$\frac{1}{e^{5N}} < 0.005$

$e^{5N} > 200$

$5N > \ln 200$

$N > \frac{\ln 200}{5}$

$N > 1.0597$

$N \geq 2$

**47.** $R_N \leq \int_{N}^{\infty} \frac{1}{x^2 + 1} \, dx = \left[ \arctan x \right]_{N}^{\infty}$

$= \frac{\pi}{2} - \arctan N < 0.001$

$-\arctan N < -1.5698$

$\arctan N > 1.5698$

$N > \tan 1.5698$

$N \geq 1004$

**49.** (a) $\displaystyle\sum_{n=2}^{\infty} \frac{1}{n^{1.1}}$. This is a convergent p-series with $p = 1.1 > 1$.

$\displaystyle\sum_{n=2}^{\infty} \frac{1}{n \ln n}$ is a divergent series. Use the Integral Test.

$\int_{2}^{\infty} \frac{1}{x \ln x} \, dx = \left[ \ln|\ln x| \right]_{2}^{\infty} = \infty$

(b) $\displaystyle\sum_{n=2}^{6} \frac{1}{n^{1.1}} = \frac{1}{2^{1.1}} + \frac{1}{3^{1.1}} + \frac{1}{4^{1.1}} + \frac{1}{5^{1.1}} + \frac{1}{6^{1.1}} \approx 0.4665 + 0.2987 + 0.2176 + 0.1703 + 0.1393$

$\displaystyle\sum_{n=2}^{6} \frac{1}{n \ln n} = \frac{1}{2 \ln 2} + \frac{1}{3 \ln 3} + \frac{1}{4 \ln 4} + \frac{1}{5 \ln 5} + \frac{1}{6 \ln 6} \approx 0.7213 + 0.3034 + 0.1803 + 0.1243 + 0.0930$

The terms of the convergent series **seem** to be larger than those of the divergent series!

(c) $\dfrac{1}{n^{1.1}} < \dfrac{1}{n \ln n}$

$n \ln n < n^{1.1}$

$\ln n < n^{0.1}$

This inequality holds when $n \geq 3.5 \times 10^{15}$. Or, $n > e^{40}$. Then $\ln e^{40} = 40 < (e^{40})^{0.1} = e^4 \approx 55$.

**51. (a)** Let $f(x) = 1/x$. $f$ is positive, continuous, and decreasing on $[1, \infty)$.

$$S_n - 1 \leq \int_1^n \frac{1}{x}\, dx$$

$$S_n - 1 \leq \ln n$$

Hence, $S_n \leq 1 + \ln n$. Similarly,

$$S_n \geq \int_1^{n+1} \frac{1}{x}\, dx = \ln(n + 1).$$

Thus, $\ln(n + 1) \leq S_n \leq 1 + \ln n$.

**(b)** Since $\ln(n + 1) \leq S_n \leq 1 + \ln n$, we have $\ln(n + 1) - \ln n \leq S_n - \ln n \leq 1$. Also, since $\ln x$ is an increasing function, $\ln(n + 1) - \ln n > 0$ for $n \geq 1$. Thus, $0 \leq S_n - \ln n \leq 1$ and the sequence $\{a_n\}$ is bounded.

**(c)** $a_n - a_{n+1} = [S_n - \ln n] - [S_{n+1} - \ln(n + 1)] = \int_n^{n+1} \frac{1}{x}\, dx - \frac{1}{n + 1} \geq 0$

Thus, $a_n \geq a_{n+1}$ and the sequence is decreasing.

**(d)** Since the sequence is bounded and monotonic, it converges to a limit, $\gamma$.

**(e)** $a_{100} = S_{100} - \ln 100 \approx 0.5822$ (Actually $\gamma \approx 0.577216$.)

**53.** $\displaystyle\sum_{n=1}^{\infty} \frac{1}{2n - 1}$

Let $f(x) = \dfrac{1}{2x - 1}$.

$f$ is positive, continuous, and decreasing for $x \geq 1$.

$$\int_1^{\infty} \frac{1}{2x - 1}\, dx = \left[ \ln \sqrt{2x - 1} \right]_1^{\infty} = \infty$$

Diverges by Theorem 8.10

**55.** $\displaystyle\sum_{n=1}^{\infty} \frac{1}{n\sqrt[4]{n}} = \sum_{n=1}^{\infty} \frac{1}{n^{5/4}}$

$p$-series with $p = \frac{5}{4}$

Converges by Theorem 8.11

**57.** $\displaystyle\sum_{n=0}^{\infty} \left(\frac{2}{3}\right)^n$

Geometric series with $r = \frac{2}{3}$

Converges by Theorem 8.6

**59.** $\displaystyle\sum_{n=1}^{\infty} \frac{n}{\sqrt{n^2 + 1}}$

$$\lim_{n \to \infty} \frac{n}{\sqrt{n^2 + 1}} = \lim_{n \to \infty} \frac{1}{\sqrt{1 + (1/n^2)}} = 1 \neq 0$$

Diverges by Theorem 8.9

**61.** $\displaystyle\sum_{n=1}^{\infty} \left(1 + \frac{1}{n}\right)^n$

$$\lim_{n \to \infty} \left(1 + \frac{1}{n}\right)^n = e \neq 0$$

Fails $n$th Term Test

Diverges by Theorem 8.9

**63.** $\displaystyle\sum_{n=2}^{\infty} \frac{1}{n(\ln n)^3}$

Let $f(x) = \dfrac{1}{x(\ln x)^3}$.

$f$ is positive, continuous and decreasing for $x \geq 2$.

$$\int_2^{\infty} \frac{1}{x(\ln x)^3}\, dx = \int_2^{\infty} (\ln x)^{-3} \frac{1}{x}\, dx = \left[ \frac{(\ln x)^{-2}}{-2} \right]_2^{\infty} = \left[ -\frac{1}{2(\ln x)^2} \right]_2^{\infty} = \frac{1}{2(\ln 2)^2}$$

Converges by Theorem 8.10. See Exercise 13.

# Section 8.4    Comparisons of Series

**1.** (a) $\displaystyle\sum_{n=1}^{\infty} \frac{6}{n^{3/2}} = \frac{6}{1} + \frac{6}{2^{3/2}} + \cdots \quad S_1 = 6$

$\displaystyle\sum_{n=1}^{\infty} \frac{6}{n^{3/2} + 3} = \frac{6}{4} + \frac{6}{2^{3/2} + 3} + \cdots \quad S_1 = \frac{3}{2}$

$\displaystyle\sum_{n=1}^{\infty} \frac{6}{n\sqrt{n^2 + 0.5}} = \frac{6}{1\sqrt{1.5}} + \frac{6}{2\sqrt{4.5}} + \cdots \quad S_1 = \frac{6}{\sqrt{1.5}} \approx 4.9$

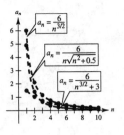

(b) The first series is a *p*-series. It converges ($p = 3/2 > 1$).

(c) The magnitude of the terms of the other two series are less than the corresponding terms at the convergent *p*-series. Hence, the other two series converge.

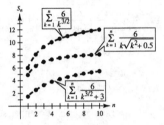

(d) The smaller the magnitude of the terms, the smaller the magnitude of the terms of the sequence of partial sums.

**3.** $\dfrac{1}{n^2 + 1} < \dfrac{1}{n^2}$

Therefore,

$$\sum_{n=1}^{\infty} \frac{1}{n^2 + 1}$$

converges by comparison with the convergent *p*-series

$$\sum_{n=1}^{\infty} \frac{1}{n^2}.$$

**5.** $\dfrac{1}{n - 1} > \dfrac{1}{n}$ for $n \geq 2$

Therefore,

$$\sum_{n=2}^{\infty} \frac{1}{n - 1}$$

diverges by comparison with the divergent *p*-series

$$\sum_{n=2}^{\infty} \frac{1}{n}.$$

**7.** $\dfrac{1}{3^n + 1} < \dfrac{1}{3^n}$

Therefore,

$$\sum_{n=0}^{\infty} \frac{1}{3^n + 1}$$

converges by comparison with the convergent geometric series

$$\sum_{n=0}^{\infty} \left(\frac{1}{3}\right)^n.$$

**9.** For $n \geq 3$, $\dfrac{\ln n}{n + 1} > \dfrac{1}{n + 1}$.

Therefore,

$$\sum_{n=1}^{\infty} \frac{\ln n}{n + 1}$$

diverges by comparison with the divergent series

$$\sum_{n=1}^{\infty} \frac{1}{n + 1}.$$

**Note:** $\displaystyle\sum_{n=1}^{\infty} \frac{1}{n + 1}$ diverges by the integral test.

**11.** For $n > 3$, $\dfrac{1}{n^2} > \dfrac{1}{n!}$.

Therefore,

$$\sum_{n=0}^{\infty} \frac{1}{n!}$$

converges by comparison with the convergent *p*-series

$$\sum_{n=1}^{\infty} \frac{1}{n^2}.$$

**13.** $\dfrac{1}{e^{n^2}} \leq \dfrac{1}{e^n}$

Therefore,

$$\sum_{n=0}^{\infty} \frac{1}{e^{n^2}}$$

converges by comparison with the convergent geometric series

$$\sum_{n=0}^{\infty} \left(\frac{1}{e}\right)^n.$$

**15.** $\lim\limits_{n\to\infty} \dfrac{n/(n^2+1)}{1/n} = \lim\limits_{n\to\infty} \dfrac{n^2}{n^2+1} = 1$

Therefore,

$$\sum_{n=1}^{\infty} \frac{n}{n^2+1}$$

diverges by a limit comparison with the divergent *p*-series

$$\sum_{n=1}^{\infty} \frac{1}{n}.$$

**17.** $\lim\limits_{n\to\infty} \dfrac{1/\sqrt{n^2+1}}{1/n} = \lim\limits_{n\to\infty} \dfrac{n}{\sqrt{n^2+1}} = 1$

Therefore,

$$\sum_{n=0}^{\infty} \frac{1}{\sqrt{n^2+1}}$$

diverges by a limit comparison with the divergent *p*-series

$$\sum_{n=1}^{\infty} \frac{1}{n}.$$

**19.** $\lim\limits_{n\to\infty} \dfrac{\dfrac{2n^2-1}{3n^5+2n+1}}{1/n^3} = \lim\limits_{n\to\infty} \dfrac{2n^5-n^3}{3n^5+2n+1} = \dfrac{2}{3}$

Therefore,

$$\sum_{n=1}^{\infty} \frac{2n^2-1}{3n^5+2n+1}$$

converges by a limit comparison with the convergent *p*-series

$$\sum_{n=1}^{\infty} \frac{1}{n^3}.$$

**21.** $\lim\limits_{n\to\infty} \dfrac{\dfrac{n+3}{n(n+2)}}{1/n} = \lim\limits_{n\to\infty} \dfrac{n^2+3n}{n^2+2n} = 1$

Therefore,

$$\sum_{n=1}^{\infty} \frac{n+3}{n(n+2)}$$

diverges by a limit comparison with the divergent *p*-series

$$\sum_{n=1}^{\infty} \frac{1}{n}.$$

**23.** $\lim\limits_{n\to\infty} \dfrac{1/\left(n\sqrt{n^2+1}\right)}{1/n^2} = \lim\limits_{n\to\infty} \dfrac{n^2}{n\sqrt{n^2+1}} = 1$

Therefore,

$$\sum_{n=1}^{\infty} \frac{1}{n\sqrt{n^2+1}}$$

converges by a limit comparison with the convergent *p*-series

$$\sum_{n=1}^{\infty} \frac{1}{n^2}.$$

**25.** $\lim\limits_{n\to\infty} \dfrac{(n^{k-1})/(n^k+1)}{1/n} = \lim\limits_{n\to\infty} \dfrac{n^k}{n^k+1} = 1$

Therefore,

$$\sum_{n=1}^{\infty} \frac{n^{k-1}}{n^k+1}$$

diverges by a limit comparison with the divergent *p*-series

$$\sum_{n=1}^{\infty} \frac{1}{n}.$$

**27.** $\lim\limits_{n\to\infty} \dfrac{\sin(1/n)}{1/n} = \lim\limits_{n\to\infty} \dfrac{(-1/n^2)\cos(1/n)}{-1/n^2}$

$$= \lim\limits_{n\to\infty} \cos\left(\frac{1}{n}\right) = 1$$

Therefore,

$$\sum_{n=1}^{\infty} \sin\left(\frac{1}{n}\right)$$

diverges by a limit comparison with the divergent *p*-series

$$\sum_{n=1}^{\infty} \frac{1}{n}.$$

**29.** $\sum\limits_{n=1}^{\infty} \dfrac{\sqrt{n}}{n} = \sum\limits_{n=1}^{\infty} \dfrac{1}{\sqrt{n}}$

Diverges

*p*-series with $p = \frac{1}{2}$

**31.** $\sum\limits_{n=1}^{\infty} \dfrac{1}{3^n+2}$

Converges

Direct comparison with $\sum\limits_{n=1}^{\infty} \left(\dfrac{1}{3}\right)^n$

**33.** $\sum\limits_{n=1}^{\infty} \dfrac{n}{2n+3}$

Diverges; *n*th Term Test

$$\lim\limits_{n\to\infty} \frac{n}{2n+3} = \frac{1}{2} \neq 0$$

**35.** $\sum\limits_{n=1}^{\infty} \dfrac{n}{(n^2+1)^2}$

Converges; integral test

**37.** $\lim_{n\to\infty} \dfrac{a_n}{1/n} = \lim_{n\to\infty} na_n$ by given conditions $\lim_{n\to\infty} na_n$ is finite and nonzero.

Therefore,

$$\sum_{n=1}^{\infty} a_n$$

diverges by a limit comparison with the $p$-series

$$\sum_{n=1}^{\infty} \frac{1}{n}.$$

**39.** $\dfrac{1}{2} + \dfrac{2}{5} + \dfrac{3}{10} + \dfrac{4}{17} + \dfrac{5}{26} + \cdots = \displaystyle\sum_{n=1}^{\infty} \frac{n}{n^2 + 1},$

which diverges since the degree of the numerator is only one less than the degree of the denominator.

**41.** $\displaystyle\sum_{n=1}^{\infty} \frac{1}{n^3 + 1}$

converges since the degree of the numerator is three less than the degree of the denominator.

**43.** $\lim_{n\to\infty} n\left(\dfrac{n^3}{5n^4 + 3}\right) = \lim_{n\to\infty} \dfrac{n^4}{5n^4 + 3} = \dfrac{1}{5} \neq 0$

Therefore,

$$\sum_{n=1}^{\infty} \frac{n^3}{5n^4 + 3} \text{ diverges.}$$

**45.** See Theorem 8.12, page 583. One example is $\displaystyle\sum_{n=1}^{\infty} \frac{1}{n^2 + 1}$ converges because

$$\frac{1}{n^2 + 1} < \frac{1}{n^2} \text{ and } \sum_{n=1}^{\infty} \frac{1}{n^2}$$

converges ($p$-series).

**47.**

For $0 < a_n < 1, 0 < a_n^2 < a_n < 1$. Hence, the lower terms are those of $\Sigma\, a_n^2$.

**49.** $\dfrac{1}{200} + \dfrac{1}{400} + \dfrac{1}{600} + \cdots = \displaystyle\sum_{n=1}^{\infty} \frac{1}{200n}$, diverges

**51.** $\dfrac{1}{201} + \dfrac{1}{204} + \dfrac{1}{209} + \dfrac{1}{216} = \displaystyle\sum_{n=1}^{\infty} \frac{1}{200 + n^2}$, converges

**53.** Some series diverge or converge very slowly. You cannot decide convergence or divergence of a series by comparing the first few terms.

**55.** False. Let $a_n = 1/n^3$ and $b_n = 1/n^2$. $0 < a_n \leq b_n$ and both

$$\sum_{n=1}^{\infty} \frac{1}{n^3} \text{ and } \sum_{n=1}^{\infty} \frac{1}{n^2}$$

converge.

**57.** True

**59.** Since $\displaystyle\sum_{n=1}^{\infty} b_n$ converges, $\lim_{n\to\infty} b_n = 0$. There exists $N$ such that $b_n < 1$ for $n > N$. Thus,

$$a_n b_n < a_n \text{ for } n > N \text{ and } \sum_{n=1}^{\infty} a_n b_n$$

converges by comparison to the convergent series $\displaystyle\sum_{i=1}^{\infty} a_n$.

**61.** $\displaystyle\sum \frac{1}{n^2}$ and $\displaystyle\sum \frac{1}{n^3}$ both converge, and hence so does $\displaystyle\sum\left(\frac{1}{n^2}\right)\left(\frac{1}{n^3}\right) = \sum \frac{1}{n^5}.$

**63.** (a) Suppose $\Sigma b_n$ converges and $\Sigma a_n$ diverges. Then there exists $N$ such that $0 < b_n < a_n$ for $n \geq N$. This means that $1 < a_n/b_n$ for $n \geq N$. Therefore, $\lim\limits_{n\to\infty} a_n/b_n \neq 0$. Thus, $\Sigma a_n$ must also converge.

(b) Suppose $\Sigma b_n$ diverges and $\Sigma a_n$ converges. Then there exists $N$ such that $0 < a_n < b_n$ for $n \geq N$. This means that $0 < a_n/b_n < 1$ for $n \geq N$. Therefore, $\lim\limits_{n\to\infty} a_n/b_n \neq \infty$. Thus, $\Sigma a_n$ must also diverge.

**65.** Start with one triangle whose sides have length 9. At the $n$th step, each side is replaced by four smaller line segments each having $\frac{1}{3}$ the length of the original side.

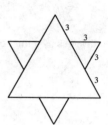

| #Sides | Length of sides |
|--------|-----------------|
| 3 | 9 |
| $3 \cdot 4$ | $9\left(\frac{1}{3}\right)$ |
| $3 \cdot 4^2$ | $9\left(\frac{1}{3}\right)^2$ |
| $\vdots$ | |
| $3 \cdot 4^n$ | $9\left(\frac{1}{3}\right)^n$ |

At the $n$th step there are $3 \cdot 4^n$ sides, each of length $9\left(\frac{1}{3}\right)^n$. At the next step, there are $3 \cdot 4^n$ new triangles of side $9\left(\frac{1}{3}\right)^{n+1}$. The area of an equilateral triangle of side $x$ is $\frac{1}{4}\sqrt{3}\, x^2$. Thus, the new triangles each have area

$$9\frac{\sqrt{3}}{4}\left(\frac{1}{3^{n+1}}\right)^2 = \frac{\sqrt{3}}{4}\frac{1}{3^{2n}}.$$

The area of the $3 \cdot 4^n$ new triangles is

$$(3 \cdot 4^n)\left(\frac{\sqrt{3}}{4}\frac{1}{3^{2n}}\right) = \frac{3\sqrt{3}}{4}\left(\frac{4}{9}\right)^n.$$

The total area is the infinite sum

$$\frac{9\sqrt{3}}{4} + \sum_{n=0}^{\infty}\frac{3\sqrt{3}}{4}\left(\frac{4}{9}\right)^n = \frac{9\sqrt{3}}{4} + \frac{3\sqrt{3}}{4}\left(\frac{1}{1-4/9}\right) = \frac{9\sqrt{3}}{4} + \frac{3\sqrt{3}}{4}\left(\frac{9}{5}\right) = \frac{18\sqrt{3}}{5}.$$

The perimeter is infinite, since at step $n$ there are $3 \cdot 4^n$ sides of length $9\left(\frac{1}{3}\right)^n$. Thus, the perimeter at step $n$ is $27\left(\frac{4}{3}\right)^n \to \infty$.

# Section 8.5    Alternating Series

**1.** $\displaystyle\sum_{n=1}^{\infty}\frac{6}{n^2} = \frac{6}{1} + \frac{6}{4} + \frac{6}{9} + \cdots$

$S_1 = 6, S_2 = 7.5$

Matches (b)

**3.** $\displaystyle\sum_{n=1}^{\infty}\frac{10}{n2^n} = \frac{10}{2} + \frac{10}{8} + \cdots$

$S_1 = 5, S_2 = 6.25$

Matches (c)

**5.** $\displaystyle\sum_{n=1}^{\infty}\frac{(-1)^{n-1}}{2n-1} = \frac{\pi}{4} \approx 0.7854$

(a)

| $n$ | 1 | 2 | 3 | 4 | 5 | 6 | 7 | 8 | 9 | 10 |
|-----|---|---|---|---|---|---|---|---|---|----|
| $S_n$ | 1 | 0.6667 | 0.8667 | 0.7238 | 0.8349 | 0.7440 | 0.8209 | 0.7543 | 0.8131 | 0.7605 |

(b)

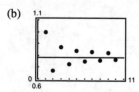

(c) The points alternate sides of the horizontal line that represents the sum of the series. The distance between successive points and the line decreases.

(d) The distance in part (c) is always less than the magnitude of the next term of the series.

**7.** $\displaystyle\sum_{n=1}^{\infty} \frac{(-1)^{n-1}}{n^2} = \frac{\pi^2}{12} \approx 0.8225$

(a)

| $n$ | 1 | 2 | 3 | 4 | 5 | 6 | 7 | 8 | 9 | 10 |
|-----|---|------|--------|--------|--------|--------|--------|--------|--------|--------|
| $S_n$ | 1 | 0.75 | 0.8611 | 0.7986 | 0.8386 | 0.8108 | 0.8312 | 0.8156 | 0.8280 | 0.8180 |

(b)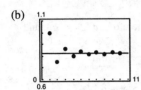

(c) The points alternate sides of the horizontal line that represents the sum of the series. The distance between successive points and the line decreases.

(d) The distance in part (c) is always less than the magnitude of the next term in the series.

**9.** $\displaystyle\sum_{n=1}^{\infty} \frac{(-1)^{n+1}}{n}$

$a_{n+1} = \dfrac{1}{n+1} < \dfrac{1}{n} = a_n$

$\displaystyle\lim_{n\to\infty} \frac{1}{n} = 0$

Converges by Theorem 8.14.

**11.** $\displaystyle\sum_{n=1}^{\infty} \frac{(-1)^{n+1}}{2n-1}$

$a_{n+1} = \dfrac{1}{2(n+1)-1} < \dfrac{1}{2n-1} = a_n$

$\displaystyle\lim_{n\to\infty} \frac{1}{2n-1} = 0$

Converges by Theorem 8.14

**13.** $\displaystyle\sum_{n=1}^{\infty} \frac{(-1)^n n^2}{n^2+1}$

$\displaystyle\lim_{n\to\infty} \frac{n^2}{n^2+1} = 1$

Diverges by the $n$th Term Test

**15.** $\displaystyle\sum_{n=1}^{\infty} \frac{(-1)^n}{\sqrt{n}}$

$a_{n+1} = \dfrac{1}{\sqrt{n+1}} < \dfrac{1}{\sqrt{n}} = a_n$

$\displaystyle\lim_{n\to\infty} \frac{1}{\sqrt{n}} = 0$

Converges by Theorem 8.14

**17.** $\displaystyle\sum_{n=1}^{\infty} \frac{(-1)^{n+1}(n+1)}{\ln(n+1)}$

$\displaystyle\lim_{n\to\infty} \frac{n+1}{\ln(n+1)} = \lim_{n\to\infty} \frac{1}{1/(n+1)} = \lim_{n\to\infty} (n+1) = \infty$

Diverges by the $n$th Term Test

**19.** $\displaystyle\sum_{n=1}^{\infty} \sin\left[\frac{(2n-1)\pi}{2}\right] = \sum_{n=1}^{\infty} (-1)^{n+1}$

Diverges by the $n$th Term Test

**21.** $\displaystyle\sum_{n=1}^{\infty} \cos n\pi = \sum_{n=1}^{\infty} (-1)^n$

Diverges by the $n$th Term Test

**23.** $\displaystyle\sum_{n=0}^{\infty} \frac{(-1)^n}{n!}$

$a_{n+1} = \dfrac{1}{(n+1)!} < \dfrac{1}{n!} = a_n$

$\displaystyle\lim_{n\to\infty} \frac{1}{n!} = 0$

Converges by Theorem 8.14

**25.** $\displaystyle\sum_{n=1}^{\infty} \frac{(-1)^{n+1}\sqrt{n}}{n+2}$

$a_{n+1} = \dfrac{\sqrt{n+1}}{(n+1)+2} < \dfrac{\sqrt{n}}{n+2}$ for $n \geq 2$

$\displaystyle\lim_{n\to\infty} \frac{\sqrt{n}}{n+2} = 0$

Converges by Theorem 8.14

**27.** $\displaystyle\sum_{n=1}^{\infty} \frac{(-1)^{n+1}(2)}{e^n - e^{-n}} = \sum_{n=1}^{\infty} \frac{(-1)^{n+1}(2e^n)}{e^{2n}-1}$

Let $f(x) = \dfrac{2e^x}{e^{2x}-1}$. Then

$f'(x) = \dfrac{-2e^x(e^{2x}+1)}{(e^{2x}-1)^2} < 0.$

Thus, $f(x)$ is decreasing. Therefore, $a_{n+1} < a_n$, and

$$\lim_{n\to\infty} \frac{2e^n}{e^{2n}-1} = \lim_{n\to\infty} \frac{2e^n}{2e^{2n}} = \lim_{n\to\infty} \frac{1}{e^n} = 0.$$

The series converges by Theorem 8.14.

**29.** $S_6 = \displaystyle\sum_{n=1}^{6} \frac{3(-1)^{n+1}}{n^2} = 2.4325$

$|R_6| = |S - S_6| \leq a_7 = \dfrac{3}{49} \approx 0.0612;\ 2.3713 \leq S \leq 2.4937$

**31.** $S_6 = \displaystyle\sum_{n=0}^{5} \frac{2(-1)^n}{n!} \approx 0.7333$

$|R_6| = |S - S_6| \leq a_7 = \dfrac{2}{6!} = 0.002778;\ 0.7305 \leq S \leq 0.7361$

**33.** $\displaystyle\sum_{n=0}^{\infty} \frac{(-1)^n}{n!}$

(a) By Theorem 8.15,

$$|R_N| \leq a_{N+1} = \frac{1}{(N+1)!} < 0.001.$$

This inequality is valid when $N = 6$.

(b) We may approximate the series by

$$\sum_{n=0}^{6} \frac{(-1)^n}{n!} = 1 - 1 + \frac{1}{2} - \frac{1}{6} + \frac{1}{24} - \frac{1}{120} + \frac{1}{720}$$

$$\approx 0.368.$$

(7 terms. Note that the sum begins with $n = 0$.)

**35.** $\displaystyle\sum_{n=0}^{\infty} \frac{(-1)^n}{(2n+1)!}$

(a) By Theorem 8.15,

$$|R_N| \leq a_{N+1} = \frac{1}{[2(N+1)+1]!} < 0.001.$$

This inequality is valid when $N = 2$.

(b) We may approximate the series by

$$\sum_{n=0}^{2} \frac{(-1)^n}{(2n+1)!} = 1 - \frac{1}{6} + \frac{1}{120} \approx 0.842.$$

(3 terms. Note that the sum begins with $n = 0$.)

**37.** $\displaystyle\sum_{n=1}^{\infty} \frac{(-1)^{n+1}}{n}$

(a) By Theorem 8.15,

$$|R_N| \leq a_{N+1} = \frac{1}{N+1} < 0.001.$$

This inequality is valid when $N = 1000$.

(b) We may approximate the series by

$$\sum_{n=1}^{1000} \frac{(-1)^{n+1}}{n} = 1 - \frac{1}{2} + \frac{1}{3} - \frac{1}{4} + \cdots - \frac{1}{1000}$$

$$\approx 0.693.$$

(1000 terms)

**39.** $\displaystyle\sum_{n=1}^{\infty} \frac{(-1)^{n+1}}{2n^3 - 1}$

By Theorem 8.15,

$$|R_N| \leq a_{N+1} = \frac{1}{2(N+1)^3 - 1} < 0.001.$$

This inequality is valid when $N = 7$.

**41.** $\displaystyle\sum_{n=1}^{\infty} \frac{(-1)^{n+1}}{(n+1)^2}$

$\displaystyle\sum_{n=1}^{\infty} \frac{1}{(n+1)^2}$ converges by comparison to the $p$-series

$$\sum_{n=1}^{\infty} \frac{1}{n^2}.$$

Therefore, the given series converge absolutely.

**45.** $\displaystyle\sum_{n=1}^{\infty} \frac{(-1)^{n+1} n^2}{(n+1)^2}$

$$\lim_{n\to\infty} \frac{n^2}{(n+1)^2} = 1$$

Therefore, the series diverges by the $n$th Term Test.

**49.** $\displaystyle\sum_{n=2}^{\infty} \frac{(-1)^n n}{n^3 - 1}$

$$\sum_{n=2}^{\infty} \frac{n}{n^3 - 1}$$

converges by a limit comparison to the convergent $p$-series

$$\sum_{n=2}^{\infty} \frac{1}{n^2}.$$

Therefore, the given series converges absolutely.

**53.** $\displaystyle\sum_{n=0}^{\infty} \frac{\cos n\pi}{n+1} = \sum_{n=0}^{\infty} \frac{(-1)^n}{n+1}$

The given series converges by the Alternating Series Test, but

$$\sum_{n=0}^{\infty} \frac{|\cos n\pi|}{n+1} = \sum_{n=0}^{\infty} \frac{1}{n+1}$$

diverges by a limit comparison to the divergent harmonic series,

$$\sum_{n=1}^{\infty} \frac{1}{n}.$$

$\displaystyle\lim_{n\to\infty} \frac{|\cos n\pi|/(n+1)}{1/n} = 1$, therefore the series converges conditionally.

**43.** $\displaystyle\sum_{n=1}^{\infty} \frac{(-1)^{n+1}}{\sqrt{n}}$

The given series converges by the Alternating Series Test, but does not converge absolutely since

$$\sum_{n=1}^{\infty} \frac{1}{\sqrt{n}}$$

is a divergent $p$-series. Therefore, the series converges conditionally.

**47.** $\displaystyle\sum_{n=2}^{\infty} \frac{(-1)^n}{\ln(n)}$

The given series converges by the Alternating Series Test, but does not converge absolutely since the series

$$\sum_{n=2}^{\infty} \frac{1}{\ln n}$$

diverges by comparison to the harmonic series

$$\sum_{n=1}^{\infty} \frac{1}{n}.$$

Therefore, the series converges conditionally.

**51.** $\displaystyle\sum_{n=0}^{\infty} \frac{(-1)^n}{(2n+1)!}$

$$\sum_{n=0}^{\infty} \frac{1}{(2n+1)!}$$

is convergent by comparison to the convergent geometric series

$$\sum_{n=0}^{\infty} \left(\frac{1}{2}\right)^n$$

since

$$\frac{1}{(2n+1)!} < \frac{1}{2^n} \text{ for } n > 0.$$

Therefore, the given series converges absolutely.

**55.** $\displaystyle\sum_{n=1}^{\infty} \frac{\cos n\pi}{n^2} = \sum_{n=1}^{\infty} \frac{(-1)^n}{n^2}$

$\displaystyle\sum_{n=1}^{\infty} \frac{1}{n^2}$ is a convergent $p$-series. Therefore, the given series converges absolutely.

**57.** An alternating series is a series whose terms alternate in sign. See Theorem 8.14.

**59.** $\sum a_n$ is absolutely convergent if $\sum |a_n|$ converges.

$\sum a_n$ is conditionally convergent if $\sum |a_n|$ diverges, but $\sum a_n$ converges.

**61.** (b).  The partial sums alternate above and below the horizontal line representing the sum.

**63.** Since $\displaystyle\sum_{n=1}^{\infty} |a_n|$ converges we have

$$\lim_{n \to \infty} |a_n| = 0.$$

Thus, there must exist an $N > 0$ such that $|a_N| < 1$ for all $n > N$ and it follows that $a_n{}^2 \le |a_n|$ for all $n > N$. Hence, by the Comparison Test,

$$\sum_{n=1}^{\infty} a_n{}^2$$

converges. Let $a_n = 1/n$ to see that the converse is false.

**65.** $\displaystyle\sum_{n=1}^{\infty} \frac{1}{n^2}$ converges, hence so does $\displaystyle\sum_{n=1}^{\infty} \frac{1}{n^4}$.

**67.** False

Let $a_n = \dfrac{(-1)^n}{n}$.

**69.** $\displaystyle\sum_{n=1}^{\infty} \frac{10}{n^{3/2}} = 10 \sum_{n=1}^{\infty} \frac{1}{n^{3/2}}$ convergent $p$-series

**71.** Diverges by $n$th Term Test. $\displaystyle\lim_{n \to \infty} a_n = \infty$

**73.** Convergent Geometric Series $\left(r = \frac{7}{8} < 1\right)$

**75.** Convergent Geometric Series $\left(r = \dfrac{1}{\sqrt{e}}\right)$ or Integral Test

**77.** Converges (absolutely) by Alternating Series Test

**79.** The first term of the series is zero, not one. You cannot regroup series terms arbitrarily.

# Section 8.6    The Ratio and Root Tests

**1.** $\dfrac{(n+1)!}{(n-2)!} = \dfrac{(n+1)(n)(n-1)(n-2)!}{(n-2)!}$

$\qquad\qquad = (n+1)(n)(n-1)$

**3.** Use the Principle of Mathematical Induction. When $k = 1$, the formula is valid since $1 = \dfrac{(2(1))!}{2^1 \cdot 1!}$. Assume that

$$1 \cdot 3 \cdot 5 \cdots (2n-1) = \frac{(2n)!}{2^n n!}$$

and show that

$$1 \cdot 3 \cdot 5 \cdots (2n-1)(2n+1) = \frac{(2n+2)!}{2^{n+1}(n+1)!}.$$

**—CONTINUED—**

**3.** **—CONTINUED—**

To do this, note that:

$$1 \cdot 3 \cdot 5 \cdots (2n - 1)(2n + 1) = [1 \cdot 3 \cdot 5 \cdots (2n - 1)](2n + 1)$$

$$= \frac{(2n)!}{2^n n!} \cdot (2n + 1)$$

$$= \frac{(2n)!(2n + 1)}{2^n n!} \cdot \frac{(2n + 2)}{2(n + 1)}$$

$$= \frac{(2n)!(2n + 1)(2n + 2)}{2^{n+1} n!(n + 1)}$$

$$= \frac{(2n + 2)!}{2^{n+1}(n + 1)}$$

The formula is valid for all $n \geq 1$.

**5.** $\displaystyle\sum_{n=1}^{\infty} n\left(\frac{3}{4}\right)^n = 1\left(\frac{3}{4}\right) + 2\left(\frac{9}{16}\right) + \cdots$

$S_1 = \frac{3}{4}, S_2 \approx 1.875$

Matches (d)

**7.** $\displaystyle\sum_{n=1}^{\infty} \frac{(-3)^{n+1}}{n!} = 9 - \frac{3^3}{2} + \cdots$

$S_1 = 9$

Matches (f)

**9.** $\displaystyle\sum_{n=1}^{\infty} \left(\frac{4n}{5n - 3}\right)^n = \frac{4}{2} + \left(\frac{8}{7}\right)^2 + \cdots$

$S_1 = 2$

Matches (a)

**11.** (a) Ratio Test: $\displaystyle\lim_{n\to\infty} \left|\frac{a_{n+1}}{a_n}\right| = \lim_{n\to\infty} \frac{(n + 1)^2(5/8)^{n+1}}{n^2(5/8)^n} = \lim_{n\to\infty} \left(\frac{n + 1}{n}\right)^2 \frac{5}{8} = \frac{5}{8} < 1.$ Converges

(b)

| $n$ | 5 | 10 | 15 | 20 | 25 |
|---|---|---|---|---|---|
| $S_n$ | 9.2104 | 16.7598 | 18.8016 | 19.1878 | 19.2491 |

(c)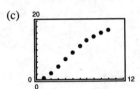

(d) The sum is approximately 19.26.

(e) The more rapidly the terms of the series approach 0, the more rapidly the sequence of the partial sums approaches the sum of the series.

**13.** $\displaystyle\sum_{n=0}^{\infty} \frac{n!}{3^n}$

$$\lim_{n\to\infty} \left|\frac{a_{n+1}}{a_n}\right| = \lim_{n\to\infty} \left|\frac{(n + 1)!}{3^{n+1}} \cdot \frac{3^n}{n!}\right|$$

$$= \lim_{n\to\infty} \frac{n + 1}{3} = \infty$$

Therefore, by the Ratio Test, the series diverges.

**15.** $\displaystyle\sum_{n=1}^{\infty} n\left(\frac{3}{4}\right)^n$

$$\lim_{n\to\infty} \left|\frac{a_n + 1}{a_n}\right| = \lim_{n\to\infty} \left|\frac{(n + 1)(3/4)^{n+1}}{n(3/4)^n}\right|$$

$$= \lim_{n\to\infty} \left|\frac{3(n + 1)}{4n}\right| = \frac{3}{4}$$

Therefore, by the Ratio Test, the series converges.

**17.** $\displaystyle\sum_{n=1}^{\infty} \frac{n}{2^n}$

$$\lim_{n\to\infty} \left|\frac{a_{n+1}}{a_n}\right| = \lim_{n\to\infty} \left|\frac{n + 1}{2^{n+1}} \cdot \frac{2^n}{n}\right|$$

$$= \lim_{n\to\infty} \frac{n + 1}{2n} = \frac{1}{2}$$

Therefore, by the Ratio Test, the series converges.

**19.** $\displaystyle\sum_{n=1}^{\infty} \frac{2^n}{n^2}$

$$\lim_{n\to\infty} \left|\frac{a_{n+1}}{a_n}\right| = \lim_{n\to\infty} \left|\frac{2^{n+1}}{(n + 1)^2} \cdot \frac{n^2}{2^n}\right|$$

$$= \lim_{n\to\infty} \frac{2n^2}{(n + 1)^2} = 2$$

Therefore, by the Ratio Test, the series diverges.

**21.** $\displaystyle\sum_{n=0}^{\infty} \frac{(-1)^n 2^n}{n!}$

$$\lim_{n\to\infty}\left|\frac{a_{n+1}}{a_n}\right| = \lim_{n\to\infty}\left|\frac{2^{n+1}}{(n+1)!}\cdot\frac{n!}{2^n}\right|$$

$$= \lim_{n\to\infty}\frac{2}{n+1} = 0$$

Therefore, by the Ratio Test, the series converges.

**23.** $\displaystyle\sum_{n=1}^{\infty} \frac{n!}{n3^n}$

$$\lim_{n\to\infty}\left|\frac{a_{n+1}}{a_n}\right| = \lim_{n\to\infty}\left|\frac{(n+1)!}{(n+1)3^{n+1}}\cdot\frac{n3^n}{n!}\right|$$

$$= \lim_{n\to\infty}\frac{n}{3} = \infty$$

Therefore, by the Ratio Test, the series diverges.

**25.** $\displaystyle\sum_{n=0}^{\infty} \frac{4^n}{n!}$

$$\lim_{n\to\infty}\left|\frac{a_{n+1}}{a_n}\right| = \lim_{n\to\infty}\left|\frac{4^{n+1}}{(n+1)!}\cdot\frac{n!}{4^n}\right|$$

$$= \lim_{n\to\infty}\frac{4}{n+1} = 0$$

Therefore, by the Ratio Test, the series converges.

**27.** $\displaystyle\sum_{n=0}^{\infty} \frac{3^n}{(n+1)^n}$

$$\lim_{n\to\infty}\left|\frac{a_{n+1}}{a_n}\right| = \lim_{n\to\infty}\left|\frac{3^{n+1}}{(n+2)^{n+1}}\cdot\frac{(n+1)^n}{3^n}\right| = \lim_{n\to\infty}\frac{3(n+1)^n}{(n+2)^{n+1}} = \lim_{n\to\infty}\frac{3}{n+2}\left(\frac{n+1}{n+2}\right)^n = (0)\left(\frac{1}{e}\right) = 0$$

To find $\displaystyle\lim_{n\to\infty}\left(\frac{n+1}{n+2}\right)^n$, let $y = \displaystyle\lim_{n\to\infty}\left(\frac{n+1}{n+2}\right)^n$. Then,

$$\ln y = \lim_{n\to\infty} n\ln\left(\frac{n+1}{n+2}\right) = \lim_{n\to\infty}\frac{\ln[(n+1)/(n+2)]}{1/n} = \frac{0}{0}$$

$$\ln y = \lim_{n\to\infty}\frac{[(1)/(n+1)] - [(1)/(n+2)]}{-(1/n^2)} = -1 \text{ by L'Hôpital's Rule}$$

$$y = e^{-1} = \frac{1}{e}.$$

Therefore, by the Ratio Test, the series converges.

**29.** $\displaystyle\sum_{n=0}^{\infty} \frac{4^n}{3^n + 1}$

$$\lim_{n\to\infty}\left|\frac{a_{n+1}}{a_n}\right| = \lim_{n\to\infty}\left|\frac{4^{n+1}}{3^{n+1}+1}\cdot\frac{3^n+1}{4^n}\right| = \lim_{n\to\infty}\frac{4(3^n+1)}{3^{n+1}+1} = \lim_{n\to\infty}\frac{4(1+1/3^n)}{3+1/3^n} = \frac{4}{3}$$

Therefore, by the Ratio Test, the series diverges.

**31.** $\displaystyle\sum_{n=0}^{\infty} \frac{(-1)^{n+1}n!}{1\cdot 3\cdot 5\cdots(2n+1)}$

$$\lim_{n\to\infty}\left|\frac{a_{n+1}}{a_n}\right| = \lim_{n\to\infty}\left|\frac{(n+1)!}{1\cdot 3\cdot 5\cdots(2n+1)(2n+3)}\cdot\frac{1\cdot 3\cdot 5\cdots(2n+1)}{n!}\right| = \lim_{n\to\infty}\frac{n+1}{2n+3} = \frac{1}{2}$$

Therefore, by the Ratio Test, the series converges.

**Note:** The first few terms of this series are $\displaystyle -1 + \frac{1}{1\cdot 3} - \frac{2!}{1\cdot 3\cdot 5} + \frac{3!}{1\cdot 3\cdot 5\cdot 7} - \cdots$

**33.** (a) $\displaystyle\sum_{n=1}^{\infty} \frac{1}{n^{3/2}}$

$$\lim_{n\to\infty} \left| \frac{a_{n+1}}{a_n} \right| = \lim_{n\to\infty} \left| \frac{1}{(n+1)^{3/2}} \cdot \frac{n^{3/2}}{1} \right| = \lim_{n\to\infty} \left( \frac{n}{n+1} \right)^{3/2} = 1$$

(b) $\displaystyle\sum_{n=1}^{\infty} \frac{1}{n^{1/2}}$

$$\lim_{n\to\infty} \left| \frac{a_{n+1}}{a_n} \right| = \lim_{n\to\infty} \left| \frac{1}{(n+1)^{1/2}} \cdot \frac{n^{1/2}}{1} \right| = \lim_{n\to\infty} \left( \frac{n}{n+1} \right)^{1/2} = 1$$

**35.** $\displaystyle\sum_{n=1}^{\infty} \left( \frac{n}{2n+1} \right)^n$

$$\lim_{n\to\infty} \sqrt[n]{|a_n|} = \lim_{n\to\infty} \sqrt[n]{\left( \frac{n}{2n+1} \right)^n}$$

$$= \lim_{n\to\infty} \frac{n}{2n+1} = \frac{1}{2}$$

Therefore, by the Root Test, the series converges.

**37.** $\displaystyle\sum_{n=2}^{\infty} \frac{(-1)^n}{(\ln n)^n}$

$$\lim_{n\to\infty} \sqrt[n]{|a_n|} = \lim_{n\to\infty} \sqrt[n]{\left| \frac{(-1)^n}{(\ln n)^n} \right|}$$

$$= \lim_{n\to\infty} \frac{1}{|\ln n|} = 0$$

Therefore, by the Root Test, the series converges.

**39.** $\displaystyle\sum_{n=1}^{\infty} \left( 2\sqrt[n]{n} + 1 \right)^n$

$$\lim_{n\to\infty} \sqrt[n]{|a_n|} = \lim_{n\to\infty} \sqrt[n]{\left( 2\sqrt[n]{n} + 1 \right)^n} = \lim_{n\to\infty} \left( 2\sqrt[n]{n} + 1 \right)$$

To find $\displaystyle\lim_{n\to\infty} \sqrt[n]{n}$, let $y = \lim_{n\to\infty} \sqrt[x]{x}$. Then

$$\ln y = \lim_{n\to\infty} \left( \ln \sqrt[x]{x} \right) = \lim_{n\to\infty} \frac{1}{x} \ln x = \lim_{n\to\infty} \frac{\ln x}{x} = \lim_{n\to\infty} \frac{1/x}{1} = 0.$$

Thus, $\ln y = 0$, so $y = e^0 = 1$ and $\displaystyle\lim_{n\to\infty} \left( 2\sqrt[n]{n} + 1 \right) = 2(1) + 1 = 3$. Therefore, by the Root Test, the series diverges.

**41.** $\displaystyle\sum_{n=3}^{\infty} \frac{1}{(\ln n)^n}$

$$\lim_{n\to\infty} \sqrt[n]{|a_n|} = \lim_{n\to\infty} \sqrt[n]{\frac{1}{(\ln n)^n}} = \lim_{n\to\infty} \frac{1}{\ln n} = 0$$

Therefore, by the Root Test, the series converges.

**43.** $\displaystyle\sum_{n=1}^{\infty} \frac{(-1)^{n+1} 5}{n}$

$$a_{n+1} = \frac{5}{n+1} < \frac{5}{n} = a_n$$

$$\lim_{n\to\infty} \frac{5}{n} = 0$$

Therefore, by the Alternating Series Test, the series converges (conditional convergence).

**45.** $\displaystyle\sum_{n=1}^{\infty} \frac{3}{n\sqrt{n}} = 3\sum_{n=1}^{\infty} \frac{1}{n^{3/2}}$

This is convergent $p$-series.

**47.** $\displaystyle\sum_{n=1}^{\infty} \frac{2n}{n+1}$

$$\lim_{n\to\infty} \frac{2n}{n+1} = 2 \neq 0$$

This diverges by the $n$th Term Test for Divergence.

**49.** $\displaystyle\sum_{n=1}^{\infty} \frac{(-1)^n 3^{n-2}}{2^n} = \sum_{n=1}^{\infty} \frac{(-1)^n 3^n 3^{-2}}{2^n} = \sum_{n=1}^{\infty} \frac{1}{9}\left( -\frac{3}{2} \right)^n$

Since $|r| = \frac{3}{2} > 1$, this is a divergent geometric series.

**51.** $\displaystyle\sum_{n=1}^{\infty} \frac{10n+3}{n2^n}$

$$\lim_{n\to\infty} \frac{(10n+3)/n2^n}{1/2^n} = \lim_{n\to\infty} \frac{10n+3}{n} = 10$$

Therefore, the series converges by a limit comparison test with the geometric series

$$\sum_{n=0}^{\infty} \left( \frac{1}{2} \right)^n.$$

**53.** $\displaystyle\sum_{n=1}^{\infty} \frac{\cos(n)}{2^n}$

$$\left| \frac{\cos(n)}{2^n} \right| \leq \frac{1}{2^n}$$

Therefore, the series

$$\sum_{n=1}^{\infty} \left| \frac{\cos(n)}{2^n} \right|$$

converges by comparison with the geometric series

$$\sum_{n=0}^{\infty} \left( \frac{1}{2} \right)^n .$$

**55.** $\displaystyle\sum_{n=1}^{\infty} \frac{n7^n}{n!}$

$$\lim_{n \to \infty} \left| \frac{a_{n+1}}{a_n} \right| = \lim_{n \to \infty} \left| \frac{(n+1)7^{n+1}}{(n+1)!} \cdot \frac{n!}{n7^n} \right| = \lim_{n \to \infty} \frac{7}{n} = 0$$

Therefore, by the Ratio Test, the series converges.

**57.** $\displaystyle\sum_{n=1}^{\infty} \frac{(-1)^n \, 3^{n-1}}{n!}$

$$\lim_{n \to \infty} \left| \frac{a_{n+1}}{a_n} \right| = \lim_{n \to \infty} \left| \frac{3^n}{(n+1)!} \cdot \frac{n!}{3^{n-1}} \right| = \lim_{n \to \infty} \frac{3}{n+1} = 0$$

Therefore, by the Ratio Test, the series converges.

**59.** $\displaystyle\sum_{n=1}^{\infty} \frac{(-3)^n}{3 \cdot 5 \cdot 7 \cdots (2n+1)}$

$$\lim_{n \to \infty} \left| \frac{a_{n+1}}{a_n} \right| = \lim_{n \to \infty} \left| \frac{(-3)^{n+1}}{3 \cdot 5 \cdot 7 \cdots (2n+1)(2n+3)} \cdot \frac{3 \cdot 5 \cdot 7 \cdots (2n+1)}{(-3)^n} \right| = \lim_{n \to \infty} \frac{3}{2n+3} = 0$$

Therefore, by the Ratio Test, the series converges.

**61.** (a) and (c)

$$\sum_{n=1}^{\infty} \frac{n5^n}{n!} = \sum_{n=0}^{\infty} \frac{(n+1)5^{n+1}}{(n+1)!}$$

$$= 5 + \frac{(2)(5)^2}{2!} + \frac{(3)(5)^3}{3!} + \frac{(4)(5)^4}{4!} + \cdots$$

**63.** (a) and (b) are the same.

**65.** Replace $n$ with $n+1$.

$$\sum_{n=1}^{\infty} \frac{n}{4^n} = \sum_{n=0}^{\infty} \frac{n+1}{4^{n+1}}$$

**67.** Since

$$\frac{3^{10}}{2^{10} \, 10!} = 1.59 \times 10^{-5},$$

use 9 terms.

$$\sum_{k=1}^{9} \frac{(-3)^k}{2^k \, k!} \approx -0.7769$$

**69.** See Theorem 8.17, page 597.

**71.** No. Let $a_n = \dfrac{1}{n + 10,000}$.

The series $\displaystyle\sum_{n=1}^{\infty} \frac{1}{n + 10,000}$ diverges.

**73.** The series converges absolutely. See Theorem 8.17.

**75.** First, let

$$\lim_{n\to\infty} \sqrt[n]{|a_n|} = r < 1$$

and choose $R$ such that $0 \le r < R < 1$. There must exist some $N > 0$ such that $\sqrt[n]{|a_n|} < R$ for all $n > N$. Thus, for $n > N$, we $|a_n| < R^n$ and since the geometric series

$$\sum_{n=0}^{\infty} R^n$$

converges, we can apply the Comparison Test to conclude that

$$\sum_{n=1}^{\infty} |a_n|$$

converges which in turn implies that $\sum_{n=1}^{\infty} a_n$ converges.

Second, let

$$\lim_{n\to\infty} \sqrt[n]{|a_n|} = r > R > 1.$$

Then there must exist some $M > 0$ such that $\sqrt[n]{|a_n|} > R$ for all $n > M$. Thus, for $n > M$, we have $|a_n| > R_n > 1$ which implies that $\lim_{n\to\infty} a_n \ne 0$ which in turn implies that

$$\sum_{n=1}^{\infty} a_n \text{ diverges.}$$

# Section 8.7    Taylor Polynomials and Approximations

**1.** $y = -\frac{1}{2}x^2 + 1$

Parabola

Matches (d)

**3.** $y = e^{-1/2}[(x+1)+1]$

Linear

Matches (a)

**5.** $f(x) = \dfrac{4}{\sqrt{x}} = 4x^{-1/2}$    $f(1) = 4$

$f'(x) = -2x^{-3/2}$    $f'(1) = -2$

$P_1(x) = f(1) + f'(1)(x - 1)$

$\qquad = 4 + (-2)(x - 1)$

$P_1(x) = -2x + 6$

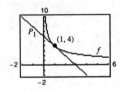

**7.** $f(x) = \sec x$    $f\left(\dfrac{\pi}{4}\right) = \sqrt{2}$

$f'(x) = \sec x \tan x$    $f'\left(\dfrac{\pi}{4}\right) = \sqrt{2}$

$P_1(x) = f\left(\dfrac{\pi}{4}\right) + f'\left(\dfrac{\pi}{4}\right)\left(x - \dfrac{\pi}{4}\right)$

$P_1(x) = \sqrt{2} + \sqrt{2}\left(x - \dfrac{\pi}{4}\right)$

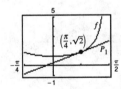

**9.** $f(x) = \dfrac{4}{\sqrt{x}} = 4x^{-1/2}$    $f(1) = 4$

$f'(x) = -2x^{-3/2}$    $f'(1) = -2$

$f''(x) = 3x^{-5/2}$    $f''(1) = 3$

$P_2 = f(1) + f'(1)(x - 1) + \dfrac{f''(1)}{2}(x - 1)^2$

$\qquad = 4 - 2(x - 1) + \dfrac{3}{2}(x - 1)^2$

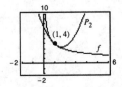

| $x$ | 0 | 0.8 | 0.9 | 1.0 | 1.1 | 1.2 | 2 |
|---|---|---|---|---|---|---|---|
| $f(x)$ | Error | 4.4721 | 4.2164 | 4.0 | 3.8139 | 3.6515 | 2.8284 |
| $P_2(x)$ | 7.5 | 4.46 | 4.215 | 4.0 | 3.815 | 3.66 | 3.5 |

**11.** $f(x) = \cos x$

$P_2(x) = 1 - \frac{1}{2}x^2$

$P_4(x) = 1 - \frac{1}{2}x^2 + \frac{1}{24}x^4$

$P_6(x) = 1 - \frac{1}{2}x^2 + \frac{1}{24}x^4 - \frac{1}{720}x^6$

(a)

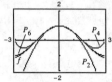

(b) $f'(x) = -\sin x \qquad P_2'(x) = -x$

$\quad f''(x) = -\cos x \qquad P_2''(x) = -1$

$\quad f''(0) = P_2''(0) = -1$

$\quad f'''(x) = \sin x \qquad P_4'''(x) = x$

$\quad f^{(4)}(x) = \cos x \qquad P_4^{(4)}(x) = 1$

$\quad f^{(4)}(0) = 1 = P_4^{(4)}(0)$

$\quad f^{(5)}(x) = -\sin x \qquad P_6^{(5)}(x) = -x$

$\quad f^{(6)}(x) = -\cos x \qquad P^{(6)}(x) = -1$

$\quad f^{(6)}(0) = -1 = P_6^{(6)}(0)$

(c) In general, $f^{(n)}(0) = P_n^{(n)}(0)$ for all $n$.

**13.** $f(x) = e^{-x} \qquad\qquad f(0) = 1$

$\quad f'(x) = -e^{-x} \qquad\quad f'(0) = -1$

$\quad f''(x) = e^{-x} \qquad\qquad f''(0) = 1$

$\quad f'''(x) = -e^{-x} \qquad\quad f'''(0) = -1$

$P_3(x) = f(0) + f'(0)x + \frac{f''(0)}{2!}x^2 + \frac{f'''(0)}{3!}x^3$

$\qquad = 1 - x + \frac{x^2}{2} - \frac{x^3}{6}$

**15.** $f(x) = e^{2x} \qquad\qquad f(0) = 1$

$\quad f'(x) = 2e^{2x} \qquad\quad f'(0) = 2$

$\quad f''(x) = 4e^{2x} \qquad\quad f''(0) = 4$

$\quad f'''(x) = 8e^{2x} \qquad\quad f'''(0) = 8$

$\quad f^{(4)}(x) = 16^{2x} \qquad f^{(4)}(0) = 16$

$P_4(x) = 1 + 2x + \frac{4}{2!}x^2 + \frac{8}{3!}x^3 + \frac{16}{4!}x^4$

$\qquad = 1 + 2x + 2x^2 + \frac{4}{3}x^3 + \frac{2}{3}x^4$

**17.** $f(x) = \sin x \qquad\qquad f(0) = 0$

$\quad f'(x) = \cos x \qquad\qquad f'(0) = 1$

$\quad f''(x) = -\sin x \qquad\quad f''(0) = 0$

$\quad f'''(x) = -\cos x \qquad\quad f'''(0) = -1$

$\quad f^{(4)}(x) = \sin x \qquad\quad f^{(4)}(0) = 0$

$\quad f^{(5)}(x) = \cos x \qquad\quad f^{(5)}(0) = 1$

$P_5(x) = 0 + (1)x + \frac{0}{2!}x^2 + \frac{-1}{3!}x^3 + \frac{0}{4!}x^4 + \frac{1}{5!}x^5$

$\qquad = x - \frac{1}{6}x^3 + \frac{1}{120}x^5$

**19.** $f(x) = xe^x \qquad\qquad f(0) = 0$

$\quad f'(x) = xe^x + e^x \qquad\quad f'(0) = 1$

$\quad f''(x) = xe^x + 2e^x \qquad f''(0) = 2$

$\quad f'''(x) = xe^x + 3e^x \qquad f'''(0) = 3$

$\quad f^{(4)}(x) = xe^x + 4e^x \qquad f^{(4)}(0) = 4$

$P_4(x) = 0 + x + \frac{2}{2!}x^2 + \frac{3}{3!}x^3 + \frac{4}{4!}x^4$

$\qquad = x + x^2 + \frac{1}{2}x^3 + \frac{1}{6}x^4$

**21.** $f(x) = \dfrac{1}{x+1} \qquad\qquad f(0) = 1$

$\quad f'(x) = -\dfrac{1}{(x+1)^2} \qquad\quad f'(0) = -1$

$\quad f''(x) = \dfrac{2}{(x+1)^2} \qquad\quad f''(0) = 2$

$\quad f'''(x) = \dfrac{-6}{(x+1)^4} \qquad\quad f'''(0) = -6$

$\quad f^{(4)}(x) = \dfrac{24}{(x+1)^5} \qquad f^{(4)}(0) = 24$

$P_4(x) = 1 - x + \frac{2}{2!}x^2 + \frac{-6}{3!}x^3 + \frac{24}{4!}x^4$

$\qquad = 1 - x + x^2 - x^3 + x^4$

**23.** $f(x) = \sec x \qquad\qquad f(0) = 1$

$\quad f'(x) = \sec x \tan x \qquad\qquad f'(0) = 0$

$\quad f''(x) = \sec^3 x + \sec x \tan^2 x \qquad f''(0) = 1$

$P_2(x) = 1 + 0x + \frac{1}{2!}x^2 = 1 + \frac{1}{2}x^2$

**25.**  $f(x) = \dfrac{1}{x}$        $f(1) = 1$

$f'(x) = -\dfrac{1}{x^2}$      $f'(1) = -1$

$f''(x) = \dfrac{2}{x^3}$        $f''(1) = 2$

$f'''(x) = -\dfrac{6}{x^4}$      $f'''(1) = -6$

$f^{(4)}(x) = \dfrac{24}{x^5}$      $f^{(4)}(1) = 24$

$P_4(x) = 1 - (x - 1) + \dfrac{2}{2!}(x - 1)^2 + \dfrac{-6}{3!}(x - 1)^3 + \dfrac{24}{4!}(x - 1)^4$

$\qquad = 1 - (x - 1) + (x - 1)^2 - (x - 1)^3 + (x - 1)^4$

**27.**      $f(x) = \sqrt{x}$            $f(1) = 1$

$f'(x) = \dfrac{1}{2\sqrt{x}}$        $f'(1) = \dfrac{1}{2}$

$f''(x) = -\dfrac{1}{4x\sqrt{x}}$      $f''(1) = -\dfrac{1}{4}$

$f'''(x) = \dfrac{3}{8x^2\sqrt{x}}$      $f'''(1) = \dfrac{3}{8}$

$f^{(4)}(x) = -\dfrac{15}{16x^3\sqrt{x}}$      $f^{(4)}(1) = -\dfrac{15}{16}$

$P_4(x) = 1 + \dfrac{1}{2}(x - 1) - \dfrac{1}{8}(x - 1)^2$

$\qquad\qquad + \dfrac{1}{16}(x - 1)^3 - \dfrac{5}{128}(x - 1)^4$

**29.**   $f(x) = \ln x$        $f(1) = 0$

$f'(x) = \dfrac{1}{x}$        $f'(1) = 1$

$f''(x) = -\dfrac{1}{x^2}$        $f''(1) = -1$

$f'''(x) = \dfrac{2}{x^3}$        $f'''(1) = 2$

$f^{(4)}(x) = -\dfrac{6}{x^4}$        $f^{(4)}(1) = -6$

$P_4(x) = 0 + (x - 1) - \dfrac{1}{2}(x - 1)^2$

$\qquad\qquad + \dfrac{1}{3}(x - 1)^3 - \dfrac{1}{4}(x - 1)^4$

**31.**   $f(x) = \tan x$

$f'(x) = \sec^2 x$

$f''(x) = 2\sec^2 x \tan x$

$f'''(x) = 4\sec^2 x \tan^2 x + 2\sec^4 x$

$f^{(4)}(x) = 8\sec^2 x \tan^3 x + 16\sec^4 x \tan x$

$f^{(5)}(x) = 16\sec^2 x \tan^4 x + 88\sec^4 x \tan^2 x + 16\sec^6 x$

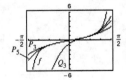

(a) $n = 3, c = 0$

$P_3(x) = 0 + x + \dfrac{0}{2!}x^2 + \dfrac{2}{3!}x^3 = x + \dfrac{1}{3}x^3$

(b) $n = 5, c = 0$

$P_5(x) = 0 + x + \dfrac{0}{2!}x^2 + \dfrac{2}{3!}x^3 + \dfrac{0}{4!}x^4 + \dfrac{16}{5!}x^5$

$\qquad = x + \dfrac{1}{3}x^3 + \dfrac{2}{15}x^5$

(c) $n = 3, c = \dfrac{\pi}{4}$

$Q_3(x) = 1 + 2\left(x - \dfrac{\pi}{4}\right) + \dfrac{4}{2!}\left(x - \dfrac{\pi}{4}\right)^2 + \dfrac{16}{3!}\left(x - \dfrac{\pi}{4}\right)^3$

$\qquad = 1 + 2\left(x - \dfrac{\pi}{4}\right) + 2\left(x - \dfrac{\pi}{4}\right)^2 + \dfrac{8}{3}\left(x - \dfrac{\pi}{4}\right)^3$

**33.** $f(x) = \sin x$

$P_1(x) = x$

$P_3(x) = x - \frac{1}{6}x^3$

$P_5(x) = x - \frac{1}{6}x^3 + \frac{1}{120}x^5$

$P_7(x) = x - \frac{1}{6}x^3 + \frac{1}{120}x^5 - \frac{1}{5040}x^7$

(a)

| $x$ | 0.00 | 0.25 | 0.50 | 0.75 | 1.00 |
|---|---|---|---|---|---|
| $\sin x$ | 0.0000 | 0.2474 | 0.4794 | 0.6816 | 0.8415 |
| $P_1(x)$ | 0.0000 | 0.2500 | 0.5000 | 0.7500 | 1.0000 |
| $P_3(x)$ | 0.0000 | 0.2474 | 0.4792 | 0.6797 | 0.8333 |
| $P_5(x)$ | 0.0000 | 0.2474 | 0.4794 | 0.6817 | 0.8417 |
| $P_7(x)$ | 0.0000 | 0.2474 | 0.4794 | 0.6816 | 0.8415 |

(b)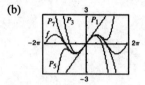

(c) As the distance increases, the accuracy decreases

**35.** $f(x) = \arcsin x$

(a) $P_3(x) = x + \dfrac{x^3}{6}$

(c)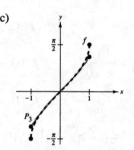

(b)

| $x$ | $-0.75$ | $-0.50$ | $-0.25$ | 0 | 0.25 | 0.50 | 0.75 |
|---|---|---|---|---|---|---|---|
| $f(x)$ | $-0.848$ | $-0.524$ | $-0.253$ | 0 | 0.253 | 0.524 | 0.848 |
| $P_3(x)$ | $-0.820$ | $-0.521$ | $-0.253$ | 0 | 0.253 | 0.521 | 0.820 |

**37.** $f(x) = \cos x$

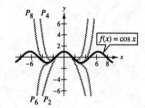

**39.** $f(x) = \ln(x^2 + 1)$

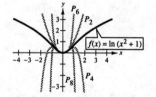

**41.** $f(x) = e^{-x} \approx 1 - x + \dfrac{x^2}{2} - \dfrac{x^3}{6}$

$f\left(\dfrac{1}{2}\right) \approx 0.6042$

**43.** $f(x) = \ln x \approx (x - 1) - \frac{1}{2}(x - 1)^2 + \frac{1}{3}(x - 1)^3 - \frac{1}{4}(x - 1)^4$

$f(1.2) \approx 0.1823$

**45.** $f(x) = \cos x; f^{(5)}(x) = -\sin x \Rightarrow$ Max on $[0, 0.3]$ is 1.

$R_4(x) \leq \dfrac{1}{5!}(0.3)^5 = 2.025 \times 10^{-5}$

**47.** $f(x) = \arcsin x; f^{(4)}(x) = \dfrac{x(6x^2 + 9)}{(1 - x^2)^{7/2}} \Longrightarrow$ Max on $[0, 0.4]$ is $f^{(4)}(0.4) \approx 7.3340$.

$$R_3(x) \le \frac{7.3340}{4!}(0.4)^4 \approx 0.00782 = 7.82 \times 10^{-3}$$

**49.** $g(x) = \sin x$

$g^{(n+1)}(x) \le 1$ for all $x$

$$R_n(x) \le \frac{1}{(n + 1)!}(0.3)^{n+1} < 0.001$$

By trial and error, $n = 3$.

**51.** $f(x) = \ln(x + 1)$

$$f^{(n+1)}(x) = \frac{(-1)^{n+1}n!}{(x + 1)^{n+1}} \Longrightarrow \text{Max on } [0, 0.5] \text{ is } n!.$$

$$R_n \le \frac{n!}{(n + 1)!}(0.5)^{n+1} = \frac{(0.5)^{n+1}}{n + 1} < 0.0001$$

By trial and error, $n = 9$. (See Example 9.) Using 9 terms, $\ln(1.5) \approx 0.4055$.

**53.** $\qquad f(x) = e^x \approx 1 + x + \dfrac{x^2}{2} + \dfrac{x^3}{6}, \; x < 0$

$$R_3(x) = \frac{e^z}{4!}x^4 < 0.001$$

$$e^z x^4 < 0.024$$

$$xe^{z/4} < 0.3936$$

$$x < \frac{0.3936}{e^{z/4}} < 0.3936, \; z < 0$$

$-0.3936 < x < 0$

**55.** The graph of the approximating polynomial $P$ and the elementary function $f$ both pass through the point $(c, f(c))$ and the slopes of $P$ and $f$ agree at $(c, f(c))$. Depending on the degree of $P$, the $n$th derivatives of $P$ and $f$ agree at $(c, f(c))$.

**57.** See definition on page 607.

**59.** The accuracy increases as the degree increases (for values within the interval of convergence).

**61.** (a) $f(x) = e^x$

$$P_4(x) = 1 + x + \frac{1}{2}x^2 + \frac{1}{6}x^3 + \frac{1}{24}x^4$$

$g(x) = xe^x$

$$Q_5(x) = x + x^2 + \frac{1}{2}x^3 + \frac{1}{6}x^4 + \frac{1}{24}x^5$$

$$Q_5(x) = x\,P_4(x)$$

(b) $f(x) = \sin x$

$$P_5(x) = x - \frac{x^3}{3!} + \frac{x^5}{5!}$$

$g(x) = x \sin x$

$$Q_6(x) = x\,P_5(x) = x^2 - \frac{x^4}{3!} + \frac{x^6}{5!}$$

(c) $g(x) = \dfrac{\sin x}{x} = \dfrac{1}{x}P_5(x) = 1 - \dfrac{x^2}{3!} + \dfrac{x^4}{5!}$

**63.** (a) $Q_2(x) = -1 + \dfrac{\pi^2(x + 2)^2}{32}$

(b) $R_2(x) = -1 + \dfrac{\pi^2(x - 6)^2}{32}$

(c) No. The polynomial will be linear.
   Translations are possible at $x = -2 + 8n$.

**65.** Let $f$ be an even function and $P_n$ be the $n$th Maclaurin polynomial for $f$. Since $f$ is even, $f'$ is odd, $f''$ is even, $f'''$ is odd, etc. (see Exercise 45). All of the odd derivatives of $f$ are odd and thus, all of the odd powers of $x$ will have coefficients of zero. $P_n$ will only have terms with even powers of $x$.

**67.** As you move away from $x = c$, the Taylor Polynomial becomes less and less accurate.

# Section 8.8    Power Series

**1.** Centered at 0

**3.** Centered at 2

**5.** $\displaystyle\sum_{n=0}^{\infty} (-1)^n \frac{x^n}{n+1}$

$$L = \lim_{n\to\infty} \left| \frac{u_{n+1}}{u_n} \right| = \lim_{n\to\infty} \left| \frac{(-1)^{n+1}x^{n+1}}{n+2} \cdot \frac{n+1}{(-1)^n x^n} \right|$$

$$= \lim_{n\to\infty} \left| \frac{n+1}{n+2} \right| |x| = |x|$$

$$|x| < 1 \Rightarrow R = 1$$

**7.** $\displaystyle\sum_{n=1}^{\infty} \frac{(2x)^n}{n^2}$

$$L = \lim_{n\to\infty} \left| \frac{u_{n+1}}{u_n} \right| = \lim_{n\to\infty} \left| \frac{(2x)^{n+1}}{(n+1)^2} \cdot \frac{n^2}{(2x)^n} \right|$$

$$= \lim_{n\to\infty} \left| \frac{2n^2 x}{(n+1)^2} \right| = 2|x|$$

$$2|x| < 1 \Rightarrow R = \frac{1}{2}$$

**9.** $\displaystyle\sum_{n=0}^{\infty} \frac{(2x)^{2n}}{(2n)!}$

$$L = \lim_{n\to\infty} \left| \frac{u_n + 1}{u_n} \right| = \lim_{n\to\infty} \left| \frac{(2x)^{2n+2}/(2n+2)!}{(2x)^{2n}/(2n)!} \right|$$

$$= \lim_{n\to\infty} \left| \frac{(2x)^2}{(2n+2)(2n+1)} \right| = 0$$

Thus, the series converges for all $x$. $R = \infty$.

**11.** $\displaystyle\sum_{n=0}^{\infty} \left( \frac{x}{2} \right)^n$

Since the series is geometric, it converges only if $|x/2| < 1$ or $-2 < x < 2$.

**13.** $\displaystyle\sum_{n=1}^{\infty} \frac{(-1)^n x^n}{n}$

$$\lim_{n\to\infty} \left| \frac{u_{n+1}}{u_n} \right| = \lim_{n\to\infty} \left| \frac{(-1)^{n+1}x^{n+1}}{n+1} \cdot \frac{n}{(-1)^n x^n} \right|$$

$$= \lim_{n\to\infty} \left| \frac{nx}{n+1} \right| = |x|$$

Interval: $-1 < x < 1$

When $x = 1$, the alternating series $\displaystyle\sum_{n=1}^{\infty} \frac{(-1)^n}{n}$ converges.

When $x = -1$, the $p$-series $\displaystyle\sum_{n=1}^{\infty} \frac{1}{n}$ diverges.

Therefore, the interval of convergence is $-1 < x \le 1$.

**15.** $\displaystyle\sum_{n=0}^{\infty} \frac{x^n}{n!}$

$$\lim_{n\to\infty} \left| \frac{u_{n+1}}{u_n} \right| = \lim_{n\to\infty} \left| \frac{x^{n+1}}{(n+1)!} \cdot \frac{n!}{x^n} \right|$$

$$= \lim_{n\to\infty} \left| \frac{x}{n+1} \right| = 0$$

The series converges for all $x$. Therefore, the interval of convergence is $-\infty < x < \infty$.

**17.** $\displaystyle\sum_{n=0}^{\infty} (2n)! \left( \frac{x}{2} \right)^n$

$$\lim_{n\to\infty} \left| \frac{u_{n+1}}{u_n} \right| = \lim_{n\to\infty} \left| \frac{(2n+2)! x^{n+1}}{2^{n+1}} \cdot \frac{2^n}{(2n)! x^n} \right| = \lim_{n\to\infty} \left| \frac{(2n+2)(2n+1)x}{2} \right| = \infty$$

Therefore, the series converges only for $x = 0$.

**19.** $\displaystyle\sum_{n=1}^{\infty} \frac{(-1)^{n+1} x^n}{4^n}$

Since the series is geometric, it converges only if $|x/4| < 1$ or $-4 < x < 4$.

**21.** $\displaystyle\sum_{n=1}^{\infty} \frac{(-1)^{n+1}(x-5)^n}{n5^n}$

$$\lim_{n\to\infty}\left|\frac{u_{n+1}}{u_n}\right| = \lim_{n\to\infty}\left|\frac{(-1)^{n+2}(x-5)^{n+1}}{(n+1)5^{n+1}}\cdot\frac{n5^n}{(-1)^{n+1}(x-5)^n}\right| = \lim_{n\to\infty}\left|\frac{n(x-5)}{5(n+1)}\right| = \frac{1}{5}|x-5|$$

$R=5$

Center: $x=5$

Interval: $-5 < x-5 < 5$ or $0 < x < 10$

When $x=0$, the $p$-series $\displaystyle\sum_{n=1}^{\infty}\frac{-1}{n}$ diverges.

When $x=10$, the alternating series $\displaystyle\sum_{n=1}^{\infty}\frac{(-1)^{n+1}}{n}$ converges.

Therefore, the interval of convergence is $0 < x \le 10$.

**23.** $\displaystyle\sum_{n=0}^{\infty} \frac{(-1)^{n+1}(x-1)^{n+1}}{n+1}$

$$\lim_{n\to\infty}\left|\frac{u_{n+1}}{u_n}\right| = \lim_{n\to\infty}\left|\frac{(-1)^{n+2}(x-1)^{n+2}}{n+2}\cdot\frac{n+1}{(-1)^{n+1}(x-1)^{n+1}}\right| = \lim_{n\to\infty}\left|\frac{(n+1)(x-1)}{n+2}\right| = |x-1|$$

$R=1$

Center: $x=1$

Interval: $-1 < x-1 < 1$ or $0 < x < 2$

When $x=0$, the series $\displaystyle\sum_{n=0}^{\infty}\frac{1}{n+1}$ diverges by the integral test.

When $x=2$, the alternating series $\displaystyle\sum_{n=0}^{\infty}\frac{(-1)^{n+1}}{n+1}$ converges.

Therefore, the interval of convergence is $0 < x \le 2$.

**25.** $\displaystyle\sum_{n=1}^{\infty} \frac{(x-c)^{n-1}}{c^{n-1}}$

$$\lim_{n\to\infty}\left|\frac{u_{n+1}}{u_n}\right| = \lim_{n\to\infty}\left|\frac{(x-c)^n}{c^n}\cdot\frac{c^{n-1}}{(x-c)^{n-1}}\right| = \frac{1}{c}|x-c|$$

$R=c$

Center: $x=c$

Interval: $-c < x-c < c$ or $0 < x < 2c$

When $x=0$, the series $\displaystyle\sum_{n=1}^{\infty}(-1)^{n-1}$ diverges.

When $x=2c$, the series $\displaystyle\sum_{n=1}^{\infty}1$ diverges.

Therefore, the interval of convergence is $0 < x < 2c$.

**27.** $\displaystyle\sum_{n=1}^{\infty} \frac{n}{n+1}(-2x)^{n-1}$

$$\lim_{n\to\infty}\left|\frac{u_{n+1}}{u_n}\right| = \lim_{n\to\infty}\left|\frac{(n+1)(-2x)^n}{n+2}\cdot\frac{n+1}{n(-2x)^{n-1}}\right|$$

$$= \lim_{n\to\infty}\left|\frac{(-2x)(n+1)^2}{n(n+2)}\right| = 2|x|$$

$R = \dfrac{1}{2}$

Interval: $-\dfrac{1}{2} < x < \dfrac{1}{2}$

When $x=-\dfrac{1}{2}$, the series $\displaystyle\sum_{n=1}^{\infty}\frac{n}{n+1}$ diverges
by the $n$th Term Test.

When $x=\dfrac{1}{2}$, the alternating series $\displaystyle\sum_{n=1}^{\infty}\frac{(-1)^{n-1}n}{n+1}$ diverges.

Therefore, the interval of convergence is $-\dfrac{1}{2} < x < \dfrac{1}{2}$.

**29.** $\displaystyle\sum_{n=0}^{\infty} \frac{x^{2n+1}}{(2n+1)!}$

$$\lim_{n\to\infty} \left| \frac{u_{n+1}}{u_n} \right| = \lim_{n\to\infty} \left| \frac{x^{2n+3}}{(2n+3)!} \cdot \frac{(2n+1)!}{x^{2n+1}} \right|$$

$$= \lim_{n\to\infty} \left| \frac{x^2}{(2n+2)(2n+3)} \right| = 0$$

Therefore, the interval of convergence is $-\infty < x < \infty$.

**31.** $\displaystyle\sum_{n=1}^{\infty} \frac{k(k+1)\cdots(k+n-1)x^n}{n!}$

$$\lim_{n\to\infty} \left| \frac{u_{n+1}}{u_n} \right| = \lim_{n\to\infty} \left| \frac{k(k+1)\cdots(k+n-1)(k+n)x^{n+1}}{(n+1)!} \cdot \frac{n!}{k(k+1)\cdots(k+n-1)x^n} \right| = \lim_{n\to\infty} \left| \frac{(k+n)x}{n+1} \right| = |x|$$

$R = 1$

When $x = \pm 1$, the series diverges and the interval of convergence is $-1 < x < 1$.

$$\left[ \frac{k(k+1)\cdots(k+n-1)}{1 \cdot 2 \cdots n} \geq 1 \right]$$

**33.** $\displaystyle\sum_{n=1}^{\infty} \frac{(-1)^{n+1}3 \cdot 7 \cdot 11 \cdots (4n-1)(x-3)^n}{4^n}$

$$\lim_{n\to\infty} \left| \frac{u_{n+1}}{u_n} \right| = \lim_{n\to\infty} \left| \frac{(-1)^{n+2} \cdot 3 \cdot 7 \cdot 11 \cdots (4n-1)(4n+3)(x-3)^{n+1}}{4^{n+1}} \cdot \frac{4^n}{(-1)^{n+1} \cdot 3 \cdot 7 \cdot 11 \cdots (4n-1)(x-3)^n} \right|$$

$$= \lim_{n\to\infty} \left| \frac{(4n+3)(x-3)}{4} \right| = \infty$$

$R = 0$

Center: $x = 3$

Therefore, the series converges only for $x = 3$.

**35.** (a) $\displaystyle f(x) = \sum_{n=0}^{\infty} \left(\frac{x}{2}\right)^n, -2 < x < 2$   (Geometric)

(b) $\displaystyle f'(x) = \sum_{n=1}^{\infty} \left(\frac{n}{2}\right)\left(\frac{x}{2}\right)^{n-1}, -2 < x < 2$

(c) $\displaystyle f''(x) = \sum_{n=2}^{\infty} \left(\frac{n}{2}\right)\left(\frac{n-1}{2}\right)\left(\frac{x}{2}\right)^{n-2}, -2 < x < 2$

(d) $\displaystyle \int f(x)\, dx = \sum_{n=0}^{\infty} \frac{2}{n+1}\left(\frac{x}{2}\right)^{n+1}, -2 \leq x < 2$

**37.** (a) $\displaystyle f(x) = \sum_{n=0}^{\infty} \frac{(-1)^{n+1}(x-1)^{n+1}}{n+1}, 0 < x \leq 2$

(b) $\displaystyle f'(x) = \sum_{n=0}^{\infty} (-1)^{n+1}(x-1)^n, 0 < x < 2$

(c) $\displaystyle f''(x) = \sum_{n=1}^{\infty} (-1)^{n+1}n(x-1)^{n-1}, 0 < x < 2$

(d) $\displaystyle \int f(x)\, dx = \sum_{n=1}^{\infty} \frac{(-1)^{n+1}(x-1)^{n+2}}{(n+1)(n+2)}, 0 \leq x \leq 2$

**39.** $\displaystyle g(1) = \sum_{n=0}^{\infty} \left(\frac{1}{3}\right)^n = 1 + \frac{1}{3} + \frac{1}{9} + \cdots$

$S_1 = 1, S_2 = 1.33$. Matches (c)

**41.** $\displaystyle g(3.1) = \sum_{n=0}^{\infty} \left(\frac{3.1}{3}\right)^n$ diverges. Matches (b)

**43.** A series of the form

$$\sum_{n=0}^{\infty} a_n(x-c)^n$$

is called a power series centered at $c$.

**45.** A single point, $a_n$ interval, or the entire real line.

**47.** (a) $f(x) = \sum_{n=0}^{\infty} \frac{(-1)^n x^{2n+1}}{(2n+1)!}$, $-\infty < x < \infty$     (See Exercise 29.)

$g(x) = \sum_{n=0}^{\infty} \frac{(-1)^n x^{2n}}{(2n)!}$, $-\infty < x < \infty$

(b) $f'(x) = \sum_{n=0}^{\infty} \frac{(-1)^n x^{2n}}{(2n)!} = g(x)$

(c) $g'(x) = \sum_{n=1}^{\infty} \frac{(-1)^n x^{2n-1}}{(2n-1)!} = \sum_{n=0}^{\infty} \frac{(-1)^{n+1} x^{2n+1}}{(2n+1)!} = -\sum_{n=0}^{\infty} \frac{(-1)^n x^{2n+1}}{(2n+1)!} = -f(x)$

(d) $f(x) = \sin x$ and $g(x) = \cos x$

**49.**

$$y = \sum_{n=0}^{\infty} \frac{x^{2n}}{2^n \, n!}$$

$$y' = \sum_{n=1}^{\infty} \frac{2nx^{2n-1}}{2^n \, n!}$$

$$y'' = \sum_{n=1}^{\infty} \frac{2n(2n-1)x^{2n-2}}{2^n \, n!}$$

$$y'' - xy' - y = \sum_{n=1}^{\infty} \frac{2n(2n-1)x^{2n-2}}{2^n \, n!} - \sum_{n=1}^{\infty} \frac{2nx^{2n}}{2^n \, n!} - \sum_{n=0}^{\infty} \frac{x^{2n}}{2^n \, n!}$$

$$= \sum_{n=1}^{\infty} \frac{2n(2n-1)x^{2n-2}}{2^n \, n!} - \sum_{n=0}^{\infty} \frac{(2n+1)x^{2n}}{2^n \, n!}$$

$$= \sum_{n=0}^{\infty} \left[ \frac{(2n+2)(2n+1)x^{2n}}{2^{n+1}(n+1)!} - \frac{(2n+1)x^{2n}}{2^n \, n!} \cdot \frac{2(n+1)}{2(n+1)} \right]$$

$$= \sum_{n=0}^{\infty} \frac{2(n+1)x^{2n}[(2n+1) - (2n+1)]}{2^{n+1}(n+1)!} = 0$$

**51.** $J_0(x) = \sum_{k=0}^{\infty} \frac{(-1)^k x^{2k}}{2^{2k} (k!)^2}$

(a) $\lim_{k\to\infty} \left| \frac{u_{k+1}}{u_k} \right| = \lim_{k\to\infty} \left| \frac{(-1)^{k+1} x^{2k+2}}{2^{2k+2}[(k+1)!]^2} \cdot \frac{2^{2k}(k!)^2}{(-1)^k x^{2k}} \right| = \lim_{k\to\infty} \left| \frac{(-1)x^2}{2^2(k+1)^2} \right| = 0$

Therefore, the interval of convergence is $-\infty < x < \infty$.

(b)

$$J_0 = \sum_{k=0}^{\infty} (-1)^k \frac{x^{2k}}{4^k (k!)^2}$$

$$J_0' = \sum_{k=1}^{\infty} (-1)^k \frac{2kx^{2k-1}}{4^k (k!)^2} = \sum_{k=0}^{\infty} (-1)^{k+1} \frac{(2k+2) x^{2k+1}}{4^{k+1}[(k+1)!]^2}$$

$$J_0'' = \sum_{k=1}^{\infty} (-1)^k \frac{2k(2k-1)x^{2k-2}}{4^k (k!)^2} = \sum_{k=0}^{\infty} (-1)^{k+1} \frac{(2k+2)(2k+1)x^{2k}}{4^{k+1}[(k+1)!]^2}$$

$$x^2 J_0'' + x J_0' + x^2 J_0 = \sum_{k=0}^{\infty} (-1)^{k+1} \frac{2(2k+1) x^{2k+2}}{4^{k+1}(k+1)!k!} + \sum_{k=0}^{\infty} (-1)^{k+1} \frac{2x^{2k+2}}{4^{k+1}(k+1)!k!} + \sum_{k=0}^{\infty} (-1)^k \frac{x^{2k+2}}{4^k (k!)^2}$$

$$= \sum_{k=0}^{\infty} \frac{(-1)^k x^{2k+2}}{4^k (k!)^2} \left[ (-1)\frac{2(2k+1)}{4(k+1)} + (-1)\frac{2}{4(k+1)} + 1 \right]$$

$$= \sum_{k=0}^{\infty} \frac{(-1)^k x^{2k+2}}{4^k (k!)^2} \left[ \frac{-4k-2}{4k+4} - \frac{2}{4k+4} + \frac{4k+4}{4k+4} \right] = 0$$

**—CONTINUED—**

**51.** **—CONTINUED—**

(c) $P_6(x) = 1 - \dfrac{x^2}{4} + \dfrac{x^4}{64} - \dfrac{x^6}{2304}$

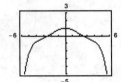

(d) $\displaystyle\int_0^1 J_0\,dx = \int_0^1 \sum_{k=0}^{\infty} \frac{(-1)^k\,x^{2k}}{4^k\,(k!)^2}\,dx$

$$= \left[ \sum_{k=0}^{\infty} \frac{(-1)^k\,x^{2k+1}}{4^k(k!)^2(2k+1)} \right]_0^1$$

$$= \sum_{k=0}^{\infty} \frac{(-1)^k}{4^k(k!)^2(2k+1)}$$

$$= 1 - \frac{1}{12} + \frac{1}{320} \approx 0.92$$

(exact integral is 0.9197304101)

**53.** $f(x) = \displaystyle\sum_{n=0}^{\infty} (-1)^n \frac{x^{2n}}{(2n)!} = \cos x$

(See Exercise 47.)

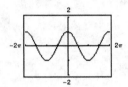

**55.** $f(x) = \displaystyle\sum_{n=0}^{\infty} (-1)^n x^n = \sum_{n=0}^{\infty} (-x)^n$

$$= \frac{1}{1-(-x)} = \frac{1}{1+x} \text{ for } -1 < x < 1$$

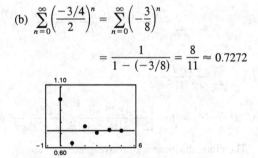

**57.** $\displaystyle\sum_{n=0}^{\infty} \left(\frac{x}{2}\right)^n$

(a) $\displaystyle\sum_{n=0}^{\infty} \left(\frac{3/4}{2}\right)^n = \sum_{n=0}^{\infty} \left(\frac{3}{8}\right)^n$

$$= \frac{1}{1-(3/8)} = \frac{8}{5} = 1.6$$

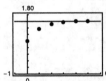

(b) $\displaystyle\sum_{n=0}^{\infty} \left(\frac{-3/4}{2}\right)^n = \sum_{n=0}^{\infty} \left(-\frac{3}{8}\right)^n$

$$= \frac{1}{1-(-3/8)} = \frac{8}{11} \approx 0.7272$$

(c) The alternating series converges more rapidly. The partial sums of the series of positive terms approach the sum from below. The partial sums of the alternating series alternate sides of the horizontal line representing the sum.

(d) $\displaystyle\sum_{n=0}^{N} \left(\frac{3}{2}\right)^n > M$

| $M$ | 10 | 100 | 1000 | 10,000 |
|-----|----|-----|------|--------|
| $N$ | 4  | 9   | 15   | 21     |

**59.** False;

$$\sum_{n=0}^{\infty} \frac{(-1)^n x^n}{n2^n}$$

converges for $x = 2$ but diverges for $x = -2$.

**61.** True; the radius of convergence is $R = 1$ for both series.

# Section 8.9    Representation of Functions by Power Series

**1.** (a) $\dfrac{1}{2-x} = \dfrac{1/2}{1-(x/2)} = \dfrac{a}{1-r}$

$$= \sum_{n=0}^{\infty} \frac{1}{2}\left(\frac{x}{2}\right)^n = \sum_{n=0}^{\infty} \frac{x^n}{2^{n+1}}$$

This series converges on $(-2, 2)$.

(b)
$$\dfrac{1}{2} + \dfrac{x}{4} + \dfrac{x^2}{8} + \dfrac{x^3}{16} + \cdots$$

$$2 - x \overline{)\,1}$$

$$\underline{1 - \dfrac{x}{2}}$$

$$\dfrac{x}{2}$$

$$\underline{\dfrac{x}{2} - \dfrac{x^2}{4}}$$

$$\dfrac{x^2}{4}$$

$$\underline{\dfrac{x^2}{4} - \dfrac{x^3}{8}}$$

$$\dfrac{x^3}{8}$$

$$\underline{\dfrac{x^3}{8} - \dfrac{x^4}{16}}$$

$$\vdots$$

**3.** (a) $\dfrac{1}{2+x} = \dfrac{1/2}{1-(-x/2)} = \dfrac{a}{1-r}$

$$= \sum_{n=0}^{\infty} \frac{1}{2}\left(-\frac{x}{2}\right)^n = \sum_{n=0}^{\infty} \frac{(-1)^n x^n}{2^{n+1}}$$

This series converges on $(-2, 2)$.

(b)
$$\dfrac{1}{2} - \dfrac{x}{4} + \dfrac{x^2}{8} - \dfrac{x^3}{16} + \cdots$$

$$2 + x \overline{)\,1}$$

$$\underline{1 + \dfrac{x}{2}}$$

$$-\dfrac{x}{2}$$

$$\underline{-\dfrac{x}{2} - \dfrac{x^2}{4}}$$

$$\dfrac{x^2}{4}$$

$$\underline{\dfrac{x^2}{4} + \dfrac{x^3}{8}}$$

$$-\dfrac{x^3}{8}$$

$$\underline{-\dfrac{x^3}{8} - \dfrac{x^4}{16}}$$

$$\vdots$$

**5.** Writing $f(x)$ in the form $a/(1-r)$, we have

$$\frac{1}{2-x} = \frac{1}{-3-(x-5)} = \frac{-1/3}{1+(1/3)(x-5)}$$

which implies that $a = -1/3$ and $r = (-1/3)(x-5)$.

Therefore, the power series for $f(x)$ is given by

$$\frac{1}{2-x} = \sum_{n=0}^{\infty} ar^n = \sum_{n=0}^{\infty} -\frac{1}{3}\left[-\frac{1}{3}(x-5)\right]^n$$

$$= \sum_{n=0}^{\infty} \frac{(x-5)^n}{(-3)^{n+1}}, \ |x-5| < 3 \text{ or } 2 < x < 8.$$

**7.** Writing $f(x)$ in the form $a/(1-r)$, we have

$$\frac{3}{2x-1} = \frac{-3}{1-2x} = \frac{a}{1-r}$$

which implies that $a = -3$ and $r = 2x$.

Therefore, the power series for $f(x)$ is given by

$$\frac{3}{2x-1} = \sum_{n=0}^{\infty} ar^n = \sum_{n=0}^{\infty} (-3)(2x)^n$$

$$= -3\sum_{n=0}^{\infty} (2x)^n, \ |2x| < 1 \text{ or } -\frac{1}{2} < x < \frac{1}{2}.$$

**9.** Writing $f(x)$ in the form $a/(1-r)$, we have

$$\frac{1}{2x-5} = \frac{-1}{11-2(x+3)}$$

$$= \frac{-1/11}{1-(2/11)(x+3)} = \frac{a}{1-r}$$

which implies that $a = -1/11$ and $r = (2/11)(x+3)$.
Therefore, the power series for $f(x)$ is given by

$$\frac{1}{2x-5} = \sum_{n=0}^{\infty} ar^n = \sum_{n=0}^{\infty} \left(-\frac{1}{11}\right)\left[\frac{2}{11}(x+3)\right]^n$$

$$= -\sum_{n=0}^{\infty} \frac{2^n(x+3)^n}{11^{n+1}},$$

$$|x+3| < \frac{11}{2} \text{ or } -\frac{17}{2} < x < \frac{5}{2}.$$

**11.** Writing $f(x)$ in the form $a/(1-r)$, we have

$$\frac{3}{x+2} = \frac{3}{2+x} = \frac{3/2}{1+(1/2)x} = \frac{a}{1-r}$$

which implies that $a = 3/2$ and $r = (-1/2)x$. Therefore, the power series for $f(x)$ is given by

$$\frac{3}{x+2} = \sum_{n=0}^{\infty} ar^n = \sum_{n=0}^{\infty} \frac{3}{2}\left(-\frac{1}{2}x\right)^n$$

$$= 3\sum_{n=0}^{\infty} \frac{(-1)^n x^n}{2^{n+1}} = \frac{3}{2}\sum_{n=0}^{\infty} \left(-\frac{x}{2}\right)^n,$$

$$|x| < 2 \text{ or } -2 < x < 2.$$

**13.** $\dfrac{3x}{x^2 + x - 2} = \dfrac{2}{x + 2} + \dfrac{1}{x - 1} = \dfrac{2}{2 + x} + \dfrac{1}{-1 + x} = \dfrac{1}{1 + (1/2)x} + \dfrac{-1}{1 - x}$

Writing $f(x)$ as a sum of two geometric series, we have

$$\frac{3x}{x^2 + x - 2} = \sum_{n=0}^{\infty} \left(-\frac{1}{2}x\right)^n + \sum_{n=0}^{\infty} (-1)(x)^n = \sum_{n=0}^{\infty} \left[\frac{1}{(-2)^n} - 1\right]x^n.$$

The interval of convergence is $-1 < x < 1$ since

$$\lim_{n\to\infty} \left|\frac{u_{n+1}}{u_n}\right| = \lim_{n\to\infty} \left|\frac{(1 - (-2)^{n+1})x^{n+1}}{(-2)^{n+1}} \cdot \frac{(-2)^n}{(1 - (-2)^n)x^n}\right| = \lim_{n\to\infty} \left|\frac{(1 - (-2)^{n+1})x}{-2 - (-2)^{n+1}}\right| = |x|.$$

**15.** $\dfrac{2}{1 - x^2} = \dfrac{1}{1 - x} + \dfrac{1}{1 + x}$

Writing $f(x)$ as a sum of two geometric series, we have

$$\frac{2}{1 - x^2} = \sum_{n=0}^{\infty} x^n + \sum_{n=0}^{\infty} (-x)^n = \sum_{n=0}^{\infty} (1 + (-1)^n)x^n = \sum_{n=0}^{\infty} 2x^{2n}.$$

The interval of convergence is $|x^2| < 1$ or $-1 < x < 1$ since $\lim_{n\to\infty} \left|\dfrac{u_{n+1}}{u_n}\right| = \lim_{n\to\infty} \left|\dfrac{2x^{2n+2}}{2x^2}\right| = |x^2|.$

**17.** $\dfrac{1}{1 + x} = \sum_{n=0}^{\infty} (-1)^n x^n$

$$\frac{1}{1 - x} = \sum_{n=0}^{\infty} (-1)^n (-x)^n = \sum_{n=0}^{\infty} (-1)^{2n} x^n = \sum_{n=0}^{\infty} x^n$$

$$h(x) = \frac{-2}{x^2 - 1} = \frac{1}{1 + x} + \frac{1}{1 - x} = \sum_{n=0}^{\infty} (-1)^n x^n + \sum_{n=0}^{\infty} x^n = \sum_{n=0}^{\infty} [(-1)^n + 1]x^n$$

$$= 2 + 0x + 2x^2 + 0x^3 + 2x^4 + 0x^5 + 2x^6 + \cdots = \sum_{n=0}^{\infty} 2x^{2n}, \ -1 < x < 1 \text{ (See Exercise 15.)}$$

**19.** By taking the first derivative, we have $\dfrac{d}{dx}\left[\dfrac{1}{x + 1}\right] = \dfrac{-1}{(x + 1)^2}.$ Therefore,

$$\frac{-1}{(x + 1)^2} = \frac{d}{dx}\left[\sum_{n=0}^{\infty} (-1)^n x^n\right] = \sum_{n=1}^{\infty} (-1)^n n x^{n-1}$$

$$= \sum_{n=0}^{\infty} (-1)^{n+1}(n + 1)x^n, \ -1 < x < 1.$$

**21.** By integrating, we have $\displaystyle\int \dfrac{1}{x + 1}\, dx = \ln(x + 1).$ Therefore,

$$\ln(x + 1) = \int\left[\sum_{n=0}^{\infty} (-1)^n x^n\right] dx = C + \sum_{n=0}^{\infty} \frac{(-1)^n x^{n+1}}{n + 1}, \ -1 < x \le 1.$$

To solve for $C$, let $x = 0$ and conclude that $C = 0$. Therefore,

$$\ln(x + 1) = \sum_{n=0}^{\infty} \frac{(-1)^n x^{n+1}}{n + 1}, \ -1 < x \le 1.$$

**23.** $\dfrac{1}{x^2 + 1} = \sum_{n=0}^{\infty} (-1)^n (x^2)^n = \sum_{n=0}^{\infty} (-1)^n x^{2n}, \ -1 < x < 1$

**25.** Since, $\dfrac{1}{x + 1} = \sum_{n=0}^{\infty} (-1)^n x^n,$ we have $\dfrac{1}{4x^2 + 1} = \sum_{n=0}^{\infty} (-1)^n (4x^2)^n = \sum_{n=0}^{\infty} (-1)^n\, 4^n x^{2n} = \sum_{n=0}^{\infty} (-1)^n (2x)^{2n}, \ -\dfrac{1}{2} < x < \dfrac{1}{2}.$

**27.** $x - \dfrac{x^2}{2} \le \ln(x+1) \le x - \dfrac{x^2}{2} + \dfrac{x^3}{3}$

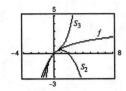

| $x$ | 0.0 | 0.2 | 0.4 | 0.6 | 0.8 | 1.0 |
|---|---|---|---|---|---|---|
| $x - \dfrac{x^2}{2}$ | 0.000 | 0.180 | 0.320 | 0.420 | 0.480 | 0.500 |
| $\ln(x+1)$ | 0.000 | 0.180 | 0.336 | 0.470 | 0.588 | 0.693 |
| $x - \dfrac{x^2}{2} + \dfrac{x^3}{3}$ | 0.000 | 0.183 | 0.341 | 0.492 | 0.651 | 0.833 |

**29.** $g(x) = x$, line, Matches (c)      **31.** $g(x) = x - \dfrac{x^3}{3} + \dfrac{x^5}{5}$, Matches (a)      **33.** $f(x) = \arctan x$ is an odd function (symmetric to the origin)

**In Exercises 35 and 37,** $\arctan x = \displaystyle\sum_{n=0}^{\infty} (-1)^n \dfrac{x^{2n+1}}{2n+1}.$

**35.** $\arctan \dfrac{1}{4} = \displaystyle\sum_{n=0}^{\infty} (-1)^n \dfrac{(1/4)^{2n+1}}{2n+1} = \sum_{n=0}^{\infty} \dfrac{(-1)^n}{(2n+1)4^{2n+1}} = \dfrac{1}{4} - \dfrac{1}{192} + \dfrac{1}{5120} + \cdots$

Since $\dfrac{1}{5120} < 0.001$, we can approximate the series by its first two terms: $\arctan \dfrac{1}{4} \approx \dfrac{1}{4} - \dfrac{1}{192} \approx 0.245.$

**37.**  $\dfrac{\arctan x^2}{x} = \displaystyle\sum_{n=0}^{\infty} (-1)^n \dfrac{x^{4n+1}}{2n+1}$

$\displaystyle\int \dfrac{\arctan x^2}{x}\, dx = \sum_{n=0}^{\infty} (-1)^n \dfrac{x^{4n+2}}{(4n+2)(2n+1)}$

$\displaystyle\int_0^{1/2} \dfrac{\arctan x^2}{x}\, dx = \sum_{n=0}^{\infty} (-1)^n \dfrac{1}{(4n+2)(2n+1)2^{4n+2}} = \dfrac{1}{8} - \dfrac{1}{1152} + \cdots$

Since $\dfrac{1}{1152} < 0.001$, we can approximate the series by its first term: $\displaystyle\int_0^{1/2} \dfrac{\arctan x^2}{x}\, dx \approx 0.125.$

**In Exercises 39 and 41, use** $\dfrac{1}{1-x} = \displaystyle\sum_{n=0}^{\infty} x^n, \; |x| < 1.$

**39.** (a) $\dfrac{1}{(1-x)^2} = \dfrac{d}{dx}\left[ \dfrac{1}{1-x} \right] = \dfrac{d}{dx}\left[ \displaystyle\sum_{n=0}^{\infty} x^n \right] = \sum_{n=1}^{\infty} n x^{n-1}, \; |x| < 1$

(b) $\dfrac{x}{(1-x)^2} = x \displaystyle\sum_{n=1}^{\infty} n x^{n-1} = \sum_{n=1}^{\infty} n x^n, \; |x| < 1$

(c) $\dfrac{1+x}{(1-x)^2} = \dfrac{1}{(1-x)^2} + \dfrac{x}{(1-x)^2} = \displaystyle\sum_{n=1}^{\infty} n(x^{n-1} + x^n), \; |x| < 1$

$\qquad\qquad\qquad = \displaystyle\sum_{n=0}^{\infty} (2n+1) x^n, \; |x| < 1$

(d) $\dfrac{x(1+x)}{(1-x)^2} = x \displaystyle\sum_{n=0}^{\infty} (2n+1) x^n = \sum_{n=0}^{\infty} (2n+1) x^{n+1}, \; |x| < 1$

**41.** $P(n) = \left( \dfrac{1}{2} \right)^n$

$E(n) = \displaystyle\sum_{n=1}^{\infty} n P(n) = \sum_{n=1}^{\infty} n \left( \dfrac{1}{2} \right)^n = \dfrac{1}{2} \sum_{n=1}^{\infty} n \left( \dfrac{1}{2} \right)^{n-1}$

$\qquad = \dfrac{1}{2} \dfrac{1}{[1 - (1/2)]^2} = 2$

Since the probability of obtaining a head on a single toss is $\dfrac{1}{2}$, it is expected that, on average, a head will be obtained in two tosses.

**43.** Replace $x$ with $(-x)$.

**45.** Replace $x$ with $(-x)$ and multiply the series by 5.

**47.** Let $\arctan x + \arctan y = \theta$. Then,

$$\tan(\arctan x + \arctan y) = \tan \theta$$

$$\frac{\tan(\arctan x) + \tan(\arctan y)}{1 - \tan(\arctan x) \tan(\arctan y)} = \tan \theta$$

$$\frac{x + y}{1 - xy} = \tan \theta$$

$$\arctan\left(\frac{x + y}{1 - xy}\right) = \theta. \text{ Therefore, } \arctan x + \arctan y = \arctan\left(\frac{x + y}{1 - xy}\right) \text{ for } xy \neq 1.$$

**49.** (a) $2 \arctan \dfrac{1}{2} = \arctan \dfrac{1}{2} + \arctan \dfrac{1}{2} = \arctan\left[\dfrac{2(1/2)}{1 - (1/2)^2}\right] = \arctan \dfrac{4}{3}$

$2 \arctan \dfrac{1}{2} - \arctan \dfrac{1}{7} = \arctan \dfrac{4}{3} + \arctan\left(-\dfrac{1}{7}\right) = \arctan\left[\dfrac{(4/3) - (1/7)}{1 + (4/3)(1/7)}\right] = \arctan \dfrac{25}{25} = \arctan 1 = \dfrac{\pi}{4}$

(b) $\pi = 8 \arctan \dfrac{1}{2} - 4 \arctan \dfrac{1}{7} \approx 8\left[\dfrac{1}{2} - \dfrac{(0.5)^3}{3} + \dfrac{(0.5)^5}{5} - \dfrac{(0.5)^7}{7}\right] - 4\left[\dfrac{1}{7} - \dfrac{(1/7)^3}{3} + \dfrac{(1/7)^5}{5} - \dfrac{(1/7)^7}{7}\right] \approx 3.14$

**51.** From Exercise 21, we have

$$\ln(x + 1) = \sum_{n=0}^{\infty} \frac{(-1)^n x^{n+1}}{n + 1} = \sum_{n=1}^{\infty} \frac{(-1)^{n-1} x^n}{n}$$

$$= \sum_{n=1}^{\infty} \frac{(-1)^{n+1} x^n}{n}.$$

Thus, $\displaystyle\sum_{n=1}^{\infty} (-1)^{n+1} \frac{1}{2^n n} = \sum_{n=1}^{\infty} \frac{(-1)^{n+1}(1/2)^n}{n}$

$$= \ln\left(\frac{1}{2} + 1\right) = \ln \frac{3}{2} \approx 0.4055$$

**53.** From Exercise 51, we have

$$\sum_{n=1}^{\infty} (-1)^{n+1} \frac{2^n}{5^n n} = \sum_{n=1}^{\infty} \frac{(-1)^{n+1}(2/5)^n}{n}$$

$$= \ln\left(\frac{2}{5} + 1\right) = \ln \frac{7}{5} \approx 0.3365.$$

**55.** From Exercise 54, we have

$$\sum_{n=0}^{\infty} (-1)^n \frac{1}{2^{2n+1}(2n + 1)} = \sum_{n=0}^{\infty} (-1)^n \frac{(1/2)^{2n+1}}{2n + 1} = \arctan \frac{1}{2} \approx 0.4636.$$

**57.** The series in Exercise 54 converges to its sum at a slower rate because its terms approach 0 at a much slower rate.

**59.** $f(x) = \displaystyle\sum_{n=1}^{\infty} (-1)^{n+1} \frac{(x - 1)^n}{n}$, $0 < x \leq 2$

$$f(0.5) = \sum_{n=1}^{\infty} (-1)^{n+1} \frac{(-0.5)^n}{n} = \sum_{n=1}^{\infty} -\frac{(1/2)^n}{n}$$

$$\sum_{n=1}^{\infty} -\frac{(1/2)^n}{n} = -0.6931$$

# Section 8.10    Taylor and Maclaurin Series

**1.** For $c = 0$, we have:

$$f(x) = e^{2x}$$

$$f^{(n)}(x) = 2^n e^{2x} \Longrightarrow f^{(n)}(0) = 2^n$$

$$e^{2x} = 1 + 2x + \frac{4x^2}{2!} + \frac{8x^3}{3!} + \frac{16x^4}{4!} + \cdots = \sum_{n=0}^{\infty} \frac{(2x)^n}{n!}$$

**3.** For $c = \pi/4$, we have:

$$f(x) = \cos(x) \qquad f\left(\frac{\pi}{4}\right) = \frac{\sqrt{2}}{2}$$

$$f'(x) = -\sin(x) \qquad f'\left(\frac{\pi}{4}\right) = -\frac{\sqrt{2}}{2}$$

$$f''(x) = -\cos(x) \qquad f''\left(\frac{\pi}{4}\right) = -\frac{\sqrt{2}}{2}$$

$$f'''(x) = \sin(x) \qquad f'''\left(\frac{\pi}{4}\right) = \frac{\sqrt{2}}{2}$$

$$f^{(4)}(x) = \cos(x) \qquad f^{(4)}\left(\frac{\pi}{4}\right) = \frac{\sqrt{2}}{2}$$

and so on. Therefore, we have:

$$\cos x = \sum_{n=0}^{\infty} \frac{f^{(n)}(\pi/4)[x - (\pi/4)]^n}{n!}$$

$$= \frac{\sqrt{2}}{2}\left[ 1 - \left(x - \frac{\pi}{4}\right) - \frac{[x - (\pi/4)]^2}{2!} + \frac{[x - (\pi/4)]^3}{3!} + \frac{[x - (\pi/4)]^4}{4!} - \cdots \right]$$

$$= \frac{\sqrt{2}}{2} \sum_{n=0}^{\infty} \frac{(-1)^{n(n+1)/2}[x - (\pi/4)]^n}{n!}.$$

[**Note:** $(-1)^{n(n+1)/2} = 1, -1, -1, 1, 1, -1, -1, 1, \ldots$]

**5.** For $c = 1$, we have,

$$f(x) = \ln x \qquad f(1) = 0$$

$$f'(x) = \frac{1}{x} \qquad f'(1) = 1$$

$$f''(x) = -\frac{1}{x^2} \qquad f''(1) = -1$$

$$f'''(x) = \frac{2}{x^3} \qquad f'''(1) = 2$$

$$f^{(4)}(x) = -\frac{6}{x^4} \qquad f^{(4)}(1) = -6$$

$$f^{(5)}(x) = \frac{24}{x^5} \qquad f^{(5)}(1) = 24$$

and so on. Therefore, we have:

$$\ln x = \sum_{n=0}^{\infty} \frac{f^{(n)}(1)(x - 1)^n}{n!}$$

$$= 0 + (x - 1) - \frac{(x-1)^2}{2!} + \frac{2(x-1)^3}{3!} - \frac{6(x-1)^4}{4!} + \frac{24(x-1)^5}{5!} - \cdots$$

$$= (x - 1) - \frac{(x-1)^2}{2} + \frac{(x-1)^3}{3} - \frac{(x-1)^4}{4} + \frac{(x-1)^5}{5} - \cdots$$

$$= \sum_{n=0}^{\infty} (-1)^n \frac{(x-1)^{n+1}}{n+1}$$

**7.** For $c = 0$, we have:

$$f(x) = \sin 2x \qquad\qquad f(0) = 0$$
$$f'(x) = 2\cos 2x \qquad\qquad f'(0) = 2$$
$$f''(x) = -4\sin 2x \qquad\qquad f''(0) = 0$$
$$f'''(x) = -8\cos 2x \qquad\qquad f'''(0) = -8$$
$$f^{(4)}(x) = 16\sin 2x \qquad\qquad f^{(4)}(0) = 0$$
$$f^{(5)}(x) = 32\cos 2x \qquad\qquad f^{(5)}(0) = 32$$
$$f^{(6)}(x) = -64\sin 2x \qquad\qquad f^{(6)}(0) = 0$$
$$f^{(7)}(x) = -128\cos 2x \qquad\qquad f^{(7)}(0) = -128$$

and so on. Therefore, we have:

$$\sin 2x = \sum_{n=0}^{\infty} \frac{f^{(n)}(0)x^n}{n!} = 0 + 2x + \frac{0x^2}{2!} - \frac{8x^3}{3!} + \frac{0x^4}{4!} + \frac{32x^5}{5!} + \frac{0x^6}{6!} - \frac{128x^7}{7!} + \cdots$$

$$= 2x - \frac{8x^3}{3!} + \frac{32x^5}{5!} - \frac{128x^7}{7!} + \cdots = \sum_{n=0}^{\infty} \frac{(-1)^n(2x)^{2n+1}}{(2n+1)!}$$

**9.** For $c = 0$, we have:

$$f(x) = \sec(x) \qquad\qquad\qquad\qquad\qquad f(0) = 1$$
$$f'(x) = \sec(x)\tan(x) \qquad\qquad\qquad\qquad f'(0) = 0$$
$$f''(x) = \sec^3(x) + \sec(x)\tan^2(x) \qquad\qquad\quad f''(0) = 1$$
$$f'''(x) = 5\sec^3(x)\tan(x) + \sec(x)\tan^3(x) \qquad\quad f'''(0) = 0$$
$$f^{(4)}(x) = 5\sec^5(x) + 18\sec^3(x)\tan^2(x) + \sec(x)\tan^4(x) \qquad f^{(4)}(0) = 5$$

$$\sec(x) = \sum_{n=0}^{\infty} \frac{f^{(n)}(0)x^n}{n!} = 1 + \frac{x^2}{2!} + \frac{5x^4}{4!} + \cdots$$

**11.** The Maclaurin series for $f(x) = \cos x$ is $\displaystyle\sum_{n=0}^{\infty} \frac{(-1)x^{2n}}{(2n)!}$.

Because $f^{(n+1)}(x) = \pm\sin x$ or $\pm\cos x$, we have $\left|f^{(n+1)}(z)\right| \leq 1$ for all $z$. Hence by Taylor's Theorem,

$$0 \leq |Rn(x)| = \left|\frac{f^{(n+1)}(z)}{(n+1)!}x^{n+1}\right| \leq \frac{|x|^{n+1}}{(n+1)!}.$$

Since $\displaystyle\lim_{n\to\infty} \frac{|x|^{n+1}}{(n+1)!} = 0$, it follows that $Rn(x) \to 0$ as $n \to \infty$. Hence, the Maclaurin series for $\cos x$ converges to $\cos x$ for all $x$.

**13.** Since $(1 + x)^{-k} = 1 - kx + \dfrac{k(k+1)x^2}{2!} - \dfrac{k(k+1)(k+2)x^3}{3!} + \cdots$, we have

$$(1+x)^{-2} = 1 - 2x + \frac{2(3)x^2}{2!} - \frac{2(3)(4)x^3}{3!} + \frac{2(3)(4)(5)x^4}{5!} - \cdots = 1 - 2x + 3x^2 - 4x^3 + 5x^4 - \cdots$$

$$= \sum_{n=0}^{\infty} (-1)^n(n+1)x^n.$$

**15.** $\dfrac{1}{\sqrt{4+x^2}} = \left(\dfrac{1}{2}\right)\left[1 + \left(\dfrac{x}{2}\right)^2\right]^{-1/2}$ and since $(1+x)^{-1/2} = 1 + \sum\limits_{n=1}^{\infty} \dfrac{(-1)^n \, 1 \cdot 3 \cdot 5 \cdots (2n-1)x^n}{2^n n!}$, we have

$$\dfrac{1}{\sqrt{4+x^2}} = \dfrac{1}{2}\left[1 + \sum_{n=1}^{\infty} \dfrac{(-1)^n \, 1 \cdot 3 \cdot 5 \cdots (2n-1)(x/2)^{2n}}{2^n n!}\right] = \dfrac{1}{2} + \sum_{n=1}^{\infty} \dfrac{(-1)^n \, 1 \cdot 3 \cdot 5 \cdots (2n-1)x^{2n}}{2^{3n+1} n!}.$$

**17.** Since $(1+x)^{1/2} = 1 + \dfrac{x}{2} + \sum\limits_{n=2}^{\infty} \dfrac{(-1)^{n+1} \, 1 \cdot 3 \cdot 5 \cdots (2n-3)x^n}{2^n n!}$   (Exercise 14)

we have $(1+x^2)^{1/2} = 1 + \dfrac{x^2}{2} + \sum\limits_{n=2}^{\infty} \dfrac{(-1)^{n+1} \, 1 \cdot 3 \cdot 5 \cdots (2n-3)x^{2n}}{2^n n!}.$

**19.** $\quad e^x = \sum\limits_{n=0}^{\infty} \dfrac{x^n}{n!} = 1 + x + \dfrac{x^2}{2!} + \dfrac{x^3}{3!} + \dfrac{x^4}{4!} + \dfrac{x^5}{5!} + \cdots$

$e^{x^2/2} = \sum\limits_{n=0}^{\infty} \dfrac{(x^2/2)^n}{n!} = \sum\limits_{n=0}^{\infty} \dfrac{x^{2n}}{2^n n!} = 1 + \dfrac{x^2}{2} + \dfrac{x^4}{2^2 2!} + \dfrac{x^6}{2^3 3!} + \dfrac{x^8}{2^4 4!} + \cdots$

**21.** $\quad \sin x = \sum\limits_{n=0}^{\infty} \dfrac{(-1)^n x^{2n+1}}{(2n+1)!} = x - \dfrac{x^3}{3!} + \dfrac{x^5}{5!} - \dfrac{x^7}{7!} + \cdots$

$\sin 2x = \sum\limits_{n=0}^{\infty} \dfrac{(-1)^n (2x)^{2n+1}}{(2n+1)!} = \sum\limits_{n=0}^{\infty} \dfrac{(-1)^n \, 2^{2n+1} x^{2n+1}}{(2n+1)!} = 2x - \dfrac{8x^3}{3!} + \dfrac{32x^5}{5!} - \dfrac{128x^7}{7!} + \cdots$

**23.** $\quad \cos x = \sum\limits_{n=0}^{\infty} \dfrac{(-1)^n x^{2n}}{(2n)!} = 1 - \dfrac{x^2}{2!} + \dfrac{x^4}{4!} - \cdots$

$\cos x^{3/2} = \sum\limits_{n=0}^{\infty} \dfrac{(-1)^n (x^{3/2})^{2n}}{(2n)!} = \sum\limits_{n=0}^{\infty} \dfrac{(-1)^n x^{3n}}{(2n)!} = 1 - \dfrac{x^3}{2!} + \dfrac{x^6}{4!} - \cdots$

**25.** $\qquad e^x = 1 + x + \dfrac{x^2}{2!} + \dfrac{x^3}{3!} + \dfrac{x^4}{4!} + \dfrac{x^5}{5!} + \cdots$

$e^{-x} = 1 - x + \dfrac{x^2}{2!} - \dfrac{x^3}{3!} + \dfrac{x^4}{4!} - \dfrac{x^5}{5!} + \cdots$

$e^x - e^{-x} = 2x + \dfrac{2x^3}{3!} + \dfrac{2x^5}{5!} + \dfrac{2x^7}{7!} + \cdots$

$\sinh(x) = \dfrac{1}{2}(e^x - e^{-x}) = x + \dfrac{x^3}{3!} + \dfrac{x^5}{5!} + \dfrac{x^7}{7!} + \cdots = \sum\limits_{n=0}^{\infty} \dfrac{x^{2n+1}}{(2n+1)!}$

**27.** $\cos^2(x) = \dfrac{1}{2}[1 + \cos(2x)]$

$= \dfrac{1}{2}\left[1 + 1 - \dfrac{(2x)^2}{2!} + \dfrac{(2x)^4}{4!} - \dfrac{(2x)^6}{6!} - \cdots\right]$

$= \dfrac{1}{2}\left[1 + \sum\limits_{n=0}^{\infty} \dfrac{(-1)^n (2x)^{2n}}{(2n)!}\right]$

**29.** $x \sin x = x\left(x - \dfrac{x^3}{3!} + \dfrac{x^5}{5!} - \cdots\right)$

$= x^2 - \dfrac{x^4}{3!} + \dfrac{x^6}{5!} - \cdots$

$= \sum\limits_{n=0}^{\infty} \dfrac{(-1)^n x^{2n+2}}{(2n+1)!}$

**31.** $\dfrac{\sin x}{x} = \dfrac{x - (x^3/3!) + (x^5/5!) - \cdots}{x}$

$= 1 - \dfrac{x^2}{2!} + \dfrac{x^4}{4!} - \cdots$

$= \sum\limits_{n=0}^{\infty} \dfrac{(-1)^n x^{2n}}{(2n+1)!}, \; x \neq 0$

**33.**
$$e^{ix} = 1 + ix + \frac{(ix)^2}{2!} + \frac{(ix)^3}{3!} + \frac{(ix)^4}{4!} + \cdots = 1 + ix - \frac{x^2}{2!} - \frac{ix^3}{3!} + \frac{x^4}{4!} + \frac{ix^5}{5!} - \frac{x^6}{6!} - \cdots$$

$$e^{-ix} = 1 - ix + \frac{(-ix)^2}{2!} + \frac{(-ix)^3}{3!} + \frac{(-ix)^4}{4!} + \cdots = 1 - ix - \frac{x^2}{2!} + \frac{ix^3}{3!} + \frac{x^4}{4!} - \frac{ix^5}{5!} - \frac{x^6}{6!} + \cdots$$

$$e^{ix} - e^{-ix} = 2ix - \frac{2ix^3}{3!} + \frac{2ix^5}{5!} - \frac{2ix^7}{7!} + \cdots$$

$$\frac{e^{ix} - e^{-ix}}{2i} = x - \frac{x^3}{3!} + \frac{x^5}{5!} - \frac{x^7}{7!} + \cdots = \sum_{n=0}^{\infty} \frac{(-1)^n x^{2n+1}}{(2n+1)!} = \sin(x)$$

**35.** $f(x) = e^x \sin x$

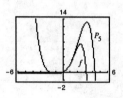

$$= \left(1 + x + \frac{x^2}{2} + \frac{x^3}{6} + \frac{x^4}{24} + \cdots\right)\left(x - \frac{x^3}{6} + \frac{x^5}{120} - \cdots\right)$$

$$= x + x^2 + \left(\frac{x^3}{2} - \frac{x^3}{6}\right) + \left(\frac{x^4}{6} - \frac{x^4}{6}\right) + \left(\frac{x^5}{120} - \frac{x^5}{12} + \frac{x^5}{24}\right) + \cdots$$

$$= x + x^2 + \frac{x^3}{3} - \frac{x^5}{30} + \cdots$$

**37.** $h(x) = \cos x \ln(1 + x)$

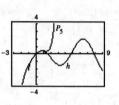

$$= \left(1 - \frac{x^2}{2} + \frac{x^4}{24} - \cdots\right)\left(x - \frac{x^2}{2} + \frac{x^3}{3} - \frac{x^4}{4} + \frac{x^5}{5} - \cdots\right)$$

$$= x - \frac{x^2}{2} + \left(\frac{x^3}{3} - \frac{x^3}{2}\right) + \left(\frac{x^4}{4} - \frac{x^4}{4}\right) + \left(\frac{x^5}{5} - \frac{x^5}{6} + \frac{x^5}{24}\right) + \cdots$$

$$= x - \frac{x^2}{2} - \frac{x^3}{6} + \frac{3x^5}{40} + \cdots$$

**39.** $g(x) = \dfrac{\sin x}{1 + x}$. Divide the series for $\sin x$ by $(1 + x)$.
$\qquad\qquad\qquad\qquad\qquad\qquad\qquad\qquad\qquad g(x) = x - x^2 + \dfrac{5x^3}{6} - \dfrac{5x^4}{6} + \cdots$

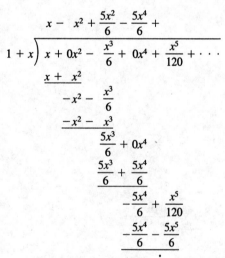

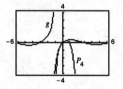

**41.** $y = x^2 - \dfrac{x^4}{3!} = x\left(x - \dfrac{x^3}{3!}\right) \approx x \sin x.$ $\qquad\qquad$ **43.** $y = x + x^2 + \dfrac{x^3}{2!} = x\left(1 + x + \dfrac{x^2}{2!}\right) \approx xe^x.$

$\qquad$ Matches (a) $\qquad\qquad\qquad\qquad\qquad\qquad\qquad\qquad$ Matches (c)

**45.** $\displaystyle\int_0^x (e^{-t^2} - 1)\, dt = \int_0^x \left[\left(\sum_{n=0}^{\infty} \frac{(-1)^n t^{2n}}{n!}\right) - 1\right] dt$

$\displaystyle = \int_0^x \left[\sum_{n=0}^{\infty} \frac{(-1)^{n+1} t^{2n+2}}{(n+1)!}\right] dt = \left[\sum_{n=0}^{\infty} \frac{(-1)^{n+1} t^{2n+3}}{(2n+3)(n+1)!}\right]_0^x = \sum_{n=0}^{\infty} \frac{(-1)^{n+1} x^{2n+3}}{(2n+3)(n+1)!}$

**47.** Since $\displaystyle \ln x = \sum_{n=0}^{\infty} \frac{(-1)^n (x-1)^{n+1}}{n+1} = (x-1) - \frac{(x-1)^2}{2} + \frac{(x-1)^3}{3} - \frac{(x-1)^4}{4} + \cdots$

we have $\displaystyle \ln 2 = 1 - \frac{1}{2} + \frac{1}{3} - \frac{1}{4} + \cdots = \sum_{n=1}^{\infty} (-1)^{n+1} \frac{1}{n} \approx 0.6931.$   (10,001 terms)

**49.** Since $\displaystyle e^x = \sum_{n=0}^{\infty} \frac{x^n}{n!} = 1 + x + \frac{x^2}{2!} + \frac{x^3}{3!} + \cdots,$

we have $\displaystyle e^2 = 1 + 2 + \frac{2^2}{2!} + \frac{2^3}{3!} + \cdots = \sum_{n=0}^{\infty} \frac{2^n}{n!} \approx 7.3891.$   (12 terms)

**51.** Since

$$\cos x = \sum_{n=0}^{\infty} \frac{(-1)^n x^{2n}}{(2n)!} = 1 - \frac{x^2}{2!} + \frac{x^4}{4!} - \frac{x^6}{6!} + \frac{x^8}{8!} - \cdots$$

$$1 - \cos x = \frac{x^2}{2!} - \frac{x^4}{4!} + \frac{x^6}{6!} - \frac{x^8}{8!} + \cdots = \sum_{n=0}^{\infty} \frac{(-1)^n x^{2n+2}}{(2n+2)!}$$

$$\frac{1 - \cos}{x} = \frac{x}{2!} - \frac{x^3}{4!} + \frac{x^5}{6!} - \frac{x^7}{8!} + \cdots = \sum_{n=0}^{\infty} \frac{(-1)^n x^{2n+1}}{(2n+2)!}$$

we have $\displaystyle \lim_{x \to 0} \frac{1 - \cos x}{x} = \lim_{x \to 0} \sum_{n=0}^{\infty} \frac{(-1) x^{2n+1}}{(2n+2)!} = 0.$

**53.** $\displaystyle \int_0^1 \frac{\sin x}{x}\, dx = \int_0^1 \left[\sum_{n=0}^{\infty} \frac{(-1)^n x^{2n}}{(2n+1)!}\right] dx = \left[\sum_{n=0}^{\infty} \frac{(-1)^n x^{2n+1}}{(2n+1)(2n+1)!}\right]_0^1 = \sum_{n=0}^{\infty} \frac{(-1)^n}{(2n+1)(2n+1)!}$

Since $1/(7 \cdot 7!) < 0.0001$, we have

$$\int_0^1 \frac{\sin x}{x}\, dx = 1 - \frac{1}{3 \cdot 3!} + \frac{1}{5 \cdot 5!} - \cdots \approx 0.9461.$$

**Note:** We are using $\displaystyle \lim_{x \to 0^+} \frac{\sin x}{x} = 1.$

**55.** $\displaystyle \int_0^{\pi/2} \sqrt{x} \cos x\, dx = \int_0^{\pi/2} \left[\sum_{n=0}^{\infty} \frac{(-1)^n x^{(4n+1)/2}}{(2n)!}\right] dx = \left[\sum_{n=0}^{\infty} \frac{(-1)^n x^{(4n+3)/2}}{\left(\frac{4n+3}{2}\right)(2n)!}\right]_0^{\pi/2} = \left[\sum_{n=0}^{\infty} \frac{(-1)^n 2 x^{(4n+3)/2}}{(4n+3)(2n)!}\right]_0^{\pi/2}$

Since $(\pi/2)^{19/2}/766{,}080 < 0.0001$, we have

$$\int_0^1 \sqrt{x} \cos x\, dx = 2\left[\frac{(\pi/2)^{3/2}}{3} - \frac{(\pi/2)^{7/2}}{14} + \frac{(\pi/2)^{11/2}}{264} - \frac{(\pi/2)^{15/2}}{10{,}800} + \frac{(\pi/2)^{19/2}}{766{,}080}\right] \approx 0.7040.$$

**57.** $\displaystyle \int_{0.1}^{0.3} \sqrt{1 + x^3}\, dx = \int_{0.1}^{0.3} \left(1 + \frac{x^3}{2} - \frac{x^6}{8} + \frac{x^9}{16} - \frac{5x^{12}}{128} + \cdots\right) dx = \left[x + \frac{x^4}{8} - \frac{x^7}{56} + \frac{x^{10}}{160} - \frac{5x^{13}}{1664} + \cdots\right]_{0.1}^{0.3}$

Since $\frac{1}{56}(0.3^7 - 0.1^7) < 0.0001$, we have

$$\int_{0.1}^{0.3} \sqrt{1 + x^3}\, dx = \left[(0.3 - 0.1) + \frac{1}{8}(0.3^4 - 0.1^4) - \frac{1}{56}(0.3^7 - 0.1^7)\right] \approx 0.2010.$$

**59.** From Exercise 19, we have

$$\frac{1}{\sqrt{2\pi}}\int_0^1 e^{-x^2/2}\,dx = \frac{1}{\sqrt{2\pi}}\int_0^1 \sum_{n=0}^\infty \frac{(-1)^n x^{2n}}{2^n n!}\,dx = \frac{1}{\sqrt{2\pi}}\left[\sum_{n=0}^\infty \frac{(-1)^n x^{2n+1}}{2^n n!(2n+1)}\right]_0^1 = \frac{1}{\sqrt{2\pi}}\sum_{n=0}^\infty \frac{(-1)^n}{2^n n!(2n+1)}$$

$$\approx \frac{1}{\sqrt{2\pi}}\left[1 - \frac{1}{2\cdot 1\cdot 3} + \frac{1}{2^2\cdot 2!\cdot 5} - \frac{1}{2^3\cdot 3!\cdot 7}\right] \approx 0.3414.$$

**61.** $f(x) = x\cos 2x = \displaystyle\sum_{n=0}^\infty \frac{(-1)^n 4^n x^{2n+1}}{(2n)!}$

$P_5(x) = x - 2x^3 + \dfrac{2x^5}{3}$

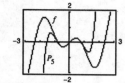

The polynomial is a reasonable approximation on the interval $\left[-\frac{3}{4}, \frac{3}{4}\right]$.

**63.** $f(x) = \sqrt{x}\ln x, c = 1$

$P_5(x) = (x-1) - \dfrac{(x-1)^3}{24} + \dfrac{(x-1)^4}{24} - \dfrac{71(x-1)^5}{1920}$

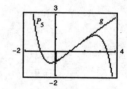

The polynomial is a reasonable approximation on the interval $\left[\frac{1}{4}, 2\right]$.

**65.** See Guidelines, page 636.

**67.** (a) Replace $x$ with $(-x)$.

    (b) Replace $x$ with $3x$.

    (c) Multiply series by $x$.

    (d) Replace $x$ with $2x$, then replace $x$ with $-2x$, and add the two together.

**69.** $y = \left(\tan\theta - \dfrac{g}{kv_0\cos\theta}\right)x - \dfrac{g}{k^2}\ln\left(1 - \dfrac{kx}{v_0\cos\theta}\right)$

$= (\tan\theta)x - \dfrac{gx}{kv_0\cos\theta} - \dfrac{g}{k^2}\left[-\dfrac{kx}{v_0\cos\theta} - \dfrac{1}{2}\left(\dfrac{kx}{v_0\cos\theta}\right)^2 - \dfrac{1}{3}\left(\dfrac{kx}{v_0\cos\theta}\right)^3 - \dfrac{1}{4}\left(\dfrac{kx}{v_o\cos\theta}\right)^4 - \cdots\right]$

$= (\tan\theta)x - \dfrac{gx}{kv_0\cos\theta} + \dfrac{gx}{kv_0\cos\theta} + \dfrac{gx^2}{2v_0^2\cos^2\theta} + \dfrac{gkx^3}{3v_0^3\cos^3\theta} + \dfrac{gk^2x^4}{4v_0^4\cos^4\theta} + \cdots\right]$

$= (\tan\theta)x + \dfrac{gx^2}{2v_0^2\cos^2\theta} + \dfrac{kgx^3}{3v_0^3\cos^3\theta} + \dfrac{k^2gx^4}{4v_0^4\cos^4\theta} + \cdots$

**71.** $f(x) = \begin{cases} e^{-1/x^2}, & x \neq 0 \\ 0, & x = 0 \end{cases}$

(a)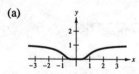

(b) $f'(0) = \displaystyle\lim_{x\to 0}\frac{f(x) - f(0)}{x - 0} = \lim_{x\to 0}\frac{e^{-1/x^2} - 0}{x}$

Let $y = \displaystyle\lim_{x\to 0}\frac{e^{-1/x^2}}{x}$. Then

$$\ln y = \lim_{x\to 0}\ln\left(\frac{e^{-1/x^2}}{x}\right) = \lim_{x\to 0^+}\left[-\frac{1}{x^2} - \ln x\right] = \lim_{x\to 0^+}\left[\frac{-1 - x^2\ln x}{x^2}\right] = -\infty.$$

Thus, $y = e^{-\infty} = 0$ and we have $f'(0) = 0$.

(c) $\displaystyle\sum_{n=0}^\infty \frac{f^{(n)}(0)}{n!}x^n = f(0) + \frac{f'(0)x}{1!} + \frac{f''(0)x^2}{2!} + \cdots = 0 \neq f(x)$

This series converges to $f$ at $x = 0$ only.

**73.** By the Ratio Test: $\displaystyle\lim_{n\to\infty}\left|\frac{x^{n+1}}{(n+1)!}\cdot\frac{n!}{x^n}\right| = \lim_{n\to\infty}\frac{|x|}{n+1} = 0$ which shows that $\displaystyle\sum_{n=0}^\infty \frac{x^n}{n!}$ converges for all $x$.

# Review Exercises for Chapter 8

**1.** $a_n = \dfrac{1}{n!}$

**3.** $a_n = 4 + \dfrac{2}{n}$: 6, 5, 4.67, . . .

Matches (a)

**5.** $a_n = 10(0.3)^{n-1}$: 10, 3, . . .

Matches (d)

**7.** $a_n = \dfrac{5n+2}{n}$

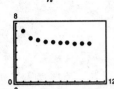

The sequence seems to converge to 5.

$$\lim_{n\to\infty} a_n = \lim_{n\to\infty} \frac{5n+2}{n}$$

$$= \lim_{n\to\infty} \left(5 + \frac{2}{n}\right) = 5$$

**9.** $\displaystyle\lim_{n\to\infty} \frac{n+1}{n^2} = 0$

Converges

**11.** $\displaystyle\lim_{n\to\infty} \frac{n^3}{n^2+1} = \infty$

**13.** $\displaystyle\lim_{n\to\infty} \left(\sqrt{n+1} - \sqrt{n}\right) = \lim_{n\to\infty} \left(\sqrt{n+1} - \sqrt{n}\right)\frac{\sqrt{n+1}+\sqrt{n}}{\sqrt{n+1}+\sqrt{n}} = \lim_{n\to\infty} \frac{1}{\sqrt{n+1}+\sqrt{n}} = 0$    Converges

**15.** $\displaystyle\lim_{n\to\infty} \frac{\sin(n)}{\sqrt{n}} = 0$

Converges

**17.** $A_n = 5000\left(1 + \dfrac{0.05}{4}\right)^n = 5000(1.0125)^n$

$n = 1, 2, 3$

(a) $A_1 = 5062.50$    $A_5 \approx 5320.41$

     $A_2 \approx 5125.78$    $A_6 \approx 5386.92$

     $A_3 \approx 5189.85$    $A_7 \approx 5454.25$

     $A_4 \approx 5254.73$    $A_8 \approx 5522.43$

(b) $A_{40} \approx 8218.10$

**19.** (a)

| $k$ | 5 | 10 | 15 | 20 | 25 |
|-----|------|-------|-------|--------|----------|
| $S_k$ | 13.2 | 113.3 | 873.8 | 6448.5 | 50,500.3 |

(c) The series diverges $\left(\text{geometric } r = \frac{3}{2} > 1\right)$

(b)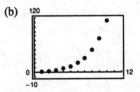

**21.** (a)

| $k$ | 5 | 10 | 15 | 20 | 25 |
|-----|--------|--------|--------|--------|--------|
| $S_k$ | 0.4597 | 0.4597 | 0.4597 | 0.4597 | 0.4597 |

(c) The series converges by the Alternating Series Test.

(b)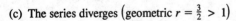

**23.** Converges. Geometric series, $r = 0.82$, $|r| < 1$.

**25.** Diverges. $n$th Term Test. $\displaystyle\lim_{n\to\infty} a_n \neq 0$.

**27.** $\displaystyle\sum_{n=0}^{\infty}\left(\frac{2}{3}\right)^n$

Geometric series with $a = 1$ and $r = \frac{2}{3}$.

$$S = \frac{a}{1-r} = \frac{1}{1-(2/3)} = \frac{1}{1/3} = 3$$

**29.** $\displaystyle\sum_{n=0}^{\infty}\left(\frac{1}{2^n} - \frac{1}{3^n}\right) = \sum_{n=0}^{\infty}\left(\frac{1}{2}\right)^n - \sum_{n=0}^{\infty}\left(\frac{1}{3}\right)^n$

$$= \frac{1}{1-(1/2)} - \frac{1}{1-(1/3)} = 2 - \frac{3}{2} = \frac{1}{2}$$

**31.** $0.\overline{09} = 0.09 + 0.0009 + 0.000009 + \cdots = 0.09(1 + 0.01 + 0.0001 + \cdots) = \displaystyle\sum_{n=0}^{\infty}(0.09)(0.01)^n = \frac{0.09}{1-0.01} = \frac{1}{11}$

**33.** $D_1 = 8$

$D_2 = 0.7(8) + 0.7(8) = 16(0.7)$

$\vdots$

$D = 8 + 16(0.7) + 16(0.7)^2 + \cdots + 16(0.7)^n + \cdots$

$$= -8 + \sum_{n=0}^{\infty} 16(0.7)^n = -8 + \frac{16}{1-0.7} = 45\frac{1}{3} \text{ meters}$$

**35.** See Exercise 86 in Section 8.2.

$$A = \frac{P(e^{rt} - 1)}{e^{r/12} - 1}$$

$$= \frac{200(e^{(0.06)(2)} - 1)}{e^{0.06/12} - 1}$$

$$\approx \$5087.14$$

**37.** $\displaystyle\int_1^{\infty} x^{-4}\ln(x)\,dx = \lim_{b \to \infty}\left[-\frac{\ln x}{3x^3} - \frac{1}{9x^3}\right]_1^b$

$$= 0 + \frac{1}{9} = \frac{1}{9}$$

By the Integral Test, the series converges.

**39.** $\displaystyle\sum_{n=1}^{\infty}\left(\frac{1}{n^2} - \frac{1}{n}\right) = \sum_{n=1}^{\infty}\frac{1}{n^2} - \sum_{n=1}^{\infty}\frac{1}{n}$

Since the second series is a divergent $p$-series while the first series is a convergent $p$-series, the difference diverges.

**41.** $\displaystyle\sum_{n=1}^{\infty}\frac{1}{\sqrt{n^3 + 2n}}$

$$\lim_{n \to \infty}\frac{1/\sqrt{n^3 + 2n}}{1/(n^{3/2})} = \lim_{n \to \infty}\frac{n^{3/2}}{\sqrt{n^3 + 2n}} = 1$$

By a limit comparison test with the convergent $p$-series

$\displaystyle\sum_{n=1}^{\infty}\frac{1}{n^{3/2}}$, the series converges.

**43.** $\displaystyle\sum_{n=1}^{\infty}\frac{1 \cdot 3 \cdot 5 \cdots (2n-1)}{2 \cdot 4 \cdot 6 \cdots (2n)}$

$$a_n = \frac{1 \cdot 3 \cdot 5 \cdots (2n-1)}{2 \cdot 4 \cdot 6 \cdots (2n)}$$

$$= \left(\frac{3}{2} \cdot \frac{5}{4} \cdots \frac{2n-1}{2n-2}\right)\frac{1}{2n} > \frac{1}{2n}$$

Since $\displaystyle\sum_{n=1}^{\infty}\frac{1}{2n} = \frac{1}{2}\sum_{n=1}^{\infty}\frac{1}{n}$ diverges (harmonic series), so does the original series.

**45.** Converges by the Alternating Series Test (Conditional convergence)

**47.** Diverges by the $n$th Term Test

**49.** $\displaystyle\sum_{n=1}^{\infty}\frac{n}{e^{n^2}}$

$$\lim_{n \to \infty}\left|\frac{a_{n+1}}{a_n}\right| = \lim_{n \to \infty}\left|\frac{n+1}{e^{(n+1)^2}} \cdot \frac{e^{n^2}}{n}\right|$$

$$= \lim_{n \to \infty}\left|\frac{e^{n^2}(n+1)}{e^{n^2 + 2n + 1}n}\right|$$

$$= \lim_{n \to \infty}\left(\frac{1}{e^{2n+1}}\right)\left(\frac{n+1}{n}\right)$$

$$= (0)(1) = 0 < 1$$

By the Ratio Test, the series converges.

**51.** $\displaystyle\sum_{n=1}^{\infty}\frac{2^n}{n^3}$

$$\lim_{n \to \infty}\left|\frac{a_{n+1}}{a_n}\right| = \lim_{n \to \infty}\left|\frac{2^{n+1}}{(n+1)^3} \cdot \frac{n^3}{2^n}\right|$$

$$= \lim_{n \to \infty}\frac{2n^3}{(n+1)^3} = 2$$

Therefore, by the Ratio Test, the series diverges.

**53. (a)** Ratio Test: $\lim\limits_{n\to\infty}\left|\dfrac{a_{n+1}}{a_n}\right| = \lim\limits_{n\to\infty}\dfrac{(n+1)(3/5)^{n+1}}{n(3/5)^n}$

$$= \lim_{n\to\infty}\left(\frac{n+1}{n}\right)\left(\frac{3}{5}\right) = \frac{3}{5} < 1$$

Converges

**(b)**

| $x$ | 5 | 10 | 15 | 20 | 25 |
|---|---|---|---|---|---|
| $S_n$ | 2.8752 | 3.6366 | 3.7377 | 3.7488 | 3.7499 |

**(c)**

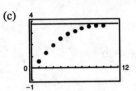

**(d)** The sum is approximately 3.75.

**55. (a)** $\displaystyle\int_N^\infty \frac{1}{x^2}\,dx = \left[-\frac{1}{x}\right]_N^\infty = \frac{1}{N}$

| $N$ | 5 | 10 | 20 | 30 | 40 |
|---|---|---|---|---|---|
| $\displaystyle\sum_{n=1}^N \frac{1}{n^2}$ | 1.4636 | 1.5498 | 1.5962 | 1.6122 | 1.6202 |
| $\displaystyle\int_N^\infty \frac{1}{x^2}\,dx$ | 0.2000 | 0.1000 | 0.0500 | 0.0333 | 0.0250 |

**(b)** $\displaystyle\int_N^\infty \frac{1}{x^5}\,dx = \left[-\frac{1}{4x^4}\right]_N^\infty = \frac{1}{4N^4}$

| $N$ | 5 | 10 | 20 | 30 | 40 |
|---|---|---|---|---|---|
| $\displaystyle\sum_{n=1}^N \frac{1}{n^5}$ | 1.0367 | 1.0369 | 1.0369 | 1.0369 | 1.0369 |
| $\displaystyle\int_N^\infty \frac{1}{x^5}\,dx$ | 0.0004 | 0.0000 | 0.0000 | 0.0000 | 0.0000 |

The series in part (b) converges more rapidly. The integral values represent the remainders of the partial sums.

**57.** $f(x) = e^{-x/2}$      $f(0) = 1$

$f'(x) = -\dfrac{1}{2}e^{-x/2}$      $f'(0) = -\dfrac{1}{2}$

$f''(x) = \dfrac{1}{4}e^{-x/2}$      $f''(0) = \dfrac{1}{4}$

$f'''(x) = -\dfrac{1}{8}e^{-x/2}$      $f'''(0) = -\dfrac{1}{8}$

$P_3(x) = f(0) + f'(0)x + f''(0)\dfrac{x^2}{2!} + f'''(0)\dfrac{x^3}{3!}$

$= 1 - \dfrac{1}{2}x + \dfrac{1}{4}\dfrac{x^2}{2!} - \dfrac{1}{8}\dfrac{x^3}{3!}$

$= 1 - \dfrac{1}{2}x + \dfrac{1}{8}x^2 - \dfrac{1}{48}x^3$

**59.** $\sin(95°) = \sin\left(\dfrac{95\pi}{180}\right) \approx \dfrac{95\pi}{180} - \dfrac{(95\pi)^3}{180^3 3!} + \dfrac{(95\pi)^5}{180^5 5!} - \dfrac{(95\pi)^7}{180^7 7!} + \dfrac{(95\pi)^9}{180^9 9!} \approx 0.996$

**61.** $\ln(1.75) \approx (0.75) - \dfrac{(0.75)^2}{2} + \dfrac{(0.75)^3}{3} - \dfrac{(0.75)^4}{4} + \dfrac{(0.75)^5}{5} - \dfrac{(0.75)^6}{6} + \cdots + \dfrac{(0.75)^{15}}{15} \approx 0.560$

**63.** $f(x) = \cos x, \ c = 0$

$$R_n(x) = \frac{f^{(n+1)}(z)}{(n+1)!}x^{n+1}$$

$$|f^{(n+1)}(z)| \le 1 \implies R_n(x) \le \frac{x^{n+1}}{(n+1)!}$$

(a) $R_n(x) \le \dfrac{(0.5)^{n+1}}{(n+1)!} < 0.001$

This inequality is true for $n = 4$.

(b) $R_n(x) \le \dfrac{(1)^{n+1}}{(n+1)!} < 0.001$

This inequality is true for $n = 6$.

(c) $R_n(x) \le \dfrac{(0.5)^{n+1}}{(n+1)!} < 0.0001$

This inequality is true for $n = 5$.

(d) $R_n(x) \le \dfrac{2^{n+1}}{(n+1)!} < 0.0001$

This inequality is true for $n = 10$.

**65.** $\displaystyle\sum_{n=0}^{\infty}\left(\frac{x}{10}\right)^n$

Geometric series which converges only if $|x/10| < 1$ or $-10 < x < 10$.

**67.** $\displaystyle\sum_{n=0}^{\infty}\frac{(-1)^n(x-2)^n}{(n+1)^2}$

$$\lim_{n\to\infty}\left|\frac{u_{n+1}}{u_n}\right| = \lim_{n\to\infty}\left|\frac{(-1)^{n+1}(x-2)^{n+1}}{(n+2)^2} \cdot \frac{(n+1)^2}{(-1)^n(x-2)^n}\right|$$

$$= |x-2|$$

$R = 1$

Center: 2

Since the series converges when $x = 1$ and when $x = 3$, the interval of convergence is $1 \le x \le 3$.

**69.** $\displaystyle\sum_{n=0}^{\infty}n!(x-2)^n$

$$\lim_{n\to\infty}\left|\frac{u_{n+1}}{u_n}\right| = \lim_{n\to\infty}\left|\frac{(n+1)!(x-2)^{n+1}}{n!(x-2)^n}\right| = \infty$$

which implies that the series converges only at the center $x = 2$.

**71.**

$$y = \sum_{n=0}^{\infty}(-1)^n\frac{x^{2n}}{4^n(n!)^2}$$

$$y' = \sum_{n=1}^{\infty}\frac{(-1)^n(2n)x^{2n-1}}{4^n(n!)^2} = \sum_{n=0}^{\infty}\frac{(-1)^{n+1}(2n+2)x^{2n+1}}{4^{n+1}[(n+1)!]^2}$$

$$y'' = \sum_{n=0}^{\infty}\frac{(-1)^{n+1}(2n+2)(2n+1)x^{2n}}{4^{n+1}[(n+1)!]^2}$$

$$x^2y'' + xy' + x^2y = \sum_{n=0}^{\infty}\frac{(-1)^{n+1}(2n+2)(2n+1)x^{2n+2}}{4^{n+1}[(n+1)!]^2} + \sum_{n=0}^{\infty}\frac{(-1)^{n+1}(2n+2)x^{2n+2}}{4^{n+1}[(n+1)!]^2} + \sum_{n=0}^{\infty}(-1)^n\frac{x^{2n+1}}{4^n(n!)^2}$$

$$= \sum_{n=0}^{\infty}\left[(-1)^{n+1}\frac{(2n+2)(2n+1)}{4^{n+1}[(n+1)!]^2} + \frac{(-1)^{n+1}(2n+2)}{4^{n+1}[(n+1)!]^2} + \frac{(-1)^n}{4^n(n!)^2}\right]x^{2n+2}$$

$$= \sum_{n=0}^{\infty}\left[\frac{(-1)^{n+1}(2n+2)(2n+1+1)}{4^{n+1}[(n+1)!]^2} + (-1)^n\frac{1}{4^n(n!)^2}\right]x^{2n+2}$$

$$= \sum_{n=0}^{\infty}\left[\frac{(-1)^{n+1}4(n+1)^2}{4^{n+1}[(n+1)!]^2} + (-1)^n\frac{1}{4^n(n!)^2}\right]x^{2n+2}$$

$$= \sum_{n=0}^{\infty}\left[\frac{(-1)^{n+1}1}{4^n(n!)^2} + (-1)^n\frac{1}{4^n(n!)^2}\right]x^{2n+2} = 0$$

**73.** $\dfrac{2}{3-x} = \dfrac{2/3}{1-(x/3)} = \dfrac{a}{1-r}$

$$\sum_{n=0}^{\infty}\frac{2}{3}\left(\frac{x}{3}\right)^n = \sum_{n=0}^{\infty}\frac{2x^n}{3^{n+1}}$$

**75.** Derivative: $\displaystyle\sum_{n=1}^{\infty}\frac{2nx^{n-1}}{3^{n+1}}$

**77.** $1 + \frac{2}{3}x + \frac{4}{9}x^2 + \frac{8}{27}x^3 + \cdots = \sum_{n=0}^{\infty} \left(\frac{2x}{3}\right)^n = \frac{1}{1-(2x/3)} = \frac{3}{3-2x}, \quad -\frac{3}{2} < x < \frac{3}{2}$

**79.** $f(x) = \sin(x)$

$f'(x) = \cos(x)$

$f''(x) = -\sin(x)$

$f'''(x) = -\cos(x), \cdots$

$\sin(x) = \sum_{n=0}^{\infty} \frac{f^{(n)}(x)[x - (3\pi/4)]^n}{n!}$

$= \frac{\sqrt{2}}{2} - \frac{\sqrt{2}}{2}\left(x - \frac{3\pi}{4}\right) - \frac{\sqrt{2}}{2 \cdot 2!}\left(x - \frac{3\pi}{4}\right)^2 + \cdots = \frac{\sqrt{2}}{2} \sum_{n=0}^{\infty} \frac{(-1)^{n(n+1)/2}[x - (3\pi/4)]^n}{n!}$

**81.** $3^x = (e^{\ln(3)})^x = e^{x \ln(3)}$ and since $e^x = \sum_{n=0}^{\infty} \frac{x^n}{n!}$, we have

$3^x = \sum_{n=0}^{\infty} \frac{(x \ln 3)^n}{n!}$

$= 1 + x \ln 3 + \frac{x^2 \ln^2 3}{2!} + \frac{x^3 \ln^3 3}{3!} + \frac{x^4 \ln^4 3}{4!} + \cdots.$

**83.** $f(x) = \frac{1}{x}$

$f'(x) = -\frac{1}{x^2}$

$f''(x) = \frac{2}{x^3}$

$f'''(x) = -\frac{6}{x^4}, \cdots$

$\frac{1}{x} = \sum_{n=0}^{\infty} \frac{f^{(n)}(-1)(x+1)^n}{n!}$

$= \sum_{n=0}^{\infty} \frac{-n!(x+1)^n}{n!} = -\sum_{n=0}^{\infty} (x+1)^n$

**85.** $(1+x)^k = 1 + kx + \frac{k(k-1)x^2}{2!} + \frac{k(k-1)(k-2)x^3}{3!} + \cdots$

$(1+x)^{1/5} = 1 + \frac{x}{5} + \frac{(1/5)(-4/5)x^2}{2!} + \frac{1/5(-4/5)(-9/5)x^3}{3!} + \cdots$

$= 1 + \frac{1}{5}x - \frac{1 \cdot 4 x^2}{5^2 2!} + \frac{1 \cdot 4 \cdot 9 x^3}{5^3 3!} - \cdots$

$= 1 + \frac{x}{5} + \sum_{n=2}^{\infty} \frac{(-1)^{n+1} 4 \cdot 9 \cdot 14 \cdots (5n-6)x^n}{5^n n!}$

$= 1 + \frac{x}{5} - \frac{2}{25}x^2 + \frac{6}{125}x^3 - \cdots$

**87.** $\ln x = \sum_{n=1}^{\infty} (-1)^{n+1} \frac{(x-1)^n}{n}, \qquad 0 < x \le 2$

$\ln\left(\frac{5}{4}\right) = \sum_{n=1}^{\infty} (-1)^{n+1}\left(\frac{(5/4)-1}{n}\right)^n$

$= \sum_{n=1}^{\infty} (-1)^{n+1} \frac{1}{4^n n} \approx 0.2231$

**89.** $e^x = \sum_{n=0}^{\infty} \frac{x^n}{n!}, \quad -\infty < x < \infty$

$e^{1/2} = \sum_{n=0}^{\infty} \frac{1}{2^n n!} \approx 1.6487$

**91.**   $\cos x = \sum\limits_{n=0}^{\infty} (-1)^n \dfrac{x^{2n}}{(2n)!}, \quad -\infty < x < \infty$

$\cos\left(\dfrac{2}{3}\right) = \sum\limits_{n=0}^{\infty} (-1)^n \dfrac{2^{2n}}{3^{2n}(2n)!} \approx 0.7859$

**93.** The series for Exercise 41 converges very slowly because the terms approach 0 at a slow rate.

**95. (a)**   $f(x) = e^{2x} \qquad f(0) = 1$

$f'(x) = 2e^{2x} \qquad f'(0) = 2$

$f''(x) = 4e^{2x} \qquad f''(0) = 4$

$f'''(x) = 8e^{2x} \qquad f'''(0) = 8$

$e^{2x} = 1 + 2x + \dfrac{4x^2}{2!} + \dfrac{8x^3}{3!} + \cdots$

$= 1 + 2x + 2x^2 + \dfrac{4}{3}x^3 + \cdots$

**(b)**   $e^x = \sum\limits_{n=0}^{\infty} \dfrac{x^n}{n!}$

$e^{2x} = \sum\limits_{n=0}^{\infty} \dfrac{(2x)^n}{n!} = 1 + 2x + \dfrac{4x^2}{2!} + \dfrac{8x^3}{3!} + \cdots$

$= 1 + 2x + 2x^2 + \dfrac{4}{3}x^3 + \cdots$

**(c)**   $e^{2x} = e^x \cdot e^x = \left(1 + x + \dfrac{x^2}{2} + \dfrac{x^3}{6} + \cdots\right)\left(1 + x + \dfrac{x^2}{2} + \dfrac{x^3}{6} + \cdots\right)$

$= 1 + (x + x) + \left(x^2 + \dfrac{x^2}{2} + \dfrac{x^2}{2}\right) + \left(\dfrac{x^3}{6} + \dfrac{x^3}{6} + \dfrac{x^3}{2} + \dfrac{x^3}{2}\right) + \cdots = 1 + 2x + 2x^2 + \dfrac{4}{3}x^3 + \cdots$

**97.**   $\sin t = \sum\limits_{n=0}^{\infty} \dfrac{(-1)^n t^{2n+1}}{(2n+1)!}$

$\dfrac{\sin t}{t} = \sum\limits_{n=0}^{\infty} \dfrac{(-1)^n t^{2n}}{(2n+1)!}$

$\displaystyle\int_0^x \dfrac{\sin t}{t}\, dt = \left[\sum\limits_{n=0}^{\infty} \dfrac{(-1)^n t^{2n+1}}{(2n+1)(2n+1)!}\right]_0^x$

$= \sum\limits_{n=0}^{\infty} \dfrac{(-1)^n x^{2n+1}}{(2n+1)(2n+1)!}$

**99.**   $\dfrac{1}{1+t} = \sum\limits_{n=0}^{\infty} (-1)^n t^n$

$\ln(1+t) = \displaystyle\int \dfrac{1}{1+t}\, dt = \sum\limits_{n=0}^{\infty} \dfrac{(-1)^n t^{n+1}}{n+1}$

$\dfrac{\ln(t+1)}{t} = \sum\limits_{n=0}^{\infty} \dfrac{(-1)^n t^n}{n+1}$

$\displaystyle\int_0^x \dfrac{\ln(t+1)}{t}\, dt = \left[\sum\limits_{n=0}^{\infty} \dfrac{(-1)^n t^{n+1}}{(n+1)^2}\right]_0^x = \sum\limits_{n=0}^{\infty} \dfrac{(-1)^n x^{n+1}}{(n+1)^2}$

**101.**   $\arctan x = x - \dfrac{x^3}{3} + \dfrac{x^5}{5} - \dfrac{x^7}{7} + \dfrac{x^9}{9} - \cdots$

$\dfrac{\arctan x}{\sqrt{x}} = \sqrt{x} - \dfrac{x^{5/2}}{3} + \dfrac{x^{9/2}}{5} - \dfrac{x^{13/2}}{7} + \dfrac{x^{17/2}}{9} - \cdots$

$\lim\limits_{x \to 0} \dfrac{\arctan x}{\sqrt{x}} = 0$

By L'Hôpital's Rule, $\lim\limits_{x\to 0} \dfrac{\arctan x}{\sqrt{x}} = \lim\limits_{x\to 0} \dfrac{\left(\dfrac{1}{1+x^2}\right)}{\left(\dfrac{1}{2\sqrt{x}}\right)} = \lim\limits_{x\to 0} \dfrac{2\sqrt{x}}{1+x^2} = 0.$

# Problem Solving for Chapter 8

**1. (a)**   $1\left(\dfrac{1}{3}\right) + 2\left(\dfrac{1}{9}\right) + 4\left(\dfrac{1}{27}\right) + \cdots = \sum\limits_{n=0}^{\infty} \dfrac{1}{3}\left(\dfrac{2}{3}\right)^n = \dfrac{1/3}{1 - (2/3)} = 1$

**(b)**   $0, \dfrac{1}{3}, \dfrac{2}{3}, 1,$ etc.

**(c)**   $\lim\limits_{n\to\infty} C_n = 1 - \sum\limits_{n=0}^{\infty} \dfrac{1}{3}\left(\dfrac{2}{3}\right)^n = 1 - 1 = 0$

**3.** If there are $n$ rows, then $a_n = \dfrac{n(n+1)}{2}$.

For one circle,

$$a_1 = 1 \text{ and } r_1 = \frac{1}{3}\left(\frac{\sqrt{3}}{2}\right) = \frac{\sqrt{3}}{6} = \frac{1}{2\sqrt{3}}$$

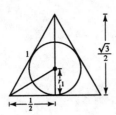

For three circles,

$$a_2 = 3 \text{ and } 1 = 2\sqrt{3}r_2 + 2r_2$$

$$r_2 = \frac{1}{2 + 2\sqrt{3}}$$

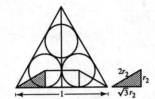

For six circles,

$$a_3 = 6 \text{ and } 1 = 2\sqrt{3}r_3 + 4r_3$$

$$r_3 = \frac{1}{2\sqrt{3} + 4}$$

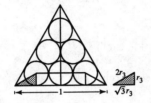

Continuing this pattern, $r_n = \dfrac{1}{2\sqrt{3} + 2(n-1)}$.

$$\text{Total Area} = (\pi r_n{}^2)a_n = \pi\left(\frac{1}{2\sqrt{3} + 2(n-1)}\right)^2 \frac{n(n+1)}{2}$$

$$A_n = \frac{\pi}{2}\,\frac{n(n+1)}{\left[2\sqrt{3} + 2(n+1)^2\right]}$$

$$\lim_{n\to\infty} A_n = \frac{\pi}{2}\cdot\frac{1}{4} = \frac{\pi}{8}$$

**5.** (a) $\displaystyle\sum a_n x^n = 1 + 2x + 3x^2 + x^3 + 2x^4 + 3x^5 + \cdots$

$$= (1 + x^3 + x^6 + \cdots) + 2(x + x^4 + x^7 + \cdots) + 3(x^2 + x^5 + x^8 + \cdots)$$

$$= (1 + x^3 + x^6 + \cdots)[1 + 2x + 3x^2]$$

$$= (1 + 2x + 3x^2)\frac{1}{1 - x^3}$$

$R = 1$ because each series in the second line has $R = 1$.

(b) $\displaystyle\sum a_n x^n = (a_0 + a_1 x + \cdots + a_{p-1}x^{p-1}) + (a_0 x^p + a_1 x^{p+1} + \cdots) + \cdots$

$$= a_0(1 + x^p + \cdots) + a_1 x(1 + x^p + \cdots) + \cdots + a_{p-1}x^{p-1}(1 + x^p + \cdots)$$

$$= (a_0 + a_1 x + \cdots + a_{p-1}x^{p-1})(1 + x^p + \cdots)$$

$$= (a_0 + a_1 x + \cdots + a_{p-1}x^{p-1})\frac{1}{1 - x^p}.$$

$R = 1$

**7.**
$$e^x = 1 + x + \frac{x^2}{2!} + \cdots$$

$$xe^x = x + x^2 + \frac{x^3}{2!} + \cdots = \sum_{n=0}^{\infty} \frac{x^{n+1}}{n!}$$

$$\int xe^x \, dx = xe^x - e^x + C = \sum_{n=0}^{\infty} \frac{x^{n+2}}{(n+2)n!}$$

Letting $x = 0$, $C = 1$. Letting $x = 1$,

$$1 = \sum_{n=0}^{\infty} \frac{1}{(n+2)n!} = \frac{1}{2} + \sum_{n=1}^{\infty} \frac{1}{(n+2)n!}.$$

Thus, $\displaystyle\sum_{n=1}^{\infty} \frac{1}{(n+2)n!} = \frac{1}{2}.$

**9.** Let $a_1 = \displaystyle\int_0^{\pi} \frac{\sin x}{x} \, dx$, $a_2 = -\displaystyle\int_{\pi}^{2\pi} \frac{\sin x}{x} \, dx$, $a_3 = \displaystyle\int_{2\pi}^{3\pi} \frac{\sin x}{x} \, dx$, etc.

Then,

$$\int_0^{\infty} \frac{\sin x}{x} \, dx = a_1 - a_2 + a_3 - a_4 + \cdots.$$

Since $\displaystyle\lim_{n \to \infty} a_n = 0$ and $a_{n+1} < a_n$, this series converges.

**11. (a)** $a_1 = 3.0$

$a_2 \approx 1.73205$

$a_3 \approx 2.17533$

$a_4 \approx 2.27493$

$a_5 \approx 2.29672$

$a_6 \approx 2.30146$

$\displaystyle\lim_{n \to \infty} a_n = \frac{1 + \sqrt{13}}{2}$ [See part (b) for proof.]

**(b)** Use mathematical induction to show the sequence is increasing. Clearly, $a_2 = \sqrt{a + a_1} = \sqrt{a\sqrt{a}} > \sqrt{a} = a_1$.

Now assume $a_n > a_{n-1}$. Then

$$a_n + a > a_{n-1} + a$$
$$\sqrt{a_n + a} > \sqrt{a_{n-1} + a}$$
$$a_{n+1} > a_n.$$

Use mathematical induction to show that the sequence is bounded above by $a$. Clearly, $a_1 = \sqrt{a} < a$.

Now assume $a_n < a$. Then $a > a_n$ and $a - 1 > 1$ implies

$$a(a - 1) > a_n(1)$$
$$a^2 - a > a_n$$
$$a^2 > a_n + a$$
$$a > \sqrt{a_n + a} = a_{n+1}.$$

Hence, the sequence converges to some number $L$. To find $L$, assume $a_{n+1} \approx a_n \approx L$:

$$L = \sqrt{a + L} \implies L^2 = a + L \implies L^2 - L - a = 0$$

$$L = \frac{1 \pm \sqrt{1 + 4a}}{2}.$$

Hence, $L = \dfrac{1 + \sqrt{1 + 4a}}{2}.$

**13.** (a) $\displaystyle\sum_{n=1}^{\infty} \frac{1}{2^{n+(-1)^n}} = \frac{1}{2^{1-1}} + \frac{1}{2^{2+1}} + \frac{1}{2^{3-1}} + \frac{1}{2^{4+1}} + \frac{1}{2^{5-1}} + \cdots$

$$S_1 = \frac{1}{2^0} = 1$$

$$S_1 = 1 + \frac{1}{8} = \frac{9}{8}$$

$$S_3 = \frac{9}{8} + \frac{1}{4} = \frac{11}{8}$$

$$S_4 = \frac{11}{8} + \frac{1}{32} = \frac{45}{32}$$

$$S_5 = \frac{45}{32} + \frac{1}{16} = \frac{47}{32}$$

(b) $\dfrac{a_{n+1}}{a_n} = \dfrac{2^{n+(-1)^n}}{2^{(n+1)+(-1)^{n+1}}} = \dfrac{2^{(-1)^n}}{2^{1+(-1)^{n+1}}}$

This sequence is $\frac{1}{8}, 2, \frac{1}{8}, 2, \ldots$ which diverges.

(c) $\displaystyle\sqrt[n]{\frac{1}{2^{n+(-1)^n}}} = \left(\frac{1}{2^n \cdot 2^{(-1)^n}}\right)^{1/n}$

$$= \frac{1}{2 \cdot \sqrt[n]{2^{(-1)^n}}} \to \frac{1}{2} < 1 \text{ converges because } \{2^{(-1)^n}\} = \frac{1}{2}, 2, \frac{1}{2}, 2, \ldots \text{ and } \sqrt[n]{1/2} \to 1 \text{ and } \sqrt[n]{2} \to 1.$$

**15.** $S_6 = 130 + 70 + 40 = 240$

$S_7 = 240 + 130 + 70 = 440$

$S_8 = 440 + 240 + 130 = 810$

$S_9 = 810 + 440 + 240 = 1490$

$S_{10} = 1490 + 810 + 440 = 2740$

# CHAPTER 9
# Conics, Parametric Equations, and Polar Coordinates

# CHAPTER 9
# Conics, Parametric Equations, and Polar Coordinates

## Section 9.1  Conics and Calculus

Solutions to Odd-Numbered Exercises

**1.** $y^2 = 4x$

Vertex: $(0, 0)$

$p = 1 > 0$

Opens to the right
Matches graph (h).

**3.** $(x + 3)^2 = -2(y - 2)$

Vertex: $(-3, 2)$

$p = -\frac{1}{2} < 0$

Opens downward
Matches graph (e).

**5.** $\dfrac{x^2}{9} + \dfrac{y^2}{4} = 1$

Center: $(0, 0)$
Ellipse
Matches (f)

**7.** $\dfrac{y^2}{16} - \dfrac{x^2}{1} = 1$

Hyperbola
Center: $(0, 0)$
Vertical transverse axis.
Matches (c)

**9.** $y^2 = -6x = 4\left(-\frac{3}{2}\right)x$

Vertex: $(0, 0)$

Focus: $\left(-\frac{3}{2}, 0\right)$

Directrix: $x = \frac{3}{2}$

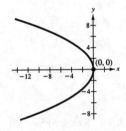

**11.** $(x + 3) + (y - 2)^2 = 0$

$$(y - 2)^2 = 4\left(-\frac{1}{4}\right)(x + 3)$$

Vertex: $(-3, 2)$

Focus: $(-3.25, 2)$

Directrix: $x = -2.75$

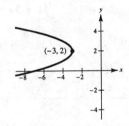

**13.** $y^2 - 4y - 4x = 0$

$$y^2 - 4y + 4 = 4x + 4$$

$$(y - 2)^2 = 4(1)(x + 1)$$

Vertex: $(-1, 2)$

Focus: $(0, 2)$

Directrix: $x = -2$

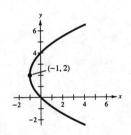

**15.** $x^2 + 4x + 4y - 4 = 0$

$$x^2 + 4x + 4 = -4y + 4 + 4$$

$$(x + 2)^2 = 4(-1)(y - 2)$$

Vertex: $(-2, 2)$

Focus: $(-2, 1)$

Directrix: $y = 3$

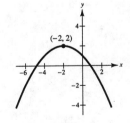

**17.** $y^2 + x + y = 0$

$y^2 + y + \frac{1}{4} = -x + \frac{1}{4}$

$\left(y + \frac{1}{2}\right)^2 = 4\left(-\frac{1}{4}\right)\left(x - \frac{1}{4}\right)$

Vertex: $\left(\frac{1}{4}, -\frac{1}{2}\right)$

Focus: $\left(0, -\frac{1}{2}\right)$

Directrix: $x = \frac{1}{2}$

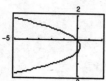

**19.** $y^2 - 4x - 4 = 0$

$y^2 = 4x + 4$

$= 4(1)(x + 1)$

Vertex: $(-1, 0)$

Focus: $(0, 0)$

Directrix: $x = -2$

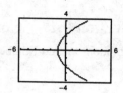

**21.**    $(y - 2)^2 = 4(-2)(x - 3)$

$y^2 - 4y + 8x - 20 = 0$

**23.**    $(x - h)^2 = 4p(y - k)$

$x^2 = 4(6)(y - 4)$

$x^2 - 24y + 96 = 0$

**25.**    $y = 4 - x^2$

$x^2 + y - 4 = 0$

**27.** Since the axis of the parabola is vertical, the form of the equation is $y = ax^2 + bx + c$. Now, substituting the values of the given coordinates into this equation, we obtain

$3 = c, 4 = 9a + 3b + c, 11 = 16a + 4b + c.$

Solving this system, we have $a = \frac{5}{3}, b = -\frac{14}{3}, c = 3$. Therefore,

$y = \frac{5}{3}x^2 - \frac{14}{3}x + 3$ or $5x^2 - 14x - 3y + 9 = 0.$

**29.** $x^2 + 4y^2 = 4$

$\frac{x^2}{4} + \frac{y^2}{1} = 1$

$a^2 = 4, b^2 = 1, c^2 = 3$

Center: $(0, 0)$

Foci: $(\pm\sqrt{3}, 0)$

Vertices: $(\pm 2, 0)$

$e = \frac{\sqrt{3}}{2}$

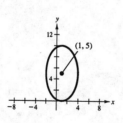

**31.** $\frac{(x - 1)^2}{9} + \frac{(y - 5)^2}{25} = 1$

$a^2 = 25, b^2 = 9, c^2 = 16$

Center: $(1, 5)$

Foci: $(1, 9), (1, 1)$

Vertices: $(1, 10), (1, 0)$

$e = \frac{4}{5}$

**33.**    $9x^2 + 4y^2 + 36x - 24y + 36 = 0$

$9(x^2 + 4x + 4) + 4(y^2 - 6y + 9) = -36 + 36 + 36$

$= 36$

$\frac{(x + 2)^2}{4} + \frac{(y - 3)^2}{9} = 1$

$a^2 = 9, b^2 = 4, c^2 = 5$

Center: $(-2, 3)$

Foci: $\left(-2, 3 \pm \sqrt{5}\right)$

Vertices: $(-2, 6), (-2, 0)$

$e = \frac{\sqrt{5}}{3}$

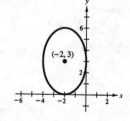

**35.** $\quad 12x^2 + 20y^2 - 12x + 40y - 37 = 0$

$$12\left(x^2 - x + \frac{1}{4}\right) + 20(y^2 + 2y + 1) = 37 + 3 + 20$$

$$= 60$$

$$\frac{[x - (1/2)]^2}{5} + \frac{(y + 1)^2}{3} = 1$$

$a^2 = 5,\ b^2 = 3,\ c^2 = 2$

Center: $\left(\dfrac{1}{2}, -1\right)$

Foci: $\left(\dfrac{1}{2} \pm \sqrt{2}, -1\right)$

Vertices: $\left(\dfrac{1}{2} \pm \sqrt{5}, -1\right)$

Solve for $y$:

$$20(y^2 + 2y + 1) = -12x^2 + 12x + 37 + 20$$

$$(y + 1)^2 = \frac{57 + 12x - 12x^2}{20}$$

$$y = -1 \pm \sqrt{\frac{57 + 12x - 12x^2}{20}}$$

(Graph each of these separately.)

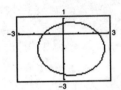

**37.** $\quad x^2 + 2y^2 - 3x + 4y + 0.25 = 0$

$$\left(x^2 - 3x + \frac{9}{4}\right) + 2(y^2 + 2y + 1) = -\frac{1}{4} + \frac{9}{4} + 2 = 4$$

$$\frac{[x - (3/2)]^2}{4} + \frac{(y + 1)^2}{2} = 1$$

$a^2 = 4,\ b^2 = 2,\ c^2 = 2$

Center: $\left(\dfrac{3}{2}, -1\right)$

Foci: $\left(\dfrac{3}{2} \pm \sqrt{2}, -1\right)$

Vertices: $\left(-\dfrac{1}{2}, -1\right), \left(\dfrac{7}{2}, -1\right)$

Solve for $y$: $\quad 2(y^2 + 2y + 1) = -x^2 + 3x - \dfrac{1}{4} + 2$

$$(y + 1)^2 = \frac{1}{2}\left(\frac{7}{4} + 3x - x^2\right)$$

$$y = -1 \pm \sqrt{\frac{7 + 12x - 4x^2}{8}}$$

(Graph each of these separately.)

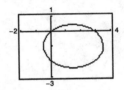

**39.** Center: $(0, 0)$
Focus: $(2, 0)$
Vertex: $(3, 0)$
Horizontal major axis

$$a = 3,\ c = 2 \implies b = \sqrt{5}$$

$$\frac{x^2}{9} + \frac{y^2}{5} = 1$$

**41.** Vertices: $(3, 1), (3, 9)$
Minor axis length: $6$
Vertical major axis
Center: $(3, 5)$

$$a = 4,\ b = 3$$

$$\frac{(x - 3)^2}{9} + \frac{(y - 5)^2}{16} = 1$$

**43.** Center: $(0, 0)$
Horizontal major axis
Points on ellipse: $(3, 1), (4, 0)$

Since the major axis is horizontal,

$$\left(\frac{x^2}{a^2}\right) + \left(\frac{y^2}{b^2}\right) = 1.$$

Substituting the values of the coordinates of the given points into this equation, we have

$$\left(\frac{9}{a^2}\right) + \left(\frac{1}{b^2}\right) = 1, \text{ and } \frac{16}{a^2} = 1.$$

The solution to this system is $a^2 = 16,\ b^2 = 16/7$.

Therefore,

$$\frac{x^2}{16} + \frac{y^2}{16/7} = 1,\ \frac{x^2}{16} + \frac{7y^2}{16} = 1.$$

**45.** $\dfrac{y^2}{1} - \dfrac{x^2}{4} = 1$

$a = 1, b = 2, c = \sqrt{5}$

Center: $(0, 0)$

Vertices: $(0, \pm 1)$

Foci: $\left(0, \pm \sqrt{5}\right)$

Asymptotes: $y = \pm \dfrac{1}{2}x$

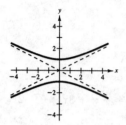

**47.** $\dfrac{(x-1)^2}{4} - \dfrac{(y+2)^2}{1} = 1$

$a = 2, b = 1, c = \sqrt{5}$

Center: $(1, -2)$

Vertices: $(-1, -2), (3, -2)$

Foci: $\left(1 \pm \sqrt{5}, -2\right)$

Asymptotes: $y = -2 \pm \dfrac{1}{2}(x - 1)$

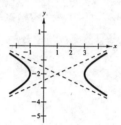

**49.** $9x^2 - y^2 - 36x - 6y + 18 = 0$

$9(x^2 - 4x + 4) - (y^2 + 6y + 9) = -18 + 36 - 9$

$$\dfrac{(x-2)^2}{1} - \dfrac{(y+3)^2}{9} = 1$$

$a = 1, b = 3, c = \sqrt{10}$

Center: $(2, -3)$

Vertices: $(1, -3), (3, -3)$

Foci: $\left(2 \pm \sqrt{10}, -3\right)$

Asymptotes: $y = -3 \pm 3(x - 2)$

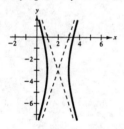

**51.** $x^2 - 9y^2 + 2x - 54y - 80 = 0$

$(x^2 + 2x + 1) - 9(y^2 + 6y + 9) = 80 + 1 - 81 = 0$

$$(x + 1)^2 - 9(y + 3)^2 = 0$$

$$y + 3 = \pm \dfrac{1}{3}(x + 1)$$

Degenerate hyperbola is two lines intersecting at $(-1, -3)$.

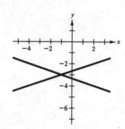

**53.** $9y^2 - x^2 + 2x + 54y + 62 = 0$

$9(y^2 + 6y + 9) - (x^2 - 2x + 1) = -62 - 1 + 81 = 18$

$$\dfrac{(y+3)^2}{2} - \dfrac{(x-1)^2}{18} = 1$$

$a = \sqrt{2}, b = 3\sqrt{2}, c = 2\sqrt{5}$

Center: $(1, -3)$

Vertices: $\left(1, -3 \pm \sqrt{2}\right)$

Foci: $\left(1, -3 \pm 2\sqrt{5}\right)$

Solve for $y$:

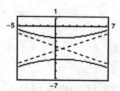

$9(y^2 + 6y + 9) = x^2 - 2x - 62 + 81$

$(y + 3)^2 = \dfrac{x^2 - 2x + 19}{9}$

$y = -3 \pm \dfrac{1}{3}\sqrt{x^2 - 2x + 19}$

(Graph each curve separately.)

**55.** $3x^2 - 2y^2 - 6x - 12y - 27 = 0$

$3(x^2 - 2x + 1) - 2(y^2 + 6y + 9) = 27 + 3 - 18 = 12$

$$\dfrac{(x-1)^2}{4} - \dfrac{(y+3)^2}{6} = 1$$

$a = 2, b = \sqrt{6}, c = \sqrt{10}$

Center: $(1, -3)$

Vertices: $(-1, -3), (3, -3)$

Foci: $\left(1 \pm \sqrt{10}, -3\right)$

Solve for $y$:

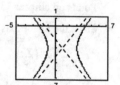

$2(y^2 + 6y + 9) = 3x^2 - 6x - 27 + 18$

$(y + 3)^2 = \dfrac{3x^2 - 6x - 9}{2}$

$y = -3 \pm \sqrt{\dfrac{3(x^2 - 2x - 3)}{2}}$

(Graph each curve separately.)

**57.** Vertices: $(\pm 1, 0)$

Asymptotes: $y = \pm 3x$

Horizontal transverse axis

Center: $(0, 0)$

$$a = 1, \pm\frac{b}{a} = \pm\frac{b}{1} = \pm 3 \implies b = 3$$

Therefore, $\dfrac{x^2}{1} - \dfrac{y^2}{9} = 1$.

**59.** Vertices: $(2, \pm 3)$

Point on graph: $(0, 5)$

Vertical transverse axis

Center: $(2, 0)$

$a = 3$

Therefore, the equation is of the form

$$\frac{y^2}{9} - \frac{(x - 2)^2}{b^2} = 1.$$

Substituting the coordinates of the point $(0, 5)$, we have

$$\frac{25}{9} - \frac{4}{b^2} = 1 \quad \text{or} \quad b^2 = \frac{9}{4}.$$

Therefore, the equation is $\dfrac{y^2}{9} - \dfrac{(x - 2)^2}{9/4} = 1$.

**61.** Center: $(0, 0)$

Vertex: $(0, 2)$

Focus: $(0, 4)$

Vertical transverse axis

$$a = 2, c = 4, b^2 = c^2 - a^2 = 12$$

Therefore, $\dfrac{y^2}{4} - \dfrac{x^2}{12} = 1$.

**63.** Vertices: $(0, 2), (6, 2)$

Asymptotes: $y = \dfrac{2}{3}x, y = 4 - \dfrac{2}{3}x$

Horizontal transverse axis

Center: $(3, 2)$

$a = 3$

Slopes of asymptotes: $\pm\dfrac{b}{a} = \pm\dfrac{2}{3}$

Thus, $b = 2$. Therefore,

$$\frac{(x - 3)^2}{9} - \frac{(y - 2)^2}{4} = 1.$$

**65. (a)** $\dfrac{x^2}{9} - y^2 = 1, \dfrac{2x}{9} - 2yy' = 0, \dfrac{x}{9y} = y'$

At $x = 6$: $y = \pm\sqrt{3}, y' = \dfrac{\pm 6}{9\sqrt{3}} = \dfrac{\pm 2\sqrt{3}}{9}$

At $\left(6, \sqrt{3}\right)$: $y - \sqrt{3} = \dfrac{2\sqrt{3}}{9}(x - 6)$

$\quad$ or $2x - 3\sqrt{3}y - 3 = 0$

At $\left(6, -\sqrt{3}\right)$: $y + \sqrt{3} = \dfrac{-2\sqrt{3}}{9}(x - 6)$

$\quad$ or $2x + 3\sqrt{3}y - 3 = 0$

**(b)** From part (a) we know that the slopes of the normal lines must be $\mp 9/\left(2\sqrt{3}\right)$.

At $\left(6, \sqrt{3}\right)$: $y - \sqrt{3} = -\dfrac{9}{2\sqrt{3}}(x - 6)$

$\quad$ or $9x + 2\sqrt{3}y - 60 = 0$

At $\left(6, -\sqrt{3}\right)$: $y + \sqrt{3} = \dfrac{9}{2\sqrt{3}}(x - 6)$

$\quad$ or $9x - 2\sqrt{3}y - 60 = 0$

**67.** $x^2 + 4y^2 - 6x + 16y + 21 = 0$

$A = 1, C = 4$

$AC = 4 > 0$

Ellipse

**69.** $y^2 - 4y - 4x = 0$

$A = 0, C = 1$

Parabola

**71.** $4x^2 + 4y^2 - 16y + 15 = 0$

$A = C = 4$

Circle

**73.** $9x^2 + 9y^2 - 36x + 6y + 34 = 0$

$A = C = 9$

Circle

**75.** $\qquad 3x^2 - 6x + 3 = 6 + 2y^2 + 4y + 2$

$3x^2 - 2y^2 - 6x - 4y - 5 = 0$

$A = 3, C = -2, AC < 0$

Hyperbola

**77.** (a) A parabola is the set of all points $(x, y)$ that are equidistant from a fixed line (directrix) and a fixed point (focus) not on the line.

(b) $(x - h)^2 = 4p(y - k)$ or $(y - k)^2 = 4p(x - h)$

(c) See Theorem 9.2.

**79.** (a) A hyperbola is the set of all points $(x, y)$ for which the absolute value of the difference between the distances from two distance fixed points (foci) is constant.

(b) $\dfrac{(x - h)^2}{a^2} - \dfrac{(y - k)^2}{b^2} = 1$ or $\dfrac{(y - k)^2}{a^2} - \dfrac{(x - h)^2}{b^2} = 1$

(c) $y = k \pm \dfrac{b}{a}(x - h)$ or $y = k \pm \dfrac{a}{b}(x - h)$

**81.** Assume that the vertex is at the origin.

$$x^2 = 4py$$

$$(3)^2 = 4p(1)$$

$$\frac{9}{4} = p$$

The pipe is located $\frac{9}{4}$ meters from the vertex.

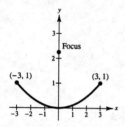

**83.** $y = ax^2$

$y' = 2ax$

The equation of the tangent line is

$$y - ax_0{}^2 = 2ax_0(x - x_0) \text{ or } y = 2ax_0 x - ax_0{}^2.$$

Let $y = 0$. Then:

$$-ax_0{}^2 = 2ax_0 x - 2ax_0{}^2$$

$$ax_0{}^2 = 2ax_0 x$$

Therefore, $\dfrac{x_0}{2} = x$ is the x-intercept.

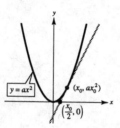

**85.** (a) Consider the parabola $x^2 = 4py$. Let $m_0$ be the slope of the one tangent line at $(x_1, y_1)$ and therefore, $-1/m_0$ is the slope of the second at $(x_2, y_2)$. From the derivative given in Exercise 32 we have:

$$m_0 = \frac{1}{2p}x_1 \text{ or } x_1 = 2pm_0$$

$$\frac{-1}{m_0} = \frac{1}{2p}x_2 \text{ or } x_2 = \frac{-2p}{m_0}$$

Substituting these values of $x$ into the equation $x^2 = 4py$, we have the coordinates of the points of tangency $(2pm_0, pm_0{}^2)$ and $(-2p/m_0, p/m_0{}^2)$ and the equations of the tangent lines are

$$(y - pm_0{}^2) = m_0(x - 2pm_0) \quad \text{and} \quad \left(y - \frac{p}{m_0{}^2}\right) = \frac{-1}{m_0}\left(x + \frac{2p}{m_0}\right).$$

The point of intersection of these lines is

$$\left(\frac{p(m_0{}^2 - 1)}{m_0}, -p\right) \text{ and is on the directrix, } y = -p.$$

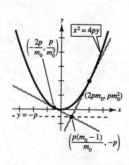

**—CONTINUED—**

**85.** **—CONTINUED—**

(b) $x^2 - 4x - 4y + 8 = 0$

$(x - 2)^2 = 4(y - 1)$.  Vertex $(2, 1)$

$$2x - 4 - 4\frac{dy}{dx} = 0$$

$$\frac{dy}{dx} = \frac{1}{2}x - 1$$

At $(-2, 5)$, $dy/dx = -2$. At $\left(3, \frac{5}{4}\right)$, $dy/dx = \frac{1}{2}$.

Tangent line at $(-2, 5)$: $y - 5 = -2(x + 2) \implies 2x + y - 1 = 0$.

Tangent line at $\left(3, \frac{5}{4}\right)$: $y - \frac{5}{4} = \frac{1}{2}(x - 3) \implies 2x - 4y - 1 = 0$.

Since $m_1 m_2 = (-2)\left(\frac{1}{2}\right) = -1$, the lines are perpendicular.

Point of intersection: $-2x + 1 = \frac{1}{2}x - \frac{1}{4}$

$$-\frac{5}{2}x = -\frac{5}{4}$$

$$x = \frac{1}{2}$$

$$y = 0$$

Directrix: $y = 0$ and the point of intersection $\left(\frac{1}{2}, 0\right)$ lies on this line.

**87.** $y = x - x^2$

$$\frac{dy}{dx} = 1 - 2x$$

At $(x_1, y_1)$ on the mountain, $m = 1 - 2x_1$. Also, $m = \dfrac{y_1 - 1}{x_1 + 1}$.

$$\frac{y_1 - 1}{x_1 + 1} = 1 - 2x_1$$

$$(x_1 - x_1{}^2) - 1 = (1 - 2x_1)(x_1 + 1)$$

$$-x_1{}^2 + x_1 - 1 = -2x_1{}^2 - x_1 + 1$$

$$x_1{}^2 + 2x_1 - 2 = 0$$

$$x_1 = \frac{-2 \pm \sqrt{2^2 - 4(1)(-2)}}{2(1)} = \frac{-2 \pm 2\sqrt{3}}{2} = -1 \pm \sqrt{3}$$

Choosing the positive value for $x_1$, we have $x_1 = -1 + \sqrt{3}$.

$$m = 1 - 2\left(-1 + \sqrt{3}\right) = 3 - 2\sqrt{3}$$

$$m = \frac{0 - 1}{x_0 + 1} = -\frac{1}{x_0 + 1}$$

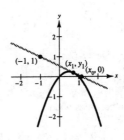

Thus, $-\dfrac{1}{x_0 + 1} = 3 - 2\sqrt{3}$

$$\frac{-1}{3 - 2\sqrt{3}} = x_0 + 1$$

$$\frac{3 + 2\sqrt{3}}{3} - 1 = x_0$$

$$\frac{2\sqrt{3}}{3} = x_0.$$

The closest the receiver can be to the hill is $\left(2\sqrt{3}/3\right) - 1 \approx 0.155$.

**89.** Parabola

Vertex: $(0, 4)$

$$x^2 = 4p(y - 4)$$

$$4^2 = 4p(0 - 4)$$

$$p = -1$$

$$x^2 = -4(y - 4)$$

$$y = 4 - \frac{x^2}{4}$$

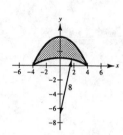

Circle

Center: $(0, k)$

Radius: 8

$$x^2 + (y - k)^2 = 64$$

$$4^2 + (0 - k)^2 = 64$$

$$k^2 = 48$$

$$k = -4\sqrt{3} \quad \text{(Center is on the negative } y\text{-axis.)}$$

$$x^2 + \left(y + 4\sqrt{3}\right)^2 = 64$$

$$y = -4\sqrt{3} \pm \sqrt{64 - x^2}$$

Since the $y$-value is positive when $x = 0$, we have $y = -4\sqrt{3} + \sqrt{64 - x^2}$.

$$A = 2\int_0^4 \left[\left(4 - \frac{x^2}{4}\right) - \left(-4\sqrt{3} + \sqrt{64 - x^2}\right)\right] dx$$

$$= 2\left[4x - \frac{x^3}{12} + 4\sqrt{3}x - \frac{1}{2}\left(x\sqrt{64 - x^2} + 64 \arcsin \frac{x}{8}\right)\right]_0^4$$

$$= 2\left[16 - \frac{64}{12} + 16\sqrt{3} - 2\sqrt{48} - 32 \arcsin \frac{1}{2}\right]$$

$$= \frac{16\left(4 + 3\sqrt{3} - 2\pi\right)}{3} \approx 15.536 \text{ square feet}$$

**91.** (a)  Assume that $y = ax^2$.

$$20 = a(60)^2 \implies a = \frac{2}{360} = \frac{1}{180} \implies y = \frac{1}{180}x^2$$

(b)  $f(x) = \dfrac{1}{180}x^2, f'(x) = \dfrac{1}{90}x$

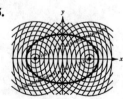

$$S = 2\int_0^{60} \sqrt{1 + \left(\frac{1}{90}x\right)^2}\, dx = \frac{2}{90}\int_0^{60} \sqrt{90^2 + x^2}\, dx$$

$$= \frac{2}{90}\frac{1}{2}\left[x\sqrt{90^2 + x^2} + 90^2 \ln\left|x + \sqrt{90^2 + x^2}\right|\right]_0^{60} \quad \text{(formula 26)}$$

$$= \frac{1}{90}\left[60\sqrt{11,700} + 90^2 \ln\left(60 + \sqrt{11,700}\right) - 90^2 \ln 90\right]$$

$$= \frac{1}{90}\left[1800\sqrt{13} + 90^2 \ln\left(60 + 30\sqrt{13}\right) - 90^2 \ln 90\right]$$

$$= 20\sqrt{13} + 90 \ln\left(\frac{60 + 30\sqrt{13}}{90}\right)$$

$$= 10\left[2\sqrt{13} + 9 \ln\left(\frac{2 + \sqrt{13}}{3}\right)\right] \approx 128.4 \text{ m}$$

**93.** $x^2 = 4py, p = \dfrac{1}{4}, \dfrac{1}{2}, 1, \dfrac{3}{2}, 2$

As $p$ increases, the graph becomes wider.

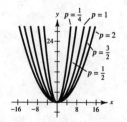

**95.**

**97.** $a = \dfrac{5}{2}, b = 2, c = \sqrt{\left(\dfrac{5}{2}\right)^2 - (2)^2} = \dfrac{3}{2}$

The tacks should be placed 1.5 feet from the center. The string should be $2a = 5$ feet long.

**99.**     $e = \dfrac{c}{a}$

$A + P = 2a$

$\quad a = \dfrac{A + P}{2}$

$\quad c = a - P = \dfrac{A + P}{2} - P = \dfrac{A - P}{2}$

$\quad e = \dfrac{c}{a} = \dfrac{(A - P)/2}{(A + P)/2} = \dfrac{A - P}{A + P}$

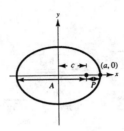

**101.** $e = \dfrac{A - P}{A + P} = \dfrac{35.34au - 0.59au}{35.34au + 0.59au} \approx 0.9672$

**103.**   $\dfrac{x^2}{10^2} + \dfrac{y^2}{5^2} = 1$

$\dfrac{2x}{10^2} + \dfrac{2yy'}{5^2} = 0$

$\qquad y' = \dfrac{-5^2 x}{10^2 y} = \dfrac{-x}{4y}$

At $(-8, 3)$: $y' = \dfrac{8}{12} = \dfrac{2}{3}$

The equation of the tangent line is $y - 3 = \frac{2}{3}(x + 8)$. It will cross the $y$-axis when $x = 0$ and $y = \frac{2}{3}(8) + 3 = \frac{25}{3}$.

**105.** $16x^2 + 9y^2 + 96x + 36y + 36 = 0$

$32x + 18yy' + 96 + 36y' = 0$

$\qquad y'(18y + 36) = -(32x + 96)$

$\qquad\qquad y' = \dfrac{-(32x + 96)}{18y + 36}$

$y' = 0$ when $x = -3$. $y'$ is undefined when $y = -2$.

At $x = -3, y = 2$ or $-6$.

Endpoints of major axis: $(-3, 2), (-3, -6)$

At $y = -2, x = 0$ or $-6$.

Endpoints of minor axis: $(0, -2), (-6, -2)$

**Note:** Equation of ellipse is $\dfrac{(x + 3)^2}{9} + \dfrac{(y + 2)^2}{16} = 1$

**107. (a)** $A = 4\displaystyle\int_0^2 \dfrac{1}{2}\sqrt{4 - x^2}\, dx = \left[ x\sqrt{4 - x^2} + 4\arcsin\left(\dfrac{x}{2}\right) \right]_0^2 = 2\pi \quad [\text{or, } A = \pi ab = \pi(2)(1) = 2\pi]$

**(b) Disk:**    $V = 2\pi\displaystyle\int_0^2 \dfrac{1}{4}(4 - x^2)\, dx = \dfrac{1}{2}\pi\left[ 4x - \dfrac{1}{3}x^3 \right]_0^2 = \dfrac{8\pi}{3}$

$y = \dfrac{1}{2}\sqrt{4 - x^2}$

$y' = \dfrac{-x}{2\sqrt{4 - x^2}}$

$\sqrt{1 + (y')^2} = \sqrt{1 + \dfrac{x^2}{16 - 4x^2}} = \sqrt{\dfrac{16 - 3x^2}{4y}}$

$S = 2(2\pi)\displaystyle\int_0^2 y\left(\dfrac{\sqrt{16 - 3x^2}}{4y}\right) dx = \dfrac{\pi}{2\sqrt{3}}\left[ \sqrt{3}x\sqrt{16 - 3x^2} + 16\arcsin\left(\dfrac{\sqrt{3}x}{4}\right) \right]_0^2 = \dfrac{2\pi}{9}(9 + 4\sqrt{3}\pi) \approx 21.48$

—CONTINUED—

**107. —CONTINUED—**

**(c) Shell:**
$$V = 2\pi \int_0^2 x\sqrt{4 - x^2}\, dx = -\pi \int_0^2 -2x(4 - x^2)^{1/2}\, dx = -\frac{2\pi}{3}\left[(4 - x^2)^{3/2}\right]_0^2 = \frac{16\pi}{3}$$

$$x = 2\sqrt{1 - y^2}$$

$$x' = \frac{-2y}{\sqrt{1 - y^2}}$$

$$\sqrt{1 + (x')^2} = \sqrt{1 + \frac{4y^2}{1 - y^2}} = \frac{\sqrt{1 + 3y^2}}{\sqrt{1 - y^2}}$$

$$S = 2(2\pi) \int_0^1 2\sqrt{1 - y^2}\, \frac{\sqrt{1 + 3y^2}}{\sqrt{1 - y^2}}\, dy = 8\pi \int_0^1 \sqrt{1 + 3y^2}\, dy$$

$$= \frac{8\pi}{2\sqrt{3}}\left[\sqrt{3}y\sqrt{1 + 3y^2} + \ln\left|\sqrt{3}y + \sqrt{1 + 3y^2}\right|\right]_0^1 = \frac{4\pi}{3}\left|6 + \sqrt{3}\ln\left(2 + \sqrt{3}\right)\right| \approx 34.69$$

**109.** From Example 5,
$$C = 4a \int_0^{\pi/2} \sqrt{1 - e^2 \sin^2 \theta}\, d\theta$$

For $\dfrac{x^2}{25} + \dfrac{y^2}{49} = 1$, we have

$$a = 7, b = 5, c = \sqrt{49 - 25} = 2\sqrt{6}, e = \frac{c}{a} = \frac{2\sqrt{6}}{7}.$$

$$C = 4(7) \int_0^{\pi/2} \sqrt{1 - \frac{24}{49} \sin^2 \theta}\, d\theta$$

$$\approx 28(1.3558) \approx 37.9614$$

**111.** Area circle $= \pi r^2 = 100\pi$
Area ellipse $= \pi ab = \pi a(10)$
$$2(100\pi) = 10\pi a \implies a = 20$$
Hence, the length of the major axis is $2a = 40$.

**113.** The transverse axis is horizontal since $(2, 2)$ and $(10, 2)$ are the foci (see definition of hyperbola).

Center: $(6, 2)$

$c = 4, 2a = 6, b^2 = c^2 - a^2 = 7$

Therefore, the equation is
$$\frac{(x - 6)^2}{9} - \frac{(y - 2)^2}{7} = 1.$$

**115.** $2a = 10 \implies a = 5$
$$c = 6 \implies b = \sqrt{11}$$

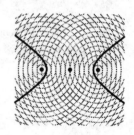

**117.** Time for sound of bullet hitting target to reach $(x, y)$: $\dfrac{2c}{v_m} + \dfrac{\sqrt{(x - c)^2 + y^2}}{v_s}$

Time for sound of rifle to reach $(x, y)$: $\dfrac{\sqrt{(x + c)^2 + y^2}}{v_s}$

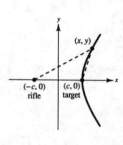

Since the times are the same, we have: $\dfrac{2c}{v_m} + \dfrac{\sqrt{(x - c)^2 + y^2}}{v_s} = \dfrac{\sqrt{(x + c)^2 + y^2}}{v_s}$

$$\frac{4c^2}{v_m^2} + \frac{4c}{v_m v_s}\sqrt{(x - c)^2 + y^2} + \frac{(x - c)^2 + y^2}{v_s^2} = \frac{(x + c)^2 + y^2}{v_s^2}$$

$$\sqrt{(x - c)^2 + y^2} = \frac{v_m^2 x - v_s^2 c}{v_s v_m}$$

$$\left(1 - \frac{v_m^2}{v_s^2}\right)x^2 + y^2 = \left(\frac{v_s^2}{v_m^2} - 1\right)c^2$$

$$\frac{x^2}{c^2 v_s^2 / v_m^2} - \frac{y^2}{c^2(v_m^2 - v_s^2)/v_m^2} = 1$$

**119.** The point $(x, y)$ lies on the line between $(0, 10)$ and $(10, 0)$. Thus, $y = 10 - x$. The point also lies on the hyperbola $(x^2/36) - (y^2/64) = 1$. Using substitution, we have:

$$\frac{x^2}{36} - \frac{(10 - x)^2}{64} = 1$$

$$16x^2 - 9(10 - x)^2 = 576$$

$$7x^2 + 180x - 1476 = 0$$

$$x = \frac{-180 \pm \sqrt{180^2 - 4(7)(-1476)}}{2(7)} = \frac{-180 \pm 192\sqrt{2}}{14} = \frac{-90 \pm 96\sqrt{2}}{7}$$

Choosing the positive value for $x$ we have:

$$x = \frac{-90 + 96\sqrt{2}}{7} \approx 6.538 \text{ and } y = \frac{160 - 96\sqrt{2}}{7} \approx 3.462$$

**121.**
$$\frac{x^2}{a^2} + \frac{2y^2}{b^2} = 1 \implies \frac{2y^2}{b^2} = 1 - \frac{x^2}{a^2}, \ c^2 = a^2 - b^2$$

$$\frac{x^2}{a^2 - b^2} - \frac{2y^2}{b^2} = 1 \implies \frac{2y^2}{b^2} = \frac{x^2}{a^2 - b^2} - 1$$

$$1 - \frac{x^2}{a^2} = \frac{x^2}{a^2 - b^2} - 1 \implies 2 = x^2\left(\frac{1}{a^2} + \frac{1}{a^2 - b^2}\right)$$

$$x^2 = \frac{2a^2(a^2 - b^2)}{2a^2 - b^2} \implies x = \pm\frac{\sqrt{2}a\sqrt{a^2 - b^2}}{\sqrt{2a^2 - b^2}} = \pm\frac{\sqrt{2}ac}{\sqrt{2a^2 - b^2}}$$

$$\frac{2y^2}{b^2} = 1 - \frac{1}{a^2}\left(\frac{2a^2c^2}{2a^2 - b^2}\right) \implies \frac{2y^2}{b^2} = \frac{b^2}{2a^2 - b^2}$$

$$y^2 = \frac{b^4}{2(2a^2 - b^2)} \implies y = \pm\frac{b^2}{\sqrt{2}\sqrt{2a^2 - b^2}}$$

There are four points of intersection: $\left(\dfrac{\sqrt{2}ac}{\sqrt{2a^2 - b^2}}, \pm\dfrac{b^2}{\sqrt{2}\sqrt{2a^2 - b^2}}\right)$, $\left(-\dfrac{\sqrt{2}ac}{\sqrt{2a^2 - b^2}}, \pm\dfrac{b^2}{\sqrt{2}\sqrt{2a^2 - b^2}}\right)$

$$\frac{x^2}{a^2} + \frac{2y^2}{b^2} = 1 \implies \frac{2x}{a^2} + \frac{4yy'}{b^2} = 0 \implies y'_e = -\frac{b^2x}{2a^2y}$$

$$\frac{x^2}{a^2 - b^2} - \frac{2y^2}{b^2} = 1 \implies \frac{2x}{c^2} - \frac{4yy'}{b^2} = 0 \implies y'_h = \frac{b^2x}{2c^2y}$$

At $\left(\dfrac{\sqrt{2}ac}{\sqrt{2a^2 - b^2}}, \dfrac{b^2}{\sqrt{2}\sqrt{2a^2 - b^2}}\right)$, the slopes of the tangent lines are:

$$y'_e = \frac{-b^2\left(\dfrac{\sqrt{2}ac}{\sqrt{2a^2 - b^2}}\right)}{2a^2\left(\dfrac{b^2}{\sqrt{2}\sqrt{2a^2 - b^2}}\right)} = -\frac{c}{a} \quad \text{and} \quad y'_h = \frac{b^2\left(\dfrac{\sqrt{2}ac}{\sqrt{2a^2 - b^2}}\right)}{2c^2\left(\dfrac{b^2}{\sqrt{2}\sqrt{2a^2 - b^2}}\right)} = \frac{a}{c}$$

Since the slopes are negative reciprocals, the tangent lines are perpendicular. Similarly, the curves are perpendicular at the other three points of intersection.

**123.** False. See the definition of a parabola.

**125.** True

**127.** False. $y^2 - x^2 + 2x + 2y = 0$ yields two intersecting lines.

**129.** True

# Section 9.2    Plane Curves and Parametric Equations

**1.** $x = \sqrt{t}, \ y = 1 - t$

(a)

| $t$ | 0 | 1 | 2 | 3 | 4 |
|---|---|---|---|---|---|
| $x$ | 0 | 1 | $\sqrt{2}$ | $\sqrt{3}$ | 2 |
| $y$ | 1 | 0 | $-1$ | $-2$ | $-3$ |

(b)

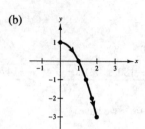

(c)

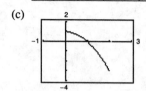

(d) $x^2 = t$

$\quad y = 1 - x^2, x \geq 0$

**3.** $x = 3t - 1$

$y = 2t + 1$

$y = 2\left(\dfrac{x+1}{3}\right) + 1$

$2x - 3y + 5 = 0$

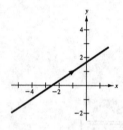

**5.** $x = t + 1$

$y = t^2$

$y = (x - 1)^2$

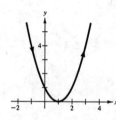

**7.** $x = t^3$

$y = \frac{1}{2}t^2$

$x = t^3$ implies $t = x^{1/3}$

$y = \frac{1}{2}x^{2/3}$

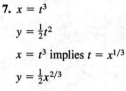

**9.** $x = \sqrt{t}, t \geq 0$

$y = t - 2$

$y = x^2 - 2, x \geq 0$

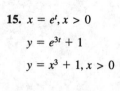

**11.** $x = t - 1$

$y = \dfrac{t}{t-1}$

$y = \dfrac{x+1}{x}$

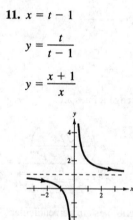

**13.** $x = 2t$

$y = |t - 2|$

$y = \left|\dfrac{x}{2} - 2\right| = \dfrac{|x-4|}{2}$

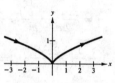

**15.** $x = e^t, x > 0$

$y = e^{3t} + 1$

$y = x^3 + 1, x > 0$

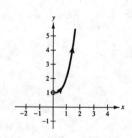

**17.**  $x = \sec \theta$

$y = \cos \theta$

$0 \le \theta < \dfrac{\pi}{2}, \dfrac{\pi}{2} < \theta \le \pi$

$xy = 1$

$y = \dfrac{1}{x}$

$|x| \ge 1, \ |y| \le 1$

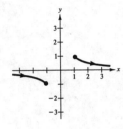

**19.**  $x = 3 \cos \theta, \ y = 3 \sin \theta$

Squaring both equations and adding, we have

$x^2 + y^2 = 9.$

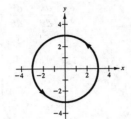

**21.**  $x = 4 \sin 2\theta$

$y = 2 \cos 2\theta$

$\dfrac{x^2}{16} = \sin^2 2\theta$

$\dfrac{y^2}{4} = \cos^2 2\theta$

$\dfrac{x^2}{16} + \dfrac{y^2}{4} = 1$

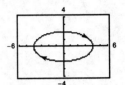

**23.**    $x = 4 + 2 \cos \theta$

$y = -1 + \sin \theta$

$\dfrac{(x-4)^2}{4} = \cos^2 \theta$

$\dfrac{(y+1)^2}{1} = \sin^2 \theta$

$\dfrac{(x-4)^2}{4} + \dfrac{(y+1)^2}{1} = 1$

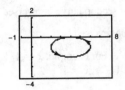

**25.**    $x = 4 + 2 \cos \theta$

$y = -1 + 4 \sin \theta$

$\dfrac{(x-4)^2}{4} = \cos^2 \theta$

$\dfrac{(y+1)^2}{16} = \sin^2 \theta$

$\dfrac{(x-4)^2}{4} + \dfrac{(y+1)^2}{16} = 1$

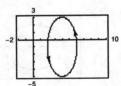

**27.**    $x = 4 \sec \theta$

$y = 3 \tan \theta$

$\dfrac{x^2}{16} = \sec^2 \theta$

$\dfrac{y^2}{9} = \tan^2 \theta$

$\dfrac{x^2}{16} - \dfrac{y^2}{9} = 1$

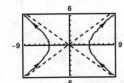

**29.**  $x = t^3$

$y = 3 \ln t$

$y = 3 \ln \sqrt[3]{x} = \ln x$

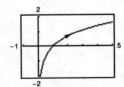

**31.**    $x = e^{-t}$

$y = e^{3t}$

$e^t = \dfrac{1}{x}$

$e^t = \sqrt[3]{y}$

$\sqrt[3]{y} = \dfrac{1}{x}$

$y = \dfrac{1}{x^3}$

$x > 0$

$y > 0$

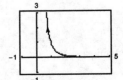

**33.** By eliminating the parameters in (a) – (d), we get $y = 2x + 1$. They differ from each other in orientation and in restricted domains. These curves are all smooth except for (b).

(a) $x = t$, $y = 2t + 1$

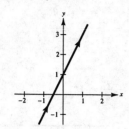

(b) $x = \cos \theta \qquad y = 2 \cos \theta + 1$

$-1 \le x \le 1 \qquad -1 \le y \le 3$

$\dfrac{dx}{d\theta} = \dfrac{dy}{d\theta} = 0$ when $\theta = 0, \pm \pi, \pm 2\pi, \ldots$.

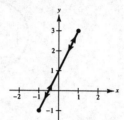

(c) $x = e^{-t} \qquad y = 2e^{-t} + 1$

$\quad\ x > 0 \qquad\ \ y > 1$

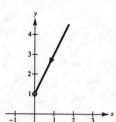

(d) $x = e^{t} \qquad y = 2e^{t} + 1$

$\quad\ x > 0 \qquad\ y > 1$

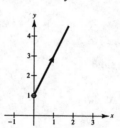

**35.** The curves are identical on $0 < \theta < \pi$. They are both smooth. Represent $y = 2(1 - x^2)$

**37.** (a)

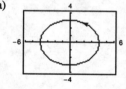

(b) The orientation of the second curve is reversed.

(c) The orientation will be reversed.

(d) Many answers possible. For example, $x = 1 + t$, $y = 1 + 2t$, and $x = 1 - t$, $x = 1 - 2t$.

**39.**
$$x = x_1 + t(x_2 - x_1)$$
$$y = y_1 + t(y_2 - y_1)$$
$$\frac{x - x_1}{x_2 - x_1} = t$$
$$y = y_1 + \left( \frac{x - x_1}{x_2 - x_1} \right)(y_2 - y_1)$$
$$y - y_1 = \frac{y_2 - y_1}{x_2 - x_1}(x - x_1)$$
$$y - y_1 = m(x - x_1)$$

**41.**
$$x = h + a \cos \theta$$
$$y = k + b \sin \theta$$
$$\frac{x - h}{a} = \cos \theta$$
$$\frac{y - k}{b} = \sin \theta$$
$$\frac{(x - h)^2}{a^2} + \frac{(y - k)^2}{b^2} = 1$$

**43.** From Exercise 39 we have
$$x = 5t$$
$$y = -2t.$$
Solution not unique

**45.** From Exercise 40 we have
$$x = 2 + 4 \cos \theta$$
$$y = 1 + 4 \sin \theta.$$
Solution not unique

**47.** From Exercise 41 we have
$$a = 5, c = 4 \implies b = 3$$
$$x = 5 \cos \theta$$
$$y = 3 \sin \theta.$$
Center: $(0, 0)$
Solution not unique

**49.** From Exercise 42 we have

$a = 4, c = 5 \implies b = 3$

$x = 4 \sec \theta$

$y = 3 \tan \theta.$

Center: $(0, 0)$
Solution not unique

**51.** $y = 3x - 2$

Example

$x = t, \qquad y = 3t - 2$

$x = t - 3, \quad y = 3t - 11$

**53.** $y = x^3$

Example

$x = t, \qquad y = t^3$

$x = \sqrt[3]{t}, \qquad y = t$

$x = \tan t, \qquad y = \tan^3 t$

**55.** $x = 2(\theta - \sin \theta)$

$y = 2(1 - \cos \theta)$

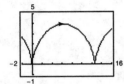

Not smooth at $\theta = 2n\pi$

**57.** $x = \theta - \frac{3}{2} \sin \theta$

$y = 1 - \frac{3}{2} \cos \theta$

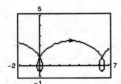

**59.** $x = 3 \cos^3 \theta$

$y = 3 \sin^3 \theta$

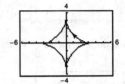

Not smooth at $(x, y) = (\pm 3, 0)$ and $(0, \pm 3)$, or $\theta = \frac{1}{2}n\pi.$

**61.** $x = 2 \cot \theta$

$y = 2 \sin^2 \theta$

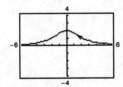

Smooth everywhere

**63.** See definition on page 665.

**65.** A plane curve $C$, represented by $x = f(t), y = g(t)$, is smooth if $f'$ and $g'$ are continuous and not simultaneously 0. See page 670.

**67.** $x = 4 \cos \theta$

$y = 2 \sin 2\theta$

Matches (d)

**69.** $x = \cos \theta + \theta \sin \theta$

$y = \sin \theta - \theta \cos \theta$

Matches (b)

**71.** When the circle has rolled $\theta$ radians, we know that the center is at $(a\theta, a)$.

$$\sin \theta = \sin(180° - \theta) = \frac{|AC|}{b} = \frac{|BD|}{b} \quad \text{or} \quad |BD| = b \sin \theta$$

$$\cos \theta = -\cos(180° - \theta) = \frac{|AP|}{-b} \quad \text{or} \quad |AP| = -b \cos \theta$$

Therefore, $x = a\theta - b \sin \theta$ and $y = a - b \cos \theta.$

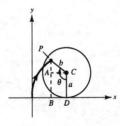

**73.** False

$x = t^2 \implies x \geq 0$

$x = t^2 \implies y \geq 0$

The graph of the parametric equations is only a portion of the line $y = x$.

**75. (a)** $100 \text{ mi/hr} = \dfrac{(100)(5280)}{3600} = \dfrac{440}{3} \text{ ft/sec}$

$$x = (v_0 \cos \theta)t = \left(\dfrac{440}{3} \cos \theta\right)t$$

$$y = h + (v_0 \sin \theta)t - 16t^2$$

$$= 3 + \left(\dfrac{440}{3} \sin \theta\right)t - 16t^2$$

**(b)**

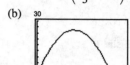

It is not a home run—when $x = 400$, $y \le 20$.

**(c)**

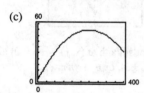

Yes, it's a home run when $x = 400$, $y > 10$.

**(d)** We need to find the angle $\theta$ (and time $t$) such that

$$x = \left(\dfrac{440}{3} \cos \theta\right)t = 400$$

$$y = 3 + \left(\dfrac{440}{3} \sin \theta\right)t - 16t^2 = 10.$$

From the first equation $t = 1200/440 \cos \theta$. Substituting into the second equation,

$$10 = 3 + \left(\dfrac{440}{3} \sin \theta\right)\left(\dfrac{1200}{440 \cos \theta}\right) - 16\left(\dfrac{1200}{440 \cos \theta}\right)^2$$

$$7 = 400 \tan \theta - 16\left(\dfrac{120}{44}\right)^2 \sec^2 \theta$$

$$= 400 \tan \theta - 16\left(\dfrac{120}{44}\right)^2 (\tan^2 \theta + 1).$$

We now solve the quadratic for $\tan \theta$:

$$16\left(\dfrac{120}{44}\right)^2 \tan^2 \theta - 400 \tan \theta + 7 + 16\left(\dfrac{120}{44}\right)^2 = 0$$

$$\tan \theta \approx 0.35185 \implies \theta \approx 19.4°$$

# Section 9.3    Parametric Equations and Calculus

**1.** $\dfrac{dy}{dx} = \dfrac{dy/dt}{dx/dt} = \dfrac{-4}{2t} = \dfrac{-2}{t}$

**3.** $\dfrac{dy}{dx} = \dfrac{dy/dt}{dx/dt} = \dfrac{-2 \cos t \sin t}{2 \sin t \cos t} = -1$

$$\left[\text{Note: } x + y = 1 \implies y = 1 - x \text{ and } \dfrac{dy}{dt} = -1\right]$$

**5.** $x = 2t, \ y = 3t - 1$

$$\dfrac{dy}{dx} = \dfrac{dy/dt}{dx/dt} = \dfrac{3}{2}$$

$$\dfrac{d^2y}{dx^2} = 0 \ \text{ Line}$$

**7.** $x = t + 1, \ y = t^2 + 3t$

$$\dfrac{dy}{dx} = \dfrac{2t + 3}{1} = 1 \text{ when } t = -1.$$

$$\dfrac{d^2y}{dx^2} = 2 \ \text{ concave upwards}$$

**9.** $x = 2 \cos \theta, \ y = 2 \sin \theta$

$$\dfrac{dy}{dx} = \dfrac{2 \cos \theta}{-2 \sin \theta} = -\cot \theta = -1 \text{ when } \theta = \dfrac{\pi}{4}.$$

$$\dfrac{d^2y}{dx^2} = \dfrac{\csc^2 \theta}{-2 \sin \theta} = \dfrac{-\csc^3 \theta}{2} = -\sqrt{2} \text{ when } \theta = \dfrac{\pi}{4}.$$

concave downward

**11.** $x = 2 + \sec \theta, \ y = 1 + 2 \tan \theta$

$$\dfrac{dy}{dx} = \dfrac{2 \sec^2 \theta}{\sec \theta \tan \theta}$$

$$= \dfrac{2 \sec \theta}{\tan \theta} = 2 \csc \theta = 4 \text{ when } \theta = \dfrac{\pi}{6}.$$

$$\dfrac{d^2y}{dx^2} = \dfrac{-2 \csc \theta \cot \theta}{\sec \theta \tan \theta}$$

$$= -2 \cot^3 \theta = -6\sqrt{3} \text{ when } \theta = \dfrac{\pi}{6}.$$

concave downward

**13.** $x = \cos^3 \theta$, $y = \sin^3 \theta$

$$\frac{dy}{dx} = \frac{3 \sin^2 \theta \cos \theta}{-3 \cos^2 \theta \sin \theta}$$

$$= -\tan \theta = -1 \text{ when } \theta = \frac{\pi}{4}.$$

$$\frac{d^2y}{dx^2} = \frac{-\sec^2 \theta}{-3 \cos^2 \theta \sin \theta} = \frac{1}{3 \cos^4 \theta \sin \theta}$$

$$= \frac{\sec^4 \theta \csc \theta}{3} = \frac{4\sqrt{2}}{3} \text{ when } \theta = \frac{\pi}{4}.$$

concave upward

**15.** $x = 2 \cot \theta$, $y = 2 \sin^2 \theta$

$$\frac{dy}{dx} = \frac{4 \sin \theta \cos \theta}{-2 \csc^2 \theta} = -2 \sin^3 \theta \cos \theta$$

At $\left(-\frac{2}{\sqrt{3}}, \frac{3}{2}\right)$, $\theta = \frac{2\pi}{3}$, and $\frac{dy}{dx} = \frac{3\sqrt{3}}{8}$.

Tangent line:    $y - \frac{3}{2} = \frac{3\sqrt{3}}{8}\left(x + \frac{2}{\sqrt{3}}\right)$

$$3\sqrt{3}x - 8y + 18 = 0$$

At $(0, 2)$, $\theta = \frac{\pi}{2}$, and $\frac{dy}{dx} = 0$.

Tangent line: $y - 2 = 0$

At $\left(2\sqrt{3}, \frac{1}{2}\right)$, $\theta = \frac{\pi}{6}$, and $\frac{dy}{dx} = -\frac{\sqrt{3}}{8}$.

Tangent line:    $y - \frac{1}{2} = -\frac{\sqrt{3}}{8}(x - 2\sqrt{3})$

$$\sqrt{3}x + 8y - 10 = 0$$

**17.** $x = 2t$, $y = t^2 - 1$, $t = 2$

(a)

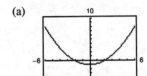

(b) At $t = 2$, $(x, y) = (4, 3)$, and

$$\frac{dx}{dt} = 2, \frac{dy}{dt} = 4, \frac{dy}{dx} = 2$$

(c) $\frac{dy}{dx} = 2$. At $(4, 3)$, $y - 3 = 2(x - 4)$

$$y = 2x - 5$$

(d)

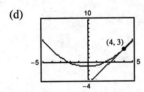

**19.** $x = t^2 - t + 2$, $y = t^3 - 3t$, $t = -1$

(a)

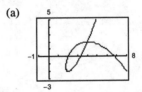

(b) At $t = -1$, $(x, y) = (4, 2)$, and

$$\frac{dx}{dt} = -3, \frac{dy}{dt} = 0, \frac{dy}{dx} = 0$$

(c) $\frac{dy}{dx} = 0$. At $(4, 2)$, $y - 2 = 0(x - 4)$

$$y = 2$$

(d)

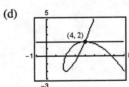

**21.** $x = 2 \sin 2t$, $y = 3 \sin t$ crosses itself at the origin, $(x, y) = (0, 0)$.

At this point, $t = 0$ or $t = \pi$.

$$\frac{dy}{dx} = \frac{3 \cos t}{4 \cos 2t}$$

At $t = 0$: $\frac{dy}{dx} = \frac{3}{4}$ and $y = \frac{3}{4}x$. Tangent Line

At $t = \pi$, $\frac{dy}{dx} = -\frac{3}{4}$ and $y = \frac{-3}{4}x$   Tangent Line

**23.** $x = \cos\theta + \theta\sin\theta$, $y = \sin\theta - \theta\cos\theta$

Horizontal tangents: $\dfrac{dy}{d\theta} = \theta\sin\theta = 0$ when $\theta = 0$, $\pi$, $2\pi$, $3\pi$, ....

Points: $(-1, [2n-1]\pi)$, $(1, 2n\pi)$ where $n$ is an integer.

Points shown: $(1, 0)$, $(-1, \pi)$, $(1, -2\pi)$

Vertical tangents: $\dfrac{dx}{d\theta} = \theta\cos\theta = 0$ when $\theta = \dfrac{\pi}{2}$, $\dfrac{3\pi}{2}$, $\dfrac{5\pi}{2}$, ....

Points: $\left( \dfrac{(-1)^{n+1}(2n-1)\pi}{2}, (-1)^{n+1} \right)$

Points shown: $\left( \dfrac{\pi}{2}, 1 \right)$, $\left( -\dfrac{3\pi}{2}, -1 \right)$, $\left( \dfrac{5\pi}{2}, 1 \right)$

**25.** $x = 1 - t$, $y = t^2$

Horizontal tangents: $\dfrac{dy}{dt} = 2t = 0$ when $t = 0$.

Point: $(1, 0)$

Vertical tangents: $\dfrac{dx}{dt} = -1 \neq 0$; none

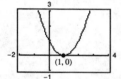

**27.** $x = 1 - t$, $y = t^3 - 3t$

Horizontal tangents: $\dfrac{dy}{dt} = 3t^2 - 3 = 0$ when $t = \pm 1$.

Points: $(0, -2)$, $(2, 2)$

Vertical tangents: $\dfrac{dx}{dt} = -1 \neq 0$; none

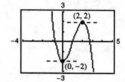

**29.** $x = 3\cos\theta$, $y = 3\sin\theta$

Horizontal tangents: $\dfrac{dy}{d\theta} = 3\cos\theta = 0$ when $\theta = \dfrac{\pi}{2}$, $\dfrac{3\pi}{2}$.

Points: $(0, 3)$, $(0, -3)$

Vertical tangents: $\dfrac{dx}{d\theta} = -3\sin\theta = 0$ when $\theta = 0$, $\pi$.

Points: $(3, 0)$, $(-3, 0)$

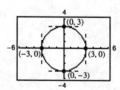

**31.** $x = 4 + 2\cos\theta$, $y = -1 + \sin\theta$

Horizontal tangents: $\dfrac{dy}{d\theta} = \cos\theta = 0$ when $\theta = \dfrac{\pi}{2}$, $\dfrac{3\pi}{2}$.

Points: $(4, 0)$, $(4, -2)$

Vertical tangents: $\dfrac{dx}{d\theta} = -2\sin\theta = 0$ when $x = 0$, $\pi$.

Points: $(6, -1)$, $(2, -1)$

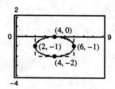

**33.** $x = \sec\theta$, $y = \tan\theta$

Horizontal tangents: $\dfrac{dy}{d\theta} = \sec^2\theta \neq 0$; none

Vertical tangents: $\dfrac{dx}{d\theta} = \sec\theta\tan\theta = 0$ when $x = 0$, $\pi$.

Points: $(1, 0)$, $(-1, 0)$

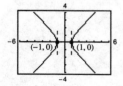

**35.** $x = t^2$, $y = 2t$, $0 \leq t \leq 2$

$\dfrac{dx}{dt} = 2t$, $\dfrac{dy}{dt} = 2$, $\left( \dfrac{dx}{dt} \right)^2 + \left( \dfrac{dy}{dt} \right)^2 = 4t^2 + 4 = 4(t^2 + 1)$

$s = 2\displaystyle\int_0^2 \sqrt{t^2 + 1}\, dt$

$= \left[ t\sqrt{t^2 + 1} + \ln\left| t + \sqrt{t^2 + 1} \right| \right]_0^2$

$= 2\sqrt{5} + \ln(2 + \sqrt{5}) \approx 5.916$

**37.** $x = e^{-t} \cos t, \ y = e^{-t} \sin t, \ 0 \le t \le \dfrac{\pi}{2}$

$$\dfrac{dx}{dt} = -e^{-t}(\sin t + \cos t), \dfrac{dy}{dt} = e^{-t}(\cos t - \sin t)$$

$$s = \int_0^{\pi/2} \sqrt{\left(\dfrac{dx}{dt}\right)^2 + \left(\dfrac{dy}{dt}\right)^2} \ dt$$

$$= \int_0^{\pi/2} \sqrt{2e^{-2t}} \ dt = -\sqrt{2} \int_0^{\pi/2} e^{-t}(-1) \ dt$$

$$= \left[ -\sqrt{2} e^{-t} \right]_0^{\pi/2} = \sqrt{2}(1 - e^{-\pi/2}) \approx 1.12$$

**39.** $x = \sqrt{t}, \ y = 3t - 1, \ \dfrac{dx}{dt} = \dfrac{1}{2\sqrt{t}}, \ \dfrac{dy}{dt} = 3$

$$S = \int_0^1 \sqrt{\dfrac{1}{4t} + 9} \ dt = \dfrac{1}{2} \int_0^1 \dfrac{\sqrt{1 + 36t}}{\sqrt{t}} \ dt$$

$$= \dfrac{1}{6} \int_0^6 \sqrt{1 + u^2} \ du$$

$$= \dfrac{1}{12} \left[ \ln\left( \sqrt{1 + u^2} + u \right) + u\sqrt{1 + u^2} \right]_0^6$$

$$= \dfrac{1}{12} \left[ \ln\left( \sqrt{37} + 6 \right) + 6\sqrt{37} \right] \approx 3.249$$

$$u = 6\sqrt{t}, \ du = \dfrac{3}{\sqrt{t}} \ dt$$

**41.** $x = a \cos^3 \theta, \ y = a \sin^3 \theta, \ \dfrac{dx}{d\theta} = -3a \cos^2 \theta \sin \theta,$

$\dfrac{dy}{d\theta} = 3a \sin^2 \theta \cos \theta$

$$S = 4 \int_0^{\pi/2} \sqrt{9a^2 \cos^4 \theta \sin^2 + 9a^2 \sin^4 \theta \cos^2 \theta} \ d\theta$$

$$= 12a \int_0^{\pi/2} \sin \theta \cos \theta \sqrt{\cos^2 \theta + \sin^2 \theta} \ d\theta$$

$$= 6a \int_0^{\pi/2} \sin 2\theta \ d\theta = \left[ -3a \cos 2\theta \right]_0^{\pi/2} = 6a$$

**43.** $x = a(\theta - \sin \theta), \ y = a(1 - \cos \theta),$

$\dfrac{dx}{d\theta} = a(1 - \cos \theta), \dfrac{dy}{d\theta} = a \sin \theta$

$$S = 2 \int_0^{\pi} \sqrt{a^2(1 - \cos \theta)^2 + a^2 \sin^2 \theta} \ d\theta$$

$$= 2\sqrt{2}a \int_0^{\pi} \sqrt{1 - \cos \theta} \ d\theta$$

$$= 2\sqrt{2}a \int_0^{\pi} \dfrac{\sin \theta}{\sqrt{1 + \cos \theta}} \ d\theta$$

$$= \left[ -4\sqrt{2}a \sqrt{1 + \cos \theta} \right]_0^{\pi} = 8a$$

**45.** $x = (90 \cos 30°)t, \ y = (90 \sin 30°)t - 16t^2$

(a)

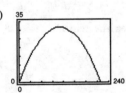

(b) Range: 219.2 ft

(c) $\dfrac{dx}{dt} = 90 \cos 30°, \dfrac{dy}{dt} = 90 \sin 30° - 32t.$

$y = 0$ for $t = \dfrac{45}{16}.$

$$s = \int_0^{45/16} \sqrt{(90 \cos 30°)^2 + (90 \sin 30° - 32t)^2} \ dt$$

$$= 230.8 \ \text{ft}$$

(d) $y = 0 \implies (90 \sin \theta)t = 16t^2 \implies t = \dfrac{90}{16} \sin \theta$

$$x = (90 \cos \theta)t = \dfrac{90^2}{16} \cos \theta \sin \theta = \dfrac{90^2}{32} \sin 2\theta$$

$$x'(\theta) = \dfrac{90^2}{32} 2 \cos 2\theta = 0 \implies \theta = 45°$$

By the First Derivative Test, $\theta = 45° \left( \dfrac{\pi}{4} \right)$ maximizes the range.

$$\dfrac{dx}{dt} = 90 \cos \theta,$$

$$\dfrac{dy}{dt} = 90 \sin \theta - 32 = 90 \sin \theta - 32 \left( \dfrac{90}{16} \sin \theta \right) = -90 \sin \theta$$

$$s = \int_0^{(90/16) \sin \theta} \sqrt{(90 \cos \theta)^2 + (-90 \sin \theta)^2} \ dt$$

$$= \int_0^{(90/16) \sin \theta} 90 \ dt = 90t \Big]_0^{(90/16) \sin \theta}$$

$$= \dfrac{90^2}{16} \sin \theta$$

$$\dfrac{ds}{d\theta} = \dfrac{90^2}{16} \cos \theta = 0 \implies \theta = \dfrac{\pi}{2}$$

By the First Derivative Test, $\theta = 90°$ maximizes the arc length.

**47.** (a)
$$x = t - \sin t$$
$$y = 1 - \cos t$$
$$0 \le t \le 2\pi$$

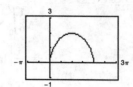

$$x = 2t - \sin(2t)$$
$$y = 1 - \cos(2t)$$
$$0 \le t \le \pi$$

(b) The average speed of the particle on the second path is twice the average speed of a particle on the first path.

(c) $x = \frac{1}{2}t - \sin(\frac{1}{2}t)$

$y = 1 - \cos(\frac{1}{2}t)$

The time required for the particle to traverse the same path is $t = 4\pi$.

**49.** $x = t$, $y = 2t$, $\dfrac{dx}{dt} = 1$, $\dfrac{dy}{dt} = 2$

(a) $S = 2\pi \displaystyle\int_0^4 2t\sqrt{1+4}\,dt = 4\sqrt{5}\pi \int_0^4 t\,dt$

$= \left[ 2\sqrt{5}\pi t^2 \right]_0^4 = 32\pi\sqrt{5}$

(b) $S = 2\pi \displaystyle\int_0^4 t\sqrt{1+4}\,dt = 2\sqrt{5}\pi \int_0^4 t\,dt$

$= \left[ \sqrt{5}\pi t^2 \right]_0^4 = 16\pi\sqrt{5}$

**51.** $x = 4\cos\theta$, $y = 4\sin\theta$, $\dfrac{dx}{d\theta} = -4\sin\theta$, $\dfrac{dy}{d\theta} = 4\cos\theta$

$S = 2\pi \displaystyle\int_0^{\pi/2} 4\cos\theta\sqrt{(-4\sin\theta)^2 + (4\cos\theta)^2}\,d\theta$

$= 32\pi \displaystyle\int_0^{\pi/2} \cos\theta\,d\theta = \left[ 32\pi\sin\theta \right]_0^{\pi/2} = 32\pi$

**53.** $x = a\cos^3\theta$, $y = a\sin^3\theta$, $\dfrac{dx}{d\theta} = -3a\cos^2\theta\sin\theta$, $\dfrac{dy}{d\theta} = 3a\sin^2\theta\cos\theta$

$S = 4\pi \displaystyle\int_0^{\pi/2} a\sin^3\theta\sqrt{9a^2\cos^4\theta\sin^2\theta + 9a^2\sin^4\theta\cos^2\theta}\,d\theta = 12a^2\pi \int_0^{\pi/2} \sin^4\theta\cos\theta\,d\theta = \frac{12\pi a^2}{5}\left[ \sin^5\theta \right]_0^{\pi/2} = \frac{12}{5}\pi a^2$

**55.** $\dfrac{dy}{dx} = \dfrac{dy/dt}{dx/dt}$

See Theorem 9.7, page 675.

**57.** One possible answer is the graph given by

$$x = t, y = -t.$$

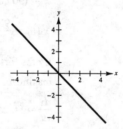

**59.** $s = \displaystyle\int_a^b \sqrt{\left(\dfrac{dx}{dt}\right)^2 + \left(\dfrac{dy}{dt}\right)^2}\,dt$

See Theorem 9.8, page 678.

**61.** $x = r\cos\phi$, $y = r\sin\phi$

$S = 2\pi \displaystyle\int_0^\theta r\sin\phi\sqrt{r^2\sin^2\phi + r^2\cos^2\phi}\,d\phi$

$= 2\pi r^2 \displaystyle\int_0^\theta \sin\phi\,d\phi$

$= \left[ -2\pi r^2 \cos\phi \right]_0^\theta$

$= 2\pi r^2(1 - \cos\theta)$

**63.** $x = \sqrt{t},\ y = 4 - t,\ 0 \le t \le 4$

$$A = \int_0^4 (4 - t)\frac{1}{2\sqrt{t}}\,dt = \frac{1}{2}\int_0^4 (4t^{-1/2} - t^{1/2})\,dt = \left[\frac{1}{2}\left(8\sqrt{t} - \frac{2}{3}t\sqrt{t}\right)\right]_0^4 = \frac{16}{3}$$

$$\bar{x} = \frac{3}{16}\int_0^4 (4 - t)\sqrt{t}\left(\frac{1}{2\sqrt{t}}\right)dt = \frac{3}{32}\int_0^4 (4 - t)\,dt = \left[\frac{3}{32}\left(4t - \frac{t^2}{2}\right)\right]_0^4 = \frac{3}{4}$$

$$\bar{y} = \frac{3}{32}\int_0^4 (4 - t)^2\frac{1}{2\sqrt{t}}\,dt = \frac{3}{64}\int_0^4 [16t^{-1/2} - 8t^{1/2} + t^{3/2}]\,dt = \frac{3}{64}\left[32\sqrt{t} - \frac{16}{3}t\sqrt{t} + \frac{2}{5}t^2\sqrt{t}\right]_0^4 = \frac{8}{5}$$

$$(\bar{x}, \bar{y}) = \left(\frac{3}{4}, \frac{8}{5}\right)$$

**65.** $x = 3\cos\theta,\ y = 3\sin\theta,\ \dfrac{dx}{d\theta} = -3\sin\theta$

$$V = 2\pi\int_{\pi/2}^0 (3\sin\theta)^2(-3\sin\theta)\,d\theta$$

$$= -54\pi\int_{\pi/2}^0 \sin^3\theta\,d\theta$$

$$= -54\pi\int_{\pi/2}^0 (1 - \cos^2\theta)\sin\theta\,d\theta$$

$$= -54\pi\left[-\cos\theta + \frac{\cos^3\theta}{3}\right]_{\pi/2}^0 = 36\pi$$

**67.** $x = 2\sin^2\theta$

$y = 2\sin^2\theta\tan\theta$

$\dfrac{dx}{d\theta} = 4\sin\theta\cos\theta$

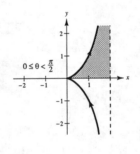

$0 \le \theta < \dfrac{\pi}{2}$

$$A = \int_0^{\pi/2} 2\sin^2\theta\tan\theta(4\sin\theta\cos\theta)\,d\theta = 8\int_0^{\pi/2} \sin^4\theta\,d\theta$$

$$= 8\left[\frac{-\sin^3\theta\cos\theta}{4} - \frac{3}{8}\sin\theta\cos\theta + \frac{3}{8}\theta\right]_0^{\pi/2} = \frac{3\pi}{2}$$

**69.** $\pi a b$ is area of ellipse (d).      **71.** $6\pi a^2$ is area of cardioid (f).      **73.** $\frac{8}{3}ab$ is area of hourglass (a).

**75.** (a) $x = \dfrac{1 - t^2}{1 + t^2},\ y = \dfrac{2t}{1 + t^2},\ -20 \le t \le 20$

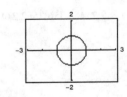

The graph is the circle $x^2 + y^2 = 1$, except the point $(-1, 0)$.

Verify: $x^2 + y^2 = \left(\dfrac{1 - t^2}{1 + t^2}\right)^2 + \left(\dfrac{2t}{1 + t^2}\right)^2 = \dfrac{1 - 2t^2 + t^4 + 4t^2}{(1 + t^2)^2} = \dfrac{(1 + t^2)^2}{(1 + t^2)^2} = 1$

(b) As $t$ increases from $-20$ to $0$, the speed increases, and as $t$ increases from $0$ to $20$, the speed decreases.

**77.** False

$$\frac{d^2y}{dx^2} = \frac{\dfrac{d}{dt}\left[\dfrac{g'(t)}{f'(t)}\right]}{f'(t)} = \frac{f'(t)g''(t) - g'(t)f''(t)}{[f'(t)]^3}$$

## Section 9.4 Polar Coordinates and Polar Graphs

**1.** $\left(4, \dfrac{\pi}{2}\right)$

$x = 4\cos\left(\dfrac{\pi}{2}\right) = 0$

$y = 4\sin\left(\dfrac{\pi}{2}\right) = 4$

$(x, y) = (0, 4)$

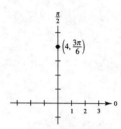

**3.** $\left(-4, -\dfrac{\pi}{3}\right)$

$x = -4\cos\left(-\dfrac{\pi}{3}\right) = -2$

$y = -4\sin\left(-\dfrac{\pi}{3}\right) = 2\sqrt{3}$

$(x, y) = \left(-2, 2\sqrt{3}\right)$

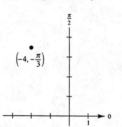

**5.** $\left(\sqrt{2}, 2.36\right)$

$x = \sqrt{2}\cos(2.36) \approx -1.004$

$y = \sqrt{2}\sin(2.36) \approx 0.996$

$(x, y) = (-1.004, 0.996)$

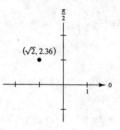

**7.** $(r, \theta) = \left(5, \dfrac{3\pi}{4}\right)$

$(x, y) = (-3.5355, 3.5355)$

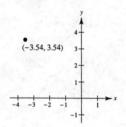

**9.** $(r, \theta) = (-3.5, 2.5)$

$(x, y) = (2.804, -2.095)$

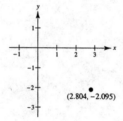

**11.** $(x, y) = (1, 1)$

$r = \pm\sqrt{2}$

$\tan\theta = 1$

$\theta = \dfrac{\pi}{4}, \dfrac{5\pi}{4}, \left(\sqrt{2}, \dfrac{\pi}{4}\right), \left(-\sqrt{2}, \dfrac{5\pi}{4}\right)$

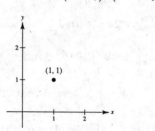

**13.** $(x, y) = (-3, 4)$

$r = \pm\sqrt{9 + 16} = \pm 5$

$\tan\theta = -\dfrac{4}{3}$

$\theta \approx 2.214, 5.356, (5, 2.214), (-5, 5.356)$

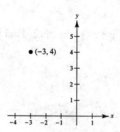

**15.** $(x, y) = (3, -2)$

$(r, \theta) = (3.606, -0.588)$

**17.** $(x, y) = \left(\dfrac{5}{2}, \dfrac{4}{3}\right)$

$(r, \theta) = (2.833, 0.490)$

**19.** (a) $(x, y) = (4, 3.5)$

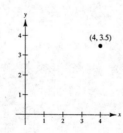

(b) $(r, \theta) = (4, 3.5)$

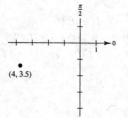

**21.** $x^2 + y^2 = a^2$

$r = a$

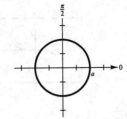

**23.**    $y = 4$

$r \sin \theta = 4$

$r = 4 \csc \theta$

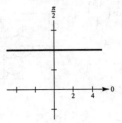

**25.**    $3x - y + 2 = 0$

$3r \cos \theta - r \sin \theta + 2 = 0$

$r(3 \cos \theta - \sin \theta) = -2$

$$r = \frac{-2}{3 \cos \theta - \sin \theta}$$

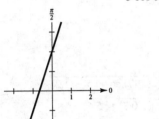

**27.**    $y^2 = 9x$

$r^2 \sin^2 \theta = 9r \cos \theta$

$$r = \frac{9 \cos \theta}{\sin^2 \theta}$$

$r = 9 \csc^2 \theta \cos \theta$

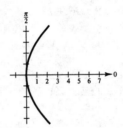

**29.**    $r = 3$

$r^2 = 9$

$x^2 + y^2 = 9$

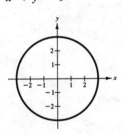

**31.**    $r = \sin \theta$

$r^2 = r \sin \theta$

$x^2 + y^2 = y$

$x^2 + \left( y - \frac{1}{2} \right)^2 = \frac{1}{4}$

$x^2 + y^2 - y = 0$

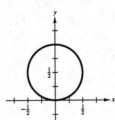

**33.**    $r = \theta$

$\tan r = \tan \theta$

$\tan \sqrt{x^2 + y^2} = \dfrac{y}{x}$

$\sqrt{x^2 + y^2} = \arctan \dfrac{y}{x}$

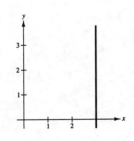

**35.**    $r = 3 \sec \theta$

$r \cos \theta = 3$

$x = 3$

$x - 3 = 0$

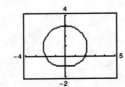

**37.** $r = 3 - 4 \cos \theta$

$0 \le \theta < 2\pi$

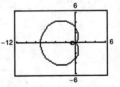

**39.** $r = 2 + \sin \theta$

$0 \le \theta < 2\pi$

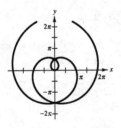

**41.** $r = \dfrac{2}{1 + \cos \theta}$

Traced out once on
$-\pi < \theta < \pi$

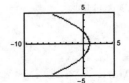

**43.** $r = 2 \cos\left(\dfrac{3\theta}{2}\right)$

$0 \le \theta < 4\pi$

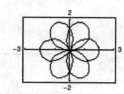

**45.** $r^2 = 4 \sin 2\theta$

$0 \le \theta < \dfrac{\pi}{2}$

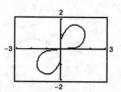

**47.**

$$r = 2(h \cos \theta + k \sin \theta)$$
$$r^2 = 2r(h \cos \theta + k \sin \theta)$$
$$r^2 = 2[h(r \cos \theta) + k(r \sin \theta)]$$
$$x^2 + y^2 = 2(hx + ky)$$
$$x^2 + y^2 - 2hx - 2ky = 0$$
$$(x^2 - 2hx + h^2) + (y^2 - 2ky + k^2) = 0 + h^2 + k^2$$
$$(x - h)^2 + (y - k)^2 = h^2 + k^2$$

Radius: $\sqrt{h^2 + k^2}$

Center: $(h, k)$

**49.** $\left(4, \dfrac{2\pi}{3}\right), \left(2, \dfrac{\pi}{6}\right)$

$$d = \sqrt{4^2 + 2^2 - 2(4)(2) \cos\left(\dfrac{2\pi}{3} - \dfrac{\pi}{6}\right)}$$

$$= \sqrt{20 - 16 \cos \dfrac{\pi}{2}} = 2\sqrt{5} \approx 4.5$$

**51.** $(2, 0.5), (7, 1.2)$

$$d = \sqrt{2^2 + 7^2 - 2(2)(7) \cos(0.5 - 1.2)}$$

$$= \sqrt{53 - 28 \cos(-0.7)} \approx 5.6$$

**53.** $r = 2 + 3 \sin \theta$

$$\dfrac{dy}{dx} = \dfrac{3 \cos \theta \sin \theta + \cos \theta(2 + 3 \sin \theta)}{3 \cos \theta \cos \theta - \sin \theta(2 + 3 \sin \theta)}$$

$$= \dfrac{2 \cos \theta(3 \sin \theta + 1)}{3 \cos 2\theta - 2 \sin \theta} = \dfrac{2 \cos \theta(3 \sin \theta + 1)}{6 \cos^2 \theta - 2 \sin \theta - 3}$$

At $\left(5, \dfrac{\pi}{2}\right), \dfrac{dy}{dx} = 0.$

At $(2, \pi), \dfrac{dy}{dx} = -\dfrac{2}{3}.$

At $\left(-1, \dfrac{3\pi}{2}\right), \dfrac{dy}{dx} = 0.$

**55.** (a), (b) $r = 3(1 - \cos \theta)$

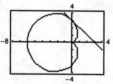

$(r, \theta) = \left(3, \dfrac{\pi}{2}\right) \implies (x, y) = (0, 3)$

Tangent line: $y - 3 = -1(x - 0)$

$$y = -x + 3$$

(c) At $\theta = \dfrac{\pi}{2}, \dfrac{dy}{dx} = -1.0.$

**57.** (a), (b) $r = 3 \sin \theta$

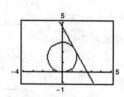

$(r, \theta) = \left(\dfrac{3\sqrt{3}}{2}, \dfrac{\pi}{3}\right) \implies (x, y) = \left(\dfrac{3\sqrt{3}}{4}, \dfrac{9}{4}\right)$

Tangent line: $y - \dfrac{9}{4} = -\sqrt{3}\left(x - \dfrac{3\sqrt{3}}{4}\right)$

$$y = -\sqrt{3}x + \dfrac{9}{2}$$

(c) At $\theta = \dfrac{\pi}{3}, \dfrac{dy}{dx} = -\sqrt{3} \approx -1.732.$

**59.**  $r = 1 - \sin \theta$

$\dfrac{dy}{d\theta} = (1 - \sin \theta) \cos \theta - \cos \theta \sin \theta$

$\quad = \cos \theta (1 - 2 \sin \theta) = 0$

$\cos \theta = 0, \sin \theta = \dfrac{1}{2} \implies \theta = \dfrac{\pi}{2}, \dfrac{3\pi}{2}, \dfrac{\pi}{6}, \dfrac{5\pi}{6}$

Horizontal tangents: $\left(2, \dfrac{3\pi}{2}\right), \left(\dfrac{1}{2}, \dfrac{\pi}{6}\right), \left(\dfrac{1}{2}, \dfrac{5\pi}{6}\right)$

$\dfrac{dx}{d\theta} = (-1 + \sin \theta) \sin \theta - \cos \theta \cos \theta$

$\quad = -\sin \theta + \sin^2 \theta + \sin^2 \theta - 1$

$\quad = 2 \sin^2 \theta - \sin \theta - 1$

$\quad = (2 \sin \theta + 1)(\sin \theta - 1) = 0$

$\sin \theta = 1, \sin \theta = -\dfrac{1}{2} \implies \theta = \dfrac{\pi}{2}, \dfrac{7\pi}{6}, \dfrac{11\pi}{6}$

Vertical tangents: $\left(\dfrac{3}{2}, \dfrac{7\pi}{6}\right), \left(\dfrac{3}{2}, \dfrac{11\pi}{6}\right)$

**61.**  $r = 2 \csc \theta + 3$

$\dfrac{dy}{d\theta} = (2 \csc \theta + 3) \cos \theta + (-2 \csc \theta \cot \theta) \sin \theta$

$\quad = 3 \cos \theta = 0$

$\theta = \dfrac{\pi}{2}, \dfrac{3\pi}{2}$

Horizontal: $\left(5, \dfrac{\pi}{2}\right), \left(1, \dfrac{3\pi}{2}\right)$

**63.**  $r = 4 \sin \theta \cos^2 \theta$

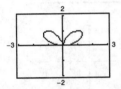

Horizontal tangents:

$\quad (0, 0), (1.4142, 0.7854), (1.4142, 2.3562)$

**65.**  $r = 2 \csc \theta + 5$

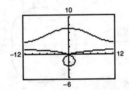

Horizontal tangents: $\left(7, \dfrac{\pi}{2}\right), \left(3, \dfrac{3\pi}{2}\right)$

**67.**

$\quad\quad\quad r = 3 \sin \theta$

$\quad\quad\quad r^2 = 3r \sin \theta$

$\quad\quad x^2 + y^2 = 3y$

$x^2 + \left(y - \dfrac{3}{2}\right)^2 = \dfrac{9}{4}$

Circle $r = \dfrac{3}{2}$

Center: $\left(0, \dfrac{3}{2}\right)$

Tangent at the pole: $\theta = 0$

**69.**  $r = 2(1 - \sin \theta)$

Cardioid

Symmetric to $y$-axis, $\theta = \dfrac{\pi}{2}$

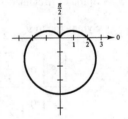

**71.**  $r = 2 \cos(3\theta)$

Rose curve with three petals

Symmetric to the polar axis

Relative extrema: $(2, 0), \left(-2, \dfrac{\pi}{3}\right), \left(2, \dfrac{2\pi}{3}\right)$

| $\theta$ | 0 | $\dfrac{\pi}{6}$ | $\dfrac{\pi}{4}$ | $\dfrac{\pi}{3}$ | $\dfrac{\pi}{2}$ | $\dfrac{2\pi}{3}$ | $\dfrac{5\pi}{6}$ | $\pi$ |
|---|---|---|---|---|---|---|---|---|
| $r$ | 2 | 0 | $-\sqrt{2}$ | $-2$ | 0 | 2 | 0 | $-2$ |

Tangents at the pole: $\theta = \dfrac{\pi}{6}, \dfrac{\pi}{2}, \dfrac{5\pi}{6}$

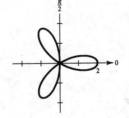

**73.** $r = 3 \sin 2\theta$

Rose curve with four petals

Symmetric to the polar axis, $\theta = \dfrac{\pi}{2}$, and pole

Relative extrema: $\left( \pm 3, \dfrac{\pi}{4} \right), \left( \pm 3, \dfrac{5\pi}{4} \right)$

Tangents at the pole: $\theta = 0, \dfrac{\pi}{2}$

$(\theta = \pi, \ 3\pi/2 \text{ give the same tangents.})$

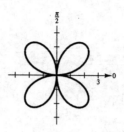

**75.** $r = 5$

Circle radius: 5

$x^2 + y^2 = 25$

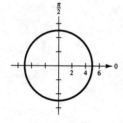

**77.** $r = 4(1 + \cos \theta)$

Cardioid

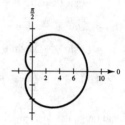

**79.** $r = 3 - 2 \cos \theta$

Limaçon

Symmetric to polar axis

| $\theta$ | 0 | $\dfrac{\pi}{3}$ | $\dfrac{\pi}{2}$ | $\dfrac{2\pi}{3}$ | $\pi$ |
|---|---|---|---|---|---|
| $r$ | 1 | 2 | 3 | 4 | 5 |

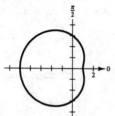

**81.**     $r = 3 \csc \theta$

$r \sin \theta = 3$

$y = 3$

Horizontal line

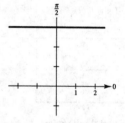

**83.** $r = 2\theta$

Spiral of Archimedes

Symmetric to $\theta = \dfrac{\pi}{2}$

| $\theta$ | 0 | $\dfrac{\pi}{4}$ | $\dfrac{\pi}{2}$ | $\dfrac{3\pi}{4}$ | $\pi$ | $\dfrac{5\pi}{4}$ | $\dfrac{3\pi}{2}$ |
|---|---|---|---|---|---|---|---|
| $r$ | 0 | $\dfrac{\pi}{2}$ | $\pi$ | $\dfrac{3\pi}{2}$ | $2\pi$ | $\dfrac{5\pi}{2}$ | $3\pi$ |

Tangent at the pole: $\theta = 0$

**85.** $r^2 = 4 \cos(2\theta)$

Lemniscate

Symmetric to the polar axis, $\theta = \dfrac{\pi}{2}$, and pole

Relative extrema: $(\pm 2, 0)$

| $\theta$ | 0 | $\dfrac{\pi}{6}$ | $\dfrac{\pi}{4}$ |
|---|---|---|---|
| $r$ | $\pm 2$ | $\pm\sqrt{2}$ | 0 |

Tangents at the pole: $\theta = \dfrac{\pi}{4}, \dfrac{3\pi}{4}$

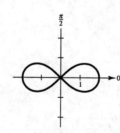

**87.** Since

$$r = 2 - \sec\theta = 2 - \frac{1}{\cos\theta},$$

the graph has polar axis symmetry and the lengths at the pole are

$$\theta = \frac{\pi}{3}, \frac{-\pi}{3}.$$

Furthermore,

$$r \Rightarrow -\infty \text{ as } \theta \Rightarrow \frac{\pi}{2}^{-}$$

$$r \Rightarrow \infty \text{ as } \theta \Rightarrow -\frac{\pi}{2}^{+}.$$

Also, $r = 2 - \dfrac{1}{\cos\theta} = 2 - \dfrac{r}{r\cos\theta} = 2 - \dfrac{r}{x}$

$$rx = 2x - r$$

$$r = \frac{2x}{1 + x}.$$

Thus, $r \Rightarrow \pm\infty$ as $x \Rightarrow -1$.

**89.** $r = \dfrac{2}{\theta}$

Hyperbolic spiral

$r \Rightarrow \infty$ as $\theta \Rightarrow 0$

$$r = \frac{2}{\theta} \Rightarrow \theta = \frac{2}{r} = \frac{2\sin\theta}{r\sin\theta} = \frac{2\sin\theta}{y}$$

$$y = \frac{2\sin\theta}{\theta}$$

$$\lim_{\theta \to 0} \frac{2\sin\theta}{\theta} = \lim_{\theta \to 0} \frac{2\cos\theta}{1} = 2$$

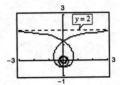

**91.** The rectangular coordinate system consists of all points of the form $(x, y)$ where $x$ is the directed distance from the $y$-axis to the point, and $y$ is the directed distance from the $x$-axis to the point. Every point has a unique representation.

The polar coordinate system uses $(r, \theta)$ to designate the location of a point.

$r$ is the directed distance to the origin and $\theta$ is the angle the point makes with the positive $x$-axis, measured clockwise.

Point do not have a unique polar representation.

**93.** $r = a$ circle

$\theta = b$ line

**95.** $r = 2 \sin\theta$ circle

Matches (c)

**97.** $r = 3(1 + \cos\theta)$

Cardioid

Matches (a)

**99.** $r = 4 \sin\theta$

(a) $0 \leq \theta \leq \dfrac{\pi}{2}$

(b) $\dfrac{\pi}{2} \leq \theta \leq \pi$

(c) $-\dfrac{\pi}{2} \leq \theta \leq \dfrac{\pi}{2}$

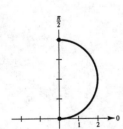

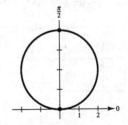

**101.** Let the curve $r = f(\theta)$ be rotated by $\phi$ to form the curve $r = g(\theta)$. If $(r_1, \theta_1)$ is a point on $r = f(\theta)$, then $(r_1, \theta_1 + \phi)$ is on $r = g(\theta)$. That is,

$$g(\theta_1 + \phi) = r_1 = f(\theta_1).$$

Letting $\theta = \theta_1 + \phi$, or $\theta_1 = \theta - \phi$, we see that

$$g(\theta) = g(\theta_1 + \phi) = f(\theta_1) = f(\theta - \phi).$$

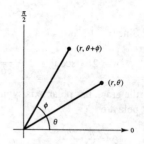

**103.** $r = 2 - \sin \theta$

(a) $r = 2 - \sin\left(\theta - \dfrac{\pi}{4}\right) = 2 - \dfrac{\sqrt{2}}{2}(\sin \theta - \cos \theta)$

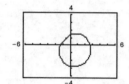

(b) $r = 2 - (-\cos \theta) = 2 + \cos \theta$

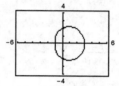

(c) $r = 2 - (-\sin \theta) = 2 + \sin \theta$

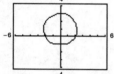

(d) $r = 2 - \cos \theta$

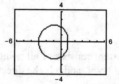

**105.** (a) $r = 1 - \sin \theta$

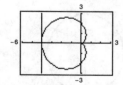

(b) $r = 1 - \sin\left(\theta - \dfrac{\pi}{4}\right)$

Rotate the graph of

$$r = 1 - \sin \theta$$

through the angle $\pi/4$.

**107.** $\tan \psi = \dfrac{r}{dr/d\theta} = \dfrac{2(1 - \cos \theta)}{2 \sin \theta}$

At $\theta = \pi$, $\tan \psi$ is undefined $\implies \psi = \dfrac{\pi}{2}$.

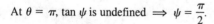

**109.** $\tan \psi = \dfrac{r}{dr/d\theta} = \dfrac{2 \cos 3\theta}{-6 \sin 3\theta}$

At $\theta = \dfrac{\pi}{6}$, $\tan \psi = 0 \implies \psi = 0$.

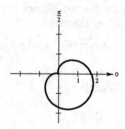

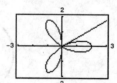

**111.**    $r = \dfrac{6}{1 - \cos \theta} = 6(1 - \cos \theta)^{-1} \Rightarrow \dfrac{dr}{d\theta} = \dfrac{6 \sin \theta}{(1 - \cos \theta)^2}$

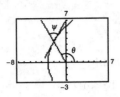

$\tan \psi = \dfrac{r}{\dfrac{dr}{d\theta}} = \dfrac{\dfrac{6}{(1 - \cos \theta)}}{\dfrac{6 \sin \theta}{(1 - \cos \theta)^2}} = \dfrac{1 - \cos \theta}{\sin \theta}$

At $\theta = \dfrac{2\pi}{3}$, $\tan \psi = \dfrac{1 - \left(-\dfrac{1}{2}\right)}{\dfrac{\sqrt{3}}{2}} = \sqrt{3}.$

$\psi = \dfrac{\pi}{3}, (60°)$

**113.** True

**115.** True

# Section 9.5    Area and Arc Length in Polar Coordinates

**1.** (a) $r = 8 \sin \theta$

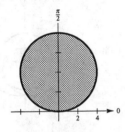

$A = \pi(4)^2 = 16\pi$

(b) $A = 2\left(\dfrac{1}{2}\right) \displaystyle\int_0^{\pi/2} \left[8 \sin \theta\right]^2 d\theta$

$= 64 \displaystyle\int_0^{\pi/2} \sin^2 \theta \, d\theta$

$= 32 \displaystyle\int_0^{\pi/2} (1 - \cos 2\theta) \, d\theta$

$= 32\left[\theta - \dfrac{\sin 2\theta}{2}\right]_0^{\pi/2} = 16\pi$

**3.** $A = 2\left[\dfrac{1}{2}\displaystyle\int_0^{\pi/6} (2 \cos 3\theta)^2 \, d\theta\right] = 2\left[\theta + \dfrac{1}{6}\sin 6\theta\right]_0^{\pi/6} = \dfrac{\pi}{3}$

**5.** $A = 2\left[\dfrac{1}{2}\displaystyle\int_0^{\pi/4} (\cos 2\theta)^2 \, d\theta\right]$

$= \dfrac{1}{2}\left[\theta + \dfrac{1}{4}\sin 4\theta\right]_0^{\pi/4} = \dfrac{\pi}{8}$

**7.** $A = 2\left[\dfrac{1}{2}\displaystyle\int_{-\pi/2}^{\pi/2} (1 - \sin \theta)^2 \, d\theta\right]$

$= \left[\dfrac{3}{2}\theta + 2\cos \theta - \dfrac{1}{4}\sin 2\theta\right]_{-\pi/2}^{\pi/2} = \dfrac{3\pi}{2}$

**9.** $A = 2\left[\dfrac{1}{2}\displaystyle\int_{2\pi/3}^{\pi} (1 + 2\cos \theta)^2 \, d\theta\right]$

$= \left[3\theta + 4\sin \theta + \sin 2\theta\right]_{2\pi/3}^{\pi} = \dfrac{2\pi - 3\sqrt{3}}{2}$

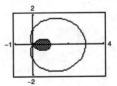

**11.** The area inside the outer loop is

$2\left[\dfrac{1}{2}\displaystyle\int_0^{2\pi/3} (1 + 2\cos \theta)^2 \, d\theta\right] = \left[3\theta + 4\sin \theta + \sin 2\theta\right]_0^{2\pi/3} = \dfrac{4\pi + 3\sqrt{3}}{2}.$

From the result of Exercise 9, the area between the loops is

$A = \left(\dfrac{4\pi + 3\sqrt{3}}{2}\right) - \left(\dfrac{2\pi - 3\sqrt{3}}{2}\right) = \pi + 3\sqrt{3}.$

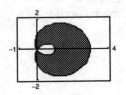

**13.** $r = 1 + \cos \theta$

$r = 1 - \cos \theta$

Solving simultaneously,

$$1 + \cos \theta = 1 - \cos \theta$$

$$2 \cos \theta = 0$$

$$\theta = \frac{\pi}{2}, \frac{3\pi}{2}.$$

Replacing $r$ by $-r$ and $\theta$ by $\theta + \pi$ in the first equation and solving, $-1 + \cos \theta = 1 - \cos \theta$, $\cos \theta = 1$, $\theta = 0$. Both curves pass through the pole, $(0, \pi)$, and $(0, 0)$, respectively.

Points of intersection: $\left(1, \frac{\pi}{2}\right), \left(1, \frac{3\pi}{2}\right), (0, 0)$

**15.** $r = 1 + \cos \theta$

$r = 1 - \sin \theta$

Solving simultaneously,

$$1 + \cos \theta = 1 - \sin \theta$$

$$\cos \theta = -\sin \theta$$

$$\tan \theta = -1$$

$$\theta = \frac{3\pi}{4}, \frac{7\pi}{4}.$$

Replacing $r$ by $-r$ and $\theta$ by $\theta + \pi$ in the first equation and solving, $-1 + \cos \theta = 1 - \sin \theta$, $\sin \theta + \cos \theta = 2$, which has no solution. Both curves pass through the pole, $(0, \pi)$, and $(0, \pi/2)$, respectively.

Points of intersection: $\left(\frac{2 - \sqrt{2}}{2}, \frac{3\pi}{4}\right), \left(\frac{2 + \sqrt{2}}{2}, \frac{7\pi}{4}\right), (0, 0)$

**17.** $r = 4 - 5 \sin \theta$

$r = 3 \sin \theta$

Solving simultaneously,

$$4 - 5 \sin \theta = 3 \sin \theta$$

$$\sin \theta = \frac{1}{2}$$

$$\theta = \frac{\pi}{6}, \frac{5\pi}{6}.$$

Both curves pass through the pole, $(0, \arcsin 4/5)$, and $(0, 0)$, respectively.

Points of intersection: $\left(\frac{3}{2}, \frac{\pi}{6}\right), \left(\frac{3}{2}, \frac{5\pi}{6}\right), (0, 0)$

**19.** $r = \frac{\theta}{2}$

$r = 2$

Solving simultaneously, we have

$$\theta/2 = 2, \theta = 4.$$

Points of intersection:

$$(2, 4), (-2, -4)$$

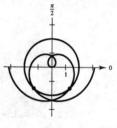

**21.** $r = 4 \sin 2\theta$

$r = 2$

$r = 4 \sin 2\theta$ is the equation of a rose curve with four petals and is symmetric to the polar axis, $\theta = \pi/2$, and the pole. Also, $r = 2$ is the equation of a circle of radius 2 centered at the pole. Solving simultaneously,

$$4 \sin 2\theta = 2$$

$$2\theta = \frac{\pi}{6}, \frac{5\pi}{6}$$

$$\theta = \frac{\pi}{12}, \frac{5\pi}{12}.$$

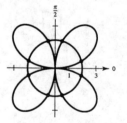

Therefore, the points of intersection for one petal are $(2, \pi/12)$ and $(2, 5\pi/12)$. By symmetry, the other points of intersection are $(2, 7\pi/12)$, $(2, 11\pi/12)$, $(2, 13\pi/12)$, $(2, 17\pi/12)$, $(2, 19\pi/12)$, and $(2, 23\pi/12)$.

**23.** $r = 2 + 3 \cos \theta$

$r = \dfrac{\sec \theta}{2}$

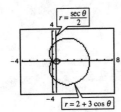

The graph of $r = 2 + 3 \cos \theta$ is a limaçon with an inner loop $(b > a)$ and is symmetric to the polar axis. The graph of $r = (\sec \theta)/2$ is the vertical line $x = 1/2$. Therefore, there are four points of intersection. Solving simultaneously,

$$2 + 3 \cos \theta = \frac{\sec \theta}{2}$$

$$6 \cos^2 \theta + 4 \cos \theta - 1 = 0$$

$$\cos \theta = \frac{-2 \pm \sqrt{10}}{6}$$

$$\theta = \arccos\left(\frac{-2 + \sqrt{10}}{6}\right) \approx 1.376$$

$$\theta = \arccos\left(\frac{-2 - \sqrt{10}}{6}\right) \approx 2.6068.$$

Points of intersection: $(-0.581, \pm 2.607), (2.581, \pm 1.376)$

**25.** $r = \cos \theta$

$r = 2 - 3 \sin \theta$

Points of intersection:

$$(0, 0), (0.935, 0.363), (0.535, -1.006)$$

The graphs reach the pole at different times ($\theta$ values).

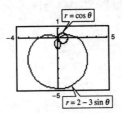

**27.** From Exercise 21, the points of intersection for one petal are $(2, \pi/12)$ and $(2, 5\pi/12)$. The area within one petal is

$$A = \frac{1}{2} \int_0^{\pi/12} (4 \sin 2\theta)^2 \, d\theta + \frac{1}{2} \int_{\pi/12}^{5\pi/12} (2)^2 \, d\theta + \frac{1}{2} \int_{5\pi/12}^{\pi/2} (4 \sin 2\theta)^2 \, d\theta$$

$$= 16 \int_0^{\pi/12} \sin^2(2\theta) \, d\theta + 2 \int_{\pi/12}^{5\pi/12} d\theta \quad \text{(by symmetry of the petal)}$$

$$= 8\left[\theta - \frac{1}{4} \sin 4\theta\right]_0^{\pi/12} + \left[2\theta\right]_{\pi/12}^{5\pi/12} = \frac{4\pi}{3} - \sqrt{3}.$$

Total area $= 4\left(\dfrac{4\pi}{3} - \sqrt{3}\right) = \dfrac{16\pi}{3} - 4\sqrt{3} = \dfrac{4}{3}\left(4\pi - 3\sqrt{3}\right)$

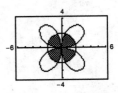

**29.** $A = 4\left[\dfrac{1}{2} \displaystyle\int_0^{\pi/2} (3 - 2 \sin \theta)^2 \, d\theta\right]$

$= 2\left[11\theta + 12 \cos \theta - \sin(2\theta)\right]_0^{\pi/2} = 11\pi - 24$

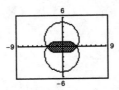

**31.** $A = 2\left[\dfrac{1}{2} \displaystyle\int_0^{\pi/6} (4 \sin \theta)^2 \, d\theta + \dfrac{1}{2} \displaystyle\int_{\pi/6}^{\pi/2} (2)^2 \, d\theta\right]$

$= 16\left[\dfrac{1}{2}\theta - \dfrac{1}{4}\sin(2\theta)\right]_0^{\pi/6} + \left[4\theta\right]_{\pi/6}^{\pi/2}$

$= \dfrac{8\pi}{3} - 2\sqrt{3} = \dfrac{2}{3}\left(4\pi - 3\sqrt{3}\right)$

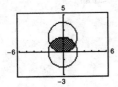

**33.** $A = 2\left[\dfrac{1}{2} \displaystyle\int_0^{\pi} [a(1 + \cos \theta)]^2 \, d\theta\right] - \dfrac{a^2\pi}{4}$

$= a^2\left[\dfrac{3}{2}\theta + 2 \sin \theta + \dfrac{\sin 2\theta}{4}\right]_0^{\pi} - \dfrac{a^2\pi}{4}$

$= \dfrac{3a^2\pi}{2} - \dfrac{a^2\pi}{4} = \dfrac{5a^2\pi}{4}$

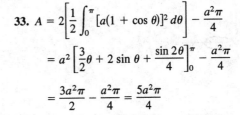

**35.** $A = \dfrac{\pi a^2}{8} + \dfrac{1}{2}\displaystyle\int_{\pi/2}^{\pi} [a(1 + \cos\theta)]^2 \, d\theta$

$= \dfrac{\pi a^2}{8} + \dfrac{a^2}{2}\displaystyle\int_{\pi/2}^{\pi} \left(\dfrac{3}{2} + 2\cos\theta + \dfrac{\cos 2\theta}{2}\right) d\theta$

$= \dfrac{\pi a^2}{8} + \dfrac{a^2}{2}\left[\dfrac{3}{2}\theta + 2\sin\theta + \dfrac{\sin 2\theta}{4}\right]_{\pi/2}^{\pi}$

$= \dfrac{\pi a^2}{8} + \dfrac{a^2}{2}\left[\dfrac{3\pi}{2} - \dfrac{3\pi}{4} - 2\right] = \dfrac{a^2}{2}[\pi - 2]$

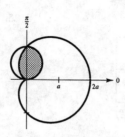

**37.** (a)  $r = a\cos^2\theta$

$r^3 = ar^2\cos^2\theta$

$(x^2 + y^2)^{3/2} = ax^2$

(b)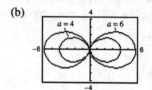

(c)  $A = 4\left(\dfrac{1}{2}\right)\displaystyle\int_0^{\pi/2} [(6\cos^2\theta)^2 - (4\cos^2\theta)^2] \, d\theta \; = 40\displaystyle\int_0^{\pi/2} \cos^4\theta \, d\theta \; = 10\displaystyle\int_0^{\pi/2} (1 + \cos 2\theta)^2 \, d\theta$

$= 10\displaystyle\int_0^{\pi/2} \left(1 + 2\cos 2\theta + \dfrac{1 - \cos 4\theta}{2}\right) d\theta = 10\left[\dfrac{3}{2}\theta + \sin 2\theta + \dfrac{1}{8}\sin 4\theta\right]_0^{\pi/2} = \dfrac{15\pi}{2}$

**39.** $r = a\cos(n\theta)$

For $n = 1$:

$r = a\cos\theta$

$A = \pi\left(\dfrac{a}{2}\right)^2 = \dfrac{\pi a^2}{4}$

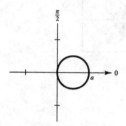

For $n = 2$:

$r = a\cos 2\theta$

$A = 8\left(\dfrac{1}{2}\right)\displaystyle\int_0^{\pi/4} (a\cos 2\theta)^2 \, d\theta = \dfrac{\pi a^2}{2}$

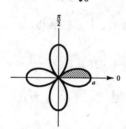

For $n = 3$:

$r = a\cos 3\theta$

$A = 6\left(\dfrac{1}{2}\right)\displaystyle\int_0^{\pi/6} (a\cos 3\theta)^2 \, d\theta = \dfrac{\pi a^2}{4}$

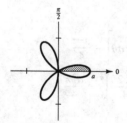

For $n = 4$:

$r = a\cos 4\theta$

$A = 16\left(\dfrac{1}{2}\right)\displaystyle\int_0^{\pi/8} (a\cos 4\theta)^2 \, d\theta = \dfrac{\pi a^2}{2}$

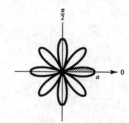

In general, the area of the region enclosed by $r = a\cos(n\theta)$ for $n = 1, 2, 3, \ldots$ is $(\pi a^2)/4$ if $n$ is odd and is $(\pi a^2)/2$ if $n$ is even.

**41.** $r = a$

$r' = 0$

$s = \int_0^{2\pi} \sqrt{a^2 + 0^2} \, d\theta = \left[ a\theta \right]_0^{2\pi} = 2\pi a$

(circumference of circle of radius $a$)

**43.** $r = 1 + \sin\theta$

$r' = \cos\theta$

$s = 2 \int_{\pi/2}^{3\pi/2} \sqrt{(1 + \sin\theta)^2 + (\cos\theta)^2} \, d\theta$

$= 2\sqrt{2} \int_{\pi/2}^{3\pi/2} \sqrt{1 + \sin\theta} \, d\theta$

$= 2\sqrt{2} \int_{\pi/2}^{3\pi/2} \frac{-\cos\theta}{\sqrt{1 - \sin\theta}} \, d\theta$

$= \left[ 4\sqrt{2} \sqrt{1 - \sin\theta} \right]_{\pi/2}^{3\pi/2}$

$= 4\sqrt{2} \left( \sqrt{2} - 0 \right) = 8$

**45.** $r = 2\theta, \ 0 \le \theta \le \dfrac{\pi}{2}$

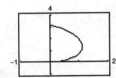

Length $\approx 4.16$

**47.** $r = \dfrac{1}{\theta}, \ \pi \le \theta \le 2\pi$

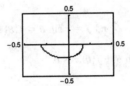

Length $\approx 0.71$

**49.** $r = \sin(3\cos\theta), \ 0 \le \theta \le \pi$

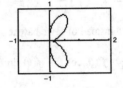

Length $\approx 4.39$

**51.** $r = 6\cos\theta$

$r' = -6\sin\theta$

$S = 2\pi \int_0^{\pi/2} 6\cos\theta \sin\theta \sqrt{36\cos^2\theta + 36\sin^2\theta} \, d\theta$

$= 72\pi \int_0^{\pi/2} \sin\theta \cos\theta \, d\theta$

$= \left[ 36\pi \sin^2\theta \right]_0^{\pi/2}$

$= 36\pi$

**53.** $r = e^{a\theta}$

$r' = ae^{a\theta}$

$S = 2\pi \int_0^{\pi/2} e^{a\theta} \cos\theta \sqrt{(e^{a\theta})^2 + (ae^{a\theta})^2} \, d\theta$

$= 2\pi\sqrt{1 + a^2} \int_0^{\pi/2} e^{2a\theta} \cos\theta \, d\theta$

$= 2\pi\sqrt{1 + a^2} \left[ \frac{e^{2a\theta}}{4a^2 + 1} (2a\cos\theta + \sin\theta) \right]_0^{\pi/2}$

$= \frac{2\pi\sqrt{1 + a^2}}{4a^2 + 1} (e^{\pi a} - 2a)$

**55.** $r = 4\cos 2\theta$

$r' = -8\sin 2\theta$

$S = 2\pi \int_0^{\pi/4} 4\cos 2\theta \sin\theta \sqrt{16\cos^2 2\theta + 64\sin^2 2\theta} \, d\theta$

$= 32\pi \int_0^{\pi/4} \cos 2\theta \sin\theta \sqrt{\cos^2 2\theta + 4\sin^2 2\theta} \, d\theta \approx 21.87$

**57.**    Area $= \dfrac{1}{2} \int_\alpha^\beta [f(\theta)]^2 d\theta = \dfrac{1}{2} \int_\alpha^\beta r^2 \, d\theta$

Arc length $= \int_\alpha^\beta \sqrt{f(\theta)^2 + f'(\theta)^2} \, d\theta = \int_\alpha^\beta \sqrt{r^2 + \left( \dfrac{dr}{d\theta} \right)^2} \, d\theta$

**59.** (a) is correct: $s \approx 33.124$.

**61.** Revolve $r = a$ about the line $r = b \sec \theta$ where $b > a > 0$.

$$f(\theta) = a$$

$$f'(\theta) = 0$$

$$S = 2\pi \int_0^{2\pi} [b - a \cos \theta] \sqrt{a^2 + 0^2}\, d\theta$$

$$= 2\pi a \Big[ b\theta - a \sin \theta \Big]_0^{2\pi}$$

$$= 2\pi a(2\pi b) = 4\pi^2 ab$$

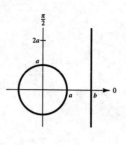

**63.** False. $f(\theta) = 1$ and $g(\theta) = -1$ have the same graphs.

**65.** In parametric form,

$$s = \int_a^b \sqrt{\left(\frac{dx}{dt}\right)^2 + \left(\frac{dy}{dt}\right)^2}\, dt.$$

Using $\theta$ instead of $t$, we have $x = r \cos \theta = f(\theta) \cos \theta$ and $y = r \sin \theta = f(\theta) \sin \theta$. Thus,

$$\frac{dx}{d\theta} = f'(\theta) \cos \theta - f(\theta) \sin \theta \text{ and } \frac{dy}{d\theta} = f'(\theta) \sin \theta + f(\theta) \cos \theta.$$

It follows that

$$\left(\frac{dx}{d\theta}\right)^2 + \left(\frac{dy}{d\theta}\right)^2 = [f(\theta)]^2 + [f'(\theta)]^2.$$

Therefore, $s = \displaystyle\int_\alpha^\beta \sqrt{[f(\theta)]^2 + [f'(\theta)]^2}\, d\theta$

# Section 9.6   Polar Equations of Conics and Kepler's Laws

**1.** $r = \dfrac{2e}{1 + e \cos \theta}$

   (a) $e = 1, r = \dfrac{2}{1 + \cos \theta}$, parabola

   (b) $e = 0.5, r = \dfrac{1}{1 + 0.5 \cos \theta} = \dfrac{2}{2 + \cos \theta}$, ellipse

   (c) $e = 1.5, r = \dfrac{3}{1 + 1.5 \cos \theta} = \dfrac{6}{2 + 3 \cos \theta}$, hyperbola

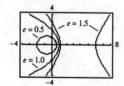

**3.** $r = \dfrac{2e}{1 - e \sin \theta}$

   (a) $e = 1, r = \dfrac{2}{1 - \sin \theta}$, parabola

   (b) $e = 0.5, r = \dfrac{1}{1 - 0.5 \sin \theta} = \dfrac{2}{2 - \sin \theta}$, ellipse

   (c) $e = 1.5, r = \dfrac{3}{1 - 1.5 \sin \theta} = \dfrac{6}{2 - 3 \sin \theta}$, hyperbola

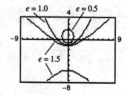

**5.** $r = \dfrac{4}{1 + e \sin \theta}$

(a)

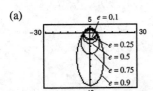

The conic is an ellipse. As $e \rightarrow 1^-$, the ellipse becomes more elliptical, and as $e \rightarrow 0^+$, it becomes more circular.

(b)

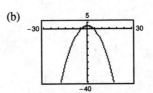

The conic is a parabola.

(c)

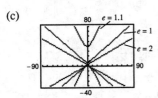

The conic is a hyperbola. As $e \rightarrow 1^+$, the hyperbolas opens more slowly, and as $e \rightarrow \infty$, they open more rapidly.

**7.** Parabola; Matches (c)

**9.** Hyperbola; Matches (a)

**11.** Ellipse; Matches (b)

**13.** $r = \dfrac{-1}{1 - \sin \theta}$

Parabola since $e = 1$

Vertex: $\left(-\dfrac{1}{2}, \dfrac{3\pi}{2}\right)$

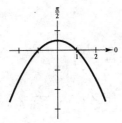

**15.** $r = \dfrac{6}{2 + \cos \theta}$

$= \dfrac{3}{1 + (1/2) \cos \theta}$

Ellipse since $e = \dfrac{1}{2} < 1$

Vertices: $(2, 0), (6, \pi)$

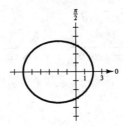

**17.** $r(2 + \sin \theta) = 4$

$r = \dfrac{4}{2 + \sin \theta}$

$= \dfrac{2}{1 + (1/2) \sin \theta}$

Ellipse since $e = \dfrac{1}{2} < 1$

Vertices: $\left(\dfrac{4}{3}, \dfrac{\pi}{2}\right), \left(4, \dfrac{3\pi}{2}\right)$

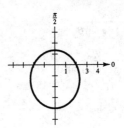

**19.** $r = \dfrac{5}{-1 + 2 \cos \theta} = \dfrac{-5}{1 - 2 \cos \theta}$

Hyperbola since $e = 2 > 1$

Vertices: $(5, 0), \left(-\dfrac{5}{3}, \pi\right)$

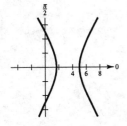

**21.** $r = \dfrac{3}{2 + 6 \sin \theta} = \dfrac{3/2}{1 + 3 \sin \theta}$

Hyperbola since $e = 3 > 1$

Vertices: $\left(\dfrac{3}{8}, \dfrac{\pi}{2}\right), \left(-\dfrac{3}{4}, \dfrac{3\pi}{2}\right)$

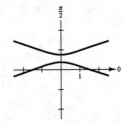

**23.** 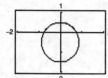  Ellipse

**25.**   Parabola

**27.** $r = \dfrac{-1}{1 - \sin\left(\theta - \dfrac{\pi}{4}\right)}$

Rotate the graph of

$$r = \frac{-1}{1 - \sin\theta}$$

counterclockwise through the angle $\dfrac{\pi}{4}$.

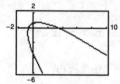

**29.** $r = \dfrac{6}{2 + \cos\left(\theta + \dfrac{\pi}{6}\right)}$

Rotate the graph of

$$r = \frac{6}{2 + \cos\theta}$$

clockwise through the angle $\dfrac{\pi}{6}$.

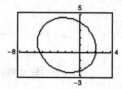

**31.** Change $\theta$ to $\theta + \dfrac{\pi}{4}$: $r = \dfrac{5}{5 + 3\cos\left(\theta + \dfrac{\pi}{4}\right)}$.

**33.** Parabola

$e = 1, x = -1, d = 1$

$$r = \frac{ed}{1 - e\cos\theta} = \frac{1}{1 - \cos\theta}$$

**35.** Ellipse

$e = \dfrac{1}{2}, y = 1, d = 1$

$$r = \frac{ed}{1 + e\sin\theta}$$

$$= \frac{1/2}{1 + (1/2)\sin\theta}$$

$$= \frac{1}{2 + \sin\theta}$$

**37.** Hyperbola

$e = 2, x = 1, d = 1$

$$r = \frac{ed}{1 + e\cos\theta} = \frac{2}{1 + 2\cos\theta}$$

**39.** Parabola

Vertex: $\left(1, -\dfrac{\pi}{2}\right)$

$e = 1, d = 2, r = \dfrac{2}{1 - \sin\theta}$

**41.** Ellipse

Vertices: $(2, 0), (8, \pi)$

$e = \dfrac{3}{5}, d = \dfrac{16}{3}$

$$r = \frac{ed}{1 + e\cos\theta}$$

$$= \frac{16/5}{1 + (3/5)\cos\theta}$$

$$= \frac{16}{5 + 3\cos\theta}$$

**43.** Hyperbola

Vertices: $\left(1, \dfrac{3\pi}{2}\right), \left(9, \dfrac{3\pi}{2}\right)$

$e = \dfrac{5}{4}, d = \dfrac{9}{5}$

$$r = \frac{ed}{1 - e\sin\theta}$$

$$= \frac{9/4}{1 - (5/4)\sin\theta}$$

$$= \frac{9}{4 - 5\sin\theta}$$

**45.** Ellipse if $0 < e < 1$, parabola if $e = 1$, hyperbola if $e > 1$.

**47.** (a) Hyperbola ($e = 2 > 1$)

    (b) Ellipse $\left(e = \dfrac{1}{2} < 1\right)$

    (c) Parabola ($e = 1$)

    (d) Rotated hyperbola ($e = 3$)

**49.** $a = 5, c = 4, e = \dfrac{4}{5}, b = 3$

$$r^2 = \frac{9}{1 - (16/25)\cos^2\theta}$$

**51.** $a = 3, b = 4, c = 5, e = \dfrac{5}{3}$

$$r^2 = \frac{-16}{1 - (25/9)\cos^2\theta}$$

**53.** $A = 2\left[\dfrac{1}{2}\displaystyle\int_0^\pi \left(\dfrac{3}{2 - \cos\theta}\right)^2 d\theta\right]$

$$= 9\int_0^\pi \frac{1}{(2 - \cos\theta)^2}\,d\theta \approx 10.88$$

**55.** Vertices: $(126{,}000, 0), (4119, \pi)$

$$a = \frac{126{,}000 + 4119}{2} = 65{,}059.5,\ c = 65{,}059.5 - 4119 = 60{,}940.5,\ e = \frac{c}{a} = \frac{40{,}627}{43{,}373},\ d = 4119\left(\frac{84{,}000}{40{,}627}\right)$$

$$r = \frac{ed}{1 - e\cos\theta} = \frac{4119(84{,}000/43{,}373)}{1 - (40{,}627/43{,}373)\cos\theta} = \frac{345{,}996{,}000}{43{,}373 - 40{,}627\cos\theta}$$

When $\theta = 60°$, $r = \dfrac{345{,}996{,}000}{23{,}059.5} \approx 15{,}004.49$.

Distance between the surface of the earth and the satellite is $r - 4000 = 11{,}004.49$ miles.

**57.** $a = 92.957 \times 10^6$ mi, $e = 0.0167$

$$r = \frac{(1 - e^2)a}{1 - e\cos\theta} = \frac{92{,}931{,}075.2223}{1 - 0.0167\cos\theta}$$

Perihelion distance: $a(1 - e) \approx 91{,}404{,}618$ mi

Aphelion distance: $a(1 + e) \approx 94{,}509{,}382$ mi

**59.** $a = 5.900 \times 10^9$ km, $e = 0.2481$

$$r = \frac{(1 - e^2)a}{1 - e\cos\theta} \approx \frac{5.537 \times 10^9}{1 - 0.2481\cos\theta}$$

Perihelion distance: $a(1 - e) = 4.436 \times 10^9$ km

Aphelion distance: $a(1 + e) = 7.364 \times 10^9$ km

**61.** $r = \dfrac{5.537 \times 10^9}{1 - 0.2481\cos\theta}$

(a) $A = \dfrac{1}{2}\displaystyle\int_0^{\pi/9}\left[\dfrac{5.537 \times 10^9}{1 - 0.2481\cos\theta}\right]^2 d\theta \approx 9.341 \times 10^{18}$ km$^2$

$$248\left[\frac{\dfrac{1}{2}\displaystyle\int_0^{\pi/9}\left[\dfrac{5.537 \times 10^9}{1 - 0.2481\cos\theta}\right]^2 d\theta}{\dfrac{1}{2}\displaystyle\int_0^{2\pi}\left[\dfrac{5.537 \times 10^9}{1 - 0.2481\cos\theta}\right]^2 d\theta}\right] \approx 21.867\ \text{yr}$$

(b) $\dfrac{1}{2}\displaystyle\int_\pi^{\alpha - \pi}\left[\dfrac{5.537 \times 10^9}{1 - 0.2481\cos\theta}\right]^2 d\theta = 9.341 \times 10^{18}$

$\alpha \approx \pi + 0.8995$ rad

In part (a) the ray swept through a smaller angle to generate the same area since the length of the ray is longer than in part (b).

(c) $r' = \dfrac{(-5.537 \times 10^9)(0.2481\sin\theta)}{(1 - 0.2481\cos\theta)^2}$

$$s = \int_0^{\pi/9}\sqrt{\left(\frac{5.537 \times 10^9}{1 - 0.2481\cos\theta}\right)^2 + \left[\frac{-1.3737297 \times 10^9 \sin\theta}{(1 - 0.2481\cos\theta)^2}\right]^2}\,d\theta \approx 2.559 \times 10^9\ \text{km}$$

$$\frac{2.559 \times 10^9\ \text{km}}{21.867\ \text{yr}} \approx 1.17 \times 10^8\ \text{km/yr}$$

$$s = \int_\pi^{\pi + 0.899}\sqrt{\left(\frac{5.537 \times 10^9}{1 - 0.2481\cos\theta}\right)^2 + \left[\frac{-1.3737297 \times 10^9 \sin\theta}{(1 - 0.2481\cos\theta)^2}\right]^2}\,d\theta \approx 4.119 \times 10^9\ \text{km}$$

$$\frac{4.119 \times 10^9\ \text{km}}{21.867\ \text{yr}} \approx 1.88 \times 10^8\ \text{km/yr}$$

**63.** $r_1 = \dfrac{ed}{1 + \sin\theta}$ and $r_2 = \dfrac{ed}{1 - \sin\theta}$

Points of intersection: $(ed, 0)$, $(ed, \pi)$

$r_1\colon \dfrac{dy}{dx} = \dfrac{\left(\dfrac{ed}{1+\sin\theta}\right)(\cos\theta) + \left(\dfrac{-ed\cos\theta}{(1+\sin\theta)^2}\right)(\sin\theta)}{\left(\dfrac{-ed}{1+\sin\theta}\right)(\sin\theta) + \left(\dfrac{-ed\cos\theta}{(1+\sin\theta)^2}\right)(\cos\theta)}$

At $(ed, 0)$, $\dfrac{dy}{dx} = -1$. At $(ed, \pi)$, $\dfrac{dy}{dx} = 1$.

$r_2\colon \dfrac{dy}{dx} = \dfrac{\left(\dfrac{ed}{1-\sin\theta}\right)(\cos\theta) + \left(\dfrac{ed\cos\theta}{(1-\sin\theta)^2}\right)(\sin\theta)}{\left(\dfrac{-ed}{1-\sin\theta}\right)(\sin\theta) + \left(\dfrac{ed\cos\theta}{(1-\sin\theta)^2}\right)(\cos\theta)}$

At $(ed, 0)$, $\dfrac{dy}{dx} = 1$. At $(ed, \pi)$, $\dfrac{dy}{dx} = -1$.

Therefore, at $(ed, 0)$ we have $m_1 m_2 = (-1)(1) = -1$, and at $(ed, \pi)$ we have $m_1 m_2 = 1(-1) = -1$. The curves intersect at right angles.

# Review Exercises for Chapter 9

**1.** Matches (d) - ellipse

**3.** Matches (a) - parabola

**5.**    $16x^2 + 16y^2 - 16x + 24y - 3 = 0$

$\left(x^2 - x + \dfrac{1}{4}\right) + \left(y^2 + \dfrac{3}{2}y + \dfrac{9}{16}\right) = \dfrac{3}{16} + \dfrac{1}{4} + \dfrac{9}{16}$

$\left(x - \dfrac{1}{2}\right)^2 + \left(y + \dfrac{3}{4}\right)^2 = 1$

Circle

Center: $\left(\dfrac{1}{2}, -\dfrac{3}{4}\right)$

Radius: 1

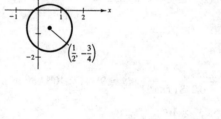

**7.**    $3x^2 - 2y^2 + 24x + 12y + 24 = 0$

$3(x^2 + 8x + 16) - 2(y^2 - 6y + 9) = -24 + 48 - 18$

$\dfrac{(x+4)^2}{2} - \dfrac{(y-3)^2}{3} = 1$

Hyperbola

Center: $(-4, 3)$

Vertices: $\left(-4 \pm \sqrt{2}, 3\right)$

Asymptotes: $y = 3 \pm \sqrt{\dfrac{3}{2}}(x + 4)$

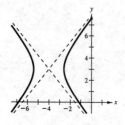

**9.**    $3x^2 + 2y^2 - 12x + 12y + 29 = 0$

$3(x^2 - 4x + 4) + 2(y^2 + 6y + 9) = -29 + 12 + 18$

$\dfrac{(x-2)^2}{1/3} + \dfrac{(y+3)^2}{1/2} = 1$

Ellipse

Center: $(2, -3)$

Vertices: $\left(2, -3 \pm \dfrac{\sqrt{2}}{2}\right)$

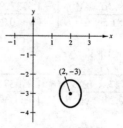

**11.** Vertex: $(0, 2)$

Directrix: $x = -3$

Parabola opens to the right

$p = 3$

$(y - 2)^2 = 4(3)(x - 0)$

$y^2 - 4y - 12x + 4 = 0$

**13.** Vertices: $(-3, 0), (7, 0)$

Foci: $(0, 0), (4, 0)$

Horizontal major axis

Center: $(2, 0)$

$a = 5, c = 2, b = \sqrt{21}$

$\dfrac{(x - 2)^2}{25} + \dfrac{y^2}{21} = 1$

**15.** Vertices: $(\pm 4, 0)$

Foci: $(\pm 6, 0)$

Center: $(0, 0)$

Horizontal transverse axis

$a = 4, c = 6, b = \sqrt{36 - 16} = 2\sqrt{5}$

$\dfrac{x^2}{16} - \dfrac{y^2}{20} = 1$

**17.** $\dfrac{x^2}{9} + \dfrac{y^2}{4} = 1, a = 3, b = 2, c = \sqrt{5}, e = \dfrac{\sqrt{5}}{3}$

By Example 5 of Section 9.1,

$$C = 12 \int_0^{\pi/2} \sqrt{1 - \left(\dfrac{5}{9}\right) \sin^2 \theta} \, d\theta \approx 15.87.$$

**19.** $y = x - 2$ has a slope of 1. The perpendicular slope is $-1$.

$y = x^2 - 2x + 2$

$\dfrac{dy}{dx} = 2x - 2 = -1$ when $x = \dfrac{1}{2}$ and $y = \dfrac{5}{4}$.

Perpendicular line: $\qquad y - \dfrac{5}{4} = -1\left(x - \dfrac{1}{2}\right)$

$$4x + 4y - 7 = 0$$

**21.** (a) $V = (\pi ab)(\text{Length}) = 12\pi(16) = 192\pi \text{ ft}^3$

(b) $F = 2(62.4) \displaystyle\int_{-3}^{3} (3 - y)\dfrac{4}{3}\sqrt{9 - y^2} \, dy = \dfrac{8}{3}(62.4)\left[3\int_{-3}^{3} \sqrt{9 - y^2} \, dy - \int_{-3}^{3} y\sqrt{9 - y^2} \, dy\right]$

$= \dfrac{8}{3}(62.4)\left[\dfrac{3}{2}\left(y\sqrt{9 - y^2} + 9 \arcsin\dfrac{y}{3}\right) + \dfrac{1}{3}(9 - y^2)^{3/2}\right]_{-3}^{3}$

$= \dfrac{8}{3}(62.4)\left[\dfrac{3}{2}\left(\dfrac{9\pi}{2}\right) - \dfrac{3}{2}\left(-\dfrac{9\pi}{2}\right)\right] = \dfrac{8}{3}(62.4)\left(\dfrac{27\pi}{2}\right) \approx 7057.274$

(c) You want $\dfrac{3}{4}$ of the total area of $12\pi$ covered. Find $h$ so that

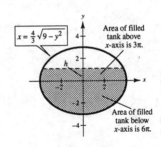

Area of filled tank above $x$-axis is $3\pi$.

$x = \dfrac{4}{3}\sqrt{9 - y^2}$

Area of filled tank below $x$-axis is $6\pi$.

$$2 \int_0^h \dfrac{4}{3}\sqrt{9 - y^2} \, dy = 3\pi$$

$$\int_0^h \sqrt{9 - y^2} \, dy = \dfrac{9\pi}{8}$$

$$\dfrac{1}{2}\left[y\sqrt{9 - y^2} + 9 \arcsin\left(\dfrac{y}{3}\right)\right]_0^h = \dfrac{9\pi}{8}$$

$$h\sqrt{9 - h^2} + 9 \arcsin\left(\dfrac{h}{3}\right) = \dfrac{9\pi}{4}.$$

By Newton's Method, $h \approx 1.212$. Therefore, the total height of the water is $1.212 + 3 = 4.212$ ft.

(d) Area of ends $= 2(12\pi) = 24\pi$

Area of sides $= (\text{Perimeter})(\text{Length})$

$= 16 \displaystyle\int_0^{\pi/2} \left(\sqrt{1 - \left(\dfrac{7}{16}\right)\sin^2 \theta}\right) d\theta(16)$ [from Example 5 of Section 9.1]

$\approx 256\left(\dfrac{\pi/2}{12}\right)\left[\sqrt{1 - \left(\dfrac{7}{16}\right)\sin^2(0)} + 4\sqrt{1 - \left(\dfrac{7}{16}\right)\sin^2\left(\dfrac{\pi}{8}\right)} + 2\sqrt{1 - \left(\dfrac{7}{16}\right)\sin^2\left(\dfrac{\pi}{4}\right)}\right.$

$\left. + 4\sqrt{1 - \left(\dfrac{7}{16}\right)\sin^2\left(\dfrac{3\pi}{8}\right)} + \sqrt{1 - \left(\dfrac{7}{16}\right)\sin^2\left(\dfrac{\pi}{2}\right)}\right] \approx 353.65$

Total area $= 24\pi + 353.65 \approx 429.05$

**23.** $x = 1 + 4t$, $y = 2 - 3t$

$$t = \frac{x-1}{4} \implies y = 2 - 3\left(\frac{x-1}{4}\right)$$

$$y = -\frac{3}{4}x + \frac{11}{4}$$

$$4y + 3x - 11 = 0$$

Line

**25.** $x = 6\cos\theta$, $y = 6\sin\theta$

$$\left(\frac{x}{6}\right)^2 + \left(\frac{y}{6}\right)^2 = 1$$

$$x^2 + y^2 = 36$$

Circle

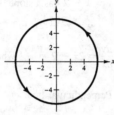

**27.** $x = 2 + \sec\theta$, $y = 3 + \tan\theta$

$$(x-2)^2 = \sec^2\theta = 1 + \tan^2\theta = 1 + (y-3)^2$$

$$(x-2)^2 - (y-3)^2 = 1$$

Hyperbola

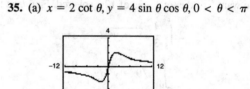

**29.** $x = 3 + (3 - (-2))t = 3 + 5t$

$y = 2 + (2 - 6)t = 2 - 4t$

(other answers possible)

**31.** $\dfrac{(x+3)^2}{16} + \dfrac{(y-4)^2}{9} = 1$

Let $\dfrac{(x+3)^2}{16} = \cos^2\theta$ and $\dfrac{(y-4)^2}{9} = \sin^2\theta$.

Then $x = -3 + 4\cos\theta$ and $y = 4 + 3\sin\theta$.

**33.** $x = \cos 3\theta + 5\cos\theta$

$y = \sin 3\theta + 5\sin\theta$

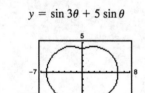

**35.** (a) $x = 2\cot\theta$, $y = 4\sin\theta\cos\theta$, $0 < \theta < \pi$

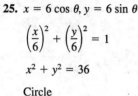

(b) $(4 + x^2)y = (4 + 4\cot^2\theta)4\sin\theta\cos\theta$

$$= 16\csc^2\theta \cdot \sin\theta \cdot \cos\theta$$

$$= 16\frac{\cos\theta}{\sin\theta}$$

$$= 8(2\cot\theta)$$

$$= 8x$$

**37.** $x = 1 + 4t$

$y = 2 - 3t$

(a) $\dfrac{dy}{dx} = -\dfrac{3}{4}$

No horizontal tangents

(b) $t = \dfrac{x-1}{4}$

$$y = 2 - \frac{3}{4}(x-1) = \frac{-3x+11}{4}$$

(c)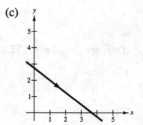

**39.** $x = \dfrac{1}{t}$

$y = 2t + 3$

(a) $\dfrac{dy}{dx} = \dfrac{2}{-1/t^2} = -2t^2$

No horizontal tangents
$(t \neq 0)$

(b) $t = \dfrac{1}{x}$

$y = \dfrac{2}{x} + 3$

(c)

**41.** $x = \dfrac{1}{2t + 1}$

$y = \dfrac{1}{t^2 - 2t}$

(a) $\dfrac{dy}{dx} = \dfrac{\dfrac{-(2t - 2)}{(t^2 - 2t)^2}}{\dfrac{-2}{(2t + 1)^2}} = \dfrac{(t - 1)(2t + 1)^2}{t^2(t - 2)^2} = 0$ when $t = 1$.

Point of horizontal tangency: $\left(\tfrac{1}{3}, -1\right)$

(b) $2t + 1 = \dfrac{1}{x} \Rightarrow t = \dfrac{1}{2}\left(\dfrac{1}{x} - 1\right)$

$y = \dfrac{1}{\dfrac{1}{2}\left(\dfrac{1 - x}{x}\right)\left[\dfrac{1}{2}\left(\dfrac{1 - x}{x}\right) - 2\right]}$

$= \dfrac{4x^2}{(1 - x)^2 - 4x(1 - x)} = \dfrac{4x^2}{(5x - 1)(x - 1)}$

(c)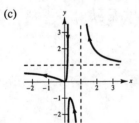

**43.** $x = 3 + 2\cos\theta$

$y = 2 + 5\sin\theta$

(a) $\dfrac{dy}{dx} = \dfrac{5\cos\theta}{-2\sin\theta} = -2.5\cot\theta = 0$ when $\theta = \dfrac{\pi}{2}, \dfrac{3\pi}{2}$.

Points of horizontal tangency: $(3, 7), (3, -3)$

(b) $\dfrac{(x - 3)^2}{4} + \dfrac{(y - 2)^2}{25} = 1$

(c)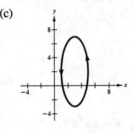

**45.** $x = \cos^3\theta$

$y = 4\sin^3\theta$

(a) $\dfrac{dy}{dx} = \dfrac{12\sin^2\theta\cos\theta}{3\cos^2\theta(-\sin\theta)} = \dfrac{-4\sin\theta}{\cos\theta} = -4\tan\theta = 0$ when $\theta = 0, \pi$.

But, $\dfrac{dy}{dt} = \dfrac{dx}{dt} = 0$ at $\theta = 0, \pi$. Hence no points of horizontal tangency.

(b) $x^{2/3} + \left(\dfrac{y}{4}\right)^{2/3} = 1$

(c)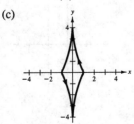

**47.** $x = \cot \theta$

$y = \sin 2\theta = 2 \sin \theta \cos \theta$

(a), (c)

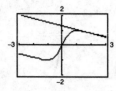

(b) At $\theta = \dfrac{\pi}{6}, \dfrac{dx}{d\theta} = -4, \dfrac{dy}{d\theta} = 1$, and $\dfrac{dy}{dx} = -\dfrac{1}{4}$

**49.** $x = r(\cos \theta + \theta \sin \theta)$

$y = r(\sin \theta - \theta \cos \theta)$

$\dfrac{dx}{d\theta} = r\theta \cos \theta$

$\dfrac{dy}{d\theta} = r\theta \sin \theta$

$s = r \displaystyle\int_0^\pi \sqrt{\theta^2 \cos^2 \theta + \theta^2 \sin^2 \theta}\, d\theta$

$= r \displaystyle\int_0^\pi \theta\, d\theta = \dfrac{r}{2}\Big[\theta^2\Big]_0^\pi = \dfrac{1}{2}\pi^2 r$

**51.** $(x, y) = (4, -4)$

$r = \sqrt{4^2 + (-4)^2} = 4\sqrt{2}$

$\theta = 7\dfrac{\pi}{4}$

$(r, \theta) = \left(4\sqrt{2}, \dfrac{7\pi}{4}\right), \left(-4\sqrt{2}, \dfrac{3\pi}{4}\right)$

$(4, -4)$

**53.**  $\quad r = 3 \cos \theta$

$r^2 = 3r \cos \theta$

$x^2 + y^2 = 3x$

$x^2 + y^2 - 3x = 0$

**55.**  $\quad r = -2(1 + \cos \theta)$

$r^2 = -2r(1 + \cos \theta)$

$x^2 + y^2 = -2\big(\pm\sqrt{x^2 + y^2}\big) - 2x$

$(x^2 + y^2 + 2x)^2 = 4(x^2 + y^2)$

**57.**  $\quad r^2 = \cos 2\theta = \cos^2 \theta - \sin^2 \theta$

$r^4 = r^2 \cos^2 \theta - r^2 \sin^2 \theta$

$(x^2 + y^2)^2 = x^2 - y^2$

**59.**  $\quad r = 4 \cos 2\theta \sec \theta$

$= 4(2 \cos^2 \theta - 1)\left(\dfrac{1}{\cos \theta}\right)$

$r \cos \theta = 8 \cos^2 \theta - 4$

$x = 8\left(\dfrac{x^2}{x^2 + y^2}\right) - 4$

$x^3 + xy^2 = 4x^2 - 4y^2$

$y^2 = x^2\left(\dfrac{4 - x}{4 + x}\right)$

**61.**  $(x^2 + y^2)^2 = ax^2 y$

$r^4 = a(r^2 \cos^2 \theta)(r \sin \theta)$

$r = a \cos^2 \theta \sin \theta$

**63.** $x^2 + y^2 = a^2\left(\arctan \dfrac{y}{x}\right)^2$

$r^2 = a^2 \theta^2$

**65.** $r = 4$

Circle of radius 4

Centered at the pole

Symmetric to polar axis,

$\theta = \pi/2$, and pole

**67.** $r = -\sec \theta = \dfrac{-1}{\cos \theta}$

$r \cos \theta = -1, x = -1$

Vertical line

**69.** $r = -2(1 + \cos\theta)$

Cardioid

Symmetric to polar axis

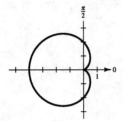

| $\theta$ | $0$ | $\dfrac{\pi}{3}$ | $\dfrac{\pi}{2}$ | $\dfrac{2\pi}{3}$ | $\pi$ |
|---|---|---|---|---|---|
| $r$ | $-4$ | $-3$ | $-2$ | $-1$ | $0$ |

**71.** $r = 4 - 3\cos\theta$

Limaçon

Symmetric to polar axis

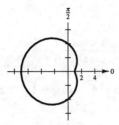

| $\theta$ | $0$ | $\dfrac{\pi}{3}$ | $\dfrac{\pi}{2}$ | $\dfrac{2\pi}{3}$ | $\pi$ |
|---|---|---|---|---|---|
| $r$ | $1$ | $\dfrac{5}{2}$ | $4$ | $\dfrac{11}{2}$ | $7$ |

**73.** $r = -3\cos(2\theta)$

Rose curve with four petals

Symmetric to polar axis, $\theta = \dfrac{\pi}{2}$, and pole

Relative extrema: $(-3, 0), \left(3, \dfrac{\pi}{2}\right), (-3, \pi), \left(3, \dfrac{3\pi}{2}\right)$

Tangents at the pole: $\theta = \dfrac{\pi}{4}, \dfrac{3\pi}{4}$

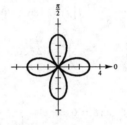

**75.** $r^2 = 4\sin^2(2\theta)$

$r = \pm 2\sin(2\theta)$

Rose curve with four petals

Symmetric to the polar axis, $\theta = \dfrac{\pi}{2}$, and pole

Relative extrema: $\left(\pm 2, \dfrac{\pi}{4}\right), \left(\pm 2, \dfrac{3\pi}{4}\right)$

Tangents at the pole: $\theta = 0, \dfrac{\pi}{2}$

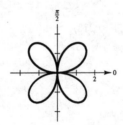

**77.** $r = \dfrac{3}{\cos[\theta - (\pi/4)]}$

Graph of $r = 3\sec\theta$ rotated through an angle of $\pi/4$

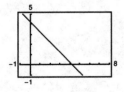

**79.** $r = 4\cos 2\theta \sec\theta$

Strophoid

Symmetric to the polar axis

$r \Longrightarrow -\infty$ as $\theta \Longrightarrow \dfrac{\pi^-}{2}$

$r \Longrightarrow -\infty$ as $\theta \Longrightarrow \dfrac{-\pi^+}{2}$

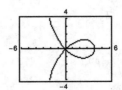

**81.** $r = 1 - 2 \cos \theta$

(a) The graph has polar symmetry and the tangents at the pole are

$$\theta = \frac{\pi}{3}, -\frac{\pi}{3}.$$

(b) $\dfrac{dy}{dx} = \dfrac{2 \sin^2 \theta + (1 - 2 \cos \theta) \cos \theta}{2 \sin \theta \cos \theta - (1 - 2 \cos \theta) \sin \theta}$

Horizontal tangents: $-4 \cos^2 \theta + \cos \theta + 2 = 0$, $\cos \theta = \dfrac{-1 \pm \sqrt{1 + 32}}{-8} = \dfrac{1 \pm \sqrt{33}}{8}$

When $\cos \theta = \dfrac{1 \pm \sqrt{33}}{8}$, $r = 1 - 2 \left( \dfrac{1 + \sqrt{33}}{8} \right) = \dfrac{3 \mp \sqrt{33}}{4}$,

$\left[ \dfrac{3 - \sqrt{33}}{4}, \arccos \left( \dfrac{1 + \sqrt{33}}{8} \right) \right] \approx (-0.686, 0.568)$

$\left[ \dfrac{3 - \sqrt{33}}{4}, -\arccos \left( \dfrac{1 + \sqrt{33}}{8} \right) \right] \approx (-0.686, -0.568)$

$\left[ \dfrac{3 + \sqrt{33}}{4}, \arccos \left( \dfrac{1 - \sqrt{33}}{8} \right) \right] \approx (2.186, 2.206)$

$\left[ \dfrac{3 + \sqrt{33}}{4}, -\arccos \left( \dfrac{1 - \sqrt{33}}{8} \right) \right] \approx (2.186, -2.206).$

Vertical tangents:

$\sin \theta (4 \cos \theta - 1) = 0$, $\sin \theta = 0$, $\cos \theta = \dfrac{1}{4}$,

$\theta = 0, \pi, \theta = \pm \arccos \left( \dfrac{1}{4} \right), (-1, 0), (3, \pi)$

$\left( \dfrac{1}{2}, \pm \arccos \dfrac{1}{4} \right) \approx (0.5, \pm 1.318)$

(c)

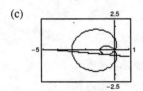

**83.** Circle: $r = 3 \sin \theta$

$\dfrac{dy}{dx} = \dfrac{3 \cos \theta \sin \theta + 3 \sin \theta \cos \theta}{3 \cos \theta \cos \theta - 3 \sin \theta \sin \theta} = \dfrac{\sin 2\theta}{\cos^2 \theta - \sin^2 \theta} = \tan 2\theta$ at $\theta = \dfrac{\pi}{6}$, $\dfrac{dy}{dx} = \sqrt{3}$

Limaçon: $r = 4 - 5 \sin \theta$

$\dfrac{dy}{dx} = \dfrac{-5 \cos \theta \sin \theta + (4 - 5 \sin \theta) \cos \theta}{-5 \cos \theta \cos \theta - (4 - 5 \sin \theta) \sin \theta}$ at $\theta = \dfrac{\pi}{6}$, $\dfrac{dy}{dx} = \dfrac{\sqrt{3}}{9}$

Let $\alpha$ be the angle between the curves:

$\tan \alpha = \dfrac{\sqrt{3} - \left( \sqrt{3}/9 \right)}{1 + (1/3)} = \dfrac{2\sqrt{3}}{3}.$

Therefore, $\alpha = \arctan \left( \dfrac{2\sqrt{3}}{3} \right) \approx 49.1°.$

**85.** $r = 1 + \cos\theta, r = 1 - \cos\theta$

The points $(1, \pi/2)$ and $(1, 3\pi/2)$ are the two points of intersection (other than the pole). The slope of the graph of $r = 1 + \cos\theta$ is

$$m_1 = \frac{dy}{dx} = \frac{r'\sin\theta + r\cos\theta}{r'\cos\theta - r\sin\theta} = \frac{-\sin^2\theta + \cos\theta(1 + \cos\theta)}{-\sin\theta\cos\theta - \sin\theta(1 + \cos\theta)}.$$

At $(1, \pi/2)$, $m_1 = -1/-1 = 1$ and at $(1, 3\pi/2)$, $m_1 = -1/1 = -1$. The slope of the graph of $r = 1 - \cos\theta$ is

$$m_2 = \frac{dy}{dx} = \frac{\sin^2\theta + \cos\theta(1 - \cos\theta)}{\sin\theta\cos\theta - \sin\theta(1 - \cos\theta)}.$$

At $(1, \pi/2)$, $m_2 = 1/-1 = -1$ and at $(1, 3\pi/2)$, $m_2 = 1/1 = 1$. In both cases, $m_1 = -1/m_2$ and we conclude that the graphs are orthogonal at $(1, \pi/2)$ and $(1, 3\pi/2)$.

**87.** $r = 2 + \cos\theta$

$$A = 2\left[\frac{1}{2}\int_0^\pi (2 + \cos\theta)^2\, d\theta\right] \approx 14.14 \quad \left(\frac{9\pi}{2}\right)$$

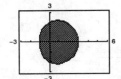

**89.** $r = \sin\theta \cdot \cos^2\theta$

$$A = 2\left[\frac{1}{2}\int_0^{\pi/2} (\sin\theta\cos^2\theta)^2\, d\theta\right]$$

$$\approx 0.10 \quad \left(\frac{\pi}{32}\right)$$

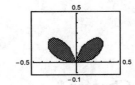

**91.** $r^2 = 4\sin 2\theta$

$$A = 2\left[\frac{1}{2}\int_0^{\pi/2} 4\sin 2\theta\, d\theta\right] = 4$$

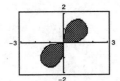

**93.** $r = 4\cos\theta, r = 2$

$$A = 2\left[\frac{1}{2}\int_0^{\pi/3} 4\, d\theta + \frac{1}{2}\int_{\pi/3}^{\pi/2} (4\cos\theta)^2\, d\theta\right] \approx 4.91$$

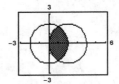

**95.** $s = 2\int_0^\pi \sqrt{a^2(1 - \cos\theta)^2 + a^2\sin^2\theta}\, d\theta$

$$= 2\sqrt{2}\, a\int_0^\pi \sqrt{1 - \cos\theta}\, d\theta = 2\sqrt{2}\, a\int_0^\pi \frac{\sin\theta}{\sqrt{1 + \cos\theta}}\, d\theta = \left[-4\sqrt{2}\, a(1 + \cos\theta)^{1/2}\right]_0^\pi = 8a$$

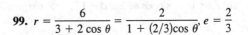

**97.** $r = \dfrac{2}{1 - \sin\theta}, e = 1$

Parabola

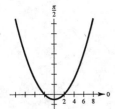

**99.** $r = \dfrac{6}{3 + 2\cos\theta} = \dfrac{2}{1 + (2/3)\cos\theta}, e = \dfrac{2}{3}$

Ellipse

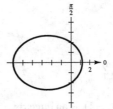

**101.** $r = \dfrac{4}{2 - 3 \sin \theta} = \dfrac{2}{1 - (3/2)\sin \theta}, \; e = \dfrac{3}{2}$

Hyperbola

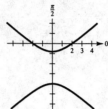

**103.** Circle

Center: $\left(5, \dfrac{\pi}{2}\right) = (0, 5)$ in rectangular coordinates

Solution point: $(0, 0)$

$$x^2 + (y - 5)^5 = 25$$
$$x^2 + y^2 - 10y = 0$$
$$r^2 - 10r \sin \theta = 0$$
$$r = 10 \sin \theta$$

**105.** Parabola

Vertex: $(2, \pi)$

Focus: $(0, 0)$

$e = 1, d = 4$

$r = \dfrac{4}{1 - \cos \theta}$

**107.** Ellipse

Vertices: $(5, 0), (1, \pi)$

Focus: $(0, 0)$

$a = 3, c = 2, e = \dfrac{2}{3}, d = \dfrac{5}{2}$

$$r = \dfrac{\left(\dfrac{2}{3}\right)\left(\dfrac{5}{2}\right)}{1 - \left(\dfrac{2}{3}\right)\cos \theta} = \dfrac{5}{3 - 2 \cos \theta}$$

# Problem Solving for Chapter 9

**1.** (a)

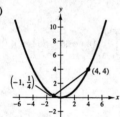

(b) $x^2 = 4y$

$2x = 4y'$

$y' = \dfrac{1}{2}x$

$y - 4 = 2(x - 4) \implies y = 2x - 4$   Tangent line at $(4, 4)$

$y - \dfrac{1}{4} = -\dfrac{1}{2}(x + 1) \implies y = -\dfrac{1}{2}x - \dfrac{1}{4}$   Tangent line at $\left(-1, \dfrac{1}{4}\right)$

Tangent lines have slopes of 2 and $-1/2 \implies$ perpendicular.

(c) Intersection:

$2x - 4 = -\dfrac{1}{2}x - \dfrac{1}{4}$

$8x - 16 = -2x - 1$

$10x = 15$

$x = \dfrac{3}{2} \implies \left(\dfrac{3}{2}, -1\right)$

Point of intersection, $(3/2, -1)$, is on directrix $y = -1$.

**3.** Consider $x^2 = 4py$ with focus $(0, p)$.

Let $p(a, b)$ be point on parabola.

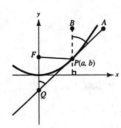

$$zx = 4py' \implies y' = \frac{x}{2p}$$

$$y - b = \frac{a}{2p}(x - a) \quad \text{Tangent line}$$

For $x = 0$, $y = b + \frac{a}{2p}(-a) = b - \frac{a^2}{2p} = b - \frac{4pb}{2p} = -b.$

Thus, $Q = (0, -b)$.

$\triangle FQP$ is isosceles because

$$|FQ| = p + b$$
$$|FP| = \sqrt{(a - 0)^2 + (b - p)^2} = \sqrt{a^2 + b^2 - 2bp + p^2}$$
$$= \sqrt{4pb + b^2 - 2bp + p^2}$$
$$= \sqrt{(b + p)^2}$$
$$= b + p.$$

Thus, $\angle FQP = \angle BPA = \angle FPQ$.

**5.** (a) In $\triangle OCB$, $\cos \theta = \dfrac{2a}{OB} \implies OB = 2a \cdot \sec \theta$.

In $\triangle OAC$, $\cos \theta = \dfrac{OA}{2a} \implies OA = 2a \cdot \cos \theta$.

$$r = OP = AB = OB - OA = 2a(\sec \theta - \cos \theta)$$
$$= 2a\left(\frac{1}{\cos \theta} - \cos \theta\right)$$
$$= 2a \cdot \frac{\sin^2 \theta}{\cos \theta}$$
$$= 2a \cdot \tan \theta \sin \theta$$

(c)
$$r = 2a \tan \theta \sin \theta$$
$$r \cos \theta = 2a \sin^2 \theta$$
$$r^3 \cos \theta = 2a\, r^2 \sin^2 \theta$$
$$(x^2 + y^2)x = 2ay^2$$
$$y^2 = \frac{x^3}{(2a - x)}$$

(b) $x = r \cos \theta = (2a \tan \theta \sin \theta)\cos \theta = 2a \sin^2 \theta$

$y = r \sin \theta = (2a \tan \theta \sin \theta)\sin \theta = 2a \tan \theta \cdot \sin^2 \theta,\ -\dfrac{\pi}{2} < \theta < \dfrac{\pi}{2}$

Let $t = \tan \theta$, $-\infty < t < \infty$.

Then $\sin^2 \theta = \dfrac{t^2}{1 + t^2}$ and $x = 2a\dfrac{t^2}{1 + t^2}$, $y = 2a\dfrac{t^3}{1 + t^2}$.

**7.** $y = a(1 - \cos \theta) \implies \cos \theta = \dfrac{a - y}{a}$

$$\theta = \arccos\left(\frac{a - y}{a}\right)$$

$x = a(\theta - \sin \theta)$

$$= a\left(\arccos\left(\frac{a - y}{a}\right) - \sin\left(\arccos\left(\frac{a - y}{a}\right)\right)\right)$$
$$= a\left(\arccos\left(\frac{a - y}{a}\right) - \frac{\sqrt{2ay - y^2}}{a}\right)$$

$x = a \cdot \arccos\left(\dfrac{a - y}{a}\right) - \sqrt{2ay - y^2},\ 0 \le y \le 2a$

**9.** For $t = \dfrac{\pi}{2}, \dfrac{3\pi}{2}, \dfrac{5\pi}{2}, \dfrac{7\pi}{2}, \ldots$

$$y = \frac{2}{\pi}, \frac{-2}{3\pi}, \frac{2}{5\pi}, \frac{-2}{7\pi}, \ldots$$

Hence, the curve has length greater that

$$S = \frac{2}{\pi} + \frac{2}{3\pi} + \frac{2}{5\pi} + \frac{2}{7\pi} + \cdots$$

$$= \frac{2}{\pi}\left(1 + \frac{1}{3} + \frac{1}{5} + \frac{1}{7} + \cdots\right)$$

$$> \frac{2}{\pi}\left(\frac{1}{2} + \frac{1}{4} + \frac{1}{6} + \frac{1}{8} + \cdots\right)$$

$$= \infty.$$

**11.** (a) Area $= \displaystyle\int_0^{\alpha} \frac{1}{2} r^2 \, d\theta$

$$= \frac{1}{2}\int_0^{\alpha} \sec^2 \theta \, d\theta$$

$x = 1$
$r = \sec\theta$

(b) $\tan \alpha = \dfrac{h}{1} \implies$ Area $= \dfrac{1}{2}(1)\tan \alpha$

$$\implies \tan \alpha = \int_0^{\alpha} \sec^2 \theta \, d\theta$$

(c) Differentiating, $\dfrac{d}{d\alpha}(\tan \alpha) = \sec^2 \alpha.$

**13.** If a dog is located at $(r, \theta)$, then its neighbor is at $\left(r, \theta + \dfrac{\pi}{2}\right)$:

$$(x, y) = (r \cos \theta, r \sin \theta) \text{ and } (x, y) = (-r \sin \theta, r \cos \theta).$$

The slope joining these points is

$$\frac{r \cos \theta - r \sin \theta}{-r \sin \theta - r \cos \theta} = \frac{\sin \theta - \cos \theta}{\sin \theta + \cos \theta} = \text{ slope of tangent line at } (r, \theta).$$

$$\frac{\dfrac{dr}{d\theta}\sin \theta + r \cos \theta}{\dfrac{dr}{d\theta}\cos \theta - r \sin \theta} = \frac{\sin \theta - \cos \theta}{\sin \theta + \cos \theta}$$

$$\implies \frac{dr}{d\theta} = -r$$

$$\frac{dr}{r} = -d\theta$$

$$\ln r = -\theta + C_1$$

$$r = e^{-\theta + C_1}$$

$$r = Ce^{-\theta}$$

$$r\left(\frac{\pi}{4}\right) = \frac{d}{\sqrt{2}} \implies r = Ce^{-\pi/4} = \frac{d}{\sqrt{2}} \implies C = \frac{d}{\sqrt{2}}e^{\pi/4}$$

Finally, $r = \dfrac{d}{\sqrt{2}}e^{((\pi/4) - \theta)}.$

**15.** (a) The first plane makes an angle of 70° with the positive $x$-axis, and is 150 miles from $P$:

$$x_1 = \cos 70°(150 - 375t)$$

$$y_1 = \sin 70°(150 - 375t)$$

Similarly for the second plane,

$$x_2 = \cos 135°(190 - 450t)$$

$$= \cos 45°(-190 + 450t)$$

$$y_2 = \sin 135°(190 - 450t)$$

$$= \sin 45°(190 - 450t)$$

(b) $d = \sqrt{(x_2 - x_1)^2 + (y_2 - y_1)^2}$

$$= [[\cos 45(-190 + 450t) - \cos 70(150 - 375t)]^2 + [\sin 45(190 - 450t) - \sin 70(150 - 375t)]^2]^{1/2}$$

(c)
280

The minimum distance is 7.59 miles when $t = 0.4145$.

**17.**

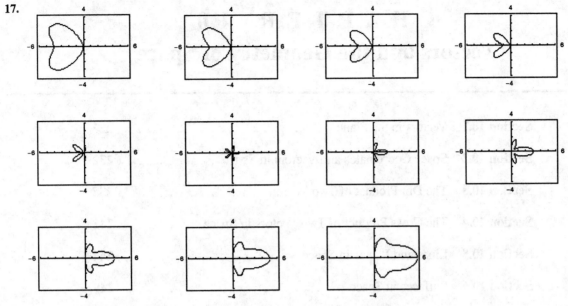

$n = 1, 2, 3, 4, 5$ produce "bells"; $n = -1, -2, -3, -4, -5$ produce "hearts".

# C H A P T E R   1 0
## Vectors and the Geometry of Space

# CHAPTER 10
# Vectors and the Geometry of Space

## Section 10.1    Vectors in the Plane

Solutions to Odd-Numbered Exercises

**1.** (a) $\mathbf{v} = \langle 5 - 1, 3 - 1 \rangle = \langle 4, 2 \rangle$

(b)

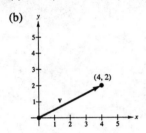

**3.** (a) $\mathbf{v} = \langle -4 - 3, -2 - (-2) \rangle = \langle -7, 0 \rangle$

(b)

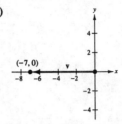

**5.** $\mathbf{u} = \langle 5 - 3, 6 - 2 \rangle = \langle 2, 4 \rangle$

$\mathbf{v} = \langle 1 - (-1), 8 - 4 \rangle = \langle 2, 4 \rangle$

$\mathbf{u} = \mathbf{v}$

**7.** $\mathbf{u} = \langle 6 - 0, -2 - 3 \rangle = \langle 6, -5 \rangle$

$\mathbf{v} = \langle 9 - 3, 5 - 10 \rangle = \langle 6, -5 \rangle$

$\mathbf{u} = \mathbf{v}$

**9.** (b) $\mathbf{v} = \langle 5 - 1, 5 - 2 \rangle = \langle 4, 3 \rangle$

(a) and (c).

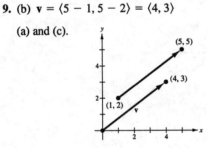

**11.** (b) $\mathbf{v} = \langle 6 - 10, -1 - 2 \rangle = \langle -4, -3 \rangle$

(a) and (c).

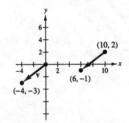

**13.** (b) $\mathbf{v} = \langle 6 - 6, 6 - 2 \rangle = \langle 0, 4 \rangle$

(a) and (c).

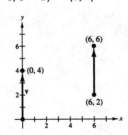

**15.** (b) $\mathbf{v} = \langle \frac{1}{2} - \frac{3}{2}, 3 - \frac{4}{3} \rangle = \langle -1, \frac{5}{3} \rangle$

(a) and (c).

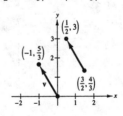

**17.** (a) $2\mathbf{v} = \langle 4, 6 \rangle$

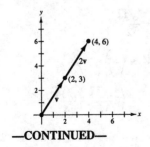

(b) $-3\mathbf{v} = \langle -6, -9 \rangle$

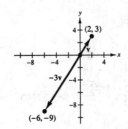

—CONTINUED—

**17. —CONTINUED—**

(c) $\frac{7}{2}\mathbf{v} = \left\langle 7, \frac{21}{2}\right\rangle$

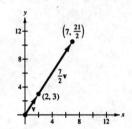

(d) $\frac{2}{3}\mathbf{v} = \left\langle \frac{4}{3}, 2\right\rangle$

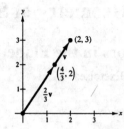

**19.**

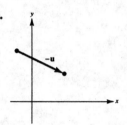

**21.**

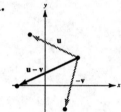

**23.** (a) $\frac{2}{3}\mathbf{u} = \frac{2}{3}\langle 4, 9\rangle = \left\langle \frac{8}{3}, 6\right\rangle$

(b) $\mathbf{v} - \mathbf{u} = \langle 2, -5\rangle - \langle 4, 9\rangle = \langle -2, -14\rangle$

(c) $2\mathbf{u} + 5\mathbf{v} = 2\langle 4, 9\rangle + 5\langle 2, -5\rangle = \langle 18, -7\rangle$

**25.** $\mathbf{v} = \frac{3}{2}(2\mathbf{i} - \mathbf{j}) = 3\mathbf{i} - \frac{3}{2}\mathbf{j}$

$\qquad = \left\langle 3, -\frac{3}{2}\right\rangle$

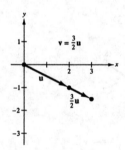

**27.** $\mathbf{v} = (2\mathbf{i} - \mathbf{j}) + 2(\mathbf{i} + 2\mathbf{j})$

$\qquad = 4\mathbf{i} + 3\mathbf{j} = \langle 4, 3\rangle$

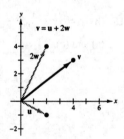

**29.** $u_1 - 4 = -1$

$\qquad u_2 - 2 = 3$

$\qquad u_1 = 3$

$\qquad u_2 = 5$

$\qquad Q = (3, 5)$

**31.** $\|\mathbf{v}\| = \sqrt{16 + 9} = 5$

**33.** $\|\mathbf{v}\| = \sqrt{36 + 25} = \sqrt{61}$

**35.** $\|\mathbf{v}\| = \sqrt{0 + 16} = 4$

**37.** $\|\mathbf{u}\| = \sqrt{3^2 + 12^2} = \sqrt{153}$

$\mathbf{v} = \dfrac{\mathbf{u}}{\|\mathbf{u}\|} = \dfrac{\langle 3, 12\rangle}{\sqrt{153}} = \left\langle \dfrac{3}{\sqrt{153}}, \dfrac{12}{\sqrt{153}}\right\rangle$

$\qquad = \left\langle \dfrac{\sqrt{17}}{17}, \dfrac{4\sqrt{17}}{17}\right\rangle$ unit vector

**39.** $\|\mathbf{u}\| = \sqrt{\left(\dfrac{3}{2}\right)^2 + \left(\dfrac{5}{2}\right)^2} = \dfrac{\sqrt{34}}{2}$

$\mathbf{v} = \dfrac{\mathbf{u}}{\|\mathbf{u}\|} = \dfrac{\langle (3/2), (5/2)\rangle}{\sqrt{34}/2} = \left\langle \dfrac{3}{\sqrt{34}}, \dfrac{5}{\sqrt{34}}\right\rangle$

$\qquad = \left\langle \dfrac{3\sqrt{34}}{34}, \dfrac{5\sqrt{34}}{34}\right\rangle$ unit vector

**41.** $\|\mathbf{u}\| = \langle 1, -1 \rangle$, $\mathbf{v} = \langle -1, 2 \rangle$

(a) $\|\mathbf{u}\| = \sqrt{1+1} = \sqrt{2}$

(b) $\|\mathbf{v}\| = \sqrt{1+4} = \sqrt{5}$

(c) $\mathbf{u} + \mathbf{v} = \langle 0, 1 \rangle$

$\|\mathbf{u} + \mathbf{v}\| = \sqrt{0+1} = 1$

(d) $\dfrac{\mathbf{u}}{\|\mathbf{u}\|} = \dfrac{1}{\sqrt{2}} \langle 1, -1 \rangle$

$\left\| \dfrac{\mathbf{u}}{\|\mathbf{u}\|} \right\| = 1$

(e) $\dfrac{\mathbf{v}}{\|\mathbf{v}\|} = \dfrac{1}{\sqrt{5}} \langle -1, 2 \rangle$

$\left\| \dfrac{\mathbf{v}}{\|\mathbf{v}\|} \right\| = 1$

(f) $\dfrac{\mathbf{u} + \mathbf{v}}{\|\mathbf{u} + \mathbf{v}\|} = \langle 0, 1 \rangle$

$\left\| \dfrac{\mathbf{u} + \mathbf{v}}{\|\mathbf{u} + \mathbf{v}\|} \right\| = 1$

**43.** $\mathbf{u} = \left\langle 1, \dfrac{1}{2} \right\rangle$, $\mathbf{v} = \langle 2, 3 \rangle$

(a) $\|\mathbf{u}\| = \sqrt{1 + \dfrac{1}{4}} = \dfrac{\sqrt{5}}{2}$

(b) $\|\mathbf{v}\| = \sqrt{4+9} = \sqrt{13}$

(c) $\mathbf{u} + \mathbf{v} = \left\langle 3, \dfrac{7}{2} \right\rangle$

$\|\mathbf{u} + \mathbf{v}\| = \sqrt{9 + \dfrac{49}{4}} = \dfrac{\sqrt{85}}{2}$

(d) $\dfrac{\mathbf{u}}{\|\mathbf{u}\|} = \dfrac{2}{\sqrt{5}} \left\langle 1, \dfrac{1}{2} \right\rangle$

$\left\| \dfrac{\mathbf{u}}{\|\mathbf{u}\|} \right\| = 1$

(e) $\dfrac{\mathbf{v}}{\|\mathbf{v}\|} = \dfrac{1}{\sqrt{13}} \langle 2, 3 \rangle$

$\left\| \dfrac{\mathbf{v}}{\|\mathbf{v}\|} \right\| = 1$

(f) $\dfrac{\mathbf{u} + \mathbf{v}}{\|\mathbf{u} + \mathbf{v}\|} = \dfrac{2}{\sqrt{85}} \left\langle 3, \dfrac{7}{2} \right\rangle$

$\left\| \dfrac{\mathbf{u} + \mathbf{v}}{\|\mathbf{u} + \mathbf{v}\|} \right\| = 1$

**45.** $\mathbf{u} = \langle 2, 1 \rangle$

$\|\mathbf{u}\| = \sqrt{5} \approx 2.236$

$\mathbf{v} = \langle 5, 4 \rangle$

$\|\mathbf{v}\| = \sqrt{41} \approx 6.403$

$\mathbf{u} + \mathbf{v} = \langle 7, 5 \rangle$

$\|\mathbf{u} + \mathbf{v}\| = \sqrt{74} \approx 8.602$

$\|\mathbf{u} + \mathbf{v}\| \le \|\mathbf{u}\| + \|\mathbf{v}\|$

**47.** $\dfrac{\mathbf{u}}{\|\mathbf{u}\|} = \dfrac{1}{\sqrt{2}} \langle 1, 1 \rangle$

$4 \left( \dfrac{\mathbf{u}}{\|\mathbf{u}\|} \right) = 2\sqrt{2} \langle 1, 1 \rangle$

$\mathbf{v} = \langle 2\sqrt{2}, 2\sqrt{2} \rangle$

**49.** $\dfrac{\mathbf{u}}{\|\mathbf{u}\|} = \dfrac{1}{2\sqrt{3}} \langle \sqrt{3}, 3 \rangle$

$2 \left( \dfrac{\mathbf{u}}{\|\mathbf{u}\|} \right) = \dfrac{1}{\sqrt{3}} \langle \sqrt{3}, 3 \rangle$

$\mathbf{v} = \langle 1, \sqrt{3} \rangle$

**51.** $\mathbf{v} = 3[(\cos 0°)\mathbf{i} + (\sin 0°)\mathbf{j}] = 3\mathbf{i} = \langle 3, 0 \rangle$

**53.** $\mathbf{v} = 2[(\cos 150°)\mathbf{i} + (\sin 150°)\mathbf{j}]$

$= -\sqrt{3}\mathbf{i} + \mathbf{j} = \langle -\sqrt{3}, 1 \rangle$

**55.** $\mathbf{u} = \mathbf{i}$

$\mathbf{v} = \dfrac{3\sqrt{2}}{2}\mathbf{i} + \dfrac{3\sqrt{2}}{2}\mathbf{j}$

$\mathbf{u} + \mathbf{v} = \left( \dfrac{2 + 3\sqrt{2}}{2} \right)\mathbf{i} + \dfrac{3\sqrt{2}}{2}\mathbf{j}$

**57.**   $\mathbf{u} = 2(\cos 4)\mathbf{i} + 2(\sin 4)\mathbf{j}$

$\mathbf{v} = (\cos 2)\mathbf{i} + (\sin 2)\mathbf{j}$

$\mathbf{u} + \mathbf{v} = (2\cos 4 + \cos 2)\mathbf{i} + (2\sin 4 + \sin 2)\mathbf{j}$

**59.** A scalar is a real number. A vector is represented by a directed line segment. A vector has both length and direction.

**61.** To normalize $\mathbf{v}$, you find a unit vector $\mathbf{u}$ in the direction of $\mathbf{v}$:

$$\mathbf{u} = \frac{\mathbf{v}}{\|\mathbf{v}\|}.$$

**For Exercises 63–67,** $a\mathbf{u} + b\mathbf{w} = a(\mathbf{i} + 2\mathbf{j}) + b(\mathbf{i} - \mathbf{j}) = (a + b)\mathbf{i} + (2a - b)\mathbf{j}$.

**63.** $\mathbf{v} = 2\mathbf{i} + \mathbf{j}$. Therefore, $a + b = 2, 2a - b = 1$. Solving simultaneously, we have $a = 1, b = 1$.

**65.** $\mathbf{v} = 3\mathbf{i}$. Therefore, $a + b = 3, 2a - b = 0$. Solving simultaneously, we have $a = 1, b = 2$.

**67.** $\mathbf{v} = \mathbf{i} + \mathbf{j}$. Therefore, $a + b = 1, 2a - b = 1$. Solving simultaneously, we have $a = \frac{2}{3}, b = \frac{1}{3}$.

**69.** $y = x^3, y' = 3x^2 = 3$ at $x = 1$.

(a) $m = 3$. Let $\mathbf{w} = \langle 1, 3 \rangle$, then

$$\frac{\mathbf{w}}{\|\mathbf{w}\|} = \pm \frac{1}{\sqrt{10}} \langle 1, 3 \rangle.$$

(b) $m = -\frac{1}{3}$. Let $\mathbf{w} = \langle 3, -1 \rangle$, then

$$\frac{\mathbf{w}}{\|\mathbf{w}\|} = \pm \frac{1}{\sqrt{10}} \langle 3, -1 \rangle.$$

**71.** $f(x) = \sqrt{25 - x^2}$

$$f'(x) = \frac{-x}{\sqrt{25 - x^2}} = \frac{-3}{4} \text{ at } x = 3.$$

(a) $m = -\frac{3}{4}$. Let $\mathbf{w} = \langle -4, 3 \rangle$, then

$$\frac{\mathbf{w}}{\|\mathbf{w}\|} = \pm \frac{1}{5} \langle -4, 3 \rangle.$$

(b) $m = \frac{4}{3}$. Let $\mathbf{w} = \langle 3, 4 \rangle$, then

$$\frac{\mathbf{w}}{\|\mathbf{w}\|} = \pm \frac{1}{5} \langle 3, 4 \rangle$$

**73.**   $\mathbf{u} = \frac{\sqrt{2}}{2}\mathbf{i} + \frac{\sqrt{2}}{2}\mathbf{j}$

$\mathbf{u} + \mathbf{v} = \sqrt{2}\mathbf{j}$

$\mathbf{v} = (\mathbf{u} + \mathbf{v}) - \mathbf{u} = -\frac{\sqrt{2}}{2}\mathbf{i} + \frac{\sqrt{2}}{2}\mathbf{j}$

**75.** Programs will vary.

**77.** $\|\mathbf{F}_1\| = 2, \theta_{\mathbf{F}_1} = 33°$

$\|\mathbf{F}_2\| = 3, \theta_{\mathbf{F}_2} = -125°$

$\|\mathbf{F}_3\| = 2.5, \theta_{\mathbf{F}_3} = 110°$

$\|\mathbf{R}\| = \|\mathbf{F}_1 + \mathbf{F}_2 + \mathbf{F}_3\| \approx 1.33$

$\theta_{\mathbf{R}} = \theta_{\mathbf{F}_1 + \mathbf{F}_2 + \mathbf{F}_3} \approx 132.5°$

**79.** (a) $180(\cos 30\mathbf{i} + \sin 30\mathbf{j}) + 275\mathbf{i} = 430.88\mathbf{i} + 90\mathbf{j}$

Direction: $\alpha = \arctan\left(\frac{90}{430.88}\right) = 0.206(= 11.8°)$

Magnitude: $\sqrt{430.88^2 + 90^2} = 440.18$ newtons

(b) $M = \sqrt{(275 + 180\cos\theta)^2 + (180\sin\theta)^2}$

$\alpha = \arctan\left[\frac{180\sin\theta}{275 + 180\cos\theta}\right]$

**—CONTINUED—**

**79. —CONTINUED—**

(c)

| $\theta$ | 0° | 30° | 60° | 90° | 120° | 150° | 180° |
|---|---|---|---|---|---|---|---|
| $M$ | 455 | 440.2 | 396.9 | 328.7 | 241.9 | 149.3 | 95 |
| $\alpha$ | 0° | 11.8° | 23.1° | 33.2° | 40.1° | 37.1° | 0 |

(d)

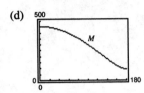
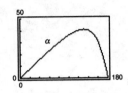

(e) $M$ decreases because the forces change from acting in the same direction to acting in the opposite direction as $\theta$ increases from 0° to 180°.

**81.** $\mathbf{F}_1 + \mathbf{F}_2 + \mathbf{F}_3 = (75 \cos 30°\mathbf{i} + 75 \sin 30°\mathbf{j}) + (100 \cos 45°\mathbf{i} + 100 \sin 45°\mathbf{j}) + (125 \cos 120°\mathbf{i} + 125 \sin 120°\mathbf{j})$

$$= \left(\frac{75}{2}\sqrt{3} + 50\sqrt{2} - \frac{125}{2}\right)\mathbf{i} + \left(\frac{75}{2} + 50\sqrt{2} + \frac{125}{2}\sqrt{3}\right)\mathbf{j}$$

$$\|\mathbf{R}\| = \|\mathbf{F}_1 + \mathbf{F}_2 + \mathbf{F}_3\| \approx 228.5 \text{ lb}$$

$$\theta_{\mathbf{R}} = \theta_{\mathbf{F}_1 + \mathbf{F}_2 + \mathbf{F}_3} \approx 71.3°$$

**83.** (a) The forces act along the same direction. $\theta = 0°$.

(b) The forces cancel out each other. $\theta = 180°$.

(c) No, the magnitude of the resultant can not be greater than the sum.

**85.** $(-4, -1), (6, 5), (10, 3)$

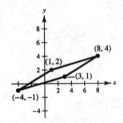
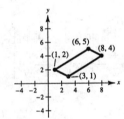
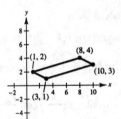

**87.** $\mathbf{u} = \vec{CB} = \|\mathbf{u}\|(\cos 30° \mathbf{i} + \sin 30° \mathbf{j})$

$\mathbf{v} = \vec{CA} = \|\mathbf{v}\|(\cos 130° \mathbf{i} + \sin 130° \mathbf{j})$

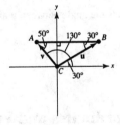

Vertical components: $\|\mathbf{u}\| \sin 30° + \|\mathbf{v}\| \sin 130° = 2000$

Horizontal components: $\|\mathbf{u}\| \cos 30° + \|\mathbf{v}\| \cos 130° = 0$

Solving this system, you obtain

$\|\mathbf{u}\| \approx 1305.5$ and $\|\mathbf{v}\| \approx 1758.8$.

**89.** Horizontal component $= \|\mathbf{v}\| \cos \theta = 1200 \cos 6° \approx 1193.43$ ft/sec

Vertical component $= \|\mathbf{v}\| \sin \theta = 1200 \sin 6° \approx 125.43$ ft/sec

**91.** $\mathbf{u} = 900[\cos 148° \, \mathbf{i} + \sin 148° \, \mathbf{j}]$

$\mathbf{v} = 100[\cos 45° \, \mathbf{i} + \sin 45° \, \mathbf{j}]$

$\mathbf{u} + \mathbf{v} = [900 \cos 148° + 100 \cos 45°]\mathbf{i} + [900 \sin 148° + 100 \sin 45°]\mathbf{j}$

$\approx -692.53 \, \mathbf{i} + 547.64 \, \mathbf{j}$

$\theta \approx \arctan\left(\dfrac{547.64}{-692.53}\right) \approx -38.34°. \quad 38.34° \text{ North of West.}$

$\|\mathbf{u} + \mathbf{v}\| = \sqrt{(-692.53)^2 + (547.64)^2} \approx 882.9 \text{ km/hr.}$

**93.** $\mathbf{F}_1 + \mathbf{F}_2 + \mathbf{F}_3 = \mathbf{0}$

$-3600\mathbf{j} + T_2(\cos 35°\mathbf{i} - \sin 35° \, \mathbf{j}) + T_3(\cos 92°\mathbf{i} + \sin 92°\mathbf{j}) = 0$

$T_2 \cos 35° + T_3 \cos 92° = 0$

$-T_2 \cos 35° + T_3 \sin 92° = 3600$

$T_2 = \dfrac{-T_3 \cos 92°}{\cos 35°} \implies \dfrac{T_3 \cos 92°}{\cos 35°} \sin 35° + T_3 \sin 92° = 3600 \text{ and } T_3(0.97495) = 3600 \implies T_3 \approx 3692.48$

Finally, $T_2 = 157.32$

**95.** Let the triangle have vertices at $(0, 0)$, $(a, 0)$, and $(b, c)$. Let $\mathbf{u}$ be the vector joining $(0, 0)$ and $(b, c)$, as indicated in the figure. Then $\mathbf{v}$, the vector joining the midpoints, is

$\mathbf{v} = \left(\dfrac{a + b}{2} - \dfrac{a}{2}\right)\mathbf{i} + \dfrac{c}{2}\mathbf{j}$

$= \dfrac{b}{2}\mathbf{i} + \dfrac{c}{2}\mathbf{j} = \dfrac{1}{2}(b\mathbf{i} + c\mathbf{j}) = \dfrac{1}{2}\mathbf{u}$

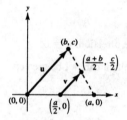

**97.** $\mathbf{w} = \|\mathbf{u}\|\mathbf{v} + \|\mathbf{v}\|\mathbf{u}$

$= \|\mathbf{u}\|[\|\mathbf{v}\| \cos \theta_v\mathbf{i} + \|\mathbf{v}\| \sin \theta_v\mathbf{j}] + \|\mathbf{v}\|[\|\mathbf{u}\| \cos \theta_u\mathbf{i} + \|\mathbf{u}\| \sin \theta_u\mathbf{j}] = \|\mathbf{u}\| \, \|\mathbf{v}\|[(\cos \theta_u + \cos \theta_v)\mathbf{i} + (\sin \theta_u + \sin \theta_v)\mathbf{j}]$

$= 2\|\mathbf{u}\| \, \|\mathbf{v}\|\left[\cos\left(\dfrac{\theta_u + \theta_v}{2}\right) \cos\left(\dfrac{\theta_u - \theta_v}{2}\right)\mathbf{i} + \sin\left(\dfrac{\theta_u + \theta_v}{2}\right) \cos\left(\dfrac{\theta_u - \theta_v}{2}\right)\mathbf{j}\right]$

$\tan \theta_w = \dfrac{\sin\left(\dfrac{\theta_u + \theta_v}{2}\right) \cos\left(\dfrac{\theta_u - \theta_v}{2}\right)}{\cos\left(\dfrac{\theta_u + \theta_v}{2}\right) \cos\left(\dfrac{\theta_u - \theta_v}{2}\right)} = \tan\left(\dfrac{\theta_u + \theta_v}{2}\right)$

Thus, $\theta_w = (\theta_u + \theta_v)/2$ and $\mathbf{w}$ bisects the angle between $\mathbf{u}$ and $\mathbf{v}$.

**99.** True

**101.** True

**103.** False

$\|a\mathbf{i} + b\mathbf{j}\| = \sqrt{2}\,|a|$

# Section 10.2 Space Coordinates and Vectors in Space

**1.**

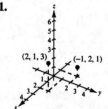

**3.**

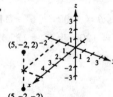

**5.** $A(2, 3, 4)$

$\quad B(-1, -2, 2)$

**7.** $x = -3, y = 4, z = 5$:  $(-3, 4, 5)$

**9.** $y = z = 0, x = 10$:  $(10, 0, 0)$

**11.** The $z$-coordinate is 0.

**13.** The point is 6 units above the $xy$-plane.

**15.** The point is on the plane parallel to the $yz$-plane that passes through $x = 4$.

**17.** The point is to the left of the $xz$-plane.

**19.** The point is on or between the planes $y = 3$ and $y = -3$.

**21.** The point $(x, y, z)$ is 3 units below the $xy$-plane, and below either quadrant I or III.

**23.** The point could be above the $xy$-plane and thus above quadrants II or IV, or below the $xy$-plane, and thus below quadrants I or III.

**25.** $d = \sqrt{(5 - 0)^2 + (2 - 0)^2 + (6 - 0)^2}$

$\quad = \sqrt{25 + 4 + 36} = \sqrt{65}$

**27.** $d = \sqrt{(6 - 1)^2 + (-2 - (-2))^2 + (-2 - 4)^2}$

$\quad = \sqrt{25 + 0 + 36} = \sqrt{61}$

**29.** $A(0, 0, 0), B(2, 2, 1), C(2, -4, 4)$

$\quad |AB| = \sqrt{4 + 4 + 1} = 3$

$\quad |AC| = \sqrt{4 + 16 + 16} = 6$

$\quad |BC| = \sqrt{0 + 36 + 9} = 3\sqrt{5}$

$\quad |BC|^2 = |AB|^2 + |AC|^2$

Right triangle

**31.** $A(1, -3, -2), B(5, -1, 2), C(-1, 1, 2)$

$\quad |AB| = \sqrt{16 + 4 + 16} = 6$

$\quad |AC| = \sqrt{4 + 16 + 16} = 6$

$\quad |BC| = \sqrt{36 + 4 + 0} = 2\sqrt{10}$

Since $|AB| = |AC|$, the triangle is isosceles.

**33.** The $z$-coordinate is changed by 5 units:

$\quad (0, 0, 5), (2, 2, 6), (2, -4, 9)$

**35.** $\left( \dfrac{5 + (-2)}{2}, \dfrac{-9 + 3}{2}, \dfrac{7 + 3}{2} \right) = \left( \dfrac{3}{2}, -3, 5 \right)$

**37.** Center: $(0, 2, 5)$

Radius: 2

$\quad (x - 0)^2 + (y - 2)^2 + (z - 5)^2 = 4$

$\quad x^2 + y^2 + z^2 - 4y - 10z + 25 = 0$

**39.** Center: $\dfrac{(2, 0, 0) + (0, 6, 0)}{2} = (1, 3, 0)$

Radius: $\sqrt{10}$

$\quad (x - 1)^2 + (y - 3)^2 + (z - 0)^2 = 10$

$\quad\quad x^2 + y^2 + z^2 - 2x - 6y = 0$

**41.** $\quad\quad\quad x^2 + y^2 + z^2 - 2x + 6y + 8z + 1 = 0$

$(x^2 - 2x + 1) + (y^2 + 6y + 9) + (z^2 + 8z + 16) = -1 + 1 + 9 + 16$

$\quad\quad\quad (x - 1)^2 + (y + 3)^2 + (z + 4)^2 = 25$

Center: $(1, -3, -4)$

Radius: 5

**43.** $9x^2 + 9y^2 + 9z^2 - 6x + 18y + 1 = 0$

$$x^2 + y^2 + z^2 - \frac{2}{3}x + 2y + \frac{1}{9} = 0$$

$$\left(x^2 - \frac{2}{3}x + \frac{1}{9}\right) + (y^2 + 2y + 1) + z^2 = -\frac{1}{9} + \frac{1}{9} + 1$$

$$\left(x - \frac{1}{3}\right)^2 + (y + 1)^2 + (z - 0)^2 = 1$$

Center: $\left(\frac{1}{3}, -1, 0\right)$

Radius: 1

**45.** $x^2 + y^2 + z^2 \le 36$

Solid ball of radius 6 centered at origin.

**47.** (a) $\mathbf{v} = (2 - 4)\mathbf{i} + (4 - 2)\mathbf{j} + (3 - 1)\mathbf{k}$

$= -2\mathbf{i} + 2\mathbf{j} + 2\mathbf{k} = \langle -2, 2, 2 \rangle$

(b)
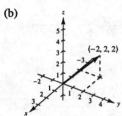

**49.** (a) $\mathbf{v} = (0 - 3)\mathbf{i} + (3 - 3)\mathbf{j} + (3 - 0)\mathbf{k}$

$= -3\mathbf{i} + 3\mathbf{k} = \langle -3, 0, 3 \rangle$

(b)
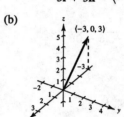

**51.** $\langle 4 - 3, 1 - 2, 6 - 0 \rangle = \langle 1, -1, 6 \rangle$

$\|\langle 1, -1, 6 \rangle\| = \sqrt{1 + 1 + 36} = \sqrt{38}$

Unit vector: $\dfrac{\langle 1, -1, 6 \rangle}{\sqrt{38}} = \left\langle \dfrac{1}{\sqrt{38}}, \dfrac{-1}{\sqrt{38}}, \dfrac{6}{\sqrt{38}} \right\rangle$

**53.** $\langle -5 - (-4), 3 - 3, 0 - 1 \rangle = \langle -1, 0, -1 \rangle$

$\|\langle -1, 0, -1 \rangle\| = \sqrt{1 + 1} = \sqrt{2}$

Unit vector: $\left\langle \dfrac{-1}{\sqrt{2}}, 0, \dfrac{-1}{\sqrt{2}} \right\rangle$

**55.** (b) $\mathbf{v} = (3 + 1)\mathbf{i} + (3 - 2)\mathbf{j} + (4 - 3)\mathbf{k}$

$= 4\mathbf{i} + \mathbf{j} + \mathbf{k} = \langle 4, 1, 1 \rangle$

(a) and (c).

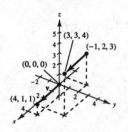

**57.** $(q_1, q_2, q_3) - (0, 6, 2) = (3, -5, 6)$

$Q = (3, 1, 8)$

**59.** (a) $2\mathbf{v} = \langle 2, 4, 4 \rangle$

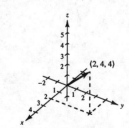

(b) $-\mathbf{v} = \langle -1, -2, -2 \rangle$

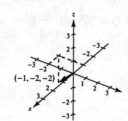

**—CONTINUED—**

**59. —CONTINUED—**

(c) $\frac{3}{2}\mathbf{v} = \langle \frac{3}{2}, 3, 3 \rangle$

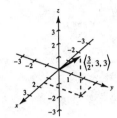

(d) $0\mathbf{v} = \langle 0, 0, 0 \rangle$

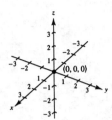

**61.** $\mathbf{z} = \mathbf{u} - \mathbf{v} = \langle 1, 2, 3 \rangle - \langle 2, 2, -1 \rangle = \langle -1, 0, 4 \rangle$

**63.** $\mathbf{z} = 2\mathbf{u} + 4\mathbf{v} - \mathbf{w} = \langle 2, 4, 6 \rangle + \langle 8, 8, -4 \rangle - \langle 4, 0, -4 \rangle = \langle 6, 12, 6 \rangle$

**65.** $2\mathbf{z} - 3\mathbf{u} = 2\langle z_1, z_2, z_3 \rangle - 3\langle 1, 2, 3 \rangle = \langle 4, 0, -4 \rangle$

$2z_1 - 3 = 4 \implies z_1 = \frac{7}{2}$

$2z_2 - 6 = 0 \implies z_2 = 3$

$2z_3 - 9 = -4 \implies z_3 = \frac{5}{2}$

$\mathbf{z} = \langle \frac{7}{2}, 3, \frac{5}{2} \rangle$

**67.** (a) and (b) are parallel since $\langle -6, -4, 10 \rangle = -2\langle 3, 2, -5 \rangle$ and $\langle 2, \frac{4}{3}, -\frac{10}{3} \rangle = \frac{2}{3}\langle 3, 2, -5 \rangle$.

**69.** $\mathbf{z} = -3\mathbf{i} + 4\mathbf{j} + 2\mathbf{k}$

(a) is parallel since $-6\mathbf{i} + 8\mathbf{j} + 4\mathbf{k} = 2\mathbf{z}$.

**71.** $P(0, -2, -5)$, $Q(3, 4, 4)$, $R(2, 2, 1)$

$\overrightarrow{PQ} = \langle 3, 6, 9 \rangle$

$\overrightarrow{PR} = \langle 2, 4, 6 \rangle$

$\langle 3, 6, 9 \rangle = \frac{3}{2}\langle 2, 4, 6 \rangle$

Therefore, $\overrightarrow{PQ}$ and $\overrightarrow{PR}$ are parallel. The points are collinear.

**73.** $P(1, 2, 4)$, $Q(2, 5, 0)$, $R(0, 1, 5)$

$\overrightarrow{PQ} = \langle 1, 3, -4 \rangle$

$\overrightarrow{PR} = \langle -1, -1, 1 \rangle$

Since $\overrightarrow{PQ}$ and $\overrightarrow{PR}$ are not parallel, the points are not collinear.

**75.** $A(2, 9, 1)$, $B(3, 11, 4)$, $C(0, 10, 2)$, $D(1, 12, 5)$

$\overrightarrow{AB} = \langle 1, 2, 3 \rangle$

$\overrightarrow{CD} = \langle 1, 2, 3 \rangle$

$\overrightarrow{AC} = \langle -2, 1, 1 \rangle$

$\overrightarrow{BD} = \langle -2, 1, 1 \rangle$

Since $\overrightarrow{AB} = \overrightarrow{CD}$ and $\overrightarrow{AC} = \overrightarrow{BD}$, the given points form the vertices of a parallelogram.

**77.** $\|\mathbf{v}\| = 0$

**79.** $\mathbf{v} = \langle 1, -2, -3 \rangle$

$\|\mathbf{v}\| = \sqrt{1 + 4 + 9} = \sqrt{14}$

**81.** $\mathbf{v} = \langle 0, 3, -5 \rangle$

$\|\mathbf{v}\| = \sqrt{0 + 9 + 25} = \sqrt{34}$

**83.** $\mathbf{u} = \langle 2, -1, 2 \rangle$

$\|\mathbf{u}\| = \sqrt{4 + 1 + 4} = 3$

(a) $\frac{\mathbf{u}}{\|\mathbf{u}\|} = \frac{1}{3}\langle 2, -1, 2 \rangle$

(b) $-\frac{\mathbf{u}}{\|\mathbf{u}\|} = -\frac{1}{3}\langle 2, -1, 2 \rangle$

**85.** $\mathbf{u} = \langle 3, 2, -5 \rangle$

$\|\mathbf{u}\| = \sqrt{9 + 4 + 25} = \sqrt{38}$

(a) $\frac{\mathbf{u}}{\|\mathbf{u}\|} = \frac{1}{\sqrt{38}}\langle 3, 2, -5 \rangle$

(b) $-\frac{\mathbf{u}}{\|\mathbf{u}\|} = -\frac{1}{\sqrt{38}}\langle 3, 2, -5 \rangle$

**87.** Programs will vary.

**89.** $c\mathbf{v} = \langle 2c, 2c, -c \rangle$

$\|c\mathbf{v}\| = \sqrt{4c^2 + 4c^2 + c^2} = 5$

$9c^2 = 25$

$c = \pm\dfrac{5}{3}$

**91.** $\mathbf{v} = 10\dfrac{\mathbf{u}}{\|\mathbf{u}\|} = 10\left\langle 0, \dfrac{1}{\sqrt{2}}, \dfrac{1}{\sqrt{2}} \right\rangle$

$= \left\langle 0, \dfrac{10}{\sqrt{2}}, \dfrac{10}{\sqrt{2}} \right\rangle$

**93.** $\mathbf{v} = \dfrac{3}{2}\dfrac{\mathbf{u}}{\|\mathbf{u}\|} = \dfrac{3}{2}\left\langle \dfrac{2}{3}, \dfrac{-2}{3}, \dfrac{1}{3} \right\rangle = \left\langle 1, -1, \dfrac{1}{2} \right\rangle$

**95.** $\mathbf{v} = 2[\cos(\pm 30°)\mathbf{j} + \sin(\pm 30°)\mathbf{k}]$

$= \sqrt{3}\mathbf{j} \pm \mathbf{k} = \langle 0, \sqrt{3}, \pm 1 \rangle$

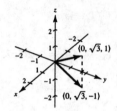

**97.**

$\mathbf{v} = \langle -3, -6, 3 \rangle$

$\dfrac{2}{3}\mathbf{v} = \langle -2, -4, 2 \rangle$

$(4, 3, 0) + (-2, -4, 2) = (2, -1, 2)$

**99. (a)**

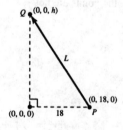

**(b)** $\mathbf{w} = a\mathbf{u} + b\mathbf{v} = a\mathbf{i} + (a + b)\mathbf{j} + b\mathbf{k} = \mathbf{0}$

$a = 0, a + b = 0, b = 0$

Thus, a and b are both zero.

**(c)** $a\mathbf{i} + (a + b)\mathbf{j} + b\mathbf{k} = \mathbf{i} + 2\mathbf{j} + \mathbf{k}$

$a = 1, b = 1$

$\mathbf{w} = \mathbf{u} + \mathbf{v}$

**(d)** $a\mathbf{i} + (a + b)\mathbf{j} + b\mathbf{k} = \mathbf{i} + 2\mathbf{j} + 3\mathbf{k}$

$a = 1, a + b = 2, b = 3$

Not possible

**101.** $d = \sqrt{(x_2 - x_1)^2 + (y_2 - y_1)^2 + (z_2 - z_1)^2}$

**103.** Two nonzero vectors $\mathbf{u}$ and $\mathbf{v}$ are parallel if $\mathbf{u} = c\mathbf{v}$ for some scalar $c$.

**105. (a)** The height of the right triangle is $h = \sqrt{L^2 - 18^2}$. The vector $\overrightarrow{PQ}$ is given by

$\overrightarrow{PQ} = \langle 0, -18, h \rangle$.

The tension vector $\mathbf{T}$ in each wire is

$\mathbf{T} = c\langle 0, -18, h \rangle$ where $ch = \dfrac{24}{3} = 8$.

Hence, $\mathbf{T} = \dfrac{8}{h}\langle 0, -18, h \rangle$ and

$T = \|\mathbf{T}\| = \dfrac{8}{h}\sqrt{18^2 + h^2} = \dfrac{8}{\sqrt{L^2 - 18^2}}\sqrt{18^2 + (L^2 - 18^2)} = \dfrac{8L}{\sqrt{L^2 - 18^2}}$

**(b)**

| $L$ | 20 | 25 | 30 | 35 | 40 | 45 | 50 |
|---|---|---|---|---|---|---|---|
| $T$ | 18.4 | 11.5 | 10 | 9.3 | 9.0 | 8.7 | 8.6 |

—CONTINUED—

**105.** —CONTINUED—

(c)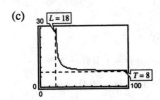

$x = 18$ is a vertical asymptote and $y = 8$ is a horizontal asymptote.

(d) $\displaystyle\lim_{L \to 18^+} \frac{8L}{\sqrt{L^2 - 18^2}} = \infty$

$\displaystyle\lim_{L \to \infty} \frac{8L}{\sqrt{L^2 - 18^2}} = \lim_{L \to \infty} \frac{8}{\sqrt{1 - (18/L)^2}} = 8$

(e) From the table, $T = 10$ implies $L = 30$ inches.

**107.** Let $\alpha$ be the angle between **v** and the coordinate axes.

$$\mathbf{v} = (\cos \alpha)\mathbf{i} + (\cos \alpha)\mathbf{j} + (\cos \alpha)\mathbf{k}$$

$$\|\mathbf{v}\| = \sqrt{3}\cos \alpha = 1$$

$$\cos \alpha = \frac{1}{\sqrt{3}} = \frac{\sqrt{3}}{3}$$

$$\mathbf{v} = \frac{\sqrt{3}}{3}(\mathbf{i} + \mathbf{j} + \mathbf{k}) = \frac{\sqrt{3}}{3}\langle 1, 1, 1\rangle$$

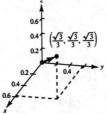

**109.** $\overrightarrow{AB} = \langle 0, 70, 115\rangle$, $\mathbf{F}_1 = C_1\langle 0, 70, 115\rangle$

$\overrightarrow{AC} = \langle -60, 0, 115\rangle$, $\mathbf{F}_2 = C_2\langle -60, 0, 115\rangle$

$\overrightarrow{AD} = \langle 45, -65, 115\rangle$, $\mathbf{F}_3 = C_3\langle 45, -65, 115\rangle$

$\mathbf{F} = \mathbf{F}_1 + \mathbf{F}_2 + \mathbf{F}_3 = \langle 0, 0, 500\rangle$

Thus:

$$-60C_2 + 45C_3 = 0$$
$$70C_1 \qquad - 65C_3 = 0$$
$$115(C_1 + C_2 + C_3) = 500$$

Solving this system yields $C_1 = \frac{104}{69}$, $C_2 = \frac{28}{23}$, and $C_3 = -\frac{112}{69}$. Thus:

$\|\mathbf{F}_1\| \approx 202.919N$

$\|\mathbf{F}_2\| \approx 157.909N$

$\|\mathbf{F}_3\| \approx 226.521N$

**111.** $d(AP) = 2d(BP)$

$$\sqrt{x^2 + (y + 1)^2 + (z - 1)^2} = 2\sqrt{(x - 1)^2 + (y - 2)^2 + z^2}$$

$$x^2 + y^2 + z^2 + 2y - 2z + 2 = 4(x^2 + y^2 + z^2 - 2x - 4y + 5)$$

$$0 = 3x^2 + 3y^2 + 3z^2 - 8x - 18y + 2z + 18$$

$$-6 + \frac{16}{9} + 9 + \frac{1}{9} = \left(x^2 - \frac{8}{3}x + \frac{16}{9}\right) + (y^2 - 6y + 9) + \left(z^2 + \frac{2}{3}z + \frac{1}{9}\right)$$

$$\frac{44}{9} = \left(x - \frac{4}{3}\right)^2 + (y - 3)^2 + \left(z + \frac{1}{3}\right)^2$$

Sphere; center: $\left(\frac{4}{3}, 3, -\frac{1}{3}\right)$, radius: $\frac{2\sqrt{11}}{3}$

# Section 10.3    The Dot Product of Two Vectors

**1.** $\mathbf{u} = \langle 3, 4 \rangle$, $\mathbf{v} = \langle 2, -3 \rangle$

(a) $\mathbf{u} \cdot \mathbf{v} = 3(2) + 4(-3) = -6$

(b) $\mathbf{u} \cdot \mathbf{u} = 3(3) + 4(4) = 25$

(c) $\|\mathbf{u}\|^2 = 25$

(d) $(\mathbf{u} \cdot \mathbf{v})\mathbf{v} = -6\langle 2, -3 \rangle = \langle -12, 18 \rangle$

(e) $\mathbf{u} \cdot (2\mathbf{v}) = 2(\mathbf{u} \cdot \mathbf{v}) = 2(-6) = -12$

**3.** $\mathbf{u} = \langle 2, -3, 4 \rangle$, $\mathbf{v} = \langle 0, 6, 5 \rangle$

(a) $\mathbf{u} \cdot \mathbf{v} = 2(0) + (-3)(6) + (4)(5) = 2$

(b) $\mathbf{u} \cdot \mathbf{u} = 2(2) + (-3)(-3) + 4(4) = 29$

(c) $\|\mathbf{u}\|^2 = 29$

(d) $(\mathbf{u} \cdot \mathbf{v})\mathbf{v} = 2\langle 0, 6, 5 \rangle = \langle 0, 12, 10 \rangle$

(e) $\mathbf{u} \cdot (2\mathbf{v}) = 2(\mathbf{u} \cdot \mathbf{v}) = 2(2) = 4$

**5.** $\mathbf{u} = 2\mathbf{i} - \mathbf{j} + \mathbf{k}$, $\mathbf{v} = \mathbf{i} - \mathbf{k}$

(a) $\mathbf{u} \cdot \mathbf{v} = 2(1) + (-1)(0) + 1(-1) = 1$

(b) $\mathbf{u} \cdot \mathbf{u} = 2(2) + (-1)(-1) + (1)(1) = 6$

(c) $\|\mathbf{u}\|^2 = 6$

(d) $(\mathbf{u} \cdot \mathbf{v})\mathbf{v} = \mathbf{v} = \mathbf{i} - \mathbf{k}$

(e) $\mathbf{u} \cdot (2\mathbf{v}) = 2(\mathbf{u} \cdot \mathbf{v}) = 2$

**7.**   $\mathbf{u} = \langle 3240, 1450, 2235 \rangle$

$\mathbf{v} = \langle 2.22, 1.85, 3.25 \rangle$

$\mathbf{u} \cdot \mathbf{v} = \$17{,}139.05$

This gives the total amount that the person earned on his products.

**9.** $\dfrac{\mathbf{u} \cdot \mathbf{v}}{\|\mathbf{u}\|\,\|\mathbf{v}\|} = \cos\theta$

$\mathbf{u} \cdot \mathbf{v} = (8)(5)\cos\dfrac{\pi}{3} = 20$

**11.** $\mathbf{u} = \langle 1, 1 \rangle$, $\mathbf{v} = \langle 2, -2 \rangle$

$\cos\theta = \dfrac{\mathbf{u} \cdot \mathbf{v}}{\|\mathbf{u}\|\,\|\mathbf{v}\|} = \dfrac{0}{\sqrt{2}\sqrt{8}} = 0$

$\theta = \dfrac{\pi}{2}$

**13.** $\mathbf{u} = 3\mathbf{i} + \mathbf{j}$, $\mathbf{v} = -2\mathbf{i} + 4\mathbf{j}$

$\cos\theta = \dfrac{\mathbf{u} \cdot \mathbf{v}}{\|\mathbf{u}\|\,\|\mathbf{v}\|} = \dfrac{-2}{\sqrt{10}\sqrt{20}} = \dfrac{-1}{5\sqrt{2}}$

$\theta = \arccos\left(-\dfrac{1}{5\sqrt{2}}\right) \approx 98.1°$

**15.** $\mathbf{u} = \langle 1, 1, 1 \rangle$, $\mathbf{v} = \langle 2, 1, -1 \rangle$

$\cos\theta = \dfrac{\mathbf{u} \cdot \mathbf{v}}{\|\mathbf{u}\|\,\|\mathbf{v}\|} = \dfrac{2}{\sqrt{3}\sqrt{6}} = \dfrac{\sqrt{2}}{3}$

$\theta = \arccos\dfrac{\sqrt{2}}{3} \approx 61.9°$

**17.** $\mathbf{u} = 3\mathbf{i} + 4\mathbf{j}$, $\mathbf{v} = -2\mathbf{j} + 3\mathbf{k}$

$\cos\theta = \dfrac{\mathbf{u} \cdot \mathbf{v}}{\|\mathbf{u}\|\,\|\mathbf{v}\|} = \dfrac{-8}{5\sqrt{13}} = \dfrac{-8\sqrt{13}}{65}$

$\theta = \arccos\left(-\dfrac{8\sqrt{13}}{65}\right) \approx 116.3°$

**19.** $\mathbf{u} = \langle 4, 0 \rangle$, $\mathbf{v} = \langle 1, 1 \rangle$

$\mathbf{u} \neq c\mathbf{v} \implies$ not parallel

$\mathbf{u} \cdot \mathbf{v} = 4 \neq 0 \implies$ not orthogonal

Neither

**21.** $\mathbf{u} = \langle 4, 3 \rangle$, $\mathbf{v} = \left\langle \dfrac{1}{2}, -\dfrac{2}{3} \right\rangle$

$\mathbf{u} \neq c\mathbf{v} \implies$ not parallel

$\mathbf{u} \cdot \mathbf{v} = 0 \implies$ orthogonal

**23.** $\mathbf{u} = \mathbf{j} + 6\mathbf{k}$, $\mathbf{v} = \mathbf{i} - 2\mathbf{j} - \mathbf{k}$

$\mathbf{u} \neq c\mathbf{v} \implies$ not parallel

$\mathbf{u} \cdot \mathbf{v} = -8 \neq 0 \implies$ not orthogonal

Neither

**25.** $\mathbf{u} = \langle 2, -3, 1 \rangle$, $\mathbf{v} = \langle -1, -1, -1 \rangle$

$\mathbf{u} \neq c\mathbf{v} \implies$ not parallel

$\mathbf{u} \cdot \mathbf{v} = 0 \implies$ orthogonal

**27.** $\mathbf{u} = \mathbf{i} + 2\mathbf{j} + 2\mathbf{k}$, $\|\mathbf{u}\| = 3$

$$\cos \alpha = \frac{1}{3}$$

$$\cos \beta = \frac{2}{3}$$

$$\cos \gamma = \frac{2}{3}$$

$$\cos^2 \alpha + \cos^2 \beta + \cos^2 \gamma = \frac{1}{9} + \frac{4}{9} + \frac{4}{9} = 1$$

**29.** $\mathbf{u} = \langle 0, 6, -4 \rangle$, $\|\mathbf{u}\| = \sqrt{52} = 2\sqrt{13}$

$$\cos \alpha = 0$$

$$\cos \beta = \frac{3}{\sqrt{13}}$$

$$\cos \gamma = -\frac{2}{\sqrt{13}}$$

$$\cos^2 \alpha + \cos^2 \beta + \cos^2 \gamma = 0 + \frac{9}{13} + \frac{4}{13} = 1$$

**31.** $\mathbf{u} = \langle 3, 2, -2 \rangle$   $\|\mathbf{u}\| = \sqrt{17}$

$$\cos \alpha = \frac{3}{\sqrt{17}} \implies \alpha \approx 0.7560 \text{ or } 43.3°$$

$$\cos \beta = \frac{2}{\sqrt{17}} \implies \beta \approx 1.0644 \text{ or } 61.0°$$

$$\cos \gamma = \frac{-2}{\sqrt{17}} \implies \gamma \approx 2.0772 \text{ or } 119.0°$$

**33.** $\mathbf{u} = \langle -1, 5, 2 \rangle$   $\|\mathbf{u}\| = \sqrt{30}$

$$\cos \alpha = \frac{-1}{\sqrt{30}} \implies \alpha \approx 1.7544 \text{ or } 100.5°$$

$$\cos \beta = \frac{5}{\sqrt{30}} \implies \beta \approx 0.4205 \text{ or } 24.1°$$

$$\cos \gamma = \frac{2}{\sqrt{30}} \implies \gamma \approx 1.1970 \text{ or } 68.6°$$

**35.** $\mathbf{F}_1$: $C_1 = \dfrac{50}{\|\mathbf{F}_1\|} \approx 4.3193$

$\mathbf{F}_2$: $C_2 = \dfrac{80}{\|\mathbf{F}_2\|} \approx 5.4183$

$\mathbf{F} = \mathbf{F}_1 + \mathbf{F}_2$

$\approx 4.3193\langle 10, 5, 3 \rangle + 5.4183\langle 12, 7, -5 \rangle$

$= \langle 108.2126, 59.5246, -14.1336 \rangle$

$\|\mathbf{F}\| \approx 124.310 \text{ lb}$

$$\cos \alpha \approx \frac{108.2126}{\|\mathbf{F}\|} \implies \alpha \approx 29.48°$$

$$\cos \beta \approx \frac{59.5246}{\|\mathbf{F}\|} \implies \beta \approx 61.39°$$

$$\cos \gamma \approx \frac{-14.1336}{\|\mathbf{F}\|} \implies \gamma \approx 96.53°$$

**37.** Let $s$ = length of a side.

$$\mathbf{v} = \langle s, s, s \rangle$$

$$\|\mathbf{v}\| = s\sqrt{3}$$

$$\cos \alpha = \cos \beta = \cos \gamma = \frac{s}{s\sqrt{3}} = \frac{1}{\sqrt{3}}$$

$$\alpha = \beta = \gamma = \arccos\left(\frac{1}{\sqrt{3}}\right) \approx 54.7°$$

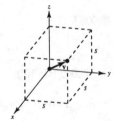

**39.** $\overrightarrow{OA} = \langle 0, 10, 10 \rangle$

$$\cos \alpha = \frac{0}{\sqrt{0^2 + 10^2 + 10^2}} = 0 \implies \alpha = 90°$$

$$\cos \beta = \cos \gamma = \frac{10}{\sqrt{0^2 + 10^2 + 10^2}}$$

$$= \frac{1}{\sqrt{2}} \implies \beta = \gamma = 45°$$

**41.** $\mathbf{w}_2 = \mathbf{u} - \mathbf{w}_1 = \langle 6, 7 \rangle - \langle 2, 8 \rangle = \langle 4, -1 \rangle$

**43.** $\mathbf{w}_2 = \mathbf{u} - \mathbf{w}_1 = \langle 0, 3, 3 \rangle - \langle -2, 2, 2 \rangle = \langle 2, 1, 1 \rangle$

**45.** $\mathbf{u} = \langle 2, 3 \rangle$, $\mathbf{v} = \langle 5, 1 \rangle$

(a) $\mathbf{w}_1 = \left(\dfrac{\mathbf{u} \cdot \mathbf{v}}{\|\mathbf{v}\|^2}\right)\mathbf{v} = \dfrac{13}{26}\langle 5, 1 \rangle = \left\langle \dfrac{5}{2}, \dfrac{1}{2} \right\rangle$

(b) $\mathbf{w}_2 = \mathbf{u} - \mathbf{w}_1 = \left\langle -\dfrac{1}{2}, \dfrac{5}{2} \right\rangle$

**47.** $\mathbf{u} = \langle 2, 1, 2 \rangle$, $\mathbf{v} = \langle 0, 3, 4 \rangle$

(a) $\mathbf{w}_1 = \left( \dfrac{\mathbf{u} \cdot \mathbf{v}}{\|\mathbf{v}\|^2} \right) \mathbf{v}$

$= \dfrac{11}{25} \langle 0, 3, 4 \rangle = \left\langle 0, \dfrac{33}{25}, \dfrac{44}{25} \right\rangle$

(b) $\mathbf{w}_2 = \mathbf{u} - \mathbf{w}_1 = \left\langle 2, -\dfrac{8}{25}, \dfrac{6}{25} \right\rangle$

**49.** $\mathbf{u} \cdot \mathbf{v} = \langle u_1, u_2, u_3 \rangle \cdot \langle v_1, v_2, v_3 \rangle = u_1 v_1 + u_2 v_2 + u_3 v_3$

**51.** (a) Orthogonal, $\theta = \dfrac{\pi}{2}$     (b) Acute, $0 < \theta < \dfrac{\pi}{2}$     (c) Obtuse, $\dfrac{\pi}{2} < \theta < \pi$

**53.** See page 738. Direction cosines of $\mathbf{v} = \langle v_1, v_2, v_3 \rangle$ are

$\cos \alpha = \dfrac{v_1}{\|\mathbf{v}\|}, \cos \beta = \dfrac{v_2}{\|\mathbf{v}\|}, \cos \gamma = \dfrac{v_3}{\|\mathbf{v}\|}.$

$\alpha$, $\beta$, and $\gamma$ are the direction angles. See Figure 10.26.

**55.** (a) $\left( \dfrac{\mathbf{u} \cdot \mathbf{v}}{\|\mathbf{v}\|^2} \right) \mathbf{v} = \mathbf{u} \Rightarrow \mathbf{u} = c\mathbf{v} \Rightarrow \mathbf{u}$ and $\mathbf{v}$ are parallel.

(b) $\left( \dfrac{\mathbf{u} \cdot \mathbf{v}}{\|\mathbf{v}\|^2} \right) \mathbf{v} = \mathbf{0} \Rightarrow \mathbf{u} \cdot \mathbf{v} = 0 \Rightarrow \mathbf{u}$ and $\mathbf{v}$ are orthogonal.

**57.** Programs will vary.

**59.** Programs will vary.

**61.** Because $\mathbf{u}$ appears to be perpendicular to $\mathbf{v}$, the projection of $\mathbf{u}$ onto $\mathbf{v}$ is $\mathbf{0}$. Analytically,

$\text{proj}_{\mathbf{v}}\, \mathbf{u} = \dfrac{\mathbf{u} \cdot \mathbf{v}}{\|\mathbf{v}\|^2} \mathbf{v} = \dfrac{\langle 2, -3 \rangle \cdot \langle 6, 4 \rangle}{\|\langle 6, 4 \rangle\|^2} \langle 6, 4 \rangle = 0 \langle 6, 4 \rangle = \mathbf{0}.$

**63.** $\mathbf{u} = \dfrac{1}{2}\mathbf{i} - \dfrac{2}{3}\mathbf{j}$. Want $\mathbf{u} \cdot \mathbf{v} = 0$.

$\mathbf{v} = 8\mathbf{i} + 6\mathbf{j}$ and $-\mathbf{v} = -8\mathbf{i} - 6\mathbf{j}$ are orthogonal to $\mathbf{u}$.

**65.** $\mathbf{u} = \langle 3, 1, -2 \rangle$. Want $\mathbf{u} \cdot \mathbf{v} = 0$.

$\mathbf{v} = \langle 0, 2, 1 \rangle$ and $-\mathbf{v} = \langle 0, -2, -1 \rangle$ are orthogonal to $\mathbf{u}$.

**67.** (a) Gravitational Force $\mathbf{F} = -48,000\,\mathbf{j}$

$\mathbf{v} = \cos 10°\, \mathbf{i} + \sin 10°\, \mathbf{j}$

$\mathbf{w}_1 = \dfrac{\mathbf{F} \cdot \mathbf{v}}{\|\mathbf{v}\|^2}\mathbf{v} = (\mathbf{F} \cdot \mathbf{v})\mathbf{v} = (-48,000)(\sin 10°)\mathbf{v}$

$\approx -8335.1(\cos 10°\, \mathbf{i} + \sin 10°\, \mathbf{j})$

$\|\mathbf{w}_1\| \approx 8335.1 \text{ lb}$

(b) $\mathbf{w}_2 = \mathbf{F} \cdot \mathbf{w}_1 = -48,000\,\mathbf{j} + 8335.1(\cos 10°\, \mathbf{i} + \sin 10°\, \mathbf{j})$

$= 8208.5\,\mathbf{i} - 46,552.6\,\mathbf{j}$

$\|\mathbf{w}_2\| \approx 47,270.8 \text{ lb}$

**69.** $\mathbf{F} = 85\left( \dfrac{1}{2}\mathbf{i} + \dfrac{\sqrt{3}}{2}\mathbf{j} \right)$

$\mathbf{v} = 10\mathbf{i}$

$W = \mathbf{F} \cdot \mathbf{v} = 425 \text{ ft} \cdot \text{lb}$

**71.** $\overrightarrow{PQ} = \langle 4, 7, 5 \rangle$

$\mathbf{v} = \langle 1, 4, 8 \rangle$

$W = \overrightarrow{PQ} \cdot \mathbf{v} = 72$

**73.** False. Let $\mathbf{u} = \langle 2, 4 \rangle$, $\mathbf{v} = \langle 1, 7 \rangle$ and $\mathbf{w} = \langle 5, 5 \rangle$. Then $\mathbf{u} \cdot \mathbf{v} = 2 + 28 = 30$ and $\mathbf{u} \cdot \mathbf{w} = 10 + 20 = 30$.

**75.** In a rhombus, $\|\mathbf{u}\| = \|\mathbf{v}\|$. The diagonals are $\mathbf{u} + \mathbf{v}$ and $\mathbf{u} - \mathbf{v}$.

$(\mathbf{u} + \mathbf{v}) \cdot (\mathbf{u} - \mathbf{v}) = (\mathbf{u} + \mathbf{v}) \cdot \mathbf{u} - (\mathbf{u} + \mathbf{v}) \cdot \mathbf{v}$

$= \mathbf{u} \cdot \mathbf{u} + \mathbf{v} \cdot \mathbf{u} - \mathbf{u} \cdot \mathbf{v} - \mathbf{v} \cdot \mathbf{v}$

$= \|\mathbf{u}\|^2 - \|\mathbf{v}\|^2 = 0$

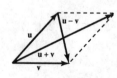

Therefore, the diagonals are orthogonal.

**77.** $\mathbf{u} = \langle \cos \alpha, \sin \alpha, 0 \rangle$, $\mathbf{v} = \langle \cos \beta, \sin \beta, 0 \rangle$

The angle between $\mathbf{u}$ and $\mathbf{v}$ is $\alpha - \beta$. (Assuming that $\alpha > \beta$). Also,

$$\cos(\alpha - \beta) = \frac{\mathbf{u} \cdot \mathbf{v}}{\|\mathbf{u}\| \|\mathbf{v}\|} = \frac{\cos \alpha \cos \beta + \sin \alpha \sin \beta}{(1)(1)} = \cos \alpha \cos \beta + \sin \alpha \sin \beta.$$

**79.** $\|\mathbf{u} - \mathbf{v}\|^2 = (\mathbf{u} - \mathbf{v}) \cdot (\mathbf{u} - \mathbf{v})$

$\qquad\qquad = (\mathbf{u} - \mathbf{v}) \cdot \mathbf{u} - (\mathbf{u} - \mathbf{v}) \cdot \mathbf{v}$

$\qquad\qquad = \mathbf{u} \cdot \mathbf{u} - \mathbf{v} \cdot \mathbf{u} - \mathbf{u} \cdot \mathbf{v} + \mathbf{v} \cdot \mathbf{v}$

$\qquad\qquad = \|\mathbf{u}\|^2 - \mathbf{u} \cdot \mathbf{v} - \mathbf{u} \cdot \mathbf{v} + \|\mathbf{v}\|^2$

$\qquad\qquad = \|\mathbf{u}\|^2 + \|\mathbf{v}\|^2 - 2\mathbf{u} \cdot \mathbf{v}$

**81.** $\|\mathbf{u} + \mathbf{v}\|^2 = (\mathbf{u} + \mathbf{v}) \cdot (\mathbf{u} + \mathbf{v})$

$\qquad\qquad = (\mathbf{u} + \mathbf{v}) \cdot \mathbf{u} + (\mathbf{u} + \mathbf{v}) \cdot \mathbf{v}$

$\qquad\qquad = \mathbf{u} \cdot \mathbf{u} + \mathbf{v} \cdot \mathbf{u} + \mathbf{u} \cdot \mathbf{v} + \mathbf{v} \cdot \mathbf{v}$

$\qquad\qquad = \|\mathbf{u}\|^2 + 2\mathbf{u} \cdot \mathbf{v} + \|\mathbf{v}\|^2$

$\qquad\qquad \leq \|\mathbf{u}\|^2 + 2\|\mathbf{u}\| \|\mathbf{v}\| + \|\mathbf{v}\|^2$ from Exercise 66

$\qquad\qquad \leq (\|\mathbf{u}\| + \|\mathbf{v}\|)^2$

Therefore, $\|\mathbf{u} + \mathbf{v}\| \leq \|\mathbf{u}\| + \|\mathbf{v}\|$.

## Section 10.4    The Cross Product of Two Vectors in Space

**1.** $\mathbf{j} \times \mathbf{i} = \begin{vmatrix} \mathbf{i} & \mathbf{j} & \mathbf{k} \\ 0 & 1 & 0 \\ 1 & 0 & 0 \end{vmatrix} = -\mathbf{k}$

**3.** $\mathbf{j} \times \mathbf{k} = \begin{vmatrix} \mathbf{i} & \mathbf{j} & \mathbf{k} \\ 0 & 1 & 0 \\ 0 & 0 & 1 \end{vmatrix} = \mathbf{i}$

**5.** $\mathbf{i} \times \mathbf{k} = \begin{vmatrix} \mathbf{i} & \mathbf{j} & \mathbf{k} \\ 1 & 0 & 0 \\ 0 & 0 & 1 \end{vmatrix} = -\mathbf{j}$

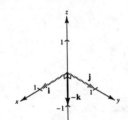

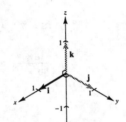

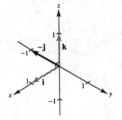

**7.** (a) $\mathbf{u} \times \mathbf{v} = \begin{vmatrix} \mathbf{i} & \mathbf{j} & \mathbf{k} \\ -2 & 3 & 4 \\ 3 & 7 & 2 \end{vmatrix} = \langle -22, 16, -23 \rangle$

(b) $\mathbf{v} \times \mathbf{u} = -(\mathbf{u} \times \mathbf{v}) = \langle 22, -16, 23 \rangle$

(c) $\mathbf{v} \times \mathbf{v} = \begin{vmatrix} \mathbf{i} & \mathbf{j} & \mathbf{k} \\ 3 & 7 & 2 \\ 3 & 7 & 2 \end{vmatrix} = 0$

**9.** (a) $\mathbf{u} \times \mathbf{v} = \begin{vmatrix} \mathbf{i} & \mathbf{j} & \mathbf{k} \\ 7 & 3 & 2 \\ 1 & -1 & 5 \end{vmatrix} = \langle 17, -33, -10 \rangle$

(b) $\mathbf{v} \times \mathbf{u} = -(\mathbf{u} \times \mathbf{v}) = \langle -17, 33, 10 \rangle$

(c) $\mathbf{v} \times \mathbf{v} = 0$

**11.** $\mathbf{u} = \langle 2, -3, 1 \rangle$, $\mathbf{v} = \langle 1, -2, 1 \rangle$

$\mathbf{u} \times \mathbf{v} = \begin{vmatrix} \mathbf{i} & \mathbf{j} & \mathbf{k} \\ 2 & -3 & 1 \\ 1 & -2 & 1 \end{vmatrix} = -\mathbf{i} - \mathbf{j} - \mathbf{k} = \langle -1, -1, -1 \rangle$

$\mathbf{u} \cdot (\mathbf{u} \times \mathbf{v}) = 2(-1) + (-3)(-1) + (1)(-1) = 0 \implies \mathbf{u} \perp \mathbf{u} \times \mathbf{v}$

$\mathbf{v} \cdot (\mathbf{u} \times \mathbf{v}) = 1(-1) + (-2)(-1) + (1)(-1) = 0 \implies \mathbf{v} \perp \mathbf{u} \times \mathbf{v}$

**13.** $\mathbf{u} = \langle 12, -3, 0 \rangle$, $\mathbf{v} = \langle -2, 5, 0 \rangle$

$$\mathbf{u} \times \mathbf{v} = \begin{vmatrix} \mathbf{i} & \mathbf{j} & \mathbf{k} \\ 12 & -3 & 0 \\ -2 & 5 & 0 \end{vmatrix} = 54\mathbf{k} = \langle 0, 0, 54 \rangle$$

$\mathbf{u} \cdot (\mathbf{u} \times \mathbf{v}) = 12(0) + (-3)(0) + 0(54)$

$\qquad = 0 \Rightarrow \mathbf{u} \perp \mathbf{u} \times \mathbf{v}$

$\mathbf{v} \cdot (\mathbf{u} \times \mathbf{v}) = -2(0) + 5(0) + 0(54)$

$\qquad = 0 \Rightarrow \mathbf{v} \perp \mathbf{u} \times \mathbf{v}$

**15.** $\mathbf{u} = \mathbf{i} + \mathbf{j} + \mathbf{k}$, $\mathbf{v} = 2\mathbf{i} + \mathbf{j} - \mathbf{k}$

$$\mathbf{u} \times \mathbf{v} = \begin{vmatrix} \mathbf{i} & \mathbf{j} & \mathbf{k} \\ 1 & 1 & 1 \\ 2 & 1 & -1 \end{vmatrix} = -2\mathbf{i} + 3\mathbf{j} - \mathbf{k} = \langle -2, 3, -1 \rangle$$

$\mathbf{u} \cdot (\mathbf{u} \times \mathbf{v}) = 1(-2) + 1(3) + 1(-1)$

$\qquad = 0 \Rightarrow \mathbf{u} \perp \mathbf{u} \times \mathbf{v}$

$\mathbf{v} \cdot (\mathbf{u} \times \mathbf{v}) = 2(-2) + 1(3) + (-1)(-1)$

$\qquad = 0 \Rightarrow \mathbf{v} \perp \mathbf{u} \times \mathbf{v}$

**17.**

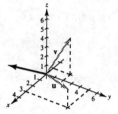

**19.**

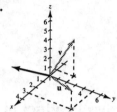

**21.** $\mathbf{u} = \langle 4, -3.5, 7 \rangle$

$\mathbf{v} = \langle -1, 8, 4 \rangle$

$\mathbf{u} \times \mathbf{v} = \left\langle -70, -23, \dfrac{57}{2} \right\rangle$

$\dfrac{\mathbf{u} \times \mathbf{v}}{\|\mathbf{u} \times \mathbf{v}\|} = \left\langle \dfrac{-140}{\sqrt{24,965}}, \dfrac{-46}{\sqrt{24,965}}, \dfrac{57}{\sqrt{24,965}} \right\rangle$

**23.** $\mathbf{u} = -3\mathbf{i} + 2\mathbf{j} - 5\mathbf{k}$

$\mathbf{v} = \dfrac{1}{2}\mathbf{i} - \dfrac{3}{4}\mathbf{j} + \dfrac{1}{10}\mathbf{k}$

$\mathbf{u} \times \mathbf{v} = \left\langle -\dfrac{71}{20}, -\dfrac{11}{5}, \dfrac{5}{4} \right\rangle$

$\dfrac{\mathbf{u} \times \mathbf{v}}{\|\mathbf{u} \times \mathbf{v}\|} = \dfrac{20}{\sqrt{7602}} \left\langle -\dfrac{71}{20}, -\dfrac{11}{5}, \dfrac{5}{4} \right\rangle$

$\qquad = \left\langle -\dfrac{71}{\sqrt{7602}}, -\dfrac{44}{\sqrt{7602}}, \dfrac{25}{\sqrt{7602}} \right\rangle$

**25.** Programs will vary.

**27.** $\mathbf{u} = \mathbf{j}$

$\mathbf{v} = \mathbf{j} + \mathbf{k}$

$$\mathbf{u} \times \mathbf{v} = \begin{vmatrix} \mathbf{i} & \mathbf{j} & \mathbf{k} \\ 0 & 1 & 0 \\ 0 & 1 & 1 \end{vmatrix} = \mathbf{i}$$

$A = \|\mathbf{u} \times \mathbf{v}\| = \|\mathbf{i}\| = 1$

**29.** $\mathbf{u} = \langle 3, 2, -1 \rangle$

$\mathbf{v} = \langle 1, 2, 3 \rangle$

$$\mathbf{u} \times \mathbf{v} = \begin{vmatrix} \mathbf{i} & \mathbf{j} & \mathbf{k} \\ 3 & 2 & -1 \\ 1 & 2 & 3 \end{vmatrix} = \langle 8, -10, 4 \rangle$$

$A = \|\mathbf{u} \times \mathbf{v}\| = \|\langle 8, -10, 4 \rangle\| = \sqrt{180} = 6\sqrt{5}$

**31.** $A(1, 1, 1,)$, $B(2, 3, 4)$, $C(6, 5, 2)$, $D(7, 7, 5)$

$\overrightarrow{AB} = \langle 1, 2, 3 \rangle$, $\overrightarrow{AC} = \langle 5, 4, 1 \rangle$, $\overrightarrow{CD} = \langle 1, 2, 3 \rangle$, $\overrightarrow{BD} = \langle 5, 4, 1 \rangle$

Since $\overrightarrow{AB} = \overrightarrow{CD}$ and $\overrightarrow{AC} = \overrightarrow{BD}$, the figure is a parallelogram. $\overrightarrow{AB}$ and $\overrightarrow{AC}$ are adjacent sides and

$$\overrightarrow{AB} \times \overrightarrow{AC} = \begin{vmatrix} \mathbf{i} & \mathbf{j} & \mathbf{k} \\ 1 & 2 & 3 \\ 5 & 4 & 1 \end{vmatrix} = -10\mathbf{i} + 14\mathbf{j} - 6\mathbf{k}.$$

$A = \|\overrightarrow{AB} \times \overrightarrow{AC}\| = \sqrt{332} = 2\sqrt{83}$

**33.** $A(0, 0, 0)$, $B(1, 2, 3)$, $C(-3, 0, 0)$

$\overrightarrow{AB} = \langle 1, 2, 3 \rangle$, $\overrightarrow{AC} = \langle -3, 0, 0 \rangle$

$$\overrightarrow{AB} \times \overrightarrow{AC} = \begin{vmatrix} \mathbf{i} & \mathbf{j} & \mathbf{k} \\ 1 & 2 & 3 \\ -3 & 0 & 0 \end{vmatrix} = -9\mathbf{j} + 6\mathbf{k}$$

$A = \dfrac{1}{2}\|\overrightarrow{AB} \times \overrightarrow{AC}\| = \dfrac{1}{2}\sqrt{117} = \dfrac{3}{2}\sqrt{13}$

**35.** $A(2, -7, 3)$, $B(-1, 5, 8)$, $C(4, 6, -1)$

$\overrightarrow{AB} = \langle -3, 12, 5 \rangle$, $\overrightarrow{AC} = \langle 2, 13, -4 \rangle$

$\overrightarrow{AB} \times \overrightarrow{AC} = \begin{vmatrix} \mathbf{i} & \mathbf{j} & \mathbf{k} \\ -3 & 12 & 5 \\ 2 & 13 & -4 \end{vmatrix} = \langle -113, -2, -63 \rangle$

Area $= \dfrac{1}{2} \| \overrightarrow{AB} \times \overrightarrow{AC} \| = \dfrac{1}{2}\sqrt{16{,}742}$

**37.** $\mathbf{F} = -20\mathbf{k}$

$\overrightarrow{PQ} = \dfrac{1}{2}(\cos 40° \mathbf{j} + \sin 40° \mathbf{k})$

$\overrightarrow{PQ} \times \mathbf{F} = \begin{vmatrix} \mathbf{i} & \mathbf{j} & \mathbf{k} \\ 0 & \cos 40°/2 & \sin 40°/2 \\ 0 & 0 & -20 \end{vmatrix} = -10 \cos 40° \mathbf{i}$

$\| \overrightarrow{PQ} \times \mathbf{F} \| = 10 \cos 40° \approx 7.66 \text{ ft} \cdot \text{lb}$

**39. (a)** $\overrightarrow{OA} = \dfrac{3}{2}\mathbf{k}$

$\mathbf{F} = -60(\sin \theta \mathbf{j} + \cos \theta \mathbf{k})$

$\overrightarrow{OA} \times \mathbf{F} = \begin{vmatrix} \mathbf{i} & \mathbf{j} & \mathbf{k} \\ 0 & 0 & 3/2 \\ 0 & -60 \sin \theta & -60 \cos \theta \end{vmatrix} = 90 \sin \theta \mathbf{i}$

$\| \overrightarrow{OA} \times \mathbf{F} \| = 90 \sin \theta$

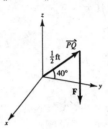

**(b)** When $\theta = 45°$: $\| \overrightarrow{OA} \times \mathbf{F} \| = 90 \left( \dfrac{\sqrt{2}}{2} \right) = 45\sqrt{2} \approx 63.64$.

**(c)** Let $T = 90 \sin \theta$.

$\dfrac{dT}{d\theta} = 90 \cos \theta = 0$ when $\theta = 90°$.

This is what we expected. When $\theta = 90°$ the pipe wrench is horizontal.

**41.** $\mathbf{u} \cdot (\mathbf{v} \times \mathbf{w}) = \begin{vmatrix} 1 & 0 & 0 \\ 0 & 1 & 0 \\ 0 & 0 & 1 \end{vmatrix} = 1$

**43.** $\mathbf{u} \cdot (\mathbf{v} \times \mathbf{w}) = \begin{vmatrix} 2 & 0 & 1 \\ 0 & 3 & 0 \\ 0 & 0 & 1 \end{vmatrix} = 6$

**45.** $\mathbf{u} \cdot (\mathbf{v} \times \mathbf{w}) = \begin{vmatrix} 1 & 1 & 0 \\ 0 & 1 & 1 \\ 1 & 0 & 1 \end{vmatrix} = 2$

$V = |\mathbf{u} \cdot (\mathbf{v} \times \mathbf{w})| = 2$

**47.** $\mathbf{u} = \langle 3, 0, 0 \rangle$

$\mathbf{v} = \langle 0, 5, 1 \rangle$

$\mathbf{w} = \langle 2, 0, 5 \rangle$

$\mathbf{u} \cdot (\mathbf{v} \times \mathbf{w}) = \begin{vmatrix} 3 & 0 & 0 \\ 0 & 5 & 1 \\ 2 & 0 & 5 \end{vmatrix} = 75$

$V = |\mathbf{u} \cdot (\mathbf{v} \times \mathbf{w})| = 75$

**49.** $\mathbf{u} \times \mathbf{v} = \langle u_1, u_2, u_3 \rangle \cdot \langle v_1, v_2, v_3 \rangle = (u_2 v_3 - u_3 v_2)\mathbf{i} - (u_1 v_3 - u_3 v_1)\mathbf{j} + (u_1 v_2 - u_2 v_1)\mathbf{k}$

**51.** The magnitude of the cross product will increase by a factor of 4.

**53.** If the vectors are ordered pairs, then the cross product does not exist. False.

**55.** True

**57.** $\mathbf{u} = \langle u_1, u_2, u_3 \rangle$, $\mathbf{v} = \langle v_1, v_2, v_3 \rangle$, $\mathbf{w} = \langle w_1, w_2, w_3 \rangle$

$$\mathbf{u} \times (\mathbf{v} + \mathbf{w}) = \begin{vmatrix} \mathbf{i} & \mathbf{j} & \mathbf{k} \\ u_1 & u_2 & u_3 \\ v_1 + w_1 & v_2 + w_2 & v_3 + w_3 \end{vmatrix}$$

$$= [u_2(v_3 + w_3) - u_3(v_2 + w_2)]\mathbf{i} - [u_1(v_3 + w_3) - u_3(v_1 + w_1)]\mathbf{j} + [u_1(v_2 + w_2) - u_2(v_1 + w_1)]\mathbf{k}$$

$$= (u_2v_3 - u_3v_2)\mathbf{i} - (u_1v_3 - u_3v_1)\mathbf{j} + (u_1v_2 - u_2v_1)\mathbf{k} + (u_2w_3 - u_3w_2)\mathbf{i} -$$
$$(u_1w_3 - u_3w_1)\mathbf{j} + (u_1w_2 - u_2w_1)\mathbf{k}$$

$$= (\mathbf{u} \times \mathbf{v}) + (\mathbf{u} \times \mathbf{w})$$

**59.** $\mathbf{u} = \langle u_1, u_2, u_3 \rangle$

$$\mathbf{u} \times \mathbf{u} = \begin{vmatrix} \mathbf{i} & \mathbf{j} & \mathbf{k} \\ u_1 & u_2 & u_3 \\ u_1 & u_2 & u_3 \end{vmatrix} = (u_2u_3 - u_3u_2)\mathbf{i} - (u_1u_3 - u_3u_1)\mathbf{j} + (u_1u_2 - u_2u_1)\mathbf{k} = \mathbf{0}$$

**61.** $\qquad \mathbf{u} \times \mathbf{v} = (u_2v_3 - u_3v_2)\mathbf{i} - (u_1v_3 - u_3v_1)\mathbf{j} + (u_1v_2 - u_2v_1)\mathbf{k}$

$(\mathbf{u} \times \mathbf{v}) \cdot \mathbf{u} = (u_2v_3 - u_3v_2)u_1 + (u_3v_1 - u_1v_3)u_2 + (u_1v_2 - u_2v_1)u_3 = 0$

$(\mathbf{u} \times \mathbf{v}) \cdot \mathbf{v} = (u_2v_3 - u_3v_2)v_1 + (u_3v_1 - u_1v_3)v_2 + (u_1v_2 - u_2v_1)v_3 = 0$

Thus, $\mathbf{u} \times \mathbf{v} \perp \mathbf{u}$ and $\mathbf{u} \times \mathbf{v} \perp \mathbf{v}$.

**63.** $\|\mathbf{u} \times \mathbf{v}\| = \|\mathbf{u}\|\,\|\mathbf{v}\| \sin \theta$

If $\mathbf{u}$ and $\mathbf{v}$ are orthogonal, $\theta = \pi/2$ and $\sin \theta = 1$. Therefore, $\|\mathbf{u} \times \mathbf{v}\| = \|\mathbf{u}\|\,\|\mathbf{v}\|$.

## Section 10.5     Lines and Planes in Space

**1.** $x = 1 + 3t$, $y = 2 - t$, $z = 2 + 5t$

(a)

(b) When $t = 0$ we have $P = (1, 2, 2)$. When $t = 3$ we have $Q = (10, -1, 17)$.

$$\overrightarrow{PQ} = \langle 9, -3, 15 \rangle$$

The components of the vector and the coefficients of $t$ are proportional since the line is parallel to $\overrightarrow{PQ}$.

(c) $y = 0$ when $t = 2$. Thus, $x = 7$ and $z = 12$.
Point: $(7, 0, 12)$

$x = 0$ when $t = -\dfrac{1}{3}$. Point: $\left(0, \dfrac{7}{3}, \dfrac{1}{3}\right)$

$z = 0$ when $t = -\dfrac{2}{5}$. Point: $\left(-\dfrac{1}{5}, \dfrac{12}{5}, 0\right)$

**3.** Point: $(0, 0, 0)$

Direction vector: $\mathbf{v} = \langle 1, 2, 3 \rangle$

Direction numbers: $1, 2, 3$

(a) Parametric: $x = t$, $y = 2t$, $z = 3t$

(b) Symmetric: $x = \dfrac{y}{2} = \dfrac{z}{3}$

**5.** Point: $(-2, 0, 3)$

Direction vector: $\mathbf{v} = \langle 2, 4, -2 \rangle$

Direction numbers: $2, 4, -2$

(a) Parametric: $x = -2 + 2t$, $y = 4t$, $z = 3 - 2t$

(b) Symmetric: $\dfrac{x + 2}{2} = \dfrac{y}{4} = \dfrac{z - 3}{-2}$

**7.** Point: $(1, 0, 1)$

   Direction vector: $\mathbf{v} = 3\mathbf{i} - 2\mathbf{j} + \mathbf{k}$

   Direction numbers: $3, -2, 1$

   (a) Parametric: $x = 1 + 3t, y = -2t, z = 1 + t$

   (b) Symmetric: $\dfrac{x-1}{3} = \dfrac{y}{-2} = \dfrac{z-1}{1}$

**9.** Points: $(5, -3, -2), \left(\dfrac{-2}{3}, \dfrac{2}{3}, 1\right)$

   Direction vector: $\mathbf{v} = \dfrac{17}{3}\mathbf{i} - \dfrac{11}{3}\mathbf{j} - 3\mathbf{k}$

   Direction numbers: $17, -11, -9$

   (a) Parametric: $x = 5 + 17t, y = -3 - 11t, z = -2 - 9t$

   (b) Symmetric: $\dfrac{x-5}{17} = \dfrac{y+3}{-11} = \dfrac{z+2}{-9}$

**11.** Points: $(2, 3, 0), (10, 8, 12)$

   Direction vector: $\langle 8, 5, 12 \rangle$

   Direction numbers: $8, 5, 12$

   (a) Parametric: $x = 2 + 8t, y = 3 + 5t, z = 12t$

   (b) Symmetric: $\dfrac{x-2}{8} = \dfrac{y-3}{5} = \dfrac{z}{12}$

**13.** Point: $(2, 3, 4)$

   Direction vector: $\mathbf{v} = \mathbf{k}$

   Direction numbers: $0, 0, 1$

   Parametric: $x = 2, y = 3, z = 4 + t$

**15.** Point: $(-2, 3, 1)$

   Direction vector: $\mathbf{v} = 4\mathbf{i} - \mathbf{k}$

   Direction numbers: $4, 0, -1$

   Parametric: $x = -2 + 4t, y = 3, z = 1 - t$

   Symmetric: $\dfrac{x+2}{4} = \dfrac{z-1}{-1}, y = 3$

   (a) On line

   (b) On line

   (c) Not on line $(y \neq 3)$

   (d) Not on line $\left(\dfrac{6+2}{4} \neq \dfrac{-2-1}{-1}\right)$

**17.** $L_1$: $\mathbf{v} = \langle -3, 2, 4 \rangle$     $(6, -2, 5)$ on line

   $L_2$: $\mathbf{v} = \langle 6, -4, -8 \rangle$     $(6, -2, 5)$ on line

   $L_3$: $\mathbf{v} = \langle -6, 4, 8 \rangle$     $(6, -2, 5)$ not on line

   $L_4$: $\mathbf{v} = \langle 6, 4, -6 \rangle$     not parallel to $L_1, L_2$, nor $L_3$

   Hence, $L_1$ and $L_2$ are identical.

   $L_1 = L_2$ and $L_3$ are parallel.

**19.** At the point of intersection, the coordinates for one line equal the corresponding coordinates for the other line. Thus,

   (i) $4t + 2 = 2s + 2$, (ii) $3 = 2s + 3$, and (iii) $-t + 1 = s + 1$.

   From (ii), we find that $s = 0$ and consequently, from (iii), $t = 0$. Letting $s = t = 0$, we see that equation (i) is satisfied and therefore the two lines intersect. Substituting zero for $s$ or for $t$, we obtain the point $(2, 3, 1)$.

   $\mathbf{u} = 4\mathbf{i} - \mathbf{k}$     (First line)

   $\mathbf{v} = 2\mathbf{i} + 2\mathbf{j} + \mathbf{k}$     (Second line)

   $\cos\theta = \dfrac{|\mathbf{u} \cdot \mathbf{v}|}{\|\mathbf{u}\| \, \|\mathbf{v}\|} = \dfrac{8 - 1}{\sqrt{17}\sqrt{9}} = \dfrac{7}{3\sqrt{17}} = \dfrac{7\sqrt{17}}{51}$

**21.** Writing the equations of the lines in parametric form we have

   $x = 3t \qquad y = 2 - t \qquad z = -1 + t$

   $x = 1 + 4s \qquad y = -2 + s \qquad z = -3 - 3s.$

   For the coordinates to be equal, $3t = 1 + 4s$ and $2 - t = -2 + s$. Solving this system yields $t = \frac{17}{7}$ and $s = \frac{11}{7}$. When using these values for $s$ and $t$, the $z$ coordinates are not equal. The lines do not intersect.

**23.** $x = 2t + 3 \qquad x = -2s + 7$

   $y = 5t - 2 \qquad y = s + 8$

   $z = -t + 1 \qquad z = 2s - 1$

   Point of intersection: $(7, 8, -1)$

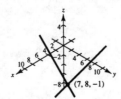

**25.** $4x - 3y - 6z = 6$

    (a) $P = (0, 0, -1)$, $Q = (0, -2, 0)$, $R = (3, 4, -1)$

        $\overrightarrow{PQ} = \langle 0, -2, 1 \rangle$, $\overrightarrow{PR} = \langle 3, 4, 0 \rangle$

    (b) $\overrightarrow{PQ} \times \overrightarrow{PR} = \begin{vmatrix} \mathbf{i} & \mathbf{j} & \mathbf{k} \\ 0 & -2 & 1 \\ 3 & 4 & 0 \end{vmatrix} = \langle -4, 3, 6 \rangle$

The components of the cross product are proportional to the coefficients of the variables in the equation. The cross product is parallel to the normal vector.

**27.** Point: $(2, 1, 2)$

    $\mathbf{n} = \mathbf{i} = \langle 1, 0, 0 \rangle$

    $1(x - 2) + 0(y - 1) + 0(z - 2) = 0$

    $x - 2 = 0$

**29.** Point: $(3, 2, 2)$

    Normal vector: $\mathbf{n} = 2\mathbf{i} + 3\mathbf{j} - \mathbf{k}$

    $2(x - 3) + 3(y - 2) - 1(z - 2) = 0$

    $2x + 3y - z = 10$

**31.** Point: $(0, 0, 6)$

    Normal vector: $\mathbf{n} = -\mathbf{i} + \mathbf{j} - 2\mathbf{k}$

    $-1(x - 0) + 1(y - 0) - 2(z - 6) = 0$

    $-x + y - 2z + 12 = 0$

    $x - y + 2z = 12$

**33.** Let $\mathbf{u}$ be the vector from $(0, 0, 0)$ to $(1, 2, 3)$:

    $\mathbf{u} = \mathbf{i} + 2\mathbf{j} + 3\mathbf{k}$

    Let $\mathbf{v}$ be the vector from $(0, 0, 0)$ to $(-2, 3, 3)$:

    $\mathbf{v} = -2\mathbf{i} + 3\mathbf{j} + 3\mathbf{k}$

    Normal vector: $\mathbf{u} \times \mathbf{v} = \begin{vmatrix} \mathbf{i} & \mathbf{j} & \mathbf{k} \\ 1 & 2 & 3 \\ -2 & 3 & 3 \end{vmatrix}$

                 $= -3\mathbf{i} + (-9)\mathbf{j} + 7\mathbf{k}$

    $-3(x - 0) - 9(y - 0) + 7(z - 0) = 0$

    $3x + 9y - 7z = 0$

**35.** Let $\mathbf{u}$ be the vector from $(1, 2, 3)$ to $(3, 2, 1)$: $\mathbf{u} = 2\mathbf{i} - 2\mathbf{k}$

Let $\mathbf{v}$ be the vector from $(1, 2, 3)$ to $(-1, -2, 2)$: $\mathbf{v} = -2\mathbf{i} - 4\mathbf{j} - \mathbf{k}$

Normal vector: $\left(\frac{1}{2}\mathbf{u}\right) \times (-\mathbf{v}) = \begin{vmatrix} \mathbf{i} & \mathbf{j} & \mathbf{k} \\ 1 & 0 & -1 \\ 2 & 4 & 1 \end{vmatrix} = 4\mathbf{i} - 3\mathbf{j} + 4\mathbf{k}$

$4(x - 1) - 3(y - 2) + 4(z - 3) = 0$

$4x - 3y + 4z = 10$

**37.** $(1, 2, 3)$, Normal vector: $\mathbf{v} = \mathbf{k}$, $1(z - 3) = 0$, $z = 3$

**39.** The direction vectors for the lines are $\mathbf{u} = -2\mathbf{i} + \mathbf{j} + \mathbf{k}$, $\mathbf{v} = -3\mathbf{i} + 4\mathbf{j} - \mathbf{k}$.

    Normal vector: $\mathbf{u} \times \mathbf{v} = \begin{vmatrix} \mathbf{i} & \mathbf{j} & \mathbf{k} \\ -2 & 1 & 1 \\ -3 & 4 & -1 \end{vmatrix} = -5(\mathbf{i} + \mathbf{j} + \mathbf{k})$

    Point of intersection of the lines: $(-1, 5, 1)$

    $(x + 1) + (y - 5) + (z - 1) = 0$

    $x + y + z = 5$

**41.** Let $\mathbf{v}$ be the vector from $(-1, 1, -1)$ to $(2, 2, 1)$: $\mathbf{v} = 3\mathbf{i} + \mathbf{j} + 2\mathbf{k}$

Let $\mathbf{n}$ be a vector normal to the plane $2x - 3y + z = 3$: $\mathbf{n} = 2\mathbf{i} - 3\mathbf{j} + \mathbf{k}$

Since $v$ and $n$ both lie in the plane $p$, the normal vector to $p$ is

$\mathbf{v} \times \mathbf{n} = \begin{vmatrix} \mathbf{i} & \mathbf{j} & \mathbf{k} \\ 3 & 1 & 2 \\ 2 & -3 & 1 \end{vmatrix} = 7\mathbf{i} + \mathbf{j} - 11\mathbf{k}$

$7(x - 2) + 1(y - 2) - 11(z - 1) = 0$

$7x + y - 11z = 5$

**43.** Let $\mathbf{u} = \mathbf{i}$ and let $\mathbf{v}$ be the vector from $(1, -2, -1)$ to $(2, 5, 6)$: $\mathbf{v} = \mathbf{i} + 7\mathbf{j} + 7\mathbf{k}$

Since $\mathbf{u}$ and $\mathbf{v}$ both lie in the plane $P$, the normal vector to $P$ is:

$$\mathbf{u} \times \mathbf{v} = \begin{vmatrix} \mathbf{i} & \mathbf{j} & \mathbf{k} \\ 1 & 0 & 0 \\ 1 & 7 & 7 \end{vmatrix} = -7\mathbf{j} + 7\mathbf{k} = -7(\mathbf{j} - \mathbf{k})$$

$[y - (-2)] - [z - (-1)] = 0$

$y - z = -1$

**45.** The normal vectors to the planes are

$$\mathbf{n}_1 = \langle 5, -3, 1 \rangle, \mathbf{n}_2 = \langle 1, 4, 7 \rangle, \cos\theta = \frac{|\mathbf{n}_1 \cdot \mathbf{n}_2|}{\|\mathbf{n}_1\| \|\mathbf{n}_2\|} = 0.$$

Thus, $\theta = \pi/2$ and the planes are orthogonal.

**47.** The normal vectors to the planes are

$$\mathbf{n}_1 = \mathbf{i} - 3\mathbf{j} + 6\mathbf{k}, \mathbf{n}_2 = 5\mathbf{i} + \mathbf{j} - \mathbf{k},$$

$$\cos\theta = \frac{|\mathbf{n}_1 \cdot \mathbf{n}_2|}{\|\mathbf{n}_1\| \|\mathbf{n}_2\|} = \frac{|5 - 3 - 6|}{\sqrt{46}\sqrt{27}} = \frac{4\sqrt{138}}{414}.$$

Therefore, $\theta = \arccos\left(\frac{4\sqrt{138}}{414}\right) \approx 83.5°$.

**49.** The normal vectors to the planes are $\mathbf{n}_1 = \langle 1, -5, -1 \rangle$ and $\mathbf{n}_2 = \langle 5, -25, -5 \rangle$. Since $\mathbf{n}_2 = 5\mathbf{n}_1$, the planes are parallel, but not equal.

**51.** $4x + 2y + 6z = 12$

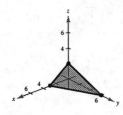

**53.** $2x - y + 3z = 4$

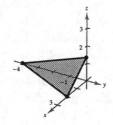

**55.** $y + z = 5$

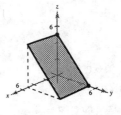

**57.** $x = 5$

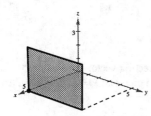

**59.** $2x + y - z = 6$

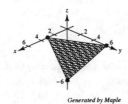

*Generated by Maple*

**61.** $-5x + 4y - 6z + 8 = 0$

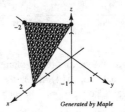

*Generated by Maple*

**63.** $P_1$: $\mathbf{n} = \langle 3, -2, 5 \rangle$    $(1, -1, 1)$ on plane

$P_2$: $\mathbf{n} = \langle -6, 4, -10 \rangle$    $(1, -1, 1)$ not on plane

$P_3$: $\mathbf{n} = \langle -3, 2, 5 \rangle$

$P_4$: $\mathbf{n} = \langle 75, -50, 125 \rangle$    $(1, -1, 1)$ on plane

$P_1$ and $P_4$ are identical.

$P_1 = P_4$ is parallel to $P_2$.

**65.** Each plane passes through the points

$(c, 0, 0), (0, c, 0),$ and $(0, 0, c).$

**67.** The normals to the planes are $\mathbf{n}_1 = 3\mathbf{i} + 2\mathbf{j} - \mathbf{k}$ and $\mathbf{n}_2 = \mathbf{i} - 4\mathbf{j} + 2\mathbf{k}$. The direction vector for the line is

$$\mathbf{n}_2 \times \mathbf{n}_1 = \begin{vmatrix} \mathbf{i} & \mathbf{j} & \mathbf{k} \\ 1 & -4 & 2 \\ 3 & 2 & -1 \end{vmatrix} = 7(\mathbf{j} + 2\mathbf{k}).$$

Now find a point of intersection of the planes.

$$\begin{aligned} 6x + 4y - 2y &= 14 \\ x - 4y + 2z &= 0 \\ 7x &= 14 \\ x &= 2 \end{aligned}$$

Substituting 2 for $x$ in the second equation, we have $-4y + 2z = -2$ or $z = 2y - 1$. Letting $y = 1$, a point of intersection is $(2, 1, 1)$.

$$x = 2, y = 1 + t, z = 1 + 2t$$

**71.** Writing the equation of the line in parametric form and substituting into the equation of the plane we have:

$$x = 1 + 3t, \ y = -1 - 2t, \ z = 3 + t$$
$$2(1 + 3t) + 3(-1 - 2t) = 10, -1 = 10, \text{ contradiction}$$

Therefore, the line does not intersect the plane.

**75.** Point: $Q(2, 8, 4)$

Plane: $2x + y + z = 5$

Normal to plane: $\mathbf{n} = \langle 2, 1, 1 \rangle$

Point in plane: $P\langle 0, 0, 5 \rangle$

Vector: $\overrightarrow{PQ} = \langle 2, 8, -1 \rangle$

$$D = \frac{|\overrightarrow{PQ} \cdot \mathbf{n}|}{\|\mathbf{n}\|} = \frac{11}{\sqrt{6}} = \frac{11\sqrt{6}}{6}$$

**79.** The normal vectors to the planes are $\mathbf{n}_1 = \langle -3, 6, 7 \rangle$ and $\mathbf{n}_2 = \langle 6, -12, -14 \rangle$. Since $\mathbf{n}_2 = -2\mathbf{n}_1$, the planes are parallel. Choose a point in each plane.

$P = (0, -1, 1)$ is a point in $-3x + 6y + 7z = 1$.

$Q = \left(\frac{25}{6}, 0, 0\right)$ is a point in $6x - 12y - 14z = 25$.

$$\overrightarrow{PQ} = \left\langle \frac{25}{6}, 1, -1 \right\rangle$$

$$D = \frac{|\overrightarrow{PQ} \cdot \mathbf{n}_1|}{\|\mathbf{n}_1\|} = \frac{|-27/2|}{\sqrt{94}} = \frac{27}{2\sqrt{94}} = \frac{27\sqrt{94}}{188}$$

**83.** The parametric equations of a line $L$ parallel to $\mathbf{v} = \langle a, b, c, \rangle$ and passing through the point $P(x_1, y_1, z_1)$ are

$$x = x_1 + at, y = y_1 + bt, z = z_1 + ct.$$

The symmetric equations are

$$\frac{x - x_1}{a} = \frac{y - y_1}{b} = \frac{z - z_1}{c}.$$

**69.** Writing the equation of the line in parametric form and substituting into the equation of the plane we have:

$$x = \frac{1}{2} + t, \ y = \frac{-3}{2} - t, \ z = -1 + 2t$$

$$2\left(\frac{1}{2} + t\right) - 2\left(\frac{-3}{2} - t\right) + (-1 + 2t) = 12, \ t = \frac{3}{2}$$

Substituting $t = 3/2$ into the parametric equations for the line we have the point of intersection $(2, -3, 2)$. The line does not lie in the plane.

**73.** Point: $Q(0, 0, 0)$

Plane: $2x + 3y + z - 12 = 0$

Normal to plane: $\mathbf{n} = \langle 2, 3, 1 \rangle$

Point in plane: $P(6, 0, 0)$

Vector $\overrightarrow{PQ} = \langle -6, 0 \ 0 \rangle$

$$D = \frac{|\overrightarrow{PQ} \cdot \mathbf{n}|}{\|\mathbf{n}\|} = \frac{|-12|}{\sqrt{14}} = \frac{6\sqrt{14}}{7}$$

**77.** The normal vectors to the planes are $\mathbf{n}_1 = \langle 1, -3, 4 \rangle$ and $\mathbf{n}_2 = \langle 1, -3, 4 \rangle$. Since $\mathbf{n}_1 = \mathbf{n}_2$, the planes are parallel. Choose a point in each plane.

$P = (10, 0, 0)$ is a point in $x - 3y + 4z = 10$.
$Q = (6, 0, 0)$ is a point in $x - 3y + 4z = 6$.

$$\overrightarrow{PQ} = \langle -4, 0, 0 \rangle, D = \frac{|\overrightarrow{PQ} \cdot \mathbf{n}_1|}{\|\mathbf{n}_1\|} = \frac{4}{\sqrt{26}} = \frac{2\sqrt{26}}{13}$$

**81.** $\mathbf{u} = \langle 4, 0, -1 \rangle$ is the direction vector for the line. $Q(1, 5, -2)$ is the given point, and $P(-2, 3, 1)$ is on the line. Hence, $\overrightarrow{PQ} = \langle 3, 2, -3 \rangle$ and

$$\overrightarrow{PQ} \times \mathbf{u} = \begin{vmatrix} \mathbf{i} & \mathbf{j} & \mathbf{k} \\ 3 & 2 & -3 \\ 4 & 0 & -1 \end{vmatrix} = \langle -2, -9, -8 \rangle$$

$$D = \frac{\|\overrightarrow{PQ} \times \mathbf{u}\|}{\|\mathbf{u}\|} = \frac{\sqrt{149}}{\sqrt{17}} = \frac{\sqrt{2533}}{17}$$

**85.** Solve the two linear equations representing the planes to find two points of intersection. Then find the line determined by the two points.

**87.** (a) Sphere

$(x - 3)^2 + (y + 2)^2 + (z - 5)^2 = 16$

$x^2 + y^2 + z^2 - 6x + 4y - 10z + 22 = 0$

(b) Parallel planes

$4x - 3y + z = 10 \pm 4\|\mathbf{n}\| = 10 \pm 4\sqrt{26}$

**89.** (a) $z = 28.7 - 1.83x - 1.09y$

| Year | 1980 | 1985 | 1990 | 1994 | 1995 | 1996 | 1997 |
|------|------|------|------|------|------|------|------|
| z (approx.) | 16.16 | 14.23 | 9.81 | 8.60 | 8.42 | 8.27 | 8.23 |

(b) An increase in $x$ or $y$ will cause a decrease in $z$. In fact, any increase in two variables will cause a decrease in the third.

(c)

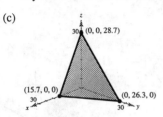

**91.** True

# Section 10.6    Surfaces in Space

**1.** Ellipsoid

Matches graph (c)

**3.** Hyperboloid of one sheet

Matches graph (f)

**5.** Elliptic paraboloid

Matches graph (d)

**7.** $z = 3$

Plane parallel to the $xy$-coordinate plane

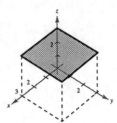

**9.** $y^2 + z^2 = 9$

The $x$-coordinate is missing so we have a cylindrical surface with rulings parallel to the $x$-axis. The generating curve is a circle.

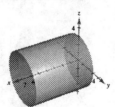

**11.** $y = x^2$

The $z$-coordinate is missing so we have a cylindrical surface with rulings parallel to the $z$-axis. The generating curve is a parabola.

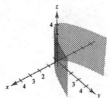

**13.** $4x^2 + y^2 = 4$

$$\frac{x^2}{1} + \frac{y^2}{4} = 1$$

The $z$-coordinate is missing so we have a cylindrical surface with rulings parallel to the $z$-axis. The generating curve is an ellipse.

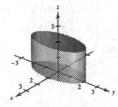

**15.** $z = \sin y$

The $x$-coordinate is missing so we have a cylindrical surface with rulings parallel to the $x$-axis. The generating curve is the sine curve.

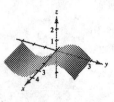

**17.** $x = x^2 + y^2$

(a) You are viewing the paraboloid from the $x$-axis: $(20, 0, 0)$

(b) You are viewing the paraboloid from above, but not on the $z$-axis: $(10, 10, 20)$

(c) You are viewing the paraboloid from the $z$-axis: $(0, 0, 20)$

(d) You are viewing the paraboloid from the $y$-axis: $(0, 20, 0)$

**19.** $\dfrac{x^2}{1} + \dfrac{y^2}{4} + \dfrac{z^2}{1} = 1$

Ellipsoid

$xy$-trace: $\dfrac{x^2}{1} + \dfrac{y^2}{4} = 1$ ellipse

$xz$-trace: $x^2 + z^2 = 1$ circle

$\dfrac{y^2}{4} + \dfrac{z^2}{1} = 1$ ellipse

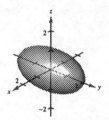

**21.** $16x^2 - y^2 + 16z^2 = 4$

$4x^2 - \dfrac{y^2}{4} + 4z^2 = 1$

Hyperboloid on one sheet

$xy$-trace: $4x^2 - \dfrac{y^2}{4} = 1$ hyperbola

$xz$-trace: $4(x^2 + z^2) = 1$ circle

$yz$-trace: $\dfrac{-y^2}{4} + 4z^2 = 1$ hyperbola

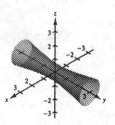

**23.** $x^2 - y + z^2 = 0$

Elliptic paraboloid

$xy$-trace: $y = x^2$

$xz$-trace: $x^2 + z^2 = 0$,

point $(0, 0, 0)$

$yz$-trace: $y = z^2$

$y = 1: x^2 + z^2 = 1$

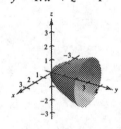

**25.** $x^2 - y^2 + z = 0$

Hyperbolic paraboloid

$xy$-trace: $y = \pm x$

$xz$-trace: $z = -x^2$

$yz$-trace: $z = y^2$

$y = \pm 1: z = 1 - x^2$

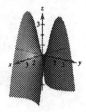

**27.** $z^2 = x^2 + \dfrac{y^2}{4}$

Elliptic Cone

$xy$-trace: point $(0, 0, 0)$

$xz$-trace: $z = \pm x$

$yz$-trace: $z = \dfrac{\pm 1}{2}y$

$z = \pm 1: x^2 + \dfrac{y^2}{4} = 1$

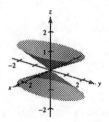

**29.**     $16x^2 + 9y^2 + 16z^2 - 32x - 36y + 36 = 0$

$16(x^2 - 2x + 1) + 9(y^2 - 4y + 4) + 16z^2 = -36 + 16 + 36$

$16(x - 1)^2 + 9(y - 2)^2 + 16z^2 = 16$

$\dfrac{(x - 1)^2}{1} + \dfrac{(y - 2)^2}{16/9} + \dfrac{z^2}{1} = 1$

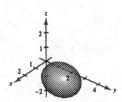

Ellipsoid with center $(1, 2, 0)$.

**31.** $z = 2 \sin x$

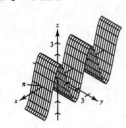

**33.** $z^2 = x^2 + 4y^2$

$z = \pm\sqrt{x^2 + 4y^2}$

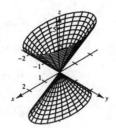

**35.** $x^2 + y^2 = \left(\dfrac{2}{z}\right)^2$

$y = \pm\sqrt{\dfrac{4}{z^2} - x^2}$

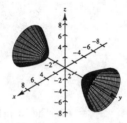

**37.** $z = 4 - \sqrt{|xy|}$

**39.** $4x^2 - y^2 + 4z^2 = -16$

$z = \pm\sqrt{\dfrac{y^2}{4} - x^2 - 4}$

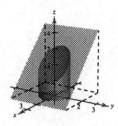

**41.** $z = 2\sqrt{x^2 + y^2}$

$z = 2$

$2\sqrt{x^2 + y^2} = 2$

$x^2 + y^2 = 1$

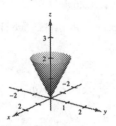

**43.** $x^2 + y^2 = 1$

$x + z = 2$

$z = 0$

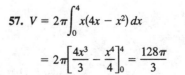

**45.** $x^2 + z^2 = [r(y)]^2$ and $z = r(y) = \pm 2\sqrt{y}$; therefore,

$x^2 + z^2 = 4y.$

**47.** $x^2 + y^2 = [r(z)]^2$ and $y = r(z) = \dfrac{z}{2}$; therefore,

$x^2 + y^2 = \dfrac{z^2}{4}, \; 4x^2 + 4y^2 = z^2.$

**49.** $y^2 + z^2 = [r(x)]^2$ and $y = r(x) = \dfrac{2}{x}$; therefore,

$y^2 + z^2 = \left(\dfrac{2}{x}\right)^2, \; y^2 + z^2 = \dfrac{4}{x^2}.$

**51.** $x^2 + y^2 - 2z = 0$

$x^2 + y^2 = \left(\sqrt{2z}\right)^2$

Equation of generating curve: $y = \sqrt{2z}$ or $x = \sqrt{2z}$

**53.** Let $C$ be a curve in a plane and let $L$ be a line not in a parallel plane. The set of all lines parallel to $L$ and intersecting $C$ is called a cylinder.

**55.** See pages 765 and 766.

**57.** $V = 2\pi \displaystyle\int_0^4 x(4x - x^2)\,dx$

$= 2\pi\left[\dfrac{4x^3}{3} - \dfrac{x^4}{4}\right]_0^4 = \dfrac{128\pi}{3}$

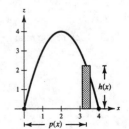

**59.** $z = \dfrac{x^2}{2} + \dfrac{y^2}{4}$

    (a) When $z = 2$ we have $2 = \dfrac{x^2}{2} + \dfrac{y^2}{4}$, or $1 = \dfrac{x^2}{4} + \dfrac{y^2}{8}$

    Major axis: $2\sqrt{8} = 4\sqrt{2}$

    Minor axis: $2\sqrt{4} = 4$

    $c^2 = a^2 - b^2, c^2 = 4, c = 2$

    Foci: $(0, \pm 2, 2)$

    (b) When $z = 8$ we have $8 = \dfrac{x^2}{2} + \dfrac{y^2}{4}$, or $1 = \dfrac{x^2}{16} + \dfrac{y^2}{32}$.

    Major axis: $2\sqrt{32} = 8\sqrt{2}$

    Minor axis: $2\sqrt{16} = 8$

    $c^2 = 32 - 16 = 16, c = 4$

    Foci: $(0, \pm 4, 8)$

**61.** If $(x, y, z)$ is on the surface, then

$$(y + 2)^2 = x^2 + (y - 2)^2 + z^2$$

$$y^2 + 4y + 4 = x^2 + y^2 - 4y + 4 + z^2$$

$$x^2 + z^2 = 8y$$

Elliptic paraboloid

Traces parallel to $xz$-plane are circles.

**63.** $\dfrac{x^2}{3963^2} + \dfrac{y^2}{3963^2} + \dfrac{z^2}{3942^2} = 1$

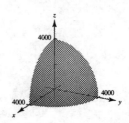

**65.** $z = \dfrac{y^2}{b^2} - \dfrac{x^2}{a^2}, z = bx + ay$

$$bx + ay = \dfrac{y^2}{b^2} - \dfrac{x^2}{a^2}$$

$$\dfrac{1}{a^2}\left(x^2 + a^2bx + \dfrac{a^4b^2}{4}\right) = \dfrac{1}{b^2}\left(y^2 - ab^2y + \dfrac{a^2b^4}{4}\right)$$

$$\dfrac{\left(x + \dfrac{a^2b}{2}\right)^2}{a^2} = \dfrac{\left(y - \dfrac{ab^2}{2}\right)^2}{b^2}$$

$$y = \pm\dfrac{b}{a}\left(x + \dfrac{a^2b}{2}\right) + \dfrac{ab^2}{2}$$

Letting $x = at$, you obtain the two intersecting lines
$x = at, y = -bt, z = 0$ and $x = at, y = bt + ab^2$
$z = 2abt + a^2b^2$.

**67.** The Klein bottle *does not* have both an "inside" and an "outside." It is formed by inserting the small open end through the side of the bottle and making it contiguous with the top of the bottle.

## Section 10.7   Cylindrical and Spherical Coordinates

**1.** $(5, 0, 2)$, cylindrical

$x = 5\cos 0 = 5$

$y = 5\sin 0 = 0$

$z = 2$

$(5, 0, 2)$, rectangular

**3.** $\left(2, \dfrac{\pi}{3}, 2\right)$, cylindrical

$x = 2\cos\dfrac{\pi}{3} = 1$

$y = 2\sin\dfrac{\pi}{3} = \sqrt{3}$

$z = 2$

$(1, \sqrt{3}, 2)$, rectangular

**5.** $\left(4, \dfrac{7\pi}{6}, 3\right)$, cylindrical

$x = 4\cos\dfrac{7\pi}{6} = -2\sqrt{3}$

$y = 4\sin\dfrac{7\pi}{6} = -2$

$z = 3$

$(-2\sqrt{3}, -2, 3)$, rectangular

**7.** $(0, 5, 1)$, rectangular

$r = \sqrt{(0)^2 + (5)^2} = 5$

$\theta = \arctan \dfrac{5}{0} = \dfrac{\pi}{2}$

$z = 1$

$\left(5, \dfrac{\pi}{2}, 1\right)$, cylindrical

**9.** $\left(1, \sqrt{3}, 4\right)$, rectangular

$r = \sqrt{1^2 + \left(\sqrt{3}\right)^2} = 2$

$\theta = \arctan\sqrt{3} = \dfrac{\pi}{3}$

$z = 4$

$\left(2, \dfrac{\pi}{3}, 4\right)$, cylindrical

**11.** $(2, -2, -4)$, rectangular

$r = \sqrt{2^2 + (-2)^2} = 2\sqrt{2}$

$\theta = \arctan(-1) = -\dfrac{\pi}{4}$

$z = -4$

$\left(2\sqrt{2}, \dfrac{-\pi}{4}, -4\right)$, cylindrical

**13.** $x^2 + y^2 + z^2 = 10$ rectangular equation

$\quad\quad r^2 + z^2 = 10$ cylindrical equation

**15.** $y = x^2$ $\quad\quad\quad\quad\quad$ rectangular equation

$r \sin \theta = (r \cos \theta)^2$

$\sin \theta = r \cos^2 \theta$

$r = \sec \theta \cdot \tan \theta$ cylindrical equation

**17.** $r = 2$

$\sqrt{x^2 + y^2} = 2$

$x^2 + y^2 = 4$

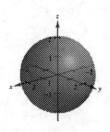

**19.** $\theta = \dfrac{\pi}{6}$

$\tan \dfrac{\pi}{6} = \dfrac{y}{x}$

$\dfrac{1}{\sqrt{3}} = \dfrac{y}{x}$

$x = \sqrt{3}\,y$

$x - \sqrt{3}\,y = 0$

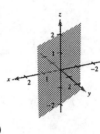

**21.** $r = 2 \sin \theta$

$r^2 = 2r \sin \theta$

$x^2 + y^2 = 2y$

$x^2 + y^2 - 2y = 0$

$x^2 + (y - 1)^2 = 1$

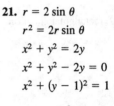

**23.** $r^2 + z^2 = 4$

$x^2 + y^2 + z^2 = 4$

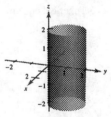

**25.** $(4, 0, 0)$, rectangular

$\rho = \sqrt{4^2 + 0^2 + 0^2} = 4$

$\theta = \arctan 0 = 0$

$\phi = \arccos 0 = \dfrac{\pi}{2}$

$\left(4, 0, \dfrac{\pi}{2}\right)$, spherical

**27.** $\left(-2, 2\sqrt{3}, 4\right)$, rectangular

$\rho = \sqrt{(-2)^2 + \left(2\sqrt{3}\right)^2 + 4^2} = 4\sqrt{2}$

$\theta = \arctan\left(-\sqrt{3}\right) = \dfrac{2\pi}{3}$

$\phi = \arccos \dfrac{1}{\sqrt{2}} = \dfrac{\pi}{4}$

$\left(4\sqrt{2}, \dfrac{2\pi}{3}, \dfrac{\pi}{4}\right)$, spherical

**29.** $\left(\sqrt{3}, 1, 2\sqrt{3}\right)$, rectangular

$\rho = \sqrt{3 + 1 + 12} = 4$

$\theta = \arctan \dfrac{1}{\sqrt{3}} = \dfrac{\pi}{6}$

$\phi = \arccos \dfrac{\sqrt{3}}{2} = \dfrac{\pi}{6}$

$\left(4, \dfrac{\pi}{6}, \dfrac{\pi}{6}\right)$, spherical

**31.** $\left(4, \dfrac{\pi}{6}, \dfrac{\pi}{4}\right)$, spherical

$x = 4 \sin \dfrac{\pi}{4} \cos \dfrac{\pi}{6} = \sqrt{6}$

$y = 4 \sin \dfrac{\pi}{4} \sin \dfrac{\pi}{6} = \sqrt{2}$

$z = 4 \cos \dfrac{\pi}{4} = 2\sqrt{2}$

$\left(\sqrt{6}, \sqrt{2}, 2\sqrt{2}\right)$, rectangular

**33.** $\left(12, \dfrac{-\pi}{4}, 0\right)$, spherical

$x = 12 \sin 0 \cos\left(\dfrac{-\pi}{4}\right) = 0$

$y = 12 \sin 0 \sin\left(\dfrac{-\pi}{4}\right) = 0$

$z = 12 \cos 0 = 12$

$(0, 0, 12)$, rectangular

**35.** $\left(5, \dfrac{\pi}{4}, \dfrac{3\pi}{4}\right)$, spherical

$x = 5 \sin \dfrac{3\pi}{4} \cos \dfrac{\pi}{4} = \dfrac{5}{2}$

$y = 5 \sin \dfrac{3\pi}{4} \sin \dfrac{\pi}{4} = \dfrac{5}{2}$

$z = 5 \cos \dfrac{3\pi}{4} = -\dfrac{5\sqrt{2}}{2}$

$\left(\dfrac{5}{2}, \dfrac{5}{2}, -\dfrac{5\sqrt{2}}{2}\right)$, rectangular

**37.** (a) Programs will vary.

(b) $(x, y, z) = (3, -4, 2)$

$(\rho, \theta, \phi) = (5.385, -0.927, 1.190)$

**39.** $x^2 + y^2 + z^2 = 36$ rectangular equation

$\rho^2 = 36$ spherical equation

**41.** $x^2 + y^2 = 9$ rectangular equation

$\rho^2 \sin^2 \phi \cos^2 \theta + \rho^2 \sin^2 \phi \sin^2 \theta = 9$

$\rho^2 \sin^2 \phi = 9$

$\rho \sin \phi = 3$

$\rho = 3 \csc \phi$ spherical equation

**43.** $\rho = 2$

$x^2 + y^2 + z^2 = 4$

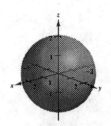

**45.** $\phi = \dfrac{\pi}{6}$

$\cos \phi = \dfrac{z}{\sqrt{x^2 + y^2 + z^2}}$

$\dfrac{\sqrt{3}}{2} = \dfrac{z}{\sqrt{x^2 + y^2 + z^2}}$

$\dfrac{3}{4} = \dfrac{z^2}{x^2 + y^2 + z^2}$

$3x^2 + 3y^2 - z^2 = 0$

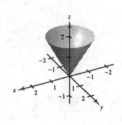

**47.** $\rho = 4 \cos \phi$

$\sqrt{x^2 + y^2 + z^2} = \dfrac{4z}{\sqrt{x^2 + y^2 + z^2}}$

$x^2 + y^2 + z^2 - 4z = 0$

$x^2 + y^2 + (z - 2)^2 = 4$

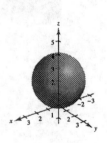

**49.** $\rho = \csc \phi$

$\rho \sin \phi = 1$

$\sqrt{x^2 + y^2} = 1$

$x^2 + y^2 = 1$

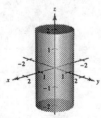

**51.** $\left(4, \dfrac{\pi}{4}, 0\right)$, cylindrical

$\rho = \sqrt{4^2 + 0^2} = 4$

$\theta = \dfrac{\pi}{4}$

$\phi = \arccos 0 = \dfrac{\pi}{2}$

$\left(4, \dfrac{\pi}{4}, \dfrac{\pi}{2}\right)$, spherical

**53.** $\left(4, \dfrac{\pi}{2}, 4\right)$, cylindrical

$\rho = \sqrt{4^2 + 4^2} = 4\sqrt{2}$

$\theta = \dfrac{\pi}{2}$

$\phi = \arccos\left(\dfrac{4}{4\sqrt{2}}\right) = \dfrac{\pi}{4}$

$\left(4\sqrt{2}, \dfrac{\pi}{2}, \dfrac{\pi}{4}\right)$, spherical

**55.** $\left(4, \dfrac{-\pi}{6}, 6\right)$, cylindrical

$\rho = \sqrt{4^2 + 6^2} = 2\sqrt{13}$

$\theta = \dfrac{-\pi}{6}$

$\phi = \arccos \dfrac{3}{\sqrt{13}}$

$\left(2\sqrt{13}, \dfrac{-\pi}{6}, \arccos \dfrac{3}{\sqrt{13}}\right)$,
spherical

**57.** $(12, \pi, 5)$, cylindrical

$\rho = \sqrt{12^2 + 5^2} = 13$

$\theta = \pi$

$\phi = \arccos \dfrac{5}{13}$

$\left(13, \pi, \arccos \dfrac{5}{13}\right)$, spherical

**59.** $\left(10, \dfrac{\pi}{6}, \dfrac{\pi}{2}\right)$, spherical

$r = 10 \sin \dfrac{\pi}{2} = 10$

$\theta = \dfrac{\pi}{6}$

$z = 10 \cos \dfrac{\pi}{2} = 0$

$\left(10, \dfrac{\pi}{6}, 0\right)$, cylindrical

**61.** $\left(36, \pi, \dfrac{\pi}{2}\right)$, spherical

$r = \rho \sin \phi = 36 \sin \dfrac{\pi}{2} = 36$

$\theta = \pi$

$z = \rho \cos \phi = 36 \cos \dfrac{\pi}{2} = 0$

$(36, \pi, 0)$, cylindrical

**63.** $\left(6, -\dfrac{\pi}{6}, \dfrac{\pi}{3}\right)$, spherical

$r = 6 \sin \dfrac{\pi}{3} = 3\sqrt{3}$

$\theta = -\dfrac{\pi}{6}$

$z = 6 \cos \dfrac{\pi}{3} = 3$

$\left(3\sqrt{3}, -\dfrac{\pi}{6}, 3\right)$, cylindrical

**65.** $\left(8, \dfrac{7\pi}{6}, \dfrac{\pi}{6}\right)$, spherical

$r = 8 \sin \dfrac{\pi}{6} = 4$

$\theta = \dfrac{7\pi}{6}$

$z = 8 \cos \dfrac{\pi}{6} = \dfrac{8\sqrt{3}}{2}$

$\left(4, \dfrac{7\pi}{6}, 4\sqrt{3}\right)$, cylindrical

| *Rectangular* | *Cylindrical* | *Spherical* |
|---|---|---|
| **67.** $(4, 6, 3)$ | $(7.211, 0.983, 3)$ | $(7.810, 0.983, 1.177)$ |
| **69.** $(4.698, 1.710, 8)$ | $\left(5, \dfrac{\pi}{9}, 8\right)$ | $(9.434, 0.349, 0.559)$ |
| **71.** $(-7.071, 12.247, 14.142)$ | $(14.142, 2.094, 14.142)$ | $\left(20, \dfrac{2\pi}{3}, \dfrac{\pi}{4}\right)$ |
| **73.** $(3, -2, 2)$ | $(3.606, -0.588, 2)$ | $(4.123, -0.588, 1.064)$ |
| **75.** $\left(\dfrac{5}{2}, \dfrac{4}{3}, \dfrac{-3}{2}\right)$ | $(2.833, 0.490, -1.5)$ | $(3.206, 0.490, 2.058)$ |
| **77.** $(-3.536, 3.536, -5)$ | $\left(5, \dfrac{3\pi}{4}, -5\right)$ | $(7.071, 2.356, 2.356)$ |
| **79.** $(2.804, -2.095, 6)$ | $(-3.5, 2.5, 6)$ | $(6.946, 5.642, 0.528)$ |

[Note: Use the cylindrical coordinates $(3.5, 5.642, 6)$]

**81.** $r = 5$

Cylinder

Matches graph (d)

**83.** $\rho = 5$

Sphere

Matches graph (c)

**85.** $r^2 = z, x^2 + y^2 = z$

Paraboloid

Matches graph (f)

**87.** Rectangular to cylindrical: $r^2 = x^2 + y^2$

$\tan \theta = \dfrac{y}{x}$

$z = z$

Cylindrical to rectangular: $x = r \cos \theta$

$y = r \sin \theta$

$z = z$

**89.** Rectangular to spherical: $\rho^2 = x^2 + y^2 + z^2$

$\tan \theta = \dfrac{y}{x}$

$\phi = \arccos\left(\dfrac{z}{\sqrt{x^2 + y^2 + z^2}}\right)$

Spherical to rectangular: $x = \rho \sin \phi \cos \theta$

$y = \rho \sin \phi \sin \theta$

$z = \rho \cos \phi$

**91.** $x^2 + y^2 + z^2 = 16$

    (a) $r^2 + z^2 = 16$

    (b) $\rho^2 = 16, \rho = 4$

**93.** $x^2 + y^2 + z^2 - 2z = 0$

    (a) $r^2 + z^2 - 2z = 0, r^2 + (z-1)^2 = 1$

    (b) $\rho^2 - 2\rho \cos \phi = 0, \rho(\rho - 2 \cos \phi) = 0,$

        $\rho = 2 \cos \phi$

**95.** $x^2 + y^2 = 4y$

    (a) $r^2 = 4r \sin \theta, \; r = 4 \sin \theta$

    (b) $\rho^2 \sin^2 \phi = 4\rho \sin \phi \sin \theta,$

        $\rho \sin \phi (\rho \sin \phi - 4 \sin \theta) = 0,$

        $\rho = \dfrac{4 \sin \theta}{\sin \phi}, \; \rho = 4 \sin \theta \csc \phi$

**97.** $x^2 - y^2 = 9$

    (a) $r^2 \cos^2 \theta - r^2 \sin^2 \theta = 9,$

        $r^2 = \dfrac{9}{\cos^2 \theta - \sin^2 \theta}$

    (b) $\rho^2 \sin^2 \phi \cos^2 \theta - \rho^2 \sin^2 \phi \sin^2 \theta = 9,$

        $\rho^2 \sin^2 \phi = \dfrac{9}{\cos^2 \theta - \sin^2 \theta},$

        $\rho^2 = \dfrac{9 \csc^2 \phi}{\cos^2 \theta - \sin^2 \theta}$

**99.** $0 \leq \theta \leq \dfrac{\pi}{2}$

    $0 \leq r \leq 2$

    $0 \leq z \leq 4$

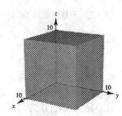

**101.** $0 \leq \theta \leq 2\pi$

    $0 \leq r \leq a$

    $r \leq z \leq a$

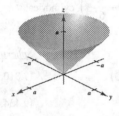

**103.** $0 \leq \theta \leq 2\pi$

    $0 \leq \phi \leq \dfrac{\pi}{6}$

    $0 \leq \rho \leq a \sec \phi$

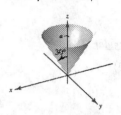

**105.** Rectangular

    $0 \leq x \leq 10$

    $0 \leq y \leq 10$

    $0 \leq z \leq 10$

**107.** Spherical

    $4 \leq \rho \leq 6$

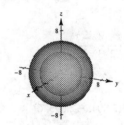

**109.** $z = \sin \theta, r = 1$

    $z = \dfrac{y}{r} = \dfrac{y}{1} = y$

The curve of intersection is the ellipse formed by the intersection of the plane $z = y$ and the cylinder $r = 1$.

## Review Exercises for Chapter 10

**1.** $P = (1, 2), \; Q = (4, 1), \; R = (5, 4)$

    (a) $\mathbf{u} = \overrightarrow{PQ} = \langle 3, -1 \rangle = 3\mathbf{i} - \mathbf{j},$

       $\mathbf{v} = \overrightarrow{PR} = \langle 4, 2 \rangle = 4\mathbf{i} + 2\mathbf{j}$

    (b) $\|\mathbf{v}\| = \sqrt{4^2 + 2^2} = 2\sqrt{5}$

    (c) $2\mathbf{u} + \mathbf{v} = \langle 6, -2 \rangle + \langle 4, 2 \rangle = \langle 10, 0 \rangle = 10\mathbf{i}$

**3.** $\mathbf{v} = \|\mathbf{v}\| \cos \theta \, \mathbf{i} + \|\mathbf{v}\| \sin \theta \, \mathbf{j} = 8 \cos 120° \, \mathbf{i} + 8 \sin 120° \, \mathbf{j}$

          $= -4\mathbf{i} + 4\sqrt{3}\mathbf{j}$

**5.** $120 \cos \theta = 100$

$$\theta = \arccos\left(\frac{5}{6}\right)$$

$$\tan \theta = \frac{2}{y} \implies y = \frac{2}{\tan \theta}$$

$$y = \frac{2}{\tan[\arccos(5/6)]} = \frac{2}{\sqrt{11}/5} = \frac{10}{\sqrt{11}} \approx 3.015 \text{ ft}$$

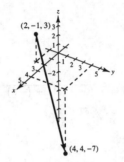

**7.** $z = 0$, $y = 4$, $x = -5$: $(-5, 4, 0)$

**9.** Looking down from the positive $x$-axis towards the $yz$-plane, the point is either in the first quadrant ($y > 0$, $z > 0$) or in the third quadrant ($y < 0$, $z < 0$). The $x$-coordinate can be any number.

**11.** $(x - 3)^2 + (y + 2)^2 + (z - 6)^2 = \left(\dfrac{15}{2}\right)^2$

**13.** $(x^2 - 4x + 4) + (y^2 - 6y + 9) + z^2 = -4 + 4 + 9$

$(x - 2)^2 + (y - 3)^2 + z^2 = 9$

Center: $(2, 3, 0)$

Radius: $3$

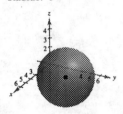

**15.** $\mathbf{v} = \langle 4 - 2, 4 + 1, -7 - 3 \rangle = \langle 2, 5, -10 \rangle$

**17.** $\mathbf{v} = \langle -1 - 3, 6 - 4, 9 + 1 \rangle = \langle -4, 2, 10 \rangle$

$\mathbf{w} = \langle 5 - 3, 3 - 4, -6 + 1 \rangle = \langle 2, -1, -5 \rangle$

Since $-2\mathbf{w} = \mathbf{v}$, the points lie in a straight line.

**19.** Unit vector: $\dfrac{\mathbf{u}}{\|\mathbf{u}\|} = \dfrac{\langle 2, 3, 5 \rangle}{\sqrt{38}} = \left\langle \dfrac{2}{\sqrt{38}}, \dfrac{3}{\sqrt{38}}, \dfrac{5}{\sqrt{38}} \right\rangle$

**21.** $P = (5, 0, 0)$, $Q = (4, 4, 0)$, $R = (2, 0, 6)$

(a) $\mathbf{u} = \overrightarrow{PQ} = \langle -1, 4, 0 \rangle = -\mathbf{i} + 4\mathbf{j}$,

$\mathbf{v} = \overrightarrow{PR} = \langle -3, 0, 6 \rangle = -3\mathbf{i} + 6\mathbf{k}$

(b) $\mathbf{u} \cdot \mathbf{v} = (-1)(-3) + 4(0) + 0(6) = 3$

(c) $\mathbf{v} \cdot \mathbf{v} = 9 + 36 = 45$

**23.** $\mathbf{u} = \langle 7, -2, 3 \rangle$, $\mathbf{v} = \langle -1, 4, 5 \rangle$

Since $\mathbf{u} \cdot \mathbf{v} = 0$, the vectors are orthogonal.

**25.** $\mathbf{u} = 5\left(\cos\dfrac{3\pi}{4}\mathbf{i} + \sin\dfrac{3\pi}{4}\mathbf{j}\right) = \dfrac{5\sqrt{2}}{2}[-\mathbf{i} + \mathbf{j}]$

$\mathbf{v} = 2\left(\cos\dfrac{2\pi}{3}\mathbf{i} + \sin\dfrac{2\pi}{3}\mathbf{j}\right) = -\mathbf{i} + \sqrt{3}\mathbf{j}$

$\mathbf{u} \cdot \mathbf{v} = \dfrac{5\sqrt{2}}{2}\left(1 + \sqrt{3}\right)$

$\|\mathbf{u}\| = 5$

$\|\mathbf{v}\| = 2$

$\cos \theta = \dfrac{|\mathbf{u} \cdot \mathbf{v}|}{\|\mathbf{u}\| \, \|\mathbf{v}\|} = \dfrac{\left(5\sqrt{2}/2\right)\left(1 + \sqrt{3}\right)}{5(2)} = \dfrac{\sqrt{2} + \sqrt{6}}{4}$

$\theta = \arccos\dfrac{\sqrt{2} + \sqrt{6}}{4} = 15°$

**27.** $\mathbf{u} = \langle 10, -5, 15 \rangle$, $\mathbf{v} = \langle -2, 1, -3 \rangle$

$\mathbf{u} = -5\mathbf{v} \implies \mathbf{u}$ is parallel to $\mathbf{v}$ and in the opposite direction.

$\theta = \pi$

**29.** There are many correct answers. For example: $v = \pm \langle 6, -5, 0 \rangle$.

In Exercises 31–39, $\mathbf{u} = \langle 3, -2, 1 \rangle$, $\mathbf{v} = \langle 2, -4, -3 \rangle$, $\mathbf{w} = \langle -1, 2, 2 \rangle$.

**31.** $\mathbf{u} \cdot \mathbf{u} = 3(3) + (-2)(-2) + (1)(1)$

$\qquad = 14 = \left( \sqrt{14} \right)^2 = \|\mathbf{u}\|^2$

**33.** $\text{proj}_{\mathbf{u}}\mathbf{w} = \left( \dfrac{\mathbf{u} \cdot \mathbf{w}}{\|\mathbf{u}\|^2} \right) \mathbf{u}$

$\qquad = -\dfrac{5}{14} \langle 3, -2, 1 \rangle$

$\qquad = \left\langle -\dfrac{15}{14}, \dfrac{10}{14}, -\dfrac{5}{14} \right\rangle$

$\qquad = \left\langle -\dfrac{15}{14}, \dfrac{5}{7}, -\dfrac{5}{14} \right\rangle$

**35.** $\mathbf{n} = \mathbf{v} \times \mathbf{w} = \begin{vmatrix} \mathbf{i} & \mathbf{j} & \mathbf{k} \\ 2 & -4 & -3 \\ -1 & 2 & 2 \end{vmatrix} = -2\mathbf{i} - \mathbf{j}$

$\|\mathbf{n}\| = \sqrt{5}$

$\dfrac{\mathbf{n}}{\|\mathbf{n}\|} = \dfrac{1}{\sqrt{5}}(-2\mathbf{i} - \mathbf{j})$

**37.** $V = |\mathbf{u} \cdot (\mathbf{v} \times \mathbf{w})|$

$\qquad = |\langle 3, -2, 1 \rangle \cdot \langle -2, -1, 0 \rangle| = |-4| = 4$

**39.** Area parallelogram $= \|\mathbf{u} \times \mathbf{v}\| = \sqrt{10^2 + 11^2 + (-8)^2}$   (See Exercises 36, 38)

$\qquad = \sqrt{285}$

**41.** $\mathbf{F} = c(\cos 20°\mathbf{j} + \sin 20°\mathbf{k})$

$\overrightarrow{PQ} = 2\mathbf{k}$

$\overrightarrow{PQ} \times \mathbf{F} = \begin{vmatrix} \mathbf{i} & \mathbf{j} & \mathbf{k} \\ 0 & 0 & 2 \\ 0 & c\cos 20° & c\sin 20° \end{vmatrix} = -2c\cos 20°\mathbf{i}$

$200 = \|\overrightarrow{PQ} \times \mathbf{F}\| = 2c\cos 20°$

$c = \dfrac{100}{\cos 20°}$

$\mathbf{F} = \dfrac{100}{\cos 20°}(\cos 20°\mathbf{j} + \sin 20°\mathbf{k}) = 100(\mathbf{j} + \tan 20°\mathbf{k})$

$\|\mathbf{F}\| = 100\sqrt{1 + \tan^2 20°} = 100\sec 20° \approx 106.4 \text{ lb}$

**43.** $\mathbf{v} = \mathbf{j}$

(a) $x = 1$, $y = 2 + t$, $z = 3$

(b) None

**45.** $3x - 3y - 7z = -4$, $x - y + 2z = 3$

Solving simultaneously, we have $z = 1$. Substituting $z = 1$ into the second equation we have $y = x - 1$. Substituting for $x$ in this equation we obtain two points on the line of intersection, $(0, -1, 1)$, $(1, 0, 1)$. The direction vector of the line of intersection is $\mathbf{v} = \mathbf{i} + \mathbf{j}$.

(a) $x = t$, $y = -1 + t$, $z = 1$

(b) $x = y + 1$, $z = 1$

**47.** The two lines are parallel as they have the same direction numbers, $-2, 1, 1$. Therefore, a vector parallel to the plane is $\mathbf{v} = -2\mathbf{i} + \mathbf{j} + \mathbf{k}$. A point on the first line is $(1, 0, -1)$ and a point on the second line is $(-1, 1, 2)$. The vector $\mathbf{u} = 2\mathbf{i} - \mathbf{j} - 3\mathbf{k}$ connecting these two points is also parallel to the plane. Therefore, a normal to the plane is

$$\mathbf{v} \times \mathbf{u} = \begin{vmatrix} \mathbf{i} & \mathbf{j} & \mathbf{k} \\ -2 & 1 & 1 \\ 2 & -1 & -3 \end{vmatrix}$$

$$= -2\mathbf{i} - 4\mathbf{j} = -2(\mathbf{i} + 2\mathbf{j}).$$

Equation of the plane: $(x - 1) + 2y = 0$

$$x + 2y = 1$$

**49.** $Q = (1, 0, 2)$

$$2x - 3y + 6z = 6$$

A point $P$ on the plane is $(3, 0, 0)$.

$$\overrightarrow{PQ} = \langle -2, 0, 2 \rangle$$

$$\mathbf{n} = \langle 2, -3, 6 \rangle$$

$$D = \frac{|\overrightarrow{PQ} \cdot \mathbf{n}|}{\|\mathbf{n}\|} = \frac{8}{7}$$

**51.** $Q(3, -2, 4)$ point

$P(5, 0, 0)$ point on plane

$\mathbf{n} = \langle 2, -5, 1 \rangle$ normal to plane

$$\overrightarrow{PQ} = \langle -2, -2, 4 \rangle$$

$$D = \frac{|\overrightarrow{PQ} \cdot \mathbf{n}|}{\|\mathbf{n}\|} = \frac{10}{\sqrt{30}} = \frac{\sqrt{30}}{3}$$

**53.** $x + 2y + 3z = 6$

Plane

Intercepts: $(6, 0, 0), \ (0, 3, 0), \ (0, 0, 2)$

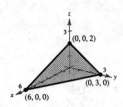

**55.** $y = \frac{1}{2}z$

Plane with rulings parallel to the $x$-axis

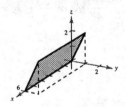

**57.** $\dfrac{x^2}{16} + \dfrac{y^2}{9} + z^2 = 1$

Ellipsoid

$xy$-trace: $\dfrac{x^2}{16} + \dfrac{y^2}{9} = 1$

$xz$-trace: $\dfrac{x^2}{16} + z^2 = 1$

$yz$-trace: $\dfrac{y^2}{9} + z^2 = 1$

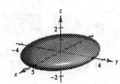

**59.** $\dfrac{x^2}{16} - \dfrac{y^2}{9} + z^2 = -1$

Hyperboloid of two sheets

$xy$-trace: $\dfrac{y^2}{4} - \dfrac{x^2}{16} = 1$

$xz$-trace: None

$yz$-trace: $\dfrac{y^2}{9} - z^2 = 1$

**61. (a)**

$$x^2 + y^2 = [r(z)]^2$$
$$= \left[\sqrt{2(z-1)}\right]^2$$
$$x^2 + y^2 - 2z + 2 = 0$$

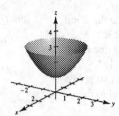

**(b)** $V = 2\pi \int_0^2 x\left[3 - \left(\frac{1}{2}x^2 + 1\right)\right] dx$

$$= 2\pi \int_0^2 \left(2x - \frac{1}{2}x^3\right) dx$$

$$= 2\pi\left[x^2 - \frac{x^4}{8}\right]_0^2$$

$$= 4\pi \approx 12.6 \text{ cm}^3$$

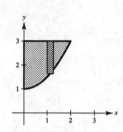

**(c)** $V = 2\pi \int_{1/2}^2 x\left[3 - \left(\frac{1}{2}x^2 + 1\right)\right] dx$

$$= 2\pi \int_{1/2}^2 \left(2x - \frac{1}{2}x^3\right) dx$$

$$= 2\pi\left[x^2 - \frac{x^4}{8}\right]_{1/2}^2$$

$$= 4\pi - \frac{31\pi}{64} = \frac{225\pi}{64} \approx 11.04 \text{ cm}^3$$

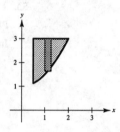

**63.** $\left(-2\sqrt{2}, 2\sqrt{2}, 2\right)$, rectangular

**(a)** $r = \sqrt{\left(-2\sqrt{2}\right)^2 + \left(2\sqrt{2}\right)^2} = 4$, $\theta = \arctan(-1) = \frac{3\pi}{4}$, $z = 2$, $\left(4, \frac{3\pi}{4}, 2\right)$, cylindrical

**(b)** $\rho = \sqrt{\left(-2\sqrt{2}\right)^2 + \left(2\sqrt{2}\right)^2 + (2)^2} = 2\sqrt{5}$, $\theta = \frac{3\pi}{4}$, $\phi = \arccos\frac{2}{2\sqrt{5}} = \arccos\frac{1}{\sqrt{5}}$, $\left(2\sqrt{5}, \frac{3\pi}{4}, \arccos\frac{\sqrt{5}}{5}\right)$, spherical

**65.** $\left(100, -\frac{\pi}{6}, 50\right)$, cylindrical

$\rho = \sqrt{100^2 + 50^2} = 50\sqrt{5}$

$\theta = -\frac{\pi}{6}$

$\phi = \arccos\left(\frac{50}{50\sqrt{5}}\right) = \arccos\left(\frac{1}{\sqrt{5}}\right) \approx 63.4°$

$\left(50\sqrt{5}, -\frac{\pi}{6}, 63.4°\right)$, spherical

**67.** $\left(25, -\frac{\pi}{4}, \frac{3\pi}{4}\right)$, spherical

$r^2 = \left(25\sin\left(\frac{3\pi}{4}\right)\right)^2 \Rightarrow r = 25\frac{\sqrt{2}}{2}$

$\theta = -\frac{\pi}{4}$

$z = \rho\cos\phi = 25\cos\frac{3\pi}{4} = -25\frac{\sqrt{2}}{2}$

$\left(25\frac{\sqrt{2}}{2}, -\frac{\pi}{4}, -\frac{25\sqrt{2}}{2}\right)$, cylindrical

**69.** $x^2 - y^2 = 2z$

**(a)** Cylindrical: $r^2\cos^2\theta - r^2\sin^2\theta = 2z$, $r^2\cos 2\theta = 2z$

**(b)** Spherical: $\rho^2\sin^2\phi\cos^2\theta - \rho^2\sin^2\phi\sin^2\theta = 2\rho\cos\phi$, $\rho\sin^2\phi\cos 2\theta - 2\cos\phi = 0$, $\rho = 2\sec 2\theta\cos\phi\csc^2\phi$

# Problem Solving for Chapter 10

**1.**
$$\mathbf{a} + \mathbf{b} + \mathbf{c} = \mathbf{0}$$
$$\mathbf{b} \times (\mathbf{a} + \mathbf{b} + \mathbf{c}) = \mathbf{0}$$
$$(\mathbf{b} \times \mathbf{a}) + (\mathbf{b} \times \mathbf{c}) = \mathbf{0}$$
$$\|\mathbf{a} \times \mathbf{b}\| = \|\mathbf{b} \times \mathbf{c}\|$$
$$\|\mathbf{b} \times \mathbf{c}\| = \|\mathbf{b}\| \, \|\mathbf{c}\| \sin A$$
$$\|\mathbf{a} \times \mathbf{b}\| = \|\mathbf{a}\| \, \|\mathbf{b}\| \sin C$$

Then,

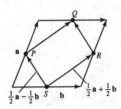

$$\frac{\sin A}{\|\mathbf{a}\|} = \frac{\|\mathbf{b} \times \mathbf{c}\|}{\|\mathbf{a}\| \, \|\mathbf{b}\| \, \|\mathbf{c}\|}$$
$$= \frac{\|\mathbf{a} \times \mathbf{b}\|}{\|\mathbf{a}\| \, \|\mathbf{b}\| \, \|\mathbf{c}\|}$$
$$= \frac{\sin C}{\|\mathbf{c}\|}.$$

The other case, $\dfrac{\sin A}{\|\mathbf{a}\|} = \dfrac{\sin B}{\|\mathbf{b}\|}$ is similar.

**3.** Label the figure as indicated.

From the figure, you see that

$$\overrightarrow{SP} = \frac{1}{2}\mathbf{a} - \frac{1}{2}\mathbf{b} = \overrightarrow{RQ} \text{ and}$$

$$\overrightarrow{SR} = \frac{1}{2}\mathbf{a} + \frac{1}{2}\mathbf{b} = \overrightarrow{PQ}.$$

Since $\overrightarrow{SP} = \overrightarrow{RQ}$ and $\overrightarrow{SR} = \overrightarrow{PQ}$, $PSRQ$ is a parallelogram.

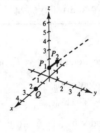

**5.** (a) $\mathbf{u} = \langle 0, 1, 1 \rangle$ direction vector of line determined by $P_1$ and $P_2$.

$$D = \frac{\|\overrightarrow{P_1Q} \times \mathbf{u}\|}{\|\mathbf{u}\|}$$

$$= \frac{\|\langle 2, 0, -1 \rangle \times \langle 0, 1, 1 \rangle\|}{\sqrt{2}}$$

$$= \frac{\|\langle 1, -2, 2 \rangle\|}{\sqrt{2}} = \frac{3}{\sqrt{2}} = \frac{3\sqrt{2}}{2}$$

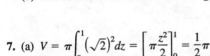

(b) The shortest distance to the line **segment** is $\|P_1Q\| = \|\langle 2, 0, -1 \rangle\| = \sqrt{5}$.

**7.** (a) $V = \pi \displaystyle\int_0^1 \left(\sqrt{2}\right)^2 dz = \left[\pi \frac{z^2}{2}\right]_0^1 = \frac{1}{2}\pi$

Note: $\dfrac{1}{2}(\text{base})(\text{altitude}) = \dfrac{1}{2}\pi(1) = \dfrac{1}{2}\pi$

(b) $\dfrac{x^2}{a^2} + \dfrac{y^2}{b^2} = z$: (slice at $z = c$)

$$\frac{x^2}{\left(\sqrt{c}a\right)^2} + \frac{y^2}{\left(\sqrt{c}b\right)^2} = 1$$

At $z = c$, figure is ellipse of area

$$\pi\left(\sqrt{c}a\right)\left(\sqrt{c}b\right) = \pi abc.$$

$$V = \int_0^k \pi abc \cdot dc = \left[\frac{\pi abc^2}{2}\right]_0^k = \frac{\pi abk^2}{2}$$

(c) $V = \dfrac{1}{2}(\pi abk)k = \dfrac{1}{2}(\text{base})(\text{height})$

**9.** (a) $\rho = 2 \sin \phi$

Torus

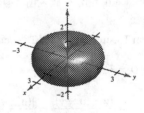

(b) $\rho = 2 \cos \phi$

Sphere

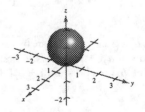

**11.** From Exercise 64, Section 10.4, $(\mathbf{u} \times \mathbf{v}) \times (\mathbf{w} \times \mathbf{z}) = [(\mathbf{u} \times \mathbf{v}) \cdot \mathbf{z}]\mathbf{w} - [(\mathbf{u} \times \mathbf{v}) \cdot \mathbf{w}]\mathbf{z}$.

**13.** (a) $\mathbf{u} = \|\mathbf{u}\|(\cos 0\,\mathbf{i} + \sin 0\,\mathbf{j}) = \|\mathbf{u}\|\mathbf{i}$

Downward force $\mathbf{w} = -\mathbf{j}$

$\mathbf{T} = \|\mathbf{T}\|(\cos(90° + \theta)\mathbf{i} + \sin(90° + \theta)\mathbf{j})$

$\qquad = \|\mathbf{T}\|(-\sin\theta\,\mathbf{i} + \cos\theta\,\mathbf{j})$

$\mathbf{0} = \mathbf{u} + \mathbf{w} + \mathbf{T} = \|\mathbf{u}\|\mathbf{i} - \mathbf{j} + \|\mathbf{T}\|(-\sin\theta\,\mathbf{i} + \cos\theta\,\mathbf{j})$

$\qquad \|\mathbf{u}\| = \sin\theta\,\|\mathbf{T}\|$

$\qquad 1 = \cos\theta\,\|\mathbf{T}\|$

If $\theta = 30°$, $\|\mathbf{u}\| = (1/2)\|\mathbf{T}\|$ and $1 = \left(\sqrt{3}/2\right)\|\mathbf{T}\|$

$\qquad \Longrightarrow \|\mathbf{T}\| = \dfrac{2}{\sqrt{3}} \approx 1.1547 \text{ lb}$

and

$\qquad \|\mathbf{u}\| = \dfrac{1}{2}\left(\dfrac{2}{\sqrt{3}}\right) \approx 0.5774 \text{ lb}$

(b) From part (a), $\|\mathbf{u}\| = \tan\theta$ and $\|\mathbf{T}\| = \sec\theta$.

Domain: $0 \le \theta \le 90°$

(c)

| $\theta$ | 0° | 10° | 20° | 30° | 40° | 50° | 60° |
|---|---|---|---|---|---|---|---|
| T | 1 | 1.0154 | 1.0642 | 1.1547 | 1.3054 | 1.5557 | 2 |
| $\|\mathbf{u}\|$ | 0 | 0.1763 | 0.3640 | 0.5774 | 0.8391 | 1.1918 | 1.7321 |

(d)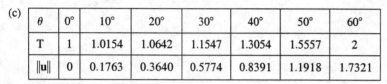

(e) Both are increasing functions.

(f) $\displaystyle\lim_{\theta \to \pi/2^-} T = \infty$ and $\displaystyle\lim_{\theta \to \pi/2^-} \|\mathbf{u}\| = \infty$.

**15.** Let $\theta = \alpha - \beta$, the angle between $\mathbf{u}$ and $\mathbf{v}$. Then

$\sin(\alpha - \beta) = \dfrac{\|\mathbf{u} \times \mathbf{v}\|}{\|\mathbf{u}\|\,\|\mathbf{v}\|} = \dfrac{\|\mathbf{v} \times \mathbf{u}\|}{\|\mathbf{u}\|\,\|\mathbf{v}\|}$.

For $\mathbf{u} = \langle \cos\alpha, \sin\alpha, 0 \rangle$ and $\mathbf{v} = \langle \cos\beta, \sin\beta, 0 \rangle$, $\|\mathbf{u}\| = \|\mathbf{v}\| = 1$ and

$\mathbf{v} \times \mathbf{u} = \begin{vmatrix} \mathbf{i} & \mathbf{j} & \mathbf{k} \\ \cos\beta & \sin\beta & 0 \\ \cos\alpha & \sin\alpha & 0 \end{vmatrix} = (\sin\alpha\cos\beta - \cos\alpha\sin\beta)\mathbf{k}$.

Thus, $\sin(\alpha - \beta) = \|\mathbf{v} \times \mathbf{u}\| = \sin\alpha\cos\beta - \cos\alpha\sin\beta$.

**17.** From Theorem 10.13 and Theorem 10.7 (6) we have

$D = \dfrac{|\overrightarrow{PQ} \cdot \mathbf{n}|}{\|\mathbf{n}\|}$

$\quad = \dfrac{|\mathbf{w} \cdot (\mathbf{u} \times \mathbf{v})|}{\|\mathbf{u} \times \mathbf{v}\|} = \dfrac{|(\mathbf{u} \times \mathbf{v}) \cdot \mathbf{w}|}{\|\mathbf{u} \times \mathbf{v}\|} = \dfrac{|\mathbf{u} \cdot (\mathbf{v} \times \mathbf{w})|}{\|\mathbf{u} \times \mathbf{v}\|}$.

**19.** $a_1, b_1, c_1$, and $a_2, b_2, c_2$ are two sets of direction numbers for the same line. The line is parallel to both $\mathbf{u} = a_1\mathbf{i} + b_1\mathbf{j} + c_1\mathbf{k}$ and $\mathbf{v} = a_2\mathbf{i} + b_2\mathbf{j} + c_2\mathbf{k}$. Therefore, $\mathbf{u}$ and $\mathbf{v}$ are parallel, and there exists a scalar $d$ such that $\mathbf{u} = d\mathbf{v}$, $a_1\mathbf{i} + b_1\mathbf{j} + c_1\mathbf{k} = d(a_2\mathbf{i} + b_2\mathbf{j} + c_2\mathbf{k})$, $a_1 = a_2d$, $b_1 = b_2d$, $c_1 = c_2d$.

# P A R T   I I

# C H A P T E R   6
## Applications of Integration

---

# C H A P T E R  6
## Applications of Integration

### Section 6.1    Area of a Region Between Two Curves

Solutions to Even-Numbered Exercises

**2.** $A = \displaystyle\int_{-2}^{2} \left[(2x + 5) - (x^2 + 2x + 1)\right] dx = \int_{-2}^{2} (-x^2 + 4)\, dx$

**4.** $A = \displaystyle\int_{0}^{1} (x^2 - x^3)\, dx$

**6.** $A = 2\displaystyle\int_{0}^{1} \left[(x - 1)^3 - (x - 1)\right] dx$

**8.** $\displaystyle\int_{-1}^{1} \left[(1 - x^2) - (x^2 - 1)\right] dx$

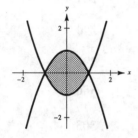

**10.** $\displaystyle\int_{2}^{3} \left[\left(\frac{x^3}{3} - x\right) - \frac{x}{3}\right] dx$

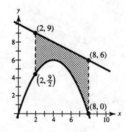

**12.** $\displaystyle\int_{-\pi/4}^{\pi/4} (\sec^2 x - \cos x)\, dx$

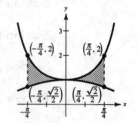

**14.** $f(x) = 2 - \frac{1}{2}x$

$g(x) = 2 - \sqrt{x}$

$A \approx 1$

Matches (a)

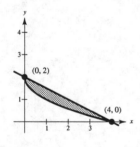

**16.** $A = \displaystyle\int_{2}^{8} \left[\left(10 - \frac{1}{2}x\right) - \left(-\frac{3}{8}x(x - 8)\right)\right] dx$

$= \displaystyle\int_{2}^{8} \left(\frac{3}{8}x^2 - \frac{7}{2}x + 10\right) dx$

$= \left[\frac{x^3}{8} - \frac{7x^2}{4} + 10x\right]_{2}^{8}$

$= (64 - 112 + 80) - (1 - 7 + 20) = 18$

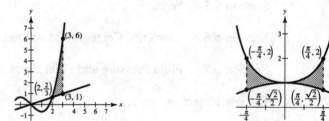

**18.** The points of intersection are given by

$$-x^2 + 4x + 1 = x + 1$$

$$-x^2 + 3x = 0$$

$$x^2 = 3x \text{ when } x = 0, 3$$

$$A = \int_0^3 [(-x^2 + 4x + 1) - (x + 1)] \, dx$$

$$= \int_0^3 (-x^2 + 3x) \, dx$$

$$= \left[ -\frac{x^3}{3} + \frac{3x^2}{2} \right]_0^3$$

$$= -9 + \frac{27}{2} = \frac{9}{2}$$

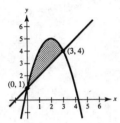

**20.** The points of intersection are given by:

$$-x^2 + 4x + 2 = x + 2$$

$$x(3 - x) = 0 \text{ when } x = 0, 3$$

$$A = \int_0^3 [f(x) - g(x)] \, dx$$

$$= \int_0^3 [(-x^2 + 4x + 2) - (x + 2)] \, dx$$

$$= \int_0^3 (-x^2 + 3x) \, dx = \left[ \frac{-x^3}{3} + \frac{3}{2}x^2 \right]_0^3 = \frac{9}{2}$$

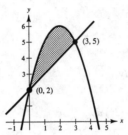

**22.** $A = \int_1^5 \left( \frac{1}{x^2} - 0 \right) dx = \left[ -\frac{1}{x} \right]_1^5 = \frac{4}{5}$

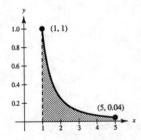

**24.** The points of intersection are given by

$$\sqrt[3]{x - 1} = x - 1$$

$$x - 1 = (x - 1)^3 = x^3 - 3x^2 + 3x - 1$$

$$x^3 - 3x^2 + 2x = 0$$

$$x(x^2 - 3x + 2) = 0$$

$$x(x - 2)(x - 1) = 0 \implies x = 0, 1, 2$$

$$A = 2 \int_0^1 [(x - 1) - \sqrt[3]{x - 1}] \, dx$$

$$= 2 \left[ \frac{x^2}{2} - x - \frac{3}{4}(x - 1)^{4/3} \right]_0^1$$

$$= 2 \left[ \left( \frac{1}{2} - 1 - 0 \right) - \left( -\frac{3}{4} \right) \right] = \frac{1}{2}$$

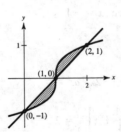

**26.** The points of intersection are given by:

$$2y - y^2 = -y$$

$$y(y - 3) = 0 \quad \text{when} \quad y = 0, 3$$

$$A = \int_0^3 [f(y) - g(y)] \, dy$$

$$= \int_0^3 [(2y - y^2) - (-y)] \, dy$$

$$= \int_0^3 (3y - y^2) \, dy = \left[\frac{3}{2}y^2 - \frac{1}{3}y^3\right]_0^3 = \frac{9}{2}$$

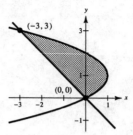

**28.** $A = \int_0^3 [f(y) - g(y)] \, dy$

$$= \int_0^3 \left[\frac{y}{\sqrt{16 - y^2}} - 0\right] dy$$

$$= -\frac{1}{2} \int_0^3 (16 - y^2)^{-1/2}(-2y) \, dy$$

$$= \left[-\sqrt{16 - y^2}\right]_0^3 = 4 - \sqrt{7} \approx 1.354$$

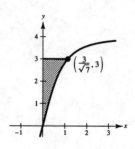

**30.** $A = \int_0^1 \left(4 - \frac{4}{2 - x}\right) dx$

$$= \left[4x + 4 \ln |2 - x|\right]_0^1$$

$$= 4 - 4 \ln 2$$

$$\approx 1.227$$

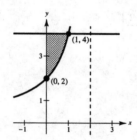

**32.** The point of intersection is given by:

$$x^3 - 2x + 1 = -2x$$

$$x^3 + 1 = 0 \quad \text{when} \quad x = -1$$

$$A = \int_{-1}^1 [f(x) - g(x)] \, dx$$

$$= \int_{-1}^1 [(x^3 - 2x + 1) - (-2x)] \, dx$$

$$= \int_{-1}^1 (x^3 + 1) \, dx = \left[\frac{x^4}{4} + x\right]_{-1}^1 = 2$$

Numerical Approximation: 2.0

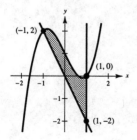

**34.** The points of intersection are given by:

$$x^4 - 2x^2 = 2x^2$$

$$x^2(x^2 - 4) = 0 \quad \text{when} \quad x = 0, \pm 2$$

$$A = 2 \int_0^2 [2x^2 - (x^4 - 2x^2)] \, dx$$

$$= 2 \int_0^2 (4x^2 - x^4) \, dx$$

$$= 2 \left[\frac{4x^3}{3} - \frac{x^5}{5}\right]_0^2 = \frac{128}{15}$$

Numerical Approximation: 8.533

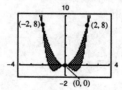

**36.** $f(x) = x^4 - 4x^2$, $g(x) = x^3 - 4x$

The points of intersection are given by:

$$x^4 - 4x^2 = x^3 - 4x$$

$$x^4 - x^3 - 4x^2 + 4x = 0$$

$$x(x-1)(x+2)(x-2) = 0 \quad \text{when} \quad x = -2, 0, 1, 2$$

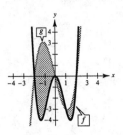

$$A = \int_{-2}^{0} [(x^3 - 4x) - (x^4 - 4x^2)]dx + \int_{0}^{1} [(x^4 - 4x^2) - (x^3 - 4x)]dx + \int_{1}^{2} [(x^3 - 4x) - (x^4 - 4x^2)]dx$$

$$= \frac{248}{30} + \frac{37}{60} + \frac{53}{60} = \frac{293}{30}$$

Numerical Approximation: $8.267 + 0.617 + 0.883 \approx 9.767$

**38.** $A = \int_{0}^{3} \left[ \frac{6x}{x^2 + 1} - 0 \right] dx$

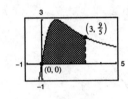

$$= \left[ 3 \ln(x^2 + 1) \right]_{0}^{3}$$

$$= 3 \ln 10$$

$$\approx 6.908$$

Numerical Approximation: 6.908

**40.** $A = \int_{0}^{4} x \sqrt{\frac{4-x}{4+x}} \, dx \approx 3.434$

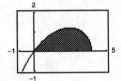

**42.** $A = \int_{-\pi/2}^{\pi/6} (\cos 2x - \sin x) \, dx$

$$= \left[ \frac{1}{2} \sin 2x + \cos x \right]_{-\pi/2}^{\pi/6}$$

$$= \left( \frac{\sqrt{3}}{4} + \frac{\sqrt{3}}{2} \right) - (0) = \frac{3\sqrt{3}}{4} \approx 1.299$$

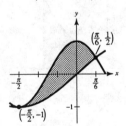

**44.** $A = \int_{0}^{1} \left[ \left( \sqrt{2} - 4 \right)x + 4 - \sec \frac{\pi x}{4} \tan \frac{\pi x}{4} \right] dx$

$$= \left[ \frac{\sqrt{2} - 4}{2} x^2 + 4x - \frac{4}{\pi} \sec \frac{\pi x}{4} \right]_{0}^{1}$$

$$= \left( \frac{\sqrt{2} - 4}{2} + 4 - \frac{4}{\pi} \sqrt{2} \right) - \left( -\frac{4}{\pi} \right)$$

$$= \frac{\sqrt{2}}{2} + 2 + \frac{4}{\pi} \left( 1 - \sqrt{2} \right) \approx 2.1797$$

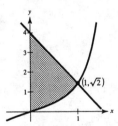

**46.** From the graph we see that $f$ and $g$ intersect twice at $x = 0$ and $x = 1$.

$$A = \int_{0}^{1} [g(x) - f(x)] \, dx$$

$$= \int_{0}^{1} [(2x + 1) - 3^x] \, dx$$

$$= \left[ x^2 + x - \frac{1}{\ln 3}(3^x) \right]_{0}^{1}$$

$$= 2 \left( 1 - \frac{1}{\ln 3} \right) \approx 0.180$$

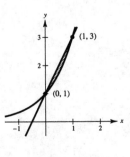

**48.** $A = \int_{0}^{\pi} [(2 \sin x + \cos 2x) - 0] \, dx$

$$= \left[ -2 \cos x + \frac{1}{2} \sin 2x \right]_{0}^{\pi} = 4$$

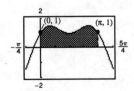

**50.** $A = \int_1^5 \left[ \frac{4 \ln x}{x} - 0 \right] dx$

$= \left[ 2(\ln x)^2 \right]_1^5 = 2(\ln 5)^2 \approx 5.181$

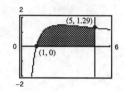

**52.** (a) $y = \sqrt{x}\, e^x$, $y = 0$, $x = 0$, $x = 1$

(b) $A = \int_0^1 \sqrt{x}\, e^x \, dx.$

No, it cannot be evaluated by hand.

(c) 1.2556

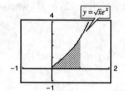

**54.** $F(x) = \int_0^x \left( \frac{1}{2} t^2 + 2 \right) dt = \left[ \frac{1}{6} t^3 + 2t \right]_0^x = \frac{x^3}{6} + 2x$

(a) $F(0) = 0$

(b) $F(4) = \frac{4^3}{6} + 2(4) = \frac{56}{3}$

(c) $F(6) = 36 + 12 = 48$

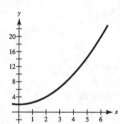

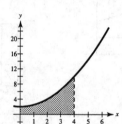

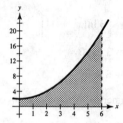

**56.** $F(y) = \int_{-1}^y 4e^{x/2} \, dx = \left[ 8e^{x/2} \right]_{-1}^y = 8e^{y/2} - 8e^{-1/2}$

(a) $F(-1) = 0$

(b) $F(0) = 8 - 8e^{-1/2} \approx 3.1478$

(c) $F(4) = 8e^2 - 8e^{-1/2} \approx 54.2602$

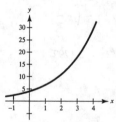

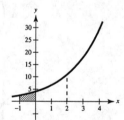

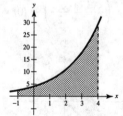

**58.** $A = \int_2^4 \left[ \left( \frac{9}{2} x - 12 \right) - (x - 5) \right] dx + \int_4^6 \left[ \left( -\frac{5}{2} x + 16 \right) - (x - 5) \right] dx$

$= \int_2^4 \left( \frac{7}{2} x - 7 \right) dx + \int_4^6 \left( -\frac{7}{2} x + 21 \right) dx$

$= \left[ \frac{7}{4} x^2 - 7x \right]_2^4 + \left[ -\frac{7}{4} x^2 + 21x \right]_4^6 = 7 + 7 = 14$

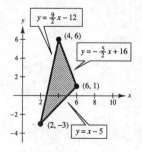

**60.** $f(x) = \dfrac{1}{x^2 + 1}$

$f'(x) = -\dfrac{2x}{(x^2 + 1)^2}$

At $\left(1, \dfrac{1}{2}\right)$, $f'(1) = -\dfrac{1}{2}$.

Tangent line:

$$y - \dfrac{1}{2} = -\dfrac{1}{2}(x - 1) \quad \text{or} \quad y = -\dfrac{1}{2}x + 1$$

The tangent line intersects $f(x) = \dfrac{1}{x^2 + 1}$ at $x = 0$.

$$A = \int_0^1 \left[ \dfrac{1}{x^2 + 1} - \left(-\dfrac{1}{2}x + 1\right) \right] dx = \left[ \arctan x + \dfrac{x^2}{4} - x \right]_0^1 = \dfrac{\pi - 3}{4} \approx 0.0354$$

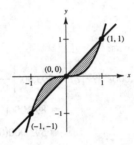

**62.** Answers will vary. See page 417.

**64.** $x^3 \geq x$ on $[-1, 0]$

$x^3 \leq x$ on $[0, 1]$

Both functions symmetric to origin

$$\int_{-1}^0 (x^3 - x)\, dx = -\int_0^1 (x^3 - x)\, dx.$$

Thus, $\displaystyle\int_{-1}^1 (x^3 - x)\, dx = 0$.

$$A = 2\int_0^1 (x - x^3)\, dx = 2\left[ \dfrac{x^2}{2} - \dfrac{x^4}{4} \right]_0^1 = \dfrac{1}{2}$$

**66.** Proposal 2 is better, since the cummulative deficit (the area under the curve) is less.

**68.** $A = 2\displaystyle\int_0^9 (9 - x)\, dx = 2\left[ 9x - \dfrac{x^2}{2} \right]_0^9 = 81$

$$2\int_0^{9-b} [(9 - x) - b]\, dx = \dfrac{81}{2}$$

$$2\int_0^{9-b} [(9 - b) - x]\, dx = \dfrac{81}{2}$$

$$2\left[ (9 - b)x - \dfrac{x^2}{2} \right]_0^{9-b} = \dfrac{81}{2}$$

$$(9 - b)(9 - b) = \dfrac{81}{2}$$

$$9 - b = \dfrac{9}{\sqrt{2}}$$

$$b = 9 - \dfrac{9}{\sqrt{2}} \approx 2.636$$

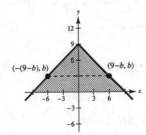

**70.** $\displaystyle\lim_{\|\Delta\|\to 0} \sum_{i=1}^{n} (4 - x_i^2)\,\Delta x$

where $x_i = -2 + \dfrac{4i}{n}$ and $\Delta x = \dfrac{4}{n}$ is the same as

$$\int_{-2}^{2} (4 - x^2)\,dx = \left[4x - \frac{x^3}{3}\right]_{-2}^{2} = \frac{32}{3}.$$

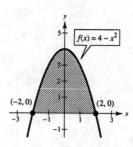

**72.** $\displaystyle\int_{0}^{5} \left[(7.21 + 0.26t + 0.02t^2) - (7.21 + 0.1t + 0.01t^2)\right] dt = \int_{0}^{5} (0.01t^2 + 0.16t)\,dt$

$$= \left[\frac{0.01t^3}{3} + \frac{0.16t^2}{2}\right]_{0}^{5}$$

$$= \frac{29}{12}\ \text{billion} \approx \$2.417\ \text{billion}$$

**74.** $5\% :\ P_1 = 893{,}000\,e^{(0.05)t}$

$3\frac{1}{2}\%:\ P_2 = 893{,}000\,e^{(0.035)t}$

Difference in profits over 5 years:

$$\int_{0}^{5} \left[893{,}000e^{0.05t} - 893{,}000e^{0.035t}\right] dt = 893{,}000\left[\frac{e^{0.05t}}{0.05} - \frac{e^{0.035t}}{0.035}\right]_{0}^{5}$$

$$\approx 893{,}000[(25.6805 - 34.0356) - (20 - 28.5714)]$$

$$\approx 893{,}000(0.2163) \approx \$193{,}156$$

**Note:** Using a graphing utility you obtain $193{,}183.

**76.** The curves intersect at the point where the slope of $y_2$ equals that of $y_1$, 1.

$$y_2 = 0.08x^2 + k \implies y_2' = 0.16x = 1 \implies x = \frac{1}{.16} = 6.25$$

(a) The value of $k$ is given by

$$y_1 = y_2$$
$$6.25 = (0.08)(6.25)^2 + k$$
$$k = 3.125.$$

(b) Area $= 2\displaystyle\int_{0}^{6.25} (y_2 - y_1)\,dx$

$$= 2\int_{0}^{6.25} (0.08x^2 + 3.125 - x)\,dx$$

$$= 2\left[\frac{0.08x^3}{3} + 3.125x - \frac{x^2}{2}\right]_{0}^{6.25}$$

$$= 2(6.510417) \approx 13.02083$$

**78.** (a) $A \approx 6.031 - 2\left[\pi\left(\dfrac{1}{16}\right)^2\right] - 2\left[\pi\left(\dfrac{1}{8}\right)^2\right] \approx 5.908$

(b) $V = 2A \approx 2(5.908) \approx 11.816\ \text{m}^3$

(c) $5000V \approx 5000(11.816) = 59{,}082\ \text{pounds}$

**80.** True

# Section 6.2    Volume: The Disk Method

**2.** $V = \pi \int_0^2 (4 - x^2)^2 \, dx = \pi \int_0^2 (x^4 - 8x^2 + 16) \, dx = \pi \left[ \dfrac{x^5}{5} - \dfrac{8x^3}{3} + 16x \right]_0^2 = \dfrac{256\pi}{15}$

**4.** $V = \pi \int_0^3 \left( \sqrt{9 - x^2} \right)^2 dx = \pi \int_0^3 (9 - x^2) \, dx$

$\qquad = \pi \left[ 9x - \dfrac{x^3}{3} \right]_0^3 = 18\pi$

**6.** $2 = 4 - \dfrac{x^2}{4}$

$\quad 8 = 16 - x^2$

$\quad x^2 = 8$

$\quad x = \pm 2\sqrt{2}$

$V = \pi \int_{-2\sqrt{2}}^{2\sqrt{2}} \left[ \left( 4 - \dfrac{x^2}{4} \right)^2 - (2)^2 \right] dx$

$\quad = 2\pi \int_0^{2\sqrt{2}} \left[ \dfrac{x^4}{16} - 2x^2 + 12 \right] dx$

$\quad = 2\pi \left[ \dfrac{x^5}{80} - \dfrac{2x^3}{3} + 12x \right]_0^{2\sqrt{2}}$

$\quad = 2\pi \left[ \dfrac{128\sqrt{2}}{80} - \dfrac{32\sqrt{2}}{3} + 24\sqrt{2} \right]$

$\quad = \dfrac{448\sqrt{2}}{15} \pi \approx 132.69$

**8.** $y = \sqrt{16 - x^2} \implies x = \sqrt{16 - y^2}$

$V = \pi \int_0^4 \left( \sqrt{16 - y^2} \right)^2 dy = \pi \int_0^4 (16 - y^2) \, dy$

$\quad = \pi \left[ 16y - \dfrac{y^3}{3} \right]_0^4 = \dfrac{128\pi}{3}$

**10.** $V = \pi \int_1^4 (-y^2 + 4y)^2 \, dy = \pi \int_1^4 (y^4 - 8y^3 + 16y^2) \, dy$

$\quad = \pi \left[ \dfrac{y^5}{5} - 2y^4 + \dfrac{16y^3}{3} \right]_1^4$

$\quad = \dfrac{459\pi}{15} = \dfrac{153\pi}{5}$

**12.** $y = 2x^2$, $y = 0$, $x = 2$

(a) $R(y) = 2$, $r(y) = \sqrt{y/2}$

$V = \pi \int_0^8 \left( 4 - \dfrac{y}{2} \right) dy = \pi \left[ 4y - \dfrac{y^2}{4} \right]_0^8 = 16\pi$

(b) $R(x) = 2x^2$, $r(x) = 0$

$V = \pi \int_0^2 4x^4 \, dx = \pi \left[ \dfrac{4x^5}{5} \right]_0^2 = \dfrac{128\pi}{5}$

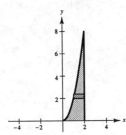

(c) $R(x) = 8$, $r(x) = 8 - 2x^2$

$V = \pi \int_0^2 [64 - (64 - 32x^2 + 4x^4)] \, dx$

$\quad = \pi \int_0^2 (32x^2 - 4x^4) \, dx = 4\pi \int_0^2 (8x^2 - x^4) \, dx$

$\quad = 4\pi \left[ \dfrac{8}{3}x^3 - \dfrac{1}{5}x^5 \right]_0^2 = \dfrac{896\pi}{15}$

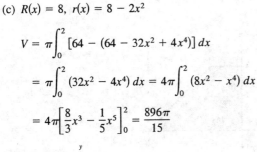

(d) $R(y) = 2 - \sqrt{y/2}$, $r(y) = 0$

$V = \pi \int_0^8 \left( 2 - \sqrt{\dfrac{y}{2}} \right)^2 dy$

$\quad = \pi \int_0^8 \left( 4 - 4\sqrt{\dfrac{y}{2}} + \dfrac{y}{2} \right) dy$

$\quad = \pi \left[ 4y - \dfrac{4\sqrt{2}}{3} y^{3/2} + \dfrac{y^2}{4} \right]_0^8 = \dfrac{16\pi}{3}$

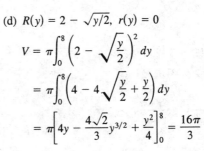

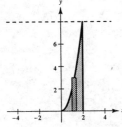

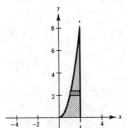

**14.** $y = 6 - 2x - x^2$, $y = x + 6$ intersect at $(-3, 3)$ and $(0, 6)$.

(a) $R(x) = 6 - 2x - x^2$, $r(x) = x + 6$

$$V = \pi \int_{-3}^{0} [(6 - 2x - x^2)^2 - (x + 6)^2] \, dx$$

$$= \pi \int_{-3}^{0} (x^4 + 4x^3 - 9x^2 - 36x) \, dx$$

$$= \pi \left[ \frac{1}{5}x^5 + x^4 - 3x^3 - 18x^2 \right]_{-3}^{0} = \frac{243\pi}{5}$$

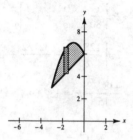

(b) $R(x) = (6 - 2x - x^2) - 3$, $r(x) = (x + 6) - 3$

$$V = \pi \int_{-3}^{0} [(3 - 2x - x^2)^2 - (x + 3)^2] \, dx$$

$$= \pi \int_{-3}^{0} (x^4 + 4x^3 - 3x^2 - 18x) \, dx$$

$$= \pi \left[ \frac{1}{5}x^5 + x^4 - x^3 - 9x^2 \right]_{-3}^{0} = \frac{108\pi}{5}$$

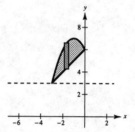

**16.** $R(x) = 4 - \dfrac{x^3}{2}$, $r(x) = 0$

$$V = \pi \int_{0}^{2} \left( 4 - \frac{x^3}{2} \right)^2 \, dx$$

$$= \pi \int_{0}^{2} \left[ 16 - 4x^3 + \frac{x^6}{4} \right] \, dx$$

$$= \pi \left[ 16x - x^4 + \frac{x^7}{28} \right]_{0}^{2}$$

$$= \pi \left[ 32 - 16 + \frac{128}{28} \right] = \frac{144}{7}\pi$$

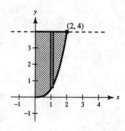

**18.** $R(x) = 4$, $r(x) = 4 - \sec x$

$$V = \pi \int_{0}^{\pi/3} [(4)^2 - (4 - \sec x)^2] \, dx$$

$$= \pi \int_{0}^{\pi/3} (8 \sec x - \sec^2 x) \, dx$$

$$= \pi \left[ 8 \ln|\sec x + \tan x| - \tan x \right]_{0}^{\pi/3}$$

$$= \pi \left[ \left( 8 \ln|2 + \sqrt{3}| - \sqrt{3} \right) - \left( 8 \ln|1 + 0| - 0 \right) \right]$$

$$= \pi \left[ 8 \ln(2 + \sqrt{3}) - \sqrt{3} \right] \approx 27.66$$

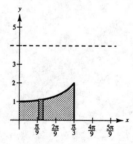

**20.** $R(y) = 6$, $r(y) = 6 - (6 - y) = y$

$$V = \pi \int_{0}^{4} [(6)^2 - (y)^2] \, dy$$

$$= \pi \left[ 36y - \frac{y^3}{3} \right]_{0}^{4} = \frac{368\pi}{3}$$

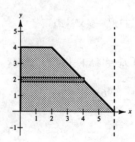

**22.** $R(y) = 6 - \dfrac{6}{y}$, $r(y) = 0$

$$V = \pi \int_2^6 \left(6 - \frac{6}{y}\right)^2 dy$$

$$= 36\pi \int_2^6 \left(1 - \frac{2}{y} + \frac{1}{y^2}\right) dy$$

$$= 36\pi \left[y - 2\ln|y| - \frac{1}{y}\right]_2^6$$

$$= 36\pi \left[\left(\frac{35}{6} - 2\ln 6\right) - \left(\frac{3}{2} - 2\ln 2\right)\right]$$

$$= 36\pi \left(\frac{13}{3} + 2\ln\frac{1}{3}\right) = 12\pi(13 - 6\ln 3) \approx 241.59$$

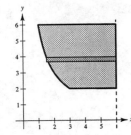

**24.** $R(x) = x\sqrt{4 - x^2}$, $r(x) = 0$

$$V = 2\pi \int_0^2 \left[x\sqrt{4 - x^2}\right]^2 dx$$

$$= 2\pi \int_0^2 (4x^2 - x^4) dx$$

$$= 2\pi \left[\frac{4x^3}{3} - \frac{x^5}{5}\right]_0^2$$

$$= \frac{128\pi}{15}$$

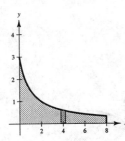

**26.** $R(x) = \dfrac{3}{x + 1}$, $r(x) = 0$

$$V = \pi \int_0^8 \left(\frac{3}{x + 1}\right)^2 dx$$

$$= 9\pi \int_0^8 (x + 1)^{-2} dx$$

$$= 9\pi \left[-\frac{1}{x + 1}\right]_0^8 = 8\pi$$

**28.** $R(x) = e^{x/2}$, $r(x) = 0$

$$V = \pi \int_0^4 (e^{x/2})^2 dx$$

$$= \pi \int_0^4 e^x dx$$

$$= \left[\pi e^x\right]_0^4$$

$$= \pi(e^4 - 1) \approx 168.38$$

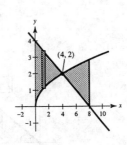

**30.** $V = \pi \int_0^4 \left[\left(4 - \frac{1}{2}x\right)^2 - (\sqrt{x})^2\right] dx + \pi \int_4^8 \left[(\sqrt{x})^2 - \left(4 - \frac{1}{2}x\right)^2\right] dx$

$$= \pi \int_0^4 \left(\frac{x^2}{4} - 5x + 16\right) dx + \pi \int_4^8 \left(-\frac{x^2}{4} + 5x - 16\right) dx$$

$$= \pi \left[\frac{x^3}{12} - \frac{5x^2}{2} + 16x\right]_0^4 + \pi \left[-\frac{x^3}{12} + \frac{5x^2}{2} - 16x\right]_4^8$$

$$= \frac{88}{3}\pi + \frac{56}{3}\pi = 48\pi$$

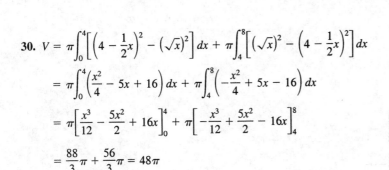

**32.** $y = 9 - x^2$, $y = 0$, $x = 2$, $x = 3$

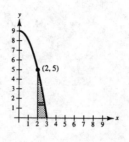

$$x = \sqrt{9 - y}$$

$$V = \pi \int_0^5 \left[ \left( \sqrt{9 - y} \right)^2 - 2^2 \right] dy$$

$$= \pi \int_0^5 (5 - y) \, dy$$

$$= \pi \left[ 5y - \frac{y^2}{2} \right]_0^5$$

$$= \pi \left( 25 - \frac{25}{2} \right) = \frac{25\pi}{2}$$

**34.** $V = \pi \int_0^{\pi/2} [\cos x]^2 \, dx \approx 2.4674$

**36.** $V = \pi \int_1^3 [\ln x]^2 \, dx \approx 3.2332$

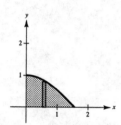

**38.** $V = \pi \int_0^5 [2 \arctan (0.2x)]^2 \, dx \approx 15.4115$

**40.** $A \approx \frac{3}{4}$

Matches (b)

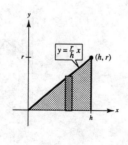

**42.** $V = \int_a^b A(x) \, dx$   or   $V = \int_c^d A(y) \, dy$

**44.** (a)

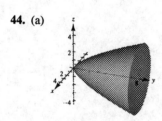

(b)

(c)

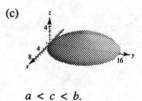

$a < c < b.$

**46.** $R(x) = \dfrac{r}{h} x$,   $r(x) = 0$

$$V = \pi \int_0^h \frac{r^2}{h^2} x^2 \, dx$$

$$= \left[ \frac{r^2 \pi}{3h^2} x^3 \right]_0^h$$

$$= \frac{r^2 \pi}{3h^2} h^3 = \frac{1}{3} \pi r^2 h$$

**48.** $x = \sqrt{r^2 - y^2}$, $R(y) = \sqrt{r^2 - y^2}$, $r(y) = 0$

$$V = \pi \int_h^r \left(\sqrt{r^2 - y^2}\right)^2 dy$$

$$= \pi \int_h^r (r^2 - y^2)\, dy$$

$$= \pi \left[ r^2 y - \frac{y^3}{3} \right]_h^r$$

$$= \pi \left[ \left( r^3 - \frac{r^3}{3} \right) - \left( r^2 h - \frac{h^3}{3} \right) \right]$$

$$= \pi \left( \frac{2r^3}{3} - r^2 h + \frac{h^3}{3} \right)$$

$$= \frac{\pi}{3} (2r^3 - 3r^2 h + h^3)$$

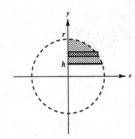

**50. (a)** $V = \pi \int_0^4 \left(\sqrt{x}\right)^2 dx = \pi \int_0^4 x\, dx = \left[ \frac{\pi x^2}{2} \right]_0^4 = 8\pi$

Let $0 < c < 4$ and set

$$\pi \int_0^c x\, dx = \left[ \frac{\pi x^2}{2} \right]_0^c = \frac{\pi c^2}{2} = 4\pi.$$

$$c^2 = 8$$

$$c = \sqrt{8} = 2\sqrt{2}$$

Thus, when $x = 2\sqrt{2}$, the solid is divided into two parts of equal volume.

**(b)** Set $\pi \int_0^c x\, dx = \frac{8\pi}{3}$ (one third of the volume). Then

$$\frac{\pi c^2}{2} = \frac{8\pi}{3},\ c^2 = \frac{16}{3},\ c = \frac{4}{\sqrt{3}} = \frac{4\sqrt{3}}{3}.$$

To find the other value, set $\pi \int_0^d x\, dx = \frac{16\pi}{3}$ (two thirds of the volume). Then

$$\frac{\pi d^2}{2} = \frac{16\pi}{3},\ d^2 = \frac{32}{3},\ d = \frac{\sqrt{32}}{\sqrt{3}} = \frac{4\sqrt{6}}{3}.$$

The $x$-values that divide the solid into three parts of equal volume are $x = \left(4\sqrt{3}\right)/3$ and $x = \left(4\sqrt{6}\right)/3$.

**52.** $y = \begin{cases} \sqrt{0.1x^3 - 2.2x^2 + 10.9x + 22.2}, & 0 \le x \le 11.5 \\ 2.95, & 11.5 < x \le 15 \end{cases}$

$$V = \pi \int_0^{11.5} \left(\sqrt{0.1x^3 - 2.2x^2 + 10.9x + 22.2}\right)^2 dx + \pi \int_{11.5}^{15} 2.95^2\, dx$$

$$= \pi \left[ \frac{0.1x^4}{4} - \frac{2.2x^3}{3} + \frac{10.9x^2}{2} + 22.2x \right]_0^{11.5} + \pi \left[ 2.95^2 x \right]_{11.5}^{15}$$

$$\approx 1031.9016 \text{ cubic centimeters}$$

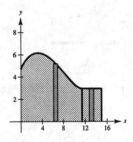

**54. (a)** First find where $y = b$ intersects the parabola:

$$b = 4 - \frac{x^2}{4}$$

$$x^2 = 16 - 4b = 4(4 - b)$$

$$x = 2\sqrt{4 - b}$$

$$V = \int_0^{2\sqrt{4-b}} \pi \left[ 4 - \frac{x^2}{4} - b \right]^2 dx + \int_{2\sqrt{4-b}}^4 \pi \left[ b - 4 + \frac{x^2}{4} \right]^2 dx$$

$$= \int_0^4 \pi \left[ 4 - \frac{x^2}{4} - b \right]^2 dx$$

$$= \pi \int_0^4 \left[ \frac{x^4}{16} - 2x^2 + \frac{bx^2}{2} + b^2 - 8b + 16 \right] dx$$

$$= \pi \left[ \frac{x^5}{80} - \frac{2x^3}{3} + \frac{bx^3}{6} + b^2 x - 8bx + 16x \right]_0^4$$

$$= \pi \left[ \frac{64}{5} - \frac{128}{3} + \frac{32}{3}b + 4b^2 - 32b + 64 \right] = \pi \left[ 4b^2 - \frac{64}{3}b + \frac{512}{15} \right]$$

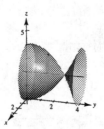

**—CONTINUED—**

**54.** —CONTINUED—

(b) graph of $V(b) = \pi\left[4b^2 - \dfrac{64}{3}b + \dfrac{512}{15}\right]$

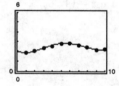

Minimum Volume is 17.87 for $b = 2.67$

(c) $V'(b) = \pi\left[8b - \dfrac{64}{3}\right] = 0 \Rightarrow b = \dfrac{64/3}{8} = \dfrac{8}{3} = 2\dfrac{2}{3}$

$V''(b) = 8\pi > 0 \Rightarrow b = \dfrac{8}{3}$ is a relative minimum.

**56.** (a) $V = \displaystyle\int_0^{10} \pi[f(x)]^2\, dx$

Simpson's Rule: $b - a = 10 - 0 = 10, \quad n = 10$

$V \approx \dfrac{\pi}{3}[(2.1)^2 + 4(1.9)^2 + 2(2.1)^2 + 4(2.35)^2 + 2(2.6)^2 + 4(2.85)^2 + 2(2.9)^2 + 4(2.7)^2 + 2(2.45)^2 + 4(2.2)^2 + (2.3)^2]$

$\approx \dfrac{\pi}{3}[178.405] \approx 186.83 \text{ cm}^3$

(b) $f(x) = 0.00249x^4 - 0.0529x^3 + 0.3314x^2 - 0.4999x + 2.112$

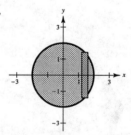

(c) $V \approx \displaystyle\int_0^{10} \pi f(x)^2\, dx \approx 186.35 \text{ cm}^3$

**58.** $V = \dfrac{1}{2}(10)(2)(3) = 30 \text{ m}^3$

**60.**

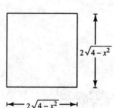

Base of Cross Section $= 2\sqrt{4 - x^2}$

(a) $A(x) = b^2 = \left(2\sqrt{4 - x^2}\right)^2$

$V = \displaystyle\int_{-2}^{2} 4(4 - x^2)\, dx$

$= 4\left[4x - \dfrac{x^3}{3}\right]_{-2}^{2} = \dfrac{128}{3}$

(b) $A(x) = \dfrac{1}{2}bh = \dfrac{1}{2}\left(2\sqrt{4 - x^2}\right)\left(\sqrt{3}\sqrt{4 - x^2}\right)$

$= \sqrt{3}\,(4 - x^2)$

$V = \sqrt{3}\displaystyle\int_{-2}^{2}(4 - x^2)\, dx$

$= \sqrt{3}\left[4x - \dfrac{x^3}{3}\right]_{-2}^{2} = \dfrac{32\sqrt{3}}{3}$

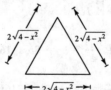

—CONTINUED—

**60.** —CONTINUED—

(c) $A(x) = \dfrac{1}{2}\pi r^2$

$$= \dfrac{\pi}{2}\left(\sqrt{4 - x^2}\right)^2 = \dfrac{\pi}{2}(4 - x^2)$$

$$V = \dfrac{\pi}{2}\int_{-2}^{2}(4 - x^2)\,dx = \dfrac{\pi}{2}\left[4x - \dfrac{x^3}{3}\right]_{-2}^{2} = \dfrac{16\pi}{3}$$

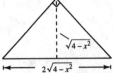

(d) $A(x) = \dfrac{1}{2}bh$

$$= \dfrac{1}{2}\left(2\sqrt{4 - x^2}\right)\left(\sqrt{4 - x^2}\right) = 4 - x^2$$

$$V = \int_{-2}^{2}(4 - x^2)\,dx = \left[4x - \dfrac{x^3}{3}\right]_{-2}^{2} = \dfrac{32}{3}$$

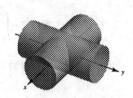

**62.** The cross sections are squares. By symmetry, we can set up an integral for an eighth of the volume and multiply by 8.

$$A(y) = b^2 = \left(\sqrt{r^2 - y^2}\right)^2$$

$$V = 8\int_{0}^{r}(r^2 - y^2)\,dy$$

$$= 8\left[r^2y - \dfrac{1}{3}y^3\right]_{0}^{r}$$

$$= \dfrac{16}{3}r^3$$

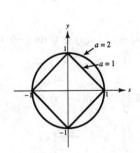

**64.** $V = \pi\displaystyle\int_{-\sqrt{R^2-r^2}}^{\sqrt{R^2-r^2}}\left[\left(\sqrt{R^2 - x^2}\right)^2 - r^2\right]dx$

$$= 2\pi\int_{0}^{\sqrt{R^2-r^2}}(R^2 - r^2 - x^2)\,dx$$

$$= 2\pi\left[(R^2 - r^2)x - \dfrac{x^3}{3}\right]_{0}^{\sqrt{R^2-r^2}}$$

$$= 2\pi\left[(R^2 - r^2)^{3/2} - \dfrac{(R^2 - r^2)^{3/2}}{3}\right]$$

$$= \dfrac{4}{3}\pi(R^2 - r^2)^{3/2}$$

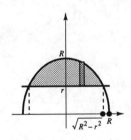

**66.** (a) When $a = 1$: $|x| + |y| = 1$ represents a square.

When $a = 2$: $|x|^2 + |y|^2 = 1$ represents a circle.

(b) $|y| = (1 - |x|^a)^{1/a}$

$$A = 2\int_{-1}^{1}(1 - |x|^a)^{1/a}\,dx = 4\int_{0}^{1}(1 - x^a)^{1/a}\,dx$$

To approximate the volume of the solid, form n slices, each of whose area is approximated by the integral above. Then sum the volumes of these n slices.

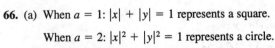

# Section 6.3    Volume:  The Shell Method

**2.** $p(x) = x$

$h(x) = 1 - x$

$V = 2\pi \displaystyle\int_0^1 x(1 - x)\,dx$

$= 2\pi \displaystyle\int_0^1 (x - x^2)\,dx = 2\pi\left[\dfrac{x^2}{2} - \dfrac{x^3}{3}\right]_0^1 = \dfrac{\pi}{3}$

**4.** $p(x) = x$

$h(x) = 8 - (x^2 + 4) = 4 - x^2$

$V = 2\pi \displaystyle\int_0^2 x(4 - x^2)\,dx$

$= 2\pi \displaystyle\int_0^2 (4x - x^3)\,dx$

$= 2\pi\left[2x^2 - \dfrac{x^4}{4}\right]_0^2 = 8\pi$

**6.** $p(x) = x$

$h(x) = \dfrac{1}{2}x^2$

$V = 2\pi \displaystyle\int_0^6 \dfrac{1}{2}x^3\,dx$

$= \left[\pi \dfrac{x^4}{4}\right]_0^6 = 324\pi$

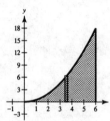

**8.** $p(x) = x$

$h(x) = 4 - x^2$

$V = 2\pi \displaystyle\int_0^2 (4x - x^3)\,dx$

$= 2\pi\left[2x^2 - \dfrac{1}{4}x^4\right]_0^2 = 8\pi$

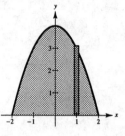

**10.** $p(x) = x$

$h(x) = 4 - 2x$

$V = 2\pi \displaystyle\int_0^2 x(4 - 2x)\,dx$

$= 2\pi \displaystyle\int_0^2 (4x - 2x^2)\,dx$

$= 2\pi\left[2x^2 - \dfrac{2}{3}x^3\right]_0^2 = \dfrac{16\pi}{3}$

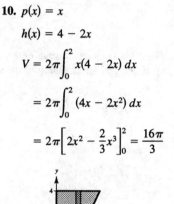

**12.** $p(x) = x$

$h(x) = \dfrac{\sin x}{x}$

$V = 2\pi \displaystyle\int_0^\pi x\left[\dfrac{\sin x}{x}\right]dx$

$= 2\pi \displaystyle\int_0^\pi \sin x\,dx = \left[-2\pi\cos x\right]_0^\pi = 4\pi$

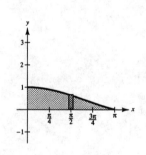

**14.** $p(y) = -y \quad (p(y) \ge 0 \text{ on } [-2, 0])$

$h(y) = 4 - (2 - y) = 2 + y$

$V = 2\pi \displaystyle\int_{-2}^0 (-y)(2 + y)\,dy$

$= 2\pi \displaystyle\int_{-2}^0 (-2y - y^2)\,dy$

$= 2\pi\left[-y^2 - \dfrac{y^3}{3}\right]_{-2}^0 = \dfrac{8\pi}{3}$

**16.** $p(y) = y$

$h(y) = 16 - y^2$

$V = 2\pi \displaystyle\int_0^4 y(16 - y^2)\,dy$

$= 2\pi \displaystyle\int_0^4 (16y - y^3)\,dy$

$= 2\pi\left[8y^2 - \dfrac{y^4}{4}\right]_0^4$

$= 2\pi[128 - 64] = 128\pi$

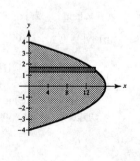

**18.** $p(x) = 2 - x$

$h(x) = 4x - x^2 - x^2 = 4x - 2x^2$

$V = 2\pi \int_0^2 (2 - x)(4x - 2x^2)\, dx$

$= 2\pi \int_0^2 (8x - 8x^2 + 2x^3)\, dx$

$= 2\pi \left[ 4x^2 - \frac{8}{3}x^3 + \frac{1}{2}x^4 \right]_0^2 = \frac{16\pi}{3}$

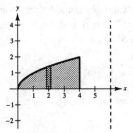

**20.** $p(x) = 6 - x$

$h(x) = \sqrt{x}$

$V = 2\pi \int_0^4 (6 - x)\sqrt{x}\, dx$

$= 2\pi \int_0^4 (6x^{1/2} - x^{3/2})\, dx$

$= 2\pi \left[ 4x^{3/2} - \frac{2}{5}x^{5/2} \right]_0^4 = \frac{192\pi}{5}$

**22. (a) Disk**

$R(x) = \frac{10}{x^2},\ r(x) = 0$

$V = \pi \int_1^5 \left( \frac{10}{x^2} \right)^2 dx$

$= 100\pi \int_1^5 x^{-4}\, dx$

$= 100\pi \left[ \frac{x^{-3}}{-3} \right]_1^5$

$= -\frac{100\pi}{3} \left[ \frac{1}{125} - 1 \right] = \frac{496}{15}\pi$

**(b) Shell**

$R(x) = x,\ r(x) = 0$

$V = 2\pi \int_1^5 x \left( \frac{10}{x^2} \right) dx$

$= 20\pi \int_1^5 \frac{1}{x}\, dx$

$= 20\pi \left[ \ln|x| \right]_1^5 = 20\pi \ln 5$

**(c) Disk**

$R(x) = 10,\ r(x) = 10 - \frac{10}{x^2}$

$V = \pi \int_1^5 \left[ 10^2 - \left( 10 - \frac{10}{x^2} \right)^2 \right] dx$

$= \pi \left[ \frac{100}{3x^3} - \frac{200}{x} \right]_1^5 = \frac{1904}{15}\pi$

**24. (a) Disk**

$R(x) = (a^{2/3} - x^{2/3})^{3/2}$

$r(x) = 0$

$V = \pi \int_{-a}^a (a^{2/3} - x^{2/3})^3\, dx$

$= 2\pi \int_0^a (a^2 - 3a^{4/3}x^{2/3} + 3a^{2/3}x^{4/3} - x^2)\, dx$

$= 2\pi \left[ a^2 x - \frac{9}{5}a^{4/3}x^{5/3} + \frac{9}{7}a^{2/3}x^{7/3} - \frac{1}{3}x^3 \right]_0^a$

$= 2\pi \left( a^3 - \frac{9}{5}a^3 + \frac{9}{7}a^3 - \frac{1}{3}a^3 \right) = \frac{32\pi a^3}{105}$

**(b)** Same as part a by symmetry

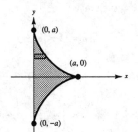

**26.** (a)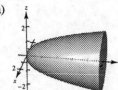

(b)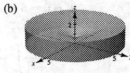

(c)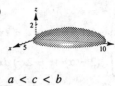

$$a < c < b$$

**28.** $2\pi \int_0^4 x\left(\frac{x}{2}\right) dx$

represents the volume of the solid generated by revolving the region bounded by $y = x/2$, $y = 0$, and $x = 4$ about the $y$-axis by using the Shell Method.

$$\pi \int_0^2 [16 - (2y)^2] \, dy = \pi \int_0^2 [(4)^2 - (2y)^2] \, dy$$

represents this same volume by using the Disk Method.

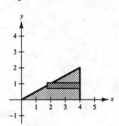

Disk Method

**30.** (a)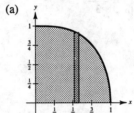

(b) $V = 2\pi \int_0^1 x\sqrt{1 - x^3} \, dx \approx 2.3222$

**32.** (a)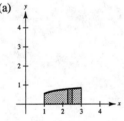

(b) $V = 2\pi \int_1^3 \frac{2x}{1 + e^{1/x}} \, dx \approx 19.0162$

**34.** $y = \tan x$, $y = 0$, $x = 0$, $x = \frac{\pi}{4}$

Volume $\approx 1$

Matches (e)

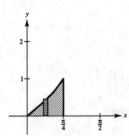

**36.** Total volume of the hemisphere is $\frac{1}{2}\left(\frac{4}{3}\right)\pi r^3 = \frac{2}{3}\pi(3)^3 = 18\pi$. By the Shell Method, $p(x) = x$, $h(x) = \sqrt{9 - x^2}$. Find $x_0$ such that

$$6\pi = 2\pi \int_0^{x_0} x\sqrt{9 - x^2} \, dx$$

$$6 = -\int_0^{x_0} (9 - x^2)^{1/2}(-2x) \, dx$$

$$= \left[-\frac{2}{3}(9 - x^2)^{3/2}\right]_0^{x_0} = 18 - \frac{2}{3}(9 - x_0^2)^{3/2}$$

$$(9 - x_0^2)^{3/2} = 18$$

$$x_0 = \sqrt{9 - 18^{2/3}} \approx 1.460.$$

Diameter: $2\sqrt{9 - 18^{2/3}} \approx 2.920$

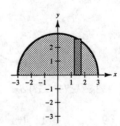

**38.** $V = 4\pi \displaystyle\int_{-r}^{r} (R - x)\sqrt{r^2 - x^2}\, dx$

$= 4\pi R \displaystyle\int_{-r}^{r} \sqrt{r^2 - x^2}\, dx - 4\pi \displaystyle\int_{-r}^{r} x\sqrt{r^2 - x^2}\, dx$

$= 4\pi R\left(\dfrac{\pi r^2}{2}\right) + \left[2\pi\left(\dfrac{2}{3}\right)(r^2 - x^2)^{3/2}\right]_{-r}^{r}$

$= 2\pi^2 r^2 R$

**40.** (a) Area region $= \displaystyle\int_0^b [ab^n - ax^n]\, dx$

$= \left[ab^n x - a\dfrac{x^{n+1}}{n+1}\right]_0^b$

$= ab^{n+1} - a\dfrac{b^{n+1}}{n+1}$

$= ab^{n+1}\left(1 - \dfrac{1}{n+1}\right) = ab^{n+1}\left(\dfrac{n}{n+1}\right)$

$R_1(n) = \dfrac{ab^{n+1}\left(\dfrac{n}{n+1}\right)}{(ab^n)b} = \dfrac{n}{n+1}$

(b) $\displaystyle\lim_{n\to\infty} R_1(n) = \lim_{n\to\infty}\dfrac{n}{n+1} = 1$

$\displaystyle\lim_{n\to\infty} (ab^n)b = \infty$

(c) **Disk Method:**

$V = 2\pi \displaystyle\int_0^b x(ab^n - ax^n)\, dx$

$= 2\pi a \displaystyle\int_0^b (xb^n - x^{n+1})\, dx$

$= 2\pi a\left[\dfrac{b^n}{2}x^2 - \dfrac{x^{n+2}}{n+2}\right]_0^b$

$= 2\pi a\left[\dfrac{b^{n+2}}{2} - \dfrac{b^{n+2}}{n+2}\right] = \pi ab^{n+2}\left(\dfrac{n}{n+2}\right)$

$R_2(n) = \dfrac{\pi ab^{n+2}\left(\dfrac{n}{n+2}\right)}{(\pi b^2)(ab^n)} = \left(\dfrac{n}{n+2}\right)$

(d) $\displaystyle\lim_{n\to\infty} R_2(n) = \lim_{n\to\infty}\left(\dfrac{n}{n+2}\right) = 1$

$\displaystyle\lim_{n\to\infty} (\pi b^2)(ab^n) = \infty$

(e) As $n \to \infty$, the graph approaches the line $x = 1$.

**42.** (a) $V = 2\pi \displaystyle\int_0^4 xf(x)\, dx$

$= \dfrac{2\pi(40)}{3(4)}[0 + 4(10)(45) + 2(20)(40) + 4(30)(20) + 0]$

$= \dfrac{20\pi}{3}[5800] \approx 121{,}475$ cubic feet

(b) Top line: $y - 50 = \dfrac{40 - 50}{20 - 0}(x - 0) = -\dfrac{1}{2}x \implies y = -\dfrac{1}{2}x + 50$

Bottom line: $y - 40 = \dfrac{0 - 40}{40 - 20}(x - 20) = -2(x - 20) \implies y = -2x + 80$

$V = 2\pi \displaystyle\int_0^{20} x\left(-\dfrac{1}{2}x + 50\right) dx + 2\pi \displaystyle\int_{20}^{40} x(-2x + 80)\, dx$

$= 2\pi \displaystyle\int_0^{20}\left(-\dfrac{1}{2}x^2 + 50x\right) dx + 2\pi \displaystyle\int_{20}^{40}(-2x^2 + 80x)\, dx$

$= 2\pi\left[-\dfrac{x^3}{6} + 25x^2\right]_0^{20} + 2\pi\left[-\dfrac{2x^3}{3} + 40x^2\right]_{20}^{40}$

$= 2\pi\left[\dfrac{26{,}000}{3}\right] + 2\pi\left[\dfrac{32{,}000}{3}\right]$

$\approx 121{,}475$ cubic feet

(Note that Simpson's Rule is exact for this problem.)

# Section 6.4 Arc Length and Surfaces of Revolution

**2.** $(1, 2), (7, 10)$

(a) $d = \sqrt{(7-1)^2 + (10-2)^2} = 10$

(b) $y = \frac{4}{3}x + \frac{2}{3}$

$y' = \frac{4}{3}$

$s = \int_1^7 \sqrt{1 + \left(\frac{4}{3}\right)^2}\, dx = \left[\frac{5}{3}x\right]_1^7 = 10$

**4.** $y = 2x^{3/2} + 3$

$y' = 3x^{1/2}, [0, 9]$

$s = \int_0^9 \sqrt{1 + 9x}\, dx$

$= \left[\frac{2}{27}(1 + 9x)^{3/2}\right]_0^9$

$= \frac{2}{27}(82^{3/2} - 1) \approx 54.929$

**6.** $y = \frac{3}{2}x^{2/3} + 4$

$y' = x^{-1/3}, [1, 27]$

$s = \int_1^{27} \sqrt{1 + \left(\frac{1}{x^{1/3}}\right)^2}\, dx$

$= \int_1^{27} \sqrt{\frac{x^{2/3} + 1}{x^{2/3}}}\, dx$

$= \frac{3}{2}\int_1^{27} \sqrt{x^{2/3} + 1}\left(\frac{2}{3x^{1/3}}\right) dx$

$= \left[\frac{3}{2} \cdot \frac{2}{3}(x^{2/3} + 1)^{3/2}\right]_1^{27}$

$= 10^{3/2} - 2^{3/2} \approx 28.794$

**8.** $y = \frac{x^5}{10} + \frac{1}{6x^3}$

$y' = \frac{1}{2}x^4 - \frac{1}{2x^4}$

$1 + (y')^2 = \left(\frac{1}{2}x^4 + \frac{1}{2x^4}\right)^2, [1, 2]$

$s = \int_a^b \sqrt{1 + (y')^2}\, dx$

$= \int_1^2 \sqrt{\left(\frac{1}{2}x^4 + \frac{1}{2x^4}\right)^2}\, dx$

$= \int_1^2 \left(\frac{1}{2}x^4 + \frac{1}{2x^4}\right) dx$

$= \left[\frac{1}{10}x^5 - \frac{1}{6x^3}\right]_1^2 = \frac{779}{240} \approx 3.246$

**10.** $y = \frac{1}{2}(e^x + e^{-x})$

$y' = \frac{1}{2}(e^x - e^{-x}), [0, 2]$

$1 + (y')^2 = \left[\frac{1}{2}(e^x + e^{-x})\right]^2, [0, 2]$

$s = \int_0^2 \sqrt{\left[\frac{1}{2}(e^x + e^{-x})\right]^2}\, dx$

$= \frac{1}{2}\int_0^2 (e^x + e^{-x})\, dx$

$= \frac{1}{2}\left[e^x - e^{-x}\right]_0^2 = \frac{1}{2}\left(e^2 - \frac{1}{e^2}\right) \approx 3.627$

**12.** (a) $y = x^2 + x - 2, -2 \le x \le 1$

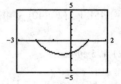

(b) $y' = 2x + 1$

$1 + (y')^2 = 1 + 4x^2 + 4x + 1$

$L = \int_{-2}^1 \sqrt{2 + 4x + 4x^2}\, dx$

(c) $L \approx 5.653$

**14.** (a) $y = \frac{1}{1 + x}, 0 \le x \le 1$

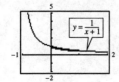

$y = \frac{1}{x + 1}$

(b) $y' = -\frac{1}{(1 + x)^2}$

$1 + (y')^2 = 1 + \frac{1}{(1 + x)^4}$

$L = \int_0^1 \sqrt{1 + \frac{1}{(1 + x)^4}}\, dx$

(c) $L \approx 1.132$

**16.** (a) $y = \cos x, -\dfrac{\pi}{2} \le x \le \dfrac{\pi}{2}$      (b)    $y' = -\sin x$     (c) 3.820

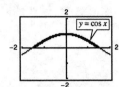

$$1 + (y')^2 = 1 + \sin^2 x$$

$$L = \int_{-\pi/2}^{\pi/2} \sqrt{1 + \sin^2 x}\, dx$$

**18.** (a) $y = \ln x, 1 \le x \le 5$     (b)    $y' = \dfrac{1}{x}$     (c) $L \approx 4.367$

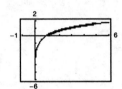

$$1 + (y')^2 = 1 + \frac{1}{x^2}$$

$$L = \int_1^5 \sqrt{1 + \frac{1}{x^2}}\, dx$$

**20.** (a) $x = \sqrt{36 - y^2}, 0 \le y \le 3$     (b) $\dfrac{dx}{dy} = \dfrac{1}{2}(36 - y^2)^{-1/2}(-2y)$     (c) $L \approx 3.142 \ (\pi!)$

$\quad\quad y = \sqrt{36 - x^2}, 3\sqrt{3} \le x \le 6$

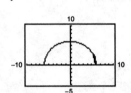

$$= \frac{-y}{\sqrt{36 - y^2}}$$

$$L = \int_0^3 \sqrt{1 + \frac{y^2}{36 - y^2}}\, dy$$

$$= \int_0^3 \frac{6}{\sqrt{36 - y^2}}\, dy$$

Alternatively, you can convert to a function of $x$.

$$y = \sqrt{36 - x^2}$$

$$y' = \frac{dy}{dx} = -\frac{x}{\sqrt{36 - x^2}}$$

$$L = \int_{3\sqrt{3}}^6 \sqrt{1 + \frac{x^2}{36 - x^2}}\, dx = \int_{3\sqrt{3}}^6 \frac{6}{\sqrt{36 - x^2}}\, dx$$

Although this integral is undefined at $x = 0$, a graphing utility still gives $L \approx 3.142$.

**22.** $\displaystyle\int_0^{\pi/4} \sqrt{1 + \left[\dfrac{d}{dx}(\tan x)\right]^2}\, dx$

$s \approx 1$

Matches (e)

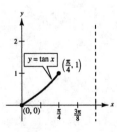

**24.** $f(x) = (x^2 - 4)^2, [0, 4]$

(a) $d = \sqrt{(4 - 0)^2 + (144 - 16)^2} \approx 128.062$

(b) $d = \sqrt{(1 - 0)^2 + (9 - 16)^2} + \sqrt{(2 - 1)^2 + (0 - 9)^2} + \sqrt{(3 - 2)^2 + (25 - 0)^2} + \sqrt{(4 - 3)^2 + (144 - 25)^2}$

$\quad\quad \approx 160.151$

(c) $s = \displaystyle\int_0^4 \sqrt{1 + [4x(x^2 - 4)]^2}\, dx \approx 159.087$

(d) 160.287

**26.** Let $y = \ln x$, $1 \le x \le e$, $y' = \dfrac{1}{x}$ and $L_1 = \displaystyle\int_1^e \sqrt{1 + \dfrac{1}{x^2}}\, dx$.

Equivalently, $x = e^y$, $0 \le y \le 1$, $\dfrac{dx}{dy} = e^y$, and $L_2 = \displaystyle\int_0^1 \sqrt{1 + e^{2y}}\, dy = \displaystyle\int_0^1 \sqrt{1 + e^{2x}}\, dx$.

Numerically, both integrals yield $L = 2.0035$

**28.**    $y = 31 - 10(e^{x/20} + e^{-x/20})$

$y' = -\dfrac{1}{2}(e^{x/20} - e^{-x/20})$

$1 + (y')^2 = 1 + \dfrac{1}{4}(e^{x/10} - 2 + e^{-x/10}) = \left[\dfrac{1}{2}(e^{x/20} + e^{-x/20})\right]^2$

$s = \displaystyle\int_{-20}^{20} \sqrt{\left[\dfrac{1}{2}(e^{x/20} + e^{-x/20})\right]^2}\, dx$

$= \dfrac{1}{2}\displaystyle\int_{-20}^{20}(e^{x/20} + e^{-x/20})\, dx = \left[10(e^{x/20} - e^{-x/20})\right]_{-20}^{20} = 20\left(e - \dfrac{1}{e}\right) \approx 47$ ft

Thus, there are $100(47) = 4700$ square feet of roofing on the barn.

**30.**   $y = 693.8597 - 68.7672 \cosh 0.0100333x$

$y' = -0.6899619478 \sinh 0.0100333x$

$s = \displaystyle\int_{-299.2239}^{299.2239} \sqrt{1 + (-0.6899619478 \sinh 0.0100333x)^2}\, dx \approx 1480$

(Use Simpson's Rule with $n = 100$ or a graphing utility.)

**32.**    $y = \sqrt{25 - x^2}$

$y' = \dfrac{-x}{\sqrt{25 - x^2}}$

$1 + (y')^2 = \dfrac{25}{25 - x^2}$

$s = \displaystyle\int_{-3}^4 \sqrt{\dfrac{25}{25 - x^2}}\, dx$

$= \displaystyle\int_{-3}^4 \dfrac{5}{\sqrt{25 - x^2}}\, dx$

$= \left[5 \arcsin \dfrac{x}{5}\right]_{-3}^4$

$= 5\left[\arcsin \dfrac{4}{5} - \arcsin\left(-\dfrac{3}{5}\right)\right] \approx 7.8540$

$\dfrac{1}{4}[2\pi(5)] \approx 7.8540 = s$

**34.**  $y = 2\sqrt{x}$

$y' = \dfrac{1}{\sqrt{x}}$, $[4, 9]$

$S = 2\pi \displaystyle\int_4^9 2\sqrt{x}\sqrt{1 + \dfrac{1}{x}}\, dx$

$= 4\pi \displaystyle\int_4^9 \sqrt{x + 1}\, dx$

$= \dfrac{8}{3}\pi(x + 1)^{3/2}\Big]_4^9$

$= \dfrac{8\pi}{3}(10^{3/2} - 5^{3/2}) \approx 171.258$

**36.**
$$y = \frac{x}{2}$$

$$y' = \frac{1}{2}$$

$$1 + (y')^2 = \frac{5}{4}, [0, 6]$$

$$S = 2\pi \int_0^6 \frac{x}{2} \sqrt{\frac{5}{4}} \, dx$$

$$= \left[ \frac{2\pi\sqrt{5}}{8} x^2 \right]_0^6 = 9\sqrt{5}\,\pi$$

**38.**  $y = 9 - x^2, [0, 3]$

$$y' = -2x$$

$$S = 2\pi \int_0^3 x\sqrt{1 + 4x^2} \, dx$$

$$= \frac{\pi}{4} \int_0^3 (1 + 4x^2)^{1/2}(8x) \, dx$$

$$= \left[ \frac{\pi}{6}(1 + 4x^2)^{3/2} \right]_0^3$$

$$= \frac{\pi}{6}(37^{3/2} - 1) \approx 117.319$$

**40.**
$$y = \ln x$$

$$y' = \frac{1}{x}$$

$$1 + (y')^2 = \frac{x^2 + 1}{x^2}, [1, e]$$

$$S = 2\pi \int_1^e x \sqrt{\frac{x^2 + 1}{x^2}} \, dx$$

$$= 2\pi \int_1^e \sqrt{x^2 + 1} \, dx \approx 22.943$$

**42.** The precalculus formula is the distance formula between two points. The representative element is

$$\sqrt{(\Delta x_i)^2 + (\Delta y_i)^2} = \sqrt{1 + \left(\frac{\Delta y_i}{\Delta x_i}\right)^2} \, \Delta x i.$$

**44.** The surface of revolution given by $f_1$ will be larger. $r(x)$ is larger for $f_1$.

**46.** $y = \sqrt{r^2 - x^2}$

$$y' = \frac{-x}{\sqrt{r^2 - x^2}}$$

$$1 + (y')^2 = \frac{r^2}{r^2 - x^2}$$

$$S = 2\pi \int_{-r}^r \sqrt{r^2 - x^2} \sqrt{\frac{r^2}{r^2 - x^2}} \, dx$$

$$= 2\pi \int_{-r}^r r \, dx = \left[ 2\pi rx \right]_{-r}^r = 4\pi r^2$$

**48.** From Exercise 47 we have:

$$S = 2\pi \int_0^a \frac{rx}{\sqrt{r^2 - x^2}} \, dx$$

$$= -r\pi \int_0^a \frac{-2x \, dx}{\sqrt{r^2 - x^2}}$$

$$= \left[ -2r\pi\sqrt{r^2 - x^2} \right]_0^a$$

$$= 2r^2\pi - 2r\pi\sqrt{r^2 - a^2}$$

$$= 2r\pi\left(r - \sqrt{r^2 - a^2}\right)$$

$$= 2\pi rh \text{ (where } h \text{ is the height of the zone)}$$

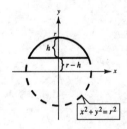

**50.** (a) We approximate the volume by summing 6 disks of thickness 3 and circumference $C_i$ equal to the average of the given circumferences:

$$V \approx \sum_{i=1}^{6} \pi r_i^2(3) = \sum_{i=1}^{6} \pi \left(\frac{C_i}{2\pi}\right)^2 (3) = \frac{3}{4\pi} \sum_{i=1}^{6} C_i^2$$

$$= \frac{3}{4\pi} \left[ \left(\frac{50 + 65.5}{2}\right)^2 + \left(\frac{65.5 + 70}{2}\right)^2 + \left(\frac{70 + 66}{2}\right)^2 + \left(\frac{66 + 58}{2}\right)^2 + \left(\frac{58 + 51}{2}\right)^2 + \left(\frac{51 + 48}{2}\right)^2 \right]$$

$$= \frac{3}{4\pi} [57.75^2 + 67.75^2 + 68^2 + 62^2 + 54.5^2 + 49.5^2]$$

$$= \frac{3}{4\pi} [21813.625] = 5207.62 \text{ cubic inches}$$

(b) The lateral surface area of a frustum of a right circular cone is $\pi s(R + r)$. For the first frustum,

$$S_1 \approx \pi \left[ 3^2 + \left(\frac{65.5 - 50}{2\pi}\right)^2 \right]^{1/2} \left[ \frac{50}{2\pi} + \frac{65.5}{2\pi} \right]$$

$$= \left(\frac{50 + 65.5}{2}\right) \left[ 9 + \left(\frac{65.5 - 50}{2\pi}\right)^2 \right]^{1/2}.$$

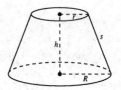

Adding the six frustums together,

$$S \approx \left(\frac{50 + 65.5}{2}\right)\left[ 9 + \left(\frac{15.5}{2\pi}\right)^2 \right]^{1/2} + \left(\frac{65.5 + 70}{2}\right)\left[ 9 + \left(\frac{4.5}{2\pi}\right)^2 \right]^{1/2} +$$

$$\left(\frac{70 + 66}{2}\right)\left[ 9 + \left(\frac{4}{2\pi}\right)^2 \right]^{1/2} + \left(\frac{66 + 58}{2}\right)\left[ 9 + \left(\frac{8}{2\pi}\right)^2 \right]^{1/2} +$$

$$\left(\frac{58 + 51}{2}\right)\left[ 9 + \left(\frac{7}{2\pi}\right)^2 \right]^{1/2} + \left(\frac{51 + 48}{2}\right)\left[ 9 + \left(\frac{3}{2\pi}\right)^2 \right]^{1/2}$$

$$\approx 224.30 + 208.96 + 208.54 + 202.06 + 174.41 + 150.37$$

$$= 1168.64$$

(c) $r = 0.00401y^3 - 0.1416y^2 + 1.232y + 7.943$

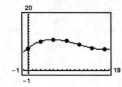

(d) $V = \displaystyle\int_0^{18} \pi r^2 \, dy \approx 5275.9 \text{ cubic inches}$

$$S = \int_0^{18} 2\pi r(y) \sqrt{1 + r'(y)^2} \, dy$$

$$\approx 1179.5 \text{ square inches}$$

**52.** Individual project, see Exercise 50, 51.

**54.** (a) $\dfrac{x^2}{9} + \dfrac{y^2}{4} = 1$

Ellipse: $y_1 = 2\sqrt{1 - \dfrac{x^2}{9}}$

$y_2 = -2\sqrt{1 - \dfrac{x^2}{9}}$

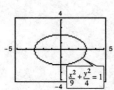

(b) $y = 2\sqrt{1 - \dfrac{x^2}{9}}, \ 0 \le x \le 3$

$$y' = 2\left(\frac{1}{2}\right)\left(1 - \frac{x^2}{9}\right)^{-1/2}\left(\frac{-2x}{9}\right)$$

$$= \frac{-2x}{9\sqrt{1 - \dfrac{x^2}{9}}} = \frac{-2x}{3\sqrt{9 - x^2}}$$

$$L = \int_0^3 \sqrt{1 + \frac{4x^2}{81 - 9x^2}} \, dx$$

(c) You cannot evaluate this definite integral, since the integrand is not defined at $x = 3$. Simpson's Rule will not work for the same reason. Also, the integrand does not have an elementary antiderivative.

**56.** Essay

# Section 6.5    Work

**2.** $W = Fd = (2800)(4) = 11,200 \text{ ft} \cdot \text{lb}$

**4.** $W = Fd = [9(2000)]\left[\frac{1}{2}(5280)\right] = 47,520,000 \text{ ft} \cdot \text{lb}$

**6.** $W = \displaystyle\int_a^b F(x)\, dx$  is the work done by a force $F$ moving an object along a straight line from $x = a$ to $x = b$.

**8.** (a) $W = \displaystyle\int_0^9 6\, dx = 54 \text{ ft} \cdot \text{lbs}$

(b) $W = \displaystyle\int_0^7 20\, dx + \int_7^9 (-10x + 90)\, dx = 140 + 20$

$\qquad = 160 \text{ ft} \cdot \text{lbs}$

(c) $W = \displaystyle\int_0^9 \frac{1}{27}x^2\, dx = \frac{x^3}{81}\Big]_0^9 = 9 \text{ ft} \cdot \text{lbs}$

(d) $W = \displaystyle\int_0^9 \sqrt{x}\, dx = \frac{2}{3}x^{3/2}\Big]_0^9 = \frac{2}{3}(27) = 18 \text{ ft} \cdot \text{lbs}$

**10.** $W = \displaystyle\int_0^{10} \frac{5}{4}x\, dx = \left[\frac{5}{8}x^2\right]_6^{10}$

$\qquad = 40 \text{ in} \cdot \text{lb} \approx 3.33 \text{ ft} \cdot \text{lb}$

**12.** $F(x) = kx$

$\qquad 800 = k(70) \implies k = \dfrac{80}{7}$

$\qquad W = \displaystyle\int_0^{70} F(x)\, dx = \int_0^{70} \frac{80}{7}x\, dx = \frac{40x^2}{7}\Big]_0^{70}$

$\qquad = 28000 \text{ n} \cdot \text{cm} = 280 \text{ Nm}$

**14.** $F(x) = kx$

$\qquad 15 = k(1) = k$

$\qquad W = 2\displaystyle\int_0^4 15x\, dx = \left[15x^2\right]_0^4$

$\qquad = 240 \text{ ft} \cdot \text{lb}$

**16.** $W = 7.5 = \displaystyle\int_0^{1/6} kx\, dx = \frac{kx^2}{2}\Big]_0^{1/6} = \frac{k}{72} \implies k = 540$

$\qquad W = \displaystyle\int_{1/6}^{5/24} 540x\, dx = 270x^2\Big]_{1/6}^{5/24} = 4.21875 \text{ ft} \cdot \text{lbs}$

**18.** $W = \displaystyle\int_{4000}^h \frac{80,000,000}{x^2}\, dx = \left[-\frac{80,000,000}{x}\right]_{4000}^h$

$\qquad = \dfrac{-80,000,000}{h} + 20,000$

$\qquad \displaystyle\lim_{h \to \infty} W = 20,000 \text{ mi/ton} \approx 2.1 \times 10^{11} \text{ ft} \cdot \text{lb}$

**20.** Weight on surface of moon: $\frac{1}{6}(12) = 2$ tons

Weight varies inversely as the square of distance from the center of the moon. Therefore,

$\qquad F(x) = \dfrac{k}{x^2}$

$\qquad 2 = \dfrac{k}{(1100)^2}$

$\qquad k = 2.42 \times 10^6$

$\qquad W = \displaystyle\int_{1100}^{1150} \frac{2.42 \times 10^6}{x^2}\, dx = \left[\frac{-2.42 \times 10^6}{x}\right]_{1100}^{1150} = 2.42 \times 10^6\left(\frac{1}{1100} - \frac{1}{1150}\right)$

$\qquad\qquad \approx 95.652 \text{ mi} \cdot \text{ton} \approx 1.01 \times 10^9 \text{ ft} \cdot \text{lb}$

**22.** The bottom half had to be pumped a greater distance then the top half.

**24.** Volume of disk: $4\pi \, \Delta y$

Weight of disk: $9800(4\pi) \, \Delta y$

Distance the disk of water is moved: $y$

$$W = \int_{10}^{12} y(9800)(4\pi) \, dy = 39,200\pi \left[ \frac{y^2}{2} \right]_{10}^{12}$$

$$= 39,200\pi(22)$$

$$= 862,400\pi \text{ newton--meters}$$

**26.** Volume of disk: $\pi \left( \frac{2}{3}y \right)^2 \Delta y$

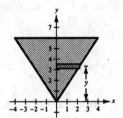

Weight of disk: $62.4\pi \left( \frac{2}{3}y \right)^2 \Delta y$

Distance: $y$

(a) $W = \dfrac{4}{9}(62.4)\pi \displaystyle\int_0^2 y^3 \, dy = \left[ \dfrac{4}{9}(62.4)\pi \left( \dfrac{1}{4}y^4 \right) \right]_0^2 \approx 110.9\pi \text{ ft} \cdot \text{lb}$

(b) $W = \dfrac{4}{9}(62.4)\pi \displaystyle\int_4^6 y^3 \, dy = \left[ \dfrac{4}{9}(62.4)\pi \left( \dfrac{1}{4}y^4 \right) \right]_4^6 \approx 7210.7\pi \text{ ft} \cdot \text{lb}$

**28.** Volume of each layer: $\dfrac{y+3}{3}(3) \, \Delta y = (y+3) \, \Delta y$

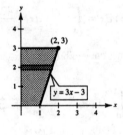

Weight of each layer: $55.6(y+3) \, \Delta y$

Distance: $6 - y$

$$W = \int_0^3 55.6(6-y)(y+3) \, dy = 55.6 \int_0^3 (18 + 3y - y^2) \, dy$$

$$= 55.6 \left[ 18y + \frac{3y^2}{2} - \frac{y^3}{3} \right]_0^3$$

$$= 3252.6 \text{ ft} \cdot \text{lb}$$

**30.** Volume of layer: $V = 12(2)\sqrt{(25/4) - y^2} \, \Delta y$

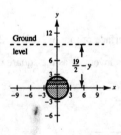

Weight of layer: $W = 42(24)\sqrt{(25/4) - y^2} \, \Delta y$

Distance: $\dfrac{19}{2} - y$

$$W = \int_{-2.5}^{2.5} 42(24) \sqrt{\frac{25}{4} - y^2} \left( \frac{19}{2} - y \right) dy$$

$$= 1008 \left[ \frac{19}{2} \int_{-2.5}^{2.5} \sqrt{\frac{25}{4} - y^2} \, dy + \int_{-2.5}^{2.5} \sqrt{\frac{25}{4} - y^2} (-y) \, dy \right]$$

The second integral is zero since the integrand is odd and the limits of integration are symmetric to the origin. The first integral represents the area of a semicircle of radius $\frac{5}{2}$. Thus, the work is

$$W = 1008 \left( \frac{19}{2} \right) \pi \left( \frac{5}{2} \right)^2 \left( \frac{1}{2} \right) = 29,925\pi \text{ ft} \cdot \text{lb} \approx 94,012.16 \text{ ft} \cdot \text{lb}.$$

**32.** The lower 10 feet of chain are raised 5 feet with a constant force.

$$W_1 = 3(10)5 = 150 \text{ ft} \cdot \text{lb}$$

The top 5 feet will be raised with variable force.

Weight of section: $3 \, \Delta y$

Distance: $5 - y$

$$W_2 = 3 \int_0^5 (5 - y) \, dy = \left[ -\frac{3}{2}(5 - y)^2 \right]_0^5 = \frac{75}{2} \text{ ft} \cdot \text{lb}$$

$$W = W_1 + W_2 = 150 + \frac{75}{2} = \frac{375}{2} \text{ ft} \cdot \text{lb}$$

**34.** The work required to lift the chain is 337.5 ft · lb (from Exercise 31). The work required to lift the 500-pound load is $W = (500)(15) = 7500$. The work required to lift the chain with a 100-pound load attached is

$$W = 337.5 + 7500 = 7837.5 \text{ ft} \cdot \text{lbs}$$

**36.** $W = 3 \int_0^6 (12 - 2y) \, dy = \left[ -\frac{3}{4}(12 - 2y)^2 \right]_0^6 = \frac{3}{4}(12)^2 = 108 \text{ ft} \cdot \text{lb}$

**38.** Work to pull up the ball: $W_1 = 500(40) = 20,000 \text{ ft} \cdot \text{lb}$

Work to pull up the cable: force is variable

Weight per section: $1 \, \Delta y$

Distance: $40 - x$

$$W_2 = \int_0^{40} (40 - x) \, dx = \left[ -\frac{1}{2}(40 - x)^2 \right]_0^{40}$$

$$= 800 \text{ ft} \cdot \text{lb}$$

$$W = W_1 + W_2 = 20,000 + 800 = 20,800 \text{ ft} \cdot \text{lb}$$

**40.** $p = \dfrac{k}{V}$

$$2500 = \frac{k}{1} \implies k = 2500$$

$$W = \int_1^3 \frac{2500}{V} \, dV = \left[ 2500 \ln V \right]_1^3$$

$$= 2500 \ln 3 \approx 2746.53 \text{ ft} \cdot \text{lb}$$

**42.** (a) $W = FD = (8000\pi)(2) = 16,000\pi \text{ ft} \cdot \text{lbs}$

(b) $W \approx \dfrac{2 - 0}{3(6)}[0 + 4(20,000) + 2(22,000) + 4(15,000) + 2(10,000) + 4(5000) + 0]$

$$\approx 24,88.889 \text{ ft} \cdot \text{lb}$$

(c) $F(x) = -16,261.36x^4 + 85,295.45x^3 - 157,738.64x^2 + 104,386.36x - 32.4675$

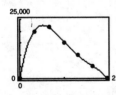

(d) $F(x) = 0$ when $x \approx 0.524$ feet. $F(x)$ is a maximum when $x \approx 0.524$ feet.

(e) $W = \displaystyle\int_0^2 F(x) \, dx \approx 25,180.5 \text{ ft} \cdot \text{lbs}$

**44.** $W = \displaystyle\int_0^4 \left( \frac{e^{x^2} - 1}{100} \right) dx \approx 11,494 \text{ ft} \cdot \text{lb}$

**46.** $W = \displaystyle\int_0^2 1000 \sinh x \, dx \approx 2762.2 \text{ ft} \cdot \text{lb}$

## Section 6.6    Moments, Centers of Mass, and Centroids

**2.** $\bar{x} = \dfrac{7(-3) + 4(-2) + 3(5) + 8(6)}{7 + 4 + 3 + 8} = \dfrac{17}{11}$

**4.** $\bar{x} = \dfrac{12(-6) + 1(-4) + 6(-2) + 3(0) + 11(8)}{12 + 1 + 6 + 3 + 11} = 0$

**6.** The center of mass is translated $k$ units as well.

**8.** $200x = 550(5 - x)$ (Person on left)

$200x = 2750 - 550x$

$750x = 2750$

$x = 3\frac{2}{3}$ feet

**10.**    $\bar{x} = \dfrac{10(1) + 2(5) + 5(-4)}{10 + 2 + 5} = 0$

$\bar{y} = \dfrac{10(-1) + 2(5) + 5(0)}{10 + 2 + 5} = 0$

$(\bar{x}, \bar{y}) = (0, 0)$

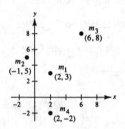

**12.**    $\bar{x} = \dfrac{12(2) + 6(-1) + \dfrac{15}{2}(6) + 15(2)}{12 + 6 + \dfrac{15}{2} + 15} = \dfrac{93}{40.5} = \dfrac{62}{27}$

$\bar{y} = \dfrac{12(3) + 6(5) + \dfrac{15}{2}(8) + 15(-2)}{12 + 6 + \dfrac{15}{2} + 15} = \dfrac{96}{40.5} = \dfrac{64}{27}$

$(\bar{x}, \bar{y}) = \left(\dfrac{62}{27}, \dfrac{64}{27}\right)$

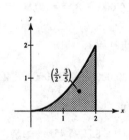

**14.**    $m = \rho \displaystyle\int_0^2 \frac{1}{2}x^2 \, dx = \left[\rho\frac{x^3}{6}\right]_0^2 = \frac{4}{3}\rho$

$M_x = \rho \displaystyle\int_0^2 \frac{1}{2}\left(\frac{1}{2}x^2\right)\left(\frac{1}{2}x^2\right) dx = \frac{\rho}{8}\int_0^2 x^4 \, dx = \left[\frac{\rho}{40}x^5\right]_0^2 = \frac{32}{40}\rho = \frac{4}{5}\rho$

$\bar{y} = \dfrac{M_x}{m} = \dfrac{\frac{4}{5}\rho}{\frac{4}{3}\rho} = \dfrac{3}{5}$

$M_y = \rho \displaystyle\int_0^2 x\left(\frac{1}{2}x^2\right) dx = \frac{1}{2}\rho\int_0^2 x^3 \, dx = \left[\frac{\rho}{8}x^4\right]_0^2 = 2\rho$

$\bar{x} = \dfrac{M_y}{m} = \dfrac{2\rho}{\frac{4}{3}\rho} = \dfrac{3}{2}$

$(\bar{x}, \bar{y}) = \left(\dfrac{3}{2}, \dfrac{3}{5}\right)$

**16.** $m = \rho \int_0^1 \left( \sqrt{x} - x \right) dx = \rho \left[ \frac{2}{3} x^{3/2} - \frac{x^2}{2} \right]_0^1 = \frac{\rho}{6}$

$M_x = \rho \int_0^1 \frac{\left( \sqrt{x} + x \right)}{2} \left( \sqrt{x} - x \right) dx = \frac{\rho}{2} \int_0^1 (x - x^2) \, dx = \frac{\rho}{2} \left[ \frac{x^2}{2} - \frac{x^3}{3} \right]_0^1 = \frac{\rho}{12}$

$\bar{y} = \frac{M_x}{m} = \frac{\rho}{12} \left( \frac{6}{\rho} \right) = \frac{1}{2}$

$M_y = \rho \int_0^1 x \left( \sqrt{x} - x \right) dx = \rho \int_0^1 (x^{3/2} - x^2) \, dx = \rho \left[ \frac{2}{5} x^{5/2} - \frac{x^3}{3} \right]_0^1 = \frac{\rho}{15}$

$\bar{x} = \frac{M_y}{m} = \frac{\rho}{15} \left( \frac{6}{\rho} \right) = \frac{2}{5}$

$(\bar{x}, \bar{y}) = \left( \frac{2}{5}, \frac{1}{2} \right)$

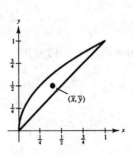

**18.** $m = \rho \int_0^9 \left[ \left( \sqrt{x} + 1 \right) - \left( \frac{1}{3} x + 1 \right) \right] dx = \rho \int_0^9 \left( \sqrt{x} - \frac{1}{3} x \right) dx$

$= \rho \left[ \frac{2}{3} x^{3/2} - \frac{x^2}{6} \right]_0^9 = \rho \left( 18 - \frac{27}{2} \right) = \frac{9}{2} \rho$

$M_x = \rho \int_0^9 \frac{\sqrt{x} + 1 + \frac{1}{3} x + 1}{2} \left( \sqrt{x} + 1 - \frac{1}{3} x - 1 \right) dx = \frac{\rho}{2} \int_0^9 \left( \sqrt{x} + \frac{1}{3} x + 2 \right) \left( \sqrt{x} - \frac{1}{3} x \right) dx$

$= \frac{\rho}{2} \int_0^9 \left( x - \frac{1}{3} x^{3/2} + \frac{1}{3} x^{3/2} - \frac{1}{9} x^2 + 2\sqrt{x} - \frac{2}{3} x \right) dx = \frac{\rho}{2} \int_0^9 \left( \frac{1}{3} x - \frac{1}{9} x^2 + 2\sqrt{x} \right) dx$

$= \frac{\rho}{2} \left[ \frac{x^2}{6} - \frac{x^3}{27} + \frac{4}{3} x^{3/2} \right]_0^9 = \frac{\rho}{2} \left[ \frac{27}{2} - 27 + 36 \right] = \frac{45}{3} \rho$

$M_y = \rho \int_0^9 x \left[ \sqrt{x} + 1 - \frac{1}{3} x - 1 \right] dx = \rho \int_0^9 \left( x^{3/2} - \frac{1}{3} x^2 \right) dx = \rho \left[ \frac{2}{5} x^{5/2} - \frac{1}{9} x^3 \right]_0^9$

$= \rho \left[ \frac{486}{5} - 81 \right] = \frac{81}{5} \rho$

$\bar{x} = \frac{M_y}{m} = \frac{\frac{81}{5} \rho}{\frac{9}{2} \rho} = \frac{18}{5}; \bar{y} = \frac{M_x}{m} = \frac{\frac{45}{4} \rho}{\frac{9}{2} \rho} = \frac{5}{2}$

$(\bar{x}, \bar{y}) = \left( \frac{18}{5}, \frac{5}{2} \right)$

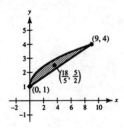

**20.**  $m = 2\rho \displaystyle\int_0^8 (4 - x^{2/3})\, dx = 2\rho \left[ 4x - \dfrac{3}{5} x^{5/3} \right]_0^8 = \dfrac{128\rho}{5}$

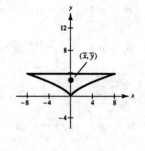

By symmetry, $M_y$ and $\bar{x} = 0$.

$M_x = 2\rho \displaystyle\int_0^8 \left( \dfrac{4 + x^{2/3}}{2} \right)(4 - x^{2/3})\, dx = \rho \left[ 16x - \dfrac{3}{7} x^{7/3} \right]_0^8 = \dfrac{512\rho}{7}$

$\bar{y} = \dfrac{512\rho}{7} \left( \dfrac{5}{128\rho} \right) = \dfrac{20}{7}$

$(\bar{x}, \bar{y}) = \left( 0, \dfrac{20}{7} \right)$

**22.**  $m = \rho \displaystyle\int_0^2 (2y - y^2)\, dy = \rho \left[ y^2 - \dfrac{y^3}{3} \right]_0^2 = \dfrac{4\rho}{3}$

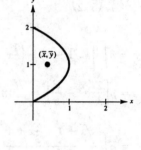

$M_y = \rho \displaystyle\int_0^2 \left( \dfrac{2y - y^2}{2} \right)(2y - y^2)\, dy = \dfrac{\rho}{2} \left[ \dfrac{4y^3}{3} - y^4 + \dfrac{y^5}{5} \right]_0^2 = \dfrac{8\rho}{15}$

$\bar{x} = \dfrac{M_y}{m} = \dfrac{8\rho}{15} \left( \dfrac{3}{4\rho} \right) = \dfrac{2}{5}$

$M_x = \rho \displaystyle\int_0^2 y(2y - y^2)\, dy = \rho \left[ \dfrac{2y^3}{3} - \dfrac{y^4}{4} \right]_0^2 = \dfrac{4\rho}{3}$

$\bar{y} = \dfrac{M_x}{m} = \dfrac{4\rho}{3} \left( \dfrac{3}{4\rho} \right) = 1$

$(\bar{x}, \bar{y}) = \left( \dfrac{2}{5}, 1 \right)$

**24.**  $m = \rho \displaystyle\int_{-1}^2 [(y + 2) - y^2]\, dy = \rho \left[ \dfrac{y^2}{2} + 2y - \dfrac{y^3}{3} \right]_{-1}^2 = \dfrac{9\rho}{2}$

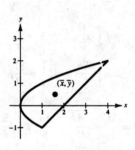

$M_y = \rho \displaystyle\int_{-1}^2 \dfrac{[(y + 2) + y^2]}{2} [(y + 2) - y^2]\, dy$

$\quad = \dfrac{\rho}{2} \displaystyle\int_{-1}^2 [(y + 2)^2 - y^4]\, dy = \dfrac{\rho}{2} \left[ \dfrac{(y + 2)^3}{3} - \dfrac{y^5}{5} \right]_{-1}^2 = \dfrac{36\rho}{5}$

$\bar{x} = \dfrac{M_y}{m} = \dfrac{36\rho}{5} \left( \dfrac{2}{9\rho} \right) = \dfrac{8}{5}$

$M_x = \rho \displaystyle\int_{-1}^2 y[(y + 2) - y^2]\, dy$

$\quad = \rho \displaystyle\int_{-1}^2 (2y + y^2 - y^3)\, dy = \rho \left[ y^2 + \dfrac{y^3}{3} - \dfrac{y^4}{4} \right]_{-1}^2 = \dfrac{9\rho}{4}$

$\bar{y} = \dfrac{M_x}{m} = \dfrac{9\rho}{4} \left( \dfrac{2}{9\rho} \right) = \dfrac{1}{2}$

$(\bar{x}, \bar{y}) = \left( \dfrac{8}{5}, \dfrac{1}{2} \right)$

**26.**  $A = \displaystyle\int_1^4 \dfrac{1}{x}\, dx = \left[ \ln|x| \right]_1^4 = \ln 4$

$M_x = \dfrac{1}{2} \displaystyle\int_1^4 \dfrac{1}{x^2}\, dx = \left[ \dfrac{1}{2} \left( -\dfrac{1}{x} \right) \right]_1^4 = \left( -\dfrac{1}{8} + \dfrac{1}{2} \right) = \dfrac{3}{8}$

$M_y = \displaystyle\int_1^4 x \left( \dfrac{1}{x} \right) dx = \left[ x \right]_1^4 = 3$

**28.** $A = \int_{-2}^{2} -(x^2 - 4)\,dx = 2\int_{0}^{2}(4 - x^2)\,dx = \left[8x - \frac{2x^3}{3}\right]_{0}^{2} = 16 - \frac{16}{3} = \frac{32}{3}$

$M_x = \frac{1}{2}\int_{-2}^{2}(x^2 - 4)(4 - x^2)\,dx = -\frac{1}{2}\int_{-2}^{2}(x^4 - 8x^2 + 16)\,dx$

$\quad = -\frac{1}{2}\left[\frac{x^5}{5} - \frac{8x^3}{3} + 16x\right]_{-2}^{2} = -\left[\frac{32}{5} - \frac{64}{3} + 32\right] = -\frac{256}{15}$

$M_y = 0$ by symmetry.

**30.** $m = \rho\int_{0}^{4} xe^{-x/2}\,dx \approx 2.3760\rho$

$M_x = \rho\int_{0}^{4}\left(\frac{xe^{-x/2}}{2}\right)(xe^{-x/2})\,dx = \frac{\rho}{2}\int_{0}^{4} x^2 e^{-x}\,dx \approx 0.7619\rho$

$M_y = \rho\int_{0}^{4} x^2 e^{-x/2}\,dx \approx 5.1732\rho$

$\bar{x} = \frac{M_y}{m} \approx 2.2$

$\bar{y} = \frac{M_x}{m} \approx 0.3$

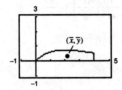

Therefore, the centroid is $(2.2, 0.3)$.

**32.** $m = \rho\int_{-2}^{2}\frac{8}{x^2 + 4}\,dx \approx 6.2832\rho$

$M_x = \rho\int_{-2}^{2}\frac{1}{2}\left(\frac{8}{x^2 + 4}\right)\left(\frac{8}{x^2 + 4}\right)\,dx = 32\rho\int_{-2}^{2}\frac{1}{(x^2 + 4)^2}\,dx \approx 5.14149\rho$

$\bar{y} = \frac{M_x}{m} \approx 0.8$

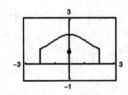

$\bar{x} = 0$ by symmetry. Therefore, the centroid is $(0, 0.8)$.

**34.** $A = bh = ac$

$\frac{1}{A} = \frac{1}{ac}$

$\bar{x} = \frac{1}{ac}\frac{1}{2}\int_{0}^{c}\left[\left(\frac{b}{c}y + a\right)^2 - \left(\frac{b}{c}y\right)^2\right]dy$

$\quad = \frac{1}{2ac}\int_{0}^{c}\left(\frac{2ab}{c}y + a^2\right)dy$

$\quad = \frac{1}{2ac}\left[\frac{ab}{c}y^2 + a^2 y\right]_{0}^{c} = \frac{1}{2ac}[abc + a^2 c] = \frac{1}{2}(b + a)$

$\bar{y} = \frac{1}{ac}\int_{0}^{c} y\left[\left(\frac{b}{c}y + a\right) - \left(\frac{b}{c}y\right)\right]dy = \left[\frac{1}{c}\frac{y^2}{2}\right]_{0}^{c} = \frac{c}{2}$

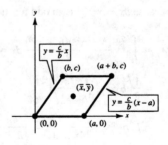

$(\bar{x}, \bar{y}) = \left(\frac{b + a}{2}, \frac{c}{2}\right)$

This is the point of intersection of the diagonals.

**36.** $\bar{x} = 0$ by symmetry

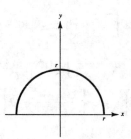

$$A = \frac{1}{2}\pi r^2$$

$$\frac{1}{A} = \frac{2}{\pi r^2}$$

$$\bar{y} = \frac{2}{\pi r^2}\frac{1}{2}\int_{-r}^{r}\left(\sqrt{r^2 - x^2}\right)^2 dx$$

$$= \frac{1}{\pi r^2}\left[r^2 x - \frac{x^3}{3}\right]_{-r}^{r} = \frac{1}{\pi r^2}\left[\frac{4r^3}{3}\right] = \frac{4r}{3\pi}$$

$$(\bar{x}, \bar{y}) = \left(0, \frac{4r}{3\pi}\right)$$

**38.** $$A = \int_0^1 [1 - (2x - x^2)]\,dx = \frac{1}{3}$$

$$\frac{1}{A} = 3$$

$$\bar{x} = 3\int_0^1 x[1 - (2x - x^2)]\,dx = 3\int_0^1 [x - 2x^2 + x^3]\,dx = 3\left[\frac{x^2}{2} - \frac{2}{3}x^3 + \frac{x^4}{4}\right]_0^1 = \frac{1}{4}$$

$$\bar{y} = 3\int_0^1 \frac{[1 + (2x - x^2)]}{2}[1 - (2x - x^2)]\,dx = \frac{3}{2}\int_0^1 [1 - (2x - x^2)^2]\,dx$$

$$= \frac{3}{2}\int_0^1 [1 - 4x^2 + 4x^3 - x^4]\,dx = \frac{3}{2}\left[x - \frac{4}{3}x^3 + x^4 - \frac{x^5}{5}\right]_0^1 = \frac{7}{10}$$

$$(\bar{x}, \bar{y}) = \left(\frac{1}{4}, \frac{7}{10}\right)$$

**40.** (a) $M_y = 0$ by symmetry

$$M_y = \int_{-\sqrt[2n]{b}}^{\sqrt[2n]{b}} x(b - x^{2n})\,dx = 0$$

because $bx - x^{2n+1}$ is an odd function.

(c) $M_x = \int_{-\sqrt[2n]{b}}^{\sqrt[2n]{b}} \frac{(b + x^{2n})(b - x^{2n})}{2}\,dx = \int_{-\sqrt[2n]{b}}^{\sqrt[2n]{b}} \frac{1}{2}(b^2 - x^{4n})\,dx$

$$= \frac{1}{2}\left(b^2 x - \frac{x^{4n+1}}{4n+1}\right)\Big]_{-\sqrt[2n]{b}}^{\sqrt[2n]{b}}$$

$$= b^2 b^{1/2n} - \frac{b^{(4n+1)/2n}}{4n+1} = \frac{4n}{4n+1}b^{(4n+1)/2n}$$

$$A = \int_{-\sqrt[2n]{b}}^{\sqrt[2n]{b}} (b - x^{2n})\,dx = 2\left[bx - \frac{x^{2n+1}}{2n+1}\right]_0^{\sqrt[2n]{b}}$$

$$= 2\left[b \cdot b^{1/2n} - \frac{b^{(2n+1)/2n}}{2n+1}\right] = \frac{4n}{2n+1}b^{(2n+1)/2n}$$

$$\bar{y} = \frac{M_x}{A} = \frac{4n\,b^{(4n+1)/2n}/(4n+1)}{4n\,b^{(24n+1)/2n}/(2n+1)} = \frac{2n+1}{4n+1}b$$

(b) $\bar{y} > \dfrac{b}{2}$ because there is more area above $y = \dfrac{b}{2}$ than below.

(d)

| $n$ | 1 | 2 | 3 | 4 |
|---|---|---|---|---|
| $\bar{y}$ | $\frac{3}{5}b$ | $\frac{5}{9}b$ | $\frac{7}{13}b$ | $\frac{9}{17}b$ |

(e) $\displaystyle\lim_{n\to\infty} \bar{y} = \lim_{n\to\infty}\frac{2n+1}{4n+1}b = \frac{1}{2}b$

(f) As $n \to \infty$, the figure gets narrower.

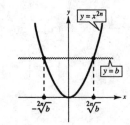

**42.** Let $f(x)$ be the top curve, given by $l + d$. The bottom curve is $d(x)$.

| $x$ | 0 | 0.5 | 1.0 | 1.5 | 2.0 |
|---|---|---|---|---|---|
| $f$ | 2.0 | 1.93 | 1.73 | 1.32 | 0 |
| $d$ | 0.50 | 0.48 | 0.43 | 0.33 | 0 |

(a) $\text{Area} = 2 \int_0^2 [f(x) - d(x)] \, dx$

$\approx 2\dfrac{2}{3(4)}[1.50 + 4(1.45) + 2(1.30) + 4(.99) + 0]$

$= \dfrac{1}{3}[13.86] = 4.62$

$M_x = \int_{-2}^2 \dfrac{f(x) + d(x)}{2}(f(x) - d(x)) \, dx$

$= \int_0^2 [f(x)^2 - d(x)^2] \, dx$

$= \dfrac{2}{3(4)}[3.75 + 4(3.4945) + 2(2.808) + 4(1.6335) + 0]$

$= \dfrac{1}{6}[29.878] = 4.9797$

$\bar{y} = \dfrac{M_x}{A} = \dfrac{4.9797}{4.62} = 1.078$

$(\bar{x}, \bar{y}) = (0, 1.078)$

(b) $f(x) = -0.1061x^4 - 0.06126x^2 + 1.9527$

$d(x) = -0.02648x^4 - 0.01497x^2 + .4862$

(c) $\bar{y} = \dfrac{M_x}{A} \approx \dfrac{4.9133}{4.59998} = 1.068$

$(\bar{x}, \bar{y}) = (0, 1.068)$

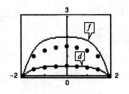

**44.** Centroids of the given regions: $\left(\dfrac{1}{2}, \dfrac{3}{2}\right)$, $\left(2, \dfrac{1}{2}\right)$, and $\left(\dfrac{7}{2}, 1\right)$

Area: $A = 3 + 2 + 2 = 7$

$\bar{x} = \dfrac{3(1/2) + 2(2) + 2(7/2)}{7} = \dfrac{25/2}{7} = \dfrac{25}{14}$

$\bar{y} = \dfrac{3(3/2) + 2(1/2) + 2(1)}{7} = \dfrac{15/2}{7} = \dfrac{15}{14}$

$(\bar{x}, \bar{y}) = \left(\dfrac{25}{14}, \dfrac{15}{14}\right)$

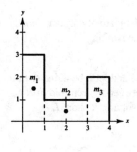

**46.** $m_1 = \dfrac{7}{8}(2) = \dfrac{7}{4}$, $P_1 = \left(0, \dfrac{7}{16}\right)$

$m_2 = \dfrac{7}{8}\left(6 - \dfrac{7}{8}\right) = \dfrac{287}{64}$, $P_2 = \left(0, \dfrac{55}{16}\right)$

By symmetry, $\bar{x} = 0$.

$\bar{y} = \dfrac{(7/4)(7/16) + (287/64)(55/16)}{(7/4) + (287/64)} = \dfrac{16,569}{6384} = \dfrac{5523}{2128}$

$(\bar{x}, \bar{y}) = \left(0, \dfrac{5523}{2128}\right) \approx (0, 2.595)$

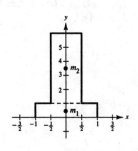

**48.** Centroids of the given regions: $(3, 0)$ and $(1, 0)$

Mass: $8 + \pi$

$$\bar{y} = 0$$

$$\bar{x} = \frac{8(1) + \pi(3)}{8 + \pi} = \frac{8 + 3\pi}{8 + \pi}$$

$$(\bar{x}, \bar{y}) = \left(\frac{8 + 3\pi}{8 + \pi}, 0\right) \approx (1.56, 0)$$

**50.** $V = 2\pi rA = 2\pi(3)(4\pi) = 24\pi^2$

**52.**
$$A = \int_2^6 2\sqrt{x - 2}\, dx = \frac{4}{3}(x - 2)^{3/2}\Big]_2^6 = \frac{32}{3}$$

$$M_y = \int_2^6 (x)2\sqrt{x - 2}\, dx = 2\int_2^6 x\sqrt{x - 2}\, dx$$

Let $u = x - 2, x = u + 2, du = dx$:

$$M_y = 2\int_0^4 (u + 2)\sqrt{u}\, du = 2\int_0^4 (u^{3/2} + 2u^{1/2})\, du = 2\left[\frac{2}{5}u^{5/2} + \frac{4}{3}u^{3/2}\right]_0^4$$

$$= 2\left[\frac{64}{5} + \frac{32}{3}\right] = \frac{704}{15}$$

$$\bar{x} = \frac{M_y}{A} = \frac{704/15}{32/3} = \frac{22}{5}$$

$$r = \bar{x} = \frac{22}{5}$$

$$V = 2\pi rA = 2\pi\left(\frac{22}{5}\right)\left(\frac{32}{3}\right) = \frac{1408\pi}{15} \approx 294.89$$

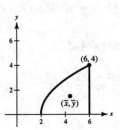

**54.** A planar lamina is a thin flat plate of constant density. The center of mass $(\bar{x}, \bar{y})$ is the balancing point on the lamina.

**56.** Let $R$ be a region in a plane and let $L$ be a line such that $L$ does not intersect the interior of $R$. If $r$ is the distance between the centroid of $R$ and $L$, then the volume $V$ of the solid of revolution formed by revolving $R$ about $L$ is

$$V = 2\pi rA$$

where $A$ is the area of $R$.

**58.** The centroid of the circle is $(1, 0)$. The distance traveled by the centroid is $2\pi$. The arc length of the circle is also $2\pi$. Therefore, $S = (2\pi)(2\pi) = 4\pi^2$.

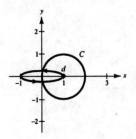

# Section 6.7    Fluid Pressure and Fluid Force

**2.** $F = PA = [62.4(5)](16) = 4992 \text{ lb}$

**4.** $F = 62.4(h + 4)(48) - (62.4)(h)(48)$

$= 62.4(4)(48) = 11{,}980.8 \text{ lb}$

**6.** $h(y) = 3 - y$

$L(y) = \dfrac{4}{3}y$

$F = 62.4 \displaystyle\int_0^3 (3 - y)\left(\dfrac{4}{3}y\right) dy$

$= \dfrac{4}{3}(62.4) \displaystyle\int_0^3 (3y - y^2) \, dy$

$= \dfrac{4}{3}(62.4) \left[\dfrac{3y^2}{2} - \dfrac{y^3}{3}\right]_0^3 = 374.4 \text{ lb}$

Force is one-third that of Exercise 5.

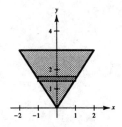

**8.** $h(y) = -y$

$L(y) = 2\sqrt{4 - y^2}$

$F = 62.4 \displaystyle\int_{-2}^0 (-y)(2)\sqrt{4 - y^2} \, dy$

$= \left[62.4\left(\dfrac{2}{3}\right)(4 - y^2)^{3/2}\right]_{-2}^0 = 332.8 \text{ lb}$

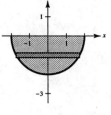

**10.** $h(y) = -y$

$L(y) = \dfrac{4}{3}\sqrt{9 - y^2}$

$F = 62.4 \displaystyle\int_{-3}^0 (-y)\dfrac{4}{3}\sqrt{9 - y^2} \, dy$

$= 62.4\left(\dfrac{2}{3}\right) \displaystyle\int_{-3}^0 (9 - y^2)^{1/2}(-2y) \, dy$

$= \left[62.4\left(\dfrac{4}{9}\right)(9 - y^2)^{3/2}\right]_{-3}^0 = 748.8 \text{ lb}$

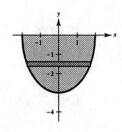

**12.** $h(y) = \left(1 + 3\sqrt{2}\right) - y$

$L_1(y) = 2y$   (lower part)

$L_2(y) = 2\left(3\sqrt{2} - y\right)$   (upper part)

$F = 2(9800)\left[\displaystyle\int_0^{3\sqrt{2}/2} \left(1 + 3\sqrt{2} - y\right)y \, dy + \displaystyle\int_{3\sqrt{2}/2}^{3\sqrt{2}} \left(1 + 3\sqrt{2} - y\right)\left(3\sqrt{2} - y\right) dy\right]$

$= 19{,}600\left[\left[\dfrac{y^2}{2} - 3\sqrt{2}y - \dfrac{y^3}{3}\right]_0^{3\sqrt{2}/2} + \left[3\sqrt{2}y + 18y + \dfrac{y^3}{3} - \dfrac{6\sqrt{2} + 1}{2}y\right]_{3\sqrt{2}/2}^{3\sqrt{2}}\right]$

$= 19{,}600\left[\dfrac{9(2\sqrt{2} + 1)}{4} + \dfrac{9(\sqrt{2} + 1)}{4}\right]$

$= 44{,}100\left(3\sqrt{2} + 2\right) \text{ Newtons}$

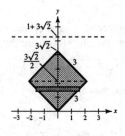

**14.** $h(y) = 6 - y$

$L(y) = 1$

$F = 9800 \int_0^5 1(6 - y)\, dy$

$\quad = 9800 \left[ 6y - \dfrac{y^2}{2} \right]_0^5 = 171{,}500 \text{ Newtons}$

**16.** $h(y) = -y$

$L(y) = 2\left( \dfrac{4}{3} \sqrt{9 - y^2} \right)$

$F = 140.7 \int_{-3}^0 (-y)(2)\left( \dfrac{4}{3} \sqrt{9 - y^2} \right) dy$

$\quad = \dfrac{(140.7)(4)}{3} \int_{-3}^0 \sqrt{9 - y^2}\,(-2y)\, dy$

$\quad = \left[ \dfrac{(140.7)(4)}{3} \left( \dfrac{2}{3} \right) (9 - y^2)^{3/2} \right]_{-3}^0 = 3376.8 \text{ lb}$

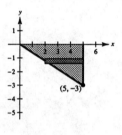

**18.** $h(y) = -y$

$L(y) = 5 + \dfrac{5}{3}y$

$F = 140.7 \int_{-3}^0 (-y)\left( 5 + \dfrac{5}{3}y \right) dy$

$\quad = 140.7 \int_{-3}^0 \left( -5y - \dfrac{5}{3}y^2 \right) dy$

$\quad = 140.7 \left[ -\dfrac{5}{2}y^2 - \dfrac{5}{9}y^3 \right]_{-3}^0$

$\quad = 140.7 \left[ \dfrac{45}{2} - 15 \right] = 1055.25 \text{ lb}$

**20.** $h(y) = \dfrac{3}{2} - y$

$L(y) = 2\left( \dfrac{1}{2} \right) \sqrt{9 - 4y^2}$

$F = 42 \int_{-3/2}^{3/2} \left( \dfrac{3}{2} - y \right) \sqrt{9 - 4y^2}\, dy = 63 \int_{-3/2}^{3/2} \sqrt{9 - 4y^2}\, dy + \dfrac{21}{4} \int_{-3/2}^{3/2} \sqrt{9 - 4y^2}\,(-8y)\, dy$

The second integral is zero since it is an odd function and the limits of integration are symmetric to the origin. The first integral is twice the area of a semicircle of radius $\frac{3}{2}$.

$\qquad \left( \sqrt{9 - 4y^2} = 2\sqrt{(9/4) - y^2} \right)$

Thus, the force is $63\left( \dfrac{9}{4}\pi \right) = 141.75\pi \approx 445.32 \text{ lb}$.

**22.** (a) $F = wk\pi r^2 = (62.4)(7)(\pi 2^2) = 1747.2\pi \text{ lbs}$

　　(b) $F = wk\pi r^2 = (62.4)(5)(\pi 3^2) = 2808\pi \text{ lbs}$

**24.** (a) $F = wkhb = (62.4)\left( \dfrac{11}{2} \right)(3)(5) = 5148 \text{ lbs}$

　　(b) $F = wkhb = (62.4)\left( \dfrac{17}{5} \right)(5)(10) = 10{,}608 \text{ lbs}$

**26.** From Exercise 21:

$$F = 64(15)\pi\left(\frac{1}{2}\right)^2 \approx 753.98 \text{ lb}$$

**28.** $h(y) = 3 - y$

Solving $y = 5x^2/(x^2 + 4)$ for $x$, you obtain
$$x = \sqrt{4y/(5 - y)}.$$

$$L(y) = 2\sqrt{\frac{4y}{5 - y}}$$

$$F = 62.4(2)\int_0^3 (3 - y)\sqrt{\frac{4y}{5 - y}}\,dy$$

$$= 2(124.8)\int_0^3 (3 - y)\sqrt{\frac{y}{5 - y}}\,dy \approx 546.265 \text{ lb}$$

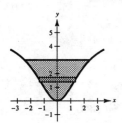

**30.** $h(y) = 12 - y$

$$L(y) = 2\frac{\sqrt{7(16 - y^2)}}{2} = \sqrt{7(16 - y^2)}$$

$$F = 62.4\int_0^4 (12 - y)\sqrt{7(16 - y^2)}\,dy$$

$$= 62.4\sqrt{7}\int_0^4 (12 - y)\sqrt{16 - y^2}\,dy \approx 21373.7 \text{ lb}$$

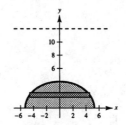

**32.** Fluid pressure is the force per unit of area exerted by a fluid over the surface of a body.

**34.** The left window experiences the greater fluid force because its centroid is lower.

# Review Exercises for Chapter 6

**2.** $A = \displaystyle\int_{1/2}^5 \left(4 - \frac{1}{x^2}\right)dx$

$$= \left[4x + \frac{1}{x}\right]_{1/2}^5 = \frac{81}{5}$$

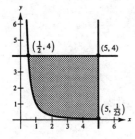

**4.** $A = \displaystyle\int_0^1 [(y^2 - 2y) - (-1)]\,dy$

$$= \int_0^1 (y^2 - 2y + 1)\,dy$$

$$= \int_0^1 (y - 1)^2\,dy$$

$$= \left[\frac{(y - 1)^3}{3}\right]_0^1 = \frac{1}{3}$$

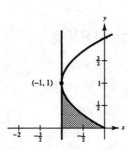

**6.** $A = \displaystyle\int_{-1}^{2} [(y+3) - (y^2+1)]\,dy$

$\qquad = \displaystyle\int_{-1}^{2} (2 + y - y^2)\,dy$

$\qquad = \left[2y + \dfrac{1}{2}y^2 - \dfrac{1}{3}y^3\right]_{-1}^{2} = \dfrac{9}{2}$

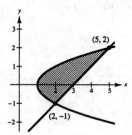

**8.** $A = 2 \displaystyle\int_{\pi/6}^{\pi/2} (2 - \csc x)\,dx$

$\qquad = 2\left[2x - \ln|\csc x - \cot x|\right]_{\pi/6}^{\pi/2}$

$\qquad = 2\left([\pi - 0] - \left[\dfrac{\pi}{3} - \ln(2 - \sqrt{3})\right]\right)$

$\qquad = 2\left[\dfrac{2\pi}{3} + \ln(2 - \sqrt{3})\right] \approx 1.555$

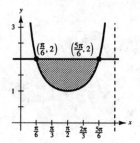

**10.** $A = \displaystyle\int_{\pi/3}^{5\pi/3} \left(\dfrac{1}{2} - \cos y\right) dy + \int_{5\pi/3}^{7\pi/3} \left(\cos y - \dfrac{1}{2}\right) dy$

$\qquad = \left[\dfrac{y}{2} - \sin y\right]_{\pi/3}^{5\pi/3} + \left[\sin y - \dfrac{y}{2}\right]_{5\pi/3}^{7\pi/3}$

$\qquad = \dfrac{\pi}{3} + 2\sqrt{3}$

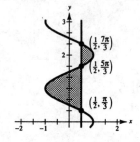

**12.** Point of intersection is given by:

$\qquad x^3 - x^2 + 4x - 3 = 0 \implies x \approx 0.783.$

$\qquad A \approx \displaystyle\int_{0}^{0.783} (3 - 4x + x^2 - x^3)\,dx$

$\qquad = \left[3x - 2x^2 + \dfrac{1}{3}x^3 - \dfrac{1}{4}x^4\right]_{0}^{0.783}$

$\qquad \approx 1.189$

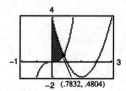

**14.** $A = 2 \displaystyle\int_{0}^{2} [2x^2 - (x^4 - 2x^2)]\,dx$

$\qquad = 2 \displaystyle\int_{0}^{2} (4x^2 - x^4)\,dx$

$\qquad = 2\left[\dfrac{4}{3}x^3 - \dfrac{1}{5}x^5\right]_{0}^{2} = \dfrac{128}{15} \approx 8.5333$

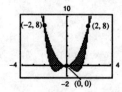

**16.** $y = \sqrt{x-1} \implies x = y^2 + 1$

$\qquad y = \dfrac{x-1}{2} \implies x = 2y + 1$

$\qquad A = \displaystyle\int_{0}^{2} [(2y+1) - (y^2+1)]\,dy$

$\qquad = \displaystyle\int_{1}^{5} \left[\sqrt{x-1} - \dfrac{x-1}{2}\right] dx$

$\qquad = \left[\dfrac{2}{3}(x-1)^{3/2} - \dfrac{1}{4}(x-1)^2\right]_{1}^{5} = \dfrac{4}{3}$

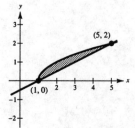

**18.** $A = \int_0^1 2\, dx + \int_1^5 \left[2 - \sqrt{x-1}\right] dx$

$x = y^2 + 1$

$A = \int_0^2 (y^2 + 1)\, dy$

$= \left[\frac{1}{3}y^3 + y\right]_0^2 = \frac{14}{3}$

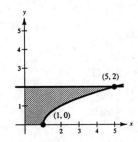

**20.** (a) $R_1(t) = 5.2834(1.2701)^t = 5.2834\, e^{0.2391t}$

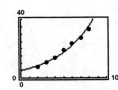

(b) $R_2(t) = 10 + 5.28\, e^{0.2t}$

Difference $= \int_{10}^{15} \left[R_1(t) - R_2(t)\right] dt \approx 171.25$ billion dollars

**22.** (a) **Shell**

$V = 2\pi \int_0^2 y^3\, dy = \left[\frac{\pi}{2}y^4\right]_0^2 = 8\pi$

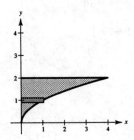

(b) **Shell**

$V = 2\pi \int_0^2 (2-y)y^2\, dy$

$= 2\pi \int_0^2 (2y^2 - y^3)\, dy$

$= 2\pi \left[\frac{2}{3}y^3 - \frac{1}{4}y^4\right]_0^2 = \frac{8\pi}{3}$

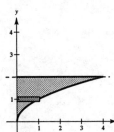

(c) **Disk**

$V = \pi \int_0^2 y^4\, dy = \left[\frac{\pi}{5}y^5\right]_0^2 = \frac{32\pi}{5}$

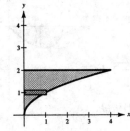

(d) **Disk**

$V = \pi \int_0^2 \left[(y^2+1)^2 - 1^2\right] dy$

$= \pi \int_0^2 (y^4 + 2y^2)\, dy$

$= \pi \left[\frac{1}{5}y^5 + \frac{2}{3}y^3\right]_0^2 = \frac{176\pi}{15}$

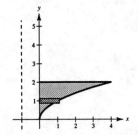

**24.** (a) **Shell**

$$V = 4\pi \int_0^a (x)\frac{b}{a}\sqrt{a^2 - x^2}\, dx$$

$$= \frac{-2\pi b}{a}\int_0^a (a^2 - x^2)^{1/2}(-2x)\, dx$$

$$= \left[\frac{-4\pi b}{3a}(a^2 - x^2)^{3/2}\right]_0^a = \frac{4}{3}\pi a^2 b$$

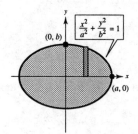

(b) **Disk**

$$V = 2\pi \int_0^a \frac{b^2}{a^2}(a^2 - x^2)\, dx$$

$$= \frac{2\pi b^2}{a^2}\left[a^2 x - \frac{1}{3}x^3\right]_0^a$$

$$= \frac{4}{3}\pi ab^2$$

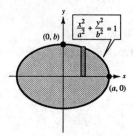

**26. Disk**

$$V = 2\pi \int_0^1 \left[\frac{1}{\sqrt{1 + x^2}}\right]^2 dx$$

$$= \left[2\pi \arctan x\right]_0^1$$

$$= 2\pi\left(\frac{\pi}{4} - 0\right)$$

$$= \frac{\pi^2}{2}$$

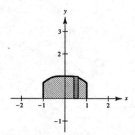

**28. Disk**

$$V = \pi \int_0^1 (e^{-x})^2 dx$$

$$= \pi \int_0^1 e^{-2x}\, dx = \left[-\frac{\pi}{2}e^{-2x}\right]_0^1$$

$$= \left(\frac{-\pi}{2e^2} + \frac{\pi}{2}\right) = \frac{\pi}{2}\left(1 - \frac{1}{e^2}\right)$$

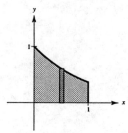

**30.** (a) **Disk**

$$V = \pi \int_{-1}^0 x^2(x + 1)\, dx$$

$$= \pi \int_{-1}^0 (x^3 + x^2)\, dx$$

$$= \pi\left[\frac{x^4}{4} + \frac{x^3}{3}\right]_{-1}^0 = \frac{\pi}{12}$$

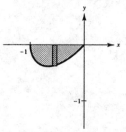

(b) **Shell**

$$u = \sqrt{x + 1}$$

$$x = u^2 - 1$$

$$dx = 2u\, du$$

$$V = 2\pi \int_{-1}^0 x^2\sqrt{x + 1}\, dx$$

$$= 4\pi \int_0^1 (u^2 - 1)^2 u^2\, du$$

$$= 4\pi \int_0^1 (u^6 - 2u^4 + u^2)\, du$$

$$= 4\pi\left[\frac{1}{7}u^7 - \frac{2}{5}u^5 + \frac{1}{3}u^3\right]_0^1 = \frac{32\pi}{105}$$

**32.** $A(x) = \frac{1}{2}bh = \frac{1}{2}\left(2\sqrt{a^2 - x^2}\right)\left(\sqrt{3}\sqrt{a^2 - x^2}\right)$

$\qquad = \sqrt{3}\,(a^2 - x^2)$

$\quad V = \sqrt{3}\displaystyle\int_{-a}^{a}(a^2 - x^2)\,dx = \sqrt{3}\left[a^2x - \frac{x^3}{3}\right]_{-a}^{a}$

$\qquad = \sqrt{3}\left(\dfrac{4a^3}{3}\right)$

Since $(4\sqrt{3}\,a^3)/3 = 10$, we have $a^3 = (5\sqrt{3})/2$. Thus,

$\quad a = \sqrt[3]{\dfrac{5\sqrt{3}}{2}} \approx 1.630$ meters.

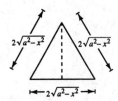

**34.** $\qquad y = \dfrac{x^3}{6} + \dfrac{1}{2x}$

$\qquad y' = \dfrac{1}{2}x^2 - \dfrac{1}{2x^2}$

$\quad 1 + (y')^2 = \left(\dfrac{1}{2}x^2 + \dfrac{1}{2x^2}\right)^2$

$\qquad s = \displaystyle\int_{1}^{3}\left(\dfrac{1}{2}x^2 + \dfrac{1}{2x^2}\right)dx = \left[\dfrac{1}{6}x^3 - \dfrac{1}{2x}\right]_{1}^{3} = \dfrac{14}{3}$

**36.** Since $f(x) = \tan x$ has $f'(x) = \sec^2 x$, this integral represents the length of the graph of $\tan x$ from $x = 0$ to $x = \pi/4$. This length is a little over 1 unit. Answers (b).

**38.** $y = 2\sqrt{x}$

$\qquad y' = \dfrac{1}{\sqrt{x}}$

$\quad 1 + (y')^2 = 1 + \dfrac{1}{x} = \dfrac{x + 1}{x}$

$\qquad S = 2\pi\displaystyle\int_{0}^{3} 2\sqrt{x}\,\sqrt{\dfrac{x+1}{x}}\,dx = 4\pi\displaystyle\int_{0}^{3}\sqrt{x+1}\,dx$

$\qquad = 4\pi\left[\left(\dfrac{2}{3}\right)(x+1)^{3/2}\right]_{0}^{3} = \dfrac{56\pi}{3}$

**40.** $\quad F = kx$

$\quad 50 = k(9) \Rightarrow k = \dfrac{50}{9}$

$\quad F = \dfrac{50}{9}x$

$\quad W = \displaystyle\int_{0}^{9}\dfrac{50}{9}x\,dx = \left[\dfrac{25}{9}x^2\right]_{0}^{9}$

$\qquad = 225 \text{ in} \cdot \text{lb} = 18.75 \text{ ft} \cdot \text{lb}$

**42.** We know that

$\quad \dfrac{dV}{dt} = \dfrac{4\text{ gal/min} - 12\text{ gal/min}}{7.481\text{ gal/ft}^3} = -\dfrac{8}{7.481}\text{ ft}^3/\text{min}$

$\quad V = \pi r^2 h = \pi\left(\dfrac{1}{9}\right)h$

$\quad \dfrac{dV}{dt} = \dfrac{\pi}{9}\left(\dfrac{dh}{dt}\right)$

$\quad \dfrac{dh}{dt} = \dfrac{9}{\pi}\left(\dfrac{dV}{dt}\right) = \dfrac{9}{\pi}\left(-\dfrac{8}{7.481}\right) \approx -3.064\text{ ft/min}.$

Depth of water: $-3.064t + 150$

Time to drain well: $t = \dfrac{150}{3.064} \approx 49$ minutes

$\quad (49)(12) = 588$ gallons pumped

Volume of water pumped in Exercise 41: 391.7 gallons

$\quad \dfrac{391.7}{52\pi} = \dfrac{588}{x\pi}$

$\qquad x = \dfrac{588(52)}{391.7} \approx 78$

Work $\approx 78\pi\,\text{ft}\cdot\text{ton}$

**44.** (a) Weight of section of cable: $4 \, \Delta x$

Distance: $200 - x$

$$W = 4 \int_0^{200} (200 - x) \, dx = \left[ -2(200 - x)^2 \right]_0^{200} = 80,000 \text{ ft} \cdot \text{lb} = 40 \text{ ft} \cdot \text{ton}$$

(b) Work to move 300 pounds 200 feet vertically: $200(300) = 60,000 \text{ ft} \cdot \text{lb} = 30 \text{ ft} \cdot \text{ton}$

Total work = work for drawing up the cable + work of lifting the load

$= 40 \text{ ft} \cdot \text{ton} + 30 \text{ ft} \cdot \text{ton} = 70 \text{ ft} \cdot \text{ton}$

**46.** $$W = \int_a^b F(x) \, dx$$

$$F(x) = \begin{cases} -(2/9)x + 6, & 0 \le x \le 9 \\ -(4/3)x + 16, & 9 \le x \le 12 \end{cases}$$

$$W = \int_0^9 \left( -\frac{2}{9}x + 6 \right) dx + \int_9^{12} \left( -\frac{4}{3}x + 16 \right) dx$$

$$= \left[ -\frac{1}{9}x^2 + 6x \right]_0^9 + \left[ -\frac{2}{3}x^2 + 16x \right]_9^{12}$$

$$= (-9 + 54) + (-96 + 192 + 54 - 144) = 51 \text{ ft} \cdot \text{lbs}$$

**48.** $$A = \int_{-1}^3 [(2x + 3) - x^2] \, dx = \left[ x^2 + 3x - \frac{1}{3}x^3 \right]_{-1}^3 = \frac{32}{3}$$

$$\frac{1}{A} = \frac{3}{32}$$

$$\bar{x} = \frac{3}{32} \int_{-1}^3 x(2x + 3 - x^2) \, dx = \frac{3}{32} \int_{-1}^3 (3x + 2x^2 - x^3) \, dx = \frac{3}{32} \left[ \frac{3}{2}x^2 + \frac{2}{3}x^3 - \frac{1}{4}x^4 \right]_{-1}^3 = 1$$

$$\bar{y} = \left( \frac{3}{32} \right) \frac{1}{2} \int_{-1}^3 [(2x + 3)^2 - x^4] \, dx = \frac{3}{64} \int_{-1}^3 (9 + 12x + 4x^2 - x^4) \, dx$$

$$= \frac{3}{64} \left[ 9x + 6x^2 + \frac{4}{3}x^3 - \frac{1}{5}x^5 \right]_{-1}^3 = \frac{17}{5}$$

$$(\bar{x}, \bar{y}) = \left( 1, \frac{17}{5} \right)$$

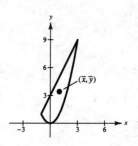

**50.** $$A = \int_0^8 \left( x^{2/3} - \frac{1}{2}x \right) dx = \left[ \frac{3}{5}x^{5/3} - \frac{1}{4}x^2 \right]_0^8 = \frac{16}{5}$$

$$\frac{1}{A} = \frac{5}{16}$$

$$\bar{x} = \frac{5}{16} \int_0^8 x \left( x^{2/3} - \frac{1}{2}x \right) dx$$

$$= \frac{5}{16} \left[ \frac{3}{8}x^{8/3} - \frac{1}{6}x^3 \right]_0^8 = \frac{10}{3}$$

$$\bar{y} = \left( \frac{5}{16} \right) \frac{1}{2} \int_0^8 \left( x^{4/3} - \frac{1}{4}x^2 \right) dx$$

$$= \frac{1}{2} \left( \frac{5}{16} \right) \left[ \frac{3}{7}x^{7/3} - \frac{1}{12}x^3 \right]_0^8 = \frac{40}{21}$$

$$(\bar{x}, \bar{y}) = \left( \frac{10}{3}, \frac{40}{21} \right)$$

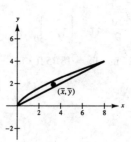

**52.** Wall at shallow end:

$$F = 62.4 \int_0^5 y(20)\, dy = \left[(1248)\frac{y^2}{2}\right]_0^5 = 15,600 \text{ lb}$$

Wall at deep end:

$$F = 62.4 \int_0^{10} y(20)\, dy = \left[(624)y^2\right]_0^{10} = 62,400 \text{ lb}$$

Side wall:

$$F_1 = 62.4 \int_0^5 y(40)\, dy = \left[(1248)y^2\right]_0^5 = 31,200 \text{ lb}$$

$$F_2 = 62.4 \int_0^5 (10 - y)8y\, dy = 62.4 \int_0^5 (80y - 8y^2)\, dy$$

$$F = F_1 + F_2 = 72,800 \text{ lb}$$

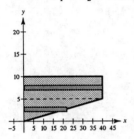

**54.** $F = 62.4(16\pi)5 = 4992\pi \text{ lb}$

# Problem Solving for Chapter 6

**2.** $R = \int_0^1 x(1 - x)\, dx = \left[\frac{x^2}{2} - \frac{x^3}{3}\right]_0^1 = \frac{1}{2} - \frac{1}{3} = \frac{1}{6}$

Let $(c, mc)$ be the intersection of the line and the parabola.

Then, $mc = c(1 - c) \implies m = 1 - c$ or $c = 1 - m$.

$$\frac{1}{2}\left(\frac{1}{6}\right) = \int_0^{1-m} (x - x^2 - mx)\, dx$$

$$\frac{1}{12} = \left[\frac{x^2}{2} - \frac{x^3}{3} - m\frac{x^2}{2}\right]_0^{1-m}$$

$$= \frac{(1 - m)^2}{2} - \frac{(1 - m)^3}{3} - m\frac{(1 - m)^2}{2}$$

$$1 = 6(1 - m)^2 - 4(1 - m)^3 - 6m(1 - m)^2$$

$$= (1 - m)^2(6 - 4(1 - m) - 6m)$$

$$= (1 - m)^2(2 - 2m)$$

$$\frac{1}{2} = (1 - m)^3$$

$$\left(\frac{1}{2}\right)^{1/3} = 1 - m$$

$$m = 1 - \left(\frac{1}{2}\right)^{1/3} \approx 0.2063$$

**4.** $8y^2 = x^2(1 - x^2)$

$$y = \pm\frac{|x|\sqrt{1 - x^2}}{2\sqrt{2}}$$

For $x > 0$, $y' = \dfrac{1 - 2x^2}{2\sqrt{2}\sqrt{1 - x^2}}$

$$S = 2(2\pi)\int_0^1 x\sqrt{1 + \left(\frac{1 - 2x^2}{2\sqrt{2}\sqrt{1 - x^2}}\right)^2}\, dx$$

$$= \frac{5\sqrt{2}\pi}{3}$$

**6.** By the Theorem of Pappus,

$$V = 2\pi r A$$

$$= 2\pi \left[ d + \frac{1}{2}\sqrt{w^2 + l^2} \right] lw$$

**8.** $f'(x)^2 = e^x$

$$f'(x) = e^{x/2}$$

$$f(x) = 2e^{x/2} + C$$

$$f(0) = 0 \implies C = -2$$

$$f(x) = 2e^{x/2} - 2$$

**10.** Let $\rho_f$ be the density of the fluid and $\rho_0$ the density of the iceberg. The buoyant force is

$$F = \rho_f g \int_{-h}^{0} A(y)\, dy$$

where $A(y)$ is a typical cross section and $g$ is the acceleration due to gravity. The weight of the object is

$$W = \rho_0 g \int_{-h}^{L-h} A(y)\, dy.$$

$$F = W$$

$$\rho_f g \int_{-h}^{0} A(y)\, dy = \rho_0 g \int_{-h}^{L-h} A(y)\, dy$$

$$\frac{\rho_0}{\rho_f} = \frac{\text{submerged volume}}{\text{total volume}} = \frac{0.92 \times 10^3}{1.03 \times 10^3} = 0.893 \text{ or } 89.3\%$$

**12.** (a) $\bar{y} = 0$ by symmetry

$$M_y = 2\int_{1}^{6} x\frac{1}{x^4}\, dx = 2\int_{1}^{6}\frac{1}{x^3}\, dx = \frac{35}{36}$$

$$m = 2\int_{1}^{6}\frac{1}{x^4}\, dx = \frac{215}{324}$$

$$\bar{x} = \frac{35/36}{215/324} = \frac{63}{43} \qquad (\bar{x}, \bar{y}) = \left(\frac{63}{43}, 0\right)$$

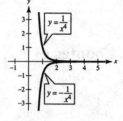

(b) $M_y = 2\int_{1}^{b}\frac{1}{x^3}\, dx = \frac{b^2 - 1}{b^2}$

$$m = 2\int_{1}^{b}\frac{1}{x^4}\, dx = \frac{2(b^3 - 1)}{3b^3}$$

$$\bar{x} = \frac{(b^2 - 1)/b^2}{2(b^3 - 1)/3b^3} = \frac{3b(b + 1)}{2(b^2 + b + 1)} \qquad (\bar{x}, \bar{y}) = \left(\frac{3b(b + 1)}{2(b^2 + b + 1)}, 0\right)$$

$$\lim_{b\to\infty} \bar{x} = \frac{3}{2} \qquad (\bar{x}, \bar{y}) = \left(\frac{3}{2}, 0\right)$$

**14.** (a) Trapezoidal: Area $\approx \frac{160}{2(8)}[0 + 2(50) + 2(54) + 2(82) + 2(82) + 2(73) + 2(75) + 2(80) + 0] = 9920$ sq ft

(b) Simpson's: Area $\approx \frac{160}{3(8)}[0 + 4(50) + 2(54) + 4(82) + 2(82) + 4(73) + 2(75) + 4(80) + 0] = 10{,}413\frac{1}{3}$ sq ft

**16.** Point of equilibrium: $1000 - 0.4x^2 = 42x$

$$x = 20, p = 840$$

$$(P_0, x_0) = (840, 20)$$

Consumer surplus $= \int_{0}^{20} [(1000 - 0.4x^2) - 840]\, dx = 2133.33$

Producer surplus $= \int_{0}^{20} [840 - 42x]\, dx = 8400$

# C H A P T E R   7
# Integration Techniques, L'Hôpital's Rule, and Improper Integrals

# C H A P T E R 7
# Integration Techniques, L'Hôpital's Rule, and Improper Integrals

## Section 7.1    Basic Integration Rules

Solutions to Even-Numbered Exercises

**2.** (a) $\dfrac{d}{dx}\Big[\ln\sqrt{x^2+1}+C\Big]=\dfrac{1}{2}\Big(\dfrac{2x}{x^2+1}\Big)=\dfrac{x}{x^2+1}$

(b) $\dfrac{d}{dx}\Big[\dfrac{2x}{(x^2+1)^2}+C\Big]=\dfrac{(x^2+1)^2(2)-(2x)(2)(x^2+1)(2x)}{(x^2+1)^4}=\dfrac{2(1-3x^2)}{(x^2+1)^3}$

(c) $\dfrac{d}{dx}[\arctan x+C]=\dfrac{1}{1+x^2}$

(d) $\dfrac{d}{dx}[\ln(x^2+1)+C]=\dfrac{2x}{x^2+1}$

$\displaystyle\int\dfrac{x}{x^2+1}\,dx$ matches (a).

**4.** (a) $\dfrac{d}{dx}[2x\sin(x^2+1)+C]=2x[\cos(x^2+1)(2x)]+2\sin(x^2+1)=2[2x^2\cos(x^2+1)+\sin(x^2+1)]$

(b) $\dfrac{d}{dx}\Big[-\dfrac{1}{2}\sin(x^2+1)+C\Big]=-\dfrac{1}{2}\cos(x^2+1)(2x)=-x\cos(x^2+1)$

(c) $\dfrac{d}{dx}\Big[\dfrac{1}{2}\sin(x^2+1)+C\Big]=\dfrac{1}{2}\cos(x^2+1)(2x)=x\cos(x^2+1)$

(d) $\dfrac{d}{dx}[-2x\sin(x^2+1)+C]=-2x[\cos(x^2+1)(2x)]-2\sin(x^2+1)=-2[2x^2\cos(x^2+1)+\sin(x^2+1)]$

$\displaystyle\int x\cos(x^2+1)\,dx$ matches (c).

**6.** $\displaystyle\int\dfrac{2t-1}{t^2-t+2}\,dt$

$u=t^2-t+2,\,du=(2t-1)\,dt$

Use $\displaystyle\int\dfrac{du}{u}.$

**8.** $\displaystyle\int\dfrac{2}{(2t-1)^2+4}\,dt$

$u=2t-1,\,du=2dt,\,a=2$

Use $\displaystyle\int\dfrac{du}{u^2+a^2}.$

**10.** $\displaystyle\int\dfrac{-2x}{\sqrt{x^2-4}}\,dx$

$u=x^2-4,\,du=2x\,dx,\,n=-\dfrac{1}{2}$

Use $\displaystyle\int u^n\,du.$

**12.** $\displaystyle\int\sec 3x\tan 3x\,dx$

$u=3x,\,du=3\,dx$

Use $\displaystyle\int\sec u\tan u\,du.$

**14.** $\displaystyle\int\dfrac{1}{x\sqrt{x^2-4}}\,dx$

$u=x,\,du=dx,\,a=2$

Use $\displaystyle\int\dfrac{du}{u\sqrt{u^2-a^2}}.$

**16.** Let $u = x - 4$, $du = dx$.

$$\int 6(x-4)^5 \, dx = 6 \int (x-4)^5 \, dx = 6 \frac{(x-4)^6}{6} + C$$
$$= (x-4)^6 + C$$

**18.** Let $u = t - 9$, $du = dt$.

$$\int \frac{2}{(t-9)^2} \, dt = 2 \int (t-9)^{-2} \, dt = \frac{-2}{t-9} + C$$

**20.** Let $u = 4 - 2x^2$, $du = -4x \, dx$.

$$\int x\sqrt{4-2x^2} \, dx = -\frac{1}{4} \int (4-2x^2)^{1/2}(-4x)dx$$
$$= -\frac{1}{6}(4-2x^2)^{3/2} + C$$

**22.** $$\int \left[ x - \frac{3}{(2x+3)^2} \right] dx = \int x \, dx - \frac{3}{2} \int (2x+3)^{-2}(2) \, dx$$
$$= \frac{x^2}{2} - \frac{3}{2}\frac{(2x+3)^{-1}}{-1} + C$$
$$= \frac{x^2}{2} + \frac{3}{2(2x+3)} + C$$

**24.** Let $u = x^2 + 2x - 4$, $du = 2(x+1) \, dx$.

$$\int \frac{x+1}{\sqrt{x^2+2x-4}} \, dx = \frac{1}{2} \int (x^2+2x-4)^{-1/2}(2)(x+1) \, dx$$
$$= \sqrt{x^2+2x-4} + C$$

**26.** $$\int \frac{2x}{x-4} \, dx = \int 2 \, dx + \int \frac{8}{x-4} \, dx = 2x + 8\ln|x-4| + C$$

**28.** $$\int \left( \frac{1}{3x-1} - \frac{1}{3x+1} \right) dx = \frac{1}{3} \int \frac{1}{3x-1}(3) \, dx - \frac{1}{3} \int \frac{1}{3x+1}(3) \, dx$$
$$= \frac{1}{3}\ln|3x-1| - \frac{1}{3}\ln|3x+1| + C = \frac{1}{3}\ln\left|\frac{3x-1}{3x+1}\right| + C$$

**30.** $$\int x\left(1+\frac{1}{x}\right)^3 = \int x\left(1 + \frac{3}{x} + \frac{3}{x^2} + \frac{1}{x^3}\right) dx = \int \left(x + 3 + \frac{3}{x} + \frac{1}{x^2}\right) dx = \frac{1}{2}x^2 + 3x + 3\ln|x| - \frac{1}{x} + C$$

**32.** $$\int \sec 4x \, dx = \frac{1}{4} \int \sec(4x)(4) \, dx$$
$$= \frac{1}{4}\ln|\sec 4x + \tan 4x| + C$$

**34.** Let $u = \cos x$, $du = -\sin x \, dx$.

$$\int \frac{\sin x}{\sqrt{\cos x}} \, dx = -\int (\cos x)^{-1/2}(-\sin x) \, dx$$
$$= -2\sqrt{\cos x} + C$$

**36.** Let $u = \cot x$, $du = -\csc^2 x \, dx$.

$$\int \csc^2 x e^{\cot x} \, dx = -\int e^{\cot x}(-\csc^2 x) \, dx = -e^{\cot x} + C$$

**38.** $$\int \frac{5}{3e^x - 2} \, dx = 5 \int \left( \frac{1}{3e^x-2} \right)\left( \frac{e^{-x}}{e^{-x}} \right) dx$$
$$= 5 \int \frac{e^{-x}}{3-2e^{-x}} \, dx$$
$$= \frac{5}{2} \int \frac{1}{3-2e^{-x}}(2e^{-x}) \, dx$$
$$= \frac{5}{2}\ln|3-2e^{-x}| + C$$

**40.** Let $u = \ln(\cos x)$, $du = \dfrac{-\sin x}{\cos x}\,dx$

$$= -\tan x\,dx$$

$$\int (\tan x)(\ln \cos x)\,dx = -\int (\ln \cos x)(-\tan x)\,dx$$

$$= \frac{-[\ln(\cos x)]^2}{2} + C$$

**42.** $\displaystyle\int \frac{1 + \cos \alpha}{\sin \alpha}\,d\alpha = \int \csc \alpha\,d\alpha + \int \cot \alpha\,d\alpha$

$$= -\ln|\csc \alpha + \cot \alpha| + \ln|\sin \alpha| + C$$

**44.** $\displaystyle\int \frac{2}{3(\sec x - 1)}\,dx = \frac{2}{3}\int \frac{1}{\sec x - 1} \cdot \left(\frac{\sec x + 1}{\sec x + 1}\right)dx$

$$= \frac{2}{3}\int \frac{\sec x + 1}{\tan^2 x}\,dx$$

$$= \frac{2}{3}\int \frac{\sec x}{\tan^2 x}\,dx + \frac{2}{3}\int \cot^2 x\,dx$$

$$= \frac{2}{3}\int \frac{\cos x}{\sin^2 x}\,dx + \frac{2}{3}\int (\csc^2 x - 1)\,dx$$

$$= \frac{2}{3}\left(-\frac{1}{\sin x}\right) - \frac{2}{3}\cot x - \frac{2}{3}x + C$$

$$= -\frac{2}{3}[\csc x + \cot x + x] + C$$

**46.** $\displaystyle\int \frac{3}{t^2 + 1}\,dt = 3\arctan t + C$

**48.** Let $u = \sqrt{3}x$, $du = \sqrt{3}\,dx$.

$$\int \frac{1}{4 + 3x^2}\,dx = \frac{1}{\sqrt{3}}\int \frac{\sqrt{3}}{4 + (\sqrt{3}x)^2}\,dx$$

$$= \frac{1}{2\sqrt{3}}\arctan\left(\frac{\sqrt{3}x}{2}\right) + C$$

**50.** Let $u = \dfrac{1}{t}$, $du = \dfrac{-1}{t^2}\,dt$.

$$\int \frac{e^{1/t}}{t^2}\,dt = -\int e^{1/t}\left(\frac{-1}{t^2}\right)dt = -e^{1/t} + C$$

**52.** $\displaystyle\int \frac{1}{(x - 1)\sqrt{4x^2 - 8x + 3}}\,dx = \int \frac{2}{[2(x - 1)]\sqrt{[2(x - 1)]^2 - 1}}\,dx = \operatorname{arcsec}|2(x - 1)| + C$

**54.** $\displaystyle\int \frac{1}{\sqrt{1 - 4x - x^2}}\,dx = \int \frac{1}{\sqrt{5 - (x^2 + 4x + 4)}}\,dx = \int \frac{1}{\sqrt{5 - (x + 2)^2}}\,dx = \arcsin\left(\frac{x + 2}{\sqrt{5}}\right) + C \quad (a = \sqrt{5})$

**56.** $\dfrac{dy}{dx} = \tan^2(2x)$, $(0, 0)$

(a)

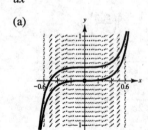

(b) $\displaystyle\int \tan^2(2x)\,dx = \int (\sec^2(2x) - 1)\,dx = \frac{1}{2}\tan(2x) - x + C$

$(0, 0)$:  $0 = C$

$$y = \frac{1}{2}\tan(2x) - x$$

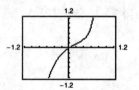

**58.**

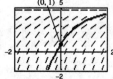

**60.** $r = \displaystyle\int \frac{(1 + e^t)^2}{e^t}\,dt = \int \frac{1 + 2e^t + e^{2t}}{e^t}\,dt$

$$= \int (e^{-t} + 2 + e^t)\,dt = -e^{-t} + 2t + e^t + C$$

**62.** Let $u = 2x, du = 2\,dx$.

$$y = \int \frac{1}{x\sqrt{4x^2 - 1}}\,dx = \int \frac{2}{2x\sqrt{(2x)^2 - 1}}\,dx$$

$$= \text{arcsec}\,|2x| + C$$

**64.** Let $u = \sin t, du = \cos t\,dt$.

$$\int_0^\pi \sin^2 t \cos t\,dt = \left[\frac{1}{3}\sin^3 t\right]_0^\pi = 0$$

**66.** Let $u = 1 - \ln x$, $du = \dfrac{-1}{x}\,dx$.

$$\int_1^e \frac{1 - \ln x}{x}\,dx = -\int_1^e (1 - \ln x)\left(\frac{-1}{x}\right)dx$$

$$= \left[-\frac{1}{2}(1 - \ln x)^2\right]_1^e = \frac{1}{2}$$

**68.** $\displaystyle\int_1^2 \frac{x - 2}{x}\,dx = \int_1^2 \left(1 - \frac{2}{x}\right)dx$

$$= \left[x - 2\ln x\right]_1^2 = 1 - \ln 4 \approx -0.386$$

**70.** $\displaystyle\int_0^4 \frac{1}{\sqrt{25 - x^2}}\,dx = \left[\arcsin\frac{x}{5}\right]_0^4 = \arcsin\frac{4}{5} \approx 0.927$

**72.** $\displaystyle\int \frac{x - 2}{x^2 + 4x + 13}\,dx = \frac{1}{2}\ln(x^2 + 4x + 13) - \frac{4}{3}\arctan\left(\frac{x + 2}{3}\right) + C$

The antiderivatives are vertical translations of each other.

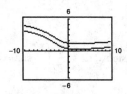

**74.** $\displaystyle\int \left(\frac{e^x + e^{-x}}{2}\right)^3\,dx = \frac{1}{24}[e^{3x} + 9e^x - 9e^{-x} - e^{-3x}] + C$

The antiderivatives are vertical translations of each other.

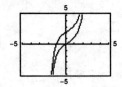

**76.** $\displaystyle\int \sec u \tan u\,du = \sec u + C$

**78.** Arctan Rule: $\displaystyle\int \frac{du}{a^2 + u^2} = \frac{1}{a}\arctan\left(\frac{4}{a}\right) + C$

**80.** They differ by a constant:

$$\sec^2 x + C_1 = (\tan^2 x + 1) + C_1 = \tan^2 x + C.$$

**82.** $f(x) = \dfrac{1}{5}(x^3 - 7x^2 + 10x)$

$$\int_0^5 f(x)\,dx < 0 \text{ because}$$

more area is below the $x$-axis than above.

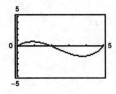

**84.** $\displaystyle\int_0^2 \frac{4}{x^2 + 1}\,dx \approx 4$

Matches (d).

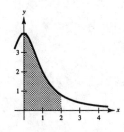

**86.** $A = \displaystyle\int_0^{\pi/2} \sin 2x\,dx$

$$= \left[-\frac{1}{2}\cos 2x\right]_0^{\pi/2} = 1$$

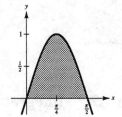

**88.** $\int_0^2 2\pi x^2 \, dx$

(a) Let $f(x) = 2\pi x^2$ over the interval $[0, 2]$.

$$A = \int_0^2 (2\pi x^2) \, dx$$

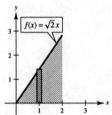

(b) Let $f(x) = \sqrt{2}\, x$ over the interval $[0, 2]$. Revolve this region about the $x$-axis.

$$V = \pi \int_0^2 (\sqrt{2}\, x)^2 \, dx$$

$$= \int_0^2 2\pi x^2 \, dx$$

(c) Let $f(x) = x$ over the interval $[0, 2]$. Revolve this region about the $y$-axis.

$$V = 2\pi \int_0^2 x(x) \, dx$$

$$= \int_0^2 2\pi x^2 \, dx$$

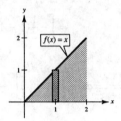

**90.** (a) $\dfrac{1}{(\pi/n) - 0} \displaystyle\int_0^{\pi/n} \sin(nx) \, dx = \dfrac{1}{\pi} \displaystyle\int_0^{\pi/n} \sin(nx)(n) \, dx = \left[ -\dfrac{1}{\pi} \cos(nx) \right]_0^{\pi/n} = \dfrac{2}{\pi}$

(b) $\dfrac{1}{3 - (-3)} \displaystyle\int_{-3}^3 \dfrac{1}{1 + x^2} \, dx = \left[ \dfrac{1}{6} \arctan x \right]_{-3}^3 = \dfrac{1}{3} \arctan 3$

**92.** $\quad y = 2\sqrt{x}$

$$y' = \dfrac{1}{\sqrt{x}}$$

$$1 + (y')^2 = 1 + \dfrac{1}{x} = \dfrac{x+1}{x}$$

$$S = 2\pi \int_0^9 2\sqrt{x} \sqrt{\dfrac{x+1}{x}} \, dx$$

$$= 2\pi \int_0^9 2\sqrt{x+1} \, dx$$

$$= \left[ 4\pi \left( \dfrac{2}{3} \right)(x+1)^{3/2} \right]_0^9$$

$$= \dfrac{8\pi}{3} \left( 10\sqrt{10} - 1 \right) \approx 256.545$$

**94.** $\quad y = x^{2/3}$

$$y' = \dfrac{2}{3x^{1/3}}$$

$$1 + (y')^2 = 1 + \dfrac{4}{9x^{2/3}}$$

$$s = \int_1^8 \sqrt{1 + \dfrac{4}{9x^{2/3}}} \, dx \approx 7.6337$$

# Section 7.2    Integration by Parts

**2.** $\dfrac{d}{dx}[x^2 \sin x + 2x \cos x - 2 \sin x] = x^2 \cos x + 2x \sin x - 2x \sin x + 2 \cos x - 2 \cos x = x^2 \cos x.$ Matches (d)

**4.** $\dfrac{d}{dx}[-x + x \ln x] = -1 + x\left(\dfrac{1}{x}\right) + \ln x = \ln x.$ Matches (a)

**6.** $\displaystyle\int x^2 e^{2x}\, dx$

$u = x^2, dv = e^{2x}\, dx$

**8.** $\displaystyle\int \ln 3x\, dx$

$u = \ln 3x, dv = dx$

**10.** $\displaystyle\int x^2 \cos x\, dx$

$u = x^2, dv = \cos x\, dx$

**12.** $dv = e^{-x}\, dx \implies v = \displaystyle\int e^{-x}\, dx = -e^{-x}$

$\quad u = x \qquad \implies du = dx$

$2\displaystyle\int \dfrac{x}{e^x}\, dx = 2\displaystyle\int x e^{-x}\, dx$

$\qquad = 2\left[-xe^{-x} - \displaystyle\int -e^{-x}\, dx\right] = 2[-xe^{-x} - e^{-x}] + C$

$\qquad = -2xe^{-x} - 2e^{-x} + C$

**14.** $\displaystyle\int \dfrac{e^{1/t}}{t^2}\, dt = -\displaystyle\int e^{1/t}\left(\dfrac{-1}{t^2}\right) dt = -e^{1/t} + C$

**16.** $dv = x^4\, dx \implies v = \dfrac{x^5}{5}$

$\quad u = \ln x \implies du = \dfrac{1}{x}\, dx$

$\displaystyle\int x^4 \ln x\, dx = \dfrac{x^5}{5} \ln x - \displaystyle\int \dfrac{x^5}{5}\left(\dfrac{1}{x}\right) dx = \dfrac{x^5}{5} \ln x - \dfrac{1}{5}\displaystyle\int x^4\, dx$

$\qquad = \dfrac{x^5}{5} \ln x - \dfrac{1}{25}x^5 + C = \dfrac{x^5}{25}(5 \ln x - 1) + C$

**18.** Let $u = \ln x,\, du = \dfrac{1}{x}\, dx.$

$\displaystyle\int \dfrac{1}{x(\ln x)^3}\, dx = \displaystyle\int (\ln x)^{-3}\left(\dfrac{1}{x}\right) dx = \dfrac{-1}{2(\ln x)^2} + C$

**20.** $dv = \dfrac{1}{x^2}\, dx \implies v = \displaystyle\int \dfrac{1}{x^2}\, dx = -\dfrac{1}{x}$

$\quad u = \ln x \implies du = \dfrac{1}{x}\, dx$

$\displaystyle\int \dfrac{\ln x}{x^2}\, dx = -\dfrac{\ln x}{x} + \displaystyle\int \dfrac{1}{x^2}\, dx = -\dfrac{\ln x}{x} - \dfrac{1}{x} + C$

**22.** $dv = \dfrac{x}{(x^2 + 1)^2}\, dx \implies v = \displaystyle\int (x^2 + 1)^{-2} x\, dx = -\dfrac{1}{2(x^2 + 1)}$

$\quad u = x^2 e^{x^2} \qquad \implies du = (2x^3 e^{x^2} + 2xe^{x^2})\, dx = 2xe^{x^2}(x^2 + 1)\, dx$

$\displaystyle\int \dfrac{x^3 e^{x^2}}{(x^2 + 1)^2}\, dx = -\dfrac{x^2 e^{x^2}}{2(x^2 + 1)} + \displaystyle\int xe^{x^2}\, dx = -\dfrac{x^2 e^{x^2}}{2(x^2 + 1)} + \dfrac{e^{x^2}}{2} + C = \dfrac{e^{x^2}}{2(x^2 + 1)} + C$

**24.** $dv = \dfrac{1}{x^2}\, dx \implies v = \displaystyle\int \dfrac{1}{x^2}\, dx = -\dfrac{1}{x}$

$\quad u = \ln 2x \implies du = \dfrac{1}{x}\, dx$

$\displaystyle\int \dfrac{\ln(2x)}{x^2}\, dx = -\dfrac{\ln(2x)}{x} + \displaystyle\int \dfrac{1}{x^2}\, dx = -\dfrac{\ln(2x)}{x} - \dfrac{1}{x} + C = -\dfrac{\ln(2x) + 1}{x} + C$

**26.** $dv = \dfrac{1}{\sqrt{2 + 3x}} dx \;\Longrightarrow\; v = \displaystyle\int (2 + 3x)^{-1/2} dx = \dfrac{2}{3}\sqrt{2 + 3x}$

$u = x \qquad\qquad \Longrightarrow du = dx$

$\displaystyle\int \dfrac{x}{\sqrt{2 + 3x}} dx = \dfrac{2x\sqrt{2 + 3x}}{3} - \dfrac{2}{3}\displaystyle\int \sqrt{2 + 3x} \, dx$

$\qquad\qquad = \dfrac{2x\sqrt{2 + 3x}}{3} - \dfrac{4}{27}(2 + 3x)^{3/2} + C = \dfrac{2\sqrt{2 + 3x}}{27}[9x - 2(2 + 3x)] + C = \dfrac{2\sqrt{2 + 3x}}{27}(3x - 4) + C$

**28.** $dv = \sin x \, dx \;\Longrightarrow\; v = -\cos x$

$u = x \qquad \Longrightarrow du = dx$

$\displaystyle\int x \sin dx = -x \cos x - \displaystyle\int -\cos x \, dx = -x \cos x + \sin x + C$

**30.** Use integration by parts twice.

(1) $u = x^2, \, du = 2x \, dx, \, dv = \cos x \, dx, \, v = \sin x$

$\displaystyle\int x^2 \cos x \, dx = x^2 \sin x - 2 \displaystyle\int x \sin x \, dx$

(2) $u = x, \, du = dx, \, dv = \sin x \, dx, \, v = -\cos x$

$\displaystyle\int x^2 \cos x \, dx = x^2 \sin x - 2\left[ -x \cos x + \displaystyle\int \cos x \, dx \right]$

$\qquad\qquad = x^2 \sin x + 2x \cos x - 2 \sin x + C$

**32.** $dv = \sec\theta \tan\theta \, d\theta \;\Longrightarrow\; v = \displaystyle\int \sec\theta \tan\theta \, d\theta = \sec\theta$

$u = \theta \qquad\qquad \Longrightarrow du = d\theta$

$\displaystyle\int \theta \sec\theta \tan\theta \, d\theta = \theta \sec\theta - \displaystyle\int \sec\theta \, d\theta$

$\qquad\qquad = \theta \sec\theta - \ln|\sec\theta + \tan\theta| + C$

**34.** $dv = dx \qquad \Longrightarrow\; v = \displaystyle\int dx = x$

$u = \arccos x \Longrightarrow du = -\dfrac{1}{\sqrt{1 - x^2}} dx$

$4 \displaystyle\int \arccos x \, dx = 4\left[ x \arccos x + \displaystyle\int \dfrac{x}{\sqrt{1 - x^2}} dx \right]$

$\qquad\qquad = 4\left[ x \arccos x - \sqrt{1 - x^2} \right] + C$

**36.** Use integration by parts twice.

(1) $dv = e^x \, dx \;\Longrightarrow\; v = \displaystyle\int e^x \, dx = e^x$

$u = \cos 2x \Longrightarrow du = -2 \sin 2x \, dx$

(2) $dv = e^x \, dx \;\Longrightarrow\; v = \displaystyle\int e^x \, dx = e^x$

$u = \sin 2x \Longrightarrow du = 2 \cos 2x \, dx$

$\displaystyle\int e^x \cos 2x \, dx = e^x \cos 2x + 2 \displaystyle\int e^x \sin 2x \, dx = e^x \cos 2x + 2\left( e^x \sin 2x - 2 \displaystyle\int e^x \cos 2x \, dx \right)$

$5 \displaystyle\int e^x \cos 2x \, dx = e^x \cos 2x + 2e^x \sin 2x$

$\displaystyle\int e^x \cos 2x \, dx = \dfrac{e^x}{5}(\cos 2x + 2 \sin 2x) + C$

**38.** $dv = dx \;\Longrightarrow\; v = x$

$u = \ln x \Longrightarrow du = \dfrac{1}{x} dx$

$y' = \ln x$

$y = \displaystyle\int \ln x \, dx = x \ln x - \displaystyle\int x\left(\dfrac{1}{x}\right) dx = x \ln x - x + C = x(-1 + \ln x) + C$

**40.** Use integration by parts twice.

(1) $dv = \sqrt{x-1}\, dx \implies v = \int (x-1)^{1/2}\, dx = \frac{2}{3}(x-1)^{3/2}$

$u = x^2 \qquad\qquad \implies du = 2x\, dx$

(2) $dv = (x-1)^{3/2}dx \implies v = \int (x-1)^{3/2}\, dx = \frac{2}{5}(x-1)^{5/2}$

$u = x \qquad\qquad \implies du = dx$

$y = \int x^2 \sqrt{x-1}\, dx$

$= \frac{2}{3}x^2(x-1)^{3/2} - \frac{4}{3}\int x(x-1)^{3/2}\, dx = \frac{2}{3}x^2(x-1)^{3/2} - \frac{4}{3}\left[\frac{2}{5}x(x-1)^{5/2} - \frac{2}{5}\int (x-1)^{5/2}\, dx\right]$

$= \frac{2}{3}x^2(x-1)^{3/2} - \frac{8}{15}x(x-1)^{5/2} + \frac{16}{105}(x-1)^{7/2} + C = \frac{2(x-1)^{3/2}}{105}(15x^2 + 12x + 8) + C$

**42.** $dv = dx \qquad \implies v = \int dx = x$

$u = \arctan\frac{x}{2} \implies du = \frac{1}{1+(x/2)^2}\left(\frac{1}{2}\right) dx = \frac{2}{4+x^2}\, dx$

$y = \int \arctan\frac{x}{2}\, dx = x\arctan\frac{x}{2} - \int \frac{2x}{4+x^2}\, dx = x\arctan\frac{x}{2} - \ln(4+x^2) + C$

**44.** (a)

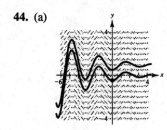

(b) $\dfrac{dy}{dx} = e^{-x/3}\sin 2x,\ \left(0, -\dfrac{18}{37}\right)$

$y = \int e^{-x/3}\sin 2x\, dx$

Use integration by parts twice.

(1) $u = \sin 2x,\ du = 2\cos 2x$

$dv = e^{-x/3}\, dx,\ v = -3e^{-x/3}$

$\int e^{-x/3}\sin 2x\, dx = -3e^{-x/3}\sin 2x + \int 6e^{-x/3}\cos 2x\, dx$

(2) $u = \cos 2x,\ du = -2\sin 2x$

$dv = e^{-x/3}\, dx,\ v = -3e^{-x/3}$

$\int e^{-x/3}\sin 2x\, dx = -3e^{-x/3}\sin 2x + 6\left[-3e^{-x/3}\cos 2x - \int 6e^{-x/3}\sin 2x\, dx\right] + C$

$37\int e^{-x/3}\sin 2x\, dx = -3e^{-x/3}\sin 2x - 18e^{-x/3}\cos 2x + C$

$y = \int e^{-x/3}\sin 2x\, dx = \frac{1}{37}\left[-3e^{-x/3}\sin 2x - 18e^{-x/3}\cos 2x\right] + C$

$\left(0, \frac{-18}{37}\right): \frac{-18}{37} = \frac{1}{37}[0 - 18] + C \implies C = 0$

$y = \frac{-1}{37}[3e^{-x/3}\sin 2x + 18e^{-x/3}\cos 2x]$

**46.** $\dfrac{dy}{dx} = \dfrac{x}{y} \sin x$, $y(0) = 4$

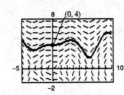

**48.** See Exercise 3.

$$\int_0^1 x^2 e^x \, dx = \left[ x^2 e^x - 2xe^x + 2e^x \right]_0^1 = e - 2 \approx 0.718$$

**50.** $dv = \sin 2x \, dx \implies v = \displaystyle\int \sin 2x \, dx = -\dfrac{1}{2} \cos 2x$

$u = x \qquad \implies du = dx$

$\displaystyle\int x \sin 2x \, dx = \dfrac{-1}{2} x \cos 2x + \dfrac{1}{2} \int \cos 2x \, dx$

$\qquad = \dfrac{-1}{2} x \cos 2x + \dfrac{1}{4} \sin 2x + C$

$\qquad = \dfrac{1}{4} (\sin 2x - 2x \cos 2x) + C$

Thus, $\displaystyle\int_0^\pi x \sin 2x \, dx = \left[ \dfrac{1}{4} (\sin 2x - 2x \cos 2x) \right]_0^\pi = -\dfrac{\pi}{2}.$

**52.** $dv = x \, dx \qquad \implies v = \displaystyle\int x \, dx = \dfrac{x^2}{2}$

$u = \arcsin x^2 \implies du = \dfrac{2x}{\sqrt{1 - x^4}} \, dx$

$\displaystyle\int x \arcsin x^2 \, dx = \dfrac{x^2}{2} \arcsin x^2 - \int \dfrac{x^3}{\sqrt{1 - x^4}} \, dx$

$\qquad = \dfrac{x^2}{2} \arcsin x^2 + \dfrac{1}{4}(2)(1 - x^4)^{1/2} + C$

$\qquad = \dfrac{1}{2}\left[ x^2 \arcsin x^2 + \sqrt{1 - x^4} \right] + C$

Thus, $\displaystyle\int_0^1 x \arcsin x^2 \, dx = \dfrac{1}{2}\left[ x^2 \arcsin x^2 + \sqrt{1 - x^4} \right]_0^1$

$\qquad\qquad = \dfrac{1}{4}(\pi - 2).$

**54.** Use integration by parts twice.

(1) $dv = e^{-x}, v = -e^{-x}, u = \cos x, du = -\sin x \, dx$

$\displaystyle\int e^{-x} \cos x \, dx = -e^{-x} \cos x - \int e^{-x} \sin x \, dx$

(2) $dv = e^{-x} \, dx, v = -e^{-x}, u = \sin x, du = \cos x \, dx$

$\displaystyle\int e^{-x} \cos x \, dx = -e^{-x} \cos x - \left[ -e^{-x} \sin x + \int e^{-x} \cos x \, dx \right] \implies 2\int e^{-x} \cos x \, dx = e^{-x} \sin x - e^{-x} \cos x$

Thus,

$$\int_0^2 e^{-x} \cos x \, dx = \left[ \dfrac{e^{-x} \sin x - e^{-x} \cos x}{2} \right]_0^2$$

$$= \dfrac{-e^{-2}}{2} [\sin 2 - \cos 2] + \dfrac{1}{2}$$

**56.** $dv = dx \qquad \implies v = \displaystyle\int dx = x$

$u = \ln(1 + x^2) \implies du = \dfrac{2x}{1 + x^2} \, dx$

$\displaystyle\int \ln(1 + x^2) \, dx = x \ln(1 + x^2) - \int \dfrac{2x^2}{1 + x^2} \, dx$

$\qquad = x \ln(1 + x^2) - 2\displaystyle\int \left[ 1 - \dfrac{1}{1 + x^2} \right] dx = x \ln(1 + x^2) - 2x + 2 \arctan x + C$

Thus, $\displaystyle\int_0^1 \ln(1 + x^2) \, dx = \left[ x \ln(1 + x^2) - 2x + 2 \arctan x \right]_0^1 = \ln 2 - 2 + \dfrac{\pi}{2}.$

**58.** $u = x, \, du = dx, \, dv = \sec^2 x \, dx, \, v = \tan x$     Hence,

$$\int x \sec^2 x \, dx = x \tan x - \int \tan x \, dx$$

$$\int_0^{\pi/4} x \sec^2 x \, dx = \Big[ x \tan x + \ln|\cos x| \Big]_0^{\pi/4}$$

$$= \left( \frac{\pi}{4} + \ln \frac{\sqrt{2}}{2} \right) - 0$$

$$= \frac{\pi}{4} - \frac{1}{2} \ln 2$$

**60.** $\displaystyle \int x^3 e^{-2x} \, dx = x^3 \left( -\frac{1}{2} e^{-2x} \right) - 3x^2 \left( \frac{1}{4} e^{-2x} \right) + 6x \left( -\frac{1}{8} e^{-2x} \right) - 6 \left( \frac{1}{16} e^{-2x} \right) + C$

$$= -\frac{1}{8} e^{-2x} (4x^3 + 6x^2 + 6x + 3) + C$$

| Alternate signs | $u$ and its derivatives | $v'$ and its antiderivatives |
|---|---|---|
| + | $x^3$ | $e^{-2x}$ |
| − | $3x^2$ | $-\frac{1}{2} e^{-2x}$ |
| + | $6x$ | $\frac{1}{4} e^{-2x}$ |
| − | $6$ | $-\frac{1}{8} e^{-2x}$ |
| + | $0$ | $\frac{1}{16} e^{-2x}$ |

**62.** $\displaystyle \int x^3 \cos 2x \, dx = x^3 \left( \frac{1}{2} \sin 2x \right) - 3x^2 \left( -\frac{1}{4} \cos 2x \right) + 6x \left( -\frac{1}{8} \sin 2x \right) - 6 \left( \frac{1}{16} \cos 2x \right) + C$

$$= \frac{1}{2} x^3 \sin 2x + \frac{3}{4} x^2 \cos 2x - \frac{3}{4} x \sin 2x - \frac{3}{8} \cos 2x + C$$

$$= \frac{1}{8} \left[ 4x^3 \sin 2x + 6x^2 \cos 2x - 6x \sin 2x - 3 \cos 2x \right] + C$$

| Alternate signs | $u$ and its derivatives | $v'$ and its antiderivatives |
|---|---|---|
| + | $x^3$ | $\cos 2x$ |
| − | $3x^2$ | $\frac{1}{2} \sin 2x$ |
| + | $6x$ | $-\frac{1}{4} \cos 2x$ |
| − | $6$ | $-\frac{1}{8} \sin 2x$ |
| + | $0$ | $\frac{1}{16} \cos 2x$ |

**64.** $\displaystyle \int x^2 (x-2)^{3/2} \, dx = \frac{2}{5} x^2 (x-2)^{5/2} - \frac{8}{35} x (x-2)^{7/2} + \frac{16}{315} (x-2)^{9/2} + C$

$$= \frac{2}{315} (x-2)^{5/2} (35x^2 + 40x + 32) + C$$

| Alternate signs | $u$ and its derivatives | $v'$ and its antiderivatives |
|---|---|---|
| + | $x^2$ | $(x-2)^{3/2}$ |
| − | $2x$ | $\frac{2}{5} (x-2)^{5/2}$ |
| + | $2$ | $\frac{4}{35} (x-2)^{7/2}$ |
| − | $0$ | $\frac{8}{315} (x-2)^{9/2}$ |

**66.** Answers will vary.
See pages 488, 493.

**68.** Yes.
$u = \ln x, \, dv = x \, dx$

**70.** No. Substitution.

**72.** No. Substitution.

**74.** $\displaystyle \int \alpha^4 \sin \pi\alpha \, d\alpha = \frac{1}{\pi^5} \left[ -(\alpha\pi)^4 \cos \pi\alpha + 4(\alpha\pi)^3 \sin \pi\alpha + 12(\alpha\pi)^2 \cos \pi\alpha - 24(\alpha\pi) \sin \pi\alpha - 24 \cos \pi\alpha \right] + C$

**76.** $\displaystyle \int_0^5 x^4 (25 - x^2)^{3/2} \, dx = \left[ \frac{1{,}171{,}875 \arcsin(x/5)}{128} - \frac{x(2x^2 + 25)(25 - x^2)^{5/2}}{16} + \frac{625 x (25 - x^2)^{3/2}}{64} + \frac{46{,}875 x \sqrt{25 - x^2}}{128} \right]_0^5$

$$\approx 14{,}381.0699$$

**78.** (a) $dv = \sqrt{4 + x}\,dx \implies v = \int (4 + x)^{1/2}\,dx = \frac{2}{3}(4 + x)^{3/2}$

$u = x \qquad \implies du = dx$

$$\int x\sqrt{4 + x}\,dx = \frac{2}{3}x(4 + x)^{3/2} - \frac{2}{3}\int (4 + x)^{3/2}\,dx$$

$$= \frac{2}{3}x(4 + x)^{3/2} - \frac{4}{15}(4 + x)^{5/2} + C = \frac{2}{15}(4 + x)^{3/2}(3x - 8) + C$$

(b) $u = 4 + x \implies x = u - 4$ and $dx = du$

$$\int x\sqrt{4 + x}\,dx = \int (u - 4)u^{1/2}du = \int (u^{3/2} - 4u^{1/2})\,du$$

$$= \frac{2}{5}u^{5/2} - \frac{8}{3}u^{3/2} + C = \frac{2}{15}u^{3/2}(3u - 20) + C$$

$$= \frac{2}{15}(4 + x)^{3/2}[3(4 + x) - 20] + C = \frac{2}{15}(4 + x)^{3/2}(3x - 8) + C$$

**80.** (a) $dv = \sqrt{4 - x}\,dx \implies v = \int (4 - x)^{1/2}\,dx$

$$= -\frac{2}{3}(4 - x)^{3/2}$$

$u = x \qquad \implies du = dx$

$$\int x\sqrt{4 - x}\,dx = -\frac{2}{3}x(4 - x)^{3/2} + \frac{2}{3}\int (4 - x)^{3/2}\,dx$$

$$= -\frac{2}{3}x(4 - x)^{3/2} - \frac{4}{15}(4 - x)^{5/2} + C$$

$$= -\frac{2}{15}(4 - x)^{3/2}[5x + 2(4 - x)] + C$$

$$= -\frac{2}{15}(4 - x)^{3/2}(3x + 8) + C$$

(b) $u = 4 - x \implies x = 4 - u$ and $dx = -du$

$$\int x\sqrt{4 - x}\,dx = -\int (4 - u)\sqrt{u}\,du$$

$$= -\int (4u^{1/2} - u^{3/2})\,du$$

$$= -\frac{8}{3}u^{3/2} + \frac{2}{5}u^{5/2} + C$$

$$= -\frac{2}{15}u^{3/2}(20 - 3u) + C$$

$$= -\frac{2}{15}(4 - x)^{3/2}[20 - 3(4 - x)] + C$$

$$= -\frac{2}{15}(4 - x)^{3/2}(3x + 8) + C$$

**82.** $n = 0$: $\int e^x\,dx = e^x + C$

$n = 1$: $\int xe^x\,dx = xe^x - e^x + C = xe^x - \int e^x\,dx$

$n = 2$: $\int x^2e^x\,dx = x^2e^x - 2xe^x + 2e^x + C$

$$= x^2e^x - 2\int xe^x\,dx$$

$n = 3$: $\int x^3e^x\,dx = x^3e^x - 3x^2e^x + 6xe^x - 6e^x + C$

$$= x^3e^x - 3\int x^2e^x\,dx$$

$n = 4$: $\int x^4e^x\,dx$

$$= x^4e^x - 4x^3e^x + 12x^2e^x - 24xe^x + 24e^x + C$$

$$= x^4e^x - 4\int x^3e^x\,dx$$

In general, $\int x^ne^x\,dx = x^ne^x - n\int x^{n-1}e^x\,dx$.

(See Exercise 86)

**84.** $dv = \cos x\,dx \implies v = \sin x$

$u = x^n \qquad \implies du = nx^{n-1}\,dx$

$$\int x^n \cos x\,dx = x^n \sin x - n\int x^{n-1}\sin x\,dx$$

**86.** $dv = e^{ax}\,dx \implies v = \frac{1}{a}e^{ax}$

$u = x^n \implies du = nx^{n-1}\,dx$

$$\int x^ne^{ax}\,dx = \frac{x^ne^{ax}}{a} - \frac{n}{a}\int x^{n-1}e^{ax}\,dx$$

**88.** Use integration by parts twice.

(1) $dv = e^{ax}\, dx \implies v = \dfrac{1}{a}e^{ax}$

    $u = \cos bx \implies du = -b\sin bx$

(2) $dv = e^{ax}\, dx \implies v = \dfrac{1}{a}e^{ax}$

    $u = \sin bx \implies du = b\cos bx$

$$\int e^{ax}\cos bx\, dx = \frac{e^{ax}\cos bx}{a} + \frac{b}{a}\int e^{ax}\sin bx\, dx = \frac{e^{ax}\cos bx}{a} + \frac{b}{a}\left[\frac{e^{ax}\sin bx}{a} - \frac{b}{a}\int e^{ax}\cos bx\, dx\right]$$

$$= \frac{e^{ax}\cos bx}{a} + \frac{be^{ax}\sin bx}{a^2} - \frac{b^2}{a^2}\int e^{ax}\cos bx\, dx$$

Therefore, $\left(1 + \dfrac{b^2}{a^2}\right)\displaystyle\int e^{ax}\cos bx\, dx = \dfrac{e^{ax}(a\cos bx + b\sin bx)}{a^2}$

$$\int e^{ax}\cos bx\, dx = \frac{e^{ax}(a\cos bx + b\sin bx)}{a^2 + b^2} + C.$$

**90.** $n = 2$ (Use formula in Exercise 84.)

$$\int x^2\cos x\, dx = x^2\sin x - 2\int x\sin x\, dx \text{ (Use formula in Exercise 83.) } (n = 1)$$

$$= x^2\sin x - 2\left[-x\cos x + \int\cos x\, dx\right] = x^2\sin x + 2x\cos x - 2\sin x + C$$

**92.** $n = 3, a = 2$ (Use formula in Exercise 86 three times.)

$$\int x^3 e^{2x}\, dx = \frac{x^3 e^{2x}}{2} - \frac{3}{2}\int x^2 e^{2x}\, dx \quad (n = 3, a = 2)$$

$$= \frac{x^3 e^{2x}}{2} - \frac{3}{2}\left[\frac{x^2 e^{2x}}{2} - \int xe^{2x}\, dx\right] \quad (n = 2, a = 2)$$

$$= \frac{x^3 e^{2x}}{2} - \frac{3x^2 e^{2x}}{4} + \frac{3}{2}\left[\frac{xe^{2x}}{2} - \frac{1}{2}\int e^{2x}\, dx\right] = \frac{x^3 e^{2x}}{2} - \frac{3x^2 e^{2x}}{4} + \frac{3xe^{2x}}{4} - \frac{3e^{2x}}{8} + C \quad (n = 1, a = 2)$$

$$= \frac{e^{2x}}{8}(4x^3 - 6x^2 + 6x - 3) + C$$

**94.** $dv = e^{-x/3}\, dx \implies v = -3e^{-x/3}$

    $u = x \qquad \implies du = dx$

$$A = \frac{1}{9}\int_0^3 xe^{-x/3}\, dx$$

$$= \frac{1}{9}\left(\left[-3xe^{-x/3}\right]_0^3 + 3\int_0^3 e^{-x/3}\, dx\right)$$

$$= \frac{1}{9}\left(\frac{-9}{e} - \left[9e^{-x/3}\right]_0^3\right)$$

$$= -\frac{1}{e} - \frac{1}{e} + 1 = 1 - \frac{2}{e} \approx 0.264$$

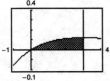

**96.** $A = \displaystyle\int_0^{\pi} x\sin x\, dx = \left[-x\cos x + \sin x\right]_0^{\pi}$

    $= \pi$ (See Exercise 83.)

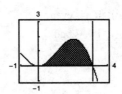

**98.** In Example 6, we showed that the centroid of an equivalent region was $(1, \pi/8)$. By symmetry, the centroid of this region is $(\pi/8, 1)$.

You can also solve this problem directly.

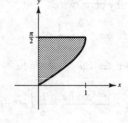

$$A = \int_0^1 \left( \frac{\pi}{2} - \arcsin x \right) dx = \left[ \frac{\pi}{2}x - x \arcsin x - \sqrt{1 - x^2} \right]_0^1 \text{ (Example 3)}$$

$$= \left( \frac{\pi}{2} - \frac{\pi}{2} - 0 \right) - (-1) = 1$$

$$\bar{x} = \frac{M_y}{A} = \int_0^1 x \left[ \frac{\pi}{2} - \arcsin x \right] dx = \frac{\pi}{8}$$

$$\bar{y} = \frac{M_x}{A} = \int_0^1 \frac{(\pi/2) + \arcsin x}{2} \left[ \frac{\pi}{2} - \arcsin x \right] dx = 1$$

**100. (a)** Average $= \int_1^2 (1.6t \ln t + 1) dt = \left[ 0.8t^2 \ln t - 0.4t^2 + t \right]_1^2 = 3.2(\ln 2) - 0.2 \approx 2.018$

**(b)** Average $= \int_3^4 (1.6t \ln t + 1) dt = \left[ 0.8t^2 \ln t - 0.4t^2 + t \right]_3^4 = 12.8(\ln 4) - 7.2(\ln 3) - 1.8 \approx 8.035$

**102.** $c(t) = 30,000 + 500t, r = 7\%, t_1 = 5$

$$P \int_0^5 (30,000 + 500t)e^{-0.07t} \, dt = 500 \int_0^5 (60 + t)e^{-0.07t} \, dt$$

Let $u = 60 + t, dv = e^{-0.07t} \, dt, du = dt, v = -\dfrac{100}{7}e^{-0.07t}$.

$$P = 500 \left\{ \left[ (60 + t)\left( -\frac{100}{7}e^{-0.07t} \right) \right]_0^5 + \frac{100}{7} \int_0^5 e^{-0.07t} \, dt \right\}$$

$$= 500 \left\{ \left[ (60 + t)\left( -\frac{100}{7}e^{-0.07t} \right) \right]_0^5 - \left[ \frac{10,000}{49}e^{-0.07t} \right]_0^5 \right\} \approx \$131,528.68$$

**104.** $\displaystyle\int_{-\pi}^{\pi} x^2 \cos nx \, dx = \left[ \frac{x^2}{n} \sin nx + \frac{2x}{n^2} \cos nx - \frac{2}{n^3} \sin nx \right]_{-\pi}^{\pi}$

$$= \frac{2\pi}{n^2} \cos n\pi + \frac{2\pi}{n^2} \cos(-n\pi)$$

$$= \frac{4\pi}{n^2} \cos n\pi$$

$$= \begin{cases} (4\pi/n^2), & \text{if } n \text{ is even} \\ -(4\pi/n^2), & \text{if } n \text{ is odd} \end{cases}$$

$$= \frac{(-1)^n 4\pi}{n^2}$$

**106.** For any integrable function, $\int f(x) \, dx = C + \int f(x) \, dx$, but this cannot be used to imply that $C = 0$.

**108.** On $\left[ 0, \dfrac{\pi}{2} \right]$, $\sin x \le 1 \implies x \sin x \le x \implies \displaystyle\int_0^{\pi/2} x \sin x \, dx \le \int_0^{\pi/2} x \, dx$.

**110.** $f'(x) = \cos\sqrt{x}, f(0) = 2$

    (a)  It cannot be solved by integration.

    (b)  You obtain the points

| $n$ | $x_n$ | $y_n$ |
|---|---|---|
| 0 | 0 | 2 |
| 1 | 0.05 | 2.05 |
| 2 | 0.10 | 2.098755 |
| 3 | 0.15 | 2.146276 |
| ⋮ | ⋮ | ⋮ |
| 80 | 4.0 | 2.8403565 |

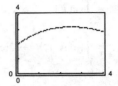

# Section 7.3    Trigonometric Integrals

**2.** (a) $y = \sec x \implies y' = \sec x \tan x = \sin x \sec^2 x.$

       Matches (iii)

    (b) $y = \cos x + \sec x \implies y' = -\sin x + \sec x \tan x$

$$= -\sin x + \sec^2 x \sin x$$
$$= \sin x(-1 + \sec^2 x)$$
$$= \sin x \tan^2 x \quad \text{Matches (i)}$$

    (c) $y = x - \tan x + \dfrac{1}{3}\tan^3 x \implies y' = 1 - \sec^2 x + \tan^2 x \sec^2 x$

$$= -\tan^2 x + \tan^2 x(1 + \tan^2 x)$$
$$= \tan^4 x \quad \text{Matches (iv)}$$

    (d) $y = 3x + 2\sin x \cos^3 x + 3\sin x \cos x \implies$

$$y' = 3 + 2\cos x(\cos^3 x) + 6\sin x \cos^2 x(-\sin x) + 3\cos^2 x - 3\sin^2 x$$
$$= 3 + 2\cos^4 x - 6\cos^2 x(1 - \cos^2 x) + 3\cos^2 x - 3(1 - \cos^2 x)$$
$$= 8\cos^4 x \quad \text{Matches (ii)}$$

**4.** $\displaystyle\int \cos^3 x \sin^4 x\, dx = \int \cos x(1 - \sin^2 x)\sin^4 x\, dx$

$$= \int (\sin^4 x - \sin^6 x)\cos x\, dx$$
$$= \frac{\sin^5 x}{5} - \frac{\sin^7 x}{7} + C$$

**6.** Let $u = \cos x,\ du = -\sin x\, dx.$

$$\int \sin^3 x\, dx = \int \sin x(1 - \cos^2 x)\, dx$$
$$= \int \cos^2 x(-\sin x)\, dx + \int \sin x\, dx$$
$$= \frac{1}{3}\cos^3 x - \cos x + C$$

**8.** Let $u = \sin\dfrac{x}{3},\ du = \dfrac{1}{3}\cos\dfrac{x}{3}\, dx.$

$$\int \cos^3 \frac{x}{3}\, dx = \int \left(\cos\frac{x}{3}\right)\left(1 - \sin^2\frac{x}{3}\right) dx$$
$$= 3\int \left(1 - \sin^2\frac{x}{3}\right)\left(\frac{1}{3}\cos\frac{x}{3}\right) dx$$
$$= 3\left(\sin\frac{x}{3} - \frac{1}{3}\sin^3\frac{x}{3}\right) + C$$
$$= 3\sin\frac{x}{3} - \sin^3\frac{x}{3} + C$$

**10.** $\displaystyle\int \frac{\sin^5 t}{\sqrt{\cos t}}\, dt = \int \sin t(1 - \cos^2 t)^2(\cos t)^{-1/2}\, dt$

$$= \int \sin t(1 - 2\cos^2 t + \cos^4 t)(\cos t)^{-1/2}\, dt$$

$$= \int [(\cos t)^{-1/2} - 2(\cos t)^{3/2} + (\cos t)^{7/2}]\sin t\, dt = -2(\cos t)^{1/2} + \frac{4}{5}(\cos t)^{5/2} - \frac{2}{9}(\cos t)^{9/2} + C$$

**12.** $\displaystyle\int \sin^2 2x\, dx = \int \frac{1 - \cos 4x}{2}\, dx = \frac{1}{2}\left(x - \frac{1}{4}\sin 4x\right) + C$

$$= \frac{1}{8}(4x - \sin 4x) + C$$

**14.** $\displaystyle\int \sin^4 2\theta\, d\theta = \int \frac{1 - \cos 4\theta}{2} \cdot \frac{1 - \cos 4\theta}{2}\, d\theta$

$$= \frac{1}{4}\int (1 - 2\cos 4\theta + \cos^2 4\theta)\, d\theta$$

$$= \frac{1}{4}\int \left(1 - 2\cos 4\theta + \frac{1 + \cos 8\theta}{2}\right) d\theta$$

$$= \frac{1}{4}\int \left(\frac{3}{2} - 2\cos 4\theta + \frac{1}{2}\cos 8\theta\right) d\theta$$

$$= \frac{1}{4}\left[\frac{3}{2}\theta - \frac{1}{2}\sin 4\theta + \frac{1}{16}\sin 8\theta\right] + C$$

$$= \frac{3}{8}\theta - \frac{1}{8}\sin 4\theta + \frac{1}{64}\sin 8\theta + C$$

**16.** Use integration by parts twice.

$$dv = \sin^2 x\, dx = \frac{1 - \cos 2x}{2} \implies v = \frac{x}{2} - \frac{\sin 2x}{4} = \frac{1}{4}(2x - \sin 2x)$$

$$u = x^2 \implies du = 2x\, dx$$

$$dv = \sin 2x\, dx \implies v = -\frac{1}{2}\cos 2x$$

$$u = x \implies du = dx$$

$$\int x^2 \sin^2 x\, dx = \frac{1}{4}x^2(2x - \sin 2x) - \frac{1}{2}\int (2x^2 - x\sin 2x)\, dx$$

$$= \frac{1}{2}x^3 - \frac{1}{4}x^2 \sin 2x - \frac{1}{3}x^3 + \frac{1}{2}\int x\sin 2x\, dx$$

$$= \frac{1}{6}x^3 - \frac{1}{4}x^2 \sin 2x + \frac{1}{2}\left[-\frac{1}{2}x\cos 2x + \frac{1}{2}\int \cos 2x\, dx\right]$$

$$= \frac{1}{6}x^3 - \frac{1}{4}x^2 \sin 2x - \frac{1}{4}x\cos 2x + \frac{1}{8}\sin 2x + C$$

$$= \frac{1}{24}(4x^3 - 6x^2 \sin 2x - 6x\cos 2x + 3\sin 2x) + C$$

**18.** Let $u = \sin x,\, du = \cos x\, dx$.

$$\int_0^{\pi/2} \cos^5 x\, dx = \int_0^{\pi/2} (1 - \sin^2 x)^2 \cos x\, dx$$

$$= \int_0^{\pi/2} (1 - 2\sin^2 x + \sin^4 x) \cos x\, dx$$

$$= \left[\sin x - \frac{2}{3}\sin^3 x + \frac{1}{5}\sin^5 x\right]_0^{\pi/2}$$

$$= \frac{8}{15}$$

**20.** $\displaystyle\int_0^{\pi/2} \sin^2 x\, dx = \frac{1}{2}\int_0^{\pi/2} (1 - \cos 2x)\, dx$

$$= \frac{1}{2}\left[x - \frac{1}{2}\sin 2x\right]_0^{\pi/2} = \frac{\pi}{4}$$

**22.** $\displaystyle\int \sec^2(2x - 1)\, dx = \frac{1}{2}\tan(2x - 1) + C$

**24.** $\displaystyle\int \sec^6 3x\, dx = \int (1 + \tan^2 3x)^2 \sec^2 3x\, dx$

$$= \int (1 + 2\tan^2 3x + \tan^4 3x)\sec^2 3x\, dx$$

$$= \frac{1}{3}\tan 3x + \frac{2}{9}\tan^3 3x + \frac{1}{15}\tan^5 3x + C$$

**26.** $\displaystyle\int \tan^2 x\, dx = \int (\sec^2 x - 1)dx = \tan x - x + C$

**28.** $\displaystyle\int \tan^3 \frac{\pi x}{2}\sec^2 \frac{\pi x}{2}\, dx = \frac{1}{2\pi}\tan^4 \frac{\pi x}{2} + C$

**30.** Let $u = \sec 2t,\ du = 2\sec 2t\tan 2t$

$$\int \tan^3 2t \cdot \sec^3 2t\, dt = \int (\sec^2 2t - 1)\sec^3 2t \cdot \tan 2t\, dt$$

$$= \int (\sec^4 2t - \sec^2 2t)(\sec 2t \tan 2t)\, dt$$

$$= \frac{\sec^5 2t}{10} - \frac{\sec^3 2t}{6} + C$$

**32.** $\displaystyle\int \tan^5 2x\sec^2 2x\, dx = \frac{1}{12}\tan^6 2x + C$

**34.** $\displaystyle\int \sec^2 \frac{x}{2}\tan \frac{x}{2}\, dx = 2\int \sec \frac{x}{2}\left(\frac{1}{2}\sec \frac{x}{2}\tan \frac{x}{2}\right) dx$

$$= \sec^2 \frac{x}{2} + C$$

or $\displaystyle\int \sec^2 \frac{x}{2}\tan \frac{x}{2}\, dx = 2\int \tan \frac{x}{2}\left(\frac{1}{2}\sec^2 \frac{x}{2}\right) dx$

$$= \tan^2 \frac{x}{2} + C$$

**36.** $\displaystyle\int \tan^3 3x\, dx = \int (\sec^2 3x - 1)\tan 3x\, dx$

$$= \frac{1}{3}\int \tan 3x(3\sec^2 3x)\, dx + \frac{1}{3}\int \frac{-3\sin 3x}{\cos 3x}\, dx$$

$$= \frac{1}{6}\tan^2 3x + \frac{1}{3}\ln|\cos 3x| + C$$

**38.** $\displaystyle\int \frac{\tan^2 x}{\sec^5 x} = \int \frac{\sin^2 x}{\cos^2 x}\cdot \cos^5 x\, dx$

$$= \int \sin^2 x \cdot \cos^3 x\, dx$$

$$= \int \sin^2 x(1 - \sin^2 x)\cos x\, dx$$

$$= \int (\sin^2 x - \sin^4 x)\cos x\, dx$$

$$= \frac{\sin^3 x}{3} - \frac{\sin^5 x}{5} + C$$

**40.** $\displaystyle s = \int \sin^2 \frac{\alpha}{2}\cos^2 \frac{\alpha}{2}\, d\alpha$

$$= \int \left(\frac{1 - \cos \alpha}{2}\right)\left(\frac{1 + \cos \alpha}{2}\right) d\alpha = \int \frac{1 - \cos^2 \alpha}{4}\, d\alpha$$

$$= \frac{1}{4}\int \sin^2 \alpha\, d\alpha = \frac{1}{8}\int (1 - \cos 2\alpha)\, d\alpha$$

$$= \frac{1}{8}\left[\theta - \frac{\sin 2\alpha}{2}\right] + C$$

$$= \frac{1}{16}(2\alpha - \sin 2\alpha) + C$$

**42.** $\displaystyle y = \int \sqrt{\tan x}\sec^4 x\, dx$

$$= \int \tan^{1/2} x(\tan^2 x + 1)\sec^2 x\, dx$$

$$= \int (\tan^{5/2} x + \tan^{1/2} x)\sec^2 x\, dx$$

$$= \frac{2}{7}\tan^{7/2} x + \frac{2}{3}\tan^{3/2} x + C$$

**44. (a)**

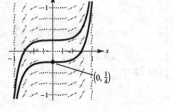
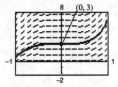

$(0, \frac{1}{4})$

**(b)** $\dfrac{dy}{dx} = \sec^2 x \tan^2 x,\ \left(0, -\dfrac{1}{4}\right)$

$y = \displaystyle\int \sec^2 x \tan^2 x\, dx \quad u = \tan x,\, du = \sec^2 x\, dx$

$y = \dfrac{\tan^3 x}{3} + C$

$\left(0, -\dfrac{1}{4}\right): \; -\dfrac{1}{4} = C \implies y = \dfrac{1}{3}\tan^3 x - \dfrac{1}{4}$

**46.** $\dfrac{dy}{dx} = 3\sqrt{y}\tan^2 x,\ y(0) = 3$

$8$  $(0, 3)$

$-1$  $1$

$-2$

**48.** $\displaystyle\int \cos 4\theta \cos(-3\theta)\, d\theta = \int \cos 4\theta \cos 3\theta\, d\theta$

$= \dfrac{1}{2}\displaystyle\int (\cos 7\theta + \cos \theta)\, d\theta$

$= \dfrac{\sin 7\theta}{14} + \dfrac{\sin \theta}{2} + C$

**50.** $\displaystyle\int \sin(-4x)\cos 3x\, dx = -\int \sin 4x \cos 3x\, dx$

$= -\dfrac{1}{2}\displaystyle\int (\sin x + \sin 7x)\, dx$

$= -\dfrac{1}{2}\left[-\cos x - \dfrac{1}{7}\cos 7x\right] + C$

$= \dfrac{1}{14}[7\cos x + \cos 7x] + C$

**52.** Let $u = \tan\dfrac{x}{2},\ du = \dfrac{1}{2}\sec^2\dfrac{x}{2}\, dx$.

$\displaystyle\int \tan^4 \dfrac{x}{2}\sec^4 \dfrac{x}{2}\, dx = \int \tan^4 \dfrac{x}{2}\left(\tan^2 \dfrac{x}{2} + 1\right)\sec^2 \dfrac{x}{2}\, dx$

$= 2\displaystyle\int \left(\tan^6 \dfrac{x}{2} + \tan^4 \dfrac{x}{2}\right)\left(\dfrac{1}{2}\sec^2 \dfrac{x}{2}\right)dx$

$= \dfrac{2}{7}\tan^7 \dfrac{x}{2} + \dfrac{2}{5}\tan^5 \dfrac{x}{2} + C$

**54.** $u = \cot 3x,\ du = -3\csc^2 3x\, dx$

$\displaystyle\int \csc^2 3x \cot 3x\, dx = -\dfrac{1}{3}\int \cot 3x(-3\csc^2 3x)\, dx$

$= -\dfrac{1}{6}\cot^2 3x + C$

**56.** $\displaystyle\int \dfrac{\cot^3 t}{\csc t}\, dt = \int \dfrac{\cos^3 t}{\sin^2 t}\, dt = \int \dfrac{(1 - \sin^2 t)\cos t}{\sin^2 t}\, dt$

$= \displaystyle\int \dfrac{\cos t}{\sin^2 t}\, dt - \int \cos t\, dt$

$= \dfrac{-1}{\sin t} - \sin t + C$

$= -\csc t - \sin t + C$

**58.** $\displaystyle\int \dfrac{\sin^2 x - \cos^2 x}{\cos x}\, dx = \int \dfrac{1 - 2\cos^2 x}{\cos x}\, dx = \int (\sec x - 2\cos x)\, dx = \ln|\sec x + \tan x| - 2\sin x + C$

**60.** $\displaystyle\int \dfrac{1 - \sec t}{\cos t - 1}\, dt = \int \dfrac{\cos t - 1}{(\cos t - 1)\cos t}\, dt$

$= \displaystyle\int \sec t\, dt = \ln|\sec t + \tan t| + C$

**62.** $\displaystyle\int_0^{\pi/3} \tan^2 x\, dx = \int_0^{\pi/3} (\sec^2 x - 1)\, dx$

$= \Big[\tan x - x\Big]_0^{\pi/3} = \sqrt{3} - \dfrac{\pi}{3}$

**64.** Let $u = \tan t,\ du = \sec^2 t\, dt$.

$\displaystyle\int_0^{\pi/4} \sec^2 t\sqrt{\tan t}\, dt = \left[\dfrac{2}{3}\tan^{3/2} t\right]_0^{\pi/4} = \dfrac{2}{3}$

**66.** $\displaystyle\int_{-\pi}^{\pi} \sin 3\theta \cos \theta\, d\theta = \dfrac{1}{2}\int_{-\pi}^{\pi} (\sin 4\theta + \sin 2\theta)\, d\theta$

$= -\dfrac{1}{2}\left[\dfrac{1}{4}\cos 4\theta + \dfrac{1}{2}\cos 2\theta\right]_{-\pi}^{\pi} = 0$

**68.** $\displaystyle\int_{-\pi/2}^{\pi/2} (\sin^2 x + 1)\, dx = \int_{-\pi/2}^{\pi/2} \left(\frac{1 - \cos 2x}{2} + 1\right) dx$

$\displaystyle = \int_{-\pi/2}^{\pi/2} \left(\frac{3}{2} - \frac{1}{2}\cos 2x\right) dx = \left[\frac{3}{2}x - \frac{1}{4}\sin 2x\right]_{-\pi/2}^{\pi/2} = \frac{3\pi}{2}$

**70.** $\displaystyle\int \sin^2 x \cos^2 x\, dx = \frac{1}{32}[4x - \sin 4x] + C$

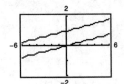

**72.** $\displaystyle\int \tan^3(1 - x)\, dx = -\frac{\tan^2(1 - x)}{2} - \ln|\cos(1 - x)| + C$

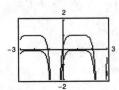

**74.** $\displaystyle\int \sec^4(1 - x)\tan(1 - x)\, dx = -\frac{\sec^4(1 - x)}{4} + C$

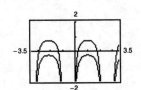

**76.** $\displaystyle\int_0^{\pi/2} (1 - \cos\theta)^2\, d\theta = \left[\frac{3}{2}\theta - 2\sin\theta + \frac{1}{4}\sin 2\theta\right]_0^{\pi/2}$

$\displaystyle = \frac{3\pi}{4} - 2$

**78.** $\displaystyle\int_0^{\pi/2} \sin^6 x\, dx = \frac{1}{8}\left[\frac{5x}{2} - 2\sin 2x + \frac{3}{8}\sin 4x + \frac{1}{6}\sin^3 2x\right]_0^{\pi/2} = \frac{5\pi}{32}$

**80.** See guidelines on page 500.

**82.** (a) Let $u = \tan x$, $du = \sec^2 x\, dx$.

$\displaystyle\int \sec^2 x \tan x\, dx = \frac{1}{2}\tan^2 x + C_1$

Or let $u = \sec x$, $du = \sec x \tan x\, dx$.

$\displaystyle\int \sec x(\sec x \tan x)\, dx = \frac{1}{2}\sec^2 x + C$

(b)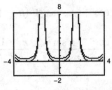

(c) $\dfrac{1}{2}\sec^2 x + C = \dfrac{1}{2}(\tan^2 x + 1) + C = \dfrac{1}{2}\tan^2 x + \left(\dfrac{1}{2} + C\right) = \dfrac{1}{2}\tan^2 x + C_2$

**84. Disks**

$R(x) = \tan x$

$r(x) = 0$

$\displaystyle V = 2\pi \int_0^{\pi/4} \tan^2 x\, dx$

$\displaystyle = 2\pi \int_0^{\pi/4} (\sec^2 x - 1)\, dx$

$\displaystyle = 2\pi \left[\tan x - x\right]_0^{\pi/4}$

$\displaystyle = 2\pi \left(1 - \frac{\pi}{4}\right) \approx 1.348$

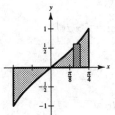

**86.** (a) $V = \pi \int_0^{\pi/2} \cos^2 x \, dx = \frac{\pi}{2} \int_0^{\pi/2} (1 + \cos 2x) \, dx = \frac{\pi}{2} \left[ x + \frac{1}{2} \sin 2x \right]_0^{\pi/2} = \frac{\pi^2}{4}$

(b) $A = \int_0^{\pi/2} \cos x \, dx = \left[ \sin x \right]_0^{\pi/2} = 1$

Let $u = x, \, dv = \cos x \, dx, \, du = dx, \, v = \sin x.$

$\bar{x} = \int_0^{\pi/2} x \cos x \, dx = \left[ x \sin x \right]_0^{\pi/2} - \int_0^{\pi/2} \sin x \, dx = \left[ x \sin x + \cos x \right]_0^{\pi/2} = \frac{\pi}{2} - 1 = \frac{\pi - 2}{2}$

$\bar{y} = \frac{1}{2} \int_0^{\pi/2} \cos^2 x \, dx$

$\quad = \frac{1}{4} \int_0^{\pi/2} (1 + \cos 2x) \, dx$

$\quad = \frac{1}{4} \left[ x + \frac{1}{2} \sin 2x \right]_0^{\pi/2} = \frac{\pi}{8}$

$(\bar{x}, \bar{y}) = \left( \frac{\pi - 2}{2}, \frac{\pi}{8} \right)$

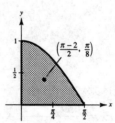

**88.** $dv = \cos x \, dx \implies v = \sin x$

$u = \cos^{n-1} x \implies du = -(n - 1)\cos^{n-2} x \sin x \, dx$

$\int \cos^n x \, dx = \cos^{n-1} x \sin x + (n - 1) \int \cos^{n-2} x \sin^2 x \, dx$

$\quad = \cos^{n-1} x \sin x + (n - 1) \int \cos^{n-2} x (1 - \cos^2 x) \, dx$

$\quad = \cos^{n-1} x \sin x + (n - 1) \int \cos^{n-2} x \, dx - (n - 1) \int \cos^n x \, dx$

Therefore, $n \int \cos^n x \, dx = \cos^{n-1} x \sin x + (n - 1) \int \cos^{n-2} x \, dx$

$\int \cos^n x \, dx = \frac{\cos^{n-1} x \sin x}{n} + \frac{n - 1}{n} \int \cos^{n-2} x \, dx.$

**90.** Let $u = \sec^{n-2} x, \, du = (n - 2)\sec^{n-2} x \tan x \, dx, \, dv = \sec^2 x \, dx, \, v = \tan x.$

$\int \sec^n x \, dx = \sec^{n-2} x \tan x - \int (n - 2) \sec^{n-2} x \tan^2 x \, dx$

$\quad = \sec^{n-2} x \tan x - (n - 2) \int \sec^{n-2} x (\sec^2 x - 1) \, dx$

$\quad = \sec^{n-2} x \tan x - (n - 2) \left[ \int \sec^n x \, dx - \int \sec^{n-2} x \, dx \right]$

$(n - 1) \int \sec^n x \, dx = \sec^{n-2} x \tan x + (n - 2) \int \sec^{n-2} x \, dx$

$\int \sec^n x \, dx = \frac{1}{n - 1} \sec^{n-2} x \tan x + \frac{n - 2}{n - 1} \int \sec^{n-2} x \, dx$

**92.** $\int \cos^4 x \, dx = \frac{\cos^3 x \sin x}{4} + \frac{3}{4} \int \cos^2 x \, dx = \frac{\cos^3 x \sin x}{4} + \frac{3}{4} \left[ \frac{\cos x \sin x}{2} + \frac{1}{2} \int dx \right]$

$\quad = \frac{1}{4} \cos^3 x \sin x + \frac{3}{8} \cos x \sin x + \frac{3}{8} x + C = \frac{1}{8} [2 \cos^3 x \sin x + 3 \cos x \sin x + 3x] + C$

**94.** $\displaystyle\int \sin^4 x \cos^2 x \, dx = -\frac{\cos^3 x \sin^3 x}{6} + \frac{1}{2}\int \cos^2 x \sin^2 x \, dx$

$\qquad = -\frac{\cos^3 x \sin^3 x}{6} + \frac{1}{2}\left[ -\frac{\cos^3 x \sin x}{4} + \frac{1}{4}\int \cos^2 x \, dx \right]$

$\qquad = -\frac{1}{6}\cos^3 x \sin^3 x - \frac{1}{8}\cos^3 x \sin x + \frac{1}{8}\left[ \frac{\cos x \sin x}{2} + \frac{x}{2} \right] + C$

$\qquad = -\frac{1}{48}\left[ 8\cos^3 x \sin^3 x + 6\cos^3 x \sin x - 3\cos x \sin x - 3x \right] + C$

**96.** (a) $n$ is odd and $n \geq 3$.

$\displaystyle\int_0^{\pi/2} \cos^n x \, dx = \left[ \frac{\cos^{n-1} x \sin x}{n} \right]_0^{\pi/2} + \frac{n-1}{n}\int_0^{\pi/2} \cos^{n-2} x \, dx$

$\qquad = \frac{n-1}{n}\left[ \left[ \frac{\cos^{n-3} x \sin x}{n-2} \right]_0^{\pi/2} + \frac{n-3}{n-2}\int_0^{\pi/2} \cos^{n-4} x \, dx \right]$

$\qquad = \frac{n-1}{n}\cdot\frac{n-3}{n-2}\left[ \left[ \frac{\cos^{n-5} x \sin x}{n-4} \right]_0^{\pi/2} + \frac{n-5}{n-4}\int_0^{\pi/2} \cos^{n-6} x \, dx \right]$

$\qquad = \frac{n-1}{n}\cdot\frac{n-3}{n-2}\cdot\frac{n-5}{n-4}\int_0^{\pi/2} \cos^{n-6} x \, dx$

$\qquad = \frac{n-1}{n}\cdot\frac{n-3}{n-2}\cdot\frac{n-5}{n-4}\cdots\int_0^{\pi/2} \cos x \, dx$

$\qquad = \left[ \frac{n-1}{n}\cdot\frac{n-3}{n-2}\cdot\frac{n-5}{n-4}\cdots(\sin x) \right]_0^{\pi/2}$

$\qquad = \frac{n-1}{n}\cdot\frac{n-3}{n-2}\cdot\frac{n-5}{n-4}\cdots 1 \quad$ (Reverse the order)

$\qquad = (1)\left(\frac{2}{3}\right)\left(\frac{4}{5}\right)\left(\frac{6}{7}\right)\cdots\left(\frac{n-1}{n}\right)$

$\qquad = \left(\frac{2}{3}\right)\left(\frac{4}{5}\right)\left(\frac{6}{7}\right)\cdots\left(\frac{n-1}{n}\right)$

(b) $n$ is even and $n \geq 2$.

$\displaystyle\int_0^{\pi/2} \cos^n x \, dx = \frac{n-1}{n}\cdot\frac{n-3}{n-2}\cdot\frac{n-5}{n-4}\cdots\int_0^{\pi/2} \cos^2 x \, dx \quad$ (From part (a).)

$\qquad = \left[ \frac{n-1}{n}\cdot\frac{n-3}{n-2}\cdot\frac{n-5}{n-4}\cdots\left(\frac{x}{2} + \frac{1}{4}\sin 2x\right) \right]_0^{\pi/2}$

$\qquad = \frac{n-1}{n}\cdot\frac{n-3}{n-2}\cdot\frac{n-5}{n-4}\cdots\frac{\pi}{4} \quad$ (Reverse the order)

$\qquad = \left(\frac{\pi}{2}\cdot\frac{1}{2}\right)\left(\frac{3}{4}\right)\left(\frac{5}{6}\right)\cdots\left(\frac{n-1}{n}\right)$

$\qquad = \left(\frac{1}{2}\right)\left(\frac{3}{4}\right)\left(\frac{5}{6}\right)\cdots\left(\frac{n-1}{n}\right)\left(\frac{\pi}{2}\right)$

# Section 7.4    Trigonometric Substitution

**2.** $\dfrac{d}{dx}\left[8\ln\left|\sqrt{x^2-16}+x\right|+\dfrac{1}{2}x\sqrt{x^2-16}+C\right]=8\left[\dfrac{(x/\sqrt{x^2-16})+1}{\sqrt{x^2-16}+x}\right]+\dfrac{1}{2}x\left(\dfrac{x}{\sqrt{x^2-16}}\right)+\dfrac{1}{2}\sqrt{x^2-16}$

$$=\frac{8(x+\sqrt{x^2-16})}{\sqrt{x^2-16}(\sqrt{x^2-16}+x)}+\frac{x^2}{2\sqrt{x^2+16}}+\frac{\sqrt{x^2-16}}{2}$$

$$=\frac{16+x^2+x^2-16}{2\sqrt{x^2-16}}$$

$$=\frac{x^2}{\sqrt{x^2-16}}$$

Indefinite integral: $\displaystyle\int\frac{x^2}{\sqrt{x^2-16}}$    Matches (d)

**4.** $\dfrac{d}{dx}\left[8\arcsin\dfrac{x-3}{4}+\dfrac{(x-3)\sqrt{7+6x-x^2}}{2}+C\right]=8\left[\dfrac{1}{\sqrt{1-[(x-3)/4]^2}}\cdot\dfrac{1}{4}\right]+\dfrac{1}{2}(x-3)\dfrac{3-x}{\sqrt{7+6x-x^2}}+\dfrac{1}{2}\sqrt{7+6x-x^2}$

$$=\frac{8}{\sqrt{16-(x-3)^2}}-\frac{(x-3)^2}{2\sqrt{16-(x-3)^2}}+\frac{\sqrt{16-(x-3)^2}}{2}$$

$$=\frac{16-(x^2-6x+9)+16-(x^2-6x+9)}{2\sqrt{16-(x-3)^2}}$$

$$=\frac{2[16-(x-3)^2]}{2\sqrt{16-(x-3)^2}}$$

$$=\sqrt{16-(x-3)^2}$$

$$=\sqrt{7+6x-x^2}$$

Indefinite integral: $\displaystyle\int\sqrt{7+6x-x^2}\,dx$    Matches (c)

**6.** Same substitution as in Exercise 5.

$$\int\frac{10}{x^2\sqrt{25-x^2}}\,dx=10\int\frac{5\cos\theta\,d\theta}{(25\sin^2\theta)(5\cos\theta)}=\frac{2}{5}\int\csc^2\theta\,d\theta=-\frac{2}{5}\cot\theta+C=\frac{-2\sqrt{25-x^2}}{5x}+C$$

**8.** Same substitution as in Exercise 5

$$\int\frac{x^2}{\sqrt{25-x^2}}\,dx=\int\frac{25\sin^2\theta}{5\cos\theta}(5\cos\theta)\,d\theta=\frac{25}{2}\int(1-\cos2\theta)\,d\theta$$

$$=\frac{25}{2}\left(\theta-\frac{1}{2}\sin2\theta\right)+C=\frac{25}{2}(\theta-\sin\theta\cos\theta)+C$$

$$=\frac{25}{2}\left[\arcsin\left(\frac{x}{5}\right)-\left(\frac{x}{5}\right)\left(\frac{\sqrt{25-x^2}}{5}\right)\right]+C=\frac{1}{2}\left[25\arcsin\left(\frac{x}{5}\right)-x\sqrt{25-x^2}\right]+C$$

**10.** Same substitution as in Exercise 9

$$\int\frac{\sqrt{x^2-4}}{x}\,dx=\int\frac{2\tan\theta}{2\sec\theta}(2\sec\theta\tan\theta)\,d\theta=2\int\tan^2\theta\,d\theta=2\int(\sec^2\theta-1)\,d\theta$$

$$=2(\tan\theta-\theta)+C=2\left[\frac{\sqrt{x^2-4}}{2}-\operatorname{arcsec}\left(\frac{x}{2}\right)\right]+C=\sqrt{x^2-4}-2\operatorname{arcsec}\left(\frac{x}{2}\right)+C$$

**12.** Same substitution as in Exercise 9

$$\int \frac{x^3}{\sqrt{x^2 - 4}}\, dx = \int \frac{8 \sec^3 \theta}{2 \tan \theta} (2 \sec \theta \tan \theta)\, d\theta = 8 \int \sec^4 \theta\, d\theta$$

$$= 8 \int (1 + \tan^2 \theta) \sec^2 \theta\, d\theta = 8\left( \tan \theta + \frac{\tan^3 \theta}{3} \right) + C = \frac{8}{3} \tan \theta (3 + \tan^2 \theta) + C$$

$$= \frac{8}{3}\left( \frac{\sqrt{x^2 - 4}}{2} \right)\left( 3 + \frac{x^2 - 4}{4} \right) + C = \frac{1}{3}\sqrt{x^2 - 4}\,(12 + x^2 - 4) + C = \frac{1}{3}\sqrt{x^2 - 4}\,(x^2 + 8) + C$$

**14.** Same substitution as in Exercise 13.

$$\int \frac{9x^3}{\sqrt{1 + x^2}}\, dx = 9 \int \frac{\tan^3 \theta}{\sec \theta} \sec^2 \theta\, d\theta = 9 \int (\sec^2 \theta - 1)\sec \theta \tan \theta\, d\theta = 9\left[ \frac{\sec^3 \theta}{3} - \sec \theta \right] + C$$

$$= 3 \sec \theta(\sec^2 \theta - 3) + C = 3\sqrt{1 + x^2}\,[(1 + x^2) - 3] + C = 3\sqrt{1 + x^2}\,(x^2 - 2) + C$$

**16.** Same substitution as in Exercise 13

$$\int \frac{x^2}{(1 + x^2)^2}\, dx = \int \frac{x^2}{\left(\sqrt{1 + x^2}\right)^4}\, dx = \int \frac{\tan^2 \theta \sec^2 \theta\, d\theta}{\sec^4 \theta} = \int \sin^2 \theta\, d\theta$$

$$= \frac{1}{2} \int (1 - \cos 2\theta)\, d\theta = \frac{1}{2}\left[ \theta - \frac{\sin 2\theta}{2} \right] = \frac{1}{2}[\theta - \sin \theta \cos \theta] + C$$

$$= \frac{1}{2}\left[ \arctan x - \left( \frac{x}{\sqrt{1 + x^2}} \right)\left( \frac{1}{\sqrt{1 + x^2}} \right) \right] + C = \frac{1}{2}\left[ \arctan x - \frac{x}{1 + x^2} \right] + C$$

**18.** Let $u = x$, $a = 1$, and $du = dx$.

$$\int \sqrt{1 + x^2}\, dx = \frac{1}{2}\left( x\sqrt{1 + x^2} + \ln\left| x + \sqrt{1 + x^2} \right| \right) + C$$

**20.** $\displaystyle \int \frac{x}{\sqrt{9 - x^2}}\, dx = -\frac{1}{2} \int (9 - x^2)^{-1/2}(-2x)\, dx$

$$= -(9 - x^2)^{1/2} + C \quad \text{(Power Rule)}$$

**22.** $\displaystyle \int \frac{1}{\sqrt{25 - x^2}}\, dx = \arcsin \frac{x}{5} + C$

**24.** Let $u = 16 - 4x^2$, $du = -8x\, dx$.

$$\int x\sqrt{16 - 4x^2}\, dx = -\frac{1}{8} \int (16 - 4x^2)^{1/2}(-8x)\, dx = \left[ -\frac{1}{12}(16 - 4x^2)^{3/2} \right] + C = -\frac{2}{3}(4 - x^2)^{3/2} + C$$

**26.** Let $u = 1 - t^2$, $du = -2t\, dt$.

$$\int \frac{t}{(1 - t^2)^{3/2}}\, dt = -\frac{1}{2} \int (1 - t^2)^{-3/2}(-2t)\, dt = \frac{1}{\sqrt{1 - t^2}} + C$$

**28.** Let $2x = 3 \tan \theta$, $dx = \dfrac{3}{2} \sec^2 \theta\, d\theta$, $\sqrt{4x^2 + 9} = 3 \sec \theta$.

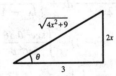

$$\int \frac{\sqrt{4x^2 + 9}}{x^4}\, dx = \int \frac{3 \sec \theta[(3/2) \sec^2 \theta\, d\theta]}{(3/2)^4 \tan^4 \theta}$$

$$= \frac{8}{9} \int \frac{\cos \theta}{\sin^4 \theta}\, d\theta$$

$$= \frac{-8}{27 \sin^3 \theta} + C$$

$$= -\frac{8}{27} \csc^3 \theta + C$$

$$= \frac{-(4x^2 + 9)^{3/2}}{27x^3} + C$$

**30.** Let $2x = 4 \tan \theta$, $dx = 2 \sec^2 \theta \, d\theta$, $\sqrt{4x^2 + 16} = 4 \sec \theta$.

$$\int \frac{1}{x \sqrt{4x^2 + 16}} \, dx = \int \frac{2 \sec^2 \theta \, d\theta}{2 \tan \theta (4 \sec \theta)}$$

$$= \frac{1}{4} \int \frac{\sec \theta}{\tan \theta} \, d\theta = \frac{1}{4} \int \csc \theta \, d\theta$$

$$= -\frac{1}{4} \ln|\csc \theta + \cot \theta| + C = -\frac{1}{4} \ln \left| \frac{\sqrt{x^2 + 4} + 2}{x} \right| + C$$

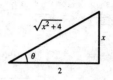

**32.** Let $x = \sqrt{3} \tan \theta$, $dx = \sqrt{3} \sec^2 \theta \, d\theta$, $x^2 + 3 = 3 \sec^2 \theta$.

$$\int \frac{1}{(x^2 + 3)^{3/2}} \, dx = \int \frac{\sqrt{3} \sec^2 \theta \, d\theta}{3\sqrt{3} \sec^3 \theta}$$

$$= \frac{1}{3} \int \cos \theta \, d\theta$$

$$= \frac{1}{3} \sin \theta + C$$

$$= \frac{x}{3\sqrt{x^2 + 3}} + C$$

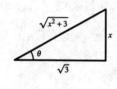

**34.** Let $u = x^2 + 2x + 2$, $du = (2x + 2) \, dx$.

$$\int (x + 1)\sqrt{x^2 + 2x + 2} \, dx = \frac{1}{2} \int (x^2 + 2x + 2)^{1/2}(2x + 2) \, dx = \frac{1}{3}(x^2 + 2x + 2)^{3/2} + C$$

**36.** Let $\sqrt{x} = \sin \theta$, $x = \sin^2 \theta$, $dx = 2 \sin \theta \cos \theta \, d\theta$, $\sqrt{1 - x} = \cos \theta$.

$$\int \frac{\sqrt{1 - x}}{\sqrt{x}} \, dx = \int \frac{\cos \theta (2 \sin \theta \cos \theta \, d\theta)}{\sin \theta}$$

$$= 2 \int \cos^2 \theta \, d\theta$$

$$= \int (1 + \cos 2\theta) \, d\theta$$

$$= (\theta + \sin \theta \cos \theta) + C$$

$$= \arcsin \sqrt{x} + \sqrt{x}\sqrt{1 - x} + C$$

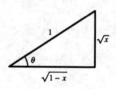

**38.** Let $x = \tan \theta$, $dx = \sec^2 \theta \, d\theta$, $x^2 + 1 = \sec^2 \theta$.

$$\int \frac{x^3 + x + 1}{x^4 + 2x^2 + 1} \, dx = \frac{1}{4} \int \frac{4x^3 + 4x}{x^4 + 2x^2 + 1} \, dx + \int \frac{1}{(x^2 + 1)^2} \, dx$$

$$= \frac{1}{4} \ln(x^4 + 2x^2 + 1) + \int \frac{\sec^2 \theta \, d\theta}{\sec^4 \theta}$$

$$= \frac{1}{2} \ln(x^2 + 1) + \frac{1}{2} \int (1 + \cos 2\theta) \, d\theta$$

$$= \frac{1}{2} \ln(x^2 + 1) + \frac{1}{2}(\theta + \sin \theta \cos \theta) + C$$

$$= \frac{1}{2} \left[ \ln(x^2 + 1) + \arctan x + \frac{x}{x^2 + 1} \right] + C$$

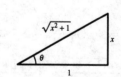

**40.** $u = \arcsin x, \implies du = \dfrac{1}{\sqrt{1 - x^2}} dx, dv = x\, dx \implies v = \dfrac{x^2}{2}$

$$\int x \arcsin x\, dx = \frac{x^2}{2} \arcsin x - \frac{1}{2} \int \frac{x^2}{\sqrt{1 - x^2}}\, dx$$

$x = \sin\theta,\, dx = \cos\theta\, d\theta,\, \sqrt{1 - x^2} = \cos\theta$

$$\int x \arcsin x\, dx = \frac{x^2}{2} \arcsin x = \frac{1}{2} \int \frac{\sin^2\theta}{\cos\theta} \cos\theta\, d\theta = \frac{x^2}{2} \arcsin x - \frac{1}{4} \int (1 - \cos 2\theta)\, d\theta$$

$$= \frac{x^2}{2} \arcsin x - \frac{1}{4}\left[ \theta - \frac{1}{2} \sin 2\theta \right] + C = \frac{x^2}{2} \arcsin x - \frac{1}{4}[\theta - \sin\theta \cos\theta] + C$$

$$= \frac{x^2}{2} \arcsin x - \frac{1}{4}\left[ \arcsin x - x\sqrt{1 - x^2} \right] + C = \frac{1}{4}\left[ (2x^2 - 1) \arcsin x + x\sqrt{1 - x^2} \right] + C$$

**42.** Let $x - 1 = \sin\theta,\, dx = \cos\theta\, d\theta,\, \sqrt{1 - (x - 1)^2} = \sqrt{2x - x^2} = \cos\theta.$

$$\int \frac{x^2}{\sqrt{2x - x^2}}\, dx = \int \frac{x^2}{\sqrt{1 - (x - 1)^2}}\, dx$$

$$= \int \frac{(1 + \sin\theta)^2 (\cos\theta\, d\theta)}{\cos\theta}$$

$$= \int (1 + 2\sin\theta + \sin^2\theta)\, d\theta$$

$$= \int \left( \frac{3}{2} + 2\sin\theta - \frac{1}{2}\cos 2\theta \right) d\theta$$

$$= \frac{3}{2}\theta - 2\cos\theta - \frac{1}{4}\sin 2\theta + C$$

$$= \frac{3}{2}\theta - 2\cos\theta - \frac{1}{2}\sin\theta\cos\theta + C$$

$$= \frac{3}{2}\arcsin(x - 1) - 2\sqrt{2x - x^2} - \frac{1}{2}(x - 1)\sqrt{2x - x^2} + C$$

$$= \frac{3}{2}\arcsin(x - 1) - \frac{1}{2}\sqrt{2x - x^2}(x + 3) + C$$

**44.** Let $x - 3 = 2\sec\theta,\, dx = 2\sec\theta\tan\theta\, d\theta,\, \sqrt{(x - 3)^2 - 4} = 2\tan\theta.$

$$\int \frac{x}{\sqrt{x^2 - 6x + 5}}\, dx = \int \frac{x}{\sqrt{(x - 3)^2 - 4}}\, dx = \int \frac{(2\sec\theta + 3)}{2\tan\theta}(2\sec\theta\tan\theta)\, d\theta$$

$$= \int (2\sec^2\theta + 3\sec\theta)\, d\theta$$

$$= 2\tan\theta + 3\ln|\sec\theta + \tan\theta| + C_1$$

$$= 2\left( \frac{\sqrt{(x - 3)^3 - 4}}{2} \right) + 3\ln\left| \frac{x - 3}{2} + \frac{\sqrt{(x - 3)^2 - 4}}{2} \right| + C_1$$

$$= \sqrt{x^2 - 6x + 5} + 3\ln\left| (x - 3) + \sqrt{x^2 - 6x + 5} \right| + C$$

**46.** Same substitution as in Exercise 45

(a) $\displaystyle \int \frac{1}{(1-t^2)^{5/2}}\, dt = \int \frac{\cos\theta\, d\theta}{\cos^5\theta} = \int \sec^4\theta\, d\theta = \int (\tan^2\theta + 1)\sec^2\theta\, d\theta$

$$= \frac{1}{3}\tan^3\theta + \tan\theta + C = \frac{1}{3}\left(\frac{t}{\sqrt{1-t^2}}\right)^3 + \frac{t}{\sqrt{1-t^2}} + C$$

Thus, $\displaystyle \int_0^{\sqrt{3}/2} \frac{1}{(1-t^2)^{5/2}}\, dt = \left[\frac{t^3}{3(1-t^2)^{3/2}} + \frac{t}{\sqrt{1-t^2}}\right]_0^{\sqrt{3}/2}$

$$= \frac{3\sqrt{3}/8}{3(1/4)^{3/2}} + \frac{\sqrt{3}/2}{\sqrt{1/4}} = \sqrt{3} + \sqrt{3} = 2\sqrt{3} \approx 3.464.$$

(b) When $t = 0$, $\theta = 0$. When $t = \sqrt{3}/2$, $\theta = \pi/3$. Thus,

$$\int_0^{\sqrt{3}/2} \frac{1}{(1-t^2)^{5/2}}\, dt = \left[\frac{1}{3}\tan^3\theta + \tan\theta\right]_0^{\pi/3} = \frac{1}{3}\left(\sqrt{3}\right)^3 + \sqrt{3} = 2\sqrt{3} \approx 3.464.$$

**48.** (a) Let $5x = 3\sin\theta$, $dx = \dfrac{3}{5}\cos\theta\, d\theta$, $\sqrt{9-25x^2} = 3\cos\theta$.

$$\int \sqrt{9-25x^2}\, dx = \int (3\cos\theta)\frac{3}{5}\cos\theta\, d\theta$$

$$= \frac{9}{5}\int \frac{1+\cos 2\theta}{2}\, d\theta$$

$$= \frac{9}{10}\left[\theta + \frac{1}{2}\sin 2\theta\right] + C$$

$$= \frac{9}{10}[\theta + \sin\theta\cos\theta] + C$$

$$= \frac{9}{10}\left[\arcsin\frac{5x}{3} + \frac{5x}{3}\cdot\frac{\sqrt{9-25x^2}}{3}\right] + C$$

Thus, $\displaystyle \int_0^{3/5} \sqrt{9-25x^2}\, dx = \frac{9}{10}\left[\arcsin\frac{5x}{3} + \frac{5x\sqrt{9-25x^2}}{9}\right]_0^{3/5} = \frac{9}{10}\left[\frac{\pi}{2}\right] = \frac{9\pi}{20}.$

(b) When $x = 0$, $\theta = 0$. When $x = \dfrac{3}{5}$, $\theta = \dfrac{\pi}{2}$.

Thus, $\displaystyle \int_0^{3/5} \sqrt{9-25x^2}\, dx = \left[\frac{9}{10}(\theta + \sin\theta\cos\theta)\right]_0^{\pi/2} = \frac{9}{10}\left(\frac{\pi}{2}\right) = \frac{9\pi}{20}.$

**50.** (a) Let $x = 3\sec\theta$, $dx = 3\sec\theta\tan\theta\, d\theta$, $\sqrt{x^2-9} = 3\tan\theta$.

$$\int \frac{\sqrt{x^2-9}}{x^2}\, dx = \int \frac{3\tan\theta}{9\sec^2\theta}3\sec\theta\tan\theta\, d\theta$$

$$= \int \frac{\tan^2\theta}{\sec\theta}\, d\theta$$

$$= \int \frac{\sin^2\theta}{\cos\theta}\, d\theta$$

$$= \int \frac{1-\cos^2\theta}{\cos\theta}\, d\theta$$

$$= \int (\sec\theta - \cos\theta)\, d\theta$$

$$= \ln|\sec\theta + \tan\theta| - \sin\theta + C$$

$$= \ln\left|\frac{x}{3} + \frac{\sqrt{x^2-9}}{3}\right| - \frac{\sqrt{x^2-9}}{x} + C$$

**—CONTINUED—**

**50.** **—CONTINUED—**

Hence, $\displaystyle\int_3^6 \frac{\sqrt{x^2-9}}{x^2}\,dx = \left[\ln\left|\frac{x}{3} + \frac{\sqrt{x^2-9}}{3}\right| - \frac{\sqrt{x^2-9}}{x}\right]_3^6 = \ln\left|2 + \sqrt{3}\right| - \frac{\sqrt{3}}{2}.$

(b) When $x = 3$, $\theta = 0$; when $x = 6$, $\theta = \dfrac{\pi}{3}$.

Hence, $\displaystyle\int_3^6 \frac{\sqrt{x^2-9}}{x^2}\,dx = \Big[\ln\left|\sec\theta + \tan\theta\right| - \sin\theta\Big]_0^{\pi/3} = \ln\left|2 + \sqrt{3}\right| - \frac{\sqrt{3}}{2}.$

**52.** $\displaystyle\int (x^2 + 2x + 11)^{3/2}\,dx = \frac{1}{4}(x+1)(x^2 + 2x + 26)\sqrt{x^2 + 2x + 11} + \frac{75}{2}\ln\left|\sqrt{x^2+2x+11} + (x+1)\right| + C$

**54.** $\displaystyle\int x^2\sqrt{x^2-4}\,dx = \frac{1}{4}x^3\sqrt{x^2-4} - \frac{1}{2}x\sqrt{x^2-4} - 2\ln\left|x + \sqrt{x^2-4}\right| + C$

**56.** (a) Substitution: $u = x^2 + 1$, $du = 2x\,dx$

(b) Trigonometric substitution: $x = \sec\theta$

**58.** (a) $x^2 + (y-k)^2 = 25$

Radius of circle $= 5$

$k^2 = 5^2 + 5^2 = 50$

$k = 5\sqrt{2}$

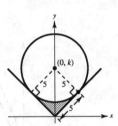

(b) Area $=$ square $- \dfrac{1}{4}$(circle)

$= 25 - \dfrac{1}{4}\pi(5)^2 = 25\left(1 - \dfrac{\pi}{4}\right)$

(c) Area $= r^2 - \dfrac{1}{4}\pi r^2 = r^2\left(1 - \dfrac{\pi}{4}\right)$

**60.** (a) Place the center of the circle at $(0, 1)$; $x^2 + (y-1)^2 = 1$. The depth $d$ satisfies $0 \le d \le 2$. The volume is

$$V = 3 \cdot 2\int_0^d \sqrt{1 - (y-1)^2}\,dy$$

$$= 6 \cdot \frac{1}{2}\Big[\arcsin(y-1) + (y-1)\sqrt{1-(y-1)^2}\Big]_0^d \quad \text{(Theorem 7.2 (1))}$$

$$= 3\Big[\arcsin(d-1) + (d-1)\sqrt{1-(d-1)^2} - \arcsin(-1)\Big]$$

$$= \frac{3\pi}{2} + 3\arcsin(d-1) + 3(d-1)\sqrt{2d - d^2}.$$

(b)

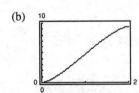

(c) The full tank holds $3\pi \approx 9.4248$ cubic meters. The horizontal lines

$$y = \frac{3\pi}{4}, \; y = \frac{3\pi}{2}, \; y = \frac{9\pi}{4}$$

intersect the curve at $d = 0.596, 1.0, 1.404$. The dip-stick would have these markings on it.

(d) $\displaystyle V = 6\int_0^d \sqrt{1-(y-1)^2}\,dy$

$\dfrac{dV}{dt} = \dfrac{dV}{dd} \cdot \dfrac{dd}{dt} = 6\sqrt{1-(d-1)^2} \cdot d'(t) = \dfrac{1}{4}$

$\Rightarrow d'(t) = \dfrac{1}{24\sqrt{1-(d-1)^2}}$

(e)

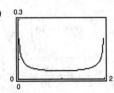

The minimum occurs at $d = 1$, which is the widest part of the tank.

**62.** Let $x - h = r \sin \theta$, $dx = r \cos \theta \, d\theta$, $\sqrt{r^2 - (x - h)^2} = r \cos \theta$.

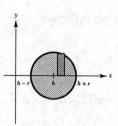

**Shell Method:**

$$V = 4\pi \int_{h-r}^{h+r} x\sqrt{r^2 - (x - h)^2} \, dx$$

$$= 4\pi \int_{-\pi/2}^{\pi/2} (h + r \sin \theta) r \cos \theta (r \cos \theta) \, d\theta = 4\pi r^2 \int_{-\pi/2}^{\pi/2} (h + r \sin \theta) \cos^2 \theta \, d\theta$$

$$= 4\pi r^2 \left[ \frac{h}{2} \int_{-\pi/2}^{\pi/2} (1 + \cos 2\theta) \, d\theta + r \int_{-\pi/2}^{\pi/2} \sin \theta \cos^2 \theta \, d\theta \right]$$

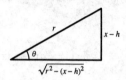

$$= 2\pi r^2 h \left[ \theta + \frac{1}{2} \sin 2\theta \right]_{-\pi/2}^{\pi/2} - \left[ 4\pi r^3 \left( \frac{\cos^3 \theta}{3} \right) \right]_{-\pi/2}^{\pi/2} = 2\pi^2 r^2 h$$

**64.** $y = \frac{1}{2}x^2$, $y' = x$, $1 + (y')^2 = 1 + x^2$

$$s = \int_0^4 \sqrt{1 + x^2} \, dx = \left[ \frac{1}{2} \left( x\sqrt{x^2 + 1} + \ln\left| x + \sqrt{x^2 + 1} \right| \right) \right]_0^4 \quad \text{(Theorem 7.2)}$$

$$= \frac{1}{2} \left[ 4\sqrt{17} + \ln\left( 4 + \sqrt{17} \right) \right] \approx 9.2936$$

**66.** (a) Along line: $d_1 = \sqrt{a^2 + a^4} = a\sqrt{1 + a^2}$

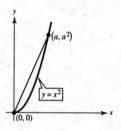

Along parabola: $y = x^2$, $y' = 2x$

$$d_2 = \int_0^a \sqrt{1 + 4x^2} \, dx$$

$$= \frac{1}{4} \left[ 2x\sqrt{4x^2 + 1} + \ln\left| 2x + \sqrt{4x^2 + 1} \right| \right]_0^a \quad \text{(Theorem 7.2)}$$

$$= \frac{1}{4} \left[ 2a\sqrt{4a^2 + 1} + \ln\left( 2a + \sqrt{4a^2 + 1} \right) \right]$$

(b) For $a = 1$, $d_1 = \sqrt{2}$ and $d_2 = \frac{\sqrt{5}}{2} + \frac{1}{4} \ln\left( 2 + \sqrt{5} \right) \approx 1.4789$.

For $a = 10$, $d_1 = 10\sqrt{101} \approx 100.4988$

$$d_2 \approx 101.0473.$$

(c) As $a$ increases, $d_2 - d_1 \to 0$.

**68.** (a)

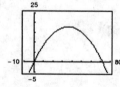

(b) $y = 0$ for $x = 72$

(c) $y = x - \dfrac{x^2}{72}$, $y' = 1 - \dfrac{x}{36}$, $1 + (y')^2 = 1 + \left( 1 - \dfrac{x}{36} \right)^2$

$$s = \int_0^{72} \sqrt{1 + \left( 1 - \frac{x}{36} \right)^2} \, dx = -36 \int_0^{72} \sqrt{1 + \left( 1 - \frac{x}{36} \right)^2} \left( -\frac{1}{36} \right) dx$$

$$= -\frac{36}{2} \left[ \left( 1 - \frac{x}{36} \right) \sqrt{1 + \left( 1 - \frac{x}{36} \right)^2} + \ln\left| \left( 1 - \frac{x}{36} \right) + \sqrt{1 + \left( 1 - \frac{x}{36} \right)^2} \right| \right]_0^{72}$$

$$= -18 \left[ \left( -\sqrt{2} + \ln\left| -1 + \sqrt{2} \right| \right) - \left( \sqrt{2} + \ln\left| 1 + \sqrt{2} \right| \right) \right] = 36\sqrt{2} + 18 \ln\left( \frac{\sqrt{2} + 1}{\sqrt{2} - 1} \right) \approx 82.641$$

**70.** First find where the curves intersect.

$$y^2 = 16 - (x - 4)^2 = \frac{1}{16}x^4$$

$$16^2 - 16(x - 4)^2 = x^4$$

$$16^2 - 16x^2 + 128x - 16^2 = x^4$$

$$x^4 + 16x^2 - 128x = 0$$

$$x(x - 4)(x^2 + 4x + 32) \implies x = 0, 4$$

$$A = \int_0^4 \frac{1}{4}x^2 dx + \frac{1}{4}\pi(4)^2 = \frac{1}{12}x^3\Big]_0^4 + 4\pi = \frac{16}{3} + 4\pi$$

$$M_y = \int_0^4 x\left[\frac{1}{4}x^2\right] dx + \int_4^8 x\sqrt{16 - (x - 4)^2}\, dx$$

$$= \frac{x^4}{16}\Big]_0^4 + \int_4^8 (x - 4)\sqrt{16 - (x - 4)^2}\, dx + \int_4^8 4\sqrt{16 - (x - 4)^2}\, dx$$

$$= 16 + \left[\frac{-1}{3}(16 - (x - 4)^2)^{3/2}\right]_4^8 + 2\left[16\arcsin\frac{x - 4}{4} + (x - 4)\sqrt{16 - (x - 4)^2}\right]_4^8$$

$$= 16 + \frac{1}{3}16^{3/2} + 2\left[16\left(\frac{\pi}{2}\right)\right] = 16 + \frac{64}{3} + 16\pi = \frac{112}{3} + 16\pi$$

$$M_x = \int_0^4 \frac{1}{2}\left(\frac{1}{4}x^2\right)^2 dx + \int_4^8 \frac{1}{2}(16 - (x - 4)^2)\, dx$$

$$= \left[\frac{1}{32}\cdot\frac{x^5}{5}\right]_0^4 + \left[8x - \frac{(x - 4)^3}{6}\right]_4^8$$

$$= \frac{32}{5} + \left(64 - \frac{64}{6}\right) - 32 = \frac{416}{15}$$

$$\bar{x} = \frac{M_y}{A} = \frac{112/3 + 16\pi}{16/3 + 4\pi} = \frac{112 + 48\pi}{16 + 12\pi} = \frac{28 + 12\pi}{4 + 3\pi} \approx 4.89$$

$$\bar{y} = \frac{M_x}{A} = \frac{416/15}{(16/3) + 4\pi} = \frac{104}{5(4 + 3\pi)} \approx 1.55$$

$$(\bar{x}, \bar{y}) \approx (4.89, 1.55)$$

**72.** Let $r = L\tan\theta$, $dr = L\sec^2\theta\, d\theta$, $r^2 + L^2 = L^2\sec^2\theta$.

$$\frac{1}{R}\int_0^R \frac{2mL}{(r^2 + L^2)^{3/2}}\, dr = \frac{2mL}{R}\int_a^b \frac{L\sec^2\theta\, d\theta}{L^3\sec^3\theta}$$

$$= \frac{2m}{RL}\int_a^b \cos\theta\, d\theta$$

$$= \left[\frac{2m}{RL}\sin\theta\right]_a^b$$

$$= \left[\frac{2m}{RL}\frac{r}{\sqrt{r^2 + L^2}}\right]_0^R$$

$$= \frac{2m}{L\sqrt{R^2 + L^2}}$$

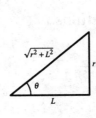

**74.** (a) $F_{\text{inside}} = 48\int_{-1}^{0.8}(0.8-y)(2)\sqrt{1-y^2}\,dy$

$$= 96\left[0.8\int_{-1}^{0.8}\sqrt{1-y^2}\,dy - \int_{-1}^{0.8}y\sqrt{1-y^2}\,dy\right]$$

$$= 96\left[\frac{0.8}{2}\left(\arcsin y + y\sqrt{1-y^2}\right) + \frac{1}{3}(1-y^2)^{3/2}\right]_{-1}^{0.8} \approx 96(1.263) \approx 121.3 \text{ lbs}$$

(b) $F_{\text{outside}} = 64\int_{-1}^{0.4}(0.4-y)(2)\sqrt{1-y^2}\,dy$

$$= 128\left[0.4\int_{-1}^{0.4}\sqrt{1-y^2}\,dy - \int_{-1}^{0.4}y\sqrt{1-y^2}\,dy\right]$$

$$= 128\left[\frac{0.4}{2}\left(\arcsin y + y\sqrt{1-y^2}\right) + \frac{1}{3}(1-y^2)^{3/2}\right]_{-1}^{0.4} \approx 92.98$$

**76.** $S = \sqrt{1520.4 + 111.2t + 15.8t^2}$

(a)

**78.** False

$$\int\frac{\sqrt{x^2-1}}{x}\,dx = \int\frac{\tan\theta}{\sec\theta}(\sec\theta\tan\theta\,d\theta)$$

$$= \int\tan^2\theta\,d\theta$$

(b) $S'(t) = \frac{1}{2}(1520.4 + 111.2t + 15.8t^2)^{-1/2}(111.2 + 31.6t)$

$S'(5) \approx 2.71$

(c) Average value $= \frac{1}{2}\int_{10}^{12}S(t)\,dt \approx 68.24$

**80.** True

$$\int_{-1}^{1}x^2\sqrt{1-x^2}\,dx = 2\int_0^1 x^2\sqrt{1-x^2}\,dx = 2\int_0^{\pi/2}(\sin^2\theta)(\cos\theta)(\cos\theta\,d\theta) = 2\int_0^{\pi/2}\sin^2\theta\cos^2\theta\,d\theta$$

# Section 7.5    Partial Fractions

**2.** $\dfrac{4x^2+3}{(x-5)^3} = \dfrac{A}{x-5} + \dfrac{B}{(x-5)^2} + \dfrac{C}{(x-5)^3}$

**4.** $\dfrac{x-2}{x^2+4x+3} = \dfrac{x-2}{(x+1)(x+3)} = \dfrac{A}{x+1} + \dfrac{B}{x+3}$

**6.** $\dfrac{2x-1}{x(x^2+1)^2} = \dfrac{A}{x} + \dfrac{Bx+C}{x^2+1} + \dfrac{Dx+E}{(x^2+1)^2}$

**8.** $\dfrac{1}{4x^2-9} = \dfrac{1}{(2x-3)(2x+3)} = \dfrac{A}{2x-3} + \dfrac{B}{2x+3}$

$1 = A(2x+3) + B(2x-3)$

When $x = \frac{3}{2}$, $1 = 6A$, $A = \frac{1}{6}$.
When $x = -\frac{3}{2}$, $1 = -6B$, $B = -\frac{1}{6}$.

$$\int\frac{1}{4x^2-9}\,dx = \frac{1}{6}\left[\int\frac{1}{2x-3}\,dx - \int\frac{1}{2x+3}\,dx\right]$$

$$= \frac{1}{12}[\ln|2x-3| - \ln|2x+3|] + C$$

$$= \frac{1}{12}\ln\left|\frac{2x-3}{2x+3}\right| + C$$

**10.** $\displaystyle\int\frac{x+1}{x^2+4x+3}\,dx = \int\frac{(x+1)}{(x+1)(x+3)}\,dx$

$$= \int\frac{1}{x+3}\,dx = \ln|x+3| + C$$

**12.** $\dfrac{5x^2 - 12x - 12}{x(x - 2)(x + 2)} = \dfrac{A}{x} + \dfrac{B}{x - 2} + \dfrac{C}{x + 2}$

$5x^2 - 12x - 12 = A(x^2 - 4) + Bx(x + 2) + Cx(x - 2)$

When $x = 0$, $-12 = -4A \implies A = 3$. When $x = 2$, $-16 = 8B \implies B = -2$. When $x = -2$, $32 = 8C \implies C = 4$.

$\displaystyle\int \dfrac{5x^2 - 12x - 12}{x^3 - 4x}\, dx = \int \dfrac{3}{x}\, dx + \int \dfrac{-2}{x - 2}\, dx + \int \dfrac{4}{x + 2}\, dx = 3\ln|x| - 2\ln|x - 2| + 4\ln|x + 2| + C$

**14.** $\dfrac{x^3 - x + 3}{x^2 + x - 2} = x - 1 + \dfrac{2x + 1}{(x + 2)(x - 1)} = x - 1 + \dfrac{A}{x + 2} + \dfrac{B}{x - 1}$

$2x + 1 = A(x - 1) + B(x + 2)$

When $x = -2$, $-3 = -3A$, $A = 1$. When $x = 1$, $3 = 3B$, $B = 1$.

$\displaystyle\int \dfrac{x^3 - x + 3}{x^2 + x - 2}\, dx = \int \left[ x - 1 + \dfrac{1}{x + 2} + \dfrac{1}{x - 1} \right] dx$

$= \dfrac{x^2}{2} - x + \ln|x + 2| + \ln|x - 1| + C = \dfrac{x^2}{2} - x + \ln|x^2 + x - 2| + C$

**16.** $\dfrac{x + 2}{x(x - 4)} = \dfrac{A}{x - 4} + \dfrac{B}{x}$

$x + 2 = Ax + B(x - 4)$

When $x = 4$, $6 = 4A$, $A = \dfrac{3}{2}$.

When $x = 0$, $2 = -4B$, $B = -\dfrac{1}{2}$.

$\displaystyle\int \dfrac{x + 2}{x^2 - 4x}\, dx = \int \left[ \dfrac{3/2}{x - 4} - \dfrac{1/2}{x} \right] dx$

$= \dfrac{3}{2}\ln|x - 4| - \dfrac{1}{2}\ln|x| + C$

**18.** $\dfrac{2x - 3}{(x - 1)^2} = \dfrac{A}{x - 1} + \dfrac{B}{(x - 1)^2}$

$2x - 3 = A(x - 1) + B$

When $x = 1$, $B = -1$. When $x = 0$, $A = 2$.

$\displaystyle\int \dfrac{2x - 3}{(x - 1)^2}\, dx = \int \left[ \dfrac{2}{x - 1} - \dfrac{1}{(x - 1)^2} \right] dx$

$= 2\ln|x - 1| + \dfrac{1}{x - 1} + C$

**20.** $\dfrac{4x^2}{x^3 + x^2 - x - 1} = \dfrac{4x^2}{x^2(x + 1) - (x + 1)} = \dfrac{4x^2}{(x^2 - 1)(x + 1)} = \dfrac{A}{x - 1} + \dfrac{B}{x + 1} + \dfrac{C}{(x + 1)^2}$

$4x^2 = A(x + 1)^2 + B(x - 1)(x + 1) + C(x - 1)$

When $x = -1$, $4 = -2C \implies C = -2$. When $x = 1$, $4 = 4A \implies A = 1$. When $x = 0$, $0 = 1 - B + 2 \implies B = 3$.

$\displaystyle\int \dfrac{4x^2}{x^3 + x^2 - x - 1}\, dx = \int \dfrac{1}{x - 1}\, dx + \int \dfrac{3}{x + 1}\, dx - \int \dfrac{2}{(x + 1)^2}\, dx$

$= \ln|x - 1| + 3\ln|x + 1| + \dfrac{2}{(x + 1)} + C$

**22.** $\dfrac{6x}{x^3 - 8} = \dfrac{6x}{(x - 2)(x^2 + 2x + 4)} = \dfrac{A}{x - 2} + \dfrac{Bx + C}{x^2 + 2x + 4}$

$6x = A(x^2 + 2x + 4) + (Bx + C)(x - 2)$

When $x = 2$, $12 = 12A \implies A = 1$. When $x = 0$, $0 = 4 - 2C \implies C = 2$. When $x = 1$, $6 = 7 + (B + 2)(-1) \implies B = -1$.

$\displaystyle\int \dfrac{6x}{x^3 - 8}\, dx = \int \dfrac{1}{x - 2}\, dx + \int \dfrac{-x + 2}{x^2 + 2x + 4}\, dx = \int \dfrac{1}{x - 2}\, dx + \int \dfrac{-x - 1}{x^2 + 2x + 4}\, dx + \int \dfrac{3}{(x^2 + 2x + 1) + 3}\, dx$

$= \ln|x - 2| - \dfrac{1}{2}\ln|x^2 + 2x + 4| + \dfrac{3}{\sqrt{3}}\arctan\left( \dfrac{x + 1}{\sqrt{3}} \right) + C$

$= \ln|x - 2| - \dfrac{1}{2}\ln|x^2 + 2x + 4| + \sqrt{3}\arctan\left( \dfrac{\sqrt{3}(x + 1)}{3} \right) + C$

**24.** $\dfrac{x^2 - x + 9}{(x^2 + 9)^2} = \dfrac{Ax + B}{x^2 + 9} + \dfrac{Cx + D}{(x^2 + 9)^2}$

$x^2 - x + 9 = (Ax + B)(x^2 + 9) + Cx + D$

$\qquad\qquad = Ax^3 + Bx^2 + (9A + C)x + (9B + D)$

By equating coefficients of like terms, we have $A = 0$, $B = 1$, $D = 0$, and $C = -1$.

$\displaystyle\int \dfrac{x^2 - x - 9}{(x^2 + 9)^2} = \int \dfrac{1}{x^2 + 9}\, dx - \int \dfrac{x}{(x^2 + 9)^2}\, dx$

$\qquad\qquad\qquad = \dfrac{1}{3} \arctan\left(\dfrac{x}{3}\right) + \dfrac{1}{2(x^2 + 9)} + C$

**26.** $\dfrac{x^2 - 4x + 7}{(x + 1)(x^2 - 2x + 3)} = \dfrac{A}{x + 1} + \dfrac{Bx + C}{x^2 - 2x + 3}$

$\qquad x^2 - 4x + 7 = A(x^2 - 2x + 3) + (Bx + C)(x + 1)$

When $x = -1$, $12 = 6A$. When $x = 0$, $7 = 3A + C$. When $x = 1$, $4 = 2A + 2B + 2C$. Solving these equations we have $A = 2$, $B = -1$, $C = 1$.

$\displaystyle\int \dfrac{x^2 - 4x + 7}{x^3 - x^2 + x + 3}\, dx = 2\int \dfrac{1}{x + 1}\, dx + \int \dfrac{-x + 1}{x^2 - 2x + 3}\, dx$

$\qquad\qquad\qquad\qquad = 2\ln|x + 1| - \dfrac{1}{2}\ln|x^2 - 2x + 3| + C$

**28.** $\dfrac{x^2 + x + 3}{(x^2 + 3)^2} = \dfrac{Ax + B}{x^2 + 3} + \dfrac{Cx + D}{(x^2 + 3)^2}$

$x^2 + x + 3 = (Ax + B)(x^2 + 3) + Cx + D$

$\qquad\qquad = Ax^3 + Bx^2 + (3A + C)x + (3B + D)$

By equating coefficients of like terms, we have $A = 0$, $B = 1$, $3A + C = 1$, $3B + D = 3$. Solving these equations we have $A = 0$, $B = 1$, $C = 1$, $D = 0$.

$\displaystyle\int \dfrac{x^2 + x + 3}{x^4 + 6x^2 + 9}\, dx = \int \left[\dfrac{1}{x^2 + 3} + \dfrac{x}{(x^2 + 3)^2}\right]\, dx$

$\qquad\qquad\qquad\qquad = \dfrac{1}{\sqrt{3}} \arctan \dfrac{x}{\sqrt{3}} - \dfrac{1}{2(x^2 + 3)} + C$

**30.** $\dfrac{x - 1}{x^2(x + 1)} = \dfrac{A}{x} + \dfrac{B}{x^2} + \dfrac{C}{x + 1}$

$\qquad x - 1 = Ax(x + 1) + B(x + 1) + Cx^2$

When $x = 0$, $B = -1$. When $x = -1$, $C = -2$. When $x = 1$, $0 = 2A + 2B + C$. Solving these equations we have $A = 2$, $B = -1$, $C = -2$.

$\displaystyle\int_1^5 \dfrac{x - 1}{x^2(x + 1)}\, dx = 2\int_1^5 \dfrac{1}{x}\, dx - \int_1^5 \dfrac{1}{x^2}\, dx - 2\int_1^5 \dfrac{1}{x + 1}\, dx$

$\qquad\qquad\qquad = \left[2\ln|x| + \dfrac{1}{x} - 2\ln|x + 1|\right]_1^5$

$\qquad\qquad\qquad = \left[2\ln\left|\dfrac{x}{x + 1}\right| + \dfrac{1}{x}\right]_1^5$

$\qquad\qquad\qquad = 2\ln\dfrac{5}{3} - \dfrac{4}{5}$

**32.** $\displaystyle\int_0^1 \frac{x^2 - x}{x^2 + x + 1}\, dx = \int_0^1 dx - \int_0^1 \frac{2x + 1}{x^2 + x + 1}\, dx = \left[x - \ln|x^2 + x + 1|\right]_0^1 = 1 - \ln 3$

**34.** $\displaystyle\int \frac{6x^2 + 1}{x^2(x - 1)^3}\, dx = 3 \ln\left|\frac{x - 1}{x}\right| + \frac{1}{x} + \frac{2}{x - 1} - \frac{7}{2(x - 1)^2} + C$

$(2, 1)$: $\displaystyle 3 \ln\left|\frac{1}{2}\right| + \frac{1}{2} + \frac{2}{1} - \frac{7}{2} + C = 1 \Rightarrow C = 2 - 3 \ln\frac{1}{2}$

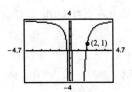

**36.** $\displaystyle\int \frac{x^3}{(x^2 - 4)^2}\, dx = \frac{1}{2} \ln|x^2 - 4| - \frac{2}{x^2 - 4} + C$

$(3, 4)$: $\displaystyle \frac{1}{2} \ln 5 - \frac{2}{5} + C = 4 \Rightarrow C = \frac{22}{5} - \frac{1}{2} \ln 5$

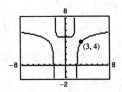

**38.** $\displaystyle\int \frac{x(2x - 9)}{x^3 - 6x^2 + 12x - 8}\, dx = 2 \ln|x - 2| + \frac{1}{x - 2} + \frac{5}{(x - 2)^2} + C$

$(3, 2)$: $0 + 1 + 5 + C = 2 \Rightarrow C = -4$

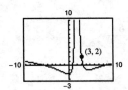

**40.** $\displaystyle\int \frac{x^2 - x + 2}{x^3 - x^2 + x - 1}\, dx = -\arctan x + \ln|x - 1| + C$

$(2, 6)$: $-\arctan 2 + 0 + C = 6 \Rightarrow C = 6 + \arctan 2$

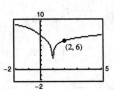

**42.** Let $u = \cos x$, $du = \sin x\, dx$.

$$\frac{1}{u(u + 1)} = \frac{A}{u} + \frac{B}{u + 1}$$

$$1 = A(u + 1) + Bu$$

When $u = 0$, $A = 1$. When $u = -1$, $B = -1$, $u = \cos x$. $du = -\sin dx$.

$$\int \frac{\sin x}{\cos x + \cos^2 x}\, dx = -\int \frac{1}{u(u + 1)}\, du$$

$$= \int \frac{1}{u + 1}\, du - \int \frac{1}{u}\, du$$

$$= \ln|u + 1| - \ln|u| + C$$

$$= \ln\left|\frac{u + 1}{u}\right| + C$$

$$= \ln\left|\frac{\cos x + 1}{\cos x}\right| + C$$

$$= \ln|1 + \sec x| + C$$

**44.** $\displaystyle\frac{1}{u(u + 1)} = \frac{A}{u} + \frac{B}{u + 1}$, $u = \tan x$, $du = \sec^2 x\, dx$

$$1 = A(u + 1) + Bu$$

When $u = 0$, $A = 1$.
When $u = -1$, $1 = -B \Rightarrow B = -1$.

$$\int \frac{\sec^2 x\, dx}{\tan x(\tan x + 1)} = \int \frac{1}{u(u + 1)}\, du$$

$$= \int \left(\frac{1}{u} - \frac{1}{u + 1}\right) du$$

$$= \ln|u| - \ln|u + 1| + C$$

$$= \ln\left|\frac{u}{u + 1}\right| + C$$

$$= \ln\left|\frac{\tan x}{\tan x + 1}\right| + C$$

**46.** Let $u = e^x$, $du = e^x dx$.

$$\frac{1}{(u^2 + 1)(u - 1)} = \frac{A}{u - 1} + \frac{Bu + C}{u^2 + 1}$$

$$1 = A(u^2 + 1) + (Bu + C)(u - 1)$$

When $u = 1$, $A = \frac{1}{2}$.

When $u = 0$, $1 = A - C$.

When $u = -1$, $1 = 2A + 2B - 2C$. Solving these equations we have $A = \frac{1}{2}$, $B = -\frac{1}{2}$, $C = -\frac{1}{2}$, $u = e^x$, $du = e^x dx$.

$$\int \frac{e^x}{(e^{2x} + 1)(e^x - 1)} dx = \int \frac{1}{(u^2 + 1)(u - 1)} du$$

$$= \frac{1}{2}\left(\int \frac{1}{u - 1} du - \int \frac{u + 1}{u^2 + 1} du\right)$$

$$= \frac{1}{2}\left(\ln|u - 1| - \frac{1}{2}\ln|u^2 + 1| - \arctan u\right) + C$$

$$= \frac{1}{4}\left(2\ln|e^x - 1| - \ln|e^{2x} + 1| - 2\arctan e^x\right) + C$$

**48.** $\dfrac{1}{a^2 - x^2} = \dfrac{A}{a - x} + \dfrac{B}{a + x}$

$$1 = A(a + x) + B(a - x)$$

When $x = a$, $A = 1/2a$.

When $x = -a$, $B = 1/2a$.

$$\int \frac{1}{a^2 - x^2} dx = \frac{1}{2a}\int\left(\frac{1}{a - x} + \frac{1}{a + x}\right) dx$$

$$= \frac{1}{2a}(-\ln|a - x| + \ln|a + x|) + C$$

$$= \frac{1}{2a}\ln\left|\frac{a + x}{a - x}\right| + C$$

**50.** $\dfrac{1}{x^2(a + bx)} = \dfrac{A}{x} + \dfrac{B}{x^2} + \dfrac{C}{a + bx}$

$$1 = Ax(a + bx) + B(a + bx) + Cx^2$$

When $x = 0$, $1 = Ba \Rightarrow B = 1/a$.

When $x = -a/b$, $1 = C(a^2/b^2) \Rightarrow C = b^2/a^2$.

When $x = 1$, $1 = (a + b)A + (a + b)B + C \Rightarrow$
$\quad A = -b/a^2$.

$$\int \frac{1}{x^2(a + bx)} dx = \int\left(\frac{-b/a^2}{x} + \frac{1/a}{x^2} + \frac{b^2/a^2}{a + bx}\right) dx$$

$$= -\frac{b}{a^2}\ln|x| - \frac{1}{ax} + \frac{b}{a^2}\ln|a + bx| + C$$

$$= -\frac{1}{ax} + \frac{b}{a^2}\ln\left|\frac{a + bx}{x}\right| + C$$

$$= -\frac{1}{ax} - \frac{b}{a^2}\ln\left|\frac{x}{a + bx}\right| + C$$

**52.** $\dfrac{dy}{dx} = \dfrac{4}{(x^2 - 2x - 3)}$, $y(0) = 5$

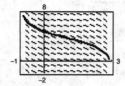

**54.** (a) $\dfrac{N(x)}{D(x)} = \dfrac{A_1}{px + q} + \dfrac{A_2}{(px + q)^2} + \cdots + \dfrac{A_m}{(px + q)^m}$

(b) $\dfrac{N(x)}{D(x)} = \dfrac{A_1 + B_1 x}{(ax^2 + bx + c)} + \cdots + \dfrac{A_n + B_n x}{(ax^2 + bx + c)^n}$

**56.** $A = 2\displaystyle\int_0^3\left(1 - \frac{7}{16 - x^2}\right) dx$

$$= 2\int_0^3 dx - 14\int_0^3 \frac{1}{16 - x^2} dx$$

$$= \left[2x - \frac{14}{8}\ln\left|\frac{4 + x}{4 - x}\right|\right]_0^3 \quad \text{(From Exercise 46)}$$

$$= 6 - \frac{7}{4}\ln 7 \approx 2.595$$

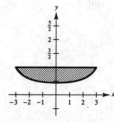

**58. (a)**

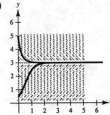

**(b)** The slope is negative because the function is decreasing.

**(c)** For $y > 0$, $\lim\limits_{t \to \infty} y(t) = 3$.

**(d)** $\dfrac{dy}{y(L-y)} = \dfrac{A}{y} + \dfrac{B}{L-y}$

$$1 = A(L-y) + By \Rightarrow A = \frac{1}{L}, B = \frac{1}{L}$$

$$\int \frac{dy}{y(L-y)} = \int k\,dt$$

$$\frac{1}{L}\left[\int \frac{1}{y}dy + \int \frac{1}{L-y}dy\right] = \int k\,dt$$

$$\frac{1}{L}\Big[\ln|y| - \ln|L-y|\Big] = kt + C_1$$

$$\ln\left|\frac{y}{L-y}\right| = k\,Lt + LC_1$$

$$C_2 e^{kLt} = \frac{y}{L-y}$$

When $t = 0$, $\dfrac{y_0}{L - y_0} = C_2 \Rightarrow \dfrac{y}{L-y} = \dfrac{y_0}{L-y_0}e^{kLt}$.

Solving for $y$, you obtain $y = \dfrac{y_0 L}{y_0 + (L - y_0)e^{-kLt}}$.

**(e)** $k = 1, L = 3$

    *(i)* $y(0) = 5$: $\quad y = \dfrac{15}{5 - 2e^{-3t}}$

    *(ii)* $y(0) = \dfrac{1}{2}$: $\quad y = \dfrac{3/2}{(1/2) + (5/2)e^{-3t}} = \dfrac{3}{1 + 5e^{-3t}}$

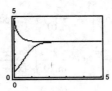

**(f)** $\dfrac{dy}{dt} = ky(L - y)$

$$\frac{d^2y}{dt^2} = k\left[y\left(\frac{-dy}{dt}\right) + (L - y)\frac{dy}{dt}\right] = 0$$

$$\Rightarrow y\frac{dy}{dt} = (L - y)\frac{dy}{dt}$$

$$\Rightarrow \quad y = \frac{L}{2}$$

From the first derivative test, this is a maximum.

**60. (a)** $V = \pi \displaystyle\int_0^3 \left(\frac{2x}{x^2+1}\right)^2 dx = 4\pi \int_0^3 \frac{x^2}{(x^2+1)^2}\,dx$

$$= 4\pi \int_0^3 \left(\frac{1}{x^2+1} - \frac{1}{(x^2+1)^2}\right)dx \qquad \text{(partial fractions)}$$

$$= 4\pi\left[\arctan x - \frac{1}{2}\left(\arctan x + \frac{x}{x^2+1}\right)\right]_0^3 \qquad \text{(trigonometric substitution)}$$

$$= 2\pi\left[\arctan x - \frac{x}{x^2+1}\right]_0^3 = 2\pi\left[\arctan 3 - \frac{3}{10}\right] \approx 5.963$$

**—CONTINUED—**

**60. —CONTINUED—**

(b) $A = \int_0^3 \frac{2x}{x^2 + 1}\, dx = \left[\ln(x^2 + 1)\right]_0^3 = \ln 10$

$\bar{x} = \frac{1}{A}\int_0^3 \frac{2x^2}{x^2 + 1}\, dx = \frac{1}{\ln 10}\int_0^3 \left(2 - \frac{2}{x^2 + 1}\right) dx$

$= \frac{1}{\ln 10}\left[2x - 2\arctan x\right]_0^3 = \frac{2}{\ln 10}[3 - \arctan 3] \approx 1.521$

$\bar{y} = \frac{1}{A}\left(\frac{1}{2}\right)\int_0^3 \left(\frac{2x}{x^2 + 1}\right)^2 dx = \frac{2}{\ln 10}\int_0^3 \frac{x^2}{(x^2 + 1)^2}\, dx$

$= \frac{2}{\ln 10}\int_0^3 \left(\frac{1}{x^2 + 1} - \frac{1}{(x^2 + 1)^2}\right) dx$  (partial fractions)

$= \frac{2}{\ln 10}\left[\arctan x - \frac{1}{2}\left(\arctan x + \frac{x}{x^2 + 1}\right)\right]_0^3$  (trigonometric substitution)

$= \frac{2}{\ln 10}\left[\frac{1}{2}\arctan x - \frac{x}{2(x^2 + 1)}\right]_0^3 = \frac{1}{\ln 10}\left[\arctan x - \frac{x}{x^2 + 1}\right]_0^3 = \frac{1}{\ln 10}\left[\arctan 3 - \frac{3}{10}\right] \approx 0.412$

$(\bar{x}, \bar{y}) \approx (1.521, 0.412)$

**62.** (a) $\dfrac{1}{(y_0 - x)(z_0 - x)} = \dfrac{A}{y_0 - x} + \dfrac{B}{z_0 - x}, A = \dfrac{1}{z_0 - y_0}, B = -\dfrac{1}{z_0 - y_0}$  (Assume $y_0 \neq z_0$)

$\dfrac{1}{z_0 - y_0}\int\left(\dfrac{1}{y_0 - x} - \dfrac{1}{z_0 - x}\right) dx = kt + C$

$\dfrac{1}{z_0 - y_0}\ln\left|\dfrac{z_0 - x}{y_0 - x}\right| = kt + C$, when $t = 0, x = 0$

$C = \dfrac{1}{z_0 - y_0}\ln\dfrac{z_0}{y_0}$

$\dfrac{1}{z_0 - y_0}\left[\ln\left|\dfrac{z_0 - x}{y_0 - x}\right| - \ln\left(\dfrac{z_0}{y_0}\right)\right] = kt$

$\ln\left[\dfrac{y_0(z_0 - x)}{z_0(y_0 - x)}\right] = (z_0 - y_0)kt$

$\dfrac{y_0(z_0 - x)}{z_0(y_0 - x)} = e^{(z_0 - y_0)kt}$

$x = \dfrac{y_0 z_0[e^{(z_0 - y_0)kt} - 1]}{z_0 e^{(z_0 - y_0)kt} - y_0}$

(b) (1) If $y_0 < z_0$, $\displaystyle\lim_{t \to \infty} x = y_0$.

(2) If $y_0 > z_0$, $\displaystyle\lim_{t \to \infty} x = z_0$.

(c) If $y_0 = z_0$, then the original equation is

$\int \dfrac{1}{(y_0 - x)^2}\, dx = \int k\, dt$

$(y_0 - x)^{-1} = kt + C_1$

$x = 0$ when $t = 0 \Rightarrow \dfrac{1}{y_0} = C_1$

$\dfrac{1}{y_0 - x} = kt + \dfrac{1}{y_0} = \dfrac{kt\, y_0 + 1}{y_0}$

$y_0 - x = \dfrac{y_0}{kt\, y_0 + 1}$

$x = y_0 - \dfrac{y_0}{kt\, y_0 + 1}$

As $t \to \infty$, $x \to y_0 = x_0$.

# Section 7.6    Integration by Tables and Other Integration Techniques

**2.** By Formula 13: $(b = 2, a = -5)$

$$\frac{2}{3}\int \frac{1}{x^2(2x-5)^2}\,dx = \frac{2}{3}\left(\frac{-1}{25}\right)\left[\frac{-5+4x}{x(-5+2x)} + \frac{4}{-5}\ln\left|\frac{x}{2x-5}\right|\right] + C$$

$$= \frac{8}{375}\ln\left|\frac{x}{2x-5}\right| - \frac{2}{75}\frac{(4x-5)}{x(2x-5)} + C$$

**4.** By Formula 29: $(a = 3)$

$$\frac{1}{3}\int \frac{\sqrt{x^2-9}}{x}\,dx = \frac{1}{3}\sqrt{x^2-9} - \text{arcsec}\frac{|x|}{3} + C$$

**6.** By Formula 41: $\displaystyle\int \frac{x}{\sqrt{9-x^4}}\,dx = \frac{1}{2}\int \frac{2x}{\sqrt{3^2-(x^2)^2}}\,dx$

$$= \frac{1}{2}\arcsin\frac{x^2}{3} + C$$

**8.** By Formulas 51 and 47: $\displaystyle\int \frac{\cos^3\sqrt{x}}{\sqrt{x}}\,dx = 2\int \cos^3\sqrt{x}\left(\frac{1}{2\sqrt{x}}\right)dx$

$$= 2\left[\frac{\cos^2\sqrt{x}\sin\sqrt{x}}{3} + \frac{2}{3}\int \cos\sqrt{x}\left(\frac{1}{2\sqrt{x}}\right)dx\right] = \frac{2}{3}\sin\sqrt{x}(\cos^2\sqrt{x} + 2) + C$$

$$u = \sqrt{x},\, du = \frac{1}{2\sqrt{x}}\,dx$$

**10.** By Formula 71:

$$\int \frac{1}{1-\tan 5x}\,dx = \frac{1}{5}\int \frac{1}{1-\tan 5x}(5)\,dx$$

$$= \frac{1}{5}\left(\frac{1}{2}\right)(u - \ln|\cos u - \sin u|) + C$$

$$= \frac{1}{10}(5x - \ln|\cos 5x - \sin 5x|) + C$$

$u = 5x,\, du = 5\,dx$

**12.** By Formula 85: $\left(a = -\frac{1}{2}, b = 2\right)$

$$\int e^{-x/2}\sin 2x\,dx = \frac{e^{-x/2}}{(1/4)+4}\left(-\frac{1}{2}\sin 2x - 2\cos 2x\right) + C$$

$$= \frac{4}{17}e^{-x/2}\left(-\frac{1}{2}\sin 2x - 2\cos 2x\right) + C$$

**14.** By Formulas 90 and 91: $\displaystyle\int (\ln x)^3\,dx = x(\ln x)^3 - 3\int (\ln x)^2\,dx$

$$= x(\ln x)^3 - 3x[2 - 2\ln x + (\ln x)^2] + C$$

$$= x[(\ln x)^3 - 3(\ln x)^2 + 6\ln x - 6] + C$$

**16.** (a) By Formula 89: $\displaystyle\int x^4 \ln x\,dx = \frac{x^5}{5^2}[-1 + (4+1)\ln x] + C = \frac{-x^5}{25} + \frac{1}{5}x^5\ln x + C$

(b) Integration by parts: $u = \ln x,\, du = \frac{1}{x}\,dx,\, dv = x^4\,dx,\, v = \frac{x^5}{5}$

$$\int x^4 \ln x\,dx = \frac{x^5}{5}\ln x - \int \frac{x^5}{5}\frac{1}{x}\,dx = \frac{x^5}{5}\ln x - \frac{x^5}{25} + C$$

**18.** (a) By Formula 24: $a = \sqrt{75}$, $x = u$, and

$$\int \frac{1}{x^2 - 75}\, dx = \frac{1}{2\sqrt{75}} \ln\left|\frac{x - \sqrt{75}}{x + \sqrt{75}}\right| + C$$

$$= \frac{\sqrt{3}}{30} \ln\left|\frac{x - \sqrt{75}}{x + \sqrt{75}}\right| + C$$

(b) Partial fractions:

$$\frac{1}{x^2 - 75} = \frac{A}{x - \sqrt{75}} + \frac{B}{x + \sqrt{75}}$$

$$1 = A(x + \sqrt{75}) + B(x - \sqrt{75})$$

$$x = \sqrt{75}:\ 1 = 2A\sqrt{75} \Rightarrow A = \frac{1}{2\sqrt{75}} = \frac{1}{10\sqrt{3}} = \frac{\sqrt{3}}{30}$$

$$x = -\sqrt{75}:\ 1 = -2B\sqrt{75} \Rightarrow B = -\frac{\sqrt{3}}{30}$$

$$\int \frac{1}{x^2 - 75}\, dx = \int \left[\frac{\sqrt{3}/30}{x - \sqrt{75}} - \frac{\sqrt{3}/30}{x + \sqrt{75}}\right] dx$$

$$= \frac{\sqrt{3}}{30} \ln\left|\frac{x - \sqrt{75}}{x + \sqrt{75}}\right| + C$$

**20.** By Formula 21: $\displaystyle\int \frac{x}{\sqrt{1 + x}}\, dx = -\frac{2}{3}(2 - x)\sqrt{1 + x} + C$

**22.** By Formula 79: $\displaystyle\int \operatorname{arcsec} 2x\, dx = \frac{1}{2}\left[2x \operatorname{arcsec} 2x - \ln\left|2x + \sqrt{4x^2 - 1}\right|\right] + C$

$u = 2x,\ du = 2\, dx$

**24.** By Formula 52: $\displaystyle\int x \sin x\, dx = \sin x - x \cos x + C$

**26.** By Formula 7: $\displaystyle\int \frac{x^2}{(3x - 5)^2}\, dx = \frac{1}{27}\left(3x - \frac{25}{3x - 5} + 10 \ln|3x - 5|\right) + C$

**28.** By Formula 14: $\displaystyle\int \frac{1}{x^2 + 2x + 2}\, dx = \frac{2}{\sqrt{4}} \arctan\left(\frac{2x + 2}{2}\right) + C = \arctan(x + 1) + C$

**30.** By Formula 56:

$$\int \frac{\theta^2}{1 - \sin \theta^3}\, d\theta = \frac{1}{3}\int \frac{1}{1 - \sin \theta^3} 3\theta^2\, d\theta$$

$$= \frac{1}{3}(\tan \theta^3 + \sec \theta^3) + C$$

**32.** By Formula 71:

$$\int \frac{e^x}{1 - \tan e^x}\, dx = \frac{1}{2}\left(e^x - \ln|\cos e^x - \sin e^x|\right) + C$$

$u = e^x,\ du = e^x\, dx$

**34.** By Formula 23: $\displaystyle\int \frac{1}{t[1 + (\ln t)^2]}\, dt = \int \frac{1}{1 + (\ln t)^2}\left(\frac{1}{t}\right) dt = \arctan(\ln t) + C$

$u = \ln t,\ du = \dfrac{1}{t}\, dt$

**36.** By Formula 26: $\displaystyle\int \sqrt{3 + x^2}\, dx = \frac{1}{2}\left(x\sqrt{x^2 + 3} + 3 \ln\left|x + \sqrt{x^2 + 3}\right|\right) + C$

**38.** By Formula 27: $\displaystyle\int x^2 \sqrt{2 + (3x)^2}\, dx = \frac{1}{27}\int (3x)^2 \sqrt{(\sqrt{2})^2 + (3x)^2}\, 3\, dx$

$$= \frac{1}{8(27)}\left[3x(18x^2 + 2)\sqrt{2 + 9x^2} - 4 \ln\left|3x + \sqrt{2 + 9x^2}\right|\right] + C$$

**40.** By Formula 77: $\displaystyle\int \sqrt{x}\,\arctan(x^{3/2})\,dx = \frac{2}{3}\int \arctan(x^{3/2})\left(\frac{3}{2}\sqrt{x}\right)dx$

$$= \frac{2}{3}\left[x^{3/2}\arctan(x^{3/2}) - \ln\sqrt{1+x^3}\right] + C$$

**42.** By Formula 45: $\displaystyle\int \frac{e^x}{(1 - e^{2x})^{3/2}}\,dx = \frac{e^x}{\sqrt{1 - e^{2x}}} + C$

$u = e^x,\, du = e^x\,dx$

**44.** By Formula 27:

$$\int (2x-3)^2\sqrt{(2x-3)^2 + 4}\,dx = \frac{1}{2}\int (2x-3)^2\sqrt{(2x-3)^2 + 4}\,(2)\,dx$$

$$= \frac{1}{8}(2x-3)[(2x-3)^2 + 2]\sqrt{(2x-3)^2 + 4} - \ln|2x - 3 + \sqrt{(2x-3)^2 + 4}| + C$$

$u = 2x - 3,\, du = 2\,dx$

**46.** By Formula 31: $\displaystyle\int \frac{\cos x}{\sqrt{\sin^2 x + 1}}\,dx = \ln|\sin x + \sqrt{\sin^2 x + 1}| + C$

$u = \sin x,\, du = \cos x\,dx$

**48.** $\displaystyle\int \sqrt{\frac{3-x}{3+x}}\,dx = \int \frac{3-x}{\sqrt{9 - x^2}}\,dx$

$$= 3\int \frac{1}{\sqrt{9 - x^2}}\,dx + \int \frac{-x}{\sqrt{9 - x^2}}\,dx$$

$$= 3\arcsin\frac{x}{3} + \sqrt{9 - x^2} + C$$

**50.** By Formula 67:

$$\int \tan^3\theta\,d\theta = \frac{\tan^2\theta}{2} - \int \tan\theta\,d\theta$$

$$= \frac{\tan^2\theta}{2} + \ln|\cos x| + C$$

**52.** Integration by parts: $w = u^n,\, dw = nu^{n-1}\,du,\, dv = \dfrac{du}{\sqrt{a + bu}},\, v = \dfrac{2}{b}\sqrt{a + bu}$

$$\int \frac{u^n}{\sqrt{a + bu}}\,du = \frac{2u^n}{b}\sqrt{a + bu} - \frac{2n}{b}\int u^{n-1}\sqrt{a + bu}\,du$$

$$= \frac{2u^n}{b}\sqrt{a + bu} - \frac{2n}{b}\int u^{n-1}\sqrt{a + bu} \cdot \frac{\sqrt{a + bu}}{\sqrt{a + bu}}\,du$$

$$= \frac{2u^n}{b}\sqrt{a + bu} - \frac{2n}{b}\int \frac{au^{n-1} + bu^n}{\sqrt{a + bu}}\,du$$

$$= \frac{2u^n}{b}\sqrt{a + bu} - \frac{2na}{b}\int \frac{u^{n-1}}{\sqrt{a + bu}}\,du - 2n\int \frac{u^n}{\sqrt{a + bu}}\,du$$

Therefore, $(2n + 1)\displaystyle\int \frac{u^n}{\sqrt{a + bu}}\,du = \frac{2}{b}\left[u^n\sqrt{a + bu} - na\int \frac{u^{n-1}}{\sqrt{a + bu}}\,du\right]$ and

$$\int \frac{u^n}{\sqrt{a + bu}} = \frac{2}{(2n + 1)b}\left[u^n\sqrt{a + bu} - na\int \frac{u^{n-1}}{\sqrt{a + bu}}\,du\right].$$

**54.** $\displaystyle\int u^n(\cos u)\,du = u^n\sin u - n\int u^{n-1}(\sin u)\,du$

$w = u^n,\, dv = \cos u\,du,\, dw = nu^{n-1}\,du,\, v = \sin u$

**56.** $\displaystyle\int (\ln u)^n \, du = u(\ln u)^n - \int n(\ln u)^{n-1}\left(\frac{1}{u}\right) u \, du = u(\ln u)^n - n\int (\ln u)^{n-1} \, du$

$w = (\ln u)^n, \, dv = du, \, dw = n(\ln u)^{n-1}\left(\dfrac{1}{u}\right) du, \, v = u$

**58.** $\displaystyle\int x\sqrt{x^2 + 2x} \, dx = \frac{1}{6}\left[2(x^2 + 2x)^{3/2} - 3(x + 1)\sqrt{x^2 + 2x} + 3\ln\left|x + 1 + \sqrt{x^2 + 2x}\right|\right] + C$

$(0, 0): \; \dfrac{1}{6}[3\ln|1|] + C = 0 \Rightarrow C = 0$

**60.** $\displaystyle\int \frac{\sqrt{2 - 2x - x^2}}{x + 1} \, dx = \sqrt{2 - 2x - x^2} - \sqrt{3}\ln\left|\frac{\sqrt{3} + \sqrt{2 - 2x - x^2}}{x + 1}\right| + C$

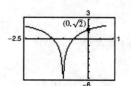

$(0, \sqrt{2}): \; \sqrt{2} - \sqrt{3}\ln\left(\sqrt{3} + \sqrt{2}\right) + C = \sqrt{2} \Rightarrow C = \sqrt{3}\ln\left(\sqrt{3} + \sqrt{2}\right)$

**62.** $\displaystyle\int \frac{\sin\theta}{(\cos\theta)(1 + \sin\theta)} \, d\theta = \frac{1}{2}\left[\frac{-\sin\theta}{1 + \sin\theta} + \ln\left|\frac{1 + \sin\theta}{\cos\theta}\right|\right] + C$

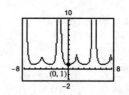

$(0, 1): \; C = 1 \Rightarrow y = \dfrac{1}{2}\left[\dfrac{-\sin\theta}{1 + \sin\theta} + \ln\left|\dfrac{1 + \sin\theta}{\cos\theta}\right|\right] + 1$

**64.** $\displaystyle\int \frac{\sin\theta}{1 + \cos^2\theta} \, d\theta = -\int \frac{-\sin\theta}{1 + (\cos\theta)^2} \, d\theta$

$\qquad\qquad\qquad\qquad = -\arctan(\cos\theta) + C$

**66.** $\displaystyle\int_0^{\pi/2} \frac{1}{3 - 2\cos\theta} \, d\theta = \int_0^1 \left[\frac{\dfrac{2u}{1 + u^2}}{3 - \dfrac{2(1 - u^2)}{1 + u^2}}\right]$

$\qquad\qquad\qquad\qquad = 2\int_0^1 \frac{1}{5u^2 + 1} \, du$

$\qquad\qquad\qquad\qquad = \left[\frac{2}{\sqrt{5}}\arctan\left(\sqrt{5}\,u\right)\right]_0^1$

$\qquad\qquad\qquad\qquad = \frac{2}{\sqrt{5}}\arctan\sqrt{5}$

$u = \tan\dfrac{\theta}{2}$

**68.** $\displaystyle\int \frac{\cos\theta}{1 + \cos\theta} \, d\theta = \int \frac{\cos\theta(1 - \cos\theta)}{(1 + \cos\theta)(1 - \cos\theta)} \, d\theta$

$\qquad\qquad = \int \frac{\cos\theta - \cos^2\theta}{\sin^2\theta} \, d\theta$

$\qquad\qquad = \int (\csc\theta\cot\theta - \cot^2\theta) \, d\theta$

$\qquad\qquad = \int (\csc\theta\cot\theta - (\csc^2\theta - 1)) \, d\theta$

$\qquad\qquad = -\csc\theta + \cot\theta + \theta + C$

**70.** $\displaystyle\int \frac{1}{\sec\theta - \tan\theta} \, d\theta = \int \frac{1}{(1/\cos\theta) - (\sin\theta/\cos\theta)} \, d\theta$

$\qquad\qquad = -\int \frac{-\cos\theta}{1 - \sin\theta} \, d\theta$

$\qquad\qquad = -\ln|1 - \sin\theta| + C$

$u = 1 - \sin\theta, \, du = -\cos\theta \, d\theta$

**72.** $A = \displaystyle\int_0^2 \dfrac{x}{1 + e^{x^2}}\, dx$

$= \dfrac{1}{2}\displaystyle\int_0^2 \dfrac{2x\, dx}{1 + e^{x^2}}$

$= \dfrac{1}{2}\left[ x^2 - \ln(1 + e^{x^2}) \right]_0^2$

$= \dfrac{1}{2}\left[ 4 - \ln(1 + e^4) \right] + \dfrac{1}{2}\ln 2$

$\approx 0.337$ square units

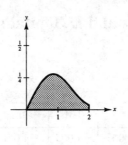

**74.** Log Rule: $\displaystyle\int \dfrac{1}{u}\, du,\ u = e^x + 1$

**76.** Integration by parts

**78.** Formula 16 with $u = e^{2x}$

**80.** A reduction formula reduces an integral to the sum of a function and a simpler integral. For example, see Formula 50, 54.

**82.** $W = \displaystyle\int_0^5 \dfrac{500x}{\sqrt{26 - x^2}}\, dx$

$= -250\displaystyle\int_0^5 (26 - x^2)^{-1/2}(-2x)\, dx$

$= \left[ -500\sqrt{26 - x^2} \right]_0^5$

$= 500\left( \sqrt{26} - 1 \right)$

$\approx 2049.51$ ft · lbs

**84.** $\dfrac{1}{2 - 0}\displaystyle\int_0^2 \dfrac{5000}{1 + e^{4.8 - 1.9t}}\, dt = \dfrac{2500}{-1.9}\displaystyle\int_0^2 \dfrac{-1.9\, dt}{1 + e^{4.8 - 1.9t}}$

$= -\dfrac{2500}{1.9}\left[ (4.8 - 1.9t) - \ln(1 + e^{4.8 - 1.9t}) \right]_0^2$

$= -\dfrac{2500}{1.9}\left[ (1 - \ln(1 + e)) - (4.8 - \ln(1 + e^{4.8})) \right]$

$= \dfrac{2500}{1.9}\left[ 3.8 + \ln\!\left( \dfrac{1 + e}{1 + e^{4.8}} \right) \right] \approx 401.4$

**86.** (a) $\displaystyle\int_0^k 6x^2 e^{-x/2}\, dx = 50$

By trial and error, $k = 5.51897$.

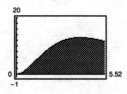

(b) $\displaystyle\int_0^{5.51897} 6x^2 e^{-x/2}\, dx$

**88.** True

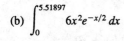

# Section 7.7 Indeterminate Forms and L'Hôpital's Rule

**2.** $\lim\limits_{x \to 0} \dfrac{1 - e^x}{x} \approx -1$

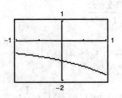

| $x$ | $-0.1$ | $-0.01$ | $-0.001$ | $0.001$ | $0.01$ | $0.1$ |
|---|---|---|---|---|---|---|
| $f(x)$ | $-0.9516$ | $-0.9950$ | $-0.9995$ | $-1.00005$ | $-1.005$ | $-1.0517$ |

**4.** $\lim\limits_{x \to \infty} \dfrac{6x}{\sqrt{3x^2 - 2x}} \approx 3.4641 \left(\text{exact: } \dfrac{6}{\sqrt{3}}\right)$

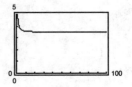

| $x$ | $1$ | $10$ | $10^2$ | $10^3$ | $10^4$ | $10^5$ |
|---|---|---|---|---|---|---|
| $f(x)$ | $6$ | $3.5857$ | $3.4757$ | $3.4653$ | $3.4642$ | $3.4641$ |

**6.** (a) $\lim\limits_{x \to -1} \dfrac{2x^2 - x - 3}{x + 1} = \lim\limits_{x \to -1} \dfrac{(2x - 3)(x + 1)}{x + 1} = \lim\limits_{x \to -1} (2x - 3) = -5$

(b) $\lim\limits_{x \to -1} \dfrac{2x^2 - x - 3}{x + 1} = \lim\limits_{x \to -1} \dfrac{(d/dx)[2x^2 - x - 3]}{(d/dx)[x + 1]} = \lim\limits_{x \to -1} \dfrac{4x - 1}{1} = -5$

**8.** (a) $\lim\limits_{x \to 0} \dfrac{\sin 4x}{2x} = \lim\limits_{x \to 0} 2\left(\dfrac{\sin 4x}{4x}\right) = 2(1) = 2$ $\qquad$ (b) $\lim\limits_{x \to 0} \dfrac{\sin 4x}{2x} = \lim\limits_{x \to 0} \dfrac{(d/dx)[\sin 4x]}{(d/dx)[2x]} = \lim\limits_{x \to 0} \dfrac{4 \cos 4x}{2} = 2$

**10.** (a) $\lim\limits_{x \to \infty} \dfrac{2x + 1}{4x^2 + x} = \lim\limits_{x \to \infty} \dfrac{(2/x) + (1/x^2)}{4 + (1/x)} = \dfrac{0}{4} = 0$

(b) $\lim\limits_{x \to \infty} \dfrac{2x + 1}{4x^2 + x} = \lim\limits_{x \to \infty} \dfrac{(d/dx)[2x + 1]}{(d/dx)[4x^2 + x]} = \lim\limits_{x \to \infty} \dfrac{2}{8x + 1} = 0$

**12.** $\lim\limits_{x \to -1} \dfrac{x^2 - x - 2}{x + 1} = \lim\limits_{x \to -1} \dfrac{2x - 1}{1} = -3$ $\qquad\qquad$ **14.** $\lim\limits_{x \to 2^-} \dfrac{\sqrt{4 - x^2}}{x - 2} = \lim\limits_{x \to 2^-} \dfrac{-x/\sqrt{4 - x^2}}{1}$

$$= \lim\limits_{x \to 2^-} \dfrac{-x}{\sqrt{4 - x^2}} = -\infty$$

**16.** $\lim\limits_{x \to 0^+} \dfrac{e^x - (1 + x)}{x^3} = \lim\limits_{x \to 0^+} \dfrac{e^x - 1}{3x^2}$ $\qquad\qquad$ **18.** $\lim\limits_{x \to 1} \dfrac{\ln x^2}{x^2 - 1} = \lim\limits_{x \to 1} \dfrac{2 \ln x}{x^2 - 1}$

$$= \lim\limits_{x \to 0^+} \dfrac{e^x}{6x} = \infty \qquad\qquad\qquad\qquad = \lim\limits_{x \to 1} \dfrac{2/x}{2x}$$

$$= \lim\limits_{x \to 1} \dfrac{1}{x^2} = 1$$

**20.** $\lim\limits_{x \to 0} \dfrac{\sin ax}{\sin bx} = \lim\limits_{x \to 0} \dfrac{a \cos ax}{b \cos bx} = \dfrac{a}{b}$ $\qquad\qquad$ **22.** $\lim\limits_{x \to 1} \dfrac{\arctan x - (\pi/4)}{x - 1} = \lim\limits_{x \to 1} \dfrac{1/(1 + x^2)}{1} = \dfrac{1}{2}$

**24.** $\lim\limits_{x \to \infty} \dfrac{x - 1}{x^2 + 2x + 3} = \lim\limits_{x \to \infty} \dfrac{1}{2x + 2} = 0$ $\qquad\qquad$ **26.** $\lim\limits_{x \to \infty} \dfrac{x^3}{x + 1} = \lim\limits_{x \to \infty} \dfrac{3x^2}{1} = \infty$

**28.** $\lim\limits_{x \to \infty} \dfrac{x^2}{e^x} = \lim\limits_{x \to \infty} \dfrac{2x}{e^x} = \lim\limits_{x \to \infty} \dfrac{2}{e^x} = 0$

**30.** $\lim\limits_{x\to\infty} \dfrac{x^2}{\sqrt{x^2+1}} = \lim\limits_{x\to\infty} \dfrac{x}{\sqrt{1+(1/x)^2}} = \infty$

**32.** $\lim\limits_{x\to\infty} \dfrac{\sin x}{x-\pi} = 0$

**Note:** Use the Squeeze Theorem for $x > \pi$.

$$-\frac{1}{x-\pi} \le \frac{\sin x}{x-\pi} \le \frac{1}{x-\pi}$$

**34.** $\lim\limits_{x\to\infty} \dfrac{\ln x^4}{x^3} = \lim\limits_{x\to\infty} \dfrac{4\ln x}{x^3} = \lim\limits_{x\to\infty} \dfrac{4/x}{3x^2}$

$\qquad = \lim\limits_{x\to\infty} \dfrac{4}{3x^3} = 0$

**36.** $\lim\limits_{x\to\infty} \dfrac{e^{x/2}}{x} = \lim\limits_{x\to\infty} \dfrac{(1/2)e^{x/2}}{1} = \infty$

**38.** (a) $\lim\limits_{x\to 0^+} x^3 \cot x = (0)(\infty)$

(b) $\lim\limits_{x\to 0^+} x^3 \cot x = \lim\limits_{x\to 0^+} \dfrac{x^3}{\tan x} = \lim\limits_{x\to 0^+} \dfrac{3x^2}{\sec^2 x} = 0$

(c)

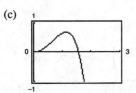

**40.** (a) $\lim\limits_{x\to\infty} \left(x\tan\dfrac{1}{x}\right) = (\infty)(0)$

(b) $\lim\limits_{x\to\infty} x\tan\dfrac{1}{x} = \lim\limits_{x\to\infty} \dfrac{\tan(1/x)}{1/x}$

$\qquad = \lim\limits_{x\to\infty} \dfrac{-(1/x^2)\sec^2(1/x)}{-(1/x^2)}$

$\qquad = \lim\limits_{x\to\infty} \sec^2\left(\dfrac{1}{x}\right) = 1$

(c)

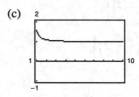

**42.** (a) $\lim\limits_{x\to 0^+} (e^x + x)^{2/x} = 1^\infty$

(b) Let $y = \lim\limits_{x\to 0^+} (e^x + x)^{2/x}$.

$\ln y = \lim\limits_{x\to 0^+} \dfrac{2\ln(e^x + x)}{x}$

$\qquad = \lim\limits_{x\to 0^+} \dfrac{2(e^x + 1)/(e^x + x)}{1} = 4$

Thus, $\ln y = 4 \implies y = e^4 \approx 54.598$.

(c)

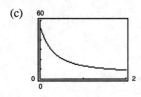

**44.** (a) $\lim\limits_{x\to\infty} \left(1 + \dfrac{1}{x}\right)^x = 1^\infty$

(b) Let $y = \lim\limits_{x\to\infty} \left(1 + \dfrac{1}{x}\right)^x$.

$\ln y = \lim\limits_{x\to\infty} \left[x\ln\left(1 + \dfrac{1}{x}\right)\right] = \lim\limits_{x\to\infty} \dfrac{\ln[1 + (1/x)]}{1/x}$

$\qquad = \lim\limits_{x\to\infty} \dfrac{\left[\dfrac{(-1/x^2)}{1 + (1/x)}\right]}{(-1/x^2)} = \lim\limits_{x\to\infty} \dfrac{1}{1 + (1/x)} = 1$

Thus, $\ln y = 1 \implies y = e^1 = e$. Therefore,

$$\lim\limits_{x\to\infty} \left(1 + \dfrac{1}{x}\right)^x = e.$$

(c)

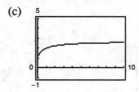

**46.** (a) $\lim\limits_{x \to \infty} (1 + x)^{1/x} = \infty^0$

(b) Let $y = \lim\limits_{x \to \infty} (1 + x)^{1/x}$.

$$\ln y = \lim_{x \to \infty} \frac{\ln(1 + x)}{x}$$

$$= \lim_{x \to \infty} \left( \frac{1/(1 + x)}{1} \right) = 0$$

Thus, $\ln y = 0 \Rightarrow y = e^0 = 1$.

Therefore, $\lim\limits_{x \to \infty} (1 + x)^{1/x} = 1$.

(c)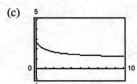

**48.** (a) $\lim\limits_{x \to 4^+} [3(x - 4)]^{x-4} = 0^0$

(b) Let $y = \lim\limits_{x \to 4^+} [3(x - 4)]^{x-4}$.

$$\ln y = \lim_{x \to 4^+} (x - 4)\ln[3(x - 4)]$$

$$= \lim_{x \to 4^+} \frac{\ln[3(x - 4)]}{1/(x - 4)}$$

$$= \lim_{x \to 4^+} \frac{1/(x - 4)}{-1/(x - 4)^2}$$

$$= \lim_{x \to 4^+} [-(x - 4)] = 0$$

Hence, $\lim\limits_{x \to 4^+} [3(x - 4)]^{x-4} = 1$.

(c)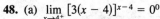

**50.** (a) $\lim\limits_{x \to 0^+} \left[ \cos\left(\frac{\pi}{2} - x\right) \right]^x = 0^0$

(b) Let $y = \lim\limits_{x \to 0^+} \left[ \cos\left(\frac{\pi}{2} - x\right) \right]^x$.

$$\ln y = \lim_{x \to 0^+} x \ln\left[ \cos\left(\frac{\pi}{2} - x\right) \right]$$

$$= 0 \cdot 0 = 0$$

Hence, $\lim\limits_{x \to 0^+} \left[ \cos\left(\frac{\pi}{2} - x\right) \right]^x = 1$.

(c)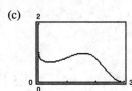

**52.** (a) $\lim\limits_{x \to 2^+} \left( \frac{1}{x^2 - 4} - \frac{\sqrt{x - 1}}{x^2 - 4} \right) = \infty - \infty$

(b) $\lim\limits_{x \to 2^+} \left( \frac{1}{x^2 - 4} - \frac{\sqrt{x - 1}}{x^2 - 4} \right) = \lim\limits_{x \to 2^+} \frac{1 - \sqrt{x - 1}}{x^2 - 4}$

$$= \lim_{x \to 2^+} \frac{-1/(2\sqrt{x - 1})}{2x}$$

$$= \lim_{x \to 2^+} \frac{-1}{4x\sqrt{x - 1}} = \frac{-1}{8}$$

(c)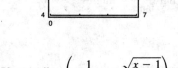

**54.** (a) $\lim\limits_{x \to 0^+} \left( \frac{10}{x} - \frac{3}{x^2} \right) = \infty - \infty$

(b) $\lim\limits_{x \to 0^+} \left( \frac{10}{x} - \frac{3}{x^2} \right) = \lim\limits_{x \to 0^+} \left( \frac{10x - 3}{x^2} \right) = -\infty$

(c)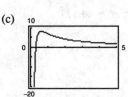

**56.** (a)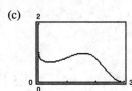

(b) Let $y = (\sin x)^x$, then $\ln y = x \ln(\sin x)$.

$$\lim_{x \to 0^+} \frac{\ln(\sin x)}{1/x} = \lim_{x \to 0^+} \frac{\cos x/\sin x}{-1/x^2} = \lim_{x \to 0^+} \frac{-x^2}{\tan x} = \lim_{x \to 0^+} \frac{-2x}{\sec^2 x} = 0$$

Therefore, since $\ln y = 0$, $y = 1$ and $\lim\limits_{x \to 0^+} (\sin x)^x = 1$.

**58. (a)**

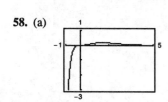

**(b)** $\lim\limits_{x\to\infty}\dfrac{x^3}{e^{2x}} = \lim\limits_{x\to\infty}\dfrac{3x^2}{2e^{2x}} = \lim\limits_{x\to\infty}\dfrac{6x}{4e^{2x}} = \lim\limits_{x\to\infty}\dfrac{6}{8e^{2x}} = 0$

**60.** See Theorem 7.4.

**62.** Let $f(x) = x + 25$ and $g(x) = x$.

**64.** $\lim\limits_{x\to\infty}\dfrac{x^3}{e^{2x}} = \lim\limits_{x\to\infty}\dfrac{3x^2}{2e^{2x}} = \lim\limits_{x\to\infty}\dfrac{6x}{4e^{2x}} = \lim\limits_{x\to\infty}\dfrac{6}{8e^{2x}} = 0$

**66.** $\lim\limits_{x\to\infty}\dfrac{(\ln x)^2}{x^3} = \lim\limits_{x\to\infty}\dfrac{(2\ln x)/x}{3x^2}$

$= \lim\limits_{x\to\infty}\dfrac{2\ln x}{3x^3}$

$= \lim\limits_{x\to\infty}\dfrac{2/x}{9x^2} = \lim\limits_{x\to\infty}\dfrac{2}{9x^3} = 0$

**68.** $\lim\limits_{x\to\infty}\dfrac{x^m}{e^{nx}} = \lim\limits_{x\to\infty}\dfrac{mx^{m-1}}{ne^{nx}}$

$= \lim\limits_{x\to\infty}\dfrac{m(m-1)x^{m-2}}{n^2 e^{nx}}$

$= \cdots = \lim\limits_{x\to\infty}\dfrac{m!}{n^m e^{nx}} = 0$

**70.**

| $x$ | 1 | 5 | 10 | 20 | 30 | 40 | 50 | 100 |
|-----|---|---|----|----|----|----|----|-----|
| $\dfrac{e^x}{x^5}$ | 2.718 | 0.047 | 0.220 | 151.614 | $4.40 \times 10^5$ | $2.30 \times 10^9$ | $1.66 \times 10^{13}$ | $2.69 \times 10^{33}$ |

**72.** $y = x^x,\ x > 0$

$\lim\limits_{x\to\infty} x^x = \infty$ and $\lim\limits_{x\to 0^+} x^x = 1$

No horizontal asymptotes

$\ln y = x\ln x$

$\dfrac{1}{y}\dfrac{dy}{dx} = x\left(\dfrac{1}{x}\right) + \ln x$

$\dfrac{dy}{dx} = x^x(1 + \ln x) = 0$

Critical number:   $x = e^{-1}$

Intervals:   $(0, e^{-1})$      $(e^{-1}, 0)$

Sign of $dy/dx$:   $-$          $+$

$y = f(x)$: Decreasing   Increasing

Relative minimum: $\left(e^{-1}, (e^{-1})^{e^{-1}}\right) = \left(\dfrac{1}{e}, \left(\dfrac{1}{e}\right)^{1/e}\right)$

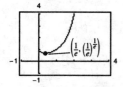

**74.** $y = \dfrac{\ln x}{x}$

Horizontal asymptote: $y = 0$ (See Exercise 29)

$\dfrac{dy}{dx} = \dfrac{x(1/x) - (\ln x)(1)}{x^2} = \dfrac{1 - \ln x}{x^2} = 0$

Critical number:   $x = e$

Intervals:   $(0, e)$          $(e, \infty)$

Sign of $dy/dx$:   $+$          $-$

$y = f(x)$: Increasing   Decreasing

Relative maximum: $\left(e, \dfrac{1}{e}\right)$

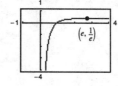

**76.** $\lim\limits_{x\to\infty}\dfrac{\sin \pi x - 1}{x} = 0$   (Numerator is bounded)

Limit is not of the form $0/0$ or $\infty/\infty$.

L'Hôpital's Rule does not apply.

**78.** $\lim\limits_{x\to\infty}\dfrac{e^{-x}}{1 + e^{-x}} = \dfrac{0}{1 + 0} = 0$

Limit is not of the form $0/0$ or $\infty/\infty$.

L'Hôpital's Rule does not apply.

**80.** $A = P\left(1 + \dfrac{r}{n}\right)^{nt}$

$\ln A = \ln P + nt \ln\left(1 + \dfrac{r}{n}\right) = \ln P + \dfrac{\ln\left(1 + \dfrac{r}{n}\right)}{\dfrac{1}{nt}}$

$\lim_{n \to \infty}\left[\dfrac{\ln\left(1 + \dfrac{r}{n}\right)}{\dfrac{1}{nt}}\right] = \lim_{n \to \infty}\left[\dfrac{-\dfrac{r}{n^2}\left(\dfrac{1}{1 + (r/n)}\right)}{-\left(\dfrac{1}{n^2 t}\right)}\right] = \lim_{n \to \infty}\left[rt\left(\dfrac{1}{1 + \dfrac{r}{n}}\right)\right] = rt$

Since $\lim_{n \to \infty} \ln A = \ln P + rt$, we have $\lim_{n \to \infty} A = e^{(\ln P = rt)} = e^{\ln P}e^{rt} = Pe^{rt}$. Alternatively,

$\lim_{n \to \infty} A = \lim_{n \to \infty} P\left(1 + \dfrac{r}{n}\right)^{nt} = \lim_{n \to \infty} P\left[\left(1 + \dfrac{r}{n}\right)^{n/r}\right]^{rt} = Pe^{rt}.$

**82.** Let $N$ be a fixed value for $n$. Then

$\lim_{x \to \infty} \dfrac{x^{N-1}}{e^x} = \lim_{x \to \infty} \dfrac{(N-1)x^{N-2}}{e^x} = \lim_{x \to \infty} \dfrac{(N-1)(N-2)x^{N-3}}{e^x} = \ldots = \lim_{x \to \infty}\left[\dfrac{(N-1)!}{e^x}\right] = 0.$   (See Exercise 68)

**84.** $f(x) = \dfrac{x^k - 1}{k}$

$k = 1, \qquad f(x) = x - 1$

$k = 0.1, \quad f(x) = \dfrac{x^{0.1} - 1}{0.1} = 10(x^{0.1} - 1)$

$k = 0.01, \quad f(x) = \dfrac{x^{0.01} - 1}{0.01} = 100(x^{0.01} - 1)$

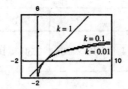

$\lim_{k \to 0^+} \dfrac{x^k - 1}{k} = \lim_{k \to 0^+} \dfrac{x^k(\ln x)}{1} = \ln x$

**86.** $f(x) = \dfrac{1}{x}, g(x) = x^2 - 4, [1, 2]$

$\dfrac{f(2) - f(1)}{g(2) - g(1)} = \dfrac{f'(c)}{g'(c)}$

$\dfrac{-1/2}{3} = \dfrac{-1/c^2}{2c}$

$-\dfrac{1}{6} = -\dfrac{1}{2c^3}$

$2c^3 = 6$

$c = \sqrt[3]{3}$

**88.** $f(x) = \ln x, g(x) = x^3, [1, 4]$

$\dfrac{f(4) - f(1)}{g(4) - g(1)} = \dfrac{f'(c)}{g'(c)}$

$\dfrac{\ln 4}{63} = \dfrac{1/c}{3c^2} = \dfrac{1}{3c^3}$

$3c^3 \ln 4 = 63$

$c^3 = \dfrac{21}{\ln 4}$

$c = \sqrt[3]{\dfrac{21}{\ln 4}} \approx 2.474$

**90.** False. If $y = e^x/x^2$, then

$y' = \dfrac{x^2 e^x - 2x e^x}{x^4} = \dfrac{x e^x(x - 2)}{x^4} = \dfrac{e^x(x - 2)}{x^3}.$

**92.** False. Let $f(x) = x$ and $g(x) = x + 1$. Then

$\lim_{x \to \infty} \dfrac{x}{x + 1} = 1$, but $\lim_{x \to \infty} [x - (x + 1)] = -1.$

**94.** $g(x) = \begin{cases} e^{-1/x^2}, & x \neq 0 \\ 0, & x = 0 \end{cases}$

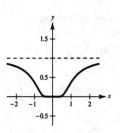

$g'(0) = \lim\limits_{x \to 0} \dfrac{g(x) - g(0)}{x - 0} = \lim\limits_{x \to 0} \dfrac{e^{-1/x^2}}{x}$

Let $y = \dfrac{e^{-1/x^2}}{x}$, then $\ln y = \ln\left(\dfrac{e^{-1/x^2}}{x}\right) = -\dfrac{1}{x^2} - \ln x = \dfrac{-1 - x^2 \ln x}{x^2}$. Since

$$\lim\limits_{x \to 0} x^2 \ln x = \lim\limits_{x \to 0} \dfrac{\ln x}{1/x^2} = \lim\limits_{x \to 0} \dfrac{1/x}{-2/x^3} = \lim\limits_{x \to 0} \left(-\dfrac{x^2}{2}\right) = 0$$

we have $\lim\limits_{x \to 0} \left(\dfrac{-1 - x^2 \ln x}{x^2}\right) = -\infty$. Thus, $\lim\limits_{x \to 0} y = e^{-\infty} = 0 \implies g'(0) = 0$.

**Note:** The graph appears to support this conclusion—the tangent line is horizontal at $(0, 0)$.

**96.** $\lim\limits_{x \to a} f(x)^{g(x)}$

$\qquad y = f(x)^{g(x)}$

$\qquad \ln y = g(x) \ln f(x)$

$\lim\limits_{x \to a} g(x) \ln f(x) = (-\infty)(-\infty) = \infty$

As $x \to a$, $\ln y \implies \infty$, and hence $y = \infty$. Thus,

$\qquad \lim\limits_{x \to a} f(x)^{g(x)} = \infty.$

**98.** $\lim\limits_{x \to 0^+} x^{\ln 2/(1 + \ln x)}$

Let $y = x^{\ln 2/(1 + \ln x)}$, then:

$$\ln y = \dfrac{\ln 2}{1 + \ln x} \cdot \ln x = \dfrac{(\ln 2)(\ln x)}{1 + \ln x}$$

$$\lim\limits_{x \to 0^+} \ln y = \lim\limits_{x \to 0^+} \dfrac{(\ln 2)(\ln x)}{1 + \ln x} = \lim\limits_{x \to 0^+} \dfrac{(\ln 2)/x}{1/x}$$

$$= \lim\limits_{x \to 0^+} (\ln 2) = \ln 2$$

Thus, $\lim\limits_{x \to \infty} y = e^{\ln 2} = 2.$

# Section 7.8    Improper Integrals

**2.** Infinite discontinuity at $x = 3$.

$$\int_3^4 \dfrac{1}{(x - 3)^{3/2}} \, dx = \lim\limits_{b \to 3^+} \int_b^4 (x - 3)^{-3/2} \, dx$$

$$= \lim\limits_{b \to 3^+} \left[-2(x - 3)^{-1/2}\right]_b^4$$

$$= \lim\limits_{b \to 3^+} \left[-2 + \dfrac{2}{\sqrt{b - 3}}\right] = \infty$$

Diverges

**4.** Infinite discontinuity at $x = 1$.

$$\int_0^2 \dfrac{1}{(x - 1)^{2/3}} \, dx = \int_0^1 \dfrac{1}{(x - 1)^{2/3}} \, dx + \int_1^2 \dfrac{1}{(x - 1)^{2/3}} \, dx$$

$$= \lim\limits_{b \to 1^-} \int_0^b \dfrac{1}{(x - 1)^{2/3}} \, dx + \lim\limits_{c \to 1^+} \int_c^2 \dfrac{1}{(x - 1)^{2/3}} \, dx$$

$$= \lim\limits_{b \to 1^-} \left[3\sqrt[3]{x - 1}\right]_0^b + \lim\limits_{c \to 1^+} \left[3\sqrt[3]{x - 1}\right]_c^2 = (0 + 3) + (3 - 0) = 6$$

Converges

**6.** Infinite limit of integration.

$$\int_{-\infty}^{0} e^{2x} \, dx = \lim_{b \to -\infty} \int_{b}^{0} e^{2x} \, dx$$

$$= \lim_{b \to -\infty} \left[ \frac{1}{2} e^{2x} \right]_{b}^{0} = \frac{1}{2} - 0 = \frac{1}{2}$$

Converges

**8.** $\int_{0}^{\infty} e^{-x} \, dx \neq 0.$ You need to evaluate the limit.

$$\lim_{b \to \infty} \int_{0}^{b} e^{-x} \, dx = \lim_{b \to \infty} \left[ -e^{-x} \right]_{0}^{b}$$

$$= \lim_{b \to \infty} \left[ -e^{-b} + 1 \right] = 1$$

**10.** $\int_{1}^{\infty} \frac{5}{x^3} \, dx = \lim_{b \to \infty} \int_{1}^{b} \frac{5}{x^3} \, dx$

$$= \lim_{b \to \infty} \left[ -\frac{5}{2} x^{-2} \right]_{1}^{b} = \frac{5}{2}$$

**12.** $\int_{1}^{\infty} \frac{4}{\sqrt[4]{x}} \, dx = \lim_{b \to \infty} \int_{1}^{b} 4x^{-1/4} \, dx$

$$= \lim_{b \to \infty} \left[ \frac{16}{3} x^{3/4} \right]_{1}^{b} = \infty \quad \text{Diverges}$$

**14.** $\int_{0}^{\infty} xe^{-x/2} \, dx = \lim_{b \to \infty} \int_{0}^{b} xe^{-x/2} \, dx = \lim_{b \to \infty} \left[ e^{-x/2}(-2x - 4) \right]_{0}^{b} = \lim_{b \to \infty} e^{-b/2}(-2b - 4) + 4 = 4$

**16.** $\int_{0}^{\infty} (x - 1)e^{-x} \, dx = \lim_{b \to \infty} \int_{0}^{b} (x - 1)e^{-x} \, dx = \lim_{b \to \infty} \left[ -xe^{-x} \right]_{0}^{b} = \lim_{b \to \infty} \left( \frac{-b}{e^b} + 0 \right) = 0$ by L'Hôpital's Rule.

**18.** $\int_{0}^{\infty} e^{-ax} \sin bx \, dx = \lim_{c \to \infty} \left[ \frac{e^{-ax}(-a \sin bx - b \cos bx)}{a^2 + b^2} \right]_{0}^{c}$

$$= 0 - \frac{-b}{a^2 + b^2} = \frac{b}{a^2 + b^2}$$

**20.** $\int_{1}^{\infty} \frac{\ln x}{x} \, dx = \lim_{b \to \infty} \int_{1}^{b} \frac{\ln x}{x} \, dx$

$$= \lim_{b \to \infty} \left[ \frac{(\ln x)^2}{2} \right]_{1}^{b} = \infty \quad \text{Diverges}$$

**22.** $\int_{0}^{\infty} \frac{x^3}{(x^2 + 1)^2} \, dx = \lim_{b \to \infty} \int_{0}^{b} \frac{x}{x^2 + 1} \, dx - \lim_{b \to \infty} \int_{0}^{b} \frac{x}{(x^2 + 1)^2} \, dx$

$$= \lim_{b \to \infty} \left[ \frac{1}{2} \ln(x^2 + 1) + \frac{1}{2(x^2 + 1)} \right]_{0}^{b}$$

$$= \infty - \frac{1}{2}$$

Diverges

**24.** $\int_{0}^{\infty} \frac{e^x}{1 + e^x} \, dx = \lim_{b \to \infty} \left[ \ln(1 + e^x) \right]_{0}^{b} = \infty - \ln 2$

Diverges

**26.** $\int_{0}^{\infty} \sin \frac{x}{2} \, dx = \lim_{b \to \infty} \left[ -2 \cos \frac{x}{2} \right]_{0}^{b}$

Diverges since $\cos \frac{x}{2}$ does not approach a limit as $x \to \infty$.

**28.** $\int_{0}^{4} \frac{8}{x} \, dx = \lim_{b \to 0^+} \int_{b}^{4} \frac{8}{x} \, dx = \lim_{b \to 0^+} \left[ 8 \ln x \right]_{b}^{4} = \infty$

Diverges

**30.** $\int_{0}^{6} \frac{4}{\sqrt{6 - x}} \, dx = \lim_{b \to 6^-} \int_{0}^{b} 4(6 - x)^{-1/2} \, dx$

$$= \lim_{b \to 6^-} \left[ -8(6 - x)^{1/2} \right]_{0}^{b}$$

$$= -8(0) + 8\sqrt{6}$$

$$= 8\sqrt{6}$$

**32.** $\int_{0}^{e} \ln x^2 \, dx = \lim_{b \to 0^+} \int_{0}^{e} 2 \ln x \, dx$

$$= \lim_{b \to 0^+} \left[ 2x \ln x - 2x \right]_{b}^{e}$$

$$= \lim_{b \to 0^+} \left[ (2e - 2e) - (2b \ln b - 2b) \right]$$

$$= 0$$

**34.** $\int_{0}^{\pi/2} \sec \theta \, d\theta = \lim_{b \to (\pi/2)} \left[ \ln|\sec \theta + \tan \theta| \right]_{0}^{b} = \infty,$

Diverges

**36.** $\int_{0}^{2} \frac{1}{\sqrt{4 - x^2}} \, dx = \lim_{b \to 2^-} \left[ \arcsin \left( \frac{x}{2} \right) \right]_{0}^{b} = \frac{\pi}{2}$

**38.** $\int_0^2 \frac{1}{4-x^2}\,dx = \lim_{b\to 2^-}\int_0^b \frac{1}{4}\left(\frac{1}{2+x}+\frac{1}{2-x}\right)dx = \lim_{b\to 2^-}\left[\frac{1}{4}\ln\left|\frac{2+x}{2-x}\right|\right]_0^b = \infty - 0$

Diverges

**40.** $\int_1^3 \frac{2}{(x-2)^{8/3}}\,dx = \int_1^2 2(x-2)^{-8/3}\,dx + \int_2^3 2(x-2)^{-8/3}\,dx$

$\qquad = \lim_{b\to 2^-}\int_1^b 2(x-2)^{-8/3}\,dx + \lim_{c\to 2^+}\int_c^3 2(x-2)^{-8/3}\,dx$

$\qquad = \lim_{b\to 2^-}\left[-\frac{6}{5}(x-2)^{-5/3}\right]_1^b + \lim_{c\to 2^+}\left[-\frac{6}{5}(x-2)^{-5/3}\right]_c^3 = \infty$

Diverges

**42.** $\int \frac{1}{x\ln x}\,dx = \ln|\ln|x|| + C$

Thus,

$\int_1^\infty \frac{1}{x\ln x}\,dx = \int_1^e \frac{1}{x\ln x}\,dx + \int_e^\infty \frac{1}{x\ln x}\,dx$

$= \lim_{b\to 1^+}\Big[\ln(\ln x)\Big]_1^e + \lim_{c\to\infty}\Big[\ln(\ln x)\Big]_e^\infty.$

Diverges

**44.** If $p=1$, $\int_0^1 \frac{1}{x}\,dx = \lim_{a\to 0^+}\ln x\Big]_a^1 = \lim_{a\to 0^+}-\ln a = \infty.$

Diverges. If $p\neq 1$,

$\int_0^1 \frac{1}{x^p}\,dx = \lim_{a\to 0^+}\left[\frac{x^{1-p}}{1-p}\right]_a^1 = \lim_{a\to 0^+}\left[\frac{1}{1-p}-\frac{a^{1-p}}{1-p}\right].$

This converges to $\frac{1}{1-p}$ if $1-p>0$ or $p<1$.

**46.** (a) Assume $\int_a^\infty g(x)\,dx = L$ (converges).

Since $0\le f(x)\le g(x)$ on $[a,\infty)$, $0\le \int_a^\infty f(x)\,dx \le \int_a^\infty g(x)\,dx = L$ and $\int_a^\infty f(x)\,dx$ converges.

(b) $\int_a^\infty g(x)\,dx$ diverges, because otherwise, by part (a), if $\int_a^\infty g(x)\,dx$ converges, then so does $\int_a^\infty f(x)\,dx.$

**48.** $\int_0^1 \frac{1}{\sqrt[3]{x}}\,dx = \frac{1}{1-(1/3)} = \frac{3}{2}$ converges.

$\left(\text{See Exercise 44, } p=\frac{1}{3}.\right)$

**50.** $\int_0^\infty x^4 e^{-x}\,dx$ converges.

(See Exercise 45.)

**52.** Since $\frac{1}{\sqrt{x-1}} \ge \frac{1}{x}$ on $[2,\infty)$ and $\int_2^\infty \frac{1}{x}\,dx$ diverges by Exercise 43, $\int_2^\infty \frac{1}{\sqrt{x-1}}\,dx$ diverges.

**54.** Since $\frac{1}{\sqrt{x}(1+x)} \le \frac{1}{x^{3/2}}$ on $[1,\infty)$ and $\int_1^\infty \frac{1}{x^{3/2}}\,dx$ converges by Exercise 43, $\int_1^\infty \frac{1}{\sqrt{x}(1+x)}\,dx$ converges.

**56.** $\frac{1}{\sqrt{x}\ln x} \ge \frac{1}{x}$ since $\sqrt{x}\ln x < x$ on $[2,\infty)$. Since $\int_2^\infty \frac{1}{x}\,dx$ diverges by Exercise 43, $\int_2^\infty \frac{1}{\sqrt{x}\ln x}\,dx$ diverges.

**58.** See the definitions, pages 540, 543.

**60.** Answers will vary.

(a) $\int_{-\infty}^\infty \frac{e^x}{1+e^{2x}}\,dx$

Converges (Example 4)

(b) $\int_{-\infty}^\infty x\,dx$

Diverges

**62.** $f(t) = t$

$F(s) = \int_0^\infty te^{-st}\,dt = \lim_{b\to\infty}\left[\frac{1}{s^2}(-st-1)e^{-st}\right]_0^b$

$\qquad = \frac{1}{s^2}, s>0$

**64.** $f(t) = e^{at}$

$$F(s) = \int_0^\infty e^{at} e^{-st}\, dt = \int_0^\infty e^{t(a-s)}\, dt$$

$$= \lim_{b\to\infty} \left[\frac{1}{a-s} e^{t(a-s)}\right]_0^b$$

$$= 0 - \frac{1}{a-s} = \frac{1}{s-a},\ s > a$$

**66.** $f(t) = \sin at$

$$F(s) = \int_0^\infty e^{-st} \sin at\, dt$$

$$= \lim_{b\to\infty} \left[\frac{e^{-st}}{s^2 + a^2}(-s \sin at - a \cos at)\right]_0^b$$

$$= 0 + \frac{a}{s^2 + a^2} = \frac{a}{s^2 + a^2},\ s > 0$$

**68.** $f(t) = \sinh at$

$$F(s) = \int_0^\infty e^{-st} \sinh at\, dt = \int_0^\infty e^{-st}\left(\frac{e^{at} - e^{-at}}{2}\right) dt = \frac{1}{2}\int_0^\infty \left[e^{t(-s+a)} - e^{t(-s-a)}\right] dt$$

$$= \lim_{b\to\infty} \frac{1}{2}\left[\frac{1}{(-s+a)} e^{t(-s+a)} - \frac{1}{(-s-a)} e^{t(-s-a)}\right]_0^b = 0 - \frac{1}{2}\left[\frac{1}{(-s+a)} - \frac{1}{(-s-a)}\right]$$

$$= \frac{-1}{2}\left[\frac{1}{(-s+a)} - \frac{1}{(-s-a)}\right] = \frac{a}{s^2 - a^2},\ s > |a|$$

**70. (a)** $A = \int_1^\infty \frac{1}{x^2}\, dx = \left[-\frac{1}{x}\right]_1^\infty = 1$

**(b) Disk:**

$$V = \pi\int_1^\infty \frac{1}{x^4}\, dx = \lim_{b\to\infty}\left[-\frac{\pi}{3x^3}\right]_1^b = \frac{\pi}{3}$$

**(c) Shell:**

$$V = 2\pi\int_1^\infty x\left(\frac{1}{x^2}\right) dx = \lim_{b\to\infty}\left[2\pi(\ln x)\right]_1^b = \infty$$

Diverges

**72.** $(x - 2)^2 + y^2 = 1$

$2(x - 2) + 2yy' = 0$

$y' = \dfrac{-(x - 2)}{y}$

$\sqrt{1 + (y')^2} = \sqrt{1 + [(x-2)^2/y^2]} = \dfrac{1}{y}$ (Assume $y > 0$.)

$$S = 4\pi\int_1^3 \frac{x}{y}\, dx = 4\pi\int_1^3 \frac{x}{\sqrt{1 - (x-2)^2}}\, dx = 4\pi\int_1^3 \left[\frac{x-2}{\sqrt{1 - (x-2)^2}} + \frac{2}{\sqrt{1 - (x-2)^2}}\right] dx$$

$$= \lim_{\substack{a\to1^+\\b\to3^-}} \left\{4\pi\left[-\sqrt{1 - (x-2)^2} + 2\arcsin(x-2)\right]_a^b\right\} = 4\pi[0 + 2\arcsin(1) - 2\arcsin(-1)] = 8\pi^2$$

**74. (a)** $F(x) = \dfrac{K}{x^2}$, $5 = \dfrac{K}{(4000)^2}$, $K = 80{,}000{,}000$

$$W = \int_{4000}^\infty \frac{80{,}000{,}000}{x^2}\, dx = \lim_{b\to\infty}\left[\frac{-80{,}000{,}000}{x}\right]_{4000}^b = 20{,}000\ \text{mi-ton}$$

**(b)** $\dfrac{W}{2} = 10{,}000 = \left[\dfrac{-80{,}000{,}000}{x}\right]_{4000}^b = \dfrac{-80{,}000{,}000}{b} + 20{,}000$

$\dfrac{80{,}000{,}000}{b} = 10{,}000$

$b = 8000$

Therefore, 4000 miles *above* the earth's surface.

**76.** (a) $\displaystyle\int_{-\infty}^{\infty} \frac{2}{5}e^{-2t/5}\,dt = \int_{0}^{\infty} \frac{2}{5}e^{-2t/5}\,dt = \lim_{b\to\infty}\left[-e^{-2t5}\right]_{0}^{b} = 1$

(b) $\displaystyle\int_{0}^{4} \frac{2}{5}e^{-2t/5}\,dt = \left[-e^{-2t/5}\right]_{0}^{4} = -e^{-8/5}+1$

$$\approx 0.7981 = 79.81\%$$

(c) $\displaystyle\int_{0}^{\infty} t\left[\frac{2}{5}e^{-2t/5}\right]dt = \lim_{b\to\infty}\left[-te^{2t/5}-\frac{5}{2}e^{-2t/5}\right]_{0}^{b} = \frac{5}{2}$

**78.** (a) $\displaystyle C = 650{,}000 + \int_{0}^{5} 25{,}000(1+0.08t)e^{-0.06t}\,dt$

$$= 650{,}000 + 25{,}000\left[-\frac{1}{0.06}e^{-0.06t} - 0.08\left(\frac{t}{0.06}e^{-0.06t} + \frac{1}{(0.06)^2}e^{-0.06t}\right)\right]_{0}^{5} \approx \$778{,}512.58$$

(b) $\displaystyle C = 650{,}000 + \int_{0}^{10} 25{,}000(1+0.08t)e^{-0.06t}\,dt$

$$= 650{,}000 + 25{,}000\left[-\frac{1}{0.06}e^{-0.06t} - 0.08\left(\frac{t}{0.06}e^{-0.06t} + \frac{1}{(0.06)^2}e^{-0.06t}\right)\right]_{0}^{10} \approx \$905{,}718.14$$

(c) $\displaystyle C = 650{,}000 + \int_{0}^{\infty} 25{,}000(1+0.08t)e^{-0.06t}\,dt$

$$= 650{,}000 + 25{,}000 \lim_{b\to\infty}\left[-\frac{t}{0.06}e^{-0.06t} - 0.08\left(\frac{t}{0.06}e^{-0.06t} + \frac{1}{(0.06)^2}e^{-0.06t}\right)\right]_{0}^{b} \approx \$1{,}622{,}222.22$$

**80.** (a) $\displaystyle\int_{1}^{\infty} \frac{1}{x}\,dx = \lim_{b\to\infty}\left[\ln|x|\right]_{1}^{b} = \infty$

$\displaystyle\int_{1}^{\infty} \frac{1}{x^2}\,dx = \lim_{b\to\infty}\left[-\frac{1}{x}\right]_{1}^{b} = 1$

$\displaystyle\int_{1}^{\infty} \frac{1}{x^n}\,dx$ will converge if $n > 1$ and will diverge if $n \le 1$.

(b) It would appear to converge.

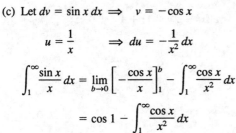

(c) Let $dv = \sin x\,dx \implies v = -\cos x$

$$u = \frac{1}{x} \implies du = -\frac{1}{x^2}\,dx$$

$$\int_{1}^{\infty} \frac{\sin x}{x}\,dx = \lim_{b\to 0}\left[-\frac{\cos x}{x}\right]_{1}^{b} - \int_{1}^{\infty} \frac{\cos x}{x^2}\,dx$$

$$= \cos 1 - \int_{1}^{\infty} \frac{\cos x}{x^2}\,dx$$

Converges

**82.** (a) Yes, the integral is not defined at $x = \pi/2$.

(c) As $n \to \infty$, the integral approaches $4(\pi/4) = \pi$.

(d) $\displaystyle I_n = \int_{0}^{\pi/2} \frac{4}{1+(\tan x)^n}\,dx$

$I_2 \approx 3.14159$

$I_4 \approx 3.14159$

$I_8 \approx 3.14159$

$I_{12} \approx 3.14159$

(b)

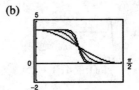

**84.** (a) $f(x) = \dfrac{1}{3\sqrt{2\pi}} e^{-(x-70)^2/18}$

$\displaystyle\int_{50}^{90} f(x)\, dx \approx 1.0$

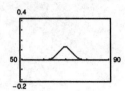

(b) $P(72 \le x < \infty) \approx 0.2525$

(c) $0.5 - P(70 \le x \le 72) \approx 0.5 - 0.2475 = 0.2525$

These are the same answers because by symmetry,

$P(70 \le x < \infty) = 0.5$

and

$0.5 = P(70 \le x < \infty)$

$\qquad = P(70 \le x \le 72) + P(72 \le x < \infty).$

**86.** False. This is equivalent to Exercise 85.

**88.** True

# Review Exercises for Chapter 7

**2.** $\displaystyle\int xe^{x^2-1}\, dx = \frac{1}{2}\int e^{x^2-1}(2x)\, dx$

$\qquad = \dfrac{1}{2} e^{x^2-1} + C$

**4.** $\displaystyle\int \frac{x}{\sqrt{1-x^2}}\, dx = -\frac{1}{2}\int (1-x^2)^{-1/2}(-2x)\, dx$

$\qquad = -\dfrac{1}{2}\dfrac{(1-x^2)^{1/2}}{1/2} + C$

$\qquad = -\sqrt{1-x^2} + C$

**6.** $\displaystyle\int 2x\sqrt{2x-3}\, dx = \int (u^4 + 3u^2)\, du = \frac{u^5}{5} + u^3 + C$

$\qquad = \dfrac{2(2x-3)^{3/2}}{5}(x+1) + C$

$u = \sqrt{2x-3},\ x = \dfrac{u^2+3}{2},\ dx = u\, du$

**8.** $\dfrac{x^4 + 2x^2 + x + 1}{x^4 + 2x^2 + 1} = 1 + \dfrac{x}{(x^2+1)^2}$

$\displaystyle\int \frac{x^4 + 2x^2 + x + 1}{(x^2+1)^2}\, dx = \int dx + \frac{1}{2}\int \frac{2x}{(x^2+1)^2}\, dx$

$\qquad = x - \dfrac{1}{2(x^2+1)} + C$

**10.** $\displaystyle\int (x^2-1)e^x\, dx = (x^2-1)e^x - 2\int xe^x\, dx = (x^2-1)e^x - 2xe^x + 2\int e^x\, dx = e^x(x^2 - 2x + 1) + 1$

(1) $dv = e^x\, dx \implies v = e^x$

$\quad u = x^2 - 1 \implies du = 2x\, dx$

(2) $dv = e^x\, dx \implies v = e^x$

$\quad u = x \implies du = dx$

**12.** $u = \arctan 2x,\ du = \dfrac{2}{1+4x^2}\, dx,\ dv = dx, v = x$

$\displaystyle\int \arctan 2x\, dx = x\arctan 2x - \int \frac{2x}{1+4x^2}\, dx$

$\qquad = x\arctan 2x - \dfrac{1}{4}\ln(1+4x^2) + C$

**14.** $\displaystyle\int \ln\sqrt{x^2-1}\, dx = \frac{1}{2}\int \ln(x^2-1)\, dx$

$\qquad = \dfrac{1}{2}x\ln|x^2-1| - \int \dfrac{x^2}{x^2-1}\, dx$

$\qquad = \dfrac{1}{2}x\ln|x^2-1| - \int dx - \int \dfrac{1}{x^2-1}\, dx$

$\qquad = \dfrac{1}{2}x\ln|x^2-1| - x - \dfrac{1}{2}\ln\left|\dfrac{x-1}{x+1}\right| + C$

$dv = dx \implies v = x$

$u = \ln(x^2-1) \implies du = \dfrac{2x}{x^2-1}\, dx$

**16.** $\displaystyle\int e^x \arctan(e^x)\,dx = e^x \arctan(e^x) - \int \frac{e^{2x}}{1 + e^{2x}}\,dx$

$$= e^x \arctan(e^x) - \frac{1}{2}\ln(1 + e^{2x}) + C$$

$dv = e^x\,dx \quad\Longrightarrow\quad v = e^x$

$u = \arctan e^x \Longrightarrow du = \dfrac{e^x}{1 + e^{2x}}\,dx$

**18.** $\displaystyle\int \sin^2 \frac{\pi x}{2}\,dx = \int \frac{1}{2}(1 - \cos \pi x)\,dx = \frac{1}{2}\left[x - \frac{1}{\pi}\sin \pi x\right] + C = \frac{1}{2\pi}[\pi x - \sin \pi x] + C$

**20.** $\displaystyle\int \tan \theta \sec^4 \theta\,d\theta = \int (\tan^3 \theta + \tan \theta) \sec^2 \theta\,d\theta = \frac{1}{4}\tan^4 \theta + \frac{1}{2}\tan^2 \theta + C_1$

or

$\displaystyle\int \tan \theta \sec^4 \theta\,d\theta = \int \sec^3 \theta(\sec \theta \tan \theta)\,d\theta = \frac{1}{4}\sec^4 \theta + C_2$

**22.** $\displaystyle\int \cos 2\theta(\sin \theta + \cos \theta)^2\,d\theta = \int (\cos^2 \theta - \sin^2 \theta)(\sin \theta + \cos \theta)^2\,d\theta$

$$= \int (\sin \theta + \cos \theta)^3(\cos \theta - \sin \theta)\,d\theta = \frac{1}{4}(\sin \theta + \cos\theta)^4 + C$$

**24.** $\displaystyle\int \frac{\sqrt{x^2 - 9}}{x}\,dx = \int \frac{3 \tan \theta}{3 \sec \theta}(3 \sec \theta \tan \theta\,d\theta)$

$$= 3\int \tan^2 \theta\,d\theta$$

$$= 3\int (\sec^2 \theta - 1)\,d\theta$$

$$= 3(\tan \theta - \theta) + C$$

$$= \sqrt{x^2 - 9} - 3 \operatorname{arcsec}\!\left(\frac{x}{3}\right) + C$$

$x = 3 \sec \theta,\ dx = 3 \sec \theta \tan \theta\,d\theta,\ \sqrt{x^2 - 9} = 3 \tan \theta$

**26.** $\displaystyle\int \sqrt{9 - 4x^2}\,dx = \frac{1}{2}\int \sqrt{9 - (2x)^2}\,(2)\,dx$

$$= \frac{1}{2}\cdot\frac{1}{2}\left[9 \arcsin \frac{2x}{3} + 2x\sqrt{9 - 4x^2}\right] + C$$

$$= \frac{9}{4}\arcsin \frac{2x}{3} + \frac{x}{2}\sqrt{9 - 4x^2} + C$$

**28.** $\displaystyle\int \frac{\sin \theta}{1 + 2\cos^2 \theta}\,d\theta = \frac{-1}{\sqrt{2}}\int \frac{1}{1 + 2\cos^2 \theta}\left(-\sqrt{2}\sin \theta\right)d\theta$

$$= \frac{-1}{\sqrt{2}}\arctan\!\left(\sqrt{2}\cos \theta\right) + C$$

$u = \sqrt{2}\cos \theta,\ du = -\sqrt{2}\sin \theta\,d\theta$

**30.** (a) $\displaystyle\int x\sqrt{4 + x}\, dx = 64\int \tan^3 \theta \sec^3 \theta\, d\theta$

$\displaystyle = 64\int (\sec^4 \theta - \sec^2 \theta)\sec \theta \tan \theta\, d\theta$

$\displaystyle = \frac{64 \sec^3 \theta}{15}(3 \sec^3 \theta - 5) + C$

$\displaystyle = \frac{2(4 + x)^{3/2}}{15}(3x - 8) + C$

$x = 4 \tan^2 \theta,\ dx = 8 \tan \theta \sec^2 \theta\, d\theta,$

$\sqrt{4 + x} = 2 \sec \theta$

(b) $\displaystyle\int x\sqrt{4 + x}\, dx = 2\int (u^4 - 4u^2)\, du$

$\displaystyle = \frac{2u^3}{15}(3u^2 - 20) + C$

$\displaystyle = \frac{2(4 + x)^{3/2}}{15}(3x - 8) + C$

$u^2 = 4 + x,\ dx = 2u\, du$

(c) $\displaystyle\int x\sqrt{4 + x}\, dx = \int (u^{3/2} - 4u^{1/2})\, du$

$\displaystyle = \frac{2u^{3/2}}{15}(3u - 20) + C$

$\displaystyle = \frac{2(4 + x)^{3/2}}{15}(3x - 8) + C$

$u = 4 + x,\ du = dx$

(d) $\displaystyle\int x\sqrt{4 + x}\, dx = \frac{2x}{3}(4 + x)^{3/2} - \frac{2}{3}\int (4 + x)^{3/2}\, dx$

$\displaystyle = \frac{2x}{3}(4 + x)^{3/2} - \frac{4}{15}(4 + x)^{5/2} + C$

$\displaystyle = \frac{2(4 + x)^{3/2}}{15}(3x - 8) + C$

$dv = \sqrt{4 + x}\, dx \implies v = \frac{2}{3}(4 + x)^{3/2}$

$u = x \qquad\qquad \implies du = dx$

**32.** $\displaystyle\frac{2x^3 - 5x^2 + 4x - 4}{x^2 - x} = 2x - 3 + \frac{4}{x} - \frac{3}{x - 1}$

$\displaystyle\int \frac{2x^3 - 5x^2 + 4x - 4}{x^2 - x}\, dx = \int \left(2x - 3 + \frac{4}{x} - \frac{3}{x - 1}\right) dx = x^2 - 3x + 4 \ln|x| - 3 \ln|x - 1| + C$

**34.** $\displaystyle\frac{4x - 2}{3(x - 1)^2} = \frac{A}{x - 1} + \frac{B}{(x - 1)^2}$

$4x - 2 = 3A(x - 1) + 3B$

Let $x = 1$:  $2 = 3B \implies B = \frac{2}{3}$

Let $x = 2$:  $6 = 3A + 3B \implies A = \frac{4}{3}$

$\displaystyle\int \frac{4x - 2}{3(x - 1)^2}\, dx = \frac{4}{3}\int \frac{1}{x - 1}\, dx + \frac{2}{3}\int \frac{1}{(x - 1)^2}\, dx = \frac{4}{3} \ln|x - 1| - \frac{2}{3(x - 1)} + C = \frac{2}{3}\left(2 \ln|x - 1| - \frac{1}{x - 1}\right) + C$

**36.** $\displaystyle\int \frac{\sec^2 \theta}{\tan \theta(\tan \theta - 1)}\, d\theta = \int \frac{1}{u(u - 1)}\, du = \int \frac{1}{u - 1}\, du - \int \frac{1}{u}\, du$

$\displaystyle = \ln|u - 1| - \ln|u| + C = \ln\left|\frac{\tan \theta - 1}{\tan \theta}\right| + C = \ln|1 - \cot \theta| + C$

$u = \tan \theta,\ du = \sec^2 \theta\, d\theta$

$\displaystyle\frac{1}{u(u - 1)} = \frac{A}{u} + \frac{B}{u - 1}$

$1 = A(u - 1) + Bu$

Let $u = 0$:  $1 = -A \implies A = -1$

Let $u = 1$:  $1 = B$

**38.** $\int \dfrac{x}{\sqrt{2+3x}}\,dx = \dfrac{-2(4-3x)}{27}\sqrt{2+3x} + C$  (Formula 21)

$$= \dfrac{6x-8}{27}\sqrt{2+3x} + C$$

**40.** $\int \dfrac{x}{1+e^{x^2}}\,dx = \dfrac{1}{2}\int \dfrac{1}{1+e^u}\,dx$  $(u = x^2)$

$$= \dfrac{1}{2}[u - \ln(1+e^u)] + C \quad \text{(Formula 84)}$$

$$= \dfrac{1}{2}[x^2 - \ln(1+e^{x^2})] + C$$

**42.** $\int \dfrac{3}{2x\sqrt{9x^2-1}}\,dx = \dfrac{3}{2}\int \dfrac{1}{3x\sqrt{(3x)^2-1}}\,3\,dx$  $(u = 3x)$

$$= \dfrac{3}{2}\operatorname{arcsec}|3x| + C \qquad \text{(Formula 33)}$$

**44.** $\int \dfrac{1}{1+\tan \pi x}\,dx = \dfrac{1}{\pi}\int \dfrac{1}{1+\tan \pi x}(\pi)dx$  $(u = \pi x)$

$$= \dfrac{1}{\pi}\dfrac{1}{2}\big[\pi x + \ln|\cos \pi x + \sin \pi x|\big] + C \quad \text{(Formula 71)}$$

**46.** $\int \tan^n x\,dx = \int \tan^{n-2}x(\sec^2 x - 1)\,dx$

$$= \int \tan^{n-2} x \sec^2 x\,dx - \int \tan^{n-2} x\,dx$$

$$= \dfrac{1}{n-1}\tan^{n-1} x - \int \tan^{n-2} x\,dx$$

**48.** $\int \dfrac{\csc\sqrt{2x}}{\sqrt{x}}\,dx = \sqrt{2}\int \csc\sqrt{2x}\left(\dfrac{1}{\sqrt{2x}}\right)dx$

$$= -\sqrt{2}\,\ln|\csc\sqrt{2x} + \cot\sqrt{2x}| + C$$

$$u = \sqrt{2x},\ du = \dfrac{1}{\sqrt{2x}}\,dx$$

**50.** $\int \sqrt{1+\sqrt{x}}\,dx = \int u(4u^3 - 4u)\,du = \int (4u^4 - 4u^2)\,du = \dfrac{4u^5}{5} - \dfrac{4u^3}{3} + C = \dfrac{4}{15}(1+\sqrt{x})^{3/2}(3\sqrt{x}-2) + C$

$$u = \sqrt{1+\sqrt{x}},\ x = u^4 - 2u^2 + 1,\ dx = (4u^3 - 4u)\,du$$

**52.** $\dfrac{3x^3 + 4x}{(x^2+1)^2} = \dfrac{Ax+B}{x^2+1} + \dfrac{Cx+D}{(x^2+1)^2}$

$$3x^3 + 4x = (Ax+B)(x^2+1) + Cx + D$$

$$= Ax^3 + Bx^2 + (A+C)x + (B+D)$$

$$A = 3, B = 0, A + C = 4 \Rightarrow C = 1,$$

$$B + D = 0 \Rightarrow D = 0$$

$$\int \dfrac{3x^3 + 4x}{(x^2+1)^2}\,dx = 3\int \dfrac{x}{x^2+1}\,dx + \int \dfrac{x}{(x^2+1)^2}\,dx$$

$$= \dfrac{3}{2}\ln(x^2+1) - \dfrac{1}{2(x^2+1)} + C$$

**54.** $\int (\sin\theta + \cos\theta)^2\,d\theta = \int (\sin^2\theta + 2\sin\theta\cos\theta + \cos^2\theta)\,d\theta$

$$= \int (1 + \sin 2\theta)\,d\theta = \theta - \dfrac{1}{2}\cos 2\theta + C = \dfrac{1}{2}(2\theta - \cos 2\theta) + C$$

**56.** $y = \int \dfrac{\sqrt{4 - x^2}}{2x} \, dx = \int \dfrac{2\cos\theta(2\cos\theta)\,d\theta}{4\sin\theta}$

$\qquad = \int (\csc\theta - \sin\theta)\,d\theta$

$\qquad = [-\ln|\csc\theta + \cos\theta| + \cos\theta] + C$

$\qquad = -\ln\left|\dfrac{2 + \sqrt{4 - x^2}}{x}\right| + \dfrac{\sqrt{4 - x^2}}{2} + C$

$x = 2\sin\theta,\ dx = 2\cos\theta\,d\theta,\ \sqrt{4 - x^2} = 2\cos\theta$

**58.** $y = \int \sqrt{1 - \cos\theta}\,d\theta = \int \dfrac{\sin\theta}{\sqrt{1 + \cos\theta}}\,d\theta = -\int (1 + \cos\theta)^{-1/2}(-\sin\theta)\,d\theta = -2\sqrt{1 + \cos\theta} + C$

$u = 1 + \cos\theta,\ du = -\sin\theta\,d\theta$

**60.** $\displaystyle\int_0^1 \dfrac{x}{(x - 2)(x - 4)}\,dx = \Big[2\ln|x - 4| - \ln|x - 2|\Big]_0^1$

$\qquad = 2\ln 3 - 2\ln 4 + \ln 2$

$\qquad = \ln\dfrac{9}{8} \approx 0.118$

**62.** $\displaystyle\int_0^2 xe^{3x}\,dx = \left[\dfrac{e^{3x}}{9}(3x - 1)\right]_0^2 = \dfrac{1}{9}(5e^6 + 1) \approx 224.238$

**64.** $\displaystyle\int_0^3 \dfrac{x}{\sqrt{1 + x}}\,dx = \left[\dfrac{-2(2 - x)}{3}\sqrt{1 + x}\right]_0^3 = \dfrac{4}{3} + \dfrac{4}{3} = \dfrac{8}{3}$

**66.** $A = \displaystyle\int_0^4 \dfrac{1}{25 - x^2}\,dx$

$\qquad = \left[-\dfrac{1}{10}\ln\left|\dfrac{x - 5}{x + 5}\right|\right]_0^4 = -\dfrac{1}{10}\ln\dfrac{1}{9} = \dfrac{1}{10}\ln 9 \approx 0.220$

**68.** By symmetry, $\bar{y} = 0$.

$\qquad A = \pi + 4\pi = 5\pi$

$\qquad \bar{x} = \dfrac{1(\pi) + 4(4\pi)}{\pi + 4\pi}$

$\qquad = \dfrac{17\pi}{5\pi} = 3.4$

$(\bar{x}, \bar{y}) = (3.4, 0)$

**70.** $s = \displaystyle\int_0^\pi \sqrt{1 + \sin^2 2x}\,dx \approx 3.82$

**72.** $\displaystyle\lim_{x \to 0} \dfrac{\sin \pi x}{\sin 2\pi x} = \lim_{x \to 0} \dfrac{\pi\cos \pi x}{2\pi\cos 2\pi x} = \dfrac{\pi}{2\pi} = \dfrac{1}{2}$

**74.** $\displaystyle\lim_{x \to \infty} xe^{-x^2} = \lim_{x \to \infty} \dfrac{x}{e^{x^2}} = \lim_{x \to \infty} \dfrac{1}{2xe^{x^2}} = 0$

**76.** $y = \displaystyle\lim_{x \to 1^+} (x - 1)^{\ln x}$

$\ln y = \displaystyle\lim_{x \to 1^+} [(\ln x)\ln(x - 1)]$

$\qquad = \displaystyle\lim_{x \to 1^+}\left[\dfrac{\ln(x - 1)}{\dfrac{1}{\ln x}}\right] = \lim_{x \to 1^+}\left[\dfrac{\dfrac{1}{x - 1}}{\left(\dfrac{1}{x}\right)\dfrac{-1}{\ln^2 x}}\right] = \lim_{x \to 1^+}\left[\dfrac{-\ln^2 x}{x - 1}\right] = \lim_{x \to 1^+}\left[\dfrac{-2\left(\dfrac{1}{x}\right)(\ln x)}{\dfrac{1}{x^2}}\right]$

$\qquad = \displaystyle\lim_{x \to 1^+} 2x(\ln x) = 0$

Since $\ln y = 0$, $y = 1$.

**78.** $\displaystyle\lim_{x \to 1^+} \left( \frac{2}{\ln x} - \frac{2}{x - 1} \right) = \lim_{x \to 1^+} \left[ \frac{2x - 2 - 2\ln x}{(\ln x)(x - 1)} \right]$

$$= \lim_{x \to 1^+} \left[ \frac{2 - (2/x)}{(x - 1)(1/x) + \ln x} \right]$$

$$= \lim_{x \to 1^+} \frac{2x - 2}{(x - 1) + x\ln x} = \lim_{x \to 1^+} \frac{2}{1 + 1 + \ln x} = 1$$

**80.** $\displaystyle\int_0^1 \frac{6}{x - 1}\, dx = \lim_{b \to 1^-} \left[ 6\ln|x - 1| \right]_0^b = -\infty$

Diverges

**82.** $\displaystyle\int_0^\infty \frac{e^{-1/x}}{x^2}\, dx = \lim_{\substack{a \to 0^+ \\ b \to \infty}} \left[ e^{-1/x} \right]_a^b = 1 - 0 = 1$

**84.** $V = \displaystyle\pi\int_0^\infty (xe^{-x})^2\, dx$

$$= \pi\int_0^\infty x^2 e^{-2x}\, dx$$

$$= \lim_{b \to \infty} \left[ -\frac{\pi e^{-2x}}{4}(2x^2 + 2x + 1) \right]_0^b = \frac{\pi}{4}$$

**86.** $\displaystyle\int_2^\infty \left[ \frac{1}{x^5} + \frac{1}{x^{10}} + \frac{1}{x^{15}} \right] dx < \int_2^\infty \frac{1}{x^5 - 1}\, dx < \int_2^\infty \left[ \frac{1}{x^5} + \frac{1}{x^{10}} + \frac{2}{x^{15}} \right] dx$

$$\lim_{b \to \infty} \left[ -\frac{1}{4x^4} - \frac{1}{9x^9} - \frac{1}{14x^{14}} \right]_2^b < \int_2^\infty \frac{1}{x^5 - 1}\, dx < \lim_{b \to \infty} \left[ -\frac{1}{4x^4} - \frac{1}{9x^9} - \frac{1}{7x^{14}} \right]_2^b$$

$$0.015846 < \int_2^\infty \frac{1}{x^5 - 1}\, dx < 0.015851$$

# Problem Solving for Chapter 7

**2.** (a) $\displaystyle\int_0^1 \ln x\, dx = \lim_{b \to 0^+} \left[ x\ln - x \right]_b^1$

$$= (-1) - \lim_{b \to 0^+} (b\ln b - b) = -1$$

**Note:** $\displaystyle\lim_{b \to 0^+} b\ln b = \lim_{b \to 0^+} \frac{\ln b}{b^{-1}} = \lim_{b \to 0^+} \frac{1/b}{-1/b^2} = 0$

$$\int_0^1 (\ln x)^2\, dx = \lim_{b \to 0^+} \left[ x(\ln x)^2 - 2x\ln x + 2x \right]_b^1$$

$$= 2 - \lim_{b \to 0^+} (b(\ln b)^2 - 2b\ln b + 2b) = 2$$

(b) Note first that $\displaystyle\lim_{b \to 0^+} b(\ln b)^n = 0$ (Mathematical induction).

Also, $\displaystyle\int (\ln x)^{n+1}\, dx = x(\ln x)^{n+1} - (n + 1)\int (\ln x)^n\, dx.$

Assume $\displaystyle\int_0^1 (\ln x)^n\, dx = (-1)^n n!.$

Then, $\displaystyle\int_0^1 (\ln x)^{n+1}\, dx = \lim_{b \to 0^+} \left[ x(\ln x)^{n+1} \right]_b^1 - (n + 1)\int_0^1 (\ln x)^n\, dx$

$$= 0 - (n + 1)(-1)^n n! = (-1)^{n+1}(n + 1)!.$$

**4.**
$$\lim_{x \to \infty} \left(\frac{x-c}{x+c}\right)^x = \frac{1}{4}$$

$$\lim_{x \to \infty} x \ln\left(\frac{x-c}{x+c}\right) = \ln\frac{1}{4}$$

$$\lim_{x \to \infty} \frac{\ln(x-c) - \ln(x+c)}{1/x} = -\ln 4$$

$$\lim_{x \to \infty} \frac{\dfrac{1}{x-c} - \dfrac{1}{x+c}}{-\dfrac{1}{x^2}} = -\ln 4$$

$$\lim_{x \to \infty} \frac{2c}{(x-c)(x+c)}(-x^2) = -\ln 4$$

$$\lim_{x \to \infty} \frac{2cx^2}{x^2 - c^2} = \ln 4$$

$$2c = \ln 4$$

$$2x = 2\ln 2$$

$$c = \ln 2$$

**6.** $\sin\theta = BD$, $\cos\theta = OD$

Area $\triangle DAB = \frac{1}{2}(DA)(BD) = \frac{1}{2}(1 - \cos\theta)\sin\theta$

Shaded area $= \dfrac{\theta}{2} - \dfrac{1}{2}(1)(BD) = \dfrac{\theta}{2} - \dfrac{1}{2}\sin\theta$

$$R = \frac{\triangle DAB}{\text{Shaded area}} = \frac{1/2(1 - \cos\theta)\sin\theta}{1/2(\theta - \sin\theta)}$$

$$\lim_{\theta \to 0^+} R = \lim_{\theta \to 0^+} \frac{(1-\cos\theta)\sin\theta}{\theta - \sin\theta} = \lim_{\theta \to 0^+} \frac{(1-\cos\theta)\cos\theta + \sin^2\theta}{1 - \cos\theta}$$

$$= \lim_{\theta \to 0^+} \frac{(1-\cos\theta)(-\sin\theta) + \cos\theta\sin\theta + 2\sin\theta\cos\theta}{\sin\theta}$$

$$= \lim_{\theta \to 0^+} \frac{-\sin\theta - 4\cos\theta\sin\theta}{\sin\theta} = \lim_{\theta \to 0} \frac{4\cos\theta - 1}{1} = 3$$

**8.** $u = \tan\dfrac{x}{2}$, $\cos x = \dfrac{1 - u^2}{1 + u^2}$, $2 + \cos x = 2 + \dfrac{1 - u^2}{1 + u^2} = \dfrac{3 + u^2}{1 + u^2}$

$$dx = \frac{2\,du}{1 + u^2}$$

$$\int_0^{\pi/2} \frac{1}{2 + \cos x}\,dx = \int_0^1 \left(\frac{1 + u^2}{3 + u^2}\right)\left(\frac{2}{1 + u^2}\right)du$$

$$= \int_0^1 \frac{2}{3 + u^2}\,du$$

$$= \left[2\frac{1}{\sqrt{3}}\arctan\left(\frac{u}{\sqrt{3}}\right)\right]_0^1$$

$$= \frac{2}{\sqrt{3}}\arctan\left(\frac{1}{\sqrt{3}}\right)$$

$$= \frac{2}{\sqrt{3}}\frac{\pi}{6} = \frac{\pi\sqrt{3}}{9} \approx 0.6046$$

**10.** Let $u = cx$, $du = c\,dx$.

$$\int_0^b e^{-c^2x^2}\,dx = \int_0^{cb} e^{-u^2}\,\frac{du}{c} = \frac{1}{c}\int_0^{cb} e^{-u^2}\,du$$

As $b \to \infty$, $cb \to \infty$. Hence, $\displaystyle\int_0^\infty e^{-c^2x^2}\,dx = \frac{1}{c}\int_0^\infty e^{-x^2}\,dx$.

$\bar{x} = 0$ by symmetry.

$$\bar{y} = \frac{M_x}{m} = \frac{2\displaystyle\int_0^\infty \frac{\left(e^{-c^2x^2}\right)}{2}\,dx}{2\displaystyle\int_0^\infty e^{-c^2x^2}\,dx}$$

$$= \frac{1}{2}\,\frac{\displaystyle\int_0^\infty e^{-2c^2x^2}\,dx}{\displaystyle\int_0^\infty e^{-c^2x^2}\,dx}$$

$$= \frac{1}{2}\,\frac{\dfrac{1}{\sqrt{2}c}\displaystyle\int_0^\infty e^{-x^2}\,dx}{\dfrac{1}{c}\displaystyle\int_0^\infty e^{-x^2}\,dx}$$

$$= \frac{1}{2\sqrt{2}} = \frac{\sqrt{2}}{4}$$

Thus, $(\bar{x}, \bar{y}) = \left(0, \dfrac{\sqrt{2}}{4}\right)$.

**12. (a)** Let $y = f^{-1}(x)$, $f(y) = x$, $dx = f'(y)\,dy$.

$$\int f^{-1}(x)\,dx = \int y f'(y)\,dy$$

$$= yf(y) - \int f(y)\,dy \qquad \begin{bmatrix} u = y,\, du = dy \\ dv = f'(y)\,dy,\, v = f(y) \end{bmatrix}$$

$$= x f^{-1}(x) - \int f(y)\,dy$$

**(b)** $f^{-1}(x) = \arcsin x = y$, $f(x) = \sin x$

$$\int \arcsin x\,dx = x\arcsin x - \int \sin y\,dy$$

$$= x\arcsin x + \cos y + C$$

$$= x\arcsin x + \sqrt{1-x^2} + C$$

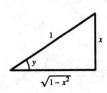

**(c)** $f(x) = e^x$, $f^{-1}(x) = \ln x = y \qquad x = 1 \iff y = 0;\, x = e \iff y = 1$

$$\int_1^e \ln x\,dx = \Big[x\ln x\Big]_1^e - \int_0^1 e^y\,dy$$

$$= e - \Big[e^y\Big]_0^1$$

$$= e - (e - 1) = 1$$

**14.** (a) Let $x = \frac{\pi}{2} - u$, $dx = du$.

$$I = \int_0^{\pi/2} \frac{\sin x}{\cos x + \sin x} dx = \int_{\pi/2}^0 \frac{\sin\left(\frac{\pi}{2} - u\right)}{\cos\left(\frac{\pi}{2} - u\right) + \sin\left(\frac{\pi}{2} - u\right)}(-du)$$

$$= \int_0^{\pi/2} \frac{\cos u}{\sin u + \cos u} du$$

Hence,

$$2I = \int_0^{\pi/2} \frac{\sin x}{\cos x + \sin x} dx + \int_0^{\pi/2} \frac{\cos x}{\sin x + \cos x} dx$$

$$= \int_0^{\pi/2} 1 \, dx = \frac{\pi}{2} \implies I = \frac{\pi}{4}.$$

(b) $$I = \int_{\pi/2}^0 \frac{\sin^n\left(\frac{\pi}{2} - u\right)}{\cos^n\left(\frac{\pi}{2} - u\right) + \sin^n\left(\frac{\pi}{2} - u\right)}(-du)$$

$$= \int_0^{\pi/2} \frac{\cos^n u}{\sin^n u + \cos^n u} du$$

Thus, $2I = \int_0^{\pi/2} 1 \, dx = \frac{\pi}{2} \implies I = \frac{\pi}{4}.$

**16.** $$\frac{N(x)}{D(x)} = \frac{P_1}{x - c_1} + \frac{P_2}{x - c_2} + \cdots + \frac{P_n}{x - c_n}$$

$$N(x) = P_1(x - c_2)(x - c_3)\ldots(x - c_n) + P_2(x - c_1)(x - c_3)\ldots(x - c_n) + \cdots + P_n(x - c_1)(x - c_2)\ldots(x - c_{n-1})$$

Let $x = c_1$: $N(c_1) = P_1(c_1 - c_2)(c_1 - c_3)\ldots(c_1 - c_n)$

$$P_1 = \frac{N(c_1)}{(c_1 - c_2)(c_1 - c_3)\ldots(c_1 - c_n)}$$

Let $x = c_2$: $N(c_2) = P_2(c_2 - c_1)(c_2 - c_3)\ldots(c_2 - c_n)$

$$P_2 = \frac{N(c_2)}{(c_2 - c_1)(c_2 - c_3)\ldots(c_2 - c_n)}$$

$\vdots$

Let $x = c_n$: $N(c_n) = P_n(c_n - c_1)(c_n - c_2)\ldots(c_n - c_{n-1})$

$$P_n = \frac{N(c_n)}{(c_n - c_1)(c_n - c_2)\ldots(c_n - c_{n-1})}$$

If $D(x) = (x - c_1)(x - c_2)(x - c_3)\ldots(x - c_n)$, then by the Product Rule

$$D'(x) = (x - c_2)(x - c_3)\ldots(x - c_n) + (x - c_1)(x - c_3)\ldots(x - c_n) + \cdots + (x - c_1)(x - c_2)(x - c_3)\ldots(x - c_{n-1})$$

and

$$D'(c_1) = (c_1 - c_2)(c_1 - c_3)\ldots(c_1 - c_n)$$
$$D'(c_2) = (c_2 - c_1)(c_2 - c_3)\ldots(c_2 - c_n)$$
$\vdots$
$$D'(c_n) = (c_n - c_1)(c_n - c_2)\ldots(c_n - c_{n-1}).$$

Thus, $P_k = N(c_k)/D'(c_k)$ for $k = 1, 2, \ldots, n$.

**18.**    $s(t) = \int \left[ -32t + 12{,}000 \ln \dfrac{50{,}000}{50{,}000 - 400t} \right] dt$

$= -16t^2 + 12{,}000 \int \left[ \ln 50{,}000 - \ln(50{,}000 - 400t) \right] dt$

$= 16t^2 + 12{,}000t \ln 50{,}000 - 12{,}000 \left[ t \ln(50{,}000 - 400t) - \int \dfrac{-400t}{50{,}000 - 400t} \, dt \right]$

$= -16t^2 + 12{,}000t \ln \dfrac{50{,}000}{50{,}000 - 400t} + 12{,}000t \int \left[ 1 - \dfrac{50{,}000}{50{,}000 - 400t} \right] dt$

$= -16t^2 + 12{,}000t \ln \dfrac{50{,}000}{50{,}000 - 400t} + 12{,}000t + 1{,}500{,}000 \ln(50{,}000 - 400t) + C$

$s(0) = 1{,}500{,}000 \ln 50{,}000 + C = 0$

$C = -1{,}500{,}000 \ln 50{,}000$

$s(t) = -16t^2 + 12{,}000t \left[ 1 + \ln \dfrac{50{,}000}{50{,}000 - 400t} \right] + 1{,}500{,}000 \ln \dfrac{50{,}000 - 400t}{50{,}000}$

When $t = 100$, $s(100) \approx 557{,}168.626$ feet

**20.** Let $u = (x - a)(x - b)$, $du = [(x - a) + (x - b)] \, dx$, $dv = f''(x) \, dx$, $v = f'(x)$.

$\displaystyle \int_a^b (x - a)(x - b) \, dx = \left[ (x - a)(x - b)f'(x) \right]_a^b - \int_a^b [(x - a) + (x - b)]f'(x) \, dx$

$\displaystyle = -\int_a^b (2x - a - b)f'(x) \, dx \qquad \left( \begin{matrix} u = 2x - a - b \\ dv = f'(x) \, dx \end{matrix} \right)$

$\displaystyle = \left[ -(2x - a - b)f(x) \right]_a^b + \int_a^b 2f(x) \, dx$

$\displaystyle = 2 \int_a^b f(x) \, dx$

# CHAPTER 8
## Infinite Series

---

# CHAPTER 8
## Infinite Series

### Section 8.1    Sequences

Solutions to Even-Numbered Exercises

**2.** $a_n = \dfrac{2n}{n+3}$

$a_1 = \dfrac{2}{4} = \dfrac{1}{2}$

$a_2 = \dfrac{4}{5}$

$a_3 = \dfrac{6}{6} = 1$

$a_4 = \dfrac{8}{7}$

$a_5 = \dfrac{10}{8} = \dfrac{5}{4}$

**4.** $a_n = \left(-\dfrac{2}{3}\right)^n$

$a_1 = -\dfrac{2}{3}$

$a_2 = \dfrac{4}{9}$

$a_3 = -\dfrac{8}{27}$

$a_4 = \dfrac{16}{81}$

$a_5 = -\dfrac{32}{243}$

**6.** $a_n = \cos\dfrac{n\pi}{2}$

$a_1 = \cos\dfrac{\pi}{2} = 0$

$a_2 = \cos\pi = -1$

$a_3 = \cos\dfrac{3\pi}{2} = 0$

$a_4 = \cos 2\pi = 1$

$a_5 = \cos\dfrac{5\pi}{2} = 0$

**8.** $a_n = (-1)^{n+1}\left(\dfrac{2}{n}\right)$

$a_1 = \dfrac{2}{1} = 2$

$a_2 = -\dfrac{2}{2} = -1$

$a_3 = \dfrac{2}{3}$

$a_4 = -\dfrac{2}{4} = -\dfrac{1}{2}$

$a_5 = \dfrac{2}{5}$

**10.** $a_n = 10 + \dfrac{2}{n} + \dfrac{6}{n^2}$

$a_1 = 10 + 2 + 6 = 18$

$a_2 = 10 + 1 + \dfrac{3}{2} = \dfrac{25}{2}$

$a_3 = 10 + \dfrac{2}{3} + \dfrac{2}{3} = \dfrac{34}{3}$

$a_4 = 10 + \dfrac{1}{2} + \dfrac{3}{8} = \dfrac{87}{8}$

$a_5 = 10 + \dfrac{2}{5} + \dfrac{6}{25} = \dfrac{266}{25}$

**12.** $a_n = \dfrac{3n!}{(n-1)!} = 3n$

$a_1 = 3(1) = 3$

$a_2 = 3(2) = 6$

$a_3 = 3(3) = 9$

$a_4 = 3(4) = 12$

$a_5 = 3(5) = 15$

**14.** $a_1 = 4,\ a_{k+1} = \left(\dfrac{k+1}{2}\right)a_k$

$a_2 = \left(\dfrac{1+1}{2}\right)a_1 = 4$

$a_3 = \left(\dfrac{2+1}{2}\right)a_2 = 6$

$a_4 = \left(\dfrac{3+1}{2}\right)a_3 = 12$

$a_5 = \left(\dfrac{4+1}{2}\right)a_4 = 30$

**16.** $a_1 = 6,\ a_{k+1} = \dfrac{1}{3}a_k^{\,2}$

$a_2 = \dfrac{1}{3}a_1^{\,2} = \dfrac{1}{3}(6^2) = 12$

$a_3 = \dfrac{1}{3}a_2^{\,2} = \dfrac{1}{3}(12^2) = 48$

$a_4 = \dfrac{1}{3}a_3^{\,2} = \dfrac{1}{3}(48^2) = 768$

$a_5 = \dfrac{1}{3}a_4^{\,2} = \dfrac{1}{3}(768)^2 = 196{,}608$

**18.** Because the sequence tends to 8 as $n$ tends to infinity, it matches (a).

**20.** This sequence increases for a few terms, then decreases $a_2 = \frac{16}{2} = 8$. Matches (b).

**22.**

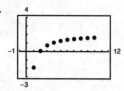

$$a_n = 2 - \frac{4}{n}, n = 1, \ldots, 10$$

**24.**

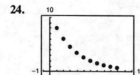

$$a_n = 8(0.75)^{n-1}, n = 1, 2, \ldots, 10$$

**26.**

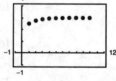

$$a_n = \frac{3n^2}{n^2 + 1}, n = 1, \ldots, 10$$

**28.** $a_n = \dfrac{n + 6}{2}$

$a_5 = \dfrac{5 + 6}{2} = \dfrac{11}{2}$

$a_6 = \dfrac{6 + 6}{2} = 6$

**30.** $a_{n+1} = 2a_n, \ a_1 = 5$

$a_5 = 2(40) = 80$

$a_6 = 2(80) = 160$

**32.** $\dfrac{25!}{23!} = \dfrac{23!(24)(25)}{23!}$

$= (24)(25) = 600$

**34.** $\dfrac{(n + 2)!}{n!} = \dfrac{n!(n + 1)(n + 2)}{n!}$

$= (n + 1)(n + 2)$

**36.** $\dfrac{(2n + 2)!}{(2n)!} = \dfrac{(2n)!(2n + 1)(2n + 2)}{(2n)!}$

$= (2n + 1)(2n + 2)$

**38.** $\displaystyle\lim_{n \to \infty} \left(5 - \frac{1}{n^2}\right) = 5 - 0 = 5$

**40.** $\displaystyle\lim_{n \to \infty} \frac{5n}{\sqrt{n^2 + 4}} = \lim_{n \to \infty} \frac{5}{\sqrt{1 + (4/n^2)}}$

$= \dfrac{5}{1} = 5$

**42.** $\displaystyle\lim_{n \to \infty} \cos\left(\frac{2}{n}\right) = 1$

**44.**

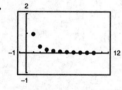

The graph seems to indicate that the sequence converges to 0. Analytically,

$$\lim_{n \to \infty} a_n = \lim_{n \to \infty} \frac{1}{n^{3/2}} = \lim_{x \to \infty} \frac{1}{x^{3/2}} = 0.$$

**46.**

The graph seems to indicate that the sequence converges to 3. Analytically,

$$\lim_{n \to \infty} a_n = \lim_{n \to \infty} \left(3 - \frac{1}{2^n}\right) = 3 - 0 = 3.$$

**48.** $\displaystyle\lim_{n \to \infty} \left[1 + (-1)^n\right]$

does not exist, (alternates between 0 and 2), diverges.

**50.** $\displaystyle\lim_{n \to \infty} \frac{\sqrt[3]{n}}{\sqrt[3]{n + 1}} = 1$, converges

**52.** $\displaystyle\lim_{n \to \infty} \frac{1 + (-1)^n}{n^2} = 0$, converges

**54.** $\displaystyle\lim_{n \to \infty} \frac{\ln \sqrt{n}}{n} = \lim_{n \to \infty} \frac{1/2 \ln n}{n}$

$= \displaystyle\lim_{n \to \infty} \frac{1}{2n} = 0$, converges

(L'Hôpital's Rule)

**56.** $\displaystyle\lim_{n \to \infty} (0.5)^n = 0$, converges

**58.** $\displaystyle\lim_{n \to \infty} \frac{(n - 2)!}{n!} = \lim_{n \to \infty} \frac{1}{n(n - 1)} = 0$, converges

**60.** $\lim\limits_{n\to\infty}\left(\dfrac{n^2}{2n+1}-\dfrac{n^2}{2n-1}\right)=\lim\limits_{n\to\infty}\dfrac{-2n^2}{4n^2-1}=-\dfrac{1}{2}$, converges

**62.** $a_n=n\sin\dfrac{1}{n}$

Let $f(x)=x\sin\dfrac{1}{x}$.

$$\lim_{x\to\infty}x\sin\frac{1}{x}=\lim_{x\to\infty}\frac{\sin(1/x)}{1/x}=\lim_{x\to\infty}\frac{(-1/x^2)\cos(1/x)}{-1/x^2}=\lim_{x\to\infty}\cos\frac{1}{x}=\cos 0=1\ \text{(L'Hôpital's Rule)}$$

or,

$$\lim_{x\to\infty}\frac{\sin(1/x)}{1/x}=\lim_{y\to 0^+}\frac{\sin(y)}{y}=1.\ \text{Therefore }\lim_{n\to\infty}n\sin\frac{1}{n}=1.$$

**64.** $\lim\limits_{n\to\infty}2^{1/n}=2^0=1$, converges    **66.** $\lim\limits_{n\to\infty}\dfrac{\cos\pi n}{n^2}=0$, converges    **68.** $a_n=4n-1$

**70.** $a_n=\dfrac{(-1)^{n-1}}{n^2}$    **72.** $a_n=\dfrac{n+2}{3n-1}$    **74.** $a_n=(-1)^n\dfrac{3^{n-2}}{2^{n-1}}$

**76.** $a_n=1+\dfrac{2^n-1}{2^n}$    **78.** $a_n=\dfrac{1}{n!}$    **80.** $a_n=\dfrac{x^{n-1}}{(n-1)!}$

$\quad\ \ =\dfrac{2^{n+1}-1}{2^n}$

**82.** Let $f(x)=\dfrac{3x}{x+2}$. Then $f'(x)=\dfrac{6}{(x+2)^2}$.

Thus, $f$ is increasing which implies $\{a_n\}$ is increasing.

$|a_n|<3$, bounded

**84.** $a_n=ne^{-n/2}$

$a_1=0.6065$

$a_2=0.7358$

$a_3=0.6694$

Not monotonic; $|a_n|\le 0.7358$, bounded

**86.** $a_n=\left(-\dfrac{2}{3}\right)^n$

$a_1=-\dfrac{2}{3}$

$a_2=\dfrac{4}{9}$

$a_3=-\dfrac{8}{27}$

Not monotonic; $|a_n|\le\dfrac{2}{3}$, bounded

**88.** $a_n=\left(\dfrac{3}{2}\right)^n<\left(\dfrac{3}{2}\right)^{n+1}=a_{n+1}$

Monotonic; $\lim\limits_{n\to\infty}a_n=\infty$, not bounded

**90.** $a_n=\dfrac{\cos n}{n}$

$a_1=0.5403$

$a_2=-0.2081$

$a_3=-0.3230$

$a_4=-0.1634$

Not monotonic; $|a_n|\le 1$, bounded

**92.** (a) $a_n = 4 - \dfrac{3}{n}$

$\left| 4 - \dfrac{3}{n} \right| < 4 \implies$ bounded

$a_n = 4 - \dfrac{3}{n} < 3 - \dfrac{4}{n+1} = a_{n+1} \implies$ monotonic

Therefore, $\{a_n\}$ converges.

(b)

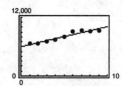

$\lim\limits_{n \to \infty} \left( 4 - \dfrac{3}{n} \right) = 4$

**94.** (a) $a_n = 4 + \dfrac{1}{2^n}$

$\left| 4 + \dfrac{1}{2^n} \right| \le 4.5 \implies \{a_n\}$ bounded

$a_n = 4 + \dfrac{1}{2^n} > 4 + \dfrac{1}{2^{n+1}}$

$= a_{n+1} \implies \{a_n\}$ monotonic

Therefore, $\{a_n\}$ converges.

(b)

$\lim\limits_{n \to \infty} \left( 4 + \dfrac{1}{2^n} \right) = 4$

**96.** $A_n = 100(101)[(1.01)^n - 1]$

(a) $A_1 = \$101.00$        (b) $A_{60} = \$8248.64$

$A_2 = \$203.01$        (c) $A_{240} = \$99,914.79$

$A_3 = \$306.04$

$A_4 = \$410.10$

$A_5 = \$515.20$

$A_6 = \$621.35$

**98.** The first sequence because every other point is below the $x$-axis.

**100.** Impossible. The sequence converges by Theorem 8.5.

**102.** Impossible. An unbounded sequence diverges.

**104.** $P_n = 16,000(1.045)^n$

$P_1 = \$16,720.00$

$P_2 = \$17,472.40$

$P_3 \approx \$18,258.66$

$P_4 \approx \$19,080.30$

$P_5 \approx \$19,938.91$

**106.** (a) $a_n = 410.9212n + 6003.8545$

(b) For 2004, $n = 14$ and $a_n = 11,757$, or $\$11,757,000,000.$

**108.** $a_n = \left( 1 + \dfrac{1}{n} \right)^n$

$a_1 = 2.0000$

$a_2 = 2.2500$

$a_3 \approx 2.3704$

$a_4 \approx 2.4414$

$a_5 \approx 2.4883$

$a_6 \approx 2.5216$

$\lim\limits_{n \to \infty} \left( 1 + \dfrac{1}{n} \right)^n = e$

**110.** Since

$\lim\limits_{n \to \infty} s_n = L > 0,$

there exists for each $\epsilon > 0$, an integer $N$ such that $|s_n - L| < \epsilon$ for every $n > N$. Let $\epsilon = L > 0$ and we have,

$|s_n - L| < L, \ -L < s_n - L < L,$ or $0 < s_n < 2L$

for each $n > N$.

**112.** If $\{a_n\}$ is bounded, monotonic and nonincreasing, then $a_1 \geq a_2 \geq a_3 \geq \cdots \geq a_n \geq \cdots$. Then

$$-a_1 \leq -a_2 \leq -a_3 \leq \cdots \leq -a_n \leq \cdots$$

is a bounded, monotonic, nondecreasing sequence which converges by the first half of the theorem. Since $\{-a_n\}$ converges, then so does $\{a_n\}$.

**114.** True

**116.** True

**118.** $x_0 = 1, x_n = \frac{1}{2}x_{n-1} + \frac{1}{x_{n-1}}, n = 1, 2, \ldots$

$x_1 = 1.5$      $x_6 = 1.414214$

$x_2 = 1.41667$      $x_7 = 1.414214$

$x_3 = 1.414216$      $x_8 = 1.414114$

$x_4 = 1.414214$      $x_9 = 1.414214$

$x_5 = 1.414214$      $x_{10} = 1.414214$

The limit of the sequence appears to be $\sqrt{2}$. In fact, this sequence is Newton's Method applied to $f(x) = x^2 - 2$.

# Section 8.2     Series and Convergence

**2.** $S_1 = \frac{1}{6} \approx 0.1667$

$S_2 = \frac{1}{6} + \frac{1}{6} \approx 0.3333$

$S_3 = \frac{1}{6} + \frac{1}{6} + \frac{3}{20} \approx 0.4833$

$S_4 = \frac{1}{6} + \frac{1}{6} + \frac{3}{20} + \frac{2}{15} \approx 0.6167$

$S_5 = \frac{1}{6} + \frac{1}{6} + \frac{3}{20} + \frac{2}{15} + \frac{5}{42} \approx 0.7357$

**4.** $S_1 = 1$

$S_2 = 1 + \frac{1}{3} \approx 1.3333$

$S_3 = 1 + \frac{1}{3} + \frac{1}{5} \approx 1.5333$

$S_4 = 1 + \frac{1}{3} + \frac{1}{5} + \frac{1}{9} \approx 1.6444$

$S_5 = 1 + \frac{1}{3} + \frac{1}{5} + \frac{1}{9} + \frac{1}{11} \approx 1.7354$

**6.** $S_1 = 1$

$S_2 = 1 - \frac{1}{2} = 0.5$

$S_3 = 1 - \frac{1}{2} + \frac{1}{6} \approx 0.6667$

$S_4 = 1 - \frac{1}{2} + \frac{1}{6} - \frac{1}{24} \approx 0.6250$

$S_5 = 1 - \frac{1}{2} + \frac{1}{6} - \frac{1}{24} + \frac{1}{120} \approx 0.6333$

**8.** $\sum_{n=0}^{\infty} \left(\frac{4}{3}\right)^n$    Geometric series

$r = \frac{4}{3} > 1$

Diverges by Theorem 8.6

**10.** $\sum_{n=0}^{\infty} 2(-1.03)^n$    Geometric series

$|r| = 1.03 > 1$

Diverges by Theorem 8.6

**12.** $\sum_{n=1}^{\infty} \frac{n}{2n + 3}$

$\lim_{n\to\infty} \frac{n}{2n + 3} = \frac{1}{2} \neq 0$

Diverges by Theorem 8.9

**14.** $\sum_{n=1}^{\infty} \frac{n}{\sqrt{n^2 + 1}}$

$\lim_{n\to\infty} \frac{n}{\sqrt{n^2 + 1}} = \lim_{n\to\infty} \frac{1}{\sqrt{1 + (1/n^2)}} = 1 \neq 0$

Diverges by Theorem 8.9

**16.** $\sum_{n=1}^{\infty} \frac{n!}{2^n}$

$\lim_{n\to\infty} \frac{n!}{2^n} = \infty$

Diverges by Theorem 8.9

**18.** $\displaystyle\sum_{n=0}^{\infty}\left(\frac{2}{3}\right)^{n} = 1 + \frac{2}{3} + \frac{4}{9} + \cdots$

$S_0 = 1, S_1 = \dfrac{5}{3}, S_2 \approx 2.11, \ldots$

Matches graph (b).

Analytically, the series is geometric:

$$\sum_{n=0}^{\infty}\left(\frac{2}{3}\right)^{n} = \frac{1}{1 - 2/3} = \frac{1}{1/3} = 3$$

**20.** $\displaystyle\sum_{n=0}^{\infty}\frac{17}{3}\left(-\frac{8}{9}\right)^{n} = \frac{17}{3}\left[1 - \frac{8}{9} + \frac{64}{81} - \cdots\right]$

$S_0 = \dfrac{17}{3}, S_1 \approx 0.63, S_3 \approx 5.1, \ldots$

Matches (d).

Analytically, the series is geometric:

$$\sum_{n=0}^{\infty}\frac{17}{3}\left(-\frac{8}{9}\right)^{n} = \frac{17/3}{1 - (-8/9)} = \frac{17/3}{17/9} = 3$$

**22.** $\displaystyle\sum_{n=1}^{\infty}\frac{1}{n(n+2)} = \sum_{n=1}^{\infty}\left(\frac{1}{2n} - \frac{1}{2(n+2)}\right) = \left(\frac{1}{2} - \frac{1}{6}\right) + \left(\frac{1}{4} - \frac{1}{8}\right) + \left(\frac{1}{6} - \frac{1}{10}\right) + \left(\frac{1}{8} - \frac{1}{12}\right) + \left(\frac{1}{10} - \frac{1}{14}\right) + \cdots$

$\displaystyle\sum_{n=1}^{\infty}\frac{1}{n(n+2)} = \lim_{n\to\infty} S_n = \lim_{n\to\infty}\left[\frac{1}{2} + \frac{1}{4} - \frac{1}{2(n+1)} - \frac{1}{2(n+2)}\right] = \frac{1}{2} + \frac{1}{4} = \frac{3}{4}$

**24.** $\displaystyle\sum_{n=0}^{\infty} 2\left(-\frac{1}{2}\right)^{n}$

Geometric series with $|r| = \left|-\frac{1}{2}\right| < 1.$

Converges by Theorem 8.6

**26.** $\displaystyle\sum_{n=0}^{\infty}(-0.6)^{n}$

Geometric series with $|r| = |-0.6| < 1.$

Converges by Theorem 8.6

**28.** (a) $\displaystyle\sum_{n=1}^{\infty}\frac{4}{n(n+4)} = \sum_{n=1}^{\infty}\left(\frac{1}{n} - \frac{1}{n+4}\right)$

$= \left(1 - \frac{1}{5}\right) + \left(\frac{1}{2} - \frac{1}{6}\right) + \left(\frac{1}{3} - \frac{1}{7}\right) + \left(\frac{1}{4} - \frac{1}{8}\right) + \left(\frac{1}{5} - \frac{1}{9}\right) + \left(\frac{1}{6} - \frac{1}{10}\right) + \cdots$

$= 1 + \frac{1}{2} + \frac{1}{3} + \frac{1}{4} = \frac{25}{12} \approx 2.0833$

(b)

| $n$ | 5 | 10 | 20 | 50 | 100 |
|---|---|---|---|---|---|
| $S_n$ | 1.5377 | 1.7607 | 1.9051 | 2.0071 | 2.0443 |

(c)

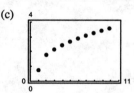

(d) The terms of the series decrease in magnitude slowly. Thus, the sequence of partial sums approaches the sum slowly.

**30.** (a) $\displaystyle\sum_{n=1}^{\infty} 3(0.85)^{n-1} = \frac{3}{1 - 0.85} = 20$  (Geometric series)

(b)

| $n$ | 5 | 10 | 20 | 50 | 100 |
|---|---|---|---|---|---|
| $S_n$ | 11.1259 | 16.0625 | 19.2248 | 19.9941 | 19.999998 |

(c)

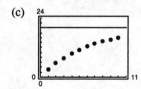

**32.** (a) $\displaystyle\sum_{n=1}^{\infty} 5\left(-\frac{1}{3}\right)^{n-1} = \frac{5}{1-(-1/3)} = \frac{15}{4} = 3.75$

(c)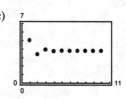

(b)

| $n$ | 5 | 10 | 20 | 50 | 100 |
|---|---|---|---|---|---|
| $S_n$ | 3.7654 | 3.7499 | 3.7500 | 3.7500 | 3.7500 |

(d) The terms of the series decrease in magnitude rapidly. Thus, the sequence of partial sums approaches the sum rapidly.

**34.** $\displaystyle\sum_{n=1}^{\infty} \frac{4}{n(n+2)} = 2\sum_{n=1}^{\infty}\left(\frac{1}{n} - \frac{1}{n+2}\right) = 2\left[\left(1 - \frac{1}{3}\right) + \left(\frac{1}{2} - \frac{1}{4}\right) + \left(\frac{1}{3} - \frac{1}{5}\right) + \cdots\right] = 2\left(1 + \frac{1}{2}\right) = 3$

**36.** $\displaystyle\sum_{n=1}^{\infty} \frac{1}{(2n+1)(2n+3)} = \frac{1}{2}\sum_{n=1}^{\infty}\left(\frac{1}{2n+1} - \frac{1}{2n+3}\right) = \frac{1}{2}\left[\left(\frac{1}{3} - \frac{1}{5}\right) + \left(\frac{1}{5} - \frac{1}{7}\right) + \left(\frac{1}{7} - \frac{1}{9}\right) + \cdots\right] = \frac{1}{2}\left(\frac{1}{3}\right) = \frac{1}{6}$

**38.** $\displaystyle\sum_{n=0}^{\infty} 6\left(\frac{4}{5}\right)^n = \frac{6}{1-(4/5)} = 30$   (Geometric)

**40.** $\displaystyle\sum_{n=0}^{\infty} 2\left(-\frac{2}{3}\right)^n = \frac{2}{1-(-2/3)} = \frac{6}{5}$

**42.** $\displaystyle\sum_{n=0}^{\infty} 8\left(\frac{3}{4}\right)^n = \frac{8}{1-(3/4)} = 32$

**44.** $\displaystyle\sum_{n=0}^{\infty} 4\left(-\frac{1}{2}\right)^n = \frac{4}{1-(-1/2)} = \frac{8}{3}$

**46.** $\displaystyle\sum_{n=1}^{\infty} [(0.7)^n + (0.9)^n] = \sum_{n=0}^{\infty}\left(\frac{7}{10}\right)^n + \sum_{n=0}^{\infty}\left(\frac{9}{10}\right)^n - 2 = \frac{1}{1-(7/10)} + \frac{1}{1-(9/10)} - 2 = \frac{10}{3} + 10 - 2 = \frac{34}{3}$

**48.** $0.81\overline{81} = \displaystyle\sum_{n=0}^{\infty} \frac{81}{100}\left(\frac{1}{100}\right)^n$

Geometric series with $a = \frac{81}{100}$ and $r = \frac{1}{100}$

$S = \dfrac{a}{1-r} = \dfrac{81/100}{1-(1/100)} = \dfrac{81}{99} = \dfrac{9}{11}$

**50.** $0.215\overline{15} = \dfrac{1}{5} + \displaystyle\sum_{n=0}^{\infty} \frac{3}{200}\left(\frac{1}{100}\right)^n$

Geometric series with $a = \frac{3}{200}$ and $r = \frac{1}{100}$

$S = \dfrac{1}{5} + \dfrac{a}{1-r} = \dfrac{1}{5} + \dfrac{3/200}{99/100} = \dfrac{71}{330}$

**52.** $\displaystyle\sum_{n=1}^{\infty} \frac{n+1}{2n-1}$

$\displaystyle\lim_{n\to\infty} \frac{n+1}{2n-1} = \frac{1}{2} \neq 0$

Diverges by Theorem 8.9

**54.** $\displaystyle\sum_{n=1}^{\infty} \frac{1}{n(n+3)} = \frac{1}{3}\sum_{n=1}^{\infty}\left(\frac{1}{n} - \frac{1}{n+3}\right)$

$\qquad = \frac{1}{3}\left[\left(1 - \frac{1}{4}\right) + \left(\frac{1}{2} - \frac{1}{5}\right) + \left(\frac{1}{3} - \frac{1}{6}\right) + \left(\frac{1}{4} - \frac{1}{7}\right) + \left(\frac{1}{5} - \frac{1}{8}\right) + \left(\frac{1}{6} - \frac{1}{9}\right) + \cdots\right]$

$\qquad = \frac{1}{3}\left(1 + \frac{1}{2} + \frac{1}{3}\right) = \frac{11}{18}, \text{ converges}$

**56.** $\displaystyle\sum_{n=1}^{\infty} \frac{3^n}{n^3}$

$\displaystyle\lim_{n\to\infty} \frac{3^n}{n^3} = \lim_{n\to\infty} \frac{(\ln 2)3^n}{3n^2} = \lim_{n\to\infty} \frac{(\ln 2)^2 3^n}{6n} = \lim_{n\to\infty} \frac{(\ln n)^3 3^n}{6} = \infty$

(by L'Hôpital's Rule) Diverges by Theorem 8.9

**58.** $\displaystyle\sum_{n=0}^{\infty} \frac{1}{4^n}$

Geometric series with $r = \frac{1}{4}$

Converges by Theorem 8.6

**60.** $\displaystyle\sum_{n=1}^{\infty} \frac{2^n}{100}$

Geometric series with $r = 2$

Diverges by Theorem 8.6

**62.** $\displaystyle\sum_{n=1}^{\infty} \left(1 + \frac{k}{n}\right)^n$

$$\lim_{n\to\infty} \left(1 + \frac{k}{n}\right)^n = e^k \neq 0$$

Diverges by Theorem 8.9

**64.** $\displaystyle\lim_{n\to\infty} a_n = 5$ means that the limit of the sequence $\{a_n\}$ is 5.

$\displaystyle\sum_{n=1}^{\infty} a_n = a_1 + a_2 + \cdots = 5$ means that the limit of the partial sums is 5.

**66.** If $\displaystyle\lim_{n\to\infty} a_n \neq 0$, then $\displaystyle\sum_{n=1}^{\infty} a_n$ diverges.

**68.** (a) $(-x/2)$ is the common ratio.

(c) $y_1 = \dfrac{2}{2 + x}$

$y_2 = 1 - \dfrac{x}{2}$

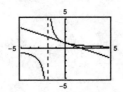

(b) $1 - \dfrac{x}{2} + \dfrac{x^2}{4} - \dfrac{x^3}{8} = \displaystyle\sum_{n=0}^{\infty} \left(-\dfrac{x}{2}\right)^n = \dfrac{1}{1 - (-x/2)}$

$$= \frac{2}{2 + x}, \ |x| < 2$$

Geometric series:

$$a = 1, r = -\frac{x}{2}, \left|-\frac{x}{2}\right| < 1 \implies |x| < 2$$

**70.** $f(x) = 2\left[\dfrac{1 - 0.8^x}{1 - 0.8}\right]$

Horizontal asymptote: $y = 10$

$\displaystyle\sum_{n=0}^{\infty} 2\left(\frac{4}{5}\right)^n$

$S = \dfrac{2}{1 - (4/5)} = 10$

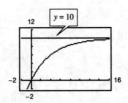

The horizontal asymptote is the sum of the series. $f(n)$ is the $n$th partial sum.

**72.**    $\dfrac{1}{2^n} < 0.0001$

$10,000 < 2^n$

This inequality is true when $n = 14$.

$(0.01)^n < 0.0001$

$10,000 < 10^n$

This inequality is true when $n = 5$. This series converges at a faster rate.

**74.** $V(t) = 225,000(1 - 0.3)^n = (0.7)^n(225,000)$

$V(5) = (0.7)^5(225,000) = \$37,815.75$

**76.** $\displaystyle\sum_{i=0}^{n-1} 100(0.60)^i = \dfrac{100[1 - 0.6^n]}{1 - 0.6}$

$$= 250(1 - 0.6^n) \quad \text{million dollars}$$

Sum = 250 million dollars

**78.** The ball in Exercise 77 takes the following times for each fall.

$s_1 = -16t^2 + 16$      $s_1 = 0$ if $t = 1$

$s_2 = -16t^2 + 16(0.81)$      $s_2 = 0$ if $t = 0.9$

$s_3 = -16t^2 + 16(0.81)^2$      $s_3 = 0$ if $t = (0.9)^2$

$\vdots$                    $\vdots$

$s_n = -16t^2 + 16(0.81)^{n-1}$      $s_n = 0$ if $t = (0.9)^{n-1}$

Beginning with $s_2$, the ball takes the same amount of time to bounce up as it takes to fall. The total elapsed time before the ball comes to rest is

$$t = 1 + 2\sum_{n=1}^{\infty} (0.9)^n = -1 + 2\sum_{n=0}^{\infty} (0.9)^n$$

$$= -1 + \frac{2}{1 - 0.9} = 19 \text{ seconds.}$$

**80.** $P(n) = \dfrac{1}{3}\left(\dfrac{2}{3}\right)^n$

$P(2) = \dfrac{1}{3}\left(\dfrac{2}{3}\right)^2 = \dfrac{4}{27}$

$\displaystyle\sum_{n=0}^{\infty} \frac{1}{3}\left(\frac{2}{3}\right)^n = \frac{1/3}{1 - (2/3)} = 1$

**82.** (a) $64 + 32 + 16 + 8 + 4 + 2 = 126$ in.$^2$

(b) $\displaystyle\sum_{n=0}^{\infty} 64\left(\frac{1}{2}\right)^n = \frac{64}{1 - (1/2)} = 128$ in.$^2$

**Note**: This is one-half of the area of the original square!

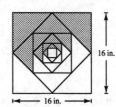

16 in.

16 in.

**84.** Surface area $= 4\pi(1)^2 + 9\left(4\pi\left(\frac{1}{3}\right)^2\right) + 9^2 \cdot 4\pi\left(\frac{1}{9}\right)^2 + \cdots = 4[\pi + \pi + \cdots] = \infty$

**86.** $\displaystyle\sum_{n=0}^{12t-1} P\left(1 + \frac{r}{12}\right)^n = \frac{P\left[1 - \left(1 + \dfrac{r}{12}\right)^{12t}\right]}{1 - \left(1 + \dfrac{r}{12}\right)}$

$= P\left(-\frac{12}{r}\right)\left[\left(1 - \left(1 + \frac{r}{12}\right)^{12t}\right)\right]$

$= P\left(\frac{12}{r}\right)\left[\left(1 + \frac{r}{12}\right)^{12t} - 1\right]$

$\displaystyle\sum_{n=0}^{12t-1} P(e^{r/12})^n = \frac{P(1 - (e^{r/12})^{12t})}{1 - e^{r/12}} = \frac{P(e^{rt} - 1)}{e^{r/12} - 1}$

**88.** $P = 75, r = 0.05, t = 25$

(a) $A = 75\left(\dfrac{12}{0.05}\right)\left[\left(1 + \dfrac{0.05}{12}\right)^{12(25)} - 1\right] \approx \$44{,}663.23$

(b) $A = \dfrac{75(e^{0.05(25)} - 1)}{e^{0.05/12} - 1} \approx \$44{,}732.85$

**90.** $P = 20, r = 0.06, t = 50$

(a) $A = 20\left(\dfrac{12}{0.06}\right)\left[\left(1 + \dfrac{0.06}{12}\right)^{12(50)} - 1\right] \approx \$75{,}743.82$

(b) $A = \dfrac{20(e^{0.06(50)} - 1)}{e^{0.06/12} - 1} \approx \$76{,}151.45$

**92.** $T = 40{,}000 + 40{,}000(1.04) + \cdots + 40{,}000(1.04)^{39}$

$= \displaystyle\sum_{n=0}^{39} 40{,}000(1.04)^n$

$= 40{,}000\left(\dfrac{1 - 1.04^{40}}{1 - 1.04}\right)$

$\approx \$3{,}801{,}020$

**94.** $x = 0.a_1a_2a_3 \ldots a_k\overline{a_1a_2a_3 \ldots a_k}$

$= 0.a_1a_2a_3 \ldots a_k\left[1 + \frac{1}{10^k} + \left(\frac{1}{10^k}\right)^2 + \left(\frac{1}{10^k}\right)^3 + \cdots\right]$

$= 0.a_1a_2a_3 \ldots a_k \displaystyle\sum_{n=0}^{\infty}\left(\frac{1}{10^k}\right)^n$

$= 0.a_1a_2a_3 \ldots a_k\left[\frac{1}{1 - (1/10^k)}\right] = $ a rational number

**96.** Let $\{S_n\}$ be the sequence of partial sums for the convergent series $\displaystyle\sum_{n=1}^{\infty} a_n = L$. Then

$\displaystyle\lim_{n \to \infty} S_n = L$ and since $R_n = \displaystyle\sum_{k=n+1}^{\infty} a_k = L - S_n$,

we have

$\displaystyle\lim_{n \to \infty} R_n = \lim_{n \to \infty}(L - S_n) = \lim_{n \to \infty} L - \lim_{n \to \infty} S_n = L - L = 0.$

**98.** If $\Sigma (a_n + b_n)$ converged, then $\Sigma (a_n + b_n) - \Sigma a_n = \Sigma b_n$ would converge, which is a contradiction.

Thus, $\Sigma (a_n + b_n)$ diverges.

**100.** True

**102.** True; $\lim\limits_{n\to\infty} \dfrac{n}{1000(n+1)} = \dfrac{1}{1000} \neq 0$

**104.** $\dfrac{1}{r} + \dfrac{1}{r^2} + \dfrac{1}{r^3} + \cdots = \sum\limits_{n=0}^{\infty} \dfrac{1}{r}\left(\dfrac{1}{r}\right)^n = \dfrac{1/r}{1-(1/r)} = \dfrac{1}{r-1}$ $\left(\text{since } \left|\dfrac{1}{r}\right| < 1\right)$

This is a geometric series which converges if $\left|\dfrac{1}{r}\right| < 1 \Leftrightarrow |r| > 1$.

# Section 8.3    The Integral Test and $p$-Series

**2.** $\sum\limits_{n=1}^{\infty} \dfrac{2}{3n+5}$

Let $f(x) = \dfrac{2}{3x+5}$.

$f$ is positive, continuous, and decreasing for $x \geq 1$.

$\int_1^\infty \dfrac{2}{3x+5}\,dx = \left[\dfrac{2}{3}\ln(3x+5)\right]_1^\infty = \infty$

Diverges by Theorem 8.10

**4.** $\sum\limits_{n=1}^{\infty} ne^{-n/2}$

Let $f(x) = xe^{-x/2}$.

$f$ is positive, continuous, and decreasing for $x \geq 3$.

Since $f'(x) = \dfrac{2-x}{2e^{x/2}} < 0$ for $x \geq 3$.

$\int_3^\infty xe^{-x/2}\,dx = \left[-2(x+2)e^{-x/2}\right]_3^\infty = 10e^{-3/2}$

Converges by Theorem 8.10

**6.** $\sum\limits_{n=1}^{\infty} \dfrac{1}{2n+1}$

Let $f(x) = \dfrac{1}{2x+1}$.

$f$ is positive, continuous, and decreasing for $x \geq 1$.

$\int_1^\infty \dfrac{1}{2x+1}\,dx = \left[\ln\sqrt{2x+1}\right]_1^\infty = \infty$

Diverges by Theorem 8.10

**8.** $\sum\limits_{n=1}^{\infty} \dfrac{n}{n^2+3}$

Let $f(x) = \dfrac{x}{x^2+3}$.

$f(x)$ is positive, continuous, and decreasing for $x \geq 2$ since

$f'(x) = \dfrac{3-x^2}{(x^2+3)} < 0$ for $x \geq 2$.

$\int_1^\infty \dfrac{x}{x^2+3}\,dx = \left[\ln\sqrt{x^2+3}\right]_1^\infty = \infty$

Diverges by Theorem 8.10

**10.** $\sum\limits_{n=1}^{\infty} n^k e^{-n}$

Let $f(x) = \dfrac{x^k}{e^x}$.

$f$ is positive, continuous, and decreasing for $x > k$ since

$f'(x) = \dfrac{x^{k-1}(k-x)}{e^x} < 0$

for $x > k$. We use integration by parts.

$\int_1^\infty x^k e^{-x}\,dx = \left[-x^k e^{-x}\right]_1^\infty + k\int_1^\infty x^{k-1} e^{-x}\,dx$

$= \dfrac{1}{e} + \dfrac{k}{e} + \dfrac{k(k-1)}{e} + \cdots + \dfrac{k!}{e}$

Converges by Theorem 8.10

**12.** $\sum\limits_{n=1}^{\infty} \dfrac{1}{n^{1/3}}$

Let $f(x) = \dfrac{1}{x^{1/3}}$.

$f$ is positive, continuous, and decreasing for $x \geq 1$.

$\int_1^\infty \dfrac{1}{x^{1/3}}\,dx = \left[\dfrac{3}{2}x^{2/3}\right]_1^\infty = \infty$

Diverges by Theorem 8.10

**14.** $\displaystyle\sum_{n=1}^{\infty} \frac{3}{n^{5/3}}$

Convergent $p$-series with $p = \dfrac{5}{3} > 1$

**16.** $\displaystyle\sum_{n=1}^{\infty} \frac{1}{n^2}$

Convergent $p$-series with $p = 2 > 1$

**18.** $\displaystyle\sum_{n=1}^{\infty} \frac{1}{n^{2/3}}$

Divergent $p$-series with $p = \frac{2}{3} < 1$

**20.** $\displaystyle\sum_{n=1}^{\infty} \frac{1}{n^{\pi}}$

Convergent $p$-series with $p = \pi > 1$

**22.** $\displaystyle\sum_{n=1}^{\infty} \frac{2}{n} = \frac{2}{1} + \frac{2}{2} + \frac{2}{3} + \cdots$

$S_1 = 2$

$S_2 = 3$

$S_3 \approx 3.67$

Matches (d)

Diverges—harmonic series

**24.** $\displaystyle\sum_{n=1}^{\infty} \frac{2}{n^2} = 2 + \frac{2}{2^2} + \frac{2}{3^2} + \cdots$

$S_1 = 2$

$S_2 = 2.5$

$S_3 \approx 2.722$

Matches (c)

Converges—$p$-series with $p = 2 > 1$.

**26. (a)**

| $n$ | 5 | 10 | 20 | 50 | 100 |
|-----|-----|-----|-----|-----|-----|
| $S_n$ | 3.7488 | 3.75 | 3.75 | 3.75 | 3.75 |

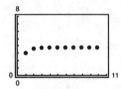

The partial sums approach the sum 3.75 very rapidly.

**(b)**

| $n$ | 5 | 10 | 20 | 50 | 100 |
|-----|-----|-----|-----|-----|-----|
| $S_n$ | 1.4636 | 1.5498 | 1.5962 | 1.6251 | 1.635 |

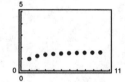

The partial sums approach the sum $\dfrac{\pi^2}{6} \approx 1.6449$ slower than the series in part (a).

**28.** $\displaystyle\xi(x) = \sum_{n=1}^{\infty} n^{-x} = \sum_{n=1}^{\infty} \frac{1}{n^x}$

Converges for $x > 1$ by Theorem 8.11.

**30.** $\displaystyle\sum_{n=2}^{\infty} \frac{\ln n}{n^p}$

If $p = 1$, then the series diverges by the Integral Test. If $p \neq 1$,

$$\int_2^{\infty} \frac{\ln x}{x^p}\,dx = \int_2^{\infty} x^{-p} \ln x\,dx = \left[ \frac{x^{-p+1}}{(-p+1)^2} \left[ -1 + (-p+1)\ln x \right] \right]_2^{\infty}. \text{ (Use Integration by Parts.)}$$

Converges for $-p + 1 < 0$ or $p > 1$.

**32.** A series of the form $\displaystyle\sum_{n=1}^{\infty} \frac{1}{n^p}$ is a $p$-series, $p > 0$.

The $p$-series converges if $p > 1$ and diverges if $0 < p \leq 1$.

**34.** The harmonic series $\displaystyle\sum_{n=1}^{\infty} \frac{1}{n}$.

**36.** From Exercise 35, we have:

$$0 \le S - S_N \le \int_N^\infty f(x)\, dx$$

$$S_N \le S \le S_N + \int_N^\infty f(x)\, dx$$

$$\sum_{n=1}^N a_n \le S \le \sum_{n=1}^N a_n + \int_N^\infty f(x)\, dx$$

**38.** $S_4 = 1 + \dfrac{1}{2^5} + \dfrac{1}{3^5} + \dfrac{1}{4^5} \approx 1.0363$

$$R_4 \le \int_4^\infty \frac{1}{x^5}\, dx = \left[ -\frac{1}{4x^4} \right]_4^\infty \approx 0.0010$$

$$1.0363 \le \sum_{n=1}^\infty \frac{1}{n^5} \le 1.0363 + 0.0010 = 1.0373$$

**40.** $S_{10} = \dfrac{1}{2(\ln 2)^3} + \dfrac{1}{3(\ln 3)^3} + \dfrac{1}{4(\ln 4)^3} + \cdots + \dfrac{1}{11(\ln 11)^3} \approx 1.9821$

$$R_{10} \le \int_{10}^\infty \frac{1}{(x+1)[\ln(x+1)]^3}\, dx = \left[ -\frac{1}{2[\ln(x+1)]^2} \right]_{10}^\infty = \frac{1}{2(\ln 11)^3} \approx 0.0870$$

$$1.9821 \le \sum_{n=1}^\infty \frac{1}{(n+1)[\ln(n+1)]^3} \le 1.9821 + 0.0870 = 2.0691$$

**42.** $S_4 = \dfrac{1}{e} + \dfrac{1}{e^2} + \dfrac{1}{e^3} + \dfrac{1}{e^4} \approx 0.5713$

$$R_4 \le \int_4^\infty e^{-x}\, dx = \left[ -e^{-x} \right]_4^\infty \approx 0.0183$$

$$0.5713 \le \sum_{n=0}^\infty e^{-n} \le 0.5713 + 0.0183 = 0.5896$$

**44.** $0 \le R_N \le \displaystyle\int_N^\infty \frac{1}{x^{3/2}}\, dx = \left[ -\frac{2}{x^{1/2}} \right]_N^\infty = \frac{2}{\sqrt{N}} < 0.001$

$$N^{-1/2} < 0.0005$$

$$\sqrt{N} > 2000$$

$$N \ge 4{,}000{,}000$$

**46.** $R_N \le \displaystyle\int_N^\infty e^{-x/2}\, dx = \left[ -2e^{-x/2} \right]_N^\infty = \dfrac{2}{e^{N/2}} < 0.001$

$$\frac{2}{e^{N/2}} < 0.001$$

$$e^{N/2} > 2000$$

$$\frac{N}{2} > \ln 2000$$

$$N > 2 \ln 2000 \approx 15.2$$

$$N \ge 16$$

**48.** $R_n \le \displaystyle\int_N^\infty \frac{2}{x^2 + 5}\, dx = 2\left[ \frac{1}{\sqrt{5}} \arctan\left( \frac{x}{\sqrt{5}} \right) \right]_N^\infty$

$$= \frac{2}{\sqrt{5}}\left( \frac{\pi}{2} - \arctan\left( \frac{N}{\sqrt{5}} \right) \right) < 0.001$$

$$\frac{\pi}{2} - \arctan\left( \frac{N}{\sqrt{5}} \right) < 0.001118$$

$$1.56968 < \arctan\left( \frac{N}{\sqrt{5}} \right)$$

$$\frac{N}{\sqrt{5}} > \tan 1.56968$$

$$N \ge 2004$$

**50.** (a) $\displaystyle\int_{10}^\infty \frac{1}{x^p}\, dx = \left[ \frac{x^{-p+1}}{-p+1} \right]_{10}^\infty = \frac{1}{(p-1)10^{p-1}},\ p > 1$

(b) $f(x) = \dfrac{1}{x^p}$

$$R_{10}(p) = \sum_{n=11}^\infty \frac{1}{n^p} \le \text{Area under the graph of } f \text{ over the interval } [10, \infty)$$

(c) The horizontal asymptote is $y = 0$. As $n$ increases, the error decreases.

**52.** $\displaystyle\sum_{n=2}^\infty \ln\left( 1 - \frac{1}{n^2} \right) = \sum_{n=2}^\infty \ln\left( \frac{n^2 - 1}{n^2} \right) = \sum_{n=2}^\infty \ln \frac{(n+1)(n-1)}{n^2} = \sum_{n=2}^\infty \left[ \ln(n+1) + \ln(n-1) - 2\ln n \right]$

$$= (\ln 3 + \ln 1 - 2\ln 2) + (\ln 4 + \ln 2 - 2\ln 3) + (\ln 5 + \ln 3 - 2\ln 4) + (\ln 6 + \ln 4 - 2\ln 5)$$

$$+ (\ln 7 + \ln 5 - 2\ln 6) + (\ln 8 + \ln 6 - 2\ln 7) + (\ln 9 + \ln 7 - 2\ln 8) + \cdots = -\ln 2$$

**54.** $\displaystyle\sum_{n=2}^{\infty} \frac{1}{n\sqrt{n^2-1}}$

Let $f(x) = \dfrac{1}{x\sqrt{x^2-1}}$.

$f$ is positive, continuous, and decreasing for $x \geq 2$.

$$\int_2^{\infty} \frac{1}{x\sqrt{x^2-1}}\, dx = \Big[\arcsec x\Big]_2^{\infty} = \frac{\pi}{2} - \frac{\pi}{3}$$

Converges by Theorem 8.10

**56.** $3\displaystyle\sum_{n=1}^{\infty} \frac{1}{n^{0.95}}$

$p$-series with $p = 0.95$

Diverges by Theorem 8.11

**58.** $\displaystyle\sum_{n=0}^{\infty} (1.075)^n$

Geometric series with $r = 1.075$

Diverges by Theorem 8.6

**60.** $\displaystyle\sum_{n=1}^{\infty}\left(\frac{1}{n^2} - \frac{1}{n^3}\right) = \sum_{n=1}^{\infty}\frac{1}{n^2} - \sum_{n=1}^{\infty}\frac{1}{n^3}$

Since these are both convergent $p$-series, the difference is convergent.

**62.** $\displaystyle\sum_{n=2}^{\infty} \ln(n)$

$\displaystyle\lim_{n\to\infty} \ln(n) = \infty$

Diverges by Theorem 8.9

**64.** $\displaystyle\sum_{n=2}^{\infty} \frac{\ln n}{n^3}$

Let $f(x) = \dfrac{\ln x}{x^3}$.

$f$ is positive, continuous, and decreasing for $x \geq 2$ since $f'(x) = \dfrac{1 - 3\ln x}{x^4} < 0$ for $x \geq 2$.

$$\int_2^{\infty} \frac{\ln x}{x^3}\, dx = \left[-\frac{\ln x}{2x^2}\right]_2^{\infty} + \frac{1}{2}\int_2^{\infty} \frac{1}{x^3}\, dx = \frac{\ln 2}{8} + \left[-\frac{1}{4x^2}\right]_2^{\infty} = \frac{\ln 2}{8} + \frac{1}{16} \text{ (Use Integration by Parts.)}$$

Converges by Theorem 8.10. See Exercise 14.

## Section 8.4   Comparisons of Series

**2.** (a) $\displaystyle\sum_{n=1}^{\infty} \frac{2}{\sqrt{n}} = 2 + \frac{2}{\sqrt{2}} + \cdots \quad S_1 = 2$

$\displaystyle\sum_{n=1}^{\infty} \frac{2}{\sqrt{n}-0.5} = \frac{2}{0.5} + \frac{2}{\sqrt{2}-0.5} + \cdots \quad S_1 = 4$

$\displaystyle\sum_{n=1}^{\infty} \frac{4}{\sqrt{n}+0.5} = \frac{4}{\sqrt{1.5}} + \frac{4}{\sqrt{2.5}} + \cdots \quad S_1 \approx 3.3$

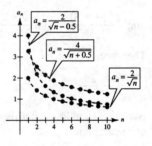

(b) The first series is a $p$-series. It diverges $\left(p = \frac{1}{2} < 1\right)$.

(c) The magnitude of the terms of the other two series are greater than the corresponding terms of the divergent $p$-series. Hence, the other two series diverge.

(d) The larger the magnitude of the terms, the larger the magnitude of the terms of the sequence of partial sums.

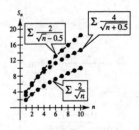

**4.** $\dfrac{1}{3n^2 + 2} < \dfrac{1}{3n^2}$

Therefore,

$$\sum_{n=1}^{\infty} \frac{1}{3n^2 + 2}$$

converges by comparison with the convergent *p*-series

$$\frac{1}{3} \sum_{n=1}^{\infty} \frac{1}{n^2}.$$

**6.** $\dfrac{1}{\sqrt{n} - 1} > \dfrac{1}{\sqrt{n}}$ for $n \geq 2$.

Therefore,

$$\sum_{n=2}^{\infty} \frac{1}{\sqrt{n} - 1}$$

diverges by comparison with the divergent *p*-series

$$\sum_{n=2}^{\infty} \frac{1}{\sqrt{n}}.$$

**8.** $\dfrac{3^n}{4^n + 5} < \left(\dfrac{3}{4}\right)^n$

Therefore,

$$\sum_{n=0}^{\infty} \frac{3^n}{4^n + 5}$$

converges by comparison with the convergent geometric series

$$\sum_{n=0}^{\infty} \left(\frac{3}{4}\right)^n.$$

**10.** $\dfrac{1}{\sqrt{n^3 + 1}} < \dfrac{1}{n^{3/2}}$

Therefore,

$$\sum_{n=1}^{\infty} \frac{1}{\sqrt{n^3 + 1}}$$

converges by comparison with the convergent *p*-series

$$\sum_{n=1}^{\infty} \frac{1}{n^{3/2}}.$$

**12.** $\dfrac{1}{4\sqrt[3]{n} - 1} > \dfrac{1}{4\sqrt[4]{n}}$

Therefore,

$$\sum_{n=1}^{\infty} \frac{1}{4\sqrt[3]{n} - 1}$$

diverges by comparison with the divergent *p*-series

$$\frac{1}{4} \sum_{n=1}^{\infty} \frac{1}{\sqrt[4]{n}}.$$

**14.** $\dfrac{4^n}{3^n - 1} > \dfrac{4^n}{3^n}$

Therefore,

$$\sum_{n=1}^{\infty} \frac{4^n}{3^n - 1}$$

diverges by comparison with the divergent geometric series

$$\sum_{n=1}^{\infty} \left(\frac{4}{3}\right)^n.$$

**16.** $\displaystyle\lim_{n \to \infty} \dfrac{2/(3^n - 5)}{1/3^n} = \lim_{n \to \infty} \dfrac{2 \cdot 3^n}{3^n - 5} = 2$

Therefore,

$$\sum_{n=1}^{\infty} \frac{2}{3^n - 5}$$

converges by a limit comparison with the convergent geometric series

$$\sum_{n=1}^{\infty} \left(\frac{1}{3}\right)^n.$$

**18.** $\displaystyle\lim_{n \to \infty} \dfrac{3/\sqrt{n^2 - 4}}{1/n} = \lim_{n \to \infty} \dfrac{3n}{\sqrt{n^2 - 4}} = 3$

Therefore,

$$\sum_{n=3}^{\infty} \frac{3}{\sqrt{n^2 - 4}}$$

diverges by a limit comparison with the divergent harmonic series

$$\sum_{n=3}^{\infty} \frac{1}{n}.$$

**20.** $\displaystyle\lim_{n \to \infty} \dfrac{\dfrac{5n - 3}{n^2 - 2n + 5}}{1/n} = \lim_{n \to \infty} \dfrac{5n^2 - 3n}{n^2 - 2n + 5} = 5$

Therefore,

$$\sum_{n=1}^{\infty} \frac{5n - 3}{n^2 - 2n + 5}$$

diverges by a limit comparison with the divergent *p*-series

$$\sum_{n=1}^{\infty} \frac{1}{n}.$$

**22.** $\displaystyle\lim_{n \to \infty} \dfrac{\dfrac{1}{n(n^2 + 1)}}{1/n^3} = \lim_{n \to \infty} \dfrac{n^3}{n^3 + n} = 1$

Therefore,

$$\sum_{n=1}^{\infty} \frac{1}{n(n^2 + 1)}$$

converges by a limit comparison with the convergent *p*-series

$$\sum_{n=1}^{\infty} \frac{1}{n^3}.$$

**24.** $\lim\limits_{n\to\infty} \dfrac{n/[(n+1)2^{n-1}]}{1/(2^{n-1})} = \lim\limits_{n\to\infty} \dfrac{n}{n+1} = 1$

Therefore,

$$\sum_{n=1}^{\infty} \frac{n}{(n+1)2^{n-1}}$$

converges by a limit comparison with the convergent geometric series

$$\sum_{n=1}^{\infty} \left(\frac{1}{2}\right)^{n-1}.$$

**26.** $\lim\limits_{n\to\infty} \dfrac{5/\left(n+\sqrt{n^2+4}\right)}{1/n} = \lim\limits_{n\to\infty} \dfrac{5n}{n+\sqrt{n^2+4}} = \dfrac{5}{2}$

Therefore,

$$\sum_{n=1}^{\infty} \frac{5}{n+\sqrt{n^2+4}}$$

diverges by a limit comparison with the divergent harmonic series

$$\sum_{n=1}^{\infty} \frac{1}{n}.$$

**28.** $\lim\limits_{n\to\infty} \dfrac{\tan(1/n)}{1/n} = \lim\limits_{n\to\infty} \dfrac{(-1/n^2)\sec^2(1/n)}{-1/n^2} = \lim\limits_{n\to\infty} \sec^2\left(\frac{1}{n}\right) = 1$

Therefore,

$$\sum_{n=1}^{\infty} \tan\left(\frac{1}{n}\right)$$

diverges by a limit comparison with the divergent $p$-series

$$\sum_{n=1}^{\infty} \frac{1}{n}.$$

**30.** $\sum\limits_{n=0}^{\infty} 5\left(-\frac{1}{5}\right)^n$

Converges

Geometric series with $r = -\frac{1}{5}$

**32.** $\sum\limits_{n=4}^{\infty} \dfrac{1}{3n^2 - 2n - 15}$

Converges

Limit comparison with $\sum\limits_{n=1}^{\infty} \dfrac{1}{n^2}$

**34.** $\sum\limits_{n=1}^{\infty} \left(\dfrac{1}{n+1} - \dfrac{1}{n+2}\right) = \left(\dfrac{1}{2} - \dfrac{1}{3}\right) + \left(\dfrac{1}{3} - \dfrac{1}{4}\right) + \left(\dfrac{1}{4} - \dfrac{1}{5}\right) + \cdots = \dfrac{1}{2}$

Converges; telescoping series

**36.** $\sum\limits_{n=1}^{\infty} \dfrac{3}{n(n+3)}$

Converges; telescoping series

$$\sum_{n=1}^{\infty} \left(\frac{1}{n} - \frac{1}{n+3}\right)$$

**38.** If $j < k - 1$, then $k - j > 1$. The $p$-series with $p = k - j$ converges and since

$$\lim_{n\to\infty} \frac{P(n)/Q(n)}{1/n^{k-j}} = L > 0,$$

the series $\sum\limits_{n=1}^{\infty} \dfrac{P(n)}{Q(n)}$ converges by the limit comparison test. Similarly, if $j \geq k - 1$, then $k - j \leq 1$ which implies that

$$\sum_{n=1}^{\infty} \frac{P(n)}{Q(n)}$$

diverges by the limit comparison test.

**40.** $\dfrac{1}{3} + \dfrac{1}{8} + \dfrac{1}{15} + \dfrac{1}{24} + \dfrac{1}{35} + \cdots = \sum\limits_{n=2}^{\infty} \dfrac{1}{n^2 - 1}$,

which converges since the degree of the numerator is two less than the degree of the denominator.

**42.** $\sum\limits_{n=1}^{\infty} \dfrac{n^2}{n^3 + 1}$

diverges since the degree of the numerator is only one less than the degree of the denominator.

**44.** $\lim\limits_{n\to\infty}\dfrac{n}{\ln n} = \lim\limits_{n\to\infty}\dfrac{1}{1/n} = \lim\limits_{n\to\infty} n = \infty \neq 0$

Therefore,

$\sum\limits_{n=2}^{\infty}\dfrac{1}{\ln n}$ diverges.

**46.** See Theorem 8.13, page 585.
One example is

$\sum\limits_{n=2}^{\infty}\dfrac{1}{\sqrt{n-1}}$ diverges because $\lim\limits_{n\to\infty}\dfrac{1/\sqrt{n-1}}{1/\sqrt{n}} = 1$

and

$\sum\limits_{n=2}^{\infty}\dfrac{1}{\sqrt{n}}$ diverges (*p*-series).

**48.** This is not correct. The beginning terms do not affect the convergence or divergence of a series.

In fact,

$\dfrac{1}{1000} + \dfrac{1}{1001} + \cdots = \sum\limits_{n=1000}^{\infty}\dfrac{1}{n}$ diverges (harmonic)

and

$1 + \dfrac{1}{4} + \dfrac{1}{9} + \cdots = \sum\limits_{n=1}^{\infty}\dfrac{1}{n^2}$ converges (*p*-series).

**50.** $\dfrac{1}{200} + \dfrac{1}{210} + \dfrac{1}{220} + \cdots = \sum\limits_{n=0}^{\infty}\dfrac{1}{200+10n}$,

diverges

**52.** $\dfrac{1}{201} + \dfrac{1}{208} + \dfrac{1}{227} + \dfrac{1}{264} + \cdots = \sum\limits_{n=1}^{\infty}\dfrac{1}{200+n^3}$,

converges

**54.** (a) $\sum\limits_{n=1}^{\infty}\dfrac{1}{(2n-1)^2} = \sum\limits_{n=1}^{\infty}\dfrac{1}{4n^2-4n+1}$

converges since the degree of the numerator is two less than the degree of the denominator. (See Exercise 38.)

(b)

| $n$ | 5 | 10 | 20 | 50 | 100 |
|-----|-----|-----|-----|-----|-----|
| $S_n$ | 1.1839 | 1.02087 | 1.2212 | 1.2287 | 1.2312 |

(c) $\sum\limits_{n=3}^{\infty}\dfrac{1}{(2n-1)^2} = \dfrac{\pi^2}{8} - S_2 \approx 0.1226$

(d) $\sum\limits_{n=10}^{\infty}\dfrac{1}{(2n-1)^2} = \dfrac{\pi^2}{8} - S_9 \approx 0.0277$

**56.** True

**58.** False. Let $a_n = 1/n$, $b_n = 1/n$, $c_n = 1/n^2$. Then, $a_n \leq b_n + c_n$, but $\sum\limits_{n=1}^{\infty} c_n$ converges.

**60.** Since $\sum\limits_{n=1}^{\infty} a_n$ converges, then $\sum\limits_{n=1}^{\infty} a_n a_n = \sum\limits_{n=1}^{\infty} a_n^2$ converges by Exercise 59.

**62.** $\sum\dfrac{1}{n^2}$ converge, and hence so does $\sum\left(\dfrac{1}{n^2}\right)^2 = \sum\dfrac{1}{n^4}$.

**64.** (a) $\sum a_n = \sum\dfrac{1}{n^3}$ and $\sum b_n = \sum\dfrac{1}{n^2}$. Since

$\lim\limits_{n\to\infty}\dfrac{a_n}{b_n} = \lim\limits_{n\to\infty}\dfrac{1/n^3}{1/n^2} = \lim\limits_{n\to\infty}\dfrac{1}{n} = 0$   and   $\sum\dfrac{1}{n^2}$

converges, so does $\sum\dfrac{1}{n^3}$.

(b) $\sum a_n = \sum\dfrac{1}{\sqrt{n}}$ and $\sum b_n = \sum\dfrac{1}{n}$. Since

$\lim\limits_{n\to\infty}\dfrac{a_n}{b_n} = \lim\limits_{n\to\infty}\dfrac{1/\sqrt{n}}{1/n} = \lim\limits_{n\to\infty}\sqrt{n} = \infty$   and   $\sum\dfrac{1}{n}$

diverges, so does $\sum\dfrac{1}{\sqrt{n}}$.

# Section 8.5    Alternating Series

**2.** $\displaystyle\sum_{n=1}^{\infty} \frac{(-1)^{n-1}6}{n^2} = \frac{6}{1} - \frac{6}{4} + \frac{6}{9} - \cdots$

$S_1 = 6, S_2 = 4.5$

Matches (d)

**4.** $\displaystyle\sum_{n=1}^{\infty} \frac{(-1)^{n-1}10}{n2^n} = \frac{10}{2} - \frac{10}{8} + \cdots$

$S_1 = 5, S_2 = 3.75$

Matches (a)

**6.** $\displaystyle\sum_{n=1}^{\infty} \frac{(-1)^{n-1}}{(n-1)!} = \frac{1}{e} \approx 0.3679$

(a)

| $n$ | 1 | 2 | 3 | 4 | 5 | 6 | 7 | 8 | 9 | 10 |
|---|---|---|---|---|---|---|---|---|---|---|
| $S_n$ | 1 | 0 | 0.5 | 0.3333 | 0.375 | 0.3667 | 0.3681 | 0.3679 | 0.3679 | 0.3679 |

(b)

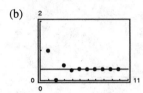

(c) The points alternate sides of the horizontal line that represents the sum of the series. The distance between successive points and the line decreases.

(d) The distance in part (c) is always less than the magnitude of the next series.

**8.** $\displaystyle\sum_{n=1}^{\infty} \frac{(-1)^{n-1}}{(2n-1)!} = \sin(1) \approx 0.8415$

(a)

| $n$ | 1 | 2 | 3 | 4 | 5 | 6 | 7 | 8 | 9 | 10 |
|---|---|---|---|---|---|---|---|---|---|---|
| $S_n$ | 1 | 0.8333 | 0.8417 | 0.8415 | 0.8415 | 0.8415 | 0.8415 | 0.8415 | 0.8415 | 0.8415 |

(b)

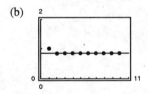

(c) The points alternate sides of the horizontal line that represents the sum of the series. The distance between successive points and the line decreases.

(d) The distance in part (c) is always less than the magnitude of the next series.

**10.** $\displaystyle\sum_{n=1}^{\infty} \frac{(-1)^{n+1}\,n}{2n-1}$

$\displaystyle\lim_{n\to\infty} \frac{n}{2n-1} = \frac{1}{2}$

Diverges by the $n$th Term Test.

**12.** $\displaystyle\sum_{n=1}^{\infty} \frac{(-1)^n}{\ln(n+1)}$

$a_{n+1} = \dfrac{1}{\ln(n+2)} < \dfrac{1}{\ln(n+1)} = a_n$

$\displaystyle\lim_{n\to\infty} \frac{1}{\ln(n+1)} = 0$

Converges by Theorem 8.14

**14.** $\displaystyle\sum_{n=1}^{\infty} \frac{(-1)^{n+1}n}{n^2+1}$

$a_{n+1} = \dfrac{n+1}{(n+1)^2+1} < \dfrac{n}{n^2+1} = a_n$

$\displaystyle\lim_{n\to\infty} \frac{n}{n^2+1} = 0$

Converges by Theorem 8.14

**16.** $\displaystyle\sum_{n=1}^{\infty} \frac{(-1)^{n+1}n^2}{n^2+5}$

$\displaystyle\lim_{n\to\infty} \frac{n^2}{n^2+5} = 1$

Diverges by $n$th Term Test

**18.** $\sum_{n=1}^{\infty} \frac{(-1)^{n+1} \ln(n+1)}{n+1}$

$$a_{n+1} = \frac{\ln[(n+1)+1]}{(n+1)+1} < \frac{\ln(n+1)}{n+1} \text{ for } n \geq 2$$

$$\lim_{n \to \infty} \frac{\ln(n+1)}{n+1} = \lim_{n \to \infty} \frac{1/(n+1)}{1} = 0$$

Converges by Theorem 8.14

**20.** $\sum_{n=1}^{\infty} \frac{1}{n} \sin\left[\frac{(2n-1)\pi}{2}\right] = \sum_{n=1}^{\infty} \frac{(-1)^{n+1}}{n}$

Converges; (see Exercise 9)

**22.** $\sum_{n=1}^{\infty} \frac{1}{n} \cos n\pi = \sum_{n=1}^{\infty} \frac{(-1)^n}{n}$

Converges; (see Exercise 9)

**24.** $\sum_{n=0}^{\infty} \frac{(-1)^n}{(2n+1)!}$

$$a_{n+1} = \frac{1}{(2n+3)!} < \frac{1}{(2n+1)!} = a_n$$

$$\lim_{n \to \infty} \frac{1}{(2n+1)!} = 0$$

Converges by Theorem 8.14

**26.** $\sum_{n=1}^{\infty} \frac{(-1)^{n+1}\sqrt{n}}{\sqrt[3]{n}}$

$$\lim_{n \to \infty} \frac{n^{1/2}}{n^{1/3}} = \lim_{n \to \infty} n^{1/6} = \infty$$

Diverges by the *n*th Term Test

**28.** $\sum_{n=1}^{\infty} \frac{2(-1)^{n+1}}{e^n + e^{-n}} = \sum_{n=1}^{\infty} \frac{(-1)^{n+1}(2e^n)}{e^{2n} + 1}$

Let $f(x) = \frac{2e^x}{e^{2x} + 1}$. Then

$$f'(x) = \frac{2e^{2x}(1 - e^{2x})}{(e^{2x} + 1)^2} < 0 \text{ for } x > 0.$$

Thus, $f(x)$ is decreasing for $x > 0$ which implies $a_{n+1} < a_n$.

$$\lim_{n \to \infty} \frac{2e^n}{e^{2n} + 1} = \lim_{n \to \infty} \frac{2e^n}{2e^{2n}} = \lim_{n \to \infty} \frac{1}{e^n} = 0$$

The series converges by Theorem 8.14.

**30.** $S_6 = \sum_{n=1}^{6} \frac{4(-1)^{n+1}}{\ln(n+1)} \approx 2.7067$

$$|R_6| = |S - S_6| \leq a_7 = \frac{4}{\ln 8} \approx 1.9236; \quad 0.7831 \leq S \leq 4.6303$$

**32.** $S_6 = \sum_{n=1}^{6} \frac{(-1)^{n+1} n}{2^n} = 0.1875$

$$|R_6| = |S - S_6| \leq a_7 = \frac{7}{2^7} \approx 0.05469; \quad 0.1328 \leq S \leq 0.2422$$

**34.** $\sum_{n=0}^{\infty} \frac{(-1)^n}{2^n n!}$

(a) By Theorem 8.15,

$$|R_n| \leq a_{N+1} = \frac{1}{2^{N+1}(N+1)!} < 0.001.$$

This inequality is valid when $N = 4$.

(b) We may approximate the series by

$$\sum_{n=0}^{4} \frac{(-1)^n}{2^n n!} = 1 - \frac{1}{2} + \frac{1}{8} - \frac{1}{48} + \frac{1}{348} \approx 0.607.$$

(5 terms. Note that the sum begins with $n = 0$.)

**36.** $\sum_{n=0}^{\infty} \frac{(-1)^n}{(2n)!}$

(a) By Theorem 8.15,

$$|R_N| \leq a_{N+1} = \frac{1}{(2N+2)!} < 0.001.$$

This inequality is valid when $N = 3$.

(b) We may approximate the series by

$$\sum_{n=0}^{3} \frac{(-1)^n}{(2n)!} = 1 - \frac{1}{2} + \frac{1}{24} - \frac{1}{720} \approx 0.540.$$

(4 terms. Note that the sum begins with $n = 0$.)

**38.** $\displaystyle\sum_{n=1}^{\infty} \frac{(-1)^{n+1}}{4^n n}$

(a) By Theorem 8.15,

$$|R_N| \le a_{N+1} = \frac{1}{4^{N+1}(N+1)} < 0.001.$$

This inequality is valid when $N = 3$.

(b) We may approximate the series by

$$\sum_{n=1}^{3} \frac{(-1)^{n+1}}{4^n n} = \frac{1}{4} - \frac{1}{32} + \frac{1}{192} \approx 0.224.$$

(3 terms)

**40.** $\displaystyle\sum_{n=1}^{\infty} \frac{(-1)^{n+1}}{n^4}$

By Theorem 8.15, $|R_N| \le a_{N+1} = \dfrac{1}{(N+1)^4} < 0.001.$

This inequality is valid when $N = 5$.

**42.** $\displaystyle\sum_{n=1}^{\infty} \frac{(-1)^{n+1}}{n+1}$

The given series converges by the Alternating Series Test, but does not converge absolutely since the series

$$\sum_{n=1}^{\infty} \frac{1}{n+1}$$

diverges by the Integral Test. Therefore, the series converge conditionally.

**44.** $\displaystyle\sum_{n=1}^{\infty} \frac{(-1)^{n+1}}{n\sqrt{n}}$

$\displaystyle\sum_{n=1}^{\infty} \frac{1}{n\sqrt{n}} = \sum_{n=1}^{\infty} \frac{1}{n^{3/2}}$ which is a convergent $p$-series.

Therefore, the given series converges absolutely.

**46.** $\displaystyle\sum_{n=1}^{\infty} \frac{(-1)^{n+1}(2n+3)}{n+10}$

$\displaystyle\lim_{n\to\infty} \frac{2n+3}{n+10} = 2$ Therefore, the series diverges by the $n$th Term Test.

**48.** $\displaystyle\sum_{n=0}^{\infty} \frac{(-1)^n}{e^{n^2}}$

$\displaystyle\sum_{n=0}^{\infty} \frac{1}{e^{n^2}}$

converges by a comparison to the convergent geometric series

$$\sum_{n=0}^{\infty} \left(\frac{1}{e}\right)^n.$$

Therefore, the given series converges absolutely.

**50.** $\displaystyle\sum_{n=1}^{\infty} \frac{(-1)^{n+1}}{n^{1.5}}$

$\displaystyle\sum_{n=1}^{\infty} \frac{1}{n^{1.5}}$ is a convergent $p$-series.

Therefore, the given series converge absolutely.

**52.** $\displaystyle\sum_{n=0}^{\infty} \frac{(-1)^n}{\sqrt{n+4}}$

The given series converges by the Alternating Series Test, but

$$\sum_{n=0}^{\infty} \frac{1}{\sqrt{n+4}}$$

diverges by a limit comparison to the divergent $p$-series

$$\sum_{n=1}^{\infty} \frac{1}{\sqrt{n}}.$$

Therefore, the given series converges conditionally.

**54.** $\displaystyle\sum_{n=1}^{\infty} (-1)^{n+1} \arctan n$

$\displaystyle\lim_{n\to\infty} \arctan n = \frac{\pi}{2} \ne 0$ Therefore, the series diverges by the $n$th Term Test.

**56.** $\displaystyle\sum_{n=1}^{\infty} \frac{\sin[(2n-1)\pi/2]}{n} = \sum_{n=1}^{\infty} \frac{(-1)^{n+1}}{n}$

The given series converges by the Alternating Series Test, but

$$\sum_{n=1}^{\infty} \left| \frac{\sin[(2n-1)\pi/2]}{n} \right| = \sum_{n=1}^{\infty} \frac{1}{n}$$

is a divergent *p*-series. Therefore, the series converges conditionally.

**58.** $|S - S_n| = |R_n| \le a_{n+1}$  (Theorem 8.15)

**60.** $\displaystyle\sum_{n=1}^{\infty} \frac{(-1)^{n+1}}{n} = 1 - \frac{1}{2} + \frac{1}{3} - \frac{1}{4} + \cdots$  (Alternating Harmonic Series)

**62.** $\displaystyle\sum_{n=1}^{\infty} \frac{(-1)^n}{n^p}$

If $p = 0$, then

$$\lim_{n\to\infty} \frac{1}{n^p} = 1$$

and the series diverges. If $p > 0$, then

$$\lim_{n\to\infty} \frac{1}{n^p} = 0 \text{ and } \frac{1}{(n+1)^p} < \frac{1}{n^p}.$$

Therefore, the series converge by the Alternating Series Test.

**64.** $\displaystyle\sum_{n=1}^{\infty} \frac{(-1)^{n-1}}{n}$ converges, but $\displaystyle\sum_{n=1}^{\infty} \frac{1}{n}$ diverges

**66.** (a) $\displaystyle\sum_{n=1}^{\infty} \frac{x^n}{n}$

converges absolutely (by comparison) for

$$-1 < x < 1,$$

since

$$\left| \frac{x^n}{n} \right| < |x^n| \text{ and } \sum x^n$$

is a convergent geometric series for $-1 < x < 1$.

(b) When $x = -1$, we have the convergent alternating series

$$\sum_{n=1}^{\infty} \frac{(-1)^n}{n}.$$

When $x = 1$, we have the divergent harmonic series

$$\frac{1}{n}.$$

Therefore,

$$\sum_{n=1}^{\infty} \frac{x^n}{n}$$

converges conditionally for $x = -1$.

**68.** True, equivalent to Theorem 8.16

**70.** $\displaystyle\sum_{n=1}^{\infty} \frac{3}{n^2 + 5}$

converges by limit comparison to convergent *p*-series

$$\sum \frac{1}{n^2}.$$

**72.** Converges by limit comparison to convergent geometric series $\displaystyle\sum \frac{1}{2^n}$.

**74.** Diverges by *n*th Term Test. $\displaystyle\lim_{n\to\infty} a_n = \frac{3}{2}$

**76.** Converges (conditionally) by Alternating Series Test.

**78.** Diverges by comparison to Divergent Harmonic Series:

$$\frac{\ln n}{n} > \frac{1}{n} \text{ for } n \ge 3.$$

# Section 8.6    The Ratio and Root Tests

**2.** $\dfrac{(2k-2)!}{(2k)!} = \dfrac{(2k-2)!}{(2k)(2k-1)(2k-2)!} = \dfrac{1}{(2k)(2k-1)}$

**4.** Use the Principle of Mathematical Induction. When $k = 3$, the formula is valid since $\dfrac{1}{1} = \dfrac{2^3 3!(3)(5)}{6!} = 1$. Assume that

$$\dfrac{1}{1 \cdot 3 \cdot 5 \cdots (2n-5)} = \dfrac{2^n n!(2n-3)(2n-1)}{(2n)!}$$

and show that

$$\dfrac{1}{1 \cdot 3 \cdot 5 \cdots (2n-5)(2n-3)} = \dfrac{2^{n+1}(n+1)!(2n-1)(2n+1)}{(2n+2)!}.$$

To do this, note that:

$$\begin{aligned}
\dfrac{1}{1 \cdot 3 \cdot 5 \cdots (2n-5)(2n-3)} &= \dfrac{1}{1 \cdot 3 \cdot 5 \cdots (2n-5)} \cdot \dfrac{1}{(2n-3)} \\
&= \dfrac{2^n n!(2n-3)(2n-1)}{(2n)!} \cdot \dfrac{1}{(2n-3)} \\
&= \dfrac{2^n n!(2n-1)}{(2n)!} \cdot \dfrac{(2n+1)(2n+2)}{(2n+1)(2n+2)} \\
&= \dfrac{2^n (2)(n+1)n!(2n-1)(2n+1)}{(2n)!(2n+1)(2n+2)} \\
&= \dfrac{2^{n+1}(n+1)!(2n-1)(2n+1)}{(2n+2)!}
\end{aligned}$$

The formula is valid for all $n \geq 3$.

**6.** $\displaystyle\sum_{n=1}^{\infty} \left(\dfrac{3}{4}\right)^n \left(\dfrac{1}{n!}\right) = \dfrac{3}{4} + \dfrac{9}{16}\left(\dfrac{1}{2}\right) + \cdots$

$S_1 = \dfrac{3}{4}, \; S_2 \approx 1.03$

Matches (c)

**8.** $\displaystyle\sum_{n=1}^{\infty} \dfrac{(-1)^{n-1}4}{(2n)!} = \dfrac{4}{2} - \dfrac{4}{24} + \cdots$

$S_1 = 2$

Matches (b)

**10.** $\displaystyle\sum_{n=0}^{\infty} 4e^{-n} = 4 + \dfrac{4}{e} + \cdots$

$S_1 = 4$

Matches (e)

**12. (a)** Ratio Test: $\displaystyle\lim_{n\to\infty} \left|\dfrac{a_{n+1}}{a_n}\right| = \lim_{n\to\infty} \dfrac{\dfrac{(n+1)^2+1}{(n+1)!}}{\dfrac{n^2+1}{n!}} = \lim_{n\to\infty} \left(\dfrac{n^2+2n+2}{n^2+1}\right)\left(\dfrac{1}{n+1}\right) = 0 < 1.$ Converges

**(b)**

| $n$ | 5 | 10 | 15 | 20 | 25 |
|---|---|---|---|---|---|
| $S_n$ | 7.0917 | 7.1548 | 7.1548 | 7.1548 | 7.1548 |

**(c)**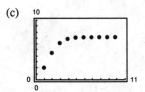

**(d)** The sum is approximately 7.15485

**(e)** The more rapidly the terms of the series approach 0, the more rapidly the sequence of the partial sums approaches the sum of the series.

**14.** $\displaystyle\sum_{n=0}^{\infty} \frac{3^n}{n!}$

$$\lim_{n\to\infty} \left|\frac{a_{n+1}}{a_n}\right| = \lim_{n\to\infty} \left|\frac{3^{n+1}}{(n+1)!} \cdot \frac{n!}{3^n}\right|$$

$$= \lim_{n\to\infty} \frac{3}{n+1} = 0$$

Therefore, by the Ratio Test, the series converges.

**16.** $\displaystyle\sum_{n=1}^{\infty} n\left(\frac{3}{2}\right)^n$

$$\lim_{n\to\infty} \left|\frac{a_{n+1}}{a_n}\right| = \lim_{n\to\infty} \left|\frac{(n+1)3^{n+1}}{2^{n+1}} \cdot \frac{2^n}{n3^n}\right|$$

$$= \lim_{n\to\infty} \frac{3(n+1)}{2n} = \frac{3}{2}$$

Therefore, by the Ratio Test, the series diverges.

**18.** $\displaystyle\sum_{n=1}^{\infty} \frac{n^3}{2^n}$

$$\lim_{n\to\infty} \left|\frac{a_n + 1}{a_n}\right| = \lim_{n\to\infty} \left|\frac{(n+1)^3/2^{n+1}}{n^3/2^n}\right|$$

$$= \lim_{n\to\infty} \left|\frac{(n+1)^3}{2n^3}\right| = \frac{1}{2}$$

Therefore, by the Ratio Test, the series converges.

**20.** $\displaystyle\sum_{n=1}^{\infty} \frac{(-1)^{n+1}(n+2)}{n(n+1)}$

$$a_{n+1} = \frac{n+3}{(n+1)(n+2)} \le \frac{n+2}{n(n+1)} = a_n$$

$$\lim_{n\to\infty} \frac{n+2}{n(n+1)} = 0$$

Therefore, by Theorem 8.14, the series converges.

**Note:** The Ratio Test is inconclusive since $\displaystyle\lim_{n\to\infty} \left|\frac{a_{n+1}}{a_n}\right| = 1$. The series converges conditionally.

**22.** $\displaystyle\sum_{n=1}^{\infty} \frac{(-1)^{n-1}(3/2)^n}{n^2}$

$$\lim_{n\to\infty} \left|\frac{a_{n+1}}{a_n}\right| = \lim_{n\to\infty} \left|\frac{(3/2)^{n+1}}{n^2+2n+1} \cdot \frac{n^2}{(3/2)^n}\right|$$

$$= \lim_{n\to\infty} \frac{3n^2}{2(n^2+2n+1)} = \frac{3}{2} > 1$$

Therefore, by the Ratio Test, the series diverges.

**24.** $\displaystyle\sum_{n=1}^{\infty} \frac{(2n)!}{n^5}$

$$\lim_{n\to\infty} \left|\frac{a_{n+1}}{a_n}\right| = \lim_{n\to\infty} \left|\frac{(2n+2)!}{(n+1)^5} \cdot \frac{n^5}{(2n)!}\right|$$

$$= \lim_{n\to\infty} \frac{(2n+2)(2n+1)n^5}{(n+1)^5} = \infty$$

Therefore, by the Ratio Test, the series diverges.

**26.** $\displaystyle\sum_{n=1}^{\infty} \frac{n^n}{n!}$

$$\lim_{n\to\infty} \left|\frac{a_{n+1}}{a_n}\right| = \lim_{n\to\infty} \left|\frac{(n+1)^{n+1}}{(n+1)!} \cdot \frac{n!}{n^n}\right|$$

$$= \lim_{n\to\infty} \frac{(n+1)(n+1)^n n!}{(n+1)n!n^n}$$

$$= \lim_{n\to\infty} \left(\frac{n+1}{n}\right)^n = e > 1$$

Therefore, by the Ratio Test, the series diverges.

**28.** $\displaystyle\sum_{n=0}^{\infty} \frac{(n!)^2}{(3n)!}$

$$\lim_{n\to\infty} \left|\frac{a_{n+1}}{a_n}\right| = \lim_{n\to\infty} \left|\frac{[(n+1)!]^2}{(3n+3)!} \cdot \frac{(3n)!}{(n!)^2}\right|$$

$$= \lim_{n\to\infty} \frac{(n+1)^2}{(3n+3)(3n+2)(3n+1)} = 0$$

Therefore, by the Ratio Test, the series converges.

**30.** $\displaystyle\sum_{n=0}^{\infty} \frac{(-1)^n 2^{4n}}{(2n+1)!}$

$$\lim_{n\to\infty} \left|\frac{a_{n+1}}{a_n}\right| = \lim_{n\to\infty} \left|\frac{2^{4n+4}}{(2n+3)!} \cdot \frac{(2n+1)!}{2^{4n}}\right| = \lim_{n\to\infty} \frac{2^4}{(2n+3)(2n+2)} = 0$$

Therefore, by the Ratio Test, the series converges.

**32.** $\displaystyle\sum_{n=1}^{\infty} \frac{(-1)^n 2 \cdot 4 \cdot 6 \cdots 2n}{2 \cdot 5 \cdot 8 \cdots (3n-1)}$

$$\lim_{n\to\infty} \left| \frac{a_{n+1}}{a_n} \right| = \lim_{n\to\infty} \left| \frac{2 \cdot 4 \cdots 2n(2n+2)}{2 \cdot 5 \cdots (3n-1)(3n+2)} \cdot \frac{2 \cdot 5 \cdots (3n-1)}{2 \cdot 4 \cdots 2n} \right| = \lim_{n\to\infty} \frac{2n+2}{3n+2} = \frac{2}{3}$$

Therefore, by the Ratio Test, the series converges.

**Note:** The first few terms of this series are    $-\dfrac{2}{2} + \dfrac{2 \cdot 4}{2 \cdot 5} - \dfrac{2 \cdot 4 \cdot 6}{2 \cdot 5 \cdot 8} + \cdots$

**34. (a)** $\displaystyle\sum_{n=1}^{\infty} \frac{1}{n^4}$

$$\lim_{n\to\infty} \left| \frac{a_{n+1}}{a_n} \right| = \lim_{n\to\infty} \left| \frac{1}{(n+1)^4} \cdot \frac{n^4}{1} \right| = \lim_{n\to\infty} \left( \frac{n}{n+1} \right)^4 = 1$$

**(b)** $\displaystyle\sum_{n=1}^{\infty} \frac{1}{n^p}$

$$\lim_{n\to\infty} \left| \frac{a_{n+1}}{a_n} \right| = \lim_{n\to\infty} \left| \frac{1}{(n+1)^p} \cdot \frac{n^p}{1} \right| = \lim_{n\to\infty} \left( \frac{n}{n+1} \right)^p = 1$$

**36.** $\displaystyle\sum_{n=1}^{\infty} \left( \frac{2n}{n+1} \right)^n$

$$\lim_{n\to\infty} \sqrt[n]{|a_n|} = \lim_{n\to\infty} \sqrt[n]{\left( \frac{2n}{n+1} \right)^n}$$

$$= \lim_{n\to\infty} \frac{2n}{n+1} = 2$$

Therefore, by the Root Test, the series diverges.

**38.** $\displaystyle\sum_{n=1}^{\infty} \left( \frac{-3n}{2n+1} \right)^{3n}$

$$\lim_{n\to\infty} \sqrt[n]{|a_n|} = \lim_{n\to\infty} \sqrt[n]{\left| \left( \frac{-3n}{2n+1} \right)^{3n} \right|}$$

$$= \lim_{n\to\infty} \left( \frac{3n}{2n+1} \right)^3 = \left( \frac{3}{2} \right)^3 = \frac{27}{8}$$

Therefore, by the Root Test, the series diverges.

**40.** $\displaystyle\sum_{n=0}^{\infty} e^{-n}$

$$\lim_{n\to\infty} \sqrt[n]{|a_n|} = \lim_{n\to\infty} \sqrt[n]{\frac{1}{e^n}} = \frac{1}{e}$$

Therefore, by the Root Test, the series converges.

**42.** $\displaystyle\sum_{n=0}^{\infty} \frac{n+1}{3^n}$

$$\lim_{n\to\infty} \sqrt[n]{|a_n|} = \lim_{n\to\infty} \sqrt[n]{\frac{n+1}{3^n}} = \lim_{n\to\infty} \frac{\sqrt[n]{n+1}}{3}$$

Let $\quad y = \displaystyle\lim_{n\to\infty} \sqrt[x]{x+1}$

$$\ln y = \lim_{n\to\infty} \left( \ln \sqrt[x]{x+1} \right)$$

$$= \lim_{n\to\infty} \frac{1}{x} \ln(x+1)$$

$$= \lim_{n\to\infty} \frac{\ln(x+1)}{x} = \frac{1}{x+1} = 0.$$

Since $\ln y = 0$, $y = e^0 = 1$, so

$$\lim_{n\to\infty} \frac{\sqrt{n+1}}{3} = \frac{1}{3}.$$

Therefore, by the Root Test, the series converges.

**44.** $\displaystyle\sum_{n=1}^{\infty} \frac{5}{n} = 5 \sum_{n=1}^{\infty} \frac{1}{n}$

This is the divergent harmonic series.

**46.** $\displaystyle\sum_{n=1}^{\infty} \left(\frac{\pi}{4}\right)^n$

Since $\pi/4 < 1$, this is convergent geometric series.

**48.** $\displaystyle\sum_{n=1}^{\infty} \frac{n}{2n^2 + 1}$

$$\lim_{n \to \infty} \frac{n/(2n^2 + 1)}{1/n} = \lim_{n \to \infty} \frac{n^2}{2n^2 + 1} = \frac{1}{2} > 0$$

This series diverges by limit comparison to the divergent harmonic series

$$\sum_{n=1}^{\infty} \frac{1}{n}.$$

**50.** $\displaystyle\sum_{n=1}^{\infty} \frac{10}{3\sqrt{n^3}}$

$$\lim_{n \to \infty} \frac{10/3n^{3/2}}{1/n^{3/2}} = \frac{10}{3}$$

Therefore, the series converges by a limit comparison test with the *p*-series

$$\sum_{n=1}^{\infty} \frac{1}{n^{3/2}}.$$

**52.** $\displaystyle\sum_{n=1}^{\infty} \frac{2^n}{4n^2 - 1}$

$$\lim_{n \to \infty} \frac{2^n}{4n^2 - 1} = \lim_{n \to \infty} \frac{(\ln 2)2^n}{8n} = \lim_{n \to \infty} \frac{(\ln 2)^2 2^n}{8} = \infty$$

Therefore, the series diverges by the *n*th Term Test for Divergence.

**54.** $\displaystyle\sum_{n=2}^{\infty} \frac{(-1)^n}{n \ln(n)}$

$$a_{n+1} = \frac{1}{(n + 1) \ln(n + 1)} \leq \frac{1}{n \ln(n)} = a_n$$

$$\lim_{n \to \infty} \frac{1}{n \ln(n)} = 0$$

Therefore, by the Alternating Series Test, the series converges.

**56.** $\displaystyle\sum_{n=1}^{\infty} \frac{\ln(n)}{n^2}$

$$\frac{\ln(n)}{n^2} \leq \frac{1}{n^{3/2}}$$

Therefore, the series converges by comparison with the *p*-series

$$\sum_{n=1}^{\infty} \frac{1}{n^{3/2}}.$$

**58.** $\displaystyle\sum_{n=1}^{\infty} \frac{(-1)^n 3^n}{n2^n}$

$$\lim_{n \to \infty} \left|\frac{a_{n+1}}{a_n}\right| = \lim_{n \to \infty} \left|\frac{3^{n+1}}{(n + 1)2^{n+1}} \cdot \frac{n2^n}{3^n}\right| = \lim_{n \to \infty} \frac{3n}{2(n + 1)} = \frac{3}{2}$$

Therefore, by the Ratio Test, the series diverges.

**60.** $\displaystyle\sum_{n=1}^{\infty} \frac{3 \cdot 5 \cdot 7 \cdots (2n + 1)}{18^n (2n - 1)n!}$

$$\lim_{n \to \infty} \left|\frac{a_{n+1}}{a_n}\right| = \lim_{n \to \infty} \left|\frac{3 \cdot 5 \cdot 7 \cdots (2n + 1)(2n + 3)}{18^{n+1}(2n + 1)(2n - 1)n!} \cdot \frac{18^n (2n - 1)n!}{3 \cdot 5 \cdot 7 \cdots (2n + 1)}\right| = \lim_{n \to \infty} \frac{(2n + 3)(2n - 1)}{18(2n + 1)(2n - 1)} = \frac{2}{18} = \frac{1}{9}$$

Therefore, by the Ratio Test, the series converge.

**62.** (b) and (c)

$$\sum_{n=0}^{\infty} (n + 1)\left(\frac{3}{4}\right)^n = \sum_{n=1}^{\infty} n\left(\frac{3}{4}\right)^{n-1}$$

$$= 1 + 2\left(\frac{3}{4}\right) + 3\left(\frac{3}{4}\right)^2 + 4\left(\frac{3}{4}\right)^3 + \cdots$$

**64.** (a) and (b) are the same.

$$\sum_{n=2}^{\infty} \frac{(-1)^n}{(n - 1)2^{n-1}} = \frac{1}{2} - \frac{1}{2 \cdot 2^2} + \frac{1}{3 \cdot 2^3} - \cdots$$

$$\sum_{n=1}^{\infty} \frac{(-1)^{n+1}}{n2^n} = \frac{1}{2} - \frac{1}{2 \cdot 2^2} + \frac{1}{3 \cdot 2^3} - \cdots$$

**66.** Replace $n$ with $n + 2$.

$$\sum_{n=2}^{\infty} \frac{2^n}{(n-2)!} = \sum_{n=0}^{\infty} \frac{2^{n+2}}{n!}$$

**68.** $\displaystyle\sum_{k=0}^{\infty} \frac{(-3)^k}{1 \cdot 3 \cdot 5 \ldots (2k+1)} = \sum_{k=0}^{\infty} \frac{(-3)^k 2^k \, k!}{(2k)!(2k+1)}$

$$= \sum_{k=0}^{\infty} \frac{(-6)^k \, k!}{(2k+1)!}$$

$$\approx 0.40967$$

(See Exercise 3 and use 10 terms, $k = 9$.)

**70.** See Theorem 8.18.

**72.** One example is $\displaystyle\sum_{n=1}^{\infty} \left( -100 + \frac{1}{n} \right)$.

**74.** Assume that

$$\lim_{n \to \infty} |a_{n+1}/a_n| = L > 1 \text{ or that } \lim_{n \to \infty} |a_{n+1}/a_n| = \infty.$$

Then there exists $N > 0$ such that $|a_{n+1}/a_n| > 1$ for all $n > N$. Therefore,

$$|a_{n+1}| > |a_n|, \quad n > N \Longrightarrow \lim_{n \to \infty} a_n \neq 0 \Longrightarrow \sum a_n \text{ diverges}$$

**76.** The differentiation test states that if

$$\sum_{n=1}^{\infty} U_n$$

is an infinite series with real terms and $f(x)$ is a real function such that $f(1/n) = U_n$ for all positive integers $n$ and $d^2 f/dx^2$ exists at $x = 0$, then

$$\sum_{n=1}^{\infty} U_n$$

converges absolutely if $f(0) = f'(0) = 0$ and diverges otherwise. Below are some examples.

| Convergent Series | Divergent Series |
|---|---|
| $\displaystyle\sum \frac{1}{n^3}, f(x) = x^3$ | $\displaystyle\sum \frac{1}{n}, f(x) = x$ |
| $\displaystyle\sum \left( 1 - \cos \frac{1}{n} \right), f(x) = 1 - \cos x$ | $\displaystyle\sum \sin \frac{1}{n}, f(x) = \sin x$ |

# Section 8.7    Taylor Polynomials and Approximations

**2.** $y = \frac{1}{8}x^4 - \frac{1}{2}x^2 + 1$

$y$-axis symmetry

Three relative extrema

Matches (c)

**4.** $y = e^{-1/2}\left[\frac{1}{3}(x-1)^3 - (x-1) + 1\right]$

Cubic

Matches (b)

**6.** $f(x) = \dfrac{4}{\sqrt[3]{x}} = 4x^{-1/3} \qquad f(8) = 2$

$f'(x) = -\dfrac{4}{3}x^{-4/3} \qquad f'(8) = -\dfrac{1}{12}$

$P_1(x) = f(8) + f'(8)(x - 8)$

$\qquad = 2 + \left(-\dfrac{1}{12}\right)(x - 8)$

$P_1(x) = -\dfrac{1}{12}x + \dfrac{8}{3}$

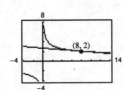

**8.** $f(x) = \tan x \qquad f\left(\dfrac{\pi}{4}\right) = 1$

$f'(x) = \sec^2 x \qquad f'\left(\dfrac{\pi}{4}\right) = 2$

$P_1 = f\left(\dfrac{\pi}{4}\right) + f'\left(\dfrac{\pi}{4}\right)\left(x - \dfrac{\pi}{4}\right)$

$\qquad = 1 + 2\left(x - \dfrac{\pi}{4}\right)$

$P_1(x) = 2x + 1 - \dfrac{\pi}{2}$

**10.** $f(x) = \sec x \qquad\qquad f\left(\dfrac{\pi}{4}\right) = \sqrt{2}$

$f'(x) = \sec x \tan x \qquad\qquad f'\left(\dfrac{\pi}{4}\right) = \sqrt{2}$

$f''(x) = \sec^3 x + \sec x \tan^2 x \qquad f''\left(\dfrac{\pi}{4}\right) = 3\sqrt{2}$

$P_2(x) = f\left(\dfrac{\pi}{4}\right) + f'\left(\dfrac{\pi}{4}\right)\left(x - \dfrac{\pi}{4}\right) + \dfrac{f''(\pi/4)}{2}\left(x - \dfrac{\pi}{4}\right)^2$

$P_2(x) = \sqrt{2} + \sqrt{2}\left(x - \dfrac{\pi}{4}\right) + \dfrac{3}{2}\sqrt{2}\left(x - \dfrac{\pi}{4}\right)^2$

| $x$ | $-2.15$ | $0.585$ | $0.685$ | $\pi/4$ | $0.885$ | $0.985$ | $1.785$ |
|-----|---------|---------|---------|---------|---------|---------|---------|
| $f(x)$ | $-1.8270$ | $1.1995$ | $1.2913$ | $1.4142$ | $1.5791$ | $1.8088$ | $-4.7043$ |
| $P_2(x)$ | $15.5414$ | $1.2160$ | $1.2936$ | $1.4142$ | $1.5761$ | $1.7810$ | $4.9475$ |

**12.** $f(x) = x^2 e^x,\ f(0) = 0$

(a) $f'(x) = (x^2 + 2x)e^x \qquad f'(0) = 0$

$\qquad f''(x) = (x^2 + 4x + 2)e^x \qquad f''(0) = 2$

$\qquad f'''(x) = (x^2 + 6x + 6)e^x \qquad f'''(0) = 6$

$\qquad f^{(4)}(x) = (x^2 + 8x + 12)e^x \qquad f^{(4)}(0) = 12$

$\qquad P_2(x) = \dfrac{2x^2}{2!} = x^2$

$\qquad P_3(x) = x^2 + \dfrac{6x^3}{3!} = x^2 + x^3$

$\qquad P_4(x) = x^2 + x^3 + \dfrac{12x^4}{4!} = x^2 + x^3 + \dfrac{x^4}{2}$

(b)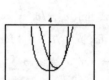

(c) $f''(0) = 2 = P_2''(0)$

$\qquad f'''(0) = 6 = P_3'''(0)$

$\qquad f^{(4)}(0) = 12 = P_4{}^{(4)}(0)$

(d) $f^{(n)}(0) = P_n{}^{(n)}(0)$

**14.** $f(x) = e^{-x} \qquad f(0) = 1$

$\quad f'(x) = -e^{-x} \qquad f'(0) = -1$

$\quad f''(x) = e^{-x} \qquad f''(0) = 1$

$\quad f'''(x) = -e^{-x} \qquad f'''(0) = -1$

$\quad f^{(4)}(x) = e^{-x} \qquad f^{(4)}(0) = 1$

$\quad f^{(5)}(x) = -e^{-x} \qquad f^{(5)}(0) = -1$

$P_5(x) = f(0) + f'(0)x + \dfrac{f''(0)}{2!}x^2 + \dfrac{f'''(0)}{3!}x^3 + \dfrac{f^{(4)}(0)}{4!}x^4 + \dfrac{f^{(5)}(0)}{5!}x^5 = 1 - x + \dfrac{x^2}{2} - \dfrac{x^3}{6} + \dfrac{x^4}{24} - \dfrac{x^5}{120}$

**16.**  $f(x) = e^{3x}$    $f(0) = 1$

$f'(x) = 3e^{3x}$    $f'(0) = 3$

$f''(x) = 9e^{3x}$    $f''(0) = 9$

$f'''(x) = 27e^{3x}$    $f'''(0) = 27$

$f^{(4)}(x) = 81e^{3x}$    $f^{(4)}(0) = 81$

$P_4(x) = 1 + 3x + \dfrac{9}{2!}x^2 + \dfrac{27}{3!}x^3 + \dfrac{81}{4!}x^4 = 1 + 3x + \dfrac{9}{2}x^2 + \dfrac{9}{2}x^3 + \dfrac{27}{8}x^4$

**18.**  $f(x) = \sin \pi x$    $f(0) = 0$

$f'(x) = \pi \cos \pi x$    $f'(0) = \pi$

$f''(x) = -\pi^2 \sin \pi x$    $f''(0) = 0$

$f'''(x) = -\pi^3 \cos \pi x$    $f'''(0) = -\pi^3$

$P_3(x) = 0 + \pi x + \dfrac{0}{2!}x^2 + \dfrac{-\pi^3}{3!}x^3 = \pi x - \dfrac{\pi^3}{6}x^3$

**20.**  $f(x) = x^2 e^{-x}$    $f(0) = 0$

$f'(x) = 2xe^{-x} - x^2 e^{-x}$    $f'(0) = 0$

$f''(x) = 2e^{-x} - 4xe^{-x} + x^2 e^{-x}$    $f''(0) = 2$

$f'''(x) = -6e^{-x} + 6xe^{-x} - x^2 e^{-x}$    $f'''(0) = -6$

$f^{(4)}(x) = 12e^{-x} - 8xe^{-x} + x^2 e^{-x}$    $f^{(4)}(0) = 12$

$P_4(x) = 0 + 0x + \dfrac{2}{2!}x^2 + \dfrac{-6}{3!}x^3 + \dfrac{12}{4!}x^4$

$\qquad = x^2 - x^3 + \dfrac{1}{2}x^4$

**22.**  $f(x) = \dfrac{x}{x+1} = \dfrac{x+1-1}{x+1} = 1 - (x+1)^{-1}$    $f(0) = 0$

$f'(x) = (x+1)^{-2}$    $f'(0) = 1$

$f''(x) = -2(x+1)^{-3}$    $f''(0) = -2$

$f'''(x) = 6(x+1)^{-4}$    $f'''(0) = 6$

$f^{(4)}(x) = -24(x+1)^{-5}$    $f^{(4)}(0) = -24$

$P_4(x) = 0 + 1(x) - \dfrac{2}{2}x^2 + \dfrac{6}{6}x^3 - \dfrac{24}{24}x^4 = x - x^2 + x^3 - x^4$

**24.**  $f(x) = \tan x$    $f(0) = 0$

$f'(x) = \sec^2 x$    $f'(0) = 1$

$f''(x) = 2\sec^2 x \tan x$    $f''(0) = 0$

$f'''(x) = 4\sec^2 x \tan^2 x + 2\sec^4 x$    $f'''(0) = 2$

$P_3(x) = 0 + 1(x) + 0 + \dfrac{2}{6}x^3 = x + \dfrac{1}{3}x^3$

**26.**  $f(x) = 2x^{-2}$    $f(2) = \dfrac{1}{2}$

$f'(x) = -4x^{-3}$    $f'(2) = -\dfrac{1}{2}$

$f''(x) = 12x^{-4}$    $f''(2) = \dfrac{3}{4}$

$f'''(x) = -48x^{-5}$    $f'''(x) = -\dfrac{3}{2}$

$f^{(4)}(x) = 240x^{-6}$    $f^{(4)}(x) = \dfrac{15}{4}$

$P_4(x) = \dfrac{1}{2} - \dfrac{1}{2}(x-2) + \dfrac{3}{8}(x-2)^2 - \dfrac{1}{4}(x-2)^3 + \dfrac{5}{32}(x-2)^4$

**28.** $f(x) = x^{1/3}$     $f(8) = 2$

$f'(x) = \dfrac{1}{3}x^{-2/3}$    $f'(8) = \dfrac{1}{12}$

$f''(x) = -\dfrac{2}{9}x^{-5/3}$    $f''(8) = -\dfrac{1}{144}$

$f'''(x) = \dfrac{10}{27}x^{-8/3}$    $f'''(8) = \dfrac{10}{27} \cdot \dfrac{1}{2^8} = \dfrac{5}{3456}$

$P_3(x) = 2 + \dfrac{1}{12}(x - 8) - \dfrac{1}{288}(x - 8)^2 + \dfrac{5}{20{,}736}(x - 8)^3$

**30.** $f(x) = x^2 \cos x$     $f(\pi) = -\pi^2$

$f'(x) = \cos x - x^2 \sin x$    $f'(\pi) = -2\pi$

$f''(x) = 2 \cos x - 4x \sin x - x^2 \cos x$   $f''(\pi) = -2 + \pi^2$

$P_2(x) = -\pi^2 - 2\pi(x - \pi) + \dfrac{(\pi^2 - 2)}{2}(x - \pi)^2$

**32.** $f(x) = \dfrac{1}{x^2 + 1}$

$f'(x) = \dfrac{-2x}{(x^2 + 1)^2}$

$f''(x) = \dfrac{2(3x^2 - 1)}{(x^2 + 1)^3}$

$f'''(x) = \dfrac{24x(1 - x^2)}{(x^2 + 1)^4}$

$f^{(4)}(x) = \dfrac{24(5x^4 - 10x^2 + 1)}{(x^2 + 1)^5}$

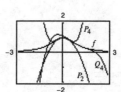

(a) $n = 2, c = 0$

$P_2(x) = 1 + 0x + \dfrac{-2}{2!}x^2 = 1 - x^2$

(b) $n = 4, c = 0$

$P_4(x) = 1 + 0x + \dfrac{-2}{2!}x^2 + \dfrac{0}{3!}x^3 + \dfrac{24}{4!}x^4 = 1 - x^2 + x^4$

(c) $n = 4, c = 1$

$Q_4(x) = \dfrac{1}{2} + \left(-\dfrac{1}{2}\right)(x - 1) + \dfrac{1/2}{2!}(x - 1)^2 + \dfrac{0}{3!}(x - 1)^3 + \dfrac{-3}{4!}(x - 1)^4 = \dfrac{1}{2} - \dfrac{1}{2}(x - 1) + \dfrac{1}{4}(x - 1)^2 - \dfrac{1}{8}(x - 1)^4$

**34.** $f(x) = \ln x$

$P_1(x) = x - 1$

$P_4(x) = (x - 1) - \dfrac{1}{2}(x - 1)^2 + \dfrac{1}{3}(x - 1)^3 - \dfrac{1}{4}(x - 1)^4$

(a)

| $x$ | 1.00 | 1.25 | 1.50 | 1.75 | 2.00 |
|---|---|---|---|---|---|
| $\ln x$ | 0.0000 | 0.2231 | 0.4055 | 0.5596 | 0.6931 |
| $P_1(x)$ | 0.0000 | 0.2500 | 0.5000 | 0.7500 | 1.0000 |
| $P_4(x)$ | 0.0000 | 0.2230 | 0.4010 | 0.5303 | 0.5833 |

(b)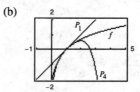

(c) As the distance increases, the accuracy decreases.

**36.** (a) $f(x) = \arctan x$

$P_3(x) = x - \dfrac{x^3}{3}$

(b)

| $x$ | $-0.75$ | $-0.50$ | $-0.25$ | 0 | 0.25 | 0.50 | 0.75 |
|---|---|---|---|---|---|---|---|
| $f(x)$ | $-0.6435$ | $-0.4636$ | $-0.2450$ | 0 | 0.2450 | 0.4636 | 0.6435 |
| $P_3(x)$ | $-0.6094$ | $-0.4583$ | $-0.2448$ | 0 | 0.2448 | 0.4583 | 0.6094 |

(c)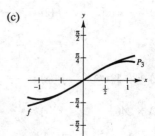

**38.** $f(x) = \arctan x$

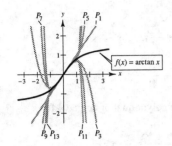

**40.** $f(x) = 4xe^{-x^2/4}$

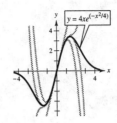

**42.** $f(x) = x^2 e^{-x} \approx x^2 - x^3 + \dfrac{1}{2}x^4$

$f\left(\dfrac{1}{5}\right) \approx 0.0328$

**44.** $f(x) = x^2 \cos x \approx -\pi^2 - 2\pi(x - \pi) + \left(\dfrac{\pi^2 - 2}{2}\right)(x - \pi)^2$

$f\left(\dfrac{7\pi}{8}\right) \approx -6.7954$

**46.** $f(x) = e^x; f^{(6)}(x) = e^x \Longrightarrow$ Max on $[0, 1]$ is $e^1$.

$R_5(x) \le \dfrac{e^1}{6!}(1)^6 \approx 0.00378 = 3.78 \times 10^{-3}$

**48.** $f(x) = \arctan x; f^{(4)}(x) = \dfrac{24x(x^2 + 1)}{(1 - x^2)^4}$

$\Longrightarrow$ Max on $[0, 0.4]$ is $f^{(4)}(0.4) \approx 22.3672$.

$R_3(x) \le \dfrac{22.3672}{4!}(0.4)^4 \approx 0.0239$

**50.**    $f(x) = e^x$

$f^{(n+1)}(x) = e^x$

Max on $[0, 0.6]$ is $e^{0.6} \approx 1.8221$.

$R_n \le \dfrac{1.8221}{(n + 1)!}(0.6)^{n+1} < 0.001$

By trial and error, $n = 5$.

**52.**    $f(x) = \cos(\pi x^2)$

$g(x) = \cos x = 1 - \dfrac{x^2}{2!} + \dfrac{x^4}{4!} - \dfrac{x^6}{6!} + \cdots$

$f(x) = g(\pi x^2)$

$= 1 - \dfrac{(\pi x^2)^2}{2!} + \dfrac{(\pi x^2)^4}{4!} - \dfrac{(\pi x^2)^6}{6!} + \cdots$

$= 1 - \dfrac{\pi^2 x^4}{2!} + \dfrac{\pi^4 x^8}{4!} - \dfrac{\pi^6 x^{12}}{6!} + \cdots$

$f(0.6) = 1 - \dfrac{\pi^2}{2!}(0.6)^4 + \dfrac{\pi^4}{4!}(0.6)^8 - \dfrac{\pi^6}{6!}(0.6)^{12} + \cdots$

Since this is an alternating series,

$R_n \le a_{n+1} = \dfrac{\pi^{2n}}{(2n)!}(0.6)^{4n} < 0.0001.$

By trial and error, $n = 4$. Using 4 terms $f(0.6) \approx 0.4257$.

**54.**    $f(x) = \sin x \approx x - \dfrac{x^3}{3!}$

$|R_3(x)| = \left|\dfrac{\sin z}{4!}x^4\right| \le \dfrac{|x^4|}{4!} < 0.001$

$x^4 < 0.024$

$|x| < 0.3936$

$-0.3936 < x < 0.3936$

**56.** $f(c) = P_2(c), f'(c) = P_2'(c),$ and $f''(c) = P_2''(c)$

**58.** See Theorem 8.19, page 611.

**60.**

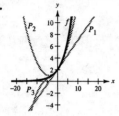

**62.** (a) $P_5(x) = x - \dfrac{x^3}{3!} + \dfrac{x^5}{5!}$ for $f(x) = \sin x$

$$P_5'(x) = 1 - \frac{x^2}{2!} + \frac{x^4}{4!}$$

This is the Maclaurin polynomial of degree 4 for $g(x) = \cos x$.

(b) $Q_6(x) = 1 - \dfrac{x^2}{2} + \dfrac{x^4}{4!} - \dfrac{x^6}{6!}$ for $\cos x$

$$Q_6'(x) = -x + \frac{x^3}{3!} - \frac{x^5}{5!} = -P_5(x)$$

(c) $R(x) = 1 + x + \dfrac{x^2}{2!} + \dfrac{x^3}{3!} + \dfrac{x^4}{4!}$

$$R'(x) = 1 + x + \frac{x^2}{2!} + \frac{x^3}{3!}$$

The first four terms are the same!

**64.** Let $f$ be an odd function and $P_n$ be the $n^{\text{th}}$ Maclaurin polynomial for $f$. Since $f$ is odd, $f'$ is even:

$$f'(-x) = \lim_{h \to 0} \frac{f(-x + h) - f(-x)}{h} = \lim_{h \to 0} \frac{-f(x - h) + f(x)}{h} = \lim_{h \to 0} \frac{f(x + (-h)) - f(x)}{-h} = f'(x).$$

Similarly, $f''$ is odd, $f'''$ is even, etc. Therefore, $f, f'', f^{(4)}$, etc. are all odd functions, which implies that $f(0) = f''(0) = \cdots = 0$. Hence, in the formula

$$P_n(x) = f(0) + f'(0)x + \frac{f''(0)x^2}{2!} + \cdots$$ all the coefficients of the even power of $x$ are zero.

**66.** Let $P_n(x) = a_0 + a_1(x - c) + a_2(x - c)^2 + \cdots + a_n(x - c)^n$ where $a_i = \dfrac{f^{(i)}(c)}{i!}$.

$$P_n(c) = a_0 = f(c)$$

For $1 \le k \le n$, $\quad P_n^{(k)}(c) = a_n k! = \left(\dfrac{f^{(k)}(c)}{k!}\right)k! = f^{(k)}(c)$.

# Section 8.8    Power Series

**2.** Centered at 0

**4.** Centered at $\pi$

**6.** $\displaystyle\sum_{n=0}^{\infty} (2x)^n$

$$L = \lim_{n \to \infty} \left| \frac{u_n + 1}{u_n} \right| = \lim_{n \to \infty} \left| \frac{(2x)^{n+1}}{(2x)^n} \right| = 2|x|$$

$$2|x| < 1 \implies R = \frac{1}{2}$$

**8.** $\displaystyle\sum_{n=0}^{\infty} \frac{(-1)^n x^n}{2^n}$

$$L = \lim_{n \to \infty} \left| \frac{u_{n+1}}{u_n} \right| = \lim_{n \to \infty} \left| \frac{(-1)^{n+1}x^{n+1}}{2^{n+1}} \cdot \frac{2^n}{(-1)^n x^n} \right|$$

$$= \frac{1}{2}|x|$$

$$\frac{1}{2}|x| < 1 \implies R = 2$$

**10.** $\sum_{n=0}^{\infty} \frac{(2n)!x^{2n}}{n!}$

$$L = \lim_{n\to\infty} \left| \frac{u_n + 1}{u_n} \right| = \lim_{n\to\infty} \left| \frac{(2n+2)!x^{2n+2}/(n+1)!}{(2n)!x^{2n}/n!} \right|$$

$$= \lim_{n\to\infty} \left| \frac{(2n+2)(2n+1)x^2}{(n+1)} \right| = \infty$$

The series only converges at $x = 0$. $R = 0$.

**12.** $\sum_{n=0}^{\infty} \left( \frac{x}{k} \right)^n$

Since the series is geometric, it converges only if $|x/k| < 1$ or $-k < x < k$.

**14.** $\sum_{n=0}^{\infty} (-1)^{n+1}(n+1)x^n$

$$\lim_{n\to\infty} \left| \frac{u_n + 1}{u_n} \right| = \lim_{n\to\infty} \left| \frac{(-1)^{n+2}(n+2)x^{n+1}}{(-1)^n(n+1)x^n} \right|$$

$$= \lim_{n\to\infty} \left| \frac{(n+2)x}{n+1} \right| = |x|$$

Interval: $-1 < x < 1$

When $x = 1$, the series $\sum_{n=0}^{\infty} (-1)^{n+1}(n+1)$ diverges.

When $x = -1$, the series $\sum_{n=0}^{\infty} -(n+1)$ diverges.

Therefore, the interval of convergence is $-1 < x < 1$.

**16.** $\sum_{n=0}^{\infty} \frac{(3x)^n}{(2n)!}$

$$\lim_{n\to\infty} \left| \frac{u_{n+1}}{u_n} \right| = \lim_{n\to\infty} \left| \frac{(3x)^{n+1}}{(2n+1)!} \cdot \frac{(2n)!}{(3x)^n} \right|$$

$$= \lim_{n\to\infty} \left| \frac{3x}{(2n+2)(2n+1)} \right| = 0$$

Therefore, the interval of convergence is $-\infty < x < \infty$.

**18.** $\sum_{n=0}^{\infty} \frac{(-1)^n x^n}{(n+1)(n+2)}$

$$\lim_{n\to\infty} \left| \frac{u_{n+1}}{u_n} \right| = \lim_{n\to\infty} \left| \frac{(-1)^{n+1}x^{n+1}}{(n+2)(n+3)} \cdot \frac{(n+1)(n+2)}{(-1)^n x^n} \right| = \lim_{n\to\infty} \left| \frac{(n+1)x}{n+3} \right| = |x|$$

Interval: $-1 < x < 1$

When $x = 1$, the alternating series $\sum_{n=0}^{\infty} \frac{(-1)^n}{(n+1)(n+2)}$ converges.

When $x = -1$, the series $\sum_{n=0}^{\infty} \frac{1}{(n+1)(n+2)}$ converges by limit comparison to $\sum_{n=1}^{\infty} \frac{1}{n^2}$.

Therefore, the interval of convergence is $-1 \le x \le 1$.

**20.** $\sum_{n=0}^{\infty} \frac{(-1)^n n!(x-4)^n}{3^n}$

$$\lim_{n\to\infty} \left| \frac{u_{n+1}}{u_n} \right| = \lim_{n\to\infty} \left| \frac{(-1)^{n+1}(n+1)!(x-4)^{n+1}}{3^{n+1}} \cdot \frac{3^n}{(-1)^n n!(x-4)^n} \right| = \lim_{n\to\infty} \left| \frac{(n+1)(x-4)}{3} \right| = \infty$$

$R = 0$

Center: $x = 4$

Therefore, the series converges only for $x = 4$.

**22.** $\displaystyle\sum_{n=0}^{\infty} \frac{(x-2)^{n+1}}{(n+1)4^{n+1}}$

$$\lim_{n\to\infty} \left|\frac{u_{n+1}}{u_n}\right| = \lim_{n\to\infty} \left|\frac{(x-2)^{n+2}}{(n+2)4^{n+2}} \cdot \frac{(n+1)4^{n+1}}{(x-2)^{n+1}}\right| = \lim_{n\to\infty} \left|\frac{(x-2)(n+1)}{4(n+2)}\right| = \frac{1}{4}|x-2|$$

$R = 4$

Center: $x = 2$

Interval: $-4 < x - 2 < 4$ or $-2 < x < 6$

When $x = -2$, the alternating series $\displaystyle\sum_{n=0}^{\infty} \frac{(-1)^{n+1}}{(n+1)}$ converges.

When $x = 6$, the series $\displaystyle\sum_{n=0}^{\infty} \frac{1}{n+1}$ diverges.

Therefore, the interval of convergence is $-2 \le x < 6$.

**24.** $\displaystyle\sum_{n=1}^{\infty} \frac{(-1)^{n+1}(x-c)^n}{nc^n}$

$$\lim_{n\to\infty} \left|\frac{u_{n+1}}{u_n}\right| = \lim_{n\to\infty} \left|\frac{(-1)^{n+2}(x-c)^{n+1}}{(n+1)c^{n+1}} \cdot \frac{nc^n}{(-1)^{n+1}(x-c)^n}\right| = \lim_{n\to\infty} \left|\frac{n(x-c)}{c(n+1)}\right| = \frac{1}{c}|x-c|$$

$R = c$

Center: $x = c$

Interval: $-c < x - c < c$ or $0 < x < 2c$

When $x = 0$, the $p$-series $\displaystyle\sum_{n=1}^{\infty} \frac{-1}{n}$ diverges.

When $x = 2c$, the alternating series $\displaystyle\sum_{n=1}^{\infty} \frac{(-1)^{n+1}}{n}$ converges. Therefore, the interval of convergence is $0 < x \le 2c$.

**26.** $\displaystyle\sum_{n=0}^{\infty} \frac{(-1)^n x^{2n+1}}{2n+1}$

$$\lim_{n\to\infty} \left|\frac{u_{n+1}}{u_n}\right| = \lim_{n\to\infty} \left|\frac{(-1)^{n+1}x^{2n+3}}{(2n+3)} \cdot \frac{(2n+1)}{(-1)^n x^{2n+1}}\right| = \lim_{n\to\infty} \left|\frac{(2n+1)}{(2n+3)}x^2\right| = |x^2|$$

$R = 1$

Interval: $-1 < x < 1$

When $x = 1$, $\displaystyle\sum_{n=0}^{\infty} \frac{(-1)^n}{2n+1}$ converges.

When $x = -1$, $\displaystyle\sum_{n=0}^{\infty} \frac{(-1)^{n+1}}{2n+1}$ converges.

Therefore, the interval of convergence is $-1 \le x \le 1$.

**28.** $\displaystyle\sum_{n=0}^{\infty} \frac{(-1)^n x^{2n}}{n!}$

$$\lim_{n\to\infty} \left|\frac{u_{n+1}}{u_n}\right| = \lim_{n\to\infty} \left|\frac{(-1)^{n+1}x^{2n+2}}{(n+1)!} \cdot \frac{n!}{(-1)^n x^{2n}}\right|$$

$$= \lim_{n\to\infty} \left|\frac{x^2}{n+1}\right| = 0$$

Therefore, the interval of convergence is $-\infty < x < \infty$.

**30.** $\displaystyle\sum_{n=1}^{\infty} \frac{n!x^n}{(2n)!}$

$$\lim_{n\to\infty} \left|\frac{u_{n+1}}{u_n}\right| = \lim_{n\to\infty} \left|\frac{(n+1)!x^{n+1}}{(2n+2)!} \cdot \frac{(2n)!}{n!x^n}\right|$$

$$= \lim_{n\to\infty} \left|\frac{(n+1)x}{(2n+2)(2n+1)}\right| = 0$$

Therefore, the interval of convergence is $-\infty < x < \infty$.

**32.** $\displaystyle\sum_{n=1}^{\infty} \frac{2 \cdot 4 \cdot 6 \cdots (2n)}{3 \cdot 5 \cdot 7 \cdots (2n+1)} (x^{2n+1})$

$\displaystyle\lim_{n\to\infty} \left| \frac{u_{n+1}}{u_n} \right| = \lim_{n\to\infty} \left| \frac{2 \cdot 4 \cdots (2n)(2n+2)x^{2n+3}}{3 \cdot 5 \cdot 7 \cdots (2n+1)(2n+3)} \cdot \frac{3 \cdot 5 \cdots (2n+1)}{2 \cdot 4 \cdots (2n)x^{2n+1}} \right| = \lim_{n\to\infty} \left| \frac{(2n+2)x^2}{(2n+3)} \right| = |x^2|$

$R = 1$

When $x = \pm 1$, the series diverges by comparing it to

$\displaystyle\sum_{n=1}^{\infty} \frac{1}{2n+1}$

which diverges. Therefore, the interval of convergence is $-1 < x < 1$.

**34.** $\displaystyle\sum_{n=1}^{\infty} \frac{n!(x-c)^n}{1 \cdot 3 \cdot 5 \cdots (2n-1)}$

$\displaystyle\lim_{n\to\infty} \left| \frac{u_{n+1}}{u_n} \right| = \lim_{n\to\infty} \left| \frac{(n+1)!(x-c)^{n+1}}{1 \cdot 3 \cdot 5 \cdots (2n-1)(2n+1)} \cdot \frac{1 \cdot 3 \cdot 5 \cdots (2n-1)}{n!(x-c)} \right| = \lim_{n\to\infty} \left| \frac{(n+1)(x-c)}{2n+1} \right| = \frac{1}{2}|x-c|$

$R = 2$

Interval: $-2 < x - c < 2$ or $c - 2 < x < c + 2$

The series diverges at the endpoints. Therefore, the interval of convergence is $c - 2 < x < c + 2$.

$\left[ \dfrac{n!(c+2-c)^n}{1 \cdot 3 \cdot 5 \cdots (2n-1)} = \dfrac{n!2^2}{1 \cdot 3 \cdot 5 \cdots (2n-1)} = \dfrac{2 \cdot 4 \cdot 6 \cdots (2n)}{1 \cdot 3 \cdot 5 \cdots (2n-1)} > 1 \right]$

**36.** (a) $f(x) = \displaystyle\sum_{n=1}^{\infty} \frac{(-1)^{n+1}(x-5)^n}{n5^n}, 0 < x \leq 10$

(b) $f'(x) = \displaystyle\sum_{n=1}^{\infty} \frac{(-1)^{n+1}(x-5)^{n-1}}{5^n}, 0 < x < 10$

(c) $f''(x) = \displaystyle\sum_{n=2}^{\infty} \frac{(-1)^{n+1}(n-1)(x-5)^{n-2}}{5^n}, 0 < x < 10$

(d) $\displaystyle\int f(x)\, dx = \sum_{n=1}^{\infty} \frac{(-1)^{n+1}(x-5)^{n+1}}{n(n+1)5^n}, 0 \leq x \leq 10$

**38.** (a) $f(x) = \displaystyle\sum_{n=1}^{\infty} \frac{(-1)^{n+1}(x-2)^n}{n}, 1 < x \leq 3$

(b) $f'(x) = \displaystyle\sum_{n=1}^{\infty} (-1)^{n+1}(x-2)^{n-1}, 1 < x < 3$

(c) $f''(x) = \displaystyle\sum_{n=2}^{\infty} (-1)^{n+1}(n-1)(x-2)^{n-2}, 1 < x < 3$

(d) $\displaystyle\int f(x)\, dx = \sum_{n=1}^{\infty} \frac{(-1)^{n+1}(x-2)^{n+1}}{n(n+1)}, 1 \leq x \leq 3$

**40.** $g(2) = \displaystyle\sum_{n=0}^{\infty} \left(\frac{2}{3}\right)^n = 1 + \frac{2}{3} + \frac{4}{9} + \cdots$

$S_1 = 1, S_2 = 1.67$. Matches (a)

**42.** $g(-2) = \displaystyle\sum_{n=0}^{\infty} \left(-\frac{2}{3}\right)^n$ alternating. Matches (d)

**44.** The set of all values of $x$ for which the power series converges is the interval of convergence. If the power series converges for all $x$, then the radius of convergence is $R = \infty$. If the power series converges at only $c$, then $R = 0$. Otherwise, according to Theorem 8.20, there exists a real number $R > 0$ (radius of convergence) such that the series converges absolutely for $|x - c| < R$ and diverges for $|x - c| > R$.

**46.** You differentiate and integrate the power series term by term. The radius of convergence remains the same. However, the interval of convergence might change.

**48.** (a) $f(x) = \displaystyle\sum_{n=0}^{\infty} \frac{x^n}{n!}, -\infty < x < \infty$     (See Exercise 11)

(b) $f'(x) = \displaystyle\sum_{n=1}^{\infty} \frac{nx^{n-1}}{n!} = \sum_{n=1}^{\infty} \frac{x^{n-1}}{(n-1)!} = \sum_{n=0}^{\infty} \frac{x^n}{n!} = f(x)$

(c) $f(x) = \displaystyle\sum_{n=1}^{\infty} \frac{x^n}{n!} = 1 + x + \frac{x^2}{2!} + \frac{x^3}{3!} + \frac{x^4}{4!} + \cdots$

$f(0) = 1$

(d) $f(x) = e^x$

**50.**
$$y = 1 + \sum_{n=1}^{\infty} \frac{(-1)^n x^{4n}}{2^{2n} n! \cdot 3 \cdot 7 \cdot 11 \cdots (4n-1)}$$

$$y' = \sum_{n=1}^{\infty} \frac{(-1)^n 4nx^{4n-1}}{2^{2n} n! \cdot 3 \cdot 7 \cdot 11 \cdots (4n-1)}$$

$$y'' = \sum_{n=1}^{\infty} \frac{(-1)^n 4n(4n-1)x^{4n-2}}{2^{2n} n! \cdot 3 \cdot 7 \cdot 11 \cdots (4n-1)} = -x^2 + \sum_{n=2}^{\infty} \frac{(-1)^n 4nx^{4n-2}}{2^{2n} n! \cdot 3 \cdot 7 \cdot 11 \cdots (4n-5)}$$

$$y'' + x^2 y = -x^2 + \sum_{n=2}^{\infty} \frac{(-1)^n 4nx^{4n-2}}{2^{2n} n! \cdot 3 \cdot 7 \cdot 11 \cdots (4n-5)} + \sum_{n=1}^{\infty} \frac{(-1)^n x^{4n+2}}{2^{2n} n! \cdot 3 \cdot 7 \cdot 11 \cdots (4n-1)} + x^2$$

$$= \sum_{n=1}^{\infty} \frac{(-1)^{n+1} 4(n+1)x^{4n+2}}{2^{2n+2}(n+1)! \cdot 3 \cdot 7 \cdot 11 \cdots (4n-1)} - \sum_{n=1}^{\infty} \frac{(-1)^{n+1} x^{4n+2}}{2^{2n} n! \cdot 3 \cdot 7 \cdot 11 \cdots (4n-1)} \frac{2^2(n+1)}{2^2(n+1)} = 0$$

**52.** $J_1(x) = x \sum_{k=0}^{\infty} \frac{(-1)^k x^{2k}}{2^{2k+1} k!(k+1)!} = \sum_{k=0}^{\infty} \frac{(-1)^k x^{2k+1}}{2^{2k+1} k!(k+1)!}$

(a) $\lim_{k \to \infty} \left| \frac{u_{k+1}}{u_k} \right| = \lim_{k \to \infty} \left| \frac{(-1)^{k+1} x^{2k+3}}{2^{2k+3}(k+1)!(k+2)!} \cdot \frac{2^{2k+1} k!(k+1)!}{(-1)^k x^{2k+1}} \right| = \lim_{k \to \infty} \left| \frac{(-1)x^2}{2^2(k+2)(k+1)} \right| = 0$

Therefore, the interval of convergence is $-\infty < x < \infty$.

(b) $J_1(x) = \sum_{k=0}^{\infty} \frac{(-1)^k x^{2k+1}}{2^{2k+1} k!(k+1!)}$

$J_1'(x) = \sum_{k=0}^{\infty} \frac{(-1)^k (2k+1)x^{2k}}{2^{2k+1} k!(k+1)!}$

$J_1''(x) = \sum_{k=1}^{\infty} \frac{(-1)^k (2k+1)(2k)x^{2k-1}}{2^{2k+1} k!(k+1)!}$

$x^2 J_1'' + x J_1' + (x^2-1)J_1 = \sum_{k=1}^{\infty} \frac{(-1)^k (2k+1)(2k)x^{2k+1}}{2^{2k+1} k!(k+1)!} + \sum_{k=0}^{\infty} \frac{(-1)^k (2k+1)x^{2k+1}}{2^{2k+1} k!(k+1)!}$

$$+ \sum_{k=0}^{\infty} \frac{(-1)^k x^{2k+3}}{2^{2k+1} k!(k+1)!} - \sum_{k=0}^{\infty} \frac{(-1)^k x^{2k+1}}{2^{2k+1} k!(k+1)!}$$

$$= \left[ \sum_{k=1}^{\infty} \frac{(-1)^k(2k+1)(2k)x^{2k+1}}{2^{2k+1} k!(k+1)!} + \frac{x}{2} + \sum_{k=1}^{\infty} \frac{(-1)^k(2k+1)x^{2k+1}}{2^{2k+1} k!(k+1)!} \right.$$

$$\left. - \frac{x}{2} - \sum_{k=1}^{\infty} \frac{(-1)^k x^{2k+1}}{2^{2k+1} k!(k+1)!} \right] + \sum_{k=0}^{\infty} \frac{(-1)^k x^{2k+3}}{2^{2k+1} k!(k+1)!}$$

$$= \sum_{k=1}^{\infty} \frac{(-1)^k x^{2k+1}[(2k+1)(2k) + (2k+1) - 1]}{2^{2k+1} k!(k+1)!} + \sum_{k=0}^{\infty} \frac{(-1)^k x^{2k+3}}{2^{2k+1} k!(k+1)!}$$

$$= \sum_{k=1}^{\infty} \frac{(-1)^k x^{2k+1} 4k(k+1)}{2^{2k+1} k!(k+1)!} + \sum_{k=0}^{\infty} \frac{(-1)^k x^{2k+3}}{2^{2k+1} k!(k+1)!}$$

$$= \sum_{k=1}^{\infty} \frac{(-1)^k x^{2k+1}}{2^{2k-1}(k-1)! k!} + \sum_{k=0}^{\infty} \frac{(-1)^k x^{2k+3}}{2^{2k+1} k!(k+1)!}$$

$$= \sum_{k=0}^{\infty} \frac{(-1)^{k+1} x^{2k+3}}{2^{2k+1} k!(k+1)!} + \sum_{k=0}^{\infty} \frac{(-1)^k x^{2k+3}}{2^{2k+1} k!(k+1)!}$$

$$= \sum_{k=0}^{\infty} \frac{(-1)^k x^{2k+3}[(-1)+1]}{2^{2k+1} k!(k+1)!} = 0$$

(c) $P_7(x) = \frac{x}{2} - \frac{1}{16}x^3 + \frac{1}{384}x^5 - \frac{1}{18,432}x^7$

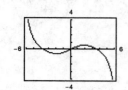

(d) $J_0'(x) = \sum_{k=0}^{\infty} \frac{(-1)^{k+1} 2(k+1)x^{2k+1}}{2^{2k+2}(k+1)!(k+1)!} = \sum_{k=0}^{\infty} \frac{(-1)^{k+1} x^{2k+1}}{2^{2k+1} k!(k+1)!}$

$-J_1(x) = -\sum_{k=0}^{\infty} \frac{(-1)^k x^{2k+1}}{2^{2k+1} k!(k+1)!} = \sum_{k=0}^{\infty} \frac{(-1)^{k+1} x^{2k+1}}{2^{2k+1} k!(k+1)!}$

**Note:** $J_0'(x) = -J_1(x)$

**54.** $f(x) = \sum_{n=0}^{\infty} (-1)^n \dfrac{x^{2n+1}}{(2n+1)!} = \sin x$

(See Exercise 47.)

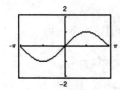

**56.** $f(x) = \sum_{n=0}^{\infty} (-1)^n \dfrac{x^{2n+1}}{2n+1} = \arctan x, \ -1 \le x \le 1$

(See Exercise 38 in Section 8.7.)

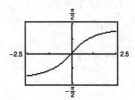

**58.** $\sum_{n=0}^{\infty} \dfrac{x^{2n+1}}{(2n+1)!} = \sum_{n=1}^{\infty} \dfrac{x^{2n-1}}{(2n-1)!}$

Replace $n$ with $n - 1$.

**60.** True; if

$$\sum_{n=0}^{\infty} a_n x^n$$

converges for $x = 2$, then we know that it must converge on $(-2, 2]$.

**62.** True

$$\int_0^1 f(x)\, dx = \int_0^1 \left( \sum_{n=0}^{\infty} a_n x^n \right) dx = \left[ \sum_{n=0}^{\infty} \dfrac{a_n x^{n+1}}{n+1} \right]_0^1 = \sum_{n=0}^{\infty} \dfrac{a_n}{n+1}$$

## Section 8.9    Representation of Functions by Power Series

**2.** (a) $f(x) = \dfrac{4}{5-x} = \dfrac{4/5}{1 - x/5} = \dfrac{a}{1-r}$

$$= \sum_{n=0}^{\infty} \dfrac{4}{5}\left(\dfrac{x}{5}\right)^n = \sum_{n=0}^{\infty} \dfrac{4x^n}{5^{n+1}}$$

This series converges on $(-5, 5)$.

(b)
$$
\begin{array}{r}
\frac{4}{5} + \frac{4}{25}x + \frac{4}{125}x^2 + \frac{4x^3}{625} + \cdots \\
5 - x \overline{) \, 4 \phantom{xxxxxxxxxxxxxxxxxxxx}} \\
4 - \frac{4}{5}x \phantom{xxxxxxxxxxxxxxx} \\
\frac{4}{5}x \phantom{xxxxxxxxxxxxxx} \\
\frac{4}{5}x - \frac{4}{25}x^2 \phantom{xxxxxxx} \\
\frac{4}{25}x^2 \phantom{xxxxxxx} \\
\frac{4}{25}x^2 - \frac{4x^3}{125} \phantom{xx} \\
\frac{4x^3}{125} \phantom{xx} \\
\frac{4x^3}{125} - \frac{4x^4}{625} \\
\vdots
\end{array}
$$

**4.** (a) $\dfrac{1}{1+x} = \dfrac{1}{1 - (-x)} = \dfrac{a}{1-r}$

$$= \sum_{n=0}^{\infty} (-x)^n = \sum_{n=0}^{\infty} (-1)^n x^n$$

This series converges on $(-1, 1)$.

(b)
$$
\begin{array}{r}
1 - x + x^2 - x^3 + \cdots \\
1 + x \overline{) \, 1 \phantom{xxxxxxxxxxxxxx}} \\
1 + x \phantom{xxxxxxxxxxx} \\
-x \phantom{xxxxxxxxxx} \\
-x - x^2 \phantom{xxxxx} \\
x^2 \phantom{xxxxx} \\
x^2 + x^3 \phantom{xx} \\
-x^3 \phantom{xx} \\
-x^3 - x^4 \\
\vdots
\end{array}
$$

**6.** Writing $f(x)$ in the form $\dfrac{a}{1-r}$, we have

$$\frac{4}{5-x} = \frac{4}{7-(x+2)} = \frac{4/7}{1-1/7(x+2)} = \frac{a}{1-r}.$$

Therefore, the power series for $f(x)$ is given by

$$\frac{4}{5-x} = \sum_{n=0}^{\infty} ar^n = \sum_{n=0}^{\infty} \frac{4}{7}\left(\frac{1}{7}(x+2)\right)^n$$

$$= \sum_{n=0}^{\infty} \frac{4(x+2)^n}{7^{n+1}}.$$

$$|x+2| < 7 \text{ or } -5 < x < 9$$

**8.** Writing $f(x)$ in the form $a/(1-r)$, we have

$$\frac{3}{2x-1} = \frac{3}{3+2(x-2)} = \frac{1}{1+(2/3)(x-2)} = \frac{a}{1-r}$$

which implies that $a = 1$ and $r = (-2/3)(x-2)$. Therefore, the power series for $f(x)$ is given by

$$\frac{3}{2x-1} = \sum_{n=0}^{\infty} ar^n = \sum_{n=0}^{\infty}\left[-\frac{2}{3}(x-2)\right]^n,$$

$$= \sum_{n=0}^{\infty} \frac{(-2)^n(x-2)^n}{3^n},$$

$$|x-2| < \frac{3}{2} \text{ or } \frac{1}{2} < x < \frac{7}{2}.$$

**10.** Writing $f(x)$ in the form $a/(1-r)$, we have

$$\frac{1}{2x-5} = \frac{1}{-5+2x} = \frac{-1/5}{1-(2/5)x} = \frac{a}{1-r}$$

which implies that $a = -1/5$ and $r = (2/5)x$. Therefore, the power series for $f(x)$ is given by

$$\frac{1}{2x-5} = \sum_{n=0}^{\infty} ar^n = \sum_{n=0}^{\infty}\left(-\frac{1}{5}\right)\left(\frac{2}{5}x\right)^n = -\sum_{n=0}^{\infty} \frac{2^n x^n}{5^{n+1}},$$

$$|x| < \frac{5}{2} \text{ or } -\frac{5}{2} < x < \frac{5}{2}.$$

**12.** Writing $f(x)$ in the form $a/(1-r)$, we have

$$\frac{4}{3x+2} = \frac{4}{8+3(x-2)} = \frac{1/2}{1+(3/8)(x-2)} = \frac{a}{1-r}$$

which implies that $a = 1/2$ and $r = (-3/8)(x-2)$. Therefore, the power series for $f(x)$ is given by

$$\frac{4}{3x+2} = \sum_{n=0}^{\infty} ar^n = \sum_{n=0}^{\infty} \frac{1}{2}\left[-\frac{3}{8}(x-2)\right]^n$$

$$= \frac{1}{2}\sum_{n=0}^{\infty} \frac{(-3)^n(x-2)^n}{8^n},$$

$$|x-2| < \frac{8}{3} \text{ or } -\frac{2}{3} < x < \frac{14}{3}.$$

**14.** $\dfrac{4x-7}{2x^2+3x-2} = \dfrac{3}{x+2} - \dfrac{2}{2x-1} = \dfrac{3}{2+x} - \dfrac{2}{-1+2x} = \dfrac{3/2}{1+(1/2)x} + \dfrac{2}{1-2x}$

Writing $f(x)$ as a sum of two geometric series, we have

$$\frac{4x-7}{2x^2+3x-2} = \sum_{n=0}^{\infty}\left(\frac{3}{2}\right)\left(-\frac{1}{2}x\right)^n + \sum_{n=0}^{\infty} 2(2x)^n = \sum_{n=0}^{\infty}\left[\frac{3(-1)^n}{2^{n+1}} + 2^{n+1}\right]x^n, |x| < \frac{1}{2} \text{ or } -\frac{1}{2} < x < \frac{1}{2}.$$

**16.** First finding the power series for $4/(4+x)$, we have

$$\frac{1}{1+(1/4)x} = \sum_{n=0}^{\infty}\left(-\frac{1}{4}x\right)^n = \sum_{n=0}^{\infty} \frac{(-1)^n x^n}{4^n}$$

Now replace $x$ with $x^2$.

$$\frac{4}{4+x^2} = \sum_{n=0}^{\infty} \frac{(-1)^n x^{2n}}{4^n}.$$

The interval of convergence is $|x^2| < 4$ or $-2 < x < 2$ since

$$\lim_{n\to\infty}\left|\frac{u_{n+1}}{u_n}\right| = \lim_{n\to\infty}\left|\frac{(-1)^{n+1}x^{2n+2}}{4^{n+1}} \cdot \frac{4^n}{(-1)^n x^{2n}}\right| = \left|-\frac{x^2}{4}\right| = \frac{|x^2|}{4}.$$

**18.** $h(x) = \dfrac{x}{x^2-1} = \dfrac{1}{2(1+x)} - \dfrac{1}{2(1-x)} = \dfrac{1}{2}\sum_{n=0}^{\infty}(-1)^n x^n - \dfrac{1}{2}\sum_{n=0}^{\infty} x^n$

$$= \frac{1}{2}\sum_{n=0}^{\infty}[(-1)^n - 1]x^n = \frac{1}{2}[0 - 2x + 0x^2 - 2x^3 + 0x^4 - 2x^5 + \cdots]$$

$$= \frac{1}{2}\sum_{n=0}^{\infty}(-2)x^{2n+1} = -\sum_{n=0}^{\infty} x^{2n+1}, 1 < x < 1$$

**20.** By taking the second derivative, we have $\dfrac{d^2}{dx^2}\left[\dfrac{1}{x+1}\right] = \dfrac{2}{(x+1)^3}$. Therefore,

$$\frac{2}{(x+1)^3} = \frac{d^2}{dx^2}\left[\sum_{n=0}^{\infty}(-1)^n x^n\right]$$

$$= \frac{d}{dx}\left[\sum_{n=1}^{\infty}(-1)^n n x^{n-1}\right] = \sum_{n=2}^{\infty}(-1)^n n(n-1)x^{n-2} = \sum_{n=0}^{\infty}(-1)^n(n+2)(n+1)x^n,\ -1 < x < 1.$$

**22.** By integrating, we have

$$\int \frac{1}{1+x}\,dx = \ln(1+x) + C_1 \text{ and } \int \frac{1}{1-x}\,dx = -\ln(1-x) + C_2.$$

$f(x) = \ln(1-x^2) = \ln(1+x) - [-\ln(1-x)]$. Therefore,

$$\ln(1-x^2) = \int \frac{1}{1+x}\,dx - \int \frac{1}{1-x}\,dx$$

$$= \int\left[\sum_{n=0}^{\infty}(-1)^n x^n\right]dx - \int\left[\sum_{n=0}^{\infty}x^n\right]dx = \left[C_1 + \sum_{n=0}^{\infty}\frac{(-1)^n x^{n+1}}{n+1}\right] - \left[C_2 + \sum_{n=0}^{\infty}\frac{x^{n+1}}{n+1}\right]$$

$$= C + \sum_{n=0}^{\infty}\frac{[(-1)^n - 1]x^{n+1}}{n+1} = C + \sum_{n=0}^{\infty}\frac{-2x^{2n+2}}{2n+2} = C + \sum_{n=0}^{\infty}\frac{(-1)x^{2n+2}}{n+1}$$

To solve for $C$, let $x = 0$ and conclude that $C = 0$. Therefore,

$$\ln(1-x^2) = -\sum_{n=0}^{\infty}\frac{x^{2n+2}}{n+1},\ -1 < x < 1$$

**24.** $\dfrac{2x}{x^2+1} = 2x\displaystyle\sum_{n=0}^{\infty}(-1)^n x^{2n}$ (See Exercise 23.)

$$= \sum_{n=0}^{\infty}(-1)^n 2x^{2n+1}$$

Since $\dfrac{d}{dx}(\ln(x^2+1)) = \dfrac{2x}{x^2+1}$, we have

$$\ln(x^2+1) = \int\left[\sum_{n=0}^{\infty}(-1)^n 2x^{2n+1}\right]dx = C + \sum_{n=0}^{\infty}\frac{(-1)^n x^{2n+2}}{n+1},\ -1 \leq x \leq 1.$$

To solve for $C$, let $x = 0$ and conclude that $C = 0$. Therefore,

$$\ln(x^2+1) = \sum_{n=0}^{\infty}\frac{(-1)^n x^{2n+2}}{n+1},\ -1 \leq x \leq 1.$$

**26.** Since $\displaystyle\int \frac{1}{4x^2+1}\,dx = \frac{1}{2}\arctan(2x)$, we can use the result of Exercise 25 to obtain

$$\arctan(2x) = 2\int \frac{1}{4x^2+1}\,dx = 2\int\left[\sum_{n=0}^{\infty}(-1)^n 4^n x^{2n}\right]dx = C + 2\sum_{n=0}^{\infty}\frac{(-1)^n 4^n x^{2n+1}}{2n+1},\ -\frac{1}{2} < x \leq \frac{1}{2}.$$

To solve for $C$, let $x = 0$ and conclude that $C = 0$. Therefore,

$$\arctan(2x) = 2\sum_{n=0}^{\infty}\frac{(-1)^n 4^n x^{2n+1}}{2n+1},\ -\frac{1}{2} < x \leq \frac{1}{2}.$$

**28.** $x - \dfrac{x^2}{2} + \dfrac{x^3}{3} - \dfrac{x^4}{4} \leq \ln(x + 1)$

$$\leq x - \frac{x^2}{2} + \frac{x^3}{3} - \frac{x^4}{4} + \frac{x^5}{5}$$

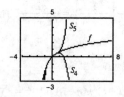

| $x$ | 0.0 | 0.2 | 0.4 | 0.6 | 0.8 | 1.0 |
|---|---|---|---|---|---|---|
| $x - \dfrac{x^2}{2} + \dfrac{x^3}{3} - \dfrac{x^4}{4}$ | 0.0 | 0.18227 | 0.33493 | 0.45960 | 0.54827 | 0.58333 |
| $\ln(x + 1)$ | 0.0 | 0.18232 | 0.33647 | 0.47000 | 0.58779 | 0.69315 |
| $x - \dfrac{x^2}{2} + \dfrac{x^3}{3} - \dfrac{x^4}{4} + \dfrac{x^5}{5}$ | 0.0 | 0.18233 | 0.33698 | 0.47515 | 0.61380 | 0.78333 |

In Exercise 35–38, $\arctan x = \displaystyle\sum_{n=0}^{\infty} (-1)^n \frac{x^{2n+1}}{2n + 1}$.

**30.** $g(x) = x - \dfrac{x^3}{3}$, cubic with 3 zeros.

Matches (d)

**32.** $g(x) = x - \dfrac{x^3}{3} + \dfrac{x^5}{5} - \dfrac{x^7}{7}$,

Matches (b)

**34.** The approximations of degree 3, 7, 11, . . . $(4n - 1, n = 1, 2, . . .)$ have relative extrema.

**In Exercises 36 and 38,** $\arctan x = \displaystyle\sum_{n=0}^{\infty} (-1)^n \frac{x^{2n+1}}{2n + 1}$.

**36.** $\arctan x^2 = \displaystyle\sum_{n=0}^{\infty} (-1)^n \frac{x^{4n+2}}{2n + 1}$

$$\int \arctan x^2 \, dx = \sum_{n=0}^{\infty} (-1)^n \frac{x^{4n+3}}{(4n + 3)(2n + 1)} + C, C = 0$$

$$\int_0^{3/4} \arctan x^2 \, dx = \sum_{n=0}^{\infty} (-1)^n \frac{(3/4)^{4n+3}}{(4n + 3)(2n + 1)}$$

$$= \sum_{n=0}^{\infty} (-1)^n \frac{3^{4n+3}}{(4n + 3)(2n + 1)4^{4n+3}}$$

$$= \frac{27}{192} - \frac{2187}{344,064} + \frac{177,147}{230,686,720}$$

Since $177,147/230,686,720 < 0.001$, we can approximate the series by its first two terms: $0.13427$

**38.** $x^2 \arctan x = \displaystyle\sum_{n=0}^{\infty} (-1)^n \frac{x^{2n+3}}{2n + 1}$

$$\int x^2 \arctan x \, dx = \sum_{n=0}^{\infty} (-1)^n \frac{x^{2n+4}}{(2n + 4)(2n + 1)}$$

$$\int_0^{1/2} x^2 \arctan x \, dx = \sum_{n=0}^{\infty} (-1)^n \frac{1}{(2n + 4)(2n + 1)2^{2n+4}} = \frac{1}{64} - \frac{1}{1152} + \cdots$$

Since $\dfrac{1}{1152} < 0.001$, we can approximate the series by its first term: $\displaystyle\int_0^{1/2} x^2 \arctan x \, dx \approx 0.015625$.

**In Exercises 40 and 42,** $\dfrac{1}{1-x} = \displaystyle\sum_{n=0}^{\infty} x^n$, $|x| 1$.

**40.** Replace $n$ with $n + 1$.

$$\sum_{n=1}^{\infty} nx^{n-1} = \sum_{n=0}^{\infty} (n+1)x^n$$

**42.** (a) $\dfrac{1}{3} \displaystyle\sum_{n=1}^{\infty} n\left(\dfrac{2}{3}\right)^n = \dfrac{2}{9} \sum_{n=1}^{\infty} n\left(\dfrac{2}{3}\right)^{n-1} = \dfrac{2}{9} \dfrac{1}{[1-(2/3)]^2} = 2$

(b) $\dfrac{1}{10} \displaystyle\sum_{n=1}^{\infty} n\left(\dfrac{9}{10}\right)^n = \dfrac{9}{100} \sum_{n=1}^{\infty} n\left(\dfrac{9}{10}\right)^{n-1}$

$$= \dfrac{9}{100} \cdot \dfrac{1}{[1-(9/10)]^2} = 9$$

**44.** Replace $x$ with $x^2$.

**46.** Integrate the series and multiply by $(-1)$.

**48.** (a) From Exercise 47, we have

$$\arctan \dfrac{120}{119} - \arctan \dfrac{1}{239} = \arctan \dfrac{120}{119} + \arctan\left(-\dfrac{1}{239}\right)$$

$$= \arctan\left[\dfrac{(120/119) + (-1/239)}{1 - (120/119)(-1/239)}\right] = \arctan\left(\dfrac{28{,}561}{28{,}561}\right) = \arctan 1 = \dfrac{\pi}{4}$$

(b) $2 \arctan \dfrac{1}{5} = \arctan \dfrac{1}{5} + \arctan \dfrac{1}{5} = \arctan\left[\dfrac{2(1/5)}{1 - (1/5)^2}\right] = \arctan \dfrac{10}{24} = \arctan \dfrac{5}{12}$

$4 \arctan \dfrac{1}{5} = 2 \arctan \dfrac{1}{5} + 2 \arctan \dfrac{1}{5} = \arctan \dfrac{5}{12} + \arctan \dfrac{5}{12} = \arctan\left[\dfrac{2(5/12)}{1 - (5/12)^2}\right] = \arctan \dfrac{120}{119}$

$4 \arctan \dfrac{1}{5} - \arctan \dfrac{1}{239} = \arctan \dfrac{120}{119} - \arctan \dfrac{1}{239} = \dfrac{\pi}{4}$ (see part (a).)

**50.** (a) $\arctan \dfrac{1}{2} + \arctan \dfrac{1}{3} = \arctan\left[\dfrac{(1/2) + (1/3)}{1 - (1/2)(1/3)}\right] = \arctan\left(\dfrac{5/6}{5/6}\right) = \dfrac{\pi}{4}$

(b) $\pi = 4\left[\arctan \dfrac{1}{2} + \arctan \dfrac{1}{3}\right]$

$$= 4\left[\dfrac{1}{2} - \dfrac{(1/2)^3}{3} + \dfrac{(1/2)^5}{5} - \dfrac{(1/2)^7}{7}\right] + 4\left[\dfrac{1}{3} - \dfrac{(1/3)^3}{3} + \dfrac{(1/3)^5}{5} - \dfrac{(1/3)^7}{7}\right]$$

$$\approx 4(0.4635) + 4(0.3217) \approx 3.14$$

**52.** From Exercise 51, we have

$$\sum_{n=1}^{\infty} (-1)^{n+1} \dfrac{1}{3^n n} = \sum_{n=1}^{\infty} \dfrac{(-1)^{n+1}(1/3)^n}{n}$$

$$= \ln\left(\dfrac{1}{3} + 1\right) = \ln \dfrac{4}{3} \approx 0.2877.$$

**54.** From Example 5, we have $\arctan x = \displaystyle\sum_{n=0}^{\infty} (-1)^n \dfrac{x^{2n+1}}{2n+1}$.

$$\sum_{n=0}^{\infty} (-1)^n \dfrac{1}{2n+1} = \sum_{n=0}^{\infty} (-1)^n \dfrac{(1)^{2n+1}}{2n+1}$$

$$= \arctan 1 = \dfrac{\pi}{4} \approx 0.7854$$

**56.** From Exercise 54, we have

$$\sum_{n=1}^{\infty} (-1)^{n+1} \dfrac{1}{3^{2n-1}(2n-1)} = \sum_{n=0}^{\infty} (-1)^n \dfrac{1}{3^{2n+1}(2n+1)}$$

$$= \sum_{n=0}^{\infty} (-1)^n \dfrac{(1/3)^{2n+1}}{2n+1}$$

$$= \arctan \dfrac{1}{3} \approx 0.3218.$$

**58.** From Example 5, we have $\arctan x = \sum_{n=0}^{\infty} (-1)^n \frac{x^{2n+1}}{2n+1}$.

$$\sum_{n=0}^{\infty} \frac{(-1)^n}{3^n(2n+1)} = \sum_{n=0}^{\infty} \frac{(-1)^n}{(\sqrt{3})^{2n}(2n+1)} \cdot \frac{\sqrt{3}}{\sqrt{3}}$$

$$= \sqrt{3} \sum_{n=0}^{\infty} \frac{(-1)^n(1/\sqrt{3})^{2n+1}}{2n+1}$$

$$= \sqrt{3} \arctan \frac{1}{\sqrt{3}}$$

$$= \sqrt{3} \left(\frac{\pi}{6}\right) = \frac{\pi}{2\sqrt{3}}$$

# Section 8.10    Taylor and Maclaurin Series

**2.** For $c = 0$, we have

$$f(x) = e^{3x}$$

$$f^{(n)}(x) = 3^n e^{3x} \implies f^{(n)}(0) = 3^n$$

$$e^{3x} = 1 + 3x + \frac{9x^2}{2!} + \frac{27x^3}{3!} + \cdots = \sum_{n=0}^{\infty} \frac{(3x)^n}{n!}$$

**4.** For $c = \pi/4$, we have:

$$f(x) = \sin x \qquad f\left(\frac{\pi}{4}\right) = \frac{\sqrt{2}}{2}$$

$$f'(x) = \cos x \qquad f'\left(\frac{\pi}{4}\right) = \frac{\sqrt{2}}{2}$$

$$f''(x) = -\sin x \qquad f''\left(\frac{\pi}{4}\right) = -\frac{\sqrt{2}}{2}$$

$$f'''(x) = -\cos x \qquad f'''\left(\frac{\pi}{4}\right) = -\frac{\sqrt{2}}{2}$$

$$f^{(4)}(x) = \sin x \qquad f^{(4)}\left(\frac{\pi}{4}\right) = \frac{\sqrt{2}}{2}$$

and so on. Therefore we have:

$$\sin x = \sum_{n=0}^{\infty} \frac{f^{(n)}(\pi/4)[x-(\pi/4)]^n}{n!}$$

$$= \frac{\sqrt{2}}{2} \left[ 1 + \left(x - \frac{\pi}{4}\right) - \frac{[x-(\pi/4)]^2}{2!} - \frac{[x-(\pi/4)]^3}{3!} + \frac{[x-(\pi/4)]^4}{4!} + \cdots \right]$$

$$= \frac{\sqrt{2}}{2} \left\{ \sum_{n=0}^{\infty} \frac{(-1)^{n(n+1)/2}[x-(\pi/4)]^{n+1}}{(n+1)!} + 1 \right\}$$

**6.** For $c = 1$, we have:

$$f(x) = e^x$$

$$f^{(n)}(x) = e^x \implies f^{(n)}(1) = e$$

$$e^x = \sum_{n=0}^{\infty} \frac{f^{(n)}(1)(x-1)^n}{n!} = e\left[ 1 + (x-1) + \frac{(x-1)^2}{2!} + \frac{(x-1)^3}{3!} + \frac{(x-1)^4}{4!} + \cdots \right] = e\sum_{n=0}^{\infty} \frac{(x-1)^n}{n!}$$

**8.** For $c = 0$, we have:

$$f(x) = \ln(x^2 + 1) \qquad\qquad f(0) = 0$$

$$f'(x) = \frac{2x}{x^2 + 1} \qquad\qquad f'(0) = 0$$

$$f''(x) = \frac{2 - 2x^2}{(x^2 + 1)^2} \qquad\qquad f''(0) = 2$$

$$f'''(x) = \frac{4x(x^2 - 3)}{(x^2 + 1)^3} \qquad\qquad f'''(0) = 0$$

$$f^{(4)}(x) = \frac{12(-x^4 + 6x^2 - 1)}{(x^2 + 1)^4} \qquad\qquad f^{(4)}(0) = -12$$

$$f^{(5)}(x) = \frac{48x(x^4 - 10x^2 + 5)}{(x^2 + 1)^5} \qquad\qquad f^{(5)}(0) = 0$$

$$f^{(6)}(x) = \frac{-240(5x^6 - 15x^4 + 15x^2 - 1)}{(x^2 + 1)^6} \qquad f^{(6)}(0) = 240$$

and so on. Therefore, we have:

$$\ln(x^2 + 1) = \sum_{n=0}^{\infty} \frac{f^{(n)}(0)x^n}{n!} = 0 + 0x + \frac{2x^2}{2!} + \frac{0x^3}{3!} - \frac{12x^4}{4!} + \frac{0x^5}{5!} + \frac{240x^6}{6!} + \cdots$$

$$= x^2 - \frac{x^4}{2} + \frac{x^6}{3} - \cdots = \sum_{n=0}^{\infty} \frac{(-1)^n x^{2n+2}}{n + 1}$$

**10.** For $c = 0$, we have;

$$f(x) = \tan(x) \qquad\qquad\qquad f(0) = 0$$

$$f'(x) = \sec^2(x) \qquad\qquad\qquad f'(0) = 1$$

$$f''(x) = 2\sec^2(x)\tan(x) \qquad\qquad\qquad f''(0) = 0$$

$$f'''(x) = 2[\sec^4(x) + 2\sec^2(x)\tan^2(x)] \qquad\qquad\qquad f'''(0) = 2$$

$$f^{(4)}(x) = 8[\sec^4(x)\tan(x) + \sec^2(x)\tan^3(x)] \qquad\qquad f^{(4)}(0) = 0$$

$$f^{(5)}(x) = 8[2\sec^6(x) + 11\sec^4(x)\tan^2(x) + 2\sec^2(x)\tan^4(x)] \qquad f^{(5)}(0) = 16$$

$$\tan(x) = \sum_{n=0}^{\infty} \frac{f^{(n)}(0)x^n}{n!} = x + \frac{2x^3}{3!} + \frac{16x^5}{5!} + \cdots = x + \frac{x^3}{3} + \frac{2}{15}x^5 + \cdots$$

**12.** The Maclaurin Series for $f(x) = e^{-2x}$ is $\displaystyle\sum_{n=0}^{\infty} \frac{(-2x)^n}{n!}$.

$f^{(n+1)}(x) = (-2)^{n+1}e^{-2x}$. Hence, by Taylor's Theorem,

$$0 \le |Rn(x)| = \left| \frac{f^{(n+1)}(z)}{(n+1)!} x^{n+1} \right| = \left| \frac{(-2)^{n+1}e^{-2z}}{(n+1)!} x^{n+1} \right|.$$

Since $\displaystyle\lim_{n\to\infty} \left| \frac{(-2)^{n+1}x^{n+1}}{(n+1)!} \right| = \lim_{n\to\infty} \left| \frac{(2x)^{n+1}}{(n+1)!} \right| = 0$, it follows that $Rn(x) \to 0$ as $n \to \infty$.

Hence, the Maclaurin Series for $e^{-2x}$ converges to $e^{-2x}$ for all $x$.

**14.** Since $(1 + x)^{-k} = 1 - kx + \dfrac{k(k + 1)x^2}{2!} - \dfrac{k(k + 1)(k + 2)x^3}{3!} + \cdots$, we have

$$\left[1 + (-x)\right]^{-1/2} = 1 + \left(\frac{1}{2}\right)x + \frac{(1/2)(3/2)x^2}{2!} + \frac{(1/2)(3/2)(5/2)x^3}{3!} + \cdots$$

$$= 1 + \frac{x}{2} + \frac{(1)(3)x^2}{2^2 2!} + \frac{(1)(3)(5)x^3}{2^3 3!} + \cdots$$

$$= 1 + \sum_{n=1}^{\infty} \frac{1 \cdot 3 \cdot 5 \cdots (2n - 1)x^n}{2^n n!}$$

**16.** Since $(1 + x)^k = 1 + kx + \dfrac{k(k - 1)x^2}{2!} + \dfrac{k(k - 1)(k - 2)x^3}{3!} + \cdots$, we have

$$(1 + x)^{1/3} = 1 + \left(\frac{1}{3}\right)x + \frac{(1/3)(-2/3)x^2}{2!} + \frac{(1/3)(-2/3)(-5/3)x^3}{3!} + \cdots$$

$$= 1 + \frac{x}{3} - \frac{2x^2}{3^2 2!} + \frac{2 \cdot 5x^3}{3^3 3!} - \frac{2 \cdot 5 \cdot 8x^4}{3^4 4!} + \cdots$$

$$= 1 + \frac{x}{3} + \sum_{n=2}^{\infty} \frac{(-1)^{n+1} 2 \cdot 5 \cdot 8 \cdots (3n - 4)}{3^n n!}.$$

**18.** Since $(1 + x)^{1/2} = 1 + \dfrac{x}{2} + \displaystyle\sum_{n=2}^{\infty} \frac{(-1)^{n+1} 1 \cdot 3 \cdot 5 \cdots (2n - 3)x^n}{2^n n!}$   (Exercise 14)

we have $(1 + x^3)^{1/2} = 1 + \dfrac{x^3}{2} + \displaystyle\sum_{n=2}^{\infty} \frac{(-1)^{n+1} 1 \cdot 3 \cdot 5 \cdots (2n - 3)x^{3n}}{2^n n!}$.

**20.**   $e^x = \displaystyle\sum_{n=0}^{\infty} \frac{x^n}{n!} = 1 + x + \frac{x^2}{2!} + \frac{x^3}{3!} + \frac{x^4}{4!} + \frac{x^5}{5!} + \cdots$

$e^{-3x} = \displaystyle\sum_{n=0}^{\infty} \frac{(-3x)^n}{n!} = \sum_{n=0}^{\infty} \frac{(-1)^n 3^n x^n}{n!} = 1 - 3x + \frac{9x^2}{2!} - \frac{27x^3}{3!} + \frac{81x^4}{4!} - \frac{243x^5}{5!} + \cdots$

**22.**   $\cos x = \displaystyle\sum_{n=0}^{\infty} \frac{(-1)^n x^{2n}}{(2n)!} = 1 - \frac{x^2}{2!} + \frac{x^4}{4!} - \frac{x^6}{6!} + \cdots$

$\cos 4x = \displaystyle\sum_{n=0}^{\infty} \frac{(-1)^n (4x)^{2n}}{(2n)!} = \sum_{n=0}^{\infty} \frac{(-1)^n 4^{2n} x^{2n}}{(2n)!}$

$\qquad = 1 - \dfrac{16x^2}{2!} + \dfrac{256x^4}{4!} - \cdots$

**24.**   $\sin x = \displaystyle\sum_{n=0}^{\infty} \frac{(-1)^n x^{2n+1}}{(2n + 1)!}$

$2 \sin x^3 = 2 \displaystyle\sum_{n=0}^{\infty} \frac{(-1)^n (x^3)^{2n+1}}{(2n + 1)!}$

$\qquad = 2\left[x^3 - \dfrac{x^9}{3!} + \dfrac{x^{15}}{5!} - \cdots\right]$

$\qquad = 2x^3 - \dfrac{2x^9}{3!} + \dfrac{2x^{15}}{5!} - \cdots$

**26.**   $e^x = 1 + x + \dfrac{x^2}{2!} + \dfrac{x^3}{3!} + \cdots$

$\qquad e^{-x} = 1 - x + \dfrac{x^2}{2!} - \dfrac{x^3}{3!} + \cdots$

$e^x + e^{-x} = 2 + \dfrac{2x^2}{2!} + \dfrac{2x^4}{4!} + \cdots$

$2 \cos h(x) = e^x + e^{-x} = \displaystyle\sum_{n=0}^{\infty} 2\frac{x^{2n}}{(2n)!}$

**28.** The formula for the binomial series gives $(1 + x)^{-1/2} = 1 + \sum_{n=1}^{\infty} \dfrac{(-1)^n 1 \cdot 3 \cdot 5 \cdots (2n - 1)x^n}{2^n n!}$, which implies that

$$(1 + x^2)^{-1/2} = 1 + \sum_{n=1}^{\infty} \frac{(-1)^n 1 \cdot 3 \cdot 5 \cdots (2n - 1)x^{2n}}{2^n n!}$$

$$\ln\left(x + \sqrt{x^2 + 1}\right) = \int \frac{1}{\sqrt{x^2 + 1}}\, dx$$

$$= x + \sum_{n=1}^{\infty} \frac{(-1)^n 1 \cdot 3 \cdot 5 \ldots (2n - 1)^{2n+1}}{2^n(2n + 1)n!}$$

$$= x - \frac{x^3}{2 \cdot 3} + \frac{1 \cdot 3x^5}{2 \cdot 4 \cdot 5} - \frac{1 \cdot 3 \cdot 5x^7}{2 \cdot 4 \cdot 6 \cdot 7} + \cdots.$$

**30.** $x \cos x = x\left(1 - \dfrac{x^2}{2!} + \dfrac{x^4}{4!} - \cdots\right)$

$$= x - \frac{x^3}{2!} + \frac{x^5}{4!} - \cdots$$

$$= \sum_{n=0}^{\infty} \frac{(-1)^n x^{2n+1}}{(2n)!}$$

**32.** $\dfrac{\arcsin x}{x} = \sum_{n=0}^{\infty} \dfrac{(2n)!x^{2n+1}}{(2^n n!)^2(2n + 1)} \cdot \dfrac{1}{x}$

$$= \sum_{n=0}^{\infty} \frac{(2n)!x^{2n}}{(2^n n!)^2(2n + 1)}, x \neq 0$$

**34.** $e^{ix} + e^{-ix} = 2 - \dfrac{2x^2}{2!} + \dfrac{2x^4}{4!} - \dfrac{2x^6}{6!} + \cdots$  (See Exercise 33.)

$$\frac{e^{ix} + e^{-ix}}{2} = 1 - \frac{x^2}{2!} + \frac{x^4}{4!} - \frac{x^6}{6!} + \cdots = \sum_{n=0}^{\infty} \frac{(-1)^n x^{2n}}{(2n)!} = \cos(x)$$

**36.** $g(x) = e^x \cos x$

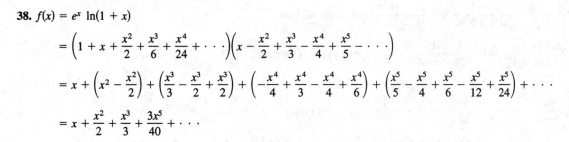

$$= \left(1 + x + \frac{x^2}{2} + \frac{x^4}{6} + \frac{x^4}{24} + \cdots\right)\left(1 - \frac{x^2}{2} + \frac{x^4}{24} - \cdots\right)$$

$$= 1 + x + \left(\frac{x^2}{2} - \frac{x^2}{2}\right) + \left(\frac{x^3}{6} - \frac{x^3}{2}\right) + \left(\frac{x^4}{24} - \frac{x^4}{4} + \frac{x^4}{24}\right) + \cdots = 1 + x - \frac{x^3}{3} - \frac{x^4}{6} + \cdots$$

**38.** $f(x) = e^x \ln(1 + x)$

$$= \left(1 + x + \frac{x^2}{2} + \frac{x^3}{6} + \frac{x^4}{24} + \cdots\right)\left(x - \frac{x^2}{2} + \frac{x^3}{3} - \frac{x^4}{4} + \frac{x^5}{5} - \cdots\right)$$

$$= x + \left(x^2 - \frac{x^2}{2}\right) + \left(\frac{x^3}{3} - \frac{x^3}{2} + \frac{x^3}{2}\right) + \left(-\frac{x^4}{4} + \frac{x^4}{3} - \frac{x^4}{4} + \frac{x^4}{6}\right) + \left(\frac{x^5}{5} - \frac{x^5}{4} + \frac{x^5}{6} - \frac{x^5}{12} + \frac{x^5}{24}\right) + \cdots$$

$$= x + \frac{x^2}{2} + \frac{x^3}{3} + \frac{3x^5}{40} + \cdots$$

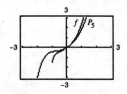

**40.** $f(x) = \dfrac{e^x}{1 + x}$. Divide the series for $e^x$ by $(1 + x)$.

$$1 + x \,\overline{\big)\, 1 + x\ + \dfrac{x^2}{2} + \dfrac{x^3}{6} + \dfrac{x^4}{24} + \dfrac{x^5}{120} + \cdots}$$

quotient: $1 + \dfrac{x^2}{2} - \dfrac{x^3}{3} + \dfrac{3x^4}{8} + \cdots$

$$\underline{1 + x}$$
$$0 + \dfrac{x^2}{2} + \dfrac{x^3}{6}$$
$$\underline{\dfrac{x^2}{2} + \dfrac{x^3}{2}}$$
$$-\dfrac{x^3}{3} + \dfrac{x^4}{24}$$
$$\underline{-\dfrac{x^3}{3} - \dfrac{x^4}{3}}$$
$$\dfrac{3x^4}{8} + \dfrac{x^5}{120}$$
$$\underline{\dfrac{3x^4}{8} + \dfrac{3x^5}{8}}$$
$$\vdots$$

$f(x) = 1 + \dfrac{x^2}{2} - \dfrac{x^3}{3} + \dfrac{3x^4}{8} - \cdots$

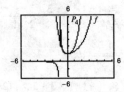

**42.** $y = x - \dfrac{x^3}{2!} + \dfrac{x^5}{4!} = x\left(1 - \dfrac{x^2}{2!} + \dfrac{x^4}{4!}\right) \approx x \cos x.$

Matches (b)

**44.** $y = x^2 - x^3 + x^4 = x^2(1 - x + x^2) \approx x^2\left(\dfrac{1}{1 + x}\right).$

Matches (d)

**46.** 
$$\int_0^x \sqrt{1 + t^3}\, dt = \int_0^x \left[1 + \dfrac{t^3}{2} + \sum_{n=2}^{\infty} \dfrac{(-1)^{n-1} 1 \cdot 3 \cdot 5 \cdots (2n - 3) t^{3n}}{2^n n!}\right] dt$$
$$= \left[t + \dfrac{t^4}{8} + \sum_{n=2}^{\infty} \dfrac{(-1)^{n-1} 1 \cdot 3 \cdot 5 \cdots (2n - 3) t^{3n+1}}{(3n + 1) 2^n n!}\right]_0^x$$
$$= x + \dfrac{x^4}{8} + \sum_{n=2}^{\infty} \dfrac{(-1)^{n-1} 1 \cdot 3 \cdot 5 \cdots (2n - 3) x^{3n+1}}{(3n + 1) 2^n n!}$$

**48.** Since $\sin(x) = \displaystyle\sum_{n=0}^{\infty} \dfrac{(-1)^n x^{2n+1}}{(2n + 1)!} = x - \dfrac{x^3}{3!} + \dfrac{x^5}{5!} - \dfrac{x^7}{7!} + \cdots$, we have

$$\sin(1) = \sum_{n=0}^{\infty} \dfrac{(-1)^n}{(2n + 1)!} = 1 - \dfrac{1}{3!} + \dfrac{1}{5!} - \dfrac{1}{7!} + \cdots \approx 0.8415. \quad \text{(4 terms)}$$

**50.** Since $e^x = \displaystyle\sum_{n=0}^{\infty} \dfrac{x^n}{n!} = 1 + x + \dfrac{x^2}{2!} + \dfrac{x^3}{3!} + \dfrac{x^4}{4!} + \dfrac{x^5}{5!} + \cdots$, we have $e^{-1} = 1 - 1 + \dfrac{1}{2!} - \dfrac{1}{3!} + \dfrac{1}{4!} - \dfrac{1}{5!} + \cdots$

and $\dfrac{e - 1}{e} = 1 - e^{-1} = 1 - \dfrac{1}{2!} + \dfrac{1}{3!} - \dfrac{1}{4!} + \dfrac{1}{5!} - \dfrac{1}{7!} + \cdots = \displaystyle\sum_{n=1}^{\infty} \dfrac{(-1)^{n-1}}{n!} \approx 0.6321. \quad \text{(6 terms)}$

**52.** Since

$$\sin x = \sum_{n=0}^{\infty} \dfrac{(-1)^n x^{2n+1}}{(2n + 1)!} = x - \dfrac{x^3}{3!} + \dfrac{x^5}{5!} - \dfrac{x^7}{7!} + \cdots$$

$$\dfrac{\sin x}{x} = 1 - \dfrac{x^2}{3!} + \dfrac{x^4}{5!} - \dfrac{x^6}{7!} + \cdots = \sum_{n=0}^{\infty} \dfrac{(-1)^n x^{2n}}{(2n + 1)!}$$

we have $\displaystyle\lim_{x \to 0} \dfrac{\sin x}{x} = \lim_{x \to 0} \sum_{n=0}^{\infty} \dfrac{(-1)^n x^{2n}}{(2n + 1)!} = 1.$

**54.** $\displaystyle\int_0^{1/2} \frac{\arctan x}{x}\, dx = \int_0^{1/2}\left(1 - \frac{x^2}{3} + \frac{x^4}{5} - \frac{x^6}{7} + \cdots\right) dx = \left[x - \frac{x^3}{3^2} + \frac{x^5}{5^2} - \frac{x^7}{7^2} + \cdots\right]_0^{1/2}$

Since $1/(9^2 2^9) < 0.0001$, we have

$$\int_0^{1/2} \frac{\arctan x}{x}\, dx \approx \left(\frac{1}{2} - \frac{1}{3^2 2^3} + \frac{1}{5^2 2^5} - \frac{1}{7^2 2^7} + \frac{1}{9^2 2^9}\right) \approx 0.4872.$$

**Note:** We are using $\displaystyle\lim_{x\to 0^+}\frac{\arctan x}{x} = 1$.

**56.** $\displaystyle\int_{0.5}^1 \cos\sqrt{x}\, dx = \int_{0.5}^1\left(1 - \frac{x}{2!} + \frac{x^2}{4!} - \frac{x^3}{6!} + \frac{x^4}{8!} - \cdots\right) dx = \left[x - \frac{x^2}{2(2!)} + \frac{x^3}{3(4!)} - \frac{x^4}{4(6!)} + \frac{x^5}{5(8!)} - \cdots\right]_{0.5}^1$

Since $\frac{1}{210,600}(1 - 0.5^5) < 0.0001$, we have

$$\int_{0.5}^1 \cos\sqrt{x}\, dx \approx \left[(1 - 0.5) - \frac{1}{4}(1 - 0.5^2) + \frac{1}{72}(1 - 0.5^3) - \frac{1}{2880}(1 - 0.5^4) + \frac{1}{201,600}(1 - 0.5)^5\right] \approx 0.3243.$$

**58.** $\displaystyle\int_0^{1/4} x\ln(x+1)\, dx = \int_0^{1/4}\left(x^2 - \frac{x^3}{2} + \frac{x^4}{3} - \frac{x^5}{4} + \cdots\right) dx$

$$= \left[\frac{x^3}{3} - \frac{x^4}{4\cdot 2} + \frac{x^5}{5\cdot 3} - \frac{x^6}{6\cdot 4} + \cdots\right]_0^{1/4}$$

Since $\dfrac{(1/4)^5}{15} < 0.0001$,

$$\int_0^{1/4} x\ln(x+1)\, dx \approx \frac{(1/4)^3}{3} - \frac{(1/4)^4}{8} \approx 0.00472.$$

**60.** From Exercise 19, we have

$$\frac{1}{\sqrt{2\pi}}\int_1^2 e^{-x^2/2}dx = \frac{1}{\sqrt{2\pi}}\int_1^2 \sum_{n=0}^\infty \frac{(-1)^n x^{2n}}{2^n n!}\, dx = \frac{1}{\sqrt{2\pi}}\left[\sum_{n=0}^\infty \frac{(-1)^n x^{2n+1}}{2^n n!(2n+1)}\right]_1^2$$

$$= \frac{1}{\sqrt{2\pi}}\sum_{n=0}^\infty \frac{(-1)^n(2^{n+1}-1)}{2^n n!(2n+1)}$$

$$\approx \frac{1}{\sqrt{2\pi}}\left[1 - \frac{7}{2\cdot 1\cdot 3} + \frac{31}{2^2\cdot 2!\cdot 5} - \frac{127}{2^3\cdot 3!\cdot 7} + \frac{511}{2^4\cdot 4!\cdot 9} - \frac{2047}{2^5\cdot 5!\cdot 11}\right.$$

$$\left. + \frac{8191}{2^6\cdot 6!\cdot 13} - \frac{32,767}{2^7\cdot 7!\cdot 15} + \frac{131,071}{2^8\cdot 8!\cdot 17} - \frac{524,287}{2^9\cdot 9!\cdot 19}\right] \approx 0.1359.$$

**62.** $f(x) = \sin\dfrac{x}{2}\ln(1+x)$

$$P_5(x) = \frac{x^2}{2} - \frac{x^3}{4} + \frac{7x^4}{48} - \frac{11x^5}{96}$$

The polynomial is a reasonable approximation on the interval $(-0.60, 0.73)$.

**64.** $f(x) = \sqrt[3]{x}\cdot\arctan x,\ c = 1$

$$P_5(x) \approx 0.7854 + 0.7618(x-1) - 0.3412\left[\frac{(x-1)^2}{2!}\right] - 0.0424\left[\frac{(x-1)^3}{3!}\right]$$

$$+ 1.3025\left[\frac{(x-1)^4}{4!}\right] - 5.5913\left[\frac{(x-1)^5}{5!}\right]$$

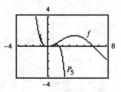

The polynomial is a reasonable approximation on the interval $(0.48, 1.75)$.

**66.** $a_{2n+1} = 0$ (odd coefficients are zero)

**68.** Answers will vary.

**70.** $\theta = 60°$, $v_0 = 64$, $k = \dfrac{1}{16}$, $g = -32$

$$y = \sqrt{3}x - \frac{32x^2}{2(64)^2(1/2)^2} - \frac{(1/16)(32)x^3}{3(64)^3(1/2)^3} - \frac{(1/16)^2(32)x^4}{4(64)^4(1/2)^4} - \cdots$$

$$= \sqrt{3}x - 32\left[\frac{2^2x^2}{2(64)^2} + \frac{2^3x^3}{3(64)^3 16} + \frac{2^4x^4}{4(64)^4(16)^2} + \cdots\right]$$

$$= \sqrt{3}x - 32\sum_{n=2}^{\infty}\frac{2^n x^n}{n(64)^n(16)^{n-2}} = \sqrt{3}x - 32\sum_{n=2}^{\infty}\frac{x^n}{n(32)^n(16)^{n-2}}$$

**72.** (a) $f(x) = \dfrac{\ln(x^2 + 1)}{x^2}$.

From Exercise 8, you obtain

$$P = \frac{1}{x^2}\sum_{n=0}^{\infty}\frac{(-1)^n x^{2n+2}}{n+1} = \sum_{n=0}^{\infty}\frac{(-1)^n x^{2n}}{n+1}$$

$$P_8 = 1 - \frac{x^2}{2} + \frac{x^4}{3} - \frac{x^6}{4} + \frac{x^8}{5}$$

(b)

(c) $F(x) = \displaystyle\int_0^x \frac{\ln(t^2 + 1)}{t^2}\,dt$

$G(x) = \displaystyle\int_0^x P_8(t)\,dt$

| $x$ | 0.25 | 0.50 | 0.75 | 1.00 | 1.50 | 2.00 |
|-----|------|------|------|------|------|------|
| $F(x)$ | 0.2475 | 0.4810 | 0.6920 | 0.8776 | 1.1798 | 1.4096 |
| $G(x)$ | 0.2475 | 0.4810 | 0.6920 | 0.8805 | 5.3064 | 652.21 |

(d) The curves are nearly identical for $0 < x < 1$. Hence, the integrals nearly agree on that interval.

**74.** Assume $e = p/q$ is rational. Let $N > q$ and form the following.

$$e - \left[1 + 1 + \frac{1}{2!} + \cdots + \frac{1}{N!}\right] = \frac{1}{(N+1)!} + \frac{1}{(N+2)!} + \cdots$$

Set $a = N!\left[e - \left(1 + 1 + \ldots + \dfrac{1}{N!}\right)\right]$, a positive integer. But,

$$a = N!\left[\frac{1}{(N+1)!} + \frac{1}{(N+2)!} + \cdots\right] = \frac{1}{N+1} + \frac{1}{(N+1)(N+2)} + \cdots < \frac{1}{N+1} + \frac{1}{(N+1)^2} + \cdots$$

$$= \frac{1}{N+1}\left[1 + \frac{1}{N+1} + \frac{1}{(N+1)^2} + \cdots\right] = \frac{1}{N+1}\left[\frac{1}{1 - \left(\dfrac{1}{N+1}\right)}\right] = \frac{1}{N}, \text{ a contradiction.}$$

# Review Exercises for Chapter 8

**2.** $a_n = \dfrac{n}{n^2 + 1}$

**4.** $a_n = 4 - \dfrac{n}{2}$: $3.5, 3, \ldots$

Matches (c)

**6.** $a_n = 6\left(-\dfrac{2}{3}\right)^{n-1}$: $6, -4, \ldots$

Matches (b)

**8.** $a_n = \sin \dfrac{n\pi}{2}$

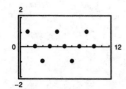

The sequence seems to diverge (oscillates).

$$\sin \frac{n\pi}{2}: \ 1, 0, -1, 0, 1, 0, \ldots$$

**10.** $\displaystyle\lim_{n\to\infty} \dfrac{1}{\sqrt{n}} = 0$

Converges

**12.** $\displaystyle\lim_{n\to\infty} \dfrac{n}{\ln(n)} = \lim_{n\to\infty} \dfrac{1}{1/n} = \infty$

Diverges

**14.** $\displaystyle\lim_{n\to\infty} \left(1 + \dfrac{1}{2n}\right)^n = \lim_{k\to\infty} \left[\left(1 + \dfrac{1}{k}\right)^k\right]^{1/2} = e^{1/2}$

Converges; $k = 2n$

**16.** Let $\quad y = (b^n + c^n)^{1/n}$

$$\ln y = \frac{\ln(b^n + c^n)}{n}$$

$$\lim_{n\to\infty} \ln y = \lim_{n\to\infty} \frac{1}{b^n + c^n}(b^n \ln b + c^n \ln c)$$

Assume $b \geq c$ and note that the terms

$$\frac{b^n \ln b + c^n \ln c}{b^n + c^n} = \frac{b^n \ln b}{b^n + c^n} + \frac{c^n \ln c}{b^n + c^n}$$

converge as $n \to \infty$. Hence $a_n$ converges.

**18.** (a) $V_n = 120{,}000(0.70)^n$, $n = 1, 2, 3, 4, 5$

(b) $V_5 = 120{,}000(0.70)^5 = \$20{,}168.40$

**20.** (a)

| $k$ | 5 | 10 | 15 | 20 | 25 |
|---|---|---|---|---|---|
| $S_k$ | 0.3917 | 0.3228 | 0.3627 | 0.3344 | 0.3564 |

(c) The series converges by the Alternating Series Test.

(b)
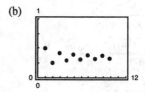

**22.** (a)

| $k$ | 5 | 10 | 15 | 20 | 25 |
|---|---|---|---|---|---|
| $S_k$ | 0.8333 | 0.9091 | 0.9375 | 0.9524 | 0.9615 |

(c) The series converges, by the limit comparison test with $\sum \dfrac{1}{n^2}$.

(b)

**24.** Diverges. Geometric series, $r = 1.82 > 1$.

**26.** Diverges. $n$th Term Test, $\displaystyle\lim_{n\to\infty} a_n = \dfrac{2}{3}$.

**28.** $\displaystyle\sum_{n=0}^{\infty} \dfrac{2^{n+2}}{3^n} = 4 \sum_{n=0}^{\infty} \left(\dfrac{2}{3}\right)^n = 4(3) = 12$

See Exercise 27.

**30.** $\displaystyle\sum_{n=0}^{\infty} \left[\left(\dfrac{2}{3}\right)^n - \dfrac{1}{(n+1)(n+2)}\right] = \sum_{n=0}^{\infty} \left(\dfrac{2}{3}\right)^n - \sum_{n=0}^{\infty} \left(\dfrac{1}{n+1} - \dfrac{1}{n+2}\right)$

$$= \frac{1}{1 - (2/3)} - \left[\left(1 - \frac{1}{2}\right) + \left(\frac{1}{2} - \frac{1}{3}\right) + \left(\frac{1}{3} - \frac{1}{4}\right) + \cdots\right] = 3 - 1 = 2$$

**32.** $0.\overline{923076} = 0.923076[1 + 0.000001 + (0.000001)^2 + \cdots]$

$$= \sum_{n=0}^{\infty} (0.923076)(0.000001)^n = \frac{0.923076}{1 - 0.000001} = \frac{923,076}{999,999} = \frac{12(76,923)}{13(76,923)} = \frac{12}{13}$$

**34.** $S = \sum_{n=0}^{39} 32,000(1.055)^n = \frac{32,000(1 - 1.055^{40})}{1 - 1.055}$

$\approx \$4,371,379.65$

**36.** See Exercise 86 in Section 8.2.

$$A = P\left(\frac{12}{r}\right)\left[\left(1 + \frac{r}{12}\right)^{12t} - 1\right]$$

$$= 100\left(\frac{12}{0.065}\right)\left[\left(1 + \frac{0.065}{12}\right)^{120} - 1\right]$$

$\approx \$16,840.32$

**38.** $\sum_{n=1}^{\infty} \frac{1}{\sqrt[4]{n^3}} = \sum_{n=1}^{\infty} \frac{1}{n^{3/4}}$

Divergent $p$-series, $p = \frac{3}{4} < 1$

**40.** $\sum_{n=1}^{\infty} \left(\frac{1}{n^2} - \frac{1}{2^n}\right) = \sum_{n=1}^{\infty} \frac{1}{n^2} - \sum_{n=1}^{\infty} \frac{1}{2^n}$

The first series is a convergent $p$-series and the second series is a convergent geometric series. Therefore, their difference converges.

**42.** $\sum_{n=1}^{\infty} \frac{n + 1}{n(n + 2)}$

$$\lim_{n \to \infty} \frac{(n + 1)/n(n + 2)}{1/n} = \lim_{n \to \infty} \frac{n + 1}{n + 2} = 1$$

By a limit comparison test with $\sum_{n=1}^{\infty} \frac{1}{n}$, the series diverges.

**44.** Since $\sum_{n=1}^{\infty} \frac{1}{3^n}$ converges, $\sum_{n=1}^{\infty} \frac{1}{3^n - 5}$ converges by the Limit Comparison Test.

**46.** $\sum_{n=1}^{\infty} \frac{(-1)^n \sqrt{n}}{n + 1}$

$$a_{n+1} = \frac{\sqrt{n + 1}}{n + 2} \leq \frac{\sqrt{n}}{n + 1} = a_n$$

$$\lim_{n \to \infty} \frac{\sqrt{n}}{n + 1} = 0$$

By the Alternating Series Test, the series converges.

**48.** Converges by the Alternating Series Test.

$$a_{n+1} = \frac{3 \ln(n + 1)}{n + 1} < \frac{3 \ln n}{n} = a_n, \ \lim_{n \to \infty} \frac{3 \ln n}{n} = 0$$

**50.** $\sum_{n=1}^{\infty} \frac{n!}{e^n}$

$$\lim_{n \to \infty} \left|\frac{a_{n+1}}{a_n}\right| = \lim_{n \to \infty} \left|\frac{(n + 1)!}{e^{n+1}} \cdot \frac{e^n}{n!}\right|$$

$$= \lim_{n \to \infty} \frac{n + 1}{e} = \infty$$

By the Ratio Test, the series diverges.

**52.** $\sum_{n=1}^{\infty} \frac{1 \cdot 3 \cdot 5 \cdots (2n - 1)}{2 \cdot 5 \cdot 8 \cdots (3n - 1)}$

$$\lim_{n \to \infty} \left|\frac{a_{n+1}}{a_n}\right| = \lim_{n \to \infty} \left|\frac{1 \cdot 3 \cdots (2n - 1)(2n + 1)}{2 \cdot 5 \cdots (3n - 1)(3n + 2)} \cdot \frac{2 \cdot 5 \cdots (3n - 1)}{1 \cdot 3 \cdots (2n - 1)}\right| = \lim_{n \to \infty} \frac{2n + 1}{3n + 2} = \frac{2}{3}$$

By the Ratio Test, the series converges.

**54.** (a) The series converges by the Alternating Series Test.

(b)

| $x$ | 5 | 10 | 15 | 20 | 25 |
|---|---|---|---|---|---|
| $S_n$ | 0.0871 | 0.0669 | 0.0734 | 0.0702 | 0.0721 |

(c)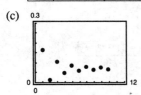

(d) The sum is approximately 0.0714.

**56.** No. Let $a_n = \dfrac{3937.5}{n^2}$, then $a_{75} = 0.7$. The series $\displaystyle\sum_{n=1}^{\infty} \dfrac{3937.5}{n^2}$ is a convergent $p$-series.

**58.** $f(x) = \tan x$ $\qquad\qquad\qquad\qquad f\left(-\dfrac{\pi}{4}\right) = -1$

$f'(x) = \sec^2 x$ $\qquad\qquad\qquad\quad\, f'\left(-\dfrac{\pi}{4}\right) = 2$

$f''(x) = 2\sec^2 x \tan x$ $\qquad\qquad f''\left(-\dfrac{\pi}{4}\right) = -4$

$f'''(x) = 4\sec^2 x \tan^2 x + 2\sec^4 x \qquad f'''\left(-\dfrac{\pi}{4}\right) = 16$

$P_3(x) = -1 + 2\left(x + \dfrac{\pi}{4}\right) - 2\left(x + \dfrac{\pi}{4}\right)^2 + \dfrac{8}{3}\left(x + \dfrac{\pi}{4}\right)^3$

**60.** $\cos(0.75) \approx 1 - \dfrac{(0.75)^2}{2!} + \dfrac{(0.75)^4}{4!} - \dfrac{(0.75)^6}{6!} \approx 0.7317$

**62.** $e^{-0.25} \approx 1 - 0.25 + \dfrac{(0.25)^2}{2!} - \dfrac{(0.25)^3}{3!} + \dfrac{(0.25)^4}{4!} \approx 0.779$

**64.** $f(x) = \cos x$

$P_4(x) = 1 - \dfrac{x^2}{2!} + \dfrac{x^4}{4!}$

$P_6(x) = 1 - \dfrac{x^2}{2!} + \dfrac{x^4}{4!} - \dfrac{x^6}{6!}$

$P_{10}(x) = 1 - \dfrac{x^2}{2!} + \dfrac{x^4}{4!} - \dfrac{x^6}{6!} + \dfrac{x^8}{8!} - \dfrac{x^{10}}{10!}$

**66.** $\displaystyle\sum_{n=0}^{\infty} (2x)^n$

Geometric series which converges only if $|2x| < 1$ or $-\dfrac{1}{2} < x < \dfrac{1}{2}$.

**68.** $\displaystyle\sum_{n=1}^{\infty} \dfrac{3^n(x-2)^n}{n}$

$\displaystyle\lim_{n\to\infty}\left|\dfrac{u_{n+1}}{u_n}\right| = \lim_{n\to\infty}\left|\dfrac{3^{n+1}(x-2)^{n+1}}{n+1} \cdot \dfrac{n}{3^n(x-2)^n}\right|$

$\qquad\qquad\qquad = 3|x-2|$

$R = \dfrac{1}{3}$

Center: 2

Since the series converges at $\frac{5}{3}$ and diverges at $\frac{7}{3}$, the interval of convergence is $\frac{5}{3} \le x < \frac{7}{3}$.

**70.** $\displaystyle\sum_{n=0}^{\infty} \dfrac{(x-2)^n}{2^n} = \sum_{n=0}^{\infty}\left(\dfrac{x-2}{2}\right)^n$

Geometric series which converges only if

$\left|\dfrac{x-2}{2}\right| < 1$ or $0 < x < 4$.

**72.**
$$y = \sum_{n=0}^{\infty} \frac{(-3)^n x^{2n}}{2^n n!}$$

$$y' = \sum_{n=1}^{\infty} \frac{(-3)^n (2n) x^{2n-1}}{2^n n!} = \sum_{n=0}^{\infty} \frac{(-3)^{n+1}(2n+2)x^{2n+1}}{2^{n+1}(n+1)!}$$

$$y'' = \sum_{n=0}^{\infty} \frac{(-3)^{n+1}(2n+2)(2n+1)x^{2n}}{2^{n+1}(n+1)!}$$

$$y'' + 3xy' + 3y = \sum_{n=0}^{\infty} \frac{(-3)^{n+1}(2n+2)(2n+1)x^{2n}}{2^{n+1}(n+1)!} + \sum_{n=0}^{\infty} \frac{(-1)^{n+1}3^{n+2}(2n+2)x^{2n+2}}{2^{n+1}(n+1)!} + \sum_{n=0}^{\infty} \frac{(-1)^n 3^{n+1} x^{2n}}{2^n n!}$$

$$= \sum_{n=0}^{\infty} \frac{(-1)^{n+1}3^{n+1}(2n+2)x^{2n}}{2^n n!} + \sum_{n=0}^{\infty} \frac{(-1)^{n+1}3^{n+2}x^{2n+2}}{2^n n!} + \sum_{n=0}^{\infty} \frac{(-1)^n 3^{n+1} x^{2n}}{2^n n!}$$

$$= \sum_{n=0}^{\infty} \frac{(-1)^n 3^{n+1} x^{2n}}{2^n n!}[-(2n+1)+1] + \sum_{n=0}^{\infty} \frac{(-1)^{n+1}3^{n+2}x^{2n+2}}{2^n n!}$$

$$= \sum_{n=0}^{\infty} \frac{(-1)^n 3^{n+1} x^{2n}}{2^n n!}(-2n) + \sum_{n=0}^{\infty} \frac{(-1)^{n+1}3^{n+2}x^{2n+2}}{2^n n!}$$

$$= \sum_{n=1}^{\infty} \frac{(-1)^{n+1}3^{n+1} x^{2n}}{2^n n!}(2n) + \sum_{n=1}^{\infty} \frac{(-1)^n 3^{n+1} x^{2n}}{2^{n-1}(n-1)!} \cdot \frac{2n}{2n}$$

$$= \sum_{n=1}^{\infty} \frac{(-1)^n 3^{n+1} x^{2n}}{2^n n!}[-2n+2n] = 0$$

**74.** $\dfrac{3}{2+x} = \dfrac{3/2}{1+(x/2)} = \dfrac{3/2}{1-(-x/2)} = \dfrac{a}{1-r}$      **76.** Integral: $\displaystyle\sum_{n=0}^{\infty} \frac{(-1)^n 3 x^{n+1}}{(n+1)2^{n+1}}$

$$\sum_{n=0}^{\infty} \frac{3}{2}\left(-\frac{x}{2}\right)^n = \sum_{n=0}^{\infty} \frac{(-1)^n 3 x^n}{2^{n+1}}$$

**78.** $8 - 2(x-3) + \dfrac{1}{2}(x-3)^2 - \dfrac{1}{8}(x-3)^3 + \cdots = \displaystyle\sum_{n=0}^{\infty} 8\left[\frac{-(x-3)}{4}\right]^n = \dfrac{8}{1-[-(x-3)/4]}$

$$= \frac{32}{4+(x-3)} = \frac{32}{1+x}, \quad -1 < x < 7$$

**80.** $f(x) = \cos x$

$f'(x) = -\sin x$

$f''(x) = -\cos x$

$f'''(x) = \sin x$

$$\cos x = \sum_{n=0}^{\infty} \frac{f^{(n)}(-\pi/4)[x+(\pi/4)]^n}{n!} = \frac{\sqrt{2}}{2} + \frac{\sqrt{2}}{2}\left(x+\frac{\pi}{4}\right) - \frac{\sqrt{2}}{2\cdot 2!}\left(x+\frac{\pi}{4}\right)^2 - \frac{\sqrt{2}}{2\cdot 3!}\left(x+\frac{\pi}{4}\right)^3 + \frac{\sqrt{2}}{2\cdot 4!}\left(x+\frac{\pi}{4}\right)^4 + \cdots$$

$$= \frac{\sqrt{2}}{2}\left[1 + \left(x+\frac{\pi}{4}\right) + \sum_{n=1}^{\infty} \frac{(-1)^{[n(n+1)]/2}[x+(\pi/4)]^{n+1}}{(n+1)!}\right]$$

**82.** $f(x) = \csc(x)$

$f'(x) = -\csc(x)\cot(x)$

$f''(x) = \csc^3(x) + \csc(x)\cot^2(x)$

$f'''(x) = -5\csc^3(x)\cot(x) - \csc(x)\cot^3(x)$

$f^{(4)}(x) = 5\csc^5(x) + 15\csc^3(x)\cot^2(x) + \csc(x)\cot^4(x)$

$$\csc(x) = \sum_{n=0}^{\infty} \frac{f^{(n)}(\pi/2)[x-(\pi/2)]^n}{n!} = 1 + \frac{1}{2!}\left(x-\frac{\pi}{2}\right)^2 + \frac{5}{4!}\left(x-\frac{\pi}{2}\right)^4 + \cdots$$

**84.**  $f(x) = x^{1/2}$

$$f'(x) = \frac{1}{2}x^{-1/2}$$

$$f''(x) = -\left(\frac{1}{2}\right)\left(\frac{1}{2}\right)x^{-3/2}$$

$$f'''(x) = \left(\frac{1}{2}\right)\left(\frac{1}{2}\right)\left(\frac{3}{2}\right)x^{-5/2}$$

$$f^{(4)}(x) = -\left(\frac{1}{2}\right)\left(\frac{1}{2}\right)\left(\frac{3}{2}\right)\left(\frac{5}{2}\right)x^{-7/2}, \cdots$$

$$\sqrt{x} = \sum_{n=0}^{\infty} \frac{f^{(n)}(4)(x-4)^n}{n!}$$

$$= 2 + \frac{(x-4)}{2^2} - \frac{(x-4)^2}{2^5 2!} + \frac{1 \cdot 3(x-4)^3}{2^8 3!} - \frac{1 \cdot 3 \cdot 5(x-4)^4}{2^{11} 4!} + \cdots$$

$$= 2 + \frac{(x-4)}{2^2} + \sum_{n=2}^{\infty} \frac{(-1)^{n+1} 1 \cdot 3 \cdot 5 \cdots (2n-3)(x-4)^n}{2^{3n-1} n!}$$

**86.**  $h(x) = (1+x)^{-3}$

$$h'(x) = -3(1+x)^{-4}$$

$$h''(x) = 12(1+x)^{-5}$$

$$h'''(x) = -60(1+x)^{-6}$$

$$h^{(4)}(x) = 360(1+x)^{-7}$$

$$h^{(5)}(x) = -2520(1+x)^{-8}$$

$$\frac{1}{(1+x)^3} = 1 - 3x + \frac{12x^2}{2!} - \frac{60x^3}{3!} + \frac{360x^4}{4!} - \frac{2520x^5}{5!} + \cdots = \sum_{n=0}^{\infty} \frac{(-1)^n (n+2)! x^n}{2 n!} = \sum_{n=0}^{\infty} \frac{(-1)^n (n+2)(n+1)x}{2}$$

**88.**  $\ln x = \sum_{n=1}^{\infty} (-1)^{n+1} \dfrac{(x-1)^n}{n}, \qquad 0 < x \le 2$

$$\ln\left(\frac{6}{5}\right) = \sum_{n=1}^{\infty} (-1)^{n+1} \left(\frac{(6/5)-1}{n}\right)^n$$

$$= \sum_{n=1}^{\infty} (-1)^{n+1} \frac{1}{5^n n} \approx 0.1823$$

**90.**  $e^x = \sum_{n=0}^{\infty} \dfrac{x^n}{n!}, \quad -\infty < x < \infty$

$$e^{2/3} = \sum_{n=0}^{\infty} \frac{(2/3)^n}{n!} = \sum_{n=0}^{\infty} \frac{2^n}{3^n n!} \approx 1.9477$$

**92.**  $\sin x = \sum_{n=0}^{\infty} (-1)^n \dfrac{x^{2n+1}}{(2n+1)!}, \quad -\infty < x < \infty$

$$\sin\left(\frac{1}{3}\right) = \sum_{n=0}^{\infty} (-1)^n \frac{1}{3^{2n+1}(2n+1)!} \approx 0.3272$$

**94.**  $e^x = \sum_{n=0}^{\infty} \dfrac{x^n}{n!} = 1 + x + \dfrac{x^2}{2!} + \cdots$

$$xe^x = \sum_{n=0}^{\infty} \frac{x^{n+1}}{n!} = x + x^2 + \frac{x^3}{2!} + \cdots$$

$$\int_0^1 xe^x \, dx = \left[xe^x - e^x\right]_0^1 = (e - e) - (0 - 1) = 1$$

$$\int_0^1 \sum_{n=0}^{\infty} \frac{x^{n+1}}{n!} \, dx = \sum_{n=0}^{\infty} \left[\frac{x^{n+2}}{(n+2)n!}\right]_0^1 = \sum_{n=0}^{\infty} \frac{1}{(n+2)n!} = 1$$

**96.** (a) $f(x) = \sin 2x$      $f(0) = 0$

$f'(x) = 2\cos 2x$      $f'(0) = 2$

$f''(x) = -4\sin 2x$      $f''(0) = 0$

$f'''(x) = -8\cos 2x$      $f'''(0) = -8$

$f^{(4)}(x) = 16\sin 2x$      $f^{(4)}(0) = 0$

$f^{(5)}(x) = 32\cos 2x$      $f^{(5)}(0) = 32$

$f^{(6)}(x) = -64\sin 2x$      $f^{(6)}(0) = 0$

$f^{(7)}(x) = -128\cos 2x$      $f^{(7)}(0) = -128$

$$\sin 2x = 0 + 2x + \frac{0x^2}{2!} - \frac{8x^3}{3!} + \frac{0x^4}{4!} + \frac{32x^5}{5!} + \frac{0x^6}{6!} - \frac{128x^7}{7!} + \cdots = 2x - \frac{4}{3}x^3 + \frac{4}{15}x^5 - \frac{8}{315}x^7 + \cdots$$

(b) $\displaystyle \sin x = \sum_{n=0}^{\infty} \frac{(-1)^n x^{2n+1}}{(2n+1)!}$

$$\sin 2x = \sum_{n=0}^{\infty} \frac{(-1)^n (2x)^{2n+1}}{(2n+1)!} = 2x - \frac{(2x)^3}{3!} + \frac{(2x)^5}{5!} - \frac{(2x)^7}{7!} + \cdots$$

$$= 2x - \frac{8x^3}{6} + \frac{32x^5}{120} - \frac{128x^7}{5040} + \cdots = 2x - \frac{4}{3}x^3 + \frac{4}{15}x^5 - \frac{8}{315}x^7 + \cdots$$

(c) $\sin 2x = 2\sin x \cos x$

$$= 2\left( x - \frac{x^3}{6} + \frac{x^5}{120} - \frac{x^7}{5040} + \cdots \right)\left( 1 - \frac{x^2}{2} + \frac{x^4}{24} - \frac{x^6}{720} + \cdots \right)$$

$$= 2\left[ x + \left( -\frac{x^3}{2} - \frac{x^3}{6} \right) + \left( \frac{x^5}{24} + \frac{x^5}{12} + \frac{x^5}{120} \right) + \left( -\frac{x^7}{720} - \frac{x^7}{144} - \frac{x^7}{240} - \frac{x^7}{5040} \right) + \cdots \right]$$

$$= 2\left[ x - \frac{2x^3}{3} + \frac{2x^5}{15} - \frac{4x^7}{315} + \cdots \right] = 2x - \frac{4}{3}x^3 + \frac{4}{15}x^5 - \frac{8}{315}x^7 + \cdots$$

**98.** $\displaystyle \cos t = \sum_{n=0}^{\infty} \frac{(-1)^n t^{2n}}{(2n)!}$

$$\cos\frac{\sqrt{t}}{2} = \sum_{n=0}^{\infty} \frac{(-1)^n t^n}{2^{2n}(2n)!}$$

$$\int_0^x \cos\frac{\sqrt{t}}{2}\,dt = \left[ \sum_{n=0}^{\infty} \frac{(-1)^n t^{n+1}}{2^{2n}(2n)!(n+1)} \right]_0^x$$

$$= \sum_{n=0}^{\infty} \frac{(-1)^n x^{n+1}}{2^{2n}(2n)!(n+1)}$$

**100.** $\displaystyle e^t = \sum_{n=0}^{\infty} \frac{t^n}{n!}$

$$e^t - 1 = \sum_{n=1}^{\infty} \frac{t^n}{n!}$$

$$\frac{e^t - 1}{t} = \sum_{n=1}^{\infty} \frac{t^{n-1}}{n!}$$

$$\int_0^x \frac{e^t - 1}{t}\,dt = \left[ \sum_{n=1}^{\infty} \frac{t^n}{n \cdot n!} \right]_0^x = \sum_{n=1}^{\infty} \frac{x^n}{n \cdot n!}$$

**102.** $\displaystyle \arcsin x = x + \frac{x^3}{2 \cdot 3} + \frac{1 \cdot 3 x^5}{2 \cdot 4 \cdot 5} + \frac{1 \cdot 3 \cdot 5 x^7}{2 \cdot 4 \cdot 6 \cdot 7} + \cdots$

$$\frac{\arcsin x}{x} = 1 + \frac{x^2}{2 \cdot 3} + \frac{1 \cdot 3 x^4}{2 \cdot 4 \cdot 5} + \frac{1 \cdot 3 \cdot 5 x^6}{2 \cdot 4 \cdot 6 \cdot 7} + \cdots$$

$$\lim_{x \to 0} \frac{\arcsin x}{x} = 1$$

By L'Hôpital's Rule, $\displaystyle \lim_{x \to 0} \frac{\arcsin x}{x} = \lim_{x \to 0} \frac{\left( \dfrac{1}{\sqrt{1-x^2}} \right)}{1} = 1.$

## Problem Solving for Chapter 8

**2.** Let $S = \sum_{n=1}^{\infty} \frac{1}{(2n-1)^2} = \frac{1}{1^2} + \frac{1}{3^2} + \frac{1}{5^2} + \cdots$

Then $\frac{\pi^2}{6} = \frac{1}{1^2} + \frac{1}{2^2} + \frac{1}{3^2} + \frac{1}{4^2} + \cdots$

$$= S + \frac{1}{2^2} + \frac{1}{4^2} + \cdots$$

$$= S + \frac{1}{2^2}\left[1 + \frac{1}{2^2} + \frac{1}{3^2} + \cdots\right]$$

$$= S + \frac{1}{2^2}\left(\frac{\pi^2}{6}\right).$$

Thus, $S = \frac{\pi^2}{6} - \frac{1}{4}\frac{\pi^2}{6} = \frac{\pi^2}{6}\left(\frac{3}{4}\right) = \frac{\pi^2}{8}.$

**4.** (a) Position the three blocks as indicated in the figure. The bottom block extends 1/6 over the edge of the table, the middle block extends 1/4 over the edge of the bottom block, and the top block extends 1/2 over the edge of the middle block.

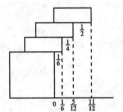

The centers of gravity are located at

bottom block: $\frac{1}{6} - \frac{1}{2} = -\frac{1}{3}$

middle block: $\frac{1}{6} + \frac{1}{4} - \frac{1}{2} = -\frac{1}{12}$

top block: $\frac{1}{6} + \frac{1}{4} + \frac{1}{2} - \frac{1}{2} = \frac{5}{12}.$

The center of gravity of the top 2 blocks is

$$\left(-\frac{1}{12} + \frac{5}{12}\right)/2 = \frac{1}{6},$$

which lies over the bottom block. The center of gravity of the 3 blocks is

$$\left(-\frac{1}{3} - \frac{1}{12} + \frac{5}{12}\right)/3 = 0$$

which lies over the table. Hence, the far edge of the top block lies

$$\frac{1}{6} + \frac{1}{4} + \frac{1}{2} = \frac{11}{12}$$

beyond the edge of the table.

(b) Yes. If there are $n$ blocks, then the edge of the top block lies $\sum_{c=1}^{n} \frac{1}{2i}$ from the edge of the table. Using 4 blocks,

$$\sum_{c=1}^{4} \frac{1}{2i} = \frac{1}{2} + \frac{1}{4} + \frac{1}{6} + \frac{1}{8} = \frac{25}{24}$$

which shows that the top block extends beyond the table.

(c) The blocks can extend any distance beyond the table because the series diverges:

$$\sum_{c=1}^{\infty} \frac{1}{2i} = \frac{1}{2}\sum_{c=1}^{\infty} \frac{1}{i} = \infty.$$

**6.** $a - \dfrac{b}{2} + \dfrac{a}{3} - \dfrac{b}{4} + \cdots = \displaystyle\sum_{n=1}^{\infty} \dfrac{(-1)^{n+1}(a+b) + (a-b)}{2n}$

If $a = b$, $\displaystyle\sum_{n=1}^{\infty} \dfrac{(-1)^{n+1}(2a)}{2n} = a \sum_{n=1}^{\infty} \dfrac{(-1)^{n+1}}{n}$ converges conditionally.

If $a \neq b$, $\displaystyle\sum_{n=1}^{\infty} \dfrac{(-1)^{n+1}(a+b)}{2n} + \sum_{n=1}^{\infty} \dfrac{a-b}{2n}$ diverges.

No values of $a$ and $b$ give absolute convergence. $a = b$ implies conditional convergence.

**8.**     $e^x = 1 + x + \dfrac{x^2}{2!} + \cdots$

$e^{x^2} = 1 + x^2 + \dfrac{x^4}{2!} + \cdots + \dfrac{x^{12}}{6!} + \cdots$

$\dfrac{f^{(12)}(0)}{12!} = \dfrac{1}{6!} \Rightarrow f^{(12)}(0) = \dfrac{12!}{6!} = 665{,}280$

**10.** (a) If $p = 1$, $\displaystyle\int_2^{\infty} \dfrac{1}{x \ln x}\, dx = \ln \ln x \Big]_2^{\infty}$ diverges.

If $p > 1$, $\displaystyle\int_2^{\infty} \dfrac{1}{x(\ln x)^p}\, dx = \lim_{b \to \infty} \left[ \dfrac{(\ln b)^{1-p}}{1-p} - \dfrac{(\ln 2)^{1-p}}{1-p} \right]$ converges.

If $p < 1$, diverges.

(b) $\displaystyle\sum_{n=4}^{\infty} \dfrac{1}{n \ln(n^2)} = \dfrac{1}{2} \sum_{n=4}^{\infty} \dfrac{1}{n \ln n}$ diverges by part (a).

**12.** Let $b_n = a_n r^n$.

$(b_n)^{1/n} = (a_n r^n)^{1/n} = a_n^{1/n} \cdot r \to Lr$ as $n \to \infty$.

$Lr < \dfrac{1}{r} r = 1$.

By the Root Test, $\sum b_n$ converges $\Rightarrow \sum a_n r^n$ converges.

**14.** (a) $\dfrac{1}{0.99} = \dfrac{1}{1 - 0.01} = \displaystyle\sum_{n=0}^{\infty} (0.01)^n$

$= 1 + 0.01 + (0.01)^2 + \cdots$

$= 1.010101 \ldots$

(b) $\dfrac{1}{0.98} = \dfrac{1}{1 - 0.02} = \displaystyle\sum_{n=0}^{\infty} (0.02)^n$

$= 1 + 0.02 + (0.02)^2 + \cdots$

$= 1 + 0.02 + 0.0004 + \cdots$

$= 1.0204081632 \ldots$

**16.** (a) Height $= 2\left[ 1 + \dfrac{1}{\sqrt{2}} + \dfrac{1}{\sqrt{3}} + \cdots \right]$

$= 2\displaystyle\sum_{n=1}^{\infty} \dfrac{1}{n^{1/2}} = \infty \quad \left( p\text{-series}, \ p = \dfrac{1}{2} < 1 \right)$

(b) $S = 4\pi\left[ 1 + \dfrac{1}{2} + \dfrac{1}{3} + \cdots \right] 4\pi \displaystyle\sum_{n=1}^{\infty} \dfrac{1}{n} = \infty$

(c) $W = \dfrac{4}{3}\pi\left[ 1 + \dfrac{1}{2^{3/2}} + \dfrac{1}{3^{3/2}} + \cdots \right]$

$= \dfrac{4}{3}\pi \displaystyle\sum_{n=1}^{\infty} \dfrac{1}{n^{3/2}}$ converges.

# CHAPTER 9
## Conics, Parametric Equations, and Polar Coordinates

---

# CHAPTER 9
## Conics, Parametric Equations, and Polar Coordinates

### Section 9.1    Conics and Calculus
Solutions to Even-Numbered Exercises

**2.** $x^2 = 8y$

Vertex: $(0, 0)$

$p = 2 > 0$

Opens upward

Matches graph (a).

**4.** $\dfrac{(x-2)^2}{16} + \dfrac{(y+1)^2}{4} = 1$

Center: $(2, -1)$

Ellipse

Matches (b)

**6.** $\dfrac{x^2}{9} + \dfrac{y^2}{9} = 1$

Circle radius 3.

Matches (g)

**8.** $\dfrac{(x-2)^2}{9} - \dfrac{y^2}{4} = 1$

Hyperbola

Center: $(-2, 0)$

Horizontal transverse axis.

Matches (d)

**10.** $x^2 + 8y = 0$

$\qquad x^2 = 4(-2)y$

Vertex: $(0, 0)$

Focus: $(0, -2)$

Directrix: $y = 2$

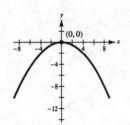

**12.** $(x-1)^2 + 8(y+2) = 0$

$\qquad (x-1)^2 = 4(-2)(y+2)$

Vertex: $(1, -2)$

Focus: $(1, -4)$

Directrix: $y = 0$

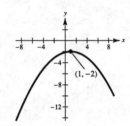

**14.** $y^2 + 6y + 8x + 25 = 0$

$\qquad y^2 + 6y + 9 = -8x - 25 + 9$

$\qquad (y+3)^2 = 4(-2)(x+2)$

Vertex: $(-2, -3)$

Focus: $(-4, -3)$

Directrix: $x = 0$

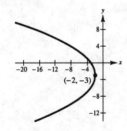

**16.** $y^2 + 4y + 8x - 12 = 0$

$\qquad y^2 + 4y + 4 = -8x + 12 + 4$

$\qquad (y+2)^2 = 4(-2)(x-2)$

Vertex: $(2, -2)$

Focus: $(0, -2)$

Directrix: $x = 4$

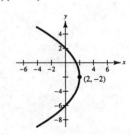

**18.**
$$y = -\tfrac{1}{6}(x^2 - 8x + 6) = -\tfrac{1}{6}(x^2 - 8x + 16 - 10)$$
$$-6y = (x - 4)^2 - 10$$
$$-6y + 10 = (x - 4)^2$$
$$(x - 4)^2 = -6\left(y - \tfrac{5}{3}\right)$$
$$(x - 4)^2 = 4\left(-\tfrac{3}{2}\right)\left(y - \tfrac{5}{3}\right)$$

Vertex: $\left(4, \tfrac{5}{3}\right)$

Focus: $\left(4, \tfrac{1}{6}\right)$

Directrix: $y = \tfrac{19}{6}$

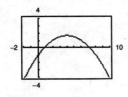

**20.** $x^2 - 2x + 8y + 9 = 0$
$$x^2 - 2x + 1 = -8y - 9 + 1$$
$$(x - 1)^2 = 4(-2)(y + 1)$$

Vertex: $(1, -1)$

Focus: $(1, -3)$

Directrix: $y = 1$

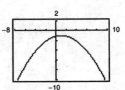

**22.**
$$(x + 1)^2 = 4(-2)(y - 2)$$
$$x^2 + 2x + 8y - 15 = 0$$

**24.** Vertex: $(0, 2)$
$$(y - 2)^2 = 4(2)(x - 0)$$
$$y^2 - 8x - 4y + 4 = 0$$

**26.**
$$y = 4 - (x - 2)^2 = 4x - x^2$$
$$x^2 - 4x + y = 0$$

**28.** From Example 2: $4p = 8$ or $p = 2$

Vertex: $(4, 0)$
$$(x - 4)^2 = 8(y - 0)$$
$$x^2 - 8x - 8y + 16 = 0$$

**30.** $5x^2 + 7y^2 = 70$
$$\frac{x^2}{14} + \frac{y^2}{10} = 1$$
$$a^2 = 14,\ b^2 = 10,\ c^2 = 4$$

Center: $(0, 0)$

Foci: $(\pm 2, 0)$

Vertices: $\left(\pm\sqrt{14}, 0\right)$

$$e = \frac{2}{\sqrt{14}} = \frac{\sqrt{14}}{7}$$

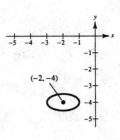

**32.** $\dfrac{(x + 2)^2}{1} + \dfrac{(y + 4)^2}{1/4} = 1$

$$a^2 = 1,\ b^2 = \frac{1}{4},\ c^2 = \frac{3}{4}$$

Center: $(-2, -4)$

Foci: $\left(-2 \pm \dfrac{\sqrt{3}}{2}, -4\right)$

Vertices: $(-1, -4),\ (-3, -4)$

$$e = \frac{\sqrt{3}}{2}$$

**34.** $16x^2 + 25y^2 - 64x + 150y + 279 = 0$
$$16(x^2 - 4x + 4) + 25(y^2 + 6y + 0) = -279 + 64 + 225$$
$$= 10$$
$$\frac{(x - 2)^2}{(5/8)} + \frac{(y + 3)^2}{(2/5)} = 1$$
$$a^2,\ \frac{5}{8},\ b^2 = \frac{2}{5},\ c^2 = a^2 - b^2 = \frac{9}{40}$$

Center: $(2, -3)$

Foci: $\left(2 \pm \dfrac{3\sqrt{10}}{20}, -3\right)$

Vertices: $\left(2 \pm \dfrac{\sqrt{10}}{4}, -3\right)$

$$e = \frac{c}{a} = \frac{3}{5}$$

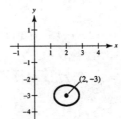

**36.**    $36x^2 + 9y^2 + 48x - 36y + 43 = 0$

$$36\left(x^2 + \frac{4}{3}x + \frac{4}{9}\right) + 9(y^2 - 4y + 4) = -43 + 16 + 36$$

$$= 9$$

$$\frac{[x + (2/3)]^2}{1/4} + \frac{(y - 2)^2}{1} = 1$$

$a^2 = 1,\ b^2 = \frac{1}{4},\ c^2 = \frac{3}{4}$

Center: $\left(-\frac{2}{3}, 2\right)$

Foci: $\left(-\frac{2}{3}, 2 \pm \frac{\sqrt{3}}{2}\right)$

Vertices: $\left(-\frac{2}{3}, 3\right), \left(-\frac{2}{3}, 1\right)$

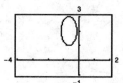

Solve for $y$:

$$9(y^2 - 4y + 4) = -36x^2 - 48x - 43 + 36$$

$$(y - 2)^2 = \frac{-(36x^2 + 48x + 7)}{9}$$

$$y = 2 \pm \frac{1}{3}\sqrt{-(36x^2 + 48x + 7)} \quad \text{(Graph each of these separately.)}$$

**38.**    $2x^2 + y^2 + 4.8x - 6.4y + 3.12 = 0$

$50x^2 + 25y^2 + 120x - 160y + 78 = 0$

$$50\left(x^2 + \frac{12}{5}x + \frac{36}{25}\right) + 25\left(y^2 - \frac{32}{5}y + \frac{256}{25}\right) = -78 + 72 + 256 = 250$$

$$\frac{[x + (6/5)]^2}{5} + \frac{[y - (16/5)]^2}{10} = 1$$

$a^2 = 10,\ b^2 = 5,\ c^2 = 5$

Center: $\left(-\frac{6}{5}, \frac{16}{5}\right)$

Foci: $\left(-\frac{6}{5}, \frac{16}{5} \pm \sqrt{5}\right)$

Vertices: $\left(-\frac{6}{5}, \frac{16}{5} \pm \sqrt{10}\right)$

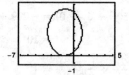

Solve for $y$:    $(y^2 - 6.4y + 10.24) = -2x^2 - 4.8x - 3.12 + 10.24$

$$(y - 3.2)^2 = 7.12 - 4x - 2x^2$$

$$y = 3.2 \pm \sqrt{7.12 - 4x - 2x^2} \quad \text{(Graph each of these separately.)}$$

**40.** Vertices: $(0, 2), (4, 2)$

Eccentricity: $\frac{1}{2}$

Horizontal major axis

Center: $(2, 2)$

$a = 2,\ c = 1 \Rightarrow b = \sqrt{3}$

$$\frac{(x - 2)^2}{4} + \frac{(y - 2)^2}{3} = 1$$

**42** Foci: $(0, \pm 5)$

Major axis length: $14$

Vertical major axis

Center: $(0, 0)$

$c = 5,\ a = 7 \Rightarrow b = \sqrt{24}$

$$\frac{x^2}{24} + \frac{y^2}{49} = 1$$

**44.** Center: $(1, 2)$

Vertical major axis

Points on ellipse: $(1, 6), (3, 2)$

From the sketch, we can see that
$h = 1, k = 2, a = 4, b = 2$

$$\frac{(x - 1)^2}{4} + \frac{(y - 2)^2}{16} = 1.$$

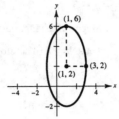

**46.** $\dfrac{x^2}{25} - \dfrac{y^2}{9} = 1$

$a = 5, b = 3, c = \sqrt{a^2 + b^2} = \sqrt{34}$

Center: $(0, 0)$

Vertices: $(\pm 5, 0)$

Foci: $\left(\pm \sqrt{34}, 0\right)$

Asymptotes: $y = \pm \dfrac{3}{5} x$

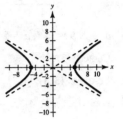

**48.** $\dfrac{(y + 1)^2}{12^2} - \dfrac{(x - 4)^2}{5^2} = 1$

$a = 12, b = 5, c = \sqrt{a^2 + b^2} = 13$

Center: $(4, -1)$
Vertices: $(4, 11), (4, -13)$
Foci: $(4, -14), (4, 12)$

Asymptotes: $y = -1 \pm \dfrac{12}{5}(x - 4)$

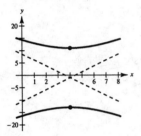

**50.** $y^2 - 9x^2 + 36x - 72 = 0$

$y^2 - 9(x^2 - 4x + 4) = 72 - 36 = 36$

$$\frac{y^2}{36} - \frac{(x - 2)^2}{4} = 1$$

$a = 6, b = 2, c = \sqrt{a^2 + b^2} = 2\sqrt{10}$

Center: $(2, 0)$

Vertices: $(2, 6), (2, -6)$

Foci: $\left(2, 2\sqrt{10}\right), \left(2, -2\sqrt{10}\right)$

Asymptotes: $y = \pm 3(x - 2)$

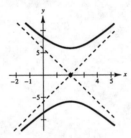

**52.** $9(x^2 + 6x + 9) - 4(y^2 - 2y + 1) = -78 + 81 - 4 = -1$

$$9(x + 3)^2 - 4(y - 1)^2 = -1$$

$$\frac{(y - 1)^2}{1/4} - \frac{(x + 3)^2}{1/9} = 1$$

$a = \dfrac{1}{2}, b = \dfrac{1}{3}, c = \dfrac{\sqrt{13}}{6}$

Center: $(-3, 1)$

Vertices: $\left(-3, \dfrac{1}{2}\right), \left(-3, \dfrac{3}{2}\right)$

Foci: $\left(-3, 1 \pm \dfrac{1}{6}\sqrt{13}\right)$

Asymptotes: $y = 1 \pm \dfrac{3}{2}(x + 3)$

**54.** $9x^2 - y^2 + 54x + 10y + 55 = 0$

$9(x^2 + 6x + 9) - (y^2 - 10y + 25) = -55 + 81 - 25$

$$= 1$$

$$\frac{(x + 3)^2}{1/9} - \frac{(y - 5)^2}{1} = 1$$

$a = \dfrac{1}{3}, b = 1, c = \dfrac{\sqrt{10}}{3}$

Center: $(-3, 5)$

Vertices: $\left(-3 \pm \dfrac{1}{3}, 5\right)$

Foci: $\left(-3 \pm \dfrac{\sqrt{10}}{3}, 5\right)$

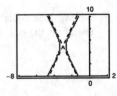

Solve for $y$:

$$y^2 - 10y + 25 = 9x^2 + 54x + 55 + 25$$

$$(y - 5)^2 = 9x^2 + 54x + 80$$

$$y = 5 \pm \sqrt{9x^2 + 54x + 80}$$

(Graph each curve separately.)

**56.**
$$3y^2 - x^2 + 6x - 12y = 0$$
$$3(y^2 - 4y + 4) - (x^2 - 6x + 9) = 0 + 12 - 9 = 3$$
$$\frac{(y-2)^2}{1} - \frac{(x-3)^2}{3} = 1$$

$a = 1, b = \sqrt{3}, c = 2$

Center: $(3, 2)$

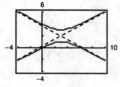

Vertices: $(3, 1), (3, 3)$

Foci: $(3, 0), (3, 4)$

Solve for $y$:
$$3(y^2 - 4y + 4) = x^2 - 6x + 12$$
$$(y - 2)^2 = \frac{x^2 - 6x + 12}{3}$$
$$y = 2 \pm \sqrt{\frac{x^2 - 6x + 12}{3}}$$

(Graph each curve separately.)

**58.** Vertices: $(0, \pm 3)$

Asymptotes: $y = \pm 3x$

Vertical transverse axis

$a = 3$

Slopes of asymptotes: $\pm \dfrac{a}{b} = \pm 3$

Thus, $b = 1$. Therefore,
$$\frac{y^2}{9} - \frac{x^2}{1} = 1.$$

**60.** Vertices: $(2, \pm 3)$

Foci: $(2, \pm 5)$

Vertical transverse axis

Center: $(2, 0)$

$a = 3, c = 5, b^2 = c^2 - a^2 = 16$

Therefore, $\dfrac{y^2}{9} - \dfrac{(x-2)^2}{16} = 1.$

**62.** Center: $(0, 0)$

Vertex: $(3, 0)$

Focus: $(5, 0)$

Horizontal transverse axis

$a = 3, c = 5, b^2 = c^2 - a^2 = 16$

Therefore, $\dfrac{x^2}{9} - \dfrac{y^2}{16} = 1.$

**64.** Focus: $(10, 0)$

Asymptotes: $y = \pm \dfrac{3}{4}x$

Horizontal transverse axis

Center: $(0, 0)$ since asymptotes intersect at the origin.

$c = 10$

Slopes of asymptotes: $\pm \dfrac{b}{a} = \pm \dfrac{3}{4}$ and $b = \dfrac{3}{4}a$

$c^2 = a^2 + b^2 = 100$

Solving these equations, we have $a^2 = 64$ and $b^2 = 36$. Therefore, the equation is
$$\frac{x^2}{64} - \frac{y^2}{36} = 1.$$

**66.** (a) $\dfrac{y^2}{4} - \dfrac{x^2}{2} = 1, y^2 - 2x^2 = 4, 2yy' - 4x = 0,$

$y' = \dfrac{4x}{2y} = \dfrac{2x}{y}$

At $x = 4$: $y = \pm 6, y' = \dfrac{\pm 2(4)}{6} = \pm \dfrac{4}{3}$

At $(4, 6)$: $y - 6 = -\dfrac{4}{3}(x - 4)$ or $4x - 3y + 2 = 0$

At $(4, -6)$: $y + 6 = -\dfrac{4}{3}(x - 4)$ or $4x + 3y + 2 = 0$

(b) From part (a) we know that the slopes of the normal lines must be $\mp 3/4$.

At $(4, 6)$: $y - 6 = -\dfrac{3}{4}(x - 4)$ or $3x + 4y - 36 = 0$

At $(4, -6)$: $y + 6 = \dfrac{3}{4}(x - 4)$ or $3x - 4y - 36 = 0$

**68.** $4x^2 - y^2 - 4x - 3 = 0$

$A = 4, C = -1$

$AC < 0$

Hyperbola

**70.** $25x^2 - 10x - 200y - 119 = 0$

$A = 25, C = 0$

Parabola

**72.** $y^2 - x - 4y - 5 = 0$

$A = 0, C = 1$

Parabola

**74.**    $2x^2 - 2xy = 3y - y^2 - 2xy$

$2x^2 + y^2 - 3y = 0$

$A = 2, C = 1, AC > 0$

Ellipse

**76.**    $9x^2 + 54x + 81 = 36 - 4(y^2 - 4y + 4)$

$9x^2 + 4y^2 + 54x - 16y + 61 = 0$

$A = 9, C = 4, AC > 0$

Ellipse

**78.** (a) An ellipse is the set of all points $(x, y)$, the sum of whose distance from two distinct fixed points (foci) is constant.

(b) $\dfrac{(x - h)^2}{a^2} + \dfrac{(y - k)^2}{b^2} = 1$ or $\dfrac{(x - h)^2}{b^2} + \dfrac{(y - k)^2}{a^2} = 1$

**80.**    $e = \dfrac{c}{a}, c = \sqrt{a^2 - b^2}\quad 0 < e < 1$

For $e \approx 0$, the ellipse is nearly circular.

For $e \approx 1$, the ellipse is elongated.

**82.** Assume that the vertex is at the origin.

(a)    $x^2 = 4py$

$8^2 = 4p\left(\dfrac{3}{100}\right)$

$\dfrac{1600}{3} = p$

$x^2 = 4\left(\dfrac{1600}{3}\right)y = \dfrac{6400}{3}y$

(b) The deflection is 1 cm when

$y = \dfrac{2}{100} \Rightarrow x = \pm\sqrt{\dfrac{128}{3}} \approx \pm 6.53$ meters.

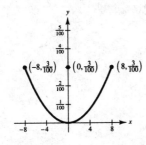

**84.** (a) Without loss of generality, place the coordinate system so that the equation of the parabola is $x^2 = 4py$ and, hence,

$y' = \left(\dfrac{1}{2p}\right)x.$

Therefore, for distinct tangent lines, the slopes are unequal and the lines intersect.

(b)    $x^2 - 4x - 4y = 0$

$2x - 4 - 4\dfrac{dy}{dx} = 0$

$\dfrac{dy}{dx} = \dfrac{1}{2}x - 1$

At $(0, 0)$, the slope is $-1$: $y = -x$. At $(6, 3)$, the slope is $2$: $y = 2x - 9$. Solving for $x$,

$-x = 2x - 9$

$-3x = -9$

$x = 3$

$y = -3.$

Point of intersection: $(3, -3)$

**86.** The focus of $x^2 = 8y = 4(2)y$ is $(0, 2)$. The distance from a point on the parabola, $(x, x^2/8)$, and the focus, $(0, 2)$, is

$d = \sqrt{(x - 0)^2 + \left(\dfrac{x^2}{8} - 2\right)^2}.$

Since $d$ is minimized when $d^2$ is minimized, it is sufficient to minimize the function

$f(x) = x^2 + \left(\dfrac{x^2}{8} - 2\right)^2.$

$f'(x) = 2x + 2\left(\dfrac{x^2}{8} - 2\right)\left(\dfrac{x}{4}\right) = \dfrac{x^3}{16} + x.$

$f'(x) = 0$ implies that

$\dfrac{x^3}{16} + x = x\left(\dfrac{x^2}{16} + 1\right) = 0 \Rightarrow x = 0.$

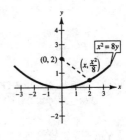

This is a minimum by the First Derivative Test. Hence, the closest point to the focus is the vertex, $(0, 0)$.

**88.** (a) $C = 0.0853t^2 + 0.2917t + 263.3559$

(b)

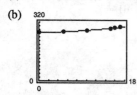

(c) $\dfrac{dC}{dt} = 0.1706t + 0.2971$

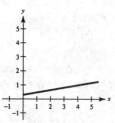

The consumption of fruits is increasing at a rate of 0.1706 pounds/year.

**90.**
$$x = \frac{1}{4}y^2$$

$$x' = \frac{1}{2}y$$

$$1 + (x')^2 = 1 + \frac{y^2}{4}$$

$$s = \int_0^4 \sqrt{1 + \left(\frac{y^2}{4}\right)}\, dy = \frac{1}{2}\int_0^4 \sqrt{4 + y^2}\, dy$$

$$= \frac{1}{4}\left[ y\sqrt{4+y^2} + 4\ln\left|y + \sqrt{4+y^2}\right| \right]_0^4$$

$$= \frac{1}{4}\left[4\sqrt{20} + 4\ln\left|4 + \sqrt{20}\right| - 4\ln 2\right]$$

$$= 2\sqrt{5} + \ln\left(2 + \sqrt{5}\right) \approx 5.916$$

**92.** $x^2 = 20y$

$$y = \frac{x^2}{20}$$

$$y' = \frac{x}{10}$$

$$S = 2\pi\int_0^r x\sqrt{1 + \left(\frac{x}{10}\right)^2}\, dx \ = 2\pi\int_0^r \frac{x\sqrt{100 + x^2}}{10}\, dx$$

$$= \left[\frac{\pi}{10}\cdot\frac{2}{3}(100 + x^2)^{3/2}\right]_0^r = \frac{\pi}{15}\left[(100 + r^2)^{3/2} - 1000\right]$$

**94.** $A = 2\int_0^h \sqrt{4py}\, dy$

$$= 4\sqrt{p}\int_0^h y^{1/2}\, dy$$

$$= \left[4\sqrt{p}\left(\frac{2}{3}\right)y^{3/2}\right]_0^h$$

$$= \frac{8}{3}\sqrt{p}\,h^{3/2}$$

**96.** (a) At the vertices we notice that the string is horizontal and has a length of $2a$.

(b) The thumbtacks are located at the foci and the length of string is the constant sum of the distances from the foci.

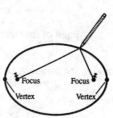

**98.**
$$e = \frac{c}{a}$$

$$0.0167 = \frac{c}{149{,}570{,}000}$$

$$c \approx 2{,}497{,}819$$

Least distance: $a - c = 147{,}072{,}181$ km

Greatest distance: $a + c = 152{,}067{,}819$ km

**100.** $e = \dfrac{A - P}{A + P}$

$$= \frac{(122{,}000 + 4000) - (119 + 4000)}{(122{,}000 + 4000) + (119 + 4000)}$$

$$= \frac{121{,}881}{130{,}119} \approx 0.9367$$

**102.**
$$\frac{x^2}{a^2} + \frac{y^2}{b^2} = 1$$

$$\frac{x^2}{a^2} + \frac{y^2}{a^2(b^2/a^2)} = 1$$

$$\frac{x^2}{a^2} + \frac{y^2}{a^2(a^2 - c^2)/a^2} = 1$$

$$\frac{x^2}{a^2} + \frac{y^2}{a^2(1 - e^2)} = 1$$

As $e \to 0$, $1 - e^2 \to 1$ and we have

$$\frac{x^2}{a^2} + \frac{y^2}{a^2} = 1 \text{ or the circle } x^2 + y^2 = a^2.$$

**104.** $\dfrac{x^2}{(4.5)^2} + \dfrac{y^2}{(2.5)^2} = 1$

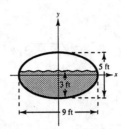

$$x^2 = (4.5)^2\left[1 - \dfrac{y^2}{(2.5)^2}\right]$$

$$x = \pm\dfrac{9}{5}\sqrt{(2.5)^2 - y^2}$$

$V = (\text{Area of bottom})(\text{Length}) + (\text{Area of top})(\text{Length})$

$V = \left[\dfrac{\pi(4.5)(2.5)}{2}\right](16) + 16\displaystyle\int_0^{0.5} \dfrac{9}{5}\sqrt{(2.5)^2 - y^2}\,dy$ (Recall: Area of ellipse is $\pi ab$.)

$= 90\pi + \dfrac{144}{5}\cdot\dfrac{1}{2}\left[y\sqrt{(2.5)^2 - y^2} + (2.5)^2 \arcsin\dfrac{y}{2.5}\right]_0^{0.5} = 90\pi + \dfrac{72}{5}\left[0.5\sqrt{6} + (2.5)^2\arcsin\dfrac{1}{5}\right] \approx 318.5 \text{ ft}^3$

**106.** $9x^2 + 4y^2 + 36x - 24y + 36 = 0$

$$18x + 8yy' + 36 - 24y' = 0$$

$$(8y - 24)y' = -(18x + 36)$$

$$y' = \dfrac{-(18x + 36)}{8y - 24}$$

$y' = 0$ when $x = -2$. $y'$ undefined when $y = 3$.
At $x = -2, y = 0$ or $6$.
Endpoints of major axis: $(-2, 0), (-2, 6)$
At $y = 3, x = 0$ or $-4$.
Endpoints of minor axis: $(0, 3), (-4, 3)$

**Note:** Equation of ellipse is $\dfrac{(x + 2)^2}{4} + \dfrac{(y - 3)^2}{9} = 1$

**108.** (a) $A = 4\displaystyle\int_0^4 \dfrac{3}{4}\sqrt{16 - x^2}\,dx = \dfrac{3}{2}\left[x\sqrt{16 - x^2} + 16\arcsin\dfrac{x}{4}\right]_0^4 = 12\pi$

(b) **Disk:** $V = 2\pi\displaystyle\int_0^4 \dfrac{9}{16}(16 - x^2)\,dx = \dfrac{9\pi}{8}\left[\left(16x - \dfrac{1}{3}x^3\right)\right]_0^4 = 48\pi$

$$y = \dfrac{3}{4}\sqrt{16 - x^2}$$

$$y' = \dfrac{-3x}{4\sqrt{16 - x^2}}$$

$$\sqrt{1 + (y')^2} = \sqrt{1 + \dfrac{9x^2}{16(16 - x^2)}}$$

$S = 2(2\pi)\displaystyle\int_0^4 \dfrac{3}{4}\sqrt{16 - x^2}\sqrt{\dfrac{16(16 - x^2) + 9x^2}{16(16 - x^2)}}\,dx = 4\pi\displaystyle\int_0^4 \dfrac{3}{4}\sqrt{16 - x^2}\dfrac{\sqrt{256 - 7x^2}}{4\sqrt{16 - x^2}}\,dx = \dfrac{3\pi}{4}\displaystyle\int_0^4 \sqrt{256 - 7x^2}\,dx$

$= \dfrac{3\pi}{8\sqrt{7}}\left[\sqrt{7}x\sqrt{256 - 7x^2} + 256\arcsin\dfrac{\sqrt{7}x}{16}\right]_0^4 = \dfrac{3\pi}{8\sqrt{7}}\left(48\sqrt{7} + 256\arcsin\dfrac{\sqrt{7}}{4}\right) \approx 138.93$

—CONTINUED—

**108.** **—CONTINUED—**

(c) **Shell:** $\quad V = 4\pi \int_0^4 x \left[ \frac{3}{4} \sqrt{16 - x^2} \right] dx = 3\pi \left[ \left( -\frac{1}{2} \right)\left( \frac{2}{3} \right)(16 - x^2)^{3/2} \right]_0^4 = 64\pi$

$$x = \frac{4}{3}\sqrt{9 - y^2}$$

$$x' = \frac{-4y}{3\sqrt{9 - y^2}}$$

$$\sqrt{1 + (x')^2} = \sqrt{1 + \frac{16y^2}{9(9 - y^2)}}$$

$$S = 2(2\pi) \int_0^3 \frac{4}{3}\sqrt{9 - y^2}\,\sqrt{\frac{9(9 - y^2) + 16y^2}{9(9 - y^2)}}\,dy$$

$$= 4\pi \int_0^3 \frac{4}{9}\sqrt{81 + 7y^2}\,dy$$

$$= \frac{16}{9}\left( \frac{\pi}{2\sqrt{7}} \right)\left[ \sqrt{7}y\sqrt{81 + 7y^2} + 81 \ln \left| \sqrt{7}y + \sqrt{81 + 7y^2} \right| \right]_0^3$$

$$= \frac{8\pi}{9\sqrt{7}}\left[ 3\sqrt{7}(12) + 81 \ln\left( 3\sqrt{7} + 12 \right) - 81 \ln 9 \right] \approx 168.53$$

**110.** (a) $\dfrac{x^2}{a^2} + \dfrac{y^2}{b^2} = 1$ $\qquad\qquad\qquad\qquad$ (b) Slope of line through $(-c, 0)$ and $(x_0, y_0)$: $m_1 = \dfrac{y_0}{x_0 + c}$

$\qquad\dfrac{2x}{a^2} + \dfrac{2yy'}{b^2} = 0$ $\qquad\qquad\qquad\qquad\qquad\qquad$ Slope of line through $(c, 0)$ and $(x_0, y_0)$: $m_2 = \dfrac{y_0}{x_0 - c}$

$\qquad\qquad y' = -\dfrac{xb^2}{ya^2}$

$\qquad$ At $P$, $y' = -\dfrac{b^2}{a^2} \cdot \dfrac{x_0}{y_0} = m.$

(c) $\tan \alpha = \dfrac{m_2 - m}{1 + m_2 m} = \dfrac{\dfrac{y_0}{x_0 - c} - \left( -\dfrac{b^2 x_0}{a^2 y_0} \right)}{1 + \left( \dfrac{y_0}{x_0 - c} \right)\left( -\dfrac{b^2 x_0}{a^2 y_0} \right)} = \dfrac{a^2 y_0^2 + b^2 x_0(x_0 - c)}{a^2 y_0(x_0 - c) - b^2 x_0 y_0}$

$\qquad\quad = \dfrac{a^2 y_0^2 + b^2 x_0^2 - b^2 x_0 c}{x_0 y_0(a^2 - b^2) - a^2 y_0 c} = \dfrac{a^2 b^2 - b^2 x_0 c}{x_0 y_0 c^2 - a^2 y_0 c} = \dfrac{b^2(a^2 - x_0 c)}{y_0 c(x_0 c - a^2)} = -\dfrac{b^2}{y_0 c}$

$\qquad\quad \alpha = \arctan\left( -\dfrac{b^2}{y_0 c} \right) = -\arctan\left( \dfrac{b^2}{y_0 c} \right)$

$\qquad \tan \beta = \dfrac{m_1 - m}{1 + m_1 m} = \dfrac{\dfrac{y_0}{x_0 + c} - \left( -\dfrac{b^2 x_0}{a^2 y_0} \right)}{1 + \left( \dfrac{y_0}{x_0 + c} \right)\left( -\dfrac{b^2 x_0}{a^2 y_0} \right)} = \dfrac{a^2 y_0^2 + b^2 x_0(x_0 + c)}{a^2 y_0(x_0 + c) - b^2 x_0 y_0}$

$\qquad\quad = \dfrac{a^2 y_0^2 + b^2 x_0^2 + b^2 x_0 c}{a^2 x_0 y_0 + a^2 c y_0 - b^2 x_0 y_0} = \dfrac{a^2 b^2 + b^2 x_0 c}{x_0 y_0(a^2 - b^2) + a^2 c y_0} = \dfrac{b^2(a^2 + x_0 c)}{y_0 c(x_0 c + a^2)} = \dfrac{b^2}{y_0 c}$

$\qquad\quad \beta = \arctan\left( \dfrac{b^2}{y_0 c} \right)$

Since $|\alpha| = |\beta|$, the tangent line to an ellipse at a point $P$ makes equal angles with the lines through $P$ and the foci.

**112.** (a) $e = \dfrac{c}{a} = \dfrac{\sqrt{a^2 + b^2}}{a} \Rightarrow (ea)^2 - a^2 = b^2$. Hence,

$$\frac{(x - h)^2}{a^2} + \frac{(y - k)^2}{b^2} = 1$$

$$\frac{(x - h)^2}{a^2} + \frac{(y - k)^2}{a^2(1 - e^2)} = 1.$$

(b) $\dfrac{(x - 2)^2}{4} + \dfrac{(y - 3)^2}{4(1 - e^2)} = 1$

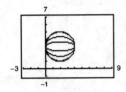

(c) As $e$ approaches 0, the ellipse approaches a circle.

**114.** The transverse axis is vertical since $(-3, 0)$ and $(-3, 3)$ are the foci.

Center: $\left(-3, \dfrac{3}{2}\right)$

$c = \dfrac{3}{2}$, $2a = 2$, $b^2 = c^2 - a^2 = \dfrac{5}{4}$

Therefore, the equation is

$$\frac{[y - (3/2)]^2}{1} - \frac{(x + 3)^2}{5/4} = 1.$$

**116.** Center: $(0, 0)$

Horizontal transverse axis

Foci: $(\pm c, 0)$

Vertices: $(\pm a, 0)$

The difference of the distances from any point on the hyperbola is constant. At a vertex, this constant difference is

$$(a + c) - (c - a) = 2a.$$

Now, for any point $(x, y)$ on the hyperbola, the difference of the distances between $(x, y)$ and the two foci must also be $2a$.

$$\sqrt{(x - c)^2 + (y - 0)^2} - \sqrt{(x + c)^2 + (y - 0)^2} = 2a$$

$$\sqrt{(x - c)^2 + y^2} = 2a + \sqrt{(x + c)^2 + y^2}$$

$$(x - c)^2 + y^2 = 4a^2 + 4a\sqrt{(x + c)^2 + y^2} + (x + c)^2 + y^2$$

$$-4xc - 4a^2 = 4a\sqrt{(x + c)^2 + y^2}$$

$$-(xc + a^2) = a\sqrt{(x + c)^2 + y^2}$$

$$x^2c^2 + 2a^2cx + a^4 = a^2[x^2 + 2cx + c^2 + y^2]$$

$$x^2(c^2 - a^2) - a^2y^2 = a^2(c^2 - a^2)$$

$$\frac{x^2}{a^2} - \frac{y^2}{c^2 - a^2} = 1$$

Since $a^2 + b^2 = c^2$, we have $(x^2/a^2) - (y^2/b^2) = 1$.

**118.** $c = 150$, $2a = 0.001(186,000)$, $a = 93$,

$b = \sqrt{150^2 - 93^2} = \sqrt{13,851}$

$$\frac{x^2}{93^2} - \frac{y^2}{13,851} = 1$$

When $y = 75$, we have

$$x^2 = 93^2\left(1 + \frac{75^2}{13,851}\right)$$

$$x \approx 110.3 \text{ miles.}$$

**120.**
$$\frac{x^2}{a^2} - \frac{y^2}{b^2} = 1$$

$$\frac{2x}{a^2} - \frac{2yy'}{b^2} = 0 \text{ or } y' = \frac{b^2x}{a^2y}$$

$$y - y_0 = \frac{b^2x_0}{a^2y_0}(x - x_0)$$

$$a^2y_0y - a^2y_0^2 = b^2x_0x - b^2x_0^2$$

$$b^2x_0^2 - a^2y_0^2 = b^2x_0x - a^2y_0y$$

$$a^2b^2 = b^2x_0x - a^2y_0y$$

$$\frac{x_0x}{a^2} - \frac{y_0y}{b^2} = 1$$

**122.**
$$Ax^2 + Cy^2 + Dx + Ey + F = 0 \quad \text{(Assume } A \neq 0 \text{ and } C \neq 0; \text{ see (b) below)}$$

$$A\left(x^2 + \frac{D}{A}x\right) + C\left(y^2 + \frac{E}{C}y\right) = -F$$

$$A\left(x^2 + \frac{D}{A}x + \frac{D^2}{4A^2}\right) + C\left(y^2 + \frac{E}{C}y + \frac{E^2}{4C^2}\right) = -F + \frac{D^2}{4A} + \frac{E^2}{4C} = R$$

$$\frac{\left[x + \left(\frac{D}{2A}\right)\right]^2}{C} + \frac{\left[y + \left(\frac{E}{2C}\right)\right]^2}{A} = \frac{R}{AC}$$

(a) If $A = C$, we have

$$\left(x + \frac{D}{2A}\right)^2 + \left(y + \frac{E}{2C}\right)^2 = \frac{R}{A}$$

which is the standard equation of a circle.

(c) If $AC > 0$, we have

$$\frac{\left[x + \left(\frac{D}{2A}\right)\right]^2}{\left|\frac{R}{A}\right|} + \frac{\left[y + \left(\frac{E}{2C}\right)\right]^2}{\left|\frac{R}{C}\right|} = 1$$

which is the equation of an ellipse.

(b) If $C = 0$, we have

$$A\left(x + \frac{D}{2A}\right)^2 = -F - Ey + \frac{D^2}{4A}.$$

If $A = 0$, we have

$$C\left(y + \frac{E}{2C}\right)^2 = -F - Dx + \frac{E^2}{4C}.$$

These are the equations of parabolas.

(d) If $AC < 0$, we have

$$\frac{\left[x + \left(\frac{D}{2A}\right)\right]^2}{\left|\frac{R}{A}\right|} - \frac{\left[y + \left(\frac{E}{2C}\right)\right]^2}{\left|\frac{R}{C}\right|} = \pm 1$$

which is the equation of a hyperbola.

**124.** True

**126.** False. The $y^4$ term should be $y^2$.

**128.** True

## Section 9.2    Plane Curves and Parametric Equations

**2.** $x = 4\cos^2\theta \qquad y = 2\sin\theta$

$0 \leq x \leq 4 \qquad -2 \leq y \leq 2$

(a)

| $\theta$ | $-\frac{\pi}{2}$ | $-\frac{\pi}{4}$ | $0$ | $\frac{\pi}{4}$ | $\frac{\pi}{2}$ |
|---|---|---|---|---|---|
| $x$ | $0$ | $2$ | $4$ | $2$ | $0$ |
| $y$ | $-2$ | $-\sqrt{2}$ | $0$ | $\sqrt{2}$ | $2$ |

(b)

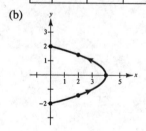

(c)

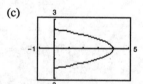

(d) $\dfrac{x}{4} = \cos^2\theta$

$\dfrac{y^2}{4} = \sin^2\theta$

$\dfrac{x}{4} + \dfrac{y^2}{4} = 1$

$x = 4 - y^2, \ -2 \leq y \leq 2$

(e) The graph would be oriented in the opposite direction.

**4.** $x = 3 - 2t$

$y = 2 + 3t$

$y = 2 + 3\left(\dfrac{3 - x}{2}\right)$

$2y + 3x - 13 = 0$

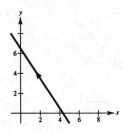

**6.** $x = 2t^2$

$y = t^4 + 1$

$y = \left(\dfrac{x}{2}\right)^2 + 1 = \dfrac{x^2}{4} + 1, x \geq 0$

For $t < 0$, the orientation is right to left.

For $t > 0$, the orientation is left to right.

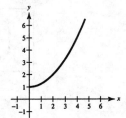

**8.** $x = t^2 + t, \; y = t^2 - t$

Subtracting the second equation from the first, we have

$x - y = 2t \quad \text{or} \quad t = \dfrac{x - y}{2}$

$y = \dfrac{(x - y)^2}{4} - \dfrac{x - y}{2}$

| $t$ | $-2$ | $-1$ | $0$ | $1$ | $2$ |
|-----|------|------|-----|-----|-----|
| $x$ | $2$  | $0$  | $0$ | $2$ | $6$ |
| $y$ | $6$  | $2$  | $0$ | $0$ | $2$ |

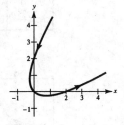

Since the discriminant is

$B^2 - 4AC = (-2)^2 - 4(1)(1) = 0,$

the graph is a rotated parabola.

**10.** $x = \sqrt[4]{t}, t \geq 0$

$y = 3 - t$

$y = 3 - x^4, x \geq 0$

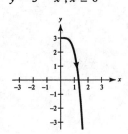

**12.** $x = 1 + \dfrac{1}{t}$

$y = t - 1$

$x = 1 + \dfrac{1}{t}$ implies $t = \dfrac{1}{x - 1}$

$y = \dfrac{1}{x - 1} - 1$

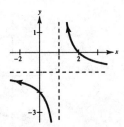

**14.** $x = |t - 1|$

$y = t + 2$

$x = |(y - 2) - 1| = |y - 3|$

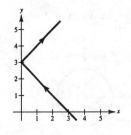

**16.** $x = e^{-t}, x > 0$

$y = e^{2t} - 1$

$y = x^{-2} - 1 = \dfrac{1}{x^2} - 1, x > 0$

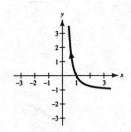

**18.**     $x = \tan^2 \theta$

$y = \sec^2 \theta$

$\sec^2 \theta = \tan^2 \theta + 1$

$y = x + 1$

$x \geq 0$

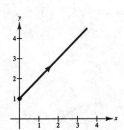

**20.**
$$x = 2 \cos \theta$$
$$y = 6 \sin \theta$$
$$\left(\frac{x}{2}\right)^2 + \left(\frac{y}{6}\right)^2 = \cos^2 + \sin^2 \theta = 1$$
$$\frac{x^2}{4} + \frac{y^2}{36} = 1 \text{ ellipse}$$

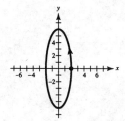

**22.**
$$x = \cos \theta$$
$$y = 2 \sin 2\theta$$
$$y = 4 \sin \theta \cos \theta$$
$$1 - x^2 = \sin^2 \theta$$
$$y = \pm 4x\sqrt{1 - x^2}$$

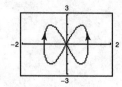

**24.**
$$x = 4 + 2 \cos \theta$$
$$y = -1 + 2 \sin \theta$$
$$(x - 4)^2 = 4 \cos^2 \theta$$
$$(y + 1)^2 = 4 \sin^2 \theta$$
$$(x - 4)^2 + (y + 1)^2 = 4$$

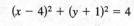
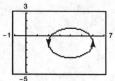

**26.**  $x = \sec \theta$
  $y = \tan \theta$
  $x^2 = \sec^2 \theta$
  $y^2 = \tan^2 \theta$

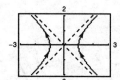

**28.**    $x = \cos^3 \theta$
    $y = \sin^3 \theta$
    $x^{2/3} = \cos^2 \theta$
    $y^{2/3} = \sin^2 \theta$

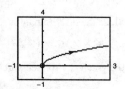

**30.** $x = \ln 2t$
  $y = t^2$
  $t = \dfrac{e^x}{2}$
  $y = \dfrac{e^{2x}}{r} = \dfrac{1}{4}e^{2x}$

**32.**  $x = e^{2t}$
  $y = e^t$
  $y^2 = x$
  $y > 0$
  $y = \sqrt{x}, x > 0$

**34.** By eliminating the parameters in (a) – (d), we get $x^2 + y^2 = 4$. They differ from each other in orientation and in restricted domains. These curves are all smooth.

(a) $x = 2 \cos \theta$, $y = 2 \sin \theta$

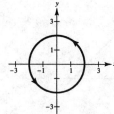

(b) $x = \dfrac{\sqrt{4t^2 - 1}}{|t|} = \sqrt{4 - \dfrac{1}{t^2}}$    $y = \dfrac{1}{t}$

$x \geq 0, \; x \neq 2$                                    $y \neq 0$

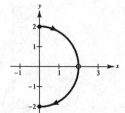

(c) $x = \sqrt{t}$    $y = \sqrt{4 - t}$
  $x \geq 0$    $y \geq 0$

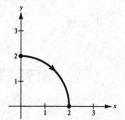

(d) $x = -\sqrt{4 - e^{2t}}$    $y = e^t$
  $-2 < x \leq 0$    $y > 0$

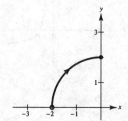

**36.** The orientations are reversed. The graphs are the same. They are both smooth.

**38.** The set of points $(x, y)$ corresponding to the rectangular equation of a set of parametric equations does not show the orientation of the curve nor any restriction on the domain of the original parametric equations.

**40.**
$$x = h + r \cos \theta$$
$$y = k + r \sin \theta$$
$$\cos \theta = \frac{x - h}{r}$$
$$\sin \theta = \frac{y - k}{r}$$
$$\cos^2 \theta + \sin^2 \theta = \frac{(x - h)^2}{r^2} + \frac{(y - k)^2}{r^2} = 1$$
$$(x - h)^2 + (y - k)^2 = r^2$$

**42.**
$$x = h + a \sec \theta$$
$$y = k + b \tan \theta$$
$$\frac{x - h}{a} = \sec \theta$$
$$\frac{y - k}{b} = \tan \theta$$
$$\frac{(x - h)^2}{a^2} - \frac{(y - k)^2}{b^2} = 1$$

**44.** From Exercise 39 we have
$$x = 1 + 4t$$
$$y = 4 - 6t.$$
Solution not unique

**46.** From Exercise 40 we have
$$x = -3 + 3 \cos \theta$$
$$y = 1 + 3 \sin \theta.$$
Solution not unique

**48.** From Exercise 41 we have
$$a = 5, c = 3 \implies b = 4$$
$$x = 4 + 5 \cos$$
$$y = 2 + 4 \sin \theta.$$
Center: $(4, 2)$
Solution not unique

**50.** From Exercise 42 we have
$$a = 1, c = 2 \implies b = \sqrt{3}$$
$$x = \sqrt{3} \tan \theta$$
$$y = \sec \theta.$$
Center: $(0, 0)$
Solution not unique
The transverse axis is vertical, therefore, $x$ and $y$ are interchanged.

**52.** $y = \dfrac{2}{x - 1}$

Example

$$x = t, y = \frac{2}{t - 1}$$
$$x = -t, y = \frac{2}{-t - 1}$$

**54.** $y = x^2$

Example

$$x = t, \qquad y = t^2$$
$$x = t^3, \qquad y = t^6$$

**56.** $x = \theta + \sin \theta$
$y = 1 - \cos \theta$

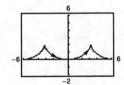

Not smooth at $x = (2n - 1)\pi$

**58.** $x = 2\theta - 4 \sin \theta$
$y = 2 - 4 \cos \theta$

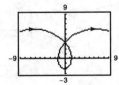

**60.** $x = 2\theta - \sin \theta$
$y = 2 - \cos \theta$

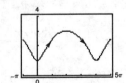

Smooth everywhere

**62.** $x = \dfrac{3t}{1 + t^3}$

$y = \dfrac{3t^2}{1 + t^3}$

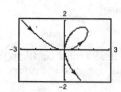

Smooth everywhere

**64.** Each point $(x, y)$ in the plane is determined by the plane curve $x = f(t)$, $y = g(t)$. For each $t$, plot $(x, y)$. As $t$ increases, the curve is traced out in a specific direction called the orientation of the curve.

**66.** (a) Matches (ii) because $-1 \leq x \leq 0$ and $1 \leq y \leq 2$.

(b) Matches (i) because $x = (y - 2)^2 - 1$ for all $y$.

**68.** $x = \cos^3 \theta$

$y = 2 \sin^2 \theta$

Matches (a)

**70.** $x = \cot \theta$

$y = 4 \sin \theta \cos \theta$

Matches (c)

**72.** Let the circle of radius 1 be centered at $C$. $A$ is the point of tangency on the line OC. $OA = 2$, $AC = 1$, $OC = 3$. $P = (x, y)$ is the point on the curve being traced out as the angle $\theta$ changes $\overparen{AB} = \overparen{AP}$. $\overparen{AB} = 2\theta$ and $\overparen{AP} = \alpha \Rightarrow \alpha = 2\theta$. Form the right triangle $\triangle CDP$. The angle $OCE = (\pi/2) - \theta$ and

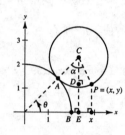

$$\angle DCP = \alpha - \left(\frac{\pi}{2} - \theta\right) = \alpha + \theta - \left(\frac{\pi}{2}\right) = 3\theta - \left(\frac{\pi}{2}\right).$$

$$x = OE + Ex = 3\sin\left(\frac{\pi}{2} - \theta\right) + \sin\left(3\theta - \frac{\pi}{2}\right) = 3\cos\theta - \cos 3\theta$$

$$y = EC - CD = 3\sin\theta - \cos\left(3\theta - \frac{\pi}{2}\right) = 3\sin\theta - \sin 3\theta$$

Hence, $x = 3\cos\theta - \cos 3\theta$, $y = 3\sin\theta - \sin 3\theta$.

**74.** False. Let $x = t^2$ and $y = t$. Then $x = y^2$ and $y$ is not a function of $x$.

**76.** (a) $x = (v_0 \cos\theta)t$

$y = h + (v_0 \sin\theta)t - 16t^2$

$$t = \frac{x}{v_0 \cos\theta} \Rightarrow y = h + (v_0 \sin\theta)\frac{x}{v_0 \cos\theta} - 16\left(\frac{x}{v_0 \cos\theta}\right)^2$$

$$y = h + (\tan\theta)x - \frac{16\sec^2\theta}{v_0^2}x^2$$

(b) $y = 5 + x - 0.005x^2 = h + (\tan\theta)x - \dfrac{16\sec^2\theta}{v_0^2}x^2$

$h = 5$, $\tan\theta = 1 \Rightarrow \theta = \dfrac{\pi}{4}$, and

$$0.005 = \frac{16\sec^2(\pi/4)}{v_0^2} = \frac{16}{v_0^2}(2)$$

$$v_0^2 = \frac{32}{0.005} = 6400 \Rightarrow v_0 = 80.$$

Hence, $x = (80\cos(45°))t$

$y = 5 + (80\sin(45°))t - 16t^2$.

(c)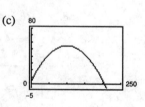

(d) Maximum height: $y = 55$ (at $x = 100$)

Range: 204.88

# Section 9.3    Parametric Equations and Calculus

**2.** $\dfrac{dy}{dx} = \dfrac{dy/dt}{dx/dt} = \dfrac{-1}{(1/3)t^{-2/3}} = -3t^{2/3}$

**4.** $\dfrac{dy}{dx} = \dfrac{dy/d\theta}{dx/d\theta} = \dfrac{(-1/2)e^{-\theta/2}}{2e^{\theta}} = -\dfrac{1}{4}e^{-3\theta/2} = \dfrac{-1}{4e^{3\theta/2}}$

**6.** $x = \sqrt{t}$, $y = 3t - 1$

$\dfrac{dy}{dx} = \dfrac{3}{1/(2\sqrt{t})} = 6\sqrt{t} = 6$   when $t = 1$.

$\dfrac{d^2y}{dx^2} = \dfrac{3/\sqrt{t}}{1/(2\sqrt{t})} = 6$  concave upwards

**8.** $x = t^2 + 3t + 2$, $y = 2t$

$\dfrac{dy}{dx} = \dfrac{2}{2t + 3} = \dfrac{2}{3}$ when $t = 0$.

$\dfrac{d^2y}{dx^2} = \dfrac{-2(2)/(2t + 3)}{2t + 3} = \dfrac{-4}{(2t + 3)^2} = \dfrac{-4}{9}$ when t = 0.

concave downward

**10.** $x = \cos\theta$, $y = 3\sin\theta$

$\dfrac{dy}{dx} = \dfrac{3\cos\theta}{-\sin\theta} = -3\cot\theta \cdot \dfrac{dy}{dx}$ is undefined when $\theta = 0$.

$\dfrac{d^2y}{dx^2} = \dfrac{3\csc^2\theta}{-\sin\theta} = \dfrac{-3}{\sin^3\theta} \cdot \dfrac{d^2y}{dx^2}$ is undefined when $\theta = 0$.

**12.** $x = \sqrt{t}$, $y = \sqrt{t - 1}$

$\dfrac{dy}{dx} = \dfrac{1/(2\sqrt{t - 1})}{1/(2\sqrt{t})}$

$= \dfrac{\sqrt{t}}{\sqrt{t - 1}} = \sqrt{2}$ when $t = 2$.

$\dfrac{d^2y}{dx^2} = \dfrac{\left[\sqrt{t-1}/(2\sqrt{t}) - \sqrt{t}(1/2\sqrt{t-1})\right]/(t-1)}{1/(2\sqrt{t})}$

$= \dfrac{-1}{(t-1)^{3/2}} = -1$ when $t = 2$.

concave downward

**14.** $x = \theta - \sin\theta$, $y = 1 - \cos\theta$

$\dfrac{dy}{dx} = \dfrac{\sin\theta}{1 - \cos\theta} = 0$ when $\theta = \pi$.

$\dfrac{d^2y}{dx^2} = \dfrac{\dfrac{[(1 - \cos\theta)\cos\theta - \sin^2\theta]}{(1 - \cos\theta)^2}}{(1 - \cos\theta)}$

$= \dfrac{-1}{(1 - \cos\theta)^2} = -\dfrac{1}{4}$ when $\theta = \pi$.

concave downward

**16.** $x = 2 - 3\cos\theta$, $y = 3 + 2\sin\theta$

$\dfrac{dy}{dx} = \dfrac{2\cos\theta}{3\sin\theta} = \dfrac{2}{3}\cot\theta$

At $(-1, 3)$, $\theta = 0$, and $\dfrac{dy}{dx}$ is undefined.

Tangent line: $x = -1$

At $(2, 5)$, $\theta = \dfrac{\pi}{2}$, and $\dfrac{dy}{dx} = 0$.

Tangent line: $y = 5$

At $\left(\dfrac{4 + 3\sqrt{3}}{2}, 2\right)$, $\theta = \dfrac{7\pi}{6}$, and $\dfrac{dy}{dx} = \dfrac{2\sqrt{3}}{3}$.

Tangent line:

$$y - 2 = \dfrac{2\sqrt{3}}{3}\left(x - \dfrac{4 + 3\sqrt{3}}{2}\right)$$

$2\sqrt{3}x - 3y - 4\sqrt{3} - 3 = 0$

**18.** $x = t - 1$, $y = \dfrac{1}{t} + 1$, $t = 1$

(a)
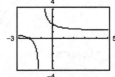

(b) At $t = 1$, $(x, y) = (0, 2)$, and

$\dfrac{dx}{dt} = 1$, $\dfrac{dy}{dt} = -1$, $\dfrac{dy}{dx} = -1$

(c) $\dfrac{dy}{dx} = -1$. At $(0, 2)$, $y - 2 = -1(x - 0)$

$y = -x + 2$

(d)
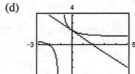

**20.** $x = 4\cos\theta,\ y = 3\sin\theta,\ \theta = \dfrac{3\pi}{4}$

(a)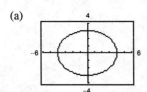

(b) At $\theta = \dfrac{3\pi}{4},\ (x, y) = \left(\dfrac{-4}{\sqrt{2}}, \dfrac{3}{\sqrt{2}}\right)$, and

$$\frac{dx}{dt} = -2\sqrt{2},\ \frac{dy}{dt} = -\frac{3\sqrt{2}}{2},\ \frac{dy}{dx} = \frac{3}{4}$$

(c) $\dfrac{dy}{dx} = \dfrac{3}{4}$. At $\left(\dfrac{-4}{\sqrt{2}}, \dfrac{3}{\sqrt{2}}\right),\quad y - \dfrac{3}{\sqrt{2}} = \dfrac{3}{4}\left(x + \dfrac{4}{\sqrt{2}}\right)$

$$y = \frac{3}{4}x + 3\sqrt{2}$$

(d)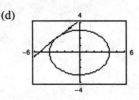

**22.** $x = t^2 - t,\ y = t^3 - 3t - 1$ crosses itself at the point $(x, y) = (2, 1)$.

At this point, $t = -1$ or $t = 2$.

$$\frac{dy}{dx} = \frac{3t^2 - 3}{2t - 1}$$

At $t = -1, \dfrac{dy}{dx} = 0$ and $y = 1$. Tangent Line

At $t = 2, \dfrac{dy}{dt} = \dfrac{9}{3} = 3$ and $y - 1 = 3(x - 2)$ or $y = 3x - 5$. Tangent Line

**24.** $x = 2\theta,\ y = 2(1 - \cos\theta)$

Horizontal tangents: $\dfrac{dy}{d\theta} = 2\sin\theta = 0$ when $\theta = 0,\ \pm\pi,\ \pm 2\pi,\ \dots$

Points: $(4n\pi, 0),\ (2[2n - 1]\pi, 4)$ where $n$ is an integer.
Points shown: $(0, 0),\ (2\pi, 4),\ (4\pi, 0)$

Vertical tangents: $\dfrac{dx}{d\theta} = 2 \neq 0$; none

**26.** $x = t + 1,\ y = t^2 + 3t$

Horizontal tangents: $\dfrac{dy}{dt} = 2t + 3 = 0$ when $t = -\dfrac{3}{2}$.

Point: $\left(-\dfrac{1}{2}, -\dfrac{9}{4}\right)$

Vertical tangents: $\dfrac{dx}{dt} = 1 \neq 0$; none

**28.** $x = t^2 - t + 2,\ y = t^3 - 3t$

Horizontal tangents: $\dfrac{dy}{dt} = 3t^2 - 3 = 0$ when $t = \pm 1$.

Points: $(2, -2),\ (4, 2)$

Vertical tangents: $\dfrac{dx}{dt} = 2t - 1 = 0$ when $t = \dfrac{1}{2}$.

Point: $\left(\dfrac{7}{4}, -\dfrac{11}{8}\right)$

**30.** $x = \cos\theta,\ y = 2\sin 2\theta$

Horizontal tangents: $\dfrac{dy}{d\theta} = 4\cos 2\theta = 0$ when $\theta = \dfrac{\pi}{4}, \dfrac{3\pi}{4}, \dfrac{5\pi}{4}, \dfrac{7\pi}{4}$.

Points: $\left(\dfrac{\sqrt{2}}{2}, 2\right), \left(-\dfrac{\sqrt{2}}{2}, -2\right), \left(-\dfrac{\sqrt{2}}{2}, 2\right), \left(\dfrac{\sqrt{2}}{2}, -2\right)$

Vertical tangents: $\dfrac{dx}{d\theta} = -\sin\theta = 0$ when $\theta = 0,\ \pi$.

Points: $(1, 0),\ (-1, 0)$

**32.** $x = 4 \cos^2 \theta$, $y = 2 \sin \theta$

Horizontal tangents: $\dfrac{dy}{d\theta} = 2 \cos \theta = 0$ when $\theta = \dfrac{\pi}{2}, \dfrac{3\pi}{2}$.

Since $dx/d\theta = 0$ at $\pi/2$ and $3\pi/2$, exclude them.

Vertical tangents: $\dfrac{dx}{d\theta} = -8 \cos \theta \sin \theta = 0$ when

$$\theta = 0, \pi.$$

Point: $(4, 0)$

**34.** $x = \cos^2 \theta$, $y = \cos \theta$

Horizontal tangents: $\dfrac{dy}{d\theta} = -\sin \theta = 0$ when $x = 0, \pi$.

Since $dx/d\theta = 0$ at these values, exclude them.

Vertical tangents: $\dfrac{dx}{d\theta} = -2 \cos \theta \sin \theta = 0$ when

$$\theta = \dfrac{\pi}{2}, \dfrac{3\pi}{2}.$$

(Exclude $0, \pi$.)

Point: $(0, 0)$

**36.** $x = t^2 + 1$, $y = 4t^3 + 3$, $-1 \le t \le 0$

$\dfrac{dx}{dt} = 2t, \dfrac{dy}{dt} = 12t^2, \left(\dfrac{dx}{dt}\right)^2 + \left(\dfrac{dy}{dt}\right)^2 = 4t^2 + 144t^4$

$s = \displaystyle\int_{-1}^{0} \sqrt{4t^2 + 144t^4}\, dt = \int_{-1}^{0} -2t\sqrt{1 + 36t^2}\, dt$

$= \left[\dfrac{-(1 + 36t^2)^{3/2}}{54}\right]_{-1}^{0} = \dfrac{-1}{54}(1 - 37^{3/2}) \approx 4.149$

**38.** $x = \arcsin t$, $y = \ln\sqrt{1 - t^2}$, $0 \le t \le \dfrac{1}{2}$

$\dfrac{dx}{dt} = \dfrac{1}{\sqrt{1 - t^2}}, \dfrac{dy}{dt} = \dfrac{1}{2}\left(\dfrac{-2t}{1 - t^2}\right) = \dfrac{t}{1 - t^2}$

$s = \displaystyle\int_{0}^{1/2} \sqrt{\left(\dfrac{dx}{dt}\right)^2 + \left(\dfrac{dy}{dt}\right)^2}\, dt$

$= \displaystyle\int_{0}^{1/2} \sqrt{\dfrac{1}{(1 - t^2)^2}}\, dt = \int_{0}^{1/2} \dfrac{1}{1 - t^2}\, dt$

$= \left[-\dfrac{1}{2} \ln\left|\dfrac{t - 1}{t + 1}\right|\right]_{0}^{1/2}$

$= -\dfrac{1}{2} \ln\left(\dfrac{1}{3}\right) = \dfrac{1}{2} \ln(3) \approx 0.549$

**40.** $x = t$, $y = \dfrac{t^5}{10} + \dfrac{1}{6t^3}$, $\dfrac{dx}{dt} = 1$, $\dfrac{dy}{dt} = \dfrac{t^4}{2} - \dfrac{1}{2t^4}$

$S = \displaystyle\int_{1}^{2} \sqrt{1 + \left(\dfrac{t^4}{2} - \dfrac{1}{2t^4}\right)^2}\, dt =$

$= \displaystyle\int_{1}^{2} \sqrt{\left(\dfrac{t^4}{2} + \dfrac{1}{2t^4}\right)^2}\, dt$

$= \displaystyle\int_{1}^{2} \left(\dfrac{t^4}{2} + \dfrac{1}{2t^4}\right) dt$

$= \left[\dfrac{t^5}{10} - \dfrac{1}{6t^3}\right]_{1}^{2} = \dfrac{779}{240}$

**42.** $x = a \cos \theta$, $y = a \sin \theta$, $\dfrac{dx}{d\theta} = -a \sin \theta$, $\dfrac{dy}{d\theta} = a \cos \theta$

$S = 4\displaystyle\int_{0}^{\pi/2} \sqrt{a^2 \sin^2 \theta + a^2 \cos^2 \theta}\, d\theta$

$= 4a\displaystyle\int_{0}^{\pi/2} d\theta = \left[4a\theta\right]_{0}^{\pi/2} = 2\pi a$

**44.** $x = \cos \theta + \theta \sin \theta$, $y = \sin \theta - \theta \cos \theta$, $\dfrac{dx}{d\theta} = \theta \cos \theta$

$\dfrac{dy}{d\theta} = \theta \sin \theta$

$S = \displaystyle\int_{0}^{2\pi} \sqrt{\theta^2 \cos^2 \theta + \theta^2 \sin^2 \theta}\, d\theta$

$= \displaystyle\int_{0}^{2\pi} \theta\, d\theta = \left[\dfrac{\theta^2}{2}\right]_{0}^{2\pi} = 2\pi^2$

**46.** $x = \dfrac{4t}{1 + t^3}$, $y = \dfrac{4t^2}{1 + t^3}$

(a) $x^3 + y^3 = 4xy$

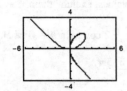

(b) $\dfrac{dy}{dt} = \dfrac{(1 + t^3)(8t) - 4t^2(3t^2)}{(1 + t^3)^2}$

$= \dfrac{4t(2 - t^3)}{(1 + t^3)^2} = 0$ when $t = 0$ or $t = \sqrt[3]{2}$.

Points: $(0, 0)$, $\left( \dfrac{4\sqrt[3]{2}}{3}, \dfrac{4\sqrt[3]{4}}{3} \right) \approx (1.6799, 2.1165)$

(c) $s = 2\displaystyle\int_0^1 \sqrt{\left[ \dfrac{4(1 - 2t^3)}{(1 + t^3)^2} \right]^2 + \left[ \dfrac{4t(2 - t^3)}{(1 + t^3)^2} \right]^2} \, dt = 2\int_0^1 \sqrt{\dfrac{16}{(1 + t^3)^4}\left[ t^8 + 4t^6 - 4t^5 - 4t^3 + 4t^2 + 1 \right]} \, dt$

$= 8\displaystyle\int_0^1 \dfrac{\sqrt{t^8 + 4t^6 - 4t^5 - 4t^3 + 4t^2 + 1}}{(1 + t^3)^2} \, dt \approx 6.557$

**48.** $x = 3\cos\theta$, $y = 4\sin\theta$

$\dfrac{dx}{d\theta} = -3\sin\theta$, $\dfrac{dy}{d\theta} = 4\cos\theta$

$s = \displaystyle\int_0^{2\pi} \sqrt{9\sin^2\theta + 16\cos^2\theta} \, d\theta \approx 22.1$

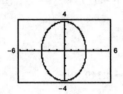

**50.** $x = t$, $y = 4 - 2t$, $\dfrac{dx}{dt} = 1$, $\dfrac{dy}{dt} = -2$

(a) $S = 2\pi\displaystyle\int_0^2 (4 - 2t)\sqrt{1 + 4} \, dt$

$= \left[ 2\sqrt{5}\pi(4t - t^2) \right]_0^2 = 8\pi\sqrt{5}$

(b) $S = 2\pi\displaystyle\int_0^2 t\sqrt{1 + 4} \, dt = \left[ \sqrt{5}\pi t^2 \right]_0^2 = 4\pi\sqrt{5}$

**52.** $x = \dfrac{1}{3}t^3$, $y = t + 1$, $1 \le t \le 2$, $y$-axis

$\dfrac{dx}{dt} = t^2$, $\dfrac{dy}{dt} = 1$

$S = 2\pi\displaystyle\int_1^2 \dfrac{1}{3}t^3\sqrt{t^4 + 1} \, dt = \dfrac{\pi}{9}\left[ (x^4 + 1)^{3/2} \right]_1^2$

$= \dfrac{\pi}{9}(17^{3/2} - 2^{3/2}) \approx 23.48$

**54.** $x = a\cos\theta$, $y = b\sin\theta$, $\dfrac{dx}{d\theta} = -a\sin\theta$, $\dfrac{dy}{d\theta} = b\cos\theta$

(a) $S = 4\pi\displaystyle\int_0^{\pi/2} b\sin\theta\sqrt{a^2\sin^2\theta + b^2\cos^2\theta} \, d\theta$

$= 4\pi\displaystyle\int_0^{\pi/2} ab\sin\theta\sqrt{1 - \left( \dfrac{a^2 - b^2}{a^2} \right)\cos^2\theta} \, d\theta = \dfrac{-4ab\pi}{e}\displaystyle\int_0^{\pi/2} (-e\sin\theta)\sqrt{1 - e^2\cos^2\theta} \, d\theta$

$= \dfrac{-2ab\pi}{e}\left[ e\cos\theta\sqrt{1 - e^2\cos^2\theta} + \arcsin(e\cos\theta) \right]_0^{\pi/2} = \dfrac{-ab\pi}{e}\left[ e\sqrt{1 - e^2} + \arcsin(e) \right]$

$= 2\pi b^2 + \left( \dfrac{2\pi a^2 b}{\sqrt{a^2 - b^2}} \right)\arcsin\left( \dfrac{\sqrt{a^2 - b^2}}{a} \right) = 2\pi b^2 + 2\pi\left( \dfrac{ab}{e} \right)\arcsin(e)$

$\left( e = \dfrac{\sqrt{a^2 - b^2}}{a} = \dfrac{c}{a}\text{: eccentricity} \right)$

**—CONTINUED—**

**54. —CONTINUED—**

(b) $S = 4\pi \displaystyle\int_0^{\pi/2} a \cos\theta \sqrt{a^2 \sin^2\theta + b^2 \cos^2\theta}\, d\theta$

$$= 4\pi \int_0^{\pi/2} a \cos\theta \sqrt{b^2 + c^2 \sin^2\theta}\, d\theta = \frac{4a\pi}{c} \int_0^{\pi/2} c \cos\theta \sqrt{b^2 + c^2 \sin^2\theta}\, d\theta$$

$$= \frac{2a\pi}{c}\left[ c \sin\theta \sqrt{b^2 + c^2 \sin^2\theta} + b^2 \ln\left|c \sin\theta + \sqrt{b^2 + c^2 \sin^2\theta}\right| \right]_0^{\pi/2}$$

$$= \frac{2a\pi}{c}\left[ c \sqrt{b^2 + c^2} + b^2 \ln\left|c + \sqrt{b^2 + c^2}\right| - b^2 \ln b \right]$$

$$= 2\pi a^2 + \frac{2\pi a b^2}{\sqrt{a^2 - b^2}} \ln\left|\frac{a + \sqrt{a^2 - b^2}}{b}\right| = 2\pi a^2 + \left(\frac{\pi b^2}{e}\right) \ln\left|\frac{1 + e}{1 - e}\right|$$

**56.** (a) 0

(b) 4

**58.** One possible answer is the graph given by

$$x = -t, \; y = -t.$$

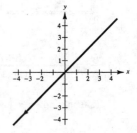

**60.** (a) $S = 2\pi \displaystyle\int_a^b g(t) \sqrt{\left(\frac{dx}{dt}\right)^2 + \left(\frac{dy}{dt}\right)^2}\, dt$

(b) $S = 2\pi \displaystyle\int_a^b f(t) \sqrt{\left(\frac{dx}{dt}\right)^2 + \left(\frac{dy}{dt}\right)^2}\, dt$

**62.** Let $y$ be a continuous function of $x$ on $a \le x \le b$. Suppose that $x = f(t)$, $y = g(t)$, and $f(t_1) = a$, $f(t_2) = b$. Then using integration by substitution, $dx = f'(t)\, dt$ and

$$\int_a^b y\, dx = \int_{t_1}^{t_2} g(t) f'(t)\, dt.$$

**64.** $x = \sqrt{4 - t}, \; y = \sqrt{t}, \; \dfrac{dx}{dt} = -\dfrac{1}{2\sqrt{4 - t}}, \; 0 \le t \le 4$

$$A = \int_4^0 \sqrt{t}\left(-\frac{1}{2\sqrt{4 - t}}\right) dt = \int_0^2 \sqrt{4 - u^2}\, du = \frac{1}{2}\left[u\sqrt{4 - u^2} + 4 \arcsin\frac{u}{2}\right]_0^2 = \pi$$

Let $u = \sqrt{4 - t}$, then $du = -1/(2\sqrt{4 - t})\, dt$ and $\sqrt{t} = \sqrt{4 - u^2}$.

$$\bar{x} = \frac{1}{\pi}\int_4^0 \sqrt{4 - t}\,\sqrt{t}\left(-\frac{1}{2\sqrt{4 - t}}\right) dt = -\frac{1}{2\pi}\int_4^0 \sqrt{t}\, dt = \left[-\frac{1}{2\pi}\frac{2}{3}t^{3/2}\right]_4^0 = \frac{8}{3\pi}$$

$$\bar{y} = \frac{1}{2\pi}\int_4^0 (\sqrt{t})^2\left(-\frac{1}{2\sqrt{4 - t}}\right) dt = -\frac{1}{4\pi}\int_4^0 \frac{t}{\sqrt{4 - t}}\, dt = -\frac{1}{4\pi}\left[\frac{-2(8 + t)}{3}\sqrt{4 - t}\right]_4^0 = \frac{8}{3\pi}$$

$$(\bar{x}, \bar{y}) = \left(\frac{8}{3\pi}, \frac{8}{3\pi}\right)$$

**66.** $x = \cos\theta, \; y = 3 \sin\theta, \; \dfrac{dx}{d\theta} = -\sin\theta$

$$V = 2\pi \int_{\pi/2}^0 (3 \sin\theta)^2 (-\sin\theta)\, d\theta$$

$$= -18\pi \int_{\pi/2}^0 \sin^3\theta\, d\theta = -18\pi\left[-\cos\theta + \frac{\cos^3\theta}{3}\right]_{\pi/2}^0 = 12\pi$$

**68.** $x = 2 \cot \theta$, $y = 2 \sin^2 \theta$, $\dfrac{dx}{d\theta} = -2 \csc^2 \theta$

$$A = 2 \int_{\pi/2}^{0} (2 \sin^2 \theta)(-2 \csc^2 \theta)\, d\theta = -8 \int_{\pi/2}^{0} d\theta = \left[ -8\theta \right]_{\pi/2}^{0} = 4\pi$$

**70.** $\frac{3}{8}\pi a^2$ is area of asteroid (b).     **72.** $2\pi a^2$ is area of deltoid (c).     **74.** $2\pi ab$ is area of teardrop (e).

**76.** (a) $y = -12 \ln\left( \dfrac{12 - \sqrt{144 - x^2}}{x} \right) - \sqrt{144 - x^2}$

$0 < x \leq 12$

(b) $x = 12 \operatorname{sech} \dfrac{t}{12}$, $y = t - 12 \tanh \dfrac{t}{12}$, $0 \leq t$

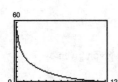

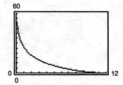

Same as the graph in (a), but has the advantage of showing the position of the object and any given time $t$.

(c) $\dfrac{dy}{dx} = \dfrac{1 - \operatorname{sech}^2(t/12)}{-\operatorname{sech}(t/12)\tan(t/12)} = -\sinh \dfrac{t}{12}$

Tangent line: $y - \left( t_0 - 12 \tanh \dfrac{t_0}{12} \right) = -\sinh \dfrac{t_0}{12} \left( x - 12 \operatorname{sech} \dfrac{t_0}{12} \right)$

$$y = t_0 - \left( \sinh \dfrac{t_0}{12} \right) x$$

$y$-intercept: $(0, t_0)$

Distance between $(0, t_0)$ and $(x, y)$: $d = \sqrt{ \left( 12 \operatorname{sech} \dfrac{t_0}{12} \right)^2 + \left( -12 \tanh \dfrac{t_0}{12} \right)^2 } = 12$

$$d = 12 \text{ for any } t \geq 0.$$

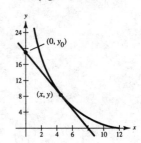

**78.** False. Both $dx/dt$ and $dy/dt$ are zero when $t = 0$. By eliminating the parameter, we have $y = x^{2/3}$ which does not have a horizontal tangent at the origin.

## Section 9.4    Polar Coordinates and Polar Graphs

**2.** $\left( -2, \dfrac{7\pi}{4} \right)$

$x = -2 \cos\left( \dfrac{7\pi}{4} \right) = -\sqrt{2}$

$y = -2 \sin\left( \dfrac{7\pi}{4} \right) = \sqrt{2}$

$(x, y) = \left( -\sqrt{2},\, \sqrt{2} \right)$

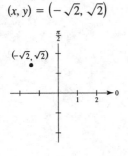

**4.** $\left( 0, -\dfrac{7\pi}{6} \right)$

$x = 0 \cos\left( -\dfrac{7\pi}{6} \right) = 0$

$y = 0 \sin\left( -\dfrac{7\pi}{6} \right) = 0$

$(x, y) = (0, 0)$

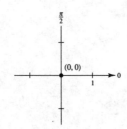

**6.** $(-3, -1.57)$

$x = -3 \cos(-1.57) \approx -0.0024$

$y = -3 \sin(-1.57) \approx 3$

$(x, y) = (-0.0024, 3)$

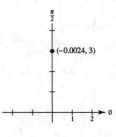

**8.** $(r, \theta) = \left(-2, \dfrac{11\pi}{6}\right)$

$(x, y) = (-1.7321, 1)$

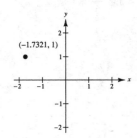

**10.** $(r, \theta) = (8.25, 1.3)$

$(x, y) = (2.2069, 7.9494)$

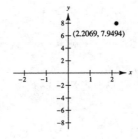

**12.** $(x, y) = (0, -5)$

$r = \pm 5$

$\tan \theta$ undefined

$\theta = \dfrac{\pi}{2}, \dfrac{3\pi}{2}, \left(5, \dfrac{3\pi}{2}\right), \left(-5, \dfrac{\pi}{2}\right)$

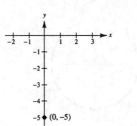

**14.** $(x, y) = (4, -2)$

$r = \pm\sqrt{16 + 4} = \pm 2\sqrt{5}$

$\tan \theta = -\dfrac{2}{4} = -\dfrac{1}{2}$

$\theta \approx -0.464$

$\left(2\sqrt{5}, -0.464\right), \left(-2\sqrt{5}, 2.678\right)$

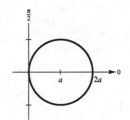

**16.** $(x, y) = \left(3\sqrt{2}, 3\sqrt{2}\right)$

$(r, \theta) = (6, 0.785)$

**18.** $(x, y) = (0, -5)$

$(r, \theta) = (5, -1.571)$

**20.** (a) Moving horizontally, the *x*-coordinate changes. Moving vertically, the *y*-coordinate changes.

(b) Both $r$ and $\theta$ values change.

(c) In polar mode, horizontal (or vertical) changes result in changes in both $r$ and $\theta$.

**22.** $x^2 + y^2 - 2ax = 0$

$r^2 - 2ar \cos \theta = 0$

$r(r - 2a \cos \theta) = 0$

$r = 2a \cos \theta$

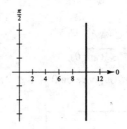

**24.** $x = 10$

$r \cos \theta = 10$

$r = 10 \sec \theta$

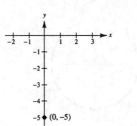

**26.** $xy = 4$

$(r \cos \theta)(r \sin \theta) = 4$

$r^2 = 4 \sec \theta \csc \theta$

$= 8 \csc 2\theta$

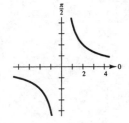

**28.** $(x^2 + y^2)^2 - 9(x^2 - y^2) = 0$

$(r^2)^2 - 9(r^2 \cos^2 \theta - r^2 \sin^2 \theta) = 0$

$r^2[r^2 - 9(\cos 2\theta)] = 0$

$r^2 = 9 \cos 2\theta$

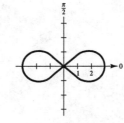

**30.** $r = -2$

$r^2 = 4$

$x^2 + y^2 = 4$

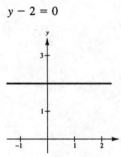

**32.** $r = 5 \cos \theta$

$r^2 = 5r \cos \theta$

$x^2 + y^2 = 5x$

$x^2 - 5x + \dfrac{25}{4} + y^2 = \dfrac{25}{4}$

$\left(x - \dfrac{5}{2}\right)^2 + y^2 = \left(\dfrac{5}{2}\right)^2$

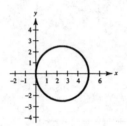

**34.** $\theta = \dfrac{5\pi}{6}$

$\tan \theta = \tan \dfrac{5\pi}{6}$

$\dfrac{y}{x} = -\dfrac{\sqrt{3}}{3}$

$y = -\dfrac{\sqrt{3}}{3}x$

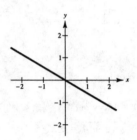

**36.** $r = 2 \csc \theta$

$r \sin \theta = 2$

$y = 2$

$y - 2 = 0$

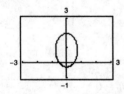

**38.** $r = 5(1 - 2 \sin \theta)$

$0 \le \theta < 2\pi$

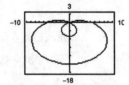

**40.** $r = 4 + 3 \cos \theta$

$0 \le \theta < 2\pi$

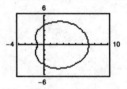

**42.** $r = \dfrac{2}{4 - 3 \sin \theta}$

Traced out once on $0 \le \theta \le 2\pi$

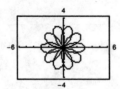

**44.** $r = 3 \sin\left(\dfrac{5\theta}{2}\right)$

$0 \le \theta < 4\pi$

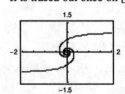

**46.** $r^2 = \dfrac{1}{\theta}.$

Graph as

$$r_1 = \dfrac{1}{\sqrt{\theta}}, r_2 = -\dfrac{1}{\sqrt{\theta}}.$$

It is traced out once on $[0, \infty)$.

**48.** (a) The rectangular coordinates of $(r_1, \theta_1)$ are $(r_1 \cos \theta_1, r_1 \sin \theta_1)$. The rectangular coordinates of $(r_2, \theta_2)$ are $(r_2 \cos \theta_2, r_2 \sin \theta_2)$.

$$d^2 = (x_2 - x_1)^2 + (y_2 - y_1)^2$$

$$= (r_2 \cos \theta_2 - r_1 \cos \theta_1)^2 + (r_2 \sin \theta_2 - r_1 \sin \theta_1)^2$$

$$= r_2^2 \cos^2 \theta_2 - 2r_1 r_2 \cos \theta_1 \cos \theta_2 + r_1^2 \cos^2 \theta_1 + r_2^2 \sin^2 \theta_2^2 - 2r_1 r_2 \sin \theta_1 \sin \theta_2 + r_1^2 \sin^2 \theta_1$$

$$= r_2^2 (\cos^2 \theta_2 + \sin^2 \theta_2) + r_1^2 (\cos^2 \theta_1 + \sin^2 \theta_1) - 2 r_1 r_2 (\cos \theta_1 \cos \theta_2 + \sin \theta_1 \sin \theta_2)$$

$$= r_1^2 + r_2^2 - 2r_1 r_2 \cos(\theta_1 - \theta_2)$$

$$d = \sqrt{r_1^2 + r_2^2 - 2r_1 r_2 \cos(\theta_1 - \theta_2)}$$

(b) If $\theta_1 = \theta_2$, the points lie on the same line passing through the origin. In this case,

$$d = \sqrt{r_1^2 + r_2^2 - 2r_1 r_2 \cos(0)}$$

$$= \sqrt{(r_1 - r_2)^2} = |r_1 - r_2|$$

(c) If $\theta_1 - \theta_2 = 90°$, then $\cos(\theta_1 - \theta_2) = 0$ and $d = \sqrt{r_1^2 + r_2^2}$, the Pythagorean Theorem!

(d) Many answers are possible. For example, consider the two points $(r_1, \theta_1) = (1, 0)$ and $(r_2, \theta_2) = (2, \pi/2)$.

$$d = \sqrt{1 + 2^2 - 2(1)(2) \cos\left(0 - \frac{\pi}{2}\right)} = \sqrt{5}$$

Using $(r_1, \theta_1) = (-1, \pi)$ and $(r_2, \theta_2) = [2, (5\pi/2)]$, $d = \sqrt{(-1)^2 + (2)^2 - 2(-1)(2) \cos\left(\pi - \frac{5\pi}{2}\right)} = \sqrt{5}$.

You always obtain the same distance.

**50.** $\left(10, \dfrac{7\pi}{6}\right)$, $(3, \pi)$

$$d = \sqrt{10^2 + 3^2 - 2(10)(3) \cos\left(\frac{7\pi}{6} - \pi\right)}$$

$$= \sqrt{109 - 60 \cos \frac{\pi}{6}} = \sqrt{109 - 30\sqrt{3}} \approx 7.6$$

**52.** $(4, 2.5)$, $(12, 1)$

$$d = \sqrt{4^2 + 12^2 - 2(4)(12) \cos(2.5 - 1)}$$

$$= \sqrt{160 - 96 \cos 1.5} \approx 12.3$$

**54.** $r = 2(1 - \sin \theta)$

$$\frac{dy}{dx} = \frac{-2 \cos \theta \sin \theta + 2 \cos \theta(1 - \sin \theta)}{-2 \cos \theta \cos \theta - 2 \sin \theta(1 - \sin \theta)}$$

At $(2, 0)$, $\dfrac{dy}{dx} = -1$.

At $\left(3, \dfrac{7\pi}{6}\right)$, $\dfrac{dy}{dx}$ is undefined.

At $\left(4, \dfrac{3\pi}{2}\right)$, $\dfrac{dy}{dx} = 0$.

**56.** (a), (b) $r = 3 - 2 \cos \theta$

$(r, \theta) = (1, 0) \Rightarrow (x, y) = (1, 0)$

Tangent line: $x = 1$

(c) At $\theta = 0$, $\dfrac{dy}{dx}$ does not exist (vertical tangent).

**58.** (a), (b) $r = 4$

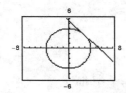

at $(r, \theta) = \left(4, \dfrac{\pi}{4}\right) \Rightarrow (x, y) = \left(2\sqrt{2}, 2\sqrt{2}\right)$

Tangent line: $y - 2\sqrt{2} = -1\left(x - 2\sqrt{2}\right)$

$$y = -x + 4\sqrt{2}$$

(c) At $\theta = \dfrac{\pi}{4}, \dfrac{dy}{dx} = -1.$

**60.** $r = a \sin \theta$

$\dfrac{dy}{d\theta} = a \sin \theta \cos \theta + a \cos \theta \sin \theta$

$\qquad = 2a \sin \theta \cos \theta = 0$

$\theta = 0, \dfrac{\pi}{2}, \pi, \dfrac{3\pi}{2}$

$\dfrac{dx}{d\theta} = -a \sin^2 \theta + a \cos^2 \theta = a(1 - 2\sin^2 \theta) = 0$

$\sin \theta = \pm\dfrac{1}{\sqrt{2}}, \quad \theta = \dfrac{\pi}{4}, \dfrac{3\pi}{4}, \dfrac{5\pi}{4}, \dfrac{7\pi}{4}$

Horizontal: $(0, 0), \left(a, \dfrac{\pi}{2}\right)$

Vertical: $\left(\dfrac{a\sqrt{2}}{2}, \dfrac{\pi}{4}\right), \left(\dfrac{a\sqrt{2}}{2}, \dfrac{3\pi}{4}\right)$

**62.** $r = a \sin \theta \cos^2 \theta$

$\dfrac{dy}{d\theta} = a \sin \theta \cos^3 \theta + \left[-2a \sin^2 \theta \cos \theta + a \cos^3 \theta\right] \sin \theta$

$\qquad = 2a\left[\sin \theta \cos^3 \theta - \sin^3 \theta \cos \theta\right]$

$\qquad = 2a \sin \theta \cos \theta (\cos^2 \theta - \sin^2 \theta) = 0$

$\theta = 0, \ \tan^2 \theta = 1, \ \theta = \dfrac{\pi}{4}, \dfrac{3\pi}{4}$

Horizontal: $\left(\dfrac{\sqrt{2}a}{4}, \dfrac{\pi}{4}\right), \left(\dfrac{\sqrt{2}a}{4}, \dfrac{3\pi}{4}\right), (0, 0)$

**64.** $r = 3 \cos 2\theta \sec \theta$

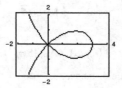

Horizontal tangents: $(2.133, \pm 0.4352)$

**66.** $r = 2 \cos(3\theta - 2)$

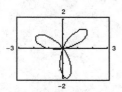

Horizontal tangents:

$\quad (1.894, 0.776), (1.755, 2.594), (1.998, -1.442)$

**68.**

$$r = 3 \cos \theta$$

$$r^2 = 3r \cos \theta$$

$$x^2 + y^2 = 3x$$

$$\left(x - \dfrac{3}{2}\right)^2 + y^2 = \dfrac{9}{4}$$

Circle: $r = \dfrac{3}{2}$

Center: $\left(\dfrac{3}{2}, 0\right)$

Tangent at pole: $\theta = \dfrac{\pi}{2}$

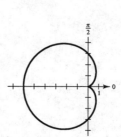

**70.** $r = 3(1 - \cos \theta)$

Cardioid

Symmetric to polar axis since $r$ is a function of $\cos \theta$.

| $\theta$ | 0 | $\dfrac{\pi}{3}$ | $\dfrac{\pi}{2}$ | $\dfrac{2\pi}{3}$ | $\pi$ |
|---|---|---|---|---|---|
| $r$ | 0 | $\dfrac{3}{2}$ | 3 | $\dfrac{9}{2}$ | 6 |

**72.** $r = -\sin(5\theta)$

Rose curve with five petals

Symmetric to $\theta = \dfrac{\pi}{2}$

Relative extrema occur when

$$\frac{dr}{d\theta} = -5\cos(5\theta) = 0 \text{ at } \theta = \frac{\pi}{10}, \frac{3\pi}{10}, \frac{5\pi}{10}, \frac{7\pi}{10}, \frac{9\pi}{10}.$$

Tangents at the pole: $\theta = 0, \dfrac{\pi}{5}, \dfrac{2\pi}{5}, \dfrac{3\pi}{5}, \dfrac{4\pi}{5}$

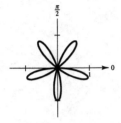

**74.** $r = 3\cos 2\theta$

Rose curve with four petals

Symmetric to the polar axis, $\theta = \dfrac{\pi}{2}$, and pole

Relative extrema: $(3, 0), \left(-3, \dfrac{\pi}{2}\right), (3, \pi), \left(-3, \dfrac{3\pi}{2}\right)$

Tangents at the pole: $\theta = \dfrac{\pi}{4}, \dfrac{3\pi}{4}$

$\theta = \dfrac{5\pi}{4}$ and $\dfrac{7\pi}{4}$ given the same tangents.

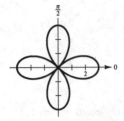

**76.** $r = 2$

Circle radius: 2

$x^2 + y^2 = 4$

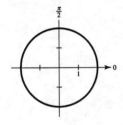

**78.** $r = 1 + \sin\theta$

Cardioid

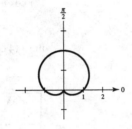

**80.** $r = 5 - 4\sin\theta$

Limaçon

Symmetric to $\theta = \dfrac{\pi}{2}$

| $\theta$ | $-\dfrac{\pi}{2}$ | $-\dfrac{\pi}{6}$ | $0$ | $\dfrac{\pi}{6}$ | $\dfrac{\pi}{2}$ |
|---|---|---|---|---|---|
| $r$ | 9 | 7 | 5 | 3 | 1 |

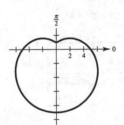

**82.** $r = \dfrac{6}{2\sin\theta - 3\cos\theta}$

$2r\sin\theta - 3r\cos\theta = 6$

$2y - 3x = 6$

Line

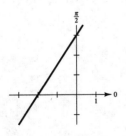

**84.** $r = \dfrac{1}{\theta}$

Hyperbolic spiral

| $\theta$ | $\dfrac{\pi}{4}$ | $\dfrac{\pi}{2}$ | $\dfrac{3\pi}{4}$ | $\pi$ | $\dfrac{5\pi}{4}$ | $\dfrac{3\pi}{2}$ |
|---|---|---|---|---|---|---|
| $r$ | $\dfrac{4}{\pi}$ | $\dfrac{2}{\pi}$ | $\dfrac{4}{3\pi}$ | $\dfrac{1}{\pi}$ | $\dfrac{4}{5\pi}$ | $\dfrac{2}{3\pi}$ |

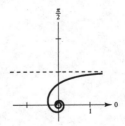

**86.** $r^2 = 4 \sin \theta$

Lemniscate

Symmetric to the polar axis, $\theta = \dfrac{\pi}{2}$, and pole

Relative extrema: $\left( \pm 2, \dfrac{\pi}{2} \right)$

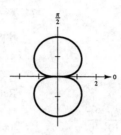

| $\theta$ | 0 | $\dfrac{\pi}{6}$ | $\dfrac{\pi}{2}$ | $\dfrac{5\pi}{6}$ | $\pi$ |
|---|---|---|---|---|---|
| $r$ | 0 | $\pm\sqrt{2}$ | $\pm 2$ | $\pm\sqrt{2}$ | 0 |

Tangent at the pole: $\theta = 0$

**88.** Since

$$r = 2 + \csc \theta = 2 + \frac{1}{\sin \theta},$$

the graphs has symmetry with respect to $\theta = \pi/2$. Furthermore,

$$r \Longrightarrow \infty \text{ as } \theta \Longrightarrow 0^+$$

$$r \Longrightarrow \infty \text{ as } \theta \Longrightarrow \pi^-.$$

Also, $r = 2 + \dfrac{1}{\sin \theta} = 2 + \dfrac{r}{\sin \theta} = 2 + \dfrac{r}{y}$

$$ry = 2y + r$$

$$r = \frac{2y}{y - 1}.$$

Thus, $r \Longrightarrow \pm\infty$ as $y \Longrightarrow 1$.

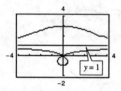

**90.** $r = 2 \cos 2\theta \sec \theta$

Strophoid

$$r \Longrightarrow -\infty \text{ as } \theta \Longrightarrow \frac{\pi^-}{2}$$

$$r \Longrightarrow \infty \text{ as } \theta \Longrightarrow \frac{-\pi^+}{2}$$

$$r = 2 \cos 2\theta \sec \theta = 2(2\cos^2 \theta - 1) \sec \theta$$

$$r \cos \theta = 4\cos^2 \theta - 2$$

$$x = 4\cos^2 \theta - 2$$

$$\lim_{\theta \to \pm\pi/2} (4\cos^2 \theta - 2) = -2$$

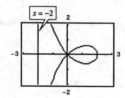

**92.** $x = r \cos \theta, y = r \sin \theta$

$$x^2 + y^2 = r^2, \tan \theta = \frac{y}{x}$$

**94.** Slope of tangent line to graph of $r = f(\theta)$ at $(r, \theta)$ is

$$\frac{dy}{dx} = \frac{f(\theta)\cos \theta + f'(\theta)\sin \theta}{-f(\theta)\sin \theta + f'(\theta)\cos \theta}.$$

If $f(\alpha) = 0$ and $f'(\alpha) \neq 0$, then $\theta = \alpha$ is tangent at the pole.

**96.** $r = 4 \cos 2\theta$

Rose curve

Matches (b)

**98.** $r = 2 \sec \theta$

Line

Matches (d)

**100.** $r = 6[1 + \cos(\theta - \phi)]$

(a) $\phi = 0, r = 6[1 + \cos\theta]$

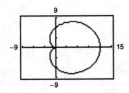

(b) $\theta = \dfrac{\pi}{4}, r = 6\left[1 + \cos\left(\theta - \dfrac{\pi}{4}\right)\right]$

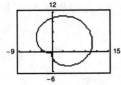

The graph of $r = 6[1 + \cos\theta]$ is rotated through the angle $\pi/4$.

(c) $\theta = \dfrac{\pi}{2}$

$$r = 6\left[1 + \cos\left(\theta - \dfrac{\pi}{2}\right)\right]$$
$$= 6\left[1 + \cos\theta\cos\dfrac{\pi}{2} + \sin\theta\sin\dfrac{\pi}{2}\right]$$
$$= 6[1 + \sin\theta]$$

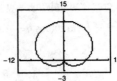

The graph of $r = 6[1 + \cos\theta]$ is rotated through the angle $\pi/2$.

**102.** (a) $\sin\left(\theta - \dfrac{\pi}{2}\right) = \sin\theta\cos\left(\dfrac{\pi}{2}\right) - \cos\theta\sin\left(\dfrac{\pi}{2}\right)$

$$= -\cos\theta$$

$$r = f\left[\sin\left(\theta - \dfrac{\pi}{2}\right)\right]$$

$$= f(-\cos\theta)$$

(b) $\sin(\theta - \pi) = \sin\theta\cos\pi - \cos\theta\sin\pi$

$$= -\sin\theta$$

$$r = f[\sin(\theta - \pi)]$$

$$= f(-\sin\theta)$$

(c) $\sin\left(\theta - \dfrac{3\pi}{2}\right) = \sin\theta\cos\left(\dfrac{3\pi}{2}\right) - \cos\theta\sin\left(\dfrac{3\pi}{2}\right)$

$$= \cos\theta$$

$$r = f\left[\sin\left(\theta - \dfrac{3\pi}{2}\right)\right] = f(\cos\theta)$$

**104.** $r = 2\sin 2\theta = 4\sin\theta\cos\theta$

(a) $r = 4\sin\left(\theta - \dfrac{\pi}{6}\right)\cos\left(\theta - \dfrac{\pi}{6}\right)$

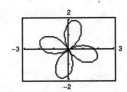

(b) $r = 4\sin\left(\theta - \dfrac{\pi}{2}\right)\cos\left(\theta - \dfrac{\pi}{2}\right) = -4\sin\theta\cos\theta$

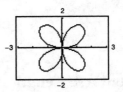

(c) $r = 4\sin\left(\theta - \dfrac{2\pi}{3}\right)\cos\left(\theta - \dfrac{2\pi}{3}\right)$

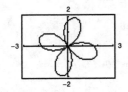

(d) $r = 4\sin(\theta - \pi)\cos(\theta - \pi) = 4\sin\theta\cos\theta$

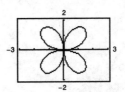

**106.** By Theorem 9.11, the slope of the tangent line through $A$ and $P$ is

$$\frac{f\cos\theta + f'\sin\theta}{-f\sin\theta + f'\cos\theta}$$

This is equal to

$$\tan(\theta + \psi) = \frac{\tan\theta + \tan\psi}{1 - \tan\theta\tan\psi} = \frac{\sin\theta + \cos\theta\tan\psi}{\cos\theta - \sin\theta\tan\psi}.$$

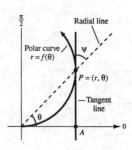

Equating the expressions and cross-multiplying, you obtain

$$(f\cos\theta + f'\sin\theta)(\cos\theta - \sin\theta\tan\psi) = (\sin\theta + \cos\theta\tan\psi)(-f\sin\theta + f'\cos\theta)$$

$$f\cos^2\theta - f\cos\theta\sin\theta\tan\psi + f'\sin\theta\cos\theta - f'\sin^2\theta\tan\psi = -f\sin^2\theta - f\sin\theta\cos\theta\tan\psi + f'\sin\theta\cos\theta + f'\cos^2\theta\tan\psi$$

$$f(\cos^2\theta + \sin^2\theta) = f'\tan\psi(\cos^2\theta + \sin^2\theta)$$

$$\tan\psi = \frac{f}{f'} = \frac{r}{dr/d\theta}.$$

**108.** $\tan\psi = \dfrac{r}{dr/d\theta} = \dfrac{3(1 - \cos\theta)}{3\sin\theta}$

At $\theta = \dfrac{3\pi}{4}$, $\tan\psi = \dfrac{1 + \left(\sqrt{2}/2\right)}{\sqrt{2}} = \dfrac{2 + \sqrt{2}}{\sqrt{2}}$.

$\psi = \arctan\left(\dfrac{2 + \sqrt{2}}{\sqrt{2}}\right) \approx 1.041 (\approx 59.64°)$

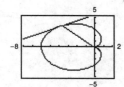

**110.** $\tan\psi = \dfrac{r}{dr/d\theta} = \dfrac{4\sin 2\theta}{8\cos 2\theta}$

At $\theta = \dfrac{\pi}{6}$, $\tan\psi = \dfrac{\sin(\pi/3)}{2\cos(\pi/3)} = \dfrac{\sqrt{3}}{2}$.

$\psi = \arctan\left(\dfrac{\sqrt{3}}{2}\right) \approx 0.7137 (\approx 40.89°)$

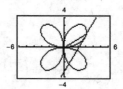

**112.** $\tan\psi = \dfrac{r}{dr/d\theta} = \dfrac{5}{0}$ undefined $\implies \psi = \dfrac{\pi}{2}$.

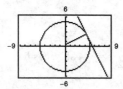

**114.** True

**116.** True

## Section 9.5    Area and Arc Length in Polar Coordinates

**2.** (a) $r = 3\cos\theta$

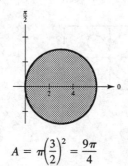

$A = \pi\left(\dfrac{3}{2}\right)^2 = \dfrac{9\pi}{4}$

(b) $A = 2\left(\dfrac{1}{2}\right)\displaystyle\int_0^{\pi/2}\left[3\cos\theta\right]^2 d\theta$

$= 9\displaystyle\int_0^{\pi/2}\cos^2\theta\, d\theta$

$= \dfrac{9}{2}\displaystyle\int_0^{\pi/2}(1 + \cos 2\theta)\, d\theta$

$= \dfrac{9}{2}\left[\theta + \dfrac{\sin 2\theta}{2}\right]_0^{\pi/2} = \dfrac{9\pi}{4}$

**4.** $A = 2\left[\dfrac{1}{2}\displaystyle\int_0^{\pi/4}(6\sin 2\theta)^2\,d\theta\right] = 36\displaystyle\int_0^{\pi/4}\sin^2 2\theta\,d\theta$

$= 36\displaystyle\int_0^{\pi/4}\dfrac{1-\cos 4\theta}{2}\,d\theta$

$= 18\left[\theta - \dfrac{\sin 4\theta}{4}\right]_0^{\pi/4}$

$= 18\left[\dfrac{\pi}{4}\right] = \dfrac{9\pi}{2}$

**6.** $A = 2\left[\dfrac{1}{2}\displaystyle\int_0^{\pi/10}(\cos 5\theta)^2\,d\theta\right]$

$= \dfrac{1}{2}\left[\theta + \dfrac{1}{10}\sin(10\,\theta)\right]_0^{\pi/10} = \dfrac{\pi}{20}$

**8.** $A = 2\left[\dfrac{1}{2}\displaystyle\int_0^{\pi/2}(1-\sin\theta)^2\,d\theta\right]$

$= \left[\dfrac{3}{2}\theta + 2\cos\theta - \dfrac{1}{4}\sin 2\theta\right]_0^{\pi/2} = \dfrac{3\pi-8}{4}$

**10.** $A = 2\left[\dfrac{1}{2}\displaystyle\int_{\arcsin(2/3)}^{\pi/2}(4-6\sin\theta)^2\,d\theta\right]$

$= \displaystyle\int_{\arcsin(2/3)}^{\pi/2}[16 - 48\sin\theta + 36\sin^2\theta]\,d\theta$

$= \displaystyle\int_{\arcsin(2/3)}^{\pi/2}\left[16 - 48\sin\theta + 36\left(\dfrac{1-\cos 2\theta}{2}\right)\right]\,d\theta$

$= \left[34\theta + 48\cos\theta - 9\sin 2\theta\right]_{\arcsin(2/3)}^{\pi/2} \approx 1.7635$

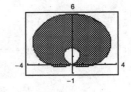

**12.** Four times the area in Exercise 11, $A = 4\left(\pi + 3\sqrt{3}\right)$. More specifically, we see that the area inside the outer loop is

$$2\left[\dfrac{1}{2}\displaystyle\int_{-\pi/6}^{\pi/2}(2(1+2\sin\theta))^2\,d\theta\right] = \displaystyle\int_{-\pi/6}^{\pi/2}(4 + 16\sin\theta + 16\sin^2\theta)\,d\theta = 8\pi + 6\sqrt{3}.$$

The area inside the inner loop is

$$2\dfrac{1}{2}\left[\displaystyle\int_{7\pi/6}^{3\pi/2}(2(1+2\sin\theta))^2\,d\theta\right] = 4\pi - 6\sqrt{3}.$$

Thus, the area between the loops is $\left(8\pi + 6\sqrt{3}\right) - \left(4\pi - 6\sqrt{3}\right) = 4\pi + 12\sqrt{3}.$

**14.** $r = 3(1 + \sin\theta)$

$r = 3(1 - \sin\theta)$

Solving simultaneously,

$3(1 + \sin\theta) = 3(1 - \sin\theta)$

$2\sin\theta = 0$

$\theta = 0,\ \pi.$

Replacing $r$ by $-r$ and $\theta$ by $\theta + \pi$ in the first equation and solving, $-3(1 - \sin\theta) = 3(1 - \sin\theta)$, $\sin\theta = 1$, $\theta = \pi/2$. Both curves pass through the pole, $(0, 3\pi/2)$, and $(0, \pi/2)$, respectively.

Points of intersection: $(3, 0)$, $(3, \pi)$, $(0, 0)$

**16.** $r = 2 - 3\cos\theta$

$r = \cos\theta$

Solving simultaneously,

$2 - 3\cos\theta = \cos\theta$

$\cos\theta = \dfrac{1}{2}$

$\theta = \dfrac{\pi}{3},\ \dfrac{5\pi}{3}.$

Both curves pass through the pole, $(0, \arccos 2/3)$, and $(0, \pi/2)$, respectively.

Points of intersection: $\left(\dfrac{1}{2}, \dfrac{\pi}{3}\right), \left(\dfrac{1}{2}, \dfrac{5\pi}{3}\right), (0, 0)$

**18.** $r = 1 + \cos \theta$

$r = 3 \cos \theta$

Solving simultaneously,

$$1 + \cos \theta = 3 \cos \theta$$

$$\cos \theta = \frac{1}{2}$$

$$\theta = \frac{\pi}{3}, \frac{5\pi}{3}.$$

Both curves pass through the pole, $(0, \pi)$, and $(0, \pi/2)$, respectively.

Points of intersection: $\left(\frac{3}{2}, \frac{\pi}{3}\right), \left(\frac{3}{2}, \frac{5\pi}{3}\right), (0, 0)$

**20.** $\theta = \frac{\pi}{4}$

$r = 2$

Line of slope 1 passing through the pole and a circle of radius 2 centered at the pole.

Points of intersection:

$$\left(2, \frac{\pi}{4}\right), \left(-2, \frac{\pi}{4}\right)$$

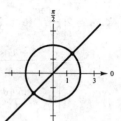

**22.** $r = 3 + \sin \theta$

$r = 2 \csc \theta$

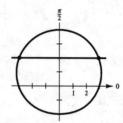

Points of intersection:

$$\left(\frac{\sqrt{17} + 3}{2}, \arcsin\left(\frac{\sqrt{17} - 3}{2}\right)\right),$$

$$\left(\frac{\sqrt{17} + 3}{2}, \pi - \arcsin\left(\frac{\sqrt{17} - 3}{2}\right)\right),$$

$(3.56, 0.596), (3.56, 2.545)$

The graph of $r = 3 + \sin \theta$ is a limaçon symmetric to $\theta = \pi/2$, and the graph of $r = 2 \csc \theta$ is the horizontal line $y = 2$. Therefore, there are two points of intersection. Solving simultaneously,

$$3 + \sin \theta = 2 \csc \theta$$

$$\sin^2 \theta + 3 \sin \theta - 2 = 0$$

$$\sin \theta = \frac{-3 \pm \sqrt{17}}{2}$$

$$\theta = \arcsin\left(\frac{\sqrt{17} - 3}{2}\right) \approx 0.596.$$

**24.** $r = 3(1 - \cos \theta)$

$r = \frac{6}{1 - \cos \theta}$

The graph of $r = 3(1 - \cos \theta)$ is a cardioid with polar axis symmetry. The graph of

$r = 6/(1 - \cos \theta)$

is a parabola with focus at the pole, vertex$(3, \pi)$, and polar axis symmetry. Therefore, there are two points of intersection. Solving simultaneously,

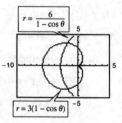

$$3(1 - \cos \theta) = \frac{6}{1 - \cos \theta}$$

$$(1 - \cos \theta)^2 = 2$$

$$\cos \theta = 1 \pm \sqrt{2}$$

$$\theta = \arccos\left(1 - \sqrt{2}\right).$$

Points of intersection: $\left(3\sqrt{2}, \arccos\left(1 - \sqrt{2}\right)\right) \approx (4.243, 1.998), \left(3\sqrt{2}, 2\pi - \arccos\left(1 - \sqrt{2}\right)\right) \approx \left(4.243, 4.285\right)$

**26.** $r = 4 \sin \theta$

$r = 2(1 + \sin \theta)$

Points of intersection: $(0, 0), \left(4, \dfrac{\pi}{2}\right)$

The graphs reach the pole at different times ($\theta$ values).

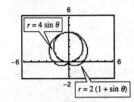

**28.** $A = 4\left[\dfrac{1}{2} \displaystyle\int_0^{\pi/2} 9(1 - \sin \theta)^2 \, d\theta\right]$

$= 18 \displaystyle\int_0^{\pi/2} (1 - \sin \theta)^2 \, d\theta = \dfrac{9}{2}(3\pi - 8)$

(from Exercise 14)

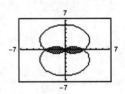

**30.** $r = 5 - 3 \sin \theta$ and $r = 5 - 3 \cos \theta$ intersect at $\theta = \pi/4$ and $\pi = 5\pi/4$.

$A = 2\left[\dfrac{1}{2} \displaystyle\int_{\pi/4}^{5\pi/4} (5 - 3 \sin \theta)^2 \, d\theta\right]$

$= \left[\dfrac{59}{2}\theta + 30 \cos \theta - \dfrac{9}{4} \sin 2\theta\right]_{\pi/4}^{5\pi/4}$

$= \left(\dfrac{59}{2}\left(\dfrac{5\pi}{4}\right) - 30\dfrac{\sqrt{2}}{2} - \dfrac{9}{4}\right) - \left(\dfrac{59}{2}\left(\dfrac{\pi}{4}\right) + 30\dfrac{\sqrt{2}}{2} - \dfrac{9}{4}\right)$

$= \dfrac{59\pi}{2} - 30\sqrt{2} \approx 50.251$

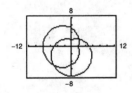

**32.** $A = 2\left[\dfrac{1}{2} \displaystyle\int_{\pi/6}^{\pi/2} (3 \sin \theta)^2 \, d\theta - \dfrac{1}{2} \displaystyle\int_{\pi/6}^{\pi/2} (2 - \sin \theta)^2 \, d\theta\right]$

$= \displaystyle\int_{\pi/6}^{\pi/2} (-4 \cos 2\theta + 4 \sin \theta) \, d\theta$

$= \left[-2 \sin(2\theta) - 4 \cos \theta\right]_{\pi/6}^{\pi/2} = 3\sqrt{3}$

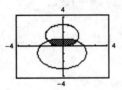

**34.** Area = Area of $r = 2a \cos \theta$ − Area of sector − twice area between $r = 2a \cos \theta$ and the lines

$\theta = \dfrac{\pi}{3}, \theta = \dfrac{\pi}{2}$.

$A = \pi a^2 - \left(\dfrac{\pi}{3}\right)a^2 - 2\left[\dfrac{1}{2} \displaystyle\int_{\pi/3}^{\pi/2} (2a \cos \theta)^2 \, d\theta\right]$

$= \dfrac{2\pi a^2}{3} - 2a^2 \displaystyle\int_{\pi/3}^{\pi/2} (1 + \cos 2\theta) \, d\theta$

$= \dfrac{2\pi a^2}{3} - 2a^2 \left[\theta + \dfrac{\sin 2\theta}{2}\right]_{\pi/3}^{\pi/2}$

$= \dfrac{2\pi a^2}{3} - 2a^2 \left[\dfrac{\pi}{2} - \dfrac{\pi}{3} - \dfrac{\sqrt{3}}{4}\right] = \dfrac{2\pi a^2 + 3\sqrt{3}a^2}{6}$

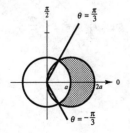

**36.** $r = a \cos \theta, r = a \sin \theta$

$\tan \theta = 1, \theta = \pi/4$

$A = 2\left[\dfrac{1}{2} \displaystyle\int_0^{\pi/2} (a \cos \theta)^2 \, d\theta\right]$

$= a^2 \displaystyle\int_0^{\pi/4} \dfrac{1 + \cos 2\theta}{2} \, d\theta$

$= \dfrac{1}{2}a^2 \left[\theta + \dfrac{\sin 2\theta}{2}\right]_0^{\pi/4}$

$= \dfrac{1}{2}a^2 \left[\dfrac{\pi}{4} + \dfrac{1}{2}\right]$

$= \dfrac{1}{4}a^2 + \dfrac{1}{8}a^2\pi$

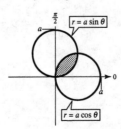

**38.** By symmetry, $A_1 = A_2$ and $A_3 = A_4$.

$$A_1 = A_2 = \frac{1}{2}\int_{-\pi/3}^{\pi/6}\left[(2a\cos\theta)^2 - (a)^2\right]d\theta + \frac{1}{2}\int_{\pi/6}^{\pi/4}\left[(2a\cos\theta)^2 - (2a\sin\theta)^2\right]d\theta$$

$$= \frac{a^2}{2}\int_{-\pi/3}^{\pi/6}(4\cos^2\theta - 1)\,d\theta + 2a^2\int_{\pi/6}^{\pi/4}\cos 2\theta\,d\theta$$

$$= \frac{a^2}{2}\Big[\theta + \sin 2\theta\Big]_{-\pi/3}^{\pi/6} + a^2\Big[\sin 2\theta\Big]_{\pi/6}^{\pi/4} = \frac{a^2}{2}\left(\frac{\pi}{2} + \sqrt{3}\right) + a^2\left(1 - \frac{\sqrt{3}}{2}\right) = a^2\left(\frac{\pi}{4} + 1\right)$$

$$A_3 = A_4 = \frac{1}{2}\left(\frac{\pi}{2}\right)a^2 = \frac{\pi a^2}{4}$$

$$A_5 = \frac{1}{2}\left(\frac{5\pi}{6}\right)a^2 - 2\left(\frac{1}{2}\right)\int_{5\pi/6}^{\pi}(2a\sin\theta)^2\,d\theta$$

$$= \frac{5\pi a^2}{12} - 2a^2\int_{5\pi/6}^{\pi}(1 - \cos 2\theta)\,d\theta$$

$$= \frac{5\pi a^2}{12} - a^2\Big[2\theta - \sin 2\theta\Big]_{5\pi/6}^{\pi} = \frac{5\pi a^2}{12} - a^2\left(\frac{\pi}{3} - \frac{\sqrt{3}}{2}\right) = a^2\left(\frac{\pi}{12} + \frac{\sqrt{3}}{2}\right)$$

$$A_6 = 2\left(\frac{1}{2}\right)\int_{0}^{\pi/6}(2a\sin\theta)^2\,d\theta + 2\left(\frac{1}{2}\right)\int_{\pi/6}^{\pi/4}a^2\,d\theta$$

$$= 2a^2\int_{0}^{\pi/6}(1 - \cos 2\theta)\,d\theta + \Big[a^2\theta\Big]_{\pi/6}^{\pi/4}$$

$$= a^2\Big[2\theta - \sin 2\theta\Big]_{0}^{\pi/6} + \frac{\pi a^2}{12} = a^2\left(\frac{\pi}{3} - \frac{\sqrt{3}}{2}\right) + \frac{\pi a^2}{12} = a^2\left(\frac{5\pi}{12} - \frac{\sqrt{3}}{2}\right)$$

$$A_7 = 2\left(\frac{1}{2}\right)\int_{\pi/6}^{\pi/4}\left[(2a\sin\theta)^2 - (a)^2\right]d\theta$$

$$= a^2\int_{\pi/6}^{\pi/4}(4\sin^2\theta - 1)\,d\theta = a^2\Big[\theta - \sin 2\theta\Big]_{\pi/6}^{\pi/4} = a^2\left(\frac{\pi}{12} - 1 + \frac{\sqrt{3}}{2}\right)$$

[**Note:** $A_1 + A_6 + A_7 + A_4 = \pi a^2 = $ area of circle of radius $a$]

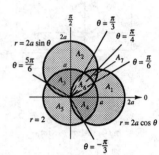

**40.**
$$r = \sec\theta - 2\cos\theta, \quad -\frac{\pi}{2} < \theta < \frac{\pi}{2}$$

$$r\cos\theta = 1 - 2\cos^2\theta$$

$$x = 1 - 2\frac{r^2\cos^2\theta}{r^2} = 1 - 2\left(\frac{x^2}{x^2 + y^2}\right)$$

$$(x^2 + y^2)x = x^2 + y^2 - 2x^2$$

$$y^2(x - 1) = -x^2 - x^3$$

$$y^2 = \frac{x^2(1 + x)}{1 - x}$$

$$A = 2\left(\frac{1}{2}\right)\int_{0}^{\pi/4}(\sec\theta - 2\cos\theta)^2\,d\theta$$

$$= \int_{0}^{\pi/4}(\sec^2\theta - 4 + 4\cos^2\theta)\,d\theta = \int_{0}^{\pi/4}(\sec^2\theta - 4 + 2(1 + \cos 2\theta))\,d\theta = \Big[\tan\theta - 2\theta + \sin 2\theta\Big]_{0}^{\pi/4} = 2 - \frac{\pi}{2}$$

**42.** $r = 2a \cos \theta$

$r' = -2a \sin \theta$

$$s = \int_{-\pi/2}^{\pi/2} \sqrt{(2a \cos \theta)^2 + (-2a \sin \theta)^2} \, d\theta$$

$$= \int_{-\pi/2}^{\pi/2} 2a \, d\theta = \Big[ 2\theta \Big]_{-\pi/2}^{\pi/2} = 2\pi a$$

**44.** $r = 8(1 + \cos \theta), \, 0 \le \theta \le 2\pi$

$r' = -8 \sin \theta$

$$s = 2 \int_0^{\pi} \sqrt{[8(1 + \cos \theta)]^2 + (-8 \sin \theta)^2} \, d\theta$$

$$= 16 \int_0^{\pi} \sqrt{1 + 2 \cos \theta + \cos^2 \theta + \sin^2 \theta} \, d\theta$$

$$= 16\sqrt{2} \int_0^{\pi} \sqrt{1 + \cos \theta} \, d\theta$$

$$= 16\sqrt{2} \int_0^{\pi} \sqrt{1 + \cos \theta} \cdot \left( \frac{\sqrt{1 - \cos \theta}}{\sqrt{1 - \cos \theta}} \right) d\theta$$

$$= 16\sqrt{2} \int_0^{\pi} \frac{\sin \theta}{\sqrt{1 - \cos \theta}} \, d\theta$$

$$= \Big[ 32\sqrt{2} \sqrt{1 - \cos \theta} \Big]_0^{\pi}$$

$$= 64$$

**46.** $r = \sec \theta, \, 0 \le \theta \le \dfrac{\pi}{3}$

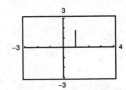

Length $\approx 1.73 \, \left( \text{exact } \sqrt{3} \right)$

**48.** $r = e^{\theta}, \, 0 \le \theta \le \pi$

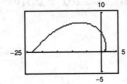

Length $\approx 31.31$

**50.** $r = 2 \sin(2 \cos \theta), \, 0 \le \theta \le \pi$

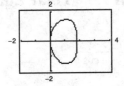

Length $\approx 7.78$

**52.** $r = a \cos \theta$

$r' = -a \sin \theta$

$$S = 2\pi \int_0^{\pi/2} a \cos \theta (\cos \theta) \sqrt{a^2 \cos \theta + a^2 \sin^2 \theta} \, d\theta$$

$$= 2\pi a^2 \int_0^{\pi/2} \cos^2 \theta \, d\theta = \pi a^2 \int_0^{\pi/2} (1 + \cos 2\theta) \, d\theta$$

$$= \left[ \pi a^2 \left( \theta + \frac{\sin 2\theta}{2} \right) \right]_0^{\pi/2} = \frac{\pi^2 a^2}{2}$$

**54.** $r = a(1 + \cos \theta)$

$r' = -a \sin \theta$

$$S = 2\pi \int_0^{\pi} a(1 + \cos \theta) \sin \theta \sqrt{a^2(1 + \cos \theta)^2 + a^2 \sin^2 \theta} \, d\theta = 2\pi a^2 \int_0^{\pi} \sin \theta (1 + \cos \theta) \sqrt{2 + 2 \cos \theta} \, d\theta$$

$$= -2\sqrt{2} \pi a^2 \int_0^{\pi} (1 + \cos \theta)^{3/2} (-\sin \theta) \, d\theta = -\frac{4\sqrt{2} \pi a^2}{5} \left[ (1 + \cos \theta)^{5/2} \right]_0^{\pi} = \frac{32 \pi a^2}{5}$$

**56.** $r = \theta$

$r' = 1$

$$S = 2\pi \int_0^{\pi} \theta \sin \theta \sqrt{\theta^2 + 1} \, d\theta \approx 42.32$$

**58.** The curves might intersect for different values of $\theta$:

See page 696.

**60.** (a) $S = 2\pi \int_{\alpha}^{\beta} f(\theta)\sin\theta \sqrt{f(\theta)^2 + f'(\theta)^2}\, d\theta$

(b) $S = 2\pi \int_{\alpha}^{\beta} f(\theta)\cos\theta \sqrt{f(\theta)^2 + f'(\theta)^2}\, d\theta$

**62.** $r = 8\cos\theta, 0 \le \theta \le \pi$

(a) $A = \dfrac{1}{2}\int_0^{\pi} r^2\, d\theta = \dfrac{1}{2}\int_0^{\pi} 64\cos^2\theta\, d\theta = 32\int_0^{\pi} \dfrac{1 + \cos 2\theta}{2}\, d\theta = 16\left[\theta + \dfrac{\sin 2\theta}{2}\right]_0^{\pi} = 16\pi$

(Area circle $= \pi r^2 = \pi 4^2 = 16\pi$)

(b)

| $\theta$ | 0.2 | 0.4 | 0.6 | 0.8 | 1.0 | 1.2 | 1.4 |
|---|---|---|---|---|---|---|---|
| $A$ | 6.32 | 12.14 | 17.06 | 20.80 | 23.27 | 24.60 | 25.08 |

(c), (d) For $\frac{1}{4}$ of area ($4\pi \approx 12.57$): 0.42

For $\frac{1}{2}$ of area ($8\pi \approx 25.13$): 1.57 ($\pi/2$)

For $\frac{3}{4}$ of area ($12\pi \approx 37.70$): 2.73

(e) No, it does not depend on the radius.

**64.** False. $f(\theta) = 0$ and $g(\theta) = \sin 2\theta$ have only one point of intersection.

## Section 9.6    Polar Equations of Conics and Kepler's Laws

**2.** $r = \dfrac{2e}{1 - e\cos\theta}$

(a) $e = 1, r = \dfrac{2}{1 - \cos\theta}$, parabola

(b) $e = 0.5, r = \dfrac{1}{1 - 0.5\cos\theta} = \dfrac{2}{2 - \cos\theta}$, ellipse

(c) $e = 1.5, r = \dfrac{3}{1 - 1.5\cos\theta} = \dfrac{6}{2 - 3\cos\theta}$, hyperbola

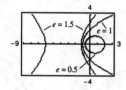

**4.** $r = \dfrac{2e}{1 + e\sin\theta}$

(a) $e = 1, r = \dfrac{2}{1 + \sin\theta}$, parabola

(b) $e = 0.5, r = \dfrac{1}{1 + 0.5\sin\theta} = \dfrac{2}{2 + \sin\theta}$, ellipse

(c) $e = 1.5, r = \dfrac{3}{1 + 1.5\sin\theta} = \dfrac{6}{2 + 3\sin\theta}$, hyperbola

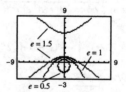

**6.** $r = \dfrac{4}{1 - 0.4\cos\theta}$

(a) Because $e = 0.4 < 1$, the conic is an ellipse with vertical directrix to the left of the pole.

(c)

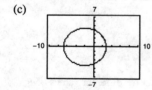
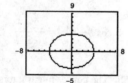

(b) $r = \dfrac{4}{1 + 0.4\cos\theta}$

The ellipse is shifted to the left. The vertical directrix is to the right of the pole

$$r = \dfrac{4}{1 - 0.4\sin\theta}.$$

The ellipse has a horizontal directrix below the pole.

**8.** Ellipse; Matches (f)          **10.** Parabola; Matches (e)          **12.** Hyperbola; Matches (d)

**14.** $r = \dfrac{6}{1 + \cos\theta}$

Parabola since $e = 1$

Vertex: $(3, 0)$

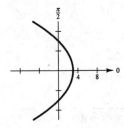

**16.** $r = \dfrac{5}{5 + 3\sin\theta} = \dfrac{1}{1 + (3/5)\sin\theta}$

Ellipse since $e = \dfrac{3}{5} < 1$

Vertices: $\left(\dfrac{5}{8}, \dfrac{\pi}{2}\right), \left(\dfrac{5}{2}, \dfrac{3\pi}{2}\right)$

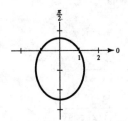

**18.** $r(3 - 2\cos\theta) = 6$

$r = \dfrac{6}{3 - 2\cos\theta}$

$= \dfrac{2}{1 - (2/3)\cos\theta}$

Ellipse since $e = \dfrac{2}{3} < 1$

Vertices: $(6, 0), \left(\dfrac{6}{5}, \pi\right)$

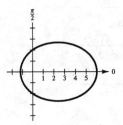

**20.** $r = \dfrac{-6}{3 + 7\sin\theta} = \dfrac{-2}{1 + (7/3)\sin\theta}$

Hyperbola since $e = \dfrac{7}{3} > 1$.

Vertices: $\left(-\dfrac{3}{5}, \dfrac{\pi}{2}\right), \left(\dfrac{3}{2}, \dfrac{3\pi}{2}\right)$

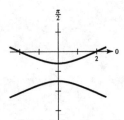

**22.** $r = \dfrac{4}{1 + 2\cos\theta}$

Hyperbola since $e = 2 > 1$

Vertices: $\left(\dfrac{4}{3}, 0\right), (-4, \pi)$

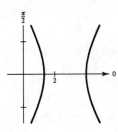

**24.**

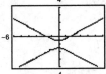    Hyperbola

**26.**

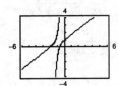    Hyperbola

**28.** $r = \dfrac{6}{1 + \cos\left(\theta - \dfrac{\pi}{3}\right)}$

Rotate the graph of $r = \dfrac{6}{1 + \cos\theta}$

counterclockwise through the angle $\dfrac{\pi}{3}$.

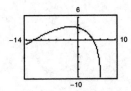

**30.** $r = \dfrac{-6}{3 + 7\sin(\theta + (2\pi/3))}$

Rotate graph of $r = \dfrac{-6}{3 + 7\sin\theta}$.

Clockwise through angle of $2\pi/3$.

**32.** Change $\theta$ to $\theta - \dfrac{\pi}{6}$: $r = \dfrac{2}{1 + \sin\left(\theta - \dfrac{\pi}{6}\right)}$

**34.** Parabola

$e = 1, y = 1, d = 1$

$$r = \frac{ed}{1 + e \sin \theta} = \frac{1}{1 + \sin \theta}$$

**36.** Ellipse

$e = \dfrac{3}{4}, y = -2, d = 2$

$$r = \frac{ed}{1 - e \sin \theta}$$

$$= \frac{2(3/4)}{1 - (3/4)\sin \theta}$$

$$= \frac{6}{4 - 3 \sin \theta}$$

**38.** Hyperbola

$e = \dfrac{3}{2}, x = -1, d = 1$

$$r = \frac{ed}{1 - e \cos \theta}$$

$$= \frac{3/2}{1 - (3/2)\cos \theta}$$

$$= \frac{3}{2 - 3 \cos \theta}$$

**40.** Parabola

Vertex: $(5, \pi)$

$e = 1, d = 10$

$$r = \frac{ed}{1 - e \cos \theta} = \frac{10}{1 - \cos \theta}$$

**42.** Ellipse

Vertices: $\left(2, \dfrac{\pi}{2}\right), \left(4, \dfrac{3\pi}{2}\right)$

$e = \dfrac{1}{3}, d = 8$

$$r = \frac{ed}{1 + e \sin \theta}$$

$$= \frac{8/3}{1 + (1/3)\sin \theta}$$

$$= \frac{8}{3 + \sin \theta}$$

**44.** Hyperbola

Vertices: $(2, 0), (10, 0)$

$e = \dfrac{3}{2}, d = \dfrac{10}{3}$

$$r = \frac{ed}{1 + e \cos \theta}$$

$$= \frac{5}{1 + (3/2)\cos \theta}$$

$$= \frac{10}{2 + 3 \cos \theta}$$

**46.** $r = \dfrac{4}{1 + \sin \theta}$ is a parabola with horizontal directrix above the pole.

(a) Parabola with vertical directrix to left pole.

(b) Parabola with horizontal directrix below pole.

(c) Parabola with vertical directrix to right of pole.

(d) Parabola (b) rotated counterclockwise $\pi/4$.

**48.** (a)

$$\frac{x^2}{a^2} + \frac{y^2}{b^2} = 1$$

$$x^2 b^2 + y^2 a^2 = a^2 b^2$$

$$b^2 r^2 \cos^2 \theta + a^2 r^2 \sin^2 \theta = a^2 b^2$$

$$r^2[b^2 \cos^2 \theta + a^2(1 - \cos^2 \theta)] = a^2 b^2$$

$$r^2[a^2 + \cos^2 \theta(b^2 - a^2)] = a^2 b^2$$

$$r^2 = \frac{a^2 b^2}{a^2 + (b^2 - a^2)\cos^2 \theta} = \frac{a^2 b^2}{a^2 - c^2 \cos^2 \theta}$$

$$= \frac{b^2}{1 - (c/a)^2 \cos^2 \theta} = \frac{b^2}{1 - e^2 \cos^2 \theta}$$

(b)

$$\frac{x^2}{a^2} - \frac{y^2}{b^2} = 1$$

$$x^2 b^2 - y^2 a^2 = a^2 b^2$$

$$b^2 r^2 \cos^2 \theta - a^2 r^2 \sin^2 \theta = a^2 b^2$$

$$r^2[b^2 \cos^2 \theta - a^2(1 - \cos^2 \theta)] = a^2 b^2$$

$$r^2[-a^2 + \cos^2 \theta(a^2 + b^2)] = a^2 b^2$$

$$r^2 = \frac{a^2 b^2}{-a^2 + c^2 \cos^2 \theta} = \frac{b^2}{-1 + (c^2/a^2)\cos^2 \theta}$$

$$= \frac{-b^2}{1 - e^2 \cos^2 \theta}$$

**50.** $a = 4, c = 5, b = 3, e = \dfrac{5}{4}$

$$r^2 = \frac{-9}{1 - (25/16) \cos^2 \theta}$$

**52.** $a = 2, b = 1, c = \sqrt{3}, e = \dfrac{\sqrt{3}}{2}$

$$r^2 = \frac{1}{1 - (3/4) \cos^2 \theta}$$

**54.** $A = 2\left[ \dfrac{1}{2} \displaystyle\int_{-\pi/2}^{\pi/2} \left( \dfrac{2}{3 - 2 \sin \theta} \right)^2 d\theta \right] = 4 \displaystyle\int_{-\pi/2}^{\pi/2} \dfrac{1}{(3 - 2 \sin \theta)^2} \, d\theta \approx 3.37$

**56.** (a) $r = \dfrac{ed}{1 - e \cos \theta}$

When $\theta = 0, r = c + a = ea + a = a(1 + e)$.

Therefore,

$$a(1 + e) = \frac{ed}{1 - e}$$

$$a(1 + e)(1 - e) = ed$$

$$a(1 - e^2) = ed.$$

Thus, $r = \dfrac{(1 - e^2)a}{1 - e \cos \theta}$.

(b) The perihelion distance is $a - c = a - ea = a(1 - e)$.

When $\theta = \pi, r = \dfrac{(1 - e^2)a}{1 + e} = a(1 - e)$.

The aphelion distance is $a + c = a + ea = a(1 + e)$.

When $\theta = 0, r = \dfrac{(1 - e^2)a}{1 - e} = a(1 + e)$.

**58.** $a = 1.427 \times 10^9$ km

$e = 0.0543$

$r = \dfrac{(1 - e^2)a}{1 - e \cos \theta} = \dfrac{1.422792505 \times 10^9}{1 - 0.0543 \cos \theta}$

Perihelion distance: $a(1 - e) = 1.3495139 \times 10^9$ km

Aphelion distance: $a(1 + e) = 1.5044861 \times 10^9$ km

**60.** $a = 36.0 \times 10^6$ mi, $e = 0.206$

$r = \dfrac{(1 - e^2)a}{1 - e \cos \theta} \approx \dfrac{34.472 \times 10^6}{1 - 0.206 \cos \theta}$

Perihelion distance: $a(1 - e) = 28.582 \times 10^6$ mi

Aphelion distance: $a(1 + e) = 43.416 \times 10^6$ mi

**62.**
$$r = a \sin \theta + b \cos \theta$$
$$r^2 = ar \sin \theta + br \cos \theta$$
$$x^2 + y^2 = ay + bx$$
$$x^2 + y^2 - bx - ay = 0 \text{ represents a circle.}$$

# Review Exercises for Chapter 9

**2.** Matches (b) - hyperbola

**4.** Matches (c) - hyperbola

**6.** $y^2 - 12y - 8x + 20 = 0$

$y^2 - 12y + 36 = 8x - 20 + 36$

$(y - 6)^2 = 4(2)(x + 2)$

Parabola

Vertex: $(-2, 6)$

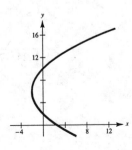

**8.** $4x^2 + y^2 - 16x + 15 = 0$

$4(x^2 - 4x + 4) + y^2 = -15 + 16$

$$\frac{(x-2)^2}{1/4} + \frac{y^2}{1} = 1$$

Ellipse

Center: $(2, 0)$

Vertices: $(2, \pm 1)$

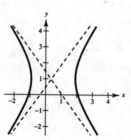

**10.**      $4x^2 - 4y^2 - 4x + 8y - 11 = 0$

$4\left(x^2 - x + \frac{1}{4}\right) - 4(y^2 - 2y + 1) = 11 + 1 - 4$

$$\frac{[x - (1/2)]^2}{2} - \frac{(y-1)^2}{2} = 1$$

Hyperbola

Center: $\left(\dfrac{1}{2}, 1\right)$

Vertices: $\left(\dfrac{1}{2} \pm \sqrt{2}, 1\right)$

Asymptotes: $y = 1 \pm \left(x - \dfrac{1}{2}\right)$

**12.** Vertex: $(4, 2)$

Focus: $(4, 0)$

Parabola opens downward

$p = -2$

$(x - 4)^2 = 4(-2)(y - 2)$

$x^2 - 8x + 8y = 0$

**14.** Center: $(0, 0)$

Solution points: $(1, 2), (2, 0)$

Substituting the values of the coordinates of the given points into

$$\left(\frac{x^2}{b^2}\right) + \left(\frac{y^2}{a^2}\right) = 1,$$

we obtain the system

$$\left(\frac{1}{b^2}\right) + \left(\frac{4}{a^2}\right) = 1, 4/b^2 = 1.$$

Solving the system, we have

$$a^2 = \frac{16}{3} \text{ and } b^2 = 4, \left(\frac{x^2}{4}\right) + \left(\frac{3y^2}{16}\right) = 1.$$

**16.** Foci: $(0, \pm 8)$

Asymptotes: $y = \pm 4x$

Center: $(0, 0)$

Vertical transverse axis

$c = 8$

$y = \dfrac{a}{b}x = 4x$ asymptote $\rightarrow a = 4b$

$b^2 = c^2 - a^2 = 64 - (4b)^2 \implies 17b^2 = 64$

$\implies b^2 = \dfrac{64}{17} \implies a^2 = \dfrac{1024}{17}$

$$\frac{y^2}{1024/17} - \frac{x^2}{64/17} = 1$$

**18.** $\dfrac{x^2}{4} + \dfrac{y^2}{25} = 1$, $a = 5$, $b = 2$, $c = \sqrt{21}$, $e = \dfrac{\sqrt{21}}{5}$

By Example 5 of Section 9.1,

$$C = 20 \int_0^{\pi/2} \sqrt{1 - \frac{21}{25}\sin^2\theta}\, d\theta \approx 23.01.$$

**20.** $y = \dfrac{1}{200}x^2$

(a) $x^2 = 200y$

   $x^2 = 4(50)y$

   Focus:  $(0, 50)$

(b)       $y = \dfrac{1}{200}x^2$

   $y' = \dfrac{1}{100}x$

   $\sqrt{1 + (y')^2} = \sqrt{1 + \dfrac{x^2}{10{,}000}}$

   $S = 2\pi \displaystyle\int_0^{100} x\sqrt{1 + \dfrac{x^2}{10{,}000}}\, dx \approx 38{,}294.49$

**22.** (a) $A = 4\displaystyle\int_0^a \dfrac{b}{a}\sqrt{a^2 - x^2}\, dx = \dfrac{4b}{a}\left(\dfrac{1}{2}\right)\left[x\sqrt{a^2 - x^2} + a^2\arcsin\left(\dfrac{x}{a}\right)\right]_0^a = \pi ab$

(b) **Disk:**  $V = 2\pi\displaystyle\int_0^b \dfrac{a^2}{b^2}(b^2 - y^2)\, dy = \dfrac{2\pi a^2}{b^2}\displaystyle\int_0^b (b^2 - y^2)\, dy = \dfrac{2\pi a^2}{b^2}\left[b^2 y - \dfrac{1}{3}y^3\right]_0^b = \dfrac{4}{3}\pi a^2 b$

   $S = 4\pi\displaystyle\int_0^b \dfrac{a}{b}\sqrt{b^2 - y^2}\left(\dfrac{\sqrt{b^4 + (a^2 - b^2)y^2}}{b\sqrt{b^2 - y^2}}\right)\, dy$

   $= \dfrac{4\pi a}{b^2}\displaystyle\int_0^b \sqrt{b^4 + c^2 y^2}\, dy = \dfrac{2\pi a}{b^2 c}\left[cy\sqrt{b^4 + c^2 y^2} + b^4\ln\left|cy + \sqrt{b^4 + c^2 y^2}\right|\right]_0^b$

   $= \dfrac{2\pi a}{b^2 c}\left[b^2 c\sqrt{b^2 + c^2} + b^4\ln\left|cb + b\sqrt{b^2 + c^2}\right| - b^4\ln(b^2)\right]$

   $= 2\pi a^2 + \dfrac{\pi a b^2}{c}\ln\left(\dfrac{c + a}{e}\right)^2 = 2\pi a^2 + \left(\dfrac{\pi b^2}{e}\right)\ln\left(\dfrac{1 + e}{1 - e}\right)$

(c) **Disk:**  $V = 2\pi\displaystyle\int_0^a \dfrac{b^2}{a^2}(a^2 - x^2)\, dx = \dfrac{2\pi b^2}{a^2}\displaystyle\int_0^a (a^2 - x^2)\, dx = \dfrac{2\pi b^2}{a^2}\left[a^2 x - \dfrac{1}{3}x^3\right]_0^a = \dfrac{4}{3}\pi a b^2$

   $S = 2(2\pi)\displaystyle\int_0^a \dfrac{b}{a}\sqrt{a^2 - x^2}\left(\dfrac{\sqrt{a^4 - (a^2 - b^2)x^2}}{a\sqrt{a^2 - x^2}}\right)\, dx$

   $= \dfrac{4\pi b}{a^2}\displaystyle\int_0^a \sqrt{a^4 - c^2 x^2}\, dx = \dfrac{2\pi b}{a^2 c}\left[cx\sqrt{a^4 - c^2 x^2} + a^4\arcsin\left(\dfrac{cx}{a^2}\right)\right]_0^a$

   $= \dfrac{a\pi b}{a^2 c}\left[a^2 c\sqrt{a^2 - c^2} + a^4\arcsin\left(\dfrac{c}{a}\right)\right] = 2\pi b^2 + 2\pi\left(\dfrac{ab}{e}\right)\arcsin(e)$

**24.** $x = t + 4,\; y = t^2$

   $t = x - 4 \implies y = (x - 4)^2$

   Parabola

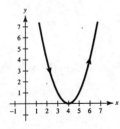

**26.** $x = 3 + 3\cos\theta,\; y = 2 + 5\sin\theta$

   $\left(\dfrac{x - 3}{3}\right)^2 + \left(\dfrac{y - 2}{5}\right)^2 = 1$

   $\dfrac{(x - 3)^2}{9} + \dfrac{(y - 2)^2}{25} = 1$

   Ellipse

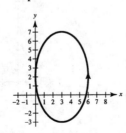

**28.** $x = 5\sin^3\theta,\; y = 5\cos^3\theta$

   $\left(\dfrac{x}{5}\right)^{2/3} + \left(\dfrac{y}{5}\right)^{2/3} = 1$

   $x^{2/3} + y^{2/3} = 5^{2/3}$

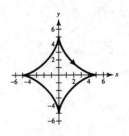

**30.** $(x - h)^2 + (y - k)^2 = r^2$

$(x - 5)^2 + (y - 3)^2 = 2^2 = 4$

**32.** $a = 4$, $c = 5$, $b^2 = c^2 - a^2 = 9$, $\dfrac{y^2}{16} - \dfrac{x^2}{9} = 1$

Let $\dfrac{y^2}{16} = \sec^2 \theta$ and $\dfrac{x^2}{9} = \tan^2 \theta$.

Then $x = 3 \tan \theta$ and $y = 4 \sec \theta$.

**34.** $x = (a - b) \cos t + b \cos \left( \dfrac{a - b}{b} t \right)$

$y = (a - b) \sin t - b \sin \left( \dfrac{a - b}{b} t \right)$

(a) $a = 2$, $b = 1$

$x = \cos t + \cos t = 2 \cos t$

$y = \sin t - \sin t = 0$

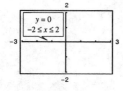

(b) $a = 3$, $b = 1$

$x = 2 \cos t + \cos 2t$

$y = 2 \sin t - \sin 2t$

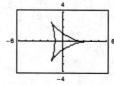

(c) $a = 4$, $b = 1$

$x = 3 \cos t + \cos 3t$

$y = 3 \sin t - \sin 3t$

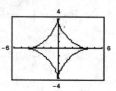

(d) $a = 10$, $b = 1$

$x = 9 \cos t + \cos 9t$

$y = 9 \sin t - \sin 9t$

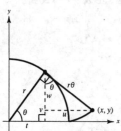

(e) $a = 3$, $b = 2$

$x = \cos t + 2 \cos \dfrac{t}{2}$

$y = \sin t - 2 \sin \dfrac{t}{2}$

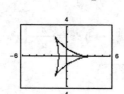

(f) $a = 4$, $b = 3$

$x = \cos t + 3 \cos \dfrac{t}{3}$

$y = \sin t - 3 \sin \dfrac{t}{3}$

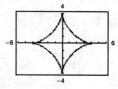

**36.** $x = t + u = r \cos \theta + r\theta \sin \theta$

$= r(\cos \theta + \theta \sin \theta)$

$y = v - w = r \sin \theta - r\theta \cos \theta$

$= r(\sin \theta - \theta \cos \theta)$

**38.** $x = t + 4$

$y = t^2$

(a) $\dfrac{dy}{dx} = \dfrac{2t}{1} = 2t = 0$ when $t = 0$.

Point of horizontal tangency: $(4, 0)$

(b) $t = x - 4$

$y = (x - 4)^2$

(c)

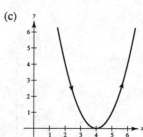

**40.** $x = \dfrac{1}{t}$

$y = t^2$

(a) $\dfrac{dy}{dx} = \dfrac{2t}{-1/t^2} = -2t^3$

No horizontal tangents $(t \neq 0)$

(b) $t = \dfrac{1}{x}$

$y = \dfrac{1}{x^2}$

(c)

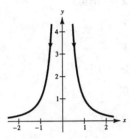

**42.** $x = 2t - 1$

$y = \dfrac{1}{t^2 - 2t}$

(a) $\dfrac{dy}{dx} = \dfrac{-(t^2 - 2t)^{-2}(2t - 2)}{2}$

$= \dfrac{1 - t}{t^2(t - 2)^2} = 0$ when $t = 1$.

Point of horizontal tangency: $(1, -1)$

(b) $t = \dfrac{x + 1}{2}$

$y = \dfrac{1}{[(x + 1)/2]^2 - 2[(x + 1)/2]} = \dfrac{4}{(x - 3)(x + 1)}$

(c)

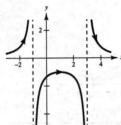

**44.** $x = 6 \cos \theta$

$y = 6 \sin \theta$

(a) $\dfrac{dy}{dx} = \dfrac{6 \cos \theta}{-6 \sin \theta} = -\cot \theta = 0$ when $\theta = \dfrac{\pi}{2}, \dfrac{3\pi}{2}$.

Points of horizontal tangency: $(0, 6), (0, -6)$

(b) $\left(\dfrac{x}{6}\right)^2 + \left(\dfrac{y}{6}\right)^2 = 1$

(c)

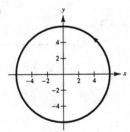

**46.** $x = e^t$

$y = e^{-t}$

(a) $\dfrac{dy}{dx} = \dfrac{-e^{-t}}{e^t} = -\dfrac{1}{e^{2t}} = -\dfrac{1}{x^2}$

No horizontal tangents

(b) $t = \ln x$

$y = e^{-\ln x} = e^{\ln(1/x)} = \dfrac{1}{x}, x > 0$

(c)

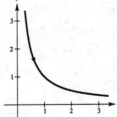

**48.** $x = 2\theta - \sin \theta$

$y = 2 - \cos \theta$

(a), (c)

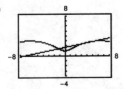

(b) At $\theta = \dfrac{\pi}{6}, \dfrac{dx}{d\theta} \approx 1.134, \left(2 - \dfrac{\sqrt{3}}{2}\right)$,

$\dfrac{dy}{dt} = 0.5$, and $\dfrac{dy}{dx} \approx 0.441$

**50.** $x = 6 \cos \theta$

$y = 6 \sin \theta$

$\dfrac{dx}{d\theta} = -6 \sin \theta$

$\dfrac{dy}{d\theta} = 6 \cos \theta$

$s = \displaystyle\int_0^\pi \sqrt{36 \sin^2 \theta + 36 \cos^2 \theta} \, d\theta = \Big[6\theta\Big]_0^\pi = 6\pi$

(one-half circumference of circle)

**52.** $(x, y) = (-1, 3)$

$$r = \sqrt{(-1)^2 + 3^2} = \sqrt{10}$$

$$\theta = \arctan(-3) \approx 1.89 \ (108.43°)$$

$$(r, \theta) = \left(\sqrt{10}, 1.89\right), \left(-\sqrt{10}, 5.03\right)$$

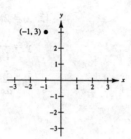

**54.**

$$r = 10$$

$$r^2 = 100$$

$$x^2 + y^2 = 100$$

**56.**

$$r = \frac{1}{2 - \cos\theta}$$

$$2r - r\cos\theta = 1$$

$$2\left(\pm\sqrt{x^2 + y^2}\right) - x = 1$$

$$4(x^2 + y^2) = (x + 1)^2$$

$$3x^2 + 4y^2 - 2x - 1 = 0$$

**58.** $r = 4\sec\left(\theta - \dfrac{\pi}{3}\right) = \dfrac{4}{\cos[\theta - (\pi/3)]}$

$$= \frac{4}{(1/2)\cos\theta + \left(\sqrt{3}/2\right)\sin\theta}$$

$$r\left(\cos\theta + \sqrt{3}\sin\theta\right) = 8$$

$$x + \sqrt{3}\,y = 8$$

**60.**

$$\theta = \frac{3\pi}{4}$$

$$\tan\theta = -1$$

$$\frac{y}{x} = -1$$

$$y = -x$$

**62.** $x^2 + y^2 - 4x = 0$

$$r^2 - 4r\cos\theta = 0$$

$$r = 4\cos\theta$$

**64.** $(x^2 + y^2)\left(\arctan\dfrac{y}{x}\right)^2 = a^2$

$$r^2\theta^2 = a^2$$

**66.** $\theta = \dfrac{\pi}{12}$

Line

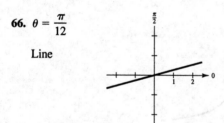

**68.** $r = 3\csc\theta, \ r\sin\theta = 3, \ y = 3$

Horizontal line

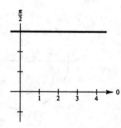

**70.** $r = 3 - 4\cos\theta$

Limaçon

Symmetric to polar axis

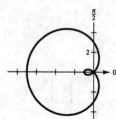

| $\theta$ | $0$ | $\dfrac{\pi}{3}$ | $\dfrac{\pi}{2}$ | $\dfrac{2\pi}{3}$ | $\pi$ |
|---|---|---|---|---|---|
| $r$ | $-1$ | $1$ | $3$ | $5$ | $7$ |

**72.** $r = 2\theta$

Spiral

Symmetric to $\theta = \pi/2$

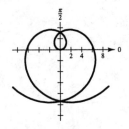

| $\theta$ | 0 | $\dfrac{\pi}{4}$ | $\dfrac{\pi}{2}$ | $\dfrac{3\pi}{4}$ | $\pi$ | $\dfrac{5\pi}{4}$ | $\dfrac{3\pi}{2}$ |
|---|---|---|---|---|---|---|---|
| $r$ | 0 | $\dfrac{\pi}{5}$ | $\pi$ | $\dfrac{3\pi}{2}$ | $2\pi$ | $\dfrac{5\pi}{2}$ | $3\pi$ |

**74.** $r = \cos(5\theta)$

Rose curve with five petals

Symmetric to polar axis

Relative extrema: $(1, 0), \left(-1, \dfrac{\pi}{5}\right), \left(1, \dfrac{2\pi}{5}\right), \left(-1, \dfrac{3\pi}{5}\right), \left(1, \dfrac{4\pi}{5}\right)$

Tangents at the pole: $\theta = \dfrac{\pi}{10}, \dfrac{3\pi}{10}, \dfrac{\pi}{2}, \dfrac{7\pi}{10}, \dfrac{9\pi}{10}$

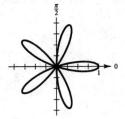

**76.** $r^2 = \cos(2\theta)$

Lemniscate

Symmetric to the polar axis

Relative extrema: $(\pm 1, 0)$

Tangents at the pole: $\theta = \dfrac{\pi}{4}, \dfrac{3\pi}{4}$

| $\theta$ | 0 | $\dfrac{\pi}{6}$ | $\dfrac{\pi}{4}$ |
|---|---|---|---|
| $r$ | $\pm 1$ | $\pm\dfrac{\sqrt{2}}{2}$ | 0 |

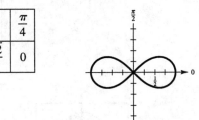

**78.** $r = 2 \sin\theta \cos^2\theta$

Bifolium

Symmetric to $\theta = \pi/2$

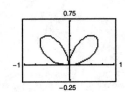

**80.** $r = 4(\sec\theta - \cos\theta)$

Semicubical parabola

Symmetric to the polar axis

$r \Rightarrow \infty$ as $\theta \Rightarrow \dfrac{\pi^-}{2}$

$r \Rightarrow \infty$ as $\theta \Rightarrow \dfrac{-\pi^+}{2}$

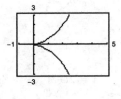

**82.** $r^2 = 4\sin(2\theta)$

(a) $2r\left(\dfrac{dr}{d\theta}\right) = 8\cos(2\theta)$

$\dfrac{dr}{d\theta} = \dfrac{4\cos(2\theta)}{r}$

Tangents at the pole: $\theta = 0, \dfrac{\pi}{2}$

(c)

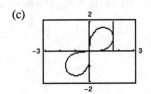

(b) $\dfrac{dy}{dx} = \dfrac{r\cos\theta + [(4\cos 2\theta \sin\theta)/r]}{-r\sin\theta + [(4\cos 2\theta \cos\theta)/r]}$

$= \dfrac{\cos(2\theta)\sin\theta + \sin(2\theta)\cos\theta}{\cos(2\theta)\cos\theta - \sin(2\theta)\sin\theta}$

Horizontal tangents:

$\dfrac{dy}{dx} = 0$ when $\cos(2\theta)\sin\theta + \sin(2\theta)\cos\theta = 0$,

$\tan\theta = -\tan(2\theta), \theta = 0, \dfrac{\pi}{3}, (0, 0), \left(\pm\sqrt{2\sqrt{3}}, \dfrac{\pi}{3}\right)$

Vertical tangents when $\cos 2\theta \cos\theta - \sin 2\theta \sin\theta = 0$:

$\tan 2\theta \tan\theta = 1, \theta = 0, \dfrac{\pi}{6}, (0, 0), \left(\pm\sqrt{2\sqrt{3}}, \dfrac{\pi}{6}\right)$

**84.** False. There are an infinite number of polar coordinate representations of a point. For example, the point $(x, y) = (1, 0)$ has polar representations $(r, \theta) = (1, 0), (1, 2\pi), (-1, \pi)$, etc.

**86.** $r = a \sin \theta, r = a \cos \theta$

The points of intersection are $\left(a/\sqrt{2}, \pi/4\right)$ and $(0, 0)$. For $r = a \sin \theta$,

$$m_1 = \frac{dy}{dx} = \frac{a \cos \theta \sin \theta + a \sin \theta \cos \theta}{a \cos^2 \theta - a \sin^2 \theta} = \frac{2 \sin \theta \cos \theta}{\cos 2\theta}.$$

At $\left(a/\sqrt{2}, \pi/4\right)$, $m_1$ is undefined and at $(0, 0)$, $m_1 = 0$. For $r = a \cos \theta$,

$$m_2 = \frac{dy}{dx} = \frac{-a \sin^2 \theta + a \cos^2 \theta}{-a \sin \theta \cos \theta - a \cos \theta \sin \theta} = \frac{\cos 2\theta}{-2 \sin \theta \cos \theta}.$$

At $\left(a/\sqrt{2}, \pi/4\right)$, $m_2 = 0$ and at $(0, 0)$, $m_2$ is undefined. Therefore, the graphs are orthogonal at $\left(a/\sqrt{2}, \pi/4\right)$ and $(0, 0)$.

**88.** $r = 5(1 - \sin \theta)$

$$A = 2\left[\frac{1}{2} \int_{\pi/2}^{3\pi/2} [5(1 - \sin \theta)]^2\right] d\theta \approx 117.81 \quad \left(75\frac{\pi}{2}\right)$$

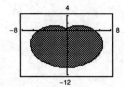

**90.** $r = 4 \sin 3\theta$

$$A = 3\left[\frac{1}{2} \int_0^{\pi/3} (4 \sin 3\theta)^2\, d\theta\right]$$

$$\approx 12.57 \quad (4\pi)$$

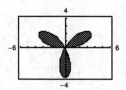

**92.** $r = 3, r^2 = 18 \sin 2\theta$

$$9 = r^2 = 18 \sin 2\theta$$

$$\sin 2\theta = \frac{1}{2}$$

$$\theta = \frac{\pi}{12}$$

$$A = 2\left[\frac{1}{2}\int_0^{\pi/12} 18 \sin 2\theta\, d\theta + \frac{1}{2}\int_{\pi/12}^{5\pi/12} 9\, d\theta + \frac{1}{2}\int_{5\pi/12}^{\pi/2} 18 \sin 2\theta\, d\theta\right]$$

$$\approx 1.2058 + 9.4248 + 1.2058 \approx 11.84$$

**94.** $r = e^\theta, 0 \le \theta \le \pi$

$$A = \frac{1}{2}\int_0^\pi (e^\theta)^2\, d\theta \approx 133.62$$

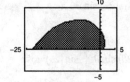

**96.** $r = a \cos 2\theta, \dfrac{dr}{d\theta} = -2a \sin 2\theta$

$$s = 8\int_0^{\pi/4} \sqrt{a^2 \cos^2 2\theta + 4a^2 \sin^2 2\theta}\, d\theta$$

$$= 8a\int_0^{\pi/4} \sqrt{1 + 3 \sin^2 2\theta}\, d\theta \quad \text{(Simpson's Rule: } n = 4)$$

$$\approx \frac{\pi a}{6}[1 + 4(1.1997) + 2(1.5811) + 4(1.8870) + 2]$$

$$\approx 9.69a$$

**98.** $r = \dfrac{2}{1 + \cos \theta}$, $e = 1$

Parabola

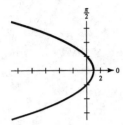

**100.** $r = \dfrac{4}{5 - 3 \sin \theta} = \dfrac{4/5}{1 - (3/5)\sin \theta}$, $e = \dfrac{3}{5}$

Ellipse

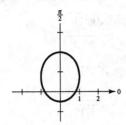

**102.** $r = \dfrac{8}{2 - 5 \cos \theta} = \dfrac{4}{1 - (5/2)\cos \theta}$, $e = \dfrac{5}{2}$

Hyperbola

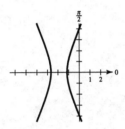

**104.** Line

Slope: $\sqrt{3}$

Solution point: $(0, 0)$

$y = \sqrt{3}\, x$, $r \sin \theta = \sqrt{3}\, r \cos \theta$,

$\tan \theta = \sqrt{3}$, $\theta = \dfrac{\pi}{3}$

**106.** Parabola

Vertex: $\left(2, \dfrac{\pi}{2}\right)$

Focus: $(0, 0)$

$e = 1$, $d = 4$

$r = \dfrac{4}{1 + \sin \theta}$

**108.** Hyperbola

Vertices: $(1, 0)$, $(7, 0)$

Focus: $(0, 0)$

$a = 3$, $c = 4$, $e = \dfrac{4}{3}$, $d = \dfrac{7}{4}$

$r = \dfrac{\left(\dfrac{4}{3}\right)\left(\dfrac{7}{4}\right)}{1 + \left(\dfrac{4}{3}\right)\cos \theta} = \dfrac{7}{3 + 4 \cos \theta}$

# Problem Solving for Chapter 9

**2.** Assume $p > 0$.

Let $y = mx + p$ be the equation of the focal chord.

First find $x$-coordinates of focal chord endpoints:

$x^2 = 4py = 4p(mx + p)$

$x^2 - 4pmx - 4p^2 = 0$

$x = \dfrac{4pm \pm \sqrt{16p^2m^2 + 16p^2}}{2} = 2pm \pm 2p\sqrt{m^2 + 1}$

$x^2 = 4py$, $2x = 4py' \implies y' = \dfrac{x}{2p}$.

(a) The slopes of the tangent lines at the endpoints are perpendicular because

$\dfrac{1}{2p}\big[2pm + 2p\sqrt{m^2 + 1}\big]\dfrac{1}{2p}\big[2pm - 2p\sqrt{m^2 + 1}\big] = \dfrac{1}{4p^2}[4p^2m^2 - 4p^2(m^2 + 1)] = \dfrac{1}{4p^2}[-4p^2] = -1$

**—CONTINUED—**

**2. —CONTINUED—**

(b) Finally, we show that the tangent lines intersect at a point on the directrix $y = -p$.

Let $b = 2pm + 2p\sqrt{m^2 + 1}$ and $c = 2pm - 2p\sqrt{m^2 + 1}$.

$$b^2 = 8p^2m^2 + 4p^2 + 8p^2m\sqrt{m^2 + 1}$$

$$c^2 = 8p^2m^2 + 4p^2 - 8p^2m\sqrt{m^2 + 1}$$

$$\frac{b^2}{4p} = 2pm^2 + p + 2pm\sqrt{m^2 + 1}$$

$$\frac{c^2}{4p} = 2pm^2 + p - 2pm\sqrt{m^2 + 1}$$

Tangent line at $x = b$:   $y - \dfrac{b^2}{4p} = \dfrac{b}{2p}(x - b) \implies y = \dfrac{bx}{2p} - \dfrac{b^2}{4p}$

Tangent line at $x = c$:   $y - \dfrac{c^2}{4p} = \dfrac{c}{2p}(x - c) \implies y = \dfrac{cx}{2p} - \dfrac{c^2}{4p}$

Intersection of tangent lines:      $\dfrac{bx}{2p} - \dfrac{b^2}{4p} = \dfrac{cx}{2p} - \dfrac{c^2}{4p}$

$$2bx - b^2 = 2cx - c^2$$

$$2x(b - c) = b^2 - c^2$$

$$2x\left(4p\sqrt{m^2 + 1}\right) = 16p^2m\sqrt{m^2 + 1}$$

$$x = 2pm$$

Finally, the corresponding $y$-value is $y - p$, which shows that the intersection point lies on the directrix.

**4.** $\dfrac{x^2}{a^2} - \dfrac{y^2}{b^2} = 1, a^2 + b^2 = c^2, MF_2 - Mf_1 = 2a$

$$y' = \frac{b^2x}{a^2y}$$

Tangent line at $M(x_0, y_0)$:      $y = y_0 = \dfrac{b^2x_0}{a^2y_0}(x - x_0)$

$$\frac{yy_0 - y_0^2}{b^2} = \frac{x_0x - x_0^2}{a^2}$$

$$\frac{x_0x}{a^2} - \frac{y_0y}{b^2} = \frac{x_0^2}{a^2} + \frac{y_0^2}{b^2}$$

$$\frac{x_0x}{a^2} - \frac{y_0y}{b^2} = 1$$

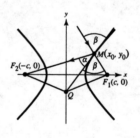

At $x = 0$, $y = -\dfrac{b^2}{y_0} \implies Q = \left(0, -\dfrac{b^2}{y_0}\right)$.

$$QF_2 = QF_1 = \sqrt{c^2 + \frac{b^4}{y_0^2}} = d$$

$$MQ = \sqrt{x_0^2 + \left(y_0 + \frac{b^2}{y_0}\right)^2} = f$$

By the Law of Cosines,

$$(F_2Q)^2 = (MF_2)^2 + (MQ)^2 - 2(MF_2)(MQ)\cos \alpha$$

$$d^2 = (MF_2)^2 + f^2 - 2f(MF_2)\cos \alpha$$

$$(F_1Q)^2 = (MF_1)^2 + f^2 - 2f(MF_1)\cos \beta$$

$$d^2 = (MF_1)^2 + f^2 - 2f(MF_1)\cos \beta.$$

$$\cos \alpha = \frac{(MF_2)^2f^2 - d^2}{2f(MF_2)}, \cos \beta = \frac{(MF_1)^2 + f^2 - d^2}{2f(MF_1)}$$

$MF_2 = MF_1 + 2a$. Let $z = MF_1$.

Slopes:   $MF_1$: $\dfrac{y_0}{x_0 - c}$; $QF_1$: $\dfrac{-b^2}{y_0c}$; $QF_2$: $\dfrac{b^2}{y_0c}$

**—CONTINUED—**

**4. —CONTINUED—**

To show $\alpha = \beta$, consider

$$[(MF_2)^2 + f^2 - d^2][2f(MF_1)] = [(MF_1)^2 + f^2 - d^2][2f(MF_2)]$$

$$\Leftrightarrow \qquad [(z + 2a)^2 + f^2 - d^2][z] = [z^2 + f^2 - d^2][z + 2a]$$

$$\Leftrightarrow \qquad z^2 + 2az = f^2 - d^2$$

$$\Leftrightarrow \qquad (x_0 - c)^2 + y_0^2 + 2az = \left(x_0^2 + \left(y_0 + \frac{b^2}{y_0}\right)^2\right) - \left(c^2 + \frac{b^4}{y_0^2}\right)$$

$$\Leftrightarrow \qquad az - x_0 c + a^2 = 0$$

$$\Leftrightarrow \qquad a\sqrt{(x_0 - c)^2 + y_0^2} = x_0 c - a^2$$

$$\Leftrightarrow \qquad x_0^2 b^2 - a^2 y_0^2 = a^2 b^2$$

$$\Leftrightarrow \qquad \frac{x_0^2}{a^2} - \frac{y_0^2}{b^2} = 1.$$

Thus, $\alpha = \beta$ and the reflective property is verified.

**6. (a)** $y^2 = \dfrac{t^2(1 - t^2)^2}{(1 + t^2)^2}, x^2 = \dfrac{(1 - t^2)^2}{(1 + t^2)^2}$

$$\frac{1 - x}{1 + x} = \frac{1 - \left(\dfrac{1 - t^2}{1 + t^2}\right)}{1 + \left(\dfrac{1 - t^2}{1 + t^2}\right)} = \frac{2t^2}{2} = t^2$$

Thus, $y^2 = x^2\left(\dfrac{1 - x}{1 + x}\right)$.

**(b)** $\qquad r^2 \sin^2 \theta = r^2 \cos^2 \theta \left(\dfrac{1 - r \cos \theta}{1 + r \cos \theta}\right)$

$$\sin^2 \theta (1 + r \cos \theta) = \cos^2 \theta (1 - r \cos \theta)$$

$$r \cos \theta \sin^2 \theta + \sin^2 \theta = \cos^2 \theta - r \cos^3 \theta$$

$$r \cos \theta(\sin^2 \theta + \cos^2 \theta) = \cos^2 \theta - \sin^2 \theta$$

$$r \cos \theta = \cos 2\theta$$

$$r = \cos 2\theta \cdot \sec \theta$$

**(c)**

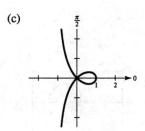

**(d)** $r(\theta) = 0$ for $\theta = \dfrac{\pi}{4}, \dfrac{3\pi}{4}$.

Thus, $y = x$ and $y = -x$ are tangent lines to curve at the origin.

**(e)** $y'(t) = \dfrac{(1 + t^2)(1 - 3t^2) - (t - t^3)(2t)}{(1 + t^2)^2} = \dfrac{1 - 4t^2 - t^4}{(1 + t^2)^2} = 0$

$$t^4 + 4t^2 - 1 = 0 \implies t^2 = -2 \pm \sqrt{5} \implies x = \frac{1 - \left(-2 \pm \sqrt{5}\right)}{1 + \left(-2 \pm \sqrt{5}\right)} = \frac{3 \mp \sqrt{5}}{-1 \pm \sqrt{5}}$$

$$= \frac{3 - \sqrt{5}}{-1 + \sqrt{5}} = \frac{\sqrt{5} - 1}{2}$$

$$\left(\frac{\sqrt{5} - 1}{2}, \pm \frac{\sqrt{5} - 1}{2}\sqrt{-2 + \sqrt{5}}\right)$$

**8.** (a)

*Generated by Mathematica*

(b) $(-x, -y) = \left(-\int_0^t \cos \frac{\pi u^2}{2}\, du, -\int_0^t \sin \frac{\pi u^2}{2}\, du\right)$ is on

the curve whenever $(x, y)$ is on the curve.

(c) $x'(t) = \cos \frac{\pi t^2}{2}, y'(t) = \sin \frac{\pi t^2}{2}, x'(t)^2 + y'(t)^2 = 1$

Thus, $s = \int_0^a dt = a.$

On $[-\pi, \pi], s = 2\pi.$

**10.** $r = \dfrac{ab}{a \sin \theta + b \cos \theta}, 0 \le \theta \le \dfrac{\pi}{2}$

$r(a \sin \theta + b \cos \theta) = ab$

$ay + bx = ab$

$\dfrac{y}{b} + \dfrac{x}{a} = 1$

Line segment

Area $= \dfrac{1}{2}ab$

**12.** Let $(r, \theta)$ be on the graph.

$$\sqrt{r^2 + 1 + 2r \cos \theta}\sqrt{r^2 + 1 - 2r \cos \theta} = 1$$

$$(r^2 + 1)^2 - 4r^2 \cos^2 \theta = 1$$

$$r^4 + 2r^2 + 1 - 4r^2 \cos^2 \theta = 1$$

$$r^2(r^2 - 4\cos^2 \theta + 2) = 0$$

$$r^2 = 4 \cos^2 \theta - 2$$

$$r^2 = 2(2 \cos^2 \theta - 1)$$

$$r^2 = 2 \cos 2\theta$$

**14.** (a) $r = 2$

Circle radius 2

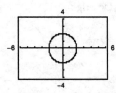

(b) $r = 2 + \cos \theta$

Convex limaçon

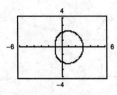

(c) $r = 2 + 2 \cos \theta$

Cardioid

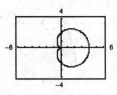

(d) $r = 2 + 3 \cos \theta$

Limaçon with
inner loop

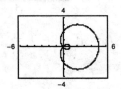

**16.** The curve is produced over the interval

$0 \le \theta \le 9\pi.$

# C H A P T E R  1 0
# Vectors and the Geometry of Space

# CHAPTER 10
# Vectors and the Geometry of Space

## Section 10.1    Vectors in the Plane

Solutions to Even-Numbered Exercises

**2.** (a) $\mathbf{v} = \langle 3 - 3, -2 - 4 \rangle = \langle 0, -6 \rangle$

(b)

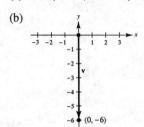

**4.** (a) $\mathbf{v} = \langle -1 - 2, 3 - 1 \rangle = \langle -3, 2 \rangle$

(b)

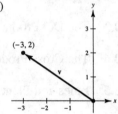

**6.** $\mathbf{u} = \langle 1 - (-4), 8 - 0 \rangle = \langle 5, 8 \rangle$

$\mathbf{v} = \langle 7 - 2, 7 - (-1) \rangle = \langle 5, 8 \rangle$

$\mathbf{u} = \mathbf{v}$

**8.** $\mathbf{u} = \langle 11 - (-4), -4 - (-1) \rangle = \langle 15, -3 \rangle$

$\mathbf{v} = \langle 25 - 0, 10 - 13 \rangle = \langle 15, -3 \rangle$

$\mathbf{u} = \mathbf{v}$

**10.** (b) $\mathbf{v} = \langle 3 - 2, 6 - (-6) \rangle = \langle 1, 12 \rangle$

(a) and (c).

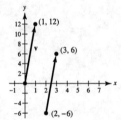

**12.** (b) $\mathbf{v} = \langle -5 - 0, -1 - (-4) \rangle = \langle -5, 3 \rangle$

(a) and (c).

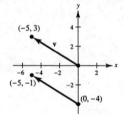

**14.** (b) $\mathbf{v} = \langle -3 - 7, -1 - (-1) \rangle = \langle -10, 0 \rangle$

(a) and (c).

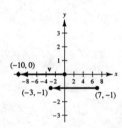

**16.** (b) $\mathbf{v} = \langle 0.84 - 0.12, 1.25 - 0.60 \rangle = \langle 0.72, 0.65 \rangle$

(a) and (c).

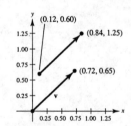

**18.** (a) $4\mathbf{v} = \langle -4, 20 \rangle$

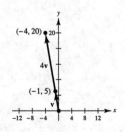

(b) $-\frac{1}{2}\mathbf{v} = \langle \frac{1}{2}, -\frac{5}{2} \rangle$

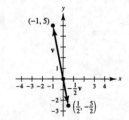

—CONTINUED—

**18.** **—CONTINUED—**

(c) $0\mathbf{v} = \langle 0, 0 \rangle$

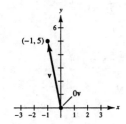

(d) $-6\mathbf{v} = \langle 6, -30 \rangle$

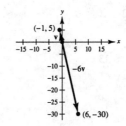

**20.** Twice as long as given vector **u**.

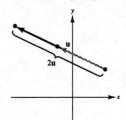

**22.**

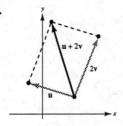

**24.** (a) $\frac{2}{3}\mathbf{u} = \frac{2}{3}\langle -3, -8 \rangle = \left\langle -2, -\frac{16}{3} \right\rangle$

    (b) $\mathbf{v} - \mathbf{u} = \langle 8, 25 \rangle - \langle -3, -8 \rangle = \langle 11, 33 \rangle$

    (c) $2\mathbf{u} + 5\mathbf{v} = 2\langle -3, -8 \rangle + 5\langle 8, 25 \rangle = \langle 34, 109 \rangle$

**26.** $\mathbf{v} = (2\mathbf{i} - \mathbf{j}) + (\mathbf{i} + 2\mathbf{j})$

    $= 3\mathbf{i} + \mathbf{j} = \langle 3, 1 \rangle$

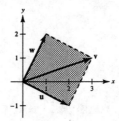

**28.** $\mathbf{v} = 5\mathbf{u} - 3\mathbf{w} = 5\langle 2, -1 \rangle - 3\langle 1, 2 \rangle = \langle 7, -11 \rangle$

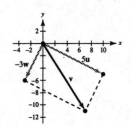

**30.** $u_1 - 3 = 4$

    $u_2 - 2 = -9$

      $u_1 = 7$

      $u_2 = -7$

      $Q = (7, -7)$

**32.** $\|\mathbf{v}\| = \sqrt{144 + 25} = 13$

**34.** $\|\mathbf{v}\| = \sqrt{100 + 9} = \sqrt{109}$

**36.** $\|\mathbf{v}\| = \sqrt{1 + 1} = \sqrt{2}$

**38.** $\|\mathbf{u}\| = \sqrt{5^2 + 15^2} = \sqrt{250} = 5\sqrt{10}$

    $\mathbf{v} = \dfrac{\mathbf{u}}{\|\mathbf{u}\|} = \dfrac{\langle 5, 15 \rangle}{5\sqrt{10}} = \left\langle \dfrac{1}{\sqrt{10}}, \dfrac{3}{\sqrt{10}} \right\rangle$ unit vector

**40.** $\|\mathbf{u}\| = \sqrt{(-6.2)^2 + (3.4)^2} = \sqrt{50} = 5\sqrt{2}$

    $\mathbf{v} = \dfrac{\mathbf{u}}{\|\mathbf{u}\|} = \dfrac{\langle -6.2, 3.4 \rangle}{5\sqrt{2}} = \left\langle \dfrac{-1.24}{\sqrt{2}}, \dfrac{0.68}{\sqrt{2}} \right\rangle$ unit vector

**42.** $\mathbf{u} = \langle 0, 1 \rangle$, $\mathbf{v} = \langle 3, -3 \rangle$

    (a) $\|\mathbf{u}\| = \sqrt{0 + 1} = 1$

    (b) $\|\mathbf{v}\| = \sqrt{9 + 9} = 3\sqrt{2}$

    (c)   $\mathbf{u} + \mathbf{v} = \langle 3, -2 \rangle$

         $\|\mathbf{u} + \mathbf{v}\| = \sqrt{9 + 4} = \sqrt{13}$

    (d)   $\dfrac{\mathbf{u}}{\|\mathbf{u}\|} = \langle 0, 1 \rangle$

         $\left\| \dfrac{\mathbf{u}}{\|\mathbf{u}\|} \right\| = 1$

    (e)   $\dfrac{\mathbf{v}}{\|\mathbf{v}\|} = \dfrac{1}{3\sqrt{2}} \langle 3, -3 \rangle$

         $\left\| \dfrac{\mathbf{v}}{\|\mathbf{v}\|} \right\| = 1$

    (f)   $\dfrac{\mathbf{u} + \mathbf{v}}{\|\mathbf{u} + \mathbf{v}\|} = \dfrac{1}{\sqrt{13}} \langle 3, -2 \rangle$

         $\left\| \dfrac{\mathbf{u} + \mathbf{v}}{\|\mathbf{u} + \mathbf{v}\|} \right\| = 1$

**44.** $\mathbf{u} = \langle 2, -4 \rangle$, $\mathbf{v} = \langle 5, 5 \rangle$

    (a) $\|\mathbf{u}\| = \sqrt{4 + 16} = 2\sqrt{5}$

    (b) $\|\mathbf{v}\| = \sqrt{25 + 25} = 5\sqrt{2}$

    (c)   $\mathbf{u} + \mathbf{v} = \langle 7, 1 \rangle$

         $\|\mathbf{u} + \mathbf{v}\| = \sqrt{49 + 1} = 5\sqrt{2}$

    (d)   $\dfrac{\mathbf{u}}{\|\mathbf{u}\|} = \dfrac{1}{2\sqrt{5}} \langle 2, -4 \rangle$

         $\left\| \dfrac{\mathbf{u}}{\|\mathbf{u}\|} \right\| = 1$

    (e)   $\dfrac{\mathbf{v}}{\|\mathbf{v}\|} = \dfrac{1}{5\sqrt{2}} \langle 5, 5 \rangle$

         $\left\| \dfrac{\mathbf{v}}{\|\mathbf{v}\|} \right\| = 1$

    (f)   $\dfrac{\mathbf{u} + \mathbf{v}}{\|\mathbf{u} + \mathbf{v}\|} = \dfrac{1}{5\sqrt{2}} \langle 7, 1 \rangle$

         $\left\| \dfrac{\mathbf{u} + \mathbf{v}}{\|\mathbf{u} + \mathbf{v}\|} \right\| = 1$

**46.**      $\mathbf{u} = \langle -3, 2 \rangle$

         $\|\mathbf{u}\| = \sqrt{13} \approx 3.606$

         $\mathbf{v} = \langle 1, -2 \rangle$

         $\|\mathbf{v}\| = \sqrt{5} \approx 2.236$

     $\mathbf{u} + \mathbf{v} = \langle -2, 0 \rangle$

     $\|\mathbf{u} + \mathbf{v}\| = 2$

     $\|\mathbf{u} + \mathbf{v}\| \leq \|\mathbf{u}\| + \|\mathbf{v}\|$

**48.**      $\dfrac{\mathbf{u}}{\|\mathbf{u}\|} = \dfrac{1}{\sqrt{2}} \langle -1, 1 \rangle$

     $4 \left( \dfrac{\mathbf{u}}{\|\mathbf{u}\|} \right) = 2\sqrt{2} \langle -1, 1 \rangle$

         $\mathbf{v} = \langle -2\sqrt{2}, 2\sqrt{2} \rangle$

**50.**      $\dfrac{\mathbf{u}}{\|\mathbf{u}\|} = \dfrac{1}{3} \langle 0, 3 \rangle$

     $3 \left( \dfrac{\mathbf{u}}{\|\mathbf{u}\|} \right) = \langle 0, 3 \rangle$

         $\mathbf{v} = \langle 0, 3 \rangle$

**52.** $\mathbf{v} = 5[(\cos 120°)\mathbf{i} + (\sin 120°)\mathbf{j}]$

       $= -\dfrac{5}{2}\mathbf{i} + \dfrac{5\sqrt{3}}{2}\mathbf{j}$

**54.** $\mathbf{v} = (\cos 3.5°)\mathbf{i} + (\sin 3.5°)\mathbf{j}$

       $\approx 0.9981\mathbf{i} + 0.0610\mathbf{j} = \langle 0.9981, 0.0610 \rangle$

**56.**      $\mathbf{u} = 4\mathbf{i}$

         $\mathbf{v} = \mathbf{i} + \sqrt{3}\mathbf{j}$

     $\mathbf{u} + \mathbf{v} = 5\mathbf{i} + \sqrt{3}\mathbf{j}$

**58.**      $\mathbf{u} = 5[\cos(-0.5)]\mathbf{i} + 5[\sin(-0.5)]\mathbf{j}$

         $= 5[\cos(0.5)]\mathbf{i} - 5[\sin(0.5)]\mathbf{j}$

         $\mathbf{v} = 5[\cos(0.5)]\mathbf{i} + 5[\sin(0.5)]\mathbf{j}$

     $\mathbf{u} + \mathbf{v} = 10[\cos(0.5)]\mathbf{i}$

**60.** See page 718:

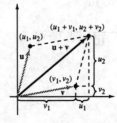
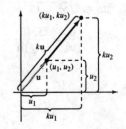

**62.** See Theorem 10.1, page 719.

**For Exercises 64–68,** $a\mathbf{u} + b\mathbf{w} = a(\mathbf{i} + 2\mathbf{j}) + b(\mathbf{i} - \mathbf{j}) = (a + b)\mathbf{i} + (2a - b)\mathbf{j}.$

**64.** $\mathbf{v} = 3\mathbf{j}.$ Therefore, $a + b = 0, 2a - b = 3.$ Solving simultaneously, we have $a = 1, b = -1.$

**66.** $\mathbf{v} = 3\mathbf{i} + 3\mathbf{j}.$ Therefore, $a + b = 3, 2a - b = 3.$ Solving simultaneously, we have $a = 2, b = 1.$

**68.** $\mathbf{v} = -\mathbf{i} + 7\mathbf{j}.$ Therefore, $a + b = -1, 2a - b = 7.$ Solving simultaneously, we have $a = 2, b = -3.$

**70.** $y = x^3, y' = 3x^2 = 12$ at $x = -2.$

(a) $m = 12.$ Let $\mathbf{w} = \langle 1, 12 \rangle,$ then

$$\frac{\mathbf{w}}{\|\mathbf{w}\|} = \pm \frac{1}{\sqrt{145}} \langle 1, 12 \rangle.$$

(b) $m = -\frac{1}{12}.$ Let $\mathbf{w} = \langle 12, -1 \rangle,$ then

$$\frac{\mathbf{w}}{\|\mathbf{w}\|} = \pm \frac{1}{\sqrt{145}} \langle 12, -1 \rangle.$$

**72.** $f(x) = \tan x$

$f'(x) = \sec^2 x = 2$ at $x = \frac{\pi}{4}.$

(a) $m = 2.$ Let $\mathbf{w} = \langle 1, 2 \rangle,$ then

$$\frac{\mathbf{w}}{\|\mathbf{w}\|} = \pm \frac{1}{\sqrt{5}} \langle 1, 2 \rangle.$$

(b) $m = -\frac{1}{2}.$ Let $\mathbf{w} = \langle -2, 1 \rangle,$ then

$$\frac{\mathbf{w}}{\|\mathbf{w}\|} = \pm \frac{1}{\sqrt{5}} \langle -2, 1 \rangle.$$

**74.** $\mathbf{u} = 2\sqrt{3}\mathbf{i} + 2\mathbf{j}$

$\mathbf{u} + \mathbf{v} = -3\mathbf{i} + 3\sqrt{3}\mathbf{j}$

$\mathbf{v} = (\mathbf{u} + \mathbf{v}) - \mathbf{u} = \left(-3 - 2\sqrt{3}\right)\mathbf{i} + \left(3\sqrt{3} - 2\right)\mathbf{j}$

**76.** magnitude $\approx 63.5$

direction $\approx -8.26°$

**78.** $\|\mathbf{F}_1\| = 2, \theta_{\mathbf{F}_1} = -10°$

$\|\mathbf{F}_2\| = 4, \theta_{\mathbf{F}_2} = 140°$

$\|\mathbf{F}_3\| = 3, \theta_{\mathbf{F}_3} = 200°$

$\|\mathbf{R}\| = \|\mathbf{F}_1 + \mathbf{F}_2 + \mathbf{F}_3\| \approx 4.09$

$\theta_{\mathbf{R}} = \theta_{\mathbf{F}_1 + \mathbf{F}_2 + \mathbf{F}_3} \approx 163.0°$

**80.** $\mathbf{F}_1 + \mathbf{F}_2 = (500 \cos 30° \mathbf{i} + 500 \sin 30° \mathbf{j}) + (200 \cos(-45°)\mathbf{i} + 200 \sin(-45°)\mathbf{j})$

$= \left(250\sqrt{3} + 100\sqrt{2}\right)\mathbf{i} + \left(250 - 100\sqrt{2}\right)\mathbf{j}$

$\|\mathbf{F}_1 + \mathbf{F}_2\| = \sqrt{\left(250\sqrt{3} + 100\sqrt{2}\right)^2 + \left(250 - 100\sqrt{2}\right)^2} \approx 584.6 \text{ lb}$

$\tan \theta = \frac{250 - 100\sqrt{2}}{250\sqrt{3} + 100\sqrt{2}} \Rightarrow \theta \approx 10.7°$

**82.** $\mathbf{F}_1 + \mathbf{F}_2 + \mathbf{F}_3 = [400(\cos(-30°)\mathbf{i} + \sin(-30°)\mathbf{j})] + [280(\cos(45°)\mathbf{i} + \sin(45°)\mathbf{j})] + [350(\cos(135°)\mathbf{i} + \sin(135°)\mathbf{j})]$

$= \left[200\sqrt{3} + 140\sqrt{2} - 175\sqrt{2}\right]\mathbf{i} + \left[-200 + 140\sqrt{2} + 175\sqrt{2}\right]\mathbf{j}$

$\|\mathbf{R}\| = \sqrt{\left(200\sqrt{3} - 35\sqrt{2}\right)^2 + \left(-200 + 315\sqrt{2}\right)^2} \approx 385.2483 \text{ newtons}$

$\theta_{\mathbf{R}} = \arctan\left(\frac{-200 + 315\sqrt{2}}{200\sqrt{3} - 35\sqrt{2}}\right) \approx 0.6908 \approx 39.6°$

**84.** $\mathbf{F}_1 = \langle 20, 0 \rangle$, $\mathbf{F}_2 = 10 \langle \cos \theta, \sin \theta \rangle$

(a) $\|\mathbf{F}_1 + \mathbf{F}_2\| = \|\langle 20 + 10 \cos \theta, 10 \sin \theta \rangle\|$

$\qquad = \sqrt{400 + 400 \cos \theta + 100 \cos^2 \theta + 100 \sin^2 \theta}$

$\qquad = \sqrt{500 + 400 \cos \theta}$

(b)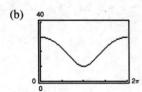

(c) The range is $10 \le \|\mathbf{F}_1 + \mathbf{F}_2\| \le 30$.

The maximum is 30, which occur at $\theta = 0$ and $\theta = 2\pi$.

The minimum is 10 at $\theta = \pi$.

(d) The minimum of the resultant is 10.

**86.** $\mathbf{u} = \langle 7 - 1, 5 - 2 \rangle = \langle 6, 3 \rangle$

$\dfrac{1}{3}\mathbf{u} = \langle 2, 1 \rangle$

$P_1 = (1, 2) + (2, 1) = (3, 3)$

$P_2 = (1, 2) + 2(2, 1) = (5, 4)$

**88.** $\theta_1 = \arctan\left(\dfrac{24}{20}\right) \approx 0.8761$ or $50.2°$

$\theta_2 = \arctan\left(\dfrac{24}{-10}\right) + \pi \approx 1.9656$ or $112.6°$

$\mathbf{u} = \|\mathbf{u}\|(\cos \theta_1 \, \mathbf{i} + \sin \theta_1 \, \mathbf{j})$

$\mathbf{v} = \|\mathbf{v}\|(\cos \theta_2 \, \mathbf{i} + \sin \theta_2 \, \mathbf{j})$

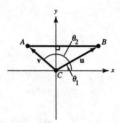

Vertical components: $\|\mathbf{u}\| \sin \theta_1 + \|\mathbf{v}\| \sin \theta_2 = 5000$

Horizontal components: $\|\mathbf{u}\| \cos \theta_1 + \|\mathbf{v}\| \cos \theta_2 = 0$

Solving this system, you obtain

$\|\mathbf{u}\| \approx 2169.4$ and $\|\mathbf{v}\| \approx 3611.2$.

**90.** To lift the weight vertically, the sum of the vertical components of $\mathbf{u}$ and $\mathbf{v}$ must be 100 and the sum of the horizontal components must be 0.

$\mathbf{u} = \|\mathbf{u}\| (\cos 60°\mathbf{i} + \sin 60°\mathbf{j})$

$\mathbf{v} = \|\mathbf{v}\| (\cos 110°\mathbf{i} + \sin 110°\mathbf{j})$

Thus, $\|\mathbf{u}\| \sin 60° + \|\mathbf{v}\| \sin 110° = 100$, or

$\|\mathbf{u}\|\left(\dfrac{\sqrt{3}}{2}\right) + \|\mathbf{v}\| \sin 110° = 100$.

And $\|\mathbf{u}\| \cos 60° + \|\mathbf{v}\| \cos 110° = 0$ or

$\|\mathbf{u}\|\left(\dfrac{1}{2}\right) + \|\mathbf{v}\| \cos 110° = 0$.

Multiplying the last equation by $\left(\sqrt{3}\right)$ and adding to the first equation gives

$\|\mathbf{u}\|(\sin 110° - \sqrt{3} \cos 110°) = 100 \implies \|\mathbf{v}\| \approx 65.27$ lb.

Then, $\|\mathbf{u}\|\left(\dfrac{1}{2}\right) + 65.27 \cos 110° = 0$ gives

$\|\mathbf{u}\| \approx 44.65$ lb.

(a) The tension in each rope: $\|\mathbf{u}\| = 44.65$ lb, $\|\mathbf{v}\| = 65.27$ lb.

(b) Vertical components: $\|\mathbf{u}\| \sin 60° \approx 38.67$ lb.

$\qquad\qquad \|\mathbf{v}\| \sin 110° \approx 61.33$ lb.

**92.**      $\mathbf{u} = 400\mathbf{i}$ (plane)

$\mathbf{v} = 50(\cos 135°\mathbf{i} + \sin 135°\mathbf{j}) = -25\sqrt{2}\mathbf{i} + 25\sqrt{2}\mathbf{j}$ (wind)

$\mathbf{u} + \mathbf{v} = \left(400 - 25\sqrt{2}\right)\mathbf{i} + 25\sqrt{2}\mathbf{j} \approx 364.64\mathbf{i} + 35.36\mathbf{j}$

$\tan \theta = \dfrac{35.36}{364.64} \implies \theta \approx 5.54°$

Direction North of East: $\approx$ N 84.46° E

Speed: $\approx$ 336.35 mph

**94.** $\|\mathbf{u}\| = \sqrt{\cos^2 \theta + \sin^2 \theta} = 1,$

$\|\mathbf{v}\| = \sqrt{\sin^2 \theta + \cos^2 \theta} = 1$

**96.** Let **u** and **v** be the vectors that determine the parallelogram, as indicated in the figure. The two diagonals are $\mathbf{u} + \mathbf{v}$ and $\mathbf{v} - \mathbf{u}$. Therefore, $\mathbf{r} = x(\mathbf{u} + \mathbf{v})$, $\mathbf{s} = y(\mathbf{v} - \mathbf{u})$. But,

$\mathbf{u} = \mathbf{r} - \mathbf{s}$

$= x(\mathbf{u} + \mathbf{v}) - y(\mathbf{v} - \mathbf{u}) = (x + y)\mathbf{u} + (x - y)\mathbf{v}.$

Therefore, $x + y = 1$ and $x - y = 0$. Solving we have $x = y = \frac{1}{2}$.

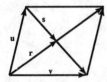

**98.** The set is a circle of radius 5, centered at the origin.

$\|\mathbf{u}\| = \|\langle x, y \rangle\| = \sqrt{x^2 + y^2} = 5 \implies x^2 + y^2 = 25$

**100.** True                     **102.** False                     **104.** True

$a = b = 0$

# Section 10.2    Space Coordinates and Vectors in Space

**2.**

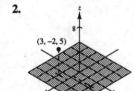

**4.**

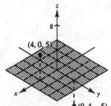

**6.** $A(2, -3, -1)$

$B(-3, 1, 4)$

**8.** $x = 7, y = -2, z = -1$:

$(7, -2, -1)$

**10.** $x = 0, y = 3, z = 2$:  $(0, 3, 2)$

**12.** The $x$-coordinate is 0.

**14.** The point is 2 units in front of the $xz$-plane.

**16.** The point is on the plane $z = -3$.

**18.** The point is behind the $yz$-plane.

**20.** The point is in front of the plane $x = 4$.

**22.** The point $(x, y, z)$ is 4 units above the $xy$-plane, and above either quadrant II or IV.

**24.** The point could be above the $xy$-plane, and thus above quadrants I or III, or below the $xy$-plane, and thus below quadrants II or IV.

**26.** $d = \sqrt{(2 - (-2))^2 + (-5 - 3)^2 + (-2 - 2)^2}$

$= \sqrt{16 + 64 + 16} = \sqrt{96} = 4\sqrt{6}$

**28.** $d = \sqrt{(4 - 2)^2 + (-5 - 2)^2 + (6 - 3)^2}$

$= \sqrt{4 + 49 + 9} = \sqrt{62}$

**30.** $A(5, 3, 4)$, $B(7, 1, 3)$, $C(3, 5, 3)$

$|AB| = \sqrt{4 + 4 + 1} = 3$

$|AC| = \sqrt{4 + 4 + 1} = 3$

$|BC| = \sqrt{16 + 16 + 0} = 4\sqrt{2}$

Since $|AB| = |AC|$, the triangle is isosceles.

**32.** $A(5, 0, 0)$, $B(0, 2, 0)$, $C(0, 0, -3)$

$|AB| = \sqrt{25 + 4 + 0} = \sqrt{29}$

$|AC| = \sqrt{25 + 0 + 9} = \sqrt{34}$

$|BC| = \sqrt{0 + 4 + 9} = \sqrt{13}$

Neither

**34.** The $y$-coordinate is changed by 3 units:

$(5, 6, 4), (7, 4, 3), (3, 8, 3)$

**36.** $\left(\dfrac{4 + 8}{2}, \dfrac{0 + 8}{2}, \dfrac{-6 + 20}{2}\right) = (6, 4, 7)$

**38.** Center: $(4, -1, 1)$

Radius: 5

$(x - 4)^2 + (y + 1)^2 + (z - 1)^2 = 25$

$x^2 + y^2 + z^2 - 8x + 2y - 2z - 7 = 0$

**40.** Center: $(-3, 2, 4)$

$r = 3$

(tangent to $yz$-plane)

$(x + 3)^2 + (y - 2)^2 + (z - 4)^2 = 9$

**42.** $x^2 + y^2 + z^2 + 9x - 2y + 10z + 19 = 0$

$\left(x^2 + 9x + \dfrac{81}{4}\right) + (y^2 - 2y + 1) + (z^2 + 10z + 25) = -19 + \dfrac{81}{4} + 1 + 25$

$\left(x + \dfrac{9}{2}\right)^2 + (y - 1)^2 + (z + 5)^2 = \dfrac{109}{4}$

Center: $\left(-\dfrac{9}{2}, 1, -5\right)$

Radius: $\dfrac{\sqrt{109}}{2}$

**44.** $4x^2 + 4y^2 + 4z^2 - 4x - 32y + 8z + 33 = 0$

$x^2 + y^2 + z^2 - x - 8y + 2z + \dfrac{33}{4} = 0$

$\left(x^2 - x + \dfrac{1}{4}\right) + (y^2 - 8y + 16) + (z^2 + 2z + 1) = -\dfrac{33}{4} + \dfrac{1}{4} + 16 + 1$

$\left(x - \dfrac{1}{2}\right)^2 + (y - 4)^2 + (z + 1)^2 = 9$

Center: $\left(\dfrac{1}{2}, 4, -1\right)$

Radius: 3

**46.**
$$x^2 + y^2 + z^2 < 4x - 6y + 8z - 13$$

$$(x^2 - 4x + 4) + (y^2 + 6y + 9) + (z^2 - 8z + 16) < 4 + 9 + 16 - 13$$

$$(x - 2)^2 + (y + 3)^2 + (z - 4)^2 < 16$$

Interior of sphere of radius 4 centered at $(2, -3, 4)$.

**48.** (a) $\mathbf{v} = (4 - 0)\mathbf{i} + (0 - 5)\mathbf{j} + (3 - 1)\mathbf{k}$

$\quad\quad = 4\mathbf{i} - 5\mathbf{j} + 2\mathbf{k} = \langle 4, -5, 2 \rangle$

(b)

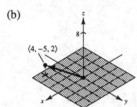

**50.** (a) $\mathbf{v} = (2 - 2)\mathbf{i} + (3 - 3)\mathbf{j} + (4 - 0)\mathbf{k}$

$\quad\quad = 4\mathbf{k} = \langle 0, 0, 4 \rangle$

(b)

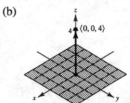

**52.** $\langle -1 - 4, 7 - (-5), -3 - 2 \rangle = \langle -5, 12, -5 \rangle$

$\|\langle -5, 12, -5 \rangle\| = \sqrt{25 + 144 + 25} = \sqrt{194}$

Unit vector: $\dfrac{\langle -5, 12, -5 \rangle}{\sqrt{194}} = \left\langle \dfrac{-5}{\sqrt{194}}, \dfrac{12}{\sqrt{194}}, \dfrac{-5}{\sqrt{194}} \right\rangle$

**54.** $\langle 2 - 1, 4 - (-2), -2 - 4 \rangle = \langle 1, 6, -6 \rangle$

$\|\langle 1, 6, -6 \rangle\| = \sqrt{1 + 36 + 36} = \sqrt{73}$

Unit vector: $\left\langle \dfrac{1}{\sqrt{73}}, \dfrac{6}{\sqrt{73}}, \dfrac{-6}{\sqrt{73}} \right\rangle$

**56.** (b) $\mathbf{v} = (-4 - 2)\mathbf{i} + (3 + 1)\mathbf{j} + (7 + 2)\mathbf{k}$

$\quad\quad = -6\mathbf{i} + 4\mathbf{j} + 9\mathbf{k} = \langle -6, 4, 9 \rangle$

(a) and (c).

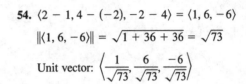

**58.** $(q_1, q_2, q_3) - \left(0, 2, \frac{5}{2}\right) = \left(1, -\frac{2}{3}, \frac{1}{2}\right)$

$Q = \left(1, -\frac{8}{3}, 3\right)$

**60.** (a) $-\mathbf{v} = \langle -2, 2, -1 \rangle$

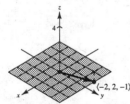

(b) $2\mathbf{v} = \langle 4, -4, 2 \rangle$

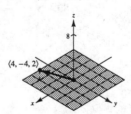

(c) $\frac{1}{2}\mathbf{v} = \left\langle 1, -1, \frac{1}{2} \right\rangle$

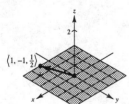

(d) $\frac{5}{2}\mathbf{v} = \left\langle 5, -5, \frac{5}{2} \right\rangle$

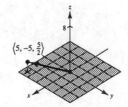

**62.** $\mathbf{z} = \mathbf{u} - \mathbf{v} + 2\mathbf{w} = \langle 1, 2, 3 \rangle - \langle 2, 2, -1 \rangle + \langle 8, 0, -8 \rangle = \langle 7, 0, -4 \rangle$

**64.** $\mathbf{z} = 5\mathbf{u} - 3\mathbf{v} - \frac{1}{2}\mathbf{w} = \langle 5, 10, 15 \rangle - \langle 6, 6, -3 \rangle - \langle 2, 0, -2 \rangle = \langle -3, 4, 20 \rangle$

**66.** $2\mathbf{u} + \mathbf{v} - \mathbf{w} + 3\mathbf{z} = 2\langle 1, 2, 3 \rangle + \langle 2, 2, -1 \rangle - \langle 4, 0, -4 \rangle + 3\langle z_1, z_2, z_3 \rangle = \langle 0, 0, 0 \rangle$

$\langle 0, 6, 9 \rangle + \langle 3z_1, 3z_2, 3z_3 \rangle = \langle 0, 0, 0 \rangle$

$0 + 3z_1 = 0 \implies z_1 = 0$

$6 + 3z_2 = 0 \implies z_2 = -2$

$9 + 3z_3 = 0 \implies z_3 = -3$

$\mathbf{z} = \langle 0, -2, -3 \rangle$

**68.** (b) and (d) are parallel since $-\mathbf{i} + \frac{4}{3}\mathbf{j} - \frac{3}{2}\mathbf{k} = -2\left(\frac{1}{2}\mathbf{i} - \frac{2}{3}\mathbf{j} + \frac{3}{4}\mathbf{k}\right)$ and $\frac{3}{4}\mathbf{i} - \mathbf{j} + \frac{9}{8}\mathbf{k} = \frac{3}{2}\left(\frac{1}{2}\mathbf{i} - \frac{2}{3}\mathbf{j} + \frac{3}{4}\mathbf{k}\right)$.

**70.** $\mathbf{z} = \langle -7, -8, 3 \rangle$

(b) is parallel since $(-z)\mathbf{z} = \langle 14, 16, -6 \rangle$.

**72.** $P(4, -2, 7), Q(-2, 0, 3), R(7, -3, 9)$

$\overrightarrow{PQ} = \langle -6, 2, -4 \rangle$

$\overrightarrow{PR} = \langle 3, -1, 2 \rangle$

$\langle 3, -1, 2 \rangle = -\frac{1}{2}\langle -6, 2, -4 \rangle$

Therefore, $\overrightarrow{PQ}$ and $\overrightarrow{PR}$ are parallel.

The points are collinear.

**74.** $P(0, 0, 0), Q(1, 3, -2), R(2, -6, 4)$

$\overrightarrow{PQ} = \langle 1, 3, -2 \rangle$

$\overrightarrow{PR} = \langle 2, -6, 4 \rangle$

Since $\overrightarrow{PQ}$ and $\overrightarrow{PR}$ are not parallel, the points are not collinear.

**76.** $A(1, 1, 3), B(9, -1, -2), C(11, 2, -9), D(3, 4, -4)$

$\overrightarrow{AB} = \langle 8, -2, -5 \rangle$

$\overrightarrow{DC} = \langle 8, -2, -5 \rangle$

$\overrightarrow{AD} = \langle 2, 3, -7 \rangle$

$\overrightarrow{BC} = \langle 2, 3, -7 \rangle$

Since $\overrightarrow{AB} = \overrightarrow{DC}$ and $\overrightarrow{AD} = \overrightarrow{BC}$, the given points form the vertices of a parallelogram.

**78.** $\|\mathbf{v}\| = \sqrt{1 + 0 + 9} = \sqrt{10}$

**80.** $\mathbf{v} = \langle -4, 3, 7 \rangle$

$\|\mathbf{v}\| = \sqrt{16 + 9 + 49} = \sqrt{74}$

**82.** $\mathbf{v} = \langle 1, 3, -2 \rangle$

$\|\mathbf{v}\| = \sqrt{1 + 9 + 4} = \sqrt{14}$

**84.** $\mathbf{u} = \langle 6, 0, 8 \rangle$

$\|\mathbf{u}\| = \sqrt{36 + 0 + 64} = 10$

(a) $\dfrac{\mathbf{u}}{\|\mathbf{u}\|} = \dfrac{1}{10}\langle 6, 0, 8 \rangle$

(b) $-\dfrac{\mathbf{u}}{\|\mathbf{u}\|} = -\dfrac{1}{10}\langle 6, 0, 8 \rangle$

**86.** $\mathbf{u} = \langle 8, 0, 0 \rangle$

$\|\mathbf{u}\| = 8$

(a) $\dfrac{\mathbf{u}}{\|\mathbf{u}\|} = \langle 1, 0, 0 \rangle$

(b) $-\dfrac{\mathbf{u}}{\|\mathbf{u}\|} = \langle -1, 0, 0 \rangle$

**88.** (a) $\mathbf{u} + \mathbf{v} = \langle 4, 7.5, -2 \rangle$

(b) $\|\mathbf{u} + \mathbf{v}\| \approx 8.732$

(c) $\|\mathbf{u}\| \approx 5.099$

(d) $\|\mathbf{v}\| \approx 9.014$

**90.** $c\mathbf{u} = \langle c, 2c, 3c \rangle$

$\|c\mathbf{u}\| = \sqrt{c^2 + 4c^2 + 9c^2} = 3$

$14c^2 = 9$

$c = \pm\dfrac{3\sqrt{14}}{14}$

**92.** $\mathbf{v} = 3\dfrac{\mathbf{u}}{\|\mathbf{u}\|} = 3\left\langle \dfrac{1}{\sqrt{3}}, \dfrac{1}{\sqrt{3}}, \dfrac{1}{\sqrt{3}} \right\rangle = \left\langle \dfrac{3}{\sqrt{3}}, \dfrac{3}{\sqrt{3}}, \dfrac{3}{\sqrt{3}} \right\rangle$

**94.** $\mathbf{v} = \sqrt{5}\dfrac{\mathbf{u}}{\|\mathbf{u}\|} = \sqrt{5}\left\langle \dfrac{-2}{\sqrt{14}}, \dfrac{3}{\sqrt{14}}, \dfrac{1}{\sqrt{14}} \right\rangle$

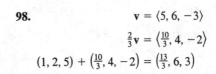

$\qquad = \left\langle \dfrac{-\sqrt{70}}{7}, \dfrac{3\sqrt{70}}{14}, \dfrac{\sqrt{70}}{14} \right\rangle$

**96.** $\mathbf{v} = 5(\cos 45°\mathbf{i} + \sin 45°\mathbf{k}) = \dfrac{5\sqrt{2}}{2}(\mathbf{i} + \mathbf{k})$ or

$\quad \mathbf{v} = 5(\cos 135°\mathbf{i} + \sin 135°\mathbf{k}) = \dfrac{5\sqrt{2}}{2}(-i + k)$

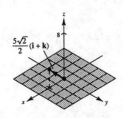

**98.** $\mathbf{v} = \langle 5, 6, -3 \rangle$

$\qquad \dfrac{2}{3}\mathbf{v} = \left\langle \dfrac{10}{3}, 4, -2 \right\rangle$

$(1, 2, 5) + \left(\dfrac{10}{3}, 4, -2\right) = \left(\dfrac{13}{3}, 6, 3\right)$

**100.** $x_0$ is directed distance to $yz$-plane.

$y_0$ is directed distance to $xz$-plane.

$z_0$ is directed distance to $xy$-plane.

**102.** $(x - x_0)^2 + (y - y_0)^2 + (z - z_0)^2 = r^2$

**104.** A sphere of radius 4 centered at $(x_1, y_1, z_1)$.

$\|\mathbf{v}\| = \|\langle x - x_2, y - y_1, z - z_1 \rangle\|$

$\qquad = \sqrt{(x - x_1)^2 + (y - y_1)^2 + (z - z_1)^2} = 4$

$(x - x_1)^2 + (y - y_1)^2 + (z - z_1)^2 = 16$  sphere

**106.** As in Exercise 105(c), $x = a$ will be a vertical asymptote. Hence, $\displaystyle\lim_{r_0 \to a^-} T = \infty$.

**108.** $\quad 550 = \|c(75\mathbf{i} - 50\mathbf{j} - 100\mathbf{k})\|$

$\quad 302{,}500 = 18{,}125c^2$

$\qquad c^2 = 16.689655$

$\qquad c \approx 4.085$

$\qquad \mathbf{F} \approx 4.085(75\mathbf{i} - 50\mathbf{j} - 100\mathbf{k})$

$\qquad \approx 306\mathbf{i} - 204\mathbf{j} - 409\mathbf{k}$

**110.** Let $A$ lie on the $y$-axis and the wall on the $x$-axis. Then

$A = (0, 10, 0)$, $B = (8, 0, 6)$, $C = (-10, 0, 6)$ and

$\overrightarrow{AB} = \langle 8, -10, 6 \rangle$, $\overrightarrow{AC} = \langle -10, -10, 6 \rangle$.

$\|\overrightarrow{AB}\| = 10\sqrt{2}$, $\|\overrightarrow{AC}\| = 2\sqrt{59}$

Thus, $\mathbf{F}_1 = 420\dfrac{\overrightarrow{AB}}{\|\overrightarrow{AB}\|}$, $\mathbf{F}_2 = 650\dfrac{\overrightarrow{AC}}{\|\overrightarrow{AC}\|}$

$\mathbf{F} = \mathbf{F}_1 + \mathbf{F}_2 \approx \langle 237.6, -297.0, 178.2 \rangle$

$\qquad + \langle -423.1, -423.1, 253.9 \rangle$

$\qquad \approx \langle -185.5, -720.1, 432.1 \rangle$

$\|\mathbf{F}\| \approx 860.0$ lb

## Section 10.3    The Dot Product of Two Vectors

**2.** $\mathbf{u} = \langle 4, 10 \rangle$, $\mathbf{v} = \langle -2, 3 \rangle$

(a) $\mathbf{u} \cdot \mathbf{v} = 4(-2) + 10(3) = 22$

(b) $\mathbf{u} \cdot \mathbf{u} = 4(4) + 10(10) = 116$

(c) $\|\mathbf{u}\|^2 = 116$

(d) $(\mathbf{u} \cdot \mathbf{v})\mathbf{v} = 22\langle -2, 3 \rangle = \langle -44, 66 \rangle$

(e) $\mathbf{u} \cdot (2\mathbf{v}) = 2(\mathbf{u} \cdot \mathbf{v}) = 2(22) = 44$

**4.** $\mathbf{u} = \mathbf{i}$, $\mathbf{v} = \mathbf{i}$

(a) $\mathbf{u} \cdot \mathbf{v} = 1$

(b) $\mathbf{u} \cdot \mathbf{u} = 1$

(c) $\|\mathbf{u}\|^2 = 1$

(d) $(\mathbf{u} \cdot \mathbf{v})\mathbf{v} = \mathbf{i}$

(e) $\mathbf{u} \cdot (2\mathbf{v}) = 2(\mathbf{u} \cdot \mathbf{v}) = 2$

**6.** $\mathbf{u} = 2\mathbf{i} + \mathbf{j} - 2\mathbf{k}, \mathbf{v} = \mathbf{i} - 3\mathbf{j} + 2\mathbf{k}$

  (a) $\mathbf{u} \cdot \mathbf{v} = 2(1) + 1(-3) + (-2)(2) = -5$

  (b) $\mathbf{u} \cdot \mathbf{u} = 2(2) + 1(1) + (-2)(-2) = 9$

  (c) $\|\mathbf{u}\|^2 = 9$

  (d) $(\mathbf{u} \cdot \mathbf{v})\mathbf{v} = -5(\mathbf{i} - 3\mathbf{j} + 2\mathbf{k}) = -5\mathbf{i} + 15\mathbf{j} - 10\mathbf{k}$

  (e) $\mathbf{u} \cdot (2\mathbf{v}) = 2(\mathbf{u} \cdot \mathbf{v}) = 2(-5) = -10$

**8.** $\mathbf{u} = \langle 3240, 1450, 2235 \rangle$

$\mathbf{v} = \langle 2.22, 1.85, 3.25 \rangle$

Increase prices by 4%: $1.04\langle 2.22, 1.85, 3.25 \rangle$.

New total amount: $1.04(\mathbf{u} \cdot \mathbf{v}) = 1.04(17,139.05)$

$\qquad\qquad\qquad\qquad = \$17,824.61$

**10.** $\dfrac{\mathbf{u} \cdot \mathbf{v}}{\|\mathbf{u}\| \, \|\mathbf{v}\|} = \cos \theta$

$\mathbf{u} \cdot \mathbf{v} = (40)(25) \cos \dfrac{5\pi}{6} = -500\sqrt{3}$

**12.** $\mathbf{u} = \langle 3, 1 \rangle, \mathbf{v} = \langle 2, -1 \rangle$

$\cos \theta = \dfrac{\mathbf{u} \cdot \mathbf{v}}{\|\mathbf{u}\| \, \|\mathbf{v}\|} = \dfrac{5}{\sqrt{10}\sqrt{5}} = \dfrac{1}{\sqrt{2}}$

$\theta = \dfrac{\pi}{4}$

**14.**    $\mathbf{u} = \cos\left(\dfrac{\pi}{6}\right)\mathbf{i} + \sin\left(\dfrac{\pi}{6}\right)\mathbf{j} = \dfrac{\sqrt{3}}{2}\mathbf{i} + \dfrac{1}{2}\mathbf{j}$

$\mathbf{v} = \cos\left(\dfrac{3\pi}{4}\right)\mathbf{i} + \sin\left(\dfrac{3\pi}{4}\right)\mathbf{j} = -\dfrac{\sqrt{2}}{2}\mathbf{i} + \dfrac{\sqrt{2}}{2}\mathbf{j}$

$\cos \theta = \dfrac{\mathbf{u} \cdot \mathbf{v}}{\|\mathbf{u}\| \, \|\mathbf{v}\|}$

$= \dfrac{\sqrt{3}}{2}\left(-\dfrac{\sqrt{2}}{2}\right) + \dfrac{1}{2}\left(\dfrac{\sqrt{2}}{2}\right) = \dfrac{\sqrt{2}}{4}\left(1 - \sqrt{3}\right)$

$\theta = \arccos\left[\dfrac{\sqrt{2}}{4}\left(1 - \sqrt{3}\right)\right] = 105°$

**16.** $\mathbf{u} = 3\mathbf{i} + 2\mathbf{j} + \mathbf{k}, \mathbf{v} = 2\mathbf{i} - 3\mathbf{j}$

$\cos \theta = \dfrac{\mathbf{u} \cdot \mathbf{v}}{\|\mathbf{u}\| \, \|\mathbf{v}\|} = \dfrac{3(2) + 2(-3) + 0}{\|\mathbf{u}\| \, \|\mathbf{v}\|} = 0$

$\theta = \dfrac{\pi}{2}$

**18.** $\mathbf{u} = 2\mathbf{i} - 3\mathbf{j} + \mathbf{k}, \mathbf{v} = \mathbf{i} - 2\mathbf{j} + \mathbf{k}$

$\cos \theta = \dfrac{\mathbf{u} \cdot \mathbf{v}}{\|\mathbf{u}\| \, \|\mathbf{v}\|}$

$= \dfrac{9}{\sqrt{14}\sqrt{6}} = \dfrac{9}{2\sqrt{21}} = \dfrac{3\sqrt{21}}{14}$

$\theta = \arccos\left(\dfrac{3\sqrt{21}}{14}\right) \approx 10.9°$

**20.** $\mathbf{u} = \langle 2, 18 \rangle, \mathbf{v} = \left\langle \dfrac{3}{2}, -\dfrac{1}{6} \right\rangle$

$\mathbf{u} \neq c\mathbf{v} \implies$ not parallel

$\mathbf{u} \cdot \mathbf{v} = 0 \implies$ orthogonal

**22.** $\mathbf{u} = -\dfrac{1}{3}(\mathbf{i} - 2\mathbf{j}), \mathbf{v} = 2\mathbf{i} - 4\mathbf{j}$

$\mathbf{u} = -\dfrac{1}{6}\mathbf{v} \implies$ parallel

**24.** $\mathbf{u} = -2\mathbf{i} + 3\mathbf{j} - \mathbf{k}, \mathbf{v} = 2\mathbf{i} + \mathbf{j} - \mathbf{k}$

$\mathbf{u} \neq c\mathbf{v} \implies$ not parallel

$\mathbf{u} \cdot \mathbf{v} = 0 \implies$ orthogonal

**26.** $\mathbf{u} = \langle \cos \theta, \sin \theta, -1 \rangle,$

$\mathbf{v} = \langle \sin \theta, -\cos \theta, 0 \rangle$

$\mathbf{u} \neq c\mathbf{v} \implies$ not parallel

$\mathbf{u} \cdot \mathbf{v} = 0 \implies$ orthogonal

**28.** $\mathbf{u} = \langle 5, 3, -1 \rangle \quad \|\mathbf{u}\| = \sqrt{35}$

$\cos \alpha = \dfrac{5}{\sqrt{35}}$

$\cos \beta = \dfrac{3}{\sqrt{35}}$

$\cos \gamma = \dfrac{-1}{\sqrt{35}}$

$\cos^2 \alpha + \cos^2 \beta + \cos^2 \gamma = \dfrac{25}{35} + \dfrac{9}{35} + \dfrac{1}{35} = 1$

**30.** $\mathbf{u} = \langle a, b, c \rangle, \|\mathbf{u}\| = \sqrt{a^2 + b^2 + c^2}$

$$\cos \alpha = \frac{a}{\sqrt{a^2 + b^2 + c^2}}$$

$$\cos \beta = \frac{b}{\sqrt{a^2 + b^2 + c^2}}$$

$$\cos \gamma = \frac{c}{\sqrt{a^2 + b^2 + c^2}}$$

$$\cos^2 \alpha + \cos^2 \beta + \cos^2 \gamma = \frac{a^2}{a^2 + b^2 + c^2} + \frac{b^2}{a^2 + b^2 + c^2} + \frac{c^2}{a^2 + b^2 + c^2} = 1$$

**32.** $\mathbf{u} = \langle -4, 3, 5 \rangle$    $\|\mathbf{u}\| = \sqrt{50} = 5\sqrt{2}$

$$\cos \alpha = \frac{-4}{5\sqrt{2}} \qquad \Rightarrow \alpha \approx 2.1721 \text{ or } 124.4°$$

$$\cos \beta = \frac{3}{5\sqrt{2}} \qquad \Rightarrow \beta \approx 1.1326 \text{ or } 64.9°$$

$$\cos \gamma = \frac{5}{5\sqrt{2}} = \frac{1}{\sqrt{2}} \Rightarrow \gamma \approx \frac{\pi}{4} \text{ or } 45°$$

**34.** $\mathbf{u} = \langle -2, 6, 1 \rangle$    $\|\mathbf{u}\| = \sqrt{41}$

$$\cos \alpha = \frac{-2}{\sqrt{41}} \Rightarrow \alpha \approx 1.8885 \text{ or } 108.2°$$

$$\cos \beta = \frac{6}{\sqrt{41}} \Rightarrow \alpha \approx 0.3567 \text{ or } 20.4°$$

$$\cos \gamma = \frac{1}{\sqrt{41}} \Rightarrow \alpha \approx 1.4140 \text{ or } 81.0°$$

**36.** $\mathbf{F}_1: C_1 = \frac{300}{\|\mathbf{F}_1\|} \approx 13.0931$

$\mathbf{F}_2: C_2 = \frac{100}{\|\mathbf{F}_2\|} \approx 6.3246$

$\mathbf{F} = \mathbf{F}_1 + \mathbf{F}_2$

$\approx 13.0931 \langle -20, -10, 5 \rangle + 6.3246 \langle 5, 15, 0 \rangle$

$= \langle -230.239, -36.062, 65.4655 \rangle$

$\|\mathbf{F}\| \approx 242.067 \text{ lb}$

$\cos \alpha \approx \frac{-230.239}{\|\mathbf{F}\|} \Rightarrow \alpha \approx 162.02°$

$\cos \beta \approx \frac{-36.062}{\|\mathbf{F}\|} \Rightarrow \beta \approx 98.57°$

$\cos \gamma \approx \frac{65.4655}{\|\mathbf{F}\|} \Rightarrow \gamma \approx 74.31°$

**38.**    $\mathbf{v}_1 = \langle s, s, s \rangle$

$\|\mathbf{v}_1\| = s\sqrt{3}$

$\mathbf{v}_2 = \langle s, s, 0 \rangle$

$\|\mathbf{v}_2\| = s\sqrt{2}$

$\cos \theta = \frac{s\sqrt{2}}{s\sqrt{3}} = \frac{\sqrt{6}}{3}$

$\theta = \arccos \frac{\sqrt{6}}{3} \approx 35.26°$

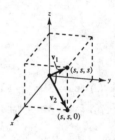

**40.** $\mathbf{F}_1 = C_1(0, 10, 10). \|\mathbf{F}_1\| = 200 = C_1 10\sqrt{2} \Rightarrow C_1 = 10\sqrt{2}$

and $\mathbf{F}_1 = \langle 0, 100\sqrt{2}, 100\sqrt{2} \rangle$

$\mathbf{F}_2 = C_2 \langle -4, -6, 10 \rangle$

$\mathbf{F}_2 = C_3 \langle 4, -6, 10 \rangle$

$\mathbf{F} = \langle 0, 0, w \rangle$

$\mathbf{F} + \mathbf{F}_1 + \mathbf{F}_2 + \mathbf{F}_3 = 0$

$-4C_2 + 4C_3 = 0 \Rightarrow C_2 = C_3$

$100\sqrt{2} - 6C_2 - 6C_3 = 0 \Rightarrow C_2 = C_3 = \frac{25\sqrt{2}}{3} N$

**42.** $\mathbf{w}_2 = \mathbf{u} - \mathbf{w}_1 = \langle 9, 7 \rangle - \langle 3, 9 \rangle = \langle 6, -2 \rangle$

**44.** $\mathbf{w}_2 = \mathbf{u} - \mathbf{w}_1 = \langle 8, 2, 0 \rangle - \langle 6, 3, -3 \rangle = \langle 2, -1, 3 \rangle$

**46.** $\mathbf{u} = \langle 2, -3 \rangle$, $\mathbf{v} = \langle 3, 2 \rangle$

    (a) $\mathbf{w}_1 = \left( \dfrac{\mathbf{u} \cdot \mathbf{v}}{\|\mathbf{v}\|^2} \right) \mathbf{v} = 0\mathbf{v} = \langle 0, 0 \rangle$

    (b) $\mathbf{w}_2 = \mathbf{u} - \mathbf{w}_1 = \langle 2, -3 \rangle$

**48.** $\mathbf{u} = \langle 1, 0, 4 \rangle$, $\mathbf{v} = \langle 3, 0, 2 \rangle$

    (a) $\mathbf{w}_1 = \left( \dfrac{\mathbf{u} \cdot \mathbf{v}}{\|\mathbf{v}\|^2} \right) \mathbf{v} = \dfrac{11}{13} \langle 3, 0, 2 \rangle = \left\langle \dfrac{33}{13}, 0, \dfrac{22}{13} \right\rangle$

    (b) $\mathbf{w}_2 = \mathbf{u} - \mathbf{w}_1 = \langle 1, 0, 4 \rangle - \left\langle \dfrac{33}{13}, 0, \dfrac{22}{13} \right\rangle$

          $= \left\langle -\dfrac{20}{13}, 0, \dfrac{30}{13} \right\rangle$

**50.** The vectors $\mathbf{u}$ and $\mathbf{v}$ are orthogonal if $\mathbf{u} \cdot \mathbf{v} = 0$.

The angle $\theta$ between $\mathbf{u}$ and $\mathbf{v}$ is given by

$$\cos \theta = \frac{\mathbf{u} \cdot \mathbf{v}}{\|\mathbf{u}\| \, \|\mathbf{v}\|}.$$

**52.** (a) and (b) are defined.

**54.** See figure 10.29, page 739.

**56.** Yes, $\left\| \dfrac{\mathbf{u} \cdot \mathbf{v}}{\|\mathbf{v}\|^2} \mathbf{v} \right\| = \left\| \dfrac{\mathbf{v} \cdot \mathbf{u}}{\|\mathbf{u}\|^2} \mathbf{u} \right\|$

    $|\mathbf{u} \cdot \mathbf{v}| \dfrac{\|\mathbf{v}\|}{\|\mathbf{v}\|^2} = |\mathbf{v} \cdot \mathbf{u}| \dfrac{\|\mathbf{u}\|}{\|\mathbf{u}\|^2}$

    $\dfrac{1}{\|\mathbf{v}\|} = \dfrac{1}{\|\mathbf{u}\|}$

    $\|\mathbf{u}\| = \|\mathbf{v}\|$

**58.** (a) $\|\mathbf{u}\| = 5$, $\|\mathbf{v}\| \approx 8.602$, $\theta \approx 91.33°$

    (b) $\|\mathbf{u}\| \approx 9.165$, $\|\mathbf{v}\| \approx 5.745$, $\theta = 90°$

**60.** (a) $\left\langle \dfrac{64}{17}, \dfrac{16}{17} \right\rangle$

    (b) $\left\langle -\dfrac{21}{26}, \dfrac{63}{26}, \dfrac{42}{13} \right\rangle$

**62.** Because $\mathbf{u}$ appears to be a multiple of $\mathbf{v}$, the projection of $\mathbf{u}$ onto $\mathbf{v}$ is $\mathbf{u}$. Analytically,

$$\text{proj}_\mathbf{v} \mathbf{u} = \frac{\mathbf{u} \cdot \mathbf{v}}{\|\mathbf{v}\|^2} \mathbf{v} = \frac{\langle -3, -2 \rangle \cdot \langle 6, 4 \rangle}{\langle 6, 4 \rangle \cdot \langle 6, 4 \rangle} \langle 6, 4 \rangle$$

$$= \frac{-26}{52} \langle 6, 4 \rangle = \langle -3, -2 \rangle = \mathbf{u}.$$

**64.** $\mathbf{u} = -8\mathbf{i} + 3\mathbf{j}$. Want $\mathbf{u} \cdot \mathbf{v} = 0$.

    $\mathbf{v} = 3\mathbf{i} + 8\mathbf{j}$ and $-\mathbf{v} = -3\mathbf{i} - 8\mathbf{j}$ are orthogonal to $\mathbf{u}$.

**66.** $\mathbf{u} = \langle 0, -3, 6 \rangle$. Want $\mathbf{u} \cdot \mathbf{v} = 0$.

    $\mathbf{v} = \langle 0, 6, 3 \rangle$ and $-\mathbf{v} = \langle 0, -6, -3 \rangle$ are orthogonal to $\mathbf{u}$.

**68.** $\overrightarrow{OA} = \langle 10, 5, 20 \rangle$, $\mathbf{v} = \langle 0, 0, 1 \rangle$

    $\text{proj}_\mathbf{v} \overrightarrow{OA} = \dfrac{20}{1^2} \langle 0, 0, 1 \rangle = \langle 0, 0, 20 \rangle$

    $\|\text{proj}_\mathbf{v} \overrightarrow{OA}\| = 20$

**70.** $\mathbf{F} = 25(\cos 20°\mathbf{i} + \sin 20°\mathbf{j})$

    $\mathbf{v} = 50\mathbf{i}$

    $W = \mathbf{F} \cdot \mathbf{v} = 1250 \cos 20° \approx 1174.6$ ft $\cdot$ lb

**72.** $\overrightarrow{PQ} = \langle -4, 2, 10 \rangle$

    $\vec{V} = \langle -2, 3, 6 \rangle$

    $W = \overrightarrow{PQ} \cdot \vec{V} = 74$

**74.** True

    $\mathbf{w} \cdot (\mathbf{u} + \mathbf{v}) = \mathbf{w} \cdot \mathbf{u} + \mathbf{w} \cdot \mathbf{v}$

                  $= 0 + 0 = 0 \Rightarrow \mathbf{w}$

    and $\mathbf{u} + \mathbf{v}$ are orthogonal.

**76. (a)**

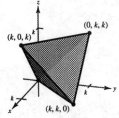

(d) $\vec{r_1} = \langle k, k, 0 \rangle - \left\langle \dfrac{k}{2}, \dfrac{k}{2}, \dfrac{k}{2} \right\rangle = \left\langle \dfrac{k}{2}, \dfrac{k}{2}, -\dfrac{k}{2} \right\rangle$

$\vec{r_2} = \langle 0, 0, 0 \rangle - \left\langle \dfrac{k}{2}, \dfrac{k}{2}, \dfrac{k}{2} \right\rangle = \left\langle -\dfrac{k}{2}, -\dfrac{k}{2}, -\dfrac{k}{2} \right\rangle$

$\cos \theta = \dfrac{-\dfrac{k^2}{4}}{\left(\dfrac{k}{2}\right)^2 \cdot 3} = -\dfrac{1}{3}$

$\theta = 109.5°$

(b) Length of each edge:

$$\sqrt{k^2 + k^2 + 0^2} = k\sqrt{2}$$

(c) $\cos \theta = \dfrac{k^2}{\left(k\sqrt{2}\right)\left(k\sqrt{2}\right)} = \dfrac{1}{2}$

$\theta = \arccos\left(\dfrac{1}{2}\right) = 60°$

**78.** The curves $y_1 = x^2$ and $y_2 = x^{1/3}$ intersect at $(0, 0)$ and at $(1, 1)$.

At $(0, 0)$: $\langle 1, 0 \rangle$ is tangent to $y_1$ and $\langle 0, 1 \rangle$ is tangent to $y_2$. The angle between these vectors is $90°$.

At $(1, 1)$: $\left(1/\sqrt{5}\right)\langle 1, 2 \rangle$ is tangent to $y_1$ and $\left(3/\sqrt{10}\right)\langle 1, 1/3 \rangle = \left(1/\sqrt{10}\right)\langle 3, 1 \rangle$ is tangent to $y_2$. To find the angle between these vectors,

$$\cos \theta = \frac{1}{\sqrt{5}} \frac{1}{\sqrt{10}}(3 + 2) = \frac{1}{\sqrt{2}} \Rightarrow \theta = 45°.$$

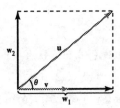

**80.** $\mathbf{u} \cdot \mathbf{v} = \|\mathbf{u}\| \|\mathbf{v}\| \cos \theta$

$|\mathbf{u} \cdot \mathbf{v}| = \left| \|\mathbf{u}\| \|\mathbf{v}\| \cos \theta \right|$

$= \|\mathbf{u}\| \|\mathbf{v}\| |\cos \theta|$

$\leq \|\mathbf{u}\| \|\mathbf{v}\|$ since $|\cos \theta| \leq 1$.

**82.** Let $\mathbf{w_1} = \text{proj}_\mathbf{v}\, \mathbf{u}$, as indicated in the figure. Because $\mathbf{w_1}$ is a scalar multiple of $\mathbf{v}$, you can write

$$\mathbf{u} = \mathbf{w_1} + \mathbf{w_2} = c\mathbf{v} + \mathbf{w_2}.$$

Taking the dot product of both sides with $\mathbf{v}$ produces

$\mathbf{u} \cdot \mathbf{v} = (c\mathbf{v} + \mathbf{w_2}) \cdot \mathbf{v} = c\mathbf{v} \cdot \mathbf{v} + \mathbf{w_2} \cdot \mathbf{v}$

$= c\|\mathbf{v}\|^2$, since $\mathbf{w_2}$ and $\mathbf{v}$ are orthogonol.

Thus, $\mathbf{u} \cdot \mathbf{v} = c\|\mathbf{v}\|^2 \Rightarrow c = \dfrac{\mathbf{u} \cdot \mathbf{v}}{\|\mathbf{v}\|^2}$ and $\mathbf{w_1} = \text{proj}_\mathbf{v}\, \mathbf{u} = c\mathbf{v} = \dfrac{\mathbf{u} \cdot \mathbf{v}}{\|\mathbf{v}\|^2}\mathbf{v}.$

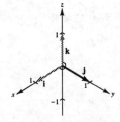

# Section 10.4    The Cross Product of Two Vectors in Space

**2.** $\mathbf{i} \times \mathbf{j} = \begin{vmatrix} \mathbf{i} & \mathbf{j} & \mathbf{k} \\ 1 & 0 & 0 \\ 0 & 1 & 0 \end{vmatrix} = \mathbf{k}$

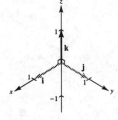

**4.** $\mathbf{k} \times \mathbf{j} = \begin{vmatrix} \mathbf{i} & \mathbf{j} & \mathbf{k} \\ 0 & 0 & 1 \\ 0 & 1 & 0 \end{vmatrix} = -\mathbf{i}$

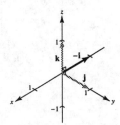

**6.** $\mathbf{k} \times \mathbf{i} = \begin{vmatrix} \mathbf{i} & \mathbf{j} & \mathbf{k} \\ 0 & 0 & 1 \\ 1 & 0 & 0 \end{vmatrix} = \mathbf{j}$

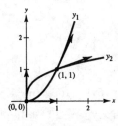

**8.** (a) $\mathbf{u} \times \mathbf{v} = \begin{vmatrix} \mathbf{i} & \mathbf{j} & \mathbf{k} \\ 3 & 0 & 5 \\ 2 & 3 & -2 \end{vmatrix} = \langle -15, 16, 9 \rangle$

(b) $\mathbf{v} \times \mathbf{u} = -(\mathbf{u} \times \mathbf{v}) = \langle 15, -16, -9 \rangle$

(c) $\mathbf{v} \times \mathbf{v} = 0$

**10.** (a) $\mathbf{u} \times \mathbf{v} = \begin{vmatrix} \mathbf{i} & \mathbf{j} & \mathbf{k} \\ 3 & -2 & -2 \\ 1 & 5 & 1 \end{vmatrix} = \langle 8, -5, 17 \rangle$

(b) $\mathbf{v} \times \mathbf{u} = -(\mathbf{u} \times \mathbf{v}) = \langle -8, 5, -17 \rangle$

(c) $\mathbf{v} \times \mathbf{v} = 0$

**12.** $\mathbf{u} = \langle -1, 1, 2 \rangle$, $\mathbf{v} = \langle 0, 1, 0 \rangle$

$\mathbf{u} \times \mathbf{v} = \begin{vmatrix} \mathbf{i} & \mathbf{j} & \mathbf{k} \\ -1 & 1 & 2 \\ 0 & 1 & 0 \end{vmatrix} = -2\mathbf{i} - \mathbf{k} = \langle -2, 0, -1 \rangle$

$\mathbf{u} \cdot (\mathbf{u} \times \mathbf{v}) = (-1)(-2) + (1)(0) + (2)(-1)$

$= 0 \Rightarrow \mathbf{u} \perp \mathbf{u} \times \mathbf{v}$

$\mathbf{v} \cdot (\mathbf{u} \times \mathbf{v}) = (0)(-2) + (1)(0) + (0)(-1)$

$= 0 \Rightarrow \mathbf{v} \perp \mathbf{u} \times \mathbf{v}$

**14.** $\mathbf{u} = \langle -10, 0, 6 \rangle$, $\mathbf{v} = \langle 7, 0, 0 \rangle$

$\mathbf{u} \times \mathbf{v} = \begin{vmatrix} \mathbf{i} & \mathbf{j} & \mathbf{k} \\ -10 & 0 & 6 \\ 7 & 0 & 0 \end{vmatrix} = 42\mathbf{j} = \langle 0, 42, 0 \rangle$

$\mathbf{u} \cdot (\mathbf{u} \times \mathbf{v}) = (-10)(0) + (0)(42) + 6(0)$

$= 0 \Rightarrow \mathbf{u} \perp \mathbf{u} \times \mathbf{v}$

$\mathbf{v} \cdot (\mathbf{u} \times \mathbf{v}) = 7(0) + (0)(42) + (0)(0)$

$= 0 \Rightarrow \mathbf{v} \perp \mathbf{u} \times \mathbf{v}$

**16.** $\mathbf{u} \times \mathbf{v} = \begin{vmatrix} \mathbf{i} & \mathbf{j} & \mathbf{k} \\ 1 & 6 & 0 \\ -2 & 1 & 1 \end{vmatrix} = 6\mathbf{i} - \mathbf{j} + 13\mathbf{k}$

$\mathbf{u} \cdot (\mathbf{u} \times \mathbf{v}) = 1(6) + 6(-1) = 0 \Rightarrow \mathbf{u} \perp (\mathbf{u} \times \mathbf{v})$

$\mathbf{v} \cdot (\mathbf{u} \times \mathbf{v}) = -2(6) + 1(-1) + 1(13) = 0 \Rightarrow \mathbf{v} \perp (\mathbf{u} \times \mathbf{v})$

**18.**

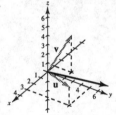

**20.**

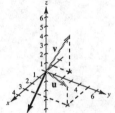

**22.** $\mathbf{u} = \langle -8, -6, 4 \rangle$

$\mathbf{v} = \langle 10, -12, -2 \rangle$

$\mathbf{u} \times \mathbf{v} = \langle 60, 24, 156 \rangle$

$\dfrac{\mathbf{u} \times \mathbf{v}}{\|\mathbf{u} \times \mathbf{v}\|} = \dfrac{1}{36\sqrt{22}} \langle 60, 24, 156 \rangle$

$= \left\langle \dfrac{5}{3\sqrt{22}}, \dfrac{2}{3\sqrt{22}}, \dfrac{13}{3\sqrt{22}} \right\rangle$

**24.**     $\mathbf{u} = \dfrac{2}{3}\mathbf{k}$

$\mathbf{v} = \dfrac{1}{2}\mathbf{i} + 6\mathbf{k}$

$\mathbf{u} \times \mathbf{v} = \left\langle 0, \dfrac{1}{3}, 0 \right\rangle$

$\dfrac{\mathbf{u} \times \mathbf{v}}{\|\mathbf{u} \times \mathbf{v}\|} = \langle 0, 1, 0 \rangle$

**26.** (a) $\mathbf{u} \times \mathbf{v} = \langle -18, -12, 48 \rangle$

$\|\mathbf{u} \times \mathbf{v}\| \approx 52.650$

(b) $\mathbf{u} \times \mathbf{v} = \langle -50, 40, -34 \rangle$

$\|\mathbf{u} \times \mathbf{v}\| \approx 72.498$

**28.** $\mathbf{u} = \mathbf{i} + \mathbf{j} + \mathbf{k}$

$\mathbf{v} = \mathbf{j} + \mathbf{k}$

$\mathbf{u} \times \mathbf{v} = \begin{vmatrix} \mathbf{i} & \mathbf{j} & \mathbf{k} \\ 1 & 1 & 1 \\ 0 & 1 & 1 \end{vmatrix} = -\mathbf{j} + \mathbf{k}$

$A = \|\mathbf{u} \times \mathbf{v}\| = \|-\mathbf{j} + \mathbf{k}\| = \sqrt{2}$

**30.** $\mathbf{u} = \langle 2, -1, 0 \rangle$

$\mathbf{v} = \langle -1, 2, 0 \rangle$

$\mathbf{u} \times \mathbf{v} = \begin{vmatrix} \mathbf{i} & \mathbf{j} & \mathbf{k} \\ 2 & -1 & 0 \\ -1 & 2 & 0 \end{vmatrix} = \langle 0, 0, 3 \rangle$

$A = \|\mathbf{u} \times \mathbf{v}\| = \|\langle 0, 0, 3 \rangle\| = 3$

**32.** $A(2, -3, 1), B(6, 5, -1), C(3, -6, 4), D(7, 2, 2)$

$\overrightarrow{AB} = \langle 4, 8, -2 \rangle, \overrightarrow{AC} = \langle 1, -3, 3 \rangle, \overrightarrow{CD} = \langle 4, 8, -2 \rangle, \overrightarrow{BD} = \langle 1, -3, 3 \rangle$

Since $\overrightarrow{AB} = \overrightarrow{CD}$ and $\overrightarrow{AC} = \overrightarrow{BD}$, the figure is a parallelogram.

$\overrightarrow{AB}$ and $\overrightarrow{AC}$ are adjacent sides and

$\overrightarrow{AB} \times \overrightarrow{AC} = \begin{vmatrix} \mathbf{i} & \mathbf{j} & \mathbf{k} \\ 4 & 8 & -2 \\ 1 & -3 & 3 \end{vmatrix} = \langle 18, -14, -20 \rangle.$

Area $= \|\overrightarrow{AB} \times \overrightarrow{AC}\| = \sqrt{920} = 2\sqrt{230}$

**34.** $A(2, -3, 4), B(0, 1, 2), C(-1, 2, 0)$

$\overrightarrow{AB} = \langle -2, 4, -2 \rangle, \overrightarrow{AC} = \langle -3, 5, -4 \rangle$

$\overrightarrow{AB} \times \overrightarrow{AC} = \begin{vmatrix} \mathbf{i} & \mathbf{j} & \mathbf{k} \\ -2 & 4 & -2 \\ -3 & 5 & -4 \end{vmatrix} = -6\mathbf{i} - 2\mathbf{j} + 2\mathbf{k}$

$A = \frac{1}{2}\|\overrightarrow{AB} \times \overrightarrow{AC}\| = \frac{1}{2}\sqrt{44} = \sqrt{11}$

**36.** $A(1, 2, 0), B(-2, 1, 0), C(0, 0, 0)$

$\overrightarrow{AB} = \langle -3, -1, 0 \rangle, \overrightarrow{AC} = \langle -1, -2, 0 \rangle$

$\overrightarrow{AB} \times \overrightarrow{AC} = \begin{vmatrix} \mathbf{i} & \mathbf{j} & \mathbf{k} \\ -3 & -1 & 0 \\ -1 & -2 & 0 \end{vmatrix} = 5\mathbf{k}$

$A = \frac{1}{2}\|\overrightarrow{AB} \times \overrightarrow{AC}\| = \frac{5}{2}$

**38.** $\mathbf{F} = -2000(\cos 30°\mathbf{j} + \sin 30°\mathbf{k}) = -1000\sqrt{3}\mathbf{j} - 1000\mathbf{k}$

$\overrightarrow{PQ} = 0.16\mathbf{k}$

$\overrightarrow{PQ} \times \mathbf{F} = \begin{vmatrix} \mathbf{i} & \mathbf{j} & \mathbf{k} \\ 0 & 0 & 0.16 \\ 0 & -1000\sqrt{3} & -1000 \end{vmatrix} = 160\sqrt{3}\mathbf{i}$

$\|\overrightarrow{PQ} \times \mathbf{F}\| = 160\sqrt{3}$ ft $\cdot$ lb

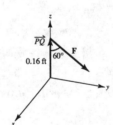

**40.** (a) $B$ is $-\frac{15}{12} = -\frac{5}{4}$ to the left of $A$, and one foot upwards:

$\overrightarrow{AB} = \frac{-5}{4}\mathbf{j} + \mathbf{k}$

$\mathbf{F} = -200(\cos\theta\mathbf{j} + \sin\theta\mathbf{k})$

(b) $\overrightarrow{AB} \times \mathbf{F} = \begin{vmatrix} \mathbf{i} & \mathbf{j} & \mathbf{k} \\ 0 & -5/4 & 1 \\ 0 & -200\cos\theta & -200\sin\theta \end{vmatrix}$

$= (250\sin\theta + 200\cos\theta)\mathbf{i}$

$\|\overrightarrow{AB} \times \mathbf{F}\| = |250\sin\theta + 200\cos\theta|$

$= 25(10\sin\theta + 8\cos\theta)$

(c) For $\theta = 30°$,

$\|\overrightarrow{AB} \times \mathbf{F}\| = 25\left(10\left(\frac{1}{2}\right) + 8\left(\frac{\sqrt{3}}{2}\right)\right)$

$= 25(5 + 4\sqrt{3}) \approx 298.2.$

(d) If $T = \|\overrightarrow{AB} \times \mathbf{F}\|$,

$\frac{dT}{d\theta} = 25(10\cos\theta - 8\sin\theta) = 0 \Rightarrow \tan\theta = \frac{5}{4}$

$\Rightarrow \theta \approx 51.34°.$

The vectors are orthogonal.

(e) The zero is $\theta \approx 141.34°$, the angle making $\overrightarrow{AB}$ parallel to $\mathbf{F}$.

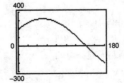

**42.** $\mathbf{u} \cdot (\mathbf{v} \times \mathbf{w}) = \begin{vmatrix} 1 & 1 & 1 \\ 2 & 1 & 0 \\ 0 & 0 & 1 \end{vmatrix} = -1$

**44.** $\mathbf{u} \cdot (\mathbf{v} \times \mathbf{w}) = \begin{vmatrix} 2 & 0 & 0 \\ 1 & 1 & 1 \\ 0 & 2 & 2 \end{vmatrix} = 0$

**46.** $\mathbf{u} \cdot (\mathbf{v} \times \mathbf{w}) = \begin{vmatrix} 1 & 3 & 1 \\ 0 & 6 & 6 \\ -4 & 0 & -4 \end{vmatrix} = -72$

$V = |\mathbf{u} \cdot (\mathbf{v} \times \mathbf{w})| = 72$

**48.** $\mathbf{u} = \langle 1, 1, 0 \rangle$

$\mathbf{v} = \langle 1, 0, 2 \rangle$

$\mathbf{w} = \langle 0, 1, 1 \rangle$

$\mathbf{u} \cdot (\mathbf{v} \times \mathbf{w}) = \begin{vmatrix} 1 & 1 & 0 \\ 1 & 0 & 2 \\ 0 & 1 & 1 \end{vmatrix} = -3$

$V = |\mathbf{u} \cdot (\mathbf{v} \times \mathbf{w})| = 3$

**50.** See Theorem 10.8, page 746.

**52.** Form the vectors for two sides of the triangle, and compute their cross product:

$$\langle x_2 - x_1, y_2 - y_1, z_2 - z_1 \rangle \times \langle x_3 - x_1, y_3 - y_1, z_3 - z_1 \rangle$$

**54.** False, let $\mathbf{u} = \langle 1, 0, 0 \rangle$, $\mathbf{v} = \langle 1, 0, 0 \rangle$, $\mathbf{w} = \langle -1, 0, 0 \rangle$.

Then,

$\mathbf{u} \times \mathbf{v} = \mathbf{u} \times \mathbf{w} = \mathbf{0}$, but $\mathbf{v} \neq \mathbf{w}$.

**56.** $\mathbf{u} = \langle u_1, u_2, u_3 \rangle$, $\mathbf{v} = \langle v_1, v_2, v_3 \rangle$, $\mathbf{w} = \langle w_1, w_2, w_3 \rangle$

$\mathbf{u} = u_1 \mathbf{i} + u_2 \mathbf{j} + u_3 \mathbf{k}$

$\mathbf{v} \times \mathbf{w} = (v_2 w_3 - v_3 w_2) \mathbf{i} - (v_1 w_3 - v_3 w_1) \mathbf{j} + (v_1 w_2 - v_2 w_1) \mathbf{k}$

$\mathbf{u} \cdot (\mathbf{v} + \mathbf{w}) = u_1(v_2 w_3 - v_3 w_2) - u_2(v_1 w_3 - v_3 w_1) + u_3(v_1 w_2 - v_2 w_1) = \begin{vmatrix} u_1 & u_2 & u_3 \\ v_1 & v_2 & v_3 \\ w_1 & w_2 & w_3 \end{vmatrix}$

**58.** $\mathbf{u} = \langle u_1, u_2, u_3 \rangle$, $\mathbf{v} = \langle v_1, v_2, v_3 \rangle$, $c$ is a scalar.

$(c\mathbf{u}) \times \mathbf{v} = \begin{vmatrix} \mathbf{i} & \mathbf{j} & \mathbf{k} \\ cu_1 & cu_2 & cu_3 \\ v_1 & v_2 & v_3 \end{vmatrix}$

$= (cu_2 v_3 - cu_3 v_2) \mathbf{i} - (cu_1 v_3 - cu_3 v_1) \mathbf{j} + (cu_1 v_2 - cu_2 v_1) \mathbf{k}$

$= c[(u_2 v_3 - u_3 v_2) \mathbf{i} - (u_1 v_3 - u_3 v_1) \mathbf{j} + (u_1 v_2 - u_2 v_1) \mathbf{k}] = c(\mathbf{u} \times \mathbf{v})$

**60.** $\mathbf{u} \cdot (\mathbf{v} \times \mathbf{w}) = \begin{vmatrix} u_1 & u_2 & u_3 \\ v_1 & v_2 & v_3 \\ w_1 & w_2 & w_3 \end{vmatrix}$

$(\mathbf{u} \times \mathbf{v}) \cdot \mathbf{w} = \mathbf{w} \cdot (\mathbf{u} \times \mathbf{v}) = \begin{vmatrix} w_1 & w_2 & w_3 \\ u_1 & u_2 & u_3 \\ v_1 & v_2 & v_3 \end{vmatrix}$

$= w_1(u_2 v_3 - v_2 u_3) - w_2(u_1 v_3 - v_1 u_3) + w_3(u_1 v_2 - v_1 u_2)$

$= u_1(v_2 w_3 - w_2 v_3) - u_2(v_1 w_3 - w_1 v_3) + u_3(v_1 w_2 - w_1 v_2)$

$= \mathbf{u} \cdot (\mathbf{v} \times \mathbf{w})$

**62.** If **u** and **v** are scalar multiples of each other, $\mathbf{u} = c\mathbf{v}$ for some scalar $c$.

$$\mathbf{u} \times \mathbf{v} = (c\mathbf{v}) \times \mathbf{v} = c(\mathbf{v} \times \mathbf{v}) = c(\mathbf{0}) = \mathbf{0}$$

If $\mathbf{u} \times \mathbf{v} = \mathbf{0}$, then $\|\mathbf{u}\| \, \|\mathbf{v}\| \sin\theta = 0$. (Assume $\mathbf{u} \neq \mathbf{0}$, $\mathbf{v} \neq \mathbf{0}$.) Thus, $\sin\theta = 0$, $\theta = 0$, and **u** and **v** are parallel. Therefore,

$\mathbf{u} = c\mathbf{v}$ for some scalar $c$.

**64.** $\mathbf{u} = \langle a_1, b_1, c_1 \rangle$, $\mathbf{v} = \langle a_2, b_2, c_2 \rangle$, $\mathbf{w} = \langle a_3, b_3, c_3 \rangle$

$$\mathbf{v} \times \mathbf{w} = \begin{vmatrix} \mathbf{i} & \mathbf{j} & \mathbf{k} \\ a_2 & b_2 & c_2 \\ a_3 & b_3 & c_3 \end{vmatrix} = (b_2c_3 - b_3c_2)\mathbf{i} - (a_2c_3 - a_3c_2)\mathbf{j} + (a_2b_3 - a_3b_2)\mathbf{k}$$

$$\mathbf{u} \times (\mathbf{v} \times \mathbf{w}) = \begin{vmatrix} \mathbf{i} & \mathbf{j} & \mathbf{k} \\ a_1 & b_1 & c_1 \\ (b_2c_3 - b_3c_2) & (a_3c_2 - a_2c_3) & (a_2b_3 - a_3b_2) \end{vmatrix}$$

$$\mathbf{u} \times (\mathbf{v} \times \mathbf{w}) = [b_1(a_2b_3 - a_3b_2) - c_1(a_3c_2 - a_2c_3)]\mathbf{i} - [a_1(a_2b_3 - a_3b_2) - c_1(b_2c_3 - b_3c_2)]\mathbf{j} +$$

$$[a_1(a_3c_2 - a_2c_3) - b_1(b_2c_3 - b_3c_2)]\mathbf{k}$$

$$= [a_2(a_1a_3 + b_1b_3 + c_1c_3) - a_3(a_1a_2 + b_1b_2 + c_1c_2)]\mathbf{i} +$$

$$[b_2(a_1a_3 + b_1b_3 + c_1c_3) - b_3(a_1a_2 + b_1b_2 + c_1c_2)]\mathbf{j} +$$

$$[c_2(a_1a_3 + b_1b_3 + c_1c_3) - c_3(a_1a_2 + b_1b_2 + c_1c_2)]\mathbf{k}$$

$$= (a_1a_3 + b_1b_3 + c_1c_3)\langle a_2, b_2, c_2 \rangle - (a_1a_2 + b_1b_2 + c_1c_2)\langle a_3, b_3, c_3 \rangle$$

$$= (\mathbf{u} \cdot \mathbf{w})\mathbf{v} - (\mathbf{u} \cdot \mathbf{v})\mathbf{w}$$

# Section 10.5　Lines and Planes in Space

**2.** $x = 2 - 3t$, $y = 2$, $z = 1 - t$

(a)

(b) When $t = 0$ we have $P = (2, 2, 1)$. When $t = 2$ we have $Q = (-4, 2, -1)$.

$$\overrightarrow{PQ} = \langle -6, 0, -2 \rangle$$

The components of the vector and the coefficients of $t$ are proportional since the line is parallel to $\overrightarrow{PQ}$.

(c) $z = 0$ when $t = 1$. Thus, $x = -1$ and $y = 2$.

Point: $(-1, 2, 0)$

$x = 0$ when $t = \dfrac{2}{3}$. Point: $\left(0, 2, \dfrac{1}{3}\right)$

**4.** Point: $(0, 0, 0)$

Direction vector: $\mathbf{v} = \left\langle -2, \dfrac{5}{2}, 1 \right\rangle$

Direction numbers: $-4, 5, 2$

(a) Parametric: $x = -4t$, $y = 5t$, $z = 2t$

(b) Symmetric: $\dfrac{x}{-4} = \dfrac{y}{5} = \dfrac{z}{2}$

**6.** Point: $(-3, 0, 2)$

Direction vector: $\mathbf{v} = \langle 0, 6, 3 \rangle$

Direction numbers: $0, 2, 1$

(a) Parametric: $x = -3$, $y = 2t$, $z = 2 + t$

(b) Symmetric: $\dfrac{y}{2} = z - 2$, $x = -3$

**8.** Point: $(-3, 5, 4)$

Directions numbers: $3, -2, 1$

(a) Parametric: $x = -3 + 3t, y = 5 - 2t, z = 4 + t$

(b) Symmetric: $\dfrac{x + 3}{3} = \dfrac{y - 5}{-2} = z - 4$

**10.** Points: $(2, 0, 2), (1, 4, -3)$

Direction vector: $\langle 1, -4, 5 \rangle$

Direction numbers: $1, -4, 5$

(a) Parametric: $x = 2 + t, y = -4t, z = 2 + 5t$

(b) Symmetric: $x - 2 = \dfrac{y}{-4} = \dfrac{z - 2}{5}$

**12.** Points: $(0, 0, 25), (10, 10, 0)$

Direction vector: $\langle 10, 10, -25 \rangle$

Direction numbers: $2, 2, -5$

(a) Parametric: $x = 2t, y = 2t, z = 25 - 5t$

(b) Symmetric: $\dfrac{x}{2} = \dfrac{y}{2} = \dfrac{z - 25}{-5}$

**14.** Point: $(2, 3, 4)$

Direction vector: $\mathbf{v} = 3\mathbf{i} + 2\mathbf{j} - \mathbf{k}$

Direction numbers: $3, 2, -1$

Parametric: $x = 2 + 3t, y = 3 + 2t, z = 4 - t$

**16.** Points: $(2, 0, -3), (4, 2, -2)$

Direction vector: $\mathbf{v} = 2\mathbf{i} + 2\mathbf{j} + \mathbf{k}$

Direction numbers: $2, 2, 1$

Parametric: $x = 2 + 2t, y = 2t, z = -3 + t$

Symmetric: $\dfrac{x - 2}{2} = \dfrac{y}{2} = \dfrac{z + 3}{1}$

(a) Not on line $\left( 1 \neq \dfrac{1}{2} \neq 1 \right)$

(b) On line

(c) Not on line $\left( \dfrac{-3}{2} = \dfrac{-3}{2} \neq -1 \right)$

**18.** $L_1$: $\mathbf{v} = \langle 4, -2, 3 \rangle$      $(8, -5, -9)$ on line

$L_2$: $\mathbf{v} = \langle 2, 1, 5 \rangle$

$L_3$: $\mathbf{v} = \langle -8, 4, -6 \rangle$      $(8, -5, -9)$ on line

$L_4$: $\mathbf{v} = \langle -2, 1, 1.5 \rangle$

$L_1$ and $L_2$ are identical.

**20.** By equating like variables, we have

(i) $-3t + 1 = 3s + 1$, (ii) $4t + 1 = 2s + 4$, and (iii) $2t + 4 = -s + 1$.

From (i) we have $s = -t$, and consequently from (ii), $t = \dfrac{1}{2}$ and from (iii), $t = -3$. The lines do not intersect.

**22.** Writing the equations of the lines in parametric form we have

$x = 2 - 3t$      $y = 2 + 6t$      $z = 3 + t$

$x = 3 + 2s$      $y = -5 + s$      $z = -2 + 4s$.

By equating like variables, we have $2 - 3t = 3 + 2s$, $2 + 6t = -5 + s$, $3 + t = -2 + 4s$. Thus, $t = -1$, $s = 1$ and the point of intersection is $(5, -4, 2)$.

$\mathbf{u} = \langle -3, 6, 1 \rangle$      (First line)

$\mathbf{v} = \langle 2, 1, 4 \rangle$      (Second line)

$\cos \theta = \dfrac{|\mathbf{u} \cdot \mathbf{v}|}{\|\mathbf{u}\| \|\mathbf{v}\|} = \dfrac{4}{\sqrt{46}\sqrt{21}} = \dfrac{4}{\sqrt{966}} = \dfrac{2\sqrt{966}}{483}$

**24.**   $x = 2t - 1$      $x = -5s - 12$

$y = -4t + 10$      $y = 3s + 11$

$z = t$      $z = -2s - 4$

Point of intersection: $(3, 2, 2)$

**26.** $2x + 3y + 4z = 4$

$P = (0, 0, 1), Q = (2, 0, 0), R = (3, 2, -2)$

(a) $\overrightarrow{PQ} = \langle 2, 0, -1 \rangle, \overrightarrow{PR} = \langle 3, 2, -3 \rangle$

(b) $\overrightarrow{PQ} \times \overrightarrow{PR} = \begin{vmatrix} \mathbf{i} & \mathbf{j} & \mathbf{k} \\ 2 & 0 & -1 \\ 3 & 2 & -3 \end{vmatrix} = \langle 2, 3, 4 \rangle$

The components of the cross product are proportional (for this choice of $P$, $Q$, and $R$, they are the same) to the coefficients of the variables in the equation. The cross product is parallel to the normal vector.

**28.** Point: $(1, 0, -3)$

$\mathbf{n} = \mathbf{k} = \langle 0, 0, 1 \rangle$

$0(x - 1) + 0(y - 0) + 1[z - (-3)] = 0$

$z + 3 = 0$

**30.** Point: $(0, 0, 0)$

Normal vector: $\mathbf{n} = -3\mathbf{i} + 2\mathbf{k}$

$-3(x - 0) + 0(y - 0) + 2(z - 0) = 0$

$-3x + 2z = 0$

**32.** Point: $(3, 2, 2)$

Normal vector: $\mathbf{v} = 4\mathbf{i} + \mathbf{j} - 3\mathbf{k}$

$4(x - 3) + (y - 2) - 3(z - 2) = 0$

$4x + y - 3z = 8$

**34.** Let $\mathbf{u}$ be vector from $(2, 3, -2)$ to $(3, 4, 2)$: $\langle 1, 1, 4 \rangle$.

Let $\mathbf{v}$ be vector from $(2, 3, -2)$ to $(1, -1, 0)$: $\langle -1, -4, 2 \rangle$.

Normal vector: $\mathbf{u} \times \mathbf{v} = \begin{vmatrix} \mathbf{i} & \mathbf{j} & \mathbf{k} \\ 1 & 1 & 4 \\ -1 & -4 & 2 \end{vmatrix} = \langle 18, -6, -3 \rangle$

$= -3\langle -6, 2, 1 \rangle$

$-6(x - 2) + 2(y - 3) + 1(z + 2) = 0$

$-6x + 2y + z = -8$

**36.** $(1, 2, 3)$, Normal vector: $\mathbf{v} = \mathbf{i}, 1(x - 1) = 0, x = 1$

**38.** The plane passes through the three points $(0, 0, 0)$, $(0, 1, 0) \left( \sqrt{3}, 0, 1 \right)$.

The vector from $(0, 0, 0)$ to $(0, 1, 0)$: $\mathbf{u} = \mathbf{j}$

The vector from $(0, 0, 0)$ to $\left( \sqrt{3}, 0, 1 \right)$: $\mathbf{v} = \sqrt{3}\mathbf{i} + \mathbf{k}$

Normal vector: $\mathbf{u} \times \mathbf{v} = \begin{vmatrix} \mathbf{i} & \mathbf{j} & \mathbf{k} \\ 0 & 1 & 0 \\ \sqrt{3} & 0 & 1 \end{vmatrix} = \mathbf{i} - \sqrt{3}\mathbf{k}$

$x - \sqrt{3}z = 0$

**40.** The direction of the line is $\mathbf{u} = 2\mathbf{i} - \mathbf{j} + \mathbf{k}$. Choose any point on the line, $[(0, 4, 0)$, for example], and let $\mathbf{v}$ be the vector from $(0, 4, 0)$ to the given point $(2, 2, 1)$:

$\mathbf{v} = 2\mathbf{i} - 2\mathbf{j} + \mathbf{k}$

Normal vector: $\mathbf{u} \times \mathbf{v} = \begin{vmatrix} \mathbf{i} & \mathbf{j} & \mathbf{k} \\ 2 & -1 & 1 \\ 2 & -2 & 1 \end{vmatrix} = \mathbf{i} - 2\mathbf{k}$

$(x - 2) - 2(z - 1) = 0$

$x - 2z = 0$

**42.** Let $\mathbf{v}$ be the vector from $(3, 2, 1)$ to $(3, 1, -5)$:

$\mathbf{v} = -\mathbf{j} - 6\mathbf{k}$

Let $\mathbf{n}$ be the normal to the given plane: $\mathbf{n} = 6\mathbf{i} + 7\mathbf{j} + 2\mathbf{k}$

Since $\mathbf{v}$ and $\mathbf{n}$ both lie in the plane $P$, the normal vector to $P$ is:

$\mathbf{v} \times \mathbf{n} = \begin{vmatrix} \mathbf{i} & \mathbf{j} & \mathbf{k} \\ 0 & -1 & -6 \\ 6 & 7 & 2 \end{vmatrix} = 40\mathbf{i} - 36\mathbf{j} + 6\mathbf{k}$

$= 2(20\mathbf{i} - 18\mathbf{j} + 3\mathbf{k})$

$20(x - 3) - 18(y - 2) + 3(z - 1) = 0$

$20x - 18y + 3z = 27$

**44.** Let $\mathbf{u} = \mathbf{k}$ and let $\mathbf{v}$ be the vector from $(4, 2, 1)$ to $(-3, 5, 7)$: $\mathbf{v} = -7\mathbf{i} + 3\mathbf{j} + 6\mathbf{k}$

Since $\mathbf{u}$ and $\mathbf{v}$ both lie in the plane $P$, the normal vector to $P$ is:

$\mathbf{u} \times \mathbf{v} = \begin{vmatrix} \mathbf{i} & \mathbf{j} & \mathbf{k} \\ 0 & 0 & 1 \\ -7 & 3 & 6 \end{vmatrix} = -3\mathbf{i} - 7\mathbf{j} = -(3\mathbf{i} + 7\mathbf{j})$

$3(x - 4) + 7(y - 2) = 0$

$3x + 7y = 26$

**46.** The normal vectors to the planes are $\mathbf{n}_1 = \langle 3, 1, -4 \rangle$, $\mathbf{n}_2 = \langle -9, -3, 12 \rangle$. Since $\mathbf{n}_2 = -3\mathbf{n}_1$, the planes are parallel, but not equal

**48.** The normal vectors to the planes are

$$\mathbf{n}_1 = 3\mathbf{i} + 2\mathbf{j} - \mathbf{k}, \ \ \mathbf{n}_2 = \mathbf{i} - 4\mathbf{j} + 2\mathbf{k},$$

$$\cos \theta = \frac{|\mathbf{n}_1 \cdot \mathbf{n}_2|}{\|\mathbf{n}_1\| \, \|\mathbf{n}_2\|} = \frac{|3 - 8 - 2|}{\sqrt{14}\sqrt{21}} = \frac{1}{\sqrt{6}}.$$

Therefore, $\theta = \arccos\left(\dfrac{1}{\sqrt{6}}\right) \approx 65.9°$.

**50.** The normal vectors to the planes are

$$\mathbf{n}_1 = \langle 2, 0, -1 \rangle, \ \mathbf{n}_2 = \langle 4, 1, 8 \rangle,$$

$$\cos \theta = \frac{|\mathbf{n}_1 \cdot \mathbf{n}_2|}{\|\mathbf{n}_1\| \, \|\mathbf{n}_2\|} = 0.$$

Thus, $\theta = \dfrac{\pi}{2}$ and the planes are orthogonal.

**52.** $3x + 6y + 2z = 6$

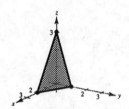

**54.** $2x - y + z = 4$

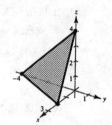

**56.** $x + 2y = 4$

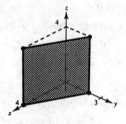

**58.** $z = 8$

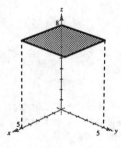

**60.** $x - 3z = 3$

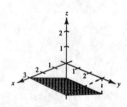

*Generated by Mathematica*

**62.** $2.1x - 4.7y - z + 3 = 0$

*Generated by Mathematica*

**64.** $P_1$: $\mathbf{n} = \langle -60, 90, 30 \rangle$ or $\langle -2, 3, 1 \rangle$    $\left(0, 0, \frac{9}{10}\right)$ on plane

$P_2$: $\mathbf{n} = \langle 6, -9, -3 \rangle$ or $\langle -2, 3, 1 \rangle$    $\left(0, 0, -\frac{2}{3}\right)$ on plane

$P_3$: $\mathbf{n} = \langle -20, 30, 10 \rangle$ or $\langle -2, 3, 1 \rangle$    $\left(0, 0, \frac{5}{6}\right)$ on plane

$P_4$: $\mathbf{n} = \langle 12, -18, 6 \rangle$ or $\langle -2, 3, -1 \rangle$

$P_1, P_2,$ and $P_3$ are parallel.

**66.** If $c = 0$, $z = 0$ is $xy$-plane.

If $c \neq 0$, $cy + z = 0 \implies y = \dfrac{-1}{c}z$ is a plane parallel to $x$-axis and passing through the points $(0, 0, 0)$ and $(0, 1, -c)$.

**68.** The normals to the planes are $\mathbf{n}_1 = \langle 6, -3, 1 \rangle$. and $\mathbf{n}_2 = \langle -1, 1, 5 \rangle$.

The direction vector for the line is

$$\mathbf{n}_1 \times \mathbf{n}_2 = \begin{vmatrix} \mathbf{i} & \mathbf{j} & \mathbf{k} \\ 6 & -3 & 1 \\ -1 & 1 & 5 \end{vmatrix} = \langle -16, -31, 3 \rangle.$$

Now find a point of intersection of the planes.

$$\begin{array}{rcl} 6x - 3y + z = 5 & \implies & 6x - 3y + z = 5 \\ -x + y + 5z = 5 & \implies & \underline{-6x + 6y + 30z = 30} \\ & & 3y + 31z = 35 \end{array}$$

Let $y = -9, z = 2 \implies x = -4 \implies (-4, -9, 2)$.

$x = -4 - 16t, y = -9 - 31t, z = 2 + 3t$

**70.** Writing the equation of the line in parametric form and substituting into the equation of the plane we have:

$$x = 1 + 4t, \ y = 2t, \ z = 3 + 6t$$

$$2(1 + 4t) + 3(2t) = -5, t = \frac{-1}{2}$$

Substituting $t = -\frac{1}{2}$ into the parametric equations for the line we have the point of intersection $(-1, -1, 0)$. The line does not lie in the plane.

**72.** Writing the equation of the line in parametric form and substituting into the equation of the plane we have:

$$x = 4 + 2t, \ y = -1 - 3t, \ z = -2 + 5t$$

$$5(4 + 2t) + 3(-1 - 3t) = 17, t = 0$$

Substituting $t = 0$ into the parametric equations for the line we have the point of intersection $(4, -1, -2)$. The line does not lie in the plane.

**74.** Point: $Q(0, 0, 0)$

Plane: $8x - 4y + z = 8$

Normal to plane: $\mathbf{n} = \langle 8, -4, 1 \rangle$

Point in plane: $P\langle 1, 0, 0 \rangle$

Vector: $\overrightarrow{PQ} = \langle -1, 0, 0 \rangle$

$$D = \frac{|\overrightarrow{PQ} \cdot \mathbf{n}|}{\|\mathbf{n}\|} = \frac{|-8|}{\sqrt{81}} = \frac{8}{9}$$

**76.** Point: $Q(3, 2, 1)$

Plane: $x - y + 2z = 4$

Normal to plane: $\mathbf{n} = \langle 1, -1, 2 \rangle$

Point in plane: $P\langle 4, 0, 0 \rangle$

Vector: $\overrightarrow{PQ} = \langle -1, 2, 1 \rangle$

$$D = \frac{|\overrightarrow{PQ} \cdot \mathbf{n}|}{\|\mathbf{n}\|} = \frac{|-1|}{\sqrt{6}} = \frac{1}{\sqrt{6}} = \frac{\sqrt{6}}{6}$$

**78.** The normal vectors to the planes are $\mathbf{n}_1 = \langle 4, -4, 9 \rangle$ and $\mathbf{n}_2 = \langle 4, -4, 9 \rangle$. Since $\mathbf{n}_1 = \mathbf{n}_2$, the planes are parallel. Choose a point in each plane.

$P = (-5, 0, 3)$ is a point in $4x - 4y + 9z = 7$.

$Q = (0, 0, 2)$ is a point in $4x - 4y + 9z = 18$.

$\overrightarrow{PQ} = \langle 5, 0, -1 \rangle$

$$D = \frac{|\overrightarrow{PQ} \cdot \mathbf{n}_1|}{\|\mathbf{n}_1\|} = \frac{11}{\sqrt{113}} = \frac{11\sqrt{113}}{113}$$

**80.** The normal vectors to the planes are $\mathbf{n}_1 = \langle 2, 0, -4 \rangle$ and $\mathbf{n}_2 = \langle 2, 0, -4 \rangle$. Since $\mathbf{n}_1 = \mathbf{n}_2$, the planes are parallel. Choose a point in each plane.

$P = (2, 0, 0)$ is a point in $2x - 4z = 4$. $Q = (5, 0, 0)$ is a point in $2x - 4z = 10$.

$$\overrightarrow{PQ} = \langle 3, 0, 0 \rangle, D = \frac{|\overrightarrow{PQ} \cdot \mathbf{n}_1|}{\|\mathbf{n}_1\|} = \frac{6}{\sqrt{20}} = \frac{3\sqrt{5}}{5}$$

**82.** $\mathbf{u} = \langle 2, 1, 2 \rangle$ is the direction vector for the line.

$P = \langle 0, -3, 2 \rangle$ is a point on the line (let $t = 0$).

$\overrightarrow{PQ} = \langle 1, 1, 2 \rangle$

$$\overrightarrow{PQ} \times \mathbf{u} = \begin{vmatrix} \mathbf{i} & \mathbf{j} & \mathbf{k} \\ 1 & 1 & 2 \\ 2 & 1 & 2 \end{vmatrix} = \langle 0, 2, -1 \rangle$$

$$D = \frac{\|\overrightarrow{PQ} \times \mathbf{u}\|}{\|\mathbf{u}\|} = \frac{\sqrt{5}}{\sqrt{9}} = \frac{\sqrt{5}}{3}$$

**84.** The equation of the plane containing $P(x_1, y_1, z_1)$ and having normal vector $\mathbf{n} = \langle a, b, c \rangle$ is

$$a(x - x_1) + b(y - y_1) + c(z - z_1) = 0.$$

You need $\mathbf{n}$ and $P$ to find the equation.

**86.** $x = a$: plane parallel to $yz$-plane containing $(a, 0, 0)$

$y = b$: plane parallel to $xz$-plane containing $(0, b, 0)$

$z = c$: plane parallel to $xy$-plane containing $(0, 0, c)$

**88.** (a) $t\mathbf{v}$ represents a line parallel to $\mathbf{v}$.

(b) $\mathbf{u} + t\mathbf{v}$ represents a line through the terminal point of $\mathbf{u}$ parallel to $\mathbf{v}$.

(c) $s\mathbf{u} + t\mathbf{v}$ represent the plane containing $\mathbf{u}$ and $\mathbf{v}$.

**90.** On one side we have the points $(0, 0, 0)$, $(6, 0, 0)$, and $(-1, -1, 8)$.

$$\mathbf{n}_1 = \begin{vmatrix} \mathbf{i} & \mathbf{j} & \mathbf{k} \\ 6 & 0 & 0 \\ -1 & -1 & 8 \end{vmatrix} = -48\mathbf{j} - 6\mathbf{k}$$

On the adjacent side we have the points $(0, 0, 0)$, $(0, 6, 0)$, and $(-1, -1, 8)$.

$$\mathbf{n}_2 = \begin{vmatrix} \mathbf{i} & \mathbf{j} & \mathbf{k} \\ 0 & 6 & 0 \\ -1 & -1 & 8 \end{vmatrix} = 48\mathbf{i} + 6\mathbf{k}$$

$$\cos\theta = \frac{|\mathbf{n}_1 \cdot \mathbf{n}_2|}{\|\mathbf{n}_1\| \, \|\mathbf{n}_2\|} = \frac{36}{2340} = \frac{1}{65}$$

$$\theta = \arccos\frac{1}{65} \approx 89.1°$$

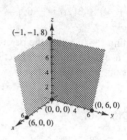

**92.** False. They may be skew lines. (See Section Project)

# Section 10.6    Surfaces in Space

**2.** Hyperboloid of two sheets

Matches graph (e)

**4.** Elliptic cone

Matches graph (b)

**6.** Hyperbolic paraboloid

Matches graph (a)

**8.** $x = 4$

Plane parallel to the
$yz$-coordinate plane

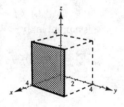

**10.** $x^2 + z^2 = 25$

The $y$-coordinate is missing so we have a cylindrical surface with rulings parallel to the $y$-axis. The generating curve is a circle.

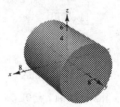

**12.** $z = 4 - y^2$

The $x$-coordinate is missing so we have a cylindrical surface with rulings parallel to the $x$-axis. The generating curve is a parabola.

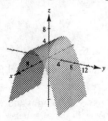

**14.** $y^2 - z^2 = 4$

$$\frac{y^2}{4} - \frac{z^2}{4} = 1$$

The $x$-coordinate is missing so we have a cylindrical surface with rulings parallel to the $x$-axis. The generating curve is a hyperbola.

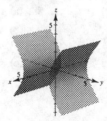

**16.** $z = e^y$

The $x$-coordinate is missing so we have a cylindrical surface with rulings parallel to the $x$-axis. The generating curve is the exponential curve.

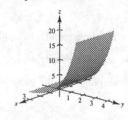

**18.** $y^2 + z^2 = 4$

    (a) From (10, 0, 0):              (b) From (0, 10, 0):              (c) From (10, 10, 10):

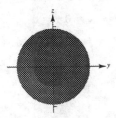 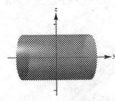 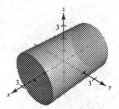

**20.** $\dfrac{x^2}{16} + \dfrac{y^2}{25} + \dfrac{z^2}{25} = 1$

Ellipsoid

$xy$-trace: $\dfrac{x^2}{16} + \dfrac{y^2}{25} = 1$ ellipse

$xz$-trace: $\dfrac{x^2}{16} + \dfrac{z^2}{25} = 1$ ellipse

$yz$-trace: $y^2 + z^2 = 25$ circle

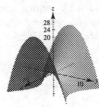

**22.** $z^2 - x^2 - \dfrac{y^2}{4} = 1$

Hyperboloid of two sheets

$xy$-trace:  none

$xz$-trace: $z^2 - x^2 = 1$ hyperbola

$yz$-trace: $z^2 - \dfrac{y^2}{4} = 1$ hyperbola

$z = \pm\sqrt{10}$: $\dfrac{x^2}{9} + \dfrac{y^2}{36} = 1$ ellipse

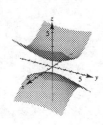

**24.** $z = x^2 + 4y^2$

Elliptic paraboloid

$xy$-trace:  point $(0, 0, 0)$

$xz$-trace: $z = x^2$ parabola

$yz$-trace: $z = 4y^2$ parabola

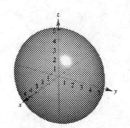

**26.** $3z = -y^2 + x^2$

Hyperbolic paraboloid

$xy$-trace: $y = \pm x$

$xz$-trace: $z = \frac{1}{3}x^2$

$yz$-trace: $z = -\frac{1}{3}y^2$

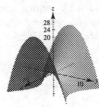

**28.** $x^2 = 2y^2 + 2z^2$

Elliptic Cone

$xy$-trace: $x = \pm\sqrt{2}\,y$

$xz$-trace: $x = \pm\sqrt{2}\,z$

$yz$-trace:  point: $(0, 0, 0)$

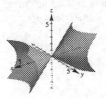

**30.**
$$9x^2 + y^2 - 9z^2 - 54x - 4y - 54z + 4 = 0$$
$$9(x^2 - 6x + 9) + (y^2 - 4y + 4) - 9(z^2 + 6z + 9) = 81 + 4 - 81$$
$$9(x - 3)^2 + (y - 2)^2 - 9(z + 3)^2 = 4$$
$$\frac{(x - 3)^2}{4/9} + \frac{(y - 2)^2}{4} - \frac{(z + 3)^2}{4/9} = 1$$

Hyperboloid of one sheet with center $(3, 2, -3)$.

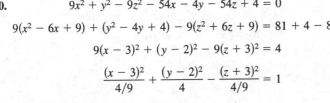

**32.** $z = x^2 + 0.5y^2$

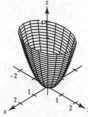

**34.** $z^2 = 4y - x^2$

    $z = \pm\sqrt{4y - x^2}$

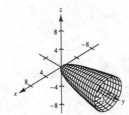

**36.** $x^2 + y^2 = e^{-z}$

    $-\ln(x^2 + y^2) = z$

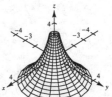

**38.** $z = \dfrac{-x}{8 + x^2 + y^2}$

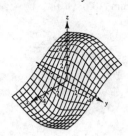

**40.** $9x^2 + 4y^2 - 8z^2 = 72$

$$z = \pm \sqrt{\dfrac{9}{8}x^2 + \dfrac{1}{2}y^2 - 9}$$

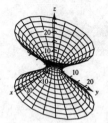

**42.** $z = \sqrt{4 - x^2}$

$y = \sqrt{4 - x^2}$

$x = 0, y = 0, z = 0$

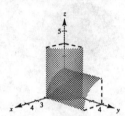

**44.** $z = \sqrt{4 - x^2 - y^2}$

$y = 2z$

$z = 0$

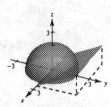

**46.** $x^2 + z^2 = [r(y)]^2$ and $z = r(y) = 3y$; therefore,

$x^2 + z^2 = 9y^2$.

**48.** $y^2 + z^2 = [r(x)]^2$ and $z = r(x) = \dfrac{1}{2}\sqrt{4 - x^2}$; therefore,

$y^2 + z^2 = \dfrac{1}{4}(4 - x^2), \; x^2 + 4y^2 + 4z^2 = 4.$

**50.** $x^2 + y^2 = [r(z)]^2$ and $y = r(z) = e^z$; therefore,

$x^2 + y^2 = e^{2z}.$

**52.** $x^2 + z^2 = \cos^2 y$

Equation of generating curve:
$x = \cos y$ or $z = \cos y$

**54.** The trace of a surface is the inter-section of the surface with a plane. You find a trace by setting one variable equal to a constant, such as $x = 0$ or $z = 2$.

**56.** About $x$-axis: $y^2 + z^2 = [r(x)]^2$

About $y$-axis: $x^2 + z^2 = [r(y)]^2$

About $z$-axis: $x^2 + y^2 = [r(z)]^2$

**58.** $V = 2\pi \displaystyle\int_0^\pi y \sin y \, dy$

$\quad = 2\pi \Big[ \sin y - y \cos y \Big]_0^\pi = 2\pi^2$

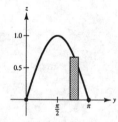

**60.** $z = \dfrac{x^2}{2} + \dfrac{y^2}{4}$

(a) When $y = 4$ we have $z = \dfrac{x^2}{2} + 4, \, 4\left(\dfrac{1}{2}\right)(z - 4) = x^2.$

Focus: $\left(0, 4, \dfrac{9}{2}\right)$

(b) When $x = 2$ we have

$z = 2 + \dfrac{y^2}{4}, \, 4(z - 2) = y^2.$

Focus: $(2, 0, 3)$

**62.** If $(x, y, z)$ is on the surface, then

$z^2 = x^2 + y^2 + (z - 4)^2$

$z^2 = x^2 + y^2 + z^2 - 8z + 16$

$8z = x^2 + y^2 + 16 \Longrightarrow z = \dfrac{x^2}{8} + \dfrac{y^2}{8} + 2$

Elliptic paraboloid shifted up 2 units. Traces parallel to $xy$-plane are circles.

**64.** $z = -0.775x^2 + 0.007y^2 + 22.15x - 0.54y - 45.4$

(a)

| Year | 1980 | 1985 | 1990 | 1995 | 1996 | 1997 |
|-------|------|------|-------|-------|-------|-------|
| $z$ | 37.5 | 72.2 | 111.5 | 185.2 | 200.1 | 214.6 |
| Model | 37.8 | 72.0 | 112.2 | 185.8 | 204.5 | 214.7 |

(b)

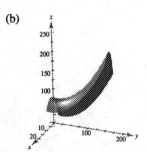

(c) For $y$ constant, the traces parallel to the $xz$-plane are concave downward. That is, for fixed $y$ (public assistance), the rate of increase of $z$ (Medicare) is decreasing with respect to $x$ (worker's compensation).

(d) The traces parallel to the $yz$-plane ($x$ constant) are concave upward. That is, for fixed $x$ (worker's compensation), the rate of increase of $z$ (Medicare) is increasing with respect to $y$ (public assistance).

**66.** Equating twice the first equation with the second equation,

$$2x^2 + 6y^2 - 4z^2 + 4y - 8 = 2x^2 + 6y^2 - 4z^2 - 3x - 2$$

$$4y - 8 = -3x - 2$$

$$3x + 4y = 6, \text{ a plane}$$

# Section 10.7   Cylindrical and Spherical Coordinates

**2.** $\left(4, \dfrac{\pi}{2}, -2\right)$, cylindrical

$x = 4\cos\dfrac{\pi}{2} = 0$

$y = 4\sin\dfrac{\pi}{2} = 4$

$z = -2$

$(0, 4, -2)$, rectangular

**4.** $\left(6, -\dfrac{\pi}{4}, 2\right)$, cylindrical

$x = 6\cos\left(-\dfrac{\pi}{4}\right) = 3\sqrt{2}$

$y = 6\sin\left(-\dfrac{\pi}{4}\right) = -3\sqrt{2}$

$z = 2$

$\left(3\sqrt{2}, -3\sqrt{2}, 2\right)$

**6.** $\left(1, \dfrac{3\pi}{2}, 1\right)$, cylindrical

$x = \cos\dfrac{3\pi}{2} = 0$

$y = \sin\dfrac{3\pi}{2} = -1$

$z = 1$

$(0, -1, 1)$, rectangular

**8.** $\left(2\sqrt{2}, -2\sqrt{2}, 4\right)$, rectangular

$r = \sqrt{\left(2\sqrt{2}\right)^2 + \left(-2\sqrt{2}\right)^2} = 4$

$\theta = \arctan(-1) = -\dfrac{\pi}{4}$

$z = 4$

$\left(4, -\dfrac{\pi}{4}, 4\right)$, cylindrical

**10.** $\left(2\sqrt{3}, -2, 6\right)$, rectangular

$r = \sqrt{12 + 4} = 4$

$\theta = \arctan\left(-\dfrac{1}{\sqrt{3}}\right) = \dfrac{5\pi}{6}$

$z = 1$

$\left(4, -\dfrac{\pi}{6}, 1\right)$, cylindrical

**12.** $(-3, 2, -1)$, rectangular

$r = \sqrt{(-3)^2 + 2^2} = \sqrt{13}$

$\theta = \arctan\left(\dfrac{-2}{3}\right) = -\arctan\dfrac{2}{3}$

$z = -1$

$\left(\sqrt{13}, -\arctan\dfrac{2}{3}, -1\right)$, cylindrical

**14.** $z = x^2 + y^2 - 2$   rectangular equation

$z = r^2 - 2$      cylindrical equation

**16.** $x^2 + y^2 = 8x$      rectangular equation

$r^2 = 8r\cos\theta$

$r = 8\cos\theta$   cylindrical equation

**18.** $z = 2$

Same

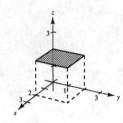

**20.** $r = \dfrac{z}{2}$

$$\sqrt{x^2 + y^2} = \dfrac{z}{2}$$

$$x^2 + y^2 - \dfrac{z^2}{4} = 0$$

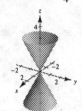

**22.** $r = 2 \cos \theta$

$$r^2 = 2r \cos \theta$$

$$x^2 + y^2 = 2x$$

$$x^2 + y^2 - 2x = 0$$

$$(x - 1)^2 + y^2 = 1$$

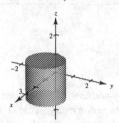

**24.** $z = r^2 \cos^2 \theta$

$z = x^2$

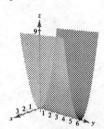

**26.** $(1, 1, 1)$, rectangular

$$\rho = \sqrt{1^2 + 1^2 + 1^2} = \sqrt{3}$$

$$\theta = \arctan 1 = \dfrac{\pi}{4}$$

$$\phi = \arccos \dfrac{1}{\sqrt{3}}$$

$$\left( \sqrt{3}, \dfrac{\pi}{4}, \arccos \dfrac{1}{\sqrt{3}} \right), \text{ spherical}$$

**28.** $\left( 2, 2, 4\sqrt{2} \right)$, rectangular

$$\rho = \sqrt{2^2 + 2^2 + \left( 4\sqrt{2} \right)^2} = 2\sqrt{10}$$

$$\theta = \arctan 1 = \dfrac{\pi}{4}$$

$$\phi = \arccos \dfrac{2}{\sqrt{5}}$$

$$\left( 2\sqrt{10}, \dfrac{\pi}{4}, \arccos \dfrac{2}{\sqrt{5}} \right), \text{ spherical}$$

**30.** $(-4, 0, 0)$, rectangular

$$\rho = \sqrt{(-4)^2 + 0^2 + 0^2} = 4$$

$$\theta = \pi$$

$$\phi = \arccos 0 = \dfrac{\pi}{2}$$

$$\left( 4, \pi, \dfrac{\pi}{2} \right), \text{ spherical}$$

**32.** $\left( 12, \dfrac{3\pi}{4}, \dfrac{\pi}{9} \right)$, spherical

$$x = 12 \sin \dfrac{\pi}{9} \cos \dfrac{3\pi}{4} \approx -2.902$$

$$y = 12 \sin \dfrac{\pi}{9} \sin \dfrac{3\pi}{4} \approx 2.902$$

$$z = 12 \cos \dfrac{\pi}{9} \approx 11.276$$

$(-2.902, 2.902, 11.276)$, rectangular

**34.** $\left( 9, \dfrac{\pi}{4}, \pi \right)$, spherical

$$x = 9 \sin \pi \cos \dfrac{\pi}{4} = 0$$

$$y = 9 \sin \pi \sin \dfrac{\pi}{4} = 0$$

$$z = 9 \cos \pi = -9$$

$(0, 0, -9)$, rectangular

**36.** $\left( 6, \pi, \dfrac{\pi}{2} \right)$, spherical

$$x = 6 \sin \dfrac{\pi}{2} \cos \pi = -6$$

$$y = 6 \sin \dfrac{\pi}{2} \sin \pi = 0$$

$$z = 6 \cos \dfrac{\pi}{2} = 0$$

$(-6, 0, 0)$, rectangular

**38.** (a) Programs will vary.

(b) $(\rho, \theta, \phi) = (5, 1, 0.5)$

$(x, y, z) = (1.295, 2.017, 4.388)$

**40.** $x^2 + y^2 - 3z^2 = 0$     rectangular equation

$x^2 + y^2 + z^2 = 4z^2$

$\rho^2 = 4\rho^2 \cos^2 \phi$

$1 = 4 \cos^2 \phi$

$\cos \phi = \dfrac{1}{2}$

$\phi = \dfrac{\pi}{3}$     (cone) spherical equation

**42.** $x = 10$     rectangular equation

$\rho \sin \phi \cos \theta = 10$

$\rho = 10 \csc \phi \sec \theta$  spherical equation

**44.** $\theta = \dfrac{3\pi}{4}$

$\tan \theta = \dfrac{y}{x}$

$-1 = \dfrac{y}{x}$

$x + y = 0$

**46.** $\phi = \dfrac{\pi}{2}$

$\cos \phi = \dfrac{z}{\sqrt{x^2 + y^2 + z^2}}$

$0 = \dfrac{z}{\sqrt{x^2 + y^2 + z^2}}$

$z = 0$

$xy$-plane

**48.** $\rho = 2 \sec \phi$

$\rho \cos \phi = 2$

$z = 2$

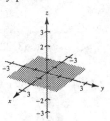

**50.** $\rho = 4 \csc \phi \sec \phi$

$= \dfrac{4}{\sin \phi \cos \theta}$

$\rho \sin \phi \cos \theta = 4$

$x = 4$

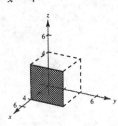

**52.** $\left(3, -\dfrac{\pi}{4}, 0\right)$, cylindrical

$\rho = \sqrt{3^2 + 0^2} = 3$

$\theta = -\dfrac{\pi}{4}$

$\phi = \arccos\left(\dfrac{0}{9}\right) = \dfrac{\pi}{2}$

$\left(3, -\dfrac{\pi}{4}, \dfrac{\pi}{2}\right)$, spherical

**54.** $\left(2, \dfrac{2\pi}{3}, -2\right)$, cylindrical

$\rho = \sqrt{2^2 + (-2)^2} = 2\sqrt{2}$

$\theta = \dfrac{2\pi}{3}$

$\phi = \arccos\left(\dfrac{-1}{\sqrt{2}}\right) = \dfrac{3\pi}{4}$

$\left(2\sqrt{2}, \dfrac{2\pi}{3}, \dfrac{3\pi}{4}\right)$, spherical

**56.** $\left(-4, \dfrac{\pi}{3}, 4\right)$, cylindrical

$\rho = \sqrt{(-4)^2 + 4^2} = 4\sqrt{2}$

$\theta = \dfrac{\pi}{3}$

$\phi = \arccos \dfrac{1}{\sqrt{2}} = \dfrac{\pi}{4}$

$\left(4\sqrt{2}, \dfrac{\pi}{3}, \dfrac{\pi}{4}\right)$, spherical

**58.** $\left(4, \dfrac{\pi}{2}, 3\right)$, cylindrical

$\rho = \sqrt{4^2 + 3^2} = 5$

$\theta = \dfrac{\pi}{2}$

$\phi = \arccos \dfrac{3}{5}$

$\left(5, \dfrac{\pi}{2}, \arccos \dfrac{3}{5}\right)$, spherical

**60.** $\left(4, \dfrac{\pi}{18}, \dfrac{\pi}{2}\right)$, spherical

$r = 4 \sin \dfrac{\pi}{2} = 4$

$\theta = \dfrac{\pi}{18}$

$z = 4 \cos \dfrac{\pi}{2} = 0$

$\left(4, \dfrac{\pi}{18}, 0\right)$, cylindrical

**62.** $\left(18, \dfrac{\pi}{3}, \dfrac{\pi}{3}\right)$, spherical

$r = \rho \sin \phi = 18 \sin \dfrac{\pi}{3} = 9$

$\theta = \dfrac{\pi}{3}$

$z = \rho \cos \phi = 18 \cos \dfrac{\pi}{3} = 9\sqrt{3}$

$\left(9, \dfrac{\pi}{3}, 9\sqrt{3}\right)$, cylindrical

**64.** $\left(5, -\dfrac{5\pi}{6}, \pi\right)$, spherical

$r = 5 \sin \pi = 0$

$\theta = -\dfrac{5\pi}{6}$

$z = 5 \cos \pi = -5$

$\left(0, -\dfrac{5\pi}{6}, -5\right)$, cylindrical

**66.** $\left(7, \dfrac{\pi}{4}, \dfrac{3\pi}{4}\right)$, spherical

$r = 7 \sin \dfrac{3\pi}{4} = \dfrac{7\sqrt{2}}{2}$

$\theta = \dfrac{\pi}{4}$

$z = 7 \cos \dfrac{3\pi}{4} = -\dfrac{7\sqrt{2}}{2}$

$\left(\dfrac{7\sqrt{2}}{2}, \dfrac{\pi}{4}, -\dfrac{7\sqrt{2}}{2}\right)$, cylindrical

| *Rectangular* | *Cylindrical* | *Spherical* |
|---|---|---|
| **68.** $(6, -2, -3)$ | $(6.325, -0.322, -3)$ | $(7.000, -0.322, 2.014)$ |
| **70.** $(7.317, -6.816, 6)$ | $(10, -0.75, 6)$ | $(11.662, -0.750, 1.030)$ |
| **72.** $(6.115, 1.561, 4.052)$ | $(6.311, 0.25, 4.052)$ | $(7.5, 0.25, 1)$ |
| **74.** $\left(3\sqrt{2}, 3\sqrt{2}, -3\right)$ | $(6, 0.785, -3)$ | $(6.708, 0.785, 2.034)$ |
| **76.** $(0, -5, 4)$ | $(5, -1.571, 4)$ | $(6.403, -1.571, 0.896)$ |
| **78.** $(-1.732, 1, 3)$ | $\left(-2, \dfrac{11\pi}{6}, 3\right)$ | $(3.606, 2.618, 0.588)$ |

$\left[\text{Note: Use the cylindrical coordinate } \left(2, \dfrac{5\pi}{6}, 3\right)\right]$

| | | |
|---|---|---|
| **80.** $(2.207, 7.949, -4)$ | $(8.25, 1.3, -4)$ | $(9.169, 1.3, 2.022)$ |

**82.** $\theta = \dfrac{\pi}{4}$

Plane

Matches graph (e)

**84.** $\phi = \dfrac{\pi}{4}$

Cone

Matches graph (a)

**86.** $\rho = 4 \sec \phi, z = \rho \cos \phi = 4$

Plane

Matches graph (b)

**88.** $r = a$   Cylinder with $z$-axis symmetry

$\theta = b$   Plane perpendicular to $xy$-plane

$z = c$   Plane parallel to $xy$-plane

**90.** $\rho = a$   Sphere

$\theta = b$   Vertical half-plane

$\phi = c$   Half-cone

**92.** $4(x^2 + y^2) = z^2$

(a) $4r^2 = z^2, 2r = z$

(b) $4(\rho^2 \sin^2 \phi \cos^2 \theta + \rho^2 \sin^2 \phi \sin^2 \theta) = \rho^2 \cos^2 \phi,$

     $4 \sin^2 \phi = \cos^2 \phi, \tan^2 \phi = \dfrac{1}{4},$

     $\tan \phi = \dfrac{1}{2}, \phi = \arctan \dfrac{1}{2}$

**94.** $x^2 + y^2 = z$

(a) $r^2 = z$

(b) $\rho^2 \sin^2 \phi = \rho \cos \phi, \rho \sin^2 \phi = \cos \phi,$

     $\rho = \dfrac{\cos \phi}{\sin^2 \phi}, \rho = \csc \phi \cot \phi$

**96.** $x^2 + y^2 = 16$

(a) $r^2 = 16, r = 4$

(b) $\rho^2 \sin^2 \phi = 16, \rho^2 \sin^2 \phi - 16 = 0,$

     $(\rho \sin \phi - 4)(\rho \sin \phi + 4) = 0, \rho = 4 \csc \phi$

**98.** $y = 4$

(a) $r \sin \theta = 4, r = 4 \csc \theta$

(b) $\rho \sin \phi \sin \theta = 4, \rho = 4 \csc \phi \csc \theta$

**100.** $-\dfrac{\pi}{2} \le \theta \le \dfrac{\pi}{2}$

$0 \le r \le 3$

$0 \le z \le r \cos \theta$

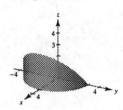

**102.** $0 \le \theta \le 2\pi$

$2 \le r \le 4$

$z^2 \le -r^2 + 6r - 8$

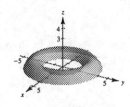

**104.** $0 \le \theta \le 2\pi$

$\dfrac{\pi}{4} \le \phi \le \dfrac{\pi}{2}$

$0 \le \rho \le 1$

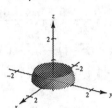

**106.** Cylindrical: $0.75 \le r \le 1.25$, $z = 8$

**108.** Cylindrical

$\dfrac{1}{2} \le r \le 3$

$0 \le \theta \le 2\pi$

$-\sqrt{9 - r^2} \le z \le \sqrt{9 - r^2}$

**110.** $\rho = 2 \sec \phi \implies \rho \cos \phi = 2 \implies z = 2$ plane

$\rho = 4$ sphere

The intersection of the plane and the sphere is a circle.

# Review Exercises for Chapter 10

**2.** $P = (-2, -1)$, $Q = (5, -1)$ $R = (2, 4)$

(a) $\mathbf{u} = \overrightarrow{PQ} = \langle 7, 0 \rangle = 7\mathbf{i}$, $\mathbf{v} = \overrightarrow{PR} = \langle 4, 5 \rangle = 4\mathbf{i} + 5\mathbf{j}$

(b) $\|\mathbf{v}\| = \sqrt{4^2 + 5^2} = \sqrt{41}$

(c) $2\mathbf{u} + \mathbf{v} = 14\mathbf{i} + (4\mathbf{i} + 5\mathbf{j}) = 18\mathbf{i} + 5\mathbf{j}$

**4.** $\mathbf{v} = \|\mathbf{v}\| \cos \theta\, \mathbf{i} + \|\mathbf{v}\| \sin \theta\, \mathbf{j} = \dfrac{1}{2} \cos 225°\, \mathbf{i} + \dfrac{1}{2} \sin 225°\, \mathbf{j}$

$= -\dfrac{\sqrt{2}}{4}\mathbf{i} + \dfrac{\sqrt{2}}{4}\mathbf{j}$

**6.** (a) The length of cable *POQ* is *L*.

$\overrightarrow{OQ} = 9\mathbf{i} - y\mathbf{j}$

$L = 2\sqrt{9^2 + y^2} \implies \sqrt{\dfrac{L^2}{4} - 81} = y$

Tension: $T = c\|\overrightarrow{OQ}\| = c\sqrt{81 + y^2}$

Also,

$cy = 250 \implies T = \dfrac{250}{y}\sqrt{81 + y^2} \implies T = \dfrac{250}{\sqrt{(L^2/4) - 81}} \cdot \dfrac{L}{2} = \dfrac{250L}{\sqrt{L^2 - 324}}$

Domain: $L > 18$ inches

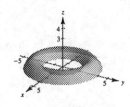

(b)

| L | 19 | 20 | 21 | 22 | 23 | 24 | 25 |
|---|-----|-----|-----|-----|-----|-----|-----|
| T | 780.9 | 573.54 | 485.36 | 434.81 | 401.60 | 377.96 | 360.24 |

(c)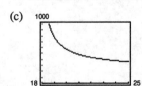

(d) The line $T = 400$ intersects the curve at

$L = 23.06$ inches.

(e) $\lim\limits_{L \to \infty} T = 250$

The maximum tension is 250 pounds in each side of the cable since the total weight is 500 pounds.

**8.** $x = z = 0,\ y = -7$: $(0, -7, 0)$

**10.** Looking towards the $xy$-plane from the positive $z$-axis. The point is either in the second quadrant ($x < 0,\ y > 0$) or in the fourth quadrant ($x > 0,\ y < 0$). The $z$-coordinate can be any number.

**12.** Center: $\left(\dfrac{0+4}{2}, \dfrac{0+6}{2}, \dfrac{4+0}{2}\right) = (2, 3, 2)$

Radius: $\sqrt{(2-0)^2 + (3-0)^2 + (2-4)^2} = \sqrt{4 + 9 + 4} = \sqrt{17}$

$(x - 2)^2 + (y - 3)^2 + (z - 2)^2 = 17$

**14.** $(x^2 - 10x + 25) + (y^2 + 6y + 9) + (z^2 - 4z + 4) = -34 + 25 + 9 + 4$

$(x - 5)^2 + (y + 3)^2 + (z - 2)^2 = 4$

Center: $(5, -3, 2)$

Radius: $2$

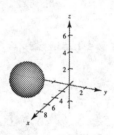

**16.** $\mathbf{v} = \langle 3 - 6, -3 - 2, 8 - 0 \rangle = \langle -3, -5, 8 \rangle$

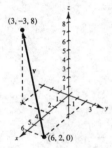

**18.** $\mathbf{v} = \langle 8 - 5, -5 + 4, 5 - 7 \rangle = \langle 3, -1, -2 \rangle$

$\mathbf{w} = \langle 11 - 5, 6 + 4, 3 - 7 \rangle = \langle 6, 10, -4 \rangle$

Since $\mathbf{v}$ and $\mathbf{w}$ are not parallel, the points do not lie in a straight line.

**20.** $8 \dfrac{\langle 6, -3, 2 \rangle}{\sqrt{49}} = \dfrac{8}{7} \langle 6, -3, 2 \rangle = \left\langle \dfrac{48}{7}, -\dfrac{24}{7}, \dfrac{16}{7} \right\rangle$

**22.** $P = (2, -1, 3),\ Q = (0, 5, 1),\ R = (5, 5, 0)$

(a) $\mathbf{u} = \overrightarrow{PQ} = \langle -2, 6, -2 \rangle = -2\mathbf{i} + 6\mathbf{j} - 2\mathbf{k}$,

$\mathbf{v} = \overrightarrow{PR} = \langle 3, 6, -3 \rangle = 3\mathbf{i} + 6\mathbf{j} - 3\mathbf{k}$

(b) $\mathbf{u} \cdot \mathbf{v} = (-2)(3) + (6)(6) + (-2)(-3) = 36$

(c) $\mathbf{v} \cdot \mathbf{v} = 9 + 36 + 9 = 54$

**24.** $\mathbf{u} = \langle -4, 3, -6 \rangle,\ \mathbf{v} = \langle 16, -12, 24 \rangle$

Since $\mathbf{v} = -4\mathbf{u}$, the vectors are parallel.

**26.** $\mathbf{u} = \langle 4, -1, 5 \rangle,\ \mathbf{v} = \langle 3, 2, -2 \rangle$

$\mathbf{u} \cdot \mathbf{v} = 0 \implies$ is orthogonal to $\mathbf{v}$.

$\theta = \dfrac{\pi}{2}$

**28.** $\mathbf{u} = \langle 1, 0, -3 \rangle$

$\mathbf{v} = \langle 2, -2, 1 \rangle$

$\mathbf{u} \cdot \mathbf{v} = -1$

$\|\mathbf{u}\| = \sqrt{10}$

$\|\mathbf{v}\| = 3$

$\cos \theta = \dfrac{|\mathbf{u} \cdot \mathbf{v}|}{\|\mathbf{u}\|\,\|\mathbf{v}\|} = \dfrac{1}{3\sqrt{10}}$

$\theta \approx 83.9°$

**30.** $W = \mathbf{F} \cdot \overrightarrow{PQ} = \|\mathbf{F}\|\,\|\overrightarrow{PQ}\| \cos \theta = (75)(8)\cos 30°$

$= 300\sqrt{3}\ \text{ft} \cdot \text{lb}$

In Exercises 32–40, $\mathbf{u} = \langle 3, -2, 1 \rangle$, $\mathbf{v} = \langle 2, -4, -3 \rangle$, $\mathbf{w} = \langle -1, 2, 2 \rangle$.

**32.** $\cos \theta = \dfrac{|\mathbf{u} \cdot \mathbf{v}|}{\|\mathbf{u}\| \, \|\mathbf{v}\|} = \dfrac{11}{\sqrt{14} \sqrt{29}}$

$\theta = \arccos\left(\dfrac{11}{\sqrt{14} \sqrt{29}}\right) \approx 56.9°$

**34.** Work $= |\mathbf{u} \cdot \mathbf{w}| = |-3 - 4 + 2| = 5$

**36.** $\mathbf{u} \times \mathbf{v} = \begin{vmatrix} \mathbf{i} & \mathbf{j} & \mathbf{k} \\ 3 & -2 & 1 \\ 2 & -4 & -3 \end{vmatrix} = 10\mathbf{i} + 11\mathbf{j} - 8\mathbf{k}$

$\mathbf{v} \times \mathbf{u} = \begin{vmatrix} \mathbf{i} & \mathbf{j} & \mathbf{k} \\ 2 & -4 & -3 \\ 3 & -2 & 1 \end{vmatrix} = -10\mathbf{i} - 11\mathbf{j} + 8\mathbf{k}$

Thus, $\mathbf{u} \times \mathbf{v} = -(\mathbf{v} \times \mathbf{u})$.

**38.** $\mathbf{u} \times (\mathbf{v} + \mathbf{w}) = \langle 3, -2, 1 \rangle \times \langle 1, -2, -1 \rangle = \begin{vmatrix} \mathbf{i} & \mathbf{j} & \mathbf{k} \\ 3 & -2 & 1 \\ 1 & -2 & -1 \end{vmatrix} = 4\mathbf{i} + 4\mathbf{j} - 4\mathbf{k}$

$\mathbf{u} \times \mathbf{v} = \begin{vmatrix} \mathbf{i} & \mathbf{j} & \mathbf{k} \\ 3 & -2 & 1 \\ 2 & -4 & -3 \end{vmatrix} = 10\mathbf{i} + 11\mathbf{j} - 8\mathbf{k}$

$\mathbf{u} \times \mathbf{w} = \begin{vmatrix} \mathbf{i} & \mathbf{j} & \mathbf{k} \\ 3 & -2 & 1 \\ -1 & 2 & 2 \end{vmatrix} = -6\mathbf{i} - 7\mathbf{j} + 4\mathbf{k}$

$(\mathbf{u} \times \mathbf{v}) + (\mathbf{u} \times \mathbf{w}) = 4\mathbf{i} + 4\mathbf{j} - 4\mathbf{k} = \mathbf{u} \times (\mathbf{v} + \mathbf{w})$

**40.** Area triangle $= \dfrac{1}{2} \|\mathbf{v} \times \mathbf{w}\| = \dfrac{1}{2} \sqrt{(-2)^2 + (-1)^2} = \dfrac{\sqrt{5}}{2}$  (See Exercise 35)

**42.** $V = |\mathbf{u} \cdot (\mathbf{v} \times \mathbf{w})| = \begin{vmatrix} 2 & 1 & 0 \\ 0 & 2 & 1 \\ 0 & -1 & 2 \end{vmatrix} = 2(5) = 10$

**44.** Direction numbers: 1, 1, 1

(a) $x = 1 + t$, $y = 2 + t$, $z = 3 + t$

(b) $x - 1 = y - 2 = z - 3$

**46.** $\mathbf{u} \times \mathbf{v} = \begin{vmatrix} \mathbf{i} & \mathbf{j} & \mathbf{k} \\ 2 & -5 & 1 \\ -3 & 1 & 4 \end{vmatrix} = -21\mathbf{i} - 11\mathbf{j} - 13\mathbf{k}$

Direction numbers: 21, 11, 13

(a) $x = 21t$, $y = 1 + 11t$, $z = 4 + 13t$

(b) $\dfrac{x}{21} = \dfrac{y - 1}{11} = \dfrac{z - 4}{13}$

**48.** $P = (-3, -4, 2)$, $Q = (-3, 4, 1)$, $R = (1, 1, -2)$

$\overrightarrow{PQ} = \langle 0, 8, -1 \rangle$, $\overrightarrow{PR} = \langle 4, 5, -4 \rangle$

$\mathbf{n} = \overrightarrow{PQ} \times \overrightarrow{PR} = \begin{vmatrix} \mathbf{i} & \mathbf{j} & \mathbf{k} \\ 0 & 8 & -1 \\ 4 & 5 & -4 \end{vmatrix} = -27\mathbf{i} - 4\mathbf{j} - 32\mathbf{k}$

$-27(x + 3) - 4(y + 4) - 32(z - 2) = 0$

$27x + 4y + 32z = -33$

**50.** The normal vectors to the planes are the same,

$$\mathbf{n} = \langle 5, -3, 1 \rangle.$$

Choose a point in the first plane, $P = (0, 0, 2)$. Choose a point in the second plane, $Q = (0, 0, -3)$.

$$\overrightarrow{PQ} = \langle 0, 0, -5 \rangle$$

$$D = \frac{|\overrightarrow{PQ} \cdot \mathbf{n}|}{\|\mathbf{n}\|} = \frac{|-5|}{\sqrt{35}} = \frac{5}{\sqrt{35}} = \frac{\sqrt{35}}{7}$$

**52.** $Q(-5, 1, 3)$ point

$\mathbf{u} = \langle 1, -2, -1 \rangle$ direction vector

$P = (1, 3, 5)$ point on line

$\overrightarrow{PQ} = \langle -6, -2, -2 \rangle$

$$\overrightarrow{PQ} \times \mathbf{u} = \begin{vmatrix} \mathbf{i} & \mathbf{j} & \mathbf{k} \\ -6 & -2 & -2 \\ 1 & -2 & -1 \end{vmatrix} = \langle -2, -8, 14 \rangle$$

$$D = \frac{\|\overrightarrow{PQ} \times \mathbf{u}\|}{\|\mathbf{u}\|} = \frac{\sqrt{264}}{\sqrt{6}} = 2\sqrt{11}$$

**54.** $y = z^2$

Since the $x$-coordinate is missing, we have a cylindrical surface with rulings parallel to the $x$-axis. The generating curve is a parabola in the $yz$-coordinate plane.

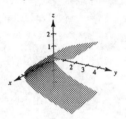

**56.** $y = \cos z$

Since the $x$-coordinate is missing, we have a cylindrical surface with rulings parallel to the $x$-axis. The generating curve is $y = \cos z$.

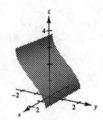

**58.** $16x^2 + 16y^2 - 9z^2 = 0$

Cone

$xy$-trace: point $(0, 0, 0)$

$xz$-trace: $z = \pm \dfrac{4x}{3}$

$yz$-trace: $z = \pm \dfrac{4y}{3}$

$z = 4, \ x^2 + y^2 = 9$

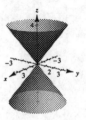

**60.** $\dfrac{x^2}{25} + \dfrac{y^2}{4} - \dfrac{z^2}{100} = 1$

Hyperboloid of one sheet

$xy$-trace: $\dfrac{x^2}{25} + \dfrac{y^2}{4} = 1$

$xz$-trace: $\dfrac{x^2}{25} - \dfrac{z^2}{100} = 1$

$yz$-trace: $\dfrac{y^2}{4} - \dfrac{z^2}{100} = 1$

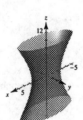

**62.** Let $y = r(x) = 2\sqrt{x}$ and revolve the curve about the $x$-axis.

**64.** $\left( \dfrac{\sqrt{3}}{4}, \dfrac{3}{4}, \dfrac{3\sqrt{3}}{2} \right)$, rectangular

(a) $r = \sqrt{\left( \dfrac{\sqrt{3}}{4} \right)^2 + \left( \dfrac{3}{4} \right)^2} = \dfrac{\sqrt{3}}{2}, \ \theta = \arctan\sqrt{3} = \dfrac{\pi}{3}, \ z = \dfrac{3\sqrt{3}}{2}, \ \left( \dfrac{\sqrt{3}}{2}, \dfrac{\pi}{2}, \dfrac{3\sqrt{3}}{2} \right)$, cylindrical

(b) $\rho = \sqrt{\left( \dfrac{\sqrt{3}}{4} \right)^2 + \left( \dfrac{3}{4} \right)^2 + \left( \dfrac{3\sqrt{3}}{2} \right)^2} = \dfrac{\sqrt{30}}{2}, \ \theta = \dfrac{\pi}{3}, \ \phi = \arccos \dfrac{3}{\sqrt{10}}, \ \left( \dfrac{\sqrt{30}}{2}, \dfrac{\pi}{3}, \arccos \dfrac{3}{\sqrt{10}} \right)$, spherical

**66.** $\left(81, -\dfrac{5\pi}{6}, 27\sqrt{3}\right)$, cylindrical

$\rho = \sqrt{6561 + 2187} = 54\sqrt{3}$

$\theta = -\dfrac{5\pi}{6}$

$\phi = \arccos\left(\dfrac{27\sqrt{3}}{54\sqrt{3}}\right) = \arccos\dfrac{1}{2} = \dfrac{\pi}{3}$

$\left(54\sqrt{3}, -\dfrac{5\pi}{6}, \dfrac{\pi}{3}\right)$, spherical

**68.** $\left(12, -\dfrac{\pi}{2}, \dfrac{2\pi}{3}\right)$, spherical

$r^2 = \left(12\sin\left(\dfrac{2\pi}{3}\right)\right)^2 \Rightarrow r = 6\sqrt{3}$

$\theta = -\dfrac{\pi}{2}$

$z = \rho\cos\phi = 12\cos\left(\dfrac{2\pi}{3}\right) = -6$

$\left(6\sqrt{3}, -\dfrac{\pi}{2}, -6\right)$, cylindrical

**70.** $x^2 + y^2 + z^2 = 16$

(a) Cylindrical: $r^2 + z^2 = 16$

(b) Spherical: $\rho = 4$

# Problem Solving for Chapter 10

**2.** $f(x) = \displaystyle\int_0^x \sqrt{t^4 + 1}\, dt$

(a)

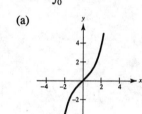

(b) $f'(x) = \sqrt{x^4 + 1}$

$f'(0) = 1 = \tan\theta$

$\theta = \dfrac{\pi}{4}$

$\mathbf{u} = \dfrac{1}{\sqrt{2}}(\mathbf{i} + \mathbf{j}) = \left\langle \dfrac{\sqrt{2}}{2}, \dfrac{\sqrt{2}}{2}\right\rangle$

(c) $\pm\left\langle \dfrac{\sqrt{2}}{2}, -\dfrac{\sqrt{2}}{2}\right\rangle$

(d) The line is $y = x$: $x = t, y = t$.

**4.** Label the figure as indicated.

$\overrightarrow{PR} = \mathbf{a} + \mathbf{b}$

$\overrightarrow{SQ} = \mathbf{b} - \mathbf{a}$

$(\mathbf{a} + \mathbf{b}) \cdot (\mathbf{b} - \mathbf{a}) = \|\mathbf{b}\|^2 - \|\mathbf{a}\|^2 = 0$, because

$\|\mathbf{a}\| = \|\mathbf{b}\|$ in a rhombus.

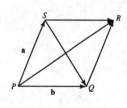

**6.** $(\mathbf{n} + \overrightarrow{PP_0}) \perp (\mathbf{n} - \overrightarrow{PP_0})$

Figure is a square.

Thus, $\|\overrightarrow{PP_0}\| = \|\mathbf{n}\|$ and the points $P$ form a circle of radius $\|\mathbf{n}\|$ in the plane with center at $P$.

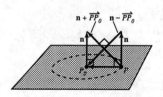

**8. (a)** $V = 2 \int_0^r \pi(r^2 - x^2)\, dx = 2\pi \left[ r^2 x - \dfrac{x^3}{3} \right]_0^r = \dfrac{4}{3}\pi r^3$

**(b)** At height $z = d > 0$,

$$\frac{x^2}{a^2} + \frac{y^2}{b^2} + \frac{d^2}{c^2} = 1$$

$$\frac{x^2}{a^2} + \frac{y^2}{b^2} = 1 - \frac{d^2}{c^2} = \frac{c^2 - d^2}{c^2}$$

$$\frac{x^2}{\dfrac{a^2(c^2 - d^2)}{c^2}} + \frac{y^2}{\dfrac{b^2(c^2 - d^2)}{c^2}} = 1.$$

$$\text{Area} = \pi \sqrt{ \left( \frac{a^2(c^2 - d^2)}{c^2} \right) \left( \frac{b^2(c^2 - d^2)}{c^2} \right) } = \frac{\pi ab}{c^2}(c^2 - d^2)$$

$$V = 2 \int_0^c \frac{\pi ab}{c^2}(c^2 - d^2)\, dd$$

$$= \frac{2\pi ab}{c^2} \left[ c^2 d - \frac{d^3}{3} \right]_0^c$$

$$= \frac{4}{3}\pi abc$$

**10. (a)** $r = 2 \cos \theta$

Cylinder

**(b)** $z = r^2 \cos 2\theta$

$z^2 = x^2 - y^2$

Hyperbolic paraboloid

**12.** $x = -t + 3, \; y = \dfrac{1}{2}t + 1, \; z = 2t - 1; \; Q = (4, 3, s)$

**(a)** $\mathbf{u} = \langle -2, 1, 4 \rangle$ direction vector for line

$P = (3, 1, -1)$ point on line

$\overrightarrow{PQ} = \langle 1, 2, s + 1 \rangle$

$$\overrightarrow{PQ} \times \mathbf{u} = \begin{vmatrix} \mathbf{i} & \mathbf{j} & \mathbf{k} \\ 1 & 2 & s + 1 \\ -2 & 1 & 4 \end{vmatrix} = (7 - s)\mathbf{i} + (-6 - 2s)\mathbf{j} + 5\mathbf{k}$$

$$D = \frac{\|\overrightarrow{PQ} \times \mathbf{u}\|}{\|\mathbf{u}\|} = \frac{\sqrt{(7 - s)^2 + (-6 - 2s)^2 + 25}}{\sqrt{21}}$$

**(b)**

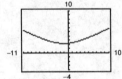

The minimum is $D \approx 2.2361$ at $s = -1$.

**(c)** Yes, there are slant asymptotes. Using $s = x$, we have

$$D(s) = \frac{1}{\sqrt{21}}\sqrt{5x^2 + 10x + 110} = \frac{\sqrt{5}}{\sqrt{21}}\sqrt{x^2 + 2x + 22}$$

$$= \frac{\sqrt{5}}{\sqrt{21}}\sqrt{(x + 1)^2 + 21} \; \rightarrow \; \pm\sqrt{\frac{5}{21}}(x + 1)$$

$$y = \pm\frac{\sqrt{105}}{21}(s + 1) \quad \text{slant asymptotes.}$$

**14.** (a) The tension $T$ is the same in each tow line.

$$6000\mathbf{i} = T(\cos 20° + \cos(-20))\mathbf{i} + T(\sin 20° + \sin(-20°))\mathbf{j}$$
$$= 2T\cos 20°\mathbf{i}$$

$$\Rightarrow T = \frac{6000}{2\cos 20°} \approx 3192.5 \text{ lbs}$$

(b) As in part (a), $6000\mathbf{i} = 2T\cos\theta$

$$\Rightarrow T = \frac{3000}{\cos\theta}$$

Domain: $0 < \theta < 90°$

(c)

| $\theta$ | 10° | 20° | 30° | 40° | 50° | 60° |
|---|---|---|---|---|---|---|
| $T$ | 3046.3 | 3192.5 | 3464.1 | 3916.2 | 4667.2 | 6000.0 |

(d)

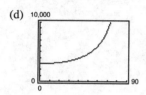

(e) As $\theta$ increases, there is less force applied in the direction of motion.

**16.** (a) Los Angeles: $(4000, -118.24°, 55.95°)$

Rio de Janeiro: $(4000, -43.22°, 112.90°)$

(b) Los Angeles: $x = 4000 \sin 55.95° \cos(-118.24°)$

$\qquad\qquad\quad y = 4000 \sin 55.95° \sin(-118.24°)$

$\qquad\qquad\quad z = 4000 \cos 55.95°$

$\qquad\qquad\quad (-1568.2, -2919.7, 2239.7)$

Rio de Janeiro: $x = (4000 \sin 112.90° \cos(-43.22°)$

$\qquad\qquad\quad y = 4000 \sin 112.90° \sin(-43.22°)$

$\qquad\qquad\quad z = 4000 \cos 112.90°$

$\qquad\qquad\quad (2685.2, -2523.3, -1556.5)$

(c) $\cos\theta = \dfrac{\mathbf{u} \cdot \mathbf{v}}{\|\mathbf{u}\| \|\mathbf{v}\|} = \dfrac{(-1568.2)(2685.2) + (-2919.7)(-2523.3) + (2239.7)(-1556.5)}{(4000)(4000)}$

$\qquad \theta \approx 91.18° \approx 1.59$ radians

(d) $s = 4000(1.59) \approx 6366$ miles

**—CONTINUED—**

**16.** —CONTINUED—

(e) For Boston and Honolulu:

a. Boston: $(4000, -71.06°, 47.64°)$

Honolulu: $(4000, -157.86°, 68.69°)$

b. Boston: $x = 4000 \sin 47.64° \cos(-71.06°)$

$y = 4000 \sin 47.64° \sin(-71.06°)$

$z = 4000 \cos 47.64°$

$(959.4, -2795.7, 2695.1)$

Honolulu: $x = (4000 \sin 68.69° \cos(-157.86°)$

$y = 4000 \sin 68.69° \sin(-157.86°)$

$z = 4000 \cos 68.69°$

$(-3451.7, -1404.4, 1453.7)$

(f) $\cos \theta = \dfrac{\mathbf{u} \cdot \mathbf{v}}{\|\mathbf{u}\| \, \|\mathbf{v}\|} = \dfrac{(959.4)(-3451.7) + (-2795.7)(-1404.4) + (2695.1)(1453.7)}{(4000)(4000)}$

$\theta \approx 73.5° \approx 1.28$ radians

(g) $s = 4000(1.28) \approx 5120$ miles

**18.** Assume one of $a, b, c$, is not zero, say $a$. Choose a point in the first plane such as $(-d_1/a, 0, 0)$. The distance between this point and the second plane is

$$D = \frac{|a(-d_1/a) + b(0) + c(0) + d_2|}{\sqrt{a^2 + b^2 + c^2}}$$

$$= \frac{|-d_1 + d_2|}{\sqrt{a^2 + b^2 + c^2}} = \frac{|d_1 - d_2|}{\sqrt{a^2 + b^2 + c^2}}.$$

**20.** Essay.